For Reference

Not to be taken from this room

The Oxford Encyclopedia of the Reformation

EDITORS

John M. Headley   James M. Kittelson   Stanford E. Lehmberg
Jill Raitt   David C. Steinmetz   Merry E. Wiesner-Hanks

ASSOCIATE EDITORS

David P. Daniel   James D. Tracy

CONSULTING EDITORS

William J. Bouwsma   Natalie Zemon Davis   Mark U. Edwards, Jr.
Robert M. Kingdon   John W. O'Malley, S.J.   Lewis W. Spitz

ADVISERS

Peter Blickle   Martin Brecht   Patrick Collinson   A. G. Dickens
Leif Grane   Hans Rudolf Guggisberg   Adolf Laube
Francis Rapp   Bernard Roussel

The Oxford Encyclopedia of the Reformation

HANS J. HILLERBRAND

EDITOR IN CHIEF

Volume 2

New York Oxford

OXFORD UNIVERSITY PRESS

1996

RENFRO LIBRARY
MARS HILL COLLEGE
MARS HILL, N.C. 28754
DISCARD

OXFORD UNIVERSITY PRESS

Oxford New York
Athens Auckland Bangkok Bombay
Calcutta Cape Town Dar es Salaam Delhi
Florence Hong Kong Istanbul Karachi
Kuala Lumpur Madras Madrid Melbourne
Mexico City Nairobi Paris Singapore
Taipei Tokyo Toronto

and associated companies in
Berlin Ibadan

Copyright © 1996 by Oxford University Press, Inc.

Published by Oxford University Press, Inc.,
198 Madison Avenue, New York, New York 10016

Oxford is a registered trademark of Oxford University Press

All rights reserved. No part of this publication
may be reproduced, stored in a retrieval system, or transmitted,
in any form or by any means, eletronic, mechanical,
photocopying, recording, or otherwise, without the prior
written permission of Oxford University Press.

Library of Congress Cataloging-in-Publication Data
The Oxford encyclopedia of the Reformation / Hans J. Hillerbrand, editor in chief
p. cm.
Includes bibliographical references and index.
ISBN 0-19-506493-3 (set : alk. paper)
1. Reformation—Encyclopedias. 2. Reformation—Biography—Encyclopedias.
3. Theology, Doctrinal—Europe—History—16th century—Encyclopedias.
4. Europe—Church history—16th century—Encyclopedias.
I. Hillerbrand, Hans J.
BR302.8.093 1996 270.6'03—dc20 95-24520 CIP

ISBN-13 978-0-19-506493-3
ISBN 0-19-506493-3 (set)
ISBN 0-19-510363-7 (vol. 2)

Grateful acknowledgment is made to the grantor of permission to use the following material in this volume. Magistracy, *article on* France: Mario Turchetti, "Religious Concord and Political Tolerance in Sixteenth- and Seventeenth-Century France," *Sixteenth Century Journal,* v 22, n 1 (Spring 1991), pp. 21–23.

Printing (last digit): 9 8 7 6 5 4 3

Printed in the United States of America
on acid-free paper

R
940.2303
O98
1996
v. 2

NOV 08 '05

D

CONTINUED

DORDRECHT. The most important city in the southernmost corner of Holland during the late sixteenth century, Dordrecht became one of the most thoroughly Reformed municipalities during the Dutch Reformation. Lying at the junction of the Maas, the Waal, and the Lek rivers, the city had emerged in the late Middle Ages as the leading trading center in the lower Maas region. Dordrecht's prominence derived largely from its staple privilege, which mandated that ships traveling down these rivers must be unloaded and their cargo stored in the city before shipment elsewhere. The defense of this commercial privilege was the central principle that shaped the magistracy's policy in the province's political machinations during the sixteenth and seventeenth centuries.

The success of the Calvinist Reformation in Dordrecht stemmed from the political support of an oligarchic magistracy that identified itself with the religious and social agenda of staunchly Reformed ministers. Before 1572 Dordrecht's city magistrates remained loyal to the central government in return for the count of Holland's continued support for the staple privilege. When the Sea Beggars captured Den Brielle in April 1572, Dordrecht's river trade came to a screeching halt, provoking a great deal of social unrest. A Protestant faction in the ruling elite, led by Adrian van Bleyenburg, Cornelis van Beveren, and Jacob Muys van Holy, used this turmoil and the anti-Spanish sentiments of the militia to stage a coup d'état in the city government. Van Bleyenburg appealed to William of Orange for assistance in June 1572, and when the Sea Beggar troops arrived, the militia refused to defend the city.

The capitulation to the Orangist side enabled the Protestant families of van Beveren, De Witt, and Muys van Holy to tighten their grip on political power and to oust their Catholic counterparts, the Oems and Drenckwaerts. In political terms, the revolt and Reformation accelerated the movement toward a closed regent oligarchy, a process that had already been underway throughout most of the sixteenth century. Unlike many city governments in Holland, the ruling elite in Dordrecht embraced the strict confessional brand of Calvinism and worked to support its aims in the city. This Protestant oligarchy retained political power at least through the 1630s, a factor that ensured Calvinism's triumph and made Dordrecht one of its strongest centers in Holland.

This cooperative environment in Dordrecht was the result of two factors: the magistracy's preference for Genevan Calvinism and the social background of Reformed church officers. Throughout the Reformation period, the magistracy called ministers from regent backgrounds and the church elected officers from the social elite in Dordrecht. From 1573 to 1579, an average of three magistrates (of fourteen) each year were elders, and an even larger component of the militia were church officers. The consistory also possessed a strong degree of representation in the magistracy. Four church officers per year served on the magistracy from 1573 to 1589. This percentage continued to rise until it peaked at nine of fourteen during the first decade of the seventeenth century.

During the same period in which the Leiden magistracy protected the Libertine minister Caspar Coolhaes from his confessional rivals, the city government in Dordrecht worked to exclude heterodox ministers. In 1582 the city council terminated the appointment of Hermannus Herbertszoon for failing to preach from the Heidelberg Catechism and for expressing latitudinarian opinions from the pulpit. The victor in this episode was Hendrik van den Corput, whom the magistrates called to Dordrecht in 1578. From a regent family in Breda, van den Corput served exiled Dutch Calvinist churches in the Palatinate before 1572. He became the leading pastor in Dordrecht during the church's formative years and worked closely with the magistracy to implant confessional Calvinism in the Dordrecht church.

The Reformed church in Dordrecht grew relatively quickly from 368 members (of a municipal population of 10,000) in 1573 to 800 members in 1580. The congregation continued to grow throughout the early seventeenth century, in part because of the influx of refugees from the southern Netherlands. It has been estimated that southern refugees made up one-third of Dordrecht's population in 1621. Reformed growth in Dordrecht manifested itself in the city's social and political institutions. The church's poor relief organ, the diaconate, displaced the traditional parish foundations as the most important charitable agency. In contrast to other cities such as Leiden, Delft, Gouda, and Haarlem, where the diaconate encountered civil resistance, Reformed poor relief in Dordrecht served the inhabitants of the entire city. Similarly, by 1591 the Reformed church effectively controlled public education within Dordrecht. It would be a mistake, however, to assume that the Calvinist church recast popular culture or reformed morals in the city. Ministers and elders were unable to make a significant dent in cultural matters that concerned them most: sabbath violations, clandestine marriages, popular amusements, and the regular litany of moral transgressions.

A cooperative relationship between the consistory and the magistracy, combined with a burgeoning membership, enabled the church to dominate the social and religious life of Dordrecht and the surrounding region. The Mennonites in Dordrecht proved to be the strongest rival confession and even took members away from the Reformed until 1600, when the Calvinist church began to attract significant numbers of Mennonites. Conversely, the Catholic church in Dordrecht had virtually no presence during the initial years of the Reformation. Priests left the area in the 1570s and the Catholic mission did not establish a foothold in Dordrecht until 1605. By the end of the 1630s, Catholicism did begin to reassert itself, claiming eighteen hundred followers served by four clergy. Despite the persistent complaints of Calvinist ministers, the Catholic revival in Dordrecht was dwarfed by Roman successes in other cities in Holland. Even the most thorny dispute within Dutch Calvinism, the Remonstrant controversy, did not play itself out dramatically in the city. A Calvinist clergy, supported by the magistracy, thwarted any significant doctrinal deviance and organization of an Arminian presence. Thus, the city of Dordrecht, like the national Synod of Dordrecht that met there in 1618/19, stands out as a landmark of Dutch Calvinism's success in Holland.

[*See also* Corput, Hendrik van den; *and* Dordrecht, Synod of.]

BIBLIOGRAPHY

Boogman, J. C. "De overgang van Gouda, Dordrecht, Leiden, en Delft in de zomer van het jaar 1572." *Tijdschrift voor Geschiedenis* 57 (1942), 81–112. One of the first studies to cast the Dutch Revolt as a civil war. Concentrates on the negotiations between the Beggar army and magistrates which led to the capitulation of these cities in 1572. Argues that most magistrates were not inclined to join the revolt.

Dooren, J. P. van, ed. *Classical Acta, 1573–1620: Particuliere Synode Zuid-Holland.* Vol. 1, *I. Classis Dordrecht, 1573–1600.* The Hague, 1980. Important compilation of the decisions of the Dordrecht classis.

Elliott, John P. "Protestantization in the Northern Netherlands; A Case Study; The Classis of Dordrecht, 1572–1640." Ph.D. diss., Columbia University, 1990. An extensive treatment of the establishment of the Calvinist Reformation in the city and classis of Dordrecht. Uses Dordrecht to argue forcefully against the views of Pieter Geyl and L. J. Rogier who contended that Calvinists used social and economic pressure to coerce people into joining the Reformed church. The best recent study of Reformation Dordrecht and one that informed this essay.

Tukker, C. A. *De Classis Dordrecht van 1573 tot 1609: Bijdrage tot de kennis van in- en extern-leven van de Gereformeerde Kerk in de periode van haar organisering.* Leiden, 1965. A very good overview of church organization in the classis of Dordrecht. Focuses on the difficulties confronting Calvinists in establishing churches in the rural region of the Lower Maas during the initial phase of the Reformation.

CHARLES H. PARKER

DORDRECHT, SYNOD OF. This Dutch national—and, in a sense, international—synod of the Reformed churches that took place in Dordrecht in 1618–1619 finally resolved the Remonstrant controversy that had divided the Dutch Reformed church between 1605 and 1618 but that traced its roots to the genesis of the Reformed church in the mid-sixteenth century. From the beginning the leading intelligentsia of the Reformed church consisted partly of theologians who were decidedly Reformed, sometimes Calvinist, and partly of theologians of a more broadly Protestant persuasion. During the decades when the Dutch Reformed church took shape, the divergences led to conflicts on doctrine, especially on predestination, as well as on the character of the church, especially on the status of the Belgic Confession, the relation of the church to the state, and the authority of synods. From 1605 all these questions converged on Arminius's rejection of the *praedestinatio ad malum.* In the Remonstrance of 1610 and the Contra-Remonstrance of 1611, both parties defined their positions clearly. From then on conciliation was impossible, and the subsequent years were full of ecclesiastical struggles. At first the Remonstrants, supported by the States of Holland and their pensionary, Johan van Oldenbarnevelt, gained the upper hand. But when in 1617 the stadtholder Maurits of Nassau sided with the Contra-Remonstrants, the tide turned. In 1618 Oldenbarnevelt was imprisoned—in 1619 he was sentenced to death—and the States-General granted permission to convene a national synod.

The synod met at Dordrecht from November 1618 to May 1619. Its influential president was the Leeuwarden minister Johannes Bogermannus, and it consisted of some one-hundred members—ministers, professors of theology, and elders—including about twenty-five representatives of foreign churches. The workload was heavy—180 sessions in 128 days—but members were well compensated. All expenses were paid by the States-General, which exerted considerable influence through their "state commissioners." The synod summoned thirteen prominent Remonstrant theologians. These men constituted themselves as a kind of counter-synod and obstructed the proceedings as much as possible. Their main spokesman was Simon Episcopius, then professor of theology at Leiden. The often-vehement discussions between the Remonstrants and synod members dealt with the status of the synod and the function of confessions. The Remonstrants maintained that the synod was a free conference, not having decisive power, and that scripture was the only authority in doctrinal matters. After five weeks of strenuous clashes with Bogermannus, the Remonstrants were dismissed.

From January to May the synod, now in good harmony, treated doctrinal questions. The "Canons of Dordrecht," or "Five Articles against the Remonstrants," were officially proclaimed as an explanation of certain points of the Belgic Confession. This extensive document defends the doctrine of double predestination and rejects the Remonstrant view of predestination as based on human faith or unbelief, as foreseen by God. Soon it gained a confessional status as one of the "formulas of concord" for the Dutch Reformed church together with the Heidelberg Catechism and the Belgic Confession.

The synod was of primary importance for the Dutch Reformed church. After 1619 there could be no doubt about the clearly Calvinist character of the church. The unity and uniformity of the church was maintained, at the expense of its broad character: two-hundred ministers were dismissed; in 1619 the Remonstrant Brotherhood was founded in exile in Antwerp; and until 1630 leading Remonstrants in the republic were persecuted. A second important decision concerned the translation of the Bible. The synod decided that an entirely new translation should be made and established general rules therefor. In 1637 the "Statenvertaling" (States' Translation) appeared, so called because the States-General bore all expenses. It influenced the Dutch language far into the nineteenth century. On the international level the synod was a showcase of Calvinist strength, and it intensified the international coherence of the Calvinist movement.

[*See also* Remonstrance of 1610.]

BIBLIOGRAPHY

Deursen, A. Th. van. *Bavianen en Slijkgeuzen: Kerk en kerkvolk ten tijde van Maurits en Oldebarnevelt.* Van Gorcum's Historische Bibliotheek no. 92. Assen, Netherlands, 1974. The character of the church and the ecclesiastical quarrels studied on the level of the local churches.

Spijker, W. van 't, et al. *De Synode van Dordrecht in 1618 en 1619.* Houten, 1987. Popular, reliable book on the synod, its causes, and the States' Translation of the Bible.

CORNELIS AUGUSTIJN

DOUAI COLLEGE. The city of Douai (Douay), located in northern France, attracted many English Catholic exiles for geographical and academic reasons: its easy access to the English channel and the opportunities presented by its new university. To reinforce English Catholicism through a constant supply of priests, William Allen, a religious exile, founded the college in 1568. It was the first establishment north of the Alps erected according to the Tridentine decrees for the formation of clergy. The first priest to return to England was Louis Barlow in 1574; the first to be martyred was Cuthbert Mayne in 1577. It is estimated that Douai sent approximately 400 priests to England by the end of Elizabeth I's reign, and the arrival of the "seminary priests" affected Elizabethan policy toward Catholics. Instead of dying the slow death of attrition, the old religion became revitalized and aggressive, and Elizabethan legislation was thus readjusted to deal with the new threat.

Although promised pensions by both Pope Gregory XIII and King Philip II, Douai's most serious problem was financial. The Spanish king was too preoccupied with the wars in the Netherlands to pay regularly. From March 1578 to June 1593 the college was transferred to Reims where it enjoyed the protection of the Dukes of Guise. In the mid-1580s the Society of Jesus assisted Allen in the solicitation of desperately needed alms. The martyrologies, carefully distributed during an appeal, informed potential Continental benefactors of the great and important work done by the seminary.

The English college aided the Catholic cause with the publication of various theological, devotional, and controversial works. Among its theologians were Richard Bristow, William Rainolds, and Gregory Martin, whose greatest contribution was his translation of the New Testament from the Vulgate (Reims, 1582). For financial reasons the translation of the Old Testament did not appear until 1609.

After Allen's final move to Rome in 1585, the government of the college passed to Richard Barrett (1588–1599) and Thomas Worthington (1599–1613). Both retained cordial relations with the Jesuits, too cordial for some members of the English secular clergy. With the Society of Jesus governing the other colleges in Rome, Seville, and Valladolid, some feared that the independence of Douai was doomed. When the long-simmering tensions between the English Jesuits and certain secular clergy (later called the Appellants) erupted over the issues of allegiance to the crown, succession to the English throne, and the nomination of an archpriest in England, the relationship soured. Matthew Kellison, president from 1613 to 1641, was warned that the secular clergy would cut off their financial support unless he ended Jesuit involvement in the college. Henceforth the once friendly relationship frequently became bitter.

The college came under the supervision of the Congregation for the Propagation of the Faith with its formation in 1622 and continued to educate both clergy and laity until the armies of the French Revolution drove it out of Douai. The college continued its work in England at Crook Hall (later Ushaw College, Durham) and at Saint Edmund's Old Hall, Ware. The seminary was later transferred to Allen Hall, Chelsea.

BIBLIOGRAPHY

Burton, Edwin H., and Thomas L. Williams, eds. *The Douay College Diaries: Third, Fourth and Fifth.* 2 vols. London, 1911.

Burton, Edwin H., and Edmond Nolan, eds. *The Douay College Diaries: The Seventh Diary.* London, 1928. The sixth diary is not extant.

Guilday, P. K. *The English Catholic Refugees on the Continent, 1558–*

1795(1914). Reprint, Farnborough, England, 1969. Best introduction to the college's history. For more detailed exposition, see the college's diaries.

Harris, P. R., ed. *Douai College Documents, 1639–1794*. London, 1972.

Knox, Thomas Francis, ed. *The First and Second Diaries of the English College, Douay*,(1878). Reprint, Farnborough, England, 1969.

THOMAS M. MCCOOG, S.J.

DRACONITES, Johann (also Drach, Trach, Draco; 1494–1566), German Lutheran reformer, professor of theology, and biblical scholar. Draconites was born in Carlstadt an der Main. He studied in Erfurt, receiving an master of arts in 1514. There he became active in the humanist circle around Eobanus Hessus and corresponded with Desiderius Erasmus. A friend and colleague of Justus Jonas, both were canons in the Erfurt collegiate church. Draconites was converted to Luther's views during the latter's visit to Erfurt on his way to Worms in 1521.

Draconites continued his studies in Wittenberg, receiving a doctorate in 1523. In the meantime, he became city pastor in Miltenberg, where he began reforms with the support of the townspeople and council. Strident opposition from the town's clergy forced him to flee. From exile he published letters of consolation to the evangelical congregation. The incident gained wider recognition when Luther wrote an open letter to the evangelical congregation there. Draconites accepted another pastorate in Waltershausen, but there too he met with little success.

In 1534 Draconites was called to the faculty at Marburg as professor of theology. He served there for fourteen years, preaching and lecturing daily. During this time he published commentaries on various books of the Old Testament and was involved in various colloquies and political meetings. He attended the Colloquy of Regensburg in 1542 at the behest of Landgrave Philipp of Hesse, but was forced to leave the city when a pamphlet he had dedicated to the Regensburg city council offended the Catholics with its aggressive advocacy of the Lutheran position.

The latter part of his tenure at Marburg was marked by theological controversy as he was accused of antinomianism by colleagues on the theological faculty. He resigned his position, in part because of this conflict but also because of his desire to devote himself to other projects, chief among them a polyglot Old Testament and a compilation and analysis of all direct and indirect messianic texts of the Old Testament to be used for the conversion of Jews, a task at which he himself had achieved some success. These commentaries were published in two large folio volumes in Lübeck in 1549 and 1550. From there he moved to Rostock, where he served as professor of theology and later as superintendent of the city's churches. Here, too, his work was steeped in controversy, this time over sabbath observances. An invitation from Duke Albert of Prussia to become superintendent of the diocese of Pomesania extricated him from the conflict in Rostock.

His heart was in his scholarly work, however, and he requested from the duke a lengthy vacation in Wittenberg to work on his polyglot Old Testament. He used his salary from the duke to fund his work and its publication and refused to take up his duties in Danzig when the duke demanded his return in 1564. Only portions of the polyglot appeared before his death in 1566. This work, on which he had labored nearly forty years, found little acceptance among his contemporaries and was of little use to scholars.

BIBLIOGRAPHY

Albrecht, Otto. *Die evangelische Gemeinde Miltenberg und ihr erster Prediger*. Halle, 1896.

Bautz, Friedrich Wilhelm. *Biographisch-bibliographisches Kirchenlexikon*. Vol. 1. Hamm, 1970, See pp. 1374–1376.

Kawerau, Gustav. "Johannes Draconites aus Carlstadt: Ein kurzes Lebensbild mit Beilagen." *Beiträge zur Bayerischen Kirchengeschichte* 3 (1897), 247–275.

D. JONATHAN GRIESER

DRAMA. From the thirteenth century, religious dramas had been written for performances in churches, monasteries, convents, and, most importantly, in the public squares of major cities in England, France, Italy, the Iberian peninsula, and the German territories. Initially tied to the celebration of the Mass or to the festivities surrounding important feasts in the Christian liturgical calendar, such as Christmas, Easter, and Corpus Christi, these sacred works gradually developed into elaborate representations of the salvation history of humankind from the fall of Lucifer to the Last Judgment. By 1500 earlier dramatizations of biblical episodes, such as the adoration of the Magi and the discovery of the empty tomb on Easter Sunday, had been incorporated into expansive plays on the entire life of Christ, replete with Old Testament scenes that prefigured New Testament events. In addition to these mystery play cycles (*mystères*), most notably the Passion and Corpus Christi plays, there were hagiographical and allegorical dramas that provided didactic, and often entertaining, manifestations of Christian truths. Audiences from all social strata, many of whom had only a superficial familiarity with Christian dogma, were thus informed of the fundamental tenets of their faith and reminded of the reward of eternal salvation that awaited all believers.

Such an effective means of public education appealed to early reformers eager to consolidate their church and to gain new adherents. Though skeptical of the social upheaval that medieval stagings usually incited, Luther and Calvin promoted public dramatic performances, albeit on a smaller scale, and encouraged schoolmasters, clerics, and preachers to compose religious plays based on scripture for the edification of the faithful. Luther was an especially outspoken proponent of biblical theater, and he often referred to the pedagogical and moral efficacy of theater in his writings. He even suggested the ideal biblical stories, all from the Apocrypha, for dramatic treatment: the books of *Judith* and *Tobit*, and the story of Susanna. *Judith* was deemed an especially appropriate topic for tragedy, while *Tobit* was considered suitable for comedy.

The world of sixteenth-century drama was exceedingly complex, and the popularity of, or disinterest in, many different types of drama varied widely within each land or language group, and among the adherents of each church. Popular forms of medieval drama did not suddenly die out, nor were they immediately replaced by the new neoclassical style promoted by Renaissance humanists that had emerged in Italy in the fourteenth century and spread northward. Rather, for much of the century, mystery plays continued to be performed, especially in Catholic lands, and coexisted with other types of medieval drama such as the miracle play and the morality play. There were also other dramatic forms at a playwright's disposal: Shrovetide farces in the German-speaking lands, allegorical civic plays of the Dutch chambers of rhetoric, and the interludes in England. All of these dramatic types mutually shaped and reshaped each other: individual scenes from the mystery plays reappeared in humanist garb; miracle plays began to adopt neoclassical conventions, such as the division into acts and the use of a chorus; and Shrovetide writers rewrote humanist works for their less educated audiences.

When Luther and Calvin sanctioned the composition of religious drama, they envisioned dramas written in imitation of the classical Greco-Roman playwrights. They were both admirers of the humanist style, and they valued the ancients for the elegance of their language and the moral content of some of their writings. But with the complex admixture of dramatic forms in the sixteenth century, humanist theater was rarely as untainted by its medieval antecedents, or as innovative, as its enthusiasts hoped. Some of the greatest Reformation plays, such as Thomas Kirchmeyer's *Pammachius* (1538), in which the pope is shown in league with the devil, combined elements from several medieval traditions with the language of Greco-Roman theater.

The Tradition and Transformation of Medieval Drama. Medieval religious drama generally consisted of one of three styles: the mystery play, the miracle play, or the morality play. Very few of these works were printed, and they were chiefly intended for public performance on major religious holidays or saints' feast days. Audiences usually included members from all social classes, though dramas presented in monasteries and convents were directed to spectators associated with a particular religious order. In the latter instance, the performers were drawn from the sponsoring institution: English Franciscans were famed for their monastic presentations, and in Italy convent theater flourished especially in Tuscan cloisters. In contrast, the mystery plays involved vast numbers of the local urban populace: patricians and merchants not only financed the staging of many Passion and Corpus Christi plays, but they often bought themselves major roles and paid for the requisite props and costumes. Local guilds also contributed to scenes indicative of their craft: for example, well-keepers were responsible for representing Noah and the Flood, and bakers staged the Last Supper. Both male and female performers presented these roles, though the preference for men prevailed; in convent theater the nuns served as both playwrights and actors.

The most elaborate forms of medieval theater were the Passion play and Corpus Christi play. These works generally consisted of forty thousand to fifty thousand verses, took days, if not weeks, to perform, and created much activity, if not chaos, in the sponsoring town. There are records of civic performances of these plays from the late thirteenth century on, but the high point of their popularity occurred in France and the German lands in the late fifteenth and early sixteenth century, and in Spain and Portugal in the mid-sixteenth century. The four complete sacred play cycles from England that survive, the Chester, York, Hegge, and Towneley cycles, originated in the late fourteenth century but were subsequently altered to suit local conditions. In these grandiose displays of human salvation history, Old and New Testament episodes, all centering on the life of Jesus and the centrality of the Redemption, were vividly and colorfully enlivened by music, parades through town, and the addition of entertaining devils and fools. Other biblical scenes conveyed clear moral messages: Herod's death exemplified the punishment of tyrants, John the Baptist glorified the office of the preacher, and young Jesus' debate with the elders in the temple exhorted youths to study. And in many works, the narrator (sometimes the playwright), directed the viewers to observe the typological significance of the Old Testament events that prefigured Jesus' life and death.

In the Protestant lands of the Reformation, the Passion plays were officially banned during the sixteenth century, but their popularity abated slowly. The reformers did not disapprove of the plays so much for doctrinal reasons but rather because of the expense and the social unrest their presentations caused. Luther, troubled by the rowdiness that accompanied Passion play performances, thought it more fitting that Christians imitate the suffering of Christ rather than lament the circumstances of his death. Melanchthon likewise regarded the plays as a threat to the civil order. In the Pomeranian town of Bahn, he recalled, the performer who played Christ was accidentally killed as he hung on the cross by the actor portraying the Roman who pierced Christ's side; as his corpse fell, he crushed two other actors; and the actor who wielded the deadly blow was subsequently murdered by a relative of the slain man. Similarly, in 1548 the Parlement of Paris banned all *mystères* because of the unruly crowds such gatherings engendered. In Elizabethan England, many of the mystery plays, despite their freedom from sectarianism, were criticized and even burned as alleged documents of rabid papism and sacrilegious embellishments of God's word.

The reformers' ban of medieval mystery plays was difficult to enforce, especially in the provinces where they enjoyed a great following. In France, the *mystères* did not effectively disappear outside Paris until the revolution, and in England, with the excision of a few overtly Catholic scenes, such as those celebrating the cult of Mary, mystery cycles were performed until the late sixteenth century. In doctrinally divided countries such as the German empire and Switzerland, the mystery plays continued in the Catholic territories and cantons, though with somewhat less extravagance and frequency. The Lucerne Passion of 1583 was renowned for its hundreds of actors and elaborate staging, but in other Catholic Alpine regions, smaller Passion plays promulgating the doctrines of the Counter-Reformation were performed into the eighteenth century. The present-day Oberammergau Passion play is a remnant of this sixteenth-century tradition.

In Catholic lands such as Spain and Portugal, the mystery plays were quickly adapted by local ecclesiastical authorities as a popular means to reinforce the doctrines challenged by Protestant reformers and to disseminate the policies of the post-Tridentine papacy. The rise of Corpus Christi plays in sixteenth-century Spain, for example, has been linked to the need for further education of a wavering populace about the Catholic interpretation of the Mass, the Eucharist, and the importance of auricular confession.

The fate of the other major forms of medieval religious drama, the miracle, or saint, play and the morality play, was much less drastic. The hagiographical miracle plays had developed alongside the mystery plays in the fourteenth and fifteenth centuries, but their performance was considerably shorter and less extravagant. Generally these works were composed by clerics, or as in the case of the Italian *sacre rappresentazioni* by lay confraternities, for presentation in public squares, private halls, and cloisters. The works were often written to celebrate the cult of a particular saint—virgin martyrs such as Saints Agnes, Barbara, Catherine of Alexandria, and Dorothea were especially popular—and they were performed on the saint's feast day. The miracle plays usually portrayed the main events in the saint's life from birth, or from their conversion to Christianity, through their public careers as preachers, benefactors of Christian charity, and most frequently, martyrs at the hands of ignorant pagans. Above all such plays were designed to dazzle their audiences with displays of the miracles performed by these saints: fifteenth-century *sacre rappresentazioni* in Florence, for example, were especially famed for their spectacular stage effects.

Obviously the reformers regarded such plays as needless celebrations of the superstitious cult of the saints, and they strove to curtail their performance. As a result, there are hardly any surviving miracle plays from the chief battlegrounds of the Reformation, the German territories and England. In France, the miracle plays continued into the sixteenth century, but they were gradually superseded by hagiographic drama written by humanist playwrights for performances in schools or public squares. The new humanist vogue also influenced saints' plays in Italy, and by the mid-sixteenth century the hagiographic dramas of clerics and nuns were all written in the style of the ancients. To be sure, the mere adaptation of the five-act form and a chorus did not guarantee a well-wrought play: most of these "neoclassical" hagiographies contained too many details of a saint's life and appeared more like a dramatized narrative rather than a unified plot. But the increased popularity of the humanist style ensured the decline of the medieval miracle play.

A similar fate befell the medieval morality play in the early sixteenth century. The morality play that had originated around 1400 in France was the most overtly didactic of all medieval dramatic forms. The characters were usually all allegorical figures representing various virtues and vices, and humans were portrayed as pilgrims on the path from sin to salvation, or at the crossroads between life and death. The most popular morality play was the Dutch/English *Elckerlijc/Everyman* (c.1510), in which, in his last hours, man realizes that his worldly friends and possessions will not accompany him beyond the grave. The motif of the spiritual preparation for death reappeared in Swiss *Totentanz* (Dance of Death) plays (c.1500) in which death gathers representatives from all social classes and professions and leads them to judgment.

With such clear didactic aims, the morality play was adopted by reformers in the early sixteenth century to disseminate their doctrine. The success of these plays was most apparent in the Low Countries, where an established tradition of allegorical moral plays had been fostered by the chambers of rhetoric (*Rederijkers*) from the fifteenth century. These chambers were amateur acting societies organized like guilds that sponsored poetic composition, public pageants, farces, and didactic allegorical drama (*spel van sinne*). Recent investigations into the activities of the *Rederijkers* have revealed that in many towns, especially Amsterdam, they used their allegorical plays to satirize the ceremonies and institutions of the Catholic church. The rabid and irreverent anticlericalism of *Rederijker* plays in Amsterdam during the 1520s and 1530s forced the civic authorities to intervene and ban the works until after mid-century, when a more conciliatory tone was adopted.

Remnants of medieval morality plays reappeared throughout the sixteenth century in other dramatic forms. In Germany and the Netherlands, several humanist Latin plays depicted Everyman, or the plight of man torn between worldly and divine love. Protestant humanist playwrights assumed a more polemical stance. Nicholas Grimald (c.1519–c.1562) and John Foxe (1516–1587) in England, and Thomas Kirchmeyer (1508–1563) in Saxony, introduced devils and allegorical figures into their Latin morality plays to lament the decline of apostolic Christianity, to decry the pope as the Antichrist, and to envision the glorious destruction of the Roman church by the reformers.

The afterlife of the medieval morality play was especially profound in early Reformation England, where it influenced the interlude, a short, moralistic play performed as a diversion in a much larger work, or separately, usually for a noble audience, as a brief entertainment. The foremost exponent of English Protestant polemical theater, John Bale (1495–1563), a renegade Carmelite, used allegorical figures in his interludes and longer dramatic pieces to rail against papal claims on the English church and Crown and the excesses of the Catholic clergy. His most famous play, *King John* (1539), written while he was in service to Thomas Cromwell, was an allegorical representation of that medieval king's fruitless struggle against the papacy with clear parallels to the contemporary conflict between Tudor England and Rome.

Early sixteenth-century Catholic playwrights continued to use the medieval morality plays for the inculcation of church doctrine. Plays celebrating the rosary and the cult of the Virgin Mary were especially popular in sixteenth-century Spain and Portugal. But the Catholic morality play as a doctrinal weapon fully matured in the hands of humanist playwrights, especially the Jesuits. They responded to the Protestant dramatic allegories of the decadence of church history by revealing the groundlessness of the reformers' objections and their senseless disregard of tradition (Andreas Fabricius, *Evangelicus fluctuans* [The Wavering Protestant], 1569). They revitalized the Everyman morality and used it to illustrate in vivid detail the damnation awaiting all who failed to adhere to the precepts of Christianity (Jacob Bidermann, *Cenodoxus*, written 1602). And they introduced allegorical figures into saints' plays and historical dramas to explicate the spiritual motivation of their protagonists.

Yet another medieval genre that played an important role in the early decades of the Reformation was the Shrovetide farce (*Fastnachtspiel*). This short, often bawdy, text had developed chiefly in the German-speaking lands during the fifteenth century (though there is also extensive evidence of such plays in France), especially in north German towns and in Bavaria and Switzerland. These plays were usually performed in the raucous atmosphere of a local tavern, but they were later transferred into public squares and halls. Their plots were derived for the most part from folk tales featuring clever peasants deceiving each other and their social betters, but the works sometimes conveyed Christian ethics or civic policy as well. During the Reformation, the traditional peasant milieu was first used with great effect by the Swiss artist-playwright Niklas Manuel (1484–1530) in his 1525 farce *Der Ablaßkrämer* (The Indulgence Peddler), in which the angry populace, tired of economic oppression by the Roman church, strings up an indulgence peddler and forces him to confess his crimes. *Fastnachtspiele* were also adapted to biblical subjects. The fervent Protestant Burkhard Waldis (c.1490–c.1556) of Riga used the Shrovetide form for his Low German prodigal son play *De Parabell vam vorlorn Szohn* (1527), in which he juxtaposed the contrite Lutheran prodigal with his Catholic older brother who remains enslaved to the attainment of salvation through good works. The most prolific Shrovetide playwright of the sixteenth century, Hans Sachs of Nuremberg (1494–1576), a loyal supporter of Luther, occasionally incorporated anticlerical criticisms into these works and into his many biblical plays, but he saved his most fiery polemics for his dialogues.

Humanist Drama and the Reform. The most significant step in the development of early modern religious theater occurred in the early 1500s in the Netherlands, where grammar school playwrights first adapted the form and language of Roman comedy to biblical subjects. There had been earlier attempts to enliven religious drama with classical language: the tenth-century nun Hrotsvitha of Gandersheim had written religious farces for her convent in the language of the Roman comedian Terence. But although her works were discovered and published by the German humanist Conradus Celtis (1459–1508), they had only a limited effect. More importantly, the Dutch schoolmaster Georgius Macropedius (1475–1558), active at schools in Utrecht and 's Hertogenbosch, first used Roman comic language with a biblical subject in his prodigal son play *Asotus* (c.1510; published 1537). Macropedius and his contemporary, Gulielmus Gnapheus (1493–1568) from the Hague, who published the most successful religious drama of the century, the prodigal son play *Acolastus* (1529), essentially created the humanist religious drama that Luther, Calvin, and their supporters would later promulgate.

Humanist school drama originated as part of the Latin-language curriculum in the grammar schools of northern Europe and rapidly became the predominant form of early modern religious theater. (The corpus of surviving plays consists of several hundred printed texts and still more in manuscript from Oxford to Dubrovnik to Évora and Uppsala, although relatively few have ever been analyzed.) Humanist teachers endorsed the study of ancient drama, chiefly Roman, as a means for students to hone their colloquial Latin skills and to develop an elegant Latin style; the annual performance of a Roman comedy or tragedy by the resident schoolboys thus became commonplace at Shrovetide or at the end of the academic year in France, England, the Low Countries, and Germany in the late fifteenth and early sixteenth century. But some schoolmen were concerned that the romantic content of Terence's plays and the blood feuds and crass emotions of the Roman tragedian Seneca might endanger the spiritual and moral education of their students, both on the stage and in the audience. Mindful of their Christian duty, writers such as Macropedius and Gnapheus decided to reform ancient theater by replacing the offensive subjects of the ancients with exemplary biblical tales. The result was the creation of two Christianized dramatic traditions, the Christian Terence—a designation coined by the prolific Haarlem school playwright Cornelius Schonaeus (1541–1611) at the end of the century—and the Christian Seneca.

When Luther and Calvin endorsed humanist theater, they hoped that the success these Latin school playwrights had enjoyed could be easily transferred into a vernacular context. Although both reformers realized the scholarly value of a thorough training in the ancients, they wanted to reach a broader audience through drama than the limited academic circles of the Latin schools. The Protestant pastors and schoolmen who began to write German-language humanist biblical drama in the 1520s and 1530s such as Joachim Greff in Saxony, who also wrote in the medieval style, and Sixt Birck (1501–1554) in Basel purposely chose episodes from the popular Passion play cycles in an attempt to win the traditional audiences of medieval theater.

The Old Testament and New Testament subjects of most sixteenth-century Latin and vernacular school plays were based on characters and events from the mystery plays: Adam and Eve, Cain and Abel, the destruction of Sodom, Abraham and Isaac, Jacob and Esau, Joseph, Jephthah, Samson, Saul, David, John the Baptist, the birth of Christ, young Jesus in the temple, the marriage feast at Cana, the raising of Lazarus, and the Last Judgment and Second Coming. In most cases the typological significance of an Old Testament plot was maintained in the humanist play—expounded usually in the chorus, or at great length in the epilogue—but many of these traditional medieval figures were ascribed a new significance. John the Baptist's popularity soared among Protestant playwrights—for example, George Buchanan, *Baptistes* (performed c.1541–1542); Nicholas Grimald, *Archipropheta* (1546–1547)—since his career provided an exemplum for many sixteenth-century preachers whose proselytizing call for reform often fell on deaf ears. Other biblical subjects such as the story of Susanna, a topic especially favored by Protestant dramatists, served a variety of purposes: as an exemplum of marital fidelity for the Saxon pastor Paul Rebhun (c.1505–1546); as a forum for proper civic conduct for the Basel schoolteacher Sixt Birck; as an indictment of the civic and aristocratic authorities for the Tübingen court humanist Nicodemus Frischlin (1547–1590). In France, where civil war raged, humanist biblical dramas almost invariably contained a political message about the legitimacy of revolution, the nature of kingship, and the proper behavior for a courtier (e.g., Jean de La Taille, *Saül le furieux*, 1572; Robert Garnier, *Les Juives*, 1604).

Humanist biblical plays were not always sectarian, and in the most accomplished religious plays of the sixteenth century the playwright transcended the boundaries of didactic school theater to explore the complexity of faith. Gulielmus Gnapheus's *Acolastus*, on the prodigal son, was an inventive amalgamation of Roman characters and motifs with the Christian allegory of forgiveness and salvation. Although Gnapheus was closely involved with the early Reformation movement in Holland, his play is devoid of any overt proselytizing, and later in the century this work was performed in many Jesuit schools. Similarly, Théodore de Bèze's *Abraham sacrifiant* (1550) investigated the natural enmity between faith and reason (a conflict that later reappeared in the seventeenth-century biblical tragedies of the Netherlander Joost van den Vondel, 1587–1679), without any unambiguous references to Calvin, with whom he was closely allied.

Most sixteenth-century humanist religious plays did not so much attempt to move the spectators as to educate them. The dramas were rife with moralistic sayings (*sententiae*), tedious sermons, repetitious plots, unidimensional characterizations, and seemingly endless debates about religious and political topics. Despite this exemplary content, humanist dramas were not universally well received by members of both churches. Besides the potentially unsettling effect that any gathering of spectators could have on a civic community during this uncertain period, the biblical plays themselves were frequently censured for their profanation of scripture and visual representation of sin. Such criticisms are generally associated with the later Puritan critique of theater in the early seventeenth century (e.g., William Prynne, *Histriomastix*, 1632), but they were already being addressed a century earlier in the dedicatory letters to printed versions of humanist school plays. Luther had rejected such criticism by claiming that the Bible too contained many sinful episodes, but other Protestants, and even some Catholics (e.g., Carlo Borromeo, the late sixteenth-century archbishop of Milan), did not share his views. In France, Protestant biblical drama was effectively halted after 1572, when the Synod of Nîmes forbade all religious plays. In the Low Countries lascivious passages from early sixteenth-century biblical drama, such as the attempted seduction of Joseph by Potiphar's wife in *Joseph* (printed 1536) by the Amsterdam humanist Cornelius Crocus, were expurgated from later printings, and even the famed Christian Terence collection of Cornelius Schonaeus (*Christianus Terentius*) that began to appear in the 1590s contained emended versions of earlier biblical plays.

The Protestant attack on theater in England, from where most such evidence survives, encompassed both secular and sacred drama, although not at first, as recent scholarship has shown. The Elizabethan reaction against theater was not the work of anti-aesthetic, killjoy Puritans (who, however, as their seventeenth-century writings make plain, shared these views), but anti-Puritan moralists such as Philip Stubbes (fl. 1583–1591) and Stephen Gosson (1554–1624), who objected to the loss of control over theatrical performances that accompanied the establishment of professional theaters in 1576. Dramatic presentations, even those in the closed confines of the university, were regarded as endangerments to both the religious and socioeconomic order. With Sunday dramatic performances, the public theaters kept the crowds away from uplifting sermons in church, while plays on weekdays seduced laborers from their work. Professional actors were likened to vagabonds, and the fact that these male performers were compelled to play female roles was considered inimical to God's division of the sexes. These objections did not decrease with the strengthening of royal censorship in the early seventeenth century under James I, for the censors searched more for subversive political rather than religious content. But with the rise of Puritan influence in Parliament, all public theaters were ordered closed in 1642.

[*See also* Art *and* Popular Religion.]

BIBLIOGRAPHY

Abbé, Derek van. *Drama in Renaissance Germany and Switzerland.* Melbourne, 1961. Literary analysis of plays up to the 1550s, with limited reference to their polemical content. Especially useful for information about the many sixteenth-century Swiss playwrights.

Andrachuk, Gregory Peter. "The *Auto Sacramental* and the Reformation." *Journal of Hispanic Philology* 10 (1985), 7–38. Detailed exploration of the use of Corpus Christi plays to disseminate post-Tridentine dogma.

Bacon, Thomas I. *Martin Luther and the Drama.* Amsterdam, 1976. Convenient compilation of most quotations from Luther's collected works about drama.

Blackburn, Ruth H. *Biblical Drama under the Tudors.* The Hague, 1971. Consists chiefly of plot summaries of sixteenth-century religious plays with little regard for the sociohistorical context.

Bryant, James C. *Tudor Drama and Religious Controversy.* Macon, Ga., 1984. Literary account of the Protestant content of sixteenth-century plays.

Holstein, Hugo. *Die Reformation im Spiegelbilde der dramatischen Literatur des sechzehnten Jahrhunderts.* Reprint, Nieuwkoop, 1967. Classic study, outdated methodologically, but still useful for many arcane historical references.

Lebègue, Raymond. *La tragédie religieuse en France: Les débuts, 1514–1573.* Paris, 1929. Classic literary-historical account with exceptionally detailed summaries of most plays.

Le Hir, Yves. *Les drames bibliques de 1541 à 1600.* Grenoble, 1974. Detailed stylistic treatment of major dramatists.

Loukovitch, Kosta. *L'évolution de la tragédie religieuse classique en France.* Reprint, Geneva, 1977. Historical survey of seventeenth-century sacred drama, with much information unavailable elsewhere.

McKendrick, Melveena M. *Theatre in Spain, 1490–1700.* Cambridge, 1989. Best English-language survey; minimal reference to sacred theater.

Parente, James A., Jr. *Religious Drama and the Humanist Tradition: Christian Theater in Germany and the Netherlands, 1500–1680.* Leiden, 1987. Discusses the nature of humanist religious drama and its afterlife in seventeenth-century neoclassical theater.

Pieri, Marzia. *La nascita del teatro moderno in Italia tra XV e XVI secolo.* Turin, 1989. Contains chapter on early modern religious drama in Italy. Useful for information concerning religious theater and other dramatic forms.

Pineas, Rainer. *Tudor and Early Stuart Anti-Catholic Drama.* Nieuwkoop, 1972. Basic overview of the polemical content of several plays.

Street, J. S. *French Sacred Drama from Bèze to Corneille: Dramatic Forms and Their Purpose in Early Modern Theater.* Cambridge, 1983. Only English-language survey of French religious drama. Focuses primarily on the literary aspects of the plays.

Tydeman, William. *The Theatre of the Middle Ages.* Cambridge, 1978. Thorough survey of the many theatrical forms, with special emphasis on performance and the socioeconomic context.

Valentin, Jean-Marie. *Le théâtre des Jésuites dans les pays de langue allemande, 1554–1680.* 3 vols. Bern, 1978. Comprehensive survey of German Jesuit drama with special regard to its sociopolitical context.

Waite, Gary K. "Vernacular Drama and the Early Urban Reformation: The Chambers of Rhetoric in Amsterdam, 1520–1550." *Journal of Medieval and Renaissance Studies* 21 (1991), 187–206. Excellent treatment of the complex ties between civic organizations and early Protestantism.

Weaver, Elissa. "Spiritual Fun: A Study of Sixteenth-Century Tuscan Convent Theater." In *Women in the Middle Ages and the Renaissance: Literary and Historical Perspectives,* edited by Mary Beth Rose, pp. 173–205. Syracuse, N.Y., 1986.

White, Paul Whitfield. *Theatre and Reformation: Protestantism, Patronage, and Playing in Tudor England.* Cambridge, 1992. Excellent literary-historical analysis of the Protestant use of drama to disseminate their doctrines.

JAMES A. PARENTE, JR.

DRYANDER, Franciscus. *See* Enzinas, Francisco de.

DUDLEY, John (1504?–1553), earl of Warwick and duke of Northumberland, English soldier, political leader, and supporter of the mid-Tudor Reformation. The son of Edmund Dudley, the disgraced minister of Henry VII, John Dudley first came into prominence as a soldier and a privy councillor during the reign of Henry VIII (r. 1509–1547). Dudley's influence was greatest after the accession of Edward VI (r. 1547–1553), when he was active in the king's council and at court. Until 1549 Dudley supported the leadership of Protector Somerset; afterward the two became political opponents. An army commanded by Dudley defeated rebels led by Robert Kett outside Norwich in 1549. Because the rebellions of that year were inspired by Protestant and Catholic extremists who threatened the government and the state church, Dudley became a vigorous advocate of law and order. He used his political influence to assist Protestant reformers who wished to move beyond the Henrician religious settlement and bring the Church of England into the mainstream of the Continental Reformation. Dudley's patronage was important in securing episcopal appointments for two leading reformers, John Hooper and John Harley. Dudley also recommended John Knox for a bishopric, but the latter declined the offer. The personal religious views of Dudley, like most of the English nobility of the period, are difficult to determine. He wrote nothing on religious questions but until his death perceived himself as a friend of the reformers. Dudley shared the conviction of most English clergy and nobles that the Anabaptists posed a threat to the country, but his opposition seems to have focused more on the Anabaptists' alleged rejection of the traditional social order than their theology.

After the king's death in 1553, Dudley unsuccessfully attempted to safeguard the Protestant church by promoting the claim of his daughter-in-law, Lady Jane Grey, to the throne. Before he was executed for treason he repudiated his former religious allegiance and stated in vague language that he accepted the Catholic religion. The government of Mary Tudor published Dudley's final words and used them to discredit him and the Protestant cause.

BIBLIOGRAPHY

Beer, Barrett L. *Northumberland: The Political Career of John Dudley, Earl of Warwick and Duke of Northumberland.* Kent, Ohio, 1973. The standard account of Northumberland's political career under Henry VIII and Edward VI.

———. "Northumberland: The Myth of the Wicked Duke and the Historical John Dudley." *Albion* 11.1 (1979), 1–14. Critical reassessment of Northumberland's historical reputation.

Bush, M. L. *The Government Policy of Protector Somerset.* Montreal, 1975. An important reappraisal of Somerset's policy and leadership during the first two years of the reign of Edward VI.

Hoak, Dale. "Rehabilitating the Duke of Northumberland: Politics and Political Control, 1549–53." In *The Mid-Tudor Polity c.1540–1560,* edited by Robert Tittler and Jennifer Loach, pp. 29–51. Totowa, N.J., 1980.

Jordan, W. K. *Edward VI: The Threshold of Power.* London, 1970.

———. *Edward VI: The Young King.* Cambridge, Mass., 1971. The most detailed account of the reign.

BARRETT L. BEER

DUIFHUIS, Hubert (c.1531–1581), Dutch "Libertine" opponent of Calvinism and reformer of the Jacobskerk in Utrecht. Born to a well-to-do family outside The Hague, Duifhuis studied at the University of Louvain. He became a priest, served as curate in the Saint Barbara Gasthuis in Delft, and in 1557 received the prestigious pastorate of the Saint Laurenskerk in Rotterdam. In the 1560s Duifhuis met Hendrik Niclaes and became attached to his spiritualist sect, the Family of Love. In 1566 Duifhuis secretly married his housekeeper, Kryntje Pietersdr. Accused of heresy, Duifhuis fled Rotterdam in 1572 and made for Cologne. There he and his friend Cornelis Jansen quarreled with Niclaes, refusing to acknowledge the latter as uniquely inspired or to submit to his authority. Other followers of Niclaes soon did the same. This group subsequently looked for inspiration to the less authoritarian Hendrik Jansen van Barrevelt, known as Hiël, another former follower of Niclaes. Duifhuis later edited Barrevelt's *Acker-schat* (c.1581) for publication.

In 1574 Duifhuis became copastor of the Jacobskerk parish in Utrecht. He began to deviate from Catholic practices in 1577, and in June 1578 he broke publicly with the Roman Catholic church. Opposed by Utrecht's five chapters, Duifhuis demanded and soon received firm commitments of support from Utrecht's city magistrates. He then went on to establish in his parish a unique church, which he and others considered Reformed yet which was distinctly un-Calvinist. It had no consistory, elders, or ecclesiastical discipline and admitted everyone to Communion. Calvinists therefore called it a "Libertine" church. Duifhuis also refused to acknowledge the authority of Calvinist classes and synods. He was hostile to catechisms and confessions of faith, denying them any binding authority. He rendered services to his parishioners on an a-confessional basis and adamantly opposed religious persecution by any power. With this exception, Duifhuis granted Christian magistrates extensive authority in religious affairs; many historians accordingly consider him an Erastian. Although Duifhuis died in 1581, the Jacobskerk survived until 1586 as an independent entity and a rival to Utrecht's Calvinist congregation. It was the only fully independent "Libertine" church in the Netherlands, realizing ideals cherished by Libertines elsewhere.

Historians have traditionally considered Duifhuis an Erasmian humanist and viewed the Jacobskerk as an attempt to find a middle path between Catholicism and Calvinism. More recent studies, however, have emphasized two other sources of Duifhuis's piety: Protestantism and spiritualism. Like other Dutch Libertines, Duifhuis turned bona fide Protestant arguments against the Dutch Calvinist establishment. For example, Duifhuis argued that Calvinist discipline was an oppressive holdover from Catholicism, a tool of clerical tyranny contrary to "Christian freedom." Meanwhile, Duifhuis exhorted people to seek salvation not through institutions but through spiritual rebirth and mystical union with God. Duifhuis thus preached a Protestant but distinctly anticonfessional message.

With the possible exception of an anonymous pamphlet, Duifhuis did not publish any writings of his own. Twenty-one of his sermons have survived in seventeenth-century transcriptions.

BIBLIOGRAPHY

Hamilton, Alastair. *The Family of Love.* Cambridge, 1981. Reveals Duifhuis's ties to the Family of Love.

Kaplan, Benjamin J. *Calvinists and Libertines: Confession and Community in Utrecht, 1578–1620.* Oxford, forthcoming. Examines Duifhuis's message, its context, and its impact.

———. "Hubert Duifhuis and the Nature of Dutch Libertinism."

Tijdschrift voor geschiedenis 105 (1992), 1–29. Emphasizes the significance of Protestantism and spiritualism in Duifhuis's piety.

Wiarda, Jan. *Huibert Duifhuis, de Prediker van Saint Jacob.* Amsterdam, 1858. Only existing monograph on Duifhuis, combining biography with a mostly formalistic analysis of Duifhuis's sermons.

BENJAMIN J. KAPLAN

DU MOULIN, Charles (also Du Molin; 1500–1566), Gallican jurisconsult who played a significant role in the development of sixteenth-century law. Born into a family of Parisian jurists, Du Moulin was educated in Paris and then earned a doctorate in law from the University of Orléans. In Paris Du Moulin enjoyed success as a legal consultant. Author of commentaries on customs, he helped codify French common law. He attacked feudal organization and undermined the hierarchical structure of society. He assumed people were free, subject only to the king, and he favored a strong monarchy. By conviction a lifelong supporter of French traditions, useful to the monarchy for enforcing its claims and institutions, he traveled in high circles.

Du Moulin read Martin Luther, Philipp Melanchthon, and Heinrich Bullinger and became a Protestant in the early 1540s. In 1551 he composed in Latin an attack on papal procedures for granting benefices in France, *Commentarius analyticus in Edictum Henrici II. . . contra parvas datas et abusus Curiae Romanae, circa beneficia Ecclesiastica . . .*, usually known in the literature by an abbreviation of the title of the French edition as *Commentaire de l'édit des petites dates.* As a result, he had to flee to Basel and then to Lausanne and Geneva where he became friends with John Calvin. In 1553 he traveled to Neuchâtel and Strasbourg and then to Tübingen, where, as professor of law, he provoked opposition because he interjected theology into his lectures. He became counselor to Count George at Montbéliard in 1554. He taught at Dôle in 1555/56 and briefly at Besançon. By 1556 Du Moulin was disenchanted with Calvinism, but he remained on good terms with Parisian Calvinists, and from 1557 to 1562 lived in Paris. In 1562, his house pillaged, he fled to Orléans.

Reformed pastors rejected his catechism (1563), which conformed more to the Augsburg Confession than to that of Geneva. Some of them accused him, falsely, of being the author of an anonymous seditious tract. He returned to Paris in 1564 and, without royal permission, attacked the decrees of the Council of Trent in print, *Conseil sur le fait du Concile de Trente.* This publication got him in trouble with the Parlement of Paris, and he was imprisoned by the court in June. He was released, with the intervention of the king, on 7 July. In 1565 he published *Collatio et unio quatuor Evangelistarum . . .* (Collation and Union of the Four Gospels . . .), intended to correct Calvin's collation of the Gospels. By now at odds with the Calvinists, he objected to consistories, synods, and dictation from Geneva. He died of asthma, perhaps a deathbed convert to Catholicism.

BIBLIOGRAPHY

Primary Source

Du Moulin, Charles. *Caroli Molinaei . . . omnia quae extant opera . . . & quàm fieri potuit diligentissimè purgata.* 5 vols. Paris, 1681. Works of Du Moulin; contains Julien Brodeau's biography.

Secondary Sources

Church, William. *Constitutional Thought in Sixteenth-Century France: A Study in the Evolution of Ideas.* Reprint, New York, 1969. Contains an analysis of Du Moulin's legal thought.

Haag, Eugène, and Émile Haag. "Du Moulin ou Du Molin." In *La France protestante ou vies des protestants français qui se sont fait un nom dans l'histoire depuis les premiers temps de la Réformation jusqu'à la reconnaissance du principe de la liberté des cultes par l'Assemblée nationale.* Vol. 4. Reprint, Geneva, 1966. See pp. 411–419 for a brief summary of the life and works of Du Moulin.

Kingdon, Robert M. *Geneva and the Consolidation of the French Protestant Movement, 1564–1572: A Contribution to the History of Congregationalism, Presbyterianism, and Calvinist Resistance Theory.* Madison, Wis., 1967. Contains a summary of Du Moulin's life and place in history, concentrating on his relationships with Geneva and the Reformed church.

Reulos, Michel. "Le jurisconsulte Charles du Moulin en conflit avec les églises réformées de France." *Bulletin de la Société de l'histoire du protestantisme français* 100 (1954), 1–12. An analysis of Du Moulin's disagreements with Calvinism and the Reformed churches.

Thireau, Jean-Louis. *Charles Du Moulin, 1500–1566: Étude sur les sources, la méthode, les idées politiques et économiques d'un juriste de la renaissance.* Geneva, 1980. Modern biography of Du Moulin and study of his works and political and economic ideas; chronological table of his correspondence.

JEANNINE E. OLSON

DUPLESSIS-MORNAY, Philippe (1549–1623), baron of La Forêt-sur-Sèvre, lord Du Plessis-Marly, theologian, diplomat, publicist, Huguenot captain, and counselor to Henry IV. Encountering both Catholic and Protestant ideas in his childhood, he received a humanist education in Paris and furthered his training in trips to Germany, Italy, and the Netherlands. At the age of twenty-three he wrote a discourse evaluating Gaspard II de Coligny's plan for military intervention in the Low Countries. Following the Saint Bartholomew's Day Massacre he at first opposed the new party of the politiques, but later, under the influence of François de la Noue, he joined the party along with Francis, duke of Alençon. In 1567, in his anonymous *Remonstrance aux États de Blois pour la paix, sous la personne d'un catholique Romain* (Entreaty for Peace to the Estates of Blois, in the Person of a Roman Catholic), he asserted that it would be in the interest of Catholics to tolerate Reformed worship. Nonetheless, from this time on Duplessis-Mornay hoped that a "holy and free, general or national" council would be convened between Protestants and Catholics, with the purpose of reforming from within the ancient edifice of the Catholic church of France. Parallel to this blueprint for general concord, he also devised a plan for union among Protestants that called for the convening of a synod at which theologians of the various Protestant denominations stemming from Protestantism would participate part. This plan went hand in hand with a proposed military league of all the Protestant princes against the Catholic forces. As a defender of the Reformed religion and of the interests of France, he opposed any foreign intervention by Roman Catholics, whether from the Holy See or from Spain. To this end he published an *Advertissement sur la réception et la publication du Concile de Trente* (Advisory on the Reception and Publication of the Council of Trent; 1583). Having entered the service of Henry, king of Navarre (Henry IV of France after 1589) in 1577, he was sent on several embassies to England, Scotland, and the Netherlands to ask Protestant princes to come to the aid of the Reformed Christians.

During this time he composed a number of important works, including *Traité de l'Église* (Treatise on the Church; 1578) in which he asserts that the Reformed faithful should separate from the church of Rome because it was heretical and schismatic and because the pope, who "under this false title tyrannizes the world, is the Anti-Christ." His *Traité sur la vérité de la religion chrétienne* (Treatise on the Truth of the Christian Religion; 1581), an extremely original work, represents an impressive effort to find in the works of classical and profane authors, both Greek and Roman, confirmation of the truths of the Christian religion already found in the religion of Israel and in the Old Testament. Thus, using arguments drawn from rationalism and from ancient philosophy (including rabbinic, Talmudic, and Cabbalistic sources), Duplessis-Mornay attempts to identify the foundations of the basic Christian truths—monotheism, the Trinity, and the immortality of the soul. From his studies he concludes "that the truth, when it is revealed, enlightens reason, and reason is thereby awakened to support the truth; reason in no way brings down faith so that we can reach it, but rather raises us up as on another's shoulders as it were, to make us see faith and take it as our guide, as the only one from whom we should learn of our salvation." It is likely that Duplessis-Mornay was also one of the main editors of the anonymous work *Vindiciae contra Tyrannos* (Claims against Tyrants; 1579).

From 1582, thanks to his talents as a negotiator and moderator, he became the most trusted adviser of Henry of Navarre in the areas of politics, strategy, economics, theology, and diplomacy. In addition to editing the instructions for Navarre and his ambassadors, he represented the king at the synods of Vitré (1582) and Montauban (1584) and at the political assembly of La Rochelle (1582), the latter of which entrusted him with responsibility for Reformed finances. In 1589, after successfully negotiating the truce between Henry III and Henry of Navarre, he was appointed governor of Saumur. After he became councillor of state under Navarre, now Henry IV, Duplessis-Mornay drafted in 1590 the two "irrevocable" edicts of union of 1585 and 1588. In view of the future religious instruction of Henry IV, Duplessis-Mornay envisaged an "expedient"—a debate between Protestant and Catholic theologians that might serve as a prelude to the "good, holy, free and legitimate" council, which was an idea he never abandoned. He was in addition one—perhaps the most important—of the Protestant negotiators of the peace that culminated in the Edict of Nantes (1598).

Also in 1598, while endeavoring to mediate and conciliate Catholics, he nonetheless published the treatise *De l'institution de l'Eucharistie en l'Église ancienne* (On the Institution of the Eucharist in the Ancient Church), in which he vigorously attacked the Roman Antichrist. This attack incurred the wrath of Henry IV and provoked a fiery response by the bishop of Evreux, Jacques Davy Du Perron, who challenged Duplessis-Mornay to defend his theses in a public debate. This debate took place at Fontainebleau on 2 April 1600 and concluded, by Catholic accounts, in a victory for the bishop.

Nevertheless, Duplessis-Mornay never ceased working for religious moderation and national reconciliation because of the problems posed by the application of the Edict of Nantes. His conception of general concord was again witnessed in his article "Pour le concile" (For the Council; 1600). He directed all his efforts toward the renewal of Protestantism and founded the academy of Saumur in 1604. After the assassination of Henry IV, he urged all Reformed Christians to remain united ("Je vous conjure . . . de vous embrasser tous" [I urge all of you . . . to embrace one another]) and railed against the Jesuits as the "parricides" of the king. In 1611 he published the *Mystère d'iniquité*, a new attack against the "omnipotence" of the pope; among other things, Duplessis-Mornay maintained that the pope had no right to impinge upon political sovereignty. He presided over the political assembly of Saumur (1611), attempting to bridge the internal dissensions of the Reformed party between the dukes of Bouillon and Roban. Despite the armed insurgence of the Protestant dukes, of which he openly disapproved, Duplessis-Mornay managed to maintain good relations with Marie de Médicis and Louis XIII.

Duplessis-Mornay advocated moderation at the assemblies of Grenoble (1615) and La Rochelle (1616), as at every other occasion. He defended his co-religionists against those who accused them of wanting to set up "a state within a state" (1613), "to diminish royal authority" (1618), and "to establish a democracy" (1619). He constantly warned the faithful against "meddling in the affairs of the state or confusing a purely religious cause with a civil one," but his advice was not heeded. He did not allow himself to become involved in the uprisings of the Protestant princes between 1615 and 1621, but his pacifist attitudes were to lead to his being dismissed from his office as governor of Saumur. Moreover, his castle was ransacked and his library was scattered. He spent the last three years of his life in his castle at La Forêt-sur-Sèvre.

BIBLIOGRAPHY

Primary Sources

Du Plessis-Mornay, Philippe. *Mémoires et correspondances.* Edited by Auguis and La Fontenelle de Vaudoré. 12 vols. Paris, 1824–1825.

———. *Mémoires de Messire Ph. de Mornay.* Amsterdam, 1651. Contains works from 1600 to 1623.

———. *Suite des Lettres et Mémoires de Messire Philippe de Mornay.* Amsterdam, 1652. Contains works from 1618 to 1623.

Secondary Sources

Dompnier, B. "Histoire religieuse chez les controversistes réformés au début du XVIIe siècle: L'apport de Du Plessis-Mornay et Rivet." In *Historiographie et Réforme,* edited by Philippe Joutard, pp. 16–36. Paris, 1977.

Herman, A. L. "Protestant Churches in a Catholic Kingdom: Political Assemblies in the Thought of Philippe Du Plessis-Mornay." *Sixteenth Century Journal* 21 (1990), 543–557.

Licques, David de. *Histoire de la vie de M. Ph. de Mornay, Seigneur du Plessis Marly, etc.* Leyde, 1647.

Mémoires de Mme de Mornay (1868–1869). Preface by F. Guizot. 2 vols. Reprint, New York, 1968.

Patry, Raoul. *Philippe du Plessis-Mornay: Un huguenot homme d'état, 1549–1623.* Paris, 1933.

MARIO TURCHETTI

Translated from French by Robert E. Shillenn

DÜRER, Albrecht (1471–1528), printmaker and painter in northern Europe during the fifteenth and sixteenth centuries. His artistic importance stems from his outstanding craftsmanship and his ability to integrate Italian Renaissance ideas on human proportion and perspective into a German context. He was also the first northern European artist to write treatises in German on art theory. A wide range of religious, mythological, and allegorical subjects are found in his prints and paintings. The woodcut series *Apocalypse* (1498), *Life of Mary* (1511), and *Passion of Christ* (1511) are indicative of his religious images. His portraiture includes images of humanist scholars, such as Desiderius Erasmus (1467?–1536) and Philipp Melanchthon (1497–1560).

Residing in Nuremberg, Dürer was trained by his goldsmith father, Albrecht Dürer the Elder (1427–1502), and by another Nuremberg painter and printmaker, Michael Wolgemut (1434/37–1519). Not content with the traditional view of the artist as a craftsman, Dürer was part of a humanist circle of Nuremberg scholars that included Willibald Pirckheimer (1470–1530) and Conradus Celtis (1459–1508). Also important to Dürer's artistic development were his bachelor's journey (1490–1494), two trips to Venice (1494–1495 and 1505–1507), and a trip to the Netherlands (1520–1521). The elector of Saxony, Frederick III (1463–1525), and the Holy Roman Emperor, Maximilian I (1459–1519), were two of his many patrons.

Dürer was acquainted with leaders of the Reformation in Nuremberg, such as Lazarus Spengler (1479–1534), Pirckheimer, and Melanchthon, and was aware of many pamphlets by Martin Luther (1483–1546). Impressed and comforted by Luther's ideas, Dürer was deeply upset when in 1521 he heard the rumor that Luther had been kidnapped. No direct evidence exists to support a hypothesis that the two men met. Until Dürer's death in 1528 he had both Catholic and Protestant patrons, and recent scholarship suggests the infeasibility of placing Dürer into either faction.

BIBLIOGRAPHY

Hutchison, Jane Campbell. *Albrecht Dürer: A Biography.* Princeton, 1990. Chronologically evaluates the surviving documentation associated with Dürer's life. Includes material about Dürer's relationship with Luther. Extensive bibliography.

Panofsky, Erwin. *The Life and Art of Albrecht Dürer.* 4th ed. Princeton, 1971. Chronologically presented interpretations of most images. Challenging Panofsky's conclusions is often the focus of recent Dürer scholarship.

Strauss, Walter L., ed. *Albrecht Dürer: Woodcuts and Wood Blocks.* New York, 1980. Over two hundred woodcuts illustrated with brief discussions. Extensive bibliography.

———. *The Intaglio Prints of Albrecht Dürer: Engravings, Etchings, and Drypoints.* New York, 1981. Over one hundred intaglio prints illustrated. Includes provenances and brief bibliography.

Strieder, Peter. *Albrecht Dürer: Paintings, Prints, Drawings.* New York, 1982. Eighty paintings placed thematically within the context of Renaissance Nuremberg.

MARY EM KIRN

DUSANUS. *See* Musculus, Wolfgang.

DUTCH BRETHREN. *See* Doopsgezinden.

DUTCH REVOLT. *See* Revolt of the Netherlands.

E

EARLY BOURGEOIS REVOLUTION. *See* Marxism.

EASTERN ORTHODOXY. After centuries of geographical attrition under the onslaught of the forces of Islam, the Byzantine empire collapsed with the fall of Constantinople on 29 May 1453. Following three days of murder, pillaging, and atrocities, Muhammad II proclaimed his policy of tolerance toward Christians. A special head tax was imposed on Christians. Although half the churches in Constantinople were converted to mosques (including the magnificent Church of Holy Wisdom, Hagia Sophia), the Orthodox church was still permitted to conduct worship and to administer its own affairs under the patriarch, who became the ethnarch of the Christian people. Within a decade Greece and the Balkans were also overrun. Thus began the "Turcocratia," the era under the "Turkish yoke," which was to last into the nineteenth century, when Greece and the Balkan states fought their way to independence from a crumbling and corrupt Ottoman empire.

The initial tolerance did not last long. Christians were a despised second class—"cattle" under Islamic law. Their condition gradually worsened, depending on the whim of the ruling sultan. There was enormous social and economic pressure to convert to Islam, while the penalty for conversion to Christianity was death. Many Christians remained faithful; more eventually converted to Islam; and some reconverted to Christianity, often publicly proclaiming their return to Christ and seeking torture and martyrdom to atone for their sin of apostasy. A new category of saints was introduced during the Turcocratia, the "New Martyrs."

Public expression of the faith was restricted or forbidden, and Christianity was to be as invisible as possible. What kept the church alive in the hearts of the faithful during these dark centuries were the liturgy, the sacraments, and the liturgical services, all rich in scriptural, spiritual, and doctrinal content. Theological education became largely a repetition of the past and existed only in some monasteries, and doctrinal and liturgical tradition was zealously adhered to. Christianity was reduced to a religion of survival. The only independent Orthodox state was now Russia, and with the fall of Constantinople, Moscow became the "Third Rome" and assumed the role of the grand protector of Orthodoxy. During a journey to Moscow, Patriarch Jeremias II in 1589 added a sixth patriarchate to the ancient pentarchy and created the first of the modern patriarchates by elevating the metropolitan of Moscow to the rank of patriarch.

Eastern Orthodoxy and Roman Catholicism. The Eastern (Orthodox) and the Western (Roman Catholic) churches had sought on a number of occasions during the Middle Ages to resolve their differences and to restore communion after the Great Schism of 1054, most notably at the councils of Lyon (1274) and Florence (1438). Florence had proclaimed a reunion, which in effect amounted to a capitulation of the Easterners, who, with the Turks at their doorstep, hoped for Western military assistance. When the emperor and the bishops returned to Constantinople, the "False Union" was overwhelmingly rejected by clergy and people, and many inhabitants of the city interpreted its subsequent fall to God's righteous chastisement upon the Byzantine Orthodox for having compromised the faith at Florence.

Now, with Orthodoxy in a debilitated condition, and with the political/military incentive for reunion having vanished, the Roman church during the sixteenth century adopted a different approach and sent skillful propagandists to the Middle East and to eastern Europe in the hope of achieving individual and group conversions rather than corporate reunion between the churches. The presence of these proselytizers, and the bitter memories of the Fourth Crusade's sack of Constantinople in 1204 and of Florence's constrained reunion, made Orthodox increasingly wary of any contact with the Roman church.

Largely through the efforts of the Jesuits in the Polish-Lithuanian Commonwealth, the first of a series of unions between Rome and pockets of Orthodox was proclaimed at Brest-Litovsk in 1596. The conditions of the union, the same terms as at Florence, were that the Orthodox must accept all Roman doctrines at variance with their own, but the Orthodox were allowed to keep their own liturgical practices and languages as well as their own distinctive customs (most notably, a married clergy). The Union of Brest-Litovsk was opposed by a minority of bishops and by the majority of priests, while many simple folk were bewildered and confused about the points of dissension and merely sought to cling tenaciously to their familiar ways. Nevertheless, the "Eastern-Rite Catholic church" had now become the legal church body in Poland, and recalcitrant Orthodox saw their property confiscated and endured enormous pressure to enter into the union.

Subsequent unions were effected during the next two centuries in the Austro-Hungarian empire, Romania, and the Middle East. Roman practices gradually were introduced and the guaranteed rights encroached upon. The existence of these "Eastern-Rite" or "Byzantine-Rite" Catholic churches persists to the present day as a source of tension between the Roman Catholic and the Eastern Orthodox church, and whether they are a model for or an obstacle to ecumenical rapprochement remains highly controversial.

Eastern Orthodoxy and Protestantism. Martin Luther was well aware of the basic issues that divided the "Greek church" (as he referred to it) and the medieval papacy: the *filioque*, papal authority, purgatory, indulgences, Communion under both kinds, the marriage of clergy, and various other doctrines and disciplines. In his conflicts with the Roman church, Luther called attention to the witness of the Greek church as an ancient and apostolic church that was in substantive agreement with certain of his positions against Rome.

In the Leipzig Disputation (1519) Luther asserted that papal supremacy was founded on medieval Western decretals and that the early church accorded the bishop of Rome only a primacy of honor; the Greek church in the past and in the present never recognized papal supremacy, so it could never then or now be considered a common doctrine of the universal church. When Johann Eck retorted that the Greeks were schismatics and heretics, Luther replied that the Greek church had produced more and better theologians than the Roman. The same reference to the Greek church appears a number of times in Luther's writings. In a letter to Georg Spalatin (1519), as in the disputations on indulgences (1518), Luther observed that "the Greeks gave an extraordinary explanation of their faith" at Florence by rejecting indulgences and purgatory as Roman innovations. Elsewhere, Luther points to the Greek church as having always offered the Communion elements of both bread and wine to the people, as having never introduced the multiplication of private daily masses, as having always employed the vernacular language in the liturgy, and as having always recognized the freedom of the clergy to be married.

Philipp Melanchthon, Luther's friend and faculty colleague, was a linguist and humanist who had profound respect for the Latin and Greek church fathers, whom he quotes fondly and frequently. This disposition inclined him to have a high regard for the Eastern church. In his extensive contributions to the Lutheran symbolical writings, most of Melanchthon's interest in the witness of the Eastern church concerned the absence there of the aforementioned Western medieval eucharistic practices to which both Luther and he objected. For example, "even today in Greek parishes there are no private Masses, but only one public Mass, and this only on Sundays and feasts. In monasteries there is a daily, though public, Mass" (*Apologie*).

Moreover, in the summer of 1559, the year before he died, Melanchthon added a new dimension and provided a foundation for later Lutheran-Orthodox relations. At that time he entertained as a house guest Demetrios Mysos, a deacon sent to Wittenberg by the Patriarch Joasaph of Constantinople to gather firsthand information about the new religious movement in Germany. The two conceived the idea of translating the Augsburg Confession into Greek. But the *Augustana Graeca* that resulted is no literal translation: while not misrepresenting Lutheran teachings, it contains numerous and extensive additions and paraphrases, sprinkled with distinctively Greek hieratic liturgical and doctrinal expressions, to present more favorably the cardinal teachings of the Reformation to a Greek Orthodox readership. The *Augustana Graeca* apparently never reached Constantinople at this time, for Mysos died on his journey home.

The Württemberg Lutherans centered at Tübingen, headed by the theologians Jakob Andreae and Lucas II Osiander, and the classicist and philhellene Martin Crusius, desired to establish contact with the Greek church. The Lutherans were convinced that they, rather than Rome, were the true apostolic and catholic church, and thus to establish contact with the venerable Greek church, to enlist its support against the papacy, and perhaps even to enter into communion with this apostolic church would have been a sensational victory. Thus in 1575 they sent the *Augustana Graeca* to Patriarch Jeremias II (d. 1595), asking his opinion. There ensued over the next six years a friendly but candid exchange of extensive doctrinal correspondence (three letters from both sides totaling over four hundred printed pages). Prominent topics discussed included the authority of scripture and tradition; the *filioque*; the nature of the church; grace, free will, and synergism; justification, faith, and good works; eucharistic practices; the priesthood and the ministry; prayers for the departed; the invocation of saints; feasts and fasting; and monasticism. Except for those doctrines and customs of the Roman church that the East had never accepted, the changes in church teaching and polity advocated by the Lutherans were rejected by the Orthodox, who thus implicitly agreed on most issues with the Catholics.

Since Luther had cited at the very dawn of the Reformation the example of the Greek church wherever it could be utilized in polemics with the Catholics, the points had already been made, and the other reformers had little left to add. Greek clerics visited western Europe and studied at Roman Catholic, Lutheran, Anglican, and Reformed universities, returning home often with either admiration or antipathy for the West. Further substantive ecumenical contacts between the churches would await later centuries.

BIBLIOGRAPHY

Benz, Ernst. *The Eastern Orthodox Church.* Chicago, 1963.

———. *Wittenberg und Byzanz: Zur Begegnung und Auseinandersetzung der Reformation und der Östlich-orthodoxen Kirche.* 2d ed. Munich, 1971.

Jorgenson, Wayne James. *The Augustana Graeca and the Correspondence between the Tübingen Lutherans and Patriarch Jeremias: Scripture and Tradition in Theological Methodology.* Ann Arbor, 1979.

Karmiris, Joannes. *Orthodoxy and Protestantism* [in Greek]. Athens, 1937.

Mastrantonis, George. *Augsburg and Constantinople.* Brookline, Mass., 1982.

Meyendorff, John. *The Orthodox Church.* Rev. ed. Crestwood, N.Y., 1960.

Schmemann, Alexander. *The Historical Road of Eastern Orthodoxy.* Reprint, Crestwood, N.Y., 1977.

Ware, Timothy Kallistos. *Eustratios Argenti: A Study of the Greek Church under Turkish Rule.* Willits, Calif., 1974.

———. *The Orthodox Church.* Rev. ed. London, 1991.

WAYNE JAMES JORGENSON

EBER, Paul (1511–1569), professor at the University of Wittenberg, pastor of the city church and general superintendent of electoral Saxony, and student and then colleague and close friend of Philipp Melanchthon. Born the son of a tailor in Kitzingen, Bavaria, Eber attended school in Ansbach and Nuremberg, where he studied with the humanist scholars Joachim Camerarius and Eobanus Hessus. Seriously injured in a fall that stunted his growth, as well as weakening and deforming his body, Eber was strong in spiritual and intellectual gifts. Support from citizens of Kitzingen and Nuremberg enabled him in 1532 to attend the University of Wittenberg, where Melanchthon soon became his mentor. He received his master of arts degree in 1536 and joined the faculty the following year, becoming professor of Latin in 1541. Also in 1541 Eber married, eventually fathering thirteen children, only four of whom survived him. As one of three professors who refused to leave Wittenberg during the Schmalkald War, Eber gained wide respect for his courage. In 1557 he became professor of Hebrew and preacher at the castle church and in 1558 succeeded Johannes Bugenhagen as pastor of the city church and general superintendent of electoral Saxony. He was promoted to doctor of theology in 1559 and joined the theology faculty.

Eber was the author of several historical and theological writings and, along with Georg Major, of a German-Latin Bible containing Martin Luther's translation and a revised Vulgate. He composed several well-known hymns, including "Wenn wir in höchsten Nöten sein." With other Philippists (adherents of Melanchthon's positions), he debated with the Gnesio-Lutherans on adiaphora, synergism, and the Eucharist. His position on Christ's presence in the sacrament changed from a Calvinist to an evangelical one. Along with Melanchthon, he participated in the Colloquy of Worms in 1557 with Calvinist theologians, and in 1568–1569 he attended the Colloquy of Altenburg. As Melanchthon's disciple, he sought to defend his mentor and to mediate between Philippists and Gnesio-Lutherans.

BIBLIOGRAPHY

Buchwald, D. Georg. *D. Paul Eber: Der Freund, Mitarbeiter und Nachfolger der Reformatoren; Ein Bild seines Lebens und Wirkens.* Leipzig, 1897.

Sixt, Christian Heinrich. *Dr. Paul Eber, der Schüler, Freund und Amtsgenosse der Reformatoren.* Heidelberg, 1843.

MARILYN J. HARRAN

ECCLESIASTICAL COURTS. *See* Courts, *article on* Church Courts.

ECCLESIASTICAL OFFICES. *See* Church Offices.

ECK, Johann (1486–1543), German Catholic theologian best known for his opposition to the Protestant reformers. Born Johann Maier in the Swabian village of Eck, he entered the University of Heidelberg in 1498 at the age of eleven. Thereafter he studied at Tübingen (master of arts, 1501), Cologne, and Freiburg (doctor of theology, 1510). In 1510 he moved to the University of Ingolstadt in Bavaria, where he received a second doctorate and assumed a position on the theology faculty. He soon became the dominant theological force at Ingolstadt and retained his position and dominance there until his death. Soon after going to Ingolstadt he became a leader in the reform of the university's philosophy curriculum. He was ordained to the priesthood in 1508 and was pastor of the Church of Our Lady in Ingolstadt from 1525 to 1532 and from 1538 to 1540.

Eck's most significant early work of theology was the *Chrysopassus* (1514), a treatise on predestination in which he argues that God predestines to rewards and punishments on the basis of foreknowledge of human merits and demerits. In this work Eck espoused positions on merit and free will that would soon be under attack from Luther and other Protestants.

Whereas at Freiburg Eck had identified himself with the nominalists, at Ingolstadt he adopted a more eclectic position among the schools. In the *Chrysopassus* he expressed a preference for the Franciscans Bonaventure (d. 1274) and Duns Scotus (d. 1308) but said he would not be a slavish disciple of any. Though willing to draw from a wide range of theologians, he was more familiar with the writings of Franciscans and nominalists than of Dominicans.

Eck's early years reveal other interests besides theology. He published works on logic (*Bursa pavonis,* 1507; *In summulas Petri Hispani,* 1516; *Elementarius dialectice,*1517) and on Aristotle (1517, 1519, 1520). He read geography and canon law. He also entered the discussion on economics, arguing that Christians may legitimately charge a modest interest on loans.

Luther's Ninety-five Theses (1517) determined the subsequent direction of Eck's career. At the request of the Bishop of Eichstätt, Gabriel von Eyb, Eck wrote a critical response to the theses, a response that was published even though Eck insisted he had intended it only for private use. Subsequent exchanges between Ingolstadt and Wittenberg led directly to the Leipzig Disputation (1519), in which Eck debated with Luther and his Wittenberg colleague Andreas Bodenstein von Karlstadt (1480–1541). Soon after, Eck journeyed to Rome and helped draft the papal bull *Exsurge Domine,* which condemned forty-one propositions drawn from Luther's works and threatened excommunication. In 1520 he and Girolamo Aleander were commissioned special nuncios to publish the bull in the empire.

Eck devoted much of the rest of his life to opposing the Protestants in Germany and Switzerland. Most of his later publications serve this purpose. Some are defenses of such specific doctrines and practices of the tradition as papal authority (*De primatu Petri,* 1520), purgatory (*De purgatorio,* 1523), penance (*De satisfactione* and *De initio poenitentiae,* both 1523), and the sacrificial character of the Mass (*De sacrificio missae,* 1526). *The Enchiridion* (published in 1525 and more than a hundred times thereafter) was a manual intended to refute a range of common Protestant "errors." It was Eck's most widely circulated work. Beginning in 1530 he published, first in German and then in Latin translation, cycles of homilies intended for use against the reformers. His German translation of the Bible, produced at least partly to counter Luther's translation, appeared in 1537.

In addition to publishing against the Protestants, Eck engaged in public disputations with them, though at times he expressed doubts about the efficacy of this tactic. Eck participated in serious theological discussion with Protestants at the imperial diets of Augsburg (1530) and Regensburg (Ratisbon, 1541), where the emperor and the princes struggled for religious unity. When the Protestant princes presented their confession (the Augsburg Confession) at Augsburg, Eck was the principal author of a response, the Confutatio, on behalf of the emperor. Though conciliatory in tone and expressing agreement with many articles of the Augsburg Confession, the Confutatio nevertheless disagreed with a number of points and contributed to the diet's rejection of the Augsburg Confession. At Regensburg, Eck found much that was acceptable in the *Book of Regensburg,* a theological platform developed mainly by the Protestant theologian Martin Bucer and the Catholic theologian Johannes Gropper. Eventually, however, Eck attacked the *Book of Regensburg* and recommended its rejection, thereby contributing again to the failure of efforts at reconciliation. Two of his late treatises, the *Apologia* of 1542 and the *Replica* of 1543, are defenses of his conduct at Regensburg, written in response to criticisms by Bucer. In 1541 Eck published *Ains Judenbüechlins verlegung,* in which he attacked the Lutheran Andreas Osiander and defended the common accusation that Jews killed Christian children and used their blood for ritual purposes.

Eck was the most influential anti-Protestant theologian of his generation. He played a major role in convincing Catholic authorities of both church and state that Luther's teachings were dangerous novelties. He helped establish an important and long-lasting connection between the dukes of Bavaria and the popes. Long an advocate of reform, in the 1530s he lent his voice to those calling for a general council. At Augsburg and Regensburg he opposed and helped undermine the efforts at reconciliation, arguing that the theological differences must not be underestimated. His writings provided anti-Protestant ammunition used by Catholic theologians and priests. He helped shape the fundamental strategy used by many Catholic controversialists for generations to come: take positions that represented a medieval consensus and, in defending them, anticipate possible Protestant objections, avoid scholastic authorities, and emphasize arguments from scripture and the church fathers.

BIBLIOGRAPHY

Primary Sources

Eck, Johann. *Enchiridion of Commonplaces against Luther and Other Enemies of the Church* (1525). Translated by Ford Lewis Battles. Grand Rapids, Mich., 1979. Eck's most influential work and one of the few English translations of his writings. Provides arguments against what Eck believed to be the principal theological errors of Luther and his associates.

Fraenkel, Pierre, ed. *Enchiridion locorum communium adversus Lutherum et alios hostes ecclesiae, 1525–1543.* Münster, 1979. Exemplary critical edition of the Enchiridion.

Secondary Sources

Bautz, Friedrich Wilhelm, ed. *Biographische-Bibliographisches Kirchenlexikon.* Hamm, 1970–. See vol. 1, pp. 1452–1454.

Iserloh, Erwin. *Johannes Eck, 1486–1543: Scholastiker, Humanist, Kontroverstheologe.* 2d ed. Münster, 1985. Most recent scholarly biography of Eck. Author's negative view of late medieval nominalism colors his evaluation of Eck as a theologian.

Iserloh, Erwin, ed. *Johannes Eck, 1486–1543, im Streit der Jahrhunderte.* Münster, 1988. Papers from an international symposium held in 1986 to mark Eck's five-hundredth birthday. Chapters concentrate on Eck's career as controversialist from 1517 onward. Most of the papers are in German, but see Nelson Minnich's chapter, "On the Origins of Eck's 'Enchiridion,'" pp. 37–73.

Moore, Walter. "Catholic Teacher and Anabaptist Pupil: The Relationship between John Eck and Balthasar Hubmaier." *Archiv für Reformationsgeschichte* 72 (1981), 68–97. Besides discussing the personal and theological relationships between Eck and Hubmaier, provides a useful introduction to Eck's early theological career and the position espoused in the *Chrysopassus.*

Verzeichnis der im deutschen Sprachbereich erschienenen Drucke des XVI. Jahrhunderts. Stuttgart, 1983–. See vol. 5, nos. 247–441.

Wiedemann, Theodor. *Dr. Johann Eck, Professor der Theologie an der Universität Ingolstadt.* Regensburg, 1865. Despite its age, still the most complete biography of Eck in any language.

WALTER L. MOORE

ECONOMICS. *See* Capitalism; Usury; Weber Thesis.

EDICT OF ______. *See under latter part of name.*

EDINBURGH. Situated in southeastern Scotland, Edinburgh by the sixteenth century was the largest burgh in the country, having a population of about twelve thousand. It was the leading economic center in Scotland and was fast becoming the center of political administration with the establishment of the Court of Session in 1532 and Parliament's meeting there on an increasingly regular basis. The town became the center of religious administration (replacing the primatial see of St. Andrews) when, after 1559, the governing body of the newly reformed church, the General Assembly of the Kirk of Scotland, made Edinburgh its principal meeting place.

The location of the town on the east coast and its function as a center of trade and government ensured the ready importation of new ideas about religious reform in the first half of the sixteenth century. As early as 1532 supporters of Martin Luther were known throughout the community, but it was not until the mid-1550s that the existence of a "privy kirk" (conventicle) was evident. Protestant preachers, including John Knox, visited Edinburgh in the 1550s, encouraging the activities of the small Protestant minority there.

The Protestant lords captured Edinburgh in June 1559, and John Knox was elected minister to the burgh. The town as a whole did not openly embrace the new religion, and the reformers were twice forced to evacuate Edinburgh during the winter of 1559/60. Even when the Protestant presence became permanent after April 1560, it established itself in what can best be described as an ambivalent, if not hostile, atmosphere.

The impact of the Reformation on Edinburgh was as much social and political as it was religious. Throughout the 1560s there was a constant tug-of-war amongst the citizens. Rival loyalties to Queen Mary, who was Catholic and conciliatory, and to John Knox, the religious leader of the community, who was Protestant and radical, resulted in continual tension within the town. The burgh was deeply divided in these allegiances, and the fracture cut across all social groups.

Following Mary's defeat at Langside (1568), Edinburgh remained the center of support for her cause. "Marians" congregated within the burgh under the leadership of Sir William Kirkcaldy of Grange, who had been appointed governor of the castle at Edinburgh after Langside. Kirkcaldy held Edinburgh castle and town in the name of Queen Mary, resisting attempts at negotiation by the king's party. Despite siege conditions the burgh continued to support the queen. It was only with the collapse of her party elsewhere and the threat of English intervention on the side of the king's men that the "Castillians" became isolated in their stand. Edinburgh town was recaptured by the king's party in the autumn of 1572, but the castle and its occupants held out in the name of Queen Mary until May 1573.

The fall of the castle meant an end to civil war and more widespread acquiescence to Protestantism throughout Edinburgh. In the next decade the town reestablished itself as the center of government, administration, and the economy, but its rapport with the regent, James, fourth earl of Morton, continued to exacerbate sociopolitical tensions.

[*See also* Cromwell, Thomas.]

BIBLIOGRAPHY

Donaldson, Gordon. *All The Queen's Men: Power and Politics in Mary Stewart's Scotland.* London, 1983. Identifies friends and enemies of Mary across all segments of Scottish society, including Edinburgh burgesses.

Lynch, Michael. *Edinburgh and the Reformation.* Edinburgh, 1982. The most comprehensive study of politics, religion, and society in sixteenth-century Edinburgh.

———. "From Privy Kirk to Burgh Church: An Alternative View of the Process of Protestantisation." In *Church, Politics and Society: Scotland, 1408–1929*, edited by Norman Macdougall, pp. 85–96. Edinburgh, 1983. A concise rendering of some of the key issues that are more fully developed in the work cited above.

Wormald, Jenny. *Court, Kirk, and Community: Scotland, 1470–1625.* The New History of Scotland, vol. 4. London, 1981. Comprehensive yet concise discussion of the social, political, intellectual, and religious environment in Scotland in the century of the Reformation.

MARY BLACK VERSCHUUR

EDUCATION. The relationship between education and the Reformation of the sixteenth century is a complex and often controversial one. In the past, historians have assumed that the Protestant emphasis on reading the vernacular Bible contributed to an educational revolution in the sixteenth century and an accompanying rise in literacy among Protestant laity. Alongside this has been a tendency to see the Counter-Reformation's impact on education and literacy as an inhibiting one. Research since the 1970s has shown, however, that the history of the interaction of education with religious reform is far more complicated—that there was already an increase in schooling and lay literacy in the late medieval period that may have contributed to the reforming impulses, and that the educational consequences of both the Catholic and Protestant reformations need to be reexamined.

Late Medieval Background. Sources for information on education are sporadic in the thirteenth century, but schools may already have grown in numbers from the eleventh century. By the fourteenth and fifteenth centuries there is evidence for schools in most towns as well as in some rural areas. The sources are widely scattered and reflect the haphazard character of pre-Reformation schooling as well as the uneven survival of documents from that period. Nonetheless, we know that in the diocese of Rouen, in Normandy, at least nineteen rural schools appear in the records between 1362 and 1500. Small towns and villages throughout Brittany had schools, although they may not have been long-lived. Documents from late medieval Champagne and the regions south of Paris show schools in dozens of rural parishes, in so many localities that scholars have concluded that there was a dense implantation of rural schools, which had, by the fifteenth century, become the norm. In western and northern England, the areas that have been most thoroughly investigated, there were several hundred schools in villages and small towns by 1500. These rural schools tended to teach an elementary form of education (reading, writing, and singing the liturgy, perhaps doing accounts), although occasionally they also offered Latin grammar.

Grammar schools were more common in the urban areas. In the fifteenth century London had perhaps a dozen Latin grammar schools. The Venetian archives have yielded the names of approximately 850 masters of schools (both elementary and grammar) from 1300 to 1430. Throughout northern and north-central Italy, cities, towns, and even tiny hamlets supported communal Latin teachers. By 1300 Genoa had a corporate college of grammar masters, attracted to Genoa because of the widespread availability of elementary education and the high fees grammar teachers could command. By 1500 there were twenty-two grammar masters in the college as well as numerous noncollegiate grammar teachers.

There is less information on elementary and secondary pre-Reformation education in Spain and Germany. Studies of lay libraries, of the book trade, and of the growth of vernacular texts and a reading public suggest that educational facilities were expanding in Spain. In 1370 Henry II of Castile established licensing procedures for masters of primary letters. By the beginning of the sixteenth century, Spanish dioceses were ordering parish priests and sacristans to teach reading, writing, and accounting, and they were examining the orthodoxy of those who did so. These are indirect indices; no one yet really knows how widespread primary or grammar schools were in late medieval Spain. In Germany, the explosive founding of new universities (sixteen between 1347 and 1506), the rising university matriculation rates in the fifteenth century, and the growing number of university-trained clergy also suggest, but do not prove, the presence of widely available elementary and secondary education.

Some of the impetus for educational expansion came from the late medieval church. Ecclesiastical reformers often linked reform with the need for better instruction of both clergy and laity. For example, Jean de Gerson, the reform-minded chancellor of Paris in the early fifteenth century, promoted legislation at the Council of Reims in 1408 that required parish visitations to ask whether parish children were being educated and whether there were schools available. In 1484 synodal constitutions from Cuenca (Spain) stipulated that all fathers send at least one son to the village sacristan to learn how to read and write.

The laity were a motivating force, sending their children to school, hiring schoolteachers, founding schools, promoting communal schools, and offering alms to scholars. In some cases, particularly in ports such as Venice and Genoa, the motivation was commercial. In many instances, lay investment in education was motivated by the need for literate, usually latinate, skills in order to participate in legal, administrative, and governmental affairs. One consequence was a dramatic increase in the demand for law and in the number of lawyers throughout Europe. In the second half of the fifteenth century, the numbers entering the clergy also increased dramatically. If tastes in books are an index, the laity may also have been motivated by the desire to read devotional works (books of hours, lives of saints), liturgical texts, and romances.

The elementary and secondary curriculum followed was remarkably similar throughout Europe, although Italian schools included more emphasis on arithmetic, bookkeeping, and the art of letter writing, while northern schools, in England for example, stressed learning the liturgy for the growing number of children in parish choirs. Some schools (abbaco schools in Italy, business schools in England, reading and writing schools in Spain and Germany) may have been conducted entirely in the vernacular. Throughout much of Europe, however, primary education began with the alphabet and simple vernacular prayers and quickly passed to Latin bits of scripture and the Latin psalter. Beginning scholars might be taught to write, often by a separate writing master. The most common elementary Latin grammar, the *Ars Minor* of Donatus, was sometimes taught in the grammar schools, sometimes as part of the elementary curriculum, and the distinction between these two levels was not always clear. Girls could attend elementary schools but rarely learned Latin grammar. The male students who went on to Latin grammar schools encountered more complex versified grammar texts, various word lists, collections of fables and myths, morality poems, a collection of moralizing Latin sentences entitled Cato's *Disticha*, readings from Virgil, Lucan, Statius, and Ovid, as well as some logic and dialectic. The revolution in the curriculum associated with the rise of humanist studies introduced newer, more classically oriented grammar texts and Latin sentences, Cicero (with an accompanying emphasis on rhetoric), Latin poets and playwrights (Terence, Plautus), and Latin historians (Livy, Caesar, Sallust), as well as the rudiments of Greek.

The humanist curriculum was first introduced in the early fifteenth century in a number of northern Italian household schools. It soon spread to Latin schools throughout Italy and then, in the late fifteenth and sixteenth century, through Europe. Italian Latin schools had become overwhelmingly secular by the fourteenth and fifteenth centuries, run by towns, villages, guilds, or privately. Outside Italy the church was somewhat more involved. Although monastic schools had been in decline from the thirteenth century, they continued to house schools, and nunneries continued to serve as places for girls to receive an education. The newer friary schools, open to the laity, emphasized higher learning—theology and philosophy—rather than grammar; the older cathedral grammar schools, while still functioning, no longer dominated the educational landscape. Throughout Europe, educational monopolies on the part of the church became increasingly difficult to enforce, with the result that late medieval schools present a mixed picture of ecclesiastical and lay patronage and control. In addition, lay schoolmasters sometimes taught in cathedral schools, while clerics might teach in lay schools or privately. At the primary level, education was often informal, with schoolmasters teaching in one locale and then, quite possibly, moving on. Increasingly, the church, through synodal legislation, required parishes to teach children the rudiments of the faith (the Lord's Prayer, Ten Commandments, seven deadly sins, seven virtues, various prayers, and parts of the psalter) and reading. The children of nobility still depended on the private education offered by household tutors, although by 1500 some of them were turning up in grammar schools, followed by some years at a university. Most schools, whether elementary or secondary, lay or ecclesiastical, private or communal, were fee paying. At the end of the fourteenth century in England, although not until the sixteenth century in Italy, individuals began to endow schools, with the result that some scholars could attend tuition free.

Historians now no longer think that expanding lay literacy and the growth of schooling were simply the result of (1) the advent of printing, (2) the rise of humanism, or (3) a consequence of the Reformation, although all these phenomena dovetailed in the sixteenth century. On the one hand, one can argue in general that Protestant allegiance followed lay literacy rather than the reverse. On the other hand, both the Protestant and Catholic reform movements, in their initial phases, promoted educational reform, the founding of schools, and training in the vernacular. Both reformations had significant impacts on the degree of governmental or ecclesiastical control exercised over education. Some of the consequences include better, more systematic training of the clergy, greater systematization of educational texts, and a continuing increase in lay literacy, as educational institutions reached more and more into rural areas. In general, the Reformation, whether Protestant or Catholic, contributed to significant changes in the relationship between church, state, schools, and schoolmasters. In part this change was because of the ideals of the reformers and in part because of the simultaneous growth of nation-states and national religions, with their appetite for trained men to serve growing bureaucracies.

Germany. German Protestant reformers stressed the importance of education. In 1520 Luther advocated education as a way of inculcating religious and civic values. For a brief time he imagined an effort of voluntary parental and community involvement, but the events of the 1520s (the Peasants' War and the rise of Anabaptism, among others) convinced him that education needed to be controlled and in the hands of secular authorities. Likewise, while Luther at first advocated unlimited access to the Bible in schools, by the late 1520s he became convinced that catechisms were the best vehicle for religious education.

Throughout Protestant Germany governments began to regulate and standardize education. Schooling became compulsory in Magdeburg in 1524, in Eisleben in 1525, and in the electorate of Saxony in 1528. In 1526 Landgrave Philipp of Hesse, in conjunction with an ecclesiastical synod, wrote an educational plan for Hesse that called for the establishment of a university (at Marburg) and for schools in all cities and villages. It included a detailed Latin curriculum with religious instruction for boys and a description of schools for girls. The qualifications and salaries of schoolmasters were detailed and the mechanics for scholarships for poor boys spelled out. The plan was instituted gradually over the next two decades. Superintendents, who were officials of the landgrave, supervised the schools at all levels, including the curriculum and discipline. A standardized curriculum was eventually established in all Hessian schools, patterned on the preparatory Latin school curriculum at Marburg.

Similar school ordinances issued from all cities and territories throughout Germany in the 1520s and 1530s, ultimately producing over one hundred different ordinances before 1600. Commonly these ordinances required parents to send their children to school, established rules for student conduct, specified common books and exams, and demanded rigorous requirements for teachers, uniform teaching methods, and standardized curricula. Teachers were examined for competence but also required to affirm their confession of faith; school inspectors as well as supervisors were appointed. There was a concerted effort to identify talented youths from poor families and to give them the wherewithal to attend school. Although these school ordinances and initiatives were often the result of joint state-church consultations, authority for the schools ultimately rested with the secular authorities.

Luther, along with other German reformers, emphasized Latin learning, which he saw as having decayed in the 1520s and 1530s. These Latin schools became a training ground for future pastors and administrative officials. Philipp Melanchthon offered a Latin curricular model that was implemented throughout Saxony in 1528 and was influential in all of Germany. At the first level students memorized Latin words and sentences, read Cato and Donatus, sang Latin hymns, and read the articles of faith and biblical extracts. German was used to instruct at this level. This use of vernacular decreased in level two, in which students studied Latin syntax and read Aesop's *Fables*, Terence, Plautus, and Latin colloquies. At the third level students encountered logic and rhetoric, readings from Virgil, Livy, Horace, Ovid, and Cicero, and some Greek. At Strasbourg the preparatory Latin gymnasium, led by Johann Sturm (1507–1589), was divided into eight rigidly hierarchical classes with strict exams for promotion. Students studied Latin grammar, rhetoric and dialectic based mainly on Cicero and Aristotle, Greek, mathematics, science, and biblical texts. Sturm's academy, geared to upgrading the quality of Protestant clergy as well as public servants, was adapted by many of the Swiss and French reformers through its influence on Calvin; as a model of classical pedagogy it also shaped the Jesuit *ratio studiorum* and schools in the Empire.

The Reformation did not revolutionize the Latin curriculum. Teachers still turned to medieval texts, to Donatus and Cato, for beginning Latin grammar. Beyond this they followed a Renaissance humanist curriculum, with the addition of some of Desiderius Erasmus's works as well as scriptural texts. Throughout Germany, however, the educational needs of a more organized and expanding school system encouraged scholars and teachers to produce new editions and translations of classical texts as well as a variety of pedagogical treatises and elementary readers and grammars.

The Reformation's impact on vernacular elementary schools is less clear than its commitment to Latin learning. Although the reformers advocated vernacular schools, schools for the poor, and schools for girls, their attention and resources went toward Latin preparatory schools and theological seminaries. Official German schools that taught reading, writing, arithmetic, and accounting were sanctioned in some places (e.g., Strasbourg) but not in others (e.g., Hesse, which was one of the first four German states to eliminate illiteracy). In addition, unauthorized vernacular schools (*Winkelschulen*, or corner schools) appeared everywhere in the sixteenth century—in towns, large villages, and even most smaller villages, with men and women teaching poorer boys and girls.

The other great educational focus of the German Reformation was on the production and teaching of the catechism. Luther produced two catechisms in 1529 (the Large and Small Catechisms) that eventually became the basis for religious instruction throughout Protestant Germany. Hundreds of other pastors and teachers produced catechisms, both printed and manuscript, in the first two generations of the reform. The catechism, which includes the basic formulas and practices of the church, became the basis for obligatory catechism classes (held largely on Sundays and devoted more to memorizing than reading the text) as well as the primary reading text in all elementary schools. In some ways the various catechisms were not that different from the late medieval primers, although they were more organized, more Protestant in content, and more widely disseminated.

Catechism instruction, legislated and investigated by the secular authorities, ensured that religious doctrine was consistently part of the curriculum. Other aspects of the curriculum (hymn singing, prayers before and after classes, worship services, as well as religiously oriented commentaries and grammar exercises) ensured that one of the major goals of the Lutheran Reformation, religious indoctrination, was promoted. Another goal, often explicitly stated, was to prepare students to become administrators in the church or state as well as pastors. Finally, the majority of reformers also promoted lay literacy and the utility of reading.

Since the mid-1970s there has been a lively debate over the degree of success or failure of these educational initiatives. On the one hand, visitation records suggest that rural areas were sometimes resistant to religious instruction and that compulsory schooling was difficult to enforce. In addition, authorities were never able to root out private schools, many of which focused on reading and writing skills rather than on religious education. On the other hand, the number of schools did increase; lay literacy (after some drawbacks in the 1520s and 1530s) grew; more and more boys went on to university; and girls' schools continued to exist, although we do not yet know whether more attended than had attended convents and elementary schools earlier. Most significantly, education became more systematized, closely governed, and examined than it had ever been.

England. Education in pre-Reformation England differed from that in Germany in the extent to which laymen, women, and clergy endowed schools and scholarships. In addition, the English vernacular, while making inroads, did not dominate the elementary curriculum as the vernacular did in Germany, nor was the vernacular Bible as much in evidence.

Between 1530 and the 1580s the English government vacillated between Catholicism and Protestantism, eventually producing an Anglican state church that was more Catholic than some Protestants wanted and too Protestant for many Catholics to live with. These fluctuations had some educational consequences but did not dramatically change the course of educational development.

The most significant educational developments occurred with the diffusion of printed texts by about 1510, which allowed for the production of mass grammars and primers, and with the introduction of a humanist curriculum by John Colet at Saint Paul's Cathedral in 1510. William Lilly, the schoolmaster of Saint Paul's from 1512 to 1522, wrote a new Latin grammar that dozens of schools quickly adopted. Overall, however, the use of Erasmian texts; of humanist texts of Latin rhetoric, poetry, and history; and of Greek spread slowly and sporadically. A suitable Greek grammar was not available until 1575, after which instruction in Greek increased rapidly.

Under Henry VIII (r. 1509–1547) the educational change most attributable to the Reformation was the dissolution of the monasteries, along with the perhaps seventy to eighty schools they housed. This dissolution was completed by 1540. Henry had planned an ambitious program of founding new dioceses, cathedrals, and schools from the proceeds. In the end, perhaps twelve new or refounded cathedral schools benefited. The destructive effects of the dissolution were real, and although Henry improved education in other areas, his efforts were ad hoc and on a smaller scale. Henry was also responsible for the greater standardization of school texts, with an amended form of Lilly's grammar legislated for use throughout England (1540–1543) and a uniform primer required in 1545. This primer, a collection of prayers similar to those used in elementary schools from the fourteenth century, contained less Latin, although a Latin version was available. It went through numerous alterations as the state's religious position evolved through the sixteenth century.

Under Henry an acceptable English translation of the Bible was made. Although Latin Bibles had been available in parish churches from the fifteenth century and therefore, theoretically, available to schoolboys and laity, only in 1538 did England begin to require all parishes to invest in an English Bible. The vernacular Bible then went through thirty separate editions by 1552; it was banned under Mary Tudor (r. 1553–1558) and required and republished many times under Queen Elizabeth I (r. 1558–1603).

Under King Edward VI (r. 1547–1553) the state took over the chantries and hospitals throughout England. Perhaps one-eighth of all chantries housed schools, as did some hospitals. Edward's commissioners were reasonably conscientious regarding the continued maintenance of the grammar schools; the elementary schools were largely ignored. Most of the grammar schools were eventually re-endowed, although often after much effort and with private resources. An upsurge of grammar school foundations in the last years of Edward's reign continued under Mary and Elizabeth; it resulted from a mixture of private and royal initiatives and eventually produced perhaps as many as four hundred grammar schools by 1600. Elementary, or petty, schools also increased, taught by parish clergy, by schoolmistresses as well as schoolmasters, and even by artisans. Based on the evidence of licenses to teach issued by the bishops, some Elizabethan dioceses had elementary schools in 50 percent of their parishes.

From 1550 on the shifts in rulers and religion hardly changed educational policies at all. Church and Crown became increasingly involved with education, and the schools came to be more rigorously supervised. Under Mary there were efforts to supervise the religious beliefs and competence of schoolmasters by requiring them to have licenses from their bishops. This policy continued, and was better enforced, under Elizabeth. Beginning in 1563 schoolmasters had to take the Oath of Supremacy. Episcopal visitations and standardized texts produced more uniformity in grammar schools than had been the case before the Reformation.

Both Catholic and Protestant regimes paid attention to the religious dimension of education. Before the Reformation schoolchildren learned to read from prayers and the psalter; they often sang in choirs; they were expected to attend Mass and say prayers; and some of their grammar texts included moral and religious materials. Sporadic ecclesiastical legislation promoted education in the Catholic faith at the parish level, reading the primer, and teaching only matters acceptable to Catholicism. In 1529 the Canterbury Convocation decreed that all religious houses have grammar instructors; that all rectors, vicars, and chantry priests instruct boys in elementary or grammar education; and that all schoolmasters teach summaries of the faith. By 1570 the church required all schoolmasters to teach selections from the Bible, to accompany boys to hear sermons, and to teach them an approved catechism. It remained standard for children to pray before and after school, to say prayers on behalf of their benefactors, and to sing hymns at service. In 1571 Alexander Nowell published a catechism that became the standard for all parish scholars.

By 1560 petty, or elementary, education was conducted in English, although it might include some elementary Latin grammar. Students learned their hornbook (a wooden tablet covered with horn that contained the alphabet), reading, writing, and accounting. They became reasonably literate after one and a half to two years and, except for a period in the 1540s and 1550s, illiteracy declined for all occupational groups, although almost imperceptibly for women and husbandmen, through the sixteenth century.

Spain. By 1550 Spain had experienced a growth in grammar education, particularly following the reign of Ferdinand and Isabella (r. 1474–1504), that occurred together with the introduction of humanism and the establishment of a printing industry. (By 1500 twenty-five towns had presses.) Private funds and municipal support created a network of grammar schools, while an unverifiable number of independent grammar masters survived on students' fees. By 1600 one contemporary estimated that there were then four thousand grammar schools in the kingdom! Similarly, elementary education (reading and writing Spanish), provided by private instructors, was available everywhere. Although documentation of the numbers of such schools is lacking, male literacy rates of 45–70 percent by 1550 in Cuenca and Toledo suggest widespread availability of elementary education, and the inquisitors, who queried individuals on where they learned their letters, reported that most had attended primary schools in their village.

Spain experienced a number of reforming movements in the late fifteenth and early sixteenth century that spilled over into the educational arena. Reform-minded bishops began to order parish catechism instruction (called Christian doctrine classes). At synods at Alcalá (1497) and Talavera (1498) Cardinal Francisco Jiménez de Cisneros ordered the clergy to explain the gospel to their parishioners every Sunday, and he attached a catechism to the decree. This concern with religious instruction had become, in the words of one historian, a "catechism craze" by the 1540s.

In order for the clergy to teach, they had to be educated. Under Queen Isabella, the Council of Aranda forbade ordaining to the priesthood those who knew no Latin. A number of bishops subsequently founded grammar schools. Cardinal Jiménez de Cisneros established the University of Alcalá de Henares in 1508, with education in Latin, Hebrew, and Greek for scholars going into the church. One of his disciples, Francisco de Contreras, advocated the establishment of schools dedicated to Christian doctrine, which he had encountered in Italy. He founded two schools, which taught singing, grammar, art, crafts, and theology. His disciple, John of Ávila (1499–1569), founded fifteen such schools as well as the University of Baeza to train future priests to preach. In his schools of Christian doctrine, the children used primers, catechisms, and confessionals in order to learn their doctrine as they learned to read and write. John of Ávila composed a catechism in rhymed couplets that the children sang. His schools of doctrine were imitated quickly throughout Spain, with parents being warned repeatedly by ecclesiastical legislation to send their children to such schools. The Jesuits, in their early years in Spain, taught catechism schools. Another institution, called "colleges of children of the doctrine" and intended specifically for orphaned boys, also spread throughout Spain. ABC primers, Spanish grammars, and reading books issued from the presses in large numbers, but increasingly it was the catechisms (pamphlets called *cartillas de leer*) that were published and used in schools. In 1556 the Toledan printer-bookseller Juan de Ayala had 73,000 in stock.

After the mid-sixteenth century, the impact of the Council of Trent, the growing influence of the Inquisition, and the coming of the Jesuits changed the educational picture substantially. Increased concern for orthodoxy meant that both elementary and grammar education were more regulated and supervised, although they continued to expand in availability. In Castile there was a continuous stream of regulations for both grammar masters and masters of primary letters. Above all, they had to prove their religious orthodoxy. In 1573 all *Conversos* were excluded from teaching as well as anyone whose forefather had been brought before the Inquisition. Inspectors reviewed school texts for doctrinal correctness and aptness. In 1592, when the Inquisition discovered some incompletely printed catechisms in Valladolid, they collected and reviewed all the catechisms they could find. In addition to royal decrees and inquisitorial investigations, municipal authorities tried, increasingly, to regulate the competence and the fees of schoolmasters by issuing licenses, although this remained nearly impossible to enforce, and private, informal schools continued to flourish, at least in the sixteenth century.

The Council of Trent (1545–1563), which promulgated decrees that every cathedral and town should possess a school taught by a priest and that every diocese should have a seminary-college for young priests, concluded with the recommendation that Jesuits be given pride of place over other teachers. Although Ignatius Loyola, in the early constitutions of the order, had made provision only for the teaching of Christian doctrine to children and for colleges to train Jesuits, he had already responded constructively to a Jesuit-founded college at Gandía in 1547 where, for the first time, Jesuits taught lay pupils along with Jesuits. By the time he died (1556) Jesuits were conducting thirty-three colleges in seven European countries. In Spain they rapidly dominated the grammar faculties attached to the universities and became the leading organizers of secondary education. Jesuit education was attractive because it was free (unless a student boarded there), and the Jesuits were willing to teach primary letters if a student needed it. In addition, they offered an organized and attractive curriculum that integrated scholastic and humanist texts along with training in morality and religion. Students at a Jesuit college learned not only grammar and philosophy but also theology, mathematics, geography, history, and astronomy, all grounded in the original Latin texts. Jesuit instructors had reputations for being well trained and dedicated. By 1600 there were Jesuit colleges in nearly all of Spain's towns and cities; Richard Kagan estimates that the Jesuits were then educating ten to fifteen thousand boys a year, the vast majority of whom were studying Latin grammar. The availability of a Latin classical education, particularly through the Jesuit colleges but also through the numerous municipal and independent schools, served as a vehicle for social mobility while at the same time ensuring religious conformity and intellectual competency among those who entered the church or the government service.

Chief among the motives for continued educational expansion in the sixteenth century, despite concerns for heterodox or heretical opinions, was the growing demand of the state for literate officials and the constant concern of the church for a more learned clergy. Only toward the beginning of the seventeenth century, as Spain's economy slid downhill, did elites in Spain try to reduce the availability of Latin grammar for fear that there would not be sufficient positions for children of the upper classes if commoners continued to rise through education.

Italy. Paul Grendler, a scholar of Italian Renaissance schooling, emphasizes the continuity in educational institutions and curricula from the fourteenth through the sixteenth century. Italian grammar schools (communal, independent, or church-supported), which were usually taught by clergy, offered a humanist curriculum. Abbaco schools, where laymen taught vernacular reading, writing, accounting, and bookkeeping, made literacy available to middle- and working-class boys. Parish schools were not common; before the Council of Trent, priests were trained informally, as apprentices to other priests. Girls were tutored at home or taught in convents and elementary schools, sometimes with female teachers.

The motivation for most education was based on the growing demand for notaries, secretaries, and public officials; merchants needed fairly high levels of literacy, and towns saw education as a way of promoting civic values and the good of the city. By the mid-sixteenth century, following the reform of the church, schools were also seen as places to teach good morals and religious doctrine, although the curriculum remained humanist. In general, the Catholic Reformation promoted an increase in educational opportunities, a shift toward endowing schools, and greater religious content in the curriculum.

The Council of Trent called for the establishment of seminaries in every diocese. Since Italy had many dioceses, it also had many seminarians, a significant percentage of whom taught in Latin schools both before and after they were ordained. These seminaries became an avenue of social mobility for the sons of craftsmen and shopkeepers.

Schools of Christian doctrine, elementary schools for all, were founded by Castellino da Castello at Milan in 1536 and spread rapidly. These schools were operated by lay confraternities and taught by laymen; they met on Sundays and religious holidays, offering reading, writing, and the fundamentals of Catholicism. Students began with a mixed Latin-Italian primer of prayers, precepts, and principles of Catholic faith and then moved on to a catechism, called the *Interrogatorio*, with a question-and-answer format. These schools were endorsed by the Council of Trent, promoted by the bishops (particularly Cardinal Carlo Borromeo, archbishop of Milan from 1560 to 1584), and advertised widely to parents. As a result, they taught thousands of children, both boys and girls.

The other significant contribution to expanding educational opportunities came from the religious orders. In the 1530s the Somaschi established orphanage schools and, later, boarding schools for the nobility; the Barnabites began to offer free Latin schools after 1605; and in the 1590s Giuseppe Calasanzio initiated the Scuole Pie movement to teach poor boys. But above all, the Jesuits, who founded their first college at Messina in 1547, offered free elementary and Latin instruction for one hundred to three hundred boys in a community. Jesuit schools numbered forty-nine in 1600, with some, like the Collegio Romano (later to become the Gregorian University) enrolling as many as fifteen hundred students. Jesuit schools received more support from princes and communes than from the ecclesiastical hierarchy, and eventually many of their foundations became elite Latin boarding schools, with a disciplined curriculum of Latin humanities, doctrinal instruction, and religious practices.

The Catholic reform affected education for women. At the elementary level more and more girls were taught reading, writing, and the catechism; they were always taught separately from boys, whether at home or in a communal school. After the Council of Trent, convent schools for girls were more strictly regulated and convents more enclosed, which made it difficult for nuns to teach as freely as before but did not inhibit wealthier families from continuing to send their daughters there.

France. Throughout the sixteenth century France was either at war or rent by warring factions. The infiltration of Erasmian and Lutheran ideas in the 1520s and 1530s, followed by the dramatic growth of Calvinism from the 1550s coupled with a diminishing enthusiasm for Catholicism that gave way to an effective Counter-Reformation, meant that France's troubles quickly took on religious colorations. To some degree education became a battleground, although the current literature on Catholic-Protestant relations in the sixteenth century ignores education, while educational studies of the sixteenth century do not focus on Catholic-Protestant issues.

The most dramatic educational development in sixteenth-century France was the widespread foundation, by municipalities supplemented by private benefactions, of public elementary and secondary institutions (called colleges). By midcentury nearly every town of sufficient size contained a public school, open to boys (and girls at the elementary level) of all classes. Staffed by a principal with five or six teachers, these schools normally taught several hundred students, dividing them into classes by age and ability. The curriculum was humanist (Latin with some Greek), entailing, as one historian puts it, "an apprenticeship with the ancients."

Clerical involvement, support, and supervision was minimal; the towns' investments were substantial in both buildings and staff. They were governed by boards of trustees that regulated them in minute detail, hired the staff, and helped enforce an educational monopoly. The numbers of these schools grew rapidly, reaching a high point in the sixteenth century and declining after 1600, when both church and Crown expressed concern that so much education was counterproductive, producing too many educated laymen. Colleges were gradually closed or placed under the authority of religious orders; even elementary schools were more restricted in their curricula, although their numbers seem to have increased in the seventeenth century.

While information on the locations and numbers of elementary schools is regional and incomplete for the late Middle Ages and the seventeenth century, it is nearly nonexistent for the sixteenth century. Royal edicts from 1560 and 1598 required all parents to send their children (both sexes) to school, and in 1576 the Estates of Blois considered levying contributions from ecclesiastical revenues to maintain elementary schoolmasters to teach Christian religion in every town and village. It is impossible to know to what degree these concerns had any impact.

The colleges usually included classes of children learning their first letters, reading and writing in both French and Latin, and they tried, as much as possible, to maintain a monopoly over this elementary level, discouraging families from teaching them at home or sending them to unlicensed teachers. Colleges also taught girls to read and write, although they usually maintained separate classes with different teachers for them.

There were certainly separate elementary schools in Paris for girls and boys; in the early seventeenth century fifty schoolmasters and twenty schoolmistresses formed a guild and were expected to teach reading, writing, arithmetic, calculating, church singing, catechism, and the elements of Latin grammar. Writing masters also had their guilds and were authorized to teach writing, spelling, and arithmetic.

The extent to which there were rural elementary schools or any religious instruction in rural areas is not yet known, although one might expect them to be more common in northern and eastern France than in south, central, or western France. There must have been extreme diversity in their standards, and many parish clergy may have attended only such schools, with perhaps some additional experience as an apprentice to the local priest.

Significant numbers of schoolteachers seem to have been attracted to Protestant reform ideas, and some colleges became vehicles for them. As a result, the colleges became a battleground among the bishops (who attempted to reassert authority), the Jesuits and other orders (who were invited in to run colleges), the municipalities (whose control over the colleges was weakened by civil war and financial exigencies), and the state (interested in greater control but not sufficiently powerful to assert it). Protestants also demanded schools of their own, modeled on the college in Geneva established by Calvin in 1559. These schools, with eight forms from reading to rhetoric, multiplied throughout France, especially with the temporary expulsion of the Jesuits from 1595 to 1604. The Ordinance of Mantes (1593) and the Edict of Nantes (1598) allowed Huguenots to erect their own schools, both secondary and primary, where they were able to teach reading from the Genevan catechism and Protestant hymn singing and to require interminable attendance at church service. Teachers in these schools had to subscribe to the Calvinist faith and obtain the consent of their local consistory to teach. With the death of Henry IV (1610) Huguenot schools encountered increasing difficulties until they deteriorated gradually because of lack of money, competition, persecution and, after the revocation of the Edict of Nantes (1685), suppression.

Although the decrees of the Council of Trent were never officially accepted in France, many of its reforms were effected under church or state initiatives. The seventeenth century, in particular, was a period rich in educational schemes put forward by Catholic orders and actively encouraged by Catholic lay societies. As early as 1562 the Jesuits were teaching in four towns. By 1565 they had moved into Paris and Lyon. Their influence on French education remained circumscribed in the sixteenth century, however (they were suspected as ultramontanes and as agents of Spanish imperialism); it expanded only in the seventeenth century when they became more closely tied with royal policy. Other Catholic reform orders—Oratorians and Doctrinaires particularly—competed with the Jesuits. The Congregation of the Oratory, founded by Pierre de Bérulle in 1611, was a company of secular, teaching priests. Its schools grew rapidly within and without France; Latin instruction was in French more than in Latin, and the curriculum stressed French history, geography, and culture. The Doctrinaires (Fathers of the Christian Doctrine) took charge of their first college in 1618 and thereafter ran thirty-nine other colleges, mostly in small and middle-sized towns in southern France. Several female orders—Angelicals, Piaristes, Filles de la Croix, Ursulines, Filles de la Pénitence—taught girls. The French Ursulines, founded by Anne de Xainctonge in 1606, established schools for poor girls in both France and Switzerland. They introduced no curricular innovations, although the order itself refused to be enclosed.

Lay *dévots* (who joined together in devotion to a particular saint or holy practice) focused on education by the seventeenth century. In Lyon the Company of the Holy Sacrament founded or reformed free primary schools for the urban poor and for peasants. Model regulations for their schools emphasized religious instruction and rigid repression of any unorthodox impulses, including profane popular customs.

Finally, the ecclesiastical hierarchy slowly but successfully, throughout the seventeenth century, established seminaries for instructing priests and pushed legislation imposing catechetical instruction on parish priests. By 1695 a royal edict declared ecclesiastical sovereignty over all schools within France.

Pedagogy. The Renaissance recovery of Pseudo-Plutarch's *On the Education of Children* and Quintilian's *Institutes* in the fifteenth century renewed interest in pedagogy. Italian humanists such as Pier Paolo Vergerio, Leonardo Bruni, and Baldassare Castiglione developed an ideology surrounding the study of the liberal arts by which the cultivation of Greek and Latin classics formed character, promoted civic values and responsibility, inculcated moral virtues, created a more versatile, well-rounded individual, and led to worldly fame and greater refinement of life. This rationale for the *studia humanitatis* revolutionized the Western educational curriculum from the time of the Reformation until the twentieth century.

Italian humanists and teachers such as Guarino da Verona (1370/74–1460) and Vittorino Ramboldoni (da Feltre, 1378–1446) raised the status of the schoolteacher by stressing the elite nature of the liberal arts (educating those who rule or advise rulers) and by drawing more systematic attention to the importance of teaching methods and a purer quality of Latin learning. They emphasized a humane, attractive pedagogy rather than a coercive one. Vergerio stressed the use of teaching strategies—discussions, reading texts aloud, teaching others—in order to learn. The use of notebooks for copying lessons was quite possibly an innovation of the Italian humanists. But some of their methods—intense repetition and memorization, exercises in pronunciation, concern with the minutiae of grammatical constructs, and the total exclusion of the vernacular—may have been more enervating than energizing.

The intellectual shift from Renaissance Italy to northern Europe of the Reformation involved significant shifts in pedagogy. There was an explosion of pedagogical writing by individuals such as Rodolphus Agricola (Roelof Huysman), Erasmus, Luther, Melanchthon, Johann Sturm, Juan Luis Vives, Roger Ascham, and Richard Mulcaster, among many others. The goals of education shifted, focusing on the inculcation of Christian piety more than the goal of worldly glory, adding more Greek and some Hebrew as well as vernacular language learning to the Latin. Although some of the northern writers focused on elite education with individualized instruction, in general they paid greater attention to public schooling, classroom teaching, a graded curriculum, and methods of instruction. Luther, along with Melanchthon, introduced an experiment in mass education that was designed to "train children in skills, discipline, and divine service . . . [to] grow into men and women capable of governing churches, land and people, households, children and servants," as he wrote in his *Eine Predigt, dass man Kinder zur Schule Halten solle* (Sermon on Keeping Children in School).

Lutheran pedagogy began from a modified Augustinian stance. Although Luther appreciated the innocence of very young children, he believed that, certainly by age seven, sinful proclivities necessitated discipline, both at home and in school. Luther's distrust of parental laxity convinced him to focus on public educational institutions and to argue that children are given to parents for God's service, not for their needs, and should therefore be sent to school even against a parent's wishes. Although Luther attacked the harsh corporal punishment common in schools, overall he promoted discipline in learning, an ordered hierarchy in the curriculum, a coherent pedagogy, and a state-run system. In contrast to late medieval schooling practices, the northern reformers also emphasized the need to separate boys and girls in school.

Reformation pedagogy is most often associated with the name of Erasmus (1467?–1536). Through his publication of popular textbooks, through his appropriation of the ideas and mantel of Rodolphus Agricola (d. 1485), and through his various writings on pedagogy (*De ratione studii*, 1511; and *De pueris instituendis*, 1529), Erasmus influenced all subsequent educational thinkers. He insisted on training children early, by age three if possible. He exhorted schoolmasters to shape young minds with praise and games, tailoring learning to individual readiness. Teaching was everything; it inculcated Christian moral habits and a facility with classical Latin (or Greek) texts. Erasmus advocated Agricola's method of collecting passages to fit preselected subject headings (*loci*), and he emphasized language and literary immersion—speaking classical Latin early, reading Latin prose prior to learning grammar, and composing Latin passages rather than preparing logical defenses. As a pedagogue, Erasmus is best remembered for his harsh criticism of contemporary schoolmasters, whose Latin he considered barbaric and whose pedagogy, he feared, consisted almost entirely of harsh, even brutal, punishments. Erasmus's methods were partially instituted in Colet's school at Saint Paul's and thoroughly installed by Johann Sturm in his gymnasium at Strasbourg, where the curriculum was structured to produce the Erasmian goal of wise piety through the method of total immersion. Sturm's emphasis on graded sequences of instruction, on teaching large numbers of students systematically and advancing them on a yearly basis, and on a curriculum culminating in scripture also showed the impact of Lutheran pedagogy.

Subsequent to Erasmus, the writings of Juan Luis Vives, Thomas Elyot, Roger Ascham, and Richard Mulcaster contributed to the developing pedagogical ideals that, although barely implemented in the sixteenth century, influenced such great thinkers as Francis Bacon and Comenius (Jan Ámos Komenský) and, subsequently, all of Western education. They advocated the use of student notebooks; training in the vernacular in addition to classical Latin; conferences between teachers or between parents and teachers; a psychological basis for teaching (in order to discern particular capacities and individual needs); attention to the site of a school (in the case of elementary schools, for example, as close to home as possible); the use of stage plays and declamatory exercises; reading of authors in the original in preference to summaries; immersion in the language with a focus on composition, double translations, and imitation rather than the rules of grammar; the greater use of colloquies and dictionaries; training schools for teachers; a gentle pedagogy that attracts; Latin learning for women; the inclusion of history; and, in science, direct observation and investigation.

It was the Jesuit order that, taking into account these pedagogical principles as well as the need for free public schooling, developed the most comprehensive school system in Europe. First in its *Ordo studiorum* (1551) and then in its *Ratio studiorum* (1599) the Jesuits laid out a sequenced curriculum (lower grammar, middle grammar, higher grammar, humanities, rhetoric, and philosophy) and explicit rules for classroom teaching with lectures, questions, written exercises, and oral repetitions, all with the goal of the greater glory of God within a Catholic setting.

Despite the confessional differences between, for example, the Jesuit colleges and the Calvinist academies, pedagogical differences were few. In general, the educationalists of the Reformation had an expansive and humane idea of the teaching process, based on the high value given to the *studia humanitatis*, whatever the classroom reality or the underlying religious goals might have been.

[*See also* Cambridge, University of; Faculty of Theology of Paris; Heidelberg, University of; Literacy; Oxford, University of; School Ordinances; Seminaries; Universities; *and* Wittenberg, University of.]

BIBLIOGRAPHY

Alexander, Michael Van Cleave. *The Growth of English Education, 1348–1648: A Social and Cultural History.* University Park, Pa., 1990.

Ascham, Roger. *The Schoolmaster* (1570). Edited by L. Ryan. Charlottesville, Va., 1967.

Barnard, H. C. *The French Tradition in Education: Ramus to Mme. Necker de Saussure* (1922). Reprint, Cambridge, 1970.

Bowen, James. *A History of Western Education,* London, 1975. See vol. 2.

Chartier, R., D. Julia, and M. M. Compere. *L'éducation en France du 16e au 18e siècles.* Paris, 1976.

Cressy, David. *Literacy and the Social Order: Reading and Writing in Tudor and Stuart England.* Cambridge, 1980.

Chrisman, Miriam. *Lay Culture, Learned Culture: Strasbourg, 1480–1599.* New Haven, 1982.

De Molen, Richard L. *Richard Mulcaster, c.1531–1611, and Educational Reform in the Renaissance.* Nieuwkoop, 1991.

Edwards, Mark U., Jr. *Printing, Propaganda, and Martin Luther.* Berkeley, 1994.

Farrell, Allan P. *The Jesuit Code of Liberal Education: Development and Scope of the Ratio Studiorum.* Milwaukee, 1938.

Furet, François, and Jacques Ozouf. *Lire et écrire: L'alphabétisation des français de Calvin à Jules Ferry.* 2 vols. Paris, 1977.

Garin, Eugenio. *Il pensiero pedagogico della umanesimo.* Florence, 1958.

Gilbert, N. W. *Renaissance Concepts of Method.* New York, 1963.

Grafton, Anthony, and Lisa Jardine. *From Humanism to the Humanities.* New York, 1986.

Green, I. "'For Children in Yeeres and Children in Understanding': The Emergence of the English Catechism under Elizabeth and the Early Stuarts." *Journal of Ecclesiastical History* 37 (1986), 397–425.

Grendler, Paul F. *Schooling in Renaissance Italy: Literacy and Learning, 1300–1600.* Baltimore, 1989.

Guilbert, Sylvette. "Les écoles rurales en Champagne au XVe siècle: Enseignement et promotion sociale." *Annales de l'Est* 34 (1982), 127–147.

Harran, Marilyn J., ed. *Luther and Learning: The Wittenberg University Luther Symposium.* Selinsgrove, Pa., 1985.

Hartfelder, Karl. *Philipp Melanchthon als Praeceptor Germaniae.* Nieuwkoop, 1964.

Huppert, George. *Public Schools in Renaissance France.* Urbana, 1984.

Jones, Michael. "Education in Brittany during the Later Middle Ages: A Survey." *Nottingham Medieval Studies* 22 (1978), 58–77.

Kagan, Richard. *Students and Society in Early Modern Spain.* Baltimore, 1974.

Kiermayr, Reinhold. "On the Education of the Pre-Reformation Clergy." *Church History* 53 (1984), 7–16.

Lawrence, J. N. H. "The Spread of Lay Literacy in Late Medieval Castile." *Bulletin of Hispanic Studies* 62 (1985), 79–94.

Luke, Carmen. *Pedagogy, Printing, and Protestantism: The Discourse on Childhood.* Albany, N.Y., 1989.

Mertz, Georg. *Das Schulwesen der deutschen Reformation.* Heidelberg, 1902.

Moog, Willy. *Geschichte der Pädagogik.* Vol. 2, *Die Pädagogik der Neuzeit von der Renaissance bis zum Ende des 17. Jahrhunderts.* 8th ed. Ratingen bei Düsseldorf, Germany, 1967.

Mora del Pozo, G. *El Colegio de Doctrinos y la enseñanza de primeras letras en Toledo; siglos xvi a xix.* Toledo, 1984.

Moran, Jo Ann Hoeppner. *The Growth of English Schooling, 1340–1548.* Princeton, 1985.

Nalle, Sara. "Literacy and Culture in Early Modern Castile." *Past and Present* 125 (1989), 65–96.

———. *God in La Mancha: Religious Reform and the People of Cuenca, 1500–1650.* Baltimore, 1992.

Orme, Nicholas. *English Schools in the Middle Ages.* London and New York, 1973.

Parker, Geoffrey. "An Educational Revolution? The Growth of Literacy and Schooling in Early Modern Europe." *Tijdschrift voor Geschiedenis* 93 (1980), 210–222.

———. "Success and Failure during the First Century of the Reformation." *Past and Present* 136 (1992), 43–82.

Petti Balbi, Giovanna. *L'insegnamento nella Liguria medievale: Scuole, maestri, libri.* Genoa, 1979.

Rabil, Albert, ed. *Renaissance Humanism: Foundations, Forms, and Legacy.* 3 vols. Philadelphia, 1988. See especially vol. 3, which has essays on humanism and education, humanism by countries, and humanism by disciplines.

Ross, James Bruce. "Venetian Schools and Teachers, Fourteenth to Early Sixteenth Century: A Survey and a Study of Giovanni Battista Egnazio." *Renaissance Quarterly* 39 (1976), 521–564.

Simon, Joan. *Education and Society in Tudor England.* Reprint, Cambridge, 1979.

Spitz, Lewis W., and Barbara Sher Tinsley. *The Reformation and Humanist Learning: Johann Sturm on Education.* Saint Louis, 1994.

Strauss, Gerald. *Luther's House of Learning: Indoctrination of the Young in the German Reformation.* Baltimore, 1978.

Strauss, Gerald, and Richard Gawthorp. "Protestantism and Literacy in Germany." *Past and Present* 104 (1984), 31–55.

Varela, J. *Modos de educación en la España de la Contrarreforma.* Madrid, 1983.

Vives, Juan Luis. *Vives: On Education* (1900). Translated by Foster Watson. Totowa, N.J., 1971.

Woodward, W. H. *Studies in Education during the Age of the Renaissance, 1400–1600* (1906). Reprint, New York, 1967.

Wright, William J. "The Impact of the Reformation on Hessian Education." *Church History* 44 (1975), 182–198.

Jo Ann Hoeppner Moran (Cruz)

EDWARD VI OF ENGLAND (1537–1553), boy-king of England and Ireland whose brief reign (1547–1553) officially marked the beginning of the Protestant Reformation. Edward VI was the son of Henry VIII and Jane Seymour, Henry's third wife; his birth (12 October 1537 at Hampton Court Palace) gave the king his only legitimate male heir, the original aim of the dynastic policy that had resulted in Henry's first divorce and his break with Rome in 1533. Edward's schooling at the hands of England's foremost scholars and theorists—his tutors included Roger Ascham, author of *The Schoolmaster*, and John Cheke, regius professor of Greek at Cambridge—followed the humanists' ideal curriculum, and at fourteen Edward, an acknowledged prodigy, was England's brightest and best-educated king: he could speak, read, and write four languages, including Greek, and possessed a textbook facility in various sciences, including geography, cosmography, and the mathematics of oceanic navigation. From a weekly succession of reformist court preachers (including Hugh Latimer, Nicholas Ridley, Thomas Becon, Martin Bucer, John Knox, and John Ponet) he absorbed the dictum that a godly prince must promote "true religion"; his notes of these sermons he recorded soberly in now-lost ledgers.

Edward was also schooled in the Aristotelian precepts of political action, and his remarkable "Chronicle," a political diary of sorts, together with his so-called state papers and memoranda in council (dating chiefly from 1551–1553), have persuaded some historians that by 1551–1552 he had precociously assumed the burdens of rule. In fact the manuscripts in question were schoolboy exercises based on papers supplied by royal secretaries; they are evidence that Edward was following, not directing, public affairs. Contemporary socioeconomic problems—vagrancy and inflation, for example—occasionally interested him; how in adulthood he would have responded to them remains unknown.

There is no evidence that Edward VI himself formulated royal policy. During his minority (scheduled to run to his eighteenth birthday in 1555) regal authority legally lay with the sixteen executors of his father's will—essentially a core of the privy council. In practice this authority, which comprehended the supreme headship of the Church of England, was wielded successively through the council by the boy's elder uncle, Edward Seymour, duke of Somerset and lord protector of the realm (1547–1549), and (after 1549) John Dudley, earl of Warwick (until 1551) and duke of Northumberland. At court political control rested on the ability of both men to plant their clients in offices in the royal household, especially in Edward's privy chamber. Dudley was so successful at this game—a man of great charm and bearing, he genuinely seems to have won Edward's trust—that even the king mistook appearances for reality: in his "speeches" in council, Edward followed scripts prepared by the duke's men, so that Dudley's wishes, said an eyewitness with only slight exaggeration, became Edward's will. This is why the scheme of 1553 to make a queen of Dudley's daughter-in-law, Jane Grey, seemed to be of Edward's own devising. Believing that the accession of his Catholic sister, Mary Tudor, presaged the coming of the Antichrist to England, Edward was persuaded to insert Jane into his "Devise" (a written instruction) for the succession only days before succumbing to tuberculosis (6 July 1553). He was buried on 8 August 1553 in Westminster Abbey in an unmarked grave. Official attempts in the 1570s to erect a tomb memorializing him as England's first Protestant "imperial" king died aborning.

Acting in Edward's name, Seymour and Dudley introduced Protestantism into England for the first time officially, authorizing a state religion based essentially on the theology of Calvin and Zwingli. A rite in English replaced that in Latin, and Communion in both kinds, signifying a commemoration of the Last Supper, supplanted the Mass. Priests, now free to marry, became salaried appointees, leading the way to the professionalization of the clergy. By 1553 the liturgy and doctrines of the reformed Church of England had been set out in a revised *Book of Common Prayer* (the clearly Protestant version of 1552 having replaced the less radical edition of 1549), an ordinal (1550), a new catechism, and the Forty-two Articles of Faith (1553).

The official Reformation often simply confirmed what in popular practice had already happened, especially in London. London's strategic geographic location enabled a minority of Protestants there (about one-fifth of the city's sixty thousand inhabitants) to exert a disproportionate influence on the formation of government policy; organized in secret cells, their faith nourished by a growing community of reformist exiles, the London "brethren" constituted a vocal "lobby" of radical activists. The domestic hub of the reformist book trade, London also briefly became an international center of Protestant thought, thanks to the arrival of numerous foreign divines, some of whom, such as Martin Bucer, Peter Martyr Vermigli, and Jan Łaski, directly influenced the formulation of new Anglican rites.

The royal injunctions of 31 July 1547 required churches to purchase a Bible, Erasmus's *Paraphrases*, and the *Homilies*, a collection of approved sermons compiled by Thomas Cranmer, archbishop of Canterbury. By banning candles, shrines, images, and processions, the injunctions also announced the government's campaign against "superstition." Despite the occasional trashing of "idols," official iconoclasm, although uncompromising and rapid, was usually orderly; to avoid the vandalism of government agents, churchwardens often paid workmen to remove statues and stained glass. Within two years a rich, pictorial aspect of medieval Christianity had vanished from the land, as windows were reglazed and church walls whitewashed in lime. Many ceremonies, some of them civic, also fell into disuse: witness the famous mystery plays and pageants on holy days. Numerous customs associated with the parish church—for example, maypoles—similarly declined almost overnight; seeking to regulate popular recreations, reformists targeted churchales (the popular festivities held in churchyards after Sunday evening prayers, occasions on which locally brewed ale was served) in particular, claiming that such gatherings threatened public order.

The injunctions of 1547 also called for the dissolution of chantries, but whereas the injunctions, at Cranmer's bidding, would have assigned confiscated endowments to charitable causes, the resulting parliamentary act (December 1547) simply assigned them to the king's use, a change in purpose Cranmer and seven bishops vehemently opposed. By mid-1548 nearly half of the estimated twenty-four hundred chantries had been sold, netting Seymour more than £110,000 for his war in Scotland. Since some urban chantries supported the teaching of children, the Crown's action forced many townsmen to petition the king to be allowed to buy back endowments in order to refound their own schools! If the dissolution thus was not quite the educational disaster once imagined, neither was Edward VI a great founder of new schools.

By lifting Henry VIII's constraints on preaching and printing (1547), Seymour opened the floodgates of religious discourse, and a torrent of Protestant propaganda, most of it aimed at the Mass, issued from press and pulpit. The violence provoked by unlicensed preachers prompted Seymour to ban all preaching on 23 September 1548; he then asked a committee of conservative and reformist bishops to produce in English a "uniform order of prayer" for the nation. In a spirit of unity designed to avert a civil war, the conservatives signed Cranmer's draft of such a rite (October 1548), on condition that the final version accommodate their objections to his new order for Communion. A subsequent disputation (December 1548) among the bishops, however, merely revealed how deep were their differences. Only by severe intimidation—forcing a sufficient number of conservatives to abstain on the final vote—did Seymour gain acceptance of the first *Book of Common Prayer* against a probable majority of bishops who opposed it. In the event, the book helped spark rebellion in southwestern England, only one of the crises that ended Seymour's protectorate (October 1549).

Politically, the language of Cranmer's *Book of Common Prayer* was designed to convince Charles V that England was still Catholic and so prevent his intervention in English affairs. When England no longer depended on the emperor's goodwill, Dudley, cloaking his greed in the rhetoric of reform, was free to resume the plunder of the church. Fiercely anti-clerical, he probably wished to destroy episcopacy. He removed seven bishops through deprivations or forced resignations, confiscating portions of their estates for himself and his cronies; only Edward VI's premature death saved from expropriation all lands attached to cathedrals. When the *Second Book of Common Prayer* (from 1 November 1552) abolished many of the instruments of Catholic ceremony—reliquaries, crosses, censers, and so on—the council ordered the confiscation of all such goods and ornaments from the parish churches. Preconfiscation sales by churchwardens anticipating the order prevented about two-thirds of this rich haul from falling into the hands of courtiers; the wardens often reinvested the proceeds in the repair of their churches.

Although Edward's last parliament rejected the *Reformatio Legum Ecclesiasticarum*, a projected modernization of canon law, Cranmer completed the reformation of doctrine with the publication (12 June 1553) of the Forty-two Articles. These featured Luther's assertion of justification by faith (article 11), Calvin's theology of predestination (article 17), and Cranmer's distinctive "Ratramnian" expression of eucharistic doctrine (article 30), similar to, but technically distinct from, that of Calvin or Zwingli. A Short Catechism compiled by John Ponet adapted the articles for use by schoolmasters. The articles appeared less than a month before the king's death and so had virtually no effect during his reign.

Edwardian reformers had outlawed Catholic doctrine and centuries-old popular religious traditions, but they had not converted the nation. The constructive phase of a state-backed Protestant Reformation necessarily awaited the missionary work of a generation of university-trained parish clergy; this was essentially an Elizabethan development. Nevertheless, because the Elizabethan Settlement rested textually on Edwardian foundations—on the 1552 *Book of Common Prayer* and the 1553 articles—the liturgical and doctrinal innovations of 1547–1553 can be said to have left a revolutionary, lasting imprint on the language and beliefs of everyone who fell heir to the reformed religious culture of Tudor England.

BIBLIOGRAPHY

Brigden, Susan. *London and the Reformation.* Oxford, 1989. Within this magisterial, deeply researched account is a one-hundred-page analysis (chaps. 10–12) suggestively connecting the Protestantism of the London clergy, people, and municipal authorities to royal religious policy, 1547–1553.

Cross, Claire. *Church and People, 1450–1660: The Triumph of the Laity in the English Church.* Reprint, London, 1987. As an introductory synthesis, Cross's 8,000 words on Edward's reign (chap. 4, pp. 81–100) supplements Dickens's discussion; counters the notion that England was Protestant by 1553.

Dickens, A. G. *The English Reformation.* Rev. ed. Reprint, University Park, Pa., 1991. Chapters 9 and 10 constitute a masterful introduction to the Edwardian Reformation, though subsequent research by others has rendered doubtful Dickens's general argument for the swift progress of grass-roots Protestantism.

Duffy, Eamon. *The Stripping of the Altars: Traditional Religion in England, c.1400–c.1580.* New Haven and London, 1992. Using parish records and the evidence of wills, Duffy persuasively chronicles (in chaps. 13–15, pp. 448–523, which cover Edward's reign) the pragmatic acceptance of official directives, not an embracing of Protestant belief.

Gasquet, Francis, and Edmund Bishop. *Edward VI and the Book of Common Prayer.* Rev. ed. London, 1928. Although superseded by research since 1965, this work by two Catholic scholars prints (pp. 395–443) the extant manuscript text of the disputation of December 1548 on the Eucharist in the House of Lords (British Library, Royal MS. 17.B.xxxix).

Hoak, Dale. *The King's Council in the Reign of Edward VI.* Cambridge, 1976. Charts the council's administration of religion generally and sets out the evidence of the making of Edward VI's state papers and Northumberland's control of information reaching the king.

Hutton, Ronald. "The Local Impact of the Tudor Reformations." In *The English Reformation Revised,* edited by Christopher Haigh, pp. 114–138. Cambridge and New York, 1987. Making original use of English churchwardens' accounts, reveals the extent of the official campaign against images and "superstitious" rituals.

Jordan, W. K. *Edward VI.* Vol. 1, *The Young King: The Protectorship of the Duke of Somerset.* Vol. 2, *The Threshold of Power: The Dominance of the Duke of Northumberland.* London, 1968 and 1970. This thousand-page, two-volume "life-and-times" narrative remains indispensable for its citation of sources, but *caveat lector:* it repeats too many outdated interpretations and, because the author occasionally misread or mistranscribed archival sources, advances unhistorical arguments.

King, John. "Freedom of the Press, Protestant Propaganda, and Protector Somerset." *Huntington Library Quarterly* 40 (1976), 1–9. Supplies statistical evidence of the dramatic outpouring of published Protestant tracts, 1547–1549.

Kreider, Alan. *English Chantries: The Road to Dissolution.* Cambridge, Mass., 1979. Systematically documents the government's transparent mercenary motives.

Nichols, J. G., ed. *Literary Remains of King Edward VI* (1857). 2 vols. Reprint, New York, 1964. Nichols's extensive introduction constitutes a scholarly biography.

Scarisbrick, J. J. *The Reformation and the English People.* Oxford, 1984. For Edward's reign, especially good on the effect of the dissolution of the chantries on urban schools.

Selwyn, D. G. "A New Version of a Mid-Sixteenth-Century Vernacular Tract on the Eucharist: A Document of the Early Edwardian Reformation?" *Journal of Ecclesiastical History* 39 (1988), 217–229. Prints important evidence of the apparent attempt in about 1548 to achieve a consensus on eucharistic doctrine among reformist and conservative divines.

Spalding, James C., ed. *The Reformation of the Ecclesiastical Laws of England, 1552.* Kirksville, Mo., 1992. A translation of the failed *Reformatio Legum Ecclesiasticarum,* showing what the Church of England could have become—canonically the most advanced of the Reformed churches.

Whiting, Robert. *The Blind Devotion of the People: Popular Religion and the English Reformation.* Cambridge, 1989. Argues the provocative thesis, on the basis of evidence from Devon and Cornwall, that passive conformity or indifference, not an active Protestantism, replaced Catholic beliefs after 1547.

DALE HOAK

EGRANUS, Sylvius (Ger., Johann Wildenauer; 1485?–1535), reform-minded German preacher and humanist. Born in Eger, Bohemia, Egranus earned his M.A. at Leipzig in 1507. After teaching there for several years, he was appointed preacher at Saint Mary's in Zwickau, Saxony. In a sermon of 1517 he attacked the cult of Saint Anne by rejecting the orthodox view that she had married Cleophas after Joachim's death. When complaints reached the bishop of Naumburg, Egranus defended himself in *Contra Calumniatores suos Apologia* (1518) and *Apologetica Responsio* (1518). Luther thereupon praised him for his evangelical zeal, while Erasmus commended his humanistic learning.

During the spring and summer of 1520 Egranus traveled widely, visiting Luther in Wittenberg and Erasmus in Louvain. Upon his return to Zwickau in October, however, he learned that Johann Eck had placed him under a ban, together with Luther. Before long he became embroiled in a controversy with the radical reformer Thomas Müntzer, who had replaced him at Saint Mary's during his prolonged absence. Attacked by both the conservatives and the demagogic Müntzer, he left Zwickau in spring 1521 and became the first reformed minister of Joachimsthal, not far from Eger. But here, too, he was reviled by the orthodox as a Lutheran and by the Lutherans as a conservative. He departed Joachimsthal in 1523, not to return until the year before his death.

Although initially sympathetic to the Reformation, Egranus soon came to oppose its fundamental tenets. He condemned Luther's position concerning the bondage of the will and vigorously rejected his doctrine of salvation by faith alone, arguing that a Christian needs charity and good works as much as faith. Like Erasmus, whom he continued to revere, he preferred to work for change within the church and thus found himself proscribed by the two warring factions.

BIBLIOGRAPHY

Clemen, Otto. "Johannes Sylvius Egranus." *Mitteilungen des Altertumsvereins für Zwickau und Umgegend* 6 (1899), 1–39, and 7 (1902), 1–32. Only thorough treatment of his life and works. A copy of this journal is in the Ratsschulbibliothek, Zwickau.

Wappler, Paul. *Thomas Münzer in Zwickau und die "Zwickauer Propheten."* Wissenschaftliche Beilage zu dem Jahresberichte des Realgymnasiums mit Realschule zu Zwickau. Zwickau, 1908. See especially pp. 7–18; deals at length with the controversy between Müntzer and Egranus. Copies of this monograph are in the Newberry Library, Chicago; British Library, London; and Ratsschulbibliothek, Zwickau.

HARRY VREDEVELD

EL DOCTOR NAVARRO. *See* Azpilcueta, Martín de.

ELECTORS. In order to solve the problem of disputed imperial successions in the Holy Roman Empire, a powerful group of princes agreed to serve as imperial electors (Ger., *Kurfürsten*) beginning in 1273. The archbishops of Mainz, Trier, and Cologne; the king of Bohemia; the count Palatine of the Rhine; the duke of Saxony; and the margrave of Brandenburg functioned as electors until 1636. Emperor Charles

IV's Golden Bull of 1356, which served as the major statement of the Empire's constitution until its dissolution in 1806, codified the procedures to be used in electing emperors and spelled out the rights and privileges of the imperial electors. Electors were granted full exemption from imperial jurisdiction and privileges with respect to coinage, customs duties, mining, and the protection of Jews.

The electors also made up the first chamber of the imperial assemblies (diets; Ger., *Reichstage*), which were fully operational by the fifteenth century. Although the Golden Bull had anticipated annual meetings of the emperor and the electors, these meetings did not materialize on a regular basis outside the sporadic meetings of the imperial diets. Some electors complained about the cost of their imperial duties, and many gave priority to ruling their own territories over imperial affairs. Efforts by Elector-Archbishop Berthold of Mainz to strengthen the powers of the electors at the expense of Emperor Maximilian I also failed. Maximilian was willing to grant the electors more power only if they were willing to pay more in order to help finance his wars.

The electoral college achieved international attention during the last year of Maximilian's reign as Pope Leo X attempted to influence the imperial election and as various magnates vied for the revived prestige of the imperial crown. Maximilian's grandson, Charles, spent at least 850,000 gulden (approximately $850 million) in his successful bid for the imperial office. Charles also had to make the traditional promises to respect the rights and privileges of the electors. This put him in a difficult position when he wanted to suppress the Lutheran movement, which was protected by Elector Frederick II of Saxony and others. The situation became even more delicate when a second electorate (Brandenburg) became Lutheran in 1525 and a third (the Palatinate) officially allowed Protestantism in 1544. Even the ecclesiastical electorate of Cologne threatened to become Protestant in 1547 and again in 1583.

In addition to the specter of a Protestant majority on the electoral college, Charles V also had to resist an effort by the elector-archbishop of Mainz, as archchancellor of the empire, to control the imperial chancellery in 1521. An attempt by Elector John of Saxony to block the election of Archduke Ferdinand as king of the Romans in 1531 also failed, as did a Habsburg family pact in 1551 to make the imperial title hereditary. Thus the imperial constitution continued to exhibit astonishing consistency throughout the sixteenth century and gave support to those who wished to limit the powers of the emperor.

The college of electors continued to elect and advise emperors as well as to serve as a parliamentary body throughout the remainder of the Reformation period and beyond. In 1623 Duke Maximilian I of Bavaria was rewarded for his leadership against the Protestants by being granted the electoral position formerly held by the rulers of the Palatinate, who had defied the authority of the convinced Catholic Emperor Ferdinand II. An eighth electoral position was granted to the Rhenish Palatinate in 1648 as part of the general settlement of the Thirty Years' War.

[*See also* Diet *and* Holy Roman Empire.]

BIBLIOGRAPHY

Bebb, Phillip N. "Golden Bull." In *The Holy Roman Empire: A Dictionary Handbook,* edited by Jonathan W. Zophy, pp. 183–186. Westport, Conn., 1980. Good starting place for a basic understanding of the constitutional position of the electors.

Becker, Winfried. *Der Kurfürstenrat: Grundzüge seiner Entwicklung in der Reichsverfassung und seine Stellung auf dem Westfälischen Friedenskongress.* Münster, 1973. An important work on how the electors functioned as a council in the first half of the seventeenth century.

Rabe, Horst. *Reich und Glaubensspaltung: Deutschland 1500–1600.* Munich, 1989. Places the electors in the broader context of imperial and Reformation history.

Rowan, Steven. "Germany: Electors." In *Dictionary of the Middle Ages,* edited by Joseph Strayer, vol. 5, pp. 491–493. New York, 1982–1989. A well written, concise summary.

JONATHAN W. ZOPHY

EL GRECO (Gk., Domenicos Theotocopulos; 1541–1614), artist. He was born on the Venetian-ruled island of Crete. Trained as an icon painter, he traveled to Venice at age seventeen to become a *madoneros,* as icon painters were called there. El Greco copied and learned from the great Venetian painters, especially Titian. In 1570 he moved to Rome, acquainting himself with the work of the leading contemporary painters there, especially Raphael and Michelangelo, as well as that of his teacher and personal friend Giulio Clovio, the great miniaturist. His friends and associates included many related to the papal offices, including Pope Pius V. Between 1572 and 1576 El Greco returned to Venice, where his work depicted scenes from the New Testament except for a few portraits and pictures of saints.

El Greco's attraction to Spain brought him to Madrid in the summer of 1577 and to Toledo by fall of that year, where he acquired important commissions. Philip II, king of Spain, commissioned *Adoration of the Holy Name of Jesus* and *Martyrdom of Saint Maurice and the Theban Legion,* both today in the Escorial. Between 1580 and 1586 he painted one of his best works, *Agony in the Garden,* now in the Toledo (Ohio) Museum of Art. It reflects Cretan, Venetian, and Spanish influences. In 1586 he painted his largest (4.8 × 3.6 m) and, to some, his most important painting, *Entombment of the Count of Orgaz,* which is located next to the main altar in the Church of Santo Tome at Toledo, Spain.

El Greco's popularity within Spanish culture in the late sixteenth and early seventeenth centuries dramatically demonstrates his acceptance by Spanish Catholic piety. In relation to the Catholic Reformation (or Counter-Reformation), El Greco entered the religious scene of Toledo more than a decade following the Council of Trent. Although none of his earlier artistic activity reflects personal engagement in the theological controversies of sixteenth-century Europe, his life prior to Toledo—early in Crete, twice in Venice, and two years in Rome—place him in contexts of lively debate. His artistic life in Spain, concentrated entirely within the life and purview of the Catholic church, produced works that served late-sixteenth-century Spanish worship (altarpieces) and correspond in visual impact to some of the instructions from the Council of Trent. He does not appear to have used his art, or allowed anyone to use his art, as propaganda for the Spanish Catholic church. Nevertheless, penance was a strong theme in many of his paintings, and his *Saint Peter in Tears* has been called a portrait of a Catholic Reformation hero.

By the end of his life, El Greco showed ever-increasing preoccupation with incorporeal matters. His late style, with its mystic associations, is expressed in the three great altars he painted for the Chapel of San Jose in Toledo in 1598–1599. As an artist in the crosscurrents of Reformation movements and thought, El Greco never wavered from his Catholic commitments.

BIBLIOGRAPHY

Bronstein, Leo. *El Greco: Domenicos Theotocopoulos*. New York, 1990.

Davies, David. "The Influence of Philosophical and Theological Ideas on the Art of El Greco in Spain." In *Actas del XXIII Congreso Internacional de Historia de Arte*, vol. 2, pp. 242–249. Granada, 1973.

El Greco of Toledo. Exhibition Catalog. Boston, 1982.

Emmrich, Irma. *El Greco*. Leipzig, 1987.

JOHN WESLEY COOK

ELIZABETH I OF ENGLAND (1533–1603), Protestant queen. To sixteenth-century Catholic apologists Elizabeth I (r. 1558–1603) was "that wicked woman," the "servant of infamy" because she restored Protestantism to England. To many contemporary Protestants she was their heroine and savior, while remaining a puzzle and a frustration because she refused to reform sufficiently the Church of England, leaving it, in their eyes, too Catholic. But none doubted that Elizabeth had a central role in the Reformation in England. By restoring Protestantism in 1559 and then refusing to sanction further changes in it she kept England on a middle way (*via media*) that frustrated many contemporaries but ripened into a distinctive form of Protestantism by the seventeenth century.

The daughter of Henry VIII and Ann Boleyn, Elizabeth and the English Reformation were born at the same time. During her teenage years in the household of Queen Katherine Parr she absorbed conservative Protestantism and much traditional piety, spending part of 1544 translating Marguerite d'Angoulême's *Miroir de l'âme pechereuse* (Mirror for Sinful Souls) and acquiring a reputation for austere faith. By the time she was twenty she had seen England move from the English Catholicism of Henry VIII through the stages of the Edwardian Reformation marked by the two *Books of Common Prayer* (1549 and 1552). Under her sister Queen Mary Tudor, Elizabeth conformed to papist Catholicism (as distinct from Henry VIII's nationalist Catholicism), but she became the center of Protestant hopes. Mary never trusted her sincerity, scrupling at Elizabeth's "heretical opinions, illegitimacy, and characteristics in which she resembled her mother." After Wyatt's Rebellion in 1554 against the Spanish match, Mary was pressured by the imperial ambassador to execute Elizabeth, but fears that Mary Stuart would inherit the throne saved her.

The presumption that Elizabeth was a Protestant and would lead England back into schism was so widespread that when she inherited the throne on 17 November 1558 she was greeted with Catholic warnings against the wolves of heresy returning from Geneva and with Protestant exuberance. Her response to these expectations was cautious and careful, confusing her contemporaries and feeding a historical debate about her personal religion and her intentions toward the church in England. She clearly intended to restore the royal supremacy over the church, but what form of Protestantism she wished to impose was less clear.

Her own faith was enigmatic. As Patrick Collinson has pointed out, opinions have ranged from belief that she was an atheistic Machiavellian to a religious zealot. The charge of atheism can be discarded, but what her theological orientation might have been is debatable. Collinson accurately describes her faith as a conservative compound of Augustinianism, Lutheranism, and Catholicism.

The Elizabethan Settlement enacted by Parliament in 1559 at Elizabeth's behest has a disputed history. Sir John Neale believed Elizabeth, who preferred to return to the conservative Protestantism of 1549, was forced by a Puritan cadre in the Commons into accepting the 1552 form of the prayer book; Winthrop Hudson and Norman Jones demonstrated that the Elizabethan Settlement was more a product of Catholic resistance in the House of Lords and argue that Elizabeth wanted the 1552 prayer book.

Whatever the queen desired for her Reformation, the settlement made her supreme governor of the church and imposed on the nation the worship prescribed by the 1552 *Book of Common Prayer* as glossed by a set of articles and injunctions issued to the visitators who imposed it in June 1559. In some ways these new rules were more conservative than those of Edward VI, placing the Communion table in the east end of the church "altar wise," and, through the "ornaments rubric," seeming to require Protestant ministers to dress like Catholic priests. Although they were issued in her name, it is not certain how much Elizabeth dictated the content of the articles and injunctions.

In the first few years of the reign many expected Elizabeth

to use her power to make further reforms of the church, since it was a "leaden mediocrity," stranded on a theological sandbar somewhere between Rome and Geneva. Indeed, Elizabeth did make some changes, but not all were to the liking of those inclining toward Swiss Protestantism. In 1560 she ordered a Latin translation of *The Book of Common Prayer* for use in colleges. She ordered a reform of the church calendar, too, so that many saints' days were restored. Refusing to sanction (but not forbidding) clerical marriage, she banned the wives and children of clergy and dons from the precincts of cathedrals and colleges. At the same time she refused to allow the persecution of Catholics, keeping the deposed Marian bishops under arrest despite demands for their deaths. To the horror of leading reformers, their queen, who had walked out of her Christmas mass in 1558 rather than witness the elevation of the Host, insisted on keeping a cross and candlesticks on the Communion table in her chapel.

A number of factors explained all this moderation. One was that Elizabeth saw herself as queen of all the English and had no intention of punishing good citizens just because they were not good Christians. In the famous phrase of Francis Bacon, Elizabeth, not liking "to make windows into men's hearts and secret thoughts . . . tempered her law so as it restraineth only manifest disobedience . . . in impugning her Majesty's supreme power" over the church. Another was that she had the political sense to see the danger inherent in the enthusiastic enforcement of religious policy—she was too aware of the violence underlying religious conviction. Christopher Haigh suggests that the Catholic resistance in Parliament and the conservatism of most of the nation frightened her; she did not wish to push her people into rebellion.

Her moderation encouraged the Catholics and frustrated the enthusiastic reformers. Catholic apologists like John Martial dedicated books to her because she kept a cross in her chapel; that provoked James Calfhill to write a book in which he had to refute Martial without offending the queen (*An Answer to John Martiall's Treatise of the Cross*, 1565). This sort of confusion continued into the late 1560s before the Revolt of the Northern Earls made it clear that Catholics were enemies to her state.

Perhaps some of her toleration toward Catholics, most visible in her refusal to allow the enforcement of the treason laws against them, was the product of her political situation. Needing the support of Spain against France, she was reluctant to alienate Philip II by being too harsh against papists. One result was that Philip II protected her from excommunication until 1570, holding out to the pope the vain hope that she might yet marry a Catholic and return England to obedience to Rome.

In the years following her excommunication, as hostility toward Spain, the plotting of Mary Stuart, and her support of the Dutch rebels increased, she became less tolerant. When seminary priests began working against her religion in 1574, she permitted them to be executed. In a proclamation of 1582 she made the mere status of seminary priest or Jesuit treason.

She had to treat Catholics carefully for pragmatic political reasons. They were too numerous and powerful. Other dangerous religious groups did not benefit from her tolerance. In 1575 she personally signed the death warrants of two Dutch Anabaptists and ordered that they be executed in Smithfield, where heretics had traditionally been burned.

Although lenient toward Catholics, she expected her bishops to enforce the articles and injunctions of 1559 even though many Protestants refused to accept them as theologically sound. This situation led to the Vestiarian Controversy, in which, under pressure from the queen, Bishop Emund Grindal of London suspended thirty-seven Protestant clerics for refusing to wear what they considered "popish rags"—the uniforms of Catholic priests. She insisted that the bishops enforce religious conformity on Protestants, but she refused to issue public orders backing them up, putting her episcopate in an anomalous position. The people they were suppressing responded by blaming the bishops and rejecting Anglican episcopacy, beginning in the late 1560s to turn to presbyterian and separatist models of church organization. Others came to be known as Puritans.

Elizabeth identified herself with her church. In statute law and, she believed, in God's law, she was its guardian and mistress, and she would not allow any infringement of her prerogative. Consequently if anyone dared to take a religious initiative without her permission she reacted swiftly and angrily. In 1562/63, when it was still expected that she would "take further order" for reform, the Convocation of Canterbury innocently prepared to finish the Reformation, proposing to Parliament a set of disciplinary reforms and a statement of belief, the Thirty-nine Articles. When introduced into Parliament, where they were known as the "alphabetical bills for religion," these reforms brought Elizabeth's wrath down on the bishops. She made clear that the bishops were not to make decisions about religion without her permission. Not until 1571 did any of these bills, including the Thirty-nine Articles, become law, leaving the English church in a disciplinary and theological limbo for the first dozen years of her reign.

As it dawned on reformers that the Queen would not complete the Reformation, they began to agitate for a purer religion, creating the Puritan movement. Elizabeth's response to their demands was consistent: she refused to concede anything officially. One important demand of the Puritans was for a better-educated, preaching clergy. In order to promote it local bands of clerics created groups, known as "prophesyings," for biblical study. Attended by laity as well as clergy, the prophesyings seemed to breach the royal prerogative and could be platforms for criticizing the establishment. Elizabeth ordered Archbishop Grindal to stop them in 1576, commenting that England already had enough preachers. After consulting his brother bishops, Grindal refused to suppress them, reminding Elizabeth she was a mortal creature and would be judged by God for hindering the duties of the bishops. Even though his argument was, as Patrick Collinson has shown, based on the unexceptionable authority of Ambrose's reminder to Theodosius that he was a son of the church, Elizabeth sequestered Grindal in 1577, refusing to let him exercise his authority. When Grindal died in 1583 he was replaced by John Whitgift. Called her "little black husband" by Elizabeth, Whitgift accepted the job of bringing the Puritans into obedience to their sovereign.

Although her friend and an ardent supporter of conformity, Whitgift, too, could run afoul of Elizabeth's prerogative in religion. When in 1595 he approved the Lambeth Articles asserting the truth of supralapsarian double predestination, the queen, finding that they went beyond the Thirty-nine Articles, ordered their immediate withdrawal.

Elizabeth's reluctance to allow innovation in her church stimulated the growth of Puritanism and Presbyterianism, but she refused to understand either their theology or their loyalty. When the Marprelate Tracts began appearing in 1587, mocking the bishops and the queen's church, Elizabeth allowed her council to abandon tolerance. Many Puritan suspects were rounded up and a few were executed. In 1593 she assented to the Conventicle Act, which ordered death for anyone who refused to attend the Anglican service or who attended a separatist meeting.

T. E. Hartley has pointed out another irony of Elizabeth's reluctance to move against her religious enemies or reform the church. It was this, he says, that created much of the tension between Elizabeth and her parliaments. Lords and Commons wanted to protect their queen and be more aggressive in defense of the reformed faith, but she insisted they could not protect her unless she asked for protection.

If by the 1590s Elizabeth was less tolerant of religious divergence than she had been, the ground of her intolerance was political. As long as people conformed quietly she never cared what they believed. Only if they acted on beliefs that threatened the state did she withdraw her protection.

Ironically, foreign Protestants saw Elizabeth as the bulwark of their faith. She herself was less enthusiastic about that role, but, under pressure from her counselors, she sent troops and money to aid Protestant rebels in Scotland, France, and the Spanish Netherlands. The origins of this habit of intervening in religious wars was the defense of the reformed religion, which meant the defense of the Elizabethan regime. But, as Wallace MacCaffrey has argued, the process by which Elizabeth emerged as champion of the gospel drained the religious content from English policy. As this happened Elizabeth and her ministers concentrated more and more on the external defense of Protestantism, either ignoring or being irritated by those who still felt stirred by religious enthusiasm.

Elizabeth's foreign policy and religious orientations came together in the many negotiations for her marriage. Under pressure to marry or declare a successor, Elizabeth spent much of the first half of her reign in negotiations with foreign princes, each with an implicit religious agenda. Elizabeth probably never intended to marry, but these negotiations were useful diplomatically and had important ramifications for domestic religious developments. For much of the 1560s talks were aimed at a match with Charles, archduke of Austria. A devout Catholic, Charles demanded the freedom to practice his religion in England, a demand that frightened English Protestants and gave Elizabeth the excuse finally to break off the negotiations. At the beginning of the 1560s it appeared that Erik XIV of Sweden might marry her, bringing Lutheranism to England to the horror of English Calvinists. When, between 1576 and 1579, François Hercules, duke of Anjou, was a candidate for royal consort his Gallican Catholicism provoked an almost hysterical response in England. John Stubbs's *The Discovery of a Gaping Gulf* and Philip Sidney's *Shepheardes Calender* were part of this hysteria, identifying England as God's elect nation whose mission could not be endangered by the marriage. The proposed Anjou match taught Elizabeth the strength of anti-Catholic prejudice and xenophobia among her people.

Elizabeth's conservative religious tastes, jealousy of her royal prerogative, and political acumen profoundly influenced the development of Anglicanism. If she had been other than she was there might never have been Puritans, and there might well have been a religious civil war in the sixteenth century.

BIBLIOGRAPHY

Erickson, Carolly. *The First Elizabeth.* Reprint, New York, 1992. A critical biography that presents Elizabeth as a whimsical, petty human being—a good corrective to the romantic tradition.

Haigh, Christopher. *Elizabeth I.* London, 1988. A collection of interpretive essays on various aspects of Elizabeth's personal rule.

Haigh, Christopher, ed. *The Reign of Elizabeth I.* London, 1984. A collection of essays on various aspects of Elizabethan history, including three on religious policy and practice.

Haugaard, William P. *Elizabeth and the English Reformation.* Cambridge, 1968. A useful account of the development of religious policy in the 1560s, it must be used with care because it rests on outdated assumptions about Elizabethan government.

Hollis, Christopher. *The Monstrous Regiment.* London, 1929. Believing Elizabeth was an atheist, Hollis wrote a Catholic study of her religious policy. Not a good book, it is the only study of her religious policy that covers the entire reign.

Jones, Norman. *The Birth of the Elizabethan Age: England in the 1560s.* Oxford, 1993. Places the establishment of Elizabeth's religious policy into context. Corrects Haugaard.

MacCaffrey, Wallace T. *The Shaping of the Elizabethan Regime.* Princeton, 1968. Narrates Elizabeth's policies from 1558 until 1572.

———. *Queen Elizabeth and the Making of Policy, 1572–1588.* Princeton, 1981. Continues the narrative up to the Armada, paying special attention to Elizabeth's relations with foreign Protestants.

———. *Elizabeth I: War and Politics, 1588–1603.* Princeton, 1992. The final volume of the trilogy, the political decay that accompanied Elizabeth's personal decay.

———. *Elizabeth I.* London, 1993. Will probably supplant Neale.

Neale, J. E. *Queen Elizabeth I.* Reprint, Chicago, 1992. Long the standard biography, it presents Elizabeth through a rosy haze of romantic nationalism.

NORMAN JONES

ELIZABETHAN SETTLEMENT. Defining the official state religion that became known as Anglicanism, the Elizabethan Settlement of 1559 made England a permanently Protestant nation. It consists of a set of statutes passed in the first Parliament of Queen Elizabeth I. The most important were the Act of Supremacy (1 Eliz. I, c. 1), which restored to the English Crown the supremacy over the church claimed by Henry VIII and Edward VI but repealed by Mary Tudor; and the Act of Uniformity (1 Eliz. I, c. 2) which reimposed *The Book of Common Prayer* of 1552 as the uniform standard of English worship. The Act of Uniformity was interpreted by the Visitation Articles and Royal Injunctions issued in June 1559 as a guide for the visitors who toured the kingdom in the summer and fall of 1559, imposing the new form of worship on the parishes, removing clergy who refused to use the new service, and cleansing the churches of "papistical" decorations. The church-state relations and the forms of worship established in 1559 became the baseline of religious change in England, creating Anglicanism. Puritanism, Separatism, and Anglo-Catholicism all grew from resistance to part or all of the settlement, making it a central event in English religious history.

For the most part, the settlement's legislation returned England to the religious position it held at the death of Edward VI. The Act of Supremacy reestablished royal supremacy over the church (which had been revoked by 1 & 2 Philip and Mary, c. 8) and canceled the Marian laws that had restored the medieval heresy statutes. It reinstated the acts of the Reformation Parliament that had abolished the papacy's jurisdiction over England and given all spiritual jurisdiction to the Crown. The Act, however, did not give the monarch the title of "Supreme Head of the Church." Responding to critics who argued that no human could head Christ's church, the new law called the monarch "Supreme Governor" of things spiritual and temporal.

The Act of Uniformity bound all English people to use the prayer book of 1552 but with two small alterations, one of which removed an attack on the pope. The other amended the words of institution in the Eucharist, making it more scripturally correct and possibly more agreeable to Henrician Catholics who wished to see in the Eucharist the transubstantiation of the Roman Mass. The act contained the Ornaments Rubric ordering that the ornaments, rites, and ceremonies of the church should be as they had been in the second year of Edward VI's reign. Innocent enough on paper, this provision provoked heated disputes in the 1560s and became central to later debates over whether Elizabeth was intending to restore Henrician Catholicism or moving closer to Calvinism.

Along with these two central statutes, there were a number of subsidiary ones that gave further form to the settlement. Most importantly, the ecclesiastical taxes known as First Fruits and Tenths were restored to the Crown. Initially given to Henry (by 26 Henry VIII, c. 3), they were returned by Mary to the restored Catholic church in the person of the primate of England. An Elizabethan act (1 Eliz. I, c. 4) placed these revenues once again at the disposal of the monarch. Reasoning that the supreme governor should control the resources of the church, another act (1 Eliz. I, c. 19) gave Elizabeth the right during vacancies to exchange lands with bishoprics. This act later slowed episcopal appointments and further impoverished the church. Following the logic of Protestantism and economics, the monasteries and chantries established under Mary were abolished (by 1 Eliz. I, c. 24), putting their revenues into the queen's pockets. A final act (1 Eliz. I, c. 22) gave Elizabeth personally the right to make rules for collegiate churches, schools, and corporations, allowing her to impose reform on institutions whose statutes might otherwise remain Catholic.

In short, the primary aim of the settlement was to restore to future English monarchs all the power over the church in England that they held before Mary Tudor returned England to obedience to the papacy. While clearly Protestant, however, it seemed to temporize between Protestantism and Catholicism. Elizabeth's refusal to be supreme head of the church, the changes in the prayer book, the Ornaments Rubric, and the absence of an act permitting the clergy to marry suggest that, although Protestant, the settlement was intended to avoid the religious extremes of both Calvinism and Roman Catholicism while finding a home close to the Lutheran establishments of the Baltic. The nature of the settlement, however, made it difficult to know what its true theological intention was, to the frustration of the faithful and historians alike.

Parliament and the Settlement. How these acts came into being and what Parliament meant by them has been debated since they were enacted. The Elizabethan Settlement created the famous Anglican *via media*, or "middle way," in reformed religion, preventing the kind of religious civil war that plagued Scotland, Holland, and France in the second half of the sixteenth century. Nonetheless, the meaning of the settlement and the religious intentions of Queen Elizabeth have been intensely debated since the 1560s. In the queen's lifetime her insistence that no further change should be allowed in religion drove many devout Protestants into dissent. In the seventeenth century the authority claimed by Archbishop William Laud rested on the settlement. In the nineteenth century the debates between High and Low Anglicans often turned around the terms and intentions of the settlement, while English Catholics sniped at the Anglicans with critiques of the historical legitimacy of the Settlement. In the early twentieth century historians carried on the partisan debate, while in the 1950s Sir John Neale created an interpretation that told the story in Cold War terms. Since the late 1970s historians have moved away from sectarian or political interpretations, concentrating on how the settlement was actually created in Parliament in order to understand what its creators were attempting to achieve.

Elizabeth's intentions in the settlement are obscure because she was attempting to avoid polarization that, she feared, would set off a religious civil war in England. She began moving the nation toward Protestantism from the first days of her reign by personal example and royal proclamation, but it required Parliament to officially change England's faith. When assembled at the end of January 1559, it was informed by Lord Keeper Nicholas Bacon that it was convened to unite the people of the realm into a uniform order of religion.

The first step in the return was the restoration of the supremacy of the Crown over the church, a bill for which was introduced in the first week of the session. A bill for "order of service and ministers in the church" and a bill for uniform worship were introduced a week later. All of these measures were joined into a single bill on 21 February. This omnibus bill, which would have given the queen the supremacy and established religious uniformity of some sort was passed by the House of Commons and sent to the House of Lords, where it met with stiff resistance from the bishops. Convocation petitioned the Lords against the bill, confirming both transubstantiation and papal supremacy, and the resistance in the House of Lords forced the bill into committee, where it was rewritten.

When it came out of committee it looked as if there would be no Elizabethan Settlement. The revised bill refused Elizabeth parliamentary recognition of the supremacy, did not restore Protestantism, and did not repeal the Marian heresy laws. The Commons reacted by passing a bill that said no one could be punished for using the religion of Edward VI, and Elizabeth, seemingly intending to dissolve Parliament before Easter, was on the verge of accepting a limited supremacy and using a royal proclamation to allow a Protestant Eucharist. Rather than a dissolution, however, the government engineered a debate between Catholics and Protestants at Westminster during the week of Easter. The Westminster Disputation ended in disaster for the Catholics, who were misled about the way in which it was to be organized. When they refused to dance to the government tune, the debate was ended, and two of the Catholic bishops were arrested and sent to the Tower of London for their disobedience.

This display of royal muscle gave the Crown just enough strength in the House of Lords to change the balance of power. New bills for supremacy and uniformity were prepared during the Easter recess, made more appealing to the enemies of the supremacy by the use of "supreme governor" in the supremacy oath and by the changed words of institution in the prayer book. These two new bills easily passed the House of Commons, but in the Lords they were forced into committee by Archbishop Nicholas Heath. Although the supremacy could not be wrecked this time, conservatives amended it so that the Commission for Ecclesiastical Causes, created by the bill in order to enforce the settlement, could not try Catholics for heresy. When the vote was taken, all the bishops in attendance and one layman voted against it, but it passed. Few lay people, even those who believed in transubstantiation, supported papal supremacy. The laity had reaped great financial benefits from the alienation of church property into their hands, and they feared having to return it to the church if the pope remained supreme.

The uniformity came much closer to defeat. A compound of the Acts of Uniformity of 1549 and 1552, it reimposed the 1552 prayer book and ordered everyone to attend church every Sunday or pay a one shilling fine. It also gave the queen the right to alter rites and ceremonies for the advancement of God's glory and the edifying of his church, a clause that gave many people hope of further reform. When the bill was put to a vote, eighteen opposed it and twenty-one voted for it, giving the bill a majority of three. If the bishops of Lincoln and Winchester had not been in the Tower of London and Abbot John Feckenham of Westminster inexplicably absent, the uniformity bill would not have passed.

The current interpretation of the creation of the Elizabethan Settlement, based on reconstruction of the events in Parliament in 1559, holds that Elizabeth intended to return the relations between the church and state in England to the standard of 1552. A Protestant herself—probably more a Lutheran than a Calvinist—she, as the lord keeper declared, wanted the supremacy and uniformity reestablished. She was supported by committed Protestants and Erastians in both houses of Parliament but bitterly resisted by the bishops in the Lords, all of whom voted against the change and were later removed from their bishoprics and imprisoned. What her enthusiastic Protestant supporters did not comprehend until later in the reign was her jealous care for her prerogative to control religion.

Passing laws does not effect change unless they are enforced. The settlement was imposed by visitors, both ecclesiastical and lay, who toured the nation in the summer and fall of 1559 administering the oath of supremacy to the clergy and asking the churchwardens to destroy Catholic church furnishings and ornaments. By the time they had finished, the prayer book was to be in use and the churches reformed. It was not as effective as hoped, but the visitation did make it clear that the new faith was required by law. The justices were called in to help, too, and slowly most of the nation became used to the new service.

Theologically the settlement was vague. Truly Protestant in inspiration, it was attached to a medieval church structure that continued to enforce the canon law of Rome unless that law contradicted the royal authority. Elizabeth's bishops, however, were for the most part heavily influenced by Swiss Protestantism and so gave the new establishment a Calvinist tinge, even as they found themselves uncomfortably defending the supremacy against Puritans and Presbyterians.

Elizabeth stuck close to the letter of the law on religion and allowed little deviation from the statutory regulations. She was deaf to the Puritans, forbidding even Parliament to discuss religion without her permission and insisting on the enforcement of the Ornaments Rubric. She even made it difficult for the bishops to acquire the disciplinary tools necessary to enforce the reform. By the time she died in 1603, still intransigent, the rhythms of the prayer book and the authority of the supreme governor were well established in the national mind. At the same time, her intransigence over changing the settlement had hardened the resistance of Puritans and Separatists and forced her bishops to take a hard line in defense of their own authority in the face of the Presbyterians, who attacked them because they had to carry out the queen's settlement.

Historiography of the Settlement. Many of the debates over the settlement center on Parliament because the intent of the Commons, Lords, and queen in Parliament set the standard by which the law must be interpreted. Unfortunately the "mind of the legislature" is particularly hard to read in 1559 because the history of the acts is confusing and obscure. The oldest historiographical tradition, represented by John Foxe, William Camden, and John Strype, held that Elizabeth intended to create the Anglican church, succeeding even though the Catholics in the House of Lords nearly scuttled her efforts. This interpretation remained standard until the early 1950s, when John Neale (1953, vol. 1) created a new orthodoxy, arguing that the settlement was a compromise between Elizabeth, who wanted only to restore the church to its state at the death of Henry VIII, and Puritans, who attempted to force the church into the Genevan mold. Consciously modeling the Puritans on the Bolsheviks, Neale argued that a tiny cadre of ideologically committed men resisted Elizabeth's intentions so stoutly in the House of Commons that she was forced to accept the 1552 *Book of Common Prayer* rather than a Henrician form of service.

Neale reached this conclusion by ignoring the House of Lords, which contained a powerful bloc of Catholic bishops who did their best to stop the enactment of the settlement, and by making some unwarranted assumptions about the religious commitments of the leaders of the government and the returned Marian exiles. In the 1970s his interpretation was attacked by Winthrop Hudson, who argued that Cambridge men like William Cecil, who led Elizabeth's government, would never have settled for less than the 1552 standard. Moreover, I found that the resistance of the bishops was of paramount importance in explaining the shape of the settlement. Michael Graves, Sir Geoffrey Elton, and several others further undermined Neale's Puritan conspiracy theory, so that his interpretation has come to be widely rejected. Current historiography holds that the settlement was intended to return the kingdom to the religion of 1552.

The Elizabethan Settlement has been subject to reinterpretation by succeeding generations of English historians because it is so central to English national identity. As religious and ideological fashions have changed, so has our understanding of the settlement. Current interpretation favors a more consensual understanding of its creation in Parliament, but that, too, has come under attack as a renewed awareness of the power of religious ideology has penetrated the academy.

[*See also* Acts of Supremacy; Acts of Uniformity; *and* Elizabeth I of England.]

BIBLIOGRAPHY

Birt, Henry Norbert. *The Elizabethan Religious Settlement.* London, 1907. An old but still useful study.

Collinson, Patrick. *The Religion of Protestants: The Church in English Society, 1559–1625.* Oxford, 1982. The Ford Lectures for 1979, these essays demonstrate the ways in which the settlement came to be a part of English life. Especially valuable on the relationship between Elizabeth and her bishops.

Frere, Walter Howard, ed. *Visitation Articles and Injunctions of the Period of the Reformation.* 3 vols. London, 1910. Vol. 3 contains the articles and injunctions that defined the settlement.

Gee, Henry. *The Elizabethan Clergy and the Settlement of Religion, 1558–1564.* Oxford, 1898. Still the best study of the effect of the settlement on the clergy.

Haugaard, William P. *Elizabeth I and the English Reformation.* Cambridge, 1968. Concentrates on the process of defining the settlement that went on in the early 1560s.

Hudson, Winthrop S. *The Cambridge Connection and the Elizabethan Settlement of 1559.* Durham, N.C., 1980. Emphasizes the personal connections between the men who ran Elizabeth's government and argues that they shared a view of religion given form in the settlement.

Jones, Norman. *Faith by Statute: Parliament and the Settlement of Religion, 1559.* London, 1982. The most detailed account of the making of the settlement.

Kitching, C. J., ed. *The Royal Visitation of 1559: Act Book of the Northern Province.* Surtees Society 187. Gateshead, U.K., 1975. Kitching's introduction provides a valuable picture of how the visitation worked and what was found in the province of York. The record for Canterbury does not survive.

Neale, John Ernest. *Elizabeth I and Her Parliaments.* 2 vols. Reprint, New York, 1966. Vol. 1 contains his now discredited account of the making of the settlement. Both volumes emphasize the attempts made to use Parliament to change the settlement.

Solt, Leo F. *Church and State in Early Modern England, 1509–1640.* Oxford, 1990. A recent and useful overview of the settlement's implications.

NORMAN JONES

ELYOT, Thomas (1490?–1546), English humanist who popularized the ideas of ancient Greece and Rome during the reign of Henry VIII. His father, Sir Richard, was a lawyer and judge. Born about 1490, probably in the county of Wiltshire, Thomas studied at Oxford and at the Middle Temple, one of the Inns of Court. He was a member of Thomas More's circle; it is likely that he met Thomas Linacre and Hans Holbein the Younger at More's home in Chelsea.

During most of the 1520s Elyot was clerk of the King's Council, a position he probably owed to the influence of Thomas Wolsey. After Wolsey's fall, Elyot also lost his office, but in 1531 he was named ambassador to Emperor Charles V. He was unable to convince Charles of the merits of Henry VIII's proceedings against Catherine of Aragon (Charles' aunt) and was recalled in 1532. He never held government office again but spent his last years in retirement at his country home near Cambridge.

Elyot's most important work is *The Boke Named the Gouernour*, published in 1531. It is possible that he put the treatise together immediately after his dismissal from the council in the hope of regaining the king's favor; it is dedicated to Henry VIII. The first chapters of the *Gouernour* set out a political theory that stresses the importance of the monarch. Later sections prescribe a classical education for members of the governing classes and discuss the virtues that such "governors" should possess. Examples drawn from the history of Greece and Rome are used to illustrate these qualities.

Elyot's greatest scholarly contribution was his Latin-English dictionary, published in 1542. It was the first dictionary aimed at giving English equivalents for the entire vocabulary of the classical Latin authors. He also wrote *The Castel of Helth*, the earliest medical manual in English to set out Galen's theory of the humors and complexions; several humanistic dialogues; and *The Defence of Good Women*, a covert statement of his support for Catherine of Aragon. Both the *Gouernour* and *The Castel of Helth* were reprinted frequently during the sixteenth century. Later editions of the dictionary were expanded and revised by Bishop Thomas Cooper.

BIBLIOGRAPHY

Primary Sources

Croft, H. H. S., ed. *The Boke Named the Gouernour.* 2 vols. London, 1880.

Lehmberg, Stanford, ed. *The Boke Named Gouernour.* London, 1962.

Secondary Sources

Dowling, Maria. *Humanism in the Age of Henry VIII.* London, 1986. Sets Elyot's work in its intellectual context.

Fox, Alistair, and John Guy, eds. *Reassessing the Henrician Age: Humanism, Politics and Reform, 1500–1550.* Oxford, 1986. Contains a valuable essay on Elyot by Alistair Fox.

Lehmberg, Stanford. *Sir Thomas Elyot, Tudor Humanist.* Austin, 1960. The standard account of Elyot's life and works.

Major, John M. *Sir Thomas Elyot and Renaissance Humanism.* Lincoln, Nebr., 1964. Emphasizes Elyot's Platonism.

Stanford E. Lehmberg

EMDEN. In the early sixteenth century the port city of Emden (with a population of about three thousand to four thousand people) was primarily important as the residence of the Cirksena counts of East Friesland (Ostfriesland). There were strong traditions of civic influence in ecclesiastical appointments, but the count from his castle controlled the nearby Grosse Kirche and appointed the city council. Count Enno (r. 1528–1540) introduced the Lutheran Reformation, but Catholicism, as well as variant forms of Protestantism, remained visible in a city already known for welcoming religious exiles, including Melchior Hoffman, who, during 1529–1530, is said to have baptized three hundred adults in the sacristy of the Grosse Kirche.

Countess Anna (r. 1540–1558) made the town council an elective body in 1545, though it was still subject to princely influence. She also veered from her late husband's religious policy by naming Jan Łaski superintendent of the Emden church (1543). Łaski introduced weekly meetings (*coetus*) of the Reformed clergy and established a board of lay elders, although its responsibilities were at this time limited to church discipline. During the years the Augsburg Interim was in effect (1548–1552), the Emdeners closed their churches rather than accept a reestablishment of Catholic ritual, and Łaski went into exile; in 1550 King Edward VI appointed him pastor of the church for Low Countries refugees in London. When Łaski returned to Emden, he brought with him members of the London congregation, especially southern Netherlanders like Maarten Micron and Jan Utenhove (both from Ghent). The reestablished consistory was now entrusted with full powers for governing the church, and the city's population grew by 30 percent between 1555 and 1562, mainly because of the influx of religious refugees from the southern Low Countries.

It was during this period that the nascent Reformed congregations of the Low Countries looked to Emden for guidance; Gaspar van der Heyden, pastor of the key Antwerp church, came to Emden for study, and Jan Arendszoon Mandenmaker received from Emden his mandate for organizing Reformed churches in Holland. Meanwhile, Emden's new printing industry, set up by refugees who had come by way of London, published as many books in south Netherlandish as in the local Low German, including a translation of the 1554 Magdeburg edition of Martin Luther's bible (1558) and the first edition of Adriaan Corneliszoon van Haemstede's Dutch martyrology (1559). Emden's importance diminished as the Netherlands congregations grew stronger, especially during the brief period (1566–1567) when there seemed a real prospect of religious liberty.

Reestablishment of Spanish control under Fernando Álvarez de Toledo, duke of Alba, brought a new wave of refugees, including, this time, many from the northern provinces of the Low Countries. Emden's Baltic trade experienced an unprecedented boom as refugees transferred their business operations here, and Dutch rebel Sea Beggars preyed on the commerce of centers still loyal to Spain, such as Amsterdam. Yet East Friesland's co-rulers, counts Edzard II (r. 1558–1599) and Johann (r. 1558–1591), were careful to keep their distance from the pirate-patriots, who did not scruple to take prizes from their natural allies. Plans for a synod of Netherlands Reformed congregations originated among southerners based in Calvinist centers such as Heidelberg and Frankenthal, but they were not entirely welcome to Hollanders based in Emden, for whom garnering all possible support for William of Orange was more important than theological precision. The Synod of Emden (1571) left room for discussion on some points, but it proved vital in defining for future Dutch Protestantism a Calvinist doctrinal standard (based on the Belgic Confession and the Heidelberg Catechism) and a Calvinist church order (based on the consistories and classes of the French church).

Once the Revolt of the Netherlands gained a foothold in Holland and Zeeland (1572), Emdeners were free to concentrate on their own affairs, just as confrontation loomed between an orthodox Lutheran co-ruler, Count Edzard II, and Menso Alting, the stout Calvinist who served as preacher at the Grosse Kirche and presiding officer of the consistory from 1575 until 1612. The Calvinist Count Johann, who shared authority with his brother, was able to shield Emden from Edzard II's practice of appointing orthodox Lutheran pastors wherever possible, but civic opposition surfaced in the creation of a body called The Forty (1589), which, unlike any of the civic bodies recognized by the counts, was chosen only by the citizens without being subject to princely approval. Upon Johann's death in 1591, Edzard II dismissed Alting from his post, banned further meetings of the consistory without his permission, and sought to place the finances of the diaconate under his control. The Forty and the consistory, however, working closely together, were strong enough to block Edzard's attempt to implement in Emden a Lutheran version of what some scholars call the Second Reformation. In two accords signed in 1595 and 1599, the count accepted Emden's religious autonomy, thus guaranteeing a future for the Reformed community built by Łaski and the London refugees.

[*See also* Calvinism; Religious Orders; *and* Social Discipline.]

BIBLIOGRAPHY

Nauta, D., J. P. van Dooren, and Otto J. deJong, eds. *De Synode van Emden, Oktober 1571*. Kampen, 1971.

Pettegree, Andrew. *Emden and the Dutch Revolt: Exile and the Development of Reformed Protestantism.* Oxford, 1992.

Schilling, Heinz. "Reformierte Kirchenzucht als Sozialdisziplinierung? Die Tätigkeit des Emdener Presbyteriums in den Jahren 1557–1562." In *Niederlande und Nordwestdeutschland. Studien zur Regional- und Stadtgeschichte Nordwestkontinentaleuropas im Mittelalter und in der Neuzeit*, edited by Wilfried Ehbrecht and Heinz Schilling, pp. 261–327. Cologne, 1983.

———. "Calvinism and Urban Republicanism: The Emden Experience." In *Civic Calvinism in Northwestern Germany and the Netherlands*, pp. 11–40. Saint Louis, 1991.

Schilling, Heinz, and Klaus-Dieter Schreiber, eds. *Die Kirchenratsprotocolle der Reformierten Gemeinde Emden, 1557–1620.* 2 vols. Cologne, 1989–1992.

JAMES D. TRACY

EMDEN, SYNOD OF. Although a product of diverse tendencies within the Netherlands Reformed community, the Synod of Emden (October 1571) had the unambiguous effect of setting a Calvinist standard for the doctrine and organization of the future Dutch Reformed church. Circular letters calling for a synod were first put out (summer 1571) by Flemish and Walloon pastors of the refugee congregations in Heidelberg and Frankenthal, but the actual organizing of the meeting was done by agents of William of Orange with the cooperation of refugees from the northern provinces (Holland in particular), who had found a haven in Emden. The men of Flanders and Wallonia were the survivors of a bitter confrontation between fierce Habsburg persecution and a community that looked to Geneva for the discipline and organization to withstand it, but Hollanders had no experience of Calvinism before 1566 and saw the need not so much for doctrinal purity (some of their ministers had kind words for the Augsburg Confession) as for political unity behind William of Orange.

If these two currents of thought did indeed clash at Emden, as the older historiography maintained, then the Calvinist party was the clear winner. Numerically dominated by delegates of Flemish and Walloon origin, the synod affirmed both the Belgic Confession (1561) and the Gallic Confession (1559) as standards of orthodoxy and recommended the use of the Geneva and Heidelberg catechisms for use in the Francophone and Netherlandish congregations, respectively. Ministers and electors were to be chosen in keeping with the practice of the Emden church, and local congregations were to be subordinated to a synodic organization, the first tier of which was the important assembly of local pastors known in northern France (and henceforth in the Netherlands) as the classis. More recent scholars have downplayed the element of friction, noting that the synod avoided taking a position on certain lesser issues where some thought purity of doctrine was at stake. The important point is that, coming fortuitously just prior to the establishment of a rebel and Protestant beachhead in Holland and Zeeland (from April 1572), the synod of Emden provided harassed leaders of a nascent official church with ready answers to basic questions. It would be years, even decades, before orthodox Calvinists achieved a clear victory over rival tendencies within the Dutch Reformed church, but it is not too much to say that Emden had pointed the way toward a Calvinist future.

BIBLIOGRAPHY

Nauta, D., and J. van Dooren, eds. *De Synode van Emden, Oktober 1571*. Kampen, 1971.

Pettegree, Andrew. *Emden and the Dutch Revolt: Exile and the Development of Reformed Protestantism*. Oxford, 1992.

Rutgers, F. L. *Acta van der Nederlandsche Synoden der Zestiende Eeuw*. The Hague, 1899. For the *acta* of the synod.

James D. Tracy

EMPIRE. The term originates from ancient Rome, where it denoted the legal power of magistrates, and, furthermore, worldwide domination by the Roman people and emperors. Beginning in the Middle Ages it came to refer to the Holy Roman Empire, which had been restored by the papacy and Otto I, crowned emperor in 962, as a continuation of Charlemagne's empire and of the ancient Roman empire. The dignity of the emperor (*Imperator Romanorum augustus* from 976) and his *Imperium Romanum* (from 1034; *sacrum* from 1157) were connected with the office of the Roman king, who was elected by German princes, and were closely associated with the Roman church. Papal consecration and coronation were constitutive elements, as was rulership over the former Italian kingdom of the Langobards and, later, over Burgundy. From the fifteenth century the addition of the phrase "of the German nation" became common. During the Middle Ages, a relationship to the Greek emperors has never been clarified; they transferred their imperial claim to their Ottoman conquerors after 1453.

Imperial theory presupposed a universal authority (also called *Monarchia*), based on the unity of the spiritual and temporal orders and their respective universal heads. The preeminence of the empire derived from the theory of the translation of the ancient Roman empire to the northern emperors, from the supremacy of Roman law granting universal jurisdiction, from its providential role as the fourth of the prophet Daniel's world empires—supposed to last until the coming of the Antichrist—and finally from the imperial duty to defend the church. Therefore only a single emperor could exist within Christianity, entrusted with the task of defending the faith and safeguarding peace and justice.

There were three major—and controversial—concepts of *Imperium:* the ecclesiastical (Innocent III), according to which it was a special dignity within the universal church and did not encroach upon the sovereignty of other rulers, who enjoyed the same rights within their territories as the emperor did in general; the hierocratic (Innocent IV), according to which the emperor was a mere servant and the pope was the true emperor in both church and world; and the dualistic (Henry VII), in which the emperor possessed independent competence in all secular matters analogous to the papal authority in the church, admitting, at least *de facto*, the existence of other subordinate powers. This concept was masterfully elaborated by Dante (d. 1321), who maintained that the world ruler depended entirely on God, that the imperial duty had been conferred on the Roman people, and that the imperial office corresponded to human destiny on earth: earthly happiness.

In reality the empire was no less subject to territorialization than were other monarchies, and finally *Imperium* came to mean the German kingdom, which possessed some rights in northern Italy and Burgundy, and where the princes strengthened their position beside the monarchical power. However, the idea of the universal empire survived among Germans and Italians (Ghibellinism) and was used by Maximilian I and Charles V in support of their dynastic power policies.

A redefinition of empire was formulated by Italian humanists of the fifteenth century. Their argument that the Roman Empire had ceased to exist with the invasion of the Goths (Flavio Biondo) had a powerful impact on the theory of translation. The classical meaning of empire, never totally forgotten, was restored—denoting either legitimate rule, any sovereign authority, or a major state that owed its growth to conquest (Leonardo Bruni).

Later understandings of empire were also influenced by the discovery of the New World. The idea of imperial unity could not survive the rise of overseas empires and, with it, expanded consciousness of the earth's dimensions. According to Francisco de Vitoria, there was no longer a single world ruler (*Relectio de Indis*, 1539).

In Germany these meanings of empire were used by Protestants as an argument against the papacy, but they insisted at the same time on the translation theory and the dignity of the German people entrusted with the empire (Philipp Melanchthon). Other national monarchies appropriated not only the humanists' interpretation of the term but also its imperial symbolism. Charles V's Spanish successors, who belonged to the Habsburg dynasty, were associated with the imperial dignity of their cousins in Vienna (*Austriacismo*). The concept of Spanish monarchy (seldom empire) derived to a great extent from imperial traditions (Tommaso Campanella). In France from the Middle Ages (Pierre Dubois) the imperial claim was based on historical ancestry in the person of Charlemagne and on the particular Christian sacredness of the French king, who should guarantee the world's unity in spiritual as well as in temporal matters (Guillaume Postel). In England the term was used to defend royal supremacy over both church and state. The monarchy was interpreted as a heritage of Constantine the Great

(Henry VIII) and as the sacred empire securing peace and justice (Elizabeth I). The concept of a kingdom of Brittany and overseas acquisitions also served as a basis for imperial claims.

[*See also* Cromwell, Thomas; Discoveries in the New World; Gattinara, Mercurino Arborio di; Habsburg, House of; Holy Roman Empire; *and* Ottoman Empire.]

BIBLIOGRAPHY

Bosbach, Franz. *Monarchia Universalis: Ein politischer Leitbegriff der frühen Neuzeit.* Göttingen, 1988.

Headley, John M. "Germany, the Empire and *Monarchia* in the Thought and Policy of Gattinara." In *Das römisch-deutsche Reich im politischen System Karls V.*, edited by Heinrich Lutz, pp. 15–33. Munich, 1982.

———. "'Eher Türckisch als Bäpstisch': Lutheran Reflections on the Problem of Empire, 1623–28." *Central European History* 20 (1987), 3–28.

Koebner, Richard. *Empire.* Cambridge, 1961; reprint, New York, 1965.

Les Grands Empires. Recueils de la Société Jean Bodin, vol. 31. Brussels, 1973.

Moraw, Peter, Karl Otmar von Aretin, Notker Hammerstein, and Werner Conze. "Reich I-V." In *Geschichtliche Grundbegriffe: Historisches Lexikon zur politisch-sozialen Sprache in Deutschland,* edited by Otto Brunner, Werner Conze, and Reinhard Koselleck, vol. 5, pp. 423–488. Stuttgart, 1984.

Yates, Frances A. *Astraea: The Imperial Theme in the Sixteenth Century.* Reprint, London and Boston, 1985.

FRANZ BOSBACH

EMSER, Hieronymus (1478–1527), German humanist and Catholic controversialist. He was probably born at Wiederstetten near Ulm and studied at Tübingen and Basel, where in 1499 he received the degree of *magister artium* and was ordained a priest; the date of his ordination is unclear, but in any case it was before 1502. In Basel he came into contact with the circle of humanists who often met at the house of the publisher Johannes Amerbach. After a period in the service of the papal legate Cardinal Raimundo Peraudi between 1502 and 1504, he pursued studies at Leipzig and obtained the baccalaureate in theology in 1505; probably in that same year he received his license in canon law.

Also in 1505 Emser accepted the invitation of Duke George of Saxony to move to Dresden to be his chaplain and official secretary. He was sent by the duke to Rome between 1506 and 1507 to promote the canonization of Bishop Benno von Meissen (who had died in 1106). Later in 1512 he published a biography of the bishop. After seven years, in 1511, he left the duke's service, with whom he nonetheless continued to maintain close relations, in order to devote himself to humanist studies. He was a friend of humanists such as Willibald Pirckheimer and Hermann von Busche and carried on a correspondence with Desiderius Erasmus, whose *Enchiridion militis christiani* he had published in Leipzig in 1515.

In 1519 he was present at the Leipzig debate between Johann Eck and Luther, with whom he had also had personal contact. From that time, with the support of Duke George and the interest of the papal nuncio Girolamo Aleandro, he devoted his energies to the debate with the reformers. The polemics with Luther, in particular, quickly took on inflamed tones. With his first pamphlet in August 1519 Emser, by maintaining that Luther was not a follower of the Hussite heresy, was in fact compelling Luther to choose between declaring himself a promoter of Hussitism or to retract his theses (*De disputatione lipsicensi . . .*). To what he considered a provocation Luther responded in one of his most violent polemical writings, *Ad aegocerotem Emserianum M. Lutheri additio*, to which Emser replied in November with *A venatione Lutherana aegocerotis assertio* (the *aegoceros* [ibex] was the heraldic emblem of Emser). In the years that followed, Emser continued to devote himself to anti-Protestant polemics, either through writings of his own or through the publishing of others' writings, to such an extent that he operated a printing press in his house between 1524 and 1526. This intense publishing activity was cut short by his premature death on 8 November 1527.

The polemical writings of Emser include twenty-six works that can be grouped as follows: the writings of 1519 on the Leipzig debate; the writings of 1520–1521 against Luther's *An den christlichen Adel*; the polemics with Andreas Bodenstein von Karlstadt on the veneration of images; his criticism in 1523 of Luther's translation of the New Testament; and his writings of 1524–1525 on the debate with Luther and also with Huldrych Zwingli. His main arguments centered on the Eucharist, the sacrificial character of the Mass, the ministerial priesthood, the interpretation of the scriptures in the light of tradition, and the magisterium of the church. Particularly biting were the criticisms he directed in 1523 against Luther's translation of the New Testament, in which he identified fourteen hundred errors and distortions. At the invitation of Duke George, Emser himself then prepared his own translation, published in 1527, the year of his death.

Emser's notoriety stems from his having been one of the first and most resolute opponents of Luther. His writings do not contain a systematic explanation of the individual points of Catholic doctrine; their weakness lies in the method itself, which consisted in refuting the adversaries' theses argument by argument. Moreover, he was by education and personal inclination a humanist. His theological preparation was inadequate for a doctrinal debate of such broad scope, despite his knowledge of the scriptures, patristics, and, within limits, the history of the church and the liturgy. Although his works were much appreciated by other Catholic controversialists such as Johann Eck and Johannes Cochlaeus (his successor in the post with the duke of Saxony), his writings fell into oblivion after his death, except for his translation of the New Testament, which saw sixty-five editions after it had been revised by Johann Dietenberger and Eck.

BIBLIOGRAPHY

Primary Source

Emser, Hieronymus. *Schriften zur Verteidigung der Messe.* Münster, 1959.

Secondary Sources

Bluhm, Heinz. "Emser's 'Emendations' of Luther's New Testament: Galatians 1." *Modern Language Notes* 81 (1966), 370–397.

Enders, Ernst Ludwig. *Luther und Emser: Ihre Streitschriften aus dem Jahre 1521.* 2 vols. Halle, 1890–1892.

Iserloh, Erwin. *Der Kampf um die Messe in den ersten Jahren der Auseinandersetzungen mit Luther.* Katholisches Leben und Kämpfen im Zeitalter der Glaubensspaltung, 10. Münster 1952.

Smolinksy, Heribert. "Reformation und Bildersturm: Hieronymus Emsers Schrifte gegen Karlstadt über die Bilderverehrung." In *Reformatio Ecclesiae: Beiträge zu kirchlichen Reformbemühungen von der alten Kirche bis zur Neuzeit,* edited by Remigius Bäumer, pp. 427–440. Paderborn, 1980.

———. *Augustin von Alveldt und Hieronymus Emser: Eine Untersuchung zur Kontroverstheologie der frühen Reformationszeit im Herzogtum Sachsen.* Reformationsgeschichtliche Studien und Texte, 122. Munich, 1983. The most recent and complete article on Emser and his writings; an exhaustive bibliography can be found on pp. 432–458.

———. "Streit um die Exegese? Die Funktion des Schriftarguments in der Kontroverstheologie des Hieronymus Emser." In *Zum Gedenken an Joseph Lortz, 1887–1975: Beiträge zur Reformationsgeschichte und Ökumene,* edited by Rolf Decot and Rainer Vinke, pp. 358–375. Veröffentlichungen des Instituts für Europäische Geschichte Mainz, Abteilung Religionsgeschichte, supplement 30. Stuttgart, 1989.

Strand, Kenneth Albert. *Reformation Bibles in the Crossfire: The Story of Jerome Emser, His Anti-Lutheran Critique and His Catholic Bible Version.* Ann Arbor, 1961.

AGOSTINO BORROMEO

Translated from Italian by Robert E. Shillenn

ENGELBREKTSSON, Olav (Nor., Engelbriktssøn; c.1480–1538), last Catholic archbishop of Norway and greatest opponent of Norway's Reformation. He was educated for the priesthood at Trondheim, received his B.A. in 1505 and his M.A. in 1507, both at Rostock, and studied further at Louvain. He became chapter dean at Trondheim in 1515 and archbishop in 1523.

As head of the Norwegian National Council, he had two tasks: to promote Norwegian independence, and to protect the Catholic church against the Reformation. Christian II was exiled from Denmark-Norway in 1523. The royal succession at that time, and again in 1533–1536 brought attempts to control Norway by installing Danish nobles in Norwegian fiefs. These attempts offered Engelbrektsson the opportunity to reverse that trend occassioned by the Kalmar Union of 1397. The kings became increasingly Lutheran, and Lutheran beginnings spread from Bergen.

Engelbrektsson knew little about the Reformation except that it afforded the opportunity for appropriating ecclesiastical property. He tried to hinder the coronation of Frederick I and the recognition of his son, Christian (III), as heir to the throne because of their Lutheran sympathies. Soon Engelbrektsson observed Frederick installing Danes in Norwegian fiefs and protecting Lutheran preachers in Bergen. Therefore, he supported Christian II's abortive attempt, in 1531, to conquer Norway. His second great effort came after Frederick's death in 1533, and during the Counts' War of succession in 1533–1536. He waited in vain for the promised support of Emperor Charles V for Christian II's son-in-law, Frederick of the Palatinate, to win the throne.

Engelbrektsson's ally in support of Norwegian independence was Vincens Lunge, a Danish nobleman who had married into the family of Lady Inger of Austraat (of Norway's most powerful noble family). But Lunge became Engelbrektsson's enemy, as both Lunge and Inger's family promoted Lutheranism and took over monasteries' lands. Engelbrektsson's forces warred with Lunge's in 1529; thereafter their efforts for Norwegian independence were increasingly interrupted by Engelbrektsson's determination to protect the Catholic church.

When Christian III won the Counts' War and demanded that Norway recognize him, Engelbrektsson convened a meeting of the National Council (whose other members realized that they had to submit to Christian) at Trondheim at Christmas, 1535. In January 1536 he had Lunge killed. He arrested the other nobles and bishops on the council and tried to arouse the populace to rise against Christian III. But Engelbrektsson was no popular leader and had done nothing to alleviate the perception that bishops were more interested in ecclesiastical and national politics than in spiritual shepherding. With no popular support or help from the count palatine or emperor, he fled to the Netherlands in 1537, en route plundering Austraat, the home and center for Lunge and Lady Inger, and carrying with him many church treasures. He died at Brabant in 1538.

Engelbrektsson was the "Antihero of Norway's Reformation," the largest figure in a reformation with no outstanding early reformer. A historiographical controversy surrounds him: Was he national hero or church hero or both? Was he incompetent, a scoundrel, or a victim of circumstances? He was probably basically honorable and capable; but he had no sense for the depth of needed church reform, lacked political astuteness and military realism, and was doomed as leader of Norway's political independence and church when both were already tottering toward their end.

BIBLIOGRAPHY

Bergsgård, Arne. "Olav Engelbriktsson." In *Norsk biografisk leksikon,* edited by Harald C. Narve-Pedersen, vol. 10, pp. 361–371. Oslo, 1949. Thorough biographical encyclopedia article; contains excellent bibliography of Scandinavian sources. Portrays Engelbrektsson neglecting nation's interests in favor of the church, though doing little for church renewal.

Christopherson, K. E. "Olav Engelbriktson: Anti-Hero of Norway's Reformation." *Journal of the American Academy of Religion* 45 suppl.

(1977), D:773–791. Most complete item in English on Archbishop Olav; portrays the varying interpretations of him.

Gjerset, Knut. *History of the Norwegian People.* 2 vols. Reprint, New York, 1969. Solid treatment of title subject. Volume 2, pp. 120–133, includes history of Engelbrektsson, with some historians' varying appraisals of him.

Koht, Halvdan. *Olav Engelbriktsson og sjølvstendetapet, 1537.* Oslo, 1951. Only full book treatment of Engelbrektsson; by Norway's outstanding historian of this century; sees Engelbrektsson as lover first of the church but also as fighter for the nation, with both causes usually in harmony.

Larsen, Karen. *A History of Norway.* Reprint, Princeton, 1970. Excellent book on title subject with good chapters on Norway's Reformation; pp. 229–232 on Engelbrektsson.

Wisløff, Carl Fr. *Norsk kirkehistorie.* 3 vols. Oslo, 1966–1971. The modern definitive work on its title subject. Volume 1 is masterfully balanced and knit together, covering Norway's Reformation. Generally follows Bergsgård's interpretation of Engelbrektsson.

KENNETH E. CHRISTOPHERSON

ENGLAND. In late medieval England relations with the universal church were governed by two conflicting facts of life. On the one hand, England had produced one of the few heretical movements of the age in Wycliffite Lollardy; on the other, kings of England had chosen to maintain relations of friendly cooperation with the papacy. In the fourteenth century indications that hostility might prevail had produced legislation (acts of provisors and praemunire) that protected English and particularly royal interests in the appointment and taxing of the clergy against papal interference, and the decades of the Great Schism, which had thrown the popes into the camp of England's French enemies, had briefly encouraged prospects of a break with Rome. Lollardy drew strength from these events, but when early in the fifteenth century it became associated with social and political protest, it lost the potential support of the Crown, who put its power behind the enforcement of orthodoxy. From Henry V onward, the kings of England repaired their relations with the pope and backed episcopal action against heresy. So Lollardy retreated into the underground; the higher clergy cooperated enthusiastically with the ordinary administration of the realm; and the relations between laity and clergy in general settled down to a peaceful coexistence. The balanced reality of church-state relations was visibly displayed in the fifteen years of Thomas Wolsey's ascendancy as lord chancellor and cardinal legate in Henry VIII's counsels (1514–1529); it appeared even more convincingly in the regular support extended by that king to the pope of Rome in his European conflicts and wars.

This description goes a trifle counter to the traditional view, which supposed that by the early sixteenth century the clergy were held in contempt by a nation increasingly anxious to free itself of the dead hand of tradition. It is now rightly agreed that pre-Reformation England was not calling loudly for the reform, and that the old order seemed more secure there than in many parts of Europe. It must nevertheless be remembered that the position of the church in England was not so solidly settled in the old way as some historians would now maintain: earlier views were by no means entirely mistaken, and England knew a sufficiency of anticlerical protest. The great wealth of the ecclesiastical institutions attracted much envious desire, and its unequal concentration in the hands of often pomp-devoted bishops and abbots stimulated thoughts about the social claims of the priesthood. Old conflicts arising out of clerical claims to immunity from the law of the state came to life again, and especially the laity of London did not forget the case of Richard Hunne (1512), murdered in the bishop of London's prison and posthumously burned for heresy. Of course, such incidents do not testify to a general turning away from the established order, any more than the extreme abuse of a pamphleteer like Simon Fish (*Supplication of the Beggars,* 1529) represents the general wave of opinion that it was once taken to be. Yet one should not ignore the spread of humanist critique of dubious traditions that helped to prepare the ground for the Reformation in the minds of a younger generation, or the infiltration of Lutheran ideas in the 1520s, especially at the universities and in London. Though the leading English Lutheran, William Tyndale, was forced to take refuge in Antwerp, where he was burned for heresy in 1536, others remained active at home, especially Robert Barnes, burned for heresy in London in 1540. It is also clear that from the beginning of Henry VIII's reign evangelical Lollardy showed signs of a positive revival, providing a possible soil for Protestant views.

More important, one should not ignore these manifestations of unrest because that is exactly what the established order did not do. Maybe England was not turning Protestant, but it felt enough vibrations to call forth some of the leading fighters against the Continental Reformation, from Henry VIII himself (*Assertio Septem Sacramentorum adversus Martinum Lutherum,* 1521), through Thomas More, commissioned to deal with Luther's reaction to that book, to John Fisher, bishop of Rochester, who in the 1520s gained a European reputation as one of the outstanding champions of orthodoxy. Once a critic himself of the condition of the church, More in effect abandoned his humanist past and turned himself into the leading lay persecutor of heresy in northern Europe, and he did find some heretics to hunt. With his and his king's encouragement, several bishops renewed their war against Lollardy and cognate heresies, incidentally testifying to their revival. In short, though the church was certainly not in a real crisis, it faced a situation shot through with warning signs: enough people, both lay and clerical, welcomed the onset of Reformed notions smuggled into England. Anyone who had followed events in Germany had at least some ground for apprehension.

Henry VIII: The Attack on the Papacy. What held the fort for Rome was, of course, the political and spiritual adherence of the governing powers, especially of Henry himself, and it was here that the breach occurred. The Reformation in England started unquestionably as a political dispute, whatever may thereafter have grown from those beginnings. It opened as a jurisdictional quarrel between the king's authority and the pope's, provoked by Henry's decision (1527) to get an annulment of his marriage to Catherine of Aragon, a marriage that he had persuaded himself contravened the law of the church. That in reality he wished to free himself to marry Anne Boleyn and secure legitimate issue from her is true but, in view of his ability to turn personal preferences into scruples of conscience, irrelevant to the argument. As the pope's old champion he had good reason to expect the necessary service from Rome: what he asked for was commonly reckoned to be within the pope's powers and had often been conceded readily to political allies. But Henry overlooked two complications. His first marriage had been legitimized by a papal bull eliminating just those obstacles that he now maintained rendered it unlawful; and at the crucial time the pope had in effect become a prisoner to Catherine's nephew, the emperor Charles V. Thus Henry's request for an annulment called papal powers in question and encountered an immovable obstacle in imperial refusal to let the pope act. Prolonged negotiations at Rome, the farce of a trial in England suspended by the papal legate, and the search for a way out of the dilemma produced deadlock but also deeply divided the governing order in England. Wolsey fell, but Thomas More, his successor as chancellor, would not help the king either. The solution finally adopted amounted to a revolution in the nature of the state and its relations with the church. It professed the sovereign independence of the English commonwealth from all exterior authority and created in the church the supremacy of the Crown.

The carefully cultivated appearance of unanimity was deceptive, however even the political reformation split the realm. The most obvious division—between those who accepted the royal supremacy and those who rejected it—signified little: the power of the monarchy and the state it ruled, organized by Thomas Cromwell's policy of lawful enforcement, won an easy victory. The victims included such outstanding men as More, Fisher, some Carthusian monks, and a few famous friars, but care was taken to avoid a reign of mere terror, and the number of people destroyed (even those caught in the northern rebellion of 1536, called the Pilgrimage of Grace) remained, by the standards of the age, within bounds. More subtle and more productive of problems for the future was the division of opinion over the foundations of the royal supremacy. Henry VIII himself claimed it as divinely ordained and vested entirely in his person, but the revolution had called for changes in the law, which meant that the supremacy came to rest on parliamentary statute and was worked out according to the concepts of the common lawyers, especially Christopher Saint German and Cromwell. In the event, the church, though outwardly unchanged, emerged as a department of the unitary state subject to the sovereignty of the king-in-Parliament and administered under the ultimate control of the regular courts that alone were capable of applying the penalties established by statute.

Henry VIII: Reform of Religion. The schism and the rejection of the papacy set the stage for a possible religious reformation but assuredly did not necessitate it. From the first it became plain that the nation contained both determined conservatives who wished to adhere to the established doctrines of the Catholic faith, and eager reformers who wished to change things in the general direction of the Protestantism that was gaining ground in much of Europe (but contained much diversity). The king adhered mainly to the first point of view, in which he had the support of all the bishops appointed before the break; but the men he had found to solve his marital problem favored the second. Cranmer was forced to leave university life for the archbishopric of Canterbury (1533–1553) so that he could declare Henry's first marriage nonexistent; he duly performed then and on later occasions. Cromwell managed the parliamentary proceedings so efficiently that Henry transferred the supreme head's authority by making him his vicegerent in spirituals (1535–1536) to run the church for him. But both Cranmer, gradually, and Cromwell, quite quickly, undertook to reform the doctrine and faith of the church by attacking transubstantiation, the worship of saints, and the doctrine of purgatory, all mainstays of popular devotion. Cromwell did the major job for the religious Reformation when he promoted and indeed financed the English translation of the Bible. Based on the work of Tyndale (whom Henry abominated), the Great Bible (1539), placed by order into every parish church, underlined the move toward a new Christianity. Throughout the 1530s the reforming leadership backed radical preachers, introduced reformers like Hugh Latimer and Nicholas Shaxton onto the bench of bishops, and strove to reduce the independence of the clergy, not least by ending the study of canon law and subjecting the church courts to the rule of statute and common law. Cromwell's *Injunctions* of 1536 and 1538 contained Lutheran elements that caused much agony among the adherents of tradition.

The most striking attack on the inherited order, the dissolution of the monasteries and secularization of their lands (1536–1540), sprang in the main from a desire to finance royal government, but it also aimed to destroy one of the mainstays of tradition. The confiscation in 1549 of the small endowments of the chantries—foundations concerned with intercessory prayers mainly for the late founders—contributed more to the second purpose than the first. From the mid-1530s onward, signs that episcopal lands would not escape unscathed began to multiply, and by the end of the century the church, once so rich, only just managed to maintain its members. The real winner was not the monarchy: hard pressed for cash, the Crown soon gave way to pressure by granting or selling off most of the lands to lay owners, mainly peers and gentry though lawyers did well too. While he lived, Cromwell protected the new acquisitions, and the real inroads began only with the collapse of royal control after the death of Henry VIII. These transfers of landed wealth had political consequences, mainly because they committed a sizable body of profiteers to the support of the reform; they had no significant social effects because the monasteries had long since been in the habit of leasing most of their lands to lay farmers. It should, however, be noted that the good causes much spoken of at the time also benefited. Four new dioceses, two major university colleges, and a number of schools drew off quite a bit of the ex-monastic endowments. The dissolution itself was carried out with genuine bureaucratic care: ex-monks received pensions (considerable for abbots and priors, only just adequate for the generality), and any debts owed by the dissolved institutions were covered by the Crown. One unexpected bonus came to the church in the supply of ex-monks to fill vacant benefices during the three decades when normal recruitment flagged under the impact of the great transformation.

Thus the political reformation did open the way for the Reformation properly so called, but the conversion did not come in a flood. Apart from the fact that the reforming party constituted a minority in the clergy and a smaller minority in the laity, two obstacles slowed things down. Henry himself refused to contemplate the kind of changes that his vicegerent favored, and he received reassurance from the specter of extreme radicalism (then commonly called Sacramentarianism) that seemed to be spreading in the wake of reform. The Lollard tradition—the brethren of More's nightmare—appeared to favor moves toward the radical ends that on the Continent produced the Anabaptist sects, and reckoned to be a threat to all established order. As it happened, Anabaptism never got a hold in England, where the only such sectaries discovered and burned were all foreign immigrants; and the small cells of extremists that in 1538–1539 troubled the peace at Calais were really as insignificant as Cromwell supposed. But such things gave their chance to champions of the old order, further driven on by personal hatred of Cromwell. Enough unrest was arising all over the country in the wake of radical preaching to cause the king to seek measures making for enforceable order, and in the circumstances order was bound to mean the reassertion of tradition. This order was achieved by the Act of Six Articles (1539), which restored pre-Reformation orthodoxy on all the debatable issues; most especially, denial of transubstantiation and the Mass was now made punishable by burning and nothing less. Recanting became more difficult and more final. Cranmer and Cromwell had to accept this arrest to the reforming movement and seemed to have done so without losing control of the ecclesiastical machinery, when the destruction of Cromwell in June 1540 by his personal enemies (especially Stephen Gardiner, bishop of Winchester) signaled the triumph of tradition.

Even so, the persecution of the reformers was patchy enough to allow the division of the nation to continue, though until Henry's death (January 1547) the official policy in the church remained positively hostile to the Reformation. In 1543 the reading of the Bible was forbidden to supposedly volatile elements (the lower orders and all women), and the *King's Book* decreed a body of doctrine that apart from the elimination of the papacy was identical with what had been called the truth before 1536. The reaction demanded some victims, especially the gallant Anne Askew, who even under torture refused to become the instrument of destruction for hidden reformers whom the conservative managers hoped to trap. Although Henry, for reasons that have never become clear, continued to look kindly on Cranmer and had his suspicions of Gardiner's ambitions, he maintained the old order in religion, the more so because his renewed wars in France and Scotland compelled cooperation with the soundly Catholic Charles V.

Edward VI and Mary Tudor. Yet this apparent triumph of the forces opposing the Reformation is in many ways misleading and has so misled some recent historians. The impetus of Cromwell's use of the vicegerency did not come to an end with his fall. Throughout Henry's last years, the official conservatism was challenged by preachers and writers, some of whom (for instance, John Bale, one of Cromwell's protégés) took refuge on the Continent; the humanist dissatisfaction with tradition continued to find expression; the monasteries remained dissolved; most incomprehensibly, the king's son and heir Edward was being educated by men of Reformed views. Nor was the political potential of the reforming party wiped out by Cromwell's fall, though it needed several years to reconstruct itself. In the intensive maneuvering at court during Henry's last months it was this faction (led by Edward Seymour, soon duke of Somerset and protector of the realm) that held the upper hand when the old king died. Though there is no reason to think that the people at large were turning eagerly toward Protestantism, the nation's leaders in the reign of Edward VI most certainly were. The boy-king himself turned out to be passionately Protestant, and Cranmer at last felt free to follow his increasing dedication to the new faith. In addition, England became a refuge for several leading European reformers (especially Martin Bucer and Peter Martyr Vermigli) whom the emperor's victory over the Lutheran princes and cities had forced to flee from home.

So the scene was set for a full-scale religious reformation, at least in the form of organization and orders from above. It was brought about by a number of measures passed through the Parliament, most especially the successive *Books of Common Prayer* (1549, 1552), of which the second embodied a positive Protestantism derived from the south German and Zwinglian varieties. In addition, in 1549 priests were allowed to marry (one reform that had met Henry VIII's relentless opposition), and the Ordinal of 1550 turned them unmistakably into ministers of the word deprived of all sacerdotal attributes. An energetic preaching campaign endeavored to persuade the people of the truth of the new dispensation. Hugh Latimer, in particular, who refused to resume the dignity and burden of the episcopal office that the Act of Six Articles had forced him to resign, became the leading spokesman for the reform of which Cranmer was the real moving spirit, assisted by Nicholas Ridley, bishop of London. In 1553 Cranmer produced a formulary of the Protestant faith in the Forty-two Articles, subscription to which was to be obligatory on all the clergy. The champions of the old order either retreated into obscurity or risked the imprisonment that befell Stephen Gardiner when he tried to stem the tide. Popular reaction varied from sullen resistance to an excessive eagerness that expressed itself in image-breaking. But on the whole, especially while young Edward occupied the throne, it looked as though the full-scale Reformation had come to stay.

Edward's early death in June 1553 revealed the error of this appearance. His successor, his elder sister Mary Tudor, had remained faithful to the papal Catholicism of her youth and was sure to reverse all reforming measures. Apprehension of this reversal produced the attempt to put Lady Jane Grey on the throne, but that coup collapsed in a few days; it is clear that the nation's manifest adherence to Mary owed a good deal to widespread dislike of the Reformation. The five years of Mary's reign witnessed the complete restoration of the old religion; aided by the returned champion of Rome, Cardinal Reginald Pole (archbishop of Canterbury), and led by Gardiner at Winchester and Edmund Bonner in London, the bulk of the episcopate supported the queen's determination to abolish the royal supremacy and all processes of reform in church and religion. Once again, the English church became part of the universal church subject to Rome. The only part of the old order not to come back were the monasteries: the secularized lands remained in the hands of their new owners, and attempts to bring back the religious orders produced almost no result. Within eighteen months of her accession, Mary seemed to have succeeded in totally expunging some twenty years from the history of England.

But this break in the English Reformation turned out to be even less securely established than the rush to reform in Edward's reign. The chief reason for its disappearance was, of course, the short time given to it: Mary's reign was just four months over five years old when she and Pole died within a few days of each other in November 1558. Now the only available heir to the throne was Mary's sister Elizabeth, daughter of Anne Boleyn and always regarded as a champion of the reforming party. In her sister's reign, she narrowly escaped death when she found herself in the Tower of London under suspicion of heresy and treason. But even without these political and personal circumstances, the fortunes of the temporary return to Rome never looked secure. Many of the leaders of the Reformation escaped abroad, to plot and prepare for a further reversal of fortunes. Mary's marriage to Philip of Burgundy, who in 1556 became king of Spain, remained unpopular in England, even though the only positive rebellion against it (led by Thomas Wyatt) failed: the marriage helped to taint Catholicism with the fear of foreign domination. Above all, the energetic persecution of Protestants—the mass burnings at Smithfield and elsewhere—proved fatal to the reputation of the regime and would have done so even without the writings of John Foxe, who turned them into one of the great themes of English history. Unused to the mass extinction of heretics, the English turned out to abominate death at the stake with a revulsion that their readiness to witness the horrors or executions for treason would not have led one to expect. Though the bulk of the victims were people of little renown, the burning of several bishops, including Cranmer, created a band of famous martyrs and gave the Reformation a new hold on popular sentiment.

The Elizabethan Settlement. The persecutions, the work of several champions of the old order backed by the queen, were a great mistake; they forever overshadowed the sacrifice of such victims of Henry VIII as Thomas More and John Fisher, and provided a springboard for the return to Protestantism that was achieved under Elizabeth by the Acts of Supremacy and Uniformity (1559), the Thirty-nine Articles (1563), and the return of the Marian exiles bringing Continental influences back to the English church. Though some have tried to maintain that Elizabeth accepted the return to the Reformation only under pressure and with much reluctance, the truth is that she meant to do so from the first; what remained to be settled was the form her Protestant church would take. By the mid-1560s it was clear that it would continue positively from the stage reached under Cranmer's guidance at the end of Edward's reign. Of course, the Protestant Church of England created in those few years needed time to win a firm hold over the faith of the people. Reformation had been achieved, but reform was to take much labor and pressure. Not until the 1580s can one speak safely of a predominantly Protestant nation of England, and by then new complications had arisen that called in question the security of the Elizabethan Settlement. Apart from the renewal of Roman Catholic agitation, not a point to be pursued here, the problems sprang from the uncertainties enshrined in the church that Elizabeth had approved and meant to maintain against all doubters.

The Church of England that emerged from the Reformation was unique in several respects. On the one hand, its organization and outward structure preserved the forms of the pre-Reformation church, except that the royal supremacy took over the role previously vested in the papacy. Even the law administered in the church courts, though ultimately under the authority of statute made by the queen-in-Parliament, in practice operated the details of the old canon law. On the other hand, the correct form of the Christian religion supposedly ministered by that church was now unquestionably Protestant, a term, however, that contained within itself various possibilities that tried to assert themselves. The first makers of the Church of England—especially Cromwell and Cranmer—believed in a *via media,* a moderate middle way between the old and the new; they had envisaged a church willing to tolerate some differences of belief especially in matters not reckoned indispensable to salvation (adiaphora) so long as uniformity prevailed in outward observance and in several fundamental articles of the faith. The Thirty-nine Articles allowed a remarkable range of interpretations. In the conditions of the sixteenth century, however, it was unlikely that this state of affairs would continue, and the Zwinglian influences on the Edwardian Reformation had already hinted at a move away from such compromises. At a time when even the church of Rome, long used to a measure of variety, closed its ranks against all deviation, it was astonishing to find a church that dreamed, however briefly, of any kind of toleration.

Though fruitful contacts with Zwinglian Zurich continued after 1560, the major influence on English theologians came increasingly to be the most extreme and relentless form of Protestantism: the Calvinism of Geneva with its rigorous doctrine of double predestination and its belief in a presbyterian government in place of the traditional episcopal system. Both these pillars of Calvinism affected the English church, but both also met resistance. The queen held her bishops to a strictly antipresbyterian line, and the traditions of free will beliefs so strong among Lollards, humanists, and the first generation of English reformers resisted the advancing victory of the predestinarians. Both these strains were to produce much conflict over the next hundred years, but it is worth notice that the dedicated Calvinist fanatics (soon dubbed Puritans) never won the war for the faith of all the people. Their exhortations made converts, but the main part of the nation (though not the loudest part) remained moderate in its reluctance to espouse those burdensome absolutes. The faith in the middle way survived, even after it was perverted during the reign of Charles I into an anti-Calvinism as aggressive as Calvinism itself. In the end, the English Reformation produced a disputatious body of ardent churchmen struggling for the sober souls of the people. The sober souls, on balance, won.

BIBLIOGRAPHY

Brigden, Susan. *London and the Reformation.* Oxford, 1989.

Collinson, Patrick. *The Elizabethan Puritan Movement.* Reprint, Oxford, 1990.

Dickens, A. G. *The English Reformation.* 2d ed. London, 1989.

Elton, G. R. *Reform and Reformation: England 1509–1558.* London and Cambridge, Mass., 1977. The most detailed general account of the period in question with a full bibliography.

———. *Policy and Police: The Enforcement of the Reformation in the Age of Thomas Cromwell.* Cambridge, 1972.

Haigh, Christopher, ed. *The English Reformation Revised.* Cambridge, 1987. A collection of essays casting doubt on the traditional interpretation.

Jones, Norman. *Faith by Statute: Parliament and the Settlement of Religion, 1559.* London, 1982.

Loades, D. M. *The Reign of Mary Tudor.* 2d ed. London, 1991.

Mozley, J. F. *John Foxe and His Book.* Reprint, New York, 1970.

Penny, D. Andrew. *Freewill or Predestination: The Battle over Saving Grace in Mid-Tudor England.* London, 1990.

Ridley, J. *Thomas Cranmer.* Reprint, London, 1966.

GEOFFREY ELTON

ENGLISH BIBLE. Although fragmentary translations had existed for centuries and Wycliffite manuscript versions survive in considerable numbers, no printed text of the English Bible existed until William Tyndale undertook its translation. Frustrated in his effort to obtain episcopal patronage in England, Tyndale went to Germany where, after authorities interrupted printing at Cologne, he secured publication of his New Testament at Worms in 1526. He acted upon the Lutheran principle of *sola scriptura,*which insisted upon the primacy of the Bible in spiritual affairs without clerical mediation, and heeded the humanistic call to return *ad fontes* by working directly from Hebrew texts and Erasmus's Greek New Testament (1516). Tyndale's avoidance of Latinate vocabulary and employment of everyday colloquial diction owes much to the Erasmian appeal in *Paraclesis* (Exhortation), the preface to the Greek New Testament, that humble plowmen and "even the lowliest women" be allowed to read or recite the Bible in their native dialect. Although publication of unauthorized versions of the scriptures would have been sufficient to incur official disapproval, Tyndale antagonized Henry VIII and the English clerical establishment by incorporating Lutheran propaganda into his prefaces and notes and even into the translations themselves. The ecclesiastical preference denoted by his usage of "congregation" instead of "church" and of "senior" or "elders instead of "priest" is notorious. Although he failed to achieve his goal of translating the entire Bible, he went on to translate the Pentateuch, *Jonah,* and other portions of the Old Testament by the time he was burnt at the stake as a heretic in 1536.

The first complete English Bible was published in 1535 in a translation compiled by Miles Coverdale from his own work and that of Tyndale. Instead of following Tyndale in the return *ad fontes,* Coverdale used Luther's German New Testament, the Vulgate, and other Latin texts. Although the volume was printed on the Continent without official authorization, the title-page border crafted by Hans Holbein the Younger implied the existence of royal consent by portraying Henry VIII in the act of handing the Bible to the bishops kneeling before him. This publication was followed in 1537 by the officially licensed "Matthew" Bible, which contains the work of Tyndale and Coverdale in an anonymous compilation by John Rogers.

These works led the way for the landmark appearance of the Great Bible in 1539 under the patronage of King Henry's vicegerent for religious affairs, Thomas Cromwell, and overseen by Coverdale. The Royal Injunctions of 1538 had ordered the purchase of "one book of the whole Bible of the largest volume, in English" by every parish church, where chained copies were freely accessible for the "reading or hearing" by parishioners. A combination of Tyndale's suspect work and that by Coverdale in the officially authorized revision that Coverdale drew from the "Matthew" Bible provides an indication of how far Cromwell and Thomas Cranmer, archbishop of Canterbury, had led England in the direction of Protestant reform, despite Henry VIII's insistence upon retaining traditional theology and the Mass. The absence of doctrinal notes and prefaces provides an index of the volume's theological conservatism. An elaborate title-page border by a member of the School of Holbein introduces this work with a portrait of the king passing the Bible to Cranmer and Cromwell for cautious dissemination to the common people at the base of the scene.

Zealous Protestants who fled to the Continent from persecution under Mary Tudor created a radically different version of the English Bible—The Geneva Bible of 1560. Prepared by William Whittingham, Anthony Gilby, and Thomas Sampson, this edition improves upon the philological scholarship in Tyndale's text and other earlier versions. Preparation of this translation for a broadly popular audience may be noted in its publication in less expensive quarto format; the use of roman type and italics instead of black letter; the provision of a variety of scholarly aids to popular understanding, such as the division of chapters into verses to facilitate quick reference and the use of concordances; and the inclusion of didactic illustrations, maps, and tables. Modern English Bibles incorporate many of the elements used in the layout of this edition. The volume's stridently Protestant annotations held out a special appeal to the Puritan readers, whose demand contributed to the publication of nearly 150 editions by the time the Genevan version went out of print in 1644. This edition was used in privacy by such poets as Shakespeare and Spenser and even by prelates like Matthew Parker, who opposed its public use.

Archbishop Parker organized the production of the Bishops' Bible (1568) for official use in church services and to counter the popular appeal of the Geneva Bible. Designed to avoid religious controversy, this edition lacks polemical notes of the kind that incurred official disfavor for the Tyndale and Genevan versions.

The Rheims-Douai Bible represented a Roman Catholic alternative to the Protestant Bibles that proliferated in England. A group of exiles at the seminary at Rheims produced a translation of the New Testament in 1582; publication of the Old Testament followed at Douai in 1609–1610. Notable for its technical vocabulary, this very literal translation of the Vulgate version lacked popular appeal.

The continuing opposition of Puritans to the Bishops' Bible led to the production of the Authorized Version of 1611 (the so-called King James Bible). A committee that originally included fifty-four members revised the Bishops' version with reference to the other English texts including the Rheims-Douai Bible. Like the Great Bible and the Bishops' Bible, the Authorized Version incorporates traditional ecclesiastical vocabulary and lacks annotations. Old-fashioned language, the archaic use of black-letter type, and the absence of illustrations contributed to a hieratic aura of sanctity that increased with the passage of time. The King James Bible is justly famous for its stylistic virtuosity, but it should be remembered that Tyndale's diction provides the foundation for all later Renaissance Bibles. If the Authorized Version has come to seem archaic, it is because Tyndale's colloquial idiom has atrophied due to the process of linguistic change. Through the Authorized Version, Tyndale's translation remained current into the nineteenth and twentieth centuries.

[*See also* Coverdale, Miles; *and* Tyndale, William.]

BIBLIOGRAPHY

Butterworth, Charles C. *The Literary Lineage of the King James Bible: 1340–1611.* Reprint, New York, 1971. Essential study of the early English printed editions.

Greenslade, S. L. "English Versions of the Bible, 1525–1611." In *The West from the Reformation to the Present Day,* edited by S. L. Greenslade, pp. 141–74. The Cambridge History of the Bible, vol. 3. Cambridge, 1963. Valuable general history.

Hammond, Gerald. *The Making of the English Bible.* Manchester, 1982. Important study of translation methods.

Herbert, A. S. *Historical Catalogue of Printed Editions of the English Bible, 1525–1961.* Rev. ed. London, 1968. Contains detailed bibliographical information that must be checked for accuracy against the original texts.

King, John N. *Tudor Royal Iconography: Literature and Art in an Age of Religious Crisis.* Princeton, 1989. Considers artistic and propagandistic aspects of illustrated title pages in Bible editions authorized by Tudor monarchs.

Pollard, Alfred W., ed. *Records of the English Bible.* Reprint, Oxford, 1974. Collects relevant historical documents.

Thompson, Craig R. *The Bible in English, 1525–1611.* Folger Booklets on Tudor and Stuart Civilization. Charlottesville, Va., 1958. Brief account containing many illustrations in facsimile.

JOHN N. KING

ENGLISH COLLEGE, VENERABLE.

See Seminaries.

ENTFELDER, Christian

ENTFELDER, Christian (fl. 1526–1547), early Anabaptist sympathizer in the spiritualist tradition of Hans Denck and Kaspar von Schwenckfeld. Little is known about

Entfelder's early life. Born into a wealthy family in the Enns Valley, Entfelder probably had legal training before his initial contact with the Anabaptists. In 1526 he appeared with Balthasar Hubmaier in Nikolsburg (Mikulov) and shortly thereafter assumed leadership of an Anabaptist congregation in Eibenschitz, Moravia. Between 1529 and 1533 Entfelder published three pamphlets. The first, appearing in 1530 during his sojourn in Strasbourg with Johannes Bünderlin, was entitled *Von den manigfaltigen im Glauben Zerspaltungen dise jar erstanden* (On the Manifold Divisions of Faith Which Have Occurred this Year). The treatise suggests a growing distance between Entfelder and the Anabaptists and offers the best insight into his speculative thought. Two other pamphlets, reflecting similar mystical themes, also survive: *Von warer Gotseligkayt* (On the True Godliness; 1530) and *Von Gottes und Christi Jesu unseres Herren Erkandtnuss* (On the Knowledge of God and Christ Jesus Our Lord; 1533).

In the tradition of medieval mysticism, particularly that of Johannes Tauler and the *Theologia Deutsch*, Entfelder's writings reflect a preoccupation with the knowledge of God. God actively reveals himself in the preexistent harmony of the created order. Through a threefold process of regeneration (purification, illumination, unification), the so-called *unio mystica*, fallen humanity could be restored to the wholeness of creation. As with the cross mysticism of Denck and Thomas Müntzer, Entfelder conceived of justification as a literal cleansing and transformation of the creaturely into a new life yielded in conformity to the life and suffering of Christ.

Entfelder's spiritualist predispositions gradually drew him away from the visible church of the Anabaptists with their strong emphases on baptism and church discipline. For a short time after 1536, Entfelder served as counselor to Albrecht von Hohenzollern. Although not identifying explicitly with any Anabaptist group, his continued sympathies to the radical Reformation may be inferred in his efforts to resettle a large group of Dutch Anabaptists to Hohenzollern lands in East Prussia in 1539. After 1547 Entfelder disappears again into obscurity. In a letter of 1560 Schwenckfeld aptly summarized Entfelder's career when he grouped him with Denck and several others as "decent, God-blessed men"—all sympathetic to the Anabaptists—but who had also avoided the separatism, legalism, and hasty zeal of the Anabaptist movement (*Corpus Schwenckfeldianorum*, vol. 17, p. 221, Pennsburg, Pa., 1960).

BIBLIOGRAPHY

Jones, Rufus M. *Spiritual Reformers in the 16th and 17th Centuries* (1914). Reprint, Gloucester, Mass., 1971. An early appreciative work, placing Entfelder in the broader context of other spiritualist writers. See especially pp. 39–45.

Packull, Werner O. *Mysticism and the Early South German–Austrian Anabaptist Movement, 1525–1531*. Scottdale, Pa., 1977. Clearly the most sophisticated analysis of Entfelder's theology. See especially pp. 163–175.

Penner, Horst. "Christian Entfelder, ein mährischer Täuferprediger." *Mennonitische Geschichtsblätter* 23 (1966), 19–23. Excellent for biographical details on Entfelder's career after 1536.

Séguenny, André, ed. *Bibliotheca Dissidentium: Répertoire des nonconformistes réligieux des seizième et dix-septième siècles.* Baden-Baden, Germany, 1980. Offers the most complete bibliography of secondary sources. See pp. 37–48.

Verzeichnis der im deutschen Sprachbereich erschienenen Drucke des XVI. Jahrhunderts. Stuttgart, 1983–. Vol. 6, nos. 1361–1368.

John D. Roth

ENZINAS, Francisco de

ENZINAS, Francisco de (also Dryander; c.1520–1552), Spanish Protestant. Born in Burgos, he went abroad in his youth, probably to Antwerp and Louvain, where he had kin. Called home by his family in 1537, he witnessed the humiliation of an elderly relative, Doctor Pedro de Lerma, chancellor of the humanist University of Alcalá de Henares, who had been arrested by the Inquisition for his preaching on such texts as "the law is not established for the just." Released on condition that he publicly retract eleven propositions as diabolically inspired, Lerma left Spain in disgust and became dean of the Faculty of Theology of Paris, where Enzinas visited him in 1541.

Enzinas enrolled at the University of Louvain in 1539. However, he deserted Louvain for the University of Wittenberg, where he matriculated in 1541, living with Philipp Melanchthon and preparing a translation of the New Testament from Greek into Spanish. He personally presented the first printed copy to Emperor Charles V on 24 November 1543 in Brussels, but in December he was accused of Lutheranism and jailed there. Enzinas spent over a year in prison and then escaped. In his memoirs (1545) he dramatically described his adventures. He never returned to Spain. Instead, he went to various Protestant cities of Germany and Switzerland (Wittenberg, Strasbourg, Constance, Zurich, and Basel). In 1546 his brother was burned at the stake in Rome as a Protestant; in the same year, Enzinas helped prepare a martyrology of his Protestant friend Juan Díaz, and in 1547 he published a vehement attack on the Council of Trent. After marrying Margaret Elter in Strasbourg in 1548, he went to England, where he was appointed to a chair of Greek at the University of Cambridge. In late 1549 he returned to Switzerland and Germany, settling in Strasbourg. Subsequently he published Spanish translations of Livy and Plutarch. He died, still a young man, in an epidemic in 1552.

BIBLIOGRAPHY

Primary Sources

Enzinas, Francisco de. *Mémoires de Francisco de Enzinas*. Edited by Ch. A. Champan. 2 vols. Brussels, 1862.

———. "Epistolae quinquaginta." *Zeitschrift für die historische Theologie*

40 (1870), 387–442. Fifty letters by Enzinas written from 1541 to 1552.

———. *Les Mémorables de Francisco de Enzinas.* Translated by Jean de Savignac. Brussels, 1963. His narrative of his adventures until 1545.

Secondary Sources

Bautz, Friedrich Wilhelm, ed. *Biographische-Bibliographisches Kirchenlexikon.* Hamm, 1970–. See vol. 1, pp. 1517–1518.

Boehmer, Edward. *Spanish Reformers of Two Centuries from 1520.* Strasbourg, 1874. See vol. 1, pp. 131–184, for a short biography and bibliography of his works.

Menéndez Pelayo, Marcelino. *Obras completas.* Santander, 1947. See vol. 37, pp. 274–276 and 280–307, for a biography that, like Boehmer's, is based primarily on Enzinas's memoir; it forms part of the author's *Historia de los heterodoxos españoles.*

Verzeichnis der im deutschen Sprachbereich erschienenen Drucke des XVI. Jahrhunderts. Stuttgart, 1983–. See vol. 6, nos. 1435–1436.

CONSTANCE J. MATHERS

EPISCOPACY. The different values given to the office of bishop by the reformers on the European continent, in the English Reformation, and in the Roman Catholic church in the sixteenth century is evident from the various ways in which the bishops in these churches, as they became established, were themselves vehicles of reform. Over against the two archbishops of Canterbury Thomas Cranmer (1489–1556) and Matthew Parker (1504–1575) stood bishops who in their own way embodied the Roman Catholic opposition to the Reformation: Cardinal Otto Truchsess von Waldburg (1514–1573), bishop of Augsburg; Cardinal Stanislaus Hosius (1505–1579), champion of the Catholic reform in Poland and Ermland; Cardinal Reginald Pole (1500–1558), the last Roman Catholic archbishop of Canterbury and sometime papal candidate; Cardinal Carlo Borromeo (1538–1584), archbishop of Milan and a model "Tridentine reform" bishop; and Francis of Sales (1567–1622), bishop of Geneva. Cranmer played an important role in the liturgical and religious reform, especially under Edward VI. Parker, whose consecration was later declared invalid by Pope Leo XIII in the bull *Apostolicae Curae* (1896, concerning the invalidity of Anglican orders) on the grounds of the Ordinal of 1552, left his mark on the synthesis developed under Queen Elizabeth I through his moderate personality (as co-author of the Thirty-nine Articles and the *Book of Advertisements*). In John Calvin's and Martin Luther's immediate spheres of influence there is no structure of order comparable to that of episcopal vehicles of Roman Catholic and Anglican reforms. Calvin completely eliminated the office of bishop from his church order. In the Lutheran Reformation, a Lutheran episcopacy existed in some countries. Bishops were not, however, necessary for the implementation of Luther's Reformation. Only in individual cases did bishops attach themselves to the Reformation in central Europe. Two archbishops of Cologne—Hermann von Wied (1477–1552) and Gebhard Truchsess von Waldburg (d.1601 as Protestant dean of Strasbourg Cathedral), nephew of the cardinal of Augsburg—both wanted to introduce the Reformation in their territories but were forced through political and military means to abdicate.

The question of the ministerial office and particularly the episcopal office was not in any way a starting point for Luther's reformation. Against the background of the heated state of church politics in the fifteenth and the early sixteenth century (reform councils of Pisa [1409], Constance [1414–1418], Basel-Ferrara-Florence [1431–1443]; together with the long-term consequences of the insignificant Conciliabulum of Pisa [1511], which, despite its insignificance, provides insight into the perception of contemporaries) and in view of the striking uncertainty regarding ecclesiology between conciliarism, on the one hand, and extreme papalism, on the other, Luther's criticism of the practice of indulgences (Ninety-five Theses) was reduced by the papal theologians Sylvester Mazzolini Prierias, Cajetan (Tomasso de Vio), and Johann Eck to the basic question of authority in the church. Luther is no systematic theologian. He was an exegete, interpreter of scripture, and polemical author who responded to specific questions and problems. In matters of ecclesiology he fought on two fronts in his writings and pronouncements—against the theologians of the old faith and Rome and against the practical errors of the spiritualists, antinomians, and Enthusiasts (Schwärmer). In the early period (from 1520) the emphasis was on the controversy with the old faith, which he termed "innovation" in reference to ecclesiology. In the later period he was concerned with establishing and consolidating his new church. With the priesthood of all believers as his point of departure, the ministerial office appeared to be secondary. Luther recognized a plurality of ministries. He mentioned "bishops, ministers, or preachers," referring to their New Testament pedigree: there must "be apostles, evangelists, prophets; they might be called whatever they wish or can who practice God's Word and work, whether from desire or ability." He described the role of these ministries as word (proclamation), baptism, the Lord's Supper, and the power of the keys in the remission of sins and in the expulsion of the obstinate from the congregation. The description of ministries in his later writings must be seen in light of his conviction of the unity of the ministerial office. In line with a significant current of Catholic theology that was still effective at the Council of Trent, Luther was of the opinion that there was no difference according to "divine law" between bishop and minister. On the question of the beginning (institution) of the ministerial office, Luther follows two lines of argument. On the one hand, he derives the ministry from the universal priesthood. The minister receives the actual ordination at baptism, but because of the necessity of following a church order he is publicly called to his office. On the other hand, alongside this argument, Luther speaks of an "institution" (foundation) of the ministerial office by Christ (on the basis, for example, of *Eph.* 4:11–14 and *1 Cor.* 12:28). He probably means not an act of institution by the earthly Jesus but an act performed through the impetus of the Spirit of the post-Easter and post-Pentecost Christ. This post-Pentecost event also needs to be objectively rooted in a church order (though this order must not obscure the gifts of the Spirit to the congregation by Christ). The increasing polemic against the papacy (the pope as Antichrist) colored his view of the episcopal ministry. Moreover, during Luther's lifetime no evangelical episcopacy existed in central Europe. Only a few bishops accepted the Reformation (Georg von Polentz, bishop of Samland, in 1524; Erhard von Queiss, bishop of Pomesanien, in 1525; Paul Speratus, his successor, in 1528; and Bartholomew Suawe, bishop of Kammin, in 1545). The institution, or ordination, of particular Lutheran bishops by Luther (Nikolaus von Amsdorf, bishop of Naumburg-Zeitz, in 1542 and Georg von Anhalt, bishop of Merseburg, 1545) did not last because of the Schmalkald War. By the end of the sixteenth century there were no more Lutheran bishops in Germany. This made possible the development of the secular rulers' assumption of the jurisdictional power of the office of the bishop, which beginning in the seventeenth century received theological and legal justification (Summepiskopat). The secular ruler becomes in certain precarious situations an "emergency bishop." In the spiritual realm the function of the bishop is assumed by the minister.

Of the reformers, Philipp Melanchthon has the most positive words for the episcopal offices. Melanchthon incisively influenced the development of the German Lutheran church as the foremost author of decisive Lutheran confessions of faith (*Confessio Augustana* [Augsburg Confession], *Apologia Confessionis Augustanae*, and *Tractus de potestate et primatu papae*). Even more than for Luther, the driving force of Melanchthon's late writings was the repudiation of Anabaptist and spiritualist criticism of the church. The definition of the church in the *Loci praecipui theologici* (1559) expressly mentions the ministry: "*Ecclesia visibilis est coetus amplectentium Evangelium Christi et recte utentium Sacramentis, in quo Deus per ministerium Evangelii est efficax*" (Robert Stupperich, ed., *Melanchthons Werke in Auswahl*, Gütersloh, 1953, vol. II/2, p. 476). Thus, article 7 of the Augsburg Confession is made more precise with reference to the ministry. The episcopal structure, the primacy of the pope, and the *ordinaria successio* of bishops are neither essence nor signs of the legitimacy of the church. These are human institutions (*ius humanum*), which are always subordinate to the gospel. The Roman church has taken over these structures from the surrounding society ("*amat enim humana ratio talem picturam Ecclesiae congruentem cum civilibus opinionibus*"; 480). The basic debate with the Roman Catholic understanding is set forth in article 28 of the Augsburg Confession and in the *Tractatus* of 1537. Melanchthon shows himself ready to compromise. Article 28 concludes the list of the "few" abuses in the Augsburg Confession ("*Tota dissensio est de paucis quibusdam abusibus*"). The article rejects the secular power of the bishops on the basis of so-called divine law but grants it on the basis of *iure humano*, independent, however, of their ecclesiastical office. As proclaimers of the gospel and administrators of the sacraments, they are owed obedience in light of *Luke* 10:16 (*de iure divino*). Whenever they contradict the gospel, specifically the article of justification by faith, they are to be opposed. The forgiveness of sins, the repudiation of false teachings, and the excommunication of public sinners through spiritual means continues to be part of their responsibility. The guardian office of the bishops is thus described in the same way as Melanchthon did with the *potestas iurisdictionis*, which is not completely equated with secular jurisdiction. Melanchthon explained the relationship between bishops and priests with reference to Jerome. The only difference that might exist between bishops and priests (presbyters) is one of human law. Bishops and ministers, or priests, fulfill the same functions except for the authority of ordination (*excepta ordinatione*). When a bishop refuses to ordain qualified candidates, the authority returns to the church. So long as bishops allow the preaching of the true faith, the episcopal structure, as a part of the order of the early church, should be preserved. In the famous proviso to his signature to the Schmalkald Articles, he declared himself to be prepared even to accept the office of the pope "on the grounds of peace and common unity."

Calvin unfolds his understanding of ministry most extensively in the fourth book of his *Institutio Religionis Christianae* (1559). Following Martin Bucer, he distinguished four forms of ministry that have always existed in the church—pastors (*pastores*), teachers (*doctores*), elders (*seniores*), and deacons (*diaconi*). He referred once to a threefold ministry (presbyter, deacon, bishop). He assigned the four offices to the threefold schema in the following way: the presbyters of the early church are the precursors of the pastors and teachers, on the one hand, and of the elders, on the other. Calvin retained the office of the deacon. In the early church the bishops headed the assembly of presbyters but purely as a time-conditioned institution based on human law. It is noteworthy that to justify his order of the four ministries he refers to the New Testament (*Eph.* 4:11; *Rom.* 12:7f; *1 Cor* 12:28) and to the pragmatic practice of the early church; he does not adopt, however, the episcopal office, which is clearly described in both the New Testament and the patristic writings. The implementation of this church order in a local church meant that the functions of the bishop, whose office had ceased to exist, were carried out by the basic ministry of the pastors. In Calvin's Geneva church leadership was exercised by the assembly of pastors and elders—the presbytery, or consistory. Teachers were catechists rather than theology teachers, as the term is understood today, so that one cannot talk about a "teaching ministry" of professors.

The deacons were subordinate to the consistory. Those holding office were united in an assembly for carrying out their functions. This scheme of things does not envision or encourage the authority of individual officeholders, thereby obligating the whole congregation. Calvin does not recognize an office that extends beyond a congregation or that encompasses the entire church, such as the institution of the episcopal office in the early church.

In Scandinavia the typical Lutheran episcopal office emerged. Particularly noteworthy are the Swedish Lutheran bishops, whose apostolic succession (in the sense of a continuous *successio ministrorum* confirmed by laying on of hands) remained uninterrupted by the Reformation. (In 1528 three bishops were consecrated by Bishop Petru Magui; in 1540 there was a short interruption of the succession, which was restored in 1575). This succession was recognized by the Anglican church. At the time Finland was a province of the archbishopric of Uppsala. Here, too, the episcopal office with apostolic succession was preserved.

In the Danish Lutheran church (as in Norway and Iceland) the episcopal office as the office of church leadership has existed since the Reformation without apostolic succession. Johannes Bugenhagen, "the reformer of the North," who was not a bishop himself, consecrated seven bishops in Copenhagen in 1537 and thus established a Lutheran episcopate. Lutheran churches with bishops (sometimes called superintendents) developed in the sixteenth century in Latvia, Estonia, Transylvania, Hungary, and Poland.

The Church of England went its own way. Throughout the different phases of the English Reformation the office of the bishop in historical succession was questioned neither theologically nor legally. Still, the place of the episcopal office in the church order needed to be newly defined in relation to the position of Rome, on the one hand, and to the objections of presbyterian and later Puritan notions, on the other. The sources of theological reflection were the Reformation emphasis on scripture and the esteem for the tradition of the early Church in Anglican spirituality. In the early days of the English Reformation the traditional threefold ministry, including that of bishop, was preserved. As the history of the Anglican church unfolded, a particular justification of the office of bishop became established, which through the Act of Uniformity (1662) and the Lambeth Quadrilateral (1888) made the episcopal structure an indispensable element of the church. The recent debate within Anglicanism centers on the question of whether the historical episcopacy is part of the definition (the *esse*) or of the ideal form (the *bene esse* or *plene esse*) of any church. Anglican apologists of the episcopacy (Archbishop John Whitgift [c.1530–1604], as well as Richard Hooker [1554–1600] in his work *Of the Laws of Ecclesiastical Polity*, particularly volumes III and VII) distinguished—in response to the argument that scripture puts forward a particular form of presbyterian church government—between "matters of faith, and in general matters necessary unto Salvation," which must be justified by a direct scriptural passage, and "matters of 'government' or 'external regiment.' " The episcopacy (like every other form of church constitution) is not explicitly prescribed in any statement of Jesus. This does not mean, however, that the episcopacy is not essential for the church. Hooker, for example, stressed in book VII of his *Ecclesiastical Polity* that the episcopacy can in some way be traced back to the apostles (be it through direct installation by the apostles or their participation in the development of this office). The episcopacy "had either divine appointment beforehand, or divine approbation afterwards, and is in that respect to be acknowledged the ordinance of God." In contrast to the Continental reformers, there is a different understanding of the term *ius divinum*, not in the sense of a divinely legitimized rule based on an explicit statement of Jesus or founded by the earthly Jesus but rather in the sense of a divine appropriation and sanctioning of a universal practice of the church. Theologians—who, in referring to Jerome, see a basic equality between priests and bishops and a difference in the *dignitas*, in the *officium*, or in the *iurisdictio* (but not in the sacrament of the *ordo*)—understand the most important role of the bishop as installing ministers in the parishes. Article 23 of the Thirty-nine Articles (1562) describes the functions of a bishop without mentioning him:

> It is not lawful for any man to take upon him the office of public preaching, or ministering the Sacraments in the Congregation, before he be lawfully called, and sent to execute the same. And those we ought to judge lawfully called and sent, which be chosen and called to this work by men who have public authority given unto them in the Congregation, to call and send Ministers into the Lord's vineyard.

Hooker summed up the majority opinion toward the end of the sixteenth century:

> A Bishop is a Minister of God, unto whom with permanent continuance, there is given not only power of administering the Word and Sacraments, which power other presbyters have; but also a further power to ordain Ecclesiastical persons, and a power of Chiefty in Government over Presbyters as well as Lay men, a power to be by way of jurisdiction a Pastor even to Pastors themselves [*Ecclesiastical Polity*, VII, 2.3].

Both priest and bishop are servants of word and sacraments. In addition, the bishop has the authority to ordain; in practice, confirmation is also his responsibility. On the level of ordination (*ordo*) the bishop is therefore distinguished by the latitude of the power of administering the sacraments. He can do what a priest can do plus ordain priests and confirm Christians. In the area of jurisdiction he has the pastoral responsibility for priests and the laity. This traditional Catholic view of the ministry of the bishop does not, however, exclude the essential equality of priest and bishop as servants of the word, the participation of the laity in leading the church (Act of Supremacy, 1534), and the synodic and collegial exercise of the bishop's office as is characteristic in the Anglican church today.

In the Roman Catholic church the sociopolitical role of the bishops in central Europe grew after the Reformation and the political consolidation of the Peace of Augsburg (1555). A theological reassessment of the office of bishop was not part of this. The sporadic declarations of the Council of Trent as a whole do not provide any complete understanding of the office of the bishop and avoid astutely any decision in the Catholic theological controversies of the time (the sacramentality of the bishop's consecration, the origin of the bishop's power of jurisdiction, and the relationship of the papacy and the episcopacy). The debate concerning the duty of bishops to reside in their dioceses and the right of the pope to authorize a dispensation from this duty illustrates that the classic ecclesiological differences (the theory of the papacy and papalism against episcopalism, Gallicanism, and Conciliarism) were still alive.

The decisions of the council underlined the *ordo* as one of the seven sacraments (ordination as a whole is a sacrament); the character indelebilis of the transfer of office; the hierarchical gradation of bishops, priests, and *ministri*; and the superiority of the bishops over and above priests. The power of ordination and confirmation was reserved for bishops alone. On the one hand, the council includes proclamation (*praedicatio Evangelii*) as the main office of the bishop. On the other hand, preaching was not included in the constitutional functions of ordination. The Tridentine decrees say nothing about the role of the general council, or synod, in the life of the church. The instruction to hold a provincial synod by the metropolitan every three years, as well as annual diocesan synods presided over by the diocesan bishop, did not gain acceptance in church practice and was soon forgotten.

Roberto Bellarmino undertook the first attempt to systematize Catholic ecclesiology in the sixteenth century in his *Disputationes de controversiis christianae fidei adversus huius temporis haereticos* (three vols., 1586–1593; expanded edition in four volumes, 1596). Influential features were his definition of church government as *monarchia temperata aristocratia et democratia* (the primacy of the pope softened by the participation of the bishops [*aristocratia*] and the faithful laity [*democratia*]), the accentuation of the visibility of the church, and the declaration that the *vinculum hierarchicum* (the unity of the faithful with the episcopacy and papacy) belongs to the visible identity of the church. Thus, the episcopal structure (alongside the common creeds and sacraments) becomes part of the definition of the church. Since Bellarmino includes in the *vinculum hierarchicum* the unity with the pope, all Christian communities outside the Roman Catholic church are not, for him, churches. In the ensuing years the ecclesiological debates in Catholicism (concerning Gallicanism, Febronianism, Josephinism, and national churches) and developments leading to Vatican I made it clear that the relationship between the pope and episcopacy remained unsolved. To distinguish itself from certain themes of the Reformation (the relationship of the individual to God, the synodical participation in the leadership of the church, and the changeability and fallibility of all church statutes), the predominant Catholic ecclesiology emphasized in successive efforts (leading to the dogma of 18 July 1870) the monarchical structure of the church and the need for a visible authority in the ministry of bishop and pope in the church constitution.

BIBLIOGRAPHY

Brecht, Martin, ed. *Martin Luther und das Bischofsamt.* Stuttgart, 1990.

Klausnitzer, Wolfgang. *Das Papstamt im Disput zwischen Lutheranern und Katholiken: Schwerpunkte von der Reformation bis zur Gegenwart.* Innsbrucker theologische Studien, vol. 20. Innsbruck, 1987.

Kühn, Ulrich. *Kirche.* Handbuch systematischer Theolgie, vol. 10. Gütersloh, 1980. Contains an analysis of the ecclesiology of the reformers.

Norris, Richard. "Episcopacy." In *The Study of Anglicanism*, edited by Stephen Sykes and John Booty, pp. 296–309. Philadelphia, 1988.

Sykes, Norman. *Old Priest and New Presbyter: The Anglican Attitudes to Episcopacy, Presbyterianism and Papacy since the Reformation.* 2d ed. Cambridge, 1957.

WOLFGANG KLAUSNITZER

Translated from German by Christoph Schuler and Lars Simpson

EPISCOPIUS, Simon (Dutch, Simon Egbertszoon Bisschop; 1583–1634), early Dutch Remonstrant leader and theologian. Born in Amsterdam, his academic talents earned him the support of former burgomaster Cornelis Bennink, enabling him to study at the States College in Leiden in 1600 and in the theological faculty in 1603. Amid the disputes between Franciscus Gomarus and Jacobus Arminius, Episcopius became an ardent partisan of Arminius. Upon earning a master of arts in 1606, he found his welcome from the city government to Amsterdam's ministry blocked by the delaying tactics of the Calvinist clergy there. He remained in Leiden to study under Gomarus and Arminius.

In 1609 he went to the new University of Franeker to study under Johannes Drusius, but there he was opposed by the Calvinist theologian Sibrandus Lubbertus. An interlude in France followed, during which he became familiar with the French language. By 1610 he was back in Holland and was one of the signatories of the Remonstrance of 1610. Later that year he was ordained as minister of the Reformed church at Bleiswijk, near Rotterdam.

In 1611, at a colloquy before the States-General, Episcopius emerged as the chief spokesman for the Remonstrants. In 1612 he was made a professor of theology at Leiden, where his inaugural oration brought new charges of heresy, first by Festus Hommius but also by his colleague J. Polyander. His tenure at Leiden was marked by constant controversy.

Back in Amsterdam there were further aggravations. In 1613 at the baptism of a child of his merchant brother, Egbert Bisschop, Episcopius was present as a witness. The officiating minister tried to bar him on the grounds of alleged heresy. A mob led by women tried to stone him. Later, a blacksmith attempted to kill him. In 1617 his brother's house was plundered by a mob incited by the Calvinist clergy. Episcopius repeatedly had to defend himself on many fronts—against the Amsterdam burgomasters, the Leiden curators, and his faculty colleagues. When he made a trip to Paris in 1615, his enemies accused him of having gone over to the Jesuits.

The controversy came to a head at the Synod of Dordrecht (1618–1619), where Episcopius as spokesman for the Remonstrants gave a speech at the twenty-third session that was praised for its power (but criticized for its length). When the synod banished the Remonstrants, Episcopius fled first to Antwerp, where he wrote the Remonstrants' Confession of Faith, published first in Dutch translation (1621) and then in his own Latin (1622). He then went to France, living in Rouen but chiefly in Paris. The death of Maurits van Nassau in 1625 ended the persecution of the Remonstrants. By 1626 Episcopius was back in Holland as minister of the Remonstrants in Rotterdam. In 1634 he became the rector of the new Remonstrant seminary in Amsterdam, serving until his death in 1634.

His many writings marked a transition of Remonstrant theology from Arminius's cautious modification of scholastic Calvinism to a development that adumbrated the Enlightenment. Where Arminius had held that human free will was entirely lost in the Fall and restored only by universal grace, Episcopius saw free will as damaged but not destroyed in the Fall. Thus humans can innately seek and know the good.

His collected writings were published, some posthumously, in two volumes (1650–1665) and in one volume (1678). His confession of faith later appeared in English translation (1684).

BIBLIOGRAPHY

Bangs, Carl. *Arminius: A Study in the Dutch Reformation.* 2d ed. Grand Rapids, Mich., 1985. See especially p. 147.

Brandt, Gerard. *The History of the Reformation and Other Ecclesiastical Transactions in and about the Low Countries . . .* (1720–1721). Reprint, New York, 1979. See vols. 2–4.

Calder, Frederick. *Memoirs of Simon Episcopius.* London and New York, 1838.

Harrison, A. W. *The Beginnings of Arminianism to the Synod of Dort.* London, 1926. See especially pp. 120ff.

Hoenderdaal, G. J. "Arminius en Episcopius." *Nederlands Archief voor Kerkgeschiedenis* 40.2 (1980), 203–235.

———. "Episcopius (Bisschop), Simon." In *Biographisch Lexicon voor de Geschiedenis van het Nederlandse Protestantism,* vol. 2, pp. 191–195. Kampen, 1983.

Nobbs, Douglas. *Theocracy and Toleration.* Cambridge, 1938. See especially pp. 91–107.

Platt, John. *Reformed Thought and Scholasticism: The Arguments for the Existence of God in Dutch Theology, 1575–1650.* Leiden, 1982.

CARL BANGS

ERASMUS, Desiderius (1467?–1536), humanist, reformer, moralist, and satirist. He was the brilliant creation of a somewhat precarious union of Netherlandish piety with the revival of classical learning initiated in quattrocento Italy. He was born in Rotterdam of unmarried parents; his mother was a widow, and his father at some stage became a priest. The father was himself a devotee of Italian humanism who knew Latin and Greek and supported himself in Rome as a scribe. Erasmus had a brother, Pieter, three years older, and the boys were orphaned by the early death of both parents about 1484/85. Little more about his origins can be said with certainty.

Their family began the schooling of the two brothers locally in Gouda, whence they came, and they were then sent (about 1478) to the more advanced school of the chapter of Saint Lebuin at Deventer, where the new learning was available and where by 1483 the headmaster was the humanist Alexander Hegius, a friend of the famous Rodolphus Agricola (Roelof Huysman). After the death of their father in 1484 the two boys were sent by their guardians to a school at 's Hertogenbosch to live, as at Deventer, in a hostel run by the Brothers of the Common Life. In 1487 both entered religious life with the Augustinian Canons, Pieter at Sion, near Delft, and Erasmus at Steyn. Although he would later claim otherwise, evidence from his own pen is abundant that the regime at Steyn was not entirely inhospitable to humanistic learning. It is also clear that the lure of classical letters was stronger than that of the cloister. After his ordination to the priesthood in 1492, he found an escape route in the service of Hendrick van Bergen, bishop of Cambrai, as Latin secretary, and never returned to Steyn. In 1485 he was allowed to go to the University of Paris to study theology, where eventually he found a key to some financial independence in the tuition of well-to-do foreigners.

Whatever he may have absorbed of the formal curriculum there, he turned increasingly to the study of classical letters and the Fathers, while his profession allowed him to develop his early treatises on education, among them his epitome of Lorenzo Valla's *Elegantiae linguae latinae* (first composed while he was still at Steyn and published without his authorization in 1529); *De copia verborum ac rerum* (Foundations of the Abundant Style; 1512), the first version of what would become his *Colloquia,* conversational discourses in Latin on a multitude of topics of the day; and his program for correct study, *De ratione studii* (1511).

In the spring of 1499 he traveled to England with his new pupil, William Blount, Baron Mountjoy, and with that journey he was effectively launched on a lifetime of travel and study, supported by patrons lay and ecclesiastical who sanctioned his desire to knit together the project of humanism and the Christian life. The result was his remedy for a reformed Christendom, the *philosophia Christi*, or "philosophy of Christ." The term distinguishes Erasmus's approach from the more familiar tradition of the "imitation of Christ": it was a patristic phrase implying a love of the wisdom found in the Word incarnate, and pointing as well to the early sources of faith that Erasmus held would provide a unique catalyst to transform the life and very being of the believer. It also reveals the stance of the Dutch reformer: that there was a primordial harmony, grounded on the Logos, between the fruits of ancient moral wisdom and the gospel of Christ.

Like many other intellectuals of the fifteenth century he turned against the speculative, systematic approach of the "moderns" to favor the "old theology," the nonscholastic tradition in which *lectio divina* and meditation upon the sacred page constituted the proper study of the theologian. Such a theology was to be used to edify the faithful through preaching and pastoral direction, rather than to construct elaborate edifices of rational conjecture. Like his master, Lorenzo Valla, Erasmus added to the older tradition the critical disciplines of classical study, insisting that the Christian life of the day could be revivified only from texts restored in the context of their historic origins. The foundation of his program thus rested on two pillars: the reform of education to proliferate the ancient, secular learning upon which a proper understanding of the key texts of the Christian life depended, and the rehabilitation and propagation of those texts through the art of printing. He intended that from these enterprises should come an informed Christian populace, lay and clerical, instructed in the service of the common good with a Christian, not a pagan notion of service.

While many other humanists of the day shared these ideals, to an extent matched by no one else Erasmus undertook to lay the foundations for all of this himself. Some of his writings on education have been mentioned already; to those must be added *De pueris instituendis* (1529) on the early, liberal education of children, and above all his *Adagia*, the collection of Greek and Latin proverbs that began as a modest work in 1500 and was expanded vastly through six editions to the end of his life, accumulating commentary on the contemporary world as it accumulated proverbs. It provided singular witness to his conviction that ancient wisdom remained a valuable guide—if a fallible one—to the conduct of the moral life, and that it had an honored place in the full revelation of God's providence in Christ. It was also a by-product of and in part the inspiration for a series of editions of Greek classical authors that is too extensive to be described here.

His works of moral instruction were many: on marriage, on Christian widowhood, on examination of conscience and confession, on prayer, on preparation for death. To these may be added a commentary on the Apostles' Creed (1533), expositions of the *Psalms* (1515–1532), paraphrases of the New Testament, and a lengthy, much-reworked treatise on preaching, *Ecclesiastes* (1535). The most important of such writings as a résumé of the *philosophia Christi* was his *Enchiridion militis Christiani*, (Handbook of the Christian Knight; 1503). This work, whose impact may seem difficult now to understand, captured the religious imagination of a large part of Europe after its second appearance (1518), being widely and repeatedly translated into a variety of languages. It was a handbook of personal discipline, largely Pauline in inspiration, strongly oriented to the lay vocation, and remote from traditions of piety derived from adapted monastic devotion. To a degree it was highly individualistic, envisaging a Christian society in which the mode of life is entirely secondary to the commitment of each of the baptized to perfection in Christ.

Toward the restoration of the sources of Christianity his first extended contribution was an edition of the letters of Jerome occupying the first four of nine volumes and prefaced by a life that is a lasting contribution to the humanist art of biography. He edited and (in the case of the Greeks) produced Latin versions of works by Basil the Great, Hilary, Cyprian, Arnobius the Younger, Chrysostom, Irenaeus, Ambrose, Origen, Lactantius, Athanasius, and Augustine. But the chief and most renowned textual work was his edition of the Greek New Testament (1516), the first in print, with a new Latin version in place of the Vulgate and annotations on the whole. The prefatory matter contained essays—the *Paraclesis*, *Methodus*, and *Apologia*—of independent importance as exhortations and guides to the study of scripture and as a defense of the undertaking.

Although much has been made of the fact that this was the first Greek text to appear in print, and that Erasmus substituted for the standard Vulgate his own Latin translation, it is clear that most of Erasmus's effort and the focus of his interest over many years lay in the *Annotations*. These were not a kind of critical apparatus but rather an independent work that is actually an extended commentary on the Vulgate Bible—the standard text of the day. Like so many of his writings, it acquired substance and controversial momentum in successive editions, attracting a corresponding intensity of criticism and praise. It seems certain that his original intention was to publish the Vulgate with this commentary, that the idea of printing a rather hastily assembled Greek text came to him only in Basel in 1515, and that the notion of producing a new Latin version in place of the Vulgate was last.

For all of its peculiarities, Erasmus's *Novum instrumentum* in its successive editions deserves its place as his best-remembered achievement. Of itself, it was a scholarly challenge to the religion of the day that was paralleled by no other work. The fresh appeal of his humanistic Latin version and the interest of the *Annotations* insured wide popularity even among those to whom the Greek remained inaccessible. The second edition of 1519 (now and henceforth titled

Novum Testamentum) was the basis of Luther's German translation, and through its being incorporated into the third edition of Robert Estienne's Greek Testament (Paris, 1550) it influenced strongly the Greek Testament of Théodore de Bèze, the standard Protestant text that in turn underlay the King James Version and the Elzevir Greek Testament of 1633, the *textus receptus*. Although it carried with it a legacy of critical problems, it was the foundation of biblical scholarship for three hundred years, until the era of higher criticism in the nineteenth century.

The prefatory material also contributed both to the success of the edition and to Erasmus's evangelical purpose. The *Paraclesis*—meaning a summons or exhortation—complemented the call to mastery of ancient wisdom in the *Antibarbari* with an exhortation to absorption in the self-revelation of God in Christ, the Word incarnate, discovered in scripture and appropriated as the inspiration and guide of life. It was in the *Paraclesis* that Erasmus introduced the term "philosophy of Christ," and it was in the *Paraclesis* that he declared that scripture should be made available in the common language of the people, "as if Christ taught such intricate doctrines that they could scarcely be understood by very few theologians or as if the strength of the Christian religion consisted in men's ignorance of it"—brave words that he would have reason later on to reconsider (John C. Olin, *Christian Humanism and the Reformation: Selected Writings of Erasmus*, p. 101, New York, 1987). Nevertheless, the *Paraclesis* reveals the essence of Erasmus's personal faith and program for reform: the universality of the Christian, baptismal vocation, the enduring moral value of pagan wisdom, the dangers of religious formalism and mere ceremonial, the perversion of theology by inappropriate (Aristotelian) philosophical instruments and the damage done thereby to the faith and peace of Christendom, and withal the scandal of laxity and of ignorance of scripture on the part of religious professionals, monks as well as theologians.

The *Methodus* was expanded in the second edition of the New Testament into the *Ratio verae theologiae*, an account of the proper approach to theology. Erasmus makes clear that, despite the sometimes edifying example of such ancients as Socrates, it is in the scriptural portrait and teaching of Christ alone that it is possible to find the complete rule of life and understanding. This is the proper object of theology, this treasure of sacred scripture understood in the historic circumstances of its day. Like so much else of Erasmus's doctrine, his hermeneutic was derived from Augustine's *De doctrina christiana*, advocating spiritual or allegorical exegesis to unlock the inwardness of the sacred text for the eye of faith; Jerome and Origen were the models. He also recommended the use of the ancient rhetorical device of "places"—*loci*—to facilitate understanding, and with *loci theologici* to harmonize the whole world of the Bible.

In the *Novum Testamentum* Erasmus emerged as an unprecedentedly formidable critic of contemporary theological and religious practice, but it was by no means the occasion for his debut in that arena. As a commentator on the common life of his day he had already put to brilliant use the literary skills of his classical training. Although he was capable of turning almost any utterance—from a personal letter to an annotation—to comic or satirical purpose, no doubt his most widely read and lasting satires were those in his *Colloquies* and the *Moriae encomium* (Praise of Folly; 1511 and, with significant alterations, 1514). In addition, some of the *Adagia* blossomed into self-sufficient essays of the genre, notably *Sileni Alcibiadis*, *Dulce bellum inexpertis*, and *Scarabeus aquilam quaerit*, along with some occasional pieces like *Querela pacis* (Complaint of Peace; 1517) and *Julius exclusus* (1517), the last probably his work, although always vehemently disowned.

A common theme in all of his satires was the scourge of war, which was also addressed in his political writings, especially the *Institutio principis Christiani* (1516), designed to instruct the youthful Prince Charles, the future Charles V. Close to this theme in many works was an unmistakable republican vein combined with radical skepticism about the moral claims of all established government. The rhetorical declamation *Moriae encomium* reveals the same concerns but forms an anthology of his satirical targets. His style was that of his master, Lucian, and if the genre was congenial to his temperament, his purpose was nevertheless deeply serious: in *Moriae encomium* the verbal play and paradox rest on a determined assertion of the claims of the *philosophia Christi*. Such satire was a powerful instrument to dissolve the encrustations of unexamined belief and practice, but it was a dangerous weapon. If the Lucianic light was meant to scatter the shades of superstition and unreflective faith, it could also sear and burn. Whatever the benefit of his provocations Erasmus became as well an impresario of disillusion, and it was this element in his writing that partly justified the otherwise doubtful allegation that he "laid the egg which Luther hatched."

Erasmus's disavowal of the systematic theology of his day meant, with his emphasis on persuasion, that his theological principles must be derived often by inference, and from a host of sources. His moralism may also mislead the inquirer into a belief that doctrine was unimportant and that he preached a humanized Christ. This was far from true, but one must approach him through his perception of what was most needed in his day. One must also be prepared to find contradictions and reconsiderations, and at all times be alert to the play of irony, which he could never for long abandon. The letter to Paul Volz that introduces the second edition of *Enchiridion* is a good example of his vision. It contains a portrait of the church original with him, which appeared also in the *Ratio*. Here the community of the faithful are ranged in three concentric circles, focussing like the rings of a target on the person of Christ. In the innermost circle are the clerics in their various ranks, whose obligation is to embrace the intense purity of the flame at the center and transmit it to those next to them. These are the secular princes with responsibility to foster and protect a truly Christian society, not to pursue their own interests. In the outermost circle are the common people who are to be nourished and encouraged by the others in seeking the one goal of life: Christ and his teaching in all its purity. Erasmus's concluding observation is also important: since the perfection of Christian service is in the interior dispositions rather than the external mode of life, it may be that the places people seem to occupy in no way reflect the true, invisible relationship of individual believers to the one transforming presence—Christ.

With this doctrine of an invisible church whose true order is known only to God, he concludes his account of a Christian commonwealth without specific institutional structure, worldly rank within it justified only by the responsibility of the powerful to the good of all. Nothing in his other pronouncements contradicts this early picture. He held that the office of the pope was not of divine origin (unlike that of the bishop) but was essential to preserve the unity of Christendom; he saw its prerogatives as those only of pastoral duty and example. He was not a conciliarist, seeing no guarantees of final authority about the teaching of Christ in any institutional order—papal, conciliar, episcopal, or congregational. Although such views would seem to echo certain tenets of Nicholas of Cusa, or Jean Gerson, or William of Ockham, his own could scarcely be classified or ordered, since his organizational principle was simply the text of scripture itself. It was precisely this, along with his rhetorical style, that drew the fire of his antagonists, especially after the appearance of the New Testament and *Moriae encomium*, so that after 1515 apologetics and polemic consumed an ever-increasing portion of his output.

No concise account can be attempted of his running combat both with Catholic and Protestant critics, but of these many controversies a representative one, the most important by far, was his historic debate with Luther. They shared much: rejection of Scholasticism, belief in the centrality of the Bible in Christian life and understanding, hatred of religious formalism and the kind of legalism represented by indulgences, emphasis on interior conversion to the following of Christ, and a desire that the reform of the church be taken in hand by the princes. As early as 1516 Luther was beginning to sense that the priorities of Erasmus were not his own, but in 1519 he was still ready to acknowledge his debt to the older man. By that time, however, worried by the storm surrounding Luther's own writings—in particular, the allegations that he, Erasmus, had contributed to Luther's views—Erasmus saw his own educational program threatened and feared that the revival of letters would be blamed. Nevertheless, he defended Luther's right to be heard and taken seriously. His most revealing worry had to do with faction; he hoped for arbitration by learned theologians under princely auspices, but Luther's tracts of 1520 made such a course of action impossible. In a letter of May 1521 to Justus Jonas intended for circulation to the whole circle of German humanists, Erasmus now protested the idea that matters of theological weight and delicacy should escape the circle of the professionals, blaming Luther "for making everything public and giving even cobblers a share in what is normally handled by scholars as mysteries reserved for the initiated" (Epistle 1202 in *Collected Works of Erasmus*, vol. 8., p. 203, Toronto, 1988). This was far from the idealism of the *Paraclesis*.

When at length, under great pressure from all sides, Erasmus decided to enter the debate, he chose an issue of great importance for his own program, that of the freedom of the will. More important than the debate itself for present purposes is the instruction it provides in Erasmus's personal theology. From the outset he had been astonishingly indifferent—as it seemed to many—to Luther's particular doctrines; his chief concern was Luther's readiness to create dissension. It was the same charge he had brought against the scholastic theologians, and it reveals the importance of concord to his personal system. While to some this attitude has seemed to mark Erasmus as a theological dilettante, his position was a weighty one. It was grounded in the traditional notion of the *consensus fidelium*, the concord of the faithful. Earlier he had used it against the complicated theology of Scholasticism; now he appealed to it against Luther's initiative. Unlike Luther, he insisted that Christians do not share in the headship of Christ as individuals; rather they are made by the Holy Spirit one among themselves. He always stressed the corporate understanding of the community of the church and did not believe that a particular revelation could take precedence over the tested experience of the body of believers through the ages. That body, moreover, was constantly instructed by the Holy Spirit, so that the self-understanding of the community of the baptized could grow, but novelties could only be vindicated by ultimate acceptance. Hence Luther's views should be respected and put to the test of time, but to advance them by aggression and discord was inadmissible. The Holy Spirit could not make itself known to a church in tumult. In this view of the essentially social character of the activity of the Holy Spirit, Erasmus's distance from Luther becomes most clear.

His part in the Reformation was the one he intended: to lay scholarly and critical foundations for a new era of scriptural and theological understanding and for a better-informed Christian populace. His personal program did not foresee and lacked entirely the popular appeal and prophetic vision of Luther, but by discrediting, probably beyond his own grasp, much of conventional religious practice he helped to pave the way for a new religious culture. His educational and scholarly initiatives survived to influence for all time all sectors of post-Reformation Christendom; his irenicism and passion for international peace are appealed to still.

BIBLIOGRAPHY

Primary Sources

Allen, P. S., ed. *Opus epistolarum.* 11 vols. and index vol. Oxford, 1906–1947. The first critical edition of Erasmus's correspondence and the foundation of the modern revival of scholarship in the field.

Collected Works of Erasmus. Toronto, 1947–. A scholarly, annotated English translation of the correspondence and most of the works, excluding editions, of which eleven volumes of correspondence and twenty-one of works have appeared to date (1994). Commonly cited as CWE.

Erasmi opera omnia. Amsterdam, 1969–. A new critical edition under the sponsorship of the International Union of Academies and the Royal Dutch Academy. Twenty volumes have appeared to date (1994). Cited as ASD. For texts not yet published by ASD the student must have recourse to the folio *Opera omnia* published in Leiden in 1703–1706 and known in the literature as LB.

Secondary Sources

Augustijn, Cornelis. *Erasmus: His Life, Works, and Influence.* Toronto, 1991. The most recent, comprehensive biography, translated from the Dutch original.

Bainton, Roland H. *Erasmus of Christendom.* Reprint, New York, 1982. A lively portrait by a scholar of Lutheranism with distinctive emphases and insights.

Bentley, Jerry H. *Humanists and Holy Writ.* Princeton, 1983. A valuable study which places Erasmus's biblical scholarship in its contemporary setting.

Boyle, Marjorie. *Erasmus on Language and Method in Theology.* Toronto, 1977.

———. *Christening Pagan Mysteries: Erasmus in Pursuit of Wisdom.* Toronto, 1981.

Chomarat, Jacques. *Grammaire et rhétorique chez Erasme.* Paris, 1981. A scholarly and comprehensive analysis of Erasmus's intellectual formation, the most important single contribution to that question in recent years.

Estes, James Martin. *Christian Magistrate and State Church: The Reforming Career of Johannes Brenz.* Toronto, 1982. An unusual appreciation of the practical influence of Erasmus's writings in the post-Lutheran religious settlement.

Margolin, Jean-Claude. *Douze années de bibliographie Érasmienne, 1950–1961.* Paris, 1963.

———. *Quatorze années de bibliographie Érasmienne, 1936–1949.* Paris, 1969.

———. *Neuf années de bibliographie Érasmienne, 1962–1970.* Paris, 1977.

McConica, James K. *Erasmus.* Oxford, 1991. A distilled account of the intellectual formation, writings, and lasting influence of Erasmus following the format of the Past Masters Series.

McSorley, Harry J. *Luther Right or Wrong?* New York, 1968. A close, critical examination by a Catholic scholar of the debate between Erasmus and Luther particularly with respect to predestination and Pelagianism, and awarding the palm to Luther.

Phillips, Margaret M. *Adagia: The "Adages" of Erasmus.* Cambridge, 1964. The only comprehensive account to date of this crucial segment of Erasmus's work by a scholar with a deep and informed sympathy with the subject.

———. *Erasmus and the Northern Renaissance.* London, 1981. A classic account of his life and times first published in 1947, last revised in 1981.

Rabil, Albert, Jr. *Erasmus and the New Testament.* San Antonio, Tex., 1972. An approach to the New Testament scholarship through the earlier intellectual formation emphasizing methodology and theology, concluding with a comparison of Erasmus and Luther on *Romans.*

Rummel, Erika. *Erasmus' Annotations on the New Testament.* Toronto, 1986. A full account of the genesis of the New Testament with particular attention to the content of the annotations and to their commentators.

———. *Erasmus and His Catholic Critics.* 2 vols. Nieuwkoop, 1989. A valuable and comprehensive survey of Erasmus's conservative critics from the appearance of *Moriae encomium* to the end of his career.

Screech, M. A. *Ecstasy and the Praise of Folly.* London, 1980. This highly individual approach to *Moriae encomium* stresses its internal structure and development, arguing for a marked commitment to Pauline ecstatic experience on Erasmus's part.

Tracy, James D. *The Politics of Erasmus.* Toronto, 1978. While the practical engagement of Erasmus in contemporary affairs is often referred to, this examination of his politics from the background of the Burgundian Netherlands gives unusual substance to his claim for attention as a political commentator and critic.

JAMES MCCONICA

ERASTIANISM.

ERASTIANISM. Named after Thomas Lüber (Lat., Erastus; 1524–1583), Erastianism held that the civil magistrate exercised all sovereignty within the state, that the church possessed no coercive power, and that excommunication should not be exercised. The origins of the theory are found in the thought of Marsilius of Padua, who argued in his *Defensor pacis* (1324) that the same people formed the church and the civil communities and that the civil government, the executive agent of the whole people, exercised coercive authority over both the ecclesiastical and civil communities. Marsilius thus stripped the church of all coercive power, including excommunication, which he placed in the hands of the local congregation.

This sort of arrangement was institutionalized in Zurich in 1525 during the Reformation with the creation of the marriage court (*Ehegericht*) under the auspices of the city government. The court became the sole instrument of discipline in Zurich; there was no excommunication *per se.* While Huldrych Zwingli favored this approach, Heinrich Bullinger was an even more vocal advocate of civil control of discipline within the Christian community. Bullinger rejected every sort of ecclesiastical jurisdiction, and he argued that the Christian magistrate was sovereign over the civil community and the church, just as the kings had been in ancient Israel. The task of the magistrate was to defend Christian morality and to protect true religion; he had the obligation to punish both sinner and heretic. This approach became the norm in the early Reformed churches.

The other Reformed program of church discipline was first proposed by Johannes Oecolampadius and then appropriated by Martin Bucer and John Calvin. They taught that the church needed a council of elders—a consistory or presbytery in addition to the civil courts—in order to discipline sinners and purify the church. This Calvinist approach assumed the necessity of a jurisdiction separate from the civil government, thus limiting the sovereignty of the magistrate.

In the late 1560s a controversy erupted in Heidelberg over

the issue of discipline. The two chief protagonists were Kaspar Olevianus and Lüber. Olevianus, a student of Calvin's and professor of theology at the university, led the Calvinists, who wanted a strict church discipline, and a consistory that could discipline and excommunicate church members independently of the civil authority. Lüber, a member of the medical faculty, was the key figure in defending the existing system, which was similar to Zurich's.

In 1568 Lüber responded to the Calvinists with 103 theses, which he later condensed to 75. He argued that no one should be excluded from the Eucharist who professed the true faith, even if that person was culpable in matters of life. Moreover, the Christian magistrate's court was sufficient to punish offenses; an ecclesiastical court to rule over or to punish the people was unnecessary. Like the kings in Israel, the Christian magistrate was sovereign; he ruled over both the civil community and the church, although he ought to consult the clergy in matters of doctrine.

Lüber sent manuscript copies of his theses to Bullinger and to Théodore de Bèze. Bullinger fully supported Lüber's position, which, in fact, was simply a restatement of his own. Bèze totally disagreed and replied to Lüber with his *Tractatus pius et moderatus de Excommunicatione.* Lüber then wrote a reply to Bèze, his "Confirmatio." Both men, however, agreed in the interest of peace not to publish their treatises. In 1589, six years after Lüber's death, both his theses and his "Confirmatio" were published in London as the *Explicatio.* It appears that Archbishop John Whitgift was instrumental in its publication. The *Explicatio* was reprinted in Amsterdam in 1649; the theses were published in an English translation in 1659 and reprinted in 1682. Bèze published the *Tractatus,* his reply to Lüber, in 1590.

Most Protestant cities and territories were "Erastian" well before the publication of the *Explicatio.* The Lutheran territories in Germany found a theorist in Johannes Brenz, who died in 1570. The Reformed church in the Netherlands was Erastian until communities were challenged by the Calvinists in the 1560s and 1570s. Until Calvin's victory in Geneva, all of the Reformed states in Switzerland followed the example of Zurich. In England royal supremacy over the church began with Henry VIII.

The basic elements of the Erastian theory, from Bullinger to Lüber, were (1) hostility toward any type of ecclesiastical jurisdiction and discipline, (2) rejection of excommunication, (3) civil control of the church, (4) the assumption of a common religion, and (5) the argument from ancient Israel. These ideas were the staple of English Erastianism.

Though the term Erastianism was not commonly used until the 1640s, Lüber's ideas had immediate impact in England after the publication of the *Explicatio.* The *Explicatio* fortified Whitgift's argument against the Presbyterians Walter Travers and Thomas Cartwright, and it influenced the argument of Richard Hooker in the eighth book of his *Laws of Ecclesiastical Polity.* While Whitgift and Hooker argued for an Erastianism based on royal supremacy, William Laud connected divine right monarchy with an ecclesiastical Erastianism. The Erastians of the 1640s, however, advocated parliamentary supremacy. Though the parties in the Long Parliament differed on the form of a national church, the majority of its members were Erastian. In the Westminster Assembly, two Erastian clergy, Thomas Coleman and John Lightfoot, were aided by other advisers and theorists, such as John Seldon, Bulstrode Whitelocke, Henry Parker, and William Prynne.

Two writers of the 1650s can also be classified as Erastians. James Harrington's more secular approach held many elements of the traditional Erastian argument. Thomas Hobbes, who reverted to earlier arguments for royal supremacy over the church, was the ultimate Erastian, though he hardly had the reverence of earlier Erastians for the Christian faith.

BIBLIOGRAPHY

Baker, J. Wayne. "In Defense of Magisterial Discipline: Bullinger's 'Tractatus de Excommunicatione' of 1568." In *Heinrich Bullinger, 1504–1575: Gesammelte Aufsätze zum 400. Todestag,* edited by Ulrich Gabler and Erland Herkenrath, vol. 1, pp. 141–159. Zurich, 1975. A study of Bullinger's unpublished treatise on excommunication and how it related to Lüber and the controversy in Heidelberg.

———. "Church Discipline and the Origins of the Reformed Schism, 1528–1531." *Andrews University Studies* 23 (1985), 3–18. Deals with the views of Zwingli, Oecolampadius, and Bullinger during the origins of the debate.

Crowley, Weldon S. "Erastianism in the Westminster Assembly." *Journal of Church and State* 15 (1973), 49–64. Concerned with showing how Erastianism developed to support parliamentary authority over church and Crown.

———. "Erastianism in the Long Parliament, 1640–1646." *Journal of Church and State* 21 (1979), 45–67. The origins of parliamentary Erastianism.

———. "Erastianism in England to 1640." *Journal of Church and State* 32 (1990), 549–566. Deals with the use of Erastus's ideas from 1589 to 1640, from Whitgift's use of Erastianism to support royal supremacy to Laud's argument for divine right monarchy and divine right episcopacy.

Erastus, Thomas. *Explicatio gravissimae quaestionis. utrum Excommunicatio. quatenus Religionem intelligentes et amplexantes, a Sacramentorum usu propter admissum facinus arcet; mandato nitatur Divino, an excogitata sit ab hominibus.* London, 1589. Lüber's treatise.

Estes, James Martin. *Christian Magistrate and State Church: The Reforming Career of Johannes Brenz.* Toronto, 1982. Excellent study of the development of Brenz's ideas about church and state and their implementation, especially in Württemberg.

Figgis, J. Neville. "Erastus and Erastianism." *Journal of Theological Studies* 2 (1901), 66–101. The authoritative discussion on Erastianism for many years; overstates the distinction between Erastus's ideas and those of later Erastians.

Walton, Robert C. "Der Streit zwischen Thomas Erastus und Caspar Olevian über die Kirchenzucht in der Kurpfalz in seiner Bedeutung fur die internationale reformierte Bewegung." *Monatshefte für Evangelische Kirchengeschichte des Rheinlandes* 37/38 (1988–1989), 205–246. Study of the background to the controversy in Heidelberg, the issues and individuals involved, and the impact of the controversy.

Wesel-Roth, Ruth. *Thomas Erastus: Ein Beitrag zur Geschichte der re-*

formierten Kirche und zur Lehre von der Staatssouveränität. Lahr, Germany, 1954. The standard work on Lüber.

J. WAYNE BAKER

ERASTUS, Thomas. *See* Lüber, Thomas.

ERDŐSI, János. *See* Sylvester, János.

ERFURT. Located in Thuringia, Erfurt (population 19,000) was an important supraregional trade and market center with a strong economic structure based on woad, a blue dye plant. Largely politically autonomous, Erfurt had acquired a territory that included some ninety villages. By 1392 the city had a university, claimed numerous religious institutions (four convents, eleven monasteries, twenty-one parish churches), and was at the center of ecclesiastical administration in the eastern part of the diocese of Mainz (suffragen bishop, general court, two archdeaconships).

After the close of the fifteenth century mediatization threatened Erfurt. The Wettins had to be recognized as protectors and the archbishop of Mainz as liege lord (treaties of Weimar and Amorbach, 1483). Constant conflicts with the territorial powers plunged the city into a debt crisis and finally into bankruptcy, which, when it came to light, triggered citizen unrest ("Crazy Year," 1509). Mainz and Saxony saw in this unrest an opportunity to expand their sovereign rights over Erfurt. Nevertheless, the competition between the two powers led to a stalemate and recognition of the treaties of 1483 (Treaty of Naumburg, 1516). The revolts were pivotal to the course of the Reformation: they altered the social structure of the governing elite and strengthened the awareness of urban values of independence and unity. A resistance formed against the archbishopric, which was seen as a threat to the city's independence, and also against the high clergy, who appeared to represent the interests of the archbishopric.

At the beginning, the Reformation in Erfurt was a movement of intellectuals. The friendship between Martin Luther and Johannes Lang guaranteed that the Erasmian-oriented humanists in Erfurt (Johannes Draconites, Justus Jonas, etc.) showed immediate interest in the *causa Lutheri*, provided publicity for it, and defended the movement vehemently ("Intimatio Erphurdiana," "Eccius dedolatus," 1520). Since, however, the humanists at the university were not firmly established, they could not open it up to the nascent Reformation, as had happened in Wittenberg. Rather, they were driven from the university and had to begin their preaching activities in the pulpits of the city. Thus, after 1521 a broad reform movement flourished that was characterized by strong anticlericalism. This was proved clearly during the first empirewide reformist "storm of the priests" (June 1521). The council knew to make use of this for its own political endeavors with regard to the clergy (restriction of privileges). Otherwise, the council pursued a course of religious-political neutrality until the Peasants' War. This allowed the pressure group led by Lang, which found support in all social strata, to engage in unrestricted activity.

In January 1522 the first desertions from the monasteries took place; in the same year the first private masses were done away with, and fasting and confession were discontinued as well. In July 1523 the first marriage of a priest took place and, for the first time, Communion under both kinds. Evangelical writings appeared without restriction, which placed Erfurt in the ranks of the six leading printing centers in the empire.

In 1524 the city council and evangelical preachers entered into a politically motivated alignment. While the preachers hoped for the support of the political authority, the city council in turn wanted to orchestrate the reform movement politically. In this way the city council also directed the revolt of the rural population (April–May 1525), for which, as Peter Blickle has stressed, the "discussions between the city and its territory" that recurred after 1521 served as the precondition. With the help of the peasants a "Reformation by coup d'état" (Robert W. Scribner) was introduced. The city declared its independence from the bishopric of Mainz, and the church in Erfurt was reorganized (prohibition of the Mass, an inventory of church property and goods, gradual closing of monasteries, Protestant order of worship services, printing and introduction of a German church order [*Teutsch kirchen Ampt*] attributed to Thomas Müntzer, the appointment and compensation of Protestant preachers).

The radical nature of the changes forced the Protestant members of the city council, led by Adolar Huttener, into reliance on the electorate of Saxony, whose evangelically motivated but eminently political entreaties for an alliance (e.g., Gotha-Torgau Alliance, 1526) jeopardized the city's independence. For that reason, after having ousted the Protestant spokesman, the council reverted back to a course of religious-political neutrality and again allowed Catholic worship (May 1526). Under the changed circumstances Lang's group of preachers lost their self-confidence and went on the defensive. Lang himself lacked the power to lead.

In 1530 the Treaty of Hammelburg, agreed on between the city council and the archbishopric, settled the issues concerning the evangelical movement in Erfurt. In this treaty the hereditary rule of Mainz was established, a limited re-Catholicization was decided, and—for the first time before the Peace of Augsburg (1555)—the reforming reorganization of the church in Erfurt was constitutionally recognized. The policy of dual confessions which had already existed in practice and was rooted in the constitutionally based dual relationship with Mainz and Saxony, gained through this treaty a solid foundation. Only after the Peace of Augsburg did the council support the institutionalization of the Protestant church, including an evangelical ministry headed by a chairman approved by the city council, the founding of the Protestant gymnasium in 1561, and the endowment of the Professor theologiae Augustanae Confessionis at the university in 1566.

BIBLIOGRAPHY

Blickle, Peter. "Die Reformation in Stadt und Landschaft Erfurt: Ein paradigmatischer Fall." In *Erfurt: Geschichte und Gegenwart*, edited by Ulman Weiß, pp. 253–273. Weimar, 1995.

Scribner, Robert W. *Reformation, Society and Humanism in Erfurt, ca. 1450–1550*. Ph.D. thesis, University of London, 1972.

———. "Civic Unity and the Reformation in Erfurt." *Past and Present* 66 (1975), 29–60.

———. "The Erasmians and the Beginning of the Reformation in Erfurt." *Journal of Religious History* 9 (1976), 3–31.

———. "Die Eigentümlichkeit der Erfurter Reformation." In *Erfurt, 742–1992; Stadtgeschichte, Universitätsgeschichte*, edited by Ulman Weiß, pp. 241-254. Weimar, 1992.

Weiß, Ulman. *Die frommen Bürger von Erfurt: Die Stadt und ihre Kirche im Spätmittelalter und in der Reformationszeit.* Weimar, 1988. See pp. 112–327.

ULMAN WEIß

Translated from German by Susan M. Sisler

ERIK XIV (1533–1577), king of Sweden, 1560–1568, son of Gustavus Vasa and Catherine of Sachsen-Lauenburg. He was highly gifted and received a solid education with Georg Norman and Dionysios Burreus as his tutors. He could sing well and played the lute, but already early in life he showed symptoms of mental disorder.

The relationship between father and son worsened during Vasa's last years. Among other things, Vasa disapproved of Erik's multifarious marriage negotiations. A planned visit to Queen Elizabeth I of England had to be cancelled because of Gustavus Vasa's death in September 1560.

In 1561, after having ascended to the throne, Erik, in the Articles of Arboga, restricted the power given to his brothers by their father. Soon thereafter he ran into a conflict with his brother John, duke of Finland, concerning the hegemony of Estonia. In 1563 Erik caused John to be arrested and convicted of high treason. Erik's political aspirations resulted eventually in war with Denmark, Lübeck, and Poland, the so-called Nordic War of 1563–1570.

In May 1567 Erik's pathological suspicion caused the killing of members of the noble Sture family. In 1568 Erik married Karen, a commoner, and legitimized his children by her. A revolt was organized by his brothers, the dukes John and Charles, together with members of the Sture family. At last Erik resigned and in 1569 a diet obliged him and his line to renounce the crown. Erik was subsequently kept prisoner in various castles until he died in 1577, probably from poisoning.

Erik continued to pursue the nonconfessional Lutheran course of his father with the Bible as the sole norm and rule of faith. Though he was familiar with the theology of Philipp Melanchthon and John Calvin, Erik nevertheless saw Luther as the true reformer. As a Renaissance prince he was not bothered by ecclesiastical questions as long as they did not affect his sovereignty. He did not continue the weakening of the episcopal authority but allowed the skillful and experienced Archbishop Laurentius Petri—a younger brother of the reformer Olaus Petri—to supervise the church. The 1560s thus saw the early development of the distinctly Swedish Lutheran church. A group of ultra-Lutheran reformers gathered around Erik wanting to weed out old church ceremonies and practices. They were supported by anti-Lutheran Calvinists. In 1564 they translated the confession of the French Huguenots into Swedish and presented the first draft of a reformed agenda in Swedish.

The king vacillated for a while between the orthodox and the Calvinist party but sided with the church meeting of 1566 in rejecting the Calvinist interpretation of the Eucharist. However, he did not abandon the Swedish line of tolerance proclaimed at Västerås in 1527. The Calvinists were allowed to retain their beliefs in so far as they did not cause general offense "as the king cannot govern conscience." Erik stayed anti-Catholic his entire life but preferred a Philippist humanistic Lutheranism.

BIBLIOGRAPHY

Andersson, Ingvar. *Erik XIV.* 4th ed., rev. and enl. Stockholm, 1979.

Holmquist, Hjalmar. *Reformationstidevarvet, 1521–1611*. Stockholm, 1933.

Kjöllerström, Sven. *Striden kring kalvinismen i Sverige under Erik XIV: En kyrkohistorisk studie.* Lund, 1935.

Roberts, Michael. *The Early Vasas: A History of Sweden, 1523–1611*. Cambridge, 1968.

INGUN MONTGOMERY

ERIKSSØN, Jørgen (1535–1604), reforming bishop of the Stavanger diocese in southwestern Norway. Little is known of Erikssøn's early life. He was born in Haderslev, in North Schleswig, Denmark. In 1559 he was appointed *rektor* of the cathedral school in the city of Bergen, in western Norway. He left Bergen in the late 1560s to continue his education at the universities of Copenhagen and Wittenberg (1568–1570). Even though King Christian III (r. 1536–1559) of Denmark and Norway had declared his lands Lutheran in 1536, the Reformation was slow to become established in Norway. In most parishes, the last Catholic priest went on to serve as the first Lutheran pastor. Little help or guidance was available to these pastors. Christian took five years to appoint a bishop for Stavanger. The work of the first Lutheran bishop, Jon Guttormssøn, was hindered by the lack of royal support and the plunder and ill will of Danish governors, all of which led to his eventual downfall. Christian then appointed eighty-year-old Jens Riber as bishop (1558–1571). Riber was unwilling and unable to provide leadership and care for the diocese.

Therefore, in 1571 Erikssøn came to a diocese that was in much worse condition than it had been when the king declared Norway Lutheran thirty-five years earlier. Much of the material resources of the diocese had been taken by the Danish governors. The bishop's task was made more difficult because of the Danish character of the Reformation. It was enforced by Danes, including the bishop himself; its literature was in the Danish language (somewhat different from Norwegian); and its regulations followed Danish custom rather than Norwegian.

With the solid support of King Frederick II of Denmark and Norway (r. 1559–1588), Erikssøn was able to establish the Reformation in the Stavanger diocese. He developed the Stavanger Latin school into an efficient instrument for the education of pastors. He also supported and trained pastors through a program of visitation. He organized an effective cathedral chapter to assist him in bringing clergy and laity under discipline, and he repaired and restored the cathedral.

As part of his ministry, Erikssøn published several works, but very little of what he wrote is original. *Om Menniskens Udkaarelse*(Concerning Human Election; 1572) is simply a translation into Danish of two lengthy passages from the Latin works of the Danish crypto-Calvinist Niels Hemmingsen. Erikssøn's chief work, *Jonae Profetis skiøne Historie* (The Prophet Jonah's Beautiful History; 1592), is a series of twenty-four sermons or theological lectures given for students at the Latin school. Its outline and much of the text are taken verbatim from *Explicatio Jonae Prophetae* (1528) by the Württemberg reformer Johannes Brenz. Other sections are composed of quotations from Hemmingsen and others. At every crucial point, however, Brenz's Lutheran theology is modified by the mildly synergistic theology of Hemmingsen and his tutor, Luther's colleague, Melanchthon. Thus even though Erikssøn has been called "Norway's Luther," the title is not really accurate. Hemmingsen, not Luther, was the bishop's primary theological mentor.

Although Erikssøn had studied at Wittenberg at the height of the theological controversies that raged among Lutherans, his writings reflect none of this turmoil. Indeed, in the preface to the sermons on Jonah, he wrote of his indebtedness to theologians on both sides of this bitter conflict, calling them all "fine builders of Christ's church," a statement many of these men would never have made about each other.

Erikssøn would not recognize or participate in the theological controversies of the day largely because he needed to give all his energy and attention to the work of rebuilding his diocese, a task he did well. Although not original, his lectures on Jonah, did bring theological and biblical studies to the pastoral candidates at the Latin school. His visitations and administrative ministry were also effective tools in bringing the Reformation to his diocese. Therefore, despite his arrival in Stavanger thirty-five years after Norway was declared Lutheran, Erikssøn is aptly known as the reforming bishop of Stavanger.

BIBLIOGRAPHY

Bang, A. Chr. *Den Norske Kirkes historie i Reformations-Aarhundredet, 1536–1600.*Kristiania (Oslo), 1895. Still the only book to cover the Reformation in Norway from a church historical perspective. However, it does not present a unified picture but deals with each diocese separately. Pp. 203–333 deal with Erikssøn. Bang's understanding of Luther's theology is clouded by nineteenth-century Lutheran orthodoxy and pietism.

Elgvin, Johannes. *En By i Kamp.* Stavanger, 1956. Pp. 75–89 of this heavily documented work evaluate the impact of Erikssøn on the city of Stavanger.

Erikssøn, Jørgen. *En Lig Predicke* (A Funeral Sermon). Copenhagen, 1578. The most original of Erikssøn's works. This and his other two works were published in Copenhagen because there was no press in Norway. They are available on microfilm at the Yale Divinity School Library. A much earlier writing, *De Fraterna Concordia,* is lost.

Quam, John E. "Jørgen Erikssøn: A Study in the Norwegian Reformation, 1571–1604." Ph.D. diss., Yale University, 1968. The only work in English on Erikssøn. Covers in detail his life and especially the literary and theological sources of his writings. Includes an extensive bibliography; also available on Michigan microfilms.

JOHN E. QUAM

ERNEST OF BAVARIA (1554–1612), third son of Albert V, head of the Wittelsbach family, and of Anne of Austria, granddaughter of the emperor Ferdinand and great-niece of Charles V. He was born 17 December 1554. Catholics and Protestants were then competing for power in the empire, and Albert V was a chief supporter of the papacy; as a result, and despite the decrees of the Council of Trent against the accumulation of ecclesiastical benefices, he was granted the episcopal seats that he claimed for his younger children. Ernest thus became bishop of Freising (1566), Hildesheim (1573), and Liège (1581), abbot of Stavelot-Malmedy (1581), and archbishop and elector of Cologne (1583), a see from which he ousted Gerhard Truchess, his reform-minded predecessor. Ernest then became bishop of Münster in 1585.

Able to speak German, Italian, and French, interested in mathematics, curious about astronomy if not astrology, a lover of hunting, dice, and women, this intelligent but lazy prince habitually allowed his advisers in Liège (Charles Billehé and Jean de Groesbeeck on political matters, Laevinus Torrentius and Jean Chapeauville on religious issues) to do his work. When necessary, he intervened at moments of crisis, particularly in matters of foreign policy, an arena in which he showed himself to be a capable diplomat.

One such instance of diplomacy took place in 1595, after the Dutch had seized the city of Huy. Ernest could not prevent the Spanish from retaking it; but when the Spanish asserted their continuing right to the city as long as Liège remained neutral, Ernest hurried to Brussels, negotiated with Philip II's ministers, and finally reclaimed his city. He succeeded in safeguarding the neutrality of Liège save for the minor concessions of the garrisoning of an increased number of Spanish troops and the selection of a governor acceptable to Spain, and for temporary concessions that were repealed by the Peace of Tongres in 1640. Another example of Ernest's diplomacy occurred in 1609, when, in response to the formation of the Protestant League, the Catholic League was organized in the empire. In his role as elector of Cologne he supported the Catholic League, while in his role as prince-bishop of Liège he remained neutral.

In matters of domestic politics, Ernest's record was mixed. At Cologne, because of excessive spending, he was almost always in conflict with his subjects; at Liège, meanwhile, he was popular thanks to his electoral settlement of 1603. According to this settlement the townspeople were granted a measure of self-government, a pawnshop was founded, and Frederick made a gift of a castle in Outre-Meuse that would become the hospital of Bavaria.

In religious matters Ernest was "a sponsor as zealous in, as he was poorly illustrative of, the Catholic Reformation." With the help of Bonhomi, nuncio of Cologne, he convened a synod in Liège (1585) during which the decrees of the Council of Trent were read; however, owing to the opposition of the Chapter of Saint-Lambert, he was unsuccessful in promulgating them. Undaunted, he founded a small seminary in 1589 at Saint-Trond, a large seminary at Liège in 1592, and finally, in 1605, a college in Louvain whose purpose was to enable the most promising of seminarians to continue their theological studies. He called on the Jesuits to found schools at Maastricht (1581), Liège (1582), and Aix-la-Chapelle (1601); he also encouraged foundations by the Capuchins (Liège, Huy, Maastricht), the Augustinian friars (Bouillon), the Recollects (Florennes), and the Poor Clares (Liège).

At the same time, he was prudent and circumspect toward the Reformation. Although he waged war on the reform movement in his electorate at Cologne, elsewhere, and especially in the diocese of Liège, his opposition was more restrained. The edicts that he promulgated (1582, 1589) did no more than impose fines and the penalty of banishment against Lutherans and Calvinists; only Anabaptism was still punishable by death. In 1595 two Anabaptist women thrown to their death in the Meuse became the last martyrs of the Reformation in the diocese of Liège. An event that took place with Ernest's approval in the principality of Stavelot-Malmedy—the trial and subsequent beheading of an accused witch, the monk Jean Del Vaulx—had such an impact that as late as the nineteenth century Marcellin la Garde included the story of Del Vaulx in his compilation of legends about the period.

Ernest died on 17 February 1612. He was succeeded by his nephew Ferdinand of Bavaria, formerly his coadjutor in Cologne (1595) and Liège (1601).

BIBLIOGRAPHY

Bax, W. *Het Protestantisme in het bisdom Luik en vooral te Maastricht, 1557–1612.* The Hague, 1941.

Dessart, H., L. E. Halkin, and J. Hoyoux. *Inventaire analytique de documents relatifs à l'histoire du diocèse de Liège sous le régime des nonces de Cologne, 1584–1606.* Brussels, 1957.

Ehses, S., and A. Meister. *Die Kölner Nuntiatur.* 2 vols. Paderborn, 1895–1899.

Fraikin, J. "Un épisode de la sorcellerie en Ardenne et en région mosellane: L'Affaire du moine de Stavelot, Dom Jean del Vaulx, 1592–1597." *Revue d'histoire ecclésiastique* 85 (1990), 650–668.

Grandsard, A. "Histoire du Grand Séminaire de Liège jusqu'au milieu du XVIIe siècle." *Bulletin de la Société d'art et d'histoire du diocèse de Liège.* 39 (1955), 86–185.

Hansotte, Georges, and Richard Forgeur. *Inventaire analytique de documents relatifs à l'histoire du diocèse de Liège sous le régime des nonces de Cologne, 1606–1634.* Brussels, 1958.

Harsin, Paul. *Études critiques sur l'histoire de la principauté de Liège. . . .* Vol. 3. Liège, 1959.

Lossen, Max. *Der kölnische Krieg.* 2 vols. Gotha, 1882–1897.

Moreau, E. de. *Histoire de l'Église en Belgique.* Vol. 5. Brussels, 1952.

Moreau, G. "L'élection du prince-évêque Ernest de Bavière." *Vieux-Liège* 86 (1950), 433–441.

Petri, Franz, and Georg Droege. *Rheinische Geschichte.* Vol. 2. 2d rev. ed. Düsseldorf, 1984.

Pirenne, H. *Histoire de Belgique.* Brussels, 1927.

Polain, E. "Ernest de Bavière, évêque et prince de Liège." *Bulletin de l'Institut archéologique liègeois* 53 (1929) 23–167.

———. "La vie à Liège sous Ernest de Bavière." *Bulletin de l'Institut archéologique liègeois* 54 (1938), 104–184.

GÉRARD MOREAU

Translated from French by Lisa S. Lustgarten

ERYTHACUS. *See* Červenka, Matthias.

ESTATES. Since the fourteenth century the term *Stand* has been used in German lands to mean "estate" or "rank," with the additional meanings of "constitution," "rule," "land," and "empire." In the fourteenth century an estate-oriented constitution emerged in Germany; in the fifteenth century it developed more fully. There were imperial and territorial estates, as well as estates-general and provincial estates. While the Estates-General were an important political force in France in the fourteenth century, the development in Germany beginning in the thirteenth century brought the consolidation of estates into groups of nobility, clergy, and townspeople. A change in the seemingly harmonious development of estates came with the early modern period, when along with the Reformation the emerging princely state changed the sociopolitical realities. This change entailed a broader meaning of "estate." It ceased being an explicitly social entity and became an ethical norm.

Martin Luther developed a theological concept of estates. Contrary to medieval thought, he did not consider society as having a threefold division. The three estates, or orders—*status ecclesiasticus, status politicus*, and *status oeconomicus*—were aspects of the life of each individual. Luther's understanding remained important in Germany until the end of the seventeenth century.

From the late Middle Ages the term *estates* applies most meaningfully and precisely to the political elites that were referred to as "the estates" until the nineteenth century. Nobility, clergy, and townspeople became institutionalized and convened in territorial diets (*Landtage*), with or without the support of the territorial ruler, to authorize taxes, and so on. As "estates" they were fundamental constitutional entities until the eighteenth century and even later. Almost everywhere in Europe the ruler, whose legitimization derived by heredity, had his counterpart in the "estates." As representatives of the realm these estates possessed considerable rights, for example, participation in governmental power, administration, and taxation.

The term *estates* also refers in the Holy Roman Empire to the so-called imperial estates (*Reichsstände*). In Germany the effective organization of the estates took place not only on the level of the empire (*Reichstag, Reichsstände*) and the large territories, but also in the mid-sized territories. The emperor and the imperial estates convened in the imperial diet. The imperial estates comprised the electors, the ecclesiastical and secular princes, and the prelates, counts, and cities who owed loyalty directly to the empire. This structure of the imperial estates remained essentially unchanged until 1806. Accordingly, a society characterized by estates was a feature of early modern Europe. The hierarchical social relationships found expression increasingly not only through poverty and wealth but also through tradition, privilege, and honor. This meant the differentiation of peasants, townspeople, and nobility as "estates." In the rigid structure imposed on society by the estates, each individual belonged to an estate by birth or privilege and could lay claim to privileges or rights associated with that estate. The elites of early modern Europe saw the distinct social differentiation of this estate-oriented society as the guarantee of the existing political order. The social consequences of this perspective were significant. The estates—nobility, townspeople, peasants—became more and more distinct, each acquiring specific social symbols, such as attire, custom, and so forth. At the same time, differentiation also occurred within the estates: in the nobility, there was the higher as well as the lower nobility, while among the townspeople the patricians occupied a special place. If the strict order of rank was violated, loss of honor and penalties resulted.

Peasants. Numerically, the peasants were the largest estate. Their labor and cultivation of the soil largely determined the daily lives of everyone, including the increasing prosperity of the upper classes of society. Socially, the peasants were highly differentiated: there were rich and poor, free and bonded peasants. The social circumstances of the peasants depended on the extent of contribution to their lord, territorial taxes, the tithe, and compulsory labor. The peasants differed greatly according to property, wealth, rank, and law, so that, by the end of the sixteenth century, there was a fixed number of rich peasants and a large number of poor ones. A well-formed family sense, a strict interpretation of inheritance laws, a pointed policy of arranged marriages across several generations, and the exercise of civic responsibilities secured the dominant position of these families in their rural community. Society at large saw the peasants mainly as subjects who were called upon to work and obey. In contrast to the townspeople, the clergy, and especially the nobility, the peasants enjoyed no political self-determination in the village. Accordingly, the early modern state was formed to a large degree without peasant participation—indeed, at their expense.

Townspeople. Numerically much smaller than the peasants, the townspeople still had a role of considerable significance for the development of trade and commerce in early modern Europe. Townspeople can be distinguished from both nobility and peasants by lifestyle, urban environment, and work. They were not a cohesive estate. This can be observed both in Europe in general and also in individual countries. Accordingly, great differences existed among the townspeople of early modern Europe. One may identify three distinct groupings in cities: patricians, merchants, and artisans. The patricians played the leadership role. Originally from families that provided city councilors and engaged in trade and commerce, the patricians succeeded in consolidating their position through their wealth as well as the acquisition of land. The merchants, the next grouping, were the dynamic force in urban society but were frequently precluded from governmental participation. The largest grouping was the artisans, the simple and common townspeople, storekeepers, and civic officials. Most of them were organized in guilds.

In early modern European cities one may distinguish three types of organization: (1) towns that possessed their own administration but were subject to territorial authorities and were thus centers of princely government; (2) free imperial cities, such as Danzig and Hamburg, that also included cohesive territories with their own administrative structures and were represented at the imperial diets; and (3) city-states that were autonomous both domestically and externally (Nuremberg).

Nobility. The nobility were the political elite of early modern Europe and retained their political and social preeminence, despite societal changes, until the end of the eighteenth and the beginning of the nineteenth century. Though numerically the smallest of the three estates, they claimed the largest land holdings, which entailed important political rights. The nobility claimed numerous prerogatives, such as the right for revenue-producing positions and exemption from ordinary taxation. Important were membership in a family, princely privileges, and connections to the ruling dynasty. The nobility was characterized by a strong class consciousness.

Clergy. The clergy, too, were a privileged estate. They enjoyed freedom from taxation, possessed, as did the nobility, their own legal system, and exercised considerable political influence. Even though the clergy as an estate survived the Reformation and retained their power until the beginning of the nineteenth century, the Reformation brought significant changes. Of particular significance was that in Protestant areas the monasteries were dissolved and the old clergy removed from office.

Organization and Functions. In early modern society the prince never ruled a territory alone. The privileged estates participated in the exercise of rule and power. They did not meet continuously but were convened by the prince. In Germany the assembly of the estates in the imperial diet occurred in three colleges, comprised of nobility, prelates, and cities (there also were four-college [or chamber] systems, where the higher nobility and "counts and lords" formed their own college; England had a two-chamber system); only rarely did the peasants have representatives. Power in the empire rested with the imperial estates.

The Golden Bull (1356) and common law provided the legal frame of reference for the constitution of the empire. These also defined the position of the ecclesiastical rulers: three of the seven electors and the majority of the members of the college of the princes were archbishops, bishops, and abbots or abbesses. They required not only installation by the emperor but also confirmation by the pope. The emperor's decisions depended on the liberality and *superioritas* ("superiority") of these estates. The emperor was elected by the seven electors—Mainz, Cologne, Trier, Palatinate, Saxony, Brandenburg, and Bohemia.

In the empire the higher nobility (*Reichsfürstenstand*) and a substantial segment of the middle and lower nobility (counts, lords, imperial knights) succeeded in establishing themselves as *Reichsunmittelbar*, meaning they were directly subject to the emperor. Constitutionally, this relation created complex realities. Large territories ruled by imperial princes with elaborate central administrations and territorial diets existed alongside small entities—all of them secure in their existence until the end of the empire. Only the princes, counts and lords, abbots and abbesses, and the imperial cities were eligible to participate in the imperial diet. The emperor convened the estates in consultation with the electors.

[*See also* Clergy; Nobility; *and* Peasants.]

BIBLIOGRAPHY

Baumgart, Peter, ed. *Ständetum und Staatsbildung in Brandenburg-Preußen.* Berlin, 1983. The relationship between estate and state formation is analyzed using Brandenburg as an illustration.

Blickle, Peter. *Die Reformation im Reich.* 2d ed. Stuttgart, 1992.

Blickel, Peter, ed. *Kommunalisierung und Christianisierung: Voraussetzungen und Folgen der Reformation, 1400–1600.* Berlin, 1989. Studies societal development between 1400 and 1600.

Dülmen, Richard van. *Fischer Weltgeschichte.* Vol. 24, *Entstehung des frühneuzeitlichen Europa, 1550–1648.* Frankfurt a.M., 1989. A good summary of early capitalist development, estates, and daily life during the Reformation in Europe.

Gerhard, Dietrich. *Ständische Vertretungen in Europa im 17. und 18. Jahrhundert.* 2d ed. Göttingen, 1974. A survey of the developments of estates in early modern Europe.

Lutz, Heinrich. *Reformation und Gegenreformation.* 3d ed. Munich, 1991. Offers a comprehensive narrative of the time together with an assessment of current scholarship and bibliography.

Münch, Paul. *Lebensformen in der Frühen Neuzeit, 1500–1800.* Frankfurt a.M., 1992. A fine study with an emphasis on the history of daily life.

Schulze, Winfried. *Ständische Gesellschaft und soziale Mobilität.* Munich, 1988. Analysis of the social development of estates.

Kristina Hübener

Translated from German by Hans J. Hillerbrand

ESTATES-GENERAL. From the thirteenth century on, the three orders of European society came to be represented in what in France, and later in the Low Countries, were called estates (*états, staten*), the First and Second consisting of the lords spiritual and temporal, the Third of deputies of designated towns. Estates might be convened in various areas but proved to be most enduring at the provincial level.

The estates were summoned by the king (or in the Low Countries by the duke of Burgundy) to assemble periodically (annually or triennially) to hear his representative explain the ruler's need for financial aid, his desire for the ratification of a treaty, and other concerns. The estates expressed their grievances, which, if accepted, could become the law of the land, after such modifications as were introduced by the royal (ducal) council.

France was not an absolute monarchy before the seventeenth century. Francis I (1515–1547), who is often credited with being its founder, could levy taxes without representation in only a part of his domain: the two ancient generalities of Languedoïl and Outre-Seine. Elsewhere he had to beg the various provincial estates for aid. The ministers of Louis XIII (1610–1643) set about to destroy the provincial estates but were only partly successful. In Brittany, Burgundy, Provence, Béarn, and Languedoc they survived.

The record of the Estates-General is more episodic. They acquired some regularity of form and function in the second half of the fourteenth century. After 1484, however, there was no assembly of the Estates-General in this now established form until 1560, though there were occasional assemblies of more limited character. Recourse in 1560 to the long-unused Estates-General was prompted by crisis: the bankrupt condition of the royal treasury after sixty-five years of unsuccessful struggle for supremacy in Italy and Europe against Charles V and Philip II of Spain, the corruption that prevented the proper functioning of each of the three orders of society, and the alarming progress of Protestantism.

In the secular sphere, the Estates-General were not ineffectual. The grievances expressed in the Estates-General at Orléans in 1560–1561, including demands for the reform of taxation, were to a notable extent embodied in the royal Ordinance of Orléans (1561), and were registered by the Parlement of Paris in September of that year. The demands of the Estates-General of Blois in 1576–1577 were similarly embodied in the Ordinance of Blois of 1579, as were those of the Estates-General of 1614–1615 in the Ordinance of 1629.

Reform of the church was called for in the first sixty-four of the 354 articles of the Third Estate at Orléans in 1560, and some of these actually became law in the Ordinance of Orléans. The advocates of reform had at first looked hopefully to the estates to redress their grievances. Calvin, in his *Christianæ Religionis Institutio* (Institutes of the Christian Religion; 1536), after insisting upon the duty of the private citizen to obey even tyrannical rulers, described the three estates of the kingdom as the divinely appointed protectors of the liberty of the people. Calvin's followers developed a theory of representative government: notably Théodore de Bèze in his *Droit des Magistrats* (1574) and François Hotman in his *Francogallia* (1573), a revisionist history of France in which he sought to show that the monarchy, until 1484, had always been limited by councils, and in recent centuries by estates. Gaspard II de Coligny, subsequently the leader of the Huguenots, was one of those at the Assembly of Notables at Fontainebleau in August 1560 who spoke vigorously in favor of convening the Estates-General. But the hopes for peaceful reform and the hopes of the government of Catherine de Médicis to preserve unity by compromise failed. After the outbreak of religious civil war in 1562, the Calvinists were never again able to exert as much influence as they had been able to muster in 1560–1561.

Though thwarted at the national level, the Calvinists continued to make use of representative institutions in those provinces where they were strong. In the eastern half of Languedoc they gained control over what they asserted were the legitimate estates of the province, but in contention with the Catholics based in Toulouse who claimed that they were the only legitimate estates. But nowhere else in France could the Huguenots claim to have come this close to the control of an entire province.

The party of reform was more successful in the Low Countries. In 1572 the followers of William of Orange were able to capture the provinces of Holland and Zeeland along with control of their estates. When in 1576 the other provinces joined in resistance to King Philip II, the government of the country fell into the hands of the Estates-General of the Netherlands. The provinces that went on to declare independence of the king were governed by their respective estates, joined together in Estates-General, in uneasy relationship with the princes of Orange.

Protestants in France had no such access to the Estates-General that assembled in 1576 and 1588, when deputies were required by King Henry III to swear an oath to the union organized by the Catholic League for the extirpation of Protestantism. After the assassination of Henry III in 1589 and in order to prevent the accession of the Protestant leader to the throne as Henry IV, the Catholic League convened their own estates in Paris in 1593. Henry outwitted them by accepting reconversion to Catholicism. His recent coreligionists could not look to the estates; their only hope now lay with the monarchy. Finally they obtained a kind of toleration in the Edict of Nantes (1598), the product of negotiations between the king and a delegation, not from any Estates-General or -Provincial, but from a Huguenot assembly. The edict recognized what had long been the fact: the existence of a state within the state, of a Calvinist community separate from the Catholic majority.

After the assassination of Henry IV, the Estates-General were convened in 1614. One of the participants, Richelieu, finding them frustrating, drew the lesson that France must be governed by an absolute monarchy, free of the vested interests represented in the estates. Though the estates of the peripheral provinces managed to escape destruction, the Estates-General were not to meet again (though they were convoked on two occasions during the Fronde, 1648–1653) until 1789.

[*See also* Diet *and* Henry IV of France.]

BIBLIOGRAPHY

Church, William F. *Constitutional Thought in Sixteenth-Century France: A Study in the Evolution of Ideas.* Reprint, New York, 1969.

Gelderen, Martin van. "The Position of the States in the Political Thought of the Dutch Revolt, 1555–1581." *Parliaments, Estates and Representation* 7.2 (1987), 163–176.

Griffiths, Gordon. *Representative Government in Western Europe in the Sixteenth Century.* Oxford, 1968. Includes chapters, with a selection of documents and bibliography, on the French Estates-General, French provincial estates, the estates of Languedoc, Huguenot assemblies, and the estates of the Netherlands.

Hayden, J. Michael. *France and the Estates-General of 1614.* Cambridge, 1974.

Koenigsberger, H. G. *Estates and Revolutions: Essays in Early Modern European History.* Ithaca, N.Y., 1971.

———. "Why Did the States General of the Netherlands Become Revolutionary in the Sixteenth Century?" *Parliaments, Estates and Representation,* 2.2 (1982), 103–111.

———. "Composite States, Representative Institutions and the American Revolution." *Historical Research: The Bulletin of the Institute of Historical Research* 62.148 (1989), 135–153. This is apparently the only theoretical attempt to explain why some states resorted to Estates-General (in addition to merely particular estates).

Major, J. Russell. *The Estates-General of 1560.* Reprint, New York, 1970.
———. *Representative Government in Early Modern France.* New Haven, 1980.
———. "French Representative Assemblies." In *Dictionary of the Middle Ages,* vol. 10, pp. 316–328. New York, 1982–1989.
———. *Representative Institutions in Renaissance France, 1421–1559.* Reprint, Westport, Conn., 1983. Shows the limited power of the Renaissance monarchy and the important role of the estates in both domestic and foreign policy.
———. *The Monarchy, the Estates and the Aristocracy in Renaissance France.* London, 1988. Includes indication of research opportunities and research published on French representative assemblies.
Villers, Robert. "Réflexions sur les premiers états généraux de France au début du XIVième siècle." *Parliaments, Estates and Representation* 4.2 (1984), 93–97.

GORDON GRIFFITHS

ESTELLA, Diego de (born Diego de San Cristobal; 1524–1578), Franciscan spiritual writer and preacher. Estella was born and raised near Pamplona, Spain, and entered the Franciscans at sixteen. After studies at Toulouse and Salamanca he went to Lisbon, where he published his first book, a panegyric of Saint John the Evangelist, in 1554. Several years later he returned to Spain and established a reputation as a fiery preacher; for a time he served as preacher at Philip II's court. His vehemence in denouncing the vices of the mighty, both lay and clerical, brought him under a prolonged investigation by the Inquisition (1565–1569), but he was allowed to resume his preaching and writing.

Details on his life, especially his last years, which were spent mainly in Salamanca, are sparse. Teresa of Ávila had him preach at the foundation of her convent in Salamanca in 1573. His main activity in these years was writing devotional works in Latin and Spanish. His vernacular works enjoyed enormous popularity, especially in Spain and Italy, but his appeal waned after 1600. In all, his books went through some 125 editions and were translated into many languages. Although Estella is often counted among the second rank of the Spanish mystics, his main audience was devout Christians in general, both lay and religious. The mystical notes in his works are muted, and his style is vivid but prolix. His main works are *Libro de la vanidad del mundo* (Toledo, 1562, greatly expanded in 1574; English translations 1584 and 1586); *Enarrationes* on Luke's gospel (Salamanca, 1574–1575), the 1578 edition of which was revised to meet objections the Inquisition raised, even though the work rebuts Protestantism; and *Meditaciones devotissimas del amor de Dios* (Salamanca, 1576; English translation 1898), enormously popular, and the best source for Estella's spirituality. His minor works include a treatise on preaching (1570) and a commentary on Psalm 136 (1576).

BIBLIOGRAPHY

Bujanda, J. M. de. *Diego de Estella, 1524–1578: Estudios de sus obras castellanas.* Rome, 1970. Recent scholarly study.
Gomis, Juan Bautista, ed. *Misticos Franciscanos Españoles.* 3 vols. Madrid, 1948–1949. The *Meditaciones* with an introduction; see especially vol. 3, pp. 41–367.
Peers, E. Allison. *Studies of the Spanish Mystics.* 2d rev. ed. London, 1951. Classic study; see especially vol. 2, pp. 218–249, 436–442.
Verzeichnis der im deutschen Sprachbereich erschienenen Drucke des XVI. Jahrhunderts. Stuttgart, 1983–. See vol. 6, nos. 3984–3995.
Zalba, J. *Fray Diego de Estella.* Pamplona, 1924.

JOHN PATRICK DONNELLY

ESTIENNE, Henri II (1531–1598), French scholarly printer and translator. Born in Paris, he became a brilliant Hellenist and a trained editor in his teens, when he cut his scholarly teeth helping his father produce the *editio princeps* of Dionysius of Halicarnassus. Several years of travel through Europe enabled him to gain access to many manuscripts of Greek texts and to make contacts with the most original scholars in France and Italy. In 1554 he printed, in Paris, the first edition of the poems ascribed to Anacreon, which had an immediate and powerful impact on French poetry; in 1555 he settled in Geneva, where he soon established his own press. In 1557 he published a new edition of Aeschylus, based on the work of the great Florentine Hellenist Pier Vettori; this edition was the first to include the full text of *Agamemnon.* From 1558 to 1568 Henri ran the family business as a whole and prospered, thanks to the support of Ulrich Fugger. His publications included several works of great ambition and accomplishment: editions of Herodotus and Thucydides; an anthology of Greek hexameter poetry (1566), in which he made the important historical point that the surviving poem of Musaeus was not the work of the legendary bard of that name but that of a much later poet; a new edition of Plato (1578), equipped with a new translation by Jean de Serres; and a magnificent five-volume *Thesaurus* of the Greek language (1572), based on original research, and so immense that it ruined Estienne financially. Some of his works and views—like his belief that the French language descended directly from Greek—now seem rather quaint, though they were normal for his time. But his prowess as a Greek scholar was exceptional, and his *Thesaurus,* in an updated edition, remains a standard reference work for classical scholars. The occasional pamphlets in which he told his public about the value and danger of the printing press express the worldview and experience of a sixteenth-century printer with matchless clarity.

A committed Calvinist, Estienne published three editions of Théodore de Bèze's folio New Testament, Antoine Chevallier's Hebrew alphabet and grammar, Immanuel Tremellius's Aramaic and Syriac grammar, and George Buchanan's poetic paraphrase of *Psalms.* Moreover, his own writings included at least one major attack on Catholic belief and practice: the *Apologie pour Hérodote* (1566). This work began as a defense of Herodotus, whose histories had been accused since ancient times of systematic exaggeration. Estienne argued that modern marvels—ranging from the strange customs observed by travelers in Muscovy and the New World to the strange legal case of Martin Guerre, the impostor who inveigled his way into another man's home and marriage and was exposed after a long trial—outdid in their weirdness those reported in Egypt and Persia by the ancient historian. In particular, he argued that the Catholic *philomesses* and *théophages* of his own day, who adored dead images and believed that they ate the body of the Lord, were far more bizarre than the Egyptians who had adored live animals. The work soon departed from its classical inspiration, though, and grew to an enormous polemic against blasphemers, "sodomites," and other sinners, written in a brilliant French prose. Though Estienne revised and reissued the original text (almost no copies of which survive) at the command of the Genevan council, he published a self-defense in the form of a pamphlet, as the result of which he was imprisoned (not for the only time).

Estienne may also have written another influential work of anti-Catholic polemic: an anonymous life of Catherine de Médicis, which appeared in 1575. The author describes his subject as nauseating and heaps up accusations of every imaginable crime. (Catherine is said to have exclaimed that she could have told him much worse things.) But the ascription remains uncertain. It is certain, however, that Estienne set himself up as a critic of the fashionable tendencies in Catholic intellectual life in his time. He wrote elaborate critiques of the "Italianization" of the French language and manners that he saw taking place at the royal court, of Italian Ciceronianism, and of the Tacitism of Justus Lipsius.

Finally, Estienne made one vital contribution to the development of late sixteenth-century irenic thought when he published his Latin translation of the *Pyrrhoniae hypotyposes* of Sextus Empiricus in 1562. This powerful expression of ancient skepticism provided vital arms to Montaigne and others, who feared that the claims of Protestant and Catholic theologians to absolute intellectual and political authority would destroy France. Montaigne took from this text the axioms that he inscribed in his library and many of the arguments of his *Apologie de Raimond Sebond* (Apology for Raymond Sebond); the staunch Calvinist Estienne thus paradoxically became a major source for the *politique* ideology of the late sixteenth century.

Estienne's poor business habits and recurrent depressions darkened his later life. He traveled incessantly, quarreled widely, and refused to let his brilliant son-in-law, Isaac Casaubon, work in his splendid library. In 1598 he died in the hospital at Lyon; tradition claims that he was destitute.

BIBLIOGRAPHY

Braden, Gordon. *The Classics and English Renaissance Poetry.* New Haven and London, 1978.

Estienne, Henri. *Apologie pour Hérodote.* Edited by P. Ristelhuber. Paris, 1879.

Gruys, J. A. *The Early Printed Editions (1518–1664) of Aeschylus.* Nieuwkoop, 1981.

Momigliano, Arnoldo. *Studies in Historiography.* London, 1966.

Mund-Dopchie, Monique. *La survie d'Eschyle à la Renaissance.* Louvain, 1984.

Pattison, Mark. *Essays.* Edited by Henry Nettleship. Oxford, 1889.

———. *Isaac Casaubon, 1559–1614.* 2d ed. Oxford, 1892.

Popkin, Richard H. *The History of Scepticism from Erasmus to Spinoza.* Berkeley and London, 1979.

Reverdin, O. "Le 'Platon' d'Henri Estienne." *Museum Helveticum* 13 (1956), 239–250.

Schreiber, Fred. *The Estiennes.* New York, 1982.

ANTHONY GRAFTON

ESTIENNE, Robert I (Lat., Stephanus; 1503?–1559), French biblical scholar, lexicographer, and printer-publisher. A fine printer and an excellent man of business, he was a distinguished Latin specialist and author of the *Thesaurus linguae latinae* and of pioneer Latin-French and French-Latin dictionaries. He was also highly competent in Greek and had at least some knowledge of Hebrew. Armed with this linguistic equipment and employing the most rigorous prevailing standards of verifying the correctness of a text, he early turned his attention to the currently accepted text of the Vulgate, the authorized Latin version of the Bible by Saint Jerome, and consulted the earliest manuscripts available in France. The result was the first critical edition of the Vulgate (1527–1528). To this he added an improved glossary of proper names and extensive indexes. His Bibles quickly gained a European-wide reputation. While in Paris he brought out five more editions of the Latin Bible as well as separate editions of the Pentateuch and the Psalms and three of the New Testament. Beginning in 1539, when he was appointed printer to the King, he produced two editions of the Hebrew Scriptures, and in 1546, 1549, and 1550 editions of the Greek Testament, based on Erasmus and the oldest manuscripts in the royal library. The 1550 edition became the received text of the Greek New Testament among scholars for some 350 years. In his Latin Bibles, he began to print a summary of the Bible itself and to provide pageheadings and subtitles, with summaries in the margins and in chapter headings. The wording of these additions held some pitfalls for an author who was not theologically trained, and his work aroused the hostility of theologians resentful of a layman's intrusion into their field and suspicious of possible "Lutheran" tendencies. The leadership of the Faculty of Theology of Paris had by then fallen into the hands of a few hard-liners who were interested only in enforcing orthodoxy and who began to campaign for a ban on Estienne's Bibles. The solution that Francis I found satisfactory—Estienne's undertaking to print the censures passed by the Faculty of Theology and to circulate them with each copy—was wholly unacceptable to the faculty, and on the accession of Henry II Estienne's position became more precarious. He fought a tenacious legal rearguard action against his enemies, but they finally obtained from the king a total ban on the sale of his Bibles (25 November 1548).

Estienne was determined not to give in, prestige and principle as well as profit being at stake. He had already sent his younger sons to be educated at Strasbourg and Lausanne, and about now he bought a house in Geneva and a controlling interest in a nearby papermill located just across the French border. He actually moved to Geneva in November 1550, leaving his brother, Charles Estienne, in charge of the firm in Paris. At Geneva he resumed printing biblical editions and produced a commentary on the Gospels entitled *Nova Glossa,* and a volume of concordances. Here too he launched the first editions of the Bible with chapters divided into numbered verses, an innovation of his that was soon adopted universally. Eventually he managed to secure a transcript of the Faculty's censures. He printed these, and his answers to them, in his *Ad censuras theologorum parisiensium . . . responsio* (Reply to the Theologians of Paris), published in 1552 in Latin and French versions. The censures are a miscellany of points arranged with little attempt at order, ranging from serious criticisms—a few of which he accepted—to mere caviling.

In the account of his dealings with the faculty and with his supporters, which serves as a preface to the *Responsio,* he demonstrates that, like many courageous and independent minds, he could be obstinate and high-handed. But there is no evidence that he had ceased to think of himself as a member of the Roman Catholic church until the faculty had made his position intolerable, or that he had been a "Nicodemite," concealing his true beliefs. Answering a censure that accused him of criticizing private masses, he said, "That could not then enter my head, I who was in those days under the spell of their fancies and in thrall to the same superstitions as other people." In Geneva, on the other hand, all his utterances are those of a convinced Protestant, and he published Latin works by Pierre Viret, Théodore de Bèze, and John Calvin, including the definitive edition of Calvin's *Institutio Christianae Religionis* (1559).

BIBLIOGRAPHY

Armstrong, Elizabeth. *Robert Estienne, Royal Printer: An Historical Study of the Elder Stephanus.* Courtenay Studies in Reformation Theology, vol. 6. Rev. and corr. ed. Appleford, England, 1986. Reproduces all the material in the first edition from Cambridge University Press, 1954 (except the appendix of documents), with additions and corrections. Contains 39 pages of new aspects of Robert Estienne, a bibliography complete to year of publication, seven additional illustrations, and a translation into English of Estienne's narrative preface to his *Ad censuras theologorum parisiensium . . . responsio.*

———. "Les rapports d'Henri Estienne avec les membres de sa famille restés ou redevenus catholiques." In *Actes du Colloque Henri Estienne organisé par le Centre V. -L. Saulnier à l'Université de Paris-Sorbonne le 12 mars 1987,* pp. 43–53. Paris, 1988.

Black, M. H. "The Printed Bible." In *The Cambridge History of the Bible: The West from the Reformation to the Present Day,* vol. 3, pp. 408–475, plates 23, 24, and 28. Cambridge, 1963.

Renouard, A. A. *Annales de l'imprimerie des Estienne* (1843). 2 vols. Reprint, Paris, 1972. Volume 1 lists all editions published by the Estienne family, necessarily incomplete, but including most of Robert Estienne's important publications, arranged chronologically. Volume 2 includes a biographical sketch, largely superseded, and the French text of his narrative preceding the *Ad censuras theologorum parisiensium. . .responsio* (see pp. 544–568).

Starnes, DeWitt T. *Robert Estienne's Influence on Lexicography.* Austin, 1963. Studies the indebtedness of works like Cruden's *Concordance* in English-speaking countries to Estienne's glossaries of proper names, concordances, and other works.

Verzeichnis der im deutschen Sprachbereich erschienenen Drucke des XVI. Jahrhunderts. Stuttgart, 1983–. See vol. 6, nos. 4025–4034.

Wright, D. F. "Robert Estienne's *Nova Glossa Ordinaria*: A Protestant Quest for a Standard Bible Commentary." In *Calvin: Erbe und Auftrag; Festschrift für Wilhelm Heinrich Neuser zum 65. Geburtstag,* edited by Willem van't Spijker, pp. 40–51. Kampen, Netherlands, 1991.

ELIZABETH ARMSTRONG

ESTONIA. On the eve of the Reformation the territory of Estonia belonged to Livonia and was divided between the Livonian Order, the bishopric of Dorpat (Tartu), and the bishopric of Ösel-Wieck (Saare-Lääne). By the middle of the sixteenth century the population reached some 250,000 and consisted of Estonians, Germans, Swedes, and Finns. In the Middle Ages nine towns were founded in Estonia, four of which belonged to the Hanseatic League.

The Reformation reached Estonia in the early 1520s, spreading primarily to the towns. In 1523 Johannes Lang preached evangelical sermons in Saint Nicholas Church, Zacharias Hasse (Leporius) in Saint Olaus Church, and Heinrich Boeckhold in Holy Spirit Church of Reval (Tallinn). At a diet of Livonian towns and vassals in Reval on 14 July 1524, three major towns—Riga, Reval, and Dorpat—formed an alliance to defend the Reformation against the archbishop of Riga, Johannes Blankenfeld. Conflicts between the citizens and the Catholic abbeys resulted in an outbreak of iconoclasm in Reval on 14 September 1524. Early in 1525 the Dominicans were expelled from Reval. From Reval the Reformation spread to other northern Estonian towns—Narva, Wesenberg (Rakvere), and Weissenstein (Paide). Dorpat was the center of the Reformation in southern Estonia. At the end of 1523 or early 1524 the evangelical preacher Hermann Marsow came from Riga to Dorpat, but Archbishop Blankenfeld forced him to leave the town.

In late 1524 the furrier Melchior Hoffman (called the "Prophet of Livonia") arrived at Dorpat and won great popularity with his message influenced by Anabaptism. An attempt to arrest Hoffman on 7 January 1525 resulted in a revolt of the citizens. Several abbeys and Catholic churches were plundered and images were destroyed. On 10 January

1525 the rebels (primarily young German merchants and some Estonians) captured the possessions of Archbishop Blankenfeld, excluding his castle, and plundered the cathedral church. But then the town magistrate seized control. The Reformation prevailed in 1525–1526 in some smaller towns, such as Fellin (Viljandi), Alt-Pernau (Old Pärnu), and Neu-Pernau (New Pärnu). Reformation ideas, combined with the echo of the German Peasants' War, caused disturbances among the Estonian peasants in the villages. The landlords and the knights of the Livonian Order partly supported the Reformation in the towns but primarily sought to seize the lands of the Catholic church. In 1525–1526 Albert, duke of Prussia (earlier grand master of the Teutonic Order), suggested the secularization of Livonia to Wolter von Plettenberg, master of the Livonian Order, but Plettenberg declined to implement the plan. By 1533 the Lutheran Reformation began to be consolidated in towns that accepted a common evangelical liturgy compiled by Johann Briessmann from Riga. Newly formed Estonian evangelical congregations in towns were granted their own churches. Evangelical preaching in Estonian was introduced in the towns, and the first printed books in Estonian were published (the first known Estonian-language publication dates from 1525). In 1535 fifteen hundred copies of an Estonian Lutheran catechism (compiled by Simon Wanradt and Johann Koell) written in Middle Low German were printed in Wittenberg at the initiative of the Reval magistrate. In 1554 a Lutheran catechism in the southern Estonian dialect (compiled and translated in Dorpat by Johann Witte[n]) was printed in Germany. In Reval and Dorpat schools were founded to educate Estonian schoolmasters and preachers. On 17 January 1554 the Livonian diet (*Landtag*) in Wolmar (Valmiera) proclaimed religious freedom. The Catholic bishops in Reval and Dorpat and some monasteries in the countryside survived. Politically the Reformation increased the decentralization and inner conflicts of Livonia on the eve of the Russo-Livonian War (1558–1561).

During the war (1558–1625) Estonian territory was divided between Sweden (northern Estonia after 1561), Denmark (Saaremaa/Ösel, 1559–1645), and Poland-Lithuania (southern Estonia, 1582–1625). In the Swedish and Danish possessions the Reformation continued, but the Counter-Reformation was introduced in southern Estonia under Polish rule. With *Constitutiones Livoniae*—issued by the king of Poland, Stephen Báthory, in 1582—the Roman Catholic church was restored, although the Augsburg Confession was not disallowed. The Catholic bishop of Livonia, with residence in Wenden (Cēsis), established Catholic churches and schools and had vicars in Wenden, Pernau, Dorpat, and Fellin. Dorpat became the center of the Counter-Reformation in southern Estonia. The Jesuits founded their *domicilium* in Dorpat in 1583 (*residentium,* 1584; *collegium,* 1585). The Jesuit mission in Livonia, conducted by Antonio Possevino between 1582 and 1587, aimed both to re-Catholicize the Estonian peasants and to establish a bridgehead for a Roman Catholic mission in Russia. A Jesuit gymnasium was founded in Dorpat in 1583, and a *seminarium interpretum* was opened in 1585. An Estonian *Cathechismus Catholicorum,* translated by Thomas Busaeus, was printed in Vilnius in 1585 (997 copies, together with Latvian and Russian editions). The active Catholic mission in southern Estonia was interrupted by the Swedish-Polish War (1600–1603). During the last decades of Polish rule in Estonia (1603–1625), the Counter-Reformation weakened. In 1625 the whole Estonian territory (except Saaremaa) became Swedish (confirmed by the Truce of Altmark in 1629). Lutheranism remained the dominant confession in Estonia and had a great influence on the formation of the Estonian national culture.

BIBLIOGRAPHY

Arbusow, Leonid. *Die Einführung der Reformation in Liv-, Est- und Kurland* (1919). Forschungen zur Reformationsgeschichte, vol. 3. Reprint, Aalen, 1964. The major work in the field. Especially valuable for its use of archival materials.

Bienemann, Friedrich. *Aus Livlands Luthertagen.* Reval, 1883. Old, but useful introduction, including publication of important documents from Tallinn city archives.

Helk, Vello. *Die Jesuiten in Dorpat, 1583–1625: Ein Vorpostender Gegenreformation in Nordosteuropa.* Odense University Studies in History and Social Sciences, vol. 44. Odense, 1977. A valuable analysis based on unpublished materials from various archives.

Kivimäe, Jüri. "Die kulturellen Einflüsse der lutherischen Reformation in Estland im 16. Jahrhundert." In *Reformation und Nationalsprachen,* edited by Burchard Brentjes and Burchard Thaler, pp. 58–82. Halle, Germany, 1983. Studies the impact of the Reformation on the printing of books in Estonian and on schools.

Kleeberg, Gerhard. "Die polnische Gegenreformation in Livland." *Schriften des Vereins für Reformationsgeschichte* 49.2 (1931), 152. A concise overview of the Counter-Reformation in Livonia.

Kurtz, Eduard. *Die Jahresberichte der Gesellschaft Jesu über ihre Wirksamkeit in Riga und Dorpat, 1583–1614.* Riga, 1925. Important publication of Jesuit reports from Livonia.

Pohrt, Otto. "Reformationsgeschichte Livlands: Ein Überblick." *Schriften des Vereins für Reformationsgeschichte* 46. 2 (1928), 145. The best overview after Arbusow's major work.

Wittram, Reinhard. "Die Reformation in Livland." In *Baltische Kirchengeschichte,* edited by Reinhard Wittram, pp. 35–56, 309–312. Göttingen, 1956. The author underlines the special character of urban reform in the context of Livonian political history.

JÜRI KIVIMÄE

ÉTIENNE, Henri II. *See* Estienne, Henri II.

ÉTIENNE, Robert I. *See* Estienne, Robert I.

EUCHARIST. No theological theme, not even justification, was more keenly debated in the Reformation era than the meaning of the central Christian rite, variously called "the Eucharist," "the Mass," "the Sacrament of the Altar," "the Breaking of Bread," "Holy Communion," or "the Lord's Supper." The endless debates were distinguished not only by acrimony (and sometimes tedium) but also by exegetical skill, historical erudition, and theological acuteness. The lines of division, however, were seldom made unambiguously clear. While disagreement rested in part on the choice of different warrants and authorities, the division was just as often over the right interpretation of the same biblical texts and the same patristic or medieval authors; and even the selfsame concepts (e.g., substance) or analogies (e.g., the sun and its rays) were invoked in contradictory senses.

It is not surprising that the sixteenth-century controversies are mirrored in scholarly disagreements among their twentieth-century interpreters. No doubt, theological subtleties that are hard to penetrate today already went over the heads of the multitude in Luther's day, and the great eucharistic colloquies (Marburg, Poissy, Montbéliard) were as much personal and political encounters as they were theological. Yet, because the theoretical divisions had liturgical consequences, no item of reform had a more immediate visual impact than eucharistic reform. Indeed, profound differences of piety were expressed in divergent eucharistic theories and practices.

The Mass and Christ's Testament. Written for the laity shortly after the outbreak of the indulgences controversy, Martin Luther's first extended discussion of the Eucharist, *Ein Sermon von dem hochwürdigen Sakrament des heiligen wahren Leichnams Christi* (A Treatise Concerning the Blessed Sacrament of the Holy and True Body of Christ; 1519), is almost entirely free of polemic against the church of Rome. True, Luther suggests that the laity ought to be given the cup as well as the bread, and he stresses the necessity for faith in using the Sacrament: to receive what the Sacrament signifies, you must *believe* that you receive it. The purpose of the Mass is precisely to strengthen faith, so that he cannot accept the medieval view of the Sacrament as an *opus operatum,* a work effective simply as done provided only that no obstacle is put in the way. But Luther apparently takes the dogma of transubstantiation for granted and simply ignores the sacrificial understanding of the Mass. The critical part of the treatise (at the end) is directed not against Rome but against the "brotherhoods," lay fraternities whose exclusiveness and self-indulgence stand in sharp opposition to the one true brotherhood, the fellowship of all saints, in which everything is shared in mutual love.

The sacramental eating and drinking, Luther explains, signify the fellowship of all saints as members of Christ's spiritual body, which is why the Sacrament is called *synaxis* in Greek and *communio* in Latin. "To receive this sacrament in bread and wine, then, is nothing else than to receive a sure sign of this fellowship and incorporation [*eyn leybung*] with Christ and all saints" (LW [*Luthers Werke*] 35:51). By it we are assured that we do not bear our burdens alone—that there is one body (*1 Cor.* 12:25–26), one loaf (*1 Cor.* 10:17). Indeed, in the Sacrament we are actually *made* one body (*eyngeleybet*) with all the saints. Luther sees the conversion of the elements into Christ's natural body and blood as an analogue to the conversion of ourselves into his spiritual body (the church). It is clearly the spiritual body that stands at the center of his exposition, and he can state explicitly: "It is more needful that you discern the spiritual than the natural body of Christ" (LW 35:62). As the apostle Paul says, it is a great "sacrament" (mystery) that Christ and the church are one flesh and blood (*Eph.* 5:31–32).

Luther had no need to renounce this conception of the blessed Sacrament entirely in later writings, and for some of the reformers incorporation was to remain the central eucharistic motif. But just one year after *Ein Sermon von dem hochwürdigen Sakrament des heiligen wahren Leichnams Christi* his thoughts on the eucharist underwent a remarkable change: in his *Ein Sermon von dem neuen Testament, das ist von der heiligen Messe* (Treatise on the New Testament That Is the Holy Mass; 1520), "testament" replaced "incorporation" as the cardinal term. The shift brought with it a sharply polemical tone; for to say that the Mass, rightly understood, is Christ's testament is to deny that it is a priestly sacrifice. Further, the dogma of transubstantiation now dropped out. Luther's challenge was to rethink the Mass by getting behind all later additions and reexamining the words of institution, since "the nearer our masses are to the first mass of Christ [the Last Supper], the better they undoubtedly are" (LW 35:81).

By "testament" Luther understands (as we say) "last will and testament": a promise made by someone about to die (cf. *Heb.* 9:16–17). God's approach to humans is in the form of a promise that evokes the response of faith, and usually he adds a sign as a kind of seal to give greater confidence in his word, as he gave Noah the rainbow, Abraham circumcision, and so on. In the first mass, shortly before his death, Christ accordingly promised forgiveness of sins to his disciples (*Mt.* 26:28) and added to his words a powerful seal and sign. Luther now takes the sign to be not the elements as such, and not eating and drinking (as in the earlier treatise), but Christ's own true body and blood under the bread and wine. But since the sign is to be grasped only in its relation to the promise, which can save without it, everything depends on the words. It is therefore a travesty of the Mass when the priest says the words to himself in Latin and turns Christ's testament into a work and a sacrifice.

Luther carried over these thoughts into his truculent *De captivitate Babylonica ecclesiae praeludium* (Prelude on the Babylonian Captivity of the Church; 1520), in which he assailed the three captivities to which the Sacrament of the bread had been subjected: the withholding of the cup from the laity, transubstantiation, and the interpretation of the Mass as a good work and a sacrifice. Transubstantiation is only one opinion among others. Pierre d'Ailly, cardinal of Cambray, proposed a better alternative when he suggested that the bread and wine, not just their accidents, might remain on the altar, though he himself was restrained from adopting it by the authority of the church. We should accept God's words in their literal sense and take "bread" to mean "bread," not "accidents of bread." "And why could not Christ include his body in the substance of the bread just as well as in the accidents?" (LW 36:32). Luther will "firmly believe not only that the body of Christ is in the bread, but that the bread is the body of Christ" (LW 36:34). But if transubstantiation is only an opinion, to be held or not as one chooses, the same cannot be said of the Roman church's teaching on the Mass as a sacrifice: this is simply an abuse, the most wicked of all abuses, and has turned the Sacrament into a profitable business. "Just as distributing a testament or accepting a promise differs diametrically from offering a sacrifice, so it is a contradiction in terms to call the mass a sacrifice, for the former is something that we receive and the latter is something that we give" (LW 36:52). Later reformers were to echo this language, even when they perceived the Sacrament as a sacred meal, not as Christ's last will and testament.

Even after Luther had become convinced that the Roman Mass was a fearful perversion of Christ's testament, he hesitated to initiate liturgical change. Others before him put together revised services in German: notably, Andreas Bodenstein von Karlstadt, Kaspar Kantz, and Thomas Müntzer. In Wittenberg it was Bodenstein who first translated theological revision into liturgical reform when Luther was absent. On Christmas Day 1521 he celebrated Mass in German wearing plain street clothes. He suppressed virtually the entire canon of the Roman Mass, left out the elevation of the elements, and placed the bread and the chalice in the hands of the communicants.

Reform of the liturgy began for Luther himself after his return from the Wartburg. He laid down the fundamental principle of reform in *Von Ordnung Gottesdients in der Gemeine* (Concerning the Order of Worship in Church; 1523): "The Word is important and not the mass. . . . We can spare everything except the Word" (LW 53:13–14). Daily masses were accordingly to be replaced by services of prayer and preaching, and the Sunday mass itself was to give due emphasis to the sermon. In his *Formula Missae et Communionis* (Order for Mass and Communion), published by the end of 1523, Luther outlined an evangelical rite in Latin. He did not intend it to be binding on the Lutheran churches; nor did he understand it as a new rite, but rather as a purification of the one in use. He excised the sacrificial language of the canon but retained the elevation of the bread and the cup, supposing that the sermon in the vernacular would prevent misinterpretation. The Sacrament was to be administered in both kinds to those who had given notice of their wish to communicate and had provided evidence of their understanding and satisfactory behavior.

More than two further years passed before Luther published a eucharistic service in the language of the people, his *Deutsche Messe und Ordnung Gottesdiensts* (German Mass and Order of Worship; 1526), in which he noted his wish eventually to have the minister stand behind the "altar," facing the people as Christ must have done at the Last Supper. By now the proliferation of German liturgies threatened to confuse the Protestant congregations, and Luther, though he repeated his warning against coerced uniformity, desired a measure of consistency at least in the form of exhortation to the communicants. The exhortation ends with the admonition to discern Christ's testament and above all to take to heart the words in which he gives his body and blood to us for the forgiveness of sins. The body and blood are the pledge and guarantee of redemption from God's wrath.

Commemoration and Spiritual Eating. New interpretations of the Eucharist followed Luther's in the mid-1520s. In a series of eucharistic tracts launched in 1524, Bodenstein rejected the bodily presence of Christ in the Lord's Supper, interpreted the rite as an act of recollection or remembrance, and proposed that when the Lord said "*This* is my body," he must have pointed at his body (not at the bread). The next year, Huldrych Zwingli published Cornelis Henricxzoen Hoen's *Epistola christiana* (Most Christian Letter; 1525), in which he had discovered the suggestion that "is" in the words "This is my body" could be taken to mean "signifies." In the symbolic theory that he spelled out the same year in his *De vera et falsa religione commentarius* (Commentary on True and False Religion; 1525), to "eat Christ's flesh" and "drink his blood" is simply to commemorate his sacrifice, to proclaim his saving deed on the cross (*1 Cor.* 11:26). In short, "eating" is believing, and to believe is to be thankful. "We therefore now understand from the very name what the Eucharist, that is, the Lord's Supper, is: namely, the thanksgiving and common rejoicing of those who declare the death of Christ" (LWZ [*Latin Works of Huldreich Zwingli*], 3:200).

Zwingli's eucharistic thought was part of a total sacramental theory, in which a sign is sharply distinguished from what it signifies and the Holy Spirit is held to impart faith directly, without means. In this view, signs are indicative or declaratory, not instrumental: a sacrament is not a means by which *God* imparts grace, but an indication *believers* give that they have already received grace and therefore belong to the church. Hence, in the Lord's Supper, the bread and wine declare that our sins were once and for all done away with by the death of Christ, for they picture the benefit of Christ's sacrifice as the food and drink of the soul. In his *Fidei expositio* (Exposition of the Faith; 1536), written in the year of his death, Zwingli presses this thought further and suggests that the outward eating of the elements indicates the parallel occurrence of an inward "feeding" on Christ by faith, who is not absent but present within. The soul holds Christ in its embrace, and he sustains and cheers it as bread and wine sustain and cheer the body (LCC [Library of Christian

Classics] 24:258–259, 263). But Zwingli's understanding of signs and signification cannot permit him to say that the outward event causes, or gives rise to, the inward.

In his own eyes, Zwingli's eucharistic doctrine had the merit of rejecting the Roman Mass without retaining the crassness of Luther's talk about an actual presence of Christ's body and blood "under" the elements—a presence excluded, in any case, by Christ's bodily ascension to heaven. If grace were bound to the sacraments, the clergy would have God at their disposal and could grant or withhold salvation at will (LWZ 2:113, 118). Indeed, the very notion of sacramental grace implies another way of salvation, in competition with the *sola fide* ("by faith alone") of the Reformation. To eat Christ's flesh, if it saves, cannot mean anything else than to believe in him (LCC 24:205). It was not clear to Zwingli that even Luther had carried through the Reformation principle consistently enough.

Zwingli had turned his attention to liturgical revision already in 1523 with his *De canone missae epichiresis* (Attack on the Canon of the Mass). Despite the belligerent title, the canon is not simply amputated (in this respect, Zwingli began more conservatively than Bodenstein or Luther); rather, it is reconstructed in four Latin prayers of Zwingli's own, which hold together eucharistic motifs, well grounded in scripture, that controversy was to put asunder. But Zwingli's German rite, *Aktion oder Brauch des Nachtmals* (Action or Use of the Lord's Supper; 1525), published in the same year as the *De vera et falsa religione commentarius*, focuses more narrowly on the motif of remembrance; indeed, he calls the rite "this memorial of Christ's passion and thanksgiving for his death." Remembrance is not construed as private meditation. On the contrary, the Zwinglian rite was designed to emphasize the true nature of the celebration as a common feast of the redeemed: the table was set in the nave, the minister (without vestments) took his place behind it, and the elements were served to the people seated in their places. It has been argued that Zwingli understood the people to have been "transubstantiated" in the first part of the service into the body of Christ (see Courvoisier). The argument is not convincing, but it has drawn attention to Zwingli's powerful sense of the church, the ecclesial body, which makes its offering of praise in the Eucharist.

From the fact that Zwingli did not ask for Communion to be available more than four times a year, one need not infer that he belittled the practice. Nevertheless, infrequent Communion meant that the Eucharist could not provide the norm of Sunday worship, which usually consisted of a preaching service. Moreover, one is bound to note the possibilities inherent in Zwingli's tendency both to spiritualize and to psychologize the Christian religion: faith is worked inwardly by the Spirit and exercised outwardly in the Sacrament by recollection. Whether this double tendency is judged theologically good or bad, it does seem to have occasioned a lesser role for the Eucharist in other Christian groups that followed one or the other (or both) of the two characteristically Zwinglian themes.

Zwingli's theology had a plain affinity with the views and practices of the evangelical Anabaptists, and the influence by no means went only one way. Although some of the Anabaptists linked the bread of the Lord's Supper with their notion of Christ's celestial flesh, for the most part they stressed thankful remembrance of his death. In addition, the distinctive nature of their communities gave prominence to the idea of fellowship, symbolized by the image of the one loaf made of many grains. The ordinance of the Lord's Supper nurtured a powerful sense of the brotherhood for which one surrendered self-will and was ready to suffer. It is arguable that among the Anabaptists the Lord's Supper could not have quite the central place assigned to it by Roman Catholics and Protestants because, to them, it was simply one of Christ's ordinances, and the celebration was usually accompanied by exercise of the ban and the ritual of foot washing. But, like the Protestants, the Anabaptists had no thought of devaluing the Eucharist; they wished only to restore it to its primitive use.

Among other groups on the left wing of the Reformation, however, the Eucharist did assume diminished importance or was even abandoned. Belief in the inwardness of the Spirit's working led Sebastian Franck to withdraw from all ecclesiastical rites, and in 1526 another spiritualist, Kaspar von Schwenckfeld, called for at least a temporary suspension of the Lord's Supper—pending a better understanding of it. In Schwenckfeld's view, the outward Supper could never do more than picture the inward transformation of the soul by a life-giving substance from the glorified Christ, and controversy over the rite had further reduced it, for the time being, to a mere distraction that should be set aside. In seventeenth-century England, the Quakers were to take a similar course: the Breaking of Bread, like foot washing and anointing the sick, had some initial usefulness as the transition was made to an inward and spiritual communion with Christ, but now the substance could stand without the figure.

The same conclusion was reached among the evangelical rationalists (antitrinitarians), though by a different route. Christ's death was not a satisfaction for sin; hence no ecclesiastical rite is needed to communicate his merits. Bernardino Ochino noted that the thief on the cross was saved without the Sacrament. It did not necessarily follow that the churches could dispense with the Eucharist, but that is in fact what sometimes happened. In a treatise on the use and purpose of the Lord's Supper, Fausto Sozzini agreed that it was instituted by the Lord himself as a perpetual commemoration of his death, by which he proved God's love for us, and that a commemoration is not a mere remembering but a public celebration. Still, though our faith may be strengthened during the celebration, the Lord's Supper itself cannot be said to strengthen faith. It is, by definition, *our* "work," and how can something we do ourselves confirm us in faith? Neither unbelievers nor believers receive anything but the bread and the wine. Despite Sozzini's talk of a *perpetual* rite, then, the Eucharist—emptied of its old sacramental meaning—lost importance in the later Socinian communities. By the seventeenth century, the English Socinians were being chided for not observing the Lord's Supper at all.

That, however, is far from being the course taken by Zwingli's own church in the years immediately following his death. A purely memorialistic interpretation of the Eucharist, with its rejection of sacramental grace, did not survive for long among the Swiss Reformed. The First Helvetic Confession (1536) asserts, partly under the influence of Martin Bucer, that the bread and wine of the Lord's Supper are "symbols by which the true communication of his body and blood is presented [*exhibeatur*] by the Lord himself" (art. 23; the German version has *gereicht und angeboten werde*). The notion of "exhibitive" signs held the promise of reconciliation. But it was not Zwingli's notion, and there is no hint of it in the Zurich liturgy. Polarization, not reconciliation, was the dominant mood of the 1520s.

Oral Reception of the Body and Blood. *De captivitate Babylonica ecclesiae praeludium* was not Luther's last word against the Roman Mass and its priesthood: he continued to see in the rival interpretations of the Eucharist, evangelical and papist, two diametrically opposed ways of approaching God. But he believed that the new interpretations of the 1520s obliged him to open a second controversial front; and in the writings of the "fanatics" he discovered the same demon that had transformed Christ's testament into a sacrifice—the *Werkteufel* ("work-devil"), who makes a good work out of the offer of grace. By 1521 he had become acquainted with Hoen's theory, to which he responded in *Von Anbeten des Sakraments das heiligen Leichnams Christi* (The Adoration of the Sacrament; 1523). He realized that an emphasis on Christ's spiritual or ecclesial body in the Sacrament might, in combination with a figurative understanding of the words of institution, entirely replace belief in the presence of Christ's natural body. Only participation in the natural body, he insisted, can bring about the fellowship of the spiritual body; the fanatics mistake a benefit of the Sacrament for the Sacrament itself (LW 36:282–287). In *Wider die himmlischen Propheten, von den Bildern und Sakrament* (Against the Heavenly Prophets; 1525), Luther then issued a massive critique of Bodenstein's views on the Lord's Supper. His one-time colleague believed that *John* 6 taught a purely inward and spiritual "eating." In Luther's judgment, Bodenstein failed to see that God confers the inward only through the outward word and sacraments. Hence Bodenstein transformed the means of grace into a devotional exercise of meditation on Christ's passion: like the papists, he made of the Sacrament a human work (LW 40:146–148, 205–206).

It was "Bodenstein's poison" that Luther detected in the eucharistic theology of Zwingli and his associates. *Sermon von dem Sakrament des Leibes und Blutes Christi, wider die Schwarmgeister* (The Sacrament of the Body and Blood of Christ against the Fanatics; 1526) expresses Luther's dismay that whereas the papists have simply failed to affirm the eucharistic gift despite their belief in the presence of Christ's body and blood, a worse error now denies the presence itself. The new preachers do not heed the words "Take, eat; this is my body, which is given for you" (Luther conflates *Mt.* 16:26 with *Lk.* 22:19) but come together merely to commemorate the Lord's death. They take away the entire *raison d'être* of the Sacrament: to individualize the promise of forgiveness, proclaimed generally and to all in the word. Though the *fruit* of the Sacrament is certainly the union of love symbolized by the one loaf, its correct *use* is to receive the body of Christ and the assurance of forgiveness that it brings (LW 36:346–354).

The next broadside against the Zwinglians, *Daß diese Wort Christi "Das ist mein Leib" noch fest stehen, wider die Schwärmgeister* (That These Words of Christ "This Is My Body" Still Stand Firm against the Fanatics; 1527), concentrates on the words of institution. The Zwinglians were persuaded that a literal interpretation of "This is my body" was absurd. Zwingli found a figure of speech in the verb "is," which (he held) means "signifies." His friend Johannes Oecolampadius, in *De genuina verborum Domini . . . expositione* (The Genuine Exposition of the Lord's Words; 1525), pointed out that the little word *is*, over which there was such a commotion, would not have appeared at all in the original "Hebrew" (Aramaic) spoken by Jesus. For his part, he preferred to locate the figure in the pronoun *this*—that is, in the bread, which is a sign of the body. Both Zwingli and Oecolampadius appealed to Augustine's teaching on signs. Luther retorted that they misunderstood Augustine, for whom a sacrament was not a sign of something absent but of something invisibly present (LW 37:104–105). In his *Vom Abendmahl Christi, Bekenntnis* (Confession concerning Christ's Supper; 1528), he argues at length that in fact there is no sign or figure (in the Zwinglian sense) at all in the words "This is my body." A single new entity comes into existence out of the bread and the body, and we can no longer properly speak of either one separately. If we are to say that there is a figure of speech in Christ's words, it can only be synecdoche—naming the part (i.e., either the bread or the body) for the whole, which is "fleshbread" (LW 37:262–268).

Luther's concern in the great polemical treatises of 1526–1527 was not to explain the mode of Christ's bodily presence in the Sacrament but to insist that, by the power of the word, the body and blood are in fact present—whether anyone believes it or not. Even the wicked receive the body and blood with their mouths, although they do it to their destruction (LW 37:86–87, 191, 238; cf. *1 Cor.* 11:29). But to demonstrate to the fanatics that "presence" need not mean a crude, local presence, Luther had recourse to some old scholastic distinctions. Christ's body and blood are not *locally* in the Sacrament, enclosed in the bread and wine. But the resurrection appearances prove that his glorified body can be present *definitively,* that is, visibly, when he so chooses, but without being circumscribed or confined to a single place. And, as God, he is present *repletively* in every place, filling all things: his divine nature imparts its supernatural presence to his humanity (LW 37:215–224). What distinguishes the Sacrament, then, is that there, through the word, he is present "for me" (LW 36:342, 37:67–68). Along with the literal interpretation of the words "This is my body," the eating of the body by the wicked—*manducatio impiorum*—and the ubiquity of the body by communication of properties became the watchwords of the Lutheran doctrine on the Lord's Supper.

In his own summary confession, Luther affirms that "in the sacrament of the altar the true body and blood of Christ are orally eaten and drunk. . . . It does not rest on man's belief or unbelief but on the Word and ordinance of God" (LW 37:367). The Zwinglian suspicion that an oral eating of Christ's flesh must mean a crass, carnal, "Capernaitic" eating (*Jn.* 6:59–60) was not well founded, though Luther's language invited the misunderstanding. On the other hand, Lutheran suspicion that any talk of the elements as signs or symbols must leave nothing but bread and wine in the Sacrament was not well founded either, although Zwingli invited misunderstanding by his negative emphasis on what one ought *not* to say about the Sacrament. The Lutheran Eucharist was not a theophagy, and the Zwinglian Eucharist was not a Pelagian workout. Nevertheless, the famous encounter in the Marburg Colloquy at the end of the decade (1529) presented a picture of intransigence on both sides, the Lutherans taking their stand on "This is my body," the Zwinglians countering that "it is the spirit that gives life; the flesh is useless" (*Jn.* 6:63).

Participation in Christ's Life-Giving Flesh. The uncompromising antagonism between Luther and Zwingli appeared to leave little common ground. But a third party emerged that tried repeatedly to strike a middle way. At first, the chief spokesman of mediation was Bucer; later, the leadership passed to Calvin. Their interpretation of the Lord's Supper was shared, in essentials, by Peter Martyr Vermigli, who, like Calvin, spent formative years in Bucer's Strasbourg; the English reformer Thomas Cranmer also belongs in spirit to their company. Among Luther's own closest associates, Philipp Melanchthon developed a cordial relationship with Bucer, which bore fruit in the Wittenberg Concord (1536) and the program for reform sponsored by Archbishop Hermann von Wied (1543). On the other side, Zwingli's successor in Zurich, Heinrich Bullinger, was drawn into the mediating camp by the negotiations with Calvin that led to the Consensus Tigurinus (concluded in 1549).

The possibility of the mediating position can be understood only if it is recognized that in the Augustinian tradition "realism" and "symbolism" need not be opposed. Zwingli's characteristic notion was that a sacramental sign is a pointer to an absent reality, or a grace that lies in the past, and for precisely this reason Luther was deeply suspicious of the distinction between sign and reality. One alternative was to argue that although a sign is not itself the reality, it nonetheless attests and brings a present reality, which the mediating theologians identified as communion with Christ or participation in his body ("incorporation"). This was the shared conviction that united them. It was clearly reflected in the language of the groundbreaking conference between Bucer and Melanchthon in December 1534: "The bread and wine are signs, *signa exhibitiva,* which being proffered and taken, the body of Christ is proffered and taken at the same time" (Wittenberg Concord, art. 2). *Exhibere* is also the word Melanchthon used in the notorious change he made in article 10 of the Augsburg Confession, which then read (in the 1540 version) "with the bread and wine the body and blood of Christ are truly proffered [*exhibeantur*]." With the fundamental concept of "exhibitive signs" other characteristic thoughts were commonly associated: for example, that Christ is present where he acts, and that the sacramental union of the bread with Christ's body persists no longer than the eucharistic celebration. Fundamental agreement did not exclude differences of expression or emphasis; it excluded only the reduction of sacramental signs to mere reminders of an absent or past reality.

Calvin's mature reflections on the Lord's Supper were occasioned by the Consensus Tigurinus, which achieved harmony among the Swiss Reformed churches but was vehemently attacked by some of the Lutherans. From the first, Calvin held Luther in higher esteem than he did Zwingli. He believed that the cardinal principle of Luther's sacramental theology was the efficacy of sacred signs, which are not empty but present what they represent; and in this Calvin felt himself to be of one mind with the German reformer. "Why would the Lord put the symbol of his body in your hands unless to assure you of a true participation in it?" (*Inst.,* 4.17.10). But he could not agree that the words "This is my body" must be construed literally, or that Christ's body is ubiquitous, or that even the wicked take the body of Christ in their mouths. For Calvin—as for Zwingli, despite their differences—Christ's ascension to heaven marked a decisive break with the manner of his presence during his earthly life. This point, he thought, the Lutheran teaching failed to take seriously enough, although he did not naively suppose that heaven is a place on the cosmological map. Yet, if the signs are not empty but efficacious, as Luther rightly insisted against Zwingli, there must be a communion with Christ's life-giving flesh in the Eucharist. The only question is how.

Now Calvin was not greatly concerned to explain how,

any more than Luther had been. "In his sacred supper [Christ] bids me take, eat, and drink his body and blood under the symbols of bread and wine. I have no doubt that he truly proffers them, and that I receive them" (*Inst.*, 4.17.32). For the rest, Calvin was prepared to marvel at what he could not comprehend. But from *Romans* 8:9–11 he did infer that participation in Christ must be a work of the Holy Spirit (*Inst.*, 4.17.12). The sacramental signs, then, are efficacious as the Spirit's instruments, who overcomes the chasm between heaven and earth. Calvin had no difficulty in asserting that the communion, communication, or participation that results is real (if "real" means "true" as opposed to deceptive or imaginary) and substantial (provided that substance is not taken for sheer physical mass). He does sometimes speak of the eucharistic gift as a life-giving virtue that flows from Christ's body; but he does not mean that the communicant receives only the virtue, not the substance, of the body. Drawing life from Christ's flesh *is* a kind of presence: from Calvin's use of the expression "the operation of the flesh," one might say that the true communication is an operative presence. The body of Christ is in any case only *locally* absent in heaven, for the person of Christ, God and man, is present everywhere. But for just this reason his body does not have to leave heaven—to change its spatial location—in order for the whole Christ to be in the Sacrament.

At stake in Calvin's eucharistic thought is not simply the mode of Christ's presence, but a total conception of how the believer is related to Christ and draws life from him. Calvin rejected Zwingli's equation of "eating" with "believing": the vital union with Christ that results from faith is by no means merely a matter of beliefs about him, or of calling to mind the benefits he has won for our salvation. We become, rather, flesh of his flesh and bone of his bone. Because this union is wholly mysterious, it can be represented only by images or metaphors. One such image is the marriage bond between husband and wife (*Eph.* 5:28–33). In *John* 6:53 Christ himself uses another, that is, eating in order to live: "Unless you eat the flesh of the Son of Man and drink his blood, you have no life in you." This "communication" certainly takes place also outside the Lord's Supper. But the *raison d'être* of the Sacrament is to serve as a kind of seal of Christ's discourse on the bread of life: "Nothing is said here that is not figured and truly given to believers in the supper" (commentary on *Jn.* 6:54). In short, the gift of the Sacrament is nourishment with the bread of life, the life-giving flesh of Christ, and it calls forth the church's ceaseless thanksgiving—not in public worship alone but also in all the duties of love for others. In the very first edition of his *Institutes*, Calvin pointed out that the Sacrament is called both "the Lord's Supper" and "the Eucharist." As the Supper by which a benevolent Father feeds his children, it is a gift of grace; as the Eucharist, it is a sacrifice of praise, the liturgical enactment of the church's entire existence as a royal priesthood (*Inst.*, 4.18.16–17; cf. *1 Pt.* 2:9).

In Reformed services of worship, the pivotal motif of a mysterious union with Christ appears with varying degrees of clarity and felicitousness. Zwinglian ideas shaped the liturgical endeavors of Oecolampadius and Guillaume Farel, but the Reformed liturgies of Geneva and Scotland were derived not from Zurich but from Strasbourg—a clear token of theological affinity. The first Protestant Eucharist in Strasbourg (1524), composed in German by Theobald Schwarz, went through several revisions before Calvin arrived to assume leadership of the French refugee congregation (1538). In the 1537 version he found a rite that precisely conveyed the mediating view of the Sacrament as no mere memorial, but an actual participation in Christ's body and blood by which he increasingly lives in us and we in him. The presiding minister prays, for instance, "He has not only offered to you [the Father] his body and blood upon the cross for our sin, but wills also to give it to us for food and drink." With a friend's help (he knew no German), Calvin put the Strasbourg rite into French, with one or two changes, in his *La Forme des Prieres* . . . (Form of Prayers . . .; original edition of 1540 is no longer extant, but Calvin released another edition in 1545). The intention of the eucharistic service is plainly expressed in the slightly simplified Geneva recension (1542) and the instruction that introduced it: the Eucharist, as a commemoration of the body and blood of the Lord, brings about an increase of the life of Christ within us. And the life of Christ consists in this: to seek and to save the lost.

The communicants at Geneva, as at Strasbourg, went forward to receive the elements, either standing or kneeling. But the Sacrament was a meal, not a sacrifice: the ministers, dressed in plain black cassocks and gowns, stood beside the table to serve the bread and wine. In the Church of Scotland, which had its own service book derived from Calvin's, the people came forward to sit at a long table placed in the chancel or nave, and they passed the elements from hand to hand.

Calvin blamed the abomination of the Mass for the practice of infrequent Communion. As Luther insisted in 1523 that Christians should not gather without preaching and prayer, so Calvin upheld the ancient rule that no meeting of the church should take place without also partaking of the Lord's Supper (and giving alms). But he could not persuade the authorities to make so startling a break with medieval custom. Quarterly Communion became the norm in Geneva and Scotland. In the liturgical legacy of both Calvin and John Knox, however, the service of worship on non-Communion Sundays was an "ante-Communion," not morning prayer with a sermon, and in Strasbourg and (probably) Geneva the entire service was conducted from the table. If Knox's *Forme of Prayers* (the *Book of Common Order* adopted in 1562) seems less forthright than its precursors in affirming the real presence, it must be read in the light of the Scots Confession (adopted in 1560), of which

Knox was also co-author. Article 21 asserts that in the right use of the Lord's Supper there takes place a "unioun and conjunction" with the body and blood of Christ Jesus.

True Presence. Debate on the eucharistic standpoint of the English Reformation has been focused, as one would expect, on Cranmer, the chief compiler of both *The Book of Common Prayer* and the Forty-two Articles (the prototype of the Anglican Articles of Religion). A new phase of the debate was initiated by Gregory Dix, who found Cranmer's eucharistic thought indistinguishable in substance from Zwingli's; it followed that Cranmer framed the Anglican rite to express a doctrine few Anglicans have ever held. Dix won some influential, if qualified, support: Cyril Richardson, in particular, added formidable evidence that Cranmer's eucharistic theology "moved within the basic framework of Zwingli's opinions." But others pointed to Cranmer's use of key words and phrases that seemed to separate him from Zwingli and to link him with Calvin, Bucer, and the "dynamic receptionists" (Timms). Similarly, the most recent study of Cranmer's doctrine of the Eucharist discovers in it the idea of a "true presence," the common possession of Bucer, Melanchthon, Bullinger, and Calvin (Brooks). The disagreement is unlikely to end there since ambiguities undeniably appear in Cranmer's utterances on the Lord's Supper, even though he himself believed his words were so simple that a child could understand them.

The attempt has been made to undercut, or at least to depreciate, the argument over Cranmer's Continental affiliations by insisting that the English reformers drew their inspiration directly from the Fathers and Schoolmen. Cranmer reports that it was Nicholas Ridley who persuaded him to renounce transubstantiation (probably in 1546), and Ridley, as he himself tells us, was led to his understanding of the Eucharist by Ratramnus's ("Bertram's") book *On the Body and Blood of the Lord.* In C. W. Dugmore's opinion, Ridley and Cranmer recovered the realist-symbolist tradition that had its roots in Augustine's theology. A "non-papist Catholic" tradition, it provided the English reformers with an alternative to the conversionist theory of Ambrose, which had been sanctioned by the "papal-catholic" dogma of transubstantiation. Perhaps it does scant justice to the English to speak as though the historical problem were merely to fit them into a Continental typology. But Cranmer did read the Continental reformers assiduously, not least Oecolampadius on the eucharistic opinions of the Fathers. Even the treatise of Ratramnus reached England in editions published by Protestants on the Continent; and it is, of course, a problem that he has been claimed as the medieval precursor of both Zwingli and Calvin. Not much can be determined about the eucharistic opinions of Ridley or Cranmer from their interest in the controversial monk of Corbie.

It is sometimes said that, when he abandoned transubstantiation, Cranmer moved into a Lutheran phase. In his translation (1548) of a Lutheran catechism, which he made from the Latin version of Justus Jonas, he appeared to endorse the view that the communicants receive the body and blood of Christ with their bodily mouths. But Cranmer later insisted that he took this language to be figurative: by figurative speech, we speak of what is done to the signs as done to what they signify. The Lutheran phase, if there was one, did not last. Cranmer arrived at an understanding of the Eucharist that excluded the Lutheran *manducatio impiorum* just as firmly as the Roman church's transubstantiation. Only faith receives the body and blood of the Lord; the wicked receive the sign, but not the thing signified.

Vermigli, Ochino, and Bucer were all living in England, by Cranmer's invitation, when the first *Book of Common Prayer* (1549) was under revision, and they might be expected to have had some influence on their host. Jan Łaski was there, too, and is sometimes held to have nudged Cranmer in a Zwinglian direction. It is difficult to determine which of the foreign guests may have won Cranmer's ear. He refused to let his adversary Stephen Gardiner drive a wedge between Bucer and himself, but his reply to Gardiner shows him reluctant to admit any real difference between Bucer and Zwingli. In a detailed critique of the 1549 prayer book (his *Censura,* which Vermigli read and approved), Bucer urged, among other things, retaining the words in the prayers of oblation and humble access that implied the true receiving of the body of the Lord. But the words were dropped from the 1552 liturgy, albeit talk of a spiritual eating and a spiritual food remained; and Cranmer's Forty-two Articles, issued the following year, expressly denied "the reall, and bodilie presence (as thei terme it) of Christes fleshe and bloude, in the Sacramente of the Lordes supper" (art. 29). These were unquestionably tokens of a shift to a more radical Protestantism in the latter part of Edward VI's reign, as was the change of the words of delivery in the Communion service. The earlier prayer book had "The body of our Lord Iesus Christ whiche was geuen for thee, preserue thy bodye and soule unto euerlasting lyfe." The revision said, "Take and eate this, in remembraunce that Christe died for the, and fede on him in thy heart by faith with thankes geuyng." In harmony with this evident shift to an explicit memorialism was the appending of the declaration on kneeling (the "black rubric") at the end of the eucharistic rite: to receive the Sacrament on one's knees did not imply "anye reall and essenciall presence," since Christ's natural flesh and blood are in heaven, not here, and cannot be in more places than one at the same time.

It would not be prudent simply to read Cranmer's mind from these changes in his church's official standards. His opinions are presumably to be sought in his major work, *A Defence of the True and Catholic Doctrine of the Sacrament of the Body and Blood of Our Saviour Christ* (1550) and in his still weightier response to Bishop Gardiner's refutation of it (the *Answer* of 1551). Unfortunately, it is precisely over these two sources (here cited from *The Remains of Thomas Cranmer*, edited by Henry Jenkyns, 4 vols., Oxford, 1833) that the controversy is liveliest. Zwingli's favorite text (*Jn.* 6:63) stands like a banner on the front page of the *Defence*. In the *Answer*, Cranmer reiterates that the Eucharist is not a sacrifice for sin, but a memorial of Christ's sacrifice and a sacrifice of laud and praise, by which we testify that we are members of Christ's (ecclesial) body. His natural body is in heaven, not in the bread, nor is he "corporally" in the communicants either (*Remains*, 3:30). Rather, Christ's benefits are in the Sacrament, and he himself is spiritually present by his divine nature. Most, perhaps all, of what Cranmer says about "eating Christ's body" means no more than "chewing" and "digesting" the fact of his sacrificial death: eating is believing.

Yet Cranmer seems constantly to press against the limits of the Zwinglian position. He insists that the signs are "pithy and efficacious"; and alongside the motif of remembrance he can set the theme of union with Christ, accompanied by Calvin's favorite expression that we become "flesh of his flesh and bone of his bones." Christ's body is really "exhibited" in the Sacrament (*Remains*, 3:201), and we can certainly speak of him as really present if "really" means "in deed and effectually," or "verily and truly" (*Remains*, 3:131, 214; cf. 4:12). He uses the sacraments, as he uses the word, like instruments "whereby he worketh, and therefore is said to be present in them" (3:38). Cranmer's confession before the papal subdelegate in September 1555 was this: "I believe, that whoso eateth and drinketh that sacrament, Christ is within them, whole Christ, his nativity, passion, resurrection, and ascension; but not that corporally sitteth in heaven" (*Remains*, 4:85). He does not seem to have judged it as important as Calvin did to distinguish between Christ's flesh and his work or benefits, nor between eating and believing. And he thought that the image of the sun's rays excluded the substance talk that Bucer and Calvin supposed it to justify. "Is the light of the candle," he asked, "the substance of the candle?" (*Remains*, 3:170; cf. 2:358). But for him, as for Calvin, the *raison d'être* of the Eucharist was to represent and to increase a feeding on Christ that occurs also outside the Sacrament (*Remains*, 3:130, 553–554; 4:37–38). Since it is the Lord himself who feeds his own, Cranmer could and did assert that the substance of the body, not only its efficacy, is present in the Lord's Supper (*Remains*, 4:13). He meant, presumably, that the substance is rightly said to be *present* where it *acts* efficaciously. "The body of Christ is effectually in the sacrament" (*Remains*, 4:11)—not, that is, in the elements but in the "ministration" (3:136–37), by which the ascended Lord himself works.

The Elizabethan Settlement both restored Cranmer's work and modified it. The denial of a "reall and bodilie presence" in the Forty-two Articles was suppressed in the Thirty-nine Articles (1563/71), which affirm instead that "the body of Christe is geuen, taken, and eaten in the Supper only after an heauenly and spirituall maner" (art. 28). Apart from the omission of the black rubric (restored with verbal changes in 1662) and the permission of vestments (albeit the question of which vestments was left uncertain in the ornaments rubric), only one change in the new *Book of Common Prayer* (1559) affected the understanding of the Eucharist: for the words of delivery, the formula of 1549 was restored and placed before the formula of 1552. Small though these changes in the articles and prayer book may seem to be, they mark exactly the direction the English divines in general followed after the accession of Elizabeth. During her reign the influence of Calvin reached its height and helped to bring about the "general agreement" of which Richard Hooker wrote in 1597 in book five of his *Laws of Ecclesiastical Polity* (chap. 67): that there is a "*real participation* of Christ and of life in his body and blood *by means of this sacrament.*" By this time, the eucharistic thinking of the established church had moved firmly into the *via media* of the Continental Reformed. But in England, as in Switzerland, theological reinterpretation of the Sacrament failed to issue in frequent Communion. The first prayer book required each parishioner to communicate at least once a year; the second, at least three times a year.

Representation of Christ's Sacrifice. Although harmony between the Lutheran and the Reformed branches of Protestantism was not achieved, and full agreement was unlikely, after Zwingli's death the two lines did converge. The Lutheran Formula of Concord (1577) certainly intended to condemn the Calvinists along with the Zwinglians (art. 7), but Calvin's blunt description of Zwingli's early teaching on the sacraments as "profane" (to Pierre Viret, 11 September 1542) makes it impossible to consider him merely a "subtle sacramentarian." Nicholas Selnecker, one of the authors of the formula, explained the Lutheran doctrine in words to which Calvin, or even Bullinger, would not have objected: "[Christ], when giving the bread, gives us simultaneously His body to eat" (cited by Sasse, p. 103). The division between the Protestants and Rome, on the other hand, appears to go much deeper.

The Council of Trent (1545–1563) did urge the faithful to receive the body of the Lord more frequently than once a year, but it remained unmoved by the plea for a vernacular rite and administration of the Sacrament to the laity in both kinds. Moreover, the council took its stand on the traditional beliefs in transubstantiation and the sacrificial nature of the Mass. The sixteenth-century debates on both these themes were, to be sure, continuous with medieval debates. But the church of Rome could hardly allow Luther's claim that transubstantiation was a matter of opinion. The Fourth Lateran Council (1215) had given it dogmatic status. Even the liberal-minded Desiderius Erasmus, who had no enthusiasm for the dogma and was tempted by Oecolampadius's case against it, refused to depart from "the consensus of the church." Trent's Decree Concerning the Most Holy Sacrament of the Eucharist (session 13, 1551) needed only to reaffirm the Lateran pronouncement that Christ's body and blood are contained in the Sacrament under the "appearances" (*sub speciebus*) of bread and wine. (In Thomas Aquinas's classic formulation, it is the "accidents" that remain, though he also uses the word "appearance" [*Summa theologiae* III, q. 75, arts. 4–5].) Transubstantiation was not negotiable.

Trent accordingly anathematized the view that the substance of the bread and wine remains together with the body and blood of the Lord. The Protestant confessions responded by condemning transubstantiation, no longer leaving it as an optional opinion. This is not to say that the Protestants simply ignored the conversionist strand in the patristic sources, but they located the change in the use or signification of the elements, not in their substance. For instance, in his *Tractatio de Sacramento Eucharistiae* (Treatise on the Sacrament of the Eucharist; 1549), Vermigli insists that a change takes place by which the natural elements become effectual signs, the Spirit working by them powerfully and in an extraordinary way (secs. 60,80; cf. Calvin, *Inst.*, 4.17.14–15). But this understanding of the eucharistic conversion, though it anticipated twentieth-century Roman Catholic theories of transignification or transfinalization, was foreign to the thinking of the Tridentine fathers.

The council's Decree Concerning the Sacrifice of the Mass (session 22) followed the session on the Eucharist more than ten years later (1562). The Mass is declared to be a truly propitiatory sacrifice by which the Lord is appeased, the same Christ who once offered himself in a bloody sacrifice being immolated bloodlessly under the visible signs. In this awe-inspiring mystery, the victim by which we are reconciled to God the Father is daily immolated on the altar by the church through the priests. But, strictly, the agent of the bloodless sacrifice is Christ himself, who is also the one victim, "the same now offering by the ministry of the priests who then offered himself on the cross, only the manner of offering being different." The Lord's intention in instituting the Mass was that, by the visible sacrifice of the Mass, the sacrifice of the cross might be "represented" (*repraesentaretur*) and its saving power applied. *Repraesentari* is perhaps best rendered "to be made present," though it is noteworthy that the catechism of the Council of Trent (*Catechismus Romanus*, 1566) uses a different term, *instaurari*, which suggests rather "to be renewed" or even "repeated." In any case, so far from derogating from it in any way, the bloodless sacrifice is the means by which the fruits of the bloody sacrifice are received, and the catechism asserts expressly that the sacrifice of the Mass is one and the same with the sacrifice of the cross.

The Protestant reformers were well acquainted with the arguments, sanctioned at Trent, by which the Roman church's apologists tried to show that the Mass was being misrepresented—as though it cast doubts on the perfect sufficiency of the death of Christ (see, e.g., Calvin, *Inst.*, 4.18.2–5). It may be that the Lutherans and the Calvinists failed to take the arguments seriously enough, despite the fact that Luther and Calvin themselves could occasionally use the language of "offering Christ to God" (Luther, *Ein Sermon von dem neuen Testament, das ist von der heiligen Messe*, LW 35:102) or "setting Christ before God" in order to propitiate him (Calvin, commentary on *Num.* 19:2–3). But it was a question of the dominant eucharistic image, even when other images were not wholly denied, and the reformers could state the issue as a stark, inescapable choice: "[The Lord] has given us a table at which to feast, not an altar on which a victim is to be offered; he has not consecrated priests to make sacrifice, but servants [*ministros*] to distribute the sacred feast" (*Inst.*, 4.18.12). The division appeared at the time to be a matter not of practical abuses, popular misconceptions, or misplaced emphasis, but of mutually exclusive doctrines. For this reason, the desire of the Tridentine fathers that Christians might at last be of one heart and mind "in this sign of unity . . . this symbol of concord" proved fruitless.

[*See also* Consubstantiation; Sacraments; *and* Transubstantiation.]

BIBLIOGRAPHY

Barclay, Alexander. *The Protestant Doctrine of the Lord's Supper: A Study in the Eucharistic Teaching of Luther, Zwingli, and Calvin.* Glasgow, 1927. Points to the affinity between Luther and Calvin but views Calvin's doctrine as the natural development of Zwingli's later thoughts on the Eucharist. Well versed in the older secondary literature.

Brooks, Peter Newman. *Thomas Cranmer's Doctrine of the Eucharist: An Essay in Historical Development.* 2d ed. Houndmills, Basingstoke, England, 1992. Argues that Cranmer held much the same doctrine of a "true presence" as did Bucer, Melanchthon, Bullinger, and Calvin. The first edition appeared in 1965.

Clark, Francis. *Eucharistic Sacrifice and the Reformation.* Reprint, Devon, England, 1980. Demonstrates that what the Protestants rejected was not simply late medieval abuses, but the eucharistic doctrine of the Roman church. First published in 1960.

Courvoisier, Jaques. *Zwingli: A Reformed Theologian.* Richmond, Va., 1963. Valuable for its emphasis on Zwingli's strong sense of the church, but questionable in its interpretation of his eucharistic thought and liturgy.

Dix, Gregory. "Dixit Cranmer et Non Timuit: A Supplement to Mr. Timms." *Church Quarterly Review* 145 (1947–1948), 145–176; 146 (1948), 44–60. Dix's response to Timms.

Dugmore, C. W. *The Mass and the English Reformers.* London, 1958. Helpful on the patristic and medieval sources of English eucharistic theology, albeit too eager to establish the independence of the English reformers from Continental Protestantism.

Gerrish, B. A. *Grace and Gratitude: The Eucharistic Theology of John Calvin.* Edinburgh and Minneapolis, 1993. Puts Calvin's doctrine of the Lord's Supper in the context of his theology as a whole and compares him with Zwingli and Luther.

McDonnell, Kilian. *John Calvin, the Church, and the Eucharist.* Princeton, 1967. A learned study of Calvin by a Roman Catholic scholar. Interprets him (debatably) in the light of the late medieval flight from secondary causality.

McLelland, Joseph C. *The Visible Words of God: An Exposition of the Sacramental Theology of Peter Martyr Vermigli, A.D. 1500–1562.* Edinburgh and Grand Rapids, Mich., 1957. One of the best studies of sixteenth-century eucharistic ideas. Establishes the "theological coincidence" between Vermigli, Bucer, and Calvin.

Payne, John B. *Erasmus: His Theology of the Sacraments.* Richmond, Va., 1970. A careful examination of a neglected aspect of the work of Erasmus. Chapter 8 presents his eucharistic theology, partly in debate with the German study by Gottfried Krodel.

Quere, Ralph Walter. *Melanchthon's Christum Cognoscere: Christ's Efficacious Presence in the Eucharistic Theology of Melanchthon.* Nieuwkoop, 1977. A dissertation that sheds light on Melanchthon's relation to Luther and explores the influence of Oecolampadius on Melanchthon's reformulation of his doctrine.

Rempel, John D. *The Lord's Supper in Anabaptism.* Scottdale, Pa., 1993. Deals with theologies of the Lord's Supper of Balthasar Hubmaier, Pilgram Marpeck, and Dirk Philips. Limited to these three Anabaptists, but offers more than was available previously.

Richardson, Cyril C. *Zwingli and Cranmer on the Eucharist: Cranmer Dixit et Contradixit.* Evanston, Ill., 1949. Finds more in Zwingli than Dix could but agrees that Cranmer did not move beyond the Zwinglian framework.

Rubin, Miri. *Corpus Christi: The Eucharist in Late Medieval Culture.* Cambridge, 1991. Explores the wide range of meanings the Eucharist had, on the eve of the Reformation, as the central cultural symbol—not just a central rite—of the Middle Ages.

Sasse, Hermann. *This Is My Body: Luther's Contention for the Real Presence in the Sacrament of the Altar.* Minneapolis, 1959. Energetically partisan, but remains one of the best studies of Luther's eucharistic theology in English.

Stephens, W. P. *The Theology of Huldrych Zwingli.* Oxford, 1986. A solid general study of the Zurich reformer with very good sections on the sacraments.

Thompson, Bard. *Liturgies of the Western Church.* Reprint, Philadelphia, 1980. An invaluable collection of liturgies in English. Well edited.

Timms, G. B. *Dixit Cranmer: A Reply to Dom Gregory.* London, 1947. Attempts to refute the interpretation of Cranmer in Gregory Dix, *The Shape of the Liturgy,* London, 1945. First published in the *Church Quarterly Review;* reprinted separately in the Alcuin Club Papers.

Williams, George Hunston. *The Radical Reformation.* 3d ed. Kirksville, Mo., 1992. Not a study of the eucharistic views of the "radical reformers" (which remains a desideratum in the secondary literature), but an indispensable general guide to their varieties and thought. The first edition was published in 1962.

Wisløff, Carl F. *The Gift of Communion: Luther's Controversy with Rome on Eucharistic Sacrifice.* Translated by Joseph M. Shaw. Minneapolis, 1964. A thorough review of Luther's statements about the eucharistic sacrifice.

B. A. GERRISH

EVANGELICAL MOVEMENTS. The central problems in interpreting the early Reformation movement (Frühe reformatorische Bewegung, 1519–1524) lie, on the one hand, in the question of its connections to pre-Reformation reform and protest movements and, on the other hand, in the question of its inner coherence. Although myriad elements flowed into the early Reformation movement from various sources, such as the monastic observant movement, reform humanism centered on the Bible, the study of the church fathers, the urban social and peasant uprisings, the critique of the church by Hussite and Waldensian circles, the struggle of the laity against clerical privileges, and the political grievance movement. The manifold survivals of late medieval motifs can thus be detected, but the attempt to derive its historical dynamic out of these late medieval traditional elements has necessarily remained unsatisfactory. Rather, what was characteristic of the early Reformation movement was its ability to take up these thoroughly heterogenous elements from late medieval reform and protest movements and, in the light of the "normative centering" (Hamm), to focus them on the Bible as the only source of theological knowledge and religious binding norms and on the grace of God that can be encountered in Christ alone.

Despite the heterogeneity of the elements and motifs that were present in the early Reformation movement from the start, this movement should be described as a coherent and unified event, albeit of historically limited stability. The dissolution of this movement—which was absolutely decisive for the process of pushing through and popularizing the Reformation and which was carried along by a consciousness of its common bond and shared opposition to the Roman church structure and its representatives in the mid 1520s—does not, however, justify the idea frequently advanced, particularly in Anglo-Saxon scholarship, that there existed various "evangelical movements" at the outset of the Reformation. Only if the early Reformation movement is understood as a unified set of realities that were carried by a partisan sense of a common bond can its historically novel and explosive dynamic be grasped.

The social vectors of the early Reformation movement are not limited to a certain stratum or a specific social context. Rather, its pervasiveness in all social milieus must be seen as an essential element of its dynamic. In the dissolution of the early Reformation movement, social dissent among the urban bourgeoisie, the knights, the peasantry, and the aristocracy was a significant contributing factor. Although adaptations in the Reformation gospel that were socially specific can be documented even in the beginnings of the early Reformation movement, the heterogenous social interests only subsequently unleashed that centripetal energy, which was discharged, for instance, in the Peasants' War and contributed to the dissolution of the early Reformation movement.

Essential in the constitution of the early Reformation movement was the emergence of a supraregional "public forum," which was a revolutionary depature from the limited communications of the late Middle Ages. This forum was aided by the growing demand of the reading public for religious pamphlets (which were increasingly available in the vernacular after 1519) leading to the production of a flood of literature that swelled mightily until 1524. Also important were the theological disputes between the representatives of the early Reformation movement and the defenders of scholastic theology and the papal church that took place before the forum of public opinion. It was the public interest in theological disputes, substantially fostered by preaching, that allowed the early Reformation movement to emerge as a collective phenomenon, pervading the German-speaking cultural sphere in just a few years.

Among the propagandists of the early Reformation movement who were active as preachers or authors, members of the clergy, including secular clergy, monks, and professors of theology, dominated. The overwhelming majority of the pamphlets that have been attributed to identifiable persons flowed from the pens of clergymen. After 1524 groups of lay authors, including women, faded even further into the background. The increasing dominance of clerical authors from the middle of the 1520s onward marks, in terms of the history of publication, the end of the early Reformation movement, which had been characterized by great social variety within its ranks.

The dissolution of the early Reformation movement can also be seen in the growing theological differences among reformers. Concerning the appropriate *modus procedendi reformationis*, fundamental alternatives had already emerged in the context of the Wittenberg disturbances of 1521–1522, first between Martin Luther and Andreas Bodenstein von Karlstadt and later between the Wittenberg theologians and those of Thomas Müntzer. The public manner in which these disputes were handled caused theological controversy to have a broader impact, which in turn had direct repercussions on the unity of the early Reformation movement. Differing interpretations of baptism and the Lord's Supper, reflected in liturgical changes, proved to be increasingly irreconcilable. It is true that the consciousness of the original common bond, particularly in the early stages of the controversy over the Lord's Supper among the reformers, played a not insignificant role. It is also true that the attempts at theological clarification, particularly in the context of the controversy over the Lord's Supper, gave impetus to the development of doctrinal variety within the Reformation, which in turn marked the end of the early Reformation movement in the sense of a movement carried by a unified party consciousness.

With the introduction of the Reformation, first in the cities and then in individual territories (i.e., the urban Reformation and the Reformation imposed by princes), we reach the end of the early Reformation movement as one characterized by great inner variety with its dominant orientation along the lines of the basic spiritual questions posed by Luther. The development of varying theological schools of thought and the different confessional ecclesial and communal organizations typify the consolidation phase of the Reformation. A variety of currents flowed into the early Reformation movement and were bound together, making possible its early success. It is only in the concept of Protestantism, with its primarily religio-political emphasis, that the consciousness of an original common bond among the multiple currents within the Reformation lives on.

BIBLIOGRAPHY

Cole, Richard G. "The Reformation in Print: German Pamphlets and Propaganda." *Archiv für Reformationsgeschichte* 66 (1975), 93–102.

Dykema, Peter, and Heiko A. Oberman, eds. *Anticlericalism in Late Medieval and Early Modern Europe.* Studies in Medieval and Reformation Thought 51. Leiden, 1993.

Guggisberg, Hans R., and Gottfried Krodel, eds. "Die Reformation in Deutschland und Europa: Interpretationen und Debatten." *Archiv für Reformationsgeschichte* supplement (1993).

Hamm, Berndt. "Reformation als normative Zentrierung von Religion und Gesellschaft." *Jahrbuch für biblische Theologie* 7 (1992), 241–279.

Hamm, Berndt, Bernd Moeller, and Dorothea Wendebourg. *Reformationstheorien: Ein kirchenhistorischer Disput über Einheit und Vielfalt der Reformation.* Göttingen, 1995.

Hsia, R. Po-Chia, ed. *The German People and the Reformation.* Ithaca, N.Y., and London, 1988.

THOMAS KAUFMANN

Translated from German by Robert E. Shillenn

EVANGELISM is the name given to a distinctive religious movement among Italians of the sixteenth century, significant especially during the 1530s and 1540s. It is not easily defined since it has also been called a religious current, a set of attitudes, a tradition, or even a word without definite meaning. In the Italian context, the term is not employed in the usual sense of zealous proclamation of the gospel by fundamentalist preachers, but in that given to it by the French scholar Pierre Imbart de la Tour in 1914 and accepted by later scholars such as the German Hubert Jedin and the Italian Delio Cantimori. They defined it as commitment to reform conceived as a process that would begin with individual Christians and then spread to the church and society. Such reform would be brought about through a return to the Gospels and Pauline epistles. Its anchor was the fact of Christ's sacrifice on the cross and the realization of its implication for the believer. While the key doctrine shared by adherents of Evangelism was justification by faith alone, the majority remained Catholic, with only a minority following the premise of *sola fides* to its logical conclusion and embracing Protestantism.

Most students of Italian religious history would probably still accept this or a similar definition of Evangelism. But beyond it opinions diverge on such issues as origin, character, extent, impact, or duration of this movement, the "evangelismo italiano del Cinquecento," a phrase that by now has acquired a rather technical meaning in the vast literature devoted to it.

The origins of Italian Evangelism go back to reform movements of the late Middle Ages, and to the Savonarolan dream of a society in full conformity with Christian moral norms. But the invasions of the peninsula by French troops in the 1490s and the terrible Sack of Rome in 1527 seemed to many contemporaries tantamount to the judgment of God on a corrupt church and society. These events did not create but certainly heightened an apocalyptic mood widespread among various groups of Italians and strengthened the conviction that a cleansing of the church and individual repentance were called for. Movements for personal and institutional reform antedated the Lutheran attack on the Catholic church but acquired momentum, even urgency, after 1517 as Lutheran and later Calvinist books reached Italy through booksellers like the Milanese Francesco Calvi, an early importer of Protestant works.

Evidence for a variety of reform impulses during the 1520s includes prophetic sermons of popular preachers, the widespread reading of works by Erasmus, and the foundation of new religious orders like the Theatines, founded in 1524, and that of the Capuchins, established in 1528. But one cannot speak of Evangelism as a recognizable movement before the period 1535–1542, when Pope Paul III repeatedly appointed prominent proponents of reform to the college of cardinals. Prelates such as Gasparo Contarini, Reginald Pole, Gian Pietro Carafa, later Pope Paul IV, Gregorio Cortese, Tommaso Badia, Giovanni Morone, Federico Fregoso, and even Pietro Bembo were highly visible church leaders; with the exception of Carafa they championed not only reform but also conciliation of Protestants and restoration of Christian unity. The name given them by contemporaries was *spirituali*, used in contrast to the "worldly," whose primary interest was in secular pursuits or power politics in church and state.

Spirituali were not confined to the highest levels of the Catholic church, however. They were found among members of loose study circles, like that of Cardinal Ercole Gonzaga in Mantua, around the charismatic Spanish reform thinker Juan de Valdés in Naples, and in the household of Cardinal Pole in Viterbo. Contrary to an older view, Evangelism was not only a phenomenon of the Italian upper classes but of the common people as well. The latter were reached primarily by sermons of Evangelical preachers, but books also played an important role in the spread of Evangelism to social groups like artisans and workers. In Venice, for example, the Bible and heterodox books were bought, read, and discussed by quite ordinary people.

The most important single work associated with Italian Evangelism was the *Beneficio di Cristo* of 1543. This little book illustrates the Christocentric spirituality of the movement together with its ambiguity. Inquisitors made sure that copies were ferreted out and burned, since the *Beneficio*, and by extension, Evangelism, tended to reduce ecclesiastical structures and sacraments to adiaphora or even irrelevance.

Although 1542, when the reorganized Roman Inquisition began its work, is sometimes regarded as decisive for the fate of Evangelism, in reality no single date marked its end. An important factor in the diminution of its role at the papal court was the unsuccessful religious Colloquy of Regensburg in 1541, to which Cardinal Contarini was sent as legate. Its failure showed how illusory the dream of healing the split between Catholics and Lutherans had become. The *spirituali* prelates gradually lost influence, not by being defeated by intransigent churchmen or by being politically outmaneuvered by old curial hands, but because their attempts at solving the crisis in the church had not worked. On a broader level, the individualistic, undogmatic spirituality of men and women belonging to Evangelical groups was perceived as antithetical to the church of the Counter-Reformation, which aimed at doctrinal uniformity, enforcement of adherence to its norms, and general participation in its liturgical functions.

Evangelism persisted until the end of the sixteenth century, with echoes into the early seventeenth, as can be seen in works of literature and art but especially in letters. Sometimes private jottings of a minor bureaucrat in Milan, Rome, or Florence reveal the depth of personal anxieties concerning questions of salvation and show that the works of Italian Evangelism continued to be read and pondered. Trials held by the Inquisition, especially in Venice, testify to the long survival of ideas characteristic of Evangelism. Despite its significance as an indigenous movement for reform, however, Evangelism never became part of the mainstream of Italian religion or culture, and it lacked organization or political support. Its memory now remains confined to works of scholarship.

[*See also* Contarini, Gasparo.]

BIBLIOGRAPHY

Gleason, Elisabeth G. "On the Nature of Italian Evangelism: Scholarship, 1953–1978." *Sixteenth Century Journal* 9.3 (1978), 3–25. Bibliography up to 1978.

Martin, John. "Salvation and Society in Sixteenth-Century Venice: Popular Evangelism in a Renaissance City." *Journal of Modern History* 60 (1988), 205–233. Thorough examination of Evangelism among the popular classes, with good bibliography.

———. *Venice's Hidden Enemies: Italian Heretics in a Renaissance City.* Berkeley, 1993.

Schutte, Anne Jacobson. "The *Lettere Volgari* and the Crisis of Evangelism in Italy." *Renaissance Quarterly* 28 (1975), 639–688. Very useful discussion of the chronological limits of Italian Evangelism.

———. "Periodization of Sixteenth-Century Italian Religious History: The Post-Cantimori Paradigm Shift." *Journal of Modern History* 61 (1989), 269–284. Wider-ranging essay with excellent bibliography.

Simoncelli, Paolo. *Evangelismo italiano del Cinquecento: Questione religiosa e nicodemismo politico.* Rome, 1979. Argument for the political nature of Evangelism, and attempt to distinguish its various constituent groups.

ELISABETH G. GLEASON

EXCOMMUNICATION refers to expulsion from the community, ecclesiastical ban, ecclesiastical outlawry, and anathema. Major and minor excommunication were established by Christ (*Mt.* 18:15ff.): "and if he refuses to listen even to the church, treat him as you would a pagan or a tax collector." Paul and John ordered their followers to have nothing to do with those who deviate from the Christian faith by their way of life (*1 Cor.* 5:3ff.) or their doctrine (*2 Thes.* 3:14f., *2 Jn.* 10f.), not to eat with them (*1 Cor.* 5:3ff.), or give them lodging or greet them (*2 Jn.* 10f.). Luther in 1519–1520 echoes such sentiments in his *Sermon von dem Bann.* According to Gabriel Biel, handing over the public fornicator to Satan (*1 Cor.* 5:4, *1 Tim.* 1:19f., *2 Tim.* 4:14) is synonymous with excommunication. Johann Eck in his *Enchiridion* cites *Titus* 3:10—"Warn a divisive person once, and then warn him a second time. After that have nothing to do with him"—and also *Romans* 8:9 and *Acts* 5:1–11; see also *Revelation* 2:20.

The word *excommunicare* was coined in Christian Latin usage in the fourth century, yet was still not found in the Vulgate. On the other hand, in view of the biblical usage, "anathema" is of special significance as a translation in the Septuagint and in the Vulgate for the Hebrew "herem" or "horma" (*Nm.* 21:3; *Dt.* 7:26, 13:17; *Jos.* 6:17, 7:1,11–13; *Jgs.* 1:17; *1 Chr.* 2:7; *Jdt.* 16:23; *Zec.* 14:11; *Mal.* 4:6; *1 Mc.* 5:5). "If anyone does not love the Lord, a curse be on him. Come, O Lord" (*1 Cor.* 16:22); "If anyone is preaching to you a gospel other than what you accepted, let him be eternally condemned!" (*Gal.* 1:8–9).

As to the transfer of the term into historical church usage, see the Council of Nicea (325), the Council of Ephesus (431), and the second Council of Constantinople. Anathema (separation from God, being thrown out, being damned) also for dead individuals was debated throughout the Middle Ages.

Curse, breaking off of personal relations, and exclusion from the Eucharist are the three elements that also characterized excommunication in the Middle Ages. The terminological distinction between "excommunicatio maior" and "excommunicatio minor," that is, between major and minor excommunication, began to develop starting in the twelfth century. Anathema was thus sometimes cited as a distinct degree of excommunication and sometimes as a solemn form of major excommunication or equated with it. The precise meaning of minor excommunication fluctuated in the fifteenth and sixteenth centuries between exclusion from reception of the Eucharist on account of a mortal sin and exclusion from attendance at the Eucharist and the greeting of peace (not, however, from preaching or the liturgy of the hours), as well as exclusion from church burial on the basis of fellowship with excommunicated individuals or other kinds of serious misconduct (such as usury, oppression of the poor, robbery, simony), or sometimes exclusion from the fellowship of believers without exclusion from the sacraments as a punishment for minor infractions (particularly those committed by clerics).

Theological Definition of Excommunication in the Late Middle Ages and at the Time of the Reformation. In the *Vocabularius theologiae* (Hagenau, 1517), Johannes Altenstaig, following Gabriel Biel, offers this definition: "Dicitur autem excommunicatio, quasi extra communionem positio, exclusio vel separatio" ("Excommunication means, as it were, putting someone outside the community, exclusion or separation"). Citing Alexander of Hales and Bonaventura, Altenstaig then differentiates three levels of community or communion: a purely spiritual and internal community, in compliance with the command of love, from which no one may be excluded, whether he be a believer or an unbeliever, inasmuch as everyone is our neighbor; a purely physical community in legitimate external dealings—*osculum, colloquium, convivium, oratio, salutatio* ("kiss/embrace," "conversation," "eating together," "speech," "greeting")—particularly public speech, participation both in the sacrament and at the table of bodily sustenance (*mensa corporalis refectionis*), which is ruled out by "excommunicatio maior," and "excommunicatio minor"; an intermediary kind of excommunication, "excommunicatio minor," which excludes a person from fellowship in the reception of the sacraments, particularly the Eucharist.

According to the *Summa Theologica* of Antoninus Pierozzi, archbishop of Florence (d. 1459), "excommunicatio maior," which is also called "anathema," excludes a person from the threefold "communion/community of the faithful" ("communio fidelium"): from human contact (in conversation or speech, food, greeting, and the like); from the reception of the sacraments; and from participation in the spiritual goods of the church. This last notion is disputed by Gabriel Biel, among others, and Luther, who in his *Sermon von dem Bann* contends that "to excommunicate is not, as some maintain, to deliver a soul to the devil and to deprive it of the prayers and all the good works of Christians," but merely "a deprivation of the external sacrament or of dealings with people." In his *Enchiridion* Eck takes issue with two assertions of Luther: that the excommunication pronounced by an ecclesiastical judge is merely an excommunication after the fact, since every person already previously excommunicates himself through sin (this was also Gabriel Biel's position); and that excommunication is to be loved. The tensions evident here have carried over into the present debate within Catholicism over the meaning of excommunication in the new Code of Canon Law (see Lüdicke). It is presupposed here that excommunication is both the actual censure as well as the sentence handed down by the judge. The problem here is the distinction between penance and excommunication, between "forum conscientiae" and "forum judiciale," that is, between internal and external forum. Thus an archdeacon who is not a priest, in contrast to a parish priest who is not a higher ecclesiastical superior, can absolve someone from the penalty of excommunication but cannot forgive sin "in foro penitentiali." Absolution from excommunication is accordingly the precondition for admission to sacramental confession (once again debated in the context of the reform of the Code). Connected with this is the question whether excommunication means only the revocation of membership rights in the church—for example, receiving the sacraments, entering church buildings, entering a religious order, accepting ecclesiastical benefices, performing valid legal acts, holding church offices, having the right to demand that contracts be carried out (here the question in dispute was more or less whether a monetary debt must be paid back if the creditor has been excommunicated in the meantime), receiving a church burial, and being named in the liturgy of the church—or whether excommunication also entails exclusion from the kingdom of God. According to Eck, a person who commits mortal sin excommunicates himself; however, such a person, although deprived of divine grace, still remains attached to the body of the church, albeit as a withered member. But in the case of "excommunicatio maior," a person is cut off from the body, although still not in such a way that he does not belong to the church at all, because for as long as he has the true faith, he is still a part of the church. Rather he is cut off inasmuch as he is deprived of having a share in the intercessory prayers of the church. In the annotations of P. Tilmanni there is a further clarification: although excommunication takes away a person's share in the communion of the saints (and thereby the prayers of the church), it replaces this share with love. The inner communion, whereby the members are joined in love with Christ, is only lost through sin and not through excommunication.

The goal ("causa finalis") of excommunication as a medicinal punishment is cure, edification, and not destruction. The condition for a just excommunication is that the excommunicator intends to give correction out of love, not to inflict injury out of hate or greed or prejudice against one's opponents. "Excommunicatio maior" is not to be imposed for relatively minor infractions but rather for grave sins that cannot be otherwise corrected, that is, particularly in the case of obstinacy ("contumacia"). A threefold warning is required. However, the member "who will not accept the medicine is to be cut off from the body with the hot iron of excommunication, so that the other members of the body will not be infected with the virulent disease that is like a poison" (*Pontificale Romanum, Forma excommunicationis maioris*). A pagan or a Jew cannot be excommunicated, while the Pope can be excommunicated only for heresy, according to Antoninus. In canon law and in the eucharistic bulls the grounds given for excommunication are, among others, attacks against the Curia Romana, the papacy, the cardinals, clerics, churches, pilgrims; malfeasance by inquisitors, clerics, mendicant friars; and support for the Saracens, heresy. (Antoninus cites eighty-one grounds.)

Critique of the Practice of Excommunication. In contrast to the positive aspects of the practice of excommunication—for instance, against those who violate the peace or who oppress the poor—excommunication and interdict (prohibition of the celebration of the liturgy and the administration of the sacraments for a given place or even regions) were used to further ecclesiastical political interests (such as the excommunication of Emperor Louis the Bavarian by Pope John XXII). The mutual excommunications resulting from the Western Schism, the use of excommunication in monetary matters (e.g., to secure the repayment of loans), and in general the rash and all-too-frequent use of the threat of excommunication for matters of lesser importance led to a situation in which this sword of the Church was more scorned than feared. Luther's excommunication stands out in view of its public effect, but Luther's was not an isolated case. Among others, the founders of the Capuchin order were excommunicated, and the papal legate Girolamo Aleandro was under excommunication for a time because of financial matters.

In chapter 3 of its Decree on Reform (session 25, December 1563), the Council of Trent ordered all ecclesiastical judges to refrain from the use of ecclesiastical censure or interdict, except where a material or personal execution of the judgment is impossible, and even then only after two warnings. Any exertion of influence by secular authorities is to be rejected.

The Question of Excommunication in the Contemporary Lutheran-Catholic Dialogue. Although the Council of Trent uses the set expression "anathema sit," there is no determined form of excommunication connected with it. On the other hand, the *Damnamus* used in Lutheran confessional documents actually meant the breaking off of eucharistic communion between the Christian churches. The clarification of this question is therefore of particular significance for the restoration of ecclesiastical communion. Thus the concluding document of the second phase of dialogue between the Lutheran World Federation and the Roman Catholic church (*Facing Unity*, 1984) stresses the necessity for "invalidating the doctrinal condemnations." For instance, it declares that the mutual condemnations with respect to the question of the efficacy of the sacraments ("ex opere operato") do not really apply to the actual confessional position of each side. This is likewise the case for the Lutheran rejection of the Mass as a sacrifice and the Catholic rejection of the denial of Christ's real presence in the Eucharist. From 1981 to 1985 the ecumenical study group of evangelical and Catholic theologians studied the mutual condemnations by Catholics and reformers in the sixteenth century with respect to the doctrine of justification, the sacraments, and church offices. The result was a conclusion that certain condemnations were based on misunderstandings, while others were aimed at extreme positions of the other side, but were not concerned with the confessions of the respective churches. Some condemnations no longer apply to the other partner; in other questions it was recognized that there was a common view in the matter itself but that terminology differed; still other questions required further clarification. "Where the interpretation of the justification of the sinner is concerned, the mutual sixteenth-century condemnation which we have discussed no longer applies to our partner today in any sense that could divide the churches" (see Lehmann and Pannenberg 27.68). It is hoped that the churches will agree to this result.

On this basis even the question of the excommunication of Martin Luther would have to be reexamined, and all the more so because the question of his memory in the church—see the bull *Exsurge Domine* concerning the prohibition on reading Luther's writings—and the question of the position of the followers of his teaching remain unresolved.

BIBLIOGRAPHY

Anker, Karl. *Bann und Interdict im 14. und 15. Jahrhundert als Voraussetzung der Reformation.* Tübingen, 1919. Documented with many instances when excommunication was ignored.

Aymans, Winfried, Karl-Theodor Geringer, and Heribert Shmitz, eds. *Schriften zum kanonischen Recht.* Paderborn, 1989. See particularly the contribution regarding ecclesiastical excommunication in the light of the distinction between the external and internal forums.

Bäumer, Remigius, ed. *Lutherprozeß und Lutherbann: Vorgeschichte, Ergebnis, Nachwirkung.* Münster, 1972.

Beinert, Wolfgang. "Anathema." In *Lexikon für Theologie und Kirche,* 3d ed., vol. 1, pp. 604–605. Freiburg, 1993.

Doskocil, Walter. "Exkommunikation." In *Reallexikon für Antike und Christentum,* vol. 7, p. 1–22. Stuttgart, 1969.

Fabisch, Peter, and Erwin Iserloh, eds. *Dokumente zur Causa Lutheri 1517–1521.* Münster 1988–1991. Most recent edition of the bull *Exsurge Domine* that threatened excommunication, the bull of excommunication *Decet Romanum Pontificem,* and the Edict of Worms.

Fransen, Piet F. "Réflexions sur l'anathème au concille de Trente." *Ephemerides theologicae Lovanienses* 29 (1953), 657–672.

Krämer, Peter. "Anathema." In *Lexikon für Theologie und Kirche,* 3d ed., vol. 1, p. 605. Freiburg, 1993. From a canonical standpoint.

Lehmann, Karl, and Wolfhart Pannenberg, eds. *Lehrverurteilungen: Kirchentrennend?* 3 vols. Dialog der Kirchen, vols. 4–6. Freiburg and Göttingen, 1986–1990. Vol. 2 contains significant contributions to the question of excommunication by Lehmann, Pannenberg, and Wenz (study of the "damnamus" in the Lutheran confessional documents).

———. *The Condemnations of the Reformation Era: Do They Still Divide?* Edited and translated by Margaret Kohl. Minneapolis, 1990. Translation of vol. I of the previous title. Statement of the Ecumenical Study Group of Protestant and Catholic Theologians.

Link, Christoph. "Bann V: Reformation und Neuzeit." In *Theologische Realenzyklopädie,* vol. 5, pp. 182–190. Berlin and New York, 1980.

Logan, F. Donald. "Excommunication." In *Dictionary of the Middle Ages,* edited by Joseph R. Strayer, vol. 4, p. 536. New York, 1984.

Lüdicke, Klaus, ed. *Münsterischer Kommentar zum Codex Iuris Canonicis. unter besonderer Berucksichtigung der Rechtslage in Deutschland, Osterreich und der Schweiz.* Essen, 1993. The most recent overview of the canonical discussion within the Catholic church regarding excommunication. Contains bibliography.

Marzoa Rodríguez, Angel. *La censura de excomunicación: Estudio de su naturaleza jurídica en ss. XIII-XV.* Pamplona, 1985. Deals principally with Thomas Aquinas and the Decretalists.

May, Georg: "Bann IV: Alte Kirche und Mittelalter." In *Theologische Realenzyklopädie,* vol. 5, pp. 170–182. Berlin and New York, 1980.

Payer, Pierre J. "Penance and Penitentials." In *Dictionary of the Middle Ages,* edited by Joseph R. Strayer, vol. 9, pp. 487–493. New York, 1987.

Pfaff, Karl. "Beiträge zur Geschichte der Abendmahlsbulle vom 16.-18. Jahrhundert." *Römische Quartalschrift* 38 (1930), 23–76. Studies the changes in the sentences of excommunication that were published in the bull *In Coena Domini.*

Tomos Agapis: Documentation for the Dialogue of Love between the Holy See and the Ecumenical Patriarchate 1958–1976. Pro Oriente Foundation. Innsbruck, 1978. Concerning the mutual revocation of sentences of excommunication by the Roman Catholic and Eastern Orthodox churches (7 December 1965).

Zapp, Hartmut. "Bann." In *Lexikon des Mittelalters,* vol. 1, p. 1416. Munich, 1980.

———. "Exkommunikation." In *Lexikon des Mittelalters,* vol. 4, p. 170. Munich, 1989.

VINZENZ PFNÜR

Translated from German by Robert E. Shillenn

EXORCISM. *See* Possession and Exorcism.

EXPLORATIONS. *See* America; Discoveries in the New World; Missions.

F

FABER, Johannes Augustanus (1470?–1530), German Dominican humanist, preacher, and administrator. Faber, who was probably born in Augsburg, devoted himself to study from his youth. After entering the Dominican order he pursued theological studies in Italy, earning a doctorate. In 1505 he was teaching scripture at Padua. In 1507 he returned home to Augsburg, where he was elected prior and devoted himself to rebuilding the Dominican church. To finance the project he obtained a papal indulgence, whose instructions, published in 1513, specify that people applying the indulgence to themselves must visit churches, make a donation, and go to confession. Those applying the indulgence to the dead need make only the donation, without confession. The poor need make no donation. The indulgence brought Faber into conflict with Emperor Maximilian I, who forbade its preaching and confiscated its income. In 1515 Faber defended indulgences against an Augsburg parish priest, Johannes Speiser, in Bologna; Faber argued that it was wicked to deny the pope's power to grant indulgences for monetary donations. The dispute foreshadowed Luther's controversy with Johann Tetzel.

Upon his return to Augsburg, Faber was named imperial counselor and began building a convent and a school to teach Latin and Greek, both with imperial patronage. Faber, named vicar general for the Dominicans in south Germany and Switzerland in 1511, tried to reorient the studies of young Dominicans away from Scholasticism and toward humanistic studies and the church fathers. Predictably this attempt stirred opposition. In 1520 Faber went to Belgium to win support from Charles V and visited Erasmus at Louvain. Later he and Erasmus became enemies. Faber was initially friendly to Luther, and his sermons at the Diet of Worms in 1521 infuriated nuncio Girolamo Alexander. But Faber soon turned against Luther, as did many other older humanists. In 1524 Luther's sympathizers forced Faber to leave Augsburg. Little is known of his last six years.

BIBLIOGRAPHY

Coulon, R. *Dictionnaire de théologie catholique.* Paris, 1913. See vol. 5, pt. 2, pp. 2046–2050. Concentrates on Faber's theology.

Dillis, T. A. "Johannes Faber." In *Lebensbilder aus dem Bayerischen Schwaben,* edited by G. von Pölniz, vol. 5, pp. 93–111. Munich, 1952. Biographical sketch.

Paulus, Nikolaus. *Die deutschen Dominkaner im Kampf gegen Luther, 1518–1563.* Freiburg, 1903.

Vincke, Rainer. "Johannes Faber." In *Contemporaries of Erasmus,* edited by Peter G. Bietenholz and Thomas B. Deutscher, vol. 2, pp. 4–5. Toronto, Buffalo, and London, 1986. Short account that stresses his relations with Eramus.

JOHN PATRICK DONNELLY

FABRI, Johann (Ger. Heigerlin; 1478–1541), German theologian, bishop of Vienna, adviser to Archduke Ferdinand. Fabri was born in Leutkirch in Swabia. His name is based on a Latinization of his father's (Peter Heigerlin) occupation as a blacksmith. After early schooling at Constance and Ulm he studied theology and law first at Tübingen, where he was ordained, and then at Freiburg, where he received a doctorate in civil and canon law. After several years of priestly work at Lindau, Leutkirch, Basel, and Constance, he was named vicar-general of Constance in 1518. His published early sermons, *Declamationes divinae de humanae vitae miseria* (Augsburg, 1520), reveal a strong humanist bent.

Initially favorable to Luther, Fabri turned against him after the Leipzig Debate of 1519; the gentle tone of Fabri's first polemical work, *Opus adversus. . . dogmata Martini Lutheri* (1522), gradually turned to open hostility in his later writings. His relations with Zwingli were also friendly at first but soured as Zwingli's theology developed. He debated against Zwingli at Zurich in 1523, later attacked him in *Christliche Beweisung über sechs Artikel Ulrich Zwinglis* (1526), and helped solidify Swiss Catholic opposition to him. Fabri also wrote books against Balthasar Hubmaier (1528) and Kaspar von Schwenckfeld (1529).

Archduke Ferdinand, the later emperor, named Fabri adviser in 1523 and his confessor in 1524; Fabri used these posts to encourage Ferdinand's adherence to Catholicism and opposition to Protestantism. In 1530 Fabri became bishop of Vienna. He proved a zealous pastor and preacher as well as a scholar who became a fierce opponent of Protestantism, censoring books for Ferdinand and trying to preserve the universities for orthodoxy.

In his youth Fabri enjoyed good relations with Erasmus, but these cooled as Fabri became more militant, especially in persecuting Anabaptists. Fabri's eighty-one writings are mainly sermons or attacks on Protestantism. His work as bishop and writer made him a precursor of the Austrian Counter-Reformation.

BIBLIOGRAPHY

Primary Source

Fabri, Johann. *Malleus in haeresim Lutheranum.* Cologne, 1524.

Secondary Sources

Bautz, Friedrich Wilhelm, ed. *Biographische-Bibliographisches Kirchenlexikon.* Hamm, 1970–. See vol. 1, pp. 1588–1589.

Immenkötter, Herbert. "Fabri, Johann." In *Theologische Realenzyklopädie,* vol. 10, pp. 784–788. Berlin and New York. Detailed encyclopedia article.

Janz, Denis. "Johannes Fabri." In *Contemporaries of Erasmus,* edited by Peter G. Bietenholz and Thomas B. Deutscher, vol. 3, pp. 5–8. Toronto, Buffalo, and London, 1986. Best account in English.

Radey, Christian. "Dr. Johann Fabri, Bishof von Wien, 1530–1541: Wegbereiter der katholische Reform, Rat König Ferdinands." Ph.D. diss., University of Vienna, 1976.

JOHN PATRICK DONNELLY

FACULTY OF THEOLOGY OF PARIS. Often conveniently but inaccurately termed "the Sorbonne," the Faculty of Theology of the University of Paris played a decisive role in curbing the Reformation in France. With statutes and privileges granted by the Holy See and by the kings of France, it was the leading school of theology in western Europe and was active in ecclesiastical and political affairs from the early thirteenth century until the suppression of the university in 1792. It influenced the development of doctrine and law by its decisions on dogmatic and moral issues, many of which were submitted to its judgment by officials of church and state. The Faculty's influence soared during the era of conciliarism but declined in the last phase of the Hundred Years' War. Staunch conservatism in theological matters, conciliarism, and Gallicanism all remained permanent traits of Faculty policy.

Faculty statutes required twelve to fourteen years of study and disputation on the Bible and on theological issues treated in the *Sententiarum libri quatuor* (Book of Sentences). Most secular candidates studied at the two largest colleges, Navarre and the Sorbonne, while students belonging to mendicant orders took classes in their own *studia;* but academic disputations and the granting of the license and doctorate in theology were the exclusive prerogative of the Faculty itself. All graduate doctors were ordained priests; about half were members of religious orders. The number of graduates doubled in the sixteenth century, from twenty every second year to forty.

After the installation of the first Parisian printing press at the Collège de Sorbonne in 1472, Paris theologians like John Mair, Josse van Clichtove, Francisco de Vitoria, Pieter Crockaert, Jérôme de Hangest, Robert Céneau, and Jacques Almain published works of scholastic theology. These traditional studies flourished so well that the Faculty successfully opposed the inroads of humanism in the university and led the censure of new biblical studies of Johannes Reuchlin, Lefèvre d'Étaples, and Erasmus. The combined opposition of the Faculty of Theology and the Parlement of Paris (the supreme court of justice in France) to the Concordat of Bologna (1516–1517), although unsuccessful, cemented a close working relationship between Faculty and Parlement, restoring to the Faculty the political influence lost a century earlier.

Scarcely three weeks before the Faculty of Theology's formal condemnation of Martin Luther (15 April 1521), the Parlement of Paris decreed that all books dealing with religion must be submitted to the doctrinal scrutiny of the Faculty. The Faculty reactivated the office of syndic, vacant for 150 years, in order to expedite the case of Luther which had been submitted to its arbitration. Noël Beda, an indefatigable traditionalist, held this office for fourteen years and set an enduring standard of opposition to religious innovation. During the next four decades, the Parlement regularly sought the Faculty's judgment about the orthodoxy of preachers and authors. In turn, the Faculty frequently spurred the Parlement into action on such matters. This collaboration ultimately resulted in the Faculty's twenty-six Articles of Faith (1543) and in the first printed Index of Prohibited Books to be issued anywhere (1544). Not intended as a new creed, the articles reaffirmed those points of Catholic dogma and piety that were being challenged by Protestant preachers. The six Paris Indexes condemned a total of 528 books by 120 major and minor figures, as well as many anonymous works, and influenced similar Indexes in other European cities. The active enforcement of the Articles of Faith and the Indexes by the French kings crowned the work of the Faculty of Theology with official status and assured the continuation in France of traditional religious orthodoxy as defined by the Faculty.

The 1521 condemnation of Luther was followed quickly by censures of books and sermons of Melanchthon, Lefèvre d'Étaples, Louis de Berquin, Martial Mazurier, Pierre Caroli, Aimé Maigret, Michel d'Arande, and others. The French royal court repeatedly intervened to protect humanists and reformers; however, during the captivity of Francis I (1525–1526) the Faculty and the Parlement were able to shut down the evangelical reforms promoted in the diocese of Meaux by Bishop Guillaume Briçonnet. In 1527 they forbade the publication of vernacular translations and new versions of the Latin Bible. Louis de Berquin, spared from prosecution in 1523 and 1527 by royal protection, was executed by the Parlement as a relapsed heretic in 1529. The formal censure of Erasmus, voted by the Faculty in 1526 and ratified by the whole university in 1527, was published in 1531.

The years 1533 and 1534 were crucial and decisive. Noël Beda and other theologians were exiled for their opposition to the Lenten sermons of Gérard Roussel, who was a protégé of the king's sister Marguerite of Navarre. She and Roussel were then the targets of a satirical play in the university, and her book *Miroir de l'âme pécheresse* appeared on a list of censured books. Beda, recalled from exile to refute spurious Protestant propaganda (January 1534), instead attacked the *lecteurs royaux* (Collège de France). For all these reasons, the humanists and reformers thought they had finally brought the Faculty and its traditionalist allies to heel. However, as a result of the evangelical sermon of Nicolas Cop (1 November 1533), Francis I pressed the willing Parlement to prosecute the "Lutheran sect." From this time on, the Parlement's registers increasingly abound with signs of cooperation with the Faculty of Theology on religious matters. Following the *Affaire des placards* (17 October 1534) and similar blasphemous pamphlets in January 1535, the king personally issued two draconian decrees of censorship and repeatedly urged the Parlement to bring religious dissenters to justice. In 1535, the Faculty advised the king against "futile" dialogues with German reformers. A major decree of censorship (1 July 1542) gave expanded powers to the Faculty of Theology to combat Protestant books pouring in from Strasbourg and Geneva. Francis himself claimed credit for the Faculty's Articles of Faith. Henry II allowed the Faculty to censor the Bibles of Robert I Estienne (November 1548), and renewed his confidence in the Faculty in several decrees and edicts—notably the Edict of Châteaubriand (1551). The Faculty approved and worked with the Parlement's new inquisitorial court, the Chambre Ardente (1549–1551). In 1561, on the eve of the Wars of Religion, representatives of Paris institutions staged massive public demonstrations in support of traditional orthodoxy as defined by the Faculty of Theology. During the tragic conflicts to come, the Faculty spoke out frequently and forcefully against religious change and political compromise, and continued to exercise significant theological influence after the restoration of peace.

[*See also* Beda, Noël; Chambre Ardente; Châteaubriand, Edict of; Collège de France; Education; Paris; *and* Universities.]

BIBLIOGRAPHY

Primary Sources

Clerval, J.-Alexandre, ed. *Registre des procès-verbaux de la Faculté de théologie de Paris.* De 1505 à 1523. Archives de l'Histoire religieuse de la France. Paris, 1917. Annotated proceedings of the Faculty of Theology's meetings, 1505–1523.

Duplessis d'Argentré, Charles, ed. *Collectio judiciorum de novis erroribus qui... in Ecclesia proscripti sunt et notati.* 3 vols. Paris, 1728–1736. Original documents of the Faculty of Theology's doctrinal judgments and decrees.

Farge, James K., ed. *Registre des procès-verbaux de la Faculté de théologie de l'Université de Paris.* De janvier 1524 à novembre 1533. Paris, 1990. Continuation of Clerval's edition of the proceedings of the Faculty of Theology's meetings and conclusions for the period 1524–1533.

———. *Le parti conservateur au XVIe siècle: Université et Parlement de Paris à l'époque de la Renaissance et de la Réforme.* Documents et inédits du Collège de France. Paris, 1992. Documents illustrating the conservative mentality of the Faculty of Theology and the Parlement and their opposition to humanism and the Reformation.

———. *Registre des conclusions de la Faculté de théologie de l'Université de Paris, de novembre 1533 à mars 1550.* Paris, 1994. Continuation of the earlier volume, giving conclusions for the period from November 1534 to March 1550.

Secondary Sources

Bujanda, J.-M. de, Francis Higman, and James K. Farge. *Index de l'Université de Paris: 1544, 1545, 1547, 1549, 1551, 1556.* Index des livres interdits, vol. 1. Sherbrooke, Que., 1985. Identifies all 528 books that were censured by the Faculty of Theology from 1544 to 1556.

Farge, James K. *Biographical Register of Paris Doctors of Theology, 1500–1536.* Subsidia Mediaevalia 10. Toronto, 1980. Biobibliographical sketches of all 474 graduates of the Faculty of Theology during the early years of the Reformation.

———. *Orthodoxy and Reform in Early Reformation France: The Faculty of Theology of Paris, 1500–1543.* Studies in Medieval and Reformation Thought, vol. 32. Leiden, 1985. Only comprehensive study of the Faculty of Theology based on primary sources.

Féret, P.-Y. *La Faculté de théologie de Paris et ses docteurs les plus célèbres.* Époque moderne, 7 vols. Paris, 1900–1910. Pioneering study, but limited by its failure to use essential archival documents.

Renaudet, Augustin. *Préréforme et humanisme à Paris pendant les premières guerres d'Italie, 1494–1517.* 2d ed. Paris, 1953; reprint, Geneva, 1981. A thorough, still indispensable study of the intellectual scene in Paris on the eve of the Reformation.

JAMES K. FARGE, C.S.B.

FAITH. The most easily identified theological controversy of the sixteenth century was the doctrine of justification. At the heart of that controversy, however, was the underlying debate about the true nature of faith. In the process of defending what they believed to be the biblical doctrine of justification, the reformers transformed the traditional meaning of faith. Their Catholic opponents, including the Tridentine theologians, rejected this concept of saving faith and thereby retained the traditional understanding of justification.

The issue was often debated exegetically and centered about a number of biblical passages: *I Corinthians* 3:12–15, which depicted how human works would be tested and rewarded; *I Corinthians* 13:13, which named the theological virtues of faith, hope, and love; *Romans* 1:17, 3:28, and 4:9, which stated that the human being (Abraham) was justified by faith without works of the law; *James* 2:24, which explained that one is justified by works and not by faith alone; *Galatians* 4:6, which described the sigh of the faithful as "Abba Father"; *John* 6:44, where Jesus explained that no one can come to him unless drawn by the Father; *Ecclesiastes* 9:1, which states that a man does not know whether he is worthy of love or hatred; and *Hebrews* 11:1, where faith is described as the "substance of things hoped for and the evidence of things not seen." On the basis of these verses both Catholic and Protestant theologians struggled to define faith and to understand its role in salvation.

At least as early as Saint Augustine's *Faith, Hope, and Love* (*Enchiridion*), faith was understood within the context of the three theological virtues. Medieval theologians proceeded to define and distinguish between various aspects of faith. Faith was considered from two fundamental perspectives: *fides quae* referred to the content of faith, while *fides qua* referred to the subjective act of faith or that by which one believes. There were other important distinctions that further defined various aspects of faith. *Fides implicita* was the faith appropriate for laypersons and denoted a habitual belief in what the church taught. *Fides explicita* was the conscious or explicit assent of the mind to Catholic truth and was expected of "those responsible for teaching others," the clergy. Aquinas taught, for example, that all Christians were bound to believe explicitly in such articles of faith as the incarnation and the Trinity but only implicitly with regard to other articles of faith. *Fides acquisita* was faith acquired through natural means. *Fides infusa* was the faith supernaturally infused into the soul and comprised one of the three theological virtues. *Fides demonum* was the historical objective faith held even by demons. Of central importance was the distinction between *fides informis* and *fides formata*. Unformed faith was faith not formed by love and able to coexist with mortal sin. Formed faith was faith formed by and active in love (*fides caritate formata*).

The concepts of formed and unformed faith came under the most direct attack in the Reformation. *Romans* 4:9 was interpreted in conjunction with *1 Corinthians* 3:12–15 and *1 Corinthians* 13:13 in order to prove that the faith that saved was a faith active in works of love. The distinction between formed and unformed faith rested on a crucial distinction, made by medieval theologians, between the justice of Christ and the justice of God. The justice of Christ was granted in baptism and renewed in the sacrament of penance. This grace both pardoned past sin and gradually transformed sinners so that they might become pleasing to God. The Christian was a *viator* ("pilgrim") traveling from the justice of Christ toward the final justice of God. Only by cooperating with grace could the Christian do the meritorious works that enabled him to stand before God. To meet the demands of God's final justice, the justice of Christ had to be completed by the righteousness of the believer. In medieval discussions this completion took place whether through the ontological elevation of the individual into a state of grace or through the acceptation of human deeds beyond their intrinsic worth. In any event, only faith formed by love could justify the sinner.

In his study of *Romans* 1:17 Luther discovered the "righteousness of God" was not the righteousness by which God punished sinners but that by which he made the sinner righteous. This exegetical discovery led Luther to believe that the justice of Christ and the justice of God were granted simultaneously. Most importantly, the sinner was justified by faith alone as the life of Abraham and Paul's letters to the Romans and the Galatians made abundantly clear.

The doctrine of justification by faith alone required Luther and his fellow reformers to define the nature of this justifying faith and to distinguish it from the scholastic formulations. It could not be true, for example, that the faith that justified was a mere historical or demon's faith. In fact this saving faith did not conform to any of the traditional categories. Above all else, this faith was not a faith perfected by love; indeed, it was precisely this entanglement of faith and love in formed faith that the reformers were most determined to unravel. They believed the traditional emphasis on love led to the doctrines of merit that had completely undermined the free grace of the gospel. As Luther so pithily stated, "Where they speak of love, we speak of faith."

In order to "speak of faith," Luther frequently turned to *Hebrews* 11:1 and the life of Abraham as recorded in *Genesis* and interpreted by Paul. In these passages he found that the faith that justified was a trust (*fiducia*) in the seemingly impossible promises of God. For Luther, *Hebrews* 11:1 showed that faith was trust in the divine promise even when that promise was hidden under a contrary and contradictory appearance. According to Luther, Abraham was the absolute believer because he consistently believed God's promises no matter how much they contradicted empirical reality, reason, and common sense. Living prior to the law, Abraham was justified not by any work of obedience but because he believed God, who gave him a promise. Luther explained that Abraham's story included nothing about preparation or faith formed by love but only the fact that God spoke and Abraham believed. Therefore, as Luther explained, faith alone was reckoned to Abraham as righteousness. In Luther's theology, believers reenacted Abraham's faith every time they believed God's promise to save by faith despite the remaining traces of sin in the soul. For Luther, trusting God's promise meant that justification rested on faith, not on holiness. To cling to God's word of justification by faith was to trust a promise that contradicted reason, the conscience, and the law.

Luther also specified the Christocentric nature of saving faith. In justification sins were "covered" and the righteousness of Christ was imputed to the believer. The Christian was "reckoned righteous" on the basis of an imputed or alien righteousness, namely, the righteousness of Christ. Luther's most famous analogy for describing how God granted righteousness and freedom to the soul through faith in Christ was the marriage analogy. Using a distinction based on Roman law, Luther distinguished between property and possession. In marriage the property of each partner became the possession of the other. The marriage between Christ and the Christian was effected by faith. The property of Christ, which was righteousness, became the possession of the believer. Likewise, the property of the believer, which was sin, became the possession of Christ. Christ took on human sin and freed the faithful from the curse of the law. The faith that saved the believer, therefore, was always a faith directed to the all-sufficient work of Christ. This justifying faith was a divinely granted ability or gift that enabled the sinner to appropriate the promise of salvation offered only through Christ.

Zwingli and Calvin reiterated many of the same themes found in Luther's discussions about justification by faith. Both stressed the complete sufficiency of Christ's atoning work and concluded that the justice of Christ needed no completion or supplementation by the inherent righteousness of the Christian; faith alone justified the sinner before God. But the doctrine of justification by faith alone bequeathed to the reformers the problem of how to explain the nature and the effect of this saving faith. Always distinguishing the faith that justifies from unformed, acquired, or implicit faith, Reformation theologians attempted to find a new vocabulary that depicted faith as active, as a transformative power that radically changed one's understanding of the relationship to God and to the neighbor. In order to forge this new vocabulary, the reformers had to return to two questions that had long been a part of the theological tradition: What was the relationship between faith and love? And did faith include the certainty of salvation?

Having denied the priority of love in justification, Luther, Zwingli, and Calvin tried to articulate the way in which faith was, indeed, active in love. This problem became increasingly acute after Catholic criticism was leveled at the Protestants and after the outbreak of the antinomian controversy with Johann Agricola (c.1536) and the Lutheran controversy sparked by the publication of Andreas Osiander's treatise *De Justificatione* (1550). Luther had established for Reformation thought that the Christian is justified by faith alone, not by a faith perfected by love. Moreover, he insisted that this faith resulted in a spiritual freedom from the curse of the law. Nonetheless, Luther never identified the freedom of faith as a freedom from good works. On the contrary, he insisted that although good works never contributed to justification, works of love would flow naturally from faith. In the relationship to God, the believer stood in a passive relationship and only received the righteousness of faith. But in the relationship to society, the believer was active toward those who needed good works, namely, the neighbor. In Luther's view, faith was inherently active and would spontaneously result in works of love. Having already been justified by faith, the Christian was finally free to serve the neighbor through an active and living faith.

Zwingli and Calvin also focused on the relationship between faith and works. More so than Luther, they believed that faith needed structure and constant instruction in the will of God. The law, which remained the perfect rule of righteousness, was intended primarily for the life of sanctification. Zwingli argued that the law was the eternal and permanent will of God and was directed to the inner life of the believer. Furthermore, Zwingli explained, the law was comprehended in Paul's words in *Romans* 13:9, "Love thy neighbor as thyself." Therefore *1 Corinthians* 13:3 referred not to justification but sanctification so that those who served under Christ did works of love. Calvin also stressed the importance of the law in the life of faith. The spiritual freedom effected by justification was a faith that manifested itself through obedience to the law. This obedience bridled the mind within the limits of "legitimate worship" and gradually restored the believer to the image of God. While the life of sanctification contributed nothing to the preceding justification, faith nevertheless would be active in repentance and in works of love toward the neighbor. In short, Zwingli and Calvin stressed the rather structured internal change or renewal of human nature wrought by faith.

The transformative power of faith extended not only to the question of faith and love but primarily to one's understanding of God. For Luther, Zwingli, and Calvin, faith transformed the believer's perception of the divine will, thereby granting subjective certainty of salvation. Medieval theology had never granted even to formed faith the subjective certitude of salvation. As *Ecclesiastes* 9:1 stated, no one could know whether he was worthy of love or hatred. Without a special revelation, the Christian could have only an objective and conjectural certainty. The Christian could know with certainty that God would save the elect. Moreover, from the signs of grace in one's own life, the believer could conjecture that he or she was among that elect group. But no final or absolute certainty of salvation was granted to the *viator* before death.

Reformation theology was, in part, a reaction against this uncertainty of salvation. The reformers insisted that justifying faith transformed the individual's perception of the divine will. As Calvin repeatedly stated, it was insufficient to believe that God existed unless one knew the nature of the divine will toward oneself. The Reformed counterpart to *Ecclesiastes* 9:1 was *Galatians* 4:6: "And because you are sons, God has sent the Spirit of his son into your hearts crying 'Abba Father.' " The term *Father* became, for the reformers, a critical epistemological or perceptual term because to see God as Father was not the work of reason or the conscience but only the work of faith. Fundamentally, Luther, Zwingli, and Calvin believed that faith radically changed one's perception of God from an exacting judge to a benevolent and merciful Father. This new perspective was granted in faith by the Holy Spirit, who was the giver of assurance and certainty. As Luther said in his 1535 lectures on *Galatians*, "Now that the plague of uncertainty with which the entire church of the pope is infected, is driven away, let us believe for a certainty that God is favorably disposed toward us. . . ."

Zwingli's clearest exposition of faith is found in his 1530 sermon "On Providence," where he, too, seized on the letter to the Hebrews to explain the nature of faith. His explanation was almost entirely concerned with certainty. Interpreting *Hebrews* 11:1 in conjunction with *Hebrews* 10:22, he defined faith as a "full, clear, and sure knowledge of God and hope in him." Repeatedly Zwingli defined faith in terms of a confidence and security of the soul and a certainty that was inwardly experienced. Zwingli explained this experiential knowledge of faith by stressing the connection between election and faith. He argued that since faith was the gift of the Holy Spirit that followed election, the person who had faith was certain of his or her predestination. For Zwingli the biblical phrase that described the certainty of faith was *John* 6:44: "No one comes to Christ unless the Father draws him."

Calvin also understood faith in terms of an inner knowledge that changed this perception of God's will. Faith was a "sure and firm" knowledge, a "tranquil confidence," a "solid constancy of persuasion," and a "sure and fixed certainty" of God's benevolent will. Calvin's clearest definition of faith occurs in *Christianae religionis Institutio* III.ii.7: "Now we shall possess a right definition of faith if we call it a firm and certain knowledge of God's benevolence toward us, founded upon the truth of the freely given promise in Christ, both revealed to our minds and sealed upon our hearts through the Holy Spirit." Distinguishing Catholic views of faith from that found in scripture, Calvin made a distinction between "uneasy doubting" and "sure tranquillity." According to Calvin, "There is no right faith except when we dare with tranquil hearts to stand in God's sight. This boldness arises only out of a sure confidence in divine benevolence and salvation." Like Luther, Calvin turned to *Galatians* 5:6 to explain that only the saved have the confidence to cry "Abba Father." And, like Luther, Calvin saw in this cry the inner seal of certainty effected in the heart by the Holy Spirit.

Throughout the many sixteenth-century polemics, Catholic theologians challenged this conception of faith. In 1532 Cajetan attacked the "Lutherans" because they enlarged the term *faith* so that it included the conviction by which the sinner approaching the sacrament believed that he or she was justified by divine mercy through Christ. Cajetan insisted that the forgiveness of sins occurred not by unformed faith but by faith informed by charity. In the *Enchiridion*, Johann Eck cited *1 Corinthians* 13:13 to defend the traditional priority of love. Citing *Galatians* 5:6, Eck concluded by arguing that Paul did not say any faith whatsoever sufficed to save the Christian, but only that faith that worked by love.

After the failure of the doctrine of double justification at the Colloquy of Regensburg and the Council of Trent, there was no incentive for Tridentine theologians to enlarge or to change the concept of justifying faith. Thus we find that the Tridentine theologians both rejected justification by faith alone and condemned any notion that faith included the absolute or final certainty of salvation. The decrees of the sixth session of the Council of Trent (1547) made clear that justification included both the remission of sins and the sanctification or inner renewal of the human being. Chapter 7 also explained that only the faith that works through love could justify the sinner. Therefore, faith cooperating with grace in good works increases the justice received through Christ.

Furthermore, in chapter 9 of the sixth session, the Council of Trent condemned the "vain confidence of heretics" who boasted of their confidence and certainty of the remission of sins. According to the Tridentine decree, the demand for holiness and the sinfulness of human nature made such certainty impossible. Therefore, Trent argued that the weakness and sinfulness of human nature required that the Christian may have "fear and apprehension" concerning his or her own grace "since no one can know with the certainty of faith which cannot be subject to error that he has obtained the grace of God." And, lest there be any doubt, canons 9–16 anathematized the doctrine as well as the belief that faith granted the certainty of salvation.

The major reformers, Luther, Zwingli, and Calvin, do not exhaust the Reformation understandings of faith. Thomas Müntzer was the first of a long line of radical Protestant reformers who rejected Luther's notions. As far as Müntzer was concerned, Luther preached an easy or "fictitious" faith, one that relied falsely on the "written Word." It was the "living Word" that provided through the Holy Spirit the true faith. This faith was experiential, entailed suffering, and was given by the Holy Spirit in the abyss of the human soul.

The Anabaptists, in turn, also rejected what they took to be the major reformers' notion of faith, that is, a faith that because it was not existential, does not produce good works in the life of the Christian believer as an inevitable consequence. Perhaps even more importantly these good works had to be visible so that the outer walk of life became an empirical testimonial to the presence of faith. In fact, the Anabaptists' notion of believers' baptism is intricately connected with the notion of visible consequences of faith.

[*See also* Justification.]

BIBLIOGRAPHY

Primary Sources

Barth, Peter, and Wilhelm Miesel, eds. *Ioannis Calvini opera selecta*. 5 vols. Munich, 1926–1936.

Calvin, John. *Institutes of the Christian Religion.* 2 vols. Edited by J. T. McNeill, translated by F. L. Battles. Library of Christian Classics, vols. 20–21. Philadelphia, 1960.

D. Martin Luthers Werke: Kritische Gesamtausgabe. Weimer, 1883–.

Egli, E., et al., eds. *Huldreich Zwinglis sämtliche Werke.* Corpus Reformatorum, vols. 88–. Berlin, Leipzig, Zurich, 1905–.

Luther, Martin. *Luther's Works.* Vol. 26, *Lectures on Galatians, 1535.* Edited by Jaroslav Pelikan. Saint Louis, 1963.

Schuler, M. and J. Schultess, eds. *Huldrich Zwinglis Werke.* 8 vols. Zurich, 1828–1842.

Zwingli, Ulrich. *On Providence.* Edited for Samuel Macauley Jackson by William John Hinkle. Durham, N.C., 1983.

Secondary Sources

Friesen, Abraham. *Thomas Muentzer: A Destroyer of the Godless.* Berkeley, 1990.

Oberman, Heiko A. *Luther: Man between God and the Devil.* Translated by Eileen Walliser-Schwarzbart. New Haven, 1982.

Pelikan, Jaroslav. *The Christian Tradition.* Vol. 3, *Growth of Medieval Theology, 600–1300.* Chicago, 1978.

———. *The Christian Tradition.* Vol. 4, *Reformation of Church and Dogma, 1300–1700.* Chicago, 1984.

Steinmetz, David C. *Luther in Context.* Bloomington, Ind., 1986.

SUSAN E. SCHREINER

FAMILY. The term *family* derives from the Latin *familia*, meaning a household, including servants and kin of the householder. With a few qualifications, this definition, based on a common ancestry, a common dwelling, and a common enterprise, was as familiar to people in the sixteenth century as it is to people today. Whereas modern interpretations, at least in the Western world, focus on the nuclear unit, excluding other inhabitants of the domicile and relegating more distant relatives to a secondary status, reformers understood as family all those sharing the householder's roof and subject to the householder's authority, including spouse, children, servants, and employees. Thus the family of the sixteenth century was and remained a biological, political, social, and economic unit, a community of interests and emotions. The Reformation neither invented nor altered it.

Protestants and other reform-minded individuals perceived, however, a crisis in the family. As proof, they evoked a number of telltale signs: the debasement of domestic life heard in popular tales and allegories; the collapse of public morality reflected in increased litigation; and the particular prejudices of a celibate Catholic clergy communicated in theology and law. Indeed, the family might have seemed an institution under siege.

For Luther and his followers, established religious attitudes were the key to understanding and repairing the disrepute into which marriage and the family had fallen. The elevation of celibacy as an ideal spiritual state drew the Catholic clergy into a posture of sexual hypocrisy that was legendary on the eve of the Reformation. Reports of fallen nuns and fornicating monks entertained taverngoers and outraged reformers across Europe. Moreover, Protestants believed that the praise of celibacy encouraged false fears of family life, concerns regarding its many temptations to sin, and its few opportunities for salvation. There were, after all, precious few married saints. No less problematical than celibacy in their eyes were Catholic marital regulations. On the one hand the doctrine that present consent constituted an indissoluble bond between prospective spouses led directly to a plague of clandestine marriages that weakened parental authority and debilitated the domestic economy. On the other hand the canon of marital impedimenta complicated the creation of valid unions and encouraged complaint and litigation that ruined many otherwise acceptable relationships. Corrupted by sin and graft, marriage no longer conformed to a Christian institution.

Against the degradation of family life, Protestants raised the contractual marriage and the patriarchal family. Men and women entered a relationship by mutual consent and with explicit knowledge of the community for the express purposes of begetting children and keeping house. Within this union and the household and family that followed it, all members were subject to the benign authority of the husband-father-master. Marriage and family replaced celibacy as the divinely ordained setting for a Christian life and salvation.

Catholic reformers and preachers had praised marriage and family as worthy callings for men and women throughout the Middle Ages. The Bamburger canon Albrecht von Eyb idealized them in his small encomium *Ehebüchlein* (1472) in sentimental terms of complete amity and unity. Aware of the need to capture the experience of their listeners as the basis of effective homiletics, fifteenth-century penitential preachers especially discussed family life in highly realistic and sympathetic terms that Protestants would appropriate a century later.

What set the efforts of Protestant reformers apart was the merit attributed to marriage and family relative to celibacy. Even those Catholic intellectuals who were willing to see the family in positive terms bowed to the force of tradition and insisted that celibacy was the higher spiritual state. Ignatius Loyola urged his followers to praise matrimony highly but chastity more highly (*Esercitii Spirituali*, 1548). Beginning with Luther, reformers countered that celibacy was a gift of God, but a gift reserved for those few saints blessed with the fortitude to live lives of abstinence. More excellent was marriage, divinely ordained as the sole setting in which human sexuality could be practiced without sin. Luther made clear that God created and ordained that men and women were inescapably driven by their natures to be fruitful and multiply and that people must marry, therefore, to keep from falling into unchastity, fornication, and adultery (*Vom ehelichen Leben*, 1522). People who felt unsuited for lives of celibacy—and that was nearly everybody—should marry immediately in the faith that this was consistent with God's will and that God would provide both spouse and sustenance.

All sixteenth-century reformers followed Luther's lead. Both Zwingli and Calvin adopted language highly reminiscent of Luther's, rejecting celibacy and accepting marriage and family as an ideal spiritual estate. Radical reformed sects, especially the Anabaptists, developed their own theory of a covenantal marriage quite distinct from the contractual union of their church opponents but agreed that marriage was to be preferred to celibacy and that its highest good was the increase of the community of the faithful.

Yet the dictum that all people should marry to avoid the sins of the flesh hardly served as a functional, positive model of familial life. It remained, therefore, for those pastors charged with the care of souls to develop and disseminate a detailed image of the Christian family, one that incorporated the ideal but corresponded to the real. From the vast corpus of published marriage sermons (*Ehepredigten* and *Ehebücher*) and housekeeping handbooks (the so-called *hausväterliche Literatur*) the family emerged as an affective unit, a social unit, and an economic unit.

Modern scholars have long sought to identify the modern family in terms of the emotional ties binding its various members. Thus the premodern family was thought to be largely without affection. Various reasons have been alleged, depending on which factors were thought to dictate the texture of domestic life. High infant mortality increased both the risks of childbearing and the frequency of loss, supposedly encouraging parents to shield themselves from grief by maintaining a certain detachment from their children. Or the highly elastic, subsistence economy that characterized the period encouraged the selection of spouses based on economic calculation. Alternatively, political uncertainties and ambitions made marriage an implement of clan solidarity and alliance. Not until the early modern period—sometime between 1500 and 1800—with the emergence of expansive demographic and economic regimes, the absolute state's enforcement of political stability, and the Reformation's emphasis on amicable domestic relationships—did affection and emotion come to predicate family life.

All these observations have some truth. Yet calculation has never precluded love. Many kinds of evidence testify directly to the abiding fondness between spouses and between parents and children and to the palpable devastation caused by their deaths.

Protestant reformers assumed a degree of affection within the family. In a sermon on *Genesis* 2:18–24 Luther described a wife as a companionable helpmate to her husband. Noting the symbolism of Christ and church, Zwingli wrote that husband and wife should particularly love and tolerate one another. Calvin concurred, urging spouses to treat one another soberly and modestly as befit Christians.

These are tepid testimonials at best, and they raise the question of meaning. For example, the cloying, demonstrative affection of von Eyb's *Ehebüchlein*, with its sweet kisses and domestic monadism, is far removed from the restrained, stylized amity of Calvin's *Institutes.* Yet the leading reformers of the sixteenth century had something less rarified and more humane in mind. They identified affection not with physical attraction, which could not form the pretext for an enduring Christian relationship, but instead with shared experience and common values.

The vast printed literature on marriage and family echoed these values. For example, Cyriakus Spangenberg, a conservative Lutheran pastor, wrote in his *Haußtafel* (1567) that husband and wife should love (*lieben*) one another and that their love should be strictly monogamous. Fidelity was understood both on the basis of Protestant teachings with regard to human sexuality and on the basis of the gospel's mandate against adultery. In his closer exploration of the mutual affection of husband and wife, Spangenberg cast it more fully in terms of moral and material responsibilities. A husband should care for his wife and her property; he should provide for her and rule over her; and he should instruct her in her domestic duties and see that she carried them out. A wife should obey, fear, honor, and support her husband. Parents owed their children material sustenance, Christian instruction, and reasonable correction. To this, children should respond with gratitude, obedience, submission, and patience. Yet Spangenberg and most other pastors understood love not merely in terms of a system of arid duties and debts. Physical attraction and emotional dependence were a natural part of these relationships but were neither discussed nor encouraged because of their basis in sin. Hence attention turned to those other elements of domestic life that also contributed to the solidarity and affection of a family. Love did not precede marriage and the family but rather developed within them.

Love developed within the context of the husband's authority as well. Spangenberg called on husbands to rule (*regieren*) and instruct their wives and on fathers to instruct and correct their children. Wives and children were bound by their duty to obey, honor, and fear the paterfamilias. Although his authority was absolute, it was not unlimited. The responsibilities to love, improve, and sustain those within his domain limited his power as patriarch. Unrestrained abuse or violence had no place in a Christian family; recourse to these things yielded to reason and equity. Physical punishments served only as a last resort because "with beating, brawling, and raging one accomplishes little."

However limited or moderated and regardless of its success or failure, patriarchy clearly served the purposes of the Protestant Reformation. The renewal of family life, intended by Luther and others, relied very much on the ability of the householder to govern all within his walls. To this end, every reformer argued the virtues of paternal authority. Johannes

Coler put the matter simply in his *Oeconomia* (1592): "The household is a monarchy . . . only one rules." Only under the patriarch's firm but mild hand could the family and household prosper spiritually and materially. Without his guidance, constantly instructing and correcting, neither wife nor children nor servants would stay firm in the discipline and piety that were to be the heart of family life. Without his direction, assigning work and exercising ceaseless vigilance over its completion, that community of fortune and solidarity of enterprise that alone assured the family's survival and prosperity would be lost. Thus patriarchy was key to the family's role as a social and as an economic unit.

In the sixteenth century families were the fundamental unit of society. They formed the basis for political representation, fiscal planning, public work, and legal accountability. But they were more than simple components of the whole. The family also spun webs of symmetrical social relations. These amounted to networks of power and obligation, simultaneously connecting the members of a single household and the households of a neighborhood or community. The prescribed purpose of these relationships was twofold: the acculturation of individuals and their integration in society.

Protestant reformers understood the function of the family in terms of accustoming persons to established authority and aligning their behavior with accepted standards. By word and deed, father and mother, master and mistress instructed all those under their sway. They provided guidance to children and servants in every facet of human discourse, from Christian doctrine and social mores to household chores and artisanal techniques.

The family was the first school of religion. Before the young began catechism their parents introduced them to the rhythms of life within a church. The ideal Christian family prayed at home, attended worship services, and set a model for Christian comportment every day. Children were a gift of God; parents had to teach them their faith.

The family was also the first school of society. In his *Hausfrid* (1553), the Lutheran pastor Paulus Rebhun observed that peaceful parents brought forth peaceful children, who became in turn peaceful citizens. The ideal citizen was nothing other than the housefather who ruled his wife with reason, his children with authority, and his servants with dominion in order to create a household in which all were modest and obedient. Submission to superior authority was the express duty of every Christian.

The family was the first school of economy as well. Spangenberg wrote in terms of a familial hierarchy: the husband instructed his wife in all matters of housekeeping and managed the household as a whole; the wife trained her servants and children in the necessary skills and saw that they completed their specific tasks; the servants and children avoided idleness and accepted correction willingly. This division of domestic labor encouraged discipline and industry, preparing the young for lives of work and self-sufficiency. The family inculcated those qualities and skills that preserved and perpetuated the family itself over a lifetime and over generations.

The process of acculturation also served to integrate the family to the society of which it was a part. Not just the authority of husband over wife or parent over child but rather all authority in the sixteenth century was thought to be patriarchal, modeled on the relationship between God and his creation. Spangenberg's *Haußtafel* included chapters on the clergy and the laity, on rulers and their subjects, and on masters and their laborers; the same ideals governing relations in the domestic hierarchy governed relations in the social hierarchy. The duties of honor, obedience, deference, and submission applied in the world with the same force that they applied in the household. In short, the society Protestants sought to reform and renew reified those relations forged and fostered in the family.

Although reformers stressed the duties implicit in family life, the relations they prescribed were, in fact, always reciprocal. Members were bound by sets of mutual obligations. Spangenberg organized his entire treatise in the form of a discourse between superiors and inferiors—how those in authority should behave and how those under authority should respond. Thus domestic paternalism would be limited by its mutuality. This applied as well to the ranked society of orders of which the family was a part. Succeeding generations were to be molded from infancy to display deference, obedience, and subservience, but they would also be accustomed to protection, sustenance, and solicitude.

Ironically, Protestant prescriptive literature had revolutionary implications despite its reactionary purpose. The reformers had intended to stabilize family life by promoting the authority of the paterfamilias. As they empowered him with rights, however, they bound him with responsibilities and suggested that a failure to fulfill the latter substantially abrogated the former. Because social and political authority in the age of the Reformation were understood in the same terms, its holders commanded deference and submission only so long as they protected and sustained their subjects. Failure to do so violated their God-given offices and exposed them to understandable if not forgivable resistance. The long litany of riot and rebellion in the sixteenth century—from walkouts to bread riots to husband beatings to peasant revolts—bears eloquent testimony to the real limitations of patriarchy and to the frailty of those who wielded it. It is altogether possible that families were staging grounds for defiance as well as obedience, something no moralist or theologian of that age would have countenanced.

Whether the family successfully fulfilled its social function of acculturation and integration cannot be determined. Much evidence exists, however, to suggest that its efficacy was limited. As noted, legal records are replete with domestic disputes of every sort and give no evidence of increased discipline or morality after the Reformation. Studies of Protestant church visitations have unearthed a wealth of testimony to the irreligion, violence, and neglect of domestic life in the sixteenth century. Even the plague of witchcraft persecutions, which victimized unmarried and elderly women above all, may be traced in part to a failure of the family to provide for its marginal members. Many instances can be cited in defense of the reformed family as a social unit, but the preaching of Protestants remained prescriptive rather than descriptive.

One marriage sermon noted that parents should give their children four things, not least of which was material sustenance. Though Luther explicitly deprecated the significance attached to property, urging people to wed regardless and trust to Providence, other reformers seem to have grasped its importance in family life. They understood the family among other things as a community of fortune, an economic unit characterized ideally by a solidarity of enterprise, an emphasis on accumulation, and the imperative of work.

All members of the family, including servants and employees, labored to the same end and drew their sustenance from the same source. Spangenberg insisted that even household servants (*Gesinde*) work industriously and loyally, that is, that they consider their master's property and prosperity as their own. In return, the employer ought to be fair: he should never tyrannize his servants and should give promptly what he owed them. This principle applied no less to the narrower family circle, where parents were to instill a habit of work in the young such that they would eventually become self-supporting and independent, and children were to complete such tasks as they were given readily and willingly.

Yet, though all labored alike, not all labor was alike. All observers and commentators of the sixteenth century recognized and recommended Aristotle's basic division of labor, in which women restricted their activities to the domestic sphere and left market activities to their men. These statements acknowledged, however, that wives were intimately engaged in the family business, buying raw materials, laboring in the shops, selling finished products, and occasionally wielding the authority of masters in their own right. Pastors and preachers regardless of confession found such behavior inappropriate. These tasks belonged rightly to the housefather alone. He bore the responsibility of providing for the family; with it came the right to assign tasks and to distribute resources. Thus solidarity of enterprise was an economic expression of the patriarchy that marked all domestic relations.

The singleness of purpose that united the ideal Christian household provided not only for present necessities but also against future exigencies. Solidarity of enterprise, therefore, served more than the need for basic subsistence. It also made possible the goal of accumulation that characterized the community of fortune.

Sermon literature constantly emphasized the need for thrift and frugality. Moderation in food and clothing, work and rest, and discipline and indulgence served to extend the family economy. To accumulate (*erübrigen*) was a frequent term in the writings of domestic moralists. Coler noted that the ideal household accumulated its resources in order to provide for its members and to serve its church and its community. Rebhun referred to the example of Christ and the Church to argue the sanctity of frugality that enabled a housefather to provide for his family during his life and after his death regardless of his status or wealth. Even Spangenberg praised material thrift, providing adequately but not excessively, as the mundane expression of a spiritual thrift that hindered anger and violence. In frugality, then, the Christian family possessed a sure means of survival, a way to accumulate property and secure its well-being without the risk of damnation.

If accumulation relied on frugality, it also required work. In fact, work was the activity that most clearly defined the family of the sixteenth century. For all reformers, it was the basis of such affection as existed between husband and wife or parents and children. Spangenberg and others never tired of referring to the fondness that was born of common enterprises and burdens, of shared joys and sorrows. Work also determined the social position and function of the family. The housefather's trade had much to do with his status and the status of his dependents in their community. Furthermore, much of the acculturation and integration that occurred within the household took the form of precise duties or obligations carried out within a traditional division of labor. Coler urged that wives, servants, and children be kept from idleness in order that they might grow and improve in sobriety, frugality, sincerity, and honesty (*Nüchternheit*, *Sparsamkeit*, *Aufrichtigkeit*, and *Redlichkeit*). In the young the habit of industry would eventually bring those social benefits that were the quintessence of citizenship: self-sufficiency, property, and domesticity. Finally, work identified the family as an economic unit. It united members in a common endeavor, provided for their needs, and contributed to their wealth and property. The master's trade determined some of the tasks carried out by members of the household. A weaver might set his family and servants to work, spinning and soaking thread, warping looms, or even weaving cloth. A shopkeeper or merchant might rely on his family to keep accounts, sell goods, or deliver sales. Beyond certain profession-specific variations, however, all families participated to a greater or lesser extent in the activities of shop or store. The family understood itself and was understood as a unit of production and, more modestly perhaps, consumption in the age of the Reformation.

The ultimate goal of a family's labor was always property

in some form and measure. Property constituted a household's only material security in an age of unstable economies. It was also an essential reflection of status in a ranked society of orders. Perhaps most importantly for the people of that period, property assured a family's continuity over time. Transferred between generations in the form of dowries and inheritances, it was an enduring monument to the previous generation's energy and expertise, a gift of fortune to posterity.

The transfer of property serves as a reminder that the family was before all else a demographic unit. The emotional texture, social function, and economic activity of any household were influenced directly by its size and shape, which were determined in turn by the forces of nuptiality, fertility, and mortality.

Scholars have pointed to the so-called European pattern of marriage, that is, the high instance of celibacy and relative late age at marriage among young men and women, as one reason for the small size of families in the Western world and for their proclivity to accumulate capital. Because women tended to marry late or not at all, the probability of their bearing children was lower and their period at risk tended to be limited to the ages after peak fecundity. Hence reduced nuptiality among Western women tended to lower fertility and limit family size despite a regime of natural fertility.

Once fertility behavior began, children tended to be born about every eighteen months to two years. Internatal periodicity seems to have been largely a function of abstinence, primitive contraception (chiefly *coitus interruptus*), and amenorrhea due to nursing. Even with delayed marriages and repressed or sublimated sexuality, however, fertility on this level would have produced catastrophically large families were it not for socially determined patterns of mortality and rearing.

Infant and child mortality was universally high in the sixteenth century but especially so among poor and rural families, a function of child-rearing practices marked by primitive hygiene and incomplete nutrition. Though generally urged by medical and moral philosophers as well as by midwives and doctors as the best protection against the dangers of disease and malnutrition, maternal nursing was not universally practiced. There is little agreement as to how widespread wetnursing was, but it seems clear that families at all levels of society sought these services, some driven by the need to work and secure a livelihood, others compelled by the dictates of class and custom. How this altered family size—for it both increased mortality and increased fecundity—has not been explained fully. The consequences of rearing are somewhat clearer. Infants may or may not have been put out to nurse, but children in general spent a relatively limited time—perhaps no more than ten years—in the bosoms of their families. In elite families these young people might have been cossetted and indulged but in artisanal families they were more frequently put to work in household and workshop or left to their own devices. By the age of twelve to fifteen most girls had been placed in service and boys apprenticed, thus permanently abandoning their biological parents and becoming *famulae* (*-i*) in their masters' households. Subject to so wide an array of factors, therefore, family size tended to vary extraordinarily according to status, occupation, and life cycle, making generalizations about this period all but useless.

Adult mortality also affected both the size and content of the family. For example, the disparity of ages at marriage between men and women, especially among urban families, often meant that one spouse died, leaving the other to support their children and possibly to remarry. Traditions of rough music aimed at couples of too dissimilar ages, the popular ballads and broadsides satirizing these unions, and the folkloric tradition of the evil step-parent all testify that this was a regular demographic feature of the early modern household. Thus not only natural and human catastrophes, which were all too common at the time, but simple biological processes conspired to dissolve families. Whether these circumstances prevented the development of emotional attachments, as some have alleged, is doubtful. But they must have made material loss and emotional bereavement familiar experiences. It is no surprise, therefore, that needy widows and orphans were universally acknowledged as deserving poor. Certainly the vast majority of families in the sixteenth century must have passed through phases of truncation and reformation.

The sixteenth century witnessed plagues, epidemics, and warfare, all of which transformed the family at least temporarily by changing rates of nuptiality, fertility, and mortality. Nonetheless, scholars have not succeeded in comprehending exactly how or why households responded to these phenomena as they did. By the same token, statements that the Reformation created the modern family or even altered the premodern family are not persuasive unless the nature of the modern family is clearly defined and the evidence of it is unequivocally identified. The notion that the Reformation somehow sanctified the family through a corpus of prescriptive literature must be rejected, therefore, without some indication of the reception of these ideals. Luther and his followers merely moved marriage to the center of a stylized religious life and made the family an object of concern and consideration. In this, at least, the Reformation succeeded.

[*See also* Celibacy and Virginity; Marriage; *and* Women.]

BIBLIOGRAPHY

Davis, Natalie Z. "Ghosts, Kin, and Progeny: Some Features of Family Life in Early Modern France." *Daedalus* 106 (Spring 1977), 87–117. Fascinating and useful essay on the family as a cultural institution.

Demos, John. *A Little Commonwealth: Family Life in Plymouth Colony.* New York, 1970. Most recent study of Puritan family life uses techniques of social and cultural history to extend findings of Morgan and others.

Goody, Jack. *The Development of the Family and Marriage in Europe.* Cambridge, 1983. Anthropological study of changing cultural and social aspects of marriage.

Herlihy, David, and Christiane Klapisch-Zuber. *Tuscans and Their Families: A Study of the Florentine Catasto of 1427.* Chicago, 1976. This is a path-breaking statistical study of urban families during the Renaissance.

Howell, Martha. *Women, Production and Patriarchy in Late Medieval Cities.* Chicago, 1986. Close study of women in the labor forces of several late medieval cities; useful for insights on connection between marriage and women's work.

Hunt, David. *Parents and Children in History.* New York, 1970. Psychohistorical study of childhood and childrearing during the medieval and early modern period, above all in France.

Klapisch-Zuber, Christiane. *Women, Family, and Ritual in Renaissance Italy.* Chicago, 1985. Applies the statistical findings on Tuscan families to social and cultural issues with particular relevance to women in and out of the family.

Laslett, Peter. *The World We Have Lost.* London, 1965. Path-breaking call to assess the demographic and economic realities of family life as the basis for further study of the experience of family life.

———. *Family Life and Illicit Love in Earlier Generations.* Corr. ed. Cambridge, 1980. Collection of essays applies and extends the techniques urged in *The World We Have Lost.*

Laslett, Peter, ed. *Household and Family in Past Time.* Cambridge, 1974. Collection of essays on aspects of demographic history of the family between the Middle Ages and the modern age.

Levine, David. *Family Formation in an Age of Nascent Capitalism.* New York, 1977. Demographic study of the early modern marriage and family using the techniques of family reconstitution on English parishes.

———. *Reproducing Families: The Political Economy of English Population History.* Cambridge, 1987. Essay argues persuasively that family structure is determined largely by changes in work processes and economic systems.

Medick, Hans, and David Sabean, eds. *Interest and Emotion: Essays on the Study of Family and Kinship.* Cambridge, 1984. Collection of essays questions from a variety of perspectives the traditional assumption that interest and emotion were irreconcilable in the premodern family.

Mitterauer, Michael, and Reinhard Sieder. *The European Family: Patriarchy to Partnership from the Middle Ages to the Present.* Chicago, 1983. Very useful overview of current scholarship on marriage and family.

Ozment, Steven E. *When Fathers Ruled: Family Life in Reformation Europe.* Cambridge, Mass., 1983. Study of marriage and family as objects of reform weakened by reliance on prescriptive literature.

Roper, Lyndal. *The Holy Household: Women and Morals in Reformation Augsburg.* Oxford, 1989. Recent study of the consequences for women of the Reformation in Augsburg offers interesting insights on the extension of patriarchy and its impact on family life.

Safley, Thomas Max. *Let No Man Put Asunder: The Control of Marriage in the German Southwest; A Comparative Study, 1550–1600.* Kirksville, Mo., 1984. Concise study of impact of Protestant and Reformed legislation on the institutions of marriage and family in Catholic and Protestant communities in southern Germany and Switzerland.

Shorter, Edward. *The Making of the Modern Family.* New York, 1975. Classic statement on emergence of modern family that places too much emphasis on affection and sexuality and is weakened by gender biases.

Stone, Lawrence. *The Family, Sex and Marriage in England, 1500–1800.* New York, 1977. Monumental study of marriage and family in early modern England sets the terms of the debate over the history of the modern family.

Wiesner, Merry. *Working Women in Renaissance Germany.* New Brunswick, N.J., 1986. A study of the changing status of women in the workshops and marketplaces of German cities with conclusions on the domestic economy of the family in the sixteenth century.

Wrigley, E. A., ed. *An Introduction to English Historical Demography.* London, 1966. Essential overview of the demographic history of early modern England with essential findings on marriage and family life.

THOMAS MAX SAFLEY

FAMILY OF LOVE. This religious sect was founded by the spiritualist prophet and visionary Hendrik Niclaes (1502–1580) during the 1540s. Niclaes believed that a second fall of humanity had followed Christ's sacrifice on the cross, and the last age of time had arrived in which God had sent Niclaes as another "new man" to enlighten the world and make humankind once again one with God. All who failed to answer this last call to righteousness would be damned, Niclaes believed.

Born in Westphalia, Niclaes lived in Amsterdam from 1531 to 1540. He claimed to have received a revelation from God that led him to found the Family of Love. God instructed Niclaes to take three elders, write down the truth, go to a land of piety, and proclaim the kingdom of love. Niclaes moved to Emden, where he lived for twenty years as a wealthy merchant, wrote his first works, and organized his followers into a religious community. He traveled widely on business, spreading his religious ideas as he broadened his commercial contacts. The Family of Love (also called House, Service, or Community of Love) was originally an open group that recognized Niclaes as inspired prophet and messiah. Members met together to educate each other through the reading and discussion of Niclaes's works and to attempt to achieve a perfect imitation of Christ that would lead to *vergoding*—the union with God that Niclaes had achieved.

The Family of Love included members from various confessions, and its purpose was to prepare for a new age in which religious ceremonies would be meaningless and humankind would once again be one with God. The sect was intended as a model of what the true community of believers would be like in the new age of love: a nonconfessional institution ruled by toleration, love of neighbor, mutual admonishment, and mutual aid. From Niclaes's own wealth and bequests left to the sect by admirers, a large fund of money was collected that was used to support the printing of Niclaes's works and the spread of his ideas. From this chest loans were made to members in professional distress, including purely commercial loans. Niclaes originally saw the community as an invisible church uniting all true believers, with its organization secret because the outside world was not yet in agreement with its ideas. He himself remained a Catholic and like other members continued to attend the services and to follow the practices of his own confessional group until the Family of Love replaced it.

One of Niclaes's earliest followers was Hendrik Jansen van Barrefelt, an Anabaptist weaver from Gelderland who lived with Niclaes in Emden and supervised the printing and distribution of his writings. Another early follower was Augustine van Hasselt, a Münsterite Anabaptist whom Niclaes saved from poverty in Groningen and set up as a printer of Familist works. In 1555 Christoffel Plantijn set up a press in Antwerp with the financial backing of Niclaes and became the major printer of the prophet's works until 1566. A humanist circle gathered around Plantijn that was influenced by Niclaes and formed a center for Familism in Antwerp. The Familism of the Antwerp humanists was not, however, Niclaes's doctrine in its original and pure form. Plantijn and his friends rejected ceremonies and adopted the ideal of the invisible church, along with an ethical code based on Christian precepts but not bound by any specific confessional position. They were willing to overlook Niclaes's claims to divine inspiration and obedience, which they found distasteful, in favor of his ideal of religious concord.

In 1570 Niclaes moved to Cologne, partly in response to a new revelation that instructed him to go to a "land of peace" with twenty-four elders to revise his writings and better organize his sect. In Cologne Niclaes organized the Family of Love into a visible church on the model of Rome, with a priestly heirarchy headed by himself as infallible bishop, along with a system of tithes, religious services, fast days, and special religious assemblies. This transformation of the sect led to a split in 1573 when Barrefelt, Plantijn, van Hasselt, Hubert Duifhuis, and Cornelis Jansen questioned Niclaes's claim to divine inspiration and demand for exclusive obedience and criticized his new emphasis on externals. Barrefelt upheld the ideal of the invisible church and went on to elaborate his own spiritualistic ideas in a series of writings after 1573. Most of the Antwerp humanists followed Barrefelt in his break with Niclaes, who continued to write and to gather followers in Cologne. The death of Niclaes in 1580, Plantijn in 1589, and Barrefelt in about 1594 effectively brought an end to Familism on the Continent, although some groups remained active in England until 1606.

BIBLIOGRAPHY

Hamilton, Alastair. *The Family of Love.* Cambridge, 1981. The only book-length overview of the subject.

Heal, Felicity. "The Family of Love in the Diocese of Ely." *Studies in Church History* 9 (1972), 213–222.

Hitchcock, J. A. "A Confession of the Family of Love." *Bulletin of the Institute of Historical Research* 43 (1970), 85.

Kirsop, Wallace. "The Family of Love in France." *Journal of Religious History* 3 (1964), 103–118.

Martin, F. L. "The Family of Love in England: Conforming Millenarians." *Sixteenth Century Journal* 3.2 (1972), 99–108.

Moss, Jean Dietz. "Additional Light on the Family of Love." *Bulletin of the Institute of Historical Research* 67 (1974), 103–105.

———. "Variations on a Theme: The Family of Love in Renaissance England." *Renaissance Quarterly* 31 (1978), 186–196.

ANDREW FIX

FAREL, Guillaume (1489–1565), pioneering French reformer. Born in 1489 in Gap, in southeastern France, Farel studied in Paris under J. Lefèvre d'Étaples and became a teacher in the Collège Cardinal Lemoine. Although not a priest, he took part in the evangelization of the Meaux diocese from 1521; but in 1523, finding the Meaux reform not radical enough, he moved to Basel, where he demanded a disputation. He and Desiderius Erasmus developed a mutual hostility; it is believed that Erasmus persuaded the city government to have Farel expelled. Farel went to Montbéliard, where he preached and celebrated Communion (his "ordination" being based on divine vocation, the call of Johannes Oecolampadius, and that of Duke Ulrich of Württemberg, count of Montbéliard). From there he went to Metz and Strasbourg, where he met the Strasbourg reformers. In 1527 he set up as a teacher in Aigle, which is now in the Swiss canton of Vaud but was then a Bernese "colony"; here he began the evangelization of French-speaking Switzerland. A peripatetic mission led him to Lausanne, Orbe, Grandson, Yverdon, and Neuchâtel; after a sometimes violent campaign he persuaded the citizens of Neuchâtel to adopt the Reformation (1530). In 1532 he made his first visit to Geneva and only just escaped with his life. At the Synod of Chanforans, in Piedmont, he brought the Waldensians fully into the Reformation movement and collected eight hundred crowns from them to finance the production of a Bible in French.

Several visits to Geneva culminated in a disputation in the convent of Rive in June 1535, the suspension of Roman Catholic worship in August 1535, the destruction of images, and, on 21 May 1536, the adoption of the Reformation by the General Council of Geneva. Two months later it was Farel who persuaded John Calvin to join in the task of reforming the city. Farel led the deputation of reformers at the Dispute of Lausanne in October 1536, which led to the establishment of the Reformation in that city and the surrounding region of Vaud. In Geneva Farel and Calvin drew up draft versions of *Ecclesiastical Ordinances* and *Confession of Faith* (1537), which, the council decreed, should be sworn to by all inhabitants of the city. The measure was highly unpopular and contributed to the election in February 1538 of four *syndics* (chief magistrates) hostile to the pastors. When the city authorities ordered the pastors to conform to Bernese eucharistic practices, Farel and Calvin refused to celebrate Communion on Easter Sunday 1538, and they were banished from Geneva.

In July 1538 Farel was invited to become pastor of Neuchâtel; he remained in that post for twenty-seven years until his death. He maintained close contacts with the leaders of the south German and Swiss Reformation through his extensive correspondence, and he made frequent journeys to numerous Reformed communities in Switzerland, Germany, and France to give advice and support. It was an illness contracted at the age of 76 on a winter journey to Metz, in northern France, that led to his death.

Farel was the pioneer of the French Reformation in many respects. From Meaux to Geneva and Neuchâtel via Strasbourg and Metz, he was involved in the beginnings of the Reformation. He wrote the first French Reformation tract (*Pater noster et le credo en français*, 1524), the first extensive statement of Reformed doctrine in French (*Sommaire et briefve declaration*, c.1529), and the first French Reformed liturgy (*Maniere et fasson*, 1528?). He had a remarkable gift for recruiting the right helper for the right place: he installed the first printer devoted to the Reformation cause in Neuchâtel, (Pierre de Wingle) in 1533 and the first Reformed printer in Geneva (Jean Girard), in 1536. He persuaded Pierre Viret and Calvin to become pastors, in 1531 and 1536, respectively. He is the true father of the French Reformation.

Farel was a preacher of deep spirituality and passionate eloquence, though none of his sermons survive. He lacked the intellectual incisiveness of Calvin and willingly advised the readers of his *Sommaire* to turn to Calvin's *Institutes* instead. His doctrines were close to those of Huldrych Zwingli: his Communion liturgy (in the *Maniere et fasson*), and his eucharistic teaching (for example, in *De la tressaincte cene de nostre Seigneur*, c.1532, attributed to him and Viret), lay stress on the Lord's Supper as a memorial of Christ's sacrifice and an expression of the unity of the faithful. After Calvin joined him in Geneva, he wrote the revised edition of the liturgy (*Ordre et maniere*, 1538) which added the concept of the communication of Christ's spiritual body and blood (probably under the influence of Calvin). His bibliography runs to fifteen titles, all in French. Most of his writings are verbose and poorly constructed; his *Sommaire*, however, with its brief, assertive chapters, remains a clear statement of the main points at issue in the early Reformation. One of the purest expressions of the spirituality and devotional ardor of the reformers is his *Pater noster* (Lord's Prayer), composed in the form of a prayer while being at the same time a commentary on the Lord's Prayer and Apostles' Creed (the latter translated and adapted from Martin Luther's *Betbüchlein;* it is the first known translation of Luther into French). With discreet modifications to tone down the doctrinal emphases on the total depravity of man and justification by faith alone, Farel's text became the basis of a popular French Catholic devotional tract, the *Livre de vraye et parfaicte oraison,* which had at least fifteen editions before 1545.

BIBLIOGRAPHY

Primary Sources

Farel, Guillaume. *Le Pater noster et le credo en françois*. Edited by F. Higman. Textes littéraires Français no. 306. Geneva, 1982. Farel's first and most widely read work. The introduction traces the history of editions of the text.

———. *Summaire et briefve declaration d'aucuns lieux fort necessaires à ung chascun chrestien pour mettre sa fiance en Dieu et ayder son prochain.* Edited by Arthur-L. Hofer. Neuchâtel, 1980. Gives the original text, and a transcription into modern French, on facing pages. A brief but useful introduction.

Secondary Sources

Barthel, Pierre, Rémy Scheurer, and Richard Stauffer, eds. *Actes du colloque Guillaume Farel, Neuchâtel, 29 septembre-1er octobre 1980*. 2 vols. Cahiers de la Revue de Théologie et de Philosophie no. 9. Geneva, 1983. Collection of articles on Farel's contacts with other reformers, his thought, and (vol. 2) a repertory of Farel's correspondence and bibliography of his printed works which entirely supersedes the information in the *Farel Biography.*

Guillaume Farel, 1489–1565: Biographie nouvelle écrite . . . par un groupe d'historiens, professeurs et pasteurs de Suisse, de France et d'Italie. Neuchâtel, 1930. Basic biographical source, richly illustrated, with good bibliography of Farel studies since the seventeenth century. Needs to be supplemented and updated by reference to Bartel et al.

Higman, Francis. "Dates-clé de la réforme française: Le *Sommaire* de Guillaume Farel et *La Somme de l'escripture saincte.*" In *Bibliothèque d'Humanisme et Renaissance* 38 (1976), 237–247. Shows by bibliographical evidence that the edition of Farel's *Sommaire,* described on the title page as being from "Turin, 1525" actually dates from c.1533; several important consequences from this change of dating.

Jacobs, Elfriede. *Die Sakramentslehre Wilhelm Farels.* Zurich, 1978. Studies of Farel's theology are so rare that even partial ones need mention. Thorough study of Farel's sacramental theology, situating him in relation to Zwingli and Calvin.

FRANCIS HIGMAN

FARNESE, Alessandro (1468–1549). See Paul III.

FARNESE, Alessandro (1542–1592), duke of Parma and governor-general of the Netherlands. Born in Rome on 27 August 1545, he was the son of Ottavio Farnese and Margaret of Parma (daughter of Emperor Charles V). He went to the court of King Philip II in 1556, and in 1565 he married Princess Maria of Portugal. In the struggle against the Turks, he distinguished himself in 1571 during the battle near Lepanto (Návpaktos). In 1577 Farnese was sent by Philip II of Spain with an army to the Netherlands, and after the death of John of Austria (1 October 1578), he was appointed governor-general and commander of the Spanish army. When he took office, he controlled only the regions of Namur and Luxembourg and a number of recently reconquered Brabant cities.

Against the governor-general stood a moderately rebellious but primarily Catholic group in Walloon Flanders, Artois, and Hainaut (the "Malcontents") and also the States-General, which were trying to keep all Netherlands provinces united but were under strong pressure from radical Calvinists. Farnese handily took advantage of the opposition between the "malcontent" Catholic Walloon nobles and the radical Protestant groups in Flanders and tried to take the wind out of the sails of the States-General by reconciling a number of prominent Catholic Walloon nobles to the king. Finally the Walloon regions made peace with the king in the Treaty of Arras (May 1579).

Philip II's appointment of Margaret of Parma governess-general in the Netherlands in March 1580 led to a conflict between mother and son, as Alessandro insisted on having both the governorship and the military command. When Philip relented by naming him to both posts again (1582) and Margaret returned to Italy (1583), Alessandro embarked on a campaign to recapture the most important cities of Flanders and Brabant. This *reconquista* reached its zenith with the capitulation of Antwerp (17 August 1585). The Protestant residents of Antwerp were given four years to become Catholics or to emigrate. Those who did emigrate could take with them their possessions. After the fall of Antwerp, the royal troops scored some further successes, but then military operations came more or less to a halt. In 1586–1588 Farnese was actively involved in peace negotiations with England, but this conference failed when the English learned in the summer of 1588 that Philip II had not given up his plans to attack. Farnese had to call off an offensive to conquer the rebellious areas in the north in order to keep his troops ready to support the action of the Spanish "invincible fleet" against England (Spanish Armada; summer 1588). The failure of this expedition was an enormous blow to Spanish prestige, and in the same year Farnese failed to recapture Bergen op Zoom. In the fall of 1589 Farnese proposed to Philip a peace plan whereby limited toleration for Calvinists could be allowed in certain cities of Holland and Zeeland in exchange for submission to royal authority and public exercise of religion for the Catholics. The king however, saw nothing good in such a settlement. From 1590 until his death in December 1592, Farnese was occupied by affairs in France, where as Philip's commander he led three military expeditions in support of the Catholic League in its rebellion against the still Protestant Henry IV.

Farnese was one of the most brilliant strategists of his time. The reconciliation of the Catholic Walloon nobles, the peace negotiations with England, the transitional measures after the fall of Antwerp, and the peace plan of 1589 demonstrate that he was also a shrewd and realistic diplomat. He brought large parts of the Netherlands back under the authority of Philip II and thus laid the political foundation for the Catholic Netherlands of the seventeenth and eighteenth centuries.

BIBLIOGRAPHY

Primary Sources

Correspondance de Philippe II d'Espagne sur les affaires des Pays-Bas 1577–1598. Deuxième partie: Recueil destiné a faire suite aux travaux de L.-P.Gachard. Edited by Joseph Lefèvre. 4 vols. Brussels, 1940–1960.

Dierickx, Michel. "Les carte Farnesiane de Naples par rapport à l'histoire des anciens Pays-Bas, après l'incendie du 30 septembre 1943." *Bulletin de la Commission Royale d'Histoire* 112 (1947), 111–126. Survey of the surviving Farnesian archives at the State Archives of Naples after the fire of 1943.

Essen, Léon van der. *Les archives Farnésiennes de Parme au point de vue de l'histoire des ancien Pays-Bas catholicques.* Brussels, 1913. Inventory of the Farnesian archives concerning the Netherlands at the State Archives of Parma.

Secondary Sources

Essen, Léon van der. *Alexandre Farnèse prince de Parme gouverneur général des Pays-Bas, 1545–1592.* 5 vols. Brussels, 1933–1937. Magisterial and complete biography of Farnese.

———. *De auteur en de betekenis van de Liber relationum eorum quae gesta fuere in Belgio et alibi per serenissimum ducem Alexandrum Farnesium.* Handschrift van de Koninklijke Bibliotheek, Brussel. Antwerp, 1943. Treats Paolo Rinaldi and the significance of his Italian story about Farnese's action in the Netherlands.

———. *Kritische studie over de oorlogvoering van het Spaanse leger in de Nederlanden tijdens de XVIe eeuw.* 7 vols. Brussels, 1953–1960. Analysis of Farnese's military expeditions in the Netherlands, 1577–1584.

Fernandez Segado, F. "Alejandro Farnesio e los negociaciones de paz entre España e Inglaterra, 1586–1588." *Hispania* 45 (1986), 513–578. Discusses the negotiations with England in 1586–1588.

Janssens, Gustaaf. "Pacification générale ou réconciliation particulière? Problèmes de guerre et de paix aux Pays-Bas au début du gouvernement d'Alexandre Farnèse, 1578–1579." *Bulletin de l'Institut historique belge de Rome* 63 (1993), 251–278.

Martin, Colin, and Geoffrey Parker. *The Spanish Armada.* London, 1988.

Parete, Gonzalo, Hugo O'Donnell, Francisco Fernandez, Maria del Carmen Couceiro, and Maria de la Asunción Armada. *Los sucesos de Flanders de 1588 en relacion con la empresa de Inglaterra.* Gran Armada, vol. 3. Madrid, 1988.

Parker, Geoffrey. *The Army of Flanders and the Spanish Road, 1567–1659: The Logistics of Spanish Victory and Defeat in the Low Countries' Wars.* Cambridge, 1972.

———. *The Dutch Revolt.* Rev. ed. London and New York, 1985.

GUSTAAF JANSSENS

FARNESE, HOUSE OF. An Italian noble family prominent in the history of the sixteenth-century papacy, the Farnese, who possessed lands around Lake Bolsena in papal territory, can be traced to the eleventh century. From that time members of the family appeared as soldiers and *condottieri* in the service of Orvieto, Viterbo, and other cities. In the fifteenth century the family penetrated the Roman aristocracy, and in 1493 Alessandro Farnese (1468–1549) was made a cardinal by Alexander VI (r. 1492–1503), in part owing to the pope's liaison with Alessandro's sister, Giulia (1474–1524). In the permissive atmosphere of Renaissance

Rome Alessandro fathered four children, most notably Costanza (c.1502–1545), who married Bosio Sforza, and Pier Luigi (1503–1547). By the 1510s the cardinal developed a deeper sense of religious commitment, but family interests remained close to his heart. This was especially significant for ecclesiastical politics after his election as Paul III in October 1534.

Although Paul III did much to intensify reform efforts at Rome, his nepotism was, as Pastor and Jedin have observed, the great blemish on his pontificate. In November 1534 he raised his young grandsons Alessandro Farnese (1520–1589) and Guido Ascanio Sforza (1518–1564) to the cardinalate. He entrusted the most important military and diplomatic tasks to his son, Pier Luigi, and grandsons, and showered them with favors.

Two events especially secured the Farnese a place among the princely houses of Italy: the marriage in 1538 of Ottavio Farnese (1523–1586), a son of Pier Luigi, to Margaret (1522–1586), the natural daughter of Emperor Charles V (1500–1558), and the investiture of Pier Luigi as duke of Parma and Piacenza in 1545. The rapacity of the Farnese caused scandal and irritation and undermined relations with the imperial court during the first session of the Council of Trent (1545–1547) and the early phases of the Schmalkald War (1546–1547). The dynasty survived the death of the aged pope, however, and produced one of the greatest generals and statesmen of the Counter-Reformation: Alessandro Farnese (1542–1592), son of Ottavio and Margaret, duke of Parma, and from 1578 until his death governor of the Netherlands.

[*See also* Farnese, Alessandro; *and* Paul III.]

BIBLIOGRAPHY

Baudrillart, A., et al., eds. *Dictionnaire d'histoire et de géographie ecclésiastiques.* Paris, 1912–. See vol. 16, cols. 608–615. This volume presents an overview of the Farnese family; it also contains a thorough bibliography.

Jedin, Hubert. *A History of the Council of Trent.* Translated by E. Graf. Vol. 1. London, 1957. Provides insight into the effects of dynastic interests on papal diplomacy.

Pastor, Ludwig. *The History of the Popes from the Close of the Middle Ages.* Edited and translated by R. F. Kerr et al. 3rd ed. Vols. 11 and 12. London 1938–1953. Describes the family background and ambitions of Paul III.

THOMAS DEUTSCHER

FAUKELIUS, Hermannus (Dutch, Herman Fauckel or Faeckel; 1560?–1625), minister in Cologne and Middelburg. A native of Brugge, Faukelius studied Reformed theology in Ghent (1580) with Jacob Kimedonck and Lambert Daneau and later in Leiden with Johannes Drusius. In 1585 Faukelius was installed as a minister in Cologne, where he stayed fourteen years, although he was often in danger of persecution.

Faukelius was a gifted man. Moving to his second parish, Middelburg, where he stayed until his death, his activities often extended beyond the town. Since the classis Walcheren had regularly entrusted him with special missions, he had an important part in the preparations of the national Synod of Dordrecht and was chosen as assessor when the synod convened in 1618.

During the synod he was appointed official translator for the New Testament and substitute translator for the Old Testament. He had already published a Dutch translation of the New Testament in 1617, but his translation of the Old Testament was to remain unfinished.

The synod also placed him in charge of discussion concerning religious education and the Belgic Confession. Here too Faukelius had some previous experience. When the Synod of Zeeland at Veere (1610) had decided to revise the text of the catechism and to reconsider the Belgic Confession, it was Faukelius who assumed this task. In 1611 the revised edition was published, with the supplement *Kort begrip der Christelijke religie voor die zich willen begeven tot des Heren Heilig Avondmaal* (A concise synopsis of the Christian faith for those who want to celebrate the Lord's Supper). This little work, written by Faukelius in 1608, was used as a catechism in Middelburg and found wide acceptance. From 1637 on it was also included in the first edition of the Dutch Authorized Version (States Bible), and that is how Faukelius's *Kort begrip* found general acceptance.

Faukelius's influence at the Synod of Dordrecht—the opinions of the classis Walcheren, whose delegate he was—were well represented in the doctrinal decisions of the synod. At the end of the synod, Faukelius edited the canons concerning disputed questions, and it was Faukelius again who expressed thanks to the States-General and to the city of Dordrecht on behalf of the synod.

After his return to Middelburg the classis Walcheren asked for his help on several occasions. He headed the committee on the East Indian churches, and served on numerous other committees, including one charged to consider the position of Walloon churches in the classis. Although a staunch Contra-Remonstrant, Faukelius was a man of moderation who avoided taking extreme positions at the Synod of Dordrecht. Even in his polemical pamphlet against the Anabaptists, *Babel, dat is verwerringhe der wederdooperen onder malkander*... (Babel, that is confusion amongst the Anabaptist themselves... ; 1621), he showed appreciation of their devout manner of life, even while condemning their doctrine.

BIBLIOGRAPHY

Borsius, J. "Hermannus Faukelius, zijn leven, karakter en letterkundige verdiensten." *Nederlandsch archief voor kerkelijke geschiedenis* 4 (1844), 183–348.

Venemans, B. A. "Hermannus Faukelius." In *Biografisch Lexicon,* vol. 3, pp. 111–113. Kampen, Netherlands, 1988. Most recent bibliography.

Verzeichnis der im deutschen Sprachbereich erschienenen Drucke des XVI. Jahrhunderts. Stuttgart, 1983–. See vol. 6, no. 638.

CL. ROOZE-STOUTHAMER

FERDINAND I

FERDINAND I (1503–1564), King of Hungary and Bohemia, later Holy Roman Emperor. Ferdinand laid both the administrative and territorial foundations of the Habsburg empire in central and east central Europe. Born in Salamanca, the second son of Philip I of Austria and Joan I of Castile, he took up residence in the German lands of his house in 1521 as part of a territorial division between himself and his brother, the emperor Charles V. Following the death in 1526 of Louis II of Hungary, his brother-in-law, during the Battle of Mohács against the Turks, Ferdinand was elected king of both Hungary and Bohemia.

Though Ferdinand recognized the need for reform in the church of Rome and gathered like-minded men at his court, he opposed Protestant sectarianism on political and religious grounds. He firmly believed that Christendom could be reunified. Nevertheless, he put his own convictions aside where dynastic and military well-being was at stake. To become king of Bohemia, he accepted the establishment of Utraquism, though he suppressed other confessional movements such as the Bohemian Brethren and Anabaptist communities, which were especially strong in Moravia. The need for military aid from the German princes, both Protestant as well as Catholic, led him to religious compromises that strengthened the position of Lutheranism in the empire as a whole. Ferdinand was the driving force behind the Peace of Augsburg (1555), which recognized both Lutheran and Catholic principalities in the German lands.

Though powerless to prevent the spread of Lutheranism throughout his own territories, he fostered the survival of Catholicism in all of them. He forced his son, the future Emperor Maximilian II, who openly sympathized with evangelical causes, to swear his allegiance to Roman orthodoxy. Ferdinand brought the Jesuits to Vienna and Prague. Becoming emperor in 1558, he promoted Catholic moral and intellectual reform during the last session of the Council of Trent (1562–1563).

BIBLIOGRAPHY

Buchholtz, Franz Bernhard von. *Geschichte der Regierung Ferdinands des Ersten.* 9 vols. Introduction by Berthold Sutter. Reprint, Graz, 1971. Contains much valuable documentary material.

Fichtner, Paula Sutter. *Ferdinand I of Austria: The Politics of Dynasticism in the Age of the Reformation.* Boulder, Colo., and New York, 1982. Political narrative.

Lhotsky, Alphons. *Das Zeitalter des Hauses Österreich: Die Ersten Jahre der Regierung Ferdinands I, 1520–1527.* Vienna, Cologne and Graz, 1971. Excellent on Austrian and dynastic affairs.

PAULA SUTTER FICHTNER

FESTIVALS

FESTIVALS. In Europe around the year 1500 the annual rhythm of working life was punctuated at regular intervals by festivals of a more or less religious nature. First, there were the major feast days of the liturgical year, observed by the whole church: Easter Week, Whitsun-tide, Corpus Christi, and the twelve days of Christmas. Second, there were celebrations in honor of patron saints by their particular clients—nations, cities, guilds, fraternities: Saint George for England, Saint Denis for France, Saint Mark for Venice, Saint Barbara for gunners, Saint Crispin for cobblers, and so on. Both categories included the pre-Christian festivals that the church had incorporated into its system, notably Carnival and the rites of spring (Mayday, associated with the Virgin Mary), summer (Midsummer, associated with John the Baptist), and winter (associated with the birth of Christ).

In a society in which people worked long hours, lacking the modern concept of "leisure" or "free time," a festival was a compulsory holiday (and craftsmen were often fined for working on those days). In a society in which many people were undernourished, if not starved, a festival was, as its name implies, a "feast," a time for eating and drinking one's fill. (Bread and meat were handed out, while the fountains ran with wine instead of water.) It was also a spectacle, in which the streets and squares of major cities were transformed by temporary decorations of wooden castles or triumphal arches and tapestries were hung outside houses, as well as by the processions that wound through the squares and streets, like the one on Piazza San Marco in Venice about 1500, painted by Gentile Bellini. Pilgrimages were a kind of festival, with processions through the countryside to a particular shrine.

A festival was generally an occasion for dramatic performances, whether indoors or outdoors, formal or informal, religious or secular. No wonder many people reckoned time by the distance from major festivals. The most elaborate performances took place in large or medium-sized European cities, such as Arras, Augsburg, Barcelona, Chester, Florence, Nuremberg, Paris, Prague, Rome, Toulouse, Venice, and York. The performers included professional actors but also many amateurs, especially young adult males organized in fraternities or "abbeys of youth" of various kinds. The audience for these shows included not only the citizens but also the local peasants and even long-distance visitors (notably to the Feast of the Ascension in Venice, the *Sensa*). Villages too might have their festivals, such as the "May Games" in the Lincolnshire village of South Kyme, described in the 1601 records of the Court of Star Chamber because the earl of Lincoln considered that the players had insulted him. Among the most important occasions for festivities in town and countryside alike were Carnival, Easter, Corpus Christ, and the Feast of Saint John.

Easter. Easter was the greatest festival of the liturgical year. By the later Middle Ages it had become customary in many parts of Europe to celebrate the feast with plays. Easter plays did not always represent the Passion, and the Passion was not only represented at Easter, but the sufferings of Christ were enacted in the streets and squares of a number of European cities at this season. In Rome, for example, the arch-fraternity of the Gonfalon regularly presented a play about the Passion. The performances were not concerned with Christ alone but frequently included scenes representing Jews and devils, figures that were sometimes terrifying, sometimes comic. Although plays of this kind gradually declined in Catholic as well as Protestant Europe in the course of the sixteenth century, performances in a vaguer sense of the term persisted or even increased in importance during this period.

For example, the washing of the feet of twelve or thirteen poor people on Maunday Thursday by men of high status (including the emperor Charles V on occasion) was an extremely theatrical ritual of humility, charity, and fraternity. Again, the whole of Holy Week was in a sense one great drama played in a theater without walls, a tragicomedy of death and resurrection in which the many processions gave large numbers of people walk-on parts. Confraternities had a prominent place in these processions, which sometimes included children dressed as angels, an image of the dead Christ, and—particularly in Spain and Italy—a column of flagellants whose self-punishment was an imitation of Christ as well as a dramatic demonstration of repentance. The wealthier members of confraternities sometimes hired substitutes for this part of the proceedings. There was also a joyful element in the celebration of the resurrection, including what was known as "Easter laughter" (*risus paschalis*), the custom of ritualized joking in church.

Corpus Christi. Another favorite occasion for religious processions, pageants, and plays took place in June, the Feast of Corpus Christi. Focused on the body of Christ in the Host, this feast became increasingly popular in the later Middle Ages. It began in the city of Liège, where the pressure to found a new festival came from the devout women of the locality, supported by the Dominican friars, and it spread rapidly across Europe. In 1264 Pope Urban IV declared that the feast should be celebrated by the whole church. It was marked by public preaching, often on the theme of the Eucharist, by pageants dramatizing events from the Bible, and by processions to display the Host in its monstrance, covered with a canopy and followed by clergy and laity (especially members of religious confraternities dedicated to the Blessed Sacrament). The residents of the streets along which the procession passed would often decorate their houses with colored cloth or with tapestries. In Spain the procession often included sword dancers, dragons, and giants, and bullfights were organized to honor the occasion. By the fifteenth century, the festival was one of the most popular in the liturgical year. When the devout English laywoman Margery Kempe visited the German shrine of Wilsnack for the Feast of Corpus Christi in 1426, she found it difficult to find a bed for the night because so many people had converged on the shrine for the occasion. After the Reformation, in areas divided in religion, such as France, the celebration of the feast—which Protestants were known to hate—turned into an opportunity for Catholics to distinguish themselves publicly from heretics.

Town councils and craft guilds became increasingly involved with the festival in the course of the later Middle Ages. In English towns such as York the procession organized by the clergy was complemented by the pageants, or outdoor plays, organized by the guilds. In fifteenth-century York, the guilds performed a cycle of plays on themes ranging from the Creation to the Last Judgment in the three months leading up to the Feast of Corpus Christi itself. Each guild was responsible for a play, sometimes on a theme related to the craft: the shipwrights presented the building of Noah's ark, the vintners the marriage feast at Cana, and the bakers the Last Supper.

As the town councils and guilds became more closely involved with the festival, the rituals gradually acquired a secular as well as a religious meaning. To celebrate the occasion in style did honor to the city and its parishes or quarters. In the small town of Provins in Champagne, the feast included communal suppers in the street, thus expressing the solidarity of the neighborhood. Indeed, it has been argued, notably by Mervyn James, that the rituals represented the "social body" as much as the body of Christ, so that the city was in some sense celebrating itself. It is perhaps no accident that one of the most sumptuous as well as the best documented of the Corpus Christi pageants in Venice took place in 1606, when the city had just been laid under a papal interdict.

The Feast of Saint John. Similar remarks about the combination of religious and civic elements might be made about the festivals in honor of the patron saints of major European cities. In fifteenth-century Florence, a large city for the period (with about 40,000 inhabitants)—indeed, a city-state controlling a substantial part of Tuscany—the Feast of Saint John the Baptist, the principal patron and protector of the city, was a particularly splendid occasion. According to the liturgical calendar, the feast was supposed to take place on 24 June, but in Florence it tended to last for more than a week.

One of the main festive events was a procession from the Duomo to the Ponte Vecchio and back via Piazza della Signoria, in which monks, friars, secular clergy, choirboys, and religious confraternities took part. Through streets decorated with rich cloths and filled with spectators, they walked accompanied by music, carrying relics, and followed by floats representing religious scenes such as the birth of John and his baptism of Christ. Another major event was the offering of gifts to the saint at the high altar of his church—velvet and silk cloth, candles, and even twelve prisoners who were released in honor of the occasion.

But the festival was also a celebration of the wealth and power of the city of Florence and especially of its government. The secular part of the celebrations included an exhibition of luxury goods produced by the craftsmen of the city, notably cloth, jewels, and goldsmith's work, displayed outside the workshops, and also a race (*palio*), not unlike the race that still takes place in Siena twice a year, with colorful costumes for the horses and their riders. The civic aspect of the festival was marked by a banquet for the *Signoria*, by the role of the different wards (*gonfaloni*) of the city in the organization of the day's events, and by the arrival of deputations from the subject towns—Pisa, Arezzo, Pistoia, Volterra, Cortona, and so on—to offer tribute to the saint and thus to the city of which he was the patron. Hence the rituals may be described as an expression of the collective identity of the Florentines.

Around this core of official events carrying religious and political messages clustered a number of semiofficial or unofficial entertainments, such as performances by jugglers, tightrope walkers, and giants (impersonated by men standing on stilts). The importance of the festival for the people of Florence was described by one of them around the year 1400. "You see the whole city involved in preparing for the feast," he declared, "as if they had nothing else to do in the months before."

The Reform of Festivals. In the sixteenth century, festivals did not please everyone. Town councils saw them as an occasion for disorder, while some clergy and pious laity found them offensive on the grounds that they encouraged drunkenness, lechery, and violence. Easter laughter, like the comic interludes in passion plays, was coming to seem a scandalous mixture of the profane with the sacred, and Johannes Oecolampadius wrote a treatise against it in 1518. The place of comic devils in religious festivals was increasingly offensive to pious eyes and ears. Criticisms of festivals often were translated into action in the age of the Catholic and Protestant Reformations. In England a royal proclamation reduced the number of festivals as early as 1536.

In Protestant parts of Europe, public festivals were often abolished altogether, along with the saints in whose names they had been justified. Some reformers viewed festivals and saints alike as survivals from "popish" or even from pagan times. (Saint George was supposed to be a new version of Perseus, Saint Christopher of the giant Polyphemus, and so on.) The idea that a particular day—Sunday apart—was holier than another was sometimes denounced as "superstitious." Festivals also fell under suspicion as occasions of immorality and other forms of disorder. The godly regarded many of them as an archbishop of York viewed the local Christmas procession: "a very rude and barbarous custom" that was practiced "very undecently."

Although Luther himself was inclined to let young men continue to celebrate Carnival or Saint John's Eve, his followers were more severe. In Nuremberg, for example, Andreas Osiander preached against Carnival. In his book *Regnum Papisticum* (The Popish Kingdom; 1533), Thomas Kirchmeyer, a Bavarian Lutheran, attacked festivals as relics of Catholicism. In Lyon in 1565, the Calvinist ministers tried to prevent the Catholics of the city from dancing on the Feast of Pentecost and found themselves with a riot on their hands instead. English Puritans were opposed to plays, "May games," dancing, and other forms of festivity. Dutch Calvinist synods denounced maypoles, sword dances, and Carnival plays. The consequence of Protestant opposition, however, was not, as intended, the disappearance of festivals but rather their increasing secularization. In sixteenth-century London, for example, Corpus Christi was effectively replaced by the Lord Mayor's Show, which used secular rather than religious language to celebrate the city.

By the later sixteenth century, if not before, the Catholic clergy, too, seem to have become alarmed by what they often called the "excesses" of popular festivals. In 1534 in Evora, Portugal, for instance, the bishop prohibited religious plays because they caused scandal. In 1548 the Paris Fraternity of the Passion was forbidden to present any more religious plays. In Lyon in 1577, the bishop forbade churches to be used for dances, fairs, or plays. In Milan in 1579, Carlo Borromeo denounced the custom of decorating the piazza with "pagan" maypoles and branches on Mayday and recommended the erection of a crucifix instead. In Pisa in 1598, the custom of celebrating the Feast of the Assumption with sword dances and bathing in the sea "in the presence of women" provoked clerical criticism.

In Spain a clerical campaign against popular festivals was launched soon after the end of the Council of Trent. Thus the council of Toledo (1565) denounced the feast of the boy bishop and the custom of celebrating Corpus Christi with bullfights and also forbade the clergy to wear masks, while the council of Valencia in the same year forbade "Moorish" festivals and also all-night festivals in churches. The synods of Burgos (1577) and Pamplona (1591) condemned what they called the "profane" elements in the Feast of Corpus Christi—the sword dances, the dragons, and the giants—and also what the clergy perceived as the "confusion" or "disorder" of the feast, notably drinking and dancing in church and the failure to separate men from women or plays from processions.

This comparative survey of religious reactions to festivals in sixteenth-century Europe suggests two main conclusions. First, objections to festivals were expressed in remarkably similar terms by Catholics and Protestants, suggesting that the fundamental objections were not so much theological as moral. The campaign against festivals reveals a significant change in attitudes to order and disorder among some groups at least (especially clergy, traders, and artisans). It is part of a change of values that the German sociologist Norbert Elias described as "the process of civilization" and the French thinker Michel Foucault as the rise of a "disciplinary society."

Second, this campaign provoked considerable resistance, a rearguard action extending over centuries. The reiteration of the condemnation of festivals in essentially the same terms in the course of the seventeenth and eighteenth centuries (if not later) suggests that the reforms were slow to take effect. At the end of the sixteenth century, the festive culture of the late Middle Ages was far from dead.

[*See also* Carnival; Devotional Practices; Flagellants; Popular Religion; *and* Saints, *article on* Cult of Saints.]

BIBLIOGRAPHY

Bercé, Yves-Marie. *Fête et révolte.* Paris, 1976.

Bernardi, Claudio. *La Drammaturgia della Settimana Santa in Italia.* Milan, 1991. Encyclopedic survey.

Chartier, Roger. *The Cultural Uses of Print in Early Modern France.* Princeton, 1987. See especially "The Fête in France," pp. 13–31.

Conor, Norreys Jephson. *Godes Peace and the Queenes.* Cambridge, 1934.

Davis, Natalie Zemon. *Society and Culture in Early Modern France.* Stanford, Calif., 1975. See especially "The Reasons of Misrule," pp. 97–123.

Jacquot, Jean, ed. *Les fêtes de la Renaissance.* 3 vols. Paris, 1956–1975. Concentrates on secular festivals but includes studies of religious festivals, especially in vol. 3, part 4.

James, Mervyn. "Ritual, Drama and Social Body in the Late Medieval English Town." *Past and Present* 98 (1983), 1–29.

Kohler, Erika. *Martin Luther und der Festbrauch.* Cologne, 1959.

Muir, Edward. *Civic Ritual in Renaissance Venice.* Princeton, 1981.

Phythian-Adams, Charles. "Ceremony and the Citizen: The Communal Year at Coventry, 1450–1550." In *Crisis and Order in English Towns*, edited by Peter Clark and Paul Slack, pp. 57–80. London, 1972.

Rubin, Miri. *Corpus Christi.* Cambridge, 1991.

Trexler, Richard. *Public Life in Renaissance Florence.* New York, 1980.

Very, Francis G. *The Spanish Corpus Christi Procession.* Valencia, Spain, 1962.

PETER BURKE

FIFTH LATERAN COUNCIL. *See* Lateran Council, Fifth.

FINLAND. Beginning in the eleventh century Christianity came to Finland from both east and west. During the thirteenth century the main (western) parts of the country were joined to Sweden and to the Roman Catholic church and the eastern regions (Karelia) to Novgorod and to the Orthodox church. The boundary between Sweden and Novgorod was drawn for the first time in 1323.

Ecclesiastically, medieval Finland was one of the seven dioceses under the archiepiscopal see of Uppsala. The bishop's see was located in Turku (Åbo). More than seventy stone churches in the southwestern part of the country still bear witness to the power and the authority of the medieval church. There were about one hundred parishes at the end of the Middle Ages. Finland had two Dominican houses, three Franciscan convents, and a Brigittine monastery.

The Finns—who numbered about 200,000 at the beginning of the modern era—spoke their own Finno-Ugric language, unrelated to any other European language. There was a Swedish-speaking minority on the west and south coasts. This explains why the clergy in the Middle Ages were native Finns: they had to preach and listen to confessions in Finnish. The basic Christian texts—Lord's Prayer, Ten Commandments, Apostles' Creed, and Ave Maria—had been translated and written in Finnish rather early. Unfortunately, no remains of these texts have been preserved.

The bishops of Turku from the middle of the fourteenth century onward were Finns. They had studied in Continental universities, the last seven bishops having studied in Paris. They also took good care always to have young Finns with university educations at hand when canons and prelates in the cathedral chapter of Turku were appointed. The first Finnish students were in Paris about 1300, and the total number of medieval students from the diocese of Turku to go to Paris was about 150.

The Reformation in Sweden was a *Fürstenreformation*, a typical princes' reformation, initiated and led by the new king, *reformator et salvator*, powerful, unscrupulous, and avaricious Gustavus Vasa (r. 1523–1560). He was little interested in theological questions but saw clearly the advantages of the new Lutheran heresy. It gave him a pretext to confiscate the property of the church and to cross its political power.

The ties to the Holy See were broken by 1523, and after that the highest ecclesiastical authority was the king. He wanted to avoid abrupt changes in church ceremonies, which could give cause for opposition and rebellion. This is why the transformation of doctrine, liturgy, church life, and organization in Sweden was smooth and slow. The episcopal structure of the church was left intact.

Vasa's eldest son, Erik XIV (r. 1560–1568), felt sympathies for Calvinism, and his second-eldest son, John III (r. 1568–1592), tried to lead Sweden to a *via media* between Lutheranism and Catholicism. John's son Sigismund, the heir of the throne and already king of Poland, was a Catholic. He was, however, compelled to agree with the decision of the Diet of Uppsala in 1593, when Sweden accepted formally the Augsburg Confession.

Sweden produced its first printed books in the vernacular at the end of the fifteenth century. The Reformation brought first the New Testament (1526), and then the entire Bible (1541), as well as liturgical books, in Swedish. Most Finns could not read Swedish, and hence they had to be translated. Thus the Reformation gave Finns their written language.

The Finnish reformer Michael Agricola is the father of Finnish literature and the Finnish written language. Agricola was born about 1510 in a Swedish-speaking peasant family in southeastern Finland. At school in Wiborg he evidently acquainted himself with the ideas of humanism and the Reformation already well known on the southern side of the Gulf of Finland, in the Baltic countries. He was a bright boy and was appointed in 1528 as the secretary of the new bishop of Turku, Martin Skytte. The bishop was a Dominican friar in his sixties, a devout Catholic, but as an Erasmian reformist he was receptive to the new ideas. During his episcopate (1528–1550), according to the Finnish Bishops' Chronicle: "the papacay collapsed in the whole of Finland, private and corner masses were abolished, holy water ran out as well as the consecration of ashes and palms, ecclesiastical chant was changed and amended."

During the 1530s the monasteries were dissolved, except for the Brigittine nunnery near Turku, which lingered until the 1590s. Celibacy was abolished. Liturgical texts were translated into Finnish and purified of "papist" elements.

The "unnecessary" property of the church—mainly landed property but also silver monstrances, chalices and patens, church bells, liturgical vestments, and the episcopal crosier—was slowly but surely confiscated. Tithes were now to be paid to the state. The clergy was henceforth paid by the Crown, which severely reduced salaries. The rural clergy lost, on average, half their income. The cathedral chapter in Turku, which at the end of the Middle Ages consisted of four prelates and eight canons, was gradually dissolved.

A positive result of the Reformation was that Finnish students were now sent directly to Wittenberg, the first of them in 1531. Eight of them had the opportunity to see and hear Martin Luther. Through 1600 a total of thirty Finnish students had studied at the Academia Leucorea, among them three later bishops of Turku and four of Wiborg. Every schoolmaster of Turku from 1535 to 1630 had studied in Wittenberg. Thus the home university of Lutheranism left its mark on the Finnish church and culture.

Agricola left for Wittenberg in 1536 and came back with a master of arts degree three years later. He attended the lectures of Luther and Philipp Melanchthon and translated, with the help of a pair of Finnish fellow students, the New Testament into Finnish—the task for which Agricola was sent to Wittenberg. Back in Finland as schoolmaster at the cathedral school in Turku, Agricola wrote the "ABC-book," the first book in the Finnish language, printed in Stockholm in 1543. In addition to the alphabet and numerals, it contains a catechism based mainly on Luther's Small Catechism.

Agricola's prayer book (1544) is his most original work. It is also the lengthiest prayer book of the Reformation (up to the 1560s), comprising more than eight hundred pages and more than six hundred prayers. Agricola used medieval sources (especially the *Missale Aboense* of 1488, the Dominican missal modified for the diocese of Turku), but also made use of evangelical prayer books. He took prayers from Luther and Melanchthon but also from Erasmus and Kaspar von Schwenckfeld.

The *magnum opus* of the Finnish Reformation, the New Testament, was published in Stockholm in 1548. Agricola and his team had translated it from the Greek text of Erasmus, the Vulgate, Luther's Bible, and the Swedish Bible of 1541.

It was Agricola's intention to translate the whole Bible, but the king refused to give a penny for the printing of the Finnish books, and the cathedral chapter of Turku was deprived of its resources. Thus it took a hundred years more: the first Finnish Bible was not printed until 1642. Nonthe-less, Agricola published the Psalter and a selection of the Old Testament prophets (1551–1552). In 1549 Agricola had published a Finnish church manual and mass, translated from the works of the Swedish reformer Olaus Petri.

Agricola's literary work—twenty-four hundred printed pages—is mainly translation and for the most part Bible translation. But the Bibles of the Reformation era were not *sola scriptura*; they had forewords, summaries, and marginal glosses. Translating those materials, Agricola made use of the works of Luther, Melanchthon, and Erasmus, but he also translated Johannes Bugenhagen, Justus Jonas, Veit Dietrich, Georg Major, Otto Brunfels, Wolfgang Capito, Herzog Albrecht von Preussen, and the Hebraist Sebastian Münster.

Comparing Agricola's Finnish translation with his mostly Latin and German sources—mainly Lutheran—one can make some interesting observations. Agricola omits most of the polemics against the Catholic church, which abound in his sources. He did not like the pope, and there is some invective, but it is the exception, not the rule. This moderation occurred evidently because the late medieval church in Finland was far from corrupt; there was no "waning of the Middle Ages." The old bishop Martin Skytte, although Catholic, was highly respected by the younger generation in the cathedral chapter of Turku, most of whom had studied in Wittenberg. Thus the Reformation in Finland was slower than on the continent or in Sweden. Agricola had no need of massive polemics. Even so, Agricola is very explicit when writing about justification by faith alone. He translates one of the crucial texts, Luther's forward to *Romans*, very carefully, word by word. And while Georg Major or Veit Dietrich, for example, just hint or point to justification by faith in their Old Testament summaries, Agricola takes the opportunity to add words to guarantee that the reader shall understand that salvation is *sola fides* and *sola gratia*.

Martin Skytte died in 1550. After a vacancy of four years, the king appointed Agricola as bishop of Turku. The diocese was no longer the same, however, for the king had divided it into two parts. The new diocese of Wiborg comprised the eastern part of Finland. The first bishop was Paavali Juusten, one of Luther's students and the author of the Finnish Bishops' Chronicle. Agricola did not approve of the division of the old diocese; the purpose of the king was evidently not to intensify the ecclesiastical administration but to reduce the power of the bishop of Turku.

Agricola died in 1557. His followers (the most prominent, Juusten, was bishop of Wiborg, 1554–1563, and of Turku, 1563–1575) had to steer the Finnish church through the tempests of the royal church policy into the era of Lutheran confessionalism.

The Finnish Reformation was a reform from above, by authoritative orders, administrative measures, and education. The scanty source material is insufficient to give a clear picture of what the ordinary people thought. There were no popular movements for the Reformation, but some local uprisings against the confiscation of church bells and against liturgical reforms did occur.

BIBLIOGRAPHY

Andersen, Niels Knud. "The Reformation in Scandinavia and the Baltic." In *The New Cambridge Modern History*, vol. 2, *The Reformation, 1520–1559*, edited by G. R. Elton. 2d ed. Cambridge, 1990.

Gummerus, Jaakko. *Michael Agricola, der Reformator Finnlands*. Schriften der Luther-Agricola Gesellschaft, 2. Helsinki, 1941.

Heininen, Simo. *Die finnischen Studenten in Wittenberg, 1531–1552*. Schriften der Luther-Agricola Gesellschaft A19. Helsinki, 1980.

Juusten, Paulus. *Catalogus et ordinaria successio episcoporum Finlandensium*. Edited by Simo Heininen. Veröffentlichungen der finnischen Gesellschaft für Kirchengeschichte 143. Helsinki, 1988.

Pirinen, Kauko. *Turun tuomiokapituli uskonpuhdistuksen murroksessa*. Helsinki, 1962.

Tarkiainen, Viljo, and Kari Tarkiainen. *Mikael Agricola*. Helsinki, 1985.

SIMO HEININEN

FISCHER, Andreas (1480–1540), theologian and leader of the Sabbatarian Anabaptists. Born in Bohemia, Fischer studied at the University of Vienna and lived for a time in Upper Austria. With Oswald Glaidt he moved to Liegnitz in Silesia, where he was a missionary of Sabbatarian Anabaptism.

By late 1528 and early 1529 Fischer superseded Glaidt as leader of the Sabbatarians in that area after Fischer and Glaidt parted company probably as a result of a disagreement concerning Glaidt's chiliasm. They would not work together again. When Fischer prepared his book *Scepastes Decalogi*, defending Sabbatarianism, the chiliastic elements of Glaidt's theology were conspicuously absent. This book shows that Fischer was theologically educated and held a covenantal theology that stressed the continuity between the Old and New Covenants.

By March 1529, Fischer had moved from Silesia into Slovakia. For the next few years he traveled between Slovakia and Moravia and had spotty success as an Anabaptist missionary. In Slovakia, where a revolt among the miners had left a simmering political situation, there was no toleration shown to religious radicals like Fischer. Despite nearly two hundred baptisms as a result of his work Fischer was not able to establish firmly rooted, permanent religious communities there. His wife was drowned for her faith. Fischer himself escaped execution only because the rope broke as he was being hanged from a castle tower.

During this time in Slovakia, Fischer was regularly charged with all sorts of heresies and irregularities—from communalism to an advocacy of plural marriage. In a letter written from Moravia to the town council of Banská Bystrica (Neusohl) in 1534, Fischer denied these false charges. Significantly, the charge of Sabbatarianism against Fischer does not appear in the sources. Perhaps those leveling the charges against Fischer were not well enough acquainted with his teachings.

Fischer returned to Moravia in about 1533. From then on, according to the Great Chronicle of the Hutterites, a faction of the Moravian Anabaptists became known as "Sabbatarians." In the great persecutions that began in 1535, Fischer appears to have gone to the town of Wiesenthal on the border between Saxony and Bohemia. He probably returned to the Nicholsburg area around 1537 and gathered what was left of a scattered Anabaptist community there. The reports of Sabbatarians in that area probably reached the ears of Martin Luther and prompted him to write his "Against the Sabbatarians" (1538).

Fischer sought a refuge for these Anabaptist migrants in Slovakia, to which he returned in 1540. Unfortunately, instead of finding a place of refuge, he was captured by the new palatine (*Oberspann*), Franz Bebek, and his men. They dragged Fischer to Bebek's castle of Krasnahorka and summarily executed him.

BIBLIOGRAPHY

Liechty, Daniel. *Andreas Fischer and the Sabbatarian Anabaptists*. Scottdale, Pa., 1988. The only extended work on Andreas Fischer available, it treats all major critical issues involved Fischer's life and work and is extensively documented.

DANIEL LIECHTY

FISCHER, Hans. *See* Bünderlin, Johann.

FISH, Simon (d. around 1531), English lawyer, polemicist, and translator. Almost everything known about Fish's life derives from John Foxe's account in which the chronology is uncertain and the stories unreliable. In 1525 Fish came to London, perhaps from Oxford, to study law. Acting the part of Wolsey in the Gray's Inn Christmas play of 1526 brought him into trouble with the cardinal, and Fish fled to William Tyndale in Antwerp. Back in London in 1527, he became a major importer of Tyndale's forbidden New Testament, and his book running impelled him into exile again in 1528.

In Antwerp Fish wrote the incendiary anticlerical tract *The Supplication for the Beggars,* the most influential pamphlet of the early English Reformation. The *Supplication* is a petition from the beggars of England to the king against the rapacity of greater beggars: the clergy, "holy, idle thieves." The beggars complain that the vast wealth seized by the clergy and their unfettered legal powers and privileges undermine and usurp royal authority and impoverish and intimidate the laity. The crimes committed by this "sinful generation" of clergy go unpunished and corrupt the people. The clergy's greatest ploy is their invention of purgatory. It is mentioned nowhere in scripture, which is why the clergy cannot allow the Bible in English. The principle of indulgences is attacked: if the pope can free one soul for money, he is a tyrant not to free all; remission of sins is given not by papal pardon but by sure faith in Christ.

The *Supplication,* with its plea for the confiscation of clerical wealth and privilege, appealed to Henry VIII, who was probably given it by Anne Boleyn. Thomas More refuted Fish's tract in *The Supplication of Souls,* which concentrated upon Fish's attack on purgatory. Fish's evangelical belief is shown more comprehensively in *The Sum of Scripture,* a translation from the Dutch of a manual of practical Protestant religion and morality, perhaps the work of Guillaume Farel. According to More, Fish recanted his Protestant belief.

BIBLIOGRAPHY

Clebsch, William A. *England's Earliest Protestants, 1520–1535.* New Haven and London, 1964.

Foxe, John. *Acts and Monuments.* Edited by Josiah Pratt. London, 1870. See vol. 4, pp. 656–666.

Haas, Steven W. "Simon Fish, William Tyndale, and Sir Thomas More's 'Lutheran Conspiracy.' " *Journal of Ecclesiastical History* 23 (1972), 125–136.

SUSAN BRIGDEN

FISHER, John (1469–1535), bishop of Rochester and chancellor of the University of Cambridge (1504–1535), patron of humanist education, polemical theologian, and Roman Catholic saint. Having studied arts and theology at Cambridge in the later fifteenth century, he became chief adviser and spiritual director to Lady Margaret Beaufort, Henry VII's mother. He diverted her patronage toward Cambridge, where he persuaded her to found two colleges, Christ's in 1506 and Saint John's in 1511. This powerful connection furthered his career, and in 1504 Henry VII appointed him bishop of Rochester, while the university elected him chancellor. Already influenced by the new humanist scholarship, he brought Erasmus to Cambridge in 1511 as the university's first lecturer in Greek. The statutes that Fisher gave Saint John's in 1516 cast it in the humanist mold of the "trilingual college," providing for the teaching of Hebrew and Greek as well as Latin. Fisher himself embarked on the study of both Greek and Hebrew in his forties, and Erasmus attributed to his example the ease with which "good letters" were accepted at Cambridge.

Fisher's career as a polemical theologian began in 1519 with three books against Jacques Lefèvre d'Étaples on the identity of Mary Magdalene, a debate that revolved around the relations among scripture, tradition, and church authority. This position has been seen as a change of front by one who had previously supported his humanist friends Johannes Reuchlin and Erasmus in the controversies over Hebrew books and the *Novum Instrumentum,* the 1516 edition of Erasmus's Greek/Latin New Testament. But Fisher argued against Lefèvre not as a scholastic but as a humanist among colleagues. Two years later, following Henry VIII's lead, he decided to refute Luther. In a sermon of May 1521 Fisher launched an attack that, by concentrating on the principles of *sola fides* and *sola scriptura,* represented the first Catholic response to get to the heart of Luther's message. This critique was expanded in his *Assertionis Lutheranae confutatio* (1523), which included an analysis of how Luther's other doctrines derived logically from his views on faith and scripture, and used Augustine's anti-Pelagian works to impugn Luther's claim to Augustinian authority. This work was followed in 1525 with defenses of the Catholic doctrines of the priesthood and of the sacrifice of the Mass (the latter in the form of a vindication of Henry's book against Luther). In 1527 his defense of the real presence against Johannes Oecolampadius was published as *De veritate corporis.*

Fisher was an eclectic theologian, drawing heavily on Greek and Latin fathers as well as revealing (largely implicitly) his scholastic formation. Among the remarkable features of his theology were a firmly Augustinian doctrine of justification by grace alone and a eucharistic theology that, though Thomist in outline, was permeated by a patristic erudition especially reliant on John Chrysostom and Cyril of Alexandria. His papalism, which coexisted with a respect for general councils, was largely conventional. Although his contributions to the debate on scripture and tradition had some value, his reconciliation of the two was not coherent. His greatest works, the *Confutatio* and the *De veritate,* were widely reprinted and circulated. His critique of Luther on faith and of Oecolampadius on the Eucharist profoundly influenced subsequent Catholic polemic and the debates at the Council of Trent.

From 1527 Fisher was preoccupied with Henry VIII's struggle to escape his marriage to Catherine of Aragon. As England's premier theologian, he was among the first to be consulted and soon decided that the marriage was valid. Fisher was the most active and influential supporter of the queen's cause, leading domestic resistance until the divorce became a *fait accompli* in 1533. He was equally prominent in resisting Henry's attacks on the independence of the Church of England in the early 1530s. In 1534 he was condemned to life imprisonment in the Act of Attainder against the Holy Maid of Kent, Elizabeth Barton, an English visionary who had foretold divine vengeance on Henry. Refusing the oath to the succession, he was sent to the Tower. Like Thomas More he was subjected to interrogations designed to trap him into denying the royal supremacy, now a treasonable offense. Unlike More, he fell into the trap. News that Pope Paul III had made him a cardinal precipitated his trial. Convicted on 17 June, he was executed on 22 June 1535 and attained almost instant recognition in Catholic Europe as a martyr for the unity of the church, papal primacy, and the indissolubility of marriage. His heroic end further enhanced the credit attached to his theological writings, and he became a role model for the Counter-Reformation episcopate.

BIBLIOGRAPHY

Bradshaw, Brendan, and Eamon Duffy, eds. *Humanism, Reform and the Reformation: The Career of Bishop John Fisher*. Cambridge, 1989. Ten studies of aspects of his career, exploring his intellectual and political outlook and context.

Rex, Richard. *The Theology of John Fisher*. Cambridge, 1991. Sets Fisher's theology in the context of Renaissance and Reformation debates, against medieval background.

Reynolds, E. E. *Saint John Fisher*. 2d rev. ed. Wheathampstead, England, 1972. Best biography in English, though thin on theology.

Rouschausse, Jean. *La Vie et l'Oeuvre de John Fisher Evêque de Rochester*. Nieuwkoop, Netherlands, 1973. Fullest biography.

Surtz, Edward. *The Works and Days of John Fisher, 1469–1535*. Cambridge, Mass., 1967. Lengthy and repetitive study of Fisher's theology; heavy going but indispensable.

RICHARD REX

FLACIUS ILLYRICUS, Matthias (Croat., Matije Vlačić; 1520–1575), Istrian Lutheran theologian. Born near Trieste in Venetian Labin (now in Croatia), his lifelong passion for collecting manuscripts was kindled at the San Marco school in Venice under Giovanni Battista di Cipelli (called Egnazio from his native city), whose curriculum was determined by members of the academy of Aldo Mannucci, celebrated publisher of Latin and Greek classics. His guardian's brother, Baldo Lupetina, Franciscan provincial in Venice and later a martyr to the Inquisition, advised him to study at Wittenberg.

After study at Basel and Tübingen, he matriculated at the University of Wittenberg in 1541; in 1544 he was appointed professor of Hebrew. His theology has been criticized for echoing the Aristotelianism of Melanchthon's Wittenberg curriculum. But he was also influenced by Luther, both in the lecture hall and, during a period of despair, in pastoral care: "I am not an untested Christian, which Doctor Martin Luther especially wanted to have in a theologian."

Following his 1547 victory over the Lutheran princes in the Schmalkald War, Emperor Charles V imposed a religious law, the Augsburg Interim, which became a source of discord among Luther's followers. Melanchthon urged a conciliatory policy, but Flacius, for whom it was a "situation of confession" *(casus confessionis)*, urged across-the-board resistance. To resist the imperial government more strongly, he left Wittenberg for Magdeburg, "God's Chancery," still unconquered after the late war. His fiery publications there stirred up public opinion against the elector Moritz of Saxony, who in 1552 led a successful attack against his former ally, the emperor. The Princes' Revolt reversed the verdict of the Schmalkald War and laid the basis for the 1555 Peace of Augsburg and religious freedom for the lands of the Reformation.

Political stability achieved, Flacius embarked on two projects to strengthen the Lutheran Reformation movement, a church history and a collection of Bible study aids. Flacius is known as the father of church history for organizing (not writing) the *Magdeburg Centuries,* the first comprehensive church history since Eusebius in the fourth century. The *Centuries* offer a "cornucopia" of primary historical sources, assembled in an extensive search "from Scotland to Constantinople." There is growing agreement that English reformers (John Foxe, John Jewel) used Flacius's easily usable *Catalogus testium veritatis,* a smaller source collection, in crafting Elizabethan political ideology. Flacius's search for manuscripts resulted in several important first editions, among them Firmicus Maternus's *De errore profanarum religionum,* rare evidence of late Roman religions, and *Otfrids Evangelienbuch,* an early monument of the German language.

For his 1567 *Clavis scripturae sacrae* (popularly called the "Golden Key"), Flacius has been recognized as the father of hermeneutics, as later carried on by Friedrich Schleiermacher, Wilhelm Dilthey, and Hans Georg Gadamer. According to Gadamer (p. 4), Flacius's assumption of the hermeneutical legitimacy of the biblical canon has been justified by the recent development of the concept of *kerygma.* Like Paul Ricoeur (Baur, p. 47), Flacius's rules permit understanding of the *Seinswelt* of texts. According to more recent authors (King, Shuger, Waswo) the *Clavis* also influenced contemporary literature.

Following Luther's teaching on the bound will, Flacius rejected the doctrine of free will. Believing with Luther that a human being is unitary (a *totus homo*), he also rejected the philosophical distinction between human's substance and accidence, since talk of accidence would allow for free will. As sinners, human beings have lost the image of God (the ability to know God truly and to obey him—*facultas cognitionis et obedientiae Dei*); it follows that the unconverted have the image of Satan and that "sin is man's substance." He made this famous statement during a disputation at Weimar in 1560 and later in his *Clavis* in the tract "Concerning Original Sin or the Names and Essence of the Old Adam." In his theocentric anthropology human substance is bound up with volition—"man *is* his relationship to God, in yes or no" (Baur, p. 46).

Unwilling, however, to write off the human race as diabolical, Flacius distinguished between *forma substantialis*, the bearer of the image of God (or, in fallen humanity, the image of Satan), and *substantialia materialis*, the bearer of some good, despite corruption. The distinction was lost, however, on those theologians who pronounced his doctrine as "unusual" *(inusitata)* and denounced a "Flacian heresy." "That he could be so execrated by his Lutheran contemporaries because of this thesis shows how little Luther's most important insights were understood even within his own church, and how thoroughly they had been forgotten only two decades after his death" (Karl Barth, *Church Dogmatics*, 1936, vol. 3, pt. 2, p. 27).

His extensive polemical writings functioned as a principle of stability in the turbulent period following Luther's death and were largely responsible for defeating the religious movements of Andreas Osiander and Kaspar von Schwenckfeld. The Flacian Controversy, resolved in the 1577 Formula of Concord, had a political background. The curious caricatures on the barrel of the "Flacian cannon" at the Coburg castle ordered by the elector of Saxony Augustus, showing Flacius chained to a demon while pursuing riches and a bishop's miter, commemorates a defamation campaign. What certain princes called a "new papacy" was the struggle of the Flacian party, based in the northern Hanseatic cities, for the independence of the church. In article 1 of the 1577 Formula of Concord, the formulators rejected his terminology, under pressure "at all costs to put Flacius in the wrong" (Ritschl, vol. 2, p. 453). But for the most part, the formula accepted his Lutheran positions against those of Melanchthon.

The Philippists were instrumental in depriving him of a professorship at Jena following his sabotage of the 1557 imperial religious colloquy at Worms. They also helped defeat his program to reform the University curriculum on the basis of his *De materiis metisque scientarum & erroribus philosophiae in rebus divinis* (On the Materials and Limits of the Sciences and the Errors of Philosophy in Divine Matters). At Regensburg he attempted unsuccessfully to found a university. Called to revolutionary Antwerp in 1566, he laid foundations for a "Martinist" church. Although the three Martinist churches were destroyed in 1567 in the Council of Blood of Fernando Álvarez de Toledo, duke of Alba, Flacius's church order contributed to adapting evangelical Lutheranism to pluralist society and eventually to that of North America. After a period of refuge from his princely persecutors in Strasbourg (1567–1573), he died in Frankfurt am Main on 11 March 1575, just days before being banished.

BIBLIOGRAPHY

Baur, Jorg. "Flacius—Radikal Theologie." In *Matthias Flacius Illyricus, 1575–1975* (Schriftenreihe des Regensburger Osteuropainstituts 2) pp. 37–49. Regensburg, 1975.

Gadamer, Hans-Georg. *Rhetorik und Hermeneutik.* Göttingen, 1976.

Hase, Hans Christoph von. *Die Gestalt der Kirche Luthers: Der Casus Confessionis im Kampf des Matthias Flacius gegen das Interim von 1548.* Göttingen, 1940. At Union Seminary, von Hase, cousin of Bonhoeffer, looked for a theoretical basis for participating in the German Kirchenkampf against the Nazis, and found Flacius's *casus confessionis.* His book was the last theological work published by Vandenhoeck & Ruprecht before the Nazis forbade printing of theological works.

King, John N. *English Reformation Literature: The Tudor Origins of the Protestant Tradition.* Princeton, 1982.

Mirković, Mijo. *Matija Vlačić Ilirik.* 2 vols. 2d ed. Pula and Rijeka, Croatia, 1960–1962. In Serbo-Croat, with new bibliography and introduction by Josip Bratulić, who is critical of Mirković's romantic view of his countryman.

Olson, Oliver K. *The 'Missa Illyrica' and the Liturgical Thought of Flacius Illyricus.* Ph.D. diss., Universität Hamburg, 1966. Available at Yale University Library.

———. "Matthias Flacius Illyricus." In *Shapers of Religious Traditions in Germany, Switzerland, and Poland, 1560–1600,* edited by Jill Raitt. New Haven, 1981. Most recent biographical article in English; a full-length biography is planned by the author.

———. "Matthias Flacius Illyricus." In *Theologische Realenzyklopädie,* vol. 11, pp. 206–214. Berlin, 1983. With bibliography of sources in European languages.

Preger, Wilhelm. *Matthias Flacius Illyricus und seine Zeit.* 2 vols. Erlangen, 1859–1861. Still the standard biography; excellent analyses of theological issues.

Ritschl, Otto. *Geschichte des Protestantismus.* 4 vols. Leipzig and Göttingen, 1908.

Schultz, Robert C. "Original Sin: Accident or Substance: The Paradoxical Significance of F[ormula] C[oncordiae] I, 53–62 in Historical Context." In *Discord, Dialogue, and Concord: Studies in the Lutheran Reformation's Formula of Concord,* edited by Lewis W. Spitz and Wenzel Lohff, pp. 38–57. Philadelphia, 1977.

Verzeichnis der im deutschen Sprachbereich erschienenen Drucke des XVI. Jahrhunderts. Stuttgart, 1983–. See vol. 7, nos. 1244–1581.

OLIVER K. OLSON

FLAGELLANTS. First appearing in public when an Italian hermit organized processions of laymen in 1260, flagellation had been performed as a penitential ritual in monasteries long before then. The flagellant movement spread through northern and central Italy, even crossing the Alps, but it had a radically different history in transalpine Christendom, where it soon acquired songs, uniforms, and a markedly anticlerical twist. The most notorious flagellant movement appeared in the Holy Roman Empire during the outbreak of the Black Death in 1348. Employing an elaborate and remarkably standardized ritual (which lost all efficacy if a priest or a woman interrupted it), members whipped themselves in order to turn away God's wrath from Christendom and apparently instigated the worst massacres of Jews in medieval Germany. Flagellation was sharply condemned by a papal bull in 1349 and outlawed in France, and groups of flagellants were arrested and sometimes executed by papal inquisitors in many regions of the empire during the late fourteenth and fifteenth century. The practice never revived in northern Europe.

In late medieval Italy, on the other hand, public flagellants were easily domesticated by the ecclesiastical hierarchy and rapidly institutionalized into confraternities. Brotherhoods of *disciplinati* or *battuti* remained a part of Italian civic life for many centuries, making ritual processions especially at times of public distress or civic strife, as well as on some holy days. Drawn from all parts of the population, they wore penitential garments that concealed their faces but exposed their backs as they whipped themselves. Surviving statutes from Renaissance Florence suggest that actual flagellation was ordinarily done in darkened rooms at private confraternal meetings. At Venice the flagellant groups had evolved by 1500 into five (later six) highly prestigious educational and charitable organizations known as *Scuole grandi.*

Although white-robed and hooded processions of flagellant brotherhoods of the "True Cross" ultimately endured longest at Spanish Holy Week celebrations, such confraternities arose there only during the sixteenth century. Even so, they caught on vigorously: numerous brotherhoods were founded in the 1520s and 1530s, becoming a regular feature of civic penitential processions by midcentury. Unlike confraternities dedicated to particular saints, which often permitted fewer than a hundred members, Spanish brotherhoods of the True Cross were extremely large. Jaén, a moderate-sized city, had five flagellant fraternities, all founded between 1540 and 1594, two of which boasted more than a thousand members. Processions of uniformed and disguised penitents equipped with ritual scourges also remained popular throughout post-Tridentine Italy and southern France; Bergamo and its district contained seventy groups of *disciplinati* in 1575. Public scourging explicitly paralleled Christ's passion. Carlo Borromeo emphasized its symbolism by ordering participants to wear cords tied with seven knots in memory of Christ's wounds. Actual flagellation, however, became rarer. At Venice the prestigious *Scuole grandi* continued their regular processions, although after 1576 they hired poor men to march with them and perform flagellation.

Though popular in Italy and Spain, flagellant processions shocked northern Catholic sensibilities. When Henri III introduced this practice at Paris during Lent in 1583, he enrolled courtiers and magistrates in his Congregation of Penitents and had the royal musicians accompany them. Their procession, however, was denounced from the pulpit of Notre-Dame, mocked by street poets, and even parodied by court lackeys wearing handkerchiefs. (By way of contrast, a miracle was reported during a flagellant procession in Catalonia seven years later).

Eventually its popularity declined, even in Spain. Madrid's largest flagellant brotherhood, the Soledad, declined from 2,400 members in 1568 to only 800 in 1658, most of whom were not flagellants. (It was still, however, the largest Holy Week procession in Madrid.) A century later, in 1767, the enlightened government of Charles III prohibited public flagellation, although the Holy Week processions continued. In Francisco Franco's Spain during the 1970s, one town in La Rioja still included public flagellation by a brotherhood of the True Cross in its Good Friday procession.

BIBLIOGRAPHY

Christian, William A. *Local Religion in Sixteenth-Century Spain.* Princeton, 1981.

Cohn, Norman. *The Pursuit of the Millenium.* London, 1957.

Henderson, John. "The Flagellant Movement and Flagellant Confraternities in Central Italy, 1260–1400." *Studies in Church History* 15 (1978), 147–160.

Pullan, Brian. *Rich and Poor in Renaissance Venice.* Oxford, 1971. See especially pp. 34–52.

Weissman, Ronald. *Ritual Brotherhood in Renaissance Florence.* New York, 1982. See especially pp. 50–58, 72–76, and 92–95.

E. WILLIAM MONTER

FLAMINIO, Marcantonio (1498–1550), Italian humanist and poet born in Serravalle (now Vittorio Veneto) near Venice. Schooled by his humanist father, Giovanni Antonio, Marcantonio showed his precocity in the first publication of his Latin poetry in 1515. This led to contacts with humanists in Naples, Rome, and Urbino in the course of a journey at age sixteen, probably undertaken in the vain hope of finding employment. From 1515 to 1517 he studied at Bologna, where he was especially influenced by Achille Bocchi, poet and professor of rhetoric, and where he formed a lifelong friendship with the Bolognese patrician Ludovico Beccadelli, later the bishop of Ragusa and secretary to Cardinal Gasparo Contarini. Transferring to the University of Padua in 1517, Flaminio continued his contacts with humanists, among whom the Netherlandish Latinist Christophe de Longueil (Ital., Longolio) stands out. While in Padua, he met the Genoese nobleman Stefano Sauli, who became his patron, enabling him to lead "the sweet life of a parasite," as he himself half-jokingly expressed it. His growing *corpus* of elegant Latin poetry included epigrams, odes, and sonnets. Flaminio followed Sauli to Genoa and in 1522 to Rome as a member of his *familia,* and through him met influential humanists and churchmen such as the Benedictine Gregorio Cortese. In 1524 Flaminio was a member of the Roman Oratory of Divine Love, having joined men like

Gian Pietro Carafa, later Pope Paul IV, and Gaetano da Thiene, the founders of the Theatine order.

Around this time Flaminio left Sauli's household for that of Gian Matteo Giberti, papal datary under Clement VII and bishop of Verona, remaining in the austere bishop's *familia* until 1538. The household resembled an academy, and Flaminio took part in the life of prayer, study, and discussion of religious questions with men who shared his and Giberti's concern for reform of the church. Among them were the Hebraist Johan van Kampen, the bishop's secretary Francesco della Torre, the poet Adamo Fumano, and Galeazzo Florimonte, humanist, courtier, and later bishop of Aquino. During the decade in Verona Flaminio made contact with Venetian reform circles, foremost among which was the loose group of *spirituali*, or proponents of personal and ecclesiastical reform, who met in the monastery of San Giorgio Maggiore when Gregorio Cortese was its abbot. Besides Contarini, it included Carafa, who had fled Rome after the sack of 1527, and occasionally Reginald Pole, cousin of Henry VIII of England and later cardinal.

To the period in Verona belong Flaminio's paraphrases of the twelfth book of Aristotle's *Metaphysics* and of thirty-two psalms, published respectively in 1536 and 1538. By the latter date he had already decided to turn to a life of Christian meditation and was reading books by northern reformers. Moving to Naples for a stay of three years, he became part of a circle of reform-minded men and women gathered around the Spaniard Juan de Valdés. Among them was the Florentine Pietro Carnesecchi, who testified at his trial before the Roman Inquisition that Flaminio revised the *Beneficio di Cristo* by Benedetto Fontanini of Mantua, the most important work associated with Italian reform thought. Flaminio shared Valdés's indifference to church ritual and ceremonies and his doubts about Catholic sacramental theology. He knew Calvin's *Institutes* by 1541, when he became a member of Cardinal Pole's household in Viterbo. A number of Valdés's followers had moved there after their master's death to continue their study of the Bible, reading of theological works (including those by northern reformers like Bucer), and religious discussions. That Flaminio preferred a life of withdrawal can be seen both by his refusal to accompany Cardinal Contarini to the Colloquy of Regensburg in 1541, and by his turning down the post of secretary during the first session of the Council of Trent. He died in Rome on 17 February 1550 in the presence of Cardinal Carafa, who, according to Beccadelli, asked for and received the dying man's confession of Catholic faith.

Flaminio's life and work exemplify the ambivalence and doubts shared by many intellectuals of his generation. Despite his humanist education and fame as a poet he remained dependent on patrons. Although drawn to the ideas of northern reformers, he developed his own spirituality centered on the benefits of Christ's death for the Christian and in the end was unwilling to break with the Roman church, either because he accepted its teaching or out of fear of exile and poverty. His complex and ambiguous thought continues to offer remarkable insight into the exterior and interior world of an Italian *spirituale*.

BIBLIOGRAPHY

Primary Source

Flaminio, Marcantonio. *Lettere*. Edited by Alessandro Pastore. Rome, 1978. Indispensable edition of Flaminio's surviving correspondence.

Secondary Sources

Fenlon, Dermot. *Heresy and Obedience in Tridentine Italy: Cardinal Pole and the Counter-Reformation*. Cambridge, 1972. Excellent analysis of the *spirituali* and *zelanti* in their larger context.

Maddison, Carol. *Marcantonio Flaminio: Poet, Humanist, Reformer*. London, 1965. Only modern work in English, focusing on Flaminio as poet.

Pastore, Alessandro. *Marcantonio Flaminio: Fortune e sfortune di un chierico nell'Italia del Cinquecento*. Milan, 1981. Best recent biography, good bibliography.

ELISABETH G. GLEASON

FLANDERS (Dutch, Vlaanderen) was one of the seventeen provinces that constituted the Habsburg Netherlands in the mid-sixteenth century. Because of the international renown of Flemish towns such as Ghent and Brugge, Flanders was widely used in the later Middle Ages, especially by foreign merchants, as a synonym for the Low Countries. This article, however, relates to Flanders proper.

Following the death of Louis of Male in 1384, Philip of Burgundy (d. 1404) governed the province in the name of his wife, Margaret of Male. Flanders thus passed to the house of Burgundy and, after the death of Mary of Burgundy in 1482, to the house of Habsburg, who retained possession until 1794. The river Scheldt, which runs through Flanders, marked the ancient boundary between the possessions of the French kings and the Holy Roman Empire, so that the county was divided between "Crown" and "Imperial" Flanders. In 1529 the French king, Francis I, surrendered his seigneurial rights in Crown Flanders. The northerly part of Flanders, bordering the Westerscheldt estuary, however, was conquered by the United Provinces in the early seventeenth century and incorporated as Staats-Vlaanderen (Zeeuws-Vlaanderen) in the Dutch Republic. In the early modern period the county was divided for administrative purposes, apart from the chief towns of Ghent, Brugge, and Ieper, into twenty-one districts, seventeen for Flanders "Flamingant" and four for "Walloon Flanders." The Council of Flanders was responsible for the administration of justice and government in both parts, but the smaller, largely French-speaking region, dominated by the towns of Lille and Douai, constituted a separate province, much of which was absorbed into France under Louis XIV.

During the later Middle Ages the textile industry of Flanders underwent major changes. The large Flemish towns, which owed their wealth to the manufacture of cloth from English wool, faced a critical situation when the English expanded their own cloth industry significantly. The growth of the so-called new draperies flourished in the small towns and villages of the Flemish Westkwartier outside the effective control of the cloth manufacturing towns. The Flemish towns were finally eclipsed in the late fifteenth century by the rapid expansion of Antwerp. The Reformation in Flanders can be divided into seven phases, as outlined below.

1520–1529: **Christian Humanism and Evangelical Dissent.** Despite the economic difficulties experienced by the Flemish towns, they continued to sustain a vigorous lay culture. The patricians and merchants took a fashionable interest in Erasmian humanism, which placed a high value on the religion of the spirit and tended to frown on the traditional piety fostered by the mendicant orders. The numerous and popular *rederijkerskamers* ("chambers of rhetoric") allowed townspeople to explore controversial religious matters without overtly expressing a preference for the new, and forbidden, doctrines of Luther and other Protestant reformers. Interest in evangelical ideas was not restricted to well-traveled merchants and the intelligentsia. Artisans, too, showed their appreciation. When Luther's books were burned at Ghent in 1521, a local baker expressed his evangelical opinions, for which he was prosecuted. At this early stage sympathetic clergy disseminated evangelical ideas from the pulpit but also in private gatherings. Though sternly forbidden by law as seditious conventicles, these private meetings supplemented rather than replaced the services in the churches. Sectarianism was scarcely conceivable in the 1520s.

1529–1545: **Repression and Early Sectarianism.** After 1529 the severity of repression increased markedly: only two heretics had been executed in Flanders between 1524 and 1529, yet over fifty were put to death by 1545. At Lille six heretics received capital sentences in 1533. The intensity of this bout of persecution reflects contemporaries' concern about Anabaptism, in both the empire and Switzerland and more particularly in the northern Netherlands and Westphalia. In fact Flanders was little affected by Münsterite Anabaptism, though some fugitives from the north did seek refuge in the county, only to be hunted down in 1538. Brussels and the ecclesiastical authorities took offense at the religious message of plays performed by rhetoricians for a festival held in Ghent in 1539. Participating chambers had to respond to the question "What is the greatest comfort for a dying man?" Not one of the nineteen chambers represented, several of which came from outside Flanders, mentioned the sacrament of the altar, and five showed marked evangelical sympathies by upholding justification by faith alone and by attacking images.

1545–1565: **Flemish Protestants in Exile and "Under the Cross."** Fierce repression in 1545 almost resulted in the elimination of heresy in the county. But by driving others to seek refuge in flight abroad, these measures ironically assisted the survival and, indeed, confessional development of dissent. Some dissidents withdrew to the relative anonymity of Antwerp, where in 1554–1555 the first Calvinist congregations were established for the French- and Dutch-speaking communities. Others settled in England: Jan Łaski set up a stranger church at London in 1550, and another was established at Sandwich in 1561, most of whose members came from the Westkwartier. Yet others took up residence at Emden in east Friesland, which, after the closure of the London Dutch church on the accession of Mary Tudor, became the "mother church" of reformed Protestantism in the Low Countries as well as the foremost center for the printing of Dutch Calvinist literature. In the French-speaking parts Protestants looked first to Strasbourg and subsequently to Geneva; in the early 1550s Protestants from French Flanders, at Brugge in search of work, disseminated Calvinist literature. The confessionalization of the Flemish Reformation accelerated when Anabaptist elders like Gillis van Aken and Leenaert Bouwens, operating chiefly from Antwerp but also from the northern Netherlands, established congregations in the chief towns as well as in southwest Flanders in and around Kortrijk.

In the closing years of the Habsburg-Valois conflict, the central government mounted another onslaught on heresy. Of the 264 religious dissidents put to death in Flanders before 1566, almost two-fifths were executed between 1557 and 1564, most of whom were Anabaptists. At the same time Calvinism made considerable inroads among the textile workers in the industrialized countryside of the Westkwartier, especially at Hondschoote and Armentières and in the adjacent Pays de L'Alleu. A tension now developed between the moderate Calvinist leadership, well represented in the consistories of the stranger churches abroad, and radicals, who were not prepared to endure the repression. Radicals in England, and especially at Sandwich, organized a successful jail break in 1561 and a public service at Boeschepe in the Westkwartier in July 1562. The activities of these militants have been regarded as marking the "start of the armed resistance against Spain," but the limited objectives of the participants and the localized nature of the violence scarcely warrant this description.

1566–1567: **Open-air Preachings, Image Breaking, and Insurrection.** When a small circle of Calvinists among the gentry organized the Compromise of the Nobility late in 1565, Calvinism in the Netherlands became a player in the political arena. In April 1566 the lesser nobility, including several from Flanders, asked Margaret of Parma to suspend the Inquisition and develop a new religious policy for the country with the assistance of the Estates-General. In fact the campaign against heresy had already stalled after 1564. This turn of events encouraged Flemish Protestants in exile, often in England, to return. By late May 1566 large crowds had begun to attend sermons delivered by lay preachers around Ieper, and from there the practice spread quickly to the rest of Flanders and beyond. Unfortunately little is known about the content and style of these sermons, though some were evidently seditious.

On 10 August 1566 Jacob de Buyzere, who had recently returned from Sandwich where he served as minister, led an onslaught on the statues in a monastery at Steenvoorde in the Westkwartier. Within a week bands of iconoclasts sacked churches in many parts of Flanders: more than one hundred churches and religious houses were reportedly attacked in the Westkwartier alone. On 20 August the image breaking began in Antwerp and copycat riots followed elsewhere in Flanders. Among the most serious was the iconoclasm at Ghent, where on 22 August some fifty churches, religious houses, and chapels were attacked. Meanwhile the organization of Reformed churches went on apace, and by the autumn consistories had been chosen in many Flemish towns and villages.

Though large numbers attended the open-air services, it is probable that only a comparatively small proportion were convinced Calvinists. After the attacks on the churches the Calvinists forfeited the support of both the nobility and the townspeople in general. As the government slowly recovered its nerve and, with it, the political initiative, the Calvinist minority in Flanders, as elsewhere, looked increasingly beleaguered, and those who took up arms against the government were routed. By April 1567 law and order had been restored throughout Flanders, and those implicated in the events of the "Wonder Year," as contemporaries referred to 1566, had to choose exile, abjuration, or returning to the small underground congregations "under the cross."

1567–1577: From the Council of Troubles to the Coup d'État of 1577. This decade represents the least-known period in the history of the Flemish Reformation. Fernando Álvarez de Toledo, duke of Alba, who arrived in the Low Countries in August 1567, established a special tribunal to investigate the disturbances of the previous year and to punish the ringleaders. The Council of Troubles, known popularly as the Council of Blood, indicted some twelve thousand persons throughout the Low Countries, of whom approximately one-third came from Flanders and French Flanders: Ieper, Ronse, Ghent, and Bailleul alone accounted for one-tenth of all those cited before the council. From 1567 to 1568 a band of fanatical antipapists, the *Bosgeuzen* ("wood beggars"), operating from England, sought to incite the inhabitants of the Westkwartier to rebellion, but the ringleaders were captured in the autumn of 1568 and put to death.

Several Calvinist ministers from Flanders attended the first national synod of the Reformed churches from the Low Countries held at Emden in October 1571, when the congregations "under the cross" in Flanders were grouped in classes. Almost nothing is known of the underground Calvinist congregations in the county at this time. During 1577 the Reformed church at Ghent was served by three ministers, which would suggest a sizable following. Though the authorities were preoccupied with the Calvinists, the Anabaptists in Flanders were treated harshly when they were discovered, and twenty were put to death at Brugge between 1568 and 1573.

1578–1585: The Calvinist Republic at Ghent. The mutinies in the "Spanish" army in the summer and autumn of 1576 obliged the "loyal" provinces to reach an understanding with the "rebel" provinces of Holland and Zeeland. Under the terms of this agreement, known as the Pacification of Ghent, signed on 8 November 1576, only the Catholic religion could be practiced in the "loyal" provinces. But since the edicts against heresy were suspended, religious dissidents in the southern Netherlands could act more boldly, and Calvinist services were reported from 1577. A coup d'état in Ghent in October 1577 brought Jan van Hembyze to power and established a regime that strongly favored the Calvinists.

Events moved swiftly. By March 1578 the Calvinists of Ghent ventured to preach in public, in May the mendicant orders were expelled from the city, and at the beginning of June the Calvinists began to preach in the churches. The revolutionary regime in Ghent sought to secure a dominant political position for the town in Flanders, and the Reformed ministers and congregations became the means to ensure compliance with this policy. This explains the remarkably rapid expansion of the Reformed churches. Before the end of 1578 fifty Reformed ministers were active in Flanders, and by early 1579 the county had been divided into fifteen classes. Since education was seen as the key to the future success of Calvinism in Flanders, a school of divinity was duly established in Ghent that despite its short-lived existence enjoyed a considerable reputation. At Brugge, too, the Calvinist regime, though less intolerant than its counterpart in Ghent, sought to impose the new religion on the surrounding region. The records of the Reformed synods of Flanders have survived. When using these to assess the success or failure of the Reformed churches in Flanders, and especially in the countryside, it is important to bear in mind that this religious experiment lasted for only three or four years, a quite insufficient period in which to efface traditional religious attachments.

William of Orange strongly opposed the politico-religious extremism of Ghent, which threatened to undermine his fragile anti-Spanish alliance. In August 1579 William did succeed in forcing Hembyze and Peter Dathenus to withdraw from Ghent, but the precarious military situation and the unpopularity of his Anjou policy in Flanders restricted William's room for maneuver. Anjou's attempt to seize control of Antwerp and several Flemish towns in January 1583 not only discredited the Valois prince but undermined William's standing in Ghent. Hembyze and Dathenus returned to Ghent, only to enter into secret negotiations with Alessandro Farnese, duke of Parma. Though Hembyze paid for his treachery with his life, Ghent was unable to withstand the duke of Parma's military pressure, and on 17 September the town surrendered, bringing to an end this attempt to make Ghent the Geneva of Flanders. Brugge and Ieper had already capitulated to the duke of Parma earlier in 1584; after the fall of Antwerp in August 1585, royalist troops once more virtually controlled Flanders.

1585–1609: **Protestant Emigration from Flanders.** Committed Protestants in the towns of Flanders faced a difficult and uncertain future. Though the duke of Parma was prepared to grant them a period of grace to settle their affairs, they had eventually either to return to the Catholic church or go into exile. According to one recent estimate as many as 175,000 southern Netherlanders may have migrated, at least in part for religious reasons, between 1540 and 1630. The greater part left to settle in Holland in the 1580s and 1590s, though some stragglers delayed their departure until after the end of the Twelve Years' Truce in 1621. The scale of the emigration aggravated the problems faced by the Flemish towns after their recapture by Parma. Textile workers migrated wholesale from Hondschoote to Leiden in Holland in 1582; one-third of the houses at Ghent were up for sale or available to rent in 1585.

Under the rule of the devout archdukes (1598–1633) and their successors, the Counter-Reformation was gradually implemented in Flanders as elsewhere in the southern Netherlands. Frequent catechization, close supervision of the schools, regular archidiaconal and episcopal pastoral visitations, and a more highly disciplined priesthood reduced religious dissent to negligible proportions. Many "heretics" who had no wish to pull up their roots made their peace with the Catholic church, and those dissidents who remained did not, for obvious reasons, proselytize.

In a few villages, however, a dissident tradition continued. Protestants living close to the border with the Dutch Republic could count on the support of their co-religionists and, no less importantly, the protection of the States-General of the United Provinces. The persistence of Protestantism at Sint-Maria Horebeke and in a handful of other villages around Audenarde, known collectively as the "Flemish Mount of Olives," may also be attributable to an unofficial understanding between the authorities on both sides not to harry the religious minorities within their borders.

[*See also* Anabaptists; Belgic Confession; Calvinism; *and* William of Orange.]

BIBLIOGRAPHY

Backhouse, Marcel Floris. "Beeldenstorm en Bosgeuzen in het Westkwartier, 1566–1568: Bijdrage tot de geschiedenis van de godsdiensttroebelen der Zuidelijke Nederlanden in de 16e eeuw." *Handelingen van de Koninklijke Geschied- en Oudheidkundige Kring van Kortriik* 38 (1971), 5–173. Best account of the activities of the Wood-Beggars who descended on the Flemish coast from England.

Coussemaker, Edmond de. *Troubles religieux du XVIe siècle dans la Flandre maritime, 1560–1570* (1876). 4 vols. Sources on the Reformation in the Flemish Westkwartier.

Crew, Phyllis Mack. *Calvinist Preaching and Iconoclasm in the Netherlands, 1544–1569.* Cambridge, 1978. Claims that in the topsy-turvey world of 1566, charismatic Calvinist ministers could appear to their auditors as men with authority.

Decavele, Johan. *De dageraad van de reformatie in Vlaanderen, 1520–1565.* 2 vols. Brussels, 1975. Fundamental study of the Reformation in Flanders until the outbreak of the revolt, with invaluable appendices. Especially strong on the socioeconomic profile of Protestantism.

Decavele, Johan, ed. *Het eind van een rebelse droom: Opstellen over het calvinistisch bewind te Gent, 1577–1584.* Ghent, 1984. Essays on the Calvinist Republic of Ghent.

Delmotte, M. "Het calvinisme in de verschillende bevolkingslagen te Gent, 1566–1567." *Tijdschrift voor geschiedenis* 76 (1963), 145–176. Sophisticated analysis of the socioeconomic position of the Calvinists and the image-breakers at Ghent.

Deyon, Solange, and Alain Lottin. *Les "casseurs" de l' été 1566: L'iconoclasme dans le Nord de la France.* N.p., 1981. Despite the misleading title, a clear and thoughtful analysis of the causes of the image-breaking and of the motives of the iconoclasts in Hainault, Artois, and French Flanders.

DuPlessis, Robert S. *Lille and the Dutch Revolt: Urban Stability in an Era of Revolution, 1500–1582.* Cambridge, 1991. The Lille magistrates reduced the risk of urban disorder by checking the growth of large-scale capitalist concerns and by paying careful attention to poor relief.

Janssen, H. Q. De. *Kerkhervorming in Vlaanderen.* 2 vols. Arnhem, 1868. Includes the acts of the reformed classes and synods held in Flanders, 1578–1583.

Pettegree, Andrew. *Emden and the Dutch Revolt: Exile and the Development of Reformed Protestantism.* Oxford, 1992. Explains the importance of Emden for the survival, organization, and development of Reformed Protestantism in the Low Countries.

Scheerder, Jozef. *De beeldenstorm.* 2d rev. ed. Bussum, Netherlands, 1978. Useful account of the image-breaking, with an excellent bibliography.

Verheyden, A. L. E. *Anabaptism in Flanders, 1530–1650.* Scottdale, Pa., 1961. Useful for those who do not read Dutch.

ALASTAIR C. DUKE

FOECKEL, Herman. *See* Faukelius, Hermannus.

FONTANINI, Benedetto. *See* Benedetto da Mantova.

FONTANUS, Johannes (Ger., Johannes Puts; 1545–1615), Reformed minister at Arnhem (1578–1615). Son of Engelbert Puts of Soller (near Düren), he enrolled as a student of theology under the name Fontanus at Geneva (1564) and at Heidelberg (1567), where his most important teacher was Zacharias Ursinus. His work as a Reformed minister and teacher of theology at the grammar school at Neuhausen near Worms (1568–2576) ended when the Lutheran Louis succeeded his father as Count Palatine. He was subsequently appointed teacher of theology at the convent of Keppel near Siegen by Count John of Nassau, the eldest brother of William of Nassau. In June 1578 Fontanus arrived in Gelderland in the company of John of Nassau, who had been appointed stadtholder of the province in March 1578, and by October 1578 he had become a minister of the Reformed congregation in Arnhem.

After the main churches had ceased Catholic worship in 1579, Fontanus, together with the municipal authorities of Arnhem, tried to remove Catholicism from public life and to get his congregation to accept strict, Calvinist discipline in life and religion. On 23 April 1581 the celebration of Mass was banned, and in 1587 all citizens and inhabitants of the town were obliged to attend the sermons of Reformed ministers on Sundays and holidays.

Between 1579 and 1610 Fontanus was nine times made president of the provincial synod and was also given various oversight responsibilities to establish the new church in Gelderland. In this capacity Fontanus tested the Reformed convictions of "ministers of the word" and fired them when he found them wanting. He also gave strict instructions to schoolmasters, sextons, and organists. Through his efforts, Arnhem's Latin school was renewed and reformed in 1591. In 1600 he also devoted himself to the foundation of a university at Harderwijk.

Fontanus was involved in the process of Calvinization in several places: Wageningen in 1579, Zutphen in 1580, Nijkerk in 1593, Nijmegen in 1595, 's Heerenberg in 1600, and the area of Meuse and Waal and the Tieler- and Bommelerwaard in 1606. While striving to establish the Reformed religion and enforce new (elitist) standards and values, Fontanus was often confronted with the fact that Catholicism and popular culture were still firmly embedded in the population of Gelderland. The new faith initially met with little or no enthusiasm. In parts of the province reformational activities were also obstructed for years by the uncertain political situation and the fluctuating fortunes of war.

Fontanus was of the opinion that the Belgic Confession and the Heidelberg Catechism had to be maintained in full, and he fiercely rejected the views of the Arminians. In 1606, when the States-General decided to call a national synod to resolve the issue, Fontanus presided over a preparatory convention (May 1607) that tried but failed to agree on an agenda. In the years that followed Fontanus kept advocating a national synod. Together with Willem Baudartius, minister at Zutphen, he was one of Gelderland's delegates to the States-General at The Hague, where, on 27 September 1612, ministers from various provinces presented an appeal for a national synod to be called as soon as possible. Meanwhile he fought against the appointment of Conradus Vorstius at Leiden, and led the Counter-Remonstrant campaign against Arminian ministers in Gelderland. Shortly before his death peace among the ministers was restored by a resolution drawn up by the local government banning two Remonstrant ministers from expressing—either privately or in the pulpit—ideas that clashed with the accepted doctrines of the Reformed church as set down in the Belgic Confession and the Heidelberg Catechism.

Fontanus was married twice. His first wife, a sister of Pieter Versteghe, Arnhem's town clerk, bore him two daughters, Sara and Sybilla. The eldest married Eilardus Mehenius, a minister at Harderwijk, and Sybilla became the wife of Gerardus Versteeg, a minister at Oud-Beierland. In 1609 Fontanus married Wilhelma van Haerdt. Both his wives were probably involved in the French school at Arnhem, for which Fontanus made his house available.

BIBLIOGRAPHY

Itterzon, G. P. van. "Fontanus Johannes." In *Biografisch Lexicon voor de Geschiedenis van het Nederlandse Protestantisme,* vol. 2, p. 201–203. Kampen, Netherlands, 1983.

Janssen, A. E. M, and J. A. M. M. Janssen. "Enkele notities uit de correspondenties van Johannes Fontanus." In *Bijdragen en Mededelingen van Gelre LXXI,* p. 81–99. Arnhem, Netherlands, 1980. Critical analysis of literature and sources.

Spiertz, M. G, and R. W. A. Megens. *Gids voor de studie van Reformatie en Katholieke Herleving in Gelderland 1520–1650.* Utrecht, 1986.

Verzeichnis der im deutschen Sprachbereich erschienenen Drucke des XVI. Jahrhunderts. Stuttgart, 1983–. See vol. 7, nos. 1839–1844.

Wiggers, A., M. G. Spiertz, and G. J. Mentink. *Gids voor de studie van Reformatie en Katholieke Herleving in Gelderland 1500–1700.* Utrecht, 1988.

MATHIEU SPIERTZ

FORMULA OF CONCORD. Composed in 1577, this formula was the last of the sixteenth-century Lutheran confessional writings. During Luther's lifetime tensions emerged among his followers over the proper interpretation of his teaching. His associate Philipp Melanchthon and his student Johann Agricola publicly disputed Agricola's antinomian positions. In the 1530s and 1540s Melanchthon and another of Luther's earliest supporters, Nikolaus von Amsdorf, differed on the role of good works in salvation, the role of the human will in conversion, the relationship of Lutheran churches to the papacy and medieval practice, and the Lord's Supper. The Schmalkald War (1546–1547) and the imposition of the re-Catholicizing Augsburg Interim (1548), along with the subsequent formulation of the Leipzig Interim by Melanchthon and his associates in electoral Saxony (1548), transformed these tensions into open polemics among Luther's followers. The deaths of the living authorities of first-generation Lutheranism—Luther (1546) and Melanchthon (1560)—impelled their followers to find a new authority to govern interpretation of the scriptures. *Corpora doctrinae* (collections of defining confessional documents) appeared in many Lutheran territories during the 1560s to fill this gap and to solve the controversies that were besetting the churches.

The chief confrontations occurred between two parties of former Wittenberg students—the more radically "Lutheran," subsequently labeled Gnesio-Lutheran, and the more conservative Philippists (closer to medieval teaching and church life), so called because they adhered more closely to Melanchthon's views (although both parties were heavily influenced by Melanchthon). Both these parties opposed the doctrine of justification formulated by another follower of Luther, Andreas Osiander. At the side of these disputes stood the party of Württemberg theologians, who finally played a decisive role in ending the disputes, and a majority of Lutheran pastors who did not become actively involved in them.

These disputes centered on three issues: (1) the Leipzig Interim and its principle of adiaphorism; (2) the proposition of Georg Major that "good works are necessary for salvation" and related questions on the nature of the gospel and the third use of the law; and (3) synergism and the related definition of original sin. Disputes over the Lord's Supper and related christological questions grew out of Joachim Westphal's defense of Lutheran sacramental theology against John Calvin and others (1552), as well as out of the disputes between the Württemberg Lutherans and the Calvinist theologians of the Palatinate which climaxed at the Colloquy of Maulbronn (1564).

These disputes had hardly begun before both theologians and Lutheran princes began efforts to end them. In general, the Gnesio-Lutheran and Philippist parties had opposing approaches to establishing concord among the Lutherans. The Philippists favored an "amnesty," or forgetting of past differences, and a statement of common confession in only the most general terms, without condemnations of false teachings and false teachers. They believed only the princes could impose a satisfactory settlement. The Gnesio-Lutherans wanted specific and detailed theses and antitheses, setting forth pure biblical teaching and condemning both false teachers and false teachings. They rejected a primary role for the princes in reaching theological agreement, insisting that it must be accomplished by a synod of theologians.

Duke Christoph of Württemberg began his efforts to bring the disputing theologians into harmony in 1553. Matthias Flacius Illyricus, leader of the Gnesio-Lutherans, offered "Gentle Proposals" for concord in 1556 and tried through the good offices of Lower Saxon friends to effect reconciliation with Melanchthon and his colleagues through the colloquy of Coswig in 1557. The situation worsened at a 1557 colloquy with Catholics held in Worms, where the two Lutheran parties failed to make a common front against the Catholic colloquists. In 1558 the princes concluded a general agreement, along the Philippist model, in the Frankfurt Recess; this only evoked the sharp criticism of the Gnesio-Lutheran party and, in ducal Saxony, the publication of a *Book of Confutation*, a detailed condemnation of heresies, including positions held by Philippists. In 1561 the Lutheran princes met at Naumburg; the situation was complicated by the efforts of Elector Frederick III of the Palatinate to find room within the churches of the Augsburg Confession for his calvinizing tendencies. The Naumburg diet pledged its participants to the Unaltered Augsburg Confession, but it also granted the Altered Augsburg Confession the status of a legitimate interpretation of the original. In 1568–1569 representatives of Philippist electoral Saxony and Gnesio-Lutheran ducal Saxony met in the Altenburg Colloquy, a series of discussions that widened the gap between the two parties.

In 1568 Duke Julius of Braunschweig-Wolfenbüttel began the introduction of the Reformation in his lands. To assist him he assembled a team of theologians—led by Martin Chemnitz of Braunschweig, Nicholas Selnecker of electoral Saxony, and Jakob Andreae of Württemberg—whose cooperation laid the groundwork for their later work together on the Formula of Concord. At the same time, while he served in the north, Andreae continued diplomatic efforts that Duke Christoph had launched more than a decade earlier on behalf of Lutheran concord. Andreae visited a large number of towns and princely courts in this endeavor (1568–1570), attempting to establish harmony among the Lutherans with a brief, Philippist-style formula cast in five articles on justification, good works, free will, adiaphora, and the Lord's Supper. His mission culminated in a meeting at Zerbst (1570), which failed to establish a satisfactory solution to the controversies. Soon thereafter the differences between his "ubiquitist" Christology and that of the Philippist Wittenbergers ruptured their relationship permanently.

In 1573 Andreae forged a new attempt to establish Lutheran concord with his *Six Sermons on the Divisions among the Theologians of the Augsburg Confession.* These sermons offer a detailed confession of the faith on the issues of justification, good works, original sin and free will, adiaphora, the proper definition of law and gospel and related questions, and Christology. Apart from the last sermon (concerning the person of Christ, in which Andreae castigates the Wittenberg faculty explicitly in the text), the condemnation of false teachers is placed judiciously in marginal notes. The sermons nonetheless meet this Gnesio-Lutheran requirement in doing so. Andreae also affirms the positions of the main body of Gnesio-Lutherans, as he rejects both the radical Flacian doctrine of original sin and the Philippist positions on synergism, good works, the definition of the gospel, and the Lord's Supper and Christology.

Andreae sent his *Six Sermons* to other leading Lutheran churchmen. Chemnitz, David Chytraeus of Rostock, and Joachim Westphal of Hamburg, leaders among the north German theologians, rejected the homiletic form of the sermons as unsuitable for a document of concord. They also feared that his abrasive personality had antagonized so many people that any document with his name attached would not serve the cause of concord. They suggested that the Württemberg theologians as a body offer a proposal for solving the disputes framed in theses and antitheses. Andreae himself composed such a document, the Swabian Concord (1574). The north German theologians, led by Chemnitz and Chytraeus, reworked its text into the Swabian-Saxon Concord (1575). Dissatisfied with its form, Andreae supported the effort of Duke Ulrich of Württemberg, Count Georg Ernst of Henneberg, and Margrave Karl of Baden to draft another formula for concord. Their theologians met at Maulbronn Abbey in January 1576 and composed the Maulbronn Formula.

Two years earlier Elector August had uncovered the secret efforts of radical Philippists to move the public teaching in his lands away from Luther's understanding of the real presence in the Lord's Supper. He began searching for a new formulation to govern teaching and church life in his domains. His theologians advised him, at a conference at Lichtenburg (February 1576), on a course that resulted in his cooperating with Julius of Braunschweig-Wolfenbüttel and Elector Johann Georg of Brandenburg in the preparation of the Formula of Concord. He enlisted Andreae to assist Nicholas Selnecker in the reform of his own lands; these two were joined by Chemnitz, Chytraeus, and two Brandenburg theologians, Andreas Musculus and Christoph Corner. At a meeting at Torgau (28 May-7 June 1576), they composed a text that was circulated to Lutheran governments and theologians throughout Germany. On the basis of critical reactions the Torgau text was revised at two meetings at Bergen Abbey near Magdeburg (March 1577 by Andreae, Chemnitz, and Selnecker and May 1577 by all six Torgau negotiators). The Bergen book became the Solid Declaration of the Formula of Concord. Andreae had already prepared an epitome of the Torgau book, which was also incorporated into the Formula of Concord.

The Formula of Concord is, in fact, a representation of the Lutheran theology that developed out of the exchange between the thought of Martin Luther and Philipp Melanchthon. Although the main body of Gnesio-Lutherans found that its teaching met their positions at every point, the formulations were composed in such a manner as to attract the moderate Philippists as well. Thus, the Formula of Concord successfully brought together more than two-thirds of the Lutherans of its day. Chemnitz and Chytraeus, both devoted disciples of Melanchthon, were primarily responsible for crafting this exposition of Luther's theology within the methodological framework of Melanchthon and for preserving certain accents and concerns of Melanchthon's approach to teaching the biblical message.

The formula begins with an introductory orientation that sets forth the absolute authority of scripture and the nature of the authority of the Lutheran confessions for the teaching of the church. Articles 1 (on original sin) and 2 (free will) deal with aspects of the synergistic controversy and reject the concept that the human will makes any contribution whatsoever to its own conversion to faith in Christ. The first article affirms the teaching of Flacius that the will is totally corrupt and unable to turn itself to God but rejects his use of the Aristotelian terminology of substance for original sin. His expressions "original sin is the substance of the fallen human creature, not merely an accident" and "the fallen human creature is in the image of Satan" are condemned.

Article 3 affirms Luther's and Melanchthon's forensic concept of justification against the ontological concept of justification advanced by Andreas Osiander and against medieval Roman Catholic views of justification. Article 4 affirms the necessity of good works for the Christian life while rejecting both Georg Major's proposition "good works are necessary for salvation" and the radical Gnesio-Lutheran repetition by Nikolaus von Amsdorf of Luther's "good works are harmful to salvation." In article 5 the formulators concede that Philippist students of Melanchthon were not wrong in defining "Gospel" as the whole preaching of Christ, both for repentance and for the forgiveness of sins, but they maintain that the proper understanding of "Gospel" focuses only on God's gracious bestowal of the forgiveness of sins and new life in Christ. Article 6 brings together the opposing views of Musculus and of the other members of the team of authors on the use of the law in the Christian life. It affirms Musculus's view that Christians act without the compulsion of the law, "out of a free and merry spirit," while at the same time insisting that the law functions in the Christian life to curb and to crush sin and also to provide instruction and insight for Christian decision making.

Articles 7–9 arose out of intra-Lutheran controversies over the Lord's Supper and related christological questions and are aimed above all at the rejection of the "Crypto-Philippism" of electoral Saxony in the years leading up to 1574; however, in affirming Lutheran teaching on the real presence of Christ's body and blood in the Lord's Supper and on the communication of the attributes of Christ's two natures against the Crypto-Philippists, the Formula of Concord rejects the Calvinist positions advanced in the Palatinate and other German lands. Article 7 (the Lord's Supper) affirms Luther's understanding of the sacramental presence of Christ's body and blood in the elements of bread and wine, partaken through the mouth by both believers and unbelievers alike. Article 8 (the person of Christ) avoids Andreae's concept of the "ubiquity" of Christ's human body, teaching instead Chemnitz's view that according to "the communication of attributes" Christ's divine and human natures so share their characteristics that his human body may be present wherever, whenever, and in whatever form God wills (multivolipresence). Article 9 addresses minor intra-Lutheran controversies on Christ's descent into hell, as well as phrasing from the Heidelberg Catechism on the subject.

The adiaphoristic controversy laid the basis for article 10, which affirms the Gnesio-Lutheran principle that, in a time when confession of the faith is necessary, nothing is an adiaphoron. Article 11 addresses the doctrine of election, attempting to clarify Luther's law/gospel approach to predestination within the context of several small controversies over the subject (that of Johannes Marbach and Girolamo Zanchi at Strasbourg in 1563 and of Cyriakus Spangenberg in the late 1560s). Article 12 condemns errors of non-Lutheran sects, including the Anabaptists, the Schwenckfelders, and the antitrinitarians.

The Formula of Concord was written to present the proper interpretation of the Augsburg Confession and thus end the controversies over the proper definition of Luther's teaching and legacy, which had divided the adherents of the Augsburg Confession both politically and theologically. It satisfactorily concluded the older controversies that had begun in the 1550s (such as the Osiandrian, synergistic, Majoristic, and adiaphoristic controversies). Those controversies, however, which arose within Lutheranism in the 1560s and 1570s, namely, the Flacian controversy over original sin and the Crypto-Philippist controversy over the Lord's Supper and Christology (as distinct from earlier disputes between Lutherans and Reformed over these issues), were not ended by the formula. Criticism of article I by the radical Flacians and of articles 7 and 8 by both Crypto-Philippists and Reformed theologians continued into the 1580s. For in gathering together the main body of Gnesio-Lutherans, moderate Philippists, Württembergers, and many others outside these parties, the formula had definitively rejected the positions of these groups.

The Formula of Concord was incorporated—along with the ancient ecumenical creeds (Apostles', Nicene, and Athanasian) and those documents that had won widest recognition as defining documents for Lutheran theology (the Augsburg Confession, its Apology, the Schmalkald Articles, the Treatise on the Power and Primacy of the Pope, and Luther's two catechisms)—into the *Book of Concord.* Jakob Andreae composed a preface for the entire *Book of Concord* in 1579; its explanation of the origins of the Formula of Concord and of its approach to Lutheran concord helped win adherents for the book.

From 1577 to 1580 Andreae and others worked tirelessly to bring as many adherents of the Augsburg Confession into the Concordianist settlement as possible. A synod was to be held in Magdeburg to express support for the formula, but this plan did not materialize. The death of Frederick III of the Palatinate brought his son Ludwig VI to the position of elector there; skillful negotiations, which included the formulation of the preface to the *Book of Concord,* brought Ludwig into the company of the other two temporal electors in support of the formula. They were joined by the majority of Lutheran governments and more than eight thousand pastors. For political reasons Duke Julius finally held Braunschweig-Wolfenbüttel outside the settlement, although his theologians agreed for the most part with its teaching. Some churches, such as those in Anhalt and Bremen, opposed the doctrinal positions of the formula (e.g., on Christology and the Lord's Supper). Others withheld support for tactical reasons (e.g., Strasbourg) or because they believed that the theology of Philipp Melanchthon had been slighted in its final formulation (e.g., Pomerania and Holstein). Resisted in some areas because the local *corpus doctrinae* had been designed for the specific need of the territory, the book became a substitute for the *corpora doctrinae* that most Lutheran governments had adopted during the 1560s and 1570s for the regulation of church life. The book was published 25 June 1580, on the fiftieth anniversary of the presentation of the Augsburg Confession. Printing of the text ensued in several places, resulting in discrepancies in the text that also provoked controversy.

The new item in the book, the Formula of Concord, attracted surprisingly little public critique. With just a few exceptions, even those German Lutheran churches that refused to accept the book avoided public condemnation of its teaching. Nonetheless, in 1583 Chemnitz, Selnecker, and Timotheus Kirchner published an *Apology of the Book of Concord,* a collection of four treatises that defended the teaching of the formula against criticism from Christoph Irenaeus, a Flacian theologian; from a variety of Reformed theologians, particularly those of the Palatinate and Bremen (on the Lord's Supper and Christology); and from the Nuremberg lay theologian Christoph Herdesian (on the authority of Luther and the Augsburg Confession). In electoral Saxony and in other lands the introduction of the *Book of Concord* as the regulating definition of Lutheran teaching served to strengthen the control of the secular prince or city council over the church, as these early modern governments attempted to consolidate their absolutist rule over their lands.

In the *Book of Concord* the majority of German Lutheran churches found their substitute for medieval popes and councils as the authoritative source and guide (later designated *norma normata*) for the interpretation of the scriptures (the *norma normans*). Lutheran theologians of subsequent centuries did not often cite the *Book of Concord,* but it remained the prime orientation for the Lutheran theological enterprise—a hermeneutical guide, as well as a source for defining fundamental doctrine. Taken less seriously in the age of the Enlightenment, it found renewed significance in the confessional revival of the nineteenth century, a significance that continued in the life of many Lutheran churches throughout the world even into the twentieth century.

[*See also* Andreae, Jakob; Gnesio-Lutherans; Lutheranism; Melanchthon, Philipp; *and* Philippists.]

BIBLIOGRAPHY

Bente, F. *Historical Introductions to the Symbolical Books of the Evangelical Luthern Church* (1921). Saint Louis, 1965. The most thorough treatment in English of the historical context of the Formula of Concord, reflecting the contributions and biases of the best European scholarship of the period.

Brecht, Martin, and Reinhard Schwarz. *Bekenntnis und Einheit der Kirche: Studien zum Konkordienbuch.* Stuttgart, 1980. Twenty-one essays analyze historical and doctrinal issues connected with the *Book of Concord.*

Dingel, Irene. "Concordia und Kontroverse: Das Ringen um konfessionelle Pluralität und bekenntnismäßige Einheit im Spiegel der öffentlichen Diskussionen um Konkordienformel und Konkordienbuch." Habilitation thesis, Ruprecht-Karls-Universität Heidelberg, 1993. A thorough analysis of the reactions to the Formula and Book of Concord.

Ebel, Jobst Christian. *Wort und Geist bei den Verfassern der Konkordienformel.* Munich, 1981.

The Formula of Concord: Quadricentennial Essays. Sixteenth Century Journal 8.4 (1977). Eight essays treat the formula's historical setting and its place in the life of the church.

Frank, F. H. R. *Die Theologie der Concordienformel historisch-dogmatisch entwickelt.* 4 vols. Erlangen, 1858–1865. The classic exposition of the subject.

Gensichen, Hans Werner. *We Condemn: How Luther and 16th-Century Lutheranism Condemned False Doctrine.* Translated by Herbert J. A. Bouman. Saint Louis, 1967. On the basis of secondary sources, the Lutheran condemnation of false doctrine is placed in its historical context and analyzed.

Green, Lowell C. *The Formula of Concord: An Historical and Bibliographical Guide.* Saint Louis, 1977. An introduction to the documents and literature.

Gritsch, Eric W., and Robert W. Jenson. *Lutheranism: The Theological Movement and Its Confessional Writings.* Philadelphia, 1976. A synthetic presentation of the historical context and doctrinal content of the *Book of Concord.*

Jungkuntz, Theodore R. *Formulators of the Formula of Concord: Four Architects of Lutheran Unity.* Saint Louis, 1977. Brief biographical sketches of Andreae, Chemnitz, Chytraeus, and Selnecker, based on secondary sources.

Koch, Ernst. "Konkordienbuch" and "Konkordienformel." In *Theologische Realenzyklopädie*, vol. 19, pp. 472–476 and 476–483. Berlin and New York, 1990. A thorough overview of the topics.

Kolb, Robert. *Andreae and the Formula of Concord: Six Sermons on the Way to Lutheran Unity.* Saint Louis, 1977. A translation of the *Six Sermons* of 1573, with an extensive introduction.

———. *Confessing the Faith: Reformers Define the Church, 1530–1580.* Saint Louis, 1991. The development of the concept of confessing the faith that culminated in the Formula and *Book of Concord* is explored in detail.

Mager, Inge. *Die Konkordienformel im Fürstentum Braunschweig-Wolfenbüttel.* Göttingen, 1993.

Mildenberger, Friedrich. *Theoloqy of the Lutheran Confessions.* Translated by Erwin Lueker. Philadelphia, 1986.

Schlink, Edmund. *Theology of the Lutheran Confessions.* Translated by Paul F. Koehneke and Herbert J. A. Bouman. Reprint, Philadelphia, 1975. The classic twentieth-century exposition of Lutheran confessional theology.

Schöne, Jobst. *Bekenntnis zur Wahrheit: Aufsätze über die Kondordienformel.* Erlangen, 1978. Thirteen essays treat doctrinal issues raised by the Formula of Concord.

Spitz, Lewis W., and Wenzel Lohff, eds. *Discord, Dialogue, and Concord: Studies in the Lutheran Reformation's Formula of Concord.* Philadelphia, 1977. Thirteen essays explore the content and reactions to the Formula of Concord.

Tschackert, Paul. *Die Entstehung der lutherischen und der reformierten Kirchenlehre samt ihren innerprotestantischen Gegensätzen* (1910). Göttingen, 1979. Detailed analysis of the developments leading to the Formula and *Book of Concord.*

ROBERT KOLB

FORTY-TWO ARTICLES. *See* Articles of Religion.

FOXE, Edward (1496?–1538), bishop of Hereford from 1535 to 1538, royal almoner, and chief architect of the propaganda campaign to secure Henry VIII's divorce from Catherine of Aragon. After attending Cambridge Foxe entered the service of Thomas Wolsey, the king's chief minister, around 1527. In early 1528 he and Stephen Gardiner traveled to Rome and secured a commission from pope Clement VII to try the divorce case in England. He was elected provost of King's College, Cambridge, in September. At Waltham in August 1529 Foxe and Thomas Cranmer devised the strategy Henry would use to render his marriage to Catherine invalid—soliciting university opinion on the issue instead of seeking remedy in canon law. Foxe was instrumental in obtaining repudiation of the royal marriage at both Cambridge and Oxford universities (1530).

Along with John Stokesley and Nicolas de Burgo, Foxe compiled the *Collectanea satis copiosa* (c.1530), an unpublished assemblage of evidence supporting the king's position, which included legal judgments, chronicles, scriptures, and patristic and conciliarist opinions. This work helped convince Henry that historically England had been and still was an empire that gave him both spiritual and temporal jurisdiction (*regnum* and *sacerdotum*) within his kingdom, thereby making the pope's approval for the divorce unnecessary. This argument was continued in his *De vera differentia regiae potestatis et ecclesiae*, published in 1534, with a second edition appearing in 1538 and an English translation ten years later. Once the position was adopted officially, Foxe assisted Henry in 1532 in forcing the Submission of the Clergy (enacted by Parliament in 1534) and in arranging a French alliance.

Foxe was a friend of Anne Boleyn and, like her, may have held Lutheran sympathies, but, during a trip to Wittenberg in 1535, he was unsuccessful in securing Martin Luther's blessing for Henry's recent maneuvers. Most likely Foxe was also a central figure in the drafting of the early Anglican doctrinal statements known as the Ten Articles (1536) and the Bishops' Book (1537). Until his death on 8 May 1538,

Foxe helped Cranmer and Thomas Cromwell lead the effort for a political (parliamentary) settlement of the divorce, royal supremacy, and related issues.

BIBLIOGRAPHY

Guy, John. "Thomas Cromwell and the Intellectual Origins of the Henrician Revolution." In *Reassessing the Henrician Age: Humanism, Politics and Reform 1500–1550*, edited by Alistair Fox and John Guy, pp. 151–78. Oxford, 1986. Not much has been written on Foxe, but this study examines his role in the efforts to legitimate Henry VIII's divorce and the royal supremacy.

Nicholson, G. D. "The Nature and Function of Historical Argument in the Henrician Reformation." Ph.D. diss., University of Cambridge, 1977. Best discussion of Foxe's career in government service.

Oakley, Francis. "Edward Foxe, Matthew Paris, and the Royal *Potestas Ordinis*." *Sixteenth Century Journal* 18 (1987), 347–353. Demonstrates that a mistranslation of a portion of *De vera differentia* has incorrectly found Foxe claiming a royal right to consecrate bishops, thereby giving him a more radical reputation than is warranted.

BEN LOWE

FOXE, John (1517–1587), English Protestant church historian. He is invariably described as "the martyrologist" (a title he disowned), and his greatest published work, *Actes and Monuments*, was popularly called *The Book of Martyrs*. No other book, after the English Bible and *The Book of Common Prayer*, had more influence on the religious self-consciousness of England as a largely Protestant nation. As a church history it was nearly universal in its scope but drew the particular attention of its readers to a dense and enthralling account of the persecution of English Protestants in the reign of Mary Tudor.

Foxe was born in Boston, Lincolnshire, and educated at Oxford, where he became a fellow of Magdalen College in 1538. His intellectual formation was that of a humanist, and he was erudite in the three biblical languages and the author of Latin plays in the manner of Terence. As a convinced Protestant, he was forced to withdraw from Oxford in the later years of Henry VIII and to find private employment, first with the Lucy family of Charlecote, Warwickshire (where he found his wife), and then in the household of the duchess of Richmond, the widow of the king's natural son. She appointed him tutor to her nephews, members of the Howard family, including the duke of Norfolk, who would be executed in 1572. In these circumstances Foxe met the learned ex-Carmelite John Bale, who stimulated his interest in church history and its inner meaning, as clarified by *Revelation*.

In Mary's reign, and after a series of narrow escapes, Foxe took refuge overseas, settling first at Frankfurt, but later and more permanently at Basel, where he made a poor living in the book trade. By this time ecclesiastical history and martyrology were beginning to absorb Foxe's intellectual interest. He had already published (at Strasbourg in 1554) a modest book in Latin called *Commentarii rerum in ecclesia gestarum*, which drew the attention of a Continental readership to the significance of events in England from the time of John Wycliffe, that morning star of reformation, up to the early sixteenth century. In 1559 he published in Basel an extended edition of this work, bringing the story forward to the reign of Mary. His friends and correspondents were now plying him with copious evidence of this latest episode in persecution, and on his return to England he set about organizing the materials that in 1563 appeared as *Actes and Monuments of these Latter and Perilous Days*, a huge folio of eighteen hundred pages, and three times the length of the 1559 book. The printer was John Day, who was responsible for a brilliant production, illustrated with stunning woodcuts.

The 1563 edition caused a sensation and provoked a bitter backlash from Catholic controversialists. These criticisms and the general public interest plunged Foxe into further prodigious labor that produced the 1570 edition, now twice the length of the 1563 edition. This version was nearly definitive, although it would be followed by further printings, with additions and rearrangements, in 1576 and 1583 (the text used by Foxe's Victorian editors). The fifth and final Elizabethan edition appeared in 1596, after the author's death.

The Book of Martyrs had long since become Foxe's life. According to his son Simeon, as he walked the streets he was hardly recognizable to those who had known him in his youth. He either refused, or was never offered, an adequate church living, although he was rewarded for his dedication of the 1563 edition to the queen with a cathedral prebend at Salisbury, and he lived and died in tight circumstances. While no Puritan, he was distanced, perhaps by the temperament of a martyrologist, from the power structures of the established church, and he lived in London as a freelance literary figure, although sought after for pastoral advice. He held unusually tolerant views for his age, and on one occasion appealed to all concerned, the queen included, for the lives of two Dutch Anabaptists, who in spite of his pleas suffered the same fate as the Marian martyrs.

In addition to *Actes and Monuments*, Foxe wrote an apocalyptic play, *Christus Triumphans*, and, his last work, an immense commentary on the book of *Revelation*. His celebrated *Sermon of Christ Crucified* was preached at Paul's Cross on Good Friday 1570. Foxe was a true son of the first great age of print in England and saw many other works through the press, including the only works of Martin Luther published in England before the nineteenth century.

BIBLIOGRAPHY

Primary Sources

Foxe, John. *Foxe's Book of Martyrs*. London, 1929.

———. *The Acts and Monuments of John Foxe*. 8 vols. Edited by George Townsend. Reprint, New York, 1965.

Secondary Sources

Collinson, Patrick. "Truth and Legend: The Veracity of John Foxe's Book of Martyrs." In *Clio's Mirror: Historiography in Britain and the Netherlands*, edited by A. C. Duke and C. A. Tamse. Zutphen, 1985.

Haller, William. *Foxe's Book of Martyrs and the Elect Nation.* London, 1963. Printed in the United States as *The Elect Nation: The Meaning and Relevance of Foxe's "Book of Martyrs,"* New York, 1963. Advances an attractive but not entirely sound case for Foxe as a source of "elect nation" and (ultimately) imperial ideas.

Helgerson, Richard. *Forms of Nationhood: The Elizabethan Writing of England.* Chicago, 1992. Includes a brilliant chapter on Foxe, Richard Hooker, and the religious "writing of England."

Knott, John R. *Discourses of Martyrdom in English Literature, 1563–1694.* Cambridge, 1993. With White, places Foxe in a broad martyrological context.

Mozley, J. F. *John Foxe and His Book.* Reprint, New York, 1970. The most scholarly account of Foxe's life, defending his integrity, almost to excess, against his nineteenth-century detractors.

Olsen, V. Norskov. *John Foxe and the Elizabethan Church.* Berkeley, 1973. A theological account of Foxe's ecclesiology.

White, Helen C. *Tudor Books of Saints and Martyrs.* Madison, Wis., 1963.

Wooden, Warren W. *John Foxe.* Boston, 1983. A pioneering literary study.

PATRICK COLLINSON

FRANCE. At the beginning of the sixteenth century, the kingdom of France was considerably smaller than it is today. Toward the east, it was effectively bounded by the Meuse and Saône rivers, leaving Lorraine and Burgundy to the empire. Lyon constituted an outlying city, bordering on Savoy and Italy. Narbonne, to the South, bordered on Roussillon, which belonged to Spain. Several foreign-controlled enclaves cut into the kingdom: the province of the Charolais, an appurtenance of the Habsburgs; the principality of Orange, which belonged to the House of Chalon, then to that of Nassau; and a papal state composed of the county of Venaissin and the city of Avignon. Several large fiefdoms still had not been brought under the sway of the French kings, among them the duchy of Brittany; the holdings of the House of Albret (the province of Foix and the Béarn, with the exception of the kingdom of Navarre) and some domains; Flanders and the Artois, which were retained by the heirs to Burgundy, the Habsburgs; and the vast possessions of the duke of Bourbon, located in the heart of the French kingdom.

This map would change during the course of the century as a result of international treaties. Flanders and the Artois were ceded, with complete sovereignty going to Charles V, in 1529. Metz, Toul, and Verdun (the "three Bishoprics"), along with their Lorraine dependencies, were occupied by France beginning in 1552. France took Calais from the English in 1558. Bresse and Bugey were annexed from the duke of Savoy in 1601.

Internal changes also occurred. The marriage of Duchess Anne to kings Charles VIII and Louis XII brought Brittany again under French sway; Brittany definitively became a part of the kingdom in 1531. The Bourbon lands were confiscated in 1524 from the constable. The title of king of Navarre, along with the Albret territory, were reunited to the Crown with the accession of Henry IV in 1589.

During the sixteenth century the population of France was approximately sixteen million, practically double that of Spain and four times that of England. France was an immense kingdom, both in temporal and spatial measurements. Although Louis XI had put in place a network of postal routes, even the most urgent news took over a week to reach Milan from Paris via Lyon, the quickest route (the defeat of Pavia on 24 February 1525, was not known in Paris until 6 March); it also took a week for news from Paris to reach Toulouse (Toulouse was apprised only on 31 August of the Saint Bartholomew's Day Massacre on 24 August 1572).

The kingdom of France was composed of provinces—which maintained extensive legal and cultural distinctions, despite the programs of unification headed by governors, parlements, and the governing classes—along with towns staunchly holding onto privileges (better maintained in the south than in the north). The Ordinance of 1539 imposed the use of French in all official documents, but local dialects remained prevalent, even though printing and an increase in literacy had already begun to edge them out.

The kings of the first half of the century enjoyed absolute authority, in large part because the Estates-General had not met between 1484 and 1558. The provincial estates continued to meet in a large number of the provinces, but with restricted powers. Foreigners were astounded by the ease with which the king of France obtained everything he desired (obedience and taxes) from his subjects. The main limitation on his power was distance. On the other hand, the principal instruments of royal power were the king's council, which ceaselessly diversified into specialized bodies, thereby increasing its power base; the parlements, which enforced the King's justice everywhere; and the standing army, which kept the nobility busy in external campaigns (notably in Italy) and which consistently improved its technical capacities (artillery), while at the same time justifying a considerable fiscal and financial pressure (through specific taxes [*taille* and *taillons*], indirect taxation, more or less forced loans, the sale of offices, and other means).

The Church. France in the sixteenth century possessed 114 bishoprics divided among 15 ecclesiastical provinces. Several metropolitan seats, notably those of Lyon and Vienne, claimed primacy; it was hopeless to try to settle these claims. To this list of provinces and dioceses, the province of Avignon, created in 1475 at the expense of Arles, must be added; Avignon's archbishopric and three bishoprics were located in the papal state. In addition, the three Lorraine bishoprics, dependent on the province of Trèves (Trier), belong to this list. Finally, the bishopric of Thérouanne, destroyed in 1553, was transferred to Boulogne and rebuilt in 1567 with its borders extensively modified to be consonant with the frontier between France and the Low Countries. Also significant was the annexation of Bugey in 1601, which brought the bishopric of Belley into the French kingdom.

The church of France was ruled by the Pragmatic Sanction, promulgated at Bourges in 1438, which served as the charter of Gallicanism. The Pragmatic Sanction affirmed the superiority of the council over the pope and stipulated that bishops were to be elected by cathedral chapters. On this last point, however, the freedom of the elections was severely curtailed by rulers who did not hesitate to impose their candidates.

As a result of such practices, the concordat concluded in 1516 at Bologna between Francis I and Pope Leo X did not really change much. The king was legally recognized as having the right to name to bishoprics and to abbeys candidates who then had to be installed by the pope, and the king was authorized to levy annual taxes (*decimes*) on ecclesiastical benefices. In exchange, the Holy See was pleased with the abrogation of the Pragmatic Sanction of 1438. The concordat was not applicable to the most recently acquired provinces (Provence and Brittany), which were deemed areas under obedience (*pays d'obédience*), but the kings lost no time in forcing the pope to grant them extensive powers over these bishoprics.

Contrary to what has long been assumed, the church of France at the beginning of the sixteenth century was not anemic. The clergy was more numerous than ever, which is not necessarily a valid criterion of vitality, since many of the reformers complained of the plethora of priests ordained with no controls, with no real vocation or training, and with no other ministry than that of the celebration of masses for the dead. More significant is the extraordinary increase in the construction and decoration of churches from the end of the fifteenth to the middle of the sixteenth century. Printing made more widely available liturgical works (missals and rituals, which increasingly employed the Roman rite), manuals for curates and collections of sermons, books of piety available to the laity, and Bibles, partial or complete, in Latin and French. Preaching was particularly active, even if it remained almost the monopoly of the mendicant orders. New orders were created, notably the Minims (introduced by Francis de Paul and encouraged by Charles VIII and his successors) and the Annonciades (founded by Jeanne of France, the repudiated spouse of Louis XII). Many abbeys and religious orders experienced reforms that were more or less permanent. Among mendicant orders, those of strict observance continued to gain in strength, but monastic orders were weakened by the practice of granting benefices to secular clergy, encouraged by the Concordat of 1516.

In retrospect, one can better assess the actions of the bishops of the sixteenth century. Not all were as zealous as Francis d'Estaing, bishop of Rodez (r. 1501–1529), but many lived within their diocese, regularly called their synod to meet there, and published regulations to guide the actions of curates (or at least had printed the regulations of their predecessors). They discussed, for example, the administration of the sacraments, religious teaching by preaching or the reading of Gerson's *Opus tripartitum*, and injunctions against dancing and other popular festivals deemed scandalous. Many of these decisions preceded the Royal Ordinance of 1539, which exhorted curates to keep careful registers of baptisms and burials.

The faithful were quite attached to parish life, in which an elite actively participated through the management of church funds and properties. Rare, however, were those who went to confession or Communion more frequently than the minimal yearly obligation. A fairly large number were excommunicated, usually as a result of debts; they did not rush to obtain absolution, except perhaps on their deathbed. The faithful, though, joined guilds, more numerous than ever, in all the cities and towns. (It was possible to join several guilds at once.) In Provence associations of penitents, imitating those of Italy, began to form. The bishops and the civil authorities were suspicious of this proliferation of associations, which often escaped their control and which cut into parish religious observance.

A burgeoning religiosity stirred the people. Everywhere relics and miraculous images were worshiped, and certain sanctuaries drew crowds of pilgrims on a national scale—among them, Nôtre-Dame de Liesse, Nôtre-Dame du Puy, Saint-Antoine de Viennois, Mont-Saint-Michel, and Sainte-Anne d'Apt. People accumulated indulgences, many of which could be obtained as a result of gifts to charitable works (for instance, the hospitals of the Quinze-Vingts in Paris or of Pont-Saint-Esprit) or for the construction of sanctuaries. The eucharistic cult developed in the form of processions at the time of the Feast of Corpus Christi, or more simply in the form of Communion at someone's deathbed. The Virgin Mary became the object of great devotion, and her Immaculate Conception was considered in France as an article of faith to be solemnly celebrated. Alongside these developments grew up a Christocentric devotion strongly oriented toward the sorrowful passion of the Savior; this belief in divine mercy helped mitigate the anguish the faithful experienced concerning the Last Judgement. The formulas of last wills and testaments, drawn up by notaries, witness to the ways in which this faith permeated the lives of believers.

The Reformation. As early as the reign of Charles VIII, reform of the church was the official order of the day. Reform had been the subject of debate at the Estates-General in 1481 and again in a special assembly convoked to discuss the topic in 1494: the aim was primarily to reform monasteries and the training of clergy.

Reform was already under way in university schools (the

College of Montaigu in Paris), in several abbeys (notably Chezal-Benoît, whose influence extended throughout the Saint-Germain-des-Prés area), and in the mendicant orders. Reform did not occur without upheaval or without legal reaction, however, especially when the powerful minister of Louis XII, Georges d'Amboise (a cardinal and papal legate as well), decided to implement authoritarian measures. These multiple reform initiatives caused heightened public awareness of religious abuses not only among the educated laity drawn from the ruling classes but also among the popular audiences of the preaching friars.

At the same time, popular opinion could not fail to be touched by the violent antipapal campaign (inaugurated by Louis XII during his struggle with Jules II) leading up to the Council of Pisa. This tumult, however, settled down with the accession of Leo X, and the Fifth Lateran Council appears to have had some positive effect on France. During this time Italy, Germany, and Spain were overrun by preachers warning of the Apocalypse, but France does not seem to have been so influenced by these preachers as were other countries, though it is not yet possible to ascertain this definitively.

Much more is known about the Parisian intellectual milieu, which was divided by those (led by Desiderius Erasmus and Jacques Lefèvre d'Étaples) who set about learning classical languages and new methods for reading the Bible and who recommended the dissemination of these abilities and techniques among all Christian people. Lefèvre d'Étaples's edition of Paul's epistles, published in 1512, should be considered the manifesto of this group (despite the author's reservations). Opposing this group, the Faculty of Theology of Paris, led by the syndic Noël Beda, resisted all innovations by espousing a particular sense of pious tradition and a rigorous Scholasticism deemed effective against certain claims of the "poets." Whether the topic of discussion was the three Marys, verses of the Exultet, or the historical veracity of Dionysius, any and all occasions were seized upon by both groups as the opportunity to engage in heated and libelous debates.

The Group of Meaux. Son of one of Charles VIII's powerful ministers and named at a very early age bishop of Lodève and abbot of Saint-Germain-des-Prés (where he installed Lefèvre d'Étaples, his former teacher), Guillaume Briçonnet was made bishop of Meaux in 1516. He undertook a mission to Italy for the king at the time when the Fifth Lateran Council was ending, and he was well known there in pious circles. Back in France in 1516, he decided to devote his time to his diocese. There he held synods and especially attempted to organize preaching. For this purpose he invited Lefèvre d'Étaples and his disciples (e.g., Gérard Roussel, Guillaume Farel, and Martial Mazurier), who had developed a system of preaching inspired by the gospel and Christian humanism in which purgatory and veneration of the saints were relegated to a secondary role. Feeling threatened in their own field, the Franciscans at Meaux protested, complaining before the Faculty of Theology and the Parlement of Paris.

This protest occurred at the time when information about Martin Luther was beginning to filter into France. As early as 1519 books by the Wittenberg doctor had arrived in France via Lyon and Basel. Luther's ideas were also spread by students and German professors, who were found in large numbers in French universities (for example, Bonifacius Amerbach in Avignon). Luther's ideas reached such religious as François Lambert—the Avignonese Franciscan who, in 1522, left his convent to go to Switzerland and Wittenberg—and various members of the laity, such as Louis de Berquin, who began to translate Luther's works. In 1521 the Faculty of Theology of Paris condemned Luther's doctrine in the same terms as had the pope, and Parlement forbade the sale and possession of his books.

This reaction spread among the group at Meaux. In 1523 Briçonnet found it necessary to purge his team, notably of Farel, who left for Basel. Two years later, after Lefèvre d'Étaples published a French New Testament and his *Epitres et évangiles pour les 52 dimanches de l'année*, both condemned by the Faculty of Theology, the entire group had to break up. Lefèvre d'Étaples and Roussel fled to Strasbourg, and Briçonnet himself escaped legal action only by requiring the priests in his diocese to return to traditional orthodoxy.

This wave of repression during 1525 was further exacerbated by the defeat at Pavia and the capture of the king and then by rumors of popular uprisings in Germany. The repression culminated in a strict decree by the Parlement of Paris in 1526 against those who read scripture in French, who held secret assemblies, and who dared to question the Catholic faith. This decree was posted in Paris, Sens, Orléans, Auxerre, Meaux, Tours, Bourges, Angers, Poitiers, Troyes, Lyon, Mâcon, "and everywhere else where it shall be needful"; this list of towns gives an idea of the diffusion of reformed ideas.

On the other hand, by order of the king, the bishops gathered in provincial councils in 1528 to condemn the doctrine of Luther and to reform the church. The only proceedings extant are those of the provinces of Bordeaux, Bourges, Lyon, and Sens; the latter are the most extensive. The council met in Paris in 1528, headed by the humanist Josse van Clichtove.

Evangelism. Evangelism is the customary term for the religious movement that arose within Erasmian humanism and Fabrist piety and that was receptive to certain strands of Luther's thought. From these sources evangelism derived a Christocentric religiosity: salvation is granted to those who believe and not to those who merit it. The evangelicals had direct recourse to scripture as their sole rule of faith; they considered as only secondary—and some as without value—the cult of the saints and relics, indulgences, and purely ecclesiastical obligations. These Christians, however, did not envision any rupture with the established church, as much because they valued Christian unity as because they were indifferent to external institutions. Isolated or in small, informal groups, these Christians deemed themselves "learned in the doctrine of the Gospel."

From the time of the dispersion of the group at Meaux, the most vital center of evangelism was that that grew up around Marguerite d'Angoulême, married in 1527 to Henry II, king of Navarre. The sister of Francis I, Marguerite maintained an extensive spiritual correspondence with Briçonnet from 1521 to 1524. Disciples of Lefèvre d'Étaples were her chaplains and preachers. In 1531 she published *Le Miroir de l'âme pêcheres,* which the doctors of the Faculty of Theology of Paris dared to censure. Marguerite's protection enabled Lefèvre d'Étaples to finish his life in peace, while some of his disciples obtained bishoprics: Michel d'Arande received Saint-Paul-Trois-Châteaux, and Roussel went to Oloron. This protection extended to universities as well, such as those at Bourges and Nîmes; to printers Simon Dubois in Alençon and Robert I Estienne in Paris, where he printed a famous Bible; and even to Clément Marot, the poet who began the translation of the *Psalms* into French.

Evangelism found its best-known expression in Rabelais's books *Pantagruel* (1532) and *Gargantua* (1534). Evangelism was also spread through sermons and books of piety. It prevailed in convents, universities, and, in proportions difficult to estimate, the populace. There was a great scandal in Paris when, in 1533, the rector of the university, Nicolas Cop, gave a speech in which he contrasted the gospel that saves with the law that damns.

The Influence of Guillaume Farel. After leaving Meaux in 1523, Farel went to Basel. From there he contacted Zwingli, whose doctrine shaped his theology, especially regarding the Eucharist. In exile Farel translated the writings of the reformers into French while awaiting the clandestine publication in Lyon in 1529 of a complete treatise on reformed Christianity entitled *Summaire et briefve declaration d'aucuns lieux fort necessaires pour mettre sa conscience en Dieu* (Summary and Brief Declaration of Several Powerful Loci Necessary to Establish One's Conscience in God). Farel called for a complete break with popish idolatry, especially as seen in the Mass.

This militant reformation took France in directions that are difficult to ascertain. Some historians, following Henri Hauser, see in this reformation the expression of a social revolt, developed notably in the workers' milieux in Lyon, Meaux, and elsewhere at a time when a weak economy was causing famine and a lowering of salaries. This thesis is certainly true in part, but it does not provide a complete account of the "pathways of heresy." A legal inquiry concerning a fuller in Troyes in 1528 provides some insight, but it is risky to generalize. This man was accused of speaking out against priests and against the Mass; concerning the Eucharist, he said that "God is God and bread is bread"; he denied the existence of purgatory and scoffed at prayers for the dead; he denied that the Virgin Mary possessed any special powers after she had brought her Son into the world; and he claimed that holy water was not as good as that from a well. All this is a strange mixture of Lutheran, Zwinglian, and popular beliefs, which may even have been influenced by the Waldensian heresy. This fuller, who knew how to read, said that he had heard many of these ideas when he was in Meaux, but where did he get the idea that there is no one in hell except evil rich men? Even though it is generally claimed that France never knew Anabaptism, this fuller from Troyes and others like him merit further investigation.

It is also necessary to look more closely at iconoclastic acts provocatively performed by zealots during the Reformation. The most spectacular occurred in Paris when a statue of the Virgin at a crossroads was broken. This created an enormous outcry, and, the perpetrators having escaped, only a procession in which the king took part could settle the situation.

During this time Farel experienced a considerable degree of success without strife. Supported by the canton of Bern, he brought the Reformation to Neuchâtel in 1530. This was the first French-speaking city to accept the Reformation, and Farel immediately invited a Lyonnais printer, Pierre de Vingle. In addition, Farel successfully rallied to the Reformation the Waldensians, heirs to a long-standing medieval heresy, who clustered in the Alps and Provence. At the Synod of Chanforan in 1532, the Waldensian preachers, called the "*barbes,*" abandoned their traditional emphasis on morality to adopt justification by faith, along with a body of doctrines and practices that Farel proposed to them in the name of the Swiss Reformation. As a result, the ex-Waldensians raised funds to have a Bible, translated into French by Pierre Robert Olivétan, printed at Neuchâtel.

From Neuchâtel as well came the pamphlets, or placards, written by Antoine Marcourt, which were ultimately posted on the walls of Paris and even on the door of the king's bedchamber. The text was a violent attack against the Mass and the eucharistic presence. The coordination of such a strike could not have been improvised; rather, it supposes the existence of an actual network, whose intent was mostly to hinder any rapprochement between royal policy (represented by the brothers Jean and Guillaume du Bellay) and the German Lutherans—a goal that was realized, since Francis I's anger took the form of a violent wave of persecution against anyone in Paris under suspicion of welcoming the new ideas. It was at this time that the student John Calvin felt it prudent to leave for Basel.

Calvinism Takes the Lead. Contrary to what many think, it was not a foregone conclusion that the French Reformation would take a Calvinist course. That this is in fact what happened is attributable to the genius of one man, to the particular city he chose, and to the felicitous events of the years 1540 to 1560.

Calvin (1509–1564) was a second-generation reformer. In his first great work, *Christianae religionis Institutio* (The Institutes of the Christian Religion; first published at Basel in 1536), he was above all a disciple of Luther. Yet Calvin quickly incorporated some of Zwingli's and especially Martin Bucer's thinking into his own theology and ecclesiology.

From 1536 Calvin's base was Geneva, which, asserting the independence it had wrested from its bishop and from the duke of Savoy, had broken with Roman Catholicism in 1535 under Farel's influence. The Francophone city was an active commercial crossroads and proud of its political institutions. Farel retained Calvin in establishing the new church there, but they were both expelled in 1538. After a stay in Strasbourg, which had significant influence on him, Calvin returned to Geneva in 1541 and achieved the adoption of his ecclesiastical ordinances, which defined his reformist program. One of Calvin's strengths was his intransigence. Scarcely accepted for about ten years by the Genevans, he nevertheless continued to strengthen his moral authority by building a power base of refugees from France and Italy. In the 1550s Geneva became the base for the Protestant conquest of France through books (e.g., Bibles, Psalters, and pamphlets printed in mass quantities) and by ministers trained in the academy, which was founded in 1558.

Throughout the kingdom of France, a hard line had been taken after 1540. In 1543 the Faculty of Theology of Paris had adopted a statement of Catholic faith in twenty-nine articles, which Francis I had published as the law of the land, a legal document to be used in specific cases against heretics. Shortly afterward, the faculty published a catalog of forbidden books (most of which had been printed in Geneva) that also received the royal sanction.

At the same time, royal power no longer hesitated to repress the new ideas. An edict of 1540 gave jurisdiction over the crime of heresy to the royal judges; henceforth persecution would be unrelenting, with the only exception being variations in intensity according to the year and the province. The repression was especially violent in Provence, where the parlement had rendered a severe decree against the Waldensians (new Calvinists) of Mérindol and neighboring villages. The decree was executed in 1545 with extreme brutality. The forces of the pontifical state joined with the royal army to destroy about twenty villages, to the acclaim of the surrounding Catholic population. In 1546 the community at Meaux, the first to be organized on the Genevan model, was destroyed; fourteen of its members died at the stake.

Under Henry II persecution continued without relief. Successive edicts, notably those of Châteaubriand (1551) and of Ecouen (1559), only further intensified punishments and reduced the rights of the accused. The parlements, which confirmed appeal sentences, outdid each other in zealous application of punishments. In Paris a special legal chamber (*chambre ardente*, a division of Parlement specializing in charges of heresy), examined 557 cases from May 1547 to March 1549, ordering sixty-one bannishments and thirty-nine condemnations to the stake. Nevertheless, these figures are happily less extensive than those of the *Légende noire* (black legend). The Parlement of Toulouse, one of the most bloodthirsty, judged 1,074 cases of heresy from 1500 to 1560 but executed only sixty-two people. In Bordeaux, of 477 suspects judged between 1541 and 1559, eighteen were condemned to death. Many of these martyrs showed an admirable constancy to the end, which greatly impressed the crowds. From 1554 Jean Crespin, a printer who had taken refuge in Geneva, published accounts of their exemplary courage in *Le Livre des Martyrs* (Book of Martyrs), which, several times completed and revised, became one of the treasures constitutive of French Protestant identity.

The persecution, however, in no way diminished the propagation of the new ideas. On the contrary, it was during the years that the persecution was the strongest that Reformed communities began to establish churches—that is to say, to celebrate services and the sacraments under the leadership of a pastor. The *Histoire ecclésiastique* (Ecclesiastical History), later compiled by Théodore de Bèze, claimed this movement began in 1555, but it is known that similar church services on the Genevan model were celebrated here and there ten years earlier. However that may be, the growth of the churches at the end of the 1550s appeared irrepressible, first in Paris and the Loire Valley and then in the towns of Normandy and the southwest.

At this stage the Calvinist model met resistance from all sides. In Poitiers several notables were critical of the Calvinist stance of open rupture with the established church. Elsewhere, in Blois, Angers, and Tours, local preachers refused to be silenced in favor of ministers arriving from Geneva; in Tours an actual schism resulted. With such tensions in mind, Calvinist ministers gathered in Poitiers in 1557 in an assembly that adopted the "political articles," a rough draft of the discipline officially adopted in Paris in 1559. The articles affirmed the precedence of ministers and deacons over elders and established synodal ties among churches.

The first "national" synod of the Reformed churches took place secretly in Paris on 25 May 1559. The ministers in attendance represented the church of Paris and some from Normandy, the Loire area, Poitou, and Saintonge. This synod adopted a confession of faith, of which the text had been solicited from Calvin (Calvin's proposal was modified in its first article to refer to the creator God, whereas Calvin had spoken of the word of God), and a church discipline, which was inspired by the Genevan model, adapting it to meet the needs of a vast kingdom: autonomy of local churches was retained but tempered by a pyramid of provincial and national synods. Thus, in 1559 the French Reformation was definitively structured and made unequivocally Calvinist.

It is difficult to measure precisely its influence. Even contemporaries were not in agreement. There is no doubt, however, that this was a movement on the rise and one that seemed unbeatable. On the national scale the best document available is the *Livre des habitants de Genève* (Book of the Inhabitants of Geneva), which recorded the names of all Protestant refugees from 1549 to 1559, but precisely because only refugees were involved, this documentation has been cast in doubt. It has to be balanced by local documents that are more or less reliable. The interpretation of such data is not devoid of ideological bias, as one can seek to prove the popular nature, indeed revolutionary character, of involvement in the Reformation or to affirm the regionalist affinities of the movement.

In general, it can be said that all the provinces were affected, but it should also be noted that Brittany, Provence, and the Massif Central were less affected than Normandy, Poitou, and Languedoc. On the other hand, this initial Protestantism was particularly centered in the cities. The large towns, especially those of northern France—Rouen, Paris, Troyes, and Lyon—saw numerous conversions, while the countryside, except in the Cévennes and perhaps in the Poitou, was hardly affected before 1560. In the towns workers made up the greatest number of converts, and without a doubt literate workers in highly skilled trades, especially printers, converted in great numbers. Yet the university population, relative to its number, provided important converts also, who, as regents of colleges or instructors in schools, spread Reformed propaganda. The clergy was represented particularly by the mendicant orders and much less by secular clergy. As for the bourgeoisie, the world of trade was little affected, but the world of appointments to offices, at least to minor posts like those of notary and legal counsel, was much more affected and had considerable influence. Finally, what was striking about the end of the 1550s was the increasingly frequent support given by the nobility, both petty and high ranking, of which the three Châtillon brothers supplied the best-known model. As seen in Paris in 1557 (the affair in the Rue Saint-Jacques) and in 1559 (the affair in Pré-aux-Clercs), the joining of the nobility to Reformed communities modified their character. Even more disturbing to royal power was the spread of Reformed ideas in the parlements: this is why Henry II reacted severely to the legal reprimand (*mercuriale*) of 1559. From this time on the support given to the Reformation by leading figures in several towns in the Midi, such as Nîmes and Saint-Antonin, was sufficient to assure its control over municipal power, which was certainly still not the case in any of the large cities in the north.

A Gallican Reform? Several times it appeared as though royal power would take in hand a reform of the church within the framework of the kingdom of France. This was the program of certain counselors of Francis I who, in 1534, invited Philipp Melanchthon to Paris after having asked advice from several other reformers. This project failed because of the Affaire des Placards.

The idea of internal reform recurred in 1551, when an open conflict concerning the principality of Parma broke out between Henry II and Pope Julius III. For the king there was no question this time of making any concessions to Protestants. On the contrary, the king promulgated an edict exacerbating the repression, but this was also directed against the pope since it was henceforth forbidden to send the pope any money or supplications. The king also threatened to call a national council to appoint a patriarch and pull away from Rome—in sum, an action much like that of Henry VIII of England. The preparations began for such a national council; bishops received the order to return to their dioceses, to visit them, to detect any traces of heresy, and to make a report to their metropolitan. Several such visits took place. At the Council of Trent, which had just reopened, Henry II ordered the reading of a solemn protest against anything that might be decided there. Things were looking quite bad when the pope, by making concessions, settled a conflict that perhaps even the king did not really want to continue.

In any event, it is certain (and would be seen as such in 1561–1562) that the French court, where several Erasmian prelates and magistrates could be found, had its own opinion about reform that was not necessarily that of Rome. Concerning doctrine, no concessions were envisioned, but these prelates would willingly close most monasteries, would indict as "superstitious" many religious manifestations (mystery plays were forbidden in Paris in 1549, and many provinces followed suit), would abolish guilds, and, especially, would block all avenues for recourse to Rome on matters of benefices or dispensations. This should all be kept in mind when seeking to understand in what spirit royal power looked upon the reopening of the Council of Trent in 1561, and, somewhat later, the reception of its decisions.

The Politico-Religious Crisis. The death of King Henry II on 10 July 1559 began a long period of weakness in the French monarchy lasting until Henry IV consolidated his power and reimposed Catholicism throughout the kingdom. The crisis essentially comprised three phases from 1559 to 1572, from 1572 to 1584, and from 1584 to 1598.

1559 to 1572. Francis II, king at sixteen years of age, allowed himself to be governed by Francis, duke of Guise, and his brother Charles, cardinal of Lorraine. Opposing them were the princes of the blood, Antoine de Bourbon, king of Navarre, and his brother Louis I Condé, who also claimed power. Cemented by religious fervor, parties formed behind these opposing ambitions, with Catholics supporting the Guises and Protestants supporting the Bourbons. The Conspiracy of Amboise (March 1560) was the first bloody episode in this struggle, but in December 1560 the death of Francis II, bringing another minor, Charles IX, to the throne, enabled his mother, Catherine de Médicis, to consolidate her power. During 1561 she tried to keep civil peace (calling a meeting of the Estates-General in Pontoise) and to find a religious compromise (at the Colloquy of Poissy), but to no avail. Finally, the Edict of Saint-Germain (January 1562) granted to Protestants freedom of conscience and, with some limitations, freedom of worship.

Hardly accepted by Catholics, who had experienced in the south at the end of the previous year a brutal wave of iconoclasm, the regime of toleration was shaken by the Massacre of Wassy (March 1562), which led Condé to incite Protestants (called Huguenots after 1560) to rebel. The Catholic camp, strengthened by the legitimacy granted them by the king, reacted violently; numerous massacres took place in the provinces, and the royal army chalked up a series of victories until the regent imposed the Peace of Amboise (March 1563), which reestablished tolerance, but on a level much less advantageous for Protestants.

Then began a period of tense religious coexistence. Catherine de Médicis had the court make a vast circuit of the kingdom (*tour de France*) to impose peace and the authority of the king everywhere. The Protestant churches began to organize. Catholics regrouped, with the French bishops participating in the Council of Trent and the Jesuits beginning their mission throughout the kingdom. Controversy tended to substitute for armed conflict.

In September 1567, however, uneasy Huguenots reopened hostilities. They were again beaten several times (the battles of Saint-Denis, Jarnac, and Moncontour), but their remaining chief, Admiral Gaspard II de Coligny, succeeded in reestablishing their political position by obtaining the Peace of Saint-Germain (1570), which reiterated that of Amboise, adding the provision of four safe places (*places de sûreté*) to be held by the Protestants.

In the eyes of the Catholic majority, these concessions were unacceptable. At Court the queen mother and most of the counselors feared that Charles IX, under Coligny's influence, might decide to send aid to the Low Countries, which were in rebellion against Philip II, king of Spain. In the summer of 1572 the Huguenot leaders gathered in Paris to celebrate the marriage of their leader, Henry of Navarre (later Henry IV), to Margaret of Valois, sister of the king. The city grumbled. On 22 August Admiral Coligny was the object of an assassination attempt apparently organized by the Guises with the consent of the queen mother. The Huguenots threatened revenge. To forestall such revenge the king's council ordered the execution of the Protestant leaders, which, put into effect on 24 August (the Feast of Saint Bartholomew), degenerated into general slaughter throughout the city. It is estimated that four thousand victims perished. Following the contradictory explanations provided by the king, violence spread to the major provincial towns—Orléans, Meaux, Angers, Lyon, Rouen, Bordeaux, and Toulouse—where massacres continued until October.

1572 to 1584. The Saint Bartholomew's Day Massacre caused a profound split. Henceforth French Protestants would no longer accuse the king's advisers but the king himself, who had broken the bonds uniting him with his subjects. Those from the south, who were now much more numerous because of the violence that those of the north had endured, organized resistance in the towns and provinces. Theorists (François Hotman and Théodore de Bèze) justified the refusal to obey the king. They had the support of the "moderate" Catholics (*politiques*) such as Henry I of Montmorency, governor of Languedoc.

Such was the situation that Charles IX, who died in 1574, left to his brother Henry III. The latter—encountering the resistance of his brother Francis, duke of Alençon and then of Anjou, who led the group called the "discontented" (*mécontents*)—was forced to accept humiliating concessions (the Peace of Monsieur in 1576 followed by a meeting of the Estates-General in Blois) without ever succeeding in asserting his authority over the long term. This king, who was decidedly better than his reputation would have it, offended the nobility by his distant air, his pacific policies, and his favoritism. On the other hand, he went through periods of intense piety that did not endear him either to the church or to the Catholic people. The most serious factor, however, was that he had no son to succeed him, and in 1584 the death of the duke of Anjou put Henry of Navarre, leader of the Huguenot party, in line as the legitimate heir to the throne according to Salic law.

1584 to 1598. The threat of a Protestant king galvanized the formation of the Catholic League, made up of provincial nobles and Parisian bourgeois, which recognized as leader Duke Henry of Guise. The league opened relations with Philip II of Spain, who provided them with money and, later, with troops. When Sixtus V excommunicated Henry of Navarre and his brother, declaring them no longer entitled to the throne, the league felt justified.

Henry III, caught between the Catholic League members and the Protestants, tried to free himself to act, but in 1588 he was forced to flee Paris during an uprising and then to call together at Blois the Estates-General, which was dominated by league members. To loosen the vise, he had the duke of Guise assassinated along with his brother Cardinal Louis II (December 1588); this resulted in the pope excommunicating Henry III and in a mass uprising of French league members. The Faculty of Theology of Paris released its subjects from obedience to the king, and a virulent campaign of sermons and pamphlets was unleashed against him. The king therefore found it necessary to cooperate with Henry of Navarre, and together they marched on Paris. While laying siege to the intransigent city, Henry III was assassinated by a Dominican monk (1 August 1589).

Henry of Navarre, now Henry IV, needed to conquer his own kingdom. Other than the Protestant minority, only the *politiques*, or "good French" (*bons Français*, those whose priority was the continuity of the monarchy as symbolized by Salic law), supported him. Among them were Catholics and numerous prelates who hoped that the king would someday convert. Several military victories (e.g., at Ivry in March 1590) and peaceful statements in favor of the established church gained time for Henry IV while his adversaries, moderate and extremist, tore each other apart (notably at the Estates-General convoked in Paris in 1593). Even so, only the king's conversion at Saint-Denis on 25 July 1593 reversed the situation in his favor. In February 1594 Henry IV was anointed king at Chartres. A month later Paris opened its gates to him. Then, in turn, princes, towns, and leaders of the league party rallied around him in exchange for privileges and the granting of requests. The hard-liners did not accept Henry IV until the pope absolved him in 1595.

To consolidate his kingdom, Henry IV had to drive out the Spanish (accomplished with the Peace of Vervins in 1598) and to reassure the Protestants, who feared they would be sacrificed. The Edict of Nantes, signed on 13 April 1598, assured Protestants freedom of conscience and of worship, guaranteeing them access to all trades and mixed tribunals (with split chambers in some parlements). Certain additional clauses gave them about a hundred *places de sûreté* and enabled them to retain a politico-military installation. On the other hand, Catholic worship was reestablished everywhere and was imposed as the religion of the king, thus reasserting Catholic institutions (e.g., respect for festivals and for Lent, as well as the levying of tithes). Despite all this, the pope protested against the Edict of Nantes, and the parlements raised myriad objections to it as well. The Parlement of Rouen did not concede until 1609.

In fact, this edict establishing religious coexistence in the kingdom was not much different from those that had been promulgated since 1562. Yet Henry IV benefited from the fatigue of the rival parties, from the anxiety that the religious troubles had caused in the ruling classes, and from an authority sufficiently strong to force them to respect his will.

The Establishment of Protestant Churches. For France's Reformed churches, the last forty years of the sixteenth century constituted a foundational period. It was then, against a background of wars and massacres but also of truces and regional hegemonies, that the geography, sociology, and religious, ethnic, and cultural character of French Protestantism took shape.

After 1562 Protestantism continued to gain converts, but nearly exclusively in the south, where it remained dominant. Elsewhere, especially in the north, Protestantism had waned, first because armed conflict had caused attrition and second as a result of the massacres of 1562, the almost as numerous massacres of 1572, and the edict of "extermination" published by the king in 1585 under pressure from the league. Even if Coligny's figure of 2,150 Protestant churches in 1562 was inflated (the historian and pastor S. Mours, having counted again more exactingly, established the total at 1,785), only 763 existed in 1598, of which only 238 were north of the line between Nantes and Geneva.

Henceforth the map of Protestantism showed several powerful strongholds—arranged in an arc around Poitou and Dauphiné and passing by Quercy, Gascony, eastern Languedoc, and the Vivarais—but these were separated by provinces that had remained for the most part Catholic. In these strongholds some large cities—La Rochelle, Montauban, Montpellier, and Nîmes—and several smaller ones were dominated by Huguenots, both politically and socially. It should not be forgotten, however, that their population was often less than that of the minority churches of the north, such as at Rouen and Paris. As for the number of faithful, it is practically impossible to determine. Even where Protestants were dominant, they were usually less numerous than Catholics. Thus, in any given small "Protestant" town and even in the principality of Orange, the ratio was one Protestant to four Catholics.

Each local congregation had a church, either a former Catholic church or a building specifically constructed and appropriately furnished. Each local church also had a minister, usually trained in Geneva, as there were as yet no educational establishments within France. (Of those founded later, the most famous was at Saumur and was created at the very end of the century by Philippe Duplessis-Mornay.) Each church, moreover, had a consistory, participation in which was increasingly limited to an elite.

The churches were grouped in colloquiums, of particular importance for pastors, and the churches sent representatives (usually the pastor and an elder from the consistory) to the provincial synod. At the end of the sixteenth century, there existed fifteen provinces, which in turn sent representatives to the national synod. This institution was important as the guardian of orthodoxy—the Synod of La Rochelle in 1571 solemnly endorsed the Confession of Faith of 1559—and of ecclesiastical discipline, which was continually being modified. The national synod also played the role of appellate court in regulating internal conflicts among churches (when they could not be settled at the provincial level) and defined a common polity. After 1567 and especially after 1572, it was most often supplanted by political assemblies, however, which explains why national synods, regularly called every year from 1561 to 1567, were no longer called by the end of the century.

At the time of the first synods, the function of the churches had been passionately debated, sparked by the ideas professed by Jean Morély and publicized by him in his *Traicté de la discipline et police chrestienne* (Treatise on Christian Discipline and Polity), which was ultimately condemned in 1565. Morély preached a more democratic regime, founded in particular on the election of pastors by the faithful. Petrus Ramus raised this question again in 1571, but the events of the Saint Bartholomew's Day Massacre, in which Ramus himself died, overrode it. At the end of the century, the synods were mostly concerned with irenic proposals, such as those of Jean de Serres.

The Catholic Renewal. From 1561 to 1594 a spectacular reestablishment of Catholicism took place in the political sphere, but behind this rise in power lay an entire process of interior renewal, not only on the institutional level but also in spiritual life. It is true that France, having participated in the last sessions of the Council of Trent, had refused to receive its decrees as laws of the land. The fear of worsening relations with Protestants, the hesitations of Gallican jurists, and Roman intransigence all conspired to prevent the promulgation of the decrees of the council, despite the urgent appeals of the clergy. The Estates-General of 1593, which had solemnly endorsed the council, was considered rebellious and without authority. Henry IV had not kept the solemn promise he had made to the pope in order to receive absolution, and the declaration of the Assembly of Clergy in 1615, much celebrated by historians, had no legal weight.

It is more important to recall that Henry III—in the Ordinance of Blois in 1580, joined with the Edict of Melun—had introduced most of the reformist programs of the council. In addition, the eight provincial councils, which were held between 1581 and 1590, all adopted the Tridentine legislation. From 1564 several bishops already had mandated at least a portion of the conciliar reforms, and others, more numerous, were to do so in the wake of provincial councils. Thus, the church of France, even before the end of the sixteenth century, was, in canonical texts at least, "tridentinized." This is confirmed by the texts of reports of visits *ad limina*, which certain bishops—a very small number, it is true—sent to Rome in obedience to the constitution of Sixtus V.

It would still be some time, however, before the reform took effect on issues as significant as the recruiting and training of clergy. Here again, the lag in the creation of seminaries was not as slow as it is made out to be; it was really that the Tridentine project was poorly matched to the needs of the church. The network of Jesuit educational institutions, rapidly put in place after 1561 until the partial expulsion of the Jesuits in 1594, was much more efficient.

The action of Jesuits in France, a little later than elsewhere, had considerable social effects. Not only did they take part in and strengthen the Catholic elite but they also began to have an effect on Protestants, to whom the reputation of Jesuit schools appealed. In Lyon and Paris the Jesuits began an abundant production of doctrinal books and books of spirituality that exposed the French to great Italian and Spanish authors.

The Capuchin monks, introduced in France in 1575, had a similar effect among the lower classes. In particular, they developed the observance of the Forty Hours. Together, religious orders also created new guilds: the penitents, already in Provence, having been introduced in Lyon and Toulouse by the Jesuit Emond Auger before he became the vindicator of the Parisian confraternity created by Henry III; Marian congregations; and the guilds of the Blessed Sacrament and of the Rosary. Some of these confraternities were institutions mobilizing anti-Huguenot sentiment.

The religious struggles and the trials accompanying them (the epidemics and famines) sparked upheaval among the people that eventually developed into unruly fervor. During the 1580s large processions traversed the kingdom, both in the south and in the north. The faithful gathered in old sanctuaries around sacred images and relics that had survived the iconoclastic furor of the Protestants (or that had been replaced). This fervor subsided when peace was restored and when the supporters of Henry IV condemned such movements as suspect.

It is a fact that the flourishing of the Catholic faith at the beginning of the seventeenth century dates from the passions at the time of the league, and it was often the same circles, even the same people (the Parisian group of Madame Acarie is the best-known example), that gave impetus to the movement. Even so, that does not mean that the *politiques* were lukewarm in their faith nor that royalist bishops and prelates were less reformist than others.

[*See also* Catholic League; Henry IV of France; Lorraine-Guise, House of; Medici, House of; Nantes, Edict of; Politiques; Valois, House of; *and* Wars of Religion.]

BIBLIOGRAPHY

Crouzet, Denis. *Les guerriers de Dieu: La violence au temps des troubles de religion, vers 1525–vers 1610.* 2 vols. Paris, 1990.

Garrison, Janine. *Les protestants au XVIe siècle.* Paris, 1988.

Greengrass, Mark. *The French Reformation.* Oxford, 1987.

Higman, Francis. *La diffusion de la Réforme en France, 1520–1565.* Geneva, 1992.

Richet, Denis. "Le royaume de France au XVIe siècle." In *De le Réforme à la Révolution: Études sur la France moderne,* pp. 343–387. Paris, 1991.

Salmon, J. H. M. *Society in Crisis: France in the Sixteenth Century.* London, 1975.

Venard, Marc. "France: XVIe siècle." In *Dictionnaire d'histoire et de géographie ecclésiastiques.* Paris, 1973. Contains a comprehensive bibliography.

———. "La grande cassure, 1520–1598." In *Histoire de la France religieuse,* edited by Jacques Le Goff and René Remond, vol. 2, pp. 185–319. Paris, 1988.

MARC VENARD

Translated from French by Catherine Randall Coats

FRANCIS I OF FRANCE (Francis of Angoulême; 1494–1547), king of France and a member of a cadet branch of the royal house of Valois. The son of Charles, count of Angoulême, and of Louise of Savoy, Francis was born at Cognac on 12 September 1494 and died at Rambouillet on

31 March 1547. He succeeded his cousin Louis XII to the French throne on 1 January 1515 and reigned for thirty-two years. He was twice married, first to Louis's daughter, Claude de France, who gave him three sons and four daughters before her death in 1524, and second to Eleanor of Portugal, sister of Emperor Charles V. Francis also had two official mistresses, one of whom, the duchess of Étampes, had considerable political influence after 1530.

In 1515 Francis invaded Italy in pursuit of a dynastic claim to the duchy of Milan inherited from his great-grandmother Valentina Visconti. He conquered the duchy after defeating the Swiss at Melegnano (Marignano). Soon afterward, he met Pope Leo X at Bologna, with whom he reached an agreement (the Concordat of Bologna) that greatly strengthened royal control of the French church. In 1519 Francis stood for election as Holy Roman Emperor but was defeated by Charles of Habsburg, who already ruled the Netherlands, Franche-Comté, and Spain. In 1521 a war, which was to last on and off for the rest of Francis's reign, broke out between him and the new emperor, Charles V. After losing Milan in 1522, Francis invaded Italy again only to be defeated and captured by Charles at the battle of Pavia in February 1525. During his captivity in Spain, which lasted until March 1526, France was ruled by his mother. Francis's almost continuous involvement in war made heavy demands on his financial resources. In addition to taxation, he relied heavily on fiscal expedients, such as the sale of offices; he also improved fiscal administration by creating a new central treasury (*Trésor de l'Épargne*).

Known as the "Father of Letters," Francis patronized the "New Learning," that is Renaissance humansim, and created royal lectureships in Greek and Hebrew from which the present Collège de France takes its origin. He was also a great builder, renovating old palaces (Blois, Saint-Germain-en-Laye, Fontainebleau) and creating new ones (Chambord, Madrid) for use by his still nomadic court, which was the most brilliant in Europe. The king's artistic patronage attracted distinguished artists from Italy, including Leonardo da Vinci, Andrea d'Agnolo (del Sarto), Giovanni Rosso, Benvenuto Cellini, Francesco Primaticcio, Sebastiano Serlio, and Giacomo Barozzi (Vignola).

Lutheranism first appeared in France in 1519. It aroused much interest among Paris theologians and claimed sympathizers at court, including the king's sister, Marguerite d'Angoulême. But the Faculty of Theology of Paris formally condemned Luther's ideas in its *Determinatio* of April 1521. The king, however, was unwilling to accept a definition of heresy covering evangelical humanism. While professing his opposition to heresy, he intervened repeatedly in the 1520s to protect certain scholars and preachers from persecution by the university's faculty of theology and the Parlement of Paris. Several were associated with a movement of evangelical reform in the diocese of Meaux initiated by Bishop Guillaume Briçonnet. He was assisted by Jacques Lefèvre d'Étaples and a group of preachers known as the *Cercle de Meaux*, comprising Gérard Roussel, Guillaume Farel, Martial Mazurier, and Pierre Caroli. The king's captivity enabled persecutors to get the upper hand, forcing Lefèvre and Roussel to seek refuge in Strasbourg, but they were allowed to resume their activities in France following Francis's release from prison. Another royal protégé was Louis de Berquin, who was twice rescued from persecution by the king but was eventually burned as a heretic while Francis's back was turned. The king's attitude toward the Reformation was also affected by the needs of his foreign policy. He sought allies against Charles V on both sides of the religious divide. Thus, in 1533 he met Pope Clement VII at Marseilles and married his son, Henry, to the pope's niece, Catherine de Médicis, while at the same time seeking the friendship of the German Protestant princes. In 1534 his agent, Guillaume du Bellay, attempted unsuccessfully to heal Germany's religious schism.

Yet Francis was opposed to any heresy that threatened public order. In 1528 he expressed his anger over the destruction of a statue of the Virgin in Paris by leading a procession to the scene of the sacrilege and commissioning a new statue. In November 1533, during the king's absence from Paris, an evangelical sermon preached by Nicolas Cop, the university's new rector, caused a public outcry and the flight from the capital of Cop and his friend, the young John Calvin, but it was the Affaire des Placards ("broadsheets") on 18 October 1534 that convinced Francis of the need for a firm stand against Protestantism. The broadsheets (written by Antoine Marcourt and printed in Switzerland), denouncing the Catholic doctrine of the Mass, reflected a shift toward "Sacramentarianism" among French Protestants. Public display of the broadsheets, one of which appeared on the door of the king's bedchamber at Amboise, provoked a fierce wave of persecution in Paris that was probably initiated by the Parlement. The king, however, endorsed the persecution by taking part in a huge antiheretical procession in Paris in January 1535. The Edict of Coucy (July 1535) has been mistakenly described as an edict of toleration, but it exempted all Sacramentarians from the conditional amnesty it extended to religious exiles. Thereafter the religious persecution gathered pace as Protestantism made deep inroads in French society, particularly among the lower clergy and urban bourgeoisie. In June 1540 the Edict of Fontainebleau gave the parlements overall control of judgments concerning heresy. In 1542 the Faculty of Theology of Paris produced the first Index of Prohibited Books, and in July 1543 it formally reaffirmed Catholic dogma, worship, and organization.

The last seven years of Francis's reign saw a steep rise in the number of heresy prosecutions. One of the chief victims was Étienne Dolet, who was burned in August 1546. The persecution reached a climax in 1544 when troops under Jean Maynier, Baron d'Oppède, wiped out several Waldensian villages in Provence. The king's attitude toward this event is uncertain. He may not have intended the massacre, but he rejected an attempt by Swiss reformers to intercede on behalf of the survivors as interference in the internal affairs of his kingdom.

BIBLIOGRAPHY

Berthoud, Gabrielle, et al., eds. *Aspects de la propagande religieuse.* Geneva, 1957.

Doucet, Roger. *Étude sur le gouvernement de François 1er dans ses rapports avec le Parlement de Paris.* Paris and Algiers, 1921–1926.

Farge, James K. *Orthodoxy and Reform in Early Reformation France: The Faculty of Theology of Paris, 1500–1543.* Leiden, 1985.

Febvre, Lucien. *Au coeur religieux du XVIe siècle.* 2d ed., rev. & enl. Paris, 1983.

Imbart de la Tour, Pierre. *Les origines de la Réforme.* 4 vols. Paris, 1905–1935.

Jourda, Pierre. *Marguerite d'Angoulême.* 2 vols. Paris, 1930.

Jacquart, Jean. *François 1er.* Paris, 1981.

Knecht, Robert Jean. "Francis I, 'Defender of the Faith'?" In *Wealth and Power in Tudor England,* edited by Eric Williams Ives, Robert Jean Knecht, and J. J. Scarisbrick. London, 1978.

———. *Renaissance Warrior and Patron: The Reign of Francis I.* Cambridge, 1994.

Lecoq, Anne-Marie. *François 1er imaginaire.* Paris, 1987.

ROBERT JEAN KNECHT

FRANCIS II OF FRANCE (1544–1560), French king. Eldest son of Henry II and Catherine de Médicis, Francis II was born on 19 January 1544 at Fontainebleau. On 21 April 1558 he married Mary Stuart, the daughter of King James V of Scotland and Mary of Guise. Francis succeeded to the throne on 10 July 1559 but reigned for only seventeen months. Though only fifteen at his accession, he was old enough by law to rule in his own right, but, because he lacked experience, the government passed into the hands of his mother, Catherine, and of the queen's uncles, Francis, second duke of Guise, and his brother, Charles, cardinal of Lorraine, who were zealous Catholics. Their main rivals were the aristocratic families of Montmorency and Bourbon. Anne de Montmorency, though no longer chief minister, continued to command an extensive clientèle. The Bourbon family was led by two brothers: Antoine, king of Navarre, and Louis I, prince of Condé, who were Protestants, or Huguenots.

Francis II's accession did not signal a change of religious policy by the crown. If anything, the savage persecution that had marked the last years of Henry II's reign was intensified. On 23 December 1559 the *parlementaire* Anne du Bourg, who had voiced Protestant opinions, was burned. More repressive legislation was enacted: on 4 September the destruction of all houses used for illegal meetings was ordered; on 9 November the death penalty was extended to anyone holding or attending such meetings; and in February 1560 nobles who failed to enforce the new laws were threatened with the loss of their judicial rights. All this was profoundly disappointing to the Huguenots, for whom the accidental death of Henry II had seemed providential and the prelude to a relaxation of their sufferings. In a letter to François Morel, pastor of the Paris church, Calvin did not rule out forceful resistance to the Guises provided it was led by Antoine of Navarre, first prince of the blood, but the latter proved unreliable. That left Condé as a possible leader of the Huguenots. In March 1560, however, he was implicated in the Conspiracy of Amboise, a plot aimed at overthrowing the Guises. News of the plot reached the ears of the Guises, who pounced on the plotters on 17 March 1560 as they converged on the king's court at Amboise. Some were ambushed and killed; others were summarily executed. The aftermath was surprisingly mild. The Edict of Amboise (2 March 1560) had already granted a pardon to all the king's subjects for religious offenses provided they would henceforth live as "good Catholics." Only pastors and conspirators were exempted from the amnesty. Francis II also ordered the release of all religious prisoners and allowed dissenters to petition him, but a circular of 31 March, banning illicit assemblies, created a problem for the Huguenots: how could they petition the king collectively without conferring together? In practice the government tolerated private gatherings.

Taking advantage of the more liberal regime, the Huguenots came into the open; some attacked Catholic churches. In May 1560 the Edict of Romorantin transferred the prosecution of heretics from the royal to ecclesiastical courts. At the same time, the punishment of seditious assemblies was entrusted to the *Présidiaux,* the newest of the royal tribunals. The edict implied liberty of conscience, but it proved a dead letter as the distinction between religious dissent and sedition was not easily made. In August 1560 the king called an assembly at Fontainebleau to consider possible remedies for the kingdom's troubles. A meeting of the Estates-General was called for 10 December. Meanwhile, civil unrest grew alarmingly, especially in Dauphiné and Provence. On 30 October Condé was arrested and sent to trial, but on 5 December, before any further action was taken, the king, who had always been a sickly youth, died. His queen returned to Scotland to make her mark in history as Mary Queen of Scots.

BIBLIOGRAPHY

Cloulas, Ivan. *Catherine de Médicis.* Paris, 1979.

Constant, Jean-Marie. *Les Guise.* Paris, 1894.

Kingdon, Robert M. *Geneva and the Coming of the Wars of Religion in France, 1555–1563.* Geneva, 1956.

Knecht, R. J. *The French Wars of Religion, 1559–1598.* London, 1989.

Lefèvre, Louis-Raymond. *Le tumulte d'Amboise.* Paris, 1949.
Pernot, Michel. *Les guerres de religion en France, 1559–1598.* Paris, 1987.
Romier, Lucien. *La conjuration d'Amboise.* Paris, 1923.
Sutherland, N. M. *The Huguenot Struggle for Recognition.* New Haven, 1980.

ROBERT JEAN KNECHT

FRANCISCANS. *See* Monasticism; Religious Orders.

FRANCISCO DE LOS ANGELES. *See* Quiñones, Francisco de.

FRANCK, Sebastian (1499–1542), German printer, chronicler, and theologian. Of all the figures of the early German Reformation, Franck is one of the most difficult to categorize. He carefully avoided identifying himself with any group of his time and, as a consequence, his career is peculiarly idiosyncratic. It was this idiosyncratic quality that limited the impact of his ideas on his own age and has made him such a fascinating figure for later epochs. Franck is significant for understanding the Reformation era because his thought and career define the margins of its intellectual and social world.

Franck was born in 1499 in the small south German imperial city of Donauwörth. He came into contact with humanism and the incipient reform movement as a part of his education and was particularly influenced by the careers of Desiderius Erasmus and Martin Luther. He encountered Luther at the famous Heidelberg Disputation of 1518. Franck, who initially had entered into the priesthood, allied himself by 1525 with the evangelical movement and took a pastoral position near Nuremberg. By 1529, Franck had given up his position, and his beliefs had evolved away from those of the magisterial reformers.

His writings from 1530 on developed and explicated a spiritualist theology that explicitly rejected the theologies of Luther, Huldrych Zwingli, and the various Anabaptists. From 1530 to 1532 Franck resided in Strasbourg, from where he was expelled on account of his controversial writings. From 1533 to 1539 he resided in the imperial city of Ulm, where he had to defend himself against the attempts of the ecclesiastical authorities of this Protestant city to expel him. Though granted citizenship in 1535, he was eventually expelled from Ulm in 1539, again as a result of his controversial publications. He then moved to Basel, where he lived until his death in 1542. Franck supported himself on and off in the printing trade, though he was impoverished for most of his life. His real calling was always as expositor of a spiritual theology that he felt he had received from God and that he believed he was called on to expose to the world.

Franck's ideas appear fully formed by about 1531 and do not change significantly afterward. Franck believed that God communicated with humans through his word, which he understood to be an image or spark of divine being existing at the center of the human essence. Franck investigated the implications of this belief in a number of different ways. His first major work—*Chronica, Zeytbuch und geschychtbibel* (Chronicle, Book of Time and Historical Bible)—was published in 1531. In this enormous work Franck traced the absence of God's word in the outward events of history. By discussing the actions of political rulers, the events of church history, and the history of heresy and heretics, Franck drew a bleak picture of the absence of being which was evident in the course of the world. By contrast, Franck found in the beliefs of many of the heretics anathematized by the Roman Catholic church evidence of God's indwelling word. For Franck the condemnation of these heretics by the church was one clear sign of their illumination, since the world ever despises the true spiritual inner word, and seeks to expel this word from its midst. Franck was a fierce critic of anything claiming to give outward form to God's inner word, be it the institutional church, an office (he was a vehement critic of the papacy), a movement (he rejected all sects within the movement for reform), a book (even the Bible), or a body of thought. During his brief career he worked out the implications of this basic idea in more than twenty publications, which ranged from sprawling historical compilations, such as the *Chronica,* to much smaller works of translation and commentary. Franck's belief in the inadequacy of the outward, physical word to contain truth discouraged him from systematizing his own ideas. Thus, his works consist almost exclusively of compilations of or commentaries upon the writings of others. Sometimes this involved the translation and exposition of a work with which he felt sympathy, such as his translation into German of Erasmus's *Encomium moriae* ("Praise of Folly"). Other times it involved compiling contradictory passages from authoritative sources and then providing a spiritual reading of the texts that overcame the contradiction, thus proving the inadequacy of the outward letter and the necessity of an inward, spiritual enlightenment to understand God's truth. The most famous example of this is *Paradoxa Ducenta Octaginta* (Two Hundred Eighty Paradoxes) of 1534, in which Franck provides the most rigorous account of his spiritual theology.

Given Franck's disdain for outward institutions and orthodoxies, it is not surprising that he earned the disapproval of sixteenth-century authorities. His expulsion from Strasbourg in 1532 was in response to the *Chronica,* within whose pages Franck managed to offend the dignity of the emperor with his account of the bloodthirsty nature of imperial rule and to raise the hackles of Erasmus by including him among the honored heretics. The complaints of the emperor and Erasmus to the city magistrates of Strasbourg led to Franck's departure. What is more surprising about

Franck's career is the extent to which he was able to recover from this censure and find a second residence in the city of Ulm, where he published a great majority of his works between 1533 and 1539. Against the advice of prominent officials, such as the city magistrates of Strasbourg and Philipp of Hesse, Franck was granted citizenship in Ulm and allowed to continue his publishing activities. This relative tolerance was a function of the flux of the early Reformation, when no clear confessional lines had been drawn. Many among the Ulm patriciate sympathized with the spiritualist theology of Kaspar von Schwenckfeld, which bore some similarities to Franck's inner word spiritualism. Thus, the definition of orthodoxy in Ulm in the 1530s was not enforced in line with Luther or Zwingli, and Franck could find a sympathetic ear for his message as long as it did not injure civic peace. Since Franck did not seek a following or try to organize a sect, he was seen as harmless and even as a useful tool by the secular magistrates. They granted him citizenship in part to emphasize their prerogative over religion in the face of attempts by the city's pastors to enforce ecclesiastical control over the community. Franck's career was made possible by these fissures in authority, which were opened by the success of reform.

Franck has been proclaimed an anomaly, a thinker whose ideas are unique in the Reformation and who would have been more at home in a later period than he was in his own day. In fact, there are clear lines that can be drawn between Franck's thought and late medieval mysticism. The writings of Johannes Tauler had a clear influence on Franck. A number of contemporaries, particularly Hans Denck, shaped Franck's views. Other lesser-known contemporaries, such as Johannes Bünderlin and Christian Entfelder, worked out spiritualist theologies quite similar to Franck's and most likely had a major role in shaping his thought. Franck fits in well with certain strains of thought within the early Reformation that have clear antecedents in the late Middle Ages. What is most striking about his ideas and career is that they did find a place in the environment of his age. Within the interstices of the movement for reform there was room for individuals who could not be categorized according to the major figures and movements of the Reformation and whose careers reveal the various trajectories taken by the initial movement for reform.

BIBLIOGRAPHY

Primary Sources

Franck, Sebastian. "A Letter to John Campanus." In *Spiritual and Anabaptist Writers,* edited by George H. Williams and Angel Mergal, pp. 147–160. Philadelphia, 1957. A good introduction to Franck's thought.

———. *Paradoxa.* Berlin, 1966.

———. *280 Paradoxes or Wondrous Sayings.* Translated by E. J. Furcha. Lewiston, N.Y., 1986. Only bits and pieces of Franck's writings have been translated into English. This is the only full work that has been translated.

Secondary Sources

Dejung, Christoph. "Sebastian Franck." In *Bibliotheca Dissidentium,* vol. 7, pp. 39–119. Baden-Baden, 1986. An essential bibliography; updates the literature and lists documentary sources for Franck's life.

Hegler, Alfred. *Geist und Schrift bei Sebastian Franck.* Freiburg, 1892. Old but still the best study of Franck's thought.

Hillerbrand, Hans. *A Fellowship of Discontent.* New York, 1967. Provides an elegantly written and accessible introduction to Franck's life and thought.

Kaczerowsky, Klaus. *Sebastian Franck: Bibliographie.* Wiesbaden, 1976. A very thorough listing of all editions of Franck's works plus secondary literature.

Ozment, Steven. *Mysticism and Dissent.* New Haven, 1973. There is relatively little literature in English on Franck. This work sets Franck into his intellectual context and is the best place to start in studying Franck.

Teufel, Eberhard. *"Landräumig": Sebastian Franck, ein Wanderer am Donau, Neckar, und Rhein.* Neustadt a.d. Aisch, Germany, 1954.

Verzeichnis der im deutschen Sprachbereich erschienenen Drucke des XVI. Jahrhunderts. Stuttgart, 1983–. See vol. 7, nos. 2064–2175.

PATRICK HAYDEN-ROY

FRANKFURT AM MAIN was an imperial and free city of great political and economic importance throughout German history. On the eve of the Reformation, Frankfurt's position in the affairs of the Holy Roman Empire depended on its prominence as the site of imperial elections (traditionally since the twelfth century, legally since 1356), as well as on the commercial significance of the annual autumn and spring fairs, which made Frankfurt one of the major centers of commodity exchange in Europe. Protection of the wealth generated by these fairs and of the privileges sustaining them was the salient political objective of Frankfurt's ruling elite, dominated from the fourteenth century by a small number of patrician families. A council (*Rat*) of forty-three members divided among three "benches," only one of which included guild representatives, conducted the city's government in a manner largely unresponsive to common aspirations, even as the highly unequal distribution of wealth polarized the populace. At the end of the fifteenth century, nearly half of Frankfurt's residents were classified as nichthäbig—worth less than twenty gulden (a sum at or near the subsistence line, in modern terms). Especially galling was a new tax rate, set in 1495, that pressed hard on the poor while it favored the rich. Popular anger turned not only against the council but also against the clergy, who, gathered in ecclesiastical foundations and chapters, were maintained by large incomes from properties and rents. The Reformation allowed these social tensions to break to the surface.

Echoes of Lutheran ideas were first heard in a circle of wealthy patricians, where humanist literary interests were cultivated and where the problem of church reform had immediate relevance to the city's relations with the local clergy and their superior, the archbishop of Mainz. In 1520 this group founded a Latin school independent of clerical supervision, naming as its head Wilhelm Nesen, formerly a student and teacher in Basel and Louvain, where he had become a follower of Erasmus. Increasingly Lutheran in his sympathies, Nesen arranged for a former monk, Hartmann Ibach, to preach the first evangelical sermons in the city in 1522.

Another source of reform pressure had a broader base. Late in 1523 the village of Bornheim refused to collect the tithe for the Frankfurt clergy, and in the summer of 1524 the congregation of Sachsenhausen demanded a voice in the appointment of their pastor. In the city itself, a new preacher at the church of Saint Catherine's convent, Dietrich Sartorius, attacked purgatory, the cult of saints, and the Catholic Mass and advocated the free choice of preachers for all congregations. As these events produced strong reactions from church authorities (with Albrecht, archbishop of Mainz, threatening to interfere with the freedom of the fairs), the council tried to mute the growing furor by ordering Sartorius to stop preaching. But this move only directed popular agitation against the government, a turn of events accelerated by the appearance in the city of a seasoned theological and political activist, the jurist Gerhard Westerburg, partisan of Andreas Bodenstein Karlstadt and Swiss Anabaptists, who joined a group of "evangelical brethren" among the burghers.

At Easter in 1525 the situation reached its crisis. Crowds occupied the city gates and chose a committee of sixty-one to speak for them, which presented a set of grievances containing forty-six points to the council on 20 April. These Frankfurt Articles, resembling in some respects the Twelve Articles of the Swabian peasants but much more far-reaching, illustrate the confluence of religious, social, and political causes in the urban reformation in Germany. They range from calls for the right to choose pastors, the closing of monasteries, and the abolition of celibacy to demands for community consultation on tax policy, price control of necessities, higher pay for day laborers, and an end to nepotism in the election of councilors. The council had to accept the articles without change, and more measures, dictated by the committee, followed. But the triumph of religious and social evangelicalism in Frankfurt was short-lived. With the defeat of the peasants, the revolt succumbed to the threat of invasion by neighboring territorial rulers. Acting once more under duress, the council abrogated the articles and nullified all political concessions.

The move to the Reformation was not reversed, however, because many patricians sympathized with it. In May 1525 Johann Agricola came from Wittenberg to advise on religious reform; in June two Protestant preachers, Johann Algesheimer and Dionysius Melander, were given pulpits. Still, for eight more years the council vacillated, temporizing between fear of the emperor and the archbishop on one side and, on the other, the increasingly strident demands for change coming from the new preachers who, after 1526, were following a Zwinglian line and had the populace behind them in their call for an end to Catholicism. Under the pressure of direct action by the crowds (in 1532 they prevented Christmas Mass from being celebrated in Saint Bartholomew's, the city's chief church), the council reluctantly gave way, abolishing processions in 1529, allowing Communion in both kinds in 1531, naming more Protestant preachers, and—in April 1533—suspending Catholic services altogether. A citizens' referendum on this action, on 21 April 1533, marks the official shift of the city to the Reformation.

But 1533 did not mean the end of Reformation struggles in Frankfurt. After long hesitation over the question of loyalty to the emperor, the city joined the Schmalkald League in 1536. But in 1548 the government had to accept the terms of the Interim, returning church properties to Catholics and muzzling Protestant preachers—a policy that brought on a devastating siege by Protestant princes in 1552. Meanwhile the preachers were locked in doctrinal quarrels between Zwinglians and Lutherans, in the course of which Johann Cellarius, a staunch Wittenberg adherent, was forced to quit the city. Luther himself attacked Frankfurt's sacramentarian bent, but it was Melanchthon's and Bucer's intervention that eventually returned the city to Lutheranism, which, notably under Hartmann Beyer, Frankfurt's chief pastor after 1546, became the dominant religious direction. Driven from England, Flemish and Dutch Calvinists arrived in the 1550s, and by 1561 Frankfurt had two Reformed congregations, to the chagrin of Lutheran preachers, who regarded them as heretics, and to the annoyance of guildsmen, who resented them as competitors. The council repeatedly restricted Calvinist activities, causing many to move on to the Palatinate. In the long run, however, Frankfurt practiced a policy of toleration—not only toward the Reformed but also toward Catholics and Jews.

[*See also* Bucer, Martin; *and* Luther, Martin.]

BIBLIOGRAPHY

Dechent, Hermann. *Kirchengeschichte von Frankfurt am Main seit der Reformation.* Vol. 1. Leipzig, 1913.

Jahns, Sigrid. *Frankfurt, Reformation und Schmalkaldischer Bund.* Studien zur Frankfurter Geschichte, vol. 9. Frankfurt, 1976.

GERALD STRAUSS

FRECHT, Martin (1494–1556), German humanist and reformer and one of the lesser-known figures of the early south German urban Reformation. He was the leading reformer in the south German imperial city of Ulm in the 1530s and 1540s. He was a close associate of the reformer Martin Bucer and shared with him the desire to institute a church order that gave to the pastorate coercive powers in enforcing morality and orthodoxy. Although he has become an obscure figure, in his own day he was highly regarded in reform circles for his erudition and staunch support of reform.

For the most part, Frecht's attempts to institute a church order with coercive authority for the pastorate were frustrated. Like many of the urban reformers, he faced in Ulm a city council that jealously guarded against any concession of power to the spiritual authorities. In the 1530s Frecht became engaged in a heated campaign to expel from Ulm Kaspar von Schwenckfeld and Sebastian Franck, two of the most prominent dissenters from the mainstream theologies of reform. In these cases and others he suffered setbacks and open rebuke from the council for his efforts, though after years of struggle he did see Franck and Schwenckfeld expelled.

In general, Frecht's career revealed the differences of opinion between secular and ecclesiastical authorities over what constituted a reformed church. As with many reformers, Frecht's frustration contributed to the vehemence of his attempts to achieve what he saw as a proper ecclesiastical order. In the end he paid for his convictions. When the troops of Charles V occupied Ulm in the late 1540s in the aftermath of the Schmalkald War, Frecht was taken from the city in chains and then imprisoned and exiled for his refusal to accept the dismantling of the reformed order in Ulm.

BIBLIOGRAPHY

Bautz, Friedrich Wilhelm, ed. *Biographische-Bibliographisches Kirchenlexikon*. Hamm, 1970–. See vol. 2, pp. 115–116.

Deetjen, Werner-Ulrich. "Licentiat Martin Frecht, Professor und Prädikant (1494–1556)." In *Die Einführung der Reformation in Ulm*, edited by Hans-Eugen Specker and Gebhard Weig, pp. 269–321. Forschungen zur Geschichte der Stadt Ulm. Reihe Dokumentation 2. Ulm, 1981.

———. "Frecht, Martin." In *Theologische Realenzyklopädie*, vol. 11, pp. 482–484. Berlin, 1983. The articles by Deetjen are virtually the only items published on Frecht; as he notes, an extended study of his life is a significant lacuna in Reformation scholarship.

Verzeichnis der im deutschen Sprachbereich erschienenen Drucke des XVI. Jahrhunderts. Stuttgart, 1983–. See vol. 7, nos. 2498.

PATRICK HAYDEN-ROY

FREDERICK I OF DENMARK AND NORWAY

FREDERICK I OF DENMARK AND NORWAY (1471–1533), king of Denmark from 1523 to 1533 and of Norway from 1524 to 1533. After his brother, King John, died in 1512, John's son Christian II succeeded to the throne of Denmark and Norway. Since the relations between Frederick and Christian II had long been tense because of Christian's aggressive policy in the duchies of Schleswig and Holstein, where Frederick sat as duke at Gottorp castle, it was logical for the nobles rebelling against Christian to initiate contact with Frederick. After Christian II had been driven into exile (1523), Frederick was crowned king. In his coronation charter Frederick had to swear that he "would never allow any heretics, Luther's disciples or others, to preach. . . against the heavenly God, the most holy faith of the church, the most holy father the pope, or the Roman Catholic Church." In spite of this, it was during Frederick's reign that the Lutheran movement succeeded in the kingdom.

Christian II's loyal circle, as well as Emperor Charles V and Catholic Germany, considered Frederick to be a usurper. He joined forces with the united Protestant powers of Saxony and Hesse. In addition, he married his daughter Dorothea to Lutheran Duke Albert of Prussia, and in 1532 he made contact with the Schmalkald League, although without becoming a member.

Domestically, Denmark was full of crises, including tensions between social classes, unrest, and a farmers' rebellion. Into all this came the evangelical movement, which began to have success from 1526. By means of a series of forceful actions, Frederick demonstrated that he intended to move away from the Curia-run Catholic church. In a conflict over the selection of the archbishop, he directly opposed Rome's candidate, and at a meeting of the council of nobles in Odense (1526) he forced through the decision that future bishopric appointments would no longer be confirmed in Rome but only by the Danish archbishop, who would be the king's man, without canonical ordination. In the bishopric appointments in the following years the king decreed that the bishops would not oppose the evangelical cause, and at a 1527 meeting of the council of nobles also in Odense, he went a step further and forbade the prelates' payment to Rome for recognition of the offices. Instead, the money would be paid to the king. He also allowed monks to leave the monasteries and to marry, but a direct edict of tolerance for the evangelicals was probably not issued, as previous research assumed. At the decisive meeting of the council of nobles in Copenhagen (1530), he declared general freedom to preach and made the Bible alone the guideline for sermon contents, but a projected discussion of religion was not realized. Moreover, from 1526 the king had issued personal letters of protection to evangelical ministers, and he refused to step in against the violent attacks on monasteries, which were increasing.

At the same time, the king supported the national council's demand that only nobles could become bishops, and he maintained the church hierarchy. He supported the bishops' tithing right and did not want to attack directly the church's economic privileges. He himself did not convert openly to Lutheranism, nor did he introduce it into the country.

It is even more difficult to talk about the king's personal conviction because direct, personal sources are lacking. An inference can be drawn from the fact that the German Lutheran theologian Hermann Bonnus, pupil of Martin Luther and Johannes Bugenhagen, was hired part-time by Frederick at Gottorp castle as tutor for one of his children. Bonnus also worked part-time (between 1526 and 1533) on a collection of twenty-two psalms in Low German, of which sixteen were by Luther. He dedicated and presented the psalms to Frederick (first printed in 1984), and he would hardly have done this if he had not known that Frederick had a positive attitude toward the Lutheran understanding of Christianity.

It is difficult to determine the intentions of the king's ecclesiastical policy. It may have been a cunning policy that mediated between the confessional representatives to keep law and order. The real goal might instead have been to establish a national Catholic church, led by the king himself and his appointed bishops, which would have stood in the loosest connection to the pope and whose teaching was to be reform-Catholicism of one kind or another. The most likely interpretation, however, is that Frederick's church policy aimed at an evangelical church as its final goal and that the king went as far as he dared within the given framework and power structure. It is important to remember that the majority in the national council were Catholic.

BIBLIOGRAPHY

Andersen, J. Oskar. *Overfor Kirkebruddet.* Copenhagen, 1917.

Grell, Ole Peter. "The City of Malmø and the Danish Reformation." *Archiv für Reformationsgeschichte* 79 (1988), 311–339.

Lausten, Martin Schwarz. *Reformationen i Danmark.* 2d ed. Copenhagen, 1992.

Scharling, Suno William. "Frederick I's kirkepolitik." *Kirkehistoriske Samlinger* (1974), 40–88.

Sjøberg, E. "Odenseprivilegiet af 1527." *Historisk Tidsskrift* 12.2 (1966–1967), 337–360.

Winge, Vibeke. "Das mittelniederdeutsche evangelische Gesangbuch König Friedrichs von Dänemark." *Jahrbuch des Vereins für niederdeutsche Sprachforschung* 107 (1984), 32–59.

MARTIN SCHWARZ LAUSTEN

FREDERICK II OF DENMARK AND NORWAY (1534–1588), king from 1559 to 1588. Born three days before his father was elected king of Denmark as Christian III, Frederick himself was elected successor in 1536. His education was carefully planned but hardly successful. Suffering from dyslexia, he never learned to write correctly. He was, however, extremely physical, a lover of hunting and military virtues, and, as such, a typical representative of the ideals of the nobility of his time. Beginning in 1554 he was gradually drawn into government affairs. His father's confidence in his capabilities was slight, however, and there was disagreement over Frederick's infatuation with a young noblewoman. In spite of repeated requests he did not go to his father's deathbed.

Although he had to sign a coronation charter that strengthened the position of the council, he succeeded in leaving his mark on government work. In 1559, together with his uncle Adolf of Gottorp, he conquered the Ditmarshes. After years of tension he attacked Sweden in 1563, probably hoping to reestablish the Scandinavian union. The war lasted until 1570 and left the country in an economically difficult state. Nevertheless, assisted by able advisers, he succeeded in consolidating the national economy. The last period of his reign was a happy time, in which Renaissance culture flourished in contrast to the more austere style of his father's reign. Several distinguished men left their mark upon developments in government affairs, education, theology, and science.

In religion Frederick was conservative. Although a sincere believer and a diligent Bible reader, he was not an original thinker, and so he was careful not to introduce any changes into the church order his father had established. In practice this meant a strict observance of a Melanchthonian, humanist line, in which the differences between Luther and Melanchthon were ignored. Theologians were ordered not to dispute on dangerous subjects, and foreigners were closely watched. In 1569 a confession in twenty-five articles was drawn up, to which all immigrants had to swear. In 1569 an authorized hymnal was issued, followed by a gradual in 1573, an ordinance for betrothal and marriage in 1582, and an official translation of the Bible in 1589.

The great leader was Niels Hemmingsen, who enjoyed a European reputation and who had a decisive influence on ecclesiastical reforms. As a consequence of the dogmatic strife in Germany, he was accused of crypto-Calvinism, and after long and painful procedures he was removed from his professorship in 1579. But no right-wing Lutheranism was desired, either. In the 1570s, when German Lutheranism tended in that direction, Frederick in spite of urgent requests from his brother-in-law, the Saxon elector, refused to follow suit. On pain of death he prohibited the importation of the *Book of Concord,* and when his sister sent him two magnificent copies, he burned them. Out of fear for Catholicism he cultivated friendly connections with non-Lutheran Protestant monarchs such as Henry of Navarre (later Henry IV of France) and Elizabeth I of England. On the whole, the "Melanchthonian orthodoxy" of his reign delayed the eventual victory of genuine Lutheran orthodoxy in Denmark.

BIBLIOGRAPHY

Jensen, Frede P. *Dansk Biografisk Leksikon.* Vol. 4, pp. 525–530. Copenhagen, 1980.

Koch, Hal and Bjørn Kornerup. *Den Danske Kirkes Historie.* Vol. 4, pp. 131–179. Copenhagen, 1959.

THORKILD C. LYBY

FREDERICK III OF SAXONY ("Frederick the Wise"; 1463–1525), elector of Saxony from 1486 to 1525. Born in Torgau in January 1463, he died in his favorite castle the "Lochau" (now Annaburg). Frederick received (for his time) a thorough education. In 1486 he succeeded, together with his brother John, to the rule of electoral Saxony. His subsequent policy clearly was to strengthen princely power in the territory at the expense of the emperor. He was initially successful, especially in introducing comprehensive administrative reform in the territory; after 1500, however, Frederick suffered a string of setbacks in his efforts to strengthen Saxony against other princes and territories, because he was not a powerful politician. Frederick has gone down in history as Martin Luther's prince under whom the Reformation had its beginning.

Upon joining the University of Wittenberg, which was founded in 1502 as a counterpart to the University of Leipzig, Luther became a subject of electoral Saxony. Frederick, who already in his lifetime was called "the Wise," showed great tactical skill in protecting Luther and thus gave the reform movement the opportunity to establish itself to the point that even military force was unable to reverse its course. Frederick prevented Luther's extradition to Rome; it was due to his negotiations that Luther was summoned to Augsburg by the cardinal-legate, Cajetan, following the diet of 1518, that he was able to appear before emperor and empire at the Diet of Worms in 1521; and that he subsequently obtained refuge in Wartburg Castle. This upright but temperamental theologian did not make it easy for the prince to provide this cautious support—he was, as Frederick stated at Worms, "much too bold." Nevertheless, Frederick often secretly provided assistance and, above all, gave advice through his legal experts.

Political and economic factors as well had a share in enabling Frederick to support a "rebellious " monk against pope and emperor. At the time the popes lacked influence in Germany, and there were limits even to imperial power in the Holy Roman Empire of the German nation. Not only did the emperor's election lie in the hands of the seven electors, but the emperor was also frequently dependent on financial grants approved at the imperial diets. Not least, the Habsburgs owed money to Frederick, who had financial claims on them going back to 1497, when he had substituted for the absent Emperor Maximilian I as head of the Imperial Court Council; in addition, Frederick had subsidized Maximilian repeatedly. Habsburg indebtedness had an impact on the outcome of secret negotiations, apparently at Worms, with Charles V—Maximilian's grandson and successor—when Frederick was able to escape being sent the Edict of Worms, which contained the imperial ban on Luther.

Frederick was clever, levelheaded, and scrupulous, and in the conduct of domestic and foreign policy he surpassed his fellow territorial princes. Thanks to the silver mines of the Erzgebirge mountains he was also among the richest, and of all the German territories his had the fewest debts. He was esteemed as the "peace lover " or *Friedensreiche*—a play on Friderich, the German version of his name—one who never resorted to arms despite repeatedly becoming involved in conflicts with neighbors. Although he was too realistic to have agreed to the proposal, the question of his candidacy was briefly debated at the imperial election of 1519.

A factor in Frederick's freedom of action was the relative unimportance of electoral Saxony in the imperial equation. Unlike the southern and western regions, it was a recent addition that, geographically and psychologically, lay on the fringe of the empire. Moreover, this was a period of flux, one in which political problems such as the Turkish threat and peasant unrest claimed considerable attention.

Still, why did Frederick show favor toward Luther's cause, and why did he protect him? Frederick was much too careful and reserved to shed light on his thoughts or true feelings, and so our answers must be purely conjectural. Certainly it must have been inconvenient for Frederick, indeed at times dangerous. His cousin, the loyal Catholic Duke George of Saxony, would have seized the electoral privileges only too gladly. From a psychological point of view, it is astonishing that a prince who in Wittenberg was accumulating one of the largest collections of relics in Europe even tolerated the presence of the reformer there.

Did competition with the archbishop of Mainz perhaps play a role? The latter was a Hohenzollern and thus belonged to the political rivals of the House of Wettin. In his Ninety-five Theses Luther had attacked his indulgence practice. Yet, the reformer rejected the idea that political motives might have been involved. He had deliberately not informed the court of his actions against indulgences.

Was it for the sake of his recently established university that Frederick protected the professor who was drawing students there in increasing numbers? In fact, Luther was finally excommunicated and ultimately became a scandal to the university. Perhaps the elector, whose sense of fairness was well known, balked at a subject's being condemned without due process. Like Luther, he repeatedly sought an objective discussion that would clarify the theological issues involved. In this respect many had pinned their hopes on the Diet of Worms, but it turned out that Luther had been summoned there merely to recant.

What is most likely is that Frederick supported and protected Luther out of religious conviction. Frederick had always been a pious man, albeit that earlier his faith had been expressed in typically medieval forms, through the performance of "good works"—his pilgrimage to the Holy Land in 1493, his many foundations at which he employed such outstanding artists as Albrecht Dürer and Lucas Cranach, his collection of relics with its 19,013 items, some of which he displayed in magnificent settings. Frederick probably owed his new understanding of the Christian faith not to his Franciscan confessor, Jacob Voigt, but to two Augustinian hermits, Johann von Paltz and especially Johann von Staupitz (who also meant much to Luther). George Spalatin,

Frederick's secretary and Luther's friend, no doubt served as a link between the two men as well. Frederick's sympathies with the evangelical faith finally became such that at the Diet of Nuremberg in autumn 1522 his retinue wore the evangelical slogan *VDMIAE—Verbum Domini manet in Aeternum*, or "The word of the Lord endures forever" (*1 Pet.* 1:25)—on the upper right sleeves of their court attire. On his deathbed Frederick received the Lord's Supper under both kinds—that is, both bread and wine—a clear confession of the new evangelical faith.

BIBLIOGRAPHY

Borth, Wilhelm. *Die Luthersache (Causa Lutheri) 1517–1524: Die Anfänge der Reformation als Frage von Politik und Recht.* Historische Studien 414. Lübeck, 1970.

Höß, Irmgard. *Georg Spalatin, 1484–1545: Ein Leben in der Zeit des Humanismus und der Reformation.* 2d ed. Weimar, 1989.

Kirn, Paul. *Friedrich der Weise und die Kirche: Seine Kirchenpolitik vor und nach Luthers Hervortreten im Jahre 1517; Dargestellt nach den Akten im thüringischen Staatsarchiv zu Weimar.* Beiträge zur Kulturgeschichte des Mittelalters und der Renaissance 30. Reprint, Hildesheim, 1972.

Ludolphy, Ingetraut. *Friedrich der Weise: Kurfürst von Sachsen 1463–1525.* Göttingen, 1984. Contains further bibliographical references.

Stephan, B. "Kurfürst Friedrich III. von Sachsen, 1463–1525." In *Kaiser. König. Kardinal. Deutsche Fürsten, 1500–1800*, pp. 26–35. Leipzig, 1991.

INGETRAUT LUDOLPHY
Translated from German by Friedemann Hebart

FREDERICK III OF THE PALATINATE (also Frederick the Pious; 1515–1576), elector of the Holy Roman Empire. Frederick was the eldest son (b. 15 February 1515) of Duke John II of Pfalz-Simmern, an impecunious branch of the famous Wittelsbach family, and Beatrix, daughter of the margrave of Baden. He was strictly educated in the Roman Catholic faith, but influenced by his wife, Maria of Brandenburg-Culmbach, whom he married in 1537, he publicly converted to Lutheranism in 1546. He succeeded his father as duke of Simmern in 1557 and became the Elector Palatine in 1559 on the death of the childless Otto Henry.

Otto Henry, who completed the country's Lutheran reformation, had cared more for scholarship than for orthodoxy and had filled the chairs at his university with the best minds he could find, indiscriminately hiring Lutherans, Philippists, and Calvinists. Frederick III reaped the trouble his predecessor had sown when a bitter controversy erupted between the leader of the Palatinate church, Tilemann Hesshus, a strict Lutheran, and William Klebitz, a deacon, over a thesis on the Lord's Supper the latter had prepared. Hesshus condemned it as Zwinglian and sacramentarian; others at the university defended it. Frederick tried in vain to mediate the controversy and ended up dismissing both (September 1559). Philipp Melanchthon, whose advice the elector had sought, approved wholeheartedly of his action. After intensive study of the issues, Frederick himself came to the conclusion that the Reformed interpretation of the Lord's Supper was the correct one. A disputation at the university (June 1560) between the Saxon theologians John Stößel and Maximilian Mörlin and the Heidelbergers Peter Boquin and Thomas Lüber increased his disenchantment with the Lutheran zealots. The elector's conversion to the Reformed creed was sealed by the Naumburg Convention (early 1561), which had been called to unite Germany's Protestants but instead demonstrated the deep divisions among them.

Frederick now dismissed all Lutheran pastors and theology professors and hired Calvinists in their stead. He named Kaspar Olevianus, who replaced the deposed Hesshus in the chair of theology, Emmanuel Tremellius, an Old Testament scholar, and Zacharias Ursinus, a student of Peter Martyr Vermigli, to the Heidelberg faculty. He also ordered the removal of art works, vestments, crucifixes, altars, baptismal fonts, organs, and other "papist idols" that had been retained in Otto Henry's moderate Lutheran reformation. In the celebration of the Lord's Supper the *fractio panis* (bread breaking) rite, a sure mark of the Reformed Communion, was introduced. Existing monasteries and other ecclesiastical foundations were secularized and their revenues used for educational and charitable activities. The Heidelberg Catechism (1563), prepared by Ursinus and Olevianus, became the new norm of doctrine. It did not include the strict teaching on predestination characteristic of other Calvinist catechisms; but, on Frederick's insistence, it did contain a precise formulation (question 80) of the difference between the Protestant and Catholic views of the Lord's Supper that condemned the Roman Mass as an "accursed idolatry." A new church order (1563), based on the Genevan and Zurich orders, and the consistory order (1564) completed the Palatinate's "Second Reformation."

While these changes found favor, especially among Calvinists abroad, they were adamantly opposed by Lutherans. The rulers of several neighboring principalities (notably Christoph of Württemberg, Wolfgang of Zweibrücken, and John Frederick of Saxony) and their theologians expressed deep concern. The Colloquy of Maulbronn (April 1564), scheduled to defuse the issue, added further to the animosity between Lutherans and Reformed. Emperor Maximilian II ordered the Palatines to annul the confessional changes made. Frederick now was in serious trouble, for if it could be formally established that his confession did not agree with the Augsburg Confession, he was in violation of imperial law and hence excluded from the peace of 1555.

The estates at the Diet of Augsburg (1566) likewise demanded the abolition of all religious innovations in the Palatinate but refused to back Emperor Maximilian in condemning Frederick for violating the Peace of Augsburg. Led by Elector August of Saxony, the Protestant princes refused to exclude the Heidelberger from the community of the

Augsburg Confession. While August rejected the Palatines' understanding of the Lord's Supper, he wanted peace to consolidate recent political gains and therefore sought to avoid any linkage of religion and politics.

The outcome of this diet not only convinced Frederick III of the truth of his faith but encouraged him to pursue his confessional interests even more vigorously. He now sided openly with his beleaguered co-religionists abroad, sending his sons to provide military assistance, Johann Casimir to the French Huguenots (in 1567/68 and 1575/76) and Christoph to the Dutch Calvinists (in 1574). In 1562 he gave Frankenthal as a place of refuge to Calvinists driven from the Netherlands. The elector's prestige crested when he achieved the seemingly impossible by betrothing his son Johann Casimir to Elizabeth, daughter of August of Saxony (1570), thereby joining the empire's leading Lutheran and Reformed ruling families. The union assured Frederick of the continued goodwill of Germany's foremost Protestant prince and hinted at the possibility of further Reformed expansion into the very heartland of Lutheranism—a hope soon dashed when Elector August suppressed crypto-Calvinism in Saxony.

At home Frederick continued his reforms by introducing in 1570 a strict church discipline and making Heidelberg a truly international center for the German Reformed movement. His efforts continued to face opposition in the Upper Palatinate, where both the estates and the administrator, the electoral prince Louis, remained loyal to the Lutheran creed. The most spectacular dissent, however, came from two antitrinitarians, Adam Neuser, a pastor in Heidelberg, and John Silvanus, inspector in Ladenburg. Frederick ordered the arrest of both after receiving proof of their heresy. Neuser managed to elude capture by fleeing to Turkey, where he converted to Islam. Silvanus was less fortunate. On the recommendation of his theologians, Frederick had him condemned to death and executed (1572). This episode cast a dark shadow on what had otherwise been a most successful reign.

Frederick III died on 26 October 1576. He was succeeded by his son Louis, who effected a brief Lutheran restoration (1576–1583) that ended when his younger brother, Johann Casimir, became elector and resumed their father's confessional policies.

BIBLIOGRAPHY

Chadwick, Owen. "The Making of a Reforming Prince: Frederick III, Elector Palatine." In *Reformation, Conformity, and Dissent: Essays in Honour of Geoffrey Nuttall*, edited by R. Buick Knox, pp. 44–69. London, 1977. Traces the history of Frederick up to the Naumburg Convention.

Clasen, Claus-Peter. *The Palatinate in European History, 1555–1618*. Oxford, 1966. Focuses on Heidelberg as the center of militant Protestantism.

Graham, W. Fred, ed. *Later Calvinism: International Perspectives*. Sixteenth Century Essays and Studies, vol. 22. Kirksville, Mo., 1994. See especially pp. 267–384. Essays address principal issues occupying the Reformed church along the Rhine.

Häusser, Ludwig. *Geschichte der rheinischen Pfalz nach ihren politischen, kirchlichen und literarischen Verhältnissen* (1856). 2d ed. 2 vols. Reprint, Pirmasens, Germany, 1970–1971. Basic for the study of the Palatinate's history.

Hollweg, Walter. *Der Augsburger Reichstag von 1566 und seine Bedeutung für die Entstehung der Reformierten Kirche und ihres Bekenntnisses*. Beiträge zur Geschichte und Lehre der Reformierten Kirche, vol. 17. Neukirchen-Vluyn, 1964. Discusses the diet of 1566 which prevented Frederick's exclusion from the Peace of Augsburg.

Kluckhohn, August, ed. *Briefe Friedrichs des Frommen, Kurfürsten von der Pfalz mit verwandten Schriftstücken*. 2 vols. Braunschweig, 1868–1872. Collection of source materials for the study of Frederick III.

Press, Volker. *Calvinismus und Territorialstaat: Regierung und Zentralbehörden der Kurpfalz 1559–1619*. Kieler Historische Studies, vol. 17. Stuttgart, 1970. Focuses on the institutions and personalities that shaped the Palatinate in the late Reformation period.

———. "Die 'Zweite Reformation' in der Kurpfalz." In *Die reformierte Konfessionalisierung in Deutschland: Das Problem der 'Zweiten Reformation'*, edited by Heinz Schilling, pp. 104–129. Schriften des Vereins für Reformationsgeschichte, 195. Gütersloh, 1986. Assesses the applicability of the term "Second Reformation" to the Palatinate.

Visser, Derk. *Zacharias Ursinus: The Reluctant Reformer; His Life and Times*. New York, 1983. Concentrates on the life and thought of one of Frederick's principal advisers.

Visser, Derk, ed. *Controversy and Conciliation: The Reformation and the Palatinate, 1559–1583*. Pittsburgh Theological Monographs. Allison Park, Pa., 1986. Collection of papers by historians and theologians presented at the 1983 colloquy commemorating the death of Zacharias Ursinus.

BODO NISCHAN

FREDERICK THE WISE. *See* Frederick III of Saxony.

FREE WILL. The question of free will, *liberum arbitrium*, in the context of the salvation process was an essential issue in Martin Luther's attack on late medieval theology and played a major role in a number of important theological controversies in the sixteenth century. All prominent Protestant reformers subscribed to Luther's view that the doctrine of justification by faith alone implied the negation of a free will in sinful humanity, through which one could by oneself turn to God's grace; but not all consented without reservation to Luther's explication of this opinion in his famous dispute with the humanist Desiderius Erasmus of Rotterdam. The relation between human will and God's grace being the key problem, the question of free will called for fundamental theological decisions concerning the concepts of God and predestination, sin and justification, the certitude of faith, and the understanding of scripture. One should note that terminological differences may sometimes explain what in the sixteenth-century debates appeared as doctrinal divergences, and that the theological negation of a free will does not necessarily imply a philosophical determinism.

Augustine and Medieval Theology. Augustine is the founder of Western theological thinking concerning freedom of the will. All theologians of the Middle Ages were faced with, and tried to solve, the fundamental problems raised by him: How can one maintain the freedom of the will and the responsibility of human beings and at the same time assert the omnipotence and foreknowledge of God? How can the will be said to be free if human beings, contrary to the teaching of Pelagius and the Pelagians, cannot live righteously or even choose to do so apart from divine grace? Augustine held that, to be saved, fallen humanity needs the aid of God's grace, which is bestowed on the elect, who from eternity have been predestined to salvation. The grace of God liberates humanity from the slavery of the willful perpetration of evil. The will of a "natural" human being can be said to be free in the sense that one does *willingly* what one cannot help doing, acting without constraint or compulsion. This freedom, then, can be described as voluntary necessity.

Careful to avoid the heresy of Pelagianism, theologians throughout the Middle Ages would maintain that salvation is the work and gift of the good, foreknowing, and omnipotent God, although dependent, nevertheless, on human meritorious acts; the reprobation of unrepentant sinners is therefore self-inflicted and not a contradiction to God's righteousness. The great thirteenth-century Franciscan theologians (Alexander of Hales, Bonaventure) as well as the Dominicans (Albertus Magnus, Thomas Aquinas) tried to explain and solve the logical problems of these apparent paradoxes by introducing a series of elaborate distinctions: primary and secondary cause, operating and cooperating grace, habitual and actual grace, conditioned and unconditioned necessity are just a few examples.

In the fourteenth and fifteenth centuries the approaches to the problem of free will were generally either Thomist or Scotist, since the theology of Duns Scotus had emerged as the Franciscan response to the theology of Thomas Aquinas. Against the Thomist emphasis on the intellect and its knowledge of a person's final good as determining the direction of one's free will stood the Scotist, or Franciscan, insistence on the volitional and affective aspect of humanity and on freedom as one's most noble characteristic. Both positions reflected distinct concepts of God. Scotism thus advocated a double voluntarism, accentuating the sovereign will of God, who at least theoretically through his absolute power (*potentia absoluta*) could dispense from the order that he through his ordained power (*potentia ordinata*) has laid down for the salvation of humanity. Whereas Thomism would emphasize that God as the primary cause is working *through* the secondary causes of created grace and free will in the process of salvation, Scotus and the Franciscans tended to stress the cooperation of the free will *with* God's grace, explained in psychological terms, and the submission of the human will to the will of God. Important to the Franciscans in this context were the ideas of a natural human being striving to do the very best (*facere quod in se est*) and of congruent merit (*meritum de congruo*), the semi-merit of natural humanity, rewarded by God by the infusion of habitual grace (*gratia gratum faciens*), thereby justifying the sinner and making possible the condign merit (*meritum de condigno*), that is to say meritorious acts really worthy of their reward, the eternal glorification.

Ockhamism and Gabriel Biel. Late medieval nominalism, the *via moderna* of scholastic theology (also named Ockhamism after the English Franciscan William of Ockham), elaborated the Scotist doctrine of free will even further. In the second half of the fifteenth century Ockhamism found an able representative in Gabriel Biel, professor at the University of Tübingen, against whom Luther directed much of his initial reaction to Scholasticism. Dismissing the idea of habitual sin, Biel asserted the freedom of natural humanity to choose or not to choose a morally good act, even to love God above all and for his own sake. Humans can thus, without the assistance of God's grace, fulfill the law of God through individual acts chosen by the will under the guidance of good reason (*recta ratio*), although one cannot fulfill it with the intention properly demanded by God. This is possible only through infused grace and love, for which one disposes oneself through *facere quod in se est*, love of God above all. The disposition of humanity is always followed by God's grace, but the infusion of grace and love, which alone makes fully meritorious acts possible, nevertheless depends solely on the discretion of the omnipotent and unchanging God, who in his sovereign freedom can do as he pleases.

Luther. Schooled in Ockhamist theology, Luther in his earliest work held a similar view of human free will, although, in his comments on Augustine (1509) and on Peter Lombard's *Libri IV Sententiarum* (1510–1511), he accentuated the primacy of God's grace, thereby alienating himself from Biel's line of thought. The most significant difference between Luther and Biel is perhaps that Luther did not allow for neutral moral acts, but claimed that all acts are either acts of love, done in grace, or mortal sins. In his first *Dictata super psalterium* (1513–1515) Luther no longer viewed the grace of God as a psychological quality opposed to the negative quality of sin, with which human will can cooperate, but as the presence of God's mercy in faith (*fides Christi*). Although still using an Ockhamist terminology, Luther realized with increasing clarity that the wisdom of scripture was quite different from that of philosophy or of *the* philosopher, Aristotle, whose impact on scholastic theology can hardly be overestimated. Lecturing on *Romans, Galatians,* and *Hebrews* (1515–1518) Luther drew on Augustine's anti-Pelagian writings, which helped him depart not only from Ockhamism but from Scholasticism altogether.

His earliest disputations, *De vitibus et voluntate hominis sine gratia* (1516) and *Contra scholasticam theologiam* (1517), as well as his *Disputatio Heidelbergae habita* (1518), contained a more direct confrontation. The thirteenth theological conclusion of the latter *Disputatio Heidelbergae habita* read: "Liberum arbitrium post peccatum res est de solo titulo, et dum facit quod in se est, peccat mortaliter" (After sin has occurred the free will is nothing but a mere name, and when doing its best it commits mortal sin). Cited as heretical in the bull *Exsurge Domine* of 1520, this sentence provides a precise formulation of Luther's new understanding of the condition of natural humanity, which also implied a new understanding of God, although to Luther the truth of the sentence was as old as the Bible (see also his *Assertio omnium articulorum*, 1520).

Scholasticism, in Luther's opinion, had lied about both God and humanity by reducing the law of God to a set of demands that could be met by natural humanity; Scholasticism also implied a depreciation of God's grace, which was seen as a supplement to nature, necessary to its perfection, and thereby actually turned into a new law. To Luther it was obvious that every thought of a free will and of *facere quod in se est* must vanish where the meaning of God's command to be loved above all is fully appreciated. Love of God (*amor dei*) is only possible as hatred of oneself (*odium sui*). Humanity always stands emptyhanded before God (*coram deo*) and his radical command, and one can oneself do nothing to change this situation. A human being is a complete sinner (*peccator*), and the only righteousness one can hope for is that of Christ realized in oneself through faith by the grace of God. Through this alien righteousness (*iustitia aliena*) humanity is found completely righteous (*iustus*) in the eyes of God. The absolute opposition of sin and grace, each of them being a determination of humanity as a whole (*totus homo*), is fundamental in Luther's theology and marks a breach with the scholastic way of thinking. Freedom, theologically speaking, is the companion of justifying grace and can only mean the participation in the divine freedom in Christ. Indeed, it is another name for faith (*fides*) as Luther has described it in his famous *Tractatus de libertate christiana* (1520).

Luther's Debate with Erasmus. Luther's statements in this tract must be seen in their apparently paradoxical but necessary inner connection with his assertions in his perhaps greatest and no doubt most disputed theological work, *De servo arbitrio* (1525), an elaborate and harsh reply to a comparatively short treatise by Erasmus, *De libero arbitrio διατριβή sine collatio* (1524). Erasmus defended himself in the two parts of his *Hyperaspistes* (1526 and 1527), to which Luther did not respond directly. Luther, who in many respects appreciated Erasmus's contribution to literature, had already in a 1516 letter to Georg Spalatin made critical remarks about Erasmus's understanding of sin as lagging behind that of the anti-Pelagian Augustine. In a letter to Johannes Lang a few months later he characterized Erasmus with the words "humana praevalent in eo plus quam divina" (in him human nature prevails against the divine) and said: "Sed aliud est iudicium eius, qui arbitrio hominis nonnihil tribuit, aliud eius, qui praeter gratiam nihil novit" (one thing is the opinion of someone who ascribes something to man's decision, quite another is that of someone who knows of nothing besides grace). As soon as he fully realized what separated him from Scholasticism, Luther seems to have seen Erasmus as siding with Scholastic theology in the question of free will.

No later than 1523 Erasmus on his part held Luther's teaching on *servum arbitrium* ("the enslaved will") to be one of his main fallacies. Erasmus insisted that man cannot be held responsible in his relationship with God unless his will to some extent is free, whereas Luther focused on the certitude of faith and on this basis asserted the slavery of the human will, the master being either God or Satan. One can argue that the discussion was not conducted on the same level by the two opponents. Erasmus defined the free will as "the power of human will, through which man can either attach himself to that which leads to eternal salvation, or turn away from it." The deliberative argument of Erasmus was based on scripture and tradition. To him it was obvious that scripture would become meaningless and even unjustifiable if a free will is not presupposed in its pronouncements on reward and retribution. One would then have to accept the monstrous thought that it is God who hardens the human heart.

What Erasmus ascribed to the free will of man was in fact very little. He did not doubt that God is the primary cause and free will a secondary cause in the process of salvation, and that humans find grace, and only grace, at the beginning and the end of the process. But in between there must be room for the decision and cooperation of the free will, although its accomplishment is nothing but a gift of God. Referring to scholastic tradition Erasmus also mentioned the distinction between conditioned and unconditioned necessity (*necessitas consequentiae, necessitas consequentis*) as a way of maintaining God's foreknowledge and the divine governing of creation without excluding the free will by asserting a pure necessitarianism.

Luther's vehement reply, with its often striking imagery, was founded on the conviction that scripture speaks with the utmost clarity in these matters, drawing a sharp borderline between sin and grace and leaving no neutral space for a free will. Luther distinguished between the things "below" humanity and those "above" humanity, the latter concerning humans in relation to God. The term *free will* can only be applied to the first order of things, although it should rather be altogether abolished, since God governs everything. As humanity's salvation, the gospel of Christ precludes any human contribution, and the many admonitions in the Bible serve to reveal the sinful state of humanity, as is always the purpose of the law. Luther related God's will to grace to his omnipotence and foreknowledge, rejecting the distinction between conditioned and unconditioned necessity, while introducing that of God concealed (*Deus absconditus*) and God revealed (*Deus revelatus*), a distinction, that he took almost to the point of splitting the idea of God's unity. Free will is solely an attribute of God, whereas human will is like a pack horse that goes wherever its rider, God or Satan, directs it.

This slavery of the will is seen as the consequence not only of the Fall but also of humanity's creatureliness. Compared to tradition this was something new and even went beyond Augustine. The concealed will of God, according to which some do not accept the revealed or incarnate God's merciful invitation to salvation, is not to be scrutinized. Not until everything is seen in the light of glory shall man understand the true wisdom and righteousness of God's decisions.

Luther, then, asserted predestination without reservation, but this does not mean that God is the author of evil or that Luther taught an absolute determinism. The evil lies in the instruments God is using, that is, in the evil human will; Luther underlined that the movement of the will is free in the sense that one is not forced (*coactus*) to do what one does but is willingly doing it. One therefore is responsible for one's sin, since God in the matter of salvation and damnation does not work without human beings.

Melanchthon. In the *Loci communes* (1521), Philipp Melanchthon opens his exposition of the fundamentals of theology with an important account of the powers of humans and of the free will followed by a paragraph about sin. Drawing on scholastic and humanist traditions, he here lays down his doctrine of the affects, which continued to play an important role in his teaching on sin and grace and marked an anthropological approach to the question of free will that was characteristically different from Luther's strictly theological concept. In Melanchthon's view the will must inevitably express itself through the affects, which constitute an overwhelming and irresistible power. Melanchthon found this point confirmed by the Pauline teaching on sin and grace and therefore maintained that in relationship with God one has no free will, since grace alone can change one's heart. In 1521 he also shared the opinion of Luther that God's omnipotence is incompatible with human free will, but this view was inconsistent with the ethical note of his theology. Not unaffected by Luther's controversy with Erasmus, Melanchthon had, by 1527, given up the thought that everything happens according to divine predestination. In his *Loci* of 1535 he spoke of three causes cooperating in human conversion: the divine Word, the Holy Spirit, and the human will; and the 1548 edition of the *Loci* even used the Erasmian formula "facultas applicandi se ad gratiam" (the faculty to attach oneself to grace) to define the free will, still presupposing the preceding effect of word and Spirit. Melanchthon considered God's gracious invitation to be universal and rejected the thought that God also predestines to damnation.

Article 18 of the *Augsburg Confession* (1530), "On Free Will," was cautiously formulated and was readily accepted by the Catholic confuters. It could be read as a formulation of Luther's view, but also a Thomist would find his opinion expressed in its wording. In the Apology of the Confession (1531) Melanchthon turned against Ockhamism, but that did not prevent his own view from actually being close to Thomism and its preoccupation with the cooperation of grace and free will. All in all on can argue that this view was similar to the Erasmian position.

The Lutheran Controversies. The controversies within Lutheranism in the sixteenth century were all intimately related to the main issue of Luther's theological reformation, the doctrine of justification. Luther was never really suspicious of Melanchthon, but after Luther's death and provoked by the Augsburg Interim (1548) and by Melanchthon's participation in the Leipzig Interim (1548), Matthias Flacius Illyricus and other Gnesio-Lutherans turned against Melanchthon and the Philippists. Among the points in dispute was the question of free will. In the first round of the Synergist controversy the views of Johannes Pfeffinger, similar to Melanchthon's teaching of the three causes, were heavily attacked and rejected as pure Scholasticism. The second round was initiated through the publication of the Weimar Confutation (1559) by Flacius Illyricus, who, against the views of Pfeffinger and Melanchthon, stressed that human will was hostile to God and without any possibility of contributing to conversion. A colleague of Flacius Illyricus at the University of Jena, Viktorin Strigel, sided with the Philippists, and at the Weimar Disputation (1560) he maintained that the free will cooperated with God's Spirit in the conversion. The disputation was rather futile and suffered from terminological ambiguity. Concerning the question of free will in the context of predestination a dispute in Strasbourg (1561–63) between the "Lutheran" Johannes Marbach and the "Calvinist" Girolamo Zanchi made it evident that a Melanchthonian view of predestination was not compatible with that of Calvin.

The Formula of Concord (1577), which was meant to end the Lutheran controversies, dealt with the question of free will as its second item and with that of predestination as its eleventh item in both the Epitome and the Solid Declaration. The synergist standpoint was repudiated, insofar as natural human beings are said to be without any faculty of attaching themselves to grace. Melanchthon's "three causes" were not accepted, but the formula also turned against the Flacian description of humanity as a stone or rock in relation to God. As to God's eternal predestination and election the formula stressed that the theologians of the Augsburg Confession never engaged in a dispute about this question. It is evident that the teaching of Calvin had made the Lutherans cautious. Double predestination was rejected and the Melanchthonian view of eternal election prevailed. Predestination extends only to the good and beloved children of God and is the cause of their salvation. The perdition of the godless results from their rejection of God's universally pronounced invitation. Lutheran orthodox theologians, from the end of the sixteenth century onward, treated the doctrinal question of the free will (*Locus de libero arbitrio*) meticulously, but in the substance of the matter they generally did not go beyond the Formula of Concord.

Reformed Protestantism and Anglicanism. Huldrych Zwingli taught a general determinism including double predestination. Since God is the first cause and the all-moving power, he also operates the human volition. Sin and evil are caused by God and are part of his plan, serving the revelation of his majestic justice. Salvation and reprobation depend on God's eternal choice, and according to Zwingli this knowledge was meant to make the elect certain of their salvation.

The same motive is found in the writings of John Calvin, especially in the last edition of his *Institutio Christianae religionis* (1559), where he elaborates on God's providence (*providentia Dei*), which encompasses all that happens including human actions and everything evil. This metaphysical necessity (*necessitas*) is not the same as coercion (*coactio externa*) and does not preclude a psychological freedom of human will, but it also means that the Fall happened according to the will of God, and that the mere thought of cooperation between human beings and God in salvation is impossible. On this background and as a biblical truth Calvin maintained that some are preordained to salvation, others to eternal damnation. According to Calvin even this double predestination, which is consistently integrated into his theology, serves the glory and glorification of God and is the ultimate guarantee of salvation through grace alone.

Among the Calvinists double predestination stayed a subject of dispute throughout and far beyond the sixteenth century. Partly because of the influence of Melanchthonian theology the Reformed creeds before 1600 were rather cautious in their doctrinal statements about the nonelect. This goes for the Anglican tradition as well. The Thirty-nine Articles of the Church of England (1563, 1571) asserted the incompetence of human will in matters of faith and good deeds toward God (article 10) and emphasized justification through faith alone, but carefully avoided adopting Calvin's teaching on double predestination (article 17).

The Radical Reformation. Several of the radical reformers embraced an anthropology that implied the notion of a free will in humans. In his treatise *Von der Freyhait des Willens* (1527) the Anabaptist Balthasar Hubmaier taught a tripartite anthropology, according to which spirit, soul, and body each has its own will. While the spirit-will of fallen humanity is intact, the body-will is totally corrupted. Having turned to the flesh the soul has lost its ability to know good from evil, but through "the sent Word" the soul-will can be restored so that it can choose to do good, and guided by the gospel of Christ men and women even attain a higher level of grace than before the Fall. Accordingly, for Hubmaier salvation through grace alone was a half-truth, and predestination was not to be discussed.

Influenced by Hans Denck, Melchior Hoffman rejected Luther's notion of predestination and of *servum arbitrium*, the unfree will, to which he had earlier subscribed, and stressed the freedom of human will and its cooperation with God. Among the spiritualist writers Sebastian Franck, critical of the ideas of predestination and original sin, followed the teaching of Erasmus, maintaining that the human will is free and capable of cooperation with the divine Spirit. Kaspar von Schwenckfeld was also skeptical of Luther's view of justification and his denial of human free will. Influenced by Franck and Paracelsus, the mystical spiritualist Valentin Weigel, who lived a quiet life as a Lutheran pastor, held that human beings, gifted with free will, through their own inner decision could solve the tormenting conflict between hatred of God and unsatisfied longing for him. Fausto Sozzini and the Socinians followed a more rationalist line of thought in their anthropology, asserting that guilt and punishment presuppose free will, and that Original Sin is a mere figment.

The Roman Catholic Response. The Council of Trent (1545–1563) treated the question of free will in the Decree on Justification (1547). Without siding definitively with either Thomism or Scotism, the council consistently asserted the cooperation of grace and human will in the process of salvation. The decree turns against Luther's words about free will as merely a name, rejects an understanding of God's omnipotence that involves double predestination, and rules out the absolute opposition of sin and grace (see the anathemas of canons 5–7). It is only logical that the certitude of faith, which was so important to the reformers, is also anathematized (canons 12–14). As a formidable recapitulation of scholastic theology in a new context the Council of Trent made the division of Western Christianity and theology crystal clear and irreversible, but it also laid the foundations of serious dissensions within Catholicism itself, as the seventeenth century would make evident.

[*See also* Grace; Justification; *and* Sin.]

BIBLIOGRAPHY

Andresen, Carl, ed. *Handbuch der Dogmen- und Theologiegeschichte.* Vol. 2, *Die Lehrentwicklung im Rahmen der Konfessionalität.* Göttingen, 1980. A collection of scholarly contributions; fine bibliographies.

Bainton, Roland Herbert. *Erasmus of Christendom.* New York and London, 1969. Full bibliography.

Boyle, Marjorie O'Rourke. *Rhetoric and Reform: Erasmus' Civil Dispute with Luther.* Harvard Historical Monographs, vol. 71. Cambridge, Mass., 1983. Approaches the dispute between Erasmus and Luther from an epistemological and rhetorical point of view.

Copleston, Frederick Charles. *A History of Medieval Philosophy.* Reprint, Notre Dame, Ind., 1990. A fine and readable survey.
Gäbler, Ulrich. *Huldrych Zwingli: Eine Einführung in sein Leben und sein Werk.* Berlin, 1985. With a bibliographical survey.
Goertz, Hans-Jürgen, ed. *Radikale Reformatoren. 21 biographische Skizzen von Thomas Müntzer bis Paracelsus.* Munich, 1978.
Grane, Leif. *Contra Gabrielem: Luthers Auseinandersetzung mit Gabriel Biel in der Disputatio Contra Scholasticam Theologiam, 1517.* Acta Theologica Danica, vol. 4. Copenhagen, 1962. An outstanding work on Gabriel Biel and on Luther's criticism of Ockhamism.
———. *Confessio Augustana.* 2d ed. Copenhagen, 1981. The best commentary on the Augsburg Confession; also available in English and German.
McSorley, Harry J. *Luthers Lehre vom unfreien Willen nach seiner Hauptschrift De servo arbitrio im Lichte der biblischen und kirchlichen Tradition.* Beiträge zur ökumenischen Theologie, vol. 1. Munich, 1967. Critical of Luther's necessitarianism, but also argues that Erasmus did not represent the Catholic tradition.
Niesel, Wilhelm. *The Theology of Calvin.* Translated by H. Knight. Reprint, London, 1980.
Oberman, Heiko Augustinus. *The Harvest of Medieval Theology: Gabriel Biel and Late Medieval Nominalism.* Cambridge, Mass., 1963. A classic in the field.
Reardon, Bernard M. G. *Religious Thought in the Reformation.* New York, 1981. A helpful guide to the theology of the most prominent reformers. Useful select bibliography.
Schwarzwäller, Klaus. *Sibboleth: Die Interpretaion von Luthers Schrift De servo arbitrio seit Theodosius Harnack; Ein Systematisch-kritischer Überblick.* Theologische Existenz Heute, vol. 153. Munich, 1969. An excellent survey of the interpretations of Luther's confutation of Erasmus.
———. *Theologia crucis: Luthers Lehre von der Prädestination nach "De servo arbitrio."* Munich, 1970. A consistent interpretation of Luther's concept of predestination.
Seeberg, Reinhold. *Lehrbuch der Dogmengeschichte.* 4 vols. Darmstadt, 1959–1974. Unmatched history of Christian theology; vols. 3 and 4 very strong on the Middle Ages and the Reformation.
Stephens, W. P. *The Theology of Huldrych Zwingli.* Oxford, 1986.
Stupperich, Robert. *Melanchthon.* Translated by R. H. Fischer. Philadelphia, 1965.
Tschackert, Paul. *Die Entstehung der lutherischen und der reformierten Kirchenlehre samt ihren innerprotestantischen Gegensätzen* (1910). Reprint, Göttingen, 1979. A gold mine of information.
Vorster, H. *Das Freiheitsverständnis bei Thomas von Aquin und Martin Luther.* Kirche und Konfession, vol. 8. Göttingen, 1962.
Williams, George Hunston. *The Radical Reformation.* Reprint, Kirksville, Mo., 1992. A highly influential scholarly work.
Williams, George Hunston, ed. *Spiritual and Anabaptist Writers: Documents Illustrative of the Radical Reformation.* Philadelphia, 1957. Classic textbook.
Zickendraht, Karl. *Der Streit zwischen Erasmus und Luther über die Willensfreiheit.* Leipzig, 1909. Still the best account of the controversy between Erasmus and Luther.

STEFFEN KJELDGAARD-PEDERSEN

FRIESLAND. In 1524 Friesland belonged to the empire of Charles V, and the province was entirely Roman Catholic. The landscape was dominated by churches and monasteries. Sixty years later the province of Friesland belonged to the independent Dutch Republic and was officially a Reformed province, with only the Reformed religion sanctioned by civic authorities.

From 1519 onward placards and many other sources mentioned the attacks of Luther on the pope and the Catholic church in general. Sixteenth-century Friesland was a cacophony of heretical voices of humanists, sacramentarians, Anabaptists (Munsterites and Mennonites), Jorists, and Schwenckfeldians, but in the end, as elsewhere in the northern Netherlands, the Reformed voice proved to be the loudest. From the 1530s the Mennonites played a dominant role, although they were persecuted severely and many were burned at the stake. From the 1560s onward the Calvinists became more and more dominant among the "protestantizing" Frisians. Partly because of the role the Calvinists played in the Revolt of the Netherlands against Spain, the Calvinists became the winning party.

On 31 March 1580 the States of Friesland adopted the resolution that has been called the constitution of the Reformed church in the province: no priest or other cleric was to conduct Catholic services in public or in secret; monasteries and convents were to be closed; the property of the Catholic church was to be used to maintain schoolmasters, Reformed ministers, and the poor; and the local authorities in the countryside (the *grietmannen*) were to remove all images from the churches and to purge them of Roman superstition and all "Popish" relics. In rural areas the major landowners were to supervise the implementation of the resolution. Victory went to the Reformed, who were transformed from the victims of persecution into the persecutors.

With Catholic worship banned and the Roman church being dismantled, a new form of church organization was required. Before 1580 there had been some 350 parishes in Friesland, each of which supported one or more priests. In that year, when many priests went into compulsory retirement, the need for church ministers to take their place was obvious. Shortly afterwards in 1585 the states decided to establish a new university in Franeker "for Christ and his church." The Reformed ministers were of enormous importance to the Calvinization of Friesland: they preached the new doctrines from the pulpit, and they were responsible for enforcing discipline on refractory members of the congregations who posed a threat to the purity of the Church. From 1580 onward, congregations grew, consistories were established, classes were formed, and synods were held. But it was a slow process. Ministers were scarce, men were reluctant to sit on the benches of the consistory, fines had to be imposed to hold the congregations to their obligations, and so on.

Calvinism in Friesland had an ambivalent face as well. On the one hand the Calvinists wanted to have congregations of members going to the Lord's Supper; on the other hand many people attended the church services but did not become members of the new church because they feared the church discipline. They were the so-called sympathizers, *liefhebbers*.

Church, state, the stadtholder as *tutor religionis*, and the university cooperated in order to impose Calvinism on the people—at least that is the general impression of Friesland. The prevailing image of Friesland is one of militant Calvinism, but this image is not true. About 1600 some 25 percent of the population in Friesland were Anabaptist. The Calvinists in general feared the influence and the magnetism of the followers of the former Frisian priest Menno Simons (1496–1561). Many people in Friesland were neutral and undecided in religious affairs. From 1580 onward in many places only 10 to 20 percent of the entire population were members of the Reformed church. The rest belonged to the Roman Catholic church (officially forbidden), the Mennonites, or the sympathizers.

The ideal to which the Reformed aspired is clear: they wanted to create a community that took religion seriously in everyday life and that would dedicate itself to the *reformatio vitae* as part of the *reformatio doctrinae*. In reality the Calvinists only partially succeeded in realizing their ideals. This is partly because of the so-called *ius patronatus* in the countryside. Landowners there appointed the church ministers, and those landowners were often Roman Catholics or sympathizers. For at least two centuries this situation caused much conflict, since many ministers were appointed who did not have the sympathy of the church members. Furthermore, many Frisians belonged to the Catholic church or to one of the many Mennonite congregations. Although we do not have statistics, it becomes clear from research that many other Frisians (and inhabitants of the Low Countries in general) declined to make a choice among the many religious denominations in a religiously pluriform society.

BIBLIOGRAPHY

Bergsma, Wiebe. "Slow to Hear God's Holy Word? Religion in Everyday Life in Early Modern Friesland." In *Experiences and Explanations: Historical and Sociological Essays on Religion in Everyday Life*, edited by L. Laeyendecker, L. G. Jansma, and C. H. A. Verhaar, pp. 59–78. Leeuwarden, 1990. Presents historical background and updates bibliography.

Woltjer, J. J. *Friesland in Hervormingstijd.* Leiden, 1962. The most impressive study of the Reformation in Friesland.

WIEBE BERGSMA

FRIIS, Peder Claussøn (1545–1614), Norwegian clergyman and reformer. He was born and raised in Egersund in southwestern Norway until he was sent to the Stavanger cathedral (Latin) school. There he took his theological training; upon the death of his father in 1566, he became his successor as the parish pastor of Sør-Audnedal. Friis is an example of many pastors in Norway who never studied overseas, in Copenhagen or elsewhere, but who were ordained on the basis of their theological training in one of Norway's cathedral schools. During the next forty-eight years, Friis was to become one of the best-known and remembered Norwegian pastors of the Reformation era. He was an ardent champion of the evangelical faith at a time when Lutheran orthodoxy was gaining ascendancy. Friis was disturbed that Roman Catholicism was still in evidence in Norway after nearly a century of evangelical preaching and teaching. In 1612, as dean of Lista, he accused several pastors of crypto-Catholicism. After a hearing, they were defrocked. (Friis was immortalized by the modern sculptor Gustav Vigeland, who carved hundreds of human figures in Frogner Park [Oslo] depicting the eternal quest of humankind. Through a large statue, Vigeland, who came from the same parish that Friis had served four centuries earlier, depicts Friis about to cast a statue of one of the saints into the river behind the Sør-Audnedal church. Friis had become so upset about his parishioners praying to the saints that it drove him to iconoclasm in his own church. Standing as it does outside of the church on the major highway through southern Norway, the statue has become a favorite stopoff point for tourists.)

Aside from his ardent preaching and teaching and his efforts to eradicate the lingering vestiges of Roman Catholicism in Norway, Friis is remembered for his efforts to regularize the church tithe and bring order to the church after a period of ecclesiastical anarchy when the old church had been set aside but the new had not yet taken root. Unlike the Oslo cathedral school that was oriented to the Greek and Roman classics, the Stavanger cathedral school sought to revive the Old Norse classics. Friis, a product of the latter school, is remembered for his translation of Snorri Sturluson's *Heimskringla* into modern Norwegian. It recounts the old sagas about the kings of Norway from the Viking era. Friis sought to awaken a sense of Norwegian national consciousness at a time of political stagnation and Danish hegemony. His description of the land and the people in his *Norrigis Bescrifuelse* aimed at both a political and a religious revival.

BIBLIOGRAPHY

Friis, Peder Claussøn. *Norske Kongers Chronica.* Copenhagen, 1633.

Storm, Gustav, ed. *Peder Clausson Samlede Skrifter.* Christiania [Oslo], 1881.

TRYGVE R. SKARSTEN

FRITH, John (1503–1533), leading English theologian and martyr. Educated at Eton and Cambridge, Frith became renowned for his learning and in 1525 was invited to the new Cardinal College, Oxford. He was already acquainted with William Tyndale, and through him converted to "the gospel." In 1528 he was imprisoned for heresy. He subsequently fled to the Continent, to collaborate with Tyndale in biblical translation and polemic. Returning from exile in July 1532 to evangelize, he was soon arrested. In the Tower of London he wrote his most influential works.

Frith was unmatched among contemporary polemicists in his detailed exegesis and sustained argument, and also in his irenicism. "There was in him," according to Foxe, "a friendly and prudent moderation in uttering the truth, joined with a learned godliness." Frith sought to avoid the controversy that divided the reformers: as long as they were all agreed that the sacrament was not to be worshiped, they might conceive of it as they wished. But he was drawn to refute the conservatives—especially Thomas More, who found him a worthy and dangerous opponent—and persuaded to provide guidance for the "brethren."

Frith mounted an attack upon the doctrine of purgatory because he found it nowhere in scripture and because it derogated from divine grace, causing redemption to rest upon human repentance. "If we must make satisfaction unto God for our sins, then would I know why Christ died." Influenced by Johannes Oecolampadius, Frith wrote "invincibly" upon the Eucharist: "I proved. . . that it [transubstantiation] was not an article of our faith, necessary to be believed under pain of damnation. Then I declared that Christ had a natural body, even as mine is (saving sin), and it could no more be in two places at once than mine can. Thirdly, I showed. . . that it was not necessary that the words ['this is my body'] should be so understood as they sound." Frith expected martyrdom for this belief, and he was martyred when he refused to recant. His radical sacramental theology and his personal example had a lasting influence.

BIBLIOGRAPHY

Primary Source

Frith, John. *The Whole Works of William Tyndale, John Frith and Dr. Barnes, Three Worthy Martyrs and Principall Teachers of This Church of England* (1573). Edited by John Foxe. Works of the English Reformers 3. London, 1831.

Secondary Sources

Bautz, Friedrich Wilhelm, ed. *Biographische-Bibliographisches Kirchenlexikon.* Hamm, 1970–. See vol. 2, p. 132.

Clebsch, William A. *England's Earliest Protestants, 1520–1535.* New Haven and London, 1964.

Foxe, John. *Acts and Monuments.* Edited by Josiah Pratt. London, 1870. See especially vol. 5, pp. 2–18, and vol. 8, pp. 695–699.

Fulop, R. E. "John Frith (1503–1533) and his Relation to the Origin of the Reformation in England." Unpubl. D.Theol. diss., Univ. of Edinburgh, 1956.

SUSAN BRIGDEN

FROBEN, Johann (Lat., Frobenius; Ger., Froeben; c.1460–26 October 1527) a Basel book printer. Froben apparently learned the trade of book printing in the shop of the Nuremberg printer Anton Koberger. His stay there is documented in 1486. Afterwards he studied in Basel, where he went as a friend and compatriot of Johann Petri and his son Adam. Johann Petri owned a printing shop in Basel and had been a citizen of the city since 1488. Through Petri, Froben met Johannes Amerbach, a well-known printer in Basel. On 13 November 1490 Froben acquired citizenship in Basel and qualified to become a guild member. He was accepted into guild membership on 13 May 1492. Already a well-known printer, he became a member of the guild "Zum Schlüssel" on 6 December 1522.

With the support of the printer and publisher Wolfgang Lachner, Froben managed to set up his own printing business. His first printed work was a simple and inconspicuous Latin Bible in 1491. His rise within the trade began when he collaborated with other prominent print shops in Basel. In 1496 he started publishing in association with Johann Petri, who also took care of the commercial affairs. From 1502 on he published in conjunction with Johannes Amerbach, "primus inter pares" among the printers in Basel. From Amerbach Froben purchased the Zum Sessel printing house in December 1507. The combination of these three book publishers made Basel into an important international center for book publishing. After Petri's death in 1511 and Amerbach's death in 1513, Froben published alone and became the most important publisher in Basel. At first even Adam Petri's printing house could not compete with him. Since Froben could not handle all the commercial and publishing matters alone—perhaps he was not interested in them—he invited Wolfgang Lachner to be his partner. (Froben had married Lachner's daughter Gertrud in 1510.)

Froben's printed works stand out for the precision of the printing, the beauty of his type, and the display of the title page. When Froben reprinted Erasmus's *Adagia*, the author was delighted with the magnificent format, particularly with the ornamental borders of the title page with the "Triumph of Humaneness" that had been designed by the artist Urs Graf. In August 1514 Erasmus traveled to Basel to meet the publisher in person. From this visit came a friendship between the two men that lasted until Froben's death. Erasmus lived at Froben's printing house, Zum Sessel, until 1527 and made a significant scholarly contribution to Froben's publishing business. In 1516 Froben published the first New Testament in the original Greek together with Erasmus's Latin translation.

Besides his connection with Erasmus, Froben kept in contact with numerous other humanist scholars, and it soon became an honor to be published by him. The publisher himself had received a humanist education and had a mastery of the ancient languages. With the exception of two works in German, Froben published only works in Latin, Greek, and Hebrew. He created a new type of Renaissance book characterized by the harmony of print and graphics, the beauty of which was never surpassed. He used the ornate Roman cursive script that the famous Italian printer Aldo Mannucci had used in Venice. Froben himself saw to the carving of the characters. Drafts for the design of the title pages were provided by famous artists such as Urs Graf (who had also worked with Amberbach in 1510), and beginning in October 1516, by Ambrosius Holbein and Hans Holbein the Younger. Metal carving became the rule for the graphics, replacing the traditional woodcarving. Typically the books published by Froben were not illustrated. Only the 1523 edition of the Lord's Prayer contained illustrations (by Hans Holbein the Younger). Well-known humanists such as Beatus Rhenanus and Wolfgang Capito helped Froben to ensure the accuracy of the Latin texts, while Konrad Pellikan proofread the Greek texts. The titles produced by Froben included editions of the church fathers, classical authors, and contemporary works by humanists, particularly by Erasmus. Thus a ten-volume edition of Jerome's writings appeared in 1516–1518 (an index in 1520), and a collection of Augustine's works was completed after Froben's death in 1528–1529. Other church fathers published included Chrysostom (1517), Cyprian (1520), Eusebius (1523), and Ambrose (1527). The classical authors published include Pliny the Elder (1525), Tacitus (1519), Seneca (1515), Velleius Paterculus (1520), and Terence (1521). In addition, grammars to aid in the interpretation of theological sources were published, including a Hebrew grammar with a dictionary by Sebastian Münster, a Chaldean (Aramaic) dictionary, and an introduction to Hebrew written by Froben himself (1527). Finally, half of all first editions of Erasmus's works were published by Froben. The *Basler Drucker und Verlegerkatalog* (Directory of Basel Printers and Publishers) lists no less than 503 editions for Froben, including those he published in association with Petri and Amerbach. At the high point of its activity around 1520, Froben's press printed some fifty titles per year.

Even before Froben's death, however, the publishing house suffered significant losses, because, on account of Erasmus's influence, it did not open itself to Reformation literature, which was generally in German. With the exception of two reprints in 1518 and 1519, Froben did not publish any works by Luther. Adam Petri, who did have an orientation toward Reformation writings, overtook Froben in the Basel publishing market. At his death, Froben had no fortune to bequeath. His older son Hieronymus continued the business. His widow later married the famous publisher Johann Herwagen.

BIBLIOGRAPHY

Benzing, Josef. *Die Buchdrucker des 16. und 17. Jahrhunderts im deutschen Sprachgebiet.* 2d ed. Wiesbaden, 1982. See vol. 1, p. 32. Extensive bibliography.

Brandler, Karl. "Johannes Frobenius: 'Ein Fürst der Buchdrucker' des 16. Jahrhunderts in Basel." *Fuldaer Geschichtsblätter* 36 (1960), 135–148. An assessment of the printer and publisher; contains biographical references.

Pfister, Arnold. "Johann Froben." In *Neue Deutsche Biographie,* vol. 5, pp. 638–640. Berlin, 1961. Extensive bibliography.

SIGRID LOOß
Translated from German by Robert E. Shillenn

FROSCH, Johann (c.1483–1533), early supporter of Martin Luther's Reformation. He received his undergraduate education at the University of Toulouse and came to Wittenberg in 1514 as a Carmelite monk. In 1516 he began his close friendship with Luther but left Wittenberg in 1517 to assume duties as prior of the Carmelite order at Saint Ann's in Augsburg. When Luther visited Augsburg in 1518 to discuss his ideas for reform with Cajetan, the papal legate, he enjoyed Frosch's warm hospitality and friendship. Frosch accompanied Luther back to Wittenberg to receive his doctorate. Soon, he was called back to Augsburg by the city council, where he served as one of the preachers at Saint Ann's with Urbanus Rhegius. On Christmas Eve 1524 Frosch and his colleague in Augsburg gave both the cup and bread to the laity during the Eucharist for the first time and became the instigators of the Reformation there. Following Luther's lead, both Frosch and Rhegius married in 1525.

In 1526 Frosch remained true to Luther's view on the Eucharist while his friends, including Rhegius, leaned toward Zwingli's position that the bread and wine were merely symbols. Tired of the controversy over the Eucharist, Frosch accepted a call in 1531 to Saint Jacob's church in the strongly Lutheran city of Nuremberg. He also preached in Saint Sebald's church. Frosch's career in Nuremberg was cut short by an early death in 1533.

Although Frosch is remembered primarily as an ardent supporter of Luther, he also left several publications, one of which is a Lutheran interpretation of the Catholic greeting Hail Mary (*Salve Regina;* 1524). He also composed several hymns, the most notable being "*Gott selbst ist unser Schutz und Macht.*" After his death a number of other musical works appeared, but recent scholarship indicates there may have been another Johann Frosch, one who was primarily a musician and not a theologian.

BIBLIOGRAPHY

Albrecht, Hans. "Johannes Frosch(ius)." In *Die Musik in Geschichte und Gegenwart,* edited by Friedrich Blume, pp. 1012–1014. Kassell and Basel, 1955. A detailed study of Frosch, with a strong bibliography of German secondary accounts.

Bautz, Friedrich Wilhelm, ed. *Biographische-Bibliographisches Kirchenlexikon.* Hamm, 1970–. See vol. 2, p. 145.

Buszin, Walter S. "Johannes Frosch." In *The Encyclopedia of the Lutheran Church,* edited by Julius Bodensieck, vol. 2, p. 891. Minneapolis, 1979. Convenient source for English readers.

Koch, Eduard Emil. "Johannes Frosch." In *Geschichte des Kirchenlieds und Kirchengesangs der Christlichen, insbesondere der deutschen evan-*

gelischen Kirche, vol. 1, pp. 405–406. Stuttgart, 1866. An older but reliable source of Frosch's creative work.

Verzeichnis der im deutschen Sprachbereich erschienenen Drucke des XVI. Jahrhunderts. Stuttgart, 1983–. See vol. 7, nos. 3143–3144.

RICHARD GLENN COLE

FROSCHAUER, Christoph (d. 1564), first printer in Zurich. He arrived in 1519 and in 1521 printed his first book, *Ein Klag des Frydens* a translation of Erasmus's *Querela Pacis*. Soon Froschauer became an ardent follower of Zwingli. He printed many of Zwingli's tracts and the work of other reformers such as Konrad Pellikan, the humanist Franciscan associate of Zwingli; Heinrich Bullinger, Zwingli's son-in-law and his successor; and Conrad Gessner, the author of the *Bibliotheca universalis,* the first printed alphabetical bibliography of Latin, Greek, and Hebrew volumes. Froschauer began the printing of another work by Gessner, the landmark edition of *Historia animalium,* the founding opus of modern zoology. The final zoological volumes were printed by Froshchauer's nephew, Christoph Froschauer II, who took over the print shop when his uncle died. A number of Froschauer's other works could be classified as Reformation polemics: relatively brief pamphlets designed for a wide if not popular audience.

Between 1524 and 1564, he published twenty-seven editions of the complete Bible, twenty of which were in vernacular German. These editions relied heavily on Luther's translations, but large segments were tanslated by preachers in Zurich; some of the editions were profusely illustrated with woodcuts by Hans Holbein. Froschauer printed a complete vernacular Bible in 1530, four years earlier than Luther's monumental Bible printed in Wittenberg.

The variety of works published by Froschauer indicates the skill of this Reformation printer. Aside from works of humanists and reformers, he gained considerable fame in the publication of the Constance songbook authored by Johannes Zwick, Ambrosius Blarer, and others, which served Protestant church singing in sixteenth-century northern Switzerland.

BIBLIOGRAPHY

Blume, Friedrich. *Protestant Church Music.* New York, 1974; London, 1975. Useful discussion of Froschauer's role in the publication of the Constance songbook.

Clair, Colin. *A History of European Printing.* New York, 1976. Provides helpful data on Froschauer's major printing accomplishments; has a relevant chapter on the history of Swiss printing in the sixteenth century.

Cole, Richard. "Reformation Printers: Unsung Heros." *Sixteenth Century Journal* 15 (1984), 327–339. Discusses literary, academic, and religious side of sixteenth-century Reformation German printers.

Götze, Alfred. *Die hochdeutschen Drucker der Reformationszeit.* Berlin, 1963. Useful for technical aspects of Froschauer's fonts.

RICHARD GLENN COLE

FUGGER, Jakob (1459–1525), the most significant representative of early German capitalism, a financier of the emperor, and an opponent of the Reformation. Born in Augsburg to a merchant family on 6 March 1459, Fugger initially pursued an ecclesiastical career in the Herrieden monastery. At the same time, he began an apprenticeship in his brother's trading company. In 1478 he left the monastery and then continued his business apprenticeship in Venice. One year later, having returned to Augsburg, he expanded the family's traditional engagement in precapitalist commodity production and trading, especially in fustian textiles. From the end of the 1480s, with a particular feel for profit opportunities, he invested in silver- and copper-mining industries in the Tirol. In so doing he entered early into close business relations with the Habsburgs. From 1494 he brought the Hungarian-Slovakian mining district under his control, which in the thirty years until his death yielded approximately 1.5 million florins profit. He used new business methods, organized an extensive intelligence service, and developed a trading network (with numerous trading posts and branches) that spanned a large part of Europe and also extended overseas.

Alongside his close connections with the Habsburgs—among other things he financed the 1508 proclamation of Maximilian I as emperor in Trent and through large bribes brought about the 1519 election of Charles V as emperor—he also formed lucrative business relationships with the Curia Romana. At the Holy See he established his own agent, who gained great influence there. Fugger banks transferred indulgence monies from the empire to Rome. High-ranking princes of the church in the Curia, as well as in the empire, were business partners of the Fuggers. With large deposits, Prince-Bishop Melchior von Meckau of Brixen was from 1508 the largest of the silent partners of the firm. In 1513/14 Fugger financed the accumulation of benefices of Albert of Brandenburg—who became the archbishop of Magdeburg, administrator of Halberstadt, and later also archbishop of Mainz, thereby becoming the highest-ranking German ecclesiastical prince—and in exchange Fugger had indulgence monies assigned to himself. In other respects as well, Fugger played a decisive role in the allocation of benefices within the empire.

This close symbiosis with the leading powers assured him political influence and support. Frequently he used, indeed forced, the emperor to help him in carrying out his economic interests. For that reason Fugger immediately positioned himself on the side of the Roman church and the emperor when Martin Luther threatened their foundation. In the summer of 1518 the papal legate Cajetan stayed in his house in Augsburg and introduced him to Luther's opponent Johann Eck. Luther's Augsburg hearing in October 1518 took place in Fugger's house. As the Reformation gained ground in Augsburg, Fugger battled its adherents, but at times he had to leave the city. In his territories—the counties of

Kirchberg, Weißenhorn, and others, which he had acquired in return for high credits—he was one of the first to rigorously execute the Edict of Worms. In 1525 he employed mercenaries against the peasant uprising in his territories. He granted loans to the Habsburgs, the Swabian League, and several princes, and he delivered copper to them for the casting of guns so that they could crush the rebellious peasants. He assigned to Luther the blame for the Peasants' War.

Fugger died on 30 December 1525, having reaffirmed on his deathbed his profession of Roman Catholic faith. His wealth amounted to nearly 2.5 million florins.

BIBLIOGRAPHY

Pölnitz, Götz. *Jakob Fugger.* 2 vols. Tübingen, 1949–1951. Comprehensive biography.

Strieder, Jakob. *Studien zur Geschichte kapitalistischer Organisationsformen: Monopole, Kartelle und Aktiengesellschaften im Mittelalter und zu Beginn der Neuzeit* (1925). 2d ed. Reprint, New York, 1971. An economic-historical approach.

———. *Jacob Fugger der Reiche.* Leipzig, 1926. Biography. Also available in English translation: *Jacob Fugger the Rich: Merchant and Banker of Augsburg, 1459–1525*, reprint, Westport, Conn., 1984.

ADOLF LAUBE

Translated from German by Susan M. Sisler

FULDANUS. *See* Krafft, Adam.

FUNERALS. The purpose of the early modern Catholic funeral rite was, as it always had been, far less to mourn the dead than to celebrate a Christian's passage into eternal life with Christ and to offer prayers on behalf of the deceased. The liturgy of the Catholic funeral had slowly evolved over the centuries; by the time of the Reformation, in fact, what was notable about Catholic practice was the absence of uniformity, even after the Council of Trent. Two sixteenth-century works that attempted to be authoritative were the Dominican Albertus Castellani's *Sacerdotale Romanum* (1523), which was largely based upon a thirteenth-century Franciscan liturgy, and the *Rituale sacramentorum Romanum* (1583) of Cardinal Julius Sanctorius, who sought a fusion of medieval and contemporary liturgical elements. The popularity of these two works notwithstanding, their ultimate influence upon contemporary practice was limited. Diocesan manuals throughout the century maintained their own forms of particularism, resulting in myriad variations. Immediately following the Council of Trent, there was little effort to impose any uniformity in funeral liturgy; that would not occur until 1614 with the promulgation of the *Roman Ritual.*

Despite local variations, sixteenth-century Catholic funeral rites generally included the following elements: the "commendation of the soul" (prayers and psalms offered for the dying Christian); cleaning and dressing the dead in preparation for burial; a wake, held either in the home or in the church, involving prayers and psalms around the body; a procession to the church, which was meant to symbolize the Christian's movement from this life to the heavenly Jerusalem; a funeral mass; the absolution, a second commendation following the mass; and burial, either within the church or in a cemetery, accompanied by the chanting of psalms. Funerals for laypeople, particularly the absolution and burial services, tended to be an abbreviated form of those for clergy. Moreover, funerals for baptized children took on their own character: manuals stated that in these cases greater emphasis should be placed on consoling the parents. Unbaptized children of Christian parents were denied Christian funeral rites; they were to be buried, at evening, outside the sanctified cemetery.

Despite his attention to other liturgies, such as baptism and Communion, Martin Luther never produced a specific funeral rite. The clearest expression of his ideas concerning that liturgy is in his "Preface to the Burial Hymns" (1542). In it Luther preserved the Catholic teaching of the funeral as a celebration of the Resurrection but discounted the practices of processions, masses for the dead, and wakes as "hocus-pocus on behalf of the dead." Equally repugnant to Luther were those Catholic graveside songs that made reference to purgatory. He therefore adapted to Catholic melodies various New Testament texts, including *Luke* 2:29–32 ("Simeon's Song"), and recommended more recent German hymns, such as *In Peace and Joy I Now Depart* and *We Lay This Body in the Grave.*

The best sources for Lutheran funeral practices are the sixteenth-century church orders. From these a general pattern emerges. Burial was not to take place too quickly after the departed's last breath; as one church order explained, this was to ensure that the Christian was indeed dead and not merely comatose. The body, covered with a cloth, would be taken to the cemetery in solemn procession accompanied by the pastors, deacons, bell ringer, schoolmaster, student acolytes, and family and friends. Although Luther had criticized the procession, many communities believed that the funeral train prompted citizens to reflect upon the Resurrection, as well as their own mortality and spiritual state. At graveside a sermon might be delivered recounting the life of the deceased and calling the living to repentance. The singing of those hymns recommended by Luther concluded the funeral service. No distinctions were to be made between clergy and laity in the length or content of Lutheran funerals; moreover, several church orders emphasized that unbaptized children, including stillbirths, were to be accorded Christian burial.

John Calvin's most direct statement on funeral liturgy, in the Genevan *Ecclesiastical Ordinances* of 1541, is terse: "The dead are to be buried decently in the place appointed. The attendance and company are left to each man's discretion." Indeed, evidence regarding Calvin's own funeral is scarce; not even the exact place of his interment is known. Despite this lack of attention to the liturgy of the Christian funeral, Calvin nonetheless valued the symbolism of the rite. In his *Christianae religionis Institutio* (Institutes of the Christian Religion), Calvin discussed at length the role of burial practices among the Old Testament patriarchs, emphasizing God's promise of resurrection. The funeral was, to Calvin, a "rare and precious aid to faith" that served as "an earnest of new life." Although one of the more cryptic among sixteenth-century theologians regarding the funeral liturgy, Calvin perhaps gave the rite's purpose its most eloquent expression in his assertion that the Christian funeral "raises our eyes from gazing upon a grave that corrupts and effaces everything, to the vision of renewal."

[*See also* Death; Sacramentals; *and* Sacraments.]

BIBLIOGRAPHY

Calvin, John. *The Institutes of the Christian Religion.* Translated by Ford Lewis Battles. Edited by John T. McNeill. Library of Christian Classics, vol. 21. Philadelphia, 1960. Contains discussion of the origin and purpose of burial rites.

———. "Draft Ecclesiastical Ordinances, 1541". In *Calvin: Theological Treatises*, pp. 56–72. Translated by J. K. S. Reid. The Library of Christian Classics, vol. 22. Philadelphia, 1964.

Luther, Martin. "Preface to the Burial Hymns, 1542." Translated by Paul Zeller Strodach. In *Luther's Works*, edited by Ulrich S. Leupold, vol. 53, pp. 325–331. Philadelphia, 1965. Luther's most direct discussion of funeral liturgy, along with recommended hymns.

Rutherford, Richard. *The Death of a Christian: The Rite of Funerals.* New York, 1980. Offers a detailed survey of Catholic funeral practices from apostolic times to the present.

Sehling, Emil. *Die evangelischen Kirchenordnungen des XVI. Jahrhunderts.* Tübingen, 1966–. A multitude of German Lutheran church orders, most containing detailed outlines of local funeral rites.

EILEEN T. DUGAN

G

GAETANO DE VIO, Tommaso. *See* Cajetan.

GAISMAIER, Michael (c.1491–1532), major political and military leader of the Peasant War in Tirol (1525–1526). Gaismaier was born near the south Tirolean town of Sterzing (Vipiteno) into an upwardly striving family engaged in mining and agriculture. Although no educational records have surfaced, his university training in law is assumed on the basis of his employment as secretary and judicial recorder for the *Landeshauptmann* ("governor") of south Tirol, Leonhard von Völs, between 1518 and 1524. That year Gaismaier was accused of misappropriating military recruitment funds, and resigned his office even though the charges against him were not proved. Through family connections, he found a position as secretary to the bishop of Brixen (Bressanonet), Sebastian Sprenz.

Gaismaier's rapid transformation from diligent bureaucrat to revolutionary remains something of a mystery. Historians continue to debate his motives in assuming leadership of the popular uprising against the bishop of Brixen which began on 10 May 1525. After peacefully handing over his employer's residence to the insurgents, Gaismaier was elected their chief spokesman and military commander.

The miners, peasants, and townspeople of Brixen hoped by their action to win a hearing from Archduke Ferdinand for their grievances against ecclesiastical rule, noble privilege, and the great commercial and banking companies that controlled the local silver- and copper-mining industries. Gaismaier and others drew up a list of thirty articles demanding fiscal, economic, and juridical relief from their feudal overlords, and the removal of intermediary political authorities between the commonalty *(gemain)* and its prince. The influence of the Reformation is apparent in the call for preaching from scripture and the abolition of clerical wealth and privilege. Yet references to the "holy martyrs," "holy sacraments," and the Virgin Mary suggest the religious framework of the articles was one of traditional piety spiked with anticlericalism rather than Reformation theology.

The appeal to Ferdinand proved fruitless, and in October 1525, after the uprising in Tirol had been forcibly put down by imperial troops, Gaismaier fled to Zurich where he found a friend and ally in Zwingli. The famous *Landesordnung* ("constitution") Gaismaier composed in exile while preparing a new uprising in 1526 bears the stamp of the Swiss reformer as well as its author's disappointed hope of reform from above.

In contrast to other peasant manifestoes of the time, the *Landesordnung* was a revolutionary blueprint for a Christian utopia in which every vestige of the old church was abandoned except for the Bible. Social distinctions were abolished and political rights shared equally in an agrarian republic of small, self-governing communes. A central authority of elected officials and biblical scholars was to supervise the economy and assure the "godliness" of the new order, which banned private commerce while permitting small-scale ownership of land and mines. Most of the twenty-eight articles deal with care for the poor and sick, land improvement, currency reform, taxes, tolls, and other mundane issues.

Despite its grounding in reformed doctrine and practice, the thrust of the *Landesordnung* was more practical than religious. The Reformation provided Gaismaier with a new principle of authority (the will of God) which both sanctioned his revolution and furnished a basis of consent for his new society. Gaismaier's plan expressed the religious mentality of his time and was deeply rooted in long-standing grievances and the expectation of a more equitable, just, and rewarding existence for his compatriots. These failed to rally when Gaismaier invaded Tirol in July 1526, and he withdrew with fifteen hundred men to seek asylum in Venice. In 1532 he was assassinated in Padua by an agent of Archduke Ferdinand.

BIBLIOGRAPHY

Bischoff-Urack, Angelika. *Michael Gaismaier: Ein Beitrag zur Sozialgeschichte des Bauernkrieges.* Innsbruck, 1983. Examines the socioeconomic background of the Gaismaier family and attempts to explain the making of a rebel in terms of disappointed expectations of upward mobility.

Bücking, Jurgen. *Michael Gaismaier: Reformer Sozialrebell Revolutionär.* Stuttgart, 1978. The socioeconomic structure of the Brixen area is painstakingly analyzed in terms of late medieval "agrarian crisis." Gaismaier is squeezed into a "model" that doesn't quite fit. Includes a useful historiographical essay showing how Gaismaier has been variously interpreted over the centuries according to changing political perspectives, including Nazism.

Dörrer, Fridolin, ed. *Die Bauernkriege und Michael Gaismaier: Protokoll des internationalen Symposion vom 15. bis 19. November 1976 in Innsbruck.* Innsbruck, 1982. Nearly every historian of the Peasant War is represented in this valuable collection of 24 papers.

Klaassen, Walter. *Michael Gaismaier: Revolutionary and Reformer.* Leiden, 1978. The only substantial work on Gaismaier in English. It makes too much of Gaismaier's religiosity, offering no compelling evidence that he "regarded himself as a new Moses." Commendable extensive bibliography.

Macek, Josef. *Der Tiroler Bauernkrieg und Michael Gaismaier.* Translated from Czech into German by R. F. Schmiedt. Berlin, 1965. The standard biography based on meticulous examination of archival sources. Indispensable despite a Marxist bias and glorified view of Gaismaier as a selfless hero of the early bourgeois revolution.

KARIN BRINKMANN BROWN

GALLARS, Nicolas des (c.1520–?), seigneur de Saules and Reformed theologian and pastor. A disciple of John Calvin, Gallars was a minister in Geneva from 1544 to 1557 and in Paris from 1557 to 1558. In 1560 he was called to London to reorganize the French church there (see his work, *Forme de police ecclésiastique instituée á Londres en l'Église des Français, s. l.,* 1561). He returned to France in the summer of 1561 to take part, with an official mandate as a Reformed theologian, in the Colloquy of Poissy, of which he gave a day-to-day account to Trockmorton, bishop of London. In 1563 he exercised his ministry in Orléans, and that year as well he presided over the fifth national synod of the Reformed churches of France, held in Paris. In 1571 he was the secretary of the seventh national synod, held in La Rochelle. Jeanne of Navarre called him in 1570 to exercise ministry in the region of Béarn.

Beginning in 1579 Gallars was professor of theology at the Academy of Lescar (Pau). He was the author of biblical commentaries (on *Exodus, Isaiah,* and the New Testament), polemical writings (against Pierre Caroli and Pierre Alexandre), and a remarkable edition (1570) of the works of Irenaeus dedicated to Edmund Grindal, archbishop of Canterbury. In the preface he states that the teaching of the apostles is sufficient for salvation; however, he concedes that knowledge of the ancient heresies is important for understanding the controversies of his time and that the lessons of the church fathers contribute to giving us the "foundations of devotion and religion." Gallars translated into French and edited several important works of Calvin (on the Lord's Supper, relics, the Libertines, and the divinity of Christ). In 1566 he polished the French edition of the *Opuscules* of Calvin in a large folio volume. He was one of the principal editors of the *Histoire ecclésiastique des Églises réformées de France* (1580).

BIBLIOGRAPHY

Collinson, Patrick."Calvinism with an Anglican Face: The Stranger Churches in Early Elizabethan London and their Superintendent." In *Reform and Reformation: England and the Continent, c.1500–c.1750,* edited by Derek Baker and C.W. Dugmore, pp. 71–102. Oxford, 1979.

MARIO TURCHETTI

Translated from French by Robert E. Shillenn

GALLICANISM. French historical texts generally classify Gallicanism as a specific characteristic of Louis XIV's reign. In fact, the word came into use after the seventeenth century, though the reality it describes considerably predates it. In France the move to impose limits on the pope's power took inspiration from the "rights of the Gallican Church," and it manifested itself in such events as Philip IV's convocation of the ecclesiastical assembly at Notre-Dame de Paris in 1302 to protest the pretensions of Pope Boniface VIII, Charles VII's attempt to apply the canons of the Council of Basel by means of the Pragmatic Sanction of Bourges, and, finally, resistance on the part of the Parlement of Paris to the Concordant of Bologna (1516). At the end of the sixteenth century, one jurist summarized these Gallican rights in two maxims:

> The first, that a Pope can neither order nor command anything, be it general or particular, concerning worldly things in the country and lands falling under the obedience and sovereignty of the very Christian king. The second, that although the Pope is recognized as sovereign in things spiritual, in France, nonetheless, absolute and infinite power has no place, but is retained and limited by the canons and rules of the previous councils of the Church received in this kingdom (P. Pithou, *Les libertez de l'Eglise gallicane,* Paris, 1594).

No one had waited for this latter-day formulation to apply these same principles. At the beginning of the sixteenth century, Pope Julius II had resolved to expel all foreigners from Italy, and he had gone to war with King Louis XII. Fearing that the pope might use spiritual arms, notably excommunication and interdiction, against the king and his kingdom, Louis XII convoked a national synod in Tours in September 1510. The ecclesiastical council declared that if the pontiff issued a sentence of interdiction, excommunication, or deposition against the prince and his subjects, such a sentence would be null and void. The same question of the pope's power over the king's worldly power resurfaced at the end of the century when Sixtus V declared Henry of Navarre (Henry IV) incapable of inheriting the crown of France. His successor, Gregory XIV, threatened excommunication on anyone defending the cause of King Henry IV, but the bishops brought together at Chartres pronounced themselves against the pontifical bulls. The Parlement of Paris, meeting in Châlons in August 1591, issued a reminder that "the French monarchy had been established by God" and forbade, under imposition of the harshest penalties, the reception of these bulls that were "directly contrary to the word of God, and to the holy decrees, councils and rights of the Gallican Church." Somewhat later the University of Paris declared that despite the pontifical pronouncements, Henry IV was nonetheless the "legitimate and true King, natural lord and heir to the kingdom of France and Navarre according to the fundamental laws of these kingdoms" and that the inhabitants of these states owed him obedience

(Pierre Dupuy, *Preuves des libertés de l'Eglise gallicane*, Paris, 1639). Moreover, it was during these controversies that the treatises were published; they were reprinted in the following century.

Occasions were plentiful for proclaiming that the pope should govern the church according to the traditional canons received in the kingdom. Francis I's decision to sign the so-called Concordat of Bologna with Pope Leo X nullified the Pragmatic Sanction of Bourges, which had aimed at reinstating the rules of the early church. The move met with tenacious resistance on the part of the Parlement of Paris. On 5 February 1517 the texts of the concordat, accompanied by the letters of patent, which prescribed registration, were taken to Parlement. The king was obeyed only after a year of strident, bitter discussions and after his pronouncement that his magistrates would pay dearly for resisting his orders any longer. Until the beginning of the following century, kings had to listen to the bishops' grievances, these latter demanding a return to episcopal elections, which the concordat had replaced with royal nomination. Fifty years later Pope Pius IV celebrated the end of the Council of Trent, which, although having met with some anxiety on the part of the papacy, reinforced pontifical prestige and power. The canons of Trent made it clear, among other things, that the bishop's judgments belonged to the pope, and it condemned the interventions of lay judges in church affairs. The Parlement of Paris immediately became hostile to an official reception of the council, which would have transformed the disciplinary decrees of Trent into the laws of the kingdom. Despite repeated entreaties by the popes, the nuncios, and even the assemblies of clergy in France, the kings never resolved to send letters of patent forcing their parlements to "receive" the council. This indecision, however, did not prevent bishops and magistrates from professing faith in the Roman church defined at Trent.

When the ecclesiastical chamber of the Estates-General of 1614 was unable to obtain the legal "reception" of the council, the bishops and other ecclesiastics of the French clergy pronounced a solemn declaration that they accepted as far as they could the Council of Trent, while at the same time, however, preserving the rights of the king and the liberties of the Gallican church (7 July 1615). On the other hand, the chamber of the Third Estate had no more success in its attempt to make the first principle of Gallican liberties a fundamental law of the state. This principle stated that, because the king received his crown only from God, there was no earthly power, be it spiritual or worldly, that could take it away from him or free his subjects from the fidelity and obedience they owed him. The Parlement of Paris had easily ruled against books by Roberto Bellarmino and Francisco Suárez, which affirmed the indirect power of the pope over the worldly power of kings, but the Third Estate ran into opposition by the clergy when it tried to proclaim the unlimited and unconditional independence of the king in worldly affairs as being in accordance with the scriptures.

This conflict, played out against the backdrop of the Estates-General of 1614, justifies the distinction between "episcopal Gallicanism" and "parliamentary Gallicanism." In fact, there would be numerous clashes between bishops and magistrates throughout the eighteenth century. Under the pretext of protecting both the kingdom and the traditional canons against the "innovations of the court of Rome," the parlements attempted to bring documents sent by Rome under their own control. They supervised theses defended at the Sorbonne. Invoking an *"appel comme d'abus,"* they intervened in trials under the jurisdiction of the church's judge, even to the point of deciding on the validity of religious vows and sacraments. To justify these practices, the Dupuy brothers, Pierre and Jacques, published in 1639 the two folios entitled *Traitez des droits et libertez de l'Eglise gallicane* (Treatise on the Rights and Liberties of the Gallican Church) and *Preuves des droits et libertez de l'Eglise gallicane* (Proofs of the Rights and Liberties of the Gallican Church). As soon as the books appeared in print, the clergy reacted. A meeting of prelates censured the two volumes, which turned the liberties of the Gallican church into constraints. In 1665 the assembly of clergy confronted Louis XIV in protest against his magistrates, who "were raising a chimerical and monstrous power that could end up overturning the State and religion."

Although the bishops often asked the king to protect them against his judges and the judges' defense of Gallican rights, they did not hesitate to turn to him to maintain what they considered their rights regarding papal authority. In 1635, upon the request of Cardinal Richelieu (Armand-Jean du Plessis), a commission of four prelates, delegated by Pope Urban VIII, deposed Bishop Saint-Pol-de-Léon. After the deaths of the cardinal and of Louis XIII, the assembly of clergy lodged a protest with the queen regent, Anne of Austria, saying that the deposition of a bishop by four apostolic commissioners ran counter not only to the customs of the kingdom but also to the Council of Trent, the concordat, and the traditional canons. The bishop was subsequently restored to his position. In 1665 the assembly of clergy reacted vehemently against a brief by Pope Alexander VII, which transferred the diocese of Paris to a bishop's control—the archbishop, Cardinal Retz (Jean-François-Paul de Gondi), having escaped a royal prison and fled to Rome. The brief had been sent on the king's request, and the royal government promised to ensure its execution. Nonetheless, the pope's nuncio, charged with communicating the document, decided to keep it hidden in order to avoid a confrontation with the episcopate of the kingdom, who saw pontifical intervention as an inversion of all of the canons.

Twenty years later the king, the bishops, and the magistrates assembled in Rome over the conflict of the *regale* (inherent rights of the monarchy), which led to the notorious *Déclaration des quatres articles* of 1682. When Pope Innocent XI openly threatened the king and the archbishop of Toulouse with church censure in 1680, the French clergy fought back with the four articles: The power of princes is entirely independent from the power of the church; the council is superior to the pope; in the government of the church, the pope must conform to the traditional canons; and the pope's decisions concerning matters of faith are infallible only after having received the consent of the entire church.

It is of some interest to note that the four articles, maintained in classical historiography as the crowning synthesis of "Gallicanism," were presented by the assembly of clergy of 1682 as a means of facilitating the return of separated Christians—of "northern princes"—to the papal throne. Furthermore, it is useful to emphasize, in the face of many erroneous interpretations, that the bishops of France, anxious to assert their own episcopal authority of divine right next to pontifical authority, energetically affirmed that they recognized in the Roman pontiff not only a precedence of honor but also a primacy of jurisdiction. Prelates and magistrates vied with each other to proclaim that they venerated the pope as the vicar of Christ, the head of the church and of all bishops and all faithful. It was only when the time came to draw practical conclusions from this principle that the accord between Roman primacy and the liberties of the Gallican church became delicate.

[*See also* France.]

BIBLIOGRAPHY

Blet, Pierre. *Le Clergé de France et la monarchie.* 2 vols. Rome, 1959.

———. *Les Assemblées du clergé et Louis XIV de 1670 à 1693.* Rome, 1972. These assemblies of the clergy, occurring every five years, offered a privileged occasion for the expression of episcopal Gallicanism.

———. *Le Clergé de France, Louis XIV, et le Saint Siège de 1695 à 1715.* Vatican, 1989.

Lecler, Joseph. "Qu'est-ce que les libertés de l'Église gallicane?" *Recherches de Sciences religieuses* 23 (1933), 385–410, 542–568; 24 (1934), 47–85.

Martimort, Aimé-Georges. *Le gallicanisme de Bossuet.* Paris, 1953. Introduction and large bibliography on all aspects of Gallicanism.

Martin, Victor. *Le gallicanisme et la réform catholique, Essai historique sur l'introduction en France des decrets du concile de Trente, 1563–1615.* Paris, 1919.

———. *Le gallicanisme politique et le clergé de France.* Paris, 1929.

———. *Les origines du gallicanisme.* Reprint, Geneva, 1978.

PIERRE BLET

Translated from French by Caroline Benforado

GALLIC CONFESSION. The forty articles of the Confession of Faith Made By Common Agreement by the French Who Desire to Live According to the Purity of the Gospel of Our Lord Jesus Christ were adopted during the course of the first National Synod of the Reformed Churches of France, which met in Paris in May 1559. It is generally called the Confession of Faith of La Rochelle because the seventh national synod, meeting in La Rochelle in 1571, officially designated it The True Confession of Faith of the Reformed Churches of France. Between 1559 and 1571, two concurrent texts circulated. The first, forty articles with a preface, was synodal: "The French Who Desire to Live according to the Purity of the Gospel . . . to the King"; the other, Genevan in origin (and conceivably written by John Calvin) was presented on the last day of the Synod of Paris somewhat later, and was introduced by the preface "The Poor Faithful Who Are Unjustly Defamed . . ."; this latter was disseminated from Geneva and Lyon.

This text is not an entirely original creation—its authors may have been inspired by a Confession to the King (Henry II) drawn up in 1557, or by the Confession of the Schoolboys (of Geneva). Nor would it remain the only one of its type; it is in fact the first of a series of similar documents drawn up during the 1560s everywhere that Calvinist churches were organizing.

The structure of the confession of faith is straightforward. Articles 1–12 refer to the knowledge, obtained from scripture, of God and man. Articles 13–19 concern the realization in Christ of the divine decree of salvation. (Its Christology has to do with the Christ of faith; that is, the doctrine of the two natures, the work of the mediator.) Articles 20–24 deal with faith, the bond by which God creates a relationship between Christ and the believer, and the condition for an ethical renewal. The doctrine of the church and the birth and maintenance of faith by preaching, clerical offices, and sacraments are developed beginning with article 25. Articles 39–40 establish the functions of laws and governing bodies: within kingdoms, republics, and principalities, hereditary or otherwise, those to whom authority is entrusted are responsible for enforcing obedience to the two tables of the law, and subjects are free to submit to temporal authority while the authority of God remains sovereign (*Mt.* 17, 24; *Acts* 4:17–19).

Numerous biblical references are attached to the confession of faith and many are incorporated into the text itself. The confession is in fact designated a summary of biblical teaching and is to be used as a standard by which to evaluate the orthodoxy of the preaching of the ministers of the word and the belief of the faithful.

The first five articles of the synodal text replaced the single article of the Genevan model, introduced by the words: "Because the foundation of belief, as Saint Paul says, is the word of God, we believe. . . ." The synodal text—more traditionally systematic, albeit that it has occasioned much discussion as to its meaning—refers successively to God and his attributes (article 1), revelation through his works and by his word (article 2), holy scripture, of which the canon is delineated here (article 3), and the source and function of scriptural authority (articles 4 and 5). The treatment of the themes and the inclusion of numerous biblical passages show that the writers of the document did not attribute any positive function to natural revelation.

The confession is first and foremost an engaged text that arose from a context of struggle. It provided the Reformed faithful with a language that enabled them to dissociate themselves from other contemporary forms of Christian expression (Catholic on the one hand; Spiritualist or Anabaptist on the other) while still assuring them of their fidelity to biblical guidelines and to the tradition of the first centuries of the church. Articles 3 and 4 bar any adherence to the former ecclesiastical tradition. The inspiration and the authority of scripture are attributed to the Holy Spirit alone, whose witness excludes the mediation of any human institution. The Apostles', Nicene, and Athanasian Creeds are affirmed as conforming to God's word. Antitrinitarian sects and heresies, once the target of Athanasius, Ambrose, and Cyril, are condemned (articles 5 and 6). Thus the document might be read as a response to the first decrees adopted by the Council of Trent. Other attacks on Catholicism are discernible (articles 24, 27, 28). The assemblies of the papacy (the absence of the term *church* is noteworthy) are places of superstition and idolatry; however, according to the Calvinist theme that the Catholic church has fallen into apostasy (that is, after having known the gospel, it perverted and rejected it), the document maintains that infant baptism—efficacious by divine promise alone—survives in the Catholic church as a small reminder of the true church (article 28). The Last Supper is clearly distinguished from the Eucharist (articles 34–37).

Unusually for this sort of text, a contemporary, Michael Servetus, is denounced as author of diabolical imaginings (article 14). Spiritualists and Anabaptists are attacked most directly in articles concerning the ministry and ethics. In articles 25, 26–31, believers are warned against interference (presumptuous mediation) by any self-designated charismatic leader. The same warning is repeated in articles 34–38, concerning the necessity and function of the sacraments, and in article 40, concerning political ethics. At the same time the ecclesiological thesis shared by Protestants is upheld, namely that only scripture can legitimize religious statements and that the local assembly gathered to receive preaching and sacraments is the privileged place in which the church emerges.

The inclusion in the text of portions of a "Discipline for the Ministry" represents a specifically Reformed aspect of the confession. This discipline accords with a divine order (article 25, 29–32), whereby the offices associated with preaching tasks (those of the ministers of the word; supervisory elders; and deacons who together make up the consistory) are founded on God's revealing himself through his word. This word, adapted to human moral and spiritual needs, must be preached regularly and publicly. The definition of offices has something of the character of canon law. Furthermore, the more fundamental articles of the discipline are based on scriptural texts.

The French Reformed tried and failed to present the newly adopted confession of faith to Francis II; later with Charles IX, they succeeded. The confession took on aspects of an apology, one that attempted to establish that the roots of the Huguenot religion were anchored within the Christian tradition and to assure the court of Huguenot loyalty. The confession was soon printed and translated into Latin, German, Italian, and Dutch. It was intended to facilitate the integration of French Protestantism into the ecclesiastical assemblies then organizing in Europe during this period of confessionalization; its main function, however, was to ensure that the French Reformed churches remained doctrinally united, both among themselves and with those of Geneva and Zurich, consolidated by the Consensus Tigurinus (1549). Ministers of the word, elders, and deacons were required to subscribe to it; it was read and solemnly ratified at the opening of each synod; political assemblies referred to it. Appended to French-language Bibles, the catechism, the Form of Prayers, and psalters, it served a pedagogical function. Owing to the elements of the discipline that were integrated into it, the confession enabled the defense of a model, fragile because unknown and contested, of nonclerical Christian observance.

Although few changes have been made to the confession of faith as adopted in 1559, the text has been the source of much contention. After first declaring the synodal text to be official, the seventh national synod (La Rochelle, 1557), at the risk of upsetting the Zurich ministers (who had been poorly informed by Théodore de Bèze), decided to retain the term *substance* in article 36; this decision was affirmed at the eighth national synod (Nîmes, 1572). Later, at the seventeenth national synod (Gap, 1603), an article (counted as the thirty-first) was added that labeled the pope the Antichrist.

The confession was reexamined at other national synods. Solemn rereading at the beginning of synodal sessions provided confirmation that the text was indeed that developed at the synod of 1559 as well as helped expose variants and imprecisions. Thus, at the seventh national synod (La Rochelle, 1571), *union* was substituted for *unity* in article 36; at the thirteenth national synod (Montauban, 1594), article 26 was likewise corrected and the formula "take, eat, drink, all of you" (from *Mat.* 26:26–27) was added to article 39. This decision was affirmed at Saumur in 1596, and then again at La Rochelle in 1607. At Tonneins in 1614, variants of articles 6, 8, and 9 were examined and agreement was reached regarding the standardized version of the quotation from *Matthew* 26 in article 39.

Proposals for additions or suppressions were sometimes entertained; these were generally taken under advisement, and then rejected. At Gap in 1603 the synod declined to add the phrase "true and pure church" to article 29; the synods of Saint-Maixent (1609) and Privas (1612) retained mention of Servetus in article 14. At La Rochelle in 1607, suggested modifications to articles 10, 18, 25, 32, 33, and 39 were rejected. In some cases interpretations were refined, as at La Rochelle in 1607, with regard to *superintendent* (article 33). Frequently the confession of faith was used to condemn personal theological opinions—as, for example, those of Piscator at La Rochelle in 1607—or to aid in deciding whether to recognize the confessions of faith drawn up in other territories. The Synod of Vitré in 1593 recognized the confession of the churches of the Low Countries, and the Synod of Alais in 1620 acknowledged the canons of the Synod of Dordrecht.

Although officially it will never be abolished, the confession of faith of 1559 fell into disuse beginning in the second half of the seventeenth century. This was confirmed when French Reformed Protestantism was reorganized beginning in the nineteenth century. At the thirtieth official synod in 1872, the first of its kind to be held since 1659, a new confession of faith was drawn up; another was drawn up in 1938 at the time of the reconstitution of the unity of the Reformed church in France. However, the confession of 1559 continues to be accepted in the Union of Independent Reformed Churches (the federation of Calvinist churches in the south of France), while the new confessions of faith refer to the old confession as a historically significant landmark in the French Reformed tradition.

BIBLIOGRAPHY

Primary Sources

Calvin, John. *I. Calvini Opera.* Corpus Reformatorum 37. Brunsvigae, 1870.

Fatio, Olivier, ed. "La Confession de foi des églises réformées de France, dite *Confession de la Rochelle.*" In *Confessions et catéchismes de la foi réformée,* pp. 113–127. Geneva, 1986.

Niesel, W., ed. *Bekenntnisschriften und Kirchenordnungen der nach Gottes Wort reformierten Kirche.* Reprint, Zurich, 1985.

Schaff, P., ed. *The Creeds of Christendom.* Vol. 3, *The Creeds of Evangelical Protestant Churches.* Grand Rapids, Mich., 1985.

Secondary Sources

Esnault, R.-H. "La Confession de foi de La Rochelle au XIXe siècle." *Etudes Théologiques et Religieuses* 34 (1959), 145–212.

Jahr, H. *Studien zur Überlieferungsgeschichte der* Confession de foi *von 1559.* Beiträge zur Geschichte und Lehre der Reformierten Kirche vol. 16. Neukirchen-Vluyn, Germany, 1964.

Millet, O. "Les Églises réformées: Confessions de foi et Églises nationales." In *Histoire du Christianisme des origines à nos jours,* edited by Marc Venard, vol. 8, pp. 95–106. Paris, 1992.

Pannier, Jacques. *Les origines de la Confession de foi et de la Discipline des Églises réformées de France.* Études d'Histoire et de Philosophie religieuses publiées par la Faculté de Théologie de Strasbourg, vol. 32. Paris, 1936.

Stauffer, R. "Briève histoire de la Confession de La Rochelle." *Bulletin de la Société de l'historie du protestantisme français* 117 (1971), 355–366.

BERNARD ROUSSEL

Translated from French by Catharine Randall Coats

GARAVITA, Pedro. *See* Peter of Alcántara.

GARDINER, Stephen (c.1497–1555), bishop of Winchester and lord chancellor of England, a conservative cleric-politician under Henry VIII, Edward VI, and Mary Tudor. Gardiner was born to humble if prosperous parents in Bury Saint Edmunds in Suffolk. Intellectually precocious, he spent part of his early life in Paris. He studied and taught canon and civil law at the University of Cambridge from 1511 to 1524, becoming master of his college, Trinity Hall, shortly afterward. At Cambridge he took part in amateur theatricals and attended the White Horse Inn, sometimes called "Little Germany," where radical undergraduates gathered to hear news about Luther. Despite being a gregarious youth, he later became embittered by the advancement of his rivals and his own constant ill health.

Gardiner was spotted by Henry VIII's chief minister, Thomas Wolsey, and entered the cardinal's household as secretary. Gardiner was principally involved in diplomacy and in pressuring the pope to grant the king's divorce from Catherine of Aragon. In 1528 he was sent to Clement VII at Orvieto, where the roofless palace in which the pope was forced to lodge after fleeing Rome made a great impression on Gardiner.

In July 1529 Gardiner passed directly into royal service as the king's principal secretary, and in September 1531 Gardiner was nominated bishop of Winchester, the wealthiest see in England. Although he reluctantly accepted the break with Rome, Gardiner continued to act as a brake on radical reform throughout the 1530's, finding himself increasingly isolated from Thomas Cromwell and Archbishop Thomas Cranmer. Able to accept reforms of the church such as the dissolution of the monasteries and the attack on the abuse of images, he was unhappy about fundamental theological change. In 1532 he risked Henry's wrath by arguing against the submission of the clergy, which effectively ended the judicial independence of the Church of England. By 1535 he had worked his way back into royal favor by writing the tract *De vera obedientia.* Gardiner argued that true obedience was due to the monarch as head of both civil and spiritual society, thus providing the most cogent of all apologies for the royal supremacy over the church. Although drawing on the example of kings from the Old Testament, the tract was also much influenced by notions of emperorship from Roman law.

Gardiner was rewarded with an embassy to France, where he stayed until 1538. After his return, the Six Articles were passed, and in 1540 Cromwell was executed. The martyrologist John Foxe intimated that Gardiner was a driving force behind these moves toward conservatism. It is just as likely that after the isolation of the 1530s, the opportunities for military adventures with the Holy Roman Emperor put Henry VIII into a less radical frame of mind. Gardiner's natural conservatism (and hatred of the French) made him once again an ideal minister for the king. In the 1540s Gardiner worked hard to achieve a closer alliance with the emperor. In 1543, on the eve of war with the emperor against France, he became involved in moves to discredit his archrival, Cranmer. He also began to write (or put his name to) works of orthodox theology, such as *A Detection of the Devil's Sophistry* (1546), in which he defended succinctly, if without originality, the miracle of the altar. For a long time, his theological works were highly regarded on the Continent as handbooks of traditional belief.

Under the boy-king Edward VI, Gardiner found it difficult to harmonize with the more overtly Protestant elements in the government, even being sent to the Fleet Prison for several months because of misgivings about the issuing of the *Book of Homilies* of 1547 during a royal minority. On 29 June 1548 Gardiner was ordered to preach before the king in London on certain prescribed topics. Although Gardiner felt he had done enough to satisfy the regime, his lack of evangelical spirit appeared to be an act of defiance and he was imprisoned once more. From the Tower he accepted *The Book of Common Prayer* of 1549 on account of its relatively orthodox treatment of the Mass, but he remained in custody. During the proceedings in 1551 that deprived him of his bishopric, Gardiner produced *An Explication and Assertion of the True Catholic Faith*, in which he attacked Cranmer's subsequent public abandonment of traditional eucharistic theology. All attempts at a *modus vivendi* ceased.

Released from the Tower in 1553, Gardiner immediately became Mary Tudor's lord chancellor and was deemed never to have lost his bishopric. He opposed the queen's marriage to Philip II of Spain but loyally served the king when he arrived in 1554. His last years were marred by ill health and his deep rivalry with William Paget, who opposed Gardiner's wish to restore papal supremacy at the earliest opportunity, as well as his plans to revive the church's right to investigate and punish heresy. Gardiner presided over the initial show trial of prominent Protestants at the start of 1555 and then busied himself in trying to negotiate peace between France and the empire.

Gardiner's life was a tragedy. Unlike the martyrs Thomas More and John Fisher, he mistakenly thought that royal supremacy would protect Catholic orthodoxy in England by preventing a full-blown Continental Reformation. Under Edward VI, he painfully realized that this was no longer the case and tried instead to rally the Church of England around traditional teaching on the Mass. Under Mary Tudor his influence waned as that of King Philip II's Spanish court increased, and he seems to have stayed aloof, for whatever reasons, from the general persecution of Protestants. He died on 12 November 1555.

BIBLIOGRAPHY

Donaldson, Peter S. *A Machiavellian Treatise*. Cambridge, 1975. Suggests Gardiner's authorship of this important political tract, refuted in Redworth.

Janelle, Pierre. *Obedience in Church and State: Three Political Tracts by Stephen Gardiner* (1930). Reprint, New York, 1968. Includes *De vera obedientia*.

Loades, David. *The Oxford Martyrs*. London, 1970. Contains substantial material about Gardiner's activities under Queen Mary.

MacCulloch, Diarmaid. "Two Dons in Politics: Thomas Cranmer and Stephen Gardiner, 1503–1533." *Historical Journal* 37 (1994), 1–22.

Muller, James Arthur. *Stephen Gardiner and the Tudor Reaction* (1926). Reprint, New York, 1970. The standard older account.

Muller, James Arthur, ed. *The Letters of Stephen Gardiner* (1933). Reprint, Westport, 1970.

Redworth, Glyn. *In Defence of the Church Catholic: The Life of Stephen Gardiner*. Oxford, 1990. Most recent study of Gardiner's career, containing new interpretations of several issues.

Verzeichnis der im deutschen Sprachbereich erschienenen Drucke des XVI. Jahrhunderts. Stuttgart, 1983–. See vol. 7, nos. 402–406.

GLYN REDWORTH

GATTINARA, Mercurino Arborio di (1465–1530), Habsburg statesman and Erasmian. He was born near Vercelli, Piedmont, on 10 June 1465 to a family of local, impecunious nobility but had relatives in the law and Savoyard ducal service. Gattinara received his degree in both civil and canon law at the University of Turin in 1493. He preferred private practice to administrative or political opportunities until he received in 1502 the appointment of legal counsel to Margaret of Habsburg, who had married Duke Philibert II the preceding year. Gattinara's command of Roman law recommended him to the highest circles of Habsburg affairs. He served Margaret and her father, Emperor Maximilian I, in a number of administrative and diplomatic capacities, represented the emperor in Spain to Ferdinand II of Aragon from July 1510 to April 1511, and became chief architect of the notorious League of Cambrai against Venice. All the while he was president of the parliament of Dôle, and hence chief administrator and judge in Franche-Comté (free county of Burgundy), from 1508 to 1516. There his rigorous application of Roman law upon a fractious nobility, together with adverse personal litigation pertaining to his country estate, led to his deposition from office. To fulfill a vow, in the autumn of 1516 he entered the monastery of Scheut near Brussels, where he remained for nine months.

When Jean le Sauvage, grand chancellor to the young Habsburg king of Spain Charles I, died in June 1518, he left this second most important office at court vacant, one that stood at the bureaucratic center of government and required a skilled jurist and experienced administrator. Furthermore, the emerging question of the future election of a Habsburg to the Holy Roman Empire, along with the imperial aspirations of the dynasty, could not be satisfactorily addressed by the narrow Flemish interests of Guillaume de Croy, Lord of Chièvres, who as grand chamberlain was the most prominent person currently in the entourage of Charles. Given the ex-president of Burgundy's preeminent legal knowledge, his awesome capacity for work, and his absolute devotion to the dynasty, Gattinara seemed the logical candidate. On 15 October 1518 he took the oath of office between the hands of Charles at Saragossa.

In Spain Gattinara decisively supported the efforts of Bartolomé de Las Casas to effect the reform of the administration of the Indies regarding the indigenous people. He promoted the election of his master as Holy Roman Emperor and presented the official justification for Charles's election. At the Calais negotiations of August–December 1521, he talked chancellors Thomas Wolsey and Antoine Duprat to a standstill. Back in Spain he was the driving force behind the conciliar reorganization of the central administration that would last until the rule of the Bourbons. In shaping policy Gattinara worked for the constriction, even dismantling of France, as well as for the European hegemony of the new Charlemagne (Charles the Great) based upon Italy as Dante's *giardin dell' imperio.* Charles himself reacted ambivalently to the imperial policy, providentialism, and pedagogy of his minister, whom he allowed to fall into debt and disfavor. But the last months of his chancellorship saw the solid accomplishments of the treaty of Barcelona with the Pope, the pacification of Italy, and the imperial coronation of Charles at Bologna. Upon his arrival in Italy Gattinara received the long-desired elevation to the cardinalate (13 August 1529). En route to the Diet of Augsburg this man who had increasingly become the white hope of the moderates, both Lutheran and Catholic, died at Innsbruck on 5 June 1530.

Gattinara's importance for the age of the Reformation stems from his representing a type—the political moderate in an age of increasing confessionalism, the responsible magistrate who found succor and direction in a broad catholicism shaped by Erasmian humanism. While at the monastery of Scheut in 1516–1517, Gattinara composed a messianic, eschatological *oratio* highly critical of an overly politicized, worldly papacy, which he expected to be cleansed imminently by an imperial pastor. While his imperial messianism and antipapalism persisted and shaped policy, his own personal deportment reflected a serious, late medieval piety, shaped first by humanist affinities and later specifically by Erasmianism. While faithful to Catholic unity, this pre-Tridentine statesman saw the pope largely as just another territorial ruler. Although he sought the ultimate extinction of Lutheranism, he believed it was possible to do it by accommodation; in framing his solution to the German Problem, he had by July 1526 claimed to find the Lutheran sect essentially based upon the truth of evangelical doctrine. Thus, he (and like-minded members of his chancellery) drew ever closer in his final years to Desiderius Erasmus, in whom Gattinara saw the paladin of orthodoxy and for whom he interceded successfully against the Louvain theologians in 1527. The absence of his usual moderation at Augsburg came as a distinct disappointment to more than one leading Protestant. Philipp Melanchthon himself identified Gattinara with a tradition of unfulfilled moderation, yet pronounced Catholic antipapalism—an interpretation that would persist in Protestant polemic and historiography into the eighteenth century.

BIBLIOGRAPHY

Primary Sources

Gattinara, Mercurino Arborio di. "Précis des conférences de Calais pour le retablissement de la paix entre François Ier et Charles V." In *Papiers d'État du Cardinal de Granvelle,* edited by Charles Weiss, vol. 1, pp. 125–241. Paris, 1841.

———. "Historia vite (sic) et gestorum per dominum magnum cancellarium. . . ." *Miscellanea di storia Italiana* 48 (1915), 233–568. Italian translation of the autobiography has recently appeared: *Mercurino Arborio di Gattinara: Autobiografia,* Rome, 1991.

———. *Pro divo Carolo. . . .* Mainz, 1527. Gattinara's considerable participation in the production of these materials is analyzed in John M. Headley's *The Emperor and His Chancellor,* Cambridge, 1983.

Secondary Sources

Bataillon, Marcel. *Erasmo y España.* Reprint, 2d ed. Madrid, 1983. Pioneered the understanding of Gattinara as a political Erasmian who influenced the emperor.

Brandi, Karl. *The Emperor Charles V.* Translated by C.V. Wedgwood. Reprint, Atlantic Highlands, N.J. 1980. Presents Gattinara as decisive in the political education and formation of the emperor.

Ferretti, Franco. *Un maestro di politica.* Milan, 1980. Effective modern biography.

Headley, John M. "Rhetoric and Reality: Messianic, Humanist and Civilian Themes in the Imperial Ethos of Gattinara." In *Prophetic Rome in the High Renaissance Period,* edited by Marjorie Reeves, pp. 241–270. Oxford, 1992. Analyzes the dimensions to Gattinara's thought and policy.

Walser, Fritz. *Die Spanischen Zentralbehörden und der Staatsrat Karls V.* Göttingen, 1959. Presents Gattinara as largely responsible for the revamping of the Spanish imperial administration.

JOHN M. HEADLEY

GEGENBACH, Pamphilus. *See* Gengenbach, Pamphilius.

GENDER. *See* Courts, *article on* Marriage Courts; Divorce; Marriage; Sexuality; Women.

GENEVA. Before the Reformation Geneva had been the capital of an ecclesiastical state ruled by a prince-bishop allied closely with the neighboring duchy of Savoy. That ecclesiastical state was large and prosperous, covering much of what is now French Savoy. Some of its prince-bishops had assumed considerable power within the area and within the international Roman Catholic church. While the bishop was sovereign, some of the police power of the principality had been turned over to the duke. Within the city of Geneva, for example, a *vidomne* appointed by the duke assisted in the prosecution and punishment of crime. In most areas, however, the purely internal government of the city had been turned over to a council of elected representatives of the local population, presided over by magistrates called syndics. Appeals to the bishop and his court were always possible. Without the Reformation this ecclesiastical state would probably have been gradually absorbed into Savoy.

In the 1520s the elected council and syndics of Geneva, encouraged by the neighboring city-states of Fribourg and Bern, with whom they established an alliance, began to assume one after another of the broader governmental powers of the bishop and duke. They took over taxation, defense, the coinage of money, diplomacy, and all jurisdiction over both criminal and civil justice, with no rights of appeal. In the end the bishop, most of the local clergy, and the agents of Savoy all left the city, although they continued to control most of the remaining parts of the diocese. Only a handful of the villages that provided food and other essentials to the city of Geneva remained under the city's control. The elected leaders of Geneva took these steps partly to gain independence from all external control and to make of Geneva a free city-state. But they took them also to advance religious change, a change encouraged by Protestant Bern, but not by Fribourg, which remained Catholic and before long dropped out of the alliance. Bern helped introduce into Geneva Protestant preachers who attacked local Catholicism and urged Genevans to embrace Protestantism. The most prominent of them was a charismatic French orator named William Farel. The Reformation in Geneva was thus the product of a revolution, with both political and religious components. These dual revolutions reached a climax in 1536, when a general assembly of the citizens voted that Geneva would henceforth live according to the gospel and the word of God, renouncing the Mass and all other papist abuses. Implicit in that resolution was the deposition of the bishop and the rejection of Savoy. A Bernese army moved into the area, surrounded Geneva, and protected it from any attempt by the bishop and duke of Savoy to regain their power. Several months later a French visitor named John Calvin was hired by the city at Farel's recommendation, to be a public lecturer charged with explaining to Genevans the implications of their religious decision.

In 1538 Farel and Calvin were both expelled from Geneva for their refusal to follow government orders; in 1541 Calvin alone was invited back and given power to shape a truly Reformed church for the city-state. In inviting him Geneva obtained a leader who combined to a rare degree the talents of a preacher and a highly trained lawyer. He could not only proclaim the word of God with eloquence and erudition but also devise and direct institutions designed to create a church of a drastically different character. One of his first acts on returning was to draft a set of ecclesiastical ordinances, which, in effect, created a constitution for the Reformed church. They were adopted by the city government with only minor amendments. These ordinances created a church that was built around four types of ministers: (1) pastors, who were to proclaim the word of God and administer the sacraments in the parish churches of the city and in the few neighboring villages remaining under city control, coordinating their activities in weekly meetings of the Compagnie des Pasteurs (Company of Pastors); (2) doctors, who were to teach the word of God, at first in informal lectures but later in the formal curriculum of an academy established in 1559; (3) elders, who were to maintain Christian discipline as members (along with the pastors) of a semijudicial body called the consistory; and (4) deacons, who were to collect alms and then distribute them to the poor, in the beginning primarily through an all-purpose charitable institution called the General Hospital.

Almost all the pastors and doctors were highly educated immigrants from France, who became salaried employees of the state. Some, most notably Calvin and his successor, Théodore de Bèze, were both pastors and doctors. Almost all the elders and deacons were either professionals or prominent local businessmen, who were chosen once a year, along with all civic officials, in the city's annual elections. Many of them received nominal payments for their work. Toward the end of Calvin's ministry, a few prominent lay immigrants were also elected to these positions.

These reforms were powerfully supported by a rapidly growing group of immigrants to Geneva who were fleeing persecution in Catholic states and attracted to the exciting experiment of creating a truly reformed community. Most of them came from France, and many were people of considerable wealth and education. They accumulated a good deal of property in Geneva and became deeply involved in many types of local business. They developed their own institutions, most notably a general fund called the *bourse française,* maintained and directed by wealthy French immigrants who were given the title of "deacon." The *bourse* was used to help those among the French refugees who needed relief, but it was also used to help various activities designed to advance the Protestant cause in France. These immigrants soon encountered stiff opposition from local citizens who resented their increasing prominence and power. This opposition crystallized into a faction of citizens led by a local patrician named Ami Perrin. Perrin and his supporters had supported the return of Calvin in 1541 and accepted without question Calvinist theology. But they objected, with growing vehemence, to the consistory's use of excommunication as a tool to control their behavior. In 1555, after a bitter controversy culminating in a riot, the refugees and their supporters among the local population decisively defeated the Perrinists and won complete control of the city government. Most of the Perrinists were driven from the city or put to death on charges of treason. From the beginning Calvin had been the most prominent single immigrant from France and the most influential single spokesman for their point of view. Once his supporters had won full control of the city, his power was absolute, if unofficial. Technically he remained a simple salaried employee of the state. His only position of preeminence was his role as moderator, or presiding officer, of the Compagnie des Pasteurs. But it was clear to all observers that he exercised more real power than had the bishop and that the institutions of both church and state almost invariably followed his instructions.

Once the Calvinist Reformation had been consolidated within Geneva, its leaders took steps to spread their program of reform into other countries. In the beginning their energies were devoted primarily to the attempt to convert neighboring France. Leading French printers—of whom the most prominent was Robert Estienne, former printer to the king of France—moved to Geneva and made it a major center for the creation and circulation of Protestant propaganda. Dozens of refugees from France were trained as Reformed pastors and sent back to their homes to convert their native communities. These efforts were so successful that a Protestant movement rapidly grew within France after 1555, winning powerful political and military support within the aristocracy. This movement provoked bitterly hostile responses from Catholic institutions and their leaders. The royal government tried to negotiate a compromise, sponsoring a conference at Poissy in 1561 of the leaders of both Catholic and Protestant parties, with the Protestants led by Théodore de Bèze, who was sent expressly from Geneva. When that attempt failed, the resulting conflict rapidly escalated into war, beginning in 1562. That war plunged France into recurring bloodshed, including further wars and massacres, of which the worst was the Saint Bartholomew's Day Massacre of 1572. This bloodshed continued with occasional interruptions for most of the rest of the century, until the enactment of the Edict of Nantes in 1598 finally restored a measure of peace to the kingdom and granted Protestants a grudging form of partial toleration.

Groups of visitors and refugees from other countries came to Geneva to hear the Calvinist message and observe the life-style that had been developed there. Many of these visitors were enormously impressed by what they heard and saw and often did their best to introduce both the message and life-style to their native countries. They included groups from England and Scotland, of which the most prominent was led by John Knox. Its members introduced Calvinism into Scotland and led in building the Puritan movement in England. Among the visitors were also many individuals from the Netherlands, of whom the most prominent were the Marnix van Sint Aldegonde brothers, who joined William of Orange in leading those provinces into the Calvinist camp. Significant groups from Italy also visited, particularly from neighboring Savoy and the city of Lucca, as well as from German Switzerland and Germany proper, particularly from the Palatinate, which turned Calvinist under the leadership of a Genevan-trained theologian named Kaspar Olevianus. There were even occasional visitors from Bohemia, Poland, and Hungary. Many of these visitors, on returning to their home countries, remained in contact with their Genevan hosts. This network of contacts made of Geneva a kind of Protestant Rome.

In 1559 the work of training Reformed leaders for other countries was given institutional shape with the creation of the Geneva academy. It supplemented the educational work of an existing college for secondary education, inherited from the Catholic past, which was updated to make the curriculum thoroughly humanistic. Within Switzerland this new academy took the place of the Lausanne school, an institution supported by the government of Bern in the nearby city of Lausanne to supply advanced education, particularly in training pastors. The Lausanne school lost most of its staff and students when they were driven out by a Bernese government that had become irritated at the variant forms of Protestantism developing in those of its lands that were French-speaking, forms that were not fully consonant with its own Zwinglian regime, which left maximum ecclesiastical authority in the hands of the secular government. The most prominent of these transfers from Lausanne to Geneva was Bèze, who became rector of the new academy. The academy built on the local college with more advanced instruction in the humanities, typical of the period, and then added professional training in the Calvinist variety of theology, built around Calvinist methods of examining and interpreting both the Hebrew and Greek texts of the Bible. Its primary function, thus, was to train Reformed pastors. In later years it added on occasion instruction in law.

Geneva's role as a Protestant Rome, however, remained precarious for several decades. On Calvin's death, Bèze, whose advanced training in law and theology was quite similar to his mentor's, succeeded him as moderator of the Geneva Compagnie des Pasteurs and as the most important single spokesman for Reformed theology. Increasingly Bèze also exercised authority similar to Calvin's within the French Reformed church and in the international Reformed movement. But the Genevan base of this headquarters of the international Reformed church was under constant threat. The Catholic monarchy in France on occasion threatened Geneva with retaliation for sponsoring "subversion" within its borders, and the Genevan government reacted by insisting on extreme caution among all its residents, particularly its pastors. The ducal government of Savoy did not forget its earlier claims to Geneva, either. Bern became disillusioned with its role as protector of Geneva and its Protestantism, and Bernese support became less certain. Some of the nearby lands also bordering Lake Geneva, notably in the Chablais, that Bern had conquered from Savoy and introduced to Protestantism early in the sixteenth century were returned to Savoy and Catholicism late in the century. Several times, particularly between 1589 and 1593, Geneva had to go to war and fight for its very existence. The last serious attack on its independence was the Savoyard attack of 1602, known as the Escalade. It was successfully repulsed, but Geneva continued to fear a Savoyard threat for decades to follow.

Geneva did, in fact, survive all these threats, and its reputation remained powerful. The city continued to serve as a center for the publication of Protestant propaganda and for the training of Protestant pastors, although this role diminished as alternative training centers were established in such places as Heidelberg, Leiden, Saumur, and Sedan. Geneva's religious leaders, most notably Bèze himself, developed a theology more closely designed for instruction within an academic milieu, which thus has come to be labeled "scholastic." They tended to resist any attempt to move Reformed theology in a more irenic direction, and thus Geneva came more and more to represent the most conservative and dogmatic form of Calvinism. That continued to be true throughout the sixteenth century and was even more emphatically true in the seventeenth century, when Genevan representatives at the Synod of Dordrecht in 1618–1620 and in the negotiations leading to the Helvetic Consensus of 1675 fought for a theological hard line on controversial details of the doctrines of predestination and biblical inspiration. Only under the influence of the eighteenth-century Enlightenment did the city's dogmatic stance soften. Yet throughout all these political and theological vicissitudes the church of Geneva continued to be respected as a mother and model to the entire Reformed movement, and to a degree it has retained this role down to the present.

[*See also* Bern; Bèze, Théodore de; Calvin, John; Church Offices, *article on* Calvinist Offices; Compagnie des Pasteurs; Consistory; Dordrecht, Synod of; Farel, Guillaume; Geneva Academy; *and* Savoy.]

BIBLIOGRAPHY

Geisendorf, Paul-F. *Bibliographie raisonnée de l'histoire de Genève, des origines à 1798*. Geneva, 1966. Provides an admirably complete bibliography of all work on Genevan history from Roman times to the French Revolution. Can be supplemented, for works published after 1966, by the annual bibliographical chronicle in the *Bulletin de la Société d'histoire et d'archéologie de Genève*.

Guichonnet, Paul, ed. *Histoire de Genève*. 3d ed. Lausanne, 1986. Excellent survey of Genevan history, with full attention to social and economic developments from its beginnings to the twentieth century.

Kingdon, Robert M. *Church and Society in Reformation Europe*. London, 1985. Contains a selection of articles on aspects of the church in Calvin's Geneva.

Martin, Paul-E., ed. *Histoire de Genève*. Geneva, 1951. Somewhat traditional survey of the political and ecclesiastical history of Geneva down to the French Revolution.

Monter, E. William. *Calvin's Geneva*. Reprint, Huntington, N.Y., 1975. Excellent introduction in English.

———. *Enforcing Morality in Early Modern Europe*. London, 1987. Collection of articles, many of which deal with the social history of Geneva.

Naef, Henri. *Les origines de la réforme à Genève*. 2 vols. Geneva and Paris, 1936, and Geneva, 1968. Extremely detailed and solid narrative of the beginnings of the Reformation in Geneva.

ROBERT M. KINGDON

GENEVA ACADEMY. In June 1559, with John Calvin's encouragement, the government of Geneva reorganized its educational system by founding a school that documents in Latin called an *academia* and French documents a *collège*. It consisted of two parts, a *Schola privata*, or private school, actually a public preparatory school for boys, designed to educate the city's youth, and a *Schola publica*, or public school, the city's first institution of higher education, designed to provide advanced training, especially in theology. This school would become the nucleus of the present University of Geneva and its library.

Some of the academy's first students and professors, including its first rector, Théodore de Bèze, came from the academy at Lausanne because of disagreements with the magistrates of Bern (who had jurisdiction over Lausanne) concerning the teaching of predestination. In 1564, within five years of its founding, Bèze wrote to Heinrich Bullinger in Zurich that there were approximately three hundred students in the *Schola publica* and twelve hundred in the *Schola privata*. Two years later Bèze wrote that there were two thousand students altogether at the annual promotion.

Over time, in Geneva, *collège* came to refer to the preparatory school and *académie* to the school of higher education. The faculty of the academy consisted initially of five lecturers, one each in Greek, Hebrew, and the arts and two in theology (Calvin and Bèze). The *collège*, divided into seven grades, included intensive training in Latin and Greek; the academy added Hebrew. The academy, which attracted an international student body, primarily prepared men to be pastors and originally granted no degrees or diplomas, only certificates testifying to studies completed, good conduct, and length of attendance. Among the well-known sixteenth-century figures who lectured there were Claude Baduel (1491?–1561), Thomas Cartwright (1535–1603), Petrus Ramus (1515–1572), and François Hotman (1524–1590). Students who came from Europe and the British Isles stayed in the homes of teachers or pastors, and, upon returning home, often entered the ministry and assumed leadership roles. The academy was crucial in the spread of Protestant Reformed Christianity.

Before the founding of the academy, Geneva had primary and secondary education but no higher education, although in 1365 Emperor Charles IV had granted the duke of Savoy a charter to found a university there. A public school was erected in 1429, the Collège de Versonnex, named after its benefactor, François de Versonnex. It disappeared in the troubles prior to the adoption of the Reformation in Geneva (1536) and was replaced by the Collège de Rive, where Sébastien Castellion (1515–1563) taught from 1541–1544. This institution was eventually absorbed into the preparatory school founded in 1559. Girls were educated apart and did not go on for higher education.

Guillaume Farel and John Calvin taught theology in the former cathedral of Saint Pierre before their banishment in 1538. After Calvin returned to Geneva from Strasbourg in 1541, he continued to lecture on theology. Many of the missionary pastors later sent from Geneva were trained in these years before the formal foundation of the academy.

In 1541, having taught in the schools of Strasbourg associated with Johann Sturm, Calvin provided, in the *Ordonnances ecclésiastiques* of Geneva, for a college to prepare young men for the ministry and for civil government. The city council of Geneva made resources available after the defeat (1555), confiscation, and sale of property of the Perrinist faction. In January 1558 the council inspected a site within the city walls where a secondary school, the Collège Calvin, now stands. Construction of the first buildings for the new academy began in 1558 and was completed in 1562.

The city constructed and maintained the buildings, paid salaries, and provided housing for the faculty. The government's efforts were supplemented by private donations, and, to help meet the costs, the council instructed the notaries of the city to encourage testators to include the new school in their wills. Genevan printers deposited in the library a copy of everything they published. In the seventeenth century the sermons of Calvin, copied down by others as he preached them, were also deposited there. The Compagnie des Pasteurs of Geneva selected professors for the academy, nominating them to the city council for appointment. Upon appointment, they became part of the Compagnie des Pasteurs.

The laws governing these Genevan schools, printed by Robert I Estienne in 1559, revealed a discipline that was strict but not severe by the standards of the time. The preparatory school required attendance at religious services, catechism classes, and daily singing of the *Psalms*. Students, organized into groups of ten, chose a group leader. Although corporal punishment was allowed, instructors who exceeded the bounds were charged with cruelty and dismissed. Classes began at dawn with prayer. At the end of the day, students and faculty assembled for public chastisement of delinquents and recitation of the Lord's Prayer, the confession of faith, and the Ten Commandments. This orderly life of disciplined study influenced the Reformed communities at the time and well into the future as young men, upon completion of their studies at the Geneva academy, moved out to become leaders of Reformed churches, contributing to the influence of Geneva and its Compagnie des Pasteurs on the world.

[*See also* Geneva.]

BIBLIOGRAPHY

Borgeaud, Charles. *Histoire de l'Université de Genève: L'Académie de Calvin, 1559–1798.* Geneva, 1900. The classic history of the Geneva academy; a large folio edition.

Doumergue, Emile. "La lutte pour l'instruction: Le Collège et l'Académie." In *Jean Calvin: Les hommes et les choses de son temps*, vol. 7, pp. 124–154. Reprint, Geneva, 1969. This chapter covers the sixteenth-century history of the College and Geneva academy.

Ganoczy, Alexandre. *La Bibliothèque de l'Académie de Calvin: Le Catalogue de 1572 et ses enseignements.* Geneva, 1969. A study of the books and authors that constituted the 1572 school library collection, nucleus of the present public library of the University of Geneva.

Kingdon, Robert M. "Training." In *Geneva and the Coming of the Wars of Religion in France, 1555–1563.* Geneva, 1956. An analysis of the Genevan training of missionary pastors sent to France and the role of the Geneva academy.

Monter, E. William. *Calvin's Geneva.* New York, 1975. See pp. 110–114 for a brief summary derived from the French sources on the Geneva academy, relying especially on Charles Borgeaud.

Schindling, Anton. *Humanistische Hochschule und freie Reichsstadt: Gymnasium und Akademie in Straßburg, 1538–1621.* Wiesbaden, 1977. See pp. 350–351 and 354 for references to Calvin's teaching in Strasbourg.

Stelling-Michaud, S. *Le livre du recteur de l'Académie de Genève, 1559–1878.* 6 vols. Geneva, 1959–1980. These volumes contain lists and biographical notices of the students who attended the Geneva academy from its inception in 1559. Vol. 1 contains the original rules governing the institution. Vol. 6 has an index of names, an index of places of origin of the students, and a list of places where students studied before or after Geneva.

Vries, Herman de. *Genève, pépinière du calvinisme hollandais.* 2 vols. Reprint, Geneva, 1980. Students from the Low Countries who studied in Geneva during the time of Théodore de Bèze and some of their correspondence.

JEANNINE E. OLSON

GENGENBACH, Pamphilius (1480?–1542), Swiss dramatist, printer, book dealer, and vigorous supporter of Luther. Gengenbach was one of the first writers in Switzerland (Basel) to adapt the German *Fastnachtspiel* ("shrovetide play") as a vehicle for serious moral-religious purposes and to view it as a means to reflect socially relevant problems of the time. He was the mediator between the Nuremberg folk-drama tradition popularized by Hans Folz, Hans Rosenplüt, and Hans Sachs and the subsequent efforts of a fellow Swiss, Niklaus Manuel, whose plays in support of Reformation ideas are equally important.

While preserving the simpler, revue-type structure in his plays, Gengenbach assumes the role of social critic, addressing in sermonlike language the weaknesses of bourgeois morality (*Der Nollhart*, 1517), the follies of love-obsessed men and women (*Die Gouchmatt*, 1516), and, in generally pessimistic tones, the reluctance of humankind to strive for moral and social improvement (*Die X Alter diser Welt*, 1515). Gengenbach incorporated older dramatic traditions into plays calling for contemporary reform by using the figure of the wise, pious hermit to contrast concern for personal salvation with acquiescence to the temptations of the world. His pleas for moral religious reform based on individual morality reflect his own involvements in and observations of the more raucous, dissipating aspects of life.

Gengenbach was also capable of a broader, philosophic view, however, that revealed insight into the sociopolitical implications of moral decay. As a printer, Gengenbach was instrumental in the publication of Johann Eberlin von Günzburg's *Fünfzehn Bundesgenossen* (1521) and other pamphlets supportive of Luther. The traditional attribution of the play *Totenfresser* (1521) and the anti-Murner satirical text *Novella*, if confirmed, would place Gengenbach even more firmly in the tradition of the popularizers of the Antichrist theme and that of the "fool" narratives associated with the Alsatian satirists Sebastian Brant and Thomas Murner and other sixteenth-century writers.

BIBLIOGRAPHY

Abbé, Derek M. van. "Development of Dramatic Form in Pamphilus Gengenbach." *Modern Language Review* 45 (1950), 46–48. Analysis of form and content of plays and dialogues.

Bautz, Friedrich Wilhelm, ed. *Biographische-Bibliographisches Kirchenlexikon*. Hamm, 1970–. See vol. 2, p. 203.

Goedeke, Karl, ed. *Pamphilius Gengenbach* (1856). Reprint, Amsterdam, 1966. Standard and most accessible source for Gengenbach's collected works.

Lendi, Karl. *Der Dichter Pamphilius Gengenbach: Beiträge zu seinem Leben und zu seinen Werken* (1926). Reprint, Nendeln, 1970. Articles placing Gengenbach in the literary and social context of his time.

Verzeichnis der im deutschen Sprachbereich erschienenen Drucke des XVI. Jahrhunderts. Stuttgart, 1983–. See vol. 7, nos. 1167–1232.

RICHARD ERNEST WALKER

GENTILE, Giovanni Valentino (d. 1566), Italian exile and anti-trinitarian. A native of Cosenza, Gentile led an obscure life until approximately 1557, when he fled Italy and took up residence in Geneva to avoid religious persecution by Catholic forces. He was part of a group of Italian expatriates whose firm opposition to both orthodox Catholicism and mainstream Protestant confessions eventually led to the creation of the so-called Socinian movement, focused around the ideas of Lelio (1525–1562) and Fausto (1539–1604) Sozzini.

Gentile promoted—along with Matteo Gribaldi (d. 1564), Giorgio Biandrata (1516–1588), and Gian Paolo Alciati (d. 1565)—antitrinitarian thought in the aftermath of the trial and execution of Michael Servetus (1509/11–1553). Because of his ties with Gribaldi, he would have been linked by John Calvin (1509–1564) to Gribaldi's criticism of the action taken against Servetus, and, following Gribaldi's expulsion from Bern in 1557, Gentile, Biandrata, and Alciati engaged in a conflict with Calvin on the nature of the relationship between the three divine persons. An anonymous text criticizing the execution of Servetus circulated and was believed to have emanated from these Italian refugees. They fled Geneva to avoid the admonition and condemnation of the city in 1558. Arrest and imprisonment in Bern followed for Gentile, and after his escape he traveled to join Biandrata in 1562 in Poland, where he became a member of a small Italian antitrinitarian community in Pinczów that included himself and Biandrata, plus Alciati and Francesco Negri (1500–1563).

Polish interest in reform had developed considerably after 1542 for social and political reasons, as well as for religious ones. Pinczów, along with Kraków, was among the main centers disseminating Reformation ideas. Although the government clearly failed to extinguish antitrinitarian thought and its support, especially among the nobility in Poland, the Edict of Parczów (1564) succeeded in driving Gentile out of the country in fear of persecution. He spent time in Moravia and Austria before returning to Bern after the death of Calvin. He was captured, tried, and decapitated there in 1566. His career became the subject of controversialist literature by such persons as Gilbert Génébrard (1537–1597), Lambert Daneau (1530–1595), and Benedict Aretius (d. 1574).

Gentile held views close to those of Gribaldi. He rejected dogmatic traditions, both ancient and contemporary, as superfluous to the essence of faith. Although his friend Alciati inclined toward a unitarian view of God, Gentile and Biandrata insisted upon a tritheist position. Gentile conceived of God the Father in Aristotelian terms as the "unmoved mover" who conferred upon the Son the work of creating the universe and upon the Holy Spirit a force that pervades and animates all of creation. Hence, among these three coeternal substances, only one (the Father) was the source of divinity, and the others were subordinate. Even at the moment of death, Gentile refused to abjure, despite the urging of friends to adopt a more moderate position. He called himself the first martyr of God the Father, suggesting that others in the past had been martyrs of the Son.

BIBLIOGRAPHY

Aretius, Benedictus. *A Short History of Valentinus Gentilis the Tritheist.* Translated by Dr. Sherlock. London, 1696. The story of his trial, condemnation, and execution, along with a description of his religious views. Originally published in Latin in 1567. Useful, but this edition was undertaken with the intention of battling the growth of tritheism in seventeenth-century England.

Caccamo, Domenico. *Eretici italiani in Moravia, Polonia, Transilvania, 1558–1611*. Chicago, 1970. An important study, aimed at explaining the originality of Italian thinkers in the doctrinal debates of the Reformation and their influence, especially for Anabaptism.

Cantimori, Delio. *Eretici italiani del Cinquecento* (1939). 3d rev. ed. Edited by Adriano Prosperi. Turin, 1992. Earlier edition available in English translation: *Italian Heretics of the Sixteenth Century*. Cambridge, Mass., 1979. The classic and still-standard treatment of Italian heretics.

———. *Italiani a Basilea e a Zurigo nel Cinquecento.* Rome, 1947.

Castiglione, T. R. "La 'impietas Valentini Gentilis' e il corrucio di Calvino." In *Ginevra e l'Italia,* edited by Delio Cantimori, pp. 149–176. Florence, 1959.

———. "Valentino contro Calvino: Il processo del 'secondo Serveto' nel 1558 a Ginevra." In *Studia nad arianizmem,* edited by L. Chmaj, pp. 59–71. Warsaw, 1959.

Church, Frederic C. *The Italian Reformers, 1534–1564* (1932). Reprint, New York, 1974. Dated and unsophisticated in ascribing Italian religious thought in this period essentially to Spanish influence, but still useful for context.

Rotondò, Antonio. *Calvin and the Italian Anti-Trinitarians.* Translated by John and Anne Tedeschi. Reformation Essays and Studies, 2. Saint Louis, 1968. Originally published as "Calvino e gli antitrinitari italiani." *Rivista storica italiana* 80 (1968), 759–784.

Ruffini, Francesco. *Studi sui riformatori italiani.* Edited by Arnaldo Bertola, Luigi Firpo, and Edoardo Ruffini. Turin, 1955. Two articles here on Matteo Gribaldi, originally published in *Rivista di storia del diritto italiano* 1 (1928), 205–269, 417–432, include information on Gentile.

WILLIAM V. HUDON

GEORGE, DUKE OF SAXONY ("the Bearded"; 1471–1539), opponent of Lutheran reform. The son of Duke Albrecht ("the Stout-hearted") and the Bohemian princess Zedena (Sidonie), he was originally destined for the clergy and therefore obtained a higher education including Latin. At the age of seventeen he was called upon to govern in place of his father during the latter's absence in the Netherlands, a task that he approached with a sense of high duty, extraordinary diligence, and a feeling for order, right, and thrift. His government was exemplary, his marriage to the Polish princess Barbara a happy one. After his father's death in 1501, he became duke of Saxony.

He felt responsible for good order in the church, was zealous in reforming monasteries, founded new ones, and put the church under princely authority; he also promoted the development of his territorial university at Leipzig. Convinced of the necessity to renew the church, he initially welcomed the appearance of Luther's Ninety-five Theses and favored their dissemination. Contrary to the sentiment of the university and its bishop, he personally hosted the Leipzig Disputation between Luther and Johann Eck in 1519. He was shocked, however, when Luther seemed to advance the views of Jan Hus, and from then on he was a strong opponent of the Lutheran "heresy." As a deeply pious man he remained a loyal member of the Church of Rome and suppressed all spontaneous expressions of Lutheran reform in his duchy. He fought vigorously against the insurgent peasants during the Peasants' War of 1525, which he regarded as the evil fruit of heresy. In the aftermath of the premature deaths of his sons John and Frederick, he attempted to thwart the introduction of the Reformation by his brother and legitimate successor Henry, who had already become an adherent of Luther; he died, however, before a different succession could be arranged. During his lifetime he had obtained the canonization of the medieval bishop Benno of Meissen to construct a bulwark against Luther's influence in his territory, had ordered the printing of a German version of the New Testament that, although based on Luther's translation, promulgated Catholic teachings, and had been involved in a continuous exchange of controversial writings with Luther. He aspired to reform the church by leaving the papacy intact but finally could not halt Luther's Reformation.

BIBLIOGRAPHY

Gess, Felician, ed. *Akten und Briefe zur Kirchenpolitik Herzog Georgs von Sachsen.* 2 vols. Reprint, Cologne, 1985.

Goerlitz, Woldemar. *Staat und Stände unter den Herzögen Albrecht und Georg.* Leipzig, 1928.

Voßler, Otto. "Herzog Georg der Bärtige und seine Ablehnung Luthers." *Historische Zeitschrift* 184 (1957), 272–291.

Werl, Elisabeth. "Herzogin Sidonie von Sachsen und ihr ältester Sohn Herzog Georg." In *Jahrbuch für deutsche Kirchengeschichte,* edited by Franz Lau, vol. 3, pp. 8–19. Berlin, 1959.

———. "Georg von Sachsen." In *Neue Deutsche Biographie,* vol. 4, pp. 224–227. Berlin, 1964.

KARLHEINZ BLASCHKE

GEORGE OF BRANDENBURG-ANSBACH (also Georg der Fromme; George the Pious; 1484–1543), margrave of Brandenburg-Ansbach. The second son of Margrave Frederick IV of Brandenburg-Ansbach, George entered the service of his uncle, Vladislav V, king of Bohemia and Hungary, in 1505 in Ofen (Buda) after a two-year stay at the court in Hesse-Kassel. After the death of Vladislav, George served as coguardian of the young king Louis II. George's first marriage—to Beatrix of Frangepan, widow of Duke John Corvinus—brought extensive lands into his possession. After the death of Beatrix in 1510, the sale of these lands enabled George to obtain some territories in Silesia, the acquisition of which had been prepared through treaties of succession with Duke Johann of Oppeln and Ratibor in 1512 and 1521. In 1523 George bought the duchy of Jägerndorf (Krnov). In 1526 he obtained custodial rights over the territories of Oderberg and Beuthen (Bytom). In his correspondence with Martin Luther beginning in 1523, George indicated his inclination toward Luther's teaching. George's residence at Jägerndorf became a center of evangelical efforts. He supported his brother Albrecht in transforming the territory of the Teutonic Order (Prussia) into a secular dukedom and encouraged the elector of Brandenburg, Joachim II, to accept the new teaching.

The Franconian territories had been cast into a severe financial crisis by Frederick IV, and thus George's older brother, Casimir, had to force the deposition of Frederick in 1515. Emperor Maximilian I bestowed the margravates on both brothers in 1516. Because George resided most of the time outside his margravate, he hardly took part in its government. With the death of Casimir in 1527, George became the sole authority in Ansbach and Kulmbach (in the latter territory as guardian for Albrecht Alcibiades, who was still a minor).

The new lord endeavored to give a new impetus to reforming efforts in both territories. Andreas Althamer was called to Ansbach as city pastor in 1528 and decisively influenced the organization of the church order. He published his *Catechism in Frag und Antwort*. In the same year, George required the clergy to preach the pure gospel. The diet decided to hold a church visitation, which was carried out in 1528–1529 in cooperation with the imperial city of Nuremberg. As a result, extensive church holdings were secularized in order to allay the territory's ever rising burden of debt. A church ordinance, worked out in cooperation with Nuremberg, went into effect 1 March 1533. It was also introduced at Jägerndorf and served as a model for other territories.

During these years George moved conspicuously into the forefront of imperial politics. During the imperial Diet of Speyer in 1529, his chancellor, George Vogler, drafted the protestation that George shared with other "Protestant" princes. At Augsburg in 1530 he joined those who signed the Augsburg Confession. Because unity of faith was more important to him than political alliance, he abstained from the joining the Schmalkald League, as did Nuremberg. Although George proved himself faithful to the emperor, Ferdinand I, as king of Bohemia, long delayed in confirming George's rights in Silesia. Only after protracted negotiations were Oppeln and Ratibor confirmed to George as custodial possessions (in the Treaty of Prague, 1531) and then only until the time when Ferdinand would dissolve these territories. The possession of Beuthen was conceded to him for two successive legitimate heirs to inherit after him, and the possession of Oderberg was given to him for three heirs. Ferdinand also renewed the bestowal of Jägerndorf. Later the Franconian Hohenzollerns lost all of these possessions to the Habsburgs.

After 1533 the tempo of reform innovations slowed in Franconian territories, in part because George resided repeatedly in Silesia and permitted himself to be represented by his brother Frederick, the Würzburg cathedral provost, who encouraged the old faith. Nevertheless, George, ever a Renaissance prince who enjoyed the pleasures of life, must receive credit for the Reformation's penetration into the Franconian territories of the Hohenzollerns. He was a hearty representative of the evangelical position in imperial politics. George's pursuit of the gospel and support of Lutheranism contributed to his appelation as "the Pious."

BIBLIOGRAPHY

Müller, Uwe. "Markgraf Georg der Fromme: Ein protestantischer Landesherr im 16. Jahrhundert." *Jahrbuch für fränkische Landesforschung* 45 (1985), 107–123.

Rudersdorf, Manfred. "Brandenburg-Ansbach und Brandenburg-Kulmbach/Bayreuth." In *Die Territorien des Reichs im Zeitalter der Reformation und Konfessionalisierung*, edited by Anton Schindling and Walter Ziegler, vol. 1, pp. 11–30. Münster, 1989.

Schornbaum, Karl. *Zur Politik des Markgrafen Georg von Brandenburg vom Beginn seiner selbstständigen Regierung bis zum Nürnberger Anstand, 1528–1532*. Munich, 1906.

GÜNTER VOGLER

Translated from German by Jeff Bach

GEORGE THE BEARDED. *See* George, Duke of Saxony.

GEORGE THE PIOUS. *See* George of Brandenburg-Ansbach.

GERBELIUS, Nikolaus (Ger., Gerbel; c.1485–1560), humanist Lutheran scholar, writer, and editor. Gerbel was born the son of a painter in Pforzheim, where he attended the Latin school, going on to study under the German humanist Conradus Celtis at the University of Vienna in 1502–1505. After teaching briefly at his hometown school, where Philipp Melanchthon was his pupil, Gerbelius attended the universities of Cologne (1506–1507) and Tübingen (1511) before receiving a doctorate in canon law from the University of Bologna in 1514. In 1515 he was appointed legal counsel and secretary to the cathedral chapter in Strasbourg, a position he held for the rest of his life.

An elegant Latin stylist and scholar in his own right, Gerbelius was highly valued by prominent humanists as a gifted editor and publisher. Between 1515 and 1520 he published editions of Ovid, Cicero, Terence, and Sallust. As friends he counted, among others, Johannes Cuspinian, Celtis, Johannes Reuchlin, Jakob Wimpfeling, and, in particular, Ulrich von Hutten. Most scholars agree that he shared in the publication of *Epistolae obscurorum virorum* of 1517. Attracted by Luther's theology and stand against Rome, Gerbelius became an early and dedicated follower. He is credited with three Latin satires written against Thomas Murner in 1520–1521. Although his unanimity with Luther alienated Gerbelius from the Strasbourg reformers Martin Bucer and Wolfgang Capito, he was instrumental in effecting a rapprochement between Strasbourg and Wittenberg in the 1530s. Luther valued his loyalty and showed his esteem by having Gerbelius stand as godfather to his oldest son.

In his later years he turned to publishing editions of ancient and medieval historical writings as well as his own history of the Holy Roman Emperors, *Icones imperatorum.* His major contribution to learning was a monumental delineation of the history, geography, language, and culture of the lands and cities of ancient Greece based on primary sources, published in 1545 under the title *In descriptionem Graeciae Sophiani.* In 1541 he became professor of history at the newly established academy in Strasbourg.

BIBLIOGRAPHY

Grimm, Heinrich. "Gerbelius." In *Neue Deutsche Biographie*, vol. 6, pp. 249–250. Berlin, 1963.

Hornung, Wilhelm. *Der Humanist Dr. Nikolaus Gerbelius, Förderer lutherischer Reformation in Straßburg.* Strasbourg, 1918.

Merker, P. *Der Verfasser des "Eccius dedolatus" und anderer Reformationsdialoge.* Halle, 1923. Argues for Gerbelius's authorship of pseudonymous Latin satires against Murner and Eck. Includes a brief biography.

Rott, Jean. "L'humaniste strasbourgeois Nicolas Gerbelius et son diaire, 1522–29." *Bulletin philologigue et historique* (1950), 69–78. Useful summary of Gerbelius's life and of his diary.

Schottenloher, Karl, ed. *Bibliographie zur deutschen Geschichte im Zeitalter der Glaubersspaltung, 1517–1585.* Stuttgart, 1957. See vol. 1. Literature to the late 1950s.

KARIN BRINKMANN BROWN

GERMAN COLLEGE. *See* Seminaries.

GERMAN LANGUAGE. The emergence of a standard German language out of the Reformation, particularly out of Luther's Bible translation, is surrounded by both popular conviction and scholarly controversy. Luther employed the term *Common German* (*Gemeindeutsch*) to describe his language. The term began to appear in the century before Luther, first as an evaluation of language level, referring to the kind of speech ordinary people might use, and later as an attempt to transcend local dialect with a generally comprehensible language system. Luther attached himself to these conventions with remarks about language, translation, and plagiarism by his disputants. He used the term *Common German* traditionally, referring to the same two features of his language: idiom on the one hand, and articulation (spelling and pronunciation) on the other. Luther evenhandedly criticized those who translated from the Latin word for word, oblivious to vernacular usage, and those who spoke in vernacular regionalisms, such as his neighbors in the Saxon countryside. In idiom his "Common German" was vernacular, a language of the people to be distinguished from Latinate, learned German; in articulation it was a compromise among the often mutually incomprehensible dialects of the German-speaking area "which both upper- and nether-landers could understand."

At the peripheries of the Germanic dialect areas, this particular intention of Luther's was never fully realized. His compromise language could not transcend the limits imposed by emerging national politics. Many Low German–speaking areas, chiefly cities, eventually yielded to a successor of Luther's German. However, in the northwest and the southwest, the Netherlands and Switzerland, Luther's German could not supplant the local languages as their speakers departed from the German body politic. Both the Dutch and the Swiss employ Bible translations linguistically detached from Luther's.

In the German heartland the needs of civil administration, commerce in general, and the book trade in particular had helped to generate a variety of "Common German" regional variants around Luther's time. These were determined by geography (e.g., trade routes), traditional local usage, and immigration. They survived well into the eighteenth century in the written language, and endure as regional coloration in spoken German even among educated speakers. Luther modeled his particular compromise on the written chancery language employed in electoral Saxony and Thuringia (Erfurt, Wittenberg, Leipzig) by his patron, Frederick the Wise, and the imperial chancery language of Maximilian I employed in upper Germany (Swabia, Bavaria, Austria). Claims for other models have been disputed, such as were made (by Konrad Burdach) for the Prague chancery of Charles IV (1347–1378)—located geographically midway between the other two, but chronologically a century too early.

Before Luther there are ample instances of effective use of the early modern successor of medieval German, Early New High German (ENHG). The rise of an unlatined urban middle class created the demand, and the art of printing began to satisfy it. German vernaculars had been employed for a wide variety of tasks: universal, regional, and city history; verse; didactic and technical prose; religious writing (meditative, homiletic, and theological); translations from the Bible; Roman classics; and Italian Renaissance belles lettres. The issues of literal (*wort zu wort:* "word by word") and substantive (*sinn zu sinn:* "meaning to meaning") translation had all been aired by humanist translators in the generations before Luther, and the German vernacular had proved itself a supple and sufficient instrument. However, it continued to suffer from a lack of literary prestige, and that remained the case even after Luther, well into the seventeenth century.

The linguistic model Luther chose for his Bible translation served his own region but had characteristics that extended well beyond it. The region lay between areas of major dialect difference, and the spoken language inclined to favor the lower German spoken to the north. The written language of the chancery, however, was designed by its scribes to deemphasize the northern inclination and to respect certain writing conventions established in the more prestigious imperial chancery of the upper German Habsburgs, in whose court Frederick the Wise served with distinction. The scribes accepted the transformation of Middle High German (MHG) long vowels (*î,û iu [long ü]* ei, au, eu: ENHG diphthongization) which had spread from the Austrian-Bavarian region across most of middle Germany before Luther. The reverse process, MHG diphthongs to long vowels (*ie, uo, üe* î, u, ü: ENHG monophthongization), took the reverse journey from middle to eastern upper Germany in the written chancery languages. The Saxon scribes favored consonant representation more like upper German than was actual spoken usage in Luther's region. The combined result was a written language that looked more than any competitor like an attempt to standardize by compromise.

In the short term orthography was less of a problem than vocabulary. Luther employed terms from his native region which were unfamiliar only a few hundred miles away in upper Germany. As early as 1523, printers unwilling to tamper with Luther's language provided glossaries to explain the differences to their local customers. The eventual disappearance of such aids is interpreted as an early sign of the acceptance of Lutheran German in terminology and the gradual disappearance of certain nativisms when they conflicted with Luther's German.

The idiomatic base of Luther's German was popular, colorful, and contemporary. He employed all the embellishments of colloquial speech, such as wordplay (*Doctor Kröte* [tortoise] for his humanist friend turned opponent, Crotus Rubeanus), metaphor (*Die Worte des Herrn . . . haben Hände und Füße,* "The words of the Lord . . . have hands and feet"), and synecdoche (*[dem] gemeinen Mann . . . aufs Maul sehen,* "to look the common man in the maw," meaning "to listen to what ordinary people actually say"). However, he similarly employed the learned rhetorical tradition of Greece and Rome, its medieval successors, and its humanist revival. Luther's transference of the rhetorical tradition to the vernacular had ample precedent in German literary prose (*Der Ackermann und der Tod* [The Ploughman from Bohemia]) and homiletics (Geiler von Kaysersberg). The rhetoric tradition was a given that provided all literate Europeans of the age, Luther no exception, with a common medium of expression.

As he had attached himself to both the Latin and vernacular traditions of prose, Luther likewise employed them in the lyric. His hymns appear in a great variety of available genres, the battle song ("Ein feste Burg"), historical folksong ("Ein neues lied wir heben an"), Te Deum ("Herr Gott, dich loben wir"), and love lyric ("Sie ist mir lieb die werde Magd"). Luther appears, however, to be among the very first literary figures of stature to experiment with classical meters in German (iambic pentameter in the German Sanctus, "Jesaia dem Propheten das geschah") in express imitation of the Roman ancients (he acknowledged Virgil).

Luther's summary of these traditions, learned and vernacular, was deliberate and self-conscious. He meant them to be renewed entirely by his passion for the gospel. In a trinitarian allegory of the old *Trivium* he called the Father "Grammar", the source of the words, the Son "Dialectic," the giver of order, and the Holy Spirit "Rhetoric," the one who gives the orator eloquence, breath, life, and the power to move hearts. As far as the formal characteristics of language are concerned—grammar, syntax, orthography, rhetoric—Luther by his own admission did not invent anything new. He did, however, bring all the principal trends together in one discourse. Those trends he did not include, such as living local dialect, eventually lost out in the contest for literacy. As far as substance, style, and experiment are concerned, he revolutionized the German language and laid the foundation for a common literary German in subsequent centuries. This applies to the entire German-speaking area, regardless of confession. Luther pointed out irascibly how his enemies were using his own German and turning it against him. The New Testament "translation" published by Johannes Emser (1527) was an outright plagiarism, "corrected" for the Vulgate but otherwise Luther's genius. The Emser version was reprinted well into the nineteenth century, assuring as much Lutheran German in Catholic as in Protestant Germany.

The means by which Luther's linguistic influence spread across German-speaking Europe were the printed broadside, the pulpit, congregational song, and, specific to the Bible translation, the home and, specific to the catechism, the schoolroom. By the end of the sixteenth century, Germans literate in the vernacular employed at least the formalisms of Luther's German. The occasional exceptions insisting on Low German or other dialect literature clearly felt under siege. In the first quarter of the seventeenth century, the victory of Luther's German over the written language was near complete. The last Low German Bible still in competition with Luther's standard German was printed in 1622.

The uninterrupted tradition of belletristic German may be said to open with the *Buch der Deutsche Poeterei* (The Book of German Prosody) of Martin Opitz (1624), in which the combination of classical poetics and vernacular tradition repeats itself. Luther is quoted in its pages as an authority on a par with Horace and Virgil. German Classicism and Romanticism fully acknowledged their debt to Luther. J. G. Herder named him the "Teacher of the German Nation" and ascribed to him the very existence of a reading public in Germany. The Romantic poet Jean Paul says of Luther's prose: it is practically a battlefield—"Few deeds equal his words" ("*wenige Taten gleichen seinen Worten*"). Goethe surveyed the diversity of Luther's language, its poetic, historic, hortatory, and didactic qualities and said of him: he handed on a mother tongue, cast as though in a single mold ("*[eine] Muttersprache, wie aus einem Guße überliefert[e]*").

BIBLIOGRAPHY

Arndt, Erwin. *Luthers deutsches Sprachschaffen: Ein Kapitel aus der Vorgeschichte der deutschen Nationalsprache und ihrer Ausdrucksformen.* Berlin, 1962.

Bacon, Thomas I. *Martin Luther and the Drama.* Amsterdam, 1976.

Beutel, Albrecht. *In dem Anfang war das Wort: Studien zu Luthers Sprachverständnis.* Tübingen, 1991.

Bluhm, Heinz. "Luther's German Bible." In *Seven-Headed Luther,* edited by Peter Newman Brooks, pp. 174–194. Oxford, 1983.

———. *Martin Luther: Creative Translator.* Reprint Saint Louis, 1984.

———. *Studies in Luther.* Bern and New York, 1987.

Borchardt, Frank L. "Luther's 'Minnesang': 'Sie ist mir lieb die werde Magd.'" In *Spectrum Medii Aevi: Essays in Early German Literature in Honor of George Fenwick Jones,* edited by William C. McDonald, pp. 41–57. Göppinger Arbeiten zur Germanistik, no. 362. Göppingen, 1983.

Bornkamm, Heinrich. *Luther als Schriftsteller.* Heidelberg, 1965.

Burdach, Konrad. *Vom Mittelalter zur Reformation: Forschung zur Geschichte der deutschen Bildung.* Halle, Germany, 1893.

Diehm, Freidrich. *Luther als Kenner deutschen Volksbrauchs und deutscher Volksüberlieferung.* Giessen, Germany, 1930.

Ebert, Helmut. *Alltagssprache und religiöse Sprache in Luthers Briefen und in seiner Bibelübersetzung: Eine satzsemantische Untersuchung am Beispiel von Aufforderunassätzen und Fragesätzen.* Frankfurt a.M. and New York, 1986.

Erben, Johannes. *Grundzüge einer Syntax der Sprache Luthers.* Deutsche Akademie der Wissenschaften zu Berlin, Veröffentlichungen des Instituts für Sprache und Literatur, vol. 2. Berlin, 1954.

Frettlöh, Regina. *Die Revisionen der Lutherbibel in wortgeschichtlicher Sicht.* Göppingen, 1986.

Hahn, Gerhart. *Evangelium als literarische Anweisung: Zu Luthers Stellung in der Geschichte des deutschen Kirchlichen Liedes.* Munich, 1981.

Junghans, Helmar. *Der junge Luther und die Humanisten.* Göttingen, 1985.

Lemmer, Manfred, ed. *Beiträge zur Sprachwirkung Martin Luthers im 17./18. Jahrhundert.* Halle, Germany, 1987.

Schröder, Werner. *Auxiliar-Ellipsen bei Geiler von Kaysersberg und bei Luther.* Stuttgart, 1985.

Sommer, Ernst. "Die Metrik in Luthers Liedern." *Jahrbuch für Liturgik und Hymnologie* 9 (1964), pp. 29–81.

Spitta, Fredrich. *Ein Feste Burg ist unser Gott: Die Lieder Luthers in ihrer Bedeutung für das evangelische Kirchenlied.* Göttingen, 1905.

Stolt, Birgit. *Die Sprachmischung in Luthers Tischreden: Studien zum Problem der Zweisprachigkeit.* Stockholm, 1964.

Tennant, Elaine C. *The Habsburg Chancery Language in Perspective.* University of California Publications in Modern Philology, no. 114. Berkeley, 1985.

Werbow, Stanley N. "Die gemeine Teutsch." *Zeitschrift für deutsche Philologie* 82 (1963), 44–83.

Wolf, Herbert. *Martin Luther: Eine Einführung in germanistische Luther-Studien.* Stuttgart, 1980.

———. *Germanistische Luther-Bibliographie: Martin Luthers deutsches Sprachschaffen im Spiegel des internationalen Schrifttums der Jahre 1880–1980.* Heidelberg, 1985.

Zimmer, Heinrich. *Martin Luther als deutscher Klassiker.* Frankfurt a.M., 1871.

FRANK L. BORCHARDT

GERSHOM, Joseph ben *See* Joselmann of Rosheim.

GESSNER, Conrad (1516–1565), Swiss naturalist, doctor, bibliographer, and humanist. He was born 16 March 1516 to a large tradesman's family in Zurich. Since the family was very poor, he lived from age five with his great-uncle Johannes Frick and then with his teacher Johann Jakob Ammann, who later urged him to study medicine. Besides Ammann, Gessner was taught by Oswald Myconius, Thomas Platter, and Peter Collin. In 1531 his father, Urs Gessner, as well as his spiritual father, Huldrych Zwingli, died in the Second Kappel War, and in the summer of 1532 he moved with the help of Myconius to Strasbourg, where he lived with Wolfgang Capito. Dissatisfied, Gessner returned after about half a year to Zurich, where he again received a scholarship. From 1533 to 1534 he studied in Bourges and Paris but then was compelled to leave France because of the Protestant persecutions. Because of an injudicious marriage in April 1535, he lost much sympathy with the Zurich church officials. Myconius, however, succeeded in reconciling him with Heinrich Bullinger, who helped him get another scholarship to study medicine in Basel.

Financial difficulties finally forced Gessner to scholarly writings. As the first fruit of these efforts, he published a Greek dictionary in 1537. In the same year, he was called to the newly founded Protestant academy in Lausanne as a professor of Greek. He spent three happy years there. During those years Gessner studied many Greek writers and collected plants. In the fall of 1540 he resumed his studies of medicine in Montpellier, completing his doctorate in Basel in March 1541. In the summer of the same year, he collected plants in the Alps, and in the following fall he published his first botanical work, the *Historia plantarum.* Since Gessner earned little as a teacher of natural history and ethics at the Carolinum, he tried to improve his financial situation by writing scholarly books and by working for the printer and publisher Christoph Froschauer, Sr. After study trips to Italy, he published in 1545 an immensely popular book, the *Bibliotheca univeralis,* the first bibliography of all Hebrew, Greek, and Latin works known up to that time. This book made him known beyond the borders of Switzerland. In the following year Gessner was granted a professorship in the theology faculty, the Prophezei, which had been founded by Zwingli. In 1551 he published the first volume of his *Historia animalium,* which brought him world fame and made him the founder of modern descriptive zoology. In 1558 came the publication of a fourth book on fish and aquatic animals. The fifth and final volume on snakes was published by his successor, Caspar Wolf, in 1587.

It was not only in the areas of bibliography and zoology that Gessner made a lasting name for himself. He also published authoritative works in the field of linguistics, as, for example, the *Mithridates* (1555), the first work of comparative linguistics. He entered the annals of classical philology as the editor of the "editio princeps" of Marcus Aurelius's *Meditationes* in 1559 and of path-breaking editions of Galen and Claudius Aelianus. His *Thesaurus Euonymi Philiatri* of 1552 became a standard work among medical prescription books and underwent many editions and translations. In his *Descriptio montis fracti* of 1555 he categorized Alpine vegetation into various main groups, which made him the founder of plant geography. Gessner's last published work, *De omni rerum fossilium genere* (1565), not only was the second work in the history of paleontology that contained pictures of fossils but also pointed out for the first time the significance of angles in crystals. Had Gessner not been taken unexpectedly by the plague on 13 December 1565, he would have made a lasting impression on botany with the planned publication of his great work on plants, the *Historia plantarum*, which remained in manuscript.

BIBLIOGRAPHY

Fischer, Hans. *Conrad Gessner, 1516–1565*. Neujahrsgabe der Naturforschenden Gesellschaft in Zurich, vol. 168. Zurich, 1966. The most recent biography of Gessner. Contains a large bibliography. No longer available in bookstores.

Fischer, Hans, ed. *Conrad Gessner, 1516–1565: Universalgelehrter, Naturforscher, Arzt*. Zurich, 1967. A collection of essays written by Swiss scholars. Includes many facsimiles from Gessner's works.

Hanhart, Johannes. *Conrad Gessner: Ein Beytrag zur Geschichte des wissenschaftlichen Strebens und der Glaubensverbesserung im 16. Jahrhundert*. Winterthur, 1824. Still the best biography. Uses many unpublished sources.

Leu, Urs B. *Conrad Gessner als Theologe: Ein Beitrag zur Zürcher Geistesgeschichte des 16. Jahrhunderts*. Bern, 1990. The first monograph to present Gessner's thought and works as they were influenced by Reformed Protestantism.

Wellisch, Hans H. *Conrad Gessner: A Bio-Bibliography*. Zug, 1984. Includes a short biography and a list of all the editions of Gessner's works. Unfortunately the list of secondary literature is incomplete. This is one of the few works on Gessner to have appeared in English.

URS B. LEU

Translated from German by Walter D. Morris

GEYER, Florian (c.1490–1525), Franconian imperial knight. Born in Giebelstadt, near Würzburg, he was the third son of Dietrich Geyer. He belonged to one of the oldest lines of nobility in Franconia. After the death of both of his older brothers, in 1512 all the rights to the Giebelstadt castle and considerable possessions in the surrounding area fell to Florian. He probably served in the army of Emperor Maximilian I in France (perhaps the report of 1513, which states that he had stayed with the king of England, relates to this). From 1515 he was in conflict with the Neumünster Stift of Würzburg because he refused to pay the required taxes from his estate. This obligation had existed since 1160 but could no longer be supported by documentary evidence. Therefore, the Würzburg state court could not decide the dispute either. The Neumünster Stift nevertheless succeeded in having Geyer excommunicated in 1517, which lasted until his death.

Various feudal lords requested Geyer's services. As vassal to Margrave Casimir of Brandenburg-Ansbach-Kulmbach, Geyer participated in the campaign of the Swabian League against Duke Ulrich of Württemberg. In connection with this service, Casimir recommended Geyer as an experienced warrior to Casimir's brother, Albrecht, grand master of the Teutonic Order. As a result, Geyer experienced the war between Poland and the order in 1519, but soon Geyer was mostly employed for diplomatic missions (trips to the imperial court and to the court of the Danish king). After a stay in his homeland, Franconia, he accompanied Albrecht in 1523 during the latter's trip through the empire and was perhaps present at Albrecht's meeting with Martin Luther and Philipp Melanchthon on 29 November 1523. Geyer reportedly embraced Lutheran teachings early on.

During the Peasants' War Geyer voluntarily joined the uprisings. Perhaps the catalyst for this decision was the requirement by the bishop of Würzburg, Konrad von Thüngen that the Franconian nobility assemble on 5 April 1525 to fight against the rebels. After 18 April Geyer can be identified as one of the leaders of the Tauber Valley peasants' army. As a knight with military experience, he may have collaborated in the formation of the military organization. Above all, however, he was entrusted by the peasants' council with negotiations to receive cities into the alliance (Kitzingen, Würzburg, and Rothenburg). These negotiations succeeded on the basis of the Tauber Valley program, which stipulated that only the gospel should be accepted as the norm, and the privileges of clergy and nobility should be curtailed. Geyer, who understood himself as a "good evangelical," identified himself with the program. After stinging defeats of the Franconian peasants, he was expelled from Rothenburg, and on the night of 9–10 June he was slain and robbed by servants of the knight Wilhelm of Grumbach at Rimpar, north of Würzburg. He served the peasants' movement with his military experience but above all with his diplomatic skills in order to promote a reform of the estates in the spirit of the gospel.

BIBLIOGRAPHY

Fuchs, Walther Peter. "Florian Geyer." In *Fränkische Lebensbilder*, vol. 3, pp. 109–140. Würzburg, 1969.

Heinemann, Wolf-Dieter. "Florian Geyer als fränkischer Ritter, sozialer Reformer und reformatorischer Christ." Ph.D. diss., Martin Luther-Universität Halle-Wittenberg, 1957.

Meyer, Manfred. "Die historische Rolle und Bedeutung Florian Geyers." *Wissenschaftliche Zeitschrift Universität Leipzig* 14.3 (1965), 479–487.

GÜNTER VOGLER

Translated from German by Jeff Bach

GHENT. As early as 1520 Lutheran doctrines were preached from the Augustinian monastery of Ghent, where

Melchior Miritsch, a friend and kindred spirit of Luther, served as prior from 1520 to 1522. The press in Ghent was also a major force in the dissemination of the new teachings. On 25 July 1521, in the presence of Charles V, over three hundred Lutheran books were publicly burned; several other book burnings followed. Between 1521 and 1535 the battle against heresy in the city was in large part a persistent effort to oppose the selling and reading of Protestant publications. Up until 1584 the printers, booksellers, and educators of Ghent played a prominent role in the spread of the new teachings, and for rather a long time a close tie clearly existed between the educated elite of Ghent and the growing evangelical movement. In these moderate groups, to which a number of rhetoricians also belonged, there was still no talk of a break with Catholicism, much less of confessional Protestantism. However, owing to the repressive hand of Charles V and, later, of Philip II, whom conservative theologians continued to support, Catholics and evangelicals were left little room to maneuver. In 1557 the inquisitor Pieter Titelmans put an end to the activities of intermediaries by driving their principal intellectual representatives, including Karel Utenhove, out of the city. Already in 1530 the first Protestant was executed. In the course of the sixteenth century 251 more executions would follow.

The first group to break completely with the official church were the Anabaptists, who first flourished around 1535, during the time of the Anabaptist kingdom at Münster. Severe persecution in 1538 put an end to their existence in Ghent. Along with the Anabaptists a loose school of evangelically inclined Sacramentarians had arisen who in their conception of the Eucharist were closely aligned with the Swiss-Zwinglian position. Harsh repression beginning in 1545 prompted a number of them to take flight. Among this first wave of emigrants were Jan Utenhove, Maarten Micron, and Karel de Coninck (Regius), each of whom—after contact with, among others, Martin Bucer—played an important role in the establishment of the Dutch exile church in London and later in Emden. After 1550 the Reformation underwent a powerful revival in Ghent, both in its Anabaptist and its Calvinist versions. Anabaptism, now under the influence of the circle around Menno Simons, found fertile soil in the social misery of the lower classes in Ghent and in the other Flemish cities. Although they adopted a consistently pacifist stance, the Anabaptists were considered to be a social threat, and they became the primary target of the Inquisitorial court of Pieter Titelmans. Their history was marked by repeated movement from one city to another and by the continuing tragedy of martyrdom: two-thirds of the heretics executed in Ghent were Anabaptists. Still, the Anabaptist community managed to survive in Ghent and the surrounding area until into the seventeenth century, when the Counter-Reformation held full sway.

Calvinism as well made inroads into Ghent toward the end of the reign of Charles V. With its carefully defined doctrine, its discipline, and its vigorous spirit, the Calvinist movement put an end to the hitherto rather tranquil image of Protestantism. This militant religion thrived during the 1560s thanks to the prevaling political, economic, and social malaise in Flanders and in Brabant. Its leadership and inspiration came primarily from the Dutch refugee churches of London, Sandwich, Emden, Wesel, and Frankenthal, and subsequently also from neighboring Huguenot France. In 1562 a Calvinist church organization was introduced into Ghent under the minister Joris Wybo, but the real breakthrough followed in the spring of 1566, largely as a result of political developments in the Netherlands. In June of that year the Ghent physician Nicasius van der Schueren and the former monk Hermannus Moded, who both had been in France, began to preach in the area around Ghent. The open-air preaching, which only continued to grow and to spread, soon provoked the iconoclastic fury and its path of destruction throughout the Netherlands. On 22–23 August 1566 the iconoclasts stormed some fifty churches, cloisters, chapels, hospitals, and beguinages in Ghent. These days were a terrible disaster for the city's artistic heritage. The Calvinists, who in the confusion that followed the iconoclasm enjoyed a limited religious freedom, managed to establish a well-organized church. According to estimates, they numbered fifteen hundred heads of families, or about thirteen percent of the total municipal population. Under the leadership of Petrus Dathenus an important synodal meeting regarding the organization of armed resistance took place in Ghent on 30 September and 1 October. Then on 27 March 1567 the city government forbade Calvinist preaching. The repression—first under Margaret of Parma, and then in all its severity through the special judicial court of Fernando Álvarez de Toledo, duke of Alba—was fierce: 127 were executed while many hundreds went into exile. Following the pacification of the city, Cornelis Jansen was installed as the first bishop of Ghent in 1568. He introduced Tridentine reforms in Ghent and in his bishopric; however, because of his early death in 1576, they did not take hold.

After a coup, a revolutionary government came to power in Ghent on 1 November 1577, and the Calvinists quickly gained the upper hand. The city became the spearhead of the resistance against Spain, adopting a far more radical position than was favored by William of Orange, the leader of the Revolt of the Netherlands. In February 1578 Calvinist preaching was instituted again. The Catholic clergy were persecuted; the exercise of Catholicism was restricted and then completely forbidden. Beginning in September 1578 the minister Petrus Dathenus assumed a leading role. He rebuilt the Calvinist ecclesiastical organization and set up a completely new educational system, including an excellent secondary school and a theological school with reputable professors, among them Lambert Daneau, a student of Théodore de Bèze. The confiscated property of the clergy financed the new church and its educational system. From

Ghent Calvinism was also imposed on all other Flemish cities. According to its political leaders, Ghent was to be the "new Geneva," at the head of a great Calvinist republic. Alessandro Farnese, duke of Parma, managed to reconquer Ghent for Spain on 17 September 1584. A few days later twenty-eight Calvinist ministers left the city. It is estimated that approximately thirty percent of Ghent's population was Protestant at this time, and the numerous Calvinists who had returned from exile were extremely influential. Beginning in 1584 approximately ten thousand Ghentenaars emigrated abroad, for religious and frequently for economic reasons as well. The rebuilding of Catholic church life would not truly begin until 1590 under Bishop Peter Damant. With the triumph of the Counter-Reformation, Ghent once again became a homogeneous Catholic city.

BIBLIOGRAPHY

Decavele, J. *De dageraad van de reformatie in Vlaanderen, 1520–1565*. 2 vols. Brussels, 1975. Examines the emergence of the Reformation in Ghent.

Decavele, Johan, ed. *Het eind van een rebelse droom*. Ghent, 1984. Considers the Calvinist rule of 1577 to 1584.

———. *Ghent: In Defense of a Rebellious City*. Antwerp, 1989. See pp. 106–130. Deals with the Reformation and Counter-Reformation of the sixteenth century.

Delmotte, Marcel. "Het calvinisme in de verschillende bevolkingslagen te Gent, 1566–1567." *Tijdschrift voor Geschiedenis* 79 (1963), 145–176. Examines the social implications of Calvinism and the iconoclasm of 1566–1567.

Despretz, Andre. "De instauratie der Gentse Calvinistische Republiek, 1577–1579." *Handelingen der Maatschappij voor Geschiedenis en Oudheidkunde te Gent* 17 (1963), 119–229. Gives a thorough analysis of the revolutionary political, religious, and social changes in Ghent from 1577 to 1579.

JOHAN DECAVELE

Translated from Dutch by Michael A. Hakkenberg

GHISLIERI, Antonio. *See* Pius V.

GIBBONS, Orlando (1583–1625), the finest Anglican composer of the early seventeenth century. He was born in Oxford, where his father, a professional musician, was a member of the town waits. From 1596 to 1598 Gibbons was a boy soprano at King's College, Cambridge, where his brother Edward was master of the choristers. Orlando later received a Mus.B. from Cambridge and a doctorate in Music from Oxford; he submitted the eight-part anthem *O Clap Your Hands* as his thesis.

Almost immediately after the accession of James I in 1603, Gibbons became a member of the Chapel Royal, probably serving as one of the two chapel organists. In 1623 he was also named organist of Westminster Abbey. In addition, he was one of the musicians of the king's privy chamber, where he played the virginals. Gibbons lived in the parish of Saint Margaret's, Westminster; his seven children were baptized in the parish church there. One of these, Christopher, also became a prominent musician.

Charles I succeeded to the English throne following James I's death in 1625, and in May of that year the court migrated to Canterbury to await the arrival of Charles's new wife, the French princess Henrietta Maria. Perhaps overcome with the strain of preparing suitable music, Gibbons suffered a stroke and died before the queen's arrival. A fine monument to Gibbons was subsequently erected in Canterbury cathedral.

Although his musical style derived from that of Thomas Tallis and William Byrd, Gibbons music is clearly of a later generation. He grew up with *The Book of Common Prayer*, not with the Latin Mass, and unlike Tallis and Byrd he never set a Latin text. His best known works are his anthems. These are of two sorts: full anthems, sometimes set for six or eight voices, such as *Hosanna to the Son of David* and *Lord, in Your Wrath Rebuke Me Not*; and verse anthems, such as *This Is the Record of John* and *See, See, the Word is Incarnate*, in which sections for a solo voice alternate with choral sections. Many of the anthems composed for the Chapel Royal were originally accompanied by viols rather than organ since these string instruments were readily available at the court and were liked by James I. Gibbons also left several sets of canticles, written in both full and verse styles. In addition, there are several hymn tunes, including the beautiful *Drop, Drop Slow Tears* for Passiontide.

Gibbons's secular works include madrigals, of which the best known is *The Silver Swan*, and keyboard works, mainly dance movements such as the pavane and galliard dedicated to James I's chief minister, Robert Cecil, earl of Salisbury. He also wrote fantasias that can be regarded as forerunners of trio sonatas. His music—elegant if not deeply spiritual—typifies the spirit of the early Stuart court.

BIBLIOGRAPHY

Fellowes, Edmund H. *Orlando Gibbons and His Family*. Rev. ed. Oxford, 1970. Still the standard monograph; a new study is needed.

Lafontaine, H. C. de. *The King's Musick* (1909). Reprint, New York, 1973. Still useful for its description of the royal musical establishment.

le Huray, Peter. *Music and the Reformation in England, 1549–1660*. Reprint, Cambridge, 1978. The best general account of music in the early Church of England.

Woodfill, Walter L. *Musicians in English Society from Elizabeth to Charles I*. Reprint, New York, 1969. Especially good on court patronage of musicians.

STANFORD E. LEHMBERG

GIBERTI, Gian Matteo (1495–1543), bishop of Verona and Catholic reformer. Born in Palermo of a rich Genoese merchant, he studied at the University of Bologna and was introduced by his father to the world of the Curia Romana. Here he quickly launched a successful career; he had the trust of Leo X and of his cousin Cardinal Giulio de' Medici, and he performed the functions of personal secretary to the pope.

After he took minor orders, he received a significant number of curial offices and ecclesiastical benefices. The death of Leo X and the election in 1522 of Adrian VI marked a pause in his career; however, the election in 1523 of his protector Giulio de' Medici, who became Pope Clement VII, caused him suddenly to become the most influential individual in the Curia. He was appointed datary, and he thus found himself in control of the most lucrative office in the Curia. He gathered around himself members of the Curia and men of letters in search of protection. Having a rather austere moral orientation, probably influenced by Savonarolan currents—for when he was very young, he had tried to become a Dominican—he must have noted the influence of the Genoese Oratory of Divine Love, founded by Ettore Vernazza. He was close to circles of the Roman Oratory of Divine Love and to the Theatines. He offered Desiderius Erasmus his protection and sought to convince him to join the fight against Martin Luther. He was hostile to Pietro Aretino, who, when attacked by Achille Della Volta, a Bolognese noble linked to Giberti, fled from Rome and took refuge in Venice.

Giberti also initiated a reform in ecclesiastical discipline among the members of the Curia and of the Roman court: clerics were obliged to wear clerical dress, shave their beards, and conduct themselves according to canonical norms. When he was appointed bishop of Verona (1524), he immediately went to be consecrated bishop and sent a well-prepared spiritual vicar to direct the diocese. Between the two political factions existing in the Curia at that time, he sided with the pro-French faction, departing from the proimperial party to which he had belonged under Leo X. In the name of what was called at that time "the freedom of Italy"—namely opposition to the excessive influence of foreign sovereigns over the Italian states—he felt compelled to ally himself with Francis I and to join the League of Cognac (1526). This pro-French policy was to end disastrously with the Sack of Rome (1527). Giberti was subsequently taken hostage by the imperial army. He luckily managed to escape and save his life, but his political career was now over. The Spanish faction never forgave him for having been the main supporter of the Franco-papal alliance. In 1529 the pope sent him to receive Charles V, but the emperor made clear his hostility toward him. In the years that followed, every time his name appeared on the list of candidates to be named cardinals, the veto of the imperial faction thwarted his chances.

Along with his political activity, Giberti had to leave the Curia. He went to Verona, where he devoted himself to running his diocese. His choice to fulfill the duty of residing in his diocese was significant and brought him to the attention of ecclesiastical circles in Italy, who were shaken by the tragedy of the Sack of Rome. Giberti, however, did not limit himself to residing in his diocese. His whole life's work as a bishop became a model for those circles convinced of the need to reform the church. The objective he pursued was to strengthen the authority of the bishop in order to reform the conduct of the clergy and to renew religious life. He surrounded himself with co-workers who were in part chosen from those he had known in the Curia, such as Marcantonio Flaminio and Tullio Crispoldi.

The Christian humanism that Giberti had cultivated in Rome in the Orti Coriciani had a significant impact on his circle in Verona. He used Venetian printing companies, particularly that of Nicolini da Sabio and the Veronese printing company of Antonio Putelleto da Portese, to publish his writings and those of his co-workers. He had a printing press with Greek letters installed in the episcopal palace for the edition of the homilies of John Chrysostom, a work inspired by the patristic evangelism so dear to Erasmus. From Giberti's first arrival in Verona in 1529, however, it was clear that he had no intention of enjoying the humanistic leisure of studies or of limiting himself to being a patron of the arts. One of his first acts was to conduct personally a pastoral visitation of his diocese: he examined the preparation of the secular clergy, and he punished and corrected in various ways those he found unprepared or living in concubinage. He visited the convents of women religious, ascertained the state of the church buildings, personally conducted a survey on how frequently the sacraments were received by the laity, and introduced a confessional into the churches to safeguard the secrecy of confessions. As a judge, he dealt with many matrimonial cases. He also gathered information on folk customs. He quickly dealt with those who enjoyed exemption from the ordinary authority of the bishop, in particular with the religious orders that were opposed to the bishop's intervening in the matter of houses of women religious and especially with the chapter of canons of the cathedral. To make his orders effective, Giberti secured papal support as well as that of the Venetian government: Clement VII and Paul III granted him authority as a *legatus de latere* ("legate from the side [of the pope]"), thanks to which he was able to overcome the obstacle of exemptions. In Venice he was able to count on the support of influential individuals, such as Gasparo Contarini. In 1536, with the naming of Contarini as a cardinal, the party favorable to church reform seemed close to victory: Giberti was called along with others to draw up the *Consilium de emendenda ecclesia* (Plan for Reforming the Church) and soon afterward was sent on a diplomatic mission with Reginald Pole to bring England back to obedience to Rome.

Meanwhile, the religious life of the diocese was being guided by Giberti toward forms that aroused the suspicions and resistance of conservative circles: laymen were preaching to the people; lessons on *Psalms* and the epistles of Paul were being held; and forms of devotion, such as frequent Communion, were being encouraged. People such as Bernardino Ochino and the "divine mother" Paola Antonia Negri were being invited. On a more strictly theological level, in Giberti's circle in 1537 a debate developed on faith and works and on predestination in which those tending toward rigid Augustinianism prevailed. After this debate Flaminio left Verona to join the circle of Juan de Valdés in Naples. With regard to the Protestant Reformation, the text of the sermons preached during the pastoral visitation of the diocese of 1530 reflects a judgment not of condemnation but of attention and interest.

The evangelism of the Verona group, however, soon reached a crisis: the failure of the colloquy of Regensburg (1541), the creation of the Roman Inquisition (1542), the death of Contarini, and the flight of Ochino forced Giberti to leave the company of the "spiritual" party in order to attempt to salvage the work of moral and disciplinary reform already accomplished in his diocese. Accused of political conspiracy with France and tried in Venice before the Council of Ten, Giberti wrote a long *Giustificazione* in which he presented the results of his work in his diocese (1542). The printing of the synodal constitutions, which took place shortly before his death (1543), was his spiritual testament.

BIBLIOGRAPHY

Fasani, Antonio. *Riforma pretridentina della diocesi di Verona: Visite pastorali del vescovo G. M. Giberti, 1525–1542*. Vincenza, 1989. An important edition of sources.

Partner, Peter. *The Pope's Men: The Papal Civil Service in the Renaissance*. Oxford, 1990. Fundamental regarding the Curia Romana during Giberti's time.

Prosperi, Adriano. *Tra evangelismo e Controriforma, G. M. Giberti, 1495–1543*. Rome, 1969.

ADRIANO PROSPERI

Translated from Italian by Robert E. Shillenn

GILES OF VITERBO (also Egidio, Antonini; 1469–1532), Italian Renaissance thinker, reforming prior general of the Augustinian order (1507–1518), and cardinal from 1517. He joined the Augustinians at Viterbo in 1493 and shortly thereafter published at Padua three works of Giles of Rome. In Florence the influence of Marsilio Ficino awakened in him an appreciation of Platonism, and not long afterward he became an outstanding member of the neo-Latin literary circle of Giovanni Pontano in Naples. He was already on his way to becoming one of the most esteemed orators and preachers of his day in central Italy, especially appreciated by Pope Julius II (r. 1503–1513). His best-known oration was the appeal for church reform at the opening of the Fifth Lateran Council on 3 May 1512. He had meanwhile learned Hebrew under Elijah Levita and became convinced that the Cabbala contained truths and prophecies providing a deeper understanding of Christianity and the course of history.

He left behind a corpus of personal and official correspondence, poems, orations, and sermons, as well as several important but curious treatises, especially his explicitly Platonizing commentary on parts of Peter Lombard's *Sentences* and his history of the world based on Cabbalistic numerology. Although little he wrote was published in his lifetime, much has appeared in print since 1969.

In 1503 Giles joined the observantist movement within the Augustinians. In 1506 Pope Julius II appointed him vicar general of the order, and in 1507 he was elected prior general by his confreres. For the next decade he worked tirelessly for the reform of the order, understood by him to mean a more exact adherence to traditional discipline. He achieved some success in halting the growing division between the conventual and observantist branches. As Martin Luther's superior general, he probably met him during his visit to Rome in 1511. Nominated a cardinal by Leo X in 1517 and appointed bishop of Viterbo by Clement VII in 1523, Giles played no further role in the order. Few records survive from the last fifteen years of his life.

BIBLIOGRAPHY

Egidio da Viterbo, O.S.A., e il suo tempo: Atti del V Convengo dell'Istituto Storico Agostiniano. Rome, 1983. A collection of ten studies, principally in English, that indicates the sweep and depth of Giles's interests.

Martin, Francis X. *Friar, Reformer, and Renaissance Scholar: Life and Work of Giles of Viterbo, 1469–1532*. Villanova, Pa., 1992. Biography, with appendixes of important studies of Giles as an Augustinian.

O'Malley, John W. *Giles of Viterbo on Church and Reform: A Study in Renaissance Thought*. Leiden, 1968. The fundamental book on Giles's intellectual culture.

O'Reilly, Clare, ed. *Giles of Viterbo OSA: Letters as Augustinian General, 1506–1517*. Rome, 1992. Critical edition, with commentary.

JOHN W. O'MALLEY

GIUSTINIANI, Tommaso (also Paolo; 1476–1528), Venetian spiritual writer, reformer of the Camaldolese, and Blessed. Born at Venice into a distinguished patrician family, he was trained in the humanities and studied philosophy and theology at the University of Padua. Around 1504 he began a long spiritual quest that led him from his student days of writing sonnets and studying scholasticism, to a Stoic interlude during an illness, and then to his retirement to a house on the island of Murano in the Venetian lagoons, where he devoted himself to prayer and the study of the Bible and church fathers. On his journey to the Holy Land in 1507, he failed to find in Bethlehem any traces of the learned solitude immortalized by Saint Jerome.

On his return to Venice in 1508, he retreated more and more from public life to his house on Murano, where he devoted himself, together with some fellow patricians, to study and spiritual concerns. Because they were reluctant to give up their individuality and independence, Giustiniani suggested that each live like a monk without actually becoming one. Hoping to formalize such a living arrangement, he visited in 1510 the Holy Hermitage of Camaldoli in the Tuscan Apennine mountains and negotiated a favorable arrangement with the hermits there. On further reflection and prayer, however, he decided that to lead a truly solitary life he should forgo all concessions and become a Camaldolese hermit. He entered the hermitage as a novice on Christmas 1510 and made his profession in August 1512. He succeeded in convincing some of his friends to join him; of these, the most important was Vincenzo Querini.

Within the order he quickly became leader of an observant movement; he hoped to restore primitive discipline by freeing the Holy Hermitage of its dependence on the cenobite monks of Fontebuono and on the prior general, Pietro Delfino, who held less rigorist views. With support from Leo X, Giustiniani persuaded the chapter meeting in Florence in April 1513 to revise the rule, unite the hermitage with the observant cenobite congregation of San Michele de Murano, and subject both to the prior of the hermitage. As *de facto* or elected leader of this congregation, Giustiniani labored to restore the eremitic life to its pristine spirit, publishing in 1520 at Fontebuono his revised constitutions, the *Eremiticae vitae regula.* With papal permission he left this congregation to found by 1523 an even more rigorist and exclusively eremitic congregation known as the Company of Saint Romualdo. To protect this new congregation from the opposition of the chapter meeting in Ravenna in 1525, Giustiniani made a number of trips to Rome. On one such visit in 1527 he was taken prisoner, tortured, and then released during the Sack of Rome. During another visit on 28 June 1528, he died, apparently of the plague, on the city's outskirts.

Apart from the rule, none of his numerous writings—at least twelve volumes of letters and spiritual treatises—were published during his lifetime. His famous epistolary exchanges with Gasparo Contarini forced that layman to clarify his thinking on the role of grace and the Christian vocation in the world. The lengthy *Libellus ad Leonem*, written with Querini in 1513, urged a comprehensive reform of the church. He also wrote against the prophets of his day, such as Amadeo (João Menezes da Silva), Girolamo Savonarola, Francesco da Meleto, and Teodoro di Giovanni da Scutari. He was a spiritual adviser to some of the early Capuchins but is most noted for his reform of the Camaldolese order.

BIBLIOGRAPHY

Primary Sources

Giustiniani, Paolo. *Trattato di ubedientia de don Paolo Giustiniani con una epistola del medesimo a M. Marc' Antonio Flaminio.* Edited by Niccolò A. Giustiniani. Venice, 1535; Padua 1753. An edition of his 1513 treatise on the twelve degrees of obedience and his 1526 letter to Flaminio on true happiness to be found in religious rather than secular life.

———. *Trattati, lettere e frammenti dai manoscritti originali dell' Archivio dei Camaldolesi di Monte Corona nell' Eremo di Frascati.* Edited by Eugenio Massa. Vol. 1, *I manoscritti originali custoditi nell' Eremo di Frascati.* Rome, 1961, 1966, 1968. Vol. 2, *I primi trattati dell' amore di Dio.* Rome, 1965, 1974. This is the modern critical edition of his writings, only two volumes having appeared so far.

———. *Letters.* In *Annales Camaldulenses Ordinis Sancti Benedicti,* edited by Giovanni-Benedetto Mittarelli and Anselmo Costadoni, vol. 9, pp., 451–596 passim. Reprint, Farnborough, 1970.

Giustiniani, Paolo, and Pietro Querini. *Libellus ad Leonem X. Pontificem Maximum.* In *Annales Camaldulenses,* edited by Giovanni-Benedetto Mittarelli and Anselmo Costadoni, vol. 9, cols. 612–719. Reprint, Farnborough, 1970.

Jedin, Hubert. "Contarini und Camaldoli." *Archivio italiano per la storia della Pietà,* 2 (1959), 51–117. Publishes some of Giustiniani's letters.

Secondary Sources

DeLuca, Giuseppe. *Letteratura di pieta a Venezia dal '300 al '600.* Edited by Vittore Branca. Saggi di "Lettere italiane" 3. Florence, 1963.

Leclerq, Jean. *Un humaniste ermite: Le bienheureux Paul Giustiniani, 1476–1528.* Rome, 1951. The most comprehensive modern study so far of his life and writings.

———. *Alone with God.* Translated by Elizabeth McCabe. New York, 1961. A work that studies Giustiniani's teachings on the eremitical life.

Massa, Eugenio. "Paolo Giustiniani." In *Bibliotheca Sanctorum,* vol. 7, cols. 2–9. Rome, 1966. A brief but excellent study of his life and thought.

NELSON H. MINNICH

GLAIDT, Oswald (1490–1546), one of the earliest Anabaptist leaders in east central Europe and the founder of the Sabbatarian wing of that movement. Glaidt was originally a Franciscan monk, but by 1520 he was working as a Lutheran in Austria. Expelled in 1525, he moved to Moravia, where he took part in a synod that attempted to unite the Lutherans with the Hussite Bohemian Brethren. He acted as the secretary for the meeting, and his first published writing was the document that this meeting produced.

Soon after Balthasar Hubmaier, the Anabaptist preacher, arrived in Moravia, Glaidt and a majority of the Lutherans there accepted his Anabaptist message and were baptized. At the same time, Glaidt published his *Enntschuldigung Osvaldi Gladit vom Chamb. Etlicher Artickel verklerung. So im von missgünnern fälschlich verkhert unnd also nach geredt wurden* (Confession of Oswald Glaidt from Cham: Some Articles Concerning Matters in Which He Has Been Falsely Accused; 1527), in which he responded to "lies spread about him" by the Franciscans in the area.

In 1527 a major dispute arose between Hubmaier, the sober biblicist, and the new arrival, the chiliastic Hans Hut. Glaidt left with Hut, and from Vienna Glaidt traveled up the Danube, baptizing those converted by Hut's preaching, including, it seems, Andreas Fischer.

Glaidt and Fischer appeared as coworkers in late 1527 in Liegnitz, Silesia, where Glaidt prepared his major theological treatise, *Vom Sabbat.* This scholarly and spirited defense of Sabbatarianism is perhaps the oldest such defense in early modern times. It combined erudite argument based on a restitutionist hermeneutic with practical concern for the life of the church. The prominence of arguments based on the Second Coming and the millennial kingdom of Christ suggests that Glaidt was still under the influence of Hut. Under Glaidt's influence, many or all of the Liegnitz Anabaptists accepted a Sabbatarian interpretation of the faith.

Glaidt returned to Moravia around 1530. There he agitated for Sabbatarianism, as is indicated by a letter from Lord von Liechtenstein to Kaspar von Schwenckfeld in Strasbourg. In 1546, Glaidt is mentioned again as a leader in the Jamnitz community of Hutterian Anabaptists.

At some point Glaidt was taken as a prisoner to Vienna. There he was questioned about and tortured for his faith. He refused to recant and in the autumn of 1546 was put to death.

BIBLIOGRAPHY

Liechty, Daniel. "Oswald Glaidt." In *Bibliotheca Dissidentium XI.* Baden Baden, 1987. The definitive work on Glaidt, which includes a complete bibliography of primary and secondary sources, archival references, facsimiles of title pages, and detailed annotation of Glaidt's writings.

DANIEL LIECHTY

GLAREANUS, Heinricus (Ger., Heinrich Loris; 1488–1563), Swiss humanist. Glareanus was born in Mollis as the son of Loris, a councillor of the nearby town of Glarus. After attending school and university in Cologne, he was awarded a master of arts in 1510. In 1512 he was appointed poet laureate by the Habsburg emperor Maximilian I. In the spring of 1514 he moved to Basel, where he became a member of the circle around Desiderius Erasmus of Rotterdam, taught Latin and Greek, and led a student hostel. Upon Erasmus's recommendation, he received a position teaching Greek at the University of Paris (where he also headed a student hostel), before returning to Basel in 1522. Glareanus dissociated himself from the Reformation, which Basel embraced in 1529, and took up a teaching post in poetry at the University of Freiburg im Breisgau, which he held until 1560. During his time in Basel, Glareanus became a recognized authority on questions of education.

Inspired by his model Strabo, he wrote *Helvetiae descriptio* in 1515, and published several works by ancient authors, including the writings of Boethius in 1546. His book *De Geographia,* which dealt with both physical geography and current knowledge of the continents, was used until the seventeenth century and followed Ptolemy and Strabo. His works written for university teaching included *Epitome de sex arithmeticas e practicae speciebus* (printed in Vienna some time after 1529). One main focus of his work was the teaching of music, and he added two pairs of modes based on C (Ionian) and A (Aeolian), the precursors of the modern major and natural minor scales, to the eight medieval church modes already in use. His views on the field of musicology were gathered together in his work *Dodecachordon,* printed in 1547.

BIBLIOGRAPHY

Fritzsche, Otto Fridolin. *Glarean: Sein Leben und seine Schriften.* Frauenfeld, 1890.

Grimm, H. "Heinrich Glareanus." In *Neue Deutsche Bibliographie,* vol. 6, pp. 425–426. Berlin, 1964.

SIEGFRIED HOYER

GNESIO-LUTHERANS. Once accused by a theological opponent of suffering from "theological rabies," the Gnesio-Lutherans were a colorful, loosely bonded group of polemicists who in the late sixteenth century held out for a theology and church practice more consistent with what they considered the true or original form of Lutheranism. The origins of Gnesio-Lutheranism lie in one of the most complex relationships in the Lutheran reform, the friendship between Martin Luther and Philipp Melanchthon. Although Melanchthon is usually placed in Luther's shadow, he and his students—who included virtually all the important theologians of second- and third-generation Lutheranism—saw his standing differently. Melanchthon was an independent theologian who, in spite of his theological alliance and at times close personal friendship with Luther, could differ with him on major issues.

There is evidence, though it is generally nuanced, of a development in Melanchthon's thinking as early as the later 1520s. But it did not lead to controversy. Through the 1530s, when he was responsible for three of the definitive confessions of Lutheranism (the Augsburg Confession, its Apology, and *De potestate et primatu papae tractatus*), Melanchthon remained, with Luther, one of the two major voices of the Lutheran reform.

More significant changes came in the later 1530s and 1540s, when Melanchthon undertook a careful reappraisal of Aristotle. Luther's apocalyptically driven, relationally oriented way of theological reflection had put him at odds with the substantialist ontology of Aristotelianism in matters of law, the human will, and the continuing earthly presence of Christ's humanity. Instead of beginning with structural assumptions about the law as guarantor of an all-pervasive order in creation, the human will as the source of freedom of movement within this order, or an ontological gulf between the divine and the human, Luther had begun relationally with the redemptive work of Christ and in effect thought backward to theological positions that relativized the law, the will, and earthly substance in matters of faith. Rethinking what he had earlier held with Luther, Melanchthon began to have serious questions on these issues.

Reasoning from the justification of the godless to the assumptions required to support it theologically, Luther concluded that if Christ justifies, the law cannot. The gospel identifies the law as a functionary that, while having some essential ancillary uses, cannot save. By the same token, if Christ saves sinners, Luther reasoned, the will implicated in sin cannot have any part in the saving. The will is not a neutral human characteristic but under alien powers that require that the self be put to death and created anew. Similarly, if Christ delivers the godless, he must necessarily be physically present with them at some point, namely, where Luther believed Christ had promised to be present, in the Sacrament of the altar.

Convinced of the essential accuracy of Luther's dialectical reasoning, Melanchthon at the same time wanted to rehabilitate Aristotle for theological purposes. So he attempted modifications, making a legal world structure a prior assumption, seeking a passive but essential role for the will, and proposing language that would allow talk of Christ's presence without apparently compromising the difference between the finite and the infinite.

A contributing factor in the controversies that followed is the way Melanchthon proposed these modifications. Instead of addressing the issues head on, he relied on political skills, setting out questions and some proposed answers through students; making subtle but dramatic changes in texts, such as an altered edition of the Augsburg Confession in 1540, without giving an accounting of himself; and so forth. The result was a distrust that fed the controversies.

The real trouble started in 1548, when Charles V, the Holy Roman Emperor, sought a pragmatic settlement following his defeat of the Lutherans in the Schmalkald War. Here Charles had succeeded where he had failed ever since Luther had faced him at the Diet of Worms: he had broken the political power base of the Lutheran reform. Some significant problems remained, however. Charles could not obtain the support of the papacy to resolve the conflict; neither could he gain the consent of the governed that was needed, even in the sixteenth century, to reap the fruits of his victory.

Charles solved the immediate political problem in electoral Saxony, which had supported the Lutheran reform from the beginning, by handing it over to the duke of Saxony, Moritz, who had been seeking to reunite the two Saxonies and had joined forces with Charles for this purpose. But that still left the theological-religious problem unsolved. So Moritz went to work with Melanchthon. Luther having died two years earlier, Melanchthon was the apparent theological leader of the Lutheran reform. His cooperation was essential to any settlement of the conflict that had begun with the reform.

Melanchthon faced a dilemma of his own, caught between Moritz, Charles, and the Lutherans. He attempted to appease, in the meantime advancing his own theological agenda. Conceding to Charles, Melanchthon argued that a Christian must honor the emperor, at the same time writing to friends deploring the necessity of concessions. Under pressure from Lutheran critics, Melanchthon argued that he was giving ground only in matters that had no clear biblical mandate. At the same time, he saw opportunity to modify some of the original formulations of Lutheranism to make them more conducive to his own subsequent theological developments.

The immediate result was the Leipzig Interim, a document that lay at the root of the next two decades of conflict within Lutheranism. In consultation with Moritz, now the elector, and some of his own students, Melanchthon drafted the first two parts of a theological statement to submit to the emperor as a confession that would govern church life and practice in Saxony. The document opens with a statement urging loyalty to the emperor and invoking the concept of adiaphora, defined as "matters of indifference that may be observed without injury to the divine scriptures."

Melanchthon's two parts concerned justification and good works. In the first, Melanchthon included the participation of the will as an essential element of justification, emphasizing the full participation of the self in faith. In the second, he argued for the necessity of good works as "so highly necessary that if they are not quickened in the heart there is no reception of divine grace." The final form of the document emerged through further negotiation, statements being added supporting the restoration of liturgical forms and churchly practices that previously had been rejected in the Lutheran reform.

The Leipzig Interim drew immediate fire from some of the cities that had been members of the Schmalkald League. But a more colorful exchange occurred in Wittenberg itself. Melanchthon's personal secretary at the time was his brilliant Croatian student, Matthias Flacius Illyricus. Ferociously opposed to any concession, Flacius Illyricus took it upon himself to resolve the difference between Melanchthon's public and private selves by publishing letters in which Melanchthon professed disgust with the concessions he was making. Since Melanchthon was under Moritz's protection, Flacius Illyricus was forced to flee the city around Easter of 1549.

Flacius Illyricus spent virtually the rest of his life on the run. He went first to Magdeburg, joining forces with Luther's old friend, Nikolaus von Amsdorf, the two becoming the most important representatives of the Gnesio-Lutherans faction. From there, Flacius Illyricus went to the University of Jena in 1557, where he taught for four years before controversy forced him out. Forty-one at the time, he spent the rest of his life in exile, moving from one brief residence to another. He died in 1575.

Although he could not match Flacius Illyricus's scholarly output, Amsdorf was equally at home in polemics. A nephew of Luther's old mentor, Johann von Staupitz, Amsdorf served on the Wittenberg faculty with Luther and was an early advocate of the Lutheran reform. He later became one of the first Lutheran bishops.

Behind Flacius Illyricus and Amsdorf were a number of lesser-known theologians and pastors who participated in the various controversies: Johann Wigand, Matthaeus Judex, and Nicolaus Gallus, pastors in Magdeburg who later dispersed to Jena and Regensburg; Andreas Poach, pastor in Erfurt later identified, with his brother-in-law Anton Otto, by the Gnesio-Lutherans themselves as Antinomians; Joachim Westphal in southern Saxony; and Tilemann Hesshus from Rostock, who later joined the faculty at Jena.

Unlike their opponents (Melanchthon's adherents, known as Philippists), the Gnesio-Lutherans were not very cohesive. The Philippists stayed in Wittenberg, though Melanchthon had supporters at other universities, such as Viktorin Strigel in Jena. The Gnesio-Lutherans, sometimes called the "Flacians" or "adiaphorists," were often at odds with political leaders, had no sure base of support or organization, and were sometimes divided among themselves.

One strong uniting factor among the Gnesio-Lutherans was their willingness to pursue controversy to the bitter end. Their claim to historical memory is rooted in a series of six controversies, each of them related closely though not always directly to Melanchthon's theological difficulties. Their claim to be reaching over Melanchthon's experimentation back to the original Lutheran consensus gave them the name "gnesio-," the pure or original Lutherans.

The first of these controversies, the adiaphorist, was the direct result of Melanchthon's use of the term in the Leipzig Interim. With Flacius Illyricus in the lead, the Gnesio-Lutherans argued adamantly that while there may religious matters without a biblical mandate that may therefore be left to the choice of the individual, an adiaphoron loses its character as such when it is placed under command. When the state or church invades matters of biblical indifference, making requirements where believers should be free to choose, the believer must by the very nature of the command resist the claim.

The second of the controversies was more extended, resulting in excesses that forced Flacius Illyricus out of a job and brought about his theological condemnation. Known as the synergist controversy, it grew out of Melanchthon's inclusion of the human will as a force in conversion. After polemical exchanges that extended through the 1550s, in 1560 Flacius Illyricus engaged the Philippist Viktorin Strigel in a public debate. Having painted himself into a theological corner with Strigel's assistance, Flacius Illyricus wound up arguing that one cannot distinguish between nature as created and human nature in sin. Strigel accused him of Manichaeanism, Flacius Illyricus lost his position at the university, and he was eventually repudiated for this teaching by the Lutheran Formula of Concord.

Melanchthon's assertion of a necessity of good works resulted in the third controversy, named for one of his adherents, Georg Major. Major had joined the Wittenberg faculty in 1545. He entered a battle from which Melanchthon backed away and found himself engaged with Nikolaus von Amsdorf, who matched him evenly in strident declarations: if Major claimed that good works are necessary to salvation, Amsdorf would gladly argue that they actually damage it.

More a series of controversies than one compact set of exchanges, the antinomian controversy extended in stages from the late 1520s into the 1570s before being settled in the Formula of Concord. It was the first public theological conflict in the Lutheran reform. In the summer of 1528 Melanchthon and Johann Agricola squared off, Agricola subsequently arguing that the law has no place in the church. Agricola joined the Wittenberg faculty in 1536 and a second stage of the controversy began, this one with Luther and lasting until 1539. Then in the 1550s a group of pastors—all of them married to nuns from the town of Nordhausen—were accused, along with Andreas Musculus, the brother-in-law of Johann Agricola, of teaching antinomianism because they questioned Melanchthon's claim to a place for the law—the so-called third use—in teaching the believer to do good works. These "later antinomians," as they are sometimes called, were opposed by both the Philippists and their other Gnesio-Lutheran colleagues. A side issue in the 1550s, more quickly settled, concerned the method of defining the law.

The fifth controversy was the crypto-Calvinist controversy. The Philippists had become more and more sympathetic to Calvinist language concerning Christ's presence in the Lord's Supper. Indeed, Melanchthon's son-in-law and others became Calvinists when the Formula of Concord sided against them. Those who did not affirm the presence of the human nature of Christ along with the divine at Communion were considered "crypto-," or hidden, Calvinists.

A theologian who succeeded in uniting the Philippists and the Gnesio-Lutherans against himself was Andreas Osiander. Pastor in Nuremberg and like many other Lutheran theologians (including Melanchthon) a sophisticated amateur astronomer, Osiander was convinced that Melanchthon had caused his own theological problems by sundering the relationship between faith and good works. Osiander attempted to reconnect the two by speaking of an indwelling of the believer by the divine nature of Christ that results in moral renewal. Both parties denounced him for arbitrarily dividing the two natures of Christ. Thus the sixth controversy is remembered as the Osiandrian.

Relations between the Gnesio-Lutherans and church and state followed a paradoxical course. Although their common penchant for polemical overkill earned them regular condemnation, the Gnesio-Lutherans succeeded in capturing Lutheranism's agenda for the generations that followed. The Formula of Concord repudiated Melanchthon's modifications, reasserting the theological consensus that Luther and Melanchthon had together forged in the earlier Lutheran confessions, all of them written between 1528 and 1537.

Similarly, while the Gnesio-Lutherans' support for resistance of the emperor kept them in some tension with other political leaders, they won enough confidence to survive. They made their imprint on the politics of the Lutheran confessions and later Lutheranism with the beginnings of a sophisticated theory of resistance that was further developed in article 11 of the formula and may well have influenced the Calvinist doctrine of the lesser magistrates. Against the background of some of Luther's early, less qualified counsel to obedience and Melanchthon's capitulation, the Gnesio-Lutherans and the Formula of Concord represent a real advance. When the state demands that obedience be rendered as a matter of faith, Christians do not have merely the right or alternative but the duty to resist.

But if the hands were Esau's, the voice was still Jacob's. Melanchthon was the teacher of the Gnesio-Lutherans as much as of the Philippists. While rejecting his modifications, the Gnesio-Lutherans and the generation that entrenched the tradition they venerated continued to carry forward Melanchthon's theological assumptions. So Lutheran orthodoxy attempted to carry off a friendship that Luther could not have accepted, between himself and Aristotle. To a surprising extent, they succeeded.

[*See also* Amsdorf, Nikolaus von; Andreae, Laurentius; Brenz, Johannes; Flacius Illyricus, Matthias; Formula of Concord; Lutheranism; *and* Philippists.]

BIBLIOGRAPHY

Primary Sources

Confessio et Apologia Pastorum & reliquorum ministrorum Ecclesiae Magdeburgenesis. Magdeburg, 1550.

Flacius Illyricus, Matthias. *Catalogus testium veritatis: Qui ante nostram aetatem reclamorunt Papae.* Basel, 1556.

Secondary Sources

Brecht, Martin, and Reinhard Schwarz, eds. *Bekenntnis und Einheit der Kirche: Studien zum Konkordienbuch.* Stuttgart, 1980.

Haikola, Lauri. *Gesetz und Evangelium bei Matthias Flacius Illyricus: Eine Untersuchung zur Lutherischen Theologie vor der Konkordien formel.* Reprint, Erlangen, 1981.

Kolb, Robert. *Nikolaus von Amsdorf (1483–1565): Popular Polemics in the Preservation of Luther's Legacy.* Nieuwkoop, 1978.

Preus, Robert D. *The Theology of Post-Reformation Lutheranism: A Study of Theological Prolegomena.* Vol. 2, *God and His Creation.* Saint Louis, 1972.

Spitz, Lewis W., and Wenzel Lohff, eds. *Discord, Dialog, and Concord: Studies in the Lutheran Reformation's Formula of Concord.* Philadelphia, 1977.

James Arne Nestingen

GODIMELUS, Claude. *See* Goudimel, Claude.

GODPARENTAGE.

The sponsorship of a child at baptism is known as godparentage. In the Middle Ages baptism was seen as a spiritual birth that created spiritual kinship between the participants in the sacrament (the baptized child, the baptizing priest, the natural parents, and the sponsors). Spiritual kinship included two relationships: a vertical one between godparent and godchild (*patrinatus*, "godparenthood") and a horizontal one between the natural parents and the sponsors (*compaternitas*, "coparenthood"). The latter relationship held greater social significance for the laity of the late Middle Ages; coparenthood created formal obligations of friendship, respect, and mutual aid. Incest taboos applied to spiritual kin: "spiritual affinity" was an impediment prohibiting marriage between godparent and godchild, between natural parents and sponsors, and between sponsors. This prohibition was extended to spouses and offspring of the participants as well.

A child had at least one godparent of each sex (*patrinus*, "godfather"; *madrina*, "godmother"); natural parents were not allowed to sponsor their own child. In the late Middle Ages the number of godparents multiplied. Ecclesiastical synods tried to limit the number to three (two of the same sex as the child, one of the opposite sex) or at most four. However, groups of six or eight godparents were common, and groups of twenty are recorded. Both Catholic and Protestant reformers criticized the laity's emphasis on the secular and social aspects of spiritual kinship, the lavishness of christening feasts and gifts, and the complex marriage impediments created by multiple godparents.

The official duties of godparents were to present the infant at the baptismal font and state its name, to make the baptismal vows on behalf of the child, and to give the child religious instruction (specifically, to teach the Apostles' Creed and the Lord's Prayer). The senior godparent of the same sex was responsible for choosing the child's name and in England usually gave it his or her own name. Godparents gave the godchild gifts at the christening feast and sometimes also later in childhood. Some mentioned godchildren in their wills.

Godparents might be chosen either to intensify existing ties of kinship or to extend social networks based on friendship or on patron-client relationships. Blood relatives were frequently chosen; even children were admitted as godparents provided they were close kin of the baptized child. However, close relatives were not chosen as godparents by merchants in Florence or by peasants in England and Germany. Here, godparents were probably more often chosen to extend social networks, either by making stronger connections to distant kin or by reinforcing ties to friends and patrons. Patrons were particularly important for nobles, but they were also significant for other social groups; peasants in England, France, and Germany frequently had one of the local gentry as a godparent. Groups of godparents often combined one or more patrons of higher status with friends and neighbors of the parents' own social level. After the Reformation, the necessity of choosing godparents from one's own faith meant that godparentage served to reinforce alliances with co-religionists.

Despite Catholic and Protestant reformers' criticisms of godparentage in its late medieval form, only Anabaptists and other sects that rejected infant baptism abolished the institution entirely. The major reformers retained baptismal sponsorship but tried to "purify" it by emphasizing the liturgical and educational functions of godparenthood and eliminating or reducing coparenthood.

Protestant reformers rejected spiritual kinship entirely. Luther denounced marriage impediments based on spiritual affinity as a device to make money. However, he considered godparents useful for religious education, particularly if the parents were dead or otherwise unable to provide instruction. The Church of England also retained godparents in their traditional form but eliminated spiritual affinity as a marriage impediment.

Calvin implied that fathers should present their own children for baptism, an argument followed by some English Puritans. The baptismal rites of the Reformed churches retained sponsors, but the duty of presenting the child was shared with the natural parents and the congregation.

Catholic reformers retained the concept of spiritual kinship but restricted its application. In 1563 the Council of Trent adopted canons limiting the number of godparents to one of each sex and specifying that marriage impediments applied only to the principal participants. These rules only gradually took effect at the local level.

During the seventeenth and eighteenth centuries, the importance of godparentage as a social institution waned in Protestant northern and western Europe, and coparenthood disappeared completely. Spiritual kinship remained significant in Catholic southern Europe, especially in Italy and Iberia, and in Latin America, where coparenthood (*compadrazgo*) remains a vital social institution today.

BIBLIOGRAPHY

Bossy, John. "Blood and Baptism: Kinship, Community and Christianity in Western Europe from the Fourteenth to the Seventeenth Centuries." In *Sanctity and Secularity: The Church and the World*, edited by Derek Baker, pp. 129–143. Studies in Church History 10. Oxford, 1973. Deals with godparentage as one of the devices used to create alliances and maintain peace within the parish community.

———. "Godparenthood: The Fortunes of a Social Institution in Early Modern Europe." In *Religion and Society in Early Modern Europe*, edited by Kaspar von Geyerz, pp. 194–201. London, 1984. Discusses the social function of godparentage in late medieval Catholicism and analyzes why the institution fell into discredit in the sixteenth century.

Hanawalt, Barbara. *The Ties That Bound: Peasant Families in Medieval England.* Oxford, 1986. Brief discussion of social aspects of godparentage, with examples drawn from legal documents.

Houlbrooke, Ralph A. *The English Family, 1450–1700*. London, 1984. Brief discussion of baptism and naming practices based on autobiographical materials; stresses changes brought about by the Reformation.

Klapisch-Zuber, Christiane. *Women, Family, and Ritual in Renaissance Italy.* Translated by Lydia G. Cochrane. Chicago, 1985. Translation of articles originally published in French in various sources. Includes discussion of godparent choice and naming practices among Florentine merchants, based on family record books.

Lynch, Joseph H. *Godparents and Kinship in Early Medieval Europe.* Princeton, 1986. The most comprehensive and authoritative treatment of spiritual kinship in Western Europe. Discusses the historiography of the institution from the Middle Ages to the present (including works by anthropologists and literary scholars); summarizes the views of sixteenth-century reformers.

Marshall, Sherrin. *The Dutch Gentry, 1500–1650*. New York, 1987. Includes statistical analysis of godparent choice based on genealogies of Dutch gentry families.

Minsk, Sidney W., and Eric R. Wolf. "An Analysis of Ritual Co-parenthood (Compadrazgo)." *Southwestern Journal of Anthropology* 6 (1950), 341–368. The historical portion of this article, long the standard reference for anthropologists, introduces the classification of godparent choice as "intensifying" or "extending" relationships. See critique in Lynch of its reliance on canon law sources and its dated concept of feudal society.

Shahar, Shulamith. *Childhood in the Middle Ages*. London, 1990. Brief discussion emphasizing emotional relationship between godparent and godchild, drawn chiefly from saints' lives and other literary sources.

JUDITH J. HURWICH

GOLDSCHMIED, Johannes. *See* Aurifaber, Johannes.

GOMARUS, Franciscus (1563–1641), Dutch Reformed minister and theologian; leading representative of a predestinarian Calvinist theology in the Netherlands and strong opponent of Arminianism. Gomarus and his family, who were from the city of Brugge in the Walloon-Flemish border region of the Low Countries, became religious refugees after they embraced the Reformed faith in the 1570s. Under Spanish pressure, Gomarus's family was forced to flee Brugge for the Palatinate in the late 1570s. Gomarus had learned Latin and Greek at an early age, and when he was fourteen he began three years of study in Strasbourg with the already famous German humanist Johannes Sturm. In 1582 and 1583 Gomarus studied at Oxford and Cambridge; at the latter he came under the influence of the Calvinist William Whitaker. In 1585 he returned to Germany and studied with the Calvinists at the University of Heidelberg; two years later he was called to serve as pastor of the refugee Walloon Reformed church in Frankfurt am Main.

Gomarus left Frankfurt in 1594 to take up a position as professor of theology at the University of Leiden; here in the early 1600s he became involved in an intense theological controversy with Jacobus Arminius over predestination. This controversy and further disappointment over the appointment of Arminius's successor, Conradus Vorstius—whose orthodoxy, particularly on the Trinity, Gomarus had challenged—led Gomarus to resign from Leiden in 1611. He served briefly as minister in the Reformed church at Middelburg and then moved to the Protestant seminary in Saumur, France (1614–1618). He ended his career as a professor of theology at the University of Groningen, a center of Calvinist orthodoxy in the northern Netherlands.

Gomarus was deeply influenced by the theology of Théodore de Bèze, Calvin's successor at Geneva, and in Gomarus's theological system supralapsarian predestination became the central doctrine. At Leiden Arminius questioned and rejected Gomarus's predestinarian theology, and in this context Gomarus's frequent writings and disputations with Arminius on predestination became especially important. The controversy began in earnest in 1604, although Gomarus had earlier challenged Arminius's appointment in theology at the university. Repeated attempts at reconciliation between Arminius and Gomarus—often sponsored by the States of Holland—failed, and from 1605 until Arminius's death in 1609 the battle was both rancorous and public. Gomarus's predestinarian Calvinism lay behind the Contra-Remonstrance of 1611, and the Contra-Remonstrant party was closely associated with Gomarus's theology even after his resignation from Leiden.

At the Synod of Dordrecht (1618/19) Gomarus represented the University of Groningen and was extremely vocal in his criticism of Arminian theology, helping secure the condemnation of the Remonstrants at this international gathering of Reformed theologians. Although the synod did not officially adopt Gomarus's extreme supralapsarianism, his predestinarian theology exercised considerable influence in the Netherlands and throughout the international Reformed community.

The Synod of Dordrecht also commissioned an official translation of the Bible for use in the Dutch Reformed church, and Gomarus was involved in the work on the Old Testament. He is perhaps best known for his polemical writings on predestination, and shortly after his death a multivolume collection of his theological works appeared (1644).

BIBLIOGRAPHY

Bangs, Carl. *Arminius: A Study in the Dutch Reformation.* 2d ed. Reprint, Grand Rapids, Mich., 1985. An excellent introduction to the theological controversy between Arminius and Gomarus.

Deursen, A. Th. van. *Bavianen en Slijkgeuzen: Kerk en Kerkvolk ten tijde van Maurits en Oldenbarnevelt.* Reprint, Franeker, 1991. Based on extensive archival research. The single best work on the development of Calvinism in the Netherlands and the significance of the Arminian controversy.

Itterzon, G. P. van. *Franciscus Gomarus.* Reprint, Groningen, 1979. The standard biography on Gomarus.

Nobbs, Douglas. *Theocracy and Toleration: A Study of Disputes in Dutch Calvinism from 1600 to 1650.* Cambridge, 1938. A detailed source of information but not readily available.

Tex, Jan den. *Oldenbarnevelt.* 2 vols. Translated by R. B. Powell. Cambridge, 1973. Excellent on the political context of the Arminian controversy.

MICHAEL A. HAKKENBERG

GOOD WORKS. With the Reformation an intense dispute broke out over the religious basis and value of good works. In the medieval church good works were, theologically speaking, those works that people who according to the Church were in a state of grace performed in order to attain eternal life. There was agreement that one could also perform morally good works without the church's conferral of grace, but these did not merit eternal life. Caritas (charity) was presupposed as the motive and regulator of religiously good and meritorious works. According to the order of charity, it is to be directed first of all toward God. Works of ecclesiastical religiosity, such as prayer, fasting, alms, and the works of the monastic life, if performed while the doer is in a state of grace, have a higher worth than other works, which are not so directly related to God. Meritorious works are required for eternal life, because on Judgment Day Christ will judge Christians according to their works. The habitual state of grace, bestowed in baptism and continually renewed through the sacrament of penance, demands to be actualized in good works willed in charity. For this reason, good works are necessary for justification. A special point of dispute in the medieval church was whether the commandments of the Decalogue as such required meritorious good works, or if the merit of the works was additionally required for eternal life. The second opinion was overwhelmingly preferred.

The question of which human works deserve to be defined as good received a new answer when Reformation theology, as a result of the notion of justification by faith alone, asserted that everything that does not proceed from faith is sin (*Rom.* 14:23). In one's responsibility before God, one therefore cannot divide works into moral works that, however, are religiously not meritorious, and religiously good works that by virtue of charity are supernaturally molded and are thus meritorious for eternal life. According to Reformation teaching, the Decalogue as such requires in its proper, deepest meaning a life of pure trust in God. The Decalogue requires works that one can perform only from a faith in the God of grace grounded in Christ. Luther emphasized that faith in Christ did not allow Christians to separate from their own religiously neutral works those works that might be morally good. In society one may be judged only according to moral standards. But before God, one may only confess to be a sinner, despite all of one's works, and only in this can one experience through the gospel God's affirmation.

Living faith brings forth good works as its "fruits" (*Mt.* 7:17; 12:23); otherwise it is not genuine faith that binds to Christ those who are conscious of their sins and trust in God's mercy. If good works are seen as fruits of faith, the metaphor "fruits" indicates that good works, which faith brings forth in unison with God's will, do not come about from a supplemental motivation and power of the human will. Good works that proceed from faith also are not meritorious with regard to eternal life. Luther makes especially clear that in the gospel present and future salvation do not split apart analogous to merit and reward. What saves one on Judgment Day is not good works but one's connection to Christ through faith. Some of Luther's students did not hold unconditionally to the unity of present and future salvation and disagreed over the question of whether good works were necessary for eternal life.

Reformation theology attacked the higher value placed on works in the monastic life. Equally it challenged the necessity of requiring good works through ecclesiastical mandates, over and above the Decalogue. All works that are done responsibly before God have the same spiritual value. Before God the work of a handmaid is worth no less than the work of any other profession. The Reformation insisted that a pastor in his vocation was simply a member of society. Since the members of monastic orders were virtually inactive with regard to charity in society, and Reformation theology rejected monastic vows for theological reasons, there was no longer any room for monastic life. The difference between religious and secular works disappeared, because men and women had to realize that they were equally responsible before God for all of their works.

Roman Catholic authors expressly contradicted the Reformation notion of good works in all the main points. The Council of Trent embodied this rejection in the *Decretum de iustificatione* (chaps. 10, 11, 16) and in the canons (canons 24–28, 32). A few works with relatively extensive expositions of the controversial issue have recently appeared in new critical editions. In chronological order of their composition they are listed here with pertinent chapters cited: Johann Eck, *Enchiridion locorum communium adversus Lutherum et alios hostes ecclesiae*, 1525, reprint, Münster, 1979, chap. 5; Nicholas Herborn, *Locorum communium adversus huius temporis haereses enchiridion*, 1529, reprint, Münster, 1927, chaps. 4–7; Johann Dietenberger, *Phimostomus scripturariorum*, 1532, reprint, Münster, 1985, chaps. 8–10; and Gasparo Contarini, *Confutatio articulorum seu quaestionum Lutheranorum*, c.1530–1535, in *Gegenreformatorische Schriften*, Münster, 1923, a. 1 and 2. The consensus of these authors concerning the doctrine of good works shows that the differences between medieval Scholastic attitudes and the anti-Reformation front were not substantial.

[*See also* Faith; Grace; *and* Justification.]

BIBLIOGRAPHY

Contarini, Gasparo. "Confutatio articulorum seu quaestionum Lutheranorum" (c.1530–1535). In *Gegenreformatorische Schriften*, edited by Friedrich Hünermann. Münster, 1923.

Dietenberger, Johannes. *Phimostomus scripturariorum* (1532). Münster, 1985. See chaps. 8–10.

Eck, Johannes. *Enchiridion locorum communium adversus Lutherum et alios hostes ecclesiae* (1525). Münster, 1979. See chap. 5.

Herborn, Nicholas. *Locorum communium adversus huius temporis haereses enchiridion* (1529). Münster, 1927. See chaps. 4–7.

REINHARD SCHWARZ

Translated from German by Jeff Bach

GOUDIMEL, Claude (Lat., Godimelus; c.1520–1572), French Protestant composer and music publisher. He was born in Besançon but nothing is known of Goudimel's youth. In 1549 he studied at the University or Paris and was appointed in 1551 as proofreader by the publisher Nicolas du Chemin. The next year he became du Chemin's partner and remained so until 1555. He resided in the Protestant city of Metz between 1557 and 1567.

Goudimel was involved in both the humanist and Calvinist movements. He met Jean de Brinon, to whom he dedicated his *Premier Livre de Psaumes* (1551). He set to music Ronsard's odes and sonnets from *Les Amours*. He sent his last letter to the German humanist Paul Schedius (Melissus) on 23 August 1572 and died in Lyon between 28 and 31 August, a victim of the Saint Bartholemew's Day Massacre.

According to his humanist wish to return "*ad fontes*," Goudimel composed *Horatian Odes* (1555). Although this work is not extant, it is mentioned by F. Salinas (*De Musica*, 1578) and Jacques-Charles Brunet (*Manuel du Libraire*, 1810). These settings probably resembled those by German musicians such as Petrus Tritonius (1507), Ludwig Senfl (1534), and Paul von Hofhaimer (1538), in the *nota contra notam* style, with the melody mainly in the tenor part, according to the principles of the *Musique mesurée à l'Antique*, taking into account the long and short syllables and thus assuring text intelligibility. The same homorhythmic and homosyllabic style is applied to some of Goudimel's *Psaumes* in paraphrases by Clément Marot (49) and Théodore de Bèze (101), with the Huguenot melody placed usually in the tenor, but sometimes in the soprano, for singing "ès-maisons" ("at home"). These compositions were borrowed by Ambrosius Lobwasser in his Psalter (Leipzig, 1573); *Dès qu'adversité nous offense* became *Zu Gott wir unsre Zuflucht haben*. Alongside this functional style, showing how humanist and church music traditions fused, Goudimel cultivated the motet and imitative counterpoint styles both with and without Genevan melodies.

As a typical sixteenth-century musician, Goudimel composed Latin Works: three magnificats, ten motets for four or five voices, five masses, as well as French secular and sacred *chansons*. The complete works of this important Protestant composer are published by Peirre Pidoux and others (Institute of Medieval Music 1967–1983).

BIBLIOGRAPHY

Egan-Buffet, Maire. *Les chansons de Claude Goudimel: Analyses modales et stylistiques*. Ottawa, 1992.

Goudimel, Claude. *Oeuvres complètes*. 14 vols. New York and Basel, 1967–1983.

Häusler, Rudolf. *Satztechnik und Form in Claude Goudimel's lateinischen Werken*. Bern, 1968. Concerns Latin masses, Magnificats, and motets and Goudimel's compositional technic.

McChesney, Lawry. *The Psalm Motets of Claude Goudimel*. Ph.D. diss., Columbia University, 1954. Deals with motets for three, four, five, and six voices on French paraphrases by Clément Marot and Théodore de Bèze.

Pidoux, Pierre. "Notes sur quelques éditions de Psaumes de Claude Goudimel." *Revue de Musicologie* 42, (1958).

Trillat, Ennemond. *Claude Goudimel, le Psautier huguenot et la Saint Barthélémy lyonnaise*. Lyon, 1949. Introduction to Goudimel's settings of the Huguenot psalter and to the events of the Saint Bartholomew's Day Massacre in Lyon (1572).

Weber, Édith, *La musique protestante de langue française*. Paris, 1979. This work is a survey of French Protestant music, mainly Huguenot psalms.

Édith Weber

GOULART, Simon (1543–1628), French Protestant minister and writer, one of the more prominent pastors of the church in Geneva. Goulart was born in the town of Senlis in the province of Picardy, France. After beginning study for a legal career, he converted to Protestantism and moved to Geneva in 1566. Soon after arriving, he was appointed pastor of the village churches of Chancy and Cartigny, located within Geneva's hinterland. He married into a prominent Genevan family and, in 1571, was assigned to the city's working-class parish of Saint Gervais, where he spent most of the rest of his career. On occasion Goulart returned to France, where he happened to be during the Saint Bartholomew's Day Massacre, and narrowly escaped with his life. He served as moderator of the Geneva Compagnie des Pasteurs from 1605 to 1612 and was acknowledged to be the company's dean, or senior member, from 1605 to 1628. He occasionally got into trouble for his harsh criticisms of city magistrates or French Protestant princes who did not, in his view, live up to the standards of their faith, but he was always able to return to full service.

Goulart was a prolific writer, and one of the most widely published leaders of the Genevan Reformation in the generation after Calvin. He was basically a popularizer rather than an original thinker and devoted most of his energies to translations and to compendia of historical and political texts. They have become sources of basic importance for the modern understanding of the early Reformation in France. The first, titled the *Mémoires de l'estat de France sous Charles neufiesme*...(Geneva, 1576 and ff.), was a collection of three volumes of treatises provoked by the Saint Bartholomew's Day Massacre, tied together with a running commentary. It was designed to persuade French Protestants to take arms against the country's monarchical government, which had supported an attempt to annihilate their movement, and to win support and sympathy in other Protestant countries for their cause. It included such classics of Protestant resistance theory as François Hotman's *Francogallia* and Théodore de Bèze's *Du droit des magistrats*, which call for a basic change in the very form of government, arguing against absolutism and for protection of human rights. In his similar *Mémoires de la Ligue*... (Geneva, 1589 and ff.), Goulart compiled treatises designed to support the campaigns of the Protestant Henry of Navarre to become Henry IV of France on the death of Henry III, last of the Valois kings, against the military resistance of the Catholic League, which was led by princes of the House of Guise and encouraged by both Spain and the papacy. Goulart also participated prominently in the compilation of the *Histoire ecclésiastique des Eglises réformées au royaume de France*. . . (Geneva, 1580 and ff.), the standard official history of the early Protestant Reformation in France, often attributed to his senior colleague, Théodore de Bèze. Among his many translations into French were works of his colleagues Bèze and Hotman.

BIBLIOGRAPHY

Bautz, Friedrich Wilhelm, ed. *Biographische-Bibliographisches Kirchenlexikon*. Hamm, 1970–. See vol. 2, p. 278.

Choisy, Eugène. *L'état chrétien calviniste à Genève au temps de Théodore de Bèze*. Geneva, 1902. Useful description of relations between the state and church in a period when Goulart was a leading actor.

Jones, Leonard Chester. *Simon Goulart, 1543–1628*. Geneva, 1917. Standard biography, based on exhaustive research and accompanied by a full bibliography of Goulart's publications.

Kingdon, Robert M. *Myths about the Saint Bartholomew's Day Massacres, 1572–1576*. Cambridge, Mass., 1988. Primarily a detailed analysis of Goulart's *Mémoires de l'Estat de France sous Charles neufiesme*.

Verzeichnis der im deutschen Sprachbereich erschienenen Drucke des XVI. Jahrhunderts. Stuttgart, 1983–. See vol. 8, nos. 2707–2708.

Robert M. Kingdon

GOVERNMENT. *See* Magistracy; Secular Magistrate, Office of.

GRACE. In general, an unmerited assistance from God, especially as it pertains to salvation, grace was a central issue for all parties in the sixteenth-century Reformation. All inherited the problematic bequeathed to the Western church by Augustine's distinctive understanding of grace as the interior transformation of the sinner by the very presence of God. Augustine's writings against Pelagius, such as *De spiritu et littera* (On the Spirit and the Letter), were background shared by all sides. Nearly all the sixteenth-century contestants favored strong versions of Augustine's insistence on the necessity of God's gracious initiative for salvation (salvation by "grace alone"); the ways parted over other conceptual and pastoral problems, none of them entirely new, posed by Augustine's legacy. Three closely related problems, each of which had a long history before becoming a flash point of controversy in the Reformation era, may provide this survey with an orientation.

First, the Christian tradition before Augustine had thought of grace primarily in terms of reconciliation and the forgiveness of sins bestowed in baptism. Augustine had no intention of contesting this, but his definition of grace as inner cleansing left an open question concerning the relationship between renewal and forgiveness.

Second, Augustine's stress on the interiority of grace generated questions about the mediation of grace. Augustine by no means questioned the centrality of the sacraments, but his theology of grace, especially combined with certain aspects of his Neoplatonic ontology, does not offer a clear account of how inward, spiritual grace can be communicated by an external, material sign.

Third, if grace is the inward working of the transcendent God, and its relationship to both forgiveness and participation in the sacraments is ambiguous, then there arises a question about the certitude of grace. It is not clear how, on Augustine's terms, one could ever be sure that God had forgiven one's sins. When this is coupled with changes in the practice of sacramental penance during the late Middle Ages, the stage is set for a serious pastoral problem of the "troubled conscience."

Martin Luther. Although the early theological development of Martin Luther (1483–1546) remains controversial, in his 1519 *Sermo de duplici iusitia* (Sermon on the Two Kinds of Righteousness) he had arrived at a concretely Christocentric account of grace and of the relationship of transformation and forgiveness. To receive grace is to receive Christ himself: "By faith in Christ the righteousness of Christ becomes ours along with all that is his, or rather he himself becomes ours" (WA 2:146). Faith takes hold of the divine-human person of Christ, who dwells in the heart of the believer, and in this union with Christ the believer receives both forgiveness and renewal at once.

In other works Luther speaks of forgiveness and renewal in terms of grace and gift (*Romans* 5:15), taking "grace" in the strict sense of "God's favor." "Grace renders one wholly pleasing so that one's person is altogether accepted, and there is no longer any place for wrath in one, while the gift heals one from sin and from all one's corruption of soul and body" (WA 8:107). God "imputes" the righteousness of Christ to those who are united with him by faith so that they are forgiven and accounted as righteous before God for Christ's sake (grace); at the same time, Christ's Spirit begins to struggle against sin within them (gift). "To be reputed righteous and to receive the Holy Spirit are the same thing" (WA 2:511). Thus, there is no forgiveness without renewal and no renewal without forgiveness, yet forgiveness is not conditioned on renewal but on the presence in the heart of the Christ who is also always the source of renewal. The ground of both is faith's engagement with the present Christ.

This engagement takes place concretely in the sinner's encounter with the external "word of promise" in preaching and sacrament. Luther accepted the medieval definition of the sacraments as "signs which confer grace" (itself a response to the Augustinian problematic), with the strong qualification that this "conferring" be understood as an act of communication that calls for faith. Luther explicates this with the concept of promise: the external word of God communicates grace by promising it, and one can accept a promise only by faith and trust. "Where there is the word of God making a promise, there the faith of the human being accepting it is necessary, so that it is clear that the beginning of our salvation is faith, which hangs on the word of the promising God" (WA 6:514).

This account of Christ present through the external word of promise, to be grasped by faith, which thereby receives both forgiveness and renewal at once, constitutes the basic structure of Luther's theology of grace. Neither of its two poles can be reduced to the other; to talk of Christ without the word or the word without Christ is to misconstrue grace fatally. Rather, one could say that union with Christ is the inner mystery of grace, while the word of promise is the form of its concrete entry into human experience. "The sound of the promise to Abraham brings Christ, and when he is grasped by faith the Holy Spirit is given immediately for Christ's sake" (WA 40/1:401).

Luther's answer to the problem of certitude, perhaps his most controversial teaching, follows the logic of this account of grace. The believer's certainty is grounded first on the identity of Christ himself as the one who is "for us" (*pro nobis*). Christ is not, Luther never tires of saying, a "new Moses," a giver of laws. The one whom faith grasps is "the Son of God who surrendered himself to redeem me out of sheer love" (WA 40/1:296). Confidence in Christ, however, becomes concrete through the word of promise, which presently bestows the gift and grace of this Christ on those who hear it.

Here again Luther exploits the logic of promise. Faced with God's present promise of forgiveness in Christ, each person who hears is obligated to believe that God speaks only the truth. Thus, one is obligated to believe not only that God is gracious in general (*fides generalis*, "faith in general") but also that he is bestowing his grace at this moment as his word promises (*fides specialis*, "specific faith"), on pain of calling God a liar. "Thus if you come to the sacrament of penance and do not believe that you are absolved in heaven, you come into judgment and damnation, because you do not believe that Christ has spoken the truth" (WA 2:13–14).

In this way *fides specialis* in the external word not only assures the conscience but also honors God's sovereign "institution" of the means of grace, his free choice to be graciously present in a particular way: just as Israel was instructed to seek God in the temple and not on the high places, so the church seeks a gracious God in the incarnate Christ and the word of promise. On Luther's account the certitude of grace is a certainty of God's institution and truthfulness, involving no introspective discernment of divine presence in the heart or of one's own transformation. Luther agrees with the medieval tradition that neither of the latter is a possible ground of assurance.

Huldrych Zwingli. The theology of Huldrych Zwingli (1484–1531) takes quite a different approach to these Augustinian issues. Zwingli agrees formally with Luther that forgiveness and transformation are inseparable and that they are defined christologically, but his material christological differences from Luther also play a role in his theology of grace. Zwingli tends to conceive of the christological determination of grace in terms of the distinction between the two natures rather than the unity of person: grace is the work of Christ as God, drawing human beings by the Holy Spirit to accept the forgiveness made possible by his past work of satisfaction in human nature and transforming them according to his human example.

Moreover, Zwingli radicalizes the Augustinian emphasis on the inwardness of grace, firmly rejecting the definition of the sacraments as signs that confer grace. Grace is conferred exclusively by the Spirit working within the sinner to bring about repentance and trust in Christ, normally (though not invariably) in a divinely willed concurrence with the preaching of the gospel. Zwingli argues in his *Commentarius de vera et falsa religione* (Commentary on True and False Religion; 1525) that to say that outward signs confer grace is to make a slave of the divine Spirit and to confuse both the material and the spiritual, the creator and the creature.

Augustine's Neoplatonism and a particular reading of the sovereignty of the biblical God interpenetrate one another in this line of thought. The crude things that constitute sacramental signs cannot reach the mind, nor can any creature share in the creator's power to renew the heart. Even the preached word serves only to present us with the object of faith but plays no role in the Spirit's inner action, which grants faith. In later writings Zwingli attempted to find a somewhat more substantial role for external signs in the life of grace, but his view remained structurally the same.

Zwingli disposes of the problem of certitude simply by reference to the experiential self-evidence of the inner work of the Spirit. It is, he insists, unthinkable that one could be unaware of so massive a change as that worked by the grace of God. The Spirit's intervention in bringing a sinner to repentance and faith is palpable and unmistakable; if one believes, one certainly knows it. The certitude of grace is founded on an introspective awareness of God's active inward presence and its transformative effect.

John Calvin. No one in the sixteenth century was closer to Luther than John Calvin (1509–1564) in conceiving of grace in terms of union with Christ through faith. As Calvin wrote in the last (1559) edition of his *Institutio Christinae religionis* (Institutes of the Christian Religion), "We await salvation from him not because he becomes visible at a distance from us, but because he makes us, grafted into his body, sharers not only in all his possessions but also in himself" (*Institutes* III/ii, 24). For Calvin grace is the undeserved kindness of God the Father for lost creatures, concretely realized in the person and work of Christ and actualized in human experience by the ministry of the Spirit; he has a special interest in the gracious work of the Spirit in its coinherence with the work of the Son (*Institutes* III/i, 1).

Calvin is likewise close to Luther in emphasizing that grace is at once forgiveness (justification) by the imputation of Christ's righteousness and transforming renewal (sanctification), both grounded in union with Christ by faith. Calvin is especially concerned with underlining the sanctifying character of grace, but, despite a common stereotype, this should not be seen as a difference in principle from Luther. Calvin is, moreover, equally insistent that forgiveness and renewal be carefully distinguished from one another and that the former should never be regarded as conditional on the latter. They are rather inseparable gifts of the free and unconditional grace of God in Christ.

Calvin underscores the utter dependence of human beings on the free initiative of divine grace with his well-known doctrine of absolute predestination (*Institutes* III/xxi-xxiv). Scholarship is unanimous, however, that predestination is by no means the systematic center of Calvin's theology; on the contrary, he seems quite indifferent to any difficulties this doctrine might seem to pose for other aspects of his theology of grace.

Calvin's view of the mediation of grace is complex and continues to be controversial among scholars. The difficulty arises chiefly from the diverse commitments that he attempts to satisfy. On the one hand, with Luther and the older tradition, he affirms the indispensable role of "external words" in the bestowal of grace; the Spirit confers grace through preaching and sacrament as "means and instruments" (*Institutes* IV/xiv, 12). On the other hand, he shares with Zwingli a view of God's transcendence that is extremely sensitive to any suggestion that God's power is bound to created realities. Therefore, he typically rejects the definition of sacraments as signs which themselves confer grace, which Calvin takes to imply that God has signed over his majestic saving power to the signs so that the "wretched minds" of human beings "come to rest in the spectacle of a bodily thing rather than in God himself" (*Institutes* IV/xiv, 14).

The middle ground that Calvin attempts to stake out is difficult to define; two moves, however, are central. First, the notion of representation seems crucial to Calvin's account of the communication of grace (*Institutes* IV/xiv, 5–6). Preaching and sacraments "represent" the grace of God to us; the sacraments have the same function as the word (*Institutes* IV/xiv, 17), adding to it only a more vivid and graphic portrayal of grace (*Institutes* IV/xiv, 6). Some scholars, such as Kilian McDonnell, suggest that the notion of representation serves Calvin's agenda through its Platonic overtones: the divine reality makes itself available through the earthly representation but is never identified with it (Kilian McDonnell, *John Calvin, the Church, and the Eucharist*, Princeton, 1967).

Second, Calvin insists that the sole operative agent in the conferral of grace through word and sacrament is the Holy Spirit. Calvin wants to say neither that the Spirit's action is only concurrent and parallel to proclamation and sacrament nor that the Spirit is "contained" in the signs (*Institutes* III/ii, 33–36; IV/xiv, 9, 17). The work of the Spirit is, so to speak, the field of energy within which the encounter of the human heart with word and sacrament has saving effect; the Spirit opens the heart to the grace represented in the sign and in turn uses the communicative capacity of the sign to impress grace on the heart.

Whereas Calvin, like Luther, insists that certitude of grace arises from confidence that God's promises are true for us (*Institutes* III/ii, 16), his position follows the contours and shares the complexities of his view of word and Spirit. For Calvin faith's certitude of grace is an acknowledgment of God's gracious promises, "confirmed and established" experientially in the heart by the Spirit (*Institutes* III/ii, 36). Although Calvin's faith does not cling to the word or sign in its externality (*contra* Luther) but to the divine grace that these represent (a distinction that Luther refuses to make), still it finds certitude of grace only by way of the external word and sacrament that the Spirit uses as instruments (*contra* Zwingli).

The Radical Reformers. Although the theology of the early Swiss Anabaptists seems to originate primarily in a radicalization of Zwingli's spiritualism, a quite distinctive theology of grace developed in the Dutch and south German wings of the radical Reformation. Anabaptist leaders, such as Melchoir Hoffman, Menno Simons, Dirk Philips, Hans Denck, and Pilgram Marpeck each developed their views differently, though certain common elements can be discerned.

Common to all was the combination of a radicalized view of the inwardness of grace with an understanding of grace as deifying transformation, the participation of the believer in the nature of God. This latter point was underscored by a tendency in Christology to emphasize the transformation of Christ's human nature by his divinity. In the case of the Dutch leaders—Hoffman, Menno, and Philips—this emphasis took the form of the so-called celestial flesh Christology, according to which Christ did not take his humanity from Mary but brought it with him as a new creation from heaven.

The point of this doctrine, made by others in a more traditionally orthodox way, is to insist that grace as union with Christ is participation in an utterly new being that cannot be assimilated into the structures of this passing age, involving an ontological change in the very nature of the believer. This participation is purely spiritual and inward, not mediated by any external signs or ceremonies, but it presses toward immediate and decisive outward expression. The first act by which inwardly deifying grace is externally expressed is baptism, by which the believer adheres voluntarily to the holy community of disciples, whose separated and obedient life witnesses to the saving power of Christ.

Questions about forgiveness and certitude were on the whole less urgent for Anabaptist theologians; indeed, they suspected that the prominence of such issues in the mainline Reformation indicated a desire to evade the rigors of discipleship. Anabaptists tended to subordinate forgiveness to transformation: God forgives the sin of those whom his transforming grace brings from darkness into light. Moreover, they were insistent that one can be certain of grace only when its renewing power brings one to a radical break with the world and its iniquity. This did not mean, however, that salvation could be achieved by human effort without grace; their position simply reflects the centrality of transformation and renewal in the Anabaptists' understanding of grace itself.

The Council of Trent. The Council of Trent (1545–1564) should not be seen as a direct Roman Catholic response to the concerns of the reformers. Communication between the various reform movements and the "old believers" broke down after the Diet of Augsburg (1530), and the bishops at Trent spared little time for detailed consideration of dissident theology. The Tridentine doctrine of grace is fundamentally pastoral in orientation, designed to provide confused Catholics with an acceptable working soteriology. Although the canons of the council condemn a number of Reformation slogans and formulas (mostly from Luther), it is seldom clear that the council fathers understood them in the sense in which the reformers intended them.

In essence, the doctrine of grace in the Tridentine *Decretum de iustificatione* (Decree on Justification) is a strong restatement of medieval Augustinianism. Grace is the renewing power of God, won for sinners by Christ's passion and bestowed in baptism (chapter 7). Christ has merited this grace and it is from him (as the body from the head and the vine from the branches) that the church continually receives it (chapter 16). Human salvation is entirely the work of grace thus conceived (chapters 1–8, 16; canons 1–3).

Forgiveness and renewal go together; those who are engrafted into Christ receive from him both remission of sins and the infusion of faith, hope, and charity (chapter 7). The council simply does not take up the concern of the reformers for a more differentiated account of forgiveness and renewal and their relation to one another; on the contrary, the suspicion is clear that the differentiation of the two in the Reformation movements amounts to an illegitimate separation (canon 11). The emphasis of the decree is on the necessarily transformative character of grace.

The council also clearly suspects all the reformers of denying the sacramental mediation of grace. Luther's stress on the necessity of the faith that accepts the promise is taken to imply that faith is self-sufficient without the sacraments (*Canones de sacramentis in genere* [Canons on the Sacraments in General], 4–6, 8). For its part, the council reiterates the traditional doctrine that the sacraments contain the grace they signify and confer that grace on all those who do not place an obstacle in the way.

The *Decretum de iustificatione* makes it clear, however, that the council does not intend the sort of semiautomatic sacramental conferral of grace without personal engagement of which the reformers accused late medieval theology and practice. Grace prepares sinners for justification by moving them freely toward God in faith, hope, and repentance (chapter 6). Baptism, the "instrumental cause" of justification, is the "sacrament of faith" (chapter 7). Faith is the "beginning of human salvation, the basis and root of all justification" (chapter 8). This emphasis on faith must be taken into account in the interpretation of Trent's teaching that the sacraments confer grace on those who do not place an obstacle in the way.

Trent interprets Reformation accounts of certitude as teaching that a subjective conviction or feeling of confidence concerning oneself is a prerequisite for salvation. This is clear from the wording of canon 14 of the *Decretum*: "If anyone says that a person is absolved from sins and justified because one believes with certainty that one is absolved and justified, or that no one is truly justified unless one believes oneself justified, and that by this faith alone absolution and justification are achieved, anathema sit."

Against this the council reaffirms the standard medieval Augustinian position. On the one hand, no one should doubt the mercy of God, the merit of Christ, and the power and effectiveness of the sacraments; on the other hand, one may have considerable fear and apprehension when one considers oneself (chapter 9). The knowledge that one has obtained grace, as a knowledge about oneself, can never have the certainty of faith. Rather than disagreeing with Luther and Calvin, the council seems simply to ask and answer the question of certitude in a less theoretically articulate, more pastorally pragmatic manner.

[*See also* Faith; Free Will; Good Works; *and* Justification.]

BIBLIOGRAPHY

Beachy, Alvin J. *The Concept of Grace in the Radical Reformation.* Nieuwkoop, 1977. The ground-breaking and controversial study that first identified a distinctive theology of grace in the radical Reformation.

Ganoczy, Alexandre. "A Note on Calvin's Trinitarian Doctrine of Grace." In *Probing the Reformed Tradition: Historical Studies in Honor of Edward A. Dowey, Jr.*, edited by Elsie Ann McKee and Brian G. Armstrong, pp. 96–107. Louisville, Ky., 1989. An important account of the way Calvin's concept of grace hangs together, by the leading Roman Catholic Calvin scholar.

Gerrish, B. A. *Grace and Gratitude: The Eucharistic Theology of John Calvin.* Minneapolis, 1993. More than a study of Calvin's sacramental theology, this fine book offers a persuasive perspective on Calvin's theology of grace as a whole.

Joest, Wilfried. *Die katholische Lehre von der Rechtfertigung und von der Gnade.* Lüneberg, Germany, 1954.

Küng, Hans. *Justification: The Doctrine of Karl Barth and a Catholic Response.* Translated by Thomas Collins et al. Reprint, Philadelphia, 1981. Part 2 is an extended exposition of the Council of Trent.

Lehmann, Karl, and Wolfhart Pannenberg, eds. *The Condemnations of the Reformation Era: Do They Still Divide?* Minneapolis, 1990. An ecumenical study by major Reformed, Lutheran, and Roman Catholic scholars; especially helpful on the ways in which participants in the sixteenth-century debates argued at cross-purposes with one another.

Mannermaa, Tuomo. *Der im Glauben gegenwärtige Christus: Rechtfertigung und Vergottung.* Translated by Hans-Christian Daniel and Juhani Forsberg. Hannover, 1989. An important new departure in Luther studies that stresses the centrality of union with the present Christ and suggests affinities between Luther and the Greek patristic tradition.

Martin-Palma, José. *Gnadenlehre: Von der Reformation bis zur Gegenwart.* Freiburg, 1980.

McCue, James F. "*Simul iustus et peccator* in Augustine, Aquinas, and Luther: Toward Putting the Debate in Context." *Journal of the American Academy of Religion* 48.1 (1980), 81–96. An illuminating account of how the "troubled conscience" became a serious pastoral problem in the Western church.

McGrath, Alister. *Justitia Dei: A History of the Christian Doctrine of Justification.* Vol. 2, *From 1500 to the Present Day.* Cambridge, 1986. Surveys the period; see especially the discussion of the Tridentine *Decretum de iustificatione* and the debates lying behind it.

Pesch, Otto Hermann, and Albrecht, Peters. *Einführung in die Lehre von Gnade und Rechtfertigung.* Reprint, Darmstadt, 1989. A study in the history of doctrine outstanding for its clear identification of conceptual issues and its incorporation of the results of ecumenical scholarship.

Stephens, W. P. *Zwingli: An Introduction to His Thought.* Oxford, 1992. A point-by-point account of Zwingli's theology in its historical development; somewhat lacking in focus, but helpfully informative. Excellent bibliography.

Wendel, François. *Calvin: The Origin and Development of His Religious Thought.* 2d ed. Translated by Philip Mairet. Durham, N.C., 1987.

Wicks, Jared. *Luther and His Spiritual Legacy.* Wilmington, Del., 1983. A superb presentation of Luther's thought for the general reader, by an influential and sympathetic Roman Catholic Luther scholar.

Williams, George H. *The Radical Reformation.* 3d ed. Kirksville, Mo., 1992. A magisterial and detailed historical study that pays considerable attention to theological issues.

Zachman, Randall C. *The Assurance of Faith: Conscience in the Theology of Martin Luther and John Calvin.* Minneapolis, 1993. Rightly stresses what Luther and Calvin have in common, but does not pay enough attention to the differences in their views of the mediation of grace.

DAVID S. YEAGO

GRADEC, Gregor Horváth Stansith de. *See* Stanšič Horváth de Gradecz, Gregor.

GRANADA, Luis de (1504–1588), Spanish Dominican. Born in Granada in 1504 in humble circumstances and orphaned at an early age, he served as page to the sons of the second marquess of Mondejar in the Alhambra, and thanks to this post, to his outstanding goodness and intellect, and to the favor of the marchioness, he obtained a humanistic education of the highest quality. At the age of twenty he became a Dominican in the monastery of Santa Cruz la Real, founded by the Catholic kings with the specific religious mission of preaching to the Christian settlers of the "reconquered" city and kingdom of Granada and converting the Muslims. The emphasis on preaching was to be the distinctive feature of Luis de Granada. His intellectual gifts made him stand out among his fellow students, and in 1529 he was elected fellow of the College of San Gregorio of Valladolid, where he again distinguished himself and received the task of preparing the edition of commentaries on Aristotle that had been written by the president of the college, Diego Astudillo. Granada finished the edition and adorned it with a humanist prologue and with a poem in Virgilian hexameters.

His destiny appeared to be a professorial chair, but his vocation was preaching and he sought to be sent as a missionary to Mexico in 1534. His superiors did not allow him to realize this dream, assigning him to Córdoba, where he rebuilt the monastery of Escalaceli, founded by Alvaro in 1423 for "reform" of the Order of Preachers. In Escalaceli he dedicated himself to the study of the holy fathers, especially Bernard and Jerome; he began his friendship with the "preacher of Andalusia," John of Ávila; and he started his career as a preacher. In 1550 he was taken away to Evora by Cardinal Enrique, future king of Portugal, and went with him to the court in Lisbon, where he lived until his death on 31 December 1588.

The literary work of Granada is distinguished by its aesthetic quality and by its ability to communicate with the reader. He is a writer who is inspirational, accessible, very rich in doctrine, and stimulating. His most famous works are *Libro de la oración*, *Guía de pecadores*, and *Memorial de la vida cristiana*. In his mature years, already nearly blind but retaining exquisite mental lucidity, he devoted himself to writing an *Introducción del símbolo de la fe*, in five volumes, which is a magnificent literary and religious edifice, an introduction to Christianity and at the same time a defense: he addressed it principally to non-Christians in an attempt to attract them to the Christian faith. The first part, which is an introduction to nature, is a beautiful study of the cosmos and of the beings that compose it, from the star to the ant, one of the best ecological works in any literature. The writings of Granada have been published in many languages, in almost six thousand editions, a figure that truly demonstrates his "capacity of preaching" and of engaging in religious dialogue with all levels of readers.

BIBLIOGRAPHY

Primary Source

Granada, Luis de. *Obras*. Edited by J. Cuervo. 14 vols. Madrid, 1906–1908.

Secondary Sources

Huerga, Alvaro. *Fray Luis de Granada: Una vida al servicio de la Iglesia*. Madrid, 1988.

Llaneza, Maximino. *Bibliografía de las obras de fray L. de G.* 4 vols. Salamanca, 1926–1930.

ALVARO HUERGA

GRANVELLE, Antoine Perrenot de (1517–1586), French prelate and adviser to Philip II of Spain. Born in Besançon on 20 August 1517, he was the son of Nicholas Perrenot de Granvelle, a leading counsellor of Emperor Charles V. Educated at Padua and Louvain, Antoine Perrenot was appointed bishop of Arras in 1538 and served the emperor and his son Philip II in various capacities until 1560. In that year Philip made Perrenot archbishop of Mechelen, which meant that, under the king's new program of church reform, he would be primate of the Netherlands. Because Philip intended him to reform not only the church but the civil administration, he was also named chief counsellor to Philip's regent, Margaret of Parma. In 1561 he was admitted to the college of cardinals as Cardinal Granvelle.

Granvelle's role as Philip's chief instrument of reform aroused great antagonism. The higher nobility of the Netherlands opposed the king's measures and almost immediately demanded the ouster of his minister. They claimed to resent Granvelle's arrogance and low birth, but in fact they feared for their own wealth and influence in an administration that was increasingly dominated by jurists and members of the lesser nobility. Philip was forced to dismiss the cardinal from his civil offices in 1564, but the episode was not forgotten and helped pave the way for the revolt of 1566.

Granvelle retired to Rome, where he represented Spanish interests and helped to negotiate the Holy League, the alliance of Spain, the papacy, and Venice, whose efforts culminated in the victory at Lepanto. When Philip imprisoned both his secretary, Antonio Pérez and Fernando Álvarez de Toledo, duke of Alba, in 1579, thereby crippling the major aristocratic factions at his court, he recalled Granvelle to Madrid and made him the first non-Spanish member of the council of state. As counsellor, Granvelle continued to urge harsh measures against the Netherlands until his death in Madrid on 21 September 1586.

BIBLIOGRAPHY

Durme, M. van. *El Cardenal Granvela.* Translated by E. Borrías Cubells and J. Pérez Ballestar. Barcelona, 1957.

Philippson, Martin. *Ein Ministerium unter Philipp II: Kardinal Granvella am spanische Hofe, 1579–1586.* Berlin, 1895.

Poullet, Edmond, and Charles Piot, eds. *Correspondence du Cardinal de Granvelle, 1556–1586.* 12 vols. Brussels, 1877–1896.

Weiss, Charles, ed. *Papiers d'état du Cardinal de Granvelle.* 9 vols. Paris, 1841–1852.

WILLIAM S. MALTBY

GRAVAMINA is the plural of Late Latin *gravamen,* which means a burden, imposition, or aggravation, a wrong inflicted; also (in medieval usage) a complaint or remonstrance, a demand for relief; hence its German equivalent *Beschwerde:* a grievance voiced, a complaint of having been *beschwert* ("burdened"). The term has special relevance to the history of the German Reformation, but its use is much older. In the late Middle Ages, the framing and presentation of gravamina (Ger., *Beschwerniss*), or grievances, became one of the chief functions of representative bodies, a practice rooted ultimately in the feudal notion of the social contract, which obligated rulers to take advice (*consilium*) and gave their subjects the right to remonstrate. In the fifteenth and sixteenth centuries, this customary *Beschwerderecht,* the right to complain and protest, was massively employed by estate bodies who used their power to vote taxes as a lever to compel rulers to note and act on their particular grievances. The French *cahiers de doléances* are the best-known historical instance of this procedure; in Germany, as in France, the various estates prepared separate tabulations of *Misstände und Gebrechen* ("wrongs and defects"), combining and redacting these lists as they made their way from village courts, parishes, town councils, and districts to the committees of territorial assemblies (*Landstände*) meeting in their diet (*Landtag*). The estates' expectation was that the recess concluding the diet would, in agreement with the territory's sovereign (*Landesherr*), undertake the redress of the most oppressive burdens. This redress did not always happen; but until the role of estates declined in the late sixteenth century and grievance procedures lapsed into routine, the lodging of gravamina was a vital constitutional function engaging all segments of the political body.

The fifteenth century also saw the presentation of grievances used as a weapon in the struggle for church reform, and it was as a politically charged protest against papacy, curia, and clergy that the issue of gravamina joined the events leading to the Reformation. At the Council of Constance (1414–1418), the German nation (along with the other nations by which this council was organized) offered its complaints and proposals as a set of *avisamenta* on eighteen points of reform chosen by the council for remedial action: annates (payments for benefices), reservations, judicial appeals to Rome, simony, indulgences, the tithe, and so on. These positions reflected the interests of the higher clergy, as did the frequent voicing of "grievances by which the German nation has hitherto been miserably weighed down [*miserabiliter gravata*]" at the subsequent Council of Basel (1431–1449), where papal taxation and appointments to benefices were much criticized, particularly after the Concordat of Vienna, negotiated in 1448 between Pope Eugenius IV and Emperor Frederick III, set aside reform measures agreed to earlier at the Council. The term *German nation,* as used on these occasions, referred mainly to German clerics participating in fifteenth-century church councils. German churchmen continued to protest Roman exploitation, as in 1479, when the clergy of the archbishoprics of Mainz, Trier, and Cologne, at a meeting in Koblenz, issued a statement in twenty-six chapters recording their objections to fiscal pressures to which they and their flocks were subjected. But "nation" soon gained much broader scope as the harm thought to have been done by Rome to the German church was raised as a battle cry in the political struggles waged by secular rulers against popes.

From 1450 the "gravamina of the German nation" were aired regularly at imperial, territorial, and municipal diets in the empire. They were brought up at receptions of papal emissaries, as on the occasion of Nicholas of Cusa's travels in Germany in 1452. They formed a large part of the grievances of imperial cities, the frequent venting of which resulted in growing urban anticlericalism in the late fifteenth century. In 1510 Emperor Maximilian I commissioned the Alsatian humanist and fervent German patriot Jakob Wimpfeling to draft a memorandum proving how "the heavy burdens imposed on the entire [Holy] Roman Empire by the riches flowing to Rome. . . may be removed." In response, Wimpfeling compiled a catalog of the—by now familiar—grievances and warned of the public furor brewing in Germany over continued exploitation by the church. Most of Wimpfeling's points had been made in the 1450s by the chancellor to the archbishop of Mainz, Martin Mayr, who, in a letter to Enea Silvio Piccolomini, the prominent churchman, diplomat, and later Pope Pius II, complained of papal violation of conciliar decrees and of the harm done to Germany by Rome's arbitrary taxation, interference in ecclesiastical appointments, the outflow of large sums of money in annates and indulgences, and simony at every level. But Wimpfeling's compilation of the *Gravamina Germanicae Nationis,* printed in 1519, reached a much wider audience. Gravamina—*Beschwerden*—was becoming a code word for anti-Roman and anticlerical feelings in Germany on the eve of the Reformation.

Once the Lutheran issue had become the focal point of the empire's relations with Rome, the gravamina were, for a time, a major point of negotiation between emperor and pope on one side and emperor and imperial estates on the other. At the Diet of Worms in 1521, when Charles V submitted a draft edict against Luther to the estates, the estates pointed in reply to the *beschwerde und missbreuch* caused in *Teutscher nacion* ("the German nation") by the Roman curia and drew up a document, intended for presentation to Rome but remaining in draft at this time, detailing "articles with which the Holy Father oppresses Germany." After 1520 such grievance statements gathered great force from Luther's publication, in the summer of that year, of his hugely popular *An den christlichen Adel deutscher Nation von des christlichen Standes Besserung* (Address to the Christian Nobility of the German Nation, Concerning the Improvement of the Christian Estate), which gave a long and savagely critical account of the injuries done by Rome to church and society in Germany. The gravamina received their final political form at the Diet of Nuremberg in 1523, where the earlier Worms draft was revised into what became the official statement of "Grievances of the Secular Estates against the Roman See and Clergy." Among the abuses to which this document objected were the constant increase in annates, proliferation of curial offices, transfer of secular cases to ecclesiastical courts, abuses of benefit of clergy, the church's avid acquisition of property, appointment of papal courtiers to German benefices, the penitentiary turned into a money making enterprise, ordination of unfit priests, clerical concubinage, excessive use of excommunication and interdict, the plague of vagrant mendicants, relic hawkers and indulgence sellers, venality of dispensation and absolution, and the pressures put on the old and sick to leave their belongings to the church. Translated into Latin, the document was sent to Rome in June 1523. It concluded with an open threat: unless the "insufferable and corrupting burdens" detailed in the preceding articles were removed in due course, the estates would be forced "to consider other appropriate ways and means to rid themselves of these impositions and oppressions."

With "other means" soon bringing about the separation of many German urban and territorial states from Rome, the gravamina subsided as a public issue after the late 1520s. Because political control over church and clergy now rested in the hands of Reformation and Counter-Reformation governments, further protests to Rome became pointless. But the smoldering resentments these protests had articulated enjoyed a long afterlife in the rich pamphlet literature of the time, where they nourished antipapal and anticlerical sentiments that Protestant authorities fostered as a way of weaning their peoples from the old religion.

[*See also* Augsburg; Diet; Luther, Martin; *and* Nuremberg.]

BIBLIOGRAPHY

Gebhardt, Bruno. *Die Gravamina der deutschen Nation gegen den römischen Hof.* 2d ed. Breslau, Germany, 1895.

Störmann, Anton. *Die städtischen Gravamina gegen den Klerus am Ausgange des Mittelalters und in der Reformationszeit.* Reformationsgeschichtliche Studien and Texte, nos. 24–26. Münster, 1916.

Wittmütz, Volkmar. *Die Gravamina der bayerischen Stände im 16. und 17. Jahrhundert als Quelle für die wirtschaftliche Situation und Entwicklung Bayerns.* Miscellanea Bavarica Monacensia, no. 26. Munich, 1970.

GERALD STRAUSS

GREBEL, Conrad (c.1498–1526), Swiss radical reformer, called the "father of Anabaptism." Conrad Grebel began public life as a passionate supporter of the Swiss reformer Huldrych Zwingli. After a failed university career in Vienna and Paris, he was converted early in 1522, and in Zurich he joined a group with Zwingli and others studying Erasmus's Greek New Testament. Grebel was at this time perhaps twenty-four years old and driven by a youthful impatience to get the process of reform moving. In July 1522 he and three others publicly interrupted and challenged monastic preachers, something Zwingli himself also did on at least one occasion. Although Grebel and his companions were publicly chastised by Zurich's city council, the action influenced the council's directive to the monks to preach strictly according to scripture. A month later Grebel wrote a Latin poem glorifying Zwingli and signing himself "Conrad Grebel, in gratitude for the gospel restored."

Grebel was an enthusiastic participant in the two public disputations of January and October 1523. Between these two events, however, Grebel's impatience at the slow pace of reform and several decisions related to it convinced him that there was a lack of will among the city's authorities to carry out the needed reforms. When in June 1523 the Zurich council decreed that tithes would continue to be obligatory, Grebel vilified members of the council with the charge that they had acted like Turks—that is, unbelievers. Shortly thereafter Zwingli, in his famous sermon "Divine and Human Justice," supported the council's decision by arguing that the tithe was part of the system of human justice, which all citizens were obligated to support. It should be noted that by this time, July 1523, there was no radical movement in Zurich opposed to Zwingli's reforms and that Conrad Grebel had until then been a fervent and faithful supporter of Zwingli.

At the second disputation, which took place in October 1523, Grebel and others also began to have their doubts about Zwingli's will to reform. During the debate Simon Stumpf, a local priest and companion of Grebel, denied Zwingli the right to put a decision about how the Mass was henceforth to be observed into the hands of the council; he added that the decision to abolish the Mass had already been made by the Holy Spirit through the Christian assembly. The minutes also reveal what appears to be a cramped biblical literalism in Grebel. For example, he demanded a decision on what kind of bread to use for the Mass and objected to water being added to the wine. Zwingli admitted that these issues were important but said they could be decided in the congregations. It was, however, not biblical literalism for its own sake that motivated Grebel. He was a "true believer," convinced that the old papal system had to be completely swept away for reform to succeed. He was following Zwingli's guiding reform principle that whatever had not been specifically commanded in scripture was to be done away with. He feared that unless every abuse, no matter how small, were removed, it would become a point of infection endangering the reform. Popes, councils, and doctors had been discredited as authorities in Zurich at the January 1523 disputation. Only the Bible, which was unchanging, could now be trusted to be a secure guide.

Arousing opposition was the council's decision of 13 December, agreed to by Zwingli, to continue the Mass for the time being because of concern that the community would otherwise fracture. Five days later Grebel judged Zwingli to be derelict in his duty as chief shepherd of Zurich for not opposing the council. Around 20 December Grebel and Stumpf came to Zwingli with a plan to resolve the impasse. They believed that the blockage lay in the council. Unanimity, they knew, was not possible, but they were convinced that those who held with Zwingli were a majority. This majority, they proposed, should elect a new council that would then carry forward the work of reform without hindrance. Zwingli rejected the plan because of its potential for conflict. Even so, at the end of 1523 Grebel and his friends accepted Zwingli's vision of church and society in which preachers and magistrates, both appointed servants of God, guided the affairs of the Christian commonwealth.

A letter of 3 September to his brother-in-law Joachim Vadian revealed Grebel's now complete disillusionment with the clerical leadership of Zurich, although Zwingli was not mentioned by name. Grebel had, however, discovered allies in Andreas Bodenstein von Karlstadt and Thomas Müntzer. Two letters to Müntzer in September 1524 reveal what the Grebel group had been thinking since the end of 1523. They were intensely anticlerical, sketching out a vision of a church of lay people who would be able to discharge their obligations as Christians because they had been taught and then baptized as adult believers. Infant baptism was identified as the sign of the clerical church *par excellence.* The group had given special attention to the question of baptism in the preceding months and was strongly influenced by the linkage between baptism and faith found in Müntzer's writings. But there was here no word about actually establishing a separatist church, for the baptism of believing adults was judged compatible with Zurich's Christian commonwealth. They apparently did not yet see that this Christian commonwealth could scarcely be reconciled with their view that the church should not be protected with the sword.

Attempts at conversation to overcome the estrangement proved fruitless because they could not agree on how to use the scriptures. The break became inevitable when in January 1525 Grebel baptized George Blaurock, who then baptized the others present in the house of Felix Mantz, another member of the group. Despite this, they continued to consider themselves to be part of the church in Zurich. The council, however, understood what had happened and pronounced all further meetings of the group illegal. Grebel, despite ill health and opposition from his family, went out to promote his understanding of the reform in Grüningen and St. Gall. He spent time in prison in Zurich, escaped, and died of the plague in May 1526.

Zwingli called Grebel the *coryphaeus,* or ringleader, of the radical opposition against him. Grebel has been credited with being the father of Anabaptism, and, in a restricted sense, inasmuch as he performed the first baptism, this is accurate.

His significance for the Reformation lies in his leadership in unfolding a vision of the emancipation of the Christian from clerical tutelage and, through baptism as an adult believer, therefore of a church of informed lay people that refused the protection of government power. These did become characteristics of what has been called Anabaptism throughout Europe.

BIBLIOGRAPHY

Primary Sources

Harder, Leland. *The Sources of Swiss Anabaptism: The Grebel Letters and Related Documents.* Classics of the Radical Reformation, vol. 4. Scottdale, Pa., 1985. All sources relating to Conrad Grebel are included in translation with introductions and commentary.

Raushenbusch, Walter, trans. *Conrad Grebel's Programmatic Letters of 1524.* Revised by John C. Wenger. Scottdale, Pa., 1970. Contains a facsimile, a transcription, and translation of Conrad Grebel's letters to Thomas Müntzer.

Secondary Sources

Bender, Harold S. *Conrad Grebel, c. 1498–1526: The Founder of the Swiss Brethren.* Reprint, Scottdale, Pa., 1971. Only full-length biography of Conrad Grebel. Contains much detail unavailable elsewhere, but Grebel's importance is too highly rated.

Fast, Heinold. "Reformation durch Provokation: Predigtstörungen in den ersten Jahren der Reformation in der Schweiz." In *Umstrittenes Täufertum,* edited by H.-J. Goertz, pp. 75–110. Göttingen, 1975. Places the radical actions of Conrad Grebel in the context of the larger Reformation and provides parallels.

———. "Conrad Grebel: The Covenant on the Cross." In *Profiles of Radical Reformers,* edited by Hans-Jürgen Goertz, pp. 118–131. Scottdale, Pa., 1982. Best single short essay on Conrad Grebel and his importance for the Reformation.

Goeters, J. F. Gerhard. "Die Vorgeschichte des Täufertums in Zürich." In *Studien zur Geschichte und Theologie der Reformation,* edited by

Luise Abramowski and J. F. G. Goeters, pp. 239–281. Neukirchen-Vluyn, Germany, 1969. Very important for the setting of the rise of radical dissent in Zurich.

Harder, Leland. "Grebel, Conrad." In *Mennonite Encyclopedia,* edited by Cornelius J. Dyck and Dennis D. Martin, vol. 5, pp. 354–356. Scottdale, Pa., 1990. Update of Bender's biography.

Klaassen, Walter. "The Rise of the Baptism of Adult Believers in Swiss Anabaptism." In *Anabaptism Revisited,* edited by Walter Klaassen, pp. 85–97. Scottdale, Pa., 1992. This essay seeks to explain why adult baptism arose and to clarify its meaning.

Williams, George H. *The Radical Reformation.* 3d ed. St. Louis, 1992. Description of Grebel's role by a prominent Reformation scholar.

WALTER KLAASSEN

GREEK ORTHODOX CHURCH. *See* Eastern Orthodoxy.

GREGORY XIII (born Ugo Boncompagni; 1502–1585), pope from 1572 to 1585. The son of a merchant family in Bologna, he received degrees there in civil and canon law in 1530. Abandoning lectureships at Bologna, he moved to Rome in 1539 and labored in the papal diplomatic corps under Paul IV (r. 1555–1559) and Pius IV (r. 1559–1565) on legations to France, the Netherlands, and Spain. He attended the last sessions (1561–1563) of the Council of Trent (1545–1563) and was appointed cardinal in 1565. The Roman people, who apparently feared the election of a Theatine loyal to the policies of Paul IV and Pius V (r. 1566–1572), greeted his election enthusiastically.

As pope, Gregory consolidated, solidified, and centralized the movement to implement the decrees of Trent. He encouraged apostolic visitations by Carlo Borromeo (1538–1584) and others but at times came into conflict with those who saw reform as an activity to be controlled by local bishops. He granted favors and subsidies to both reformed, older orders and to new religious institutions, such as the Camaldolese, Oratorians, Carmelites, Capuchins, Theatines, and Jesuits. He took the decrees concerning clerical education perhaps most seriously and established a seminary system through patronage of the Roman College and through the foundation of other national colleges (which became affiliated with the Gregorian University). He extended this work by founding colleges for the education of clerical candidates from missionary territories. Such activities reflect his intellectual interests, which he also followed by commissioning scriptural studies and editions, Carlo Sigonio's (1523–1584) history of the church, a new edition of *Corpus iuris canonici,* and reform of the calendar. Results of the latter project were issued as the Gregorian calendar in 1582.

Like his predecessors, he remained active in political and Inquisitorial matters. He did not focus the same energy on action against heterodoxy as had Paul IV and Pius V but still sought to control infiltration of heretical doctrine into Italy and ordered victory celebrations after the Saint Bartholomew's Day Massacre in 1572. He promoted a peaceful settlement of the Revolt of the Netherlands, provided financial support for anti-Huguenot action by the French Crown, favored Philip II's plan to invade England, and attempted to influence German dynastic politics. Still, convinced that heresy could not be stopped simply by force, he consistently linked such political action with intense support for ecclesiastical renewal and improved clerical education. Thus, he sent missionaries to England, Poland, Sweden, and Russia; assisted in expansion of the Capuchin order beyond Italy; and set up a commission of cardinals to aid German ecclesiastical reform.

Gregory's administration of the Papal States met with popular acclaim, as he financed all these policies (which included support for missionaries in the New World) without new taxes. He insisted instead upon full collection of the tributes due from nobles holding fiefs in the territory, which had long gone uncollected. He also increased arable land by draining marshes in the vicinity of Ravenna. This determined and forward-thinking pope was a generous patron of the arts and of architectural projects throughout Rome, including the Quirinal Palace and the Jesuit church of Gesù, in addition to public fountains and university buildings.

BIBLIOGRAPHY

Caraman, Philip. *University of the Nations: The Story of the Gregorian University With Its Associated Institutes, the Biblical and the Oriental.* New York, 1981.

Caravale, Mario and Alberto Caracciolo. *Lo Stato pontificio da Martino V a Pio IX.* Storia d'Italia, no. 14. Turin, 1978.

Ciappi, Marco Antonio. *Compendio delle herioche et gloriose attioni e vita di Gregorio XIII.* Rome, 1591.

Karttunen, L. *Grégoire XIII comme politicien et souverain.* Helsinki, 1911. A limited portrait focused on his political activities, as the title suggests.

Maffei, Giovanni Pietro. *Degli annali di Gregorio XIII.* 2 vols. Rome, 1742. The first full biography. Maffei (1535–1603) based his work on the Boncompagni archives. Although not altogether impartial, it is reliable and has been heavily used by other authors.

McCuaig, William. *Carlo Sigonio: The Changing World of the Late Renaissance.* Princeton, 1989. Chapters 1 and 4 provide information on the support and commission given by Gregory to Sigonio, as well as on the difficulties he had with censors in Gregory's curia.

Pastor, Ludwig. *The History of the Popes from the Close of the Middle Ages.* 3d ed., 40 vols. Saint Louis, 1938–1953. Volumes 19 and 20 are really a "life and times"—still the best extended study of Gregory XIII, and the only one in English. The work was originally published as *Geschichte der Päpste seit dem Ausgang des Mittelalters,* 21 vols., Freiburg, 1866–1938.

Prodi, Paolo. *The Papal Prince: One Body and Two Souls; The Papal Monarchy in Early Modern Europe.* Translated by Susan Haskins. Cambridge, 1987. Originally published as *Il sovrano pontefice: Un corpo e due anime; La monarchia papale nella prima età moderna,* Bologna, 1982.

Ranke, Leopold von. *History of the Popes.* 3 vols. New York, 1901. Less reliable than Pastor, it includes limited information on Gregory in volume 1, more on the political context of his pontificate in volume

2, and a few pertinent documents in volume 3. The work was originally published as *Die römischen Päpste, ihre Kirche und ihr Staat im sechzehnten und siebzehnten Jahrhundert*, Berlin, 1834–1836.

WILLIAM V. HUDON

GREY, Jane (1537–1554), the daughter of Henry Grey (third marquis of Dorset and later Duke of Suffolk) and Frances Brandon (the daughter of Henry VIII's younger sister, Mary) and for nine days in 1553 the titular queen of England. She was one of the best-educated girls of her time. Taught Latin and Greek by John Aylmer, the future bishop of London, she also learned modern languages and some Hebrew. Pious and scholarly, she reputedly announced at the age of thirteen that "whatsoever I do else but learning is full of grief, trouble, fear, and wholy misliking unto me."

Her father hoped that Jane might wed her young cousin, Edward VI, but, instead she was married on 21 May 1553 to Lord Guildford Dudley, the son of John Dudley, duke of Northumberland, the most powerful man in the kingdom. About the same time, Edward signed a document excluding his sisters from the throne and vesting the succession directly in Jane and her sisters. Accordingly, Jane was proclaimed queen after Edward's death on 6 July. The Catholic Mary Tudor, however, claimed the throne, and despite the efforts of Northumberland and other Protestants, Jane was soon a prisoner in the Tower of London. Although Jane was condemned to death for treason, her life was, in fact, spared until her father's involvement in Sir Thomas Wyatt's rebellion in early 1554. She was executed, with her husband, on 12 February 1554.

Jane's death at the hands of the monarch who restored England to the Roman obedience, together with her youth and learning, created an ideal model of female constancy and evangelical piety. Writings attributed to her soon appeared in print, while numerous editions of John Foxe's *Acts and Monuments,* which gave a full account of her conduct in the last months of her life, spread her fame still further. It is perhaps impossible to separate the authentic voice from the hagiographic tradition; few commentators have tried.

BIBLIOGRAPHY

Primary Sources

Grey, Jane. *An epistle of the ladye Jane, a right virtuous woman, to a learned man of late falne from the truth of Gods word. Wherunto is added the communication that she had with master Feckenham. Also another epistle to her sister, with the words she spake vpon the scaffold.* London?, 1554? Microfilm copy available from University Microfilms, Ann Arbor, 1982.

———. *The lamentacion that ladie Jane made, saiying for my fathers proclamacion now must I lese my heade.* London, c.1570.

Secondary Sources

Chapman, Hester W. *Lady Jane Grey.* Reprint, London, 1985.

Levine, Carole. "Lady Jane Grey: Protestant Queen and Martyr." In *Silent But for the Word: Tudor Women as Patrons, Translators, and Writers of Religious Works,* edited by Margaret P. Hannay. Kent, Ohio, 1985.

JENNIFER LOACH

GRIBALDI, Matteo (d. 1564), Italian jurisprudent, exile, and antitrinitarian. His family name sometimes appears as Gribaldi Mofa. Born probably at the beginning of the sixteenth century, Gribaldi grew up in a patrician family of Chieri, just southeast of Turin, perhaps with Celio Secondo Curione (1503–1569), another famous Italian heretic. An itinerant legal scholar, he taught at Perugia, Toulouse (1535–1536), Valenza (1540–1541), Grenoble (1543–1545 and 1559–1560), and Padua (1548), bringing humanist methodology to his studies. He was the author of legal tracts, and perhaps the most famous of these, *De methodo ac ratione studenti* (On the Study and Teaching of Roman Law), went through numerous editions between 1544 and 1564. His marriage to Georgine Carraxe (d. 1558) linked him to property she controlled at Farges in the territory of Bern, Switzerland. While at Padua he apparently became committed to Protestantism and engaged in correspondence with John Calvin (1509–1564), whom he may have met during one of his summer vacations at Farges.

Beginning in 1554 the relationship between Gribaldi (as well as other Italian exiles) and the community of Geneva was strained because of the fear of continuing antitrinitarianism following the execution of Michael Servetus in 1553. Gribaldi witnessed the trial of Servetus and rejected the idea that anyone should be put to death for the opinions they held. As a result, historians credit him and his followers—such as Valentino Gentile (d. 1566), Gian Paolo Alciati (d. 1565) and Giorgio Biandrata (1516–1588)—with an attempt to ensure religious freedom and toleration there. Calvin identified the continuation of antitrinitarian thought in Geneva with the three Italians and had Gribaldi permanently banned from the city in 1555. He returned to Padua but fled from there in the same year, as Venetian officials were cooperating with those in Rome in the investigation of suspected heretics. A brief stay in Tübingen ended when he was summoned before the senate of the university for interrogation concerning the Trinity. He fled to avoid their requirement that he put his views in writing. Imprisonment at Bern and then banishment followed in 1557, although he was allowed to return to his estate in Farges after the death of his wife. He died there of plague in 1564.

His brief religious writings (*Religionis christianae* and *Confessio fidei*) directly espouse the existence of three distinct gods—Father, Son, and Holy Spirit—although they also have a predestinarian character more reminiscent of traditional Calvinism. Most historians link his "tritheist" position with a desire to retain the philosophical notion of the unity of God. The trail of expulsions and condemnations he endured revealed the opposition he and his followers maintained to both orthodox Catholicism and mainstream Protestant confessions and signaled the beginning of serious problems for most Italian expatriates in Switzerland: previous sympathy for their difficulties quickly turned to aversion among local authorities. The ideas he promoted fit into the overall scheme of Italian antitrinitarianism that was capped by the work of Lelio (1525–1562) and Fausto (1539–1604) Sozzini and stood at the foundation of Unitarianism.

BIBLIOGRAPHY

Caccamo, Domenico. *Eretici italiani in Moravia, Polonia, Transilvania, 1558–1611*. Chicago, 1970. An important study, aimed at explaining the originality of Italian thinkers in the doctrinal debates of the Reformation and their influence, especially for Anabaptism.

Cantimori, Delio. *Eretici italiani del Cinquecento* (1939). 3d rev. ed. Edited by Adriano Prosperi. Turin, 1992. Earlier edition available in English translation: *Italian Heretics of the Sixteenth Century*, Cambridge, Mass., 1979. The classic and still-standard treatment of Italian heretics.

———. *Italiani a Basilea e a Zurigo nel Cinquecento*. Rome, 1947.

Cantimori, Delio, and E. Fiest, eds. *Per la storia degli eretici italiani del secolo XVI in Europa*. Rome, 1937. Collection of texts written by noteworthy Italian reformers interested in Protestant thought. Includes Gribaldi's brief texts *Religionis christianae* and *Confessio fidei*.

Church, Frederic C. *The Italian Reformers, 1534–1564* (1932). Reprint, New York, 1974. Dated and unsophisticated in ascribing Italian religious thought in this period essentially to Spanish influence, but still useful for context.

Pascal, A. "Gli antitrinitari piemontesi." *Bollettino storico-biografico subalpino* 22 (1920), 3–62.

Rotondò, Antonio. *Calvin and the Anti-Trinitarians*. Translated by John and Anne Tedeschi. Reformation Essays and Studies, 2. Saint Louis, 1968. Originally published as "Calvino e gli antitrinitari italiani." *Rivista storica italiana* 80 (1968), 759–784.

Ruffini, Francesco. *Studi sui riformatori italiani*. Edited by Arnaldo Bertola, Luigi Firpo, and Edoardo Ruffini. Turin, 1955. Section two includes two articles on Gribaldi originally published in *Rivista di storia del diritto italiano* 1 (1928), 205–269, 417–432.

Verzeichnis der im deutschen Sprachbereich erschienenen Drucke des XVI. Jahrhunderts. Stuttgart, 1983–. Vol. 8, nos. 3295–3317.

William V. Hudon

GRIEN, Hans Baldung. *See* Baldung, Hans.

GRINDAL, Edmund (c.1519–1583), English prelate, successively bishop of London, archbishop of York, and archbishop of Canterbury. He was born the son of a poor farmer in what he called the "little angle" of Saint Bees in the extreme northwest of England. Like many other northerners, he found his way into the wider world of an academic and clerical career, which began in the late 1530s at Pembroke Hall, Cambridge, where he became successively fellow, president, and master. In the years of the late Henrician religious reaction, he was ordained under the old ordinal and would later tell a group of radical Elizabethan Puritans that he regretted having said Mass. But by the reign of Edward VI Grindal had been converted to Reformed Protestantism by a reading of Heinrich Bullinger and emerged as a leader among the younger Cambridge reformers. He attracted the attention of both William Cecil and Bishop Nicholas Ridley, for whom he deputized as master of Pembroke. Grindal was deeply affected by the teaching and example of Martin Bucer, who occupied the Cambridge divinity chair in the last two years of his life. Later he would help to preserve Bucer's English writings, which in their printed form would be dedicated to him as archbishop of Canterbury. Grindal's understanding of the episcopal office was to be Bucerian, just as he later bequeathed to the English Protestant episcopate a model that was Grindalian. This model was evangelical, fraternal rather than "lordly," but strong on pastoral discipline.

As Ridley's lieutenant Grindal had been named to succeed him as bishop of London at the time of Edward VI's death. With Mary on the throne, he seems to have been deliberately consigned to the uncertain future, departing for Germany and leaving Ridley and his colleagues in Saint Paul's cathedral, John Rogers and John Bradford, to face the judgment and the flames of the Marian persecution. He spent most of the exile in and around Bucer's Strasbourg, learned German, and exercised leadership among the English exiles at the time of those "troubles of Frankfurt" about church order that anticipated the divisions within the Elizabethan church. He was much involved in the project that would lead to the Elizabethan editions of John Foxe's *Book of Martyrs*.

Grindal was one of the original group of Elizabethan bishops and as bishop of London played a leading and constructive role, helped by his friendship with Cecil, now effectively prime minister. The queen's insistence on literal adherence to a relatively conservative church settlement placed this advanced magisterial reformer in a difficult position, and, in the circumstances of the Vestiarian Controversy of the mid-1560s, strained his relations with Archbishop Matthew Parker, who alone among the senior bishops had not experienced the Marian exile. But Grindal had learned from Bucer that obstinate nonconformity over such trifles as the white linen surplice was in itself reprehensible, and it is a mistake to suppose that he had compromised his public standing as a "Puritan" bishop. His promotion, first to York in 1570, and then to Canterbury in 1576, cannot have surprised his contemporaries.

At York, Grindal effectively introduced not only the Elizabethan religious settlement but the Reformation itself to a region still conservative in its religious practice. He dealt rigorously with Catholic resistance and may have left the north with the mistaken impression that this problem was near solution. In Parliament Grindal had been active in attempts to secure more effective anti-Catholic legislation.

The high hopes with which Grindal's appointment to Canterbury was greeted in late 1575, especially in "forward"

Protestant circles, were to be dashed within little more than a year. His primacy coincided with a critical ideological contest to determine the internal and external alignments of the Elizabethan regime. There was probably a conservative conspiracy at court to destroy the archbishop. If so, the overscrupulous Grindal played into its hands. Required by the queen to order the suppression of the preaching conferences known as "prophesyings," and to curtail the number of licensed preachers, Grindal explained in a long letter modeled on the epistles of Ambrose to Emperor Theodosius, as tactless as it was courageous, why he could not comply. The upshot was his effective suspension from office by a queen who was barely restrained from depriving him altogether. There were plans for Grindal's resignation, but in 1583 he died still in office, a blind and broken man. He left a reputation for "primitive" consistency and was an acceptable figure in the estimation of such critics of episcopacy as John Milton.

BIBLIOGRAPHY

Primary Source

Grindal, Edmund. *The Remains of Edmund Grindal* (1843). Edited by W. Micholson. Reprint, New York, 1968. Essential source material.

Secondary Sources

Collinson, Patrick. *Archbishop Grindal, 1519–1583: The Struggle for a Reformed Church.* London and Berkeley, 1979. The only modern biographical study.

———. *The Religion of Protestants: The Church in English Society, 1559–1625.* Reprint, Oxford, 1984.

———. *The Elizabethan Puritan Movement.* Reprint, Oxford, 1990.

Cross, Claire. *The Royal Supremacy in the Elizabethan Church.* Cambridge, 1969. Includes a lengthy extract from Grindal's letter to the queen.

Strype, John. *The Life and Acts of the Most Reverend Father in God, Edmund Grindal* (1710). Reprint, Oxford, 1962. Its publication was precipitated by a political storm (the Sacheverell affair). Strype's account is defensive. He prints and paraphrases many documents.

PATRICK COLLINSON

GROCYN, William (1446?–1519), early English scholar of Greek, textual critic, and priest. Grocyn enjoyed an excellent early education at Winchester, and proceeded to New College, Oxford (1465; fellow in 1467). In about 1483 he was reader in divinity in Magdalen College. Having learned some Greek at Oxford, he left in 1488 to spend two years studying it intensively in Italy. On returning to Oxford in 1490 he lectured on Greek.

Grocyn published almost nothing. The four-line epigram still often credited to him was actually written in the tenth century (R. W. Chambers, *Thomas More,* London, 1935, p. 82). His only extant writing is a letter of just over one folio page included in Thomas Linacre's translation of Proclus's *De Sphaera* published by Aldo Manuzio (1499). This letter shows Grocyn's conservative preference for Aristotle over Plato and his alertness to the potentialities of the still-new art of printing, but it is not really remarkable.

The moment that could have made Grocyn a major figure in textual criticism and thus an influence on the Reformation came in late 1501. In the course of a series of lectures on the *Ecclesiastica Hierarchia* then attributed to the Dionysius who was the apostle Paul's sole convert in Athens, Grocyn came to see that the attribution must be false and honestly admitted the fact to his audience. But he did not publish his conclusions. Instead, when he found that his discovery disturbed his audience in Saint Paul's Cathedral he dropped it. Thirty years later Erasmus asserted that many still alive remembered Grocyn's conclusion, but Erasmus's own published doubts about Dionysius had made him a villain in the eyes of the orthodox (including, in this case, Luther), a fate Grocyn was not inclined to share. He lived on quietly without publishing, a highly orthodox churchman, "almost to the point of superstition," according to Erasmus. Erasmus declared in a letter to an English friend that Grocyn, then an old man, had wasted his talents.

BIBLIOGRAPHY

Burrows, Montagu. "Memoir of William Grocyn." In *Collectanea, Second Series,* edited by Montagu Burrows, pp. 332–380. Oxford, 1890. The only extended discussion in English, but inevitably old-fashioned. Contains useful documentary appendixes on Grocyn's books. Cites Erasmus's references to Grocyn.

Emden, A. B. "Grocyn, William." In *A Biographical Register of the University of Oxford to A.D. 1500,* vol. 2, pp. 827–830. Oxford, 1957–1959. Contains a compendium of documentary references to Grocyn and a list of his benefices. Especially valuable for a list of over two hundred books and manuscripts from Grocyn's large library, which gives insight into his intellectual interests.

Krusman, V. E. "William Grocyn." In *K dvadtsati-pyatiletiyu uchenopedagogicheskoĭ deyatel'nosti Ivana Mikhaĭlovicha Grevsa, 1884–1909: Sbornik stateĭ ego uchenikov* [In Honor of Twenty-five Years of Scholarship and Teaching by Ivan Mikhailovich Grevs, 1884–1909: A Collection of Essays by His Students], pp. 321–340. Saint Petersburg, 1911. No recorded copy in North America. Copies in the British Library, London; Saltykov-Shchedrin Public Library, Saint Petersburg; National Library, Prague. The only comprehensive twentieth-century interpretation of Grocyn in any language, by a widely published specialist on the beginnings of English humanism. Sees Grocyn's significance as twofold: a patron of English humanists and a teacher. Like Burrows, Krusman is puzzled by Grocyn's failure to publish, and like him attributes this fact to bad eyes, even though Grocyn was a bibliophile and an omnivorous reader.

Schulte-Herbrüggen, H. "Et in Anglia Hellas: William Grocyn und die Frühgeschichte der englischen Gräzistik." In *Roma Renascens: Beiträge zur Spätantike und Rezeptionsgeschichte; Ilona Opelt von ihren Freunden und Schülern zum 9.7.1988 in Verehrung gewidmet,* edited by Martin Wissemann, pp. 321–354. Frankfurt a.M., 1988. A detailed catalogue of Grocyn's Greek manuscripts and books, with an interpretation of their significance for his career.

JOHN B. GLEASON

GROOT, Huig de. *See* Grotius, Hugo.

GROPPER, Johannes (1503–1559), Catholic reformer, theologian, and cardinal. Born of a prominent family at Soest, Westphalia, Gropper attended the University of Cologne, where he took a doctorate in civil law in 1525; meanwhile he was teaching himself theology. He was appointed chancellor of the archbishopric of Cologne (1526) and canon of its cathedral (1534). In 1528 he drew up a plan for reorganizing the electorate/archbishopric of Cologne which he tried to avoid conflicts between civil and ecclesiastical law. He attended the Diet of Augsburg in 1530 and established friendly relations with Melanchthon.

The archbishop of Cologne, Hermann von Wied, convoked a synod to reform his electorate in 1536. In preparation Gropper composed reform regulations with an Erasmian flavor. Reflecting these reforms was a new catechism written by Gropper, *Enchiridion christianae institutionis* (Cologne, 1538), which enjoyed considerable popularity, in part because it sought common ground between Catholics and Protestants on disputed points. Gropper's catechism developed his idea of a twofold justification: an imputed justification effected by faith (obviously derived from Luther) and an inherent justification, which by itself always remained insufficient.

Gropper's mediating position recommended him to Charles V, who was seeking to find a theological compromise that would conciliate both Protestants and Catholics and avoid civil strife within the empire. Gropper supported the Colloquies of Hagenau and Worms in 1540, which Charles had called in hope of achieving reconciliation. Although these colloquies accomplished little, the emperor sponsored the Colloquy of Regensburg of 1541, the most important effort of the Reformation era to find a doctrinal consensus. The main Catholic representatives were Gropper and Johann Eck. Only Eck was a hard-liner, but his influence was offset by the conciliatory cardinal-legate, Gasparo Contarini. The main Protestant representatives were Melanchthon and Martin Bucer. Discussions centered on the twenty-three articles of the Regensburg Interim, which Gropper and Bucer had drafted. The colloquy reached agreement on most points, including a statement on justification reflecting Gropper's twofold theory. Later the Council of Trent rejected double justification. But the colloquy could not agree on the Eucharist, and it collapsed. Many participants later wrote apologies to justify their role.

Returning to Cologne, Gropper encountered the most difficult struggle of his life: Archbishop von Wied, in cooperation with Bucer, tried to convert the electorate to Lutheranism. Had he succeeded, four Protestant electors would have outvoted three Catholic ones, and German history would have taken a different course. Gropper led the university and the chapter of canons in successfully combating von Wied. Gropper appealed personally to Charles V to replace von Wied and published several works in German defending Catholicism. Gropper helped compose the Interim of Augsburg, which Charles V imposed on many Protestant territories after his victory in the First Schmalkald War. In 1551 Gropper spoke before the Council of Trent, attacking Lutheran teaching on penance. In 1555 Paul IV named him a cardinal. When Gropper died at Rome in 1559, Paul IV preached the funeral sermon. The Erasmian reformer had come almost full circle.

BIBLIOGRAPHY

Bautz, Friedrich Wilhelm, ed. *Biographische-Bibliographisches Kirchenlexikon.* Hamm, 1970–. See vol. 2, pp. 355–357.

Braunisch, Reinhard. "Gropper, Johannes, 1503–1559." In *Theologische Realenzyklopädie,* vol. 14, pp. 266–270. Berlin, 1985. The most recent account with an up-to-date bibliography.

Gulik, Wilhelm van. *Johannes Gropper, 1503–1559: Ein Beitrag zur Kirchengeschichte Deutschlands, besonders der Rheinlande im 16. Jahrhundert.* Freiburg, 1906. Detailed study, now dated.

Jedin, Hubert. *A History of the Council of Trent.* 3 vols. Trans. by Ernest Graf. London, 1957, 1961, and 1963. Volume 1 covers the Regensburg Colloquy. Volume 2 covers the doctrine of two-fold justification at Trent.

Klaiber, Wilbirgis, ed. *Katholische Kontroverstheologen und Reformer des 16. Jahrhunderts: Ein Werkverzeichnis.* Münster, 1978.

Lipgens, Walter. *Kardinal Johannes Gropper, 1503–1559, und die Anfänge der katholischen Reform in Deutschland.* Münster, 1951. Standard biography with thorough bibliography.

Schroeder, Joseph. "Gropper, John." In *The Catholic Encyclopedia,* edited by H. Herbermann et al., vol. 7, pp. 36–37. New York, 1910.

Verzeichnis der im deutschen Sprachbereich erschienenen Drucke des XVI. Jahrhunderts. Stuttgart, 1983–. See vol. 8, nos. 3389–3418.

JOHN PATRICK DONNELLY

GROSSMANN, Caspar. *See* Megander, Caspar.

GROTIUS, Hugo (also Huig de Groot; 1583–1645), Dutch jurist and Christian humanist. Born on 10 April 1583 in Delft, the "Miracle of Holland," as Grotius was called, matriculated in the University of Leiden in 1594 and was presented with the honorary doctor of laws degree at Orléans in 1599. In the same year Grotius became advocate of the Court and High Council of Holland and in 1604 was appointed Latin historiographer of Holland. Casting his lot with that of the grand pensionary Johan van Oldenbarnevlt (1547–1619), Grotius became attorney general at the courts of Holland, Westfriesland, and Zeeland in 1607 and in 1613 was appointed city pensionary of Rotterdam.

In his new function Grotius became entangled in the politico-religious struggle between liberal and orthodox Calvinists—that is, between Arminians, or Remonstrants, and Gomarists, or Counter-Remonstrants—centered on the doctrine of predestination and the authority of the state in church matters. Because of his Arminian leanings, strengthened by the office he held, Grotius rejected the Gomarist principles of absolute predestination and collateral powers for the church. Instead, he argued for the primacy of ethical principle over dogma and advocated strict supervision of the church by the state. In a series of tracts, such as *Meletius* (1611), *Ordinum Pietas* (1613), *De Imperio* (1614), and *Defenso Fidei* (1617), Grotius defended the right of the States of Holland to exert its full authority (*jus magistratus*) in ecclesiastical affairs, including the appointment of ministers, the decision of doctrinal controversies, and the prohibition of a national synod. After the coup d'état of Stadtholder Prince Maurits van Nassau (1567–1625) in 1618, however, and the convocation of the Synod of Dordrecht of 1618–1619, Remonstrantism was condemned as heterodoxy, Oldenbarnevelt was executed, and Grotius was sentenced to life imprisonment. Grotius's subsequent detention at Loevestein (1619–1621) was only of short duration thanks to a spectacular escape in a book chest provided by his resourceful wife, Maria van Reigersberch (1589–1653).

During his ensuing exile at Paris, Grotius published an apology, the *Verantwoordingh van de Wettelijcke Regieringh* (1622), while hoping for a personal rehabilitation and the revocation of the decisions of the Synod of Dordrecht. In an attempt to force the issue, Grotius decided to return to Holland in late 1631 but had to make a hasty retreat following an eviction order of the States General. Finally, cutting all ties with his beloved patria, Grotius in 1635 accepted the offer of the Swedish chancellor Axel Oxenstierna (1583–1654) to become the Swedish ambassador in Paris. Frustrated by political machinations and the declining international status of Sweden, Grotius devoted himself in the 1640s to the dissemination of his irencist and Erasmian ideal, the restoration of the *respublica christiana.* As a Christian humanist and member of an international ecumenical movement dedicated to healing the breach in the Christian community opened up by the Reformation and Counter-Reformation, Grotius argued for a *religio reformata* in the sense of a reestablishment of church order, the abolition of abuses and superstitions, and a check on the uncontrolled growth in liturgical and doctrinal matters. His plea for an integral restitution of the early church, however, was met by incomprehension on the part of his Remonstrant friends in Holland, skepticism from the Catholic side, and downright hostility from the orthodox Calvinist camp, who accused him of being a crypto-Catholic ("Grotius papizans"). Recalled from Paris in 1645, Grotius died on his way back to Stockholm at Rostock on 28 August 1645.

BIBLIOGRAPHY

Primary Sources

Grotius, Hugo. *Mare Liberum* (1609). Reprint, New York, 1972.
———. *De Antiquitate Reipublicae Batavicae.* Leiden, 1610.
———. *Ordinum Hollandiae ac Westfrisiae Pietas.* Leiden, 1613.
———. *Defenso fidei catholicae de Satisfactione Christi adversus Faustum Socinum Senensum* (1617). Edited by Edwin Rabbie. Translated by Hotze Mulder. Assen, 1990. In Latin and English.
———. *Bewys van de waere Godsdienst.* N.p., 1622.
———. *Verantwoordingh van de Wettelijcke Regieringh van Hollandt Ende West-Vrieslandt.* Hoorn, 1622.
———. *Dicta Poetarum quae apud Ioann, Stobaeum extant.* Paris, 1623.
———. *De jure Belli ac Pacis.* Paris, 1625.
———. *Inleidinghe tot de Hollandsche Rechtsgeleerdheid* (1631). Annotated and edited by F. Dovring et al., Reprint, Leiden, 1965.
———. *Commentatio ad Loca quaedam N. Testamenti quae de Antichristo agunt.* Amsterdam, 1640.
———. *Annotationum in Novum Testamentum.* 3 vols. Paris, 1641–1650.
———. *Annotata ad Consultationem Cassandri.* Leiden, 1642.
———. *Via ad pacem ecclesiasticam.* Paris, 1642.
———. *Votum pro pace ecclesiastica, contra Examen Andrae Riveti, & alios irreconciliables.* Paris, 1642.
———. *Annotata ad Vetum Testamentum.* Amsterdam, 1644.
———. *De Imperio Summarum Potestatum Circa Sacra.* Paris, 1647.
———. *Philosophorum Sententiae de fato.* Paris, 1648.
———. *Annales et Historiae De Rebus Belgicus.* Amsterdam, 1657.

Secondary Sources

Gellinek, Christian. *Hugo Grotius.* Boston, 1983. Comprehensive literary analysis of Grotius's main works written in Latin and Dutch.
Meulen, Jacob Ter, and P. J. J. Diermanse. *Bibliographie des écrits imprimés de Hugo Grotius.* The Hague, 1950. Comprehensive list of published works of Grotius in all their editions and translations.
Mothuysen, P. C., et al. *Briefwisseling van Hugo Grotius.* Rijks Geschiedkundige Publicatien, Grote Serie. 13 vols. to date. The Hague, 1928–. The correspondence of Grotius furnished with explanatory footnotes.
Nellen, H. J. M. *Hugo de Groot, 1583–1645: De loopbaan van een geleerd staatsman.* Weesp, 1985. Critique of Romein's and Fruin's biographical studies on Grotius.
Posthumus Meyjes, G. H. M. *Meletius, sive, de iis quae inter christianos conveniunt epistola.* Studies in the History of Christian Thought 40. Leiden, 1988. Critical edition of Grotius's first theological treatise discovered in the Amsterdam University Library.
Wolf, Dieter. *Die Irenik des Hugo Grotius nach ihren Prinzipien und biographisch-geistesgeschichtlichen Perspektiven.* Schriften des Instituts für Wissenschaftliche Irenik der Johann Wolfgang Goethe Universität, Frankfurt am Main, 9. Marburg, 1969. Thorough discussion of Grotius's theory of religious unity and the spiritual-religious foundations and aims of his irenicism.
The World of Hugo Grotius, 1583–1645. Proceedings of an international conference, Rotterdam, 6–9 April 1983. Amsterdam, 1984. Valuable collection of essays, in particular the articles by Posthumus Meyjes and de Jonge on Grotius's activities as irenicist and biblical exegete.

MARCUS P. M. VINK

GRUMBACH, Argula von (also von Stauff; c.1490–c.1564) Bavarian noblewoman and outspoken defender of Martin Luther's teachings. Her father gave her a Coburg Bible in 1502. After her parents' early death, Argula lived in the household of Duke Albert IV of Bavaria Munich. She served Duchess Kunigund. She married a knight, Friedrich von Grumbach, and bore four children before his death in 1532. Luther's message early attracted her and was a matter of disagreement between Argula and her loyal Catholic husband. She corresponded with Luther and other reformers.

Von Grumbach came to public attention when she protested in writing the dismissal and imprisonment of Ingolstadt instructor Arsacius Seehofer, who was accused of being a Lutheran. She kept her initial appeals secret, but the recipients allowed them to be published. They and her subsequent letters appeared in numerous editions in late 1523 and 1524. Impressive are not only her courage but also her considerable knowledge of the Bible, from which she argued, though she read and wrote only German. On 20 September 1523 she addressed the theologians of the University of Ingolstadt, calling Seehofer's evangelical beliefs correct. She offered to appear before them and defend Luther's and Philipp Melanchthon's teachings further. "Aren't you all ashamed," she wrote, "that you have had to deny all of Martin's writings?" On the same day she appealed to William IV, duke of Bavaria, to intervene: "God's Word should and must govern all things." Her audacity angered her high-ranking cousin, Adam von Törring, who was said to have remarked that her husband should "wall her up." She eloquently justified her actions. The theologians' response, represented as that of an Ingolstadt student, Johann von Landshut, took the form of mocking doggerel, to which she replied in kind: "I will not ever cease/to speak at home and in the street." She maintained that women as well as men received the Holy Spirit.

After 1524 Argula von Grumbach wrote no more for public consumption, but because of her, her husband lost his post. She held to her evangelical convictions, went to Coburg in 1530 to dine with Luther, and in 1563 was imprisoned briefly for presiding at burial services.

BIBLIOGRAPHY

Bainton, Roland H. *Women of the Reformation in Germany and Italy.* Minneapolis, 1971. See especially pp. 96–109.

Classen, Albrecht. "Footnotes to the German Canon: Maria von Wolkenstein and Argula von Grumbach." In *The Politics of Gender in Early Modern Europe,* edited by Jean R. Brink, Allison P. Coudert, and Maryanne C. Horowitz, pp. 131–47. Kirksville, Mo., 1989.

Kolde, Theodor. "Arsacius Seehofer und Argula von Grumbach." *Beiträge zur bayerischen Kirchengeschichte* 11 (1905), 49–77, 97–125, 149–187. Indispensable scholarly account rooted in the primary sources.

Russell, Paul A. *Lay Theology in the Reformation: Popular Pamphleteers in Southwest Germany, 1521–1525.* Cambridge, 1986. Reliant on Bainton, Kolde, and a close reading of von Grumbach's writings; see especially pp. 191–201.

Verzeichnis der im deutschen Sprachbereich erschienenen Drucke des XVI. Jahrhunderts. Stuttgart, 1983–. Vol. 8, nos. 3656–3687.

SUSAN C. KARANT-NUNN

GRÜNEWALD, Matthias (also Mathis Gothardt Neithardt; c.1475–1528), German painter of the sixteenth century. He was probably born in Würzburg, but nothing certain is known of his early life or training. He served two successive archbishop-electors of Mainz, whose castle was at Aschaffenburg. For the second of these, Cardinal Albert of Brandenburg, he also worked at Halle.

Aside from a few drawings, Grünewald's surviving compositions consist of oil paintings that deal almost exclusively with religious themes. By far his most important contribution consists of the remarkable set of panels painted around 1512–1515 for the Isenheim Altarpiece. This work was commissioned by the abbot of the Monastery of Saint Anthony at Isenheim. The altarpiece, in its closed state, displays at the center one of the most awe-inspiring Crucifixion scenes ever painted. Almost as famous is the visionary Resurrection, which—along with depictions of the Annunciation, Madonna and Child, and Angelic Concert—come into view when the outer wings are opened. In its final transformation the altarpiece features two compositions devoted to Saint Anthony, namesake of the Antonian order. Scholarship has found one source for the iconography of these panels in the writings of the medieval mystic Saint Bridget of Sweden. Noteworthy as well are the healing functions assigned the paintings by the Isenheim Antonians, who ran a hospital for disabling diseases.

Modern efforts to link Grünewald with the Reformation appeal primarily to the possibly fugitive nature of his movements during the years 1526–1528 and the presence of some Protestant writings on the list of belongings left at his death. These included twenty-seven sermons by Martin Luther, a New Testament, and an ambiguously titled treatise that has been variously interpreted as a collection of peasant articles or an Anabaptist tract.

BIBLIOGRAPHY

Hayum, Andrée. *The Isenheim Altarpiece: God's Medicine and the Painter's Vision.* Princeton, 1989. Emphasizes the healing function of the altarpiece in its hospital setting.

Parshall, Linda B., and Peter W. Parshall. *Art and the Reformation: An Annotated Bibliography.* Boston, 1986. See items 1049–1060.

Scheja, Georg. *The Isenheim Altarpiece.* Translated by Robert Erich Wolf. New York, 1969. Evaluates medieval theological sources for the altarpiece.

CARL C. CHRISTENSEN

GRYNAEUS, Johann Jacob (Ger., Johann Gryner, Gryn; 1540–1617), Swiss Reformed theologian and Basel University professor. Born in Bern but educated in Basel, Grynaeus studied theology at Basel with Martin Borrhaus and Simon Sulzer and at Tübingen (where he obtained his doctorate) with Jakob Heerbrand, Theodor Schnepf, and Jakob Andreae. When his father, Thomas, died of the plague in 1565, Grynaeus succeeded him as pastor at Rotelen, near Basel. A decade later he became professor of Old Testament at Basel. As a student, Grynaeus had absorbed a Lutheran position on the Lord's Supper from Sulzer, but, by the time he joined the faculty, he questioned Christ's ubiquity and rejected the Lutheran arguments on the real presence. Instead, he adopted a Reformed position and criticized the Lutheran 1577 Formula of Concord.

Facing opposition from Sulzer and others, Grynaeus gladly accepted a call in 1584 from Johann Casimir, elector of the Palatinate, to oversee the reorganization of Heidelberg University. Grynaeus promptly promoted Reformed theology in the territory. Two years later, with Sulzer now dead, Grynaeus succeeded his old professor in Basel as *Antistes*, a clerical position that made him pastor at the minster, head of Basel's clergy, archdeacon of the territory, and university professor of New Testament.

Grynaeus now exerted strong influence on Basel's theology and practice. He revamped the Latin school and saw to it that children were instructed in parishes weekly rather than only on the three feasts of Christmas, Easter, and Pentecost. Grynaeus redirected Basel's theology, shifting from a Lutheran course that had been favored by Sulzer toward a Calvinist position found in other Swiss cities. He could not persuade the city to adopt Heinrich Bullinger's 1566 Second Helvetic Confession. (Basel finally accepted it in 1644.) In 1590, however, Grynaeus did revive the 1534 Basel Confession that Sulzer had set aside. Although blind by 1612, Grynaeus preached and lectured until his death, leaving behind volumes of biblical exegesis and writings on dogmatic and practical theology.

BIBLIOGRAPHY

Primary Sources

Grynaeus, Johann Jacob. *Joannis Jacobi Grynaei vita et mors ex variis ipsius scriptis colleeta et edita*. Basel, 1618. Includes Grynaeus's own autobiography.

———. *Epistolae familiares LXV ad Christophor. Andr. Ivlivm ... Norimbergae et Altorfii*. Frankfurt, 1715. Preface includes biographical information on Grynaeus.

Secondary Sources

Hagenbach, Karl Rudolf. *Kritische Geschichte der Entstehung und der Schicksale der ersten Baslerkonfession*. Basel, 1827. See pp. 137–156. Recounts Grynaeus's efforts to reissue the 1534 Basel Confession. Also available on microfiche from the Inter Documentation Company in the collection *Reformed Protestantism*, section 1, *The Swiss Urban Reformation*, Zug, 1982.

ROBERT ROSIN

GRYNAEUS, Simon (1493–1541), German humanist, professor of Greek at the University of Basel, and, together with Oswald Myconius, leader of the Reformed church in Basel after the death of Johannes Oecolampadius (1531). Born to a peasant family in Swabia, Grynaeus was first educated in classical studies in the city school of Pforzheim, then continued his studies at the universities of Vienna and Wittenberg. In 1526 he was appointed professor of Greek at the University of Heidelberg. When invited by Oecolampadius in 1529 to teach Greek at the University of Basel, he described himself in his response as a scholar of classical literature who intended to focus on the study of medicine. With its vigorous intellectual atmosphere stimulated by humanists and printers such as Erasmus, Hieronymus Froben, and Bonifacius Amerbach, Basel provided Grynaeus ample opportunity to edit and translate classical writings.

During the 1530s Grynaeus became increasingly active in the Basel church. He helped prepare the Basel Confession (1534) and the first Helvetic Confession (1536), always seeking to reconcile Lutheran and Zwinglian views. In 1536 he began lecturing on the New Testament at the university. His correspondence with Calvin provided an important link between Geneva and Basel.

By the late 1530s Grynaeus was a spokesman for a majority of clergy who asserted repeatedly that the city council had failed to give them adequate support in their attempts to discipline the faithful by use of the ban (i.e., expulsion from the church and, in theory at least, also from guilds and city offices). The city council members, for their part, had hoped that regular meetings of the clergy (synods) under the supervision of university theologians would produce a unified and disciplined clergy. To the council's dismay, the pastors seemed to be querulous and divided. Therefore the council announced in 1539 that it, rather than the pastors, would enforce the ban. In order to insure greater unity, the council had also required in 1538 that all clergy become doctoral candidates at the university. Grynaeus, who had not earned a doctorate, was subject to this rule. He and Myconius protested bitterly, declaring that the freedom of the church was endangered, but to no avail. Grynaeus rejected the doctorate as a medieval, papal accretion that had supplanted the practice of the early church, the apostolic laying on of hands. Eventually exempted from the doctoral requirement, Grynaeus was named rector of the university on 1 May 1543, just three months before his death.

BIBLIOGRAPHY

Die Amerbachkorrespondenz. Edited by Alfred Hartmann and Beat Rudolf Jenny. 9 vols. Basel, 1942-. Letters describing Grynaeus's humanistic scholarship are in vols. 3–5. Capito and Artolf describe Grynaeus's position regarding the doctoral requirement in vol. 5, nos. 2269 and 2389.

Bietenholz, Peter G. "Simon Grynaeus." In *Contemporaries of Erasmus: A Biographical Register of the Renaissance and Reformation*, edited by Peter G Bietenholz and Thomas B. Deutscher, vol. 2, pp. 142–146. Toronto, 1986. The best recent survey of Grynaeus's career, emphasizing his humanistic contributions.

Burckhardt, Paul. *Introduction to Das Tagebuch des Johannes Gast*. Basler Chroniken, vol. 8. Basel, 1945. Summarizes the conflicts between council and clergy during the late 1530s and provides a source bibliography for that period.

Rädle, Herbert. "Simon Grynaeus, 1493–1541: Briefe: Ausgewählt, übersetzt und herausgegeben." *Basler Zeitschrift für Geschichte und*

Altertumskunde 90 (1990), 35–118. German translation of correspondence with Melanchthon, Oecolampadius, and Calvin.

Verzeichnis der im deutschen Sprachbereich erschienenen Drucke des XVI. Jahrhunderts. Stuttgart, 1983–. See vol. 8, nos. 3748–3823.

Wernle, Paul. *Calvin und Basel bis zum Tode des Myconius, 1535–1552*. Basel, 1909. Depicts Grynaeus as a primary contact between Calvin and the church in Basel.

PAUL L. NYHUS

GUALTHER, Rudolf. *See* Gwalther, Rudolf.

GUERRERO, Pedro (1510–1576), Spanish cleric, theologian, and archbishop. Born in Leza, near Logroño (Spain), Guerrero studied at the University of Alcalá de Henares, and starting in 1529 at the University of Salamanca. One of his professors at Salamanca was the famous Dominican theologian Francisco de Vitoria, whose teaching was to have a profound effect on Guerrero's intellectual development. In 1535 Guerrero became one of the chairs of theology at the University of Sigüenza, where he remained until his appointment as archbishop of Granada, which was confirmed in 1546. After his arrival in his new diocese in March of the following year, Guerrero marked out a reform agenda, anticipating some of the provisions that the Council of Trent would later make obligatory.

In March 1551 he left Granada to go to Trent, where he took part in the second period of the council (1551–1552). His theological erudition and his pastoral experience made him one of the most influential of the council fathers from Spain. During the third period of the council (1561–1563), however, he emerged as the undisputed leader of the Iberian bishops and one of the outstanding spokesmen in favor of a rigorous reform of the church. With particular fervor he endeavored to get the council to define the obligation of bishops to reside in their own dioceses as a direct divine mandate (*de iure divino*). Such a definition would have meant nullifying the papal dispensations that many of the bishops enjoyed; therefore the proposal met with fierce opposition. The proposal was not any more welcome in Rome; Pius IV ended up forbidding any further discussion of the subject.

Upon his return to Granada on 5 May 1564, Guerrero devoted his energies to implementing the decrees of the council. In 1565 he convened a provincial council, but its acts could not be promulgated because of opposition from the cathedral chapters. In 1573 he convened a diocesan synod, and this time the constitutions it approved were published in a regular manner. Through his tireless work on behalf of reform, which he also carried out through visitations of his diocese, he battled against the vices and ignorance of the clergy and endeavored to raise the level of Christian understanding among the people. He devoted particular attention to the religious instruction of the Moriscos (i.e., Christians of Muslim origin) through mass catechizing, for which he enlisted the help of the Jesuits. He died on 2 April 1576 and was buried in the cathedral of Grenada.

BIBLIOGRAPHY

Primary Source

Guerrero, Pedro. *Don Pedro Guerrero: Epistolario y documentación*. Edited by Juan López Martín. Publicaciones del Instituto español de historia eclesiástica, subsidia 13. Rome, 1974. Fundamental edition of Guerrero's letters and other documents concerning him.

Secondary Sources

Jedin, Hubert. *A History of the Council of Trent*. 4 vols. London, 1957–1961. See vol. 3 and vol. 4, pt. 2, concerning the part played by Guerrero in the second and third phases of the Council of Trent.

López Martín, Juan. "Don Pedro Guerrero com obispo del tiempo de la Contrarreforma." *Archivo Teológico Granadino* 31 (1968), 193–231.

———. *La imagen del obispo en el pensamiento teológico-pastoral de don Pedro Guerrero en Trento*. Publicaciones del Instituto español de historia eclesiástica, monografías 16. Rome, 1971.

Marín Ocete, Antonio. *El arzobispo don Pedro Guerrero y la política conciliar española en el siglo XVI*. Madrid, 1970.

AGOSTINO BORROMEO
Translated from Italian by Robert E. Shillenn

GUEVARA, Antonio de (c.1480–1545), Spanish political writer and moralist. Born into a prominent family at Treceño, he spent his youth at the court of Ferdinand and Isabella and served as a page to prince Juan until the latter's death in 1497. After joining the Franciscans in 1504, Guevara was appointed court preacher in 1521, largely because, as an avid royalist, he had opposed the *comuneros*. He was named royal chronicler to Charles V in 1526 but spent most of the next three years working with the Inquisition on its prosecution of the Valencian Moriscos and then as one of the theologians appointed to examine the writings of Desiderius Erasmus. He accompanied the emperor to Tunis in 1535 and was appointed bishop of Mondoñedo in 1537.

Guevara is best known for his books of advice to princes and courtiers. They include the popular *Vida del famosísimo Emperador Marco Aurelio con el Relox de príncipes* (1529), as well as three works published in 1539: *El despertador de cortesanos*, *Una Década de Césares*, and *Libro llamado Menosprecio de corte y alabança de aldea*. Like his *Epístolas familiares*, a series of 112 essays also published in 1539, all are noted for a florid, moralizing style that presages the baroque and for a wealth of invented quotations. He advocates an imperial monarchy based upon Roman tradition but guided by Christian principles and warns of the pitfalls of intrigue.

In his later years Guevara turned to devotional writing. His *Oratorio de religiosos y exercicio de virtuosos* and *Libro llamado Monte Calvario* are, like his earlier works, more noted for style than for depth or originality. Immensely popular in his own day, Guevara is now remembered primarily for his defense of the imperial ideal that inspired Charles V in his early years. He died at Mondoñedo in 1545.

BIBLIOGRAPHY

Costes, R. *Antonio de Guevara: Sa vie et son oeuvre.* 2 vols. Bordeaux, 1925–1926.

Gibbs, J. *La vida de Fray Antonio de Guevara.* Valladolid, Spain, 1960.

Verzeichnis der im deutschen Sprachbereich erschienenen Drucke des XVI. Jahrhunderts. Stuttgart, 1983–. See vol. 8, nos. 4008–4026.

WILLIAM S. MALTBY

GUISE, HOUSE OF. *See* Lorraine-Guise, House of.

GÜNZBURG, Johann Eberlin von (c.1455–1534), German humanist, reformer, and pamphleteer. Besides the fact that he was born in the margravate of Burgau near the Swabian city of Günzburg, not much is known of his family background; it is clear, however, that his parents were impoverished members of the lower nobility. He was educated at the universities of Basel and Freiburg im Breisgau; by the time he was thirty years old, he was a priest in the diocese of Augsburg and a member of the strict begging order of observant Franciscans. Eberlin was not suited by temperament or interest for this order of friars. He complained bitterly about long fasts, bans on luxuries, and prohibition on being in the company of women. He was convinced the monastic life was against God, God's word, and nature. Eberlin was an avid reader of Martin Luther's famous pamphlets of 1520, *An den christlichen Adel deutscher Nation von des christlichen Standes Besserung* (Address to the Christian Nobility of the German Nation), *De captivate Babylonica ecclesiae praeludium* (The Babylonian Captivity of the Church), and *Von den Freiheit eines Christen Menschen* (The Freedom of the Christian). He debated Luther's ideas with his brothers in the cloister at Ulm, and as a result he was asked to leave; he set out upon a wandering course that ultimately led him, albeit briefly, to the side of Martin Luther.

Eberlin's ideas were set forth in dozens of unique pamphlets that appeared in many editions throughout the 1520s. In 1521 he published a series of short pamphlets in the vernacular titled *Die 15 Bundgenossen* (Fifteen Comrades). In these tracts, which established his Reformation credentials, he called for reform in all areas of life. One of most the interesting examples of his early Reformation work was the eleventh pamphlet, *Wolfaria,* about a fictional land where life goes well. As was typical of social reform plans, Eberlin envisioned a state without lawyers or oppressive bodies of canon and imperial law. In every aspect of life, much responsibility was placed on the shoulders of the individual Christian. In recent years a number of scholars have tried to describe the source and meaning of Eberlin's utopian vision, employing such phrases as "aristocratic paternalism," "nascent form of democracy," "radical Lutheranism," and "precursor of National Socialism." It is likely that Eberlin was familiar with Thomas More's *Utopia* and the work of Diodorus Siculus, who in the first century summarized in his *Blessed Island* many of the egalitarian fantasies inherited by the Middle Ages.

Although Eberlin was one of the first to discuss in depth sixteenth-century social, economic, and political problems, he also had much to say about religion. "Doctor Luther has spoken as I am writing," he was careful to point out, and he was anxious to convince his readers that his three years in Wittenberg lent him special authority. He hoped the German lands would witness a revival of evangelical Christianity of the type that had prevailed before the advent of scholastic doctors. He directly attacked abuses of power by the Catholic church and the corruption within it. With satire, accusation, and indictment, he lashed out at worldly bishops, priests, wandering and begging monks, and all monastic people. One of the major contributions of Eberlin to the Lutheran Reformation was that he helped to organize Luther's religious ideas into clear and concise statements that enabled the lay reader to grasp the basic points of Lutheran theology. The central points of Lutheran teaching—the instrumentality of the scriptures in knowing Christ as the central and basic element of Christian faith, the theology of the cross, justification by faith, Luther's view of the Eucharist, the priesthood of all believers, and the ultimate authority of the Bible—are all clearly stated in his pamphlets.

In 1525 Eberlin entered the court of George II of Wertheim, who had been an early supporter of Luther and who was an enlightened ruler of his lands; after the Peasants' War of 1524–1526, he was one of the few German princes to reach a compromise with the peasants regarding certain grievances. It was in this relatively peaceful realm that Eberlin—aiming to teach his countrymen their own history—completed a translation into German of Tacitus's *Germania.* In 1530 Eberlin moved for the final time, to Leuterhausen, where he died. Although it is difficult to assess Eberlin's significance in the cause of the Reformation, most agree that he was a friend of the masses, a popular preacher, and an imaginative reformer.

BIBLIOGRAPHY

Primary Source

Günzburg, Johann Eberlin. *Ausgewählte (sämtliche) Schriften.* 3 vols. Halle, 1896–1900. Contains the majority of Eberlin's Reformation pamphlets.

Secondary Sources

Baldini, A. Enzo. "Riforma Lutherna e Utopia: Gli 'Statuti del Paese di Wolfaria' di Johann Eberlin." *Il Pensiero Politico* 19 (1986), 3–29. Contains the most recent and thorough bibliography of recent scholarship on Johann Eberlin von Günzburg.

Cole, Richard G. "The Reformation in Print: German Pamphlets and Propaganda." *Archiv für Reformationsgeschichte* 66 (1975), 93–102. Treats in detail Eberlin's use of the print medium in spreading Reformation ideas.

Riggenbach, Berhnard. *Johann Eberlin von Günzburg und sein Reform Program* (1874). Reprint, Nieuwkoop, 1967. An older but still useful monograph on Eberlin's life and work.

Sessions, Kyle C. "Christian Humanism and Freedom of a Christian: Johann Eberlin von Gunzburg to the Peasants." In *Social History of the Reformation*, edited by L. P. Buck and J. W. Zophy, pp. 137–155. Columbus, Ohio, 1972. Emphasizes Eberlin's evangelistic style.

Spitz, Lewis. "Johannes Eberlin." In *New Catholic Encyclopedia*, vol. 5, pp. 28–29. New York, 1967–1979. A good example of easily available references.

RICHARD GLENN COLE

GWALTHER, Rudolf (also Walther, Walthard, Gualther; 1519–1586), third *Antistes* (or bishop) of the Reformed Church of Zurich, following Bullinger and Zwingli in that office. Gwalther was Bullinger's student at Kappel in 1528, and later, upon taking up residence in Bullinger's house in Zurich in 1532, came to be treated almost as a son. In 1537 Gwalther traveled to England, and from 1538 to 1541, with a scholarship from Zurich, he studied at Basel, Strasbourg, Lausanne, and Marburg. He attended the Colloquy of Regensburg with the theologians from Hesse in 1541, where Calvin was also present. Upon returning to Zurich in 1541, Gwalther married Regula Zwingli, the daughter of the reformer, who also was a resident in the Bullinger household. After her death in 1565, he married Anna Blarer. In 1541 Gwalther became pastor at Schwamendingen. The following year he succeeded Leo Jud as pastor of Saint Peter's church in Zurich. For more than thirty years he worked closely with Bullinger until the latter's death in 1575. In his *Testament*, Bullinger named Gwalther his successor.

As leader of the Zurich church, Gwalther defended the Zurich version of the Protestant faith, especially against the Lutheran authors of the Formula of Concord. He was instrumental in developing good relations between the Zurich church and other Reformed churches in Europe. He had many contacts in England, where he was very influential, particularly as an advocate of the Zurich model of the state church. Gwalther's son, Rudolf, received a master of arts degree from the University of Oxford in 1574, and Gwalther regularly corresponded with English bishops and others.

Gwalther's works include Latin homilies on all the gospels, as well as on *Acts of the Apostles*, *Romans*, *Corinthians*, *Galatians*, and the twelve minor prophets. He also edited three volumes of the works of Zwingli and translated many of Zwingli's German works into Latin. Gwalther's famous work on the Antichrist (*Der Endtchrist*, 1546) was translated into several languages. He wrote poems and two works on metrics. He even tried his hand at drama (*Nabal comoedia sacra*, 1562). After his death his sermon notes on *Esther*, *Isaiah*, Psalms 1 to 94, and on all the books of the New Testament except *Revelation* were published.

BIBLIOGRAPHY

Boesch, Paul. "Rudolph Gwalthers Reise nach England im Jahr 1537." *Zwingliana* 8 (1947), 433–471. Short discussion of and a transcription of the Latin diary that Gwalther kept during his trip to England in 1537. Includes a German translation.

Giovanoli, Sandro. *Form und Funktion des Schuldramas im 16. Jahrhundert: Eine Untersuchung zu Rudolf Gwalthers "Nabal."* Bonn, 1980. A literary study of Gwalther's *Nabal comoedia sacra* of 1562.

Kressner, Helmut. *Schweizer Ursprünge des anglikanischen Staatskirchentums.* Gütersloh, 1953. Study of the influence of Zwingli, Bullinger, and Gwalther on the development of Anglican state church theory in the thought of such men as Hooker and Whitgift in late sixteenth-century England.

Zimmerman, Georg Rudolf. *Die Zürcher Kirche von der Reformation bis zum dritten Reformationsjubiläum, 1519–1819, der Zürischen Antistes geschildert.* Zurich, 1878. A study of the office of *Antistes* in the Zurich church.

J. WAYNE BAKER

H

HABSBURG, HOUSE OF. Sprawling from the Iberian Peninsula in the west to Hungary and Bohemia in the east, the European lands of the Habsburg house of Austria were the scene of some of the most crucial developments of the Reformation era. As Holy Roman Emperors in Germany from 1440 until Napoleon dissolved the empire in 1806, the Habsburgs Charles V, Ferdinand I, and Maximilian II set policies in central Europe which conditioned the development of both Lutheranism and Calvinism.

Of Alemannic origins, the Habsburgs received their Austrian patrimony in the thirteenth century under conditions that allowed them exceptional juridical independence. The earliest heads of the dynasty served as Holy Roman Emperors, but territorial divisions and rivalries among the male members of the house during the fourteenth century considerably reduced its influence among the German princes.

The election as Holy Roman Emperor of Frederick III (r. 1440–1493) permanently changed the European position of the house. Chronically short of money and almost always on the defensive militarily against the Turks, the Hungarians, and even his own brother, Archduke Albrecht VI (1418–1463), Frederick nevertheless laid the foundations of Habsburg territorial might. Expansion to the west began with the marriage in 1477 of his son Maximilian, the future Emperor Maximilian I (r. 1493–1519), to Mary of Burgundy (1457–1482), sole heir to the rich lands of her father, Duke Charles the Bold (r. 1467–1477). The marriage of Archduke Philip (1478–1506), Maximilian's son, to Juana of Castile (1479–1555) further enlarged the Spanish–central European complex that fell to their male heirs, Charles, king of Spain in 1516 and Holy Roman Emperor in 1519, and his younger brother Ferdinand. When the latter was elected king of Hungary and Bohemia in 1526 upon the death of his brother-in-law, King Louis, in combat against the Turks, the dynasty's European holdings had reached their sixteenth-century maximum.

Devout Catholics, Charles and Ferdinand had taken to heart the principles of the Erasmian reform in their youth. They therefore had much to criticize in contemporary church practice. Neither, however, sympathized with the sectarian tendencies of Protestantism. Faced with a defiant Luther at the Diet of Worms in 1521, Charles placed the imperial ban upon the reformer. Systematic Habsburg efforts to eradicate the new faith were limited, however, by the military and political needs of both the emperor and his brother. Departing from Germany in 1521 to pursue imperial and Spanish interests in Italy, Charles did not return until the Diet of Augsburg in 1530. Ferdinand, from 1522 the territorial ruler of the Austrian lands, served as his deputy. On the front line of defense against the expansion of the Ottoman empire before and after 1526, the younger man was quick to strike temporary confessional compromises with the Lutherans when armies had to be raised. It was Ferdinand's need for Protestant financial support at the Diet of Speyer in 1526 that led him to endorse the territorial exercise of either Catholicism or Lutheranism pending a settlement of religious divisions through either a national or general church council. As Catholics, however, both he and his brother had responsibilities to princes of that faith as well. Always the majority party in the imperial estates owing to the membership of the ecclesiastical principalities, Catholics charged Lutherans with abusing the arrangement agreed upon in 1526. Under pressure from this cohort, Ferdinand revoked his concession in 1529. Lutherans responded with formal "Protest," thereby giving the name to the entire movement against the Church of Rome.

Called upon repeatedly by Ferdinand for military assistance and to come to Germany and begin working toward religious reunification, Charles disappointed his brother time and again. Only after he was crowned Holy Roman Emperor in Bologna by Clement VII in 1530, did Charles return to Augsburg for a diet that year. Both confessional sides were open to conciliatory suggestions. However, the emperor would not countenance the Lutheran Augsburg Confession, prepared by Luther's associate Philipp Melanchthon. Charles's intransigence led to the conclusion of a Lutheran military confederation, the Schmalkald League, in 1531. The allies quickly weakened the territorial position of the Habsburgs in the empire by forcing Ferdinand from the duchy of Württemberg, which the dynasty had controlled since 1519. Charles himself was forced to take back some of the more stringent measures he had recommended against the Lutherans in 1530.

It was clear, however, to both Charles and others, that his moderation was only a passing expedient. By 1545, freed temporarily from concern with the Turks in the Mediterranean and France in Italy, he began to plan a military strike against the German Protestants. His formal invasion began in 1546 and ended triumphantly in April of 1547 in the Battle of Mühlberg in Saxony. The Schmalkald leaders, Elector John Frederick of Saxony and Landgrave Philipp of Hesse, were vanquished and imprisoned. In the Interim issued at the Diet of Augsburg in 1548, Charles asked Lutherans to remain within the Catholic church pending reform of the latter.

The emperor's victory, however, was short-lived. The Interim proved unworkable. A bitter family quarrel broke out in 1550 and 1551 over who would follow him in the imperial office. It was finally decided that his brother Ferdinand would succeed him, to be followed not by Ferdinand's own son, Maximilian, but by his nephew, the future Philip II (r. 1556–1598) of Spain. The agreement left Maximilian hostile to both his cousin and uncle and confirmed the suspicions of many among the imperial estates that the Habsburgs intended to turn the elective emperorship into a hereditary position. In 1552 an alliance of princes under Moritz of Saxony, who wished to free Philipp of Hesse, his father-in-law, drove the emperor from Germany altogether.

It was these circumstances and renewed Ottoman threats that prompted Ferdinand to find some local resolution of German religious divisions. Meeting with several of Moritz's allies in Passau in 1552, he agreed to revive the idea of confessional territorialism, first established at Speyer in 1526, until a national council presided over by the emperor himself agreed to more lasting arrangements. Such a gathering took place in Augsburg in 1555, but without the presence or, in the end, support of the emperor. The decision of the diet to reaffirm the notions of 1526, for which later the phrase *cuius regio, eius religio* ("he who has the rule has the religion") was employed, was accepted by Ferdinand, although he was unable to win his brother over to it. Ferdinand was also responsible for two other important pieces of religious policy announced at the diet, the so-called Ecclesiastical Reservation, which called for church lands in ecclesiastical principalities that turned Lutheran to remain under Catholic control, and the unofficial *Declaratio ferdinandea*, allowing Lutherans in the ecclesiastical principalities to practice their faith undisturbed.

Becoming emperor in 1558, Ferdinand worked simultaneously to improve the position of Catholicism in Germany and his patrimonial lands and to restore religious unity. He had already brought Jesuits both to the Austrian lands and to Bohemia and written an introduction to Peter Canisius's new catechism. Confessional reconciliation proved beyond him. With the Protestants refusing to attend the final session of the Council of Trent, he worked tirelessly to further the educational and moral reform of the church under discussion at the gathering. At the same time, under pressure from his own lands, he won permission from Pius IV to allow Communion in both kinds if he believed it necessary.

Disliked by the German princes and absorbed with concerns in the Mediterranean and western Europe, Philip II of Spain quickly lost interest in the imperial crown. It was therefore his cousin Maximilian who succeeded Ferdinand. Deeply engaged in the theological controversies of his day and openly sympathetic to the moral impulse, if not the institutional structure, of Lutheranism, the new emperor enjoyed widespread support among the Protestant electors. He took the Peace of Augsburg seriously, regarding it as a model for others to follow in resolving contemporary religious conflicts. He believed, however, that confessional pluralism in Germany stopped with Lutheranism, and took a dim view of Calvinism, especially when he came to believe that it threatened the peace of the empire during the Revolt of the Netherlands. Shocked to discover that Calvinist rebels in the Netherlands supported Duke John Frederick of Saxony's efforts to reclaim the electoral title for his Ernestine branch of the Wettin dynasty, he suppressed the move forcefully in 1567. Though appalled by the bloody St. Bartholemew's Day Massacre in 1572 in France, he was even more disturbed by the specter of religiously inspired rebellion in the kingdom. Though Maximilian encouraged reform in monasteries and convents through the *Klosterrat* ("monastery council") established in 1568, his Catholicism was tepid at best. He gave little support to the Jesuits, who otherwise enjoyed great favor in his immediate family. In general, he believed that little was to be gained through force in resolving confessional disputes. Though he worked toward the reunification of confessions in his own lands, he was a helpless witness to the spread there not only of all strands of Lutheranism but of Calvinism as well, especially in Hungary.

Charles, Ferdinand, and even the latitudinarian Maximilian II were persuaded that the soundest realm was one with no confessional divisions. All three, however, tempered their convictions with realism, bending to Protestant wishes as Habsburg political and military needs dictated. At the same time, the policies of all three men assured not only the survival of Catholicism, but its revitalization as well.

BIBLIOGRAPHY

Benecke, Gerhard. *Maximilian I, 1459–1519: An Analytical Biography.* London, 1982. Socioeconomic study.

Bibl, Viktor. *Maximilian II. Der rätselhafte Kaiser.* Hellerau bei Dresden, 1929. A sound, though undocumented, portrait.

Brandi, Karl. *The Emperor Charles V.* Translated by C. V. Wedgewood. Reprint, London, 1965. Standard work.

Evans, Robert J. W. *The Making of the Habsburg Monarchy, 1550–1700: An Interpretation.* Oxford, 1979. Sophisticated cultural synthesis that stresses the role of Counter-Reformation Catholicism in the building of the Habsburg state.

Fernandez-Alvarez, Manuel. *Charles V: Elected Emperor and Hereditary Ruler.* Translated by J. A. Lalaguna. London, 1975. Lively political-military narrative.

Fichtner, Paula Sutter. *Ferdinand I of Austria: The Politics of Dynasticism in the Age of the Reformation.* New York, 1982.

Fischer-Galati, Stephen. *Ottoman Imperialism and German Protestantism, 1521–1555*. Harvard Historical Monographs, 43. Cambridge, Mass., 1959. Interaction of Habsburg policy with Lutheranism under the pressure of Ottoman expansion.

Holtzmann, Robert. *Maximilian II. bis zu seiner Thronbesteigung, 1527–1564*. Berlin, 1903. Stresses Maximilian's Protestant sympathies. The book is not widely available.

Kohler, Alfred. *Antihabsburgische Politik in der Epoche Karls V.: Die reichsständische Opposition gegen die Wahl Ferdinands I, zum römischen König und gegen die Anerkennung seines Königtums, 1524–1534*. Schriftenreihe der historischen Kommission bei der bayerischen Akademie der Wissenschaften, 19. Göttingen, 1982. Detailed account of Habsburg-imperial politics at a crucial moment in the division of Germany into religious camps.

Lhotsky, Alphons. *Das Zeitalter des Hauses Österreich: Die Ersten Jahre der Regierung Ferdinands I, 1520–1527*. Vienna, 1971. Especially valuable for portrayal of dynastic interplay of these early years.

Lutz, Heinrich. *Christianitas Afflicta: Europa, das Reich und die päpstliche Politik im Niedergang der Hegemonie Kaiser Karls V., 1552–1556*. Göttingen, 1964. Magisterial study that integrates the collapse of Charles V's imperial program and the dynamics leading to the Peace of Augsburg.

Press, Volker. *Kaiser Karl V., König Ferdinand und die Entstehung der Reichsritterschaft*. Institut für europäische Geschichte Mainz, Vortrag 20. Wiesbaden, 1976. Case study in the flaws and goals of Charles V's imperial politics.

Rady, Martyn. *The Emperor Charles V*. London, 1988. Good narrative for a beginning student.

Schindling, Anton, and Walter Ziegler, eds. *Die Kaiser der Neuzeit, 1519–1918: Heiliges Römisches Reich, Österreich, Deutschland*. Munich, 1990.

Schulze, Winfried. *Reich und Türkengefahr im späten 16. Jahrhundert*. Munich, 1978. Wide-ranging study of impact of Ottoman threat in Habsburg lands.

Wandruszka, Adam. *The House of Habsburg: Six Hundred Years of a European Dynasty*. Translated by Cathleen Epstein and Hans Epstein. Garden City, N.Y., 1964. Concise and engaging introductory reading.

Wiesflecker, Hermann. *Kaiser Maximilian I.: Das Reich, Österreich und Europa an der Wende der Neuzeit*. 5 vols. Vienna, 1971–1986. Definitive, though repetitious, work.

PAULA SUTTER FICHTNER

HAEMSTEDE, Adriaan Corneliszoon van (c.1525–1562), Dutch theologian and martyrologist. Now recognized as one of the most influential of the first generation of Dutch Reformed writers, notably through the enduring popularity of his martyrology, in his own day Haemstede was a turbulent and controversial figure. Born in Zeeland, Haemstede came from a prosperous, probably noble, family, as did many of the first generation of reformers. He studied at Louvain University before his ordination to the priesthood in 1552. Sometime around 1555 Haemstede abandoned the old church and within a year had taken up the ministry in the small secret evangelical congregation in Antwerp. Here he soon became embroiled in a sequence of disputes with his colleague Gaspar van der Heyden and the leading lay members of the congregation, controversies that were settled only when an intensification of persecution brought the church's temporary disbandment in 1558. But also during these Antwerp years Haemstede completed the *Historie der Martelaren* (History of the Pious Martyrs; 1559), his greatest work and a literary achievement to rank alongside the better-known works of Jean Crespin and John Foxe. Closely modeled on the previously published martyr books (Ludwig Rabus and Crespin), Haemstede's work draws much of its material from these two sources, along with a number of smaller writings by John Bale. Its major historical interest lay in the new material Haemstede provided relating to Netherlandish martyrs: the moving accounts of their interrogation and suffering, which Haemstede experienced at firsthand in Antwerp, remain one of the best sources for the history of the early Dutch congregations.

Haemstede's remaining years were clouded with further controversy, notably in England, whence he had fled after the closure of the Antwerp church. Established as minister of the London Dutch church in 1559, Haemstede was first disciplined and then deposed following indiscreet remarks that were interpreted as unacceptably complaisant toward the various sectarian groups within the city's foreign community. These remarks were sufficient to rekindle doubts about Hamestede's orthodoxy, though the fact that Mennonite martyrs were rigorously excluded from his martyrology seems to give the lie to suggestions that he was an Anabaptist sympathizer. In November 1560 the London church authorities formally excommunicated Haemstede, and all efforts to have the sentence lifted, first through the intervention of the Emden church, proved vain in the face of Haemstede's stubborn determination to justify his conduct. He died in 1562, unreconciled. Despite the tribulation of his later years, Haemstede's literary achievement ensured that his work would live on in the Dutch Reformed tradition; his martyrology, repeatedly enhanced with new material after the first edition (the only one supervised by Haemstede), became one of the seminal texts of the emerging Dutch church.

BIBLIOGRAPHY

Primary Source

Haemstede, Adriaan van. *Historie der Martelaren die om de getuigenis der evangelische Waarheid hun bloed gestort hebben, vanaf Christus onze Zaligmaker tot het jaer 1655*. Edited by J. H. Landwehr. Utrecht, 1980. Contains much material not in Haemstede's original text.

Secondary Sources

Gilmont, Jean-François. "Le genèse du martyrologie d'Adrien van Haemstede." *Revue d'histoire ecclésiastique* 63 (1968), 379–414.

Jelsma, A. J. *Adriaan van Haemstede en zijn Martelaarsboek*. The Hague, 1970.

Pettegree, Andrew. *Foreign Protestant Communities in Sixteenth-Century London*. Oxford, 1986. See chapter 6 for the London disputes.

———. *Emden and the Dutch Revolt: Exile and the Development of Re-*

formed Protestantism. Oxford, 1992. See Chapter 3 for Haemstede's Antwerp ministry.

ANDREW PETTEGREE

HAGENAU, COLLOQUY OF. In 1540 Emperor Charles V embarked on the path of religious colloquies in order to achieve a settlement of the religious controversy. With regard to domestic politics in the empire, the Catholic party was in danger of losing its majority in the electoral college. With regard to foreign politics, a worsening of relations with France and the Gueldrian question, combined with the continuing Turkish menace, threatened to involve him in a war on two fronts. By settling the religious quarrels, Charles V wanted to achieve a wider scope of action internally and a stronger impetus externally. With regard to ecclesiastical politics, he was angered by the chronic failure to convene a general council. Since the meeting in Nuremberg, which had been decided on in the Peace of Frankfurt (1539), had not taken place, Charles V called a meeting in Speyer for June 1540. Because of the plague, it was moved to the Alsatian imperial city of Hagenau.

The colloquy began on 12 June. Participation was low because important rulers stayed away for fundamental objections to negotiations with enemies of the church. Therefore the imperial court was forced to make concessions. Ferdinand I attempted by all means possible to make the talks successful. The Catholic side was represented by a number of important advisers and theologians. The main Catholic demands were a renewal of negotiations on the basis of the Augsburg Confession of 1530, the Protestants' renunciation of ecclesiastical property, the recognition of the supreme court of the empire, as well as the exclusion from the Schmalkald League of the territories accepted into the league since the Peace of Nuremberg in 1532. These demands met with decisive opposition from the Protestants, some of whose leaders were absent (elector of Saxony, landgrave of Hesse, Philipp Melanchthon); they were represented by Nikolaus von Amsdorf, Thomas Blarer, Johannes Brenz, Martin Bucer, Wolfgang Capito, Andreas Osiander, and Johann Sturm, who demanded open talks on the basis of the Peace of Frankfurt. In the light of the opposing points of departure, the negotiations deadlocked over initial questions of procedure. When the plague threatened Hagenau, a move to a new location was demanded immediately. Therefore the key problems were not even addressed. The concluding document did not bring any of the main issues closer to a resolution. The only outcome was the agreement that both sides would nominate the same number of theologians for the continuation of the colloquy at a different place.

Despite this announcement, the Colloquy of Hagenau basically failed. The reasons were the absence of the most important representatives of both sides and the lack of interest in the colloquy by the old church, which feared an unsatisfactory compromise. Nonetheless, the meeting was important. As regards religion, the emerging new churches demonstrated that they wanted to continue dialogue. As regards politics, the colloquy illustrated that the emperor still had enough credit with the oppositional rulers for them not to break with him. The Colloquy of Hagenau continued in Worms and Regensburg.

[*See also* Bucer, Martin; Charles V; Schmalkald League; *and* Regensburg, Colloquy of.]

BIBLIOGRAPHY

Moses, Reinhold. *Die Religionsverhandlungen zu Hagenau und Worms 1540 und 1541.* Jena, 1889.

Neuser, Wilhelm H., ed. *Die Vorbereitung der Religionsgespräche von Worms und Regensburg 1540/41.* Texte zur Geschichte der evangelischen Theologie, 4. Neukirchen-Vluyn, 1974.

Pastor, Ludwig. *Die kirchliche Reunionsbestrebungen während der Regierung Karls V.* Freiburg, 1879. See pp. 184–198.

ALOIS SCHMID

HALLER, Berchtold (1492–1536), reformer of Bern. Born at Aldingen, near Rottweil, in Württemberg, he attended school at Rottweil and Pforzheim, matriculating at the University of Cologne in 1510, he received his masters degree in 1511. He taught briefly at Rottweil, then in 1513 moved to Bern to become an assistant to his former teacher, Rubellus. He soon became an assistant of Thomas Wyttenbach, and in 1519, preacher at the Münster in Bern. He became a canon and priest in 1520.

Haller met Zwingli for the first time in 1521. For the next ten years, Zwingli heavily influenced Haller's ideas and actions. The reform in Bern began in the early 1520s and was concluded with the Disputation of 1528. Haller was the leader throughout the process. In 1525, Haller quit saying Mass, following the lead of Zwingli at Zurich. In 1526, Haller was Bern's only representative at the Baden Disputation, a debate sponsored by the Catholic cantons to generate and consolidate opposition to the Reformed doctrine.

By late 1527 the pressure for reform in Bern was so intense that the council ordered that a disputation take place in early January 1528. Haller played a leading role in developing the ten theses for debate. The disputation, from 6–26 January, was dominated by Zwingli, and the resulting reform closely resembled that of Zurich. In 1532, in the midst of controversy after the defeat of Zurich at Kappel, Haller collaborated with Capito in writing a new church order for Bern (*Berner Synodus*). In the same year, Haller became dean of the chapter at Bern. Haller's attempt to institute reform in Solothurn in 1530 was a failure.

In the early 1530s Haller agonized over how to deal with Anabaptists. Though he had some success in a debate with the Anabaptists at Zöfingen in 1532, they continued to multiply and to be a problem in Bernese territories. He corresponded with Bullinger about the issues of the Anabaptists, church discipline, and whether heretics ought to be executed. Bullinger convinced Haller to support the Zurich type of magisterial discipline, in which excommunication was not used, but he could not convince him that heretics ought to be executed by the magistracy. Haller died on 25 February 1536.

BIBLIOGRAPHY

Baker, J. Wayne. "Church Discipline or Civil Punishment: On the Origins of the Reformed Schism, 1528–1531." *Andrews University Seminary Studies* 23 (1985), 3–18. Considers Bullinger's advice to Haller on the nature of Christian discipline.

———. "Church, State, and Dissent: The Crisis of the Swiss Reformation, 1531–1536." *Church History* 57 (1988), 135–152. Deals with Bullinger's correspondence with Haller on the issue of the Anabaptists and the death penalty for heretics.

Bautz, Friedrich Wilhelm, ed. *Biographische-Bibliographisches Kirchenlexikon.* Hamm, 1970–. See vol. 2, pp. 485–493.

Fast, Heinold, and John H. Yoder. "How to Deal with Anabaptists: An Unpublished Letter of Heinrich Bullinger." *Mennonite Quarterly Review* 33 (1959), 83–95. Translation, with commentary, of Bullinger's letter to Haller just before the disputation at Zöfingen.

Hendricks, Dan L. "The Bern Disputation: Some Observations." *Zwingliana* 14.10 (1978), 565–575. Argues that the ideas presented in the ten theses of the Bern Disputation reflected dependence on the theology of Zwingli and antagonism to the Catholic theology presented at the Baden Disputation of 1526. Emphasizes Haller's dependence on Zwingli.

Pestalozzi, Carl. *Bertold Haller: Nach handschriftlichen und gleichzeitigen Quellen.* Elberfeld, 1861. The only biography of Haller.

J. WAYNE BAKER

HAMBURG. Around 1500 the Hanseatic city of Hamburg had some fourteen thousand inhabitants. Its political position in relation to the empire and to the duchy of Holstein was unclear. In a relatively loose social structure, the council appeared to be an oligarchy of the merchants. The citizenry, which was divided into four parishes (Petri, Nikolai, Katharinen, Jacobi), included property owners and masters of the crafts guilds—a fraction of the total population. Piety typical of the time and growing criticism of the clergy—joined early with demands for a voice in the selection of ministers—determined the relationship of the community to the church, whose leadership lay in the cathedral chapter, suffragan of the Bremen archbishop. Inner ecclesiastical attempts at reform, particularly by the dean of the cathedral, Albert Krantz (d. 1517), failed. The reputation of the clergy decreased: foundations and donations fell; in 1523 the Dithmarsch church left the supremacy of the Hamburg cathedral chapter; and in a two-year controversy the burghers took the Nikolai parish school from the cathedral teachers. At the beginning of this controversy (1522) representatives of all parishes had ceremoniously announced their common opposition to any injustice on the part of the clergy and the secular authorities. Thus in a communal spirit, they had overcome the political separation of the parishes.

Soon thereafter the first traces of the Lutheran doctrine appeared. In 1522/23 a short-lived printing shop of Dutch immigrants published sixteen reformed writings, among them Luther's September New Testament in Low German translation. For a while, Hamburg became the center of Reformation propaganda in north Germany. Among the preachers of the new doctrine, the Rostock Franciscan Stephan Kempe had the greatest effect in 1523. The citizenry insisted on his remaining in the city. Other clerics bore ill will toward Kempe, but the city council tacitly tolerated him, while the cathedral chapter seemed paralyzed.

From the beginning, the sermon proved to be the most important medium of the new doctrine. In 1524 the council thwarted the attempt of the citizens to appoint Johannes Bugenhagen to the Nikolai parish, but Bugenhagen elaborated his theology in the missive "Vom Christenglauben" of 1525, which strongly influenced the reform movement. The council could not stop it with mandates. Against its weakening resistance, the citizens named Johann Zegenhagen from Magdeburg minister of Saint Nikolai in 1525, in 1526 Johann Fritze from Lübeck minister of Saint Jacobi, and in 1527 Stephan Kempe minister of Saint Katharine. Before the Reformation was formally completed, three of the four main churches had Lutheran ministers, each soon married to a former nun.

The intensification of the eucharistic controversy prompted the council, which was concerned with order and security, in May 1527 to convene a debate. The success of the Lutherans encouraged the Nikolai citizens to establish a common chest for the poor according to Luther's and Bugenhagen's model. The other parishes followed. Their poor-chest ordinance (1527) shows the evangelical-communal motives of the supporters, most of whom were members of the merchant class. The council went along with this development.

In its elections in March 1528, the council added four Lutherans instead of the planned Catholics. Resistance by Catholic crafts groups formed in the Dominican monastery of Saint Johannis. Rumors of uprisings and of pulpit polemics increased the tension, until the council decided on another debate of the disputing clergy in order to have a unified proclamation in the city (28 April 1528). It practically anticipated the outcome when it declared the Bible to be the only guide for the decision. After the clear victory of the Lutherans, the most recalcitrant Catholic priests were exiled, while others left voluntarily. This marked the breakthrough of the Reformation: the end of Catholic ceremonies, customs, masses, and feast days; of monasteries; and of the spiritual authority of the cathedral chapter.

The change also affected the political situation. While the council now called Bugenhagen to draft a new church order, the parishes expanded their 48 administrators of the common chests for the poor to a 144-member body for negotiations with the council and established a central chest for their four common chests for the poor (29 September 1528), administered by 12 *Oberalten* (named from the 48). The result of the political negotiations was the "Long Recess" (16 February 1529), which together with numerous economic-commercial regulations granted the *Oberalten* and the 144 the right to voice citizens' complaints and to act as a control group vis à vis the council, even though the latter rejected the diminishing of its right to self-determination and the opening of its financial records. The citizens' right to a voice stabilized the internal relationships and supported the authority of the council; many *Oberalten* later became members of the council. Bugenhagen's church ordinance (23 May 1529) followed the Braunschweig model: it organized the school system, particularly the new grammar school, regulated the clergy and religious services, and carried on charity work beyond its available means.

From 1528 the cathedral chapter demanded restitution before the imperial court. This lawsuit determined Hamburg politics for decades. It required the return of church goods and in 1536 Hamburg's membership in the Schmalkald League, the costs of which and its later defeat led to formidable indebtedness; it caused the council in 1563 to turn the financial administration over to the citizens. The Bremen Agreement (1561) gave the cathedral chapter autonomy and property but prohibited all influence on church and school. As the first superintendent, Johannes Aepinus guarded the purity of doctrine from 1532. In 1535 he convened in Hamburg, in reaction to Münster Anabaptism, the first north German synod of the cities of Bremen, Hamburg, Lübeck, Lüneburg, Rostock, and Stralsund, which formed a common front against Anabaptism. The new political order of Hamburg proved to be lasting: the citizens' assemblies lasted into the nineteenth century.

[*See also* Hanseatic League *and* Schmalkald League.]

BIBLIOGRAPHY

Beckey, Kurt. *Die Reformation in Hamburg*. Hamburg, 1929.

Postel, Rainer. "Reformation and Gegenreformation, 1517–1618." In *Hamburg: Geschichte der Stadt und ihrer Bewohner*, edited by Hans-Dieter Loose, vol. 1, pp. 191–258. Hamburg, 1982.

———. *Die Reformation in Hamburg, 1517–1528*. Quellen und Forschung zur Reformationsgeschichte, vol. 52. Gütersloh, 1986.

Sillem, C. H. Wilhelm. *Die Einführung der Reformation in Hamburg*. Schriften des Vereins für Reformationsgeschichte, vol. 16. Halle, 1886.

RAINER POSTEL

Translated from German by Walter D. Morris

HAMILTON, Patrick (d. 1528), Scottish reformer and martyr. Hamilton was one of the numerous Scottish scholars who went abroad to study—he was at Paris and then Louvain—and by so doing in the early sixteenth century entered the intellectual world of religious ferment. He returned to Saint Leonard's College, Saint Andrews, to study theology in 1523; the influence on him of Erasmian humanism is not clear, but Luther's markedly is. Possibly because of connections in high places, including his uncle James, earl of Arran, and James V himself, he seems to have been allowed to study and express his views with remarkable openness; there was indeed a general willingness to discuss the new ideas, however dangerous, in Saint Leonard's in the early 1520s. He was clearly popular as an exciting scholar and as a musician who composed a nine-part mass.

In 1527, however, for reasons that have not been precisely discovered, he was accused of heresy by Archbishop James Beaton. His response was to flee to the University of Marburg, where he promptly produced a Lutheran thesis on faith and good works that came to be known as "Patrick's Places," and then returned to Scotland in the autumn of that year to throw down the gauntlet by his preaching. He was arrested and burned on 29 February 1528.

His execution was, of course, sensational. There had been virtually no heresy in Scotland; only two had been burned, for Lollard views, a century earlier. The early date of Hamilton's burning, when the authorities were only beginning to show fear of heresy (an act banning the import of Lutheran literature was passed in 1525), looked like a dramatic and brutal assertion of orthodoxy. Hamilton was a notable martyr from the beginning, therefore. And as greater leniency than the execution seemed to herald became the general hallmark of the Scottish Reformation, he remained a rare symbol of the full-blown and devilish persecution that Protestant writers such as John Knox and David Calderwood sought so unconvincingly to depict.

BIBLIOGRAPHY

Cowan, Ian B. *The Scottish Reformation: Church and Society in Sixteenth-Century Scotland*. London, 1982. A very well-informed and wide-ranging discussion of the Reformation.

Sanderson, Margaret H. B. *Cardinal of Scotland: David Beaton, c.1494–1546*. Edinburgh, 1986. An excellent study of the early Reformation, with sensitive analysis of its most strenuous opponent.

JENNY WORMALD

HANSEATIC LEAGUE. A loose association of north German merchants and cities, which had emerged in the course of the thirteenth century, was the dominant trading power in northern Europe throughout the fourteenth and fifteenth centuries. The Hanseatic merchants owed their outstanding position to their function as intermediaries in the commerce between the countries bordering the Baltic Sea and western Europe. Supported by extensive trade privileges and a progressive trade organization, they had been able almost to monopolize that trade.

By the beginning of the sixteenth century, however, the situation had perceptibly changed to the disadvantage of the Hanse. Dutch and English merchants were penetrating the Baltic Sea with products of their home cloth industries and other merchandise, thus threatening the Hanseatic trade monopoly. At the same time the opposing interests of the various regional groups of cities became obvious and impeded unanimous action against the foreign rivals. Moreover, by the end of the fifteenth century, the office (*Kontor*) at Brugge, which had always been regarded as a foundation of the Hanse, existed only in name, while the office at Novgorod had been closed by Ivan III in 1494. The increasing power of the princes restricted the political independence of the Hanseatic cities, thus also limiting the ability of the Hanse to act.

Lutheran notions had entered the Hanseatic cities from 1521, and, combined with already existing political and social tensions, this resulted in new burdens for the Hanse. In 1525 the league changed its initially disapproving attitude toward the Reformation after some important cities had decided in favor of the new doctrine. From then on each of the cities was to decide matters of religion on its own. In individual Hanseatic cities the Reformation took a different course, spawning quarrels with the old (Catholic) city councils. A common element were the church orders (*Kirchenordnungen*) of Braunschweig, Hamburg, Lübeck, Hildesheim, and some Pomeranian towns that Johannes Bugenhagen (1485–1558) had drafted. The Anabaptist reign in Münster (1534/35) remained an isolated phenomenon. In Lübeck Jürgen Wullenwever tried to make use of the inconclusive religious situation in order to stop the Dutch expansion into the Baltic Sea and to restore the traditional preeminence of Lübeck by gaining control of the Sundpassage. The defeat of Lübeck in the so-called Counts' War (1534/35) helped to weaken the reputation of the Hanseatic community.

During the second half of the sixteenth century the economic and political changes in the Baltic, Russia's advance to the Baltic Sea, and the rise of the Scandinavian states further contributed to the undermining of the Hanseatic position. In 1570 the Peace of Stettin finally demonstrated that Lübeck and the Hanse had lost their former prestige. Nevertheless, the Hanse tried to regain its reputation and economic importance by renewing the inner structures of the league. In 1557 and 1579 *Konfederationsnoteln* describing the duties of the towns were passed in order to strengthen the league. By establishing the office of a Hanseatic syndic in 1556—first filled by Heinrich Sudermann (1520–1591)—the community's capacity to act was to be increased. Similarly, the reorganization of the office (*Kontor*) in London (1554), the moving of the Brugge office to Antwerp, the building of the splendid *Oosterlingenhuis* (1564–1568, a residence for Hanseatic merchants), as well as new statutes for the members of the league providing for strict rules of conduct among the merchants and an uncompromising limitation of the so-called *Butenhansen* (non-member merchants) were to give the Hanseatic trade new impetus.

But all proved to be untimely attempts that came to nothing. In 1593 the Antwerp office had to be given up, while in 1598 Elizabeth I decreed the closing of the London steelyard, prohibiting the Hanseatic merchants from any trading activities in England. Though the sixteenth century was for many Hanseatic towns an age of economic prosperity, not only for those situated along the coasts and able to participate in the flourishing trade with Iceland and the Iberian Peninsula, this prosperity was not the result of foresighted Hanseatic policy, but actually took place in contrast to traditional principles of Hanseatic trade. In the history of the Hanse the sixteenth century was an age of decay, the final deathblow being dealt in the seventeenth century in the course of the Thirty Years' War.

BIBLIOGRAPHY

Dollinger, Philippe. *Die Hanse.* 4th ed. Stuttgart, 1989.

Korell, Günter. *Jürgen Wullenwever: Sein sozialpolitisches Wirken in Lübeck und der Kampf mit den erstarkenden Mächten Nordeuropas.* Weimar, 1980.

Pitz, Ernst. "Steigende und fallende Tendenzen in Politik und Wirtschaftsleben der Hanse im 16. Jahrhundert." *Hansische Geschichtsblätter* 102 (1984), 39–77.

Postel, Rainer. "Hamburg und Lübeck im Zeitalter der Reformation." *Zeitschrift des Vereins für Lübeckische Geschichte und Altertumskunde* 59 (1979), 63–82.

Schildhauer, Johannes. *Soziale, politische und religiöse Auseinandersetzungen in den Hansestädten Stralsund, Rostock und Wismar im ersten Drittel des 16. Jahrhunderts.* Weimar, 1959.

Schildhauer, Johannes, et al. *Die Hanse.* 6th ed. Berlin, 1984.

Schilling, Heinz. "Konfessionskonflikte und hansestädtische Freiheiten im 16. und frühen 17. Jahrhundert." *Hansische Geschichtsblätter* 97 (1979), 36–59.

Wriedt, Klaus. "Heinrich Sudermann, 1520–1591." In *Rheinische Lebensbilder,* edited by Wilhelm Janssen, vol. 10. Cologne, 1985.

VOLKER HENN

HAPSBURG, HOUSE OF.

See Habsburg, House of.

HARMONY OF CONFESSIONS.

The history of the *Harmony of Confessions of Faith* (*Harmonia confessionum fidei*) is more interesting in some ways than is the volume itself. It was published anonymously in Geneva in August 1581 and wrongly attributed to "Salnar," under whose name it is listed in the Union Catalogue of the Library of Congress. In 1887 A. Bernus identified the author as Jean-François Salvard. Bernus's correction is borne out by entries in the *Registres de la Compagnie des Pasteurs de Genève,* volume 4 (1575–1582). The *Harmonia* of 1581 is a collection of the confessions of the Protestant churches of Europe and England. It was intended to prove the orthodoxy and basic unanimity of Protestants. In the *Registres* Salvard is given principal credit for producing it, although he had the help of a number of Reformed theologians, mainly Théodore de Bèze, Antoine de la Roche Chandieu, Lambert Daneau, and Simon Goulart.

The history of this document began in 1577 with the publication of the Lutheran Formula of Concord, which condemned Zwinglians and Calvinists as "sacramentarians." To deal with this problem Count Palatine Johann Casimir invited representatives of Elizabeth of England and the churches of Poland, France, and Switzerland to Frankfurt am Main in September 1577 to determine a course of action. Jean-François Salvard, then resident in Frankfurt and a delegate of the French churches, suggested gathering church confessions. Casimir preferred writing a new confession that all Protestants might sign. Girolamo Zanchi was charged with drawing up a confession based on the Augsburg Confession and Heinrich Bullinger's Second Helvetic Confession.

When the project of a new confession failed in 1579, Bèze wrote for the Compagnie des Pasteurs ("Company of Pastors") in Geneva to the pastors of Zurich informing them, among other matters, that the Genevans would send them a list of confessions drawn up by Salvard, who had moved to Geneva, to be included in a harmony of confessions. In 1581 the Compagnie des Pasteurs of Geneva approved the collection of confessions and on 23 March 1581 Salvard sent his list to Rudolf Gwalther in Zurich. The next day Bèze wrote to the Zurich pastors commenting on the *Harmonia* in detail. Gwalther answered on 4 April for the Zurich pastors, correcting two errors but approving the *Harmonia* in principle. Gwalther added that Zurich awaited the approval of other German-Swiss towns, England, Poland, and the Netherlands. The German-Swiss towns of Schaffhausen, Zurich, Bern, and Neustadt approved. Johann-Konrad Ulmer of Schaffhausen asked that the *Harmonia* be published in Latin and German so that it would be a better answer to the Lutheran *Book of Concord.* The pastors of Neustadt suggested delaying publication so that the Danish and Scottish Confessions could be included (Bèze seemed not to know of the Scottish Confession of 1561), but before this correction could be made, the *Harmonia* was published.

The work consists of a preface in the name of the Gallican and Belgic churches, a catalog of confessions included the *Harmonia,* and an admonition to the pious reader on the use of the book, followed by nineteen sections in which statements from various confessions concerning particular theological points are gathered. A rationale is given at the head of each section for the arrangement of the confessional statements and for why some do not appear there. A second section explains what may seem obscure or confusing, and any apparent contradictions are either harmonized or recognized, although the author protests that these latter are few. The 1581 *Harmonia* contains the following confessions: the Augsburg Confession (1530) with its preface and as emended in some articles, edited and published at Wittenberg, the Tetrapolitan Confession (1530), the Basel (Mulhouse) Confession (1534), the First (1536) and Second (1566) Helvetic Confessions, the Saxon Confession (1551), the Württemberg Confession (1552), the Gallican Confession (1559), the Anglican Confession (1562), the Belgic Confession (1566), and the Bohemian (Waldensian) Confession (1573). An index of confessions locates the statements drawn from each. The hope of the compilers of the *Harmonia* was that the churches might be reconciled with the help of God. That hope was frustrated. Tensions and polemical, even political, attacks grew worse between Lutheran and Reformed theologians well into the next century.

Translations and additions followed rapidly. In 1586 an English translation appeared to which the Scottish Confession had been added. In 1643 the London publisher I. Legatt produced another English translation, the title of which included the information that the 1581 edition had been subscribed by "the Kings Majestie and his houshould . . . at Edinburgh. . . ." Two centuries later (1842, 1844) Peter Hall translated the original Latin into English and added both commentary and an appendix containing the Articles of the Church of England, the Synod of Dordrecht, and the Westminster Confession.

[*See also* Bèze, Theódore de; Chandieu, Antoine de la Roche; Daneau, Lambert; Geneva; Goulart, Simon; *and* Salvard, Jean-François.]

BIBLIOGRAPHY

Bernus, Auguste. "Jean-François Salvard." *Bulletin historique et litteraire de la Société de l'histoire du protestantisme français* 36 (1887), 498–503.

Léonard, Émile G. *Histoire génerale du protestantisme.* Vol. 2, *L'Établissement, 1564–1700.* Paris, 1988. See especially pp. 27–28.

Registres de la Compagnie des Pasteurs de Genève. Vol. 4, 1575–1582. Edited by Olivier Labarthe and Bernard Lescaze. Geneva, 1974.

Salvard, Jean-François. *The Harmony of Protestant Confessions: Exhibiting the Faith of the Churches of Christ, Reformed after the Pure and Holy Doctrine of the Gospel throughout Europe* (1842). Translated by Peter Hall. Reprint, Edmonton, 1992.

JILL RAITT

HARTMANN, Adam. *See* Cratander, Andreas.

HASSLER, Hans Leo (1562–1612), organist, composer, entrepreneur; a significant figure in the transition of German sacred and secular music from Renaissance to Baroque style. Following initial musical training from his father, Hassler studied in 1584 in Venice under Andrea Gabrieli. Consequent to filling a composing commission from the Augsburg Fuggers, Hassler was appointed organist to Octavian II Fugger in 1585.

The Augsburg period brought Hassler wide recognition as a composer and organist. But his fame was accompanied by controversy. He was not popular among musical leaders of Augsburg, probably because he competed successfully in their mechanical instrument business. Hassler also became prominent, wealthy, and notorious as a financial operative, particularly in transactions with Emperor Rudolf II.

Released from his Fugger obligation by the death in 1600 of Octavian II, Hassler moved to Nuremberg to become city music director. He severed completely from Nuremberg by 1607, took citizenship in Ulm, where he had married, and pursued business interests and publication of his compositions. Elector Christian II of Saxony summoned him to Dresden as chamber organist in 1608. He had risen to kapellmeister at the time of his death from tuberculosis in 1612.

Hassler's organ mastery and aristocratic manners gained him fame and popularity during his lifetime. Nevertheless, he ranks with the best German choral and instrumental composers in the established polyphonic and polychoral Italian style. Examples are four-voice *Canzonetten* (1590); four- to twelve-voice Latin motets, *Cantiones sacrae* (1591); and four- to eight-voice *Messen* (1590).

Hassler also is noteworthy for using newer melodic-rhythmic techniques with popular idioms in the major-minor tonal system to produce works of great dignity, deep feeling, and formal beauty. Examples are *Psalm und christliche Gesäng auf die Melodeien fugweis componiert* (1607), using fugal polyphony on choral melodies; and *Kirchengesäng, simpliciter gesetzt* (1608), comprising sixty-eight four-voice choral settings of traditional Lutheran congregational songs, psalms, and catechism. Numerous hymn settings remain in evangelical hymnals.

From his secular collection, *Lustgarten newer teutscher Gesäng* (1601), comes the melody, "Mein Gmüt is mir verwirret." Contrafacted by Johann Crüger for Paul Gerhardt's passion hymn, "O Haupt voll Blut und Wunden" (1647), melody and text became enshrined as a chorale in J. S. Bach's *Saint Matthew Passion.* The hymn is universal in English hymnals as "O Sacred Head Now Wounded."

BIBLIOGRAPHY

Mehl, Johannes G. "Hans Leo Hassler von Nürnberg, 1564–1612." *Gottesdienst und Kirchenmusik* 5 (1964), 179–183. Reflects quadricentennial scholarship.

Neyses, Joseph. *Studien zur Geschichte der deutschen Motette des 16. Jahrhunderts.* Düsseldorf, 1927. Compositional and biographical study.

Wagner, Rudolph and Friedrich Blume. "Hassler, Hans Leo." In *Die Musik in Geschichte und Gegenwart,* edited by Friedrich Blume, vol. 5, pp. 1798–1808. Kassel, 1956.

KYLE C. SESSIONS

HÄTZER, Ludwig (1500?–1529), Swiss antitrinitarian reformer and translator. Born in the canton of Thurgau in about 1500, Hätzer was trained for the priesthood and served briefly as chaplain. His university training was humanistic, and in 1523 he went to Zurich, drawn there no doubt by the reformer Huldrych Zwingli, whose work had a strong humanist cast. In September 1523 Hätzer entered the debate on images by publishing a book on the subject, and not long afterward he prepared the records of the Second Zurich Disputation of October 1523 for publication. In the preface he expressed not only his confidence in scripture as the arbiter of all ecclesiastical disputes but also his strong support for Zwingli's leadership.

By mid-1524, however, Hätzer was charging that the scriptures had not been strictly enough applied in the Reformation and announced a new reformation that would produce a truly reformed church. These views put him near the radical circle of Conrad Grebel and Felix Mantz. He participated in talks between Zwingli and the Grebel group late in 1524, arguing against infant baptism, but, despite the fact that he was expelled from Zurich in January 1525 along with the Anabaptists, he had not joined their group and had not been baptized.

In the first half of 1525 Hätzer took a position as proofreader with the printer Silvan Otmar in Augsburg, where he published an ethical treatise against the practice of excessive drinking by supporters of the Reformation. The Christian's example is Christ, he wrote, not Bacchus. He also became involved in conventicle gatherings in which Zwingli's view of the Lord's Supper was supported against the Lutheran position. He clashed with the Augsburg reformer Urbanus Rhegius and was expelled from the city as a disturber of the peace.

Hätzer then spent time in Constance and Basel, but in November 1525 he returned to Zurich and was reconciled to Zwingli acknowledged in part the legitimacy of infant baptism and, following Zwingli's spiritualism, separated the gift of the Holy Spirit from the sacraments. Back in Basel, he spent time translating the works of Johannes Oecolampadius, especially several on the Lord's Supper. His introductory comments reveal strong spiritualistic leanings.

Because of a sexual offense he was forced to flee and went to Strasbourg. He found refuge with Wolfgang Capito and continued his writing activities. Being proficient in the three classical languages, he now turned his attention to translating the prophet Isaiah into German from the original. In Strasbourg he also met Michael Sattler, with whom he strongly disagreed, having moved away from Sattler's biblicism. He also met Hans Denck, with whose mysticism he was now much more in tune. Denck was expelled from Strasbourg in December 1526, and a short time later Hätzer left voluntarily, following Denck to Worms. There the two friends worked feverishly at translating the prophets into German. Building on Hätzer's earlier work, they finished the task in two months, and the work appeared in print in April 1527. It was the first translation of the prophets in German during the Reformation. The Zurich translators used it in their own work, and Luther gave it grudging recognition. Before midyear both men had once more been expelled.

From then until November 1528 Hätzer's whereabouts are unknown, but his literary activities continued. His leanings toward mysticism and an accompanying devaluing of the scriptures were evident in his new edition of the *Theologia Deutsch.* In this work he also revealed his move toward antitrinitarianism when in place of Luther's term *trinity* he used *threeness.* In a book about Jesus Christ, never published, he attacked the orthodox teaching of Christ's deity, which earned him identification as an Arian.

At the end of November 1528 he was arrested in Constance and brought to trial on charges of adultery. He was condemned to death and executed on 4 February 1529. Although the charge may have been accurate, adultery did not warrant the death penalty. The evidence suggests that the charge was used to get rid of a dangerous mystic and antitrinitarian.

Hätzer was one of a number of figures in the Reformation period who cannot be placed firmly in any of the contending religious camps. Though he did baptize several persons in Regensburg, he was never really an Anabaptist but found south German Anabaptism, with its mystic cast, the most hospitable. He helped move the controversy over images in Zurich ahead to a resolution and made a name for himself with the translation of the prophets, which filled a need at that time; within four years it was republished twelve times. Even so, he left no lasting legacy.

BIBLIOGRAPHY

Goeters, J. F. Gerhard. "Hätzer, Ludwig." In *Mennonite Encyclopedia,* edited by Cornelius J. Dyck and Dennis D. Martin, vol. 2, pp. 621–626. Scottdale, Pa., 1956. Summary of the standard biography.

———. *Ludwig Hätzer ca. 1500 bis 1529: Spiritualist und Antitrinitarier. Eine Randfigur der frühen Täuferbewegung.* Gütersloh, 1957. The authoritative biography.

Ozment, Steven. *Mysticism and Dissent: Religious Ideology and Social Protest in the Sixteenth Century.* New Haven and London, 1973. Hätzer as part of the popular mysticism of the Reformation period.

Verzeichnis der im deutschen Sprachbereich erschienenen Drucke des XVI. Jahrhunderts. Stuttgart, 1983–. See vol. 8, nos. 136–146.

Weis, Frederick. *The Life and Teachings of Ludwig Hetzer, a Leader and Martyr of the Anabaptists, 1500–1529.* Dorchester, Mass., 1930. Hätzer presented as an early martyr for Unitarianism.

WALTER KLAASSEN

HAUSMANN, Nikolaus (1478/79–1538), Lutheran reformer in Zwickau and Anhalt-Dessau. His father was city councilor and, between 1492 and 1499, Saxon master of the mint in Freiberg. Hausmann himself studied in Leipzig beginning in the summer of 1498, receiving the bachelor's degree in 1499 and the master's degree in 1503. From the middle of 1519 he preached Lutheran notions but without much impact. He established close relations with Martin Luther. After Johannes Sylvius Egranus and Thomas Müntzer left Zwickau in April 1521, Hausmann assumed the vacant position at Saint Mary's church in Zwickau (May 1521). At that time Zwickau was characterized by tensions among followers of monks loyal to Rome, the humanist reformer Egranus, Müntzer, the Zwickau Prophets, and Luther.

In collaboration with the city council, the clergy of the town, and Duke John, Hausmann led the evangelical movement without undue polemics to an orderly reform of the church. As a means of reform he focused especially on sermons (he invited Luther in 1522 and Kaspar Güttel in 1523 as guest preachers), but he also insisted on a new church order, on visitations in order to secure the economic needs of the clergy, and on a catechism. He asked Luther both for a new church order and for church visitations. Luther dedicated in 1523 his *Formula missae et communionis* to Hausmann and was from 1525 onward an advocate of visitations. In a small pamphlet in 1525 Hausmann justified the agitation of the Zwickau citizens against the monks in their city. In the same year, the city council dissolved the Franciscan monastery. Hausmann contributed significantly to Zwickau's leading role among the Saxon cities in the introduction of the Reformation.

In 1528 the Saxon elector John appointed Hausmann to be a member of a visitation committee, and in 1529 Hausmann became the first superintendent of Zwickau. He came in conflict with the city council in 1531, when the council dismissed a minister. Supported by Luther, Hausmann fought against the city council's domination of church government in Zwickau, which in 1505 had received the patronage right over the churches in the city. Elector John confirmed the action of the city council but required his approval of any future appointment or dismissal of ministers.

In September 1532 Luther recommended Hausmann, who had been dismissed from Zwickau, to be court preacher for the rulers of Anhalt-Dessau. These rulers had favored the Reformation since 1530 and had dismissed their court preacher after he had delivered a derogatory sermon against the laity who wanted the Communion cup. In close contact with the Wittenberg theologians, Hausmann introduced the Lutheran Reformation in Anhalt-Dessau in 1534. He drafted a church order for Anhalt-Dessau that Luther supported but also counseled that it not be imposed too quickly on the local congregations.

In November 1538 Duke Henry of Saxony appointed Hausmann superintendent for Freiberg, which had introduced the Reformation early in 1537. Hausmann happily accepted this assignment to his hometown and had hopes of conciliating Duke Henry and his brother Duke George of Saxony in their disagreement over the word of God.

When Hausmann delivered his first sermon in the cathedral of Freiberg on 3 November 1538, he suffered a stroke from which he died on the same day.

BIBLIOGRAPHY

Primary Source

Hausmann, Nikolaus. *Vnterrichdt vnd Warnung an die Kirche zu Zwickau.* Zwickau, 1525. Also available on microfiche from Inter Documentation Company, Zug, 1979.

Secondary Sources

Clemen, Otto. "Nicolaus Hausmann." In *Otto Clemen: Kleine Schriften zur Reformationsgeschichte, 1897–1944,* edited by Ernst Koch, vol. 8, pp. 24–27. Leipzig, 1987.

Bräuer, Helmut. *Zwickau und Martinus Luther: Die gesellschaftlichen Auseinandersetzungen um die städtische Kirchenpolitik in Zwickau, 1527–1531.* Karl-Marx-Stadt, 1983.

Karant-Nunn, Susan C. *Zwickau in Transition, 1500–1547: The Reformation as an Agent of Change.* Columbus, Ohio, 1987.

Verzeichnis der im deutschen Sprachbereich erschienenen Drucke des 16. Jahrhunderts. Stuttgart, 1987. See vol. 8, no. 814.

HELMAR JUNGHANS

Translated from German by Hans J. Hillerbrand

HEALING. *See* Medicine and Healing.

HEBLER, Matthias (d. 1571), first bishop of the Saxon Lutherans in Transylvania and advocate of early Lutheran orthodoxy. He helped to establish the authority of the office of superintendent among the Saxon Lutherans in Transylvania. Hebler was born in Krupina (Slovakia) and, after receiving his basic education in local schools, matriculated at Wittenberg in 1546, where he completed his master's. Returning to Hungary, he became a teacher in Levoča and then, in 1551, was called as a teacher to Sibiu (Hermannstadt) in Transylvania. He was ordained by Johannes Bugenhagen in Wittenberg in 1553 and was named deacon and preacher in 1554 at the behest of the Saxon Lutheran bishop, Paul Wiener, who died that year during the plague. In 1555 Hebler became town pastor and one year later was elected the superintendent (bishop) of Saxon Lutherans, in which office he served until his death in 1571.

As pastor and bishop, he was an ardent supporter of the Augsburg Confession and the theology of the Wittenberg reformers. He had to contend with the growing influence of Swiss Reformed views in eastern Hungary and Transylvania. He signed the consensus on the Lord's Supper at the synod of Cluj (Clausenberg) in 1557, and at the synod of Medias (Mediasch) in 1560 he joined with the equally firm Dionysius Alexsius, bishop of the Magyar Lutheran church in Transylvania, to obtain the repudiation of the views of Francis Dávid. The following year, he issued his *Brevis confessio de coena Domini ecclesiarum Saxonicarum et coniuntarum in Transylvania,* which set forth his Lutheran understanding of the sacrament. He also prepared other polemical tracts, which remained in manuscript, against the Reformed (collected in *Elleboron ad repurganda phanaticorum quorundam spirituum capita, qui primum in Transylvanicam Calvinismi semina spargere coeperunt*). Hebler participated in colloquies at Enyed in 1564 and at Alba Iulia (Weissenburg) in 1568 that confirmed the Lutheran stance of the Saxons of Transylvania. Shortly before his death, he was appointed to supervise a debate at Debrecen that matched supporters of Francis Dávid against those of the Calvinist Péter Somogyi Melius.

BIBLIOGRAPHY

Primary Sources

Hebler, Matthias. *Brevis confessio de coena Domini ecclesiarum Saxonicarum et conjunctarum in Transylvania.* Kronstadt, 1561.

———. *Elleboron ad repurganda phanaticorum quorundam spirituum capita, qui primum in Transylvanicam Calvinismi semina spargere coeperunt.* N.p., 1556.

Secondary Sources

Bautz, Friedrich Wilhelm, ed. "Hebler, Matthias." In *Biographisch-Bibliographisches Kirchenlexikon.* Herzberg, 1990.

Myss, Walter, ed. *Lexikon der siebenbürgischen Sachsen.* Thaur, 1993.

Schullerus, Adolf. "Die Augustana in Siebenbürgen." *Archiv des Vereins für Siebenbürgische Landesgeschichte* 41 (1923), 161–296.

Teutsch, Georg Daniel. *Die Bischöfe der evangelischen Kirche A.B. in Siebenbürgen.* Part 1, *Die Bischöfe der Jahre 1553–1867* (1933). Cologne, 1978. See pp. 11–22.

DAVID P. DANIEL

HEDIO, Caspar (also Seiler; 1494/95–1552), irenic Protestant reformer and chronicler. Born in Ettlingen, near Karlsruhe, he studied at the universities of Freiburg (1513–1516), Basel (1517–1519), and Mainz, where he became received a doctorate in theology (1523). He served as vicar and chaplain in Basel; in October 1520, at the instigation of Capito, his teacher and friend, he moved to Mainz, and the following January was appointed preacher at that city's Saint Martin's cathedral. In November 1523 he was nominated to be the main preacher at Strasbourg cathedral, a post he occupied until 1550, when the Interim was enforced. Already in Basel and Mainz, under the influence of Capito, Zwingli, and his friend Oecolampadius, he had shown himself to be favorable toward the reform movement; in Strasbourg he dared the definitive step of marriage (May 1524).

There Hedio joined Bucer and the pedagogue Johannes Sturm in building new educational structures: his activities in this area included teaching at the theological school (from 1524); helping to organize the high school (1537–1538) and serving as school inspector; creating the Saint Guillaume boarding school for poor children (1543–1544); and helping to establish the library. He also conducted church visitations not only in and around Strasbourg but also in the south German territories of Count Wilhelm von Fürstenberg (d. 1549); during the summer of 1543, he assisted Archbishop Hermann von Wied in reforming the diocese of Cologne; and he succeeded Bucer (who had taken refuge in England) as president of the *Kirchen Konvent*, an ecclesiastical authority created in 1544. Following the application of the Interim Hedio preached in the former Dominican church. He died of the plague on 17 October 1552.

Characteristically moderate, Hedio took no stand in the heated debate over the Eucharist, although he was present at the Colloquy of Marburg (1529) and signed the Tetrapolitan Confession (1530) and the Augsburg Confession (1532). He rejected any attempt to define the doctrine of real presence in the celebration of the Lord's Supper. While not opposed to stronger church discipline as advocated by Bucer, Hedio showed greater deference toward the civil authority of the magistrate and the emperor; and when the magistrate expressed opposition to Bucer's *Christlichen Gemeinschaften* (small groups of militant believers amid the established church) and to the reintroduction of excommunication, relations between Hedio and Bucer became somewhat strained. (Differences regarding the application of the Interim in Strasbourg—albeit that both disagreed with its content—were another contributing factor.) Unlike Capito, however, Hedio always stood by Bucer in the fight against Anabaptist ideas. He also engaged in polemic against the *Chronicle* (1531) of the spiritualist Sebastian Franck.

In addition, Hedio was one of the most important translators of the first half of the sixteenth century. He translated into German the works of patristic, medieval, and contemporaneous writers, among them the *Church History* of Eusebius and the *Tripartita*. The so-called *Ursberger Chronicle* he not only translated but brought up to date, and thus he can be regarded as the first Protestant chronicler as well.

BIBLIOGRAPHY

Adam, Jean. "Versuch einer Bibliographie K. Hedios." *Zeitschrift für die Geschichte des Oberrheins* 70 (1916), 424–429. Contains works by Hedio.

Bodenmann, Reinhard. "Hedio (Seiler), Caspar." In *Nouveau Dictionnaire de Biographie Alsacienne*, edited by Jean-Pierre Kintz, pt. 16, pp. 1470–1473. Strasbourg, 1990. A important bibliography.

Chrisman, Miriam U. "Caspar Hedio of Ettlingen." In *Contemporaries of Erasmus*, edited by Peter G. Bietenholz and Thomas B. Deutscher, vol. 2. Toronto, 1986.

Himmelheber, Emil. *Caspar Hedio: Ein Lebensbild aus der Reformationsgeschichte.* Karlsruhe, 1881.

Keute, Hartwig. *Reformation und Geschichte: Kaspar Hedio als Historiograph.* Göttingen, 1980.

Spindler, Charles. *Hédion: Essai biographique et litteraire.* Strasbourg, 1864.

Reinhard Bodenmann

HEIDELBERG, UNIVERSITY OF.

Founded in 1386, the University of Heidelberg was not widely renowned at the beginning of the sixteenth century. To regenerate itself, the unwieldy institution ended up being increasingly dependent on the more dynamic princely court, with which the faculty members were already connected as councillors and in other functions. Although Louis V of the Palatinate (r. 1508–1544) accepted many recommendations from various Alsatian humanists in 1521/22 for a reform of the university, the changes were largely confined to stronger control of the university by the prince. Attempts by the faculty of arts to open the study of the liberal arts to humanism met with failure since the teachers of Greek and Hebrew quickly left for more lucrative positions. The Reformation received no strong support at the university in view of the indecisive stance of the prince, even though Martin Luther had presented his theology with great success among younger listeners in the Heidelberg Disputation in 1518.

Nonetheless, the university soon came under the suspicion of Lutheran heresy. From the Interim period on, with brief interruptions, there were cautious but significant reforms under Frederick II (r. 1544–1556). The reform of the Holy Ghost Foundation (*Heiliggeiststift*) and the permission granted for laypersons to receive ecclesiastical incomes broke through the clerical character of the university for the first time. The various scholarships for the students were brought together into a *contubernium* ("common life"). In addition, the existing colleges were expanded; the Collegium Sapientiae was added to the Collegium Principis and the Dionysianum, and on the recommendation of Paul Fagius an institute for instruction in Latin and Greek was founded. What was decisive, however, was the improvement in the financial situation of the university, which occurred with the approval of the Curia Romana. This took place by transforming traditional prebend income into firm annual payments and through the incorporation of monasteries in the Palatinate that had been deserted or were threatened with extinction. The result was that the professors could be paid with a fixed salary.

The reformation of the Palatinate under Ottheinrich (r. 1556–1559) was connected in 1558 with a reform of the university that was to lay the groundwork for centuries. As a comprehensive reform of regulations, it left little room for an autonomous administration of the university. The rector was chosen by the university senate alternately from the various schools, but the deans of the schools had only a one-year term of office. The organization of the schools and the assignments of the professors in them were regulated anew, and even course content and textbooks were prescribed. A course of study in the liberal arts was no longer the prerequisite for study in the other schools, whose prestige was thus enhanced. These studies were completely dominated by German humanism. The professors of the faculty of theology were obliged to affirm their acceptance of the Augsburg

Confession and its Apology. In the school of law the primacy of secular law was asserted, while in the school of medicine firsthand factual knowledge and clinical practice were demanded. The fact that Ottheinrich donated his large collection of manuscripts and books to the university made it more attractive to scholars from all over Europe. The prince was successful in attracting outstanding professors, although they represented different schools of Protestant thought. This created controversy and paved the way for the Calvinization of the Palatinate under Frederick III (r. 1559–1576). In the years that followed the university could not escape the impact of decisions on religious affiliation by sovereigns. These decisions were often accompanied by painful interventions and hindered its otherwise rapid development into a "family university," where only relatives are chosen as professors.

As the "German" or "third" Geneva after Leiden, Heidelberg, like other universities, experienced a remarkable blossoming. The faculty came largely from countries in southern and western Europe, while the students came from all the Reformed regions of Europe. Controversies occasionally arose with the church council over ecclesiastical discipline, and there was an antitrinitarian trial. At times there were also tensions with the prince, who encouraged his successors to support the university but also to maintain control. With the Lutheranization of the Palatinate under Louis VI (r. 1576–1583), not only the professors but also most of the students had to leave the university. Part of them were taken in by the Neustädter *Hochschule*, recently founded by Louis's brother Johann Casimir. When Johann Casimir took over the regency (1583–1592), the Lutherans were dismissed, and the university once again took on a decisively Reformed orientation. Outstanding scholars represented their fields in all the schools, and the influx of students steadily increased. Along with adhering to the *Calvinismus aulicus* ("court Calvinism") that characterized Heidelberg, the university under subsequent princes made its contribution (including the theologians) to a dangerous imperial policy that under Frederick V (r. 1610–1632) led the Palatinate into a catastrophic war. This ended the first zenith of the university.

After the capture of Heidelberg in 1622, Maximilian I turned the library of the university over to Pope Gregory XV. Since then, as the Bibliotheca Palatina, it has formed a significant part of the Vatican Library. The university itself was replaced by a Catholic university, established in 1629, which did not flourish. After the capture of the city by Swedish forces in 1632, some thought was given to reopening a Protestant university, but under the protection of imperial troops a revival of the Catholic university occurred between 1635 and 1641. As a result, the reopening of the University of Heidelberg under Charles Louis (r. 1648–1680) practically amounted to the founding of a new university. The significance of the university lies in its role as a bulwark of Reformed theology in the second half of the sixteenth century.

BIBLIOGRAPHY

Die Geschichte der Universität Heidelberg: Sammelband der Vorträge des Studium Generale im Wintersemester 1985/86. Heidelberg, 1986.

Wolgast, Eike. *Die Universität Heidelberg, 1386–1986*. Berlin and New York, 1986.

Gottfried Seebaß

Translated from German by Robert E. Shillenn

HELIE, Paul (Dan., Poul/Povel Helgesen; c.1480–c.1534), Danish Catholic humanist. He is often called the "Erasmus of Denmark." Born in Varberg in the province of Halland in what is today southern Sweden, early in childhood he was given over to a monastery. Nothing is known of Helie until he became the first principal of the Carmelite college in Copenhagen. As such, he was also connected to theological studies at the University of Copenhagen. Many of Helie's students were strongly influenced by his biblical humanism and his call for ecclesiastical reform. Later they were to become leaders of the Lutheran Reformation in Scandinavia. Helie vacillated between the evangelical faith and Roman Catholicism, never becoming a Lutheran himself. As a result of this vacillation, he became known as Paul Vendekaabe ("Turncoat").

Helie became acquainted early with Luther and the reform movement emanating from Wittenberg. He acknowledged it as a much-needed positive movement and proceeded to translate a number of Luther's writings. He concurred with Luther's biblical emphasis and his attack on the moral depravity of the time. But like his mentor, Erasmus, he became increasingly horrified at Luther's attack on the Roman church, its ministry, and its sacraments. In 1524 he sided with Erasmus in the debate over free will. Reform was Helie's goal, not revolution or schism. Reform would come through a biblical renaissance as mediated by the Roman church, pope, theologians, and the guidance of the church fathers.

The Danish monarch, Christian II (r. 1513–1523), was a gifted, enlightened Renaissance prince who was at the same time impulsive and unpredictable. He desired a strong royal house and control of the Danish church. He allied himself with the rising mercantile class, thus alienating himself from the nobility and church hierarchy. In 1523 the king was toppled and had to flee to the Netherlands and eventually to Wittenberg. For a time, Helie enjoyed the king's favor, but his sermon exposing royal immorality, which he likened to that of Herod and Herodias, and his refusal to fulfill the king's request to translate Machiavelli's *The Prince*, substituting instead Erasmus's *Institutio principis Christiani*, brought down on Helie the wrath of Christian II. He was forced to flee in 1522 to Århus in Jutland. Helie had become involved in the growing opposition to Christian II that viewed the king as a tyrant who allowed the Lutheran heresy to flourish. Yet two years later, Helie translated Luther's *Betbüchlein* into Danish.

As the years progressed, Helie became more and more isolated and embittered. He who had been the first in Denmark to call for biblical reform realized after 1526 that even his own students, who were going over to the Lutheran side, did not understand his point of view. The defection of men such as Frans Vormordsen, Peter Laurentsen, and Claus Mortensen, who were to become the leaders of the Lutheran Reformation in Malmø (today Sweden), was especially galling. For a time Helie seemed to enjoy the favor of the new king, Frederick I (r. 1523–1533), but after a sermon before the king in 1526 in which he criticized Communion in both kinds and the breaking of the Lenten fast, he drifted into increasing obscurity. After the Diet of Copenhagen (1530) and the subsequent turmoil that closed the university, Helie moved to Helsingør and eventually Roskilde. The war of succession (Counts' War, 1533–1536) that erupted after Frederick's death was especially upsetting to Helie.

In 1650 a manuscript was discovered in the wall behind the altar of the church at Skiby in Sjælland (Zealand). Though anonymous, it is clearly Helie's and is known as *Skibykrøniken*. It begins with a chronicle of events from the eleventh century and becomes increasingly detailed as Helie comments on his own age, ending abruptly in midsentence in the autumn of 1534. No friend or foe bothered to complete the sentence or to enlighten posterity of Helie's demise.

Helie's formula for reform combined learning with piety. While something in Luther seemed constantly to attract him, many have contended that the example of Christian II was an insurmountable stumbling block for Helie. A prince was to be obedient to the hierarchy of the church. God's punishment could be seen in Turkey, Russia, and Bohemia. That heresy even existed was a sure sign that the coming of the Antichrist was near.

BIBLIOGRAPHY

Andersen, J. Oskar. *Paulus Helie.* Copenhagen, 1936.

Andersen, Niels K. *Confessio Hafniensis.* Copenhagen, 1954.

Heise, A. *Skibykrøniken* (1890). Reprint, Copenhagen, 1967.

Severinsen, P., et al. *Skrifter af Paulus Helie.* 7 vols. Copenhagen, 1932–1948.

Valkner, Kristen. *Paulus Helie og Christiern II.* Oslo, 1963.

TRYGVE R. SKARSTEN

HELMICHIUS, Werner (also Wernerus; 1551–1608), Dutch reformed minister. Helmichius, the son of a civil servant, was born in Utrecht; he studied theology in Geneva from 1566 and in Heidelberg from 1570. In 1576 he entered the ministry of the Dutch Reformed exile church at Frankfurt; he served as a minister in Utrecht from 1579, in Delft from 1590, and from 1602 until his death in Amsterdam.

Helmichius belonged to the first generation of leading theologians in the Dutch Republic. His career reflects the main events of the first three decades of its existence: after training abroad, a ministry in one of the exile churches; the difficult establishment of a Dutch consistorial organization; the Leicester period; and the beginning of the Arminian controversy.

At Frankfurt Helmichius was the leader of the rather small Netherlandish-speaking Reformed exile church. Like the French-speaking exile church, it consisted of Reformed exiles who were undesirable aliens in Frankfurt, and therefore had difficulties with the town council and with the Lutheran ministers. Almost from the beginning of Helmichius's ministry churches in the Dutch republic tried to engage him. After two and a half years in Frankfurt he returned to his native city, which had two Protestant churches.

Helmichius belonged to the "consistorials," the Reformed church that was governed by a consistory. Its competitor was the church of the "parochials" (parishioners), followers of Hubert Duifhuis, who aimed at transforming a Catholic parish step by step into a Protestant community. In 1586 the two churches united, owing to the efforts of the magistrates, who at that time supported the consistorials. Two years later the town council, now on the side of the adversaries of the Reformed church, fired the ministers. The entire affair was connected with the activity of Leicester as governor of the republic on behalf of Elizabeth I (1585–1587). Supported by the Reformed church Leicester tried to strengthen the central power and by doing so alienated Holland, the most powerful province. Ecclesiastical conflicts in Utrecht became intertwined with the political choice, for or against, Leicester. Leicester's departure resulted in the victory of the magistrates over the the Reformed church at Utrecht.

Helmichius's years in Delft were relatively peaceful. He acted as a mediator in several ecclesiastical controversies in Holland, each stemming from the church's effort to strengthen itself by emphazising its Calvinist character and by imposing appropriate norms on those ministers who had their roots either in the Catholic or a less definitively Reformed tradition.

In Amsterdam Helmichius worked on behalf of the churches in Holland in much the same spirit. Immediately after his arrival he became involved in the Arminian affair. Perhaps prompted by his colleague Petrus Plancius, he tried to prevent the appointment of his colleague Jacobus Arminius as a professor at Leiden. His opposition was based both on his own doctrinal position—he considered Arminius as deviating from the Reformed doctrine in many respects, not only in the matter of predestination—and on his opinion regarding the character of Arminius, whom he considered to be rash and inconsiderate. He deeply regretted the stand of Johannes Wtenbogaert, who had been an esteemed colleague in Utrecht and who now fully backed Arminius. Helmichius played an important role in the negotiations, initiated by the States-General, to convene a synod aimed at resolving the difficulties.

BIBLIOGRAPHY

Itterzon, G. P. van. "Helmichius, Wernerus." In *Biografisch Lexicon voor de Geschiedenis van het Nederlandse Protestantisme*, vol. 2, pp. 237–239. Kampen, Netherlands, 1983. Excellent biographical dictionary; includes full bibliography.

Meinert, Hermann, and Wolfram Dahmer, eds. *Das Protokollbuch der Niederländischen Reformierten Gemeinde zu Franfurt am Main, 1570–1581*. Frankfurt a.M., 1977. Useful for Helmichius's Frankfurt years, which are not covered in the article cited above.

CORNELIS AUGUSTIJN

HELTAI, Caspar (also Gaspar Helth; c.1500–1574), reformer and humanist translator and printer in Cluj (Klausenburg, Kolozsvár), Transylvania. Like Francis Dávid, Heltai was a Transylvanian German whose spiritual pilgrimage led from Catholicism through Lutheranism and Calvinism to Socinianism. Almost nothing is known of his early life except that he was probably born of German heritage in Heltau, Transylvania, sometime after 1500 but before 1515. After initial schooling in Siebenbürgen, possibly in Braşov (Kronstadt, Brassó), he matriculated at the university of Wittenberg on 13 February 1543. He was in Wittenberg only briefly, and in 1544 he was the city pastor of the German community in Cluj when it accepted the Lutheran Reformation. As the pastor of one of the major cities in Transylvania, he participated on the committee, led by Johannes Honter, that prepared the *Reformatio ecclesiarum Saxonicarum in Transylvania* (Coronae, 1547), the first Lutheran church order for all of Siebenbürgen. It appears that Heltai was probably a Philippist in his views during the 1550s, and on 13 June 1557 he signed the agreement between the Lutherans and Catholics (Klausenburg Consensus) as the senior of the Lutheran church in Cluj.

By the fall of that year, however, he had resigned his pastorate, probably to devote more energy to his paper mill and the printing establishment he had founded in 1549 with George Hoffgreff from Nuremberg, who may have begun a press of his own in 1555. Heltai was replaced by Dávid, his spiritual companion, and followed the lead of Dávid, who in 1560 accepted the Reformed position on the Lord's Supper. Heltai—whose first prints from his press were an Agenda and Luther's Catechism in Hungarian and German (1549) and who wrote with Dávid the *Confessio de Mediatore* (Wittenberg, 1555), a defense of Philipp Melanchthon against the followers of Francis Stancarus—was from 1559 (when he probably reestablished his press) to 1570, the leading publisher of Hungarian and Reformed religious materials in Transylvania. Although he started to learn Hungarian only at the age of sixteen, he so mastered it that his translations of hymns (1574), of classical works, including Aesop's Fables (1566) and the grammar of Aelius Donatus (1552), and especially of the Bible, issued in by his press in segments, contributed significantly to the development of Hungarian as a literary language. His press printed many of the confessions and doctrinal statements of the Reformed church, as well as editions of the works of the Helvetic and upper German reformers.

Between 1568 and 1570, however, Heltai again followed Dávid and left the Reformed church to become an antitrinitarian. He marked this change by issuing in 1570 his report of the colloquy between the Reformed Péter Somogyi Melius and the antitrinitarian Giorgio Biandrata; originally published in 1568, this report included a revised introduction in which he regretted calling Dávid and Biandrata innovators. Heltai probably died in 1574 during an outbreak of the plague, and the last publication he prepared was a Hungarian translation of the *Chronicle* of Antonio Bonifini (1575). The press, which continued to be run by his heirs, issued the largest number of titles of any press in Transylvania.

BIBLIOGRAPHY

Primary Sources

Borsa, Gedeon, et al., eds. *Régi Magyarországi nyomtatványok, 1473–1600*. Magyar Tudományos Akadémia and Országos Széchényi Könyvtár. Budapest, 1971. See for bibliographic information about Heltai's works and publications of his press.

Secondary Sources

Borsa, Gedeon. "Die Buchdrucker des XV. und XVI. Jahrhunderts in Ungarn." *Bibliothek und Wissenschaft* 2 (1965), 1–33.

Capesius, Bernhard. "Neue Forschung über Caspar Helth." *Forschungen zur Volks- und Landeskunde* 13 (1970), 96–97.

Klaniczay, Tibor, ed. *Handbuch der ungarischen Literatur*. Budapest, 1977. See pp. 46–58.

Soltész, Zoltánne. *A magyarországi könyvdiszitésa XVI. században*. Budapest, 1961. See pp. 158–160.

Trausch, Joseph. *Schriftsteller-Lexikon oder biographisch-literarische Denk-Blätter der siebenbürger Deutschen*. 3 vols. Kronstadt, 1868–1871. See vol. 2, pp. 101–118.

DAVID P. DANIEL

HELVETIC CONFESSIONS. The First Helvetic Confession (*Confessio Helvetica prior*) was published in 1536 as the first statement of faith uniting the Reformed cantons of Switzerland on a common theological basis. It is sometimes referred to as the Second Confession of Basel in order to distinguish it from an earlier doctrinal standard prepared by a local commission of theologians in the same city two years before. The first Basel statement, along with earlier Reformed documents such as the Ten Theses of Bern (1528), commanded only local authority in their place of origin.

The need for a united Swiss confession in the mid-1530s was stimulated by two external factors. First, Pope Paul III's call for a general council to assemble in Mantua (1537) alerted the Reformed churches of Switzerland of their need to unite under a common confessional standard. On another front, the Reformed churches had no document comparable to the Lutheran Augsburg Confession (1530) and needed to clarify their views in light of the festering eucharistic controversies.

On 30 January 1536, a number of Swiss theologians from Zurich, Bern, Basel, Schaffhausen, St. Gall, Mühlhausen, and Biel assembled in the Augustinian convent at Basel to prepare the document. It is generally held that Heinrich Bullinger had the greatest influence in shaping the confession, although Leo Jud, Oswald Myconius, Simon Grynaeus, and Caspar Megander were also assigned to work on it. It was accepted and signed by the delegates on 4 February and published immediately in Latin. Jud prepared a somewhat longer German translation. George Wishart, an early Protestant martyr of Scotland, translated the confession into English.

The Latin text of the confession contains twenty-eight articles that succinctly summarize major themes of Protestant theology. The first five articles deal with holy scripture, its interpretation, antiquity, authority, and scope. Articles 6–11 touch on the fundamental Christian doctrines of the Trinity, Christology, and soteriology. Human beings are declared to be created in the image of God but so marred by original sin as to leave them incapable of salvation apart from God's electing grace. "Our salvation is from God, from us there is nothing but sin and damnation." Articles 12–14 deal with the purpose of evangelical teaching, the divine benefits given to the believer by the Holy Spirit, and faith, which, although not based on human works, nonetheless issues in the true worship of God and manifold service to others ("operum foecundissima"). Articles 15–20 deal with issues related to the church and its ministry. Articles 21–23 present a moderate statement on the sacraments, which are said to be not merely empty signs but rather signs that convey the reality of that which they signify ("non nudis signis, sed signis simul et rebus constant"). The closing articles (24–28) touch on issues of church order, civil society, heresy, schism, and marriage.

Martin Bucer and Wolfgang Capito, reformers of Strasbourg, attended the synod that adopted the confession and hoped to use it as a vehicle of mediation with the Lutherans. Luther's initial reaction to the confession was mildly favorable, but when Bullinger and the other Swiss reformers refused to embrace Bucer's Wittenberg Concord (1536), Luther reverted to his harsh stance against the Swiss "sacramentarians." The primary significance of the First Helvetic Confession was its role in promoting unity among the Swiss Reformed churches and in providing a precedent for subsequent confessions of national authority.

The thirty-year interval between the publication of the First and Second Helvetic Confessions was an era of transition in Reformation history. The deaths of both Luther (1546) and Calvin (1564) gave rise to new leaders within their respective movements. More important still, the resurgence of Tridentine Catholicism presented the Reformed churches with a united front committed to an aggressive and well-defined Counter-Reformation. In addition to the First Helvetic Confession, other national confessions had been recently issued by Reformed churches in several countries. These include the French Gallic Confession (1559), the First Scottish Confession (1560), and the Belgic Confession (1561). But it was felt that a new confession commanding international respect was called for at this time. The immediate occasion for the Second Helvetic Confession arose out of the special needs of the Reformation in the Palatinate. In 1555 the Peace of Augsburg had established a new religious status quo between Lutherans and Catholics within the empire without granting any special prerogative to the Reformed churches. In 1563 Frederick III, elector of the Palatinate, had published the Heidelberg Catechism within his territory. This act prompted a severe attack from Lutheran partisans, who threatened to have Frederick tried for heresy at the forthcoming meeting of the imperial diet. To fortify himself against such charges, Frederick requested that Bullinger send him a complete exposition of the Reformed faith.

In 1561 Bullinger had drafted a personal confession of faith. Written during a severe illness he did not expect to survive, Bullinger intended to bequeath this document to the church at Zurich as part of his last will and testament. Although Bullinger recovered and lived on until 1575, his confession was approved by other notable theologians such as Peter Martyr Vermigli and soon gained a wider acceptance beyond Zurich. In response to Frederick's appeal, Bullinger forwarded this confession to him. It proved helpful in the preparation and defense of his orthodox faith before the imperial assembly in 1566.

Although written by a single theologian, the Second Helvetic Confession became the most comprehensive and influential of all the Reformed confessions of the sixteenth century. In addition to its initial acceptance by the Swiss cantons and the Palatinate, in whose name it was originally published, it was also adopted by the Reformed churches of France (1571), Hungary (1567), Poland (1571 and 1578), and Scotland (1566). It was also well received in Holland and England and translated into nine languages including Magyar, Italian, and Arabic.

Bullinger was well suited to write such a confession, having served as chief pastor (*Antistes*) of Zurich since the death of Zwingli in 1531. He was an indefatigable exegete, commentator, and correspondent. He was also well skilled in the intricate art of intra-Reformed diplomacy, having negotiated with Calvin himself the Consensus Tigurinus of 1549. His breadth of learning and consummate theological skill are reflected in the catholicity and moderation of this confession.

Chapters 1–2 deal with the holy scriptures, their inspiration, extent, and interpretation. The scriptures are declared to be the source not only of all true wisdom and piety but also of sound theology and church polity. The value of church tradition is acknowledged, including the teaching of councils and the writings of the Greek and Latin fathers, though all of these derivative norms are subordinated to the primary authority of the scriptures. This is the first Protestant confession to exclude specifically the apocryphal books from the canon.

Chapters 3–7 deal with the doctrines of God, providence, and creation. The traditional trinitarian dogma is reaffirmed and the Apostles' Creed endorsed ("recipimus Symbolum Apostolorum, quod veram nobis fidem tradit"). The veneration of images and the cult of the saints are declared to be unworthy media for the true worship of God. God's providence, consisting of works of preservation and governance, is taken to include the use of secondary means. God is declared the creator of all things including the angels, the devil, and humans. Each human being is said to consist of two diverse substances united in one person ("duabus ac diversis quidem substantiis in una persona"). "Soul-sleep" and pantheism are condemned.

Chapters 8–10 cover the issues of human sinfulness, free will, and predestination. Sin is said to be both inborn corruption and personal depravity. The confession condemns three errors concerning sin: the denial of Original Sin, the consideration of all sins as equal, and the characterization of God as the author of sin. In Augustinian fashion, the human will is viewed under three conditions: in its prefallen state, in its sinful captivity, and in its regenerate restoration. Despite the devastating effects of the Fall on human ability, sinful humans have not been turned into "a stone or stock" ("lapidem vel truncum"), nor has the human will ("voluntas") been converted into a mere nothing ("noluntas"). The article on predestination affirms the eternity and gratuity of God's choice of the elect. Still, we are warned not to "rashly count anyone among the reprobate." Christ's universal invitation to salvation is affirmed (*Mt.* 11:28), and Christ is declared to be "the mirror in which we behold our predestination." The experiential implications of the doctrine of election are seen in the life of prayer, baptism, the Lord's Supper, and good works. Théodore de Bèze, Calvin's successor in Geneva, objected to the original wording of the article on predestination since it seemed to be biased against a Calvinist interpretation of this doctrine. Consequently, Bullinger made two alterations in the published version of the confession in order to achieve a more solid Reformed consensus on this controverted issue.

Chapters 11–13 focus on Christology, the law, and the gospel. The Chalcedonian Christology of the early church is affirmed and the various christological heresies are again repudiated. The *communicatio idiomatum* (exchange of properties) is also affirmed, although, with an eye to the Lutheran interpretation of this patristic motif, both the suffering of Christ's divine nature and the ubiquity of his human nature are alike denied. The catholicity of the Reformed faith is affirmed in the explicit acceptance of the creeds and decrees of the first four ecumenical councils. "We retain, unchanged and entire, the Christian, Orthodox, and Catholic faith; knowing that nothing is contained in the aforesaid creeds which does not correspond with the Word of God and aid in setting forth the true faith." The distinction between law and gospel is explained in terms of the economy of salvation history.

Chapters 14–16 deal with the work of salvation in the life of the believer. Repentance is declared to be a change of a sinner's heart that the Holy Spirit produces by the word of the gospel. Priestly confession is declared unnecessary, although pastoral counseling is allowed: "We may seek counsel and comfort from a minister of the gospel in time of distress and trial." Justification is declared to be entirely by grace through faith and is explained in terms of imputation. A true faith issues in good works, which God approves and awards. "We say with Augustine that God crowns and rewards in us, not our merits, but the gifts of his grace."

Chapters 17–18 present the Reformed understanding of the church and its ministry. The church is declared to be invisible in that its membership is known only to God, but visible and militant in its earthly manifestation. The unity and holiness of the church are affirmed, while obedience to papal authority is deplored: "The Roman head preserves the tyranny and corruption in the church, and opposes and destroys all true reformation." The equality of ministers within a presbyterian polity is advocated. The chief duties of ministers are said to be the preaching of the gospel, the administration of the sacraments, the care of souls, and the maintenance of discipline.

Chapters 19–21 cover the theology and practice of the sacraments. The two sacraments of holy baptism and the Lord's Supper are said to be "sacred rights instituted by God as signs and seals of his promises for the strengthening of our faith, and as pledges on our part for our consecration to him." Infant baptism is affirmed as a sign of the covenant for the children of believers. The repetition of baptism is condemned, as are "later human additions to the primitive form of baptism" such as exorcism, baptism by midwives, the use of oil, salt, spittle, and so on. The Lord's Supper is recognized as "a grateful commemoration of the benefits of redemption, and a spiritual feast of believers instituted by Christ, wherein he nourishes us by his own flesh and blood by true faith unto eternal life." The Lutheran doctrines of Christ's corporal presence and the "eating of the unworthy" are both denied. The body of Christ is declared to be in heaven at the right hand of the Father, and "hence we must raise our hearts to Heaven" ("sursum ergo elevanda sunt corda"). Yet Christ is not absent from his people when they celebrate his Communion, but he is present "spiritually by his enlivening and vivifying operation."

Chapters 22–29 deal with a variety of topics related to practical issues of church life. These include the importance of regular public worship, singing, prayers, fasting, catechizing, burial, church property, and marriage. The concluding chapter (30) concerns the role of the civil magistrates, who are seen as God's instruments for the preservation of peace and public order as well as the punishment of evil offenders including incorrigible heretics and disturbers of the church. The Anabaptist rejection of capital punishment, war, oath taking, and the holding of civil office is repudiated.

The Second Helvetic Confession was Bullinger's most enduring legacy to the Reformed church. No other document of the Reformation era, with the exception of the Heidelberg Catechism, enjoyed such high esteem and widespread influence. Like the Consensus Tigurinus of 1549, the Second Helvetic Confession also represents the convergence of the Zwinglian and Calvinist tributaries of the Swiss Reformation. Its catholicity and moderation still commend it as a worthy guide to the theology and pastoral practice of what the Puritans in England called "the best Reformed churches."

[*See also* Bullinger, Heinrich; Consenus Tigurinus; *and* Palatinate.]

BIBLIOGRAPHY

Koch, Ernst. *Die Theologie der Confessio Helvetica Posterior*. Neukirchen-Vluyn, Germany, 1968.

Rogers, Jack. *Presbyterian Creeds: A Guide to the Book of Confessions.* Philadelphia, 1985.

Schaff, Philip. *Creeds of Christendom* (1877). 6th ed. Grand Rapids, Mich., 1990. See vol. 1, pp. 388–420.

Staedtke, Joachim, ed. *Glauben und Bekennen: Vierhundert Jahre Confessio Helvetica Posterior.* Zurich, 1966.

TIMOTHY GEORGE

HEMMINGSEN, Niels (1513–1600), Danish theologian. Some scholars consider him the greatest Scandinavian theologian of the sixteenth century. Many came to visit him from all over Europe, including James VI of Scotland, counting it a great honor to be received by him. Hemmingsen was born on the island of Lolland and was trained by biblical humanists at Roskilde and Lund. In 1537, the year after the royal decree that made Denmark-Norway into a Lutheran realm, Hemmingsen matriculated at the University of Wittenberg. At Wittenberg, Hemmingsen was strongly attracted to the biblical humanism and theology of Philipp Melanchthon. The two continued to exchange letters over the years; Hemmingsen extolled Melanchthon's method and theology all his life.

Shortly after his return to Denmark in 1542, Hemmingsen was appointed professor of Greek at the University of Copenhagen. In 1545 he was named professor of dialectics and exegesis and in 1553 professor of theology. Besides his university duties, Hemmingsen served as pastor of the Church of the Holy Spirit in Copenhagen.

Two years after becoming a theology professor, Hemmingsen published his handbook on dogmatics and ethics (*Enchiridion theologicum*), which was used as a systematic textbook for many years throughout much of Protestant Europe. Hemmingsen simply called it an introduction to Melanchthon's *Loci*. But it was quickly seen to be much more than that; it was the first attempt within Lutheran circles to set forth a work on theological ethics. In 1561 Hemmingsen published his *Evangeliepostil*, which was used as a homiletics textbook. It was reprinted many times and translated into Danish, English, and German. It was not a series of sermons on the pericope texts but rather served as outlines and models for preaching, forcing pastors into serious exegesis of the biblical text. A third work that solidified Hemmingsen's reputation abroad was his *Pastor* (1562). For many decades this served as the textbook in pastoral theology, seeking to present "all that belongs to the work of an evangelical pastor and curate of the soul's life and doctrine." Thus within ten years of having been named professor of theology, Hemmingsen had written three works that were to become textbooks in the fields of systematic theology, homiletics, and pastoral theology. Besides these works, Hemmingsen published works on methodology, marriage counseling, numerous commentaries on the New Testament and *Psalms*, as well as a work on natural law. The last was said to have greatly influenced Hugo Grotius.

Hemmingsen had a warm, irenic spirit. During the theologically fluid years of the 1540s and 1550s, he championed Melanchthon's *Variata* version of the Augsburg Confession. When the Lord's Supper controversy broke out in Germany, Christian III asked the university for an opinion. Hemmingsen drew up the *Tavle om Herrens Nadvere* (Statement on the Lord's Supper; 1557), to which all the university professors subscribed. In it they declared their unanimity with the Lutheran position and the Augsburg Confession without designating any particular version. Sometime after 1557, however, Hemmingsen's Melanchthonian sympathies veered in the direction of crypto-Calvinism and eventually outright Calvinism. In 1571 Hemmingsen attacked the Gnesio-Lutheran party and the doctrine of ubiquity in his *Demonstratio indubitatae veritatis de Domino Jesu.* In a large dogmatic work three years later (*Syntagma institutionum Christianarum*), Hemmingsen openly espoused the Calvinist doctrine of the Lord's Supper.

Complaints soon began to arise from abroad, though not from within Denmark, where Hemmingsen's prestige remained high. While seeking to rid his realm of crypto-

Calvinists, the Lutheran elector Augustus of Saxony found that some of the latter appealed to the writings of Hemmingsen. It so happened that Augustus was married to the sister of the Danish king, Frederick II. Augustus therefore appealed to his brother-in-law to rid his kingdom of Calvinist sympathizers and to suspend the teaching career of Hemmingsen. Pressure for Hemmingsen's dismissal mounted. In 1579 Frederick II felt compelled "for the sake of concord" to remove his most illustrious university professor. So great was Hemmingsen's lingering prestige, however, that the *Book of Concord* has never been accepted as the confessional basis for the Lutheran church in Denmark, Norway, or Iceland.

BIBLIOGRAPHY

Andersen, J. Oskar. "Om Niels Hemmingsens Teologi." *Kyrkohistorisk årsskrift* 41 (1941), 108–131.

Barnekow, Kjell. *Niels Hemmingsens teologiska åskådning*. Lund, 1940.

Madsen, Erik M. *Niels Hemmingsens Etik*. Copenhagen, 1946.

Skarsten, Trygve R. "The Reaction in Scandinavia to the Formula of Concord." In *Discord, Dialogue and Concord*, edited by Lewis W. Spitz and W. Lohff, pp. 136–149. Philadelphia, 1977.

TRYGVE R. SKARSTEN

HENCKEL, Johann (1480–1539), humanist and court chaplain to Queen Mary of Hungary and Bohemia. Born at Löcse (Levoca, Slovakia) in northern Hungary, Henckel was the son of German-speaking parents. In 1496 he matriculated at the University of Vienna, receiving a B.A. in 1499 and an M.A. four years later. Like many central European students, he went to Italy to further his education, attending the universities of Padua (1508) and Bologna (1509) before returning to Hungary as a doctor of canon law. In 1513 he was offered the position of parish priest of Löcse, which he accepted. He emerged from relative obscurity in 1517, when he was a member of a delegation from Löcse that greeted the recently elected king of Hungary, Louis II (r. 1516–1526). An avid book collector and scholar, Henckel was also instrumental in attracting the English humanist Leonard Cox to become headmaster of the municipal school at Löcse.

Henckel's fame for eloquence and scholarship spread and brought him to the attention of the royal court. In 1522 he was invited to Buda to become chaplain and confessor to Queen Mary. Henckel found the court to be the center of religious controversy and political instability. His predecessor as confessor to the queen, Conrad Cordatus, had been imprisoned briefly because of his Lutheran sympathies and had left Hungary for Wittenberg. In his eloquent sermons Henckel preached moderation and peace and sought the company of a group of Erasmian humanists that had formed in Buda. Although critical of the abuses of the Roman church, these Hungarian humanists looked to Erasmus, the great Dutch scholar, for guidance. In the spring of 1526 Erasmus wrote the first of many letters to Henckel praising him for his humanity, moderation, and wide-ranging scholarship.

In 1526 King Louis II died at the Battle of Mohács (29 August). His widow, Queen Mary, fled Hungary, and Henckel for a time served as parish priest at Košice (Kaschau, Kassa). János Zápolya tried to gain Henckel's support and offered him a bishopric, but he declined and in 1528 rejoined the service of Mary. At Henckel's request Erasmus sent his *Vidua christiana* to console the widowed queen, whom Henckel later accompanied to the Diet of Augsburg (1530). There a large delegation from Hungary urged the restoration of religious unity and requested aid against the Turks. Henckel believed that a reconciliation between Luther and Rome was possible. He took part in the negotiations and hoped that a unified Christendom would repulse the advancing Turks. He also had frequent contacts with Martin Bucer, Wolfgang Capito, and Philipp Melanchthon, which drew the ire of Johann Eck and subsequently caused him problems. The imperial diet ended without the restoration of sectarian peace or unified action against the Ottomans.

In 1531 Emperor Charles V appointed his sister Mary as regent of the Low Countries with the stipulation that she dismiss those in her service who fell under suspicion of harboring Lutheran sympathies, which because of his conciliatory role at Augsburg, included Henckel. With the queen's assistance, he secured a benefice in Silesia, where he became canon of Wrocław (Breslau). He was also appointed pastor of the nearby town of Schweidnitz, which he administered until 1533. Henckel died on 5 November 1539 and was buried in the cathedral of Wrocław. A number of his books have found their way to the library at Alba Iulia (Gyulafehérvár), in Transylvania. His activities at the court in Buda, his close contacts with Erasmus, and his participation at the Diet of Augsburg clearly demonstrate his tolerant, moderate, and conciliatory Christian humanist worldview.

BIBLIOGRAPHY

Bauch, Gusztáv. "Dr. Johann Henckel, der Hofprediger der Königin Maria von Ungarn." *Ungarische Revue* (1884), 559–627. First attempt at a biography of Henckel; must be used with caution owing to its many factual errors.

———. "Adalékok a reformácio és a tudományok történetéhez Magyarországon a XVI. században." *Történelmi Tár* (1885), 353–354; 519–523. Contains some of the letters of Henckel.

Domonkos, L. "Johann Henckel." In *Contemporaries of Erasmus*, edited by Peter G. Bietenholz and Thomas B. Deutscher, vol. 2, pp. 175–176. Toronto, 1985. The only accessible study in English.

Fraknói, Vilmos. *Henkel János: Mária királyné udvari papja*. Pest, 1872. Based on primary sources, but tries to deny Henckel's sympathies with the Lutheran cause.

Hudak, Adalbert. "Der Hofprediger Johannes Henckel and seine Beziehungen zu Erasmus von Rotterdam." *Kirche im Osten* 2 (1959),

106–113. The most complete and balanced attempt at a biography in any language.

Varju, Elemér. "A gyulafehérvári Batthány-könyvtfár." *Magyar könyvszemle* 7 (1899), 134–175; 209–243; 329–345. Contains information on the books belonging to Henckel.

L. S. DOMONKOS

HENRICXZOEN, Cornelis. *See* Hoen, Cornelis Henricxzoen.

HENRY II OF FRANCE (1519–1559), second son of Francis I, and king of France from 1547. Henry was seven years old when he and his older brother were sent to Spain as hostages for the ransom of their father, captured at the Battle of Pavia. Henry never forgave Charles V for what he regarded as harsh treatment during his four years in Spain. In 1534 he was wedded to Catherine de Médicis, Pope Clement VII's cousin, as part of a Franco-papal alliance. Henry never grew to love his wife but found emotional fulfillment with Diane de Poitiers, twenty years his senior, who remained his mistress to his death.

In 1536 Henry's older brother died, and he became Dauphin. Despite the coldness in the relationship between father and son, Francis provided Henry a good training in the affairs of state. When Henry ascended the throne in 1547, he quickly made a number of changes in the system of governance, in particular creating the offices of the four secretaries of state, each having responsibility for a specific aspect of administration.

The central theme of Henry's reign was the conflict with Charles V. Henry sought to injure the interests of the emperor wherever he could. For that purpose he sent armies to Italy, aided the German Lutherans, and occupied the three bishoprics of Lorraine. His rivalry with Charles also led him to try to get his candidate elected pope in 1549. When Julius III was elected and proved favorable to the Habsburgs, Henry nearly created a schism in 1553.

Henry's attitude toward the French Protestants was severe. He took seriously his oath to protect the Catholic church. Shortly after he became king, realizing that the French bishops were not making use of their authority over heretics, he created a special chamber in the Parlement of Paris to hear heresy cases. Called the *Chambre ardente* because of its zealous pursuit of heretics, it condemned thirty-seven persons to death in the three years of its existence. However, the objections of the hierarchy persuaded Henry to shut it down in 1550. He had difficulty in dealing with heresy because of the competition between the Parlement and the hierarchy over heresy prosecution. This competition rendered ineffective such harsh edicts as that of Châteaubriand (1551). What Henry especially feared about heresy was its perceived affinity with lower class sedition.

Although Henry vowed to rid France of "this Lutheran scum," war prevented him from giving full attention to the task. His conflict with the Habsburgs reached its climax with Henry's disastrous defeat at Saint-Quentin (1557) and his conquest of Calais in 1558. Philip II and Henry then agreed to the Treaty of Cateau-Cambrésis (1559), intended to free both rulers to deal with heresy in their realms. Henry's first move was to order an investigation of the Parlement of Paris, which had several members sympathetic to Protestantism. When the Parlement failed to move as quickly as he wanted, he attended in person. Stung by the criticism directed at him by several magistrates, he ordered their arrest. The most famous among them was Anne Du Bourg, who was later executed. Before Henry could pursue the Huguenots further, Fernando Álvarez de Toledo, duke of Alba, arrived in Paris as Philip's proxy for signing the peace and wedding Henry's daughter. Henry took up a lance in the great tournament arranged for the festivities. The broken end of his opponent's lance struck Henry in the face, and a splinter pierced his brain. He died ten days later. At his death he left to his fifteen-year-old son, Francis II, a realm beset with problems, including the religious divisions and a debt amounting to 43 million livres—over two and a half times the monarchy's annual income. Henry's death led to the Wars of Religion.

BIBLIOGRAPHY

Baumgartner, Frederic J. *Henry II, King of France, 1547–1559*. Durham, N.C., 1988. The only recent biography in English.

Cloulas, Ivan. *Henri II*. Paris, 1985. Particularly strong on Henry's patronage of art and culture and his fiscal policy.

Cloulas, Ivan. *Catherine de Médicis*. Paris, 1979. Good biography of Henry's queen.

Matuszek-Baudoin, M. N., ed. *Catalogue des actes de Henri II*. 3 vols. Paris, 1979–.

FREDERIC J. BAUMGARTNER

HENRY III OF FRANCE (1551–1589), king of Poland (1574) and last Valois king of France (r. 1574–1589). Of all Europe's monarchs, none suffered more from the political consequences of the Reformation than Henry III. He was the fourth son of Henry II, king of France (r. 1547–1559), and Catherine de Médicis. Brought up at the French royal court, he was educated by the Greek scholar and humanist Jacques Amyot, who stimulated his eclectic interest in the world of late Renaissance humanism. During his formative years as duke of Orléans (from 1560), he witnessed at close quarters the failure of his mother's attempts to prevent the outbreak of civil war during the minority of his brother Charles IX. He was present at the opening session of the Estates-General of Orléans in December 1560 and, nine months later, at the Colloquy of Poissy. During a tour of the kingdom, undertaken by the royal court from 1564 to 1566, he was introduced to the depth of sectarian tensions in the French polity. As heir apparent, he was a focus for intense rivalries at court. Despite ambiguous testimony to the contrary, the evidence points to his agreeing with those who held that the Huguenots represented a fundamental threat to the sacral nature of the French monarchy and to the stability and security of the kingdom. He never wavered from the Catholicism in which he had been brought up. Created duke of Anjou in 1566, he played a leading role in the second and third civil wars as lieutenant general of the realm, securing two of the few military victories enjoyed by the French crown during the civil wars (Jarnac and Moncontour, 1569). By then preeminent among the political leaders of Catholic France, he supported the pacification of 1570 (Peace of Saint-Germain), which ended dramatically with the Saint Bartholomew's Day Massacre, which began on 24 August 1572. Although there is no evidence to conclude that he was involved in the assassination of Admiral Gaspard II de Coligny (which preceded the massacre), he feared a Protestant assault on the French monarchy in the wake of the assassination. He played an ambiguous role in preparations to eliminate leading Protestants that began the massacre and led the campaign against La Rochelle and other Huguenot strongholds in its aftermath. Henry's problem as king was that he never lived up to the expectations among Catholics or outlived the suspicions among Protestants formed during these years. His consecration as king of Poland in February 1574 seemed a triumph of Valois diplomacy. In retrospect, the efforts to counteract the negative impact of the massacre on the Polish nobility during his election were barely rewarded by the 146 days of his kingship, cut short by the premature death of Charles IX on 30 May 1574, or by the adverse effects of his sudden and secret flight from Poland. He returned to a France in which the authority of the monarchy had become eroded and the dangers from religious, political, and social discord were increasingly apparent.

His reign was not so complete and tragic a failure as it has sometimes been presented. There were years of relative quiescence from civil war, particularly after the Peace of Bergerac (14 September 1577). Sectarian massacres, particularly in French cities, were generally on the wane. In an erratic fashion, the king devoted some of his energies to what he saw as the necessary and fundamental reforms of the kingdom to ensure the survival of France's traditional monarchy. He reorganized the council (1574), reformed the court (1582–1585), and instituted a new chivalric order (the Holy Spirit) to revive the loyalties of the French nobility to the Crown (1578). He reformed French coinage and customs (1577), the army (1584), and convoked the Estates-General at Blois (1576/77) to enlist its help in restructuring France. Partly on the basis of its deliberations, he promulgated the Ordinance of Blois (May 1579), which constituted a fundamental legislative framework for the French ancien régime. He never formally accepted the canons of the Council of Trent in France for fear of alienating the Gallican sovereign law courts (parlements), who would have opposed them. Instead, he gave well-publicized displays of a distinctive mystical devotion, reforming the kingdom by expiation. Influenced by his almoner, the Jesuit Émond Auger, he undertook retreats, monastic pilgrimages, and penitential processions and instituted several pious foundations.

Yet the political basis for any degree of reconstruction was fragile. Attempted reform attracted its own critics, the more so when only partially carried out. A persistent undercurrent of criticism at the expense and immorality of the court damaged the king's public credibility, even if the allegations concerning his homosexuality may have been misfounded. The advancement of favorites (*mignons*) certainly harmed his relations with the French aristocracy, whose provincial power had been much enhanced during the civil wars. The Protestant minority were never convinced that he would guarantee their rights to worship and protect them. A succession crisis provoked the last, tragic period of the reign.

The king's marriage to Louise of Vaudémont in February 1575 provided no heirs. His younger brother, Francis, duke of Anjou, died on 10 June 1584, leaving the possibility of the French throne passing to the Huguenot prince of the blood, Henry, king of Navarre (later Henry IV). The political movement known as the Holy (or Catholic) League with, as its leader, Henry III's childhood companion, Henry of Guise, rallied forces inside France and out, eventually driving Henry III from Paris in a popular insurrection known as the Day of Barricades (12–13 May 1588). With his authority evaporating, as was evident in the early deliberations of the Estates-General at Blois in October 1588, the king had the duke of Guise assassinated on 23 December 1588, followed by his brother the cardinal of Guise the next day. Almost all the major cities of the realm joined in a popular rebellion against him and, excommunicated by Pope Sixtus V in April 1589, the last Valois was assassinated on 1 August 1589 by a Dominican monk, Jacques Clément. The assassination marked the end of the Valois dynasty and the most serious political crisis facing the French monarchy in the ancien régime.

BIBLIOGRAPHY

Boucher, Jacqueline. *La cour de Henri III*. Rennes, 1986. Reassessment of the king's reign, summarizing the author's detailed doctoral thesis, published in 1981.

Chevallier, Pierre. *Henri III*. Paris, 1985. Most recent biography, with extensive additional reading.

Salmon, J. H. M. *Society in Crisis: France in the Sixteenth Century*. London, 1975. Most accessible and authoritative survey in English of the religious wars.

Sutherland, N. M. *The Huguenot Struggle for Recognition.* New Haven, 1980.

MARK GREENGRASS

HENRY IV OF FRANCE (1553–1610), known in his early days as "Henry of Navarre" and, more familiarly, as "Le vert galant," king between 1589 and 1610. Henry was the son of Jeanne of Navarre (Jeanne d'Albret), an early adherent to Protestantism. He was brought up partly by his devout mother and partly at the royal court of the Valois line, and this led to a number of religious shifts. "Converted" to Catholicism in 1562 at the court, he reverted to Protestantism when he left it in 1567, only to be forcibly reconverted after the Saint Bartholomew's Day Massacre, when he was again in Paris. In 1576, having once more left the court, he again renounced Catholicism.

During the next thirteen years Henry of Navarre established himself as the leader of the French Protestants, proving to be a redoubtable cavalry leader and an astute tactician. From this time, too, he began establishing diplomatic contacts with other Protestant leaders, particularly with Queen Elizabeth I of England and with the German Protestant princes. In 1589 King Henry III was assassinated, and Henry of Navarre succeeded to the throne as Henry IV. At first he may have hoped that he could establish his authority without abjuring Protestantism. But as time went by it became clear that this would not be possible; although many French Catholics were prepared to recognize his claim to the throne, Henry was unable to expand out of his southwestern base as long as he remained Protestant. The great towns, with Paris in the lead, were particularly obdurate in their resistance to the idea of a Protestant king.

Thus in 1593 Henry made the "perilous leap," embracing Catholicism for the third time. This shift lost him the support of many Protestants, but over the next five years he slowly succeeded in establishing his power, until in 1598 he placated, to some extent, his old friends by the concessions of the Edict of Nantes. This edict, designed as a stopgap measure, gave the Protestants a breathing space by granting them a substantial number of secure towns (*places de sûreté*) in southwest France; the royal treasury paid for their garrisons. The Edict of Nantes aroused great opposition in Catholic France, but Henry insisted on its implementation, forcing it through each of the parlements in turn, though the Parlement of Rouen held out on certain details until 1609.

After 1598 the French Protestants were more or less quiescent politically, though they sometimes held assemblies at which autonomous aspirations were expressed. Henry did his best to stifle these hopes, using his Protestant minister Maximilien de Béthune, duke of Sully, to persuade the deputies to moderate their demands and, for instance, not to use bad language about the pope. Sully played an important role in thus defusing political discontent and in acting as the leading Protestant in the realm. He and the king, if we are to believe Sully's memoirs, constantly played verbal games around their religious differences. In 1600, for instance, when the king asked if Sully would not like to kiss the ladies of the bedchamber as he gave them their annual gifts, Sully replied that he would indeed do so, but in the way one would kiss a relic—a characteristic dig at the king's new religious practices.

As time went by, Henry seems to have taken his conversion more and more seriously. He had been obliged to go through a full ceremony of abjuration in 1594 as a political necessity, but afterward seemed increasingly to relish his pre-eminent role in the Catholic church. Thus he religiously carried out the ceremony of touching for the king's evil, in which the laying on of hands by the "Most Christian King" was held to cure some cases of scrofula. In 1599, too, he encouraged a theological debate between his old companion-in-arms, Philippe Duplessis-Mornay, and the Catholic bishop of Évreux, Jacques-Davy Du Perron. The king must have know that Duplessis-Mornay would be hopelessly outclassed in such a contest, but he seemed to relish the discomfiture of the Protestant champion.

During the first decade of the seventeenth century, Henry did his best to raise the intellectual and pastoral level of the Catholic bishops in France, picking out promising young men for promotion and then supporting their efforts to reform their dioceses in the ways recommended at the Council of Trent. At court, too, he came under Counter-Reformation influences through the Jesuit Père Pierre Coton, thus giving rise to the quip that he had cotton wool ("du Coton") in his ears. These Catholicizing influences were much encouraged by Henry's Florentine queen, Marie de Médicis.

By 1603, if we are to believe Coton, Henry was a changed man: "He daily grows in piety, acknowledging that he owes everything to God. The Queen says that every day he prays for half an hour before speaking to anybody, and does the same at night. He has given up all his *fols amours*, banished sin and loose women from the court, and cannot tolerate swearing there." It sounds like a reversion to the Calvinism of his youth, though in fact Henry remained an unrepentant womanizer to the end of his life, and even made some scandalous appointments to the episcopacy. Still, we do have the impression of a man who, having changed his coat five times, was now content at the prospect of living and dying in the Catholic church.

At first glance, his foreign policy seemed to contradict this affinity for Catholicism. He remained obdurately opposed to the Habsburg empire, for having made peace with Spain in 1598, he went over to a sort of "cold war" with that power. In contrast, he maintained good relations with England, with the United Provinces, and with the Protestant German princes. It would be a mistake, however, to imagine that these political alignments derived from religious sympathies. In fact, his foreign policy was similar to that followed a quarter of a century later by Armand-Jean du Plessis, Cardinal Richelieu, who also subordinated the interests of international Catholicism to those of French nationalism. In his foreign policy, as in his domestic administration, Henry was primarily guided by a sense of how best to preserve France's fragile national unity. If this involved enmity with Spain abroad, so be it, but he was equally ready to encourage the Jesuits and other reformers within France as a means of spreading education and social relief.

In the end, Henry was a highly pragmatic person, averse to general principles and grand theories. During his early years the very survival of France seemed in doubt, and he was determined to do his best to see that such a period of chaos would never return. Fully aware of the varieties of Christian experience, he came in the end to savor the certainties of the Catholic church. But this decision did not mean either that he would deny the right of the Protestants to exist in France, or that he would subordinate France's foreign policy to any considerations based on the interests of the papacy.

BIBLIOGRAPHY

Babelon, Jean-Pierre. *Henri IV.* Paris, 1982. This account of Henry's life is the fullest recently written and, though it lacks footnotes, is thoroughly reliable.

Buisseret, David. *Henry IV.* London, 1984. A concise account, dwelling particularly on the period 1598–1610.

Garrisson, Janine. *Henry IV.* Paris, 1984. This life of Henry IV is particularly strong on his Protestant connections.

Vaissière, Pierre de. *Henri IV.* Paris, 1928. The classic life of Henry IV, written by a lawyer with a deep knowledge of the region around Pau, where Henry grew up.

David Buisseret

HENRY VIII OF ENGLAND (1491–1547), second son of Henry VII and Queen Elizabeth (daughter of Edward IV); became heir to the throne on the death of his brother Arthur in 1502 and succeeded on 22 April 1509. He had been betrothed to his brother's widow, Catherine of Aragon, in 1503, and married her after his accession, on 11 June 1509.

Having been somewhat indulged as a younger brother, as heir to the throne Henry fell victim to his father's anxieties. Arthur had been sent at the age of fifteen, a married man, to gain practical experience by governing Wales. Henry was kept under his father's eye, ("like a young girl," the Spanish ambassador reported), hardly daring to speak without his father's permission. His accession, when he was just short of eighteen years of age, represented liberation. With no adult member of his family in a position to warn or restrain him (his formidable grandmother Lady Margaret Beaufort died just after Henry VII), Henry was handed instant power at a dangerous age and exposed to the flattery of those who rejoiced at the end of the harsh and joyless last years of Henry VII. Henry's overweening sense of himself, his determination not to be checked, obviously owed a good deal to these experiences, even if the more unpleasant aspects of his character only became more pronounced as he grew older.

Henry's aim was to establish himself as a magnificent prince, not only in terms of artistic patronage and court show, but also in playing a prominent part on the European diplomatic stage and in the pursuit of military glory. Wars with France (1511–1514 and 1522–1525) involved considerable effort and expenditure, but little in the way of tangible victory, except in 1513; even then Henry's victory (the "Battle of the Spurs") in northern France was overshadowed by the defeat of the invading Scots and the death of their king, James IV, at Flodden while Henry was out of the kingdom. War was interspersed with grandiose peace projects, including the Treaty of London for "perpetual peace" in 1518 and Henry's spectacular meeting with Francis I of France at the "Field of the Cloth of Gold," near Calais, in 1520. At home there were protests at taxation in the Parliament of 1523 and a revolt over the so-called "Amicable Grant" (in effect taxation not authorized by Parliament) in 1525. But in general the first twenty years of the reign were seen as a success; there was no serious opposition, and certainly nothing in the way of armed opposition by aristocrats, in spite of the execution for alleged treason of England's greatest nobleman, Edward Stafford, duke of Buckingham, in 1521.

Thomas Wolsey. Henry worked in profitable partnership with his chief minister, Thomas Wolsey. Historians no longer accept the image of Wolsey taking all decisions while Henry devoted himself to pleasure. Major policy decisions were taken by Henry, no matter how skilled Wolsey was in implementing them or indeed in influencing decisions by controlling the flow of information and drawing up the position papers. Wolsey was useful in drawing the fire for unpopular decisions, as in 1525, when Henry withdrew the demand for the Amicable Grant, claiming ignorance of the sum asked for. Wolsey's enthusiasm for the outward display of a prince of the church added to the prestige of Henry's court; he was, after all, Henry's cardinal. Henry's position as king seemed impregnable; his ability to play the part of gracious sovereign contributed vitally to that result, as did the absence of any obvious alternative. His ability to weather the storms ahead rested on the prestige he acquired in the first twenty years.

Looking back, there seems to be some foreshadowing in these years of the revolution that was to come in the relations of church and state in England. In Henry VII's reign there had been agitation in Parliament about the number of people not in holy orders but able to claim clerical privileges before the criminal law and so escape capital punishment. In 1512 Parliament withdrew clerical immunity from such "clerks" for particularly heinous offenses. The legislation was due to be renewed in 1515. Before that happened there was popular outcry over the case of Richard Hunne, a London merchant arrested on a heresy charge who was found hanging, believed murdered, in the bishop of London's prison. Meanwhile the Lateran Council (1512–1517) had reaffirmed the church's teaching on clerical immunity. At a conference at Blackfriars in November 1515 Henry declared that, "by the ordinance and sufferance of God, we as king of England and kings of England in times past have never had any superior but God only," and warned the clergy that he would allow no more disobedience to his "decrees" than "any of our progenitors have done in times past."

The crisis that seemed to loom in 1515 came to nothing. The offending act was not renewed. As *legate a latere* Wolsey ruled both provinces of the English church through delegated papal powers. In theory this brought into the heart of the English polity an authority that had been rather distant. In practice Wolsey was papal legate because he was the king's minister; the concentration in his hands of secular and ecclesiastical power foreshadowed the royal supremacy. Occasional disputes about the boundaries between ecclesiastical and secular jurisdiction were inherent in the nature of the relationship, but there was no reason to think they would reach crisis proportions. Henry appeared to have no doubts about the spiritual office of the papacy. In 1521 he wrote (with some assistance) an answer to Luther's *De Captivitate Babylonica Ecclesiae Praelundium* (Babylonian Captivity), his *Assertio Septem Sacramentorum* (Assertion of the Seven Sacraments); this was not merely a defense of traditional Catholic doctrine and an attack on the Lutheran appeal to *sola scriptura*, the authority of scripture alone, but also a defense of Catholic unity and of the papacy as the guarantor of that unity. In return Henry was granted the papal title for which he had been angling for some time—*Fidei Defensor*, "Defender of the Faith"—to set beside that of "The Most Christian King" (of France) and "Catholic King" (of Spain).

The "Divorce." Henry's matrimonial problem was the direct cause of the English Reformation. Without it there would have been no necessity, or even likelihood, of a reformation instigated "from above" by the king. Whether or not there would have been at some stage a reformation "from below" is a matter for speculation. But if there had been it would have differed profoundly in form and content from what actually happened. The matrimonial problem drew together various issues that, left to themselves, might well have produced irritations of various sorts but hardly the explosion which actually occurred.

The origins of the matrimonial problem go back to 1503 and the procuring of a bull from Pope Julius II allowing Henry to marry Catherine, his brother's widow, even if the earlier marriage had been consummated. The bull did not pronounce on whether it had or had not been. There was also issued in 1504 a papal brief, conveyed to Queen Isabella of Castile, Catherine's mother, that differed in some details, notably in assuming a consummation; the brief was unknown in England. The delay in bringing about the new marriage (Henry VII regarded his son's hand as too useful a card in the diplomatic game to actually play it) cast some doubt on the validity of the dispensation in Europe. But this was, for the moment, stilled when Henry at last married Catherine.

Although the marriage resulted in a number of conceptions, only one child survived infancy, and she, Princess Mary, a girl. Catherine's last pregnancy was in 1517. By 1527, at the latest, Henry had determined to marry Anne Boleyn. He had persuaded himself that his failure to produce a male heir was due to God's judgment on his marriage. *Leviticus* (18:16 and 20:21) was read as forbidding marriage to a brother's widow; this was the positive law of God; the pope in such circumstances had no power to dispense; Henry was the victim of God's curse, which pronounced that such a union could not produce issue. The awkward fact that, in Mary, the marriage had produced issue was explained, to Henry's apparent satisfaction, by the argument that the Hebrew had been mistranslated and should read "son." Equally Henry contrived to explain away *Deuteronomy* (25:5), which made it a man's duty to raise up seed for his brother on his brother's widow. He also sought a papal dispensation to marry Anne in spite of previous sexual relations with her sister, an impediment very similar to that with Catherine.

The issue dragged on from 1527 to 1529, complicated by the international situation, and especially the Sack of Rome. Henry insisted essentially on the repudiation of Julius's bull, based not on some formal defect but on the pope's having acted *ultra vires*; thus he made things difficult for Pope Clement VII, who would have preferred a more low-key approach, to give Henry what he wanted without questioning matters of principle. (Henry's demand for a formal repudiation in unequivocal terms may in fact have been motivated as much by his exalted view of the papal office as by his desire to avoid domestic or international embarrassments.) Catherine, too, was stubborn in refusing suggestions that she take the veil, thereby freeing Henry without bastardizing their daughter. She insisted that her marriage to Arthur had not been consummated; though by doing so she seemed to play into Henry's hands by implicitly accepting that a consummated marriage would have been an indispensable barrier. Possibly, had Henry taken her at her word, he might have found a workable solution in terms of technicalities that would have satisfied all parties (except Catherine and Mary). Catherine also adduced the papal brief of 1504, which, being unknown to the English agents, was not covered by the commissions they were trying to extract from Rome. When at last the legatine commission under Campeggio and Wolsey got under way at Blackfriars in June 1529, Catherine, through Charles V, had persuaded the pope to revoke the case to Rome. Campeggio adjourned the court on a technicality at the end of July; it was never to reassemble.

The recall of the case to Rome fatally enmeshed the issue with that of church-state relations. Used initially against Wolsey, then against the church as a whole, was the weapon of praemunire. Stemming from fourteenth-century legislation designed originally to deal with some specific issues between king and pope, the summarizing act (of 1393) was so phrased that it threatened with perpetual imprisonment and loss of property anybody invoking any foreign jurisdiction to the detriment of the king and his courts. At the beginning of the sixteenth century it was being used as a weapon by common-lawyers in boundary disputes between the king's courts and the ordinary ecclesiastical courts in England, implying that the latter were in some sense merely offshoots of the Roman courts; these cases, however, were rarely pushed to a definite conclusion. In 1529 praemunire actions were brought against Wolsey over some specific actions of his as papal legate, allegedly in derogation of the Crown; in 1530 against selected clerics for abetting Wolsey's exercise of legatine jurisdiction (something of which the king himself was hardly guiltless); in 1531, much more drastically, against the clerical body as a whole for offending against the laws by the very process of exercising jurisdiction in church courts. In return for a pardon for these unspecified offenses, the clergy granted the king a large sum of money and recognized him as "sole protector and supreme head" of the English church and clergy, after some bargaining being allowed to add the qualification "so far as the law of Christ allows."

Parliament. In 1532 Parliament agreed to the suspension of the payment of "annates" to Rome (dues paid on appointment to bishoprics), for implementation at some future date to be determined at the royal will. At the same time there emerged in the House of Commons the "Supplication against the Ordinaries" (i.e., the judges in the spiritual courts, in effect the bishops and their deputies). This was a collection of complaints about procedures in church courts and about the more general misdemeanors of the clergy. Purporting to be a spontaneous production of the Commons, and probably incorporating various complaints that might otherwise have come to very little, the supplication was drafted by the king's new minister, Thomas Cromwell. Henry professed himself shocked to find that the clergy "be but half our subjects, yea and scarce our subjects" because of the oath sworn by prelates to the pope. An embattled Canterbury Convocation was induced to make the "Submission of the Clergy," acknowledging that it had no right to legislate except with the express permission of the king.

The process of battering both the papacy and the English clergy continued, apparently inexorably. In 1533 judicial appeals to Rome were prohibited by parliamentary act. In 1534 the Act of Supremacy declared that the king "justly and rightfully is and ought to be the supreme head of the Church of England," without qualification.

These complicated developments raise a number of questions. What initiative did Henry himself take? How far was the whole process merely a question of bringing pressure to bear on the pope to grant Henry his divorce? Or how far had the jurisdictional issue now taken on a life of its own? The argument that in Christian states the secular authority had the duty to regulate the practice of religion had been enunciated by the Lutheran William Tyndale in his *Obedience of the Christian Man* in 1528—though Tyndale (like Luther) had no sympathy for Henry's divorce proceedings. It also appeared in a collection of writings known as the *Collectanea Satis Copiosa* assembled in 1530. Kings of England were invested by God. The position was memorably expounded in the 1533 Appeals Act: "Where by divers sundry old authentic histories and chronicles it is manifestly declared. . . that this realm of England is an empire. . . governed by one supreme head and king," a "body politic, compact of all sorts and degrees of people" both spirituality and temporality owing the king "next to God a natural and humble obedience" the realm is therefore jurisdictionally self-sufficient. These arguments were devised by a set of clerics and lawyers working for the Crown; and the implementation of the program through Parliament, so clothing proceedings with the utmost solemnity and making them ostensibly an expression of the will of the realm, was probably due largely to Thomas Cromwell. But there can be little doubt that Henry himself, unused to having his will thwarted as it had been over the divorce, came to see the control of the English church as an integral part of his kingly office, a duty laid upon him by God. He had even, in 1531, tried to claim the cure of souls.

The divorce issue had been settled at last in defiance of Rome in 1533. A possible obstacle had been removed with the death in August 1532 of the aged archbishop of Canterbury, William Warham. In May his successor, Thomas Cranmer, pronounced Henry's marriage to Catherine null. Anne Boleyn was crowned as queen; in September a daughter, the future Queen Elizabeth, was born.

Thomas Cromwell. From 1534 events proceeded at breakneck speed. By the treason act of that year it became a capital offense (among much else) to speak against the royal supremacy. Thomas Cromwell was appointed the king's "vicegerent" in spiritual matters, a sign that the supremacy was not to be something vague and nominal but an active, managerial office involving the thoroughgoing supervision of all aspects of the English church. The year 1535 saw a detailed survey of the church's landed wealth, the *Valor Ecclesiasticus*, as well as the execution of Sir Thomas More, Bishop John Fisher, and a number of clerics for denying the royal supremacy. The following year saw the death of Catherine of Aragon, followed quickly by the repudiation and death of Anne Boleyn, and Henry's marriage to Jane Seymour.

The year 1536 also saw the dissolution of the smaller monasteries, by act of Parliament, following a "visitation," or inquiry into their general state, carried out under the vicegerent's aegis. Convocation under royal guidance issued a doctrinal formulary, the Ten Articles. Backed up by a set of "Injunctions" issued on the vicegerent's authority, they represented a cautious move in a Protestant direction. All this was happening at a time when the clergy were paying taxation to the Crown on an unprecedented scale and the laity were paying, unusually, a parliamentary levy of taxation in peacetime. The impression was created that the parish church and local community generally were at the mercy of royal rapacity. The result was the massive rebellion, originating in Lincolnshire and involving all the northern counties (with a good deal of sympathy in the rest of the country), known as the "Pilgrimage of Grace." Between 1537 and 1540 the remaining religious houses surrendered themselves piecemeal to the crown. The process of dissolution had more than tripled the crown's landed estate.

The year 1537 brought Henry simultaneous joy and sorrow with the birth of the long-hoped-for male heir, Prince Edward, and the death of Jane Seymour. The "Bishops' Book" was issued, tentatively Lutheran in tone, if less so than the Ten Articles. Talks were started with the German Lutherans. Two versions of the English Bible were licensed, the "Coverdale" and the "Matthew." In 1538 all churches were ordered to provide themselves with English Bibles. In 1539 the Crown issued the official "Great Bible," complete with frontispiece depicting God the Father looking on approvingly at the massive enthroned Henry handing out copies of the word of God to nobles and prelates; the common people gratefully receiving the fruits of the enterprise, shout "God save the king." But in those same years a mood of reaction was also setting in, perhaps a delayed response to the Pilgrimage of Grace. In 1539 Parliament passed the Act of Six Articles, reaffirming Catholic orthodoxy on key doctrinal issues. In January 1540 Henry married Anne of Cleves; the marriage represented an opening to the German princes, as Henry feared the possibility of a conjunction of Charles V and Francis I against him. In April Thomas Cromwell was made earl of Essex, showing, apparently, that the "Protestant" party had outfaced its enemies. But, he was arrested seven weeks later. His last service to Henry was to provide evidence of the nonconsummation of the marriage to Anne of Cleves, which was annulled on 9 July. Cromwell was executed on 28 July.

Henry's Last Years. The pace of events in Henry's last seven years was to be a little less hectic. The failure to appoint a successor to Cromwell as vicegerent may indicate a determination by Henry no longer to allow himself to be hustled. Attention shifted again to foreign affairs: war against France in alliance with the emperor—in which an unprecedently large invasion force captured Boulogne for Henry in 1544—and war in Scotland. James V, king of Scots, had died in 1542; he was succeeded by his baby daughter Mary, whose marriage to Henry's heir, Prince Edward, would create a unified Britain. For a time Henry secured the acquiescence of various parties among the Scots to the marriage; ultimately he failed, despite (or perhaps because of) the burning of Scottish towns and villages and an attempt to interest the Scots in the advantages of repudiating the papacy. Military activity on this scale was expensive; the result high taxation, the beginnings of the sale by the Crown of the immense landed estate it had acquired by the dissolution of the monasteries, and the debasement of the coinage in the interests of a quick profit.

Henry's personal life continued on its idiosyncratic way. The repudiation of Anne of Cleves in July 1540 was followed immediately by marriage to Catherine Howard (on the very day of Cromwell's execution). She in turn was executed in February 1542 for committing adultery (treason in a queen). The years 1542 and 1543 were something of a watershed in the struggle for power in England between, broadly, a group led by Thomas Howard, duke of Norfolk, and Stephen Gardiner, bishop of Winchester, old opponents of Cromwell, battling among much else for the preservation of essentially Catholic religious practices; and another which included Archbishop Cranmer and Prince Edward's uncle Edward Seymour, hoping to edge the king into resuming the Protestantizing policy of Cromwell's days. Catherine Howard's downfall (the news of her infidelities was broken to the king by Cranmer) was seen as a victory for the "Protestant" faction. In July 1543 Henry married for the last time; the bride was Catherine Parr, twice a widow, thirty-one years old, and with a taste for mildly advanced religious literature.

The "Catholics," however, fought back hard in early 1543. The "King's Book," a conservative revision of the 1537 "Bishops' Book," was published in May 1543. At the same time a parliamentary act attempted to control the publication of unorthodox books and, to damp down disruptive discussion, prohibited women and working men from reading even the officially authorized Bible. There was also a drive against heretics that, but for Henry's personal intervention, would have netted Archbishop Cranmer among its victims. The struggle was resumed at the end of 1545. Parliament was induced, with some difficulty, to agree to allow the dissolution of the chantries (endowments to provide masses for the dead), instancing not doctrinal reasons but the king's overriding need for war finance. The chantries were surveyed in 1546, although no definite steps were taken toward their abolition. Also in 1546, during peace talks with France, Henry is alleged to have announced a plan for the French to join the English in repudiating the papacy and for both countries to change the Mass into a Communion service. On the other hand, Anne Askew, a Lincolnshire gentlewoman, was burnt as a heretic under the Act of Six Articles for her beliefs about the sacrament of the altar. Before her death she was tortured under the supervision of two privy councillors (Lord Chancellor Thomas Wriothesly and Richard Riche) in an attempt to incriminate the wives of leading courtiers and perhaps the queen herself.

At the end of 1546, however, the balance swung firmly to the "Protestant" side. In December Thomas Howard, duke of Norfolk, and his son Henry Howard, earl of Surrey, (otherwise distinguished as a poet), were arrested for treason; they were charged with speculating about the nature of a regency government and, on Surrey's part, allegedly urging his sister (widow of Henry's bastard son the duke of Richmond) to try to become Henry's mistress. Shortly thereafter the king was induced to drop Stephen Gardiner from the list of councillors who were to govern the country during the minority of his son. Whether by the accident of the game of "musical chairs" (in the sense that Henry died just when the "Catholic" party was temporarily out of favor) or because of a plot involving the cynical manipulation of a dying man, the way was set for a "Protestant" regime in the new reign, under the aegis of the new king's uncle Edward Seymour, soon to be duke of Somerset. Henry died on 28 January 1547, leaving money for perpetual masses for his soul and that of Jane Seymour—a privilege of which the intended chantry legislation was about to deprive his subjects, and indeed Henry himself.

Henry VIII and the Reformation. What, then, of Henry's personal contribution to the English Reformation? Quite clearly it would not have happened, at least not in the form that it did, without the question of the validity of Henry's first marriage. Once the quarrel with the papacy was set in train, a drift in the Protestant direction seems natural. That is not to say that the "national Catholic" position as championed by Henry himself or by such bishops as Stephen Gardiner or Cuthbert Tunstall was necessarily illogical or untenable, but rather that definite if not necessarily overt Protestants such as Cranmer and Cromwell provided Henry with his most natural and full-blooded allies against the papacy and against the clerical order. And, once the opportunity of milking the church's wealth had become apparent in 1531, the temptation to proceed further and in doing so damage the institutional buttress of Catholic practice was difficult to resist.

In that sense Henry's achievement was to hold Protestantism back. Formal Catholic beliefs were enforced by law and heretics burnt, as well as papalist "traitors" executed. On the parish level the traditional Latin services remained almost unaltered in 1547, except for the reading of a chapter of scripture in English during Sunday mass and the availability of an English litany for special occasions. Church furnishings had hardly changed, except in that minority of dioceses where reforming bishops had translated the admonitions against superstitious images into an attack on images generally. The fears voiced in 1536 of a wholesale attack on the fittings of parish churches had proved groundless, though perhaps because the Pilgrimage of Grace itself had helped reverse the Protestantizing current. Iconoclasm and the confiscation of church treasures were to be the feature of the next reign.

Nevertheless the point remains that the institutional props of Catholicism had been badly undermined, and it must remain doubtful whether the Henrician compromise could have been maintained except by Henry himself. Of course, had his lead been followed, had Francis I lived to implement the scheme mooted with Henry in 1546 (if it was ever a reality, and if Francis was ever serious), had Charles V been successful with his Interim of 1548, then a moderate, possibly "Erasmian" vision of church order might have triumphed in Europe as a whole. As it was, the availability, by royal command, of the scriptures in English helped to fuel that small group of vociferous Protestants who helped force the pace in Edward's reign. The dissolution of the monasteries, the abandonment of so many great churches, the public display of fraudulently miraculous images, the (to many eyes) sacrilegious attack on relics and shrines, all helped shatter that air of impregnability, of the existing order as something natural, indeed inevitable, in which lay a great part of its strength. The rights of the clergy to celebrate the sacraments had been maintained, but their independent right of jurisdiction had been denied; a layman had been made head of the church, another layman became his active and interfering deputy, and a bishop, several abbots, and a number of monks, friars, and secular clergy had been executed (where previously all clerks were exempt from capital punishment)—shattering blows to the image of the clergy as a body set apart from, and superior to, lay society. The very fact that Parliament had pronounced on what was correct doctrine in the Act of Six Articles opened the way for its changing that doctrine in Edward's reign. None of this made Catholicism a hopeless cause; it did, however, fatally weaken its capacity to resist should the attack come, as it came in Edward's reign, from the Crown.

Henry himself was far from the decisive autocrat sometimes depicted. His policies were determined largely by the interplay of political groups, what have become known as "factions." Even Wolsey had to guard his back against groups of courtiers conspiring to influence the king against him. The unpredictability of factional politics and their dependence on changes in the king's mood are strikingly illustrated by the events of 1540, when within a space of four months Cromwell was promoted to an earldom, condemned by attainder, and executed; eight months later Henry was lamenting him as the most devoted servant he had ever had. Sometimes one has the impression, as with the Gardiner-Cranmer rivalry of the 1540s, of Henry's deliberately using faction as a means of maintaining his own authority by spreading uncertainty and suspicion. Success in influencing Henry depended on mobilizing his prejudices against one's rivals; the difficulty was in knowing which of Henry's prejudices might be activated on a given occasion. The dangers of backfire, as Gardiner discovered, were great.

On religious matters Henry's beliefs in his later years can be inferred from his suggested revisions to the Bishops' Book in 1537 (in his own hand), the King's Book, and from his will. Henry's interest does not imply theological sophistication, and Cranmer's annotations to Henry's formulations read like those of a long-suffering tutor of a not very bright pupil. Famously, Henry tried to reword the first commandment to forbid belief in any God "but me Jesu Christ." Henry's theology was not just "Catholicism without the pope," but rather a distinctly idiosyncratic brew. He did not, for instance, object to the division of the sacraments in the Bishops' Book into first- and second-order sacraments (scripturally warranted and other), although the distinction was removed in 1543. His annotations and questions about auricular confession, confirmation, and extreme unction show that he had moved a long way from the 1521 acceptance of Catholic orthodoxy on the seven sacraments. He had, unsurprisingly, a distinctly unexalted view of the priestly office and denied any other than a functional distinction between bishop and priest. However, he was more papalist than the pope on clerical celibacy, which the Six Articles held to be indelible according to the law of God. This was hard on monks and especially nuns cast adrift into the world outside the abbey gate by Henry's actions yet still forbidden to marry. Henry held firmly to the "real" presence of Christ in the eucharistic elements and to Christ's sacrifice taking place anew each time Mass was celebrated. On the other hand he seems to have developed a less "mechanistic" view of the efficacy of the Mass than some of his contemporaries. His will stipulated daily masses for his soul, but not that banking up of thousands of masses which Henry VII had decreed for himself, or Henry for Jane Seymour in 1537. His wrath was particularly directed against "sacramentaries," those who held that the Eucharist was a symbolic commemoration; protecting such heretics had been a main charge against Cromwell. He also opposed vigorously the central Lutheran doctrine of "solafideism," insisting on the necessity of such "good deeds and charitable works as scripture commandeth" for salvation. What does emerge is Henry's egotism, his extraordinarily high view of the royal office as the essentially animating and authorizing force for all matters temporal and spiritual in a Christian state. It is not surprising that he likened himself to King David and sympathized with those passages in *Psalms* in which David complains of being traduced and misunderstood.

Outwardly, however, Henry radiated self-confidence. Arguably, indeed, his apparent vindictiveness (dancing at the death of Catherine of Aragon, marrying Catherine Howard on the day of Cromwell's execution, indulging in a massive feast a week after the execution of Catherine Howard) may charitably be explained in terms of the need always to project an image of confidence. That self-confidence helps explain how he was able to bring about a revolution in the life of the country; a revolution which, although carried through without violating the formal processes of English law and with the acquiescence of Parliament, can hardly be seen as representing the will of his subjects in any positive sense. The penalties incurred by opposition and the efficiency of government in investigating rumors of discontent and sniffing out potential conspiracies explain this in part. So does the crown's ability to set group against group, to browbeat the clergy by fanning anticlericalism or by ominously protecting heretics. That the worst had not occurred by 1547, that the clergy still exercised a considerable jurisdiction, albeit under royal authority, that heresy had for the most part been kept at bay, suggest that the implicit bargain struck by the bishops in 1532–1534 had been at least a tolerable one. The Henrician state was both feared and respected. Yet that state was no abstract entity. Henry's own massive frame embodied its majesty. Henry's subjects, or a good part of them, had come to accept his vision of the king in person being held responsible by God for the ordering of his realm.

BIBLIOGRAPHY

Bowker, Margaret. *The Henrician Reformation: The Diocese of Lincoln under John Langland, 1521–1547.* Cambridge, 1981. Detailed case study of one of the largest English dioceses.

Brigden, Susan. *London and the Reformation.* Oxford and New York, 1989. Central, sensitive.

Dickens, A. G. *The English Reformation.* 2d ed. London, 1989. The classic account, revised to take issue with criticism that it exaggerates popular anticlericalism and incipient Protestantism.

Duffy, Eamon. *The Stripping of the Altars.* New Haven, 1992. The Reformation as disaster; includes detailed account of Henrician measures.

Elton, G. R. *Policy and Police: The Enforcement of the Reformation in the Age of Thomas Cromwell* (1972). Reprint, Cambridge, 1985. Emphasizes the efficiency rather than the terror of countersubversion.

Guy, John. *Tudor England.* Oxford and New York, 1988. Most detailed recent overview.

Haigh, Christopher. *English Reformation: Religion, Politics, and Society under the Tudors.* Oxford and New York, 1993. "Revisionist," combative.

Haigh, Christopher, ed. *The English Reformation Revised.* Cambridge, 1987. The editor argues for the unpopularity of the Reformation; the essays are useful on implementation on the ground.

Kelly, Henry Anagar. *The Matrimonial Trials of Henry VIII.* Stanford, Calif., 1976.

Pollard, A. F. *Henry VIII* (1902). Reprint, London, 1970. Dated but readable; takes for granted England's "national destiny" and Henry's part in it.

Redworth, Glyn. "Whatever Happened to the English Reformation?" *History Today* 37 (October, 1987), 29–35. Sees the church settlement as constructive, enlightened.

———. *In Defence of the Church Catholic: The Life of Stephen Gardiner.* Oxford, 1990. Sympathetic account of a leading "Henrician" bishop.

Rex, Richard. *Henry VIII and the English Reformation.* London, 1993.

Argues for a specific "Henrician" policy, rather than an alternation of "Catholic" and "Protestant" policies.
Scarisbrick, J. J. *Henry VIII*. London, 1968. The most substantial biography; especially good on Henry's own theological views.
———. *The Reformation and the English People*. Oxford, 1984. "Revisionist," light in tone, weighty in argument.
Smith, Lacey Baldwin. *Henry VIII: The Mask of Royalty*. London, 1971. Sees Henry as acting as manipulator.
Starkey, David. *The Reign of Henry VIII: Personalities and Politics*. London, 1985. Brief, lively, geared to "factional" interpretation; sees Henry as being manipulated.

CLIFFORD S. L. DAVIES

HENRY OF NAVARRE. *See* Henry IV of France.

HERBERTSZOON, Hermannus (Eng., Herman Herberts; c.1540–1607), Dutch Reformed minister. Herbertszoon started his life and controversial ecclesiastical career in the eastern border area of the northern Netherlands, where he successively became a Cistercian monk, Roman Catholic pastor, and Protestant minister. Unfortunately little is known about his formative years.

Herbertszoon's notoriety rests on his ministry in Dordrecht (1577–1582) and Gouda (1582–1607), considered (respectively) the most orthodox and the most libertine Reformed congregations in Holland at the time. From the beginning he was a popular preacher. In 1582, however, his orthodox colleagues were alarmed when Herbertszoon refused to preach on the Heidelberg Catechism and put forward in a sermon the opinion that humans by their own efforts could reach perfection in this life, a view opposed to the Calvinist doctrine of predestination. Disciplinary procedures were started, and Herbertszoon left for Gouda, where he had powerful friends in both the church and town council. Here he was immediately appointed minister. Persistent rumors now spread that he favored the views of the self-styled prophet Hendrik Niclaes, founder of the sect called the Family of Love, and of the Anabaptist visionary David Joris.

From 1582 to 1592 a lengthy ecclesiastical examination of Herbertszoon's orthodoxy was held. He consistently denied having objections to the Reformed confession of faith and the catechism but refused to state his convictions unequivocally. The Gouda magistrates supported him throughout these years and expressly stated that they would keep him on as minister regardless of the church's judgments.

The synod decided to excommunicate him in 1592, but the Estates of Holland forbade it. A powerful faction in the Estates strongly favored a Reformed church that offered doctrinal latitude. Herbertszoon never retracted his errors or changed his opinions. With protection from the secular power he continued his ministry in Gouda undisturbed until his death. The Synod of Dordrecht in 1618–1619 would formally make an end to the latitude the patrons of Herbertszoon had propagated. Influential seventeenth-century Remonstrant historians claimed that the Reformed church in the Netherlands had originally been much broader than what Dordrecht had made of it. With Caspar Coolhaes, Cornelis Wiggerts, and others, Herbertszoon was one of the exemplars of a former latitudinarianism to which these historians pointed.

BIBLIOGRAPHY

Berg, A. J. van den. "Herman Herberts (ca. 1540–1607) in conflict met de gereformeerde kerk." In *Kerkhistorische opstellen aangeboden aan prof. dr. J. van den Berg*, edited by C. Augustijn, P. N. Holtrop, and G. H. M. Posthumus Meyjes, pp. 20–29. Kampen, 1987. Overview of Herbertszoon's life and his relevance to the history of Dutch Calvinism; includes references to source material.
Hibben, C. C. *Gouda in Revolt: Particularism and Pacifism in the Revolt of the Netherlands, 1572–1588*. Utrecht, 1983. Shows Herbertszoon in the context of the struggles that accompanied revolt and Reformation in Holland.

JOKE SPAANS

HERBST, Hans. *See* Oporinus, Johannes.

HERGOT, Hans (d. 1527), Nuremberg printer and bookseller. Hergot is mentioned as a printer in Nuremberg sources for the first time in 1524. He probably was born in Nuremberg, though his year of birth is unknown. He was married to a member of the Kunigunde family, who looked after his business and after his death ran his print shop until 1539. Between 1524 and early 1527 this shop published at least 75 titles in German, of which one-third explicitly identified him as the printer. Hergot reprinted five editions of Luther's New Testament and printed other writings of Luther as well as those of Philipp Melanchthon, Johannes Bugenhagen, Andreas Osiander, and several Catholic authors. He was by no means a printer of radical reform tracts and pamphlets and did not propagate the ideas of either Thomas Müntzer or the early Anabaptists. Although it is true that Müntzer's major tract, *Ausgedrueckte Entbloessung des falschen Glaubens* ("Explicit Revelation of the False Faith"), was printed in October 1524 in Hergot's print shop, this happened during Hergot's absence and was carried out by his apprentices. He only learned of the temporary imprisonment of his three compositors after his return.

Hergot had to travel constantly in order to improve his financial condition through book sales. Toward the end of 1525 it would appear that Hergot was heavily in debt and could only continue his printing activities through financial support of partners. Late in 1526 he traveled to Wittenberg to ask the printers Joerg Plochinger and Hans Weiß for the repayment of loans. On his return through Catholic Saxony he was arrested in Leipzig because he carried with him the sociocritical utopian tract *Von der newen Wandlung eynes christlichen Lebens* (Concerning the New Change of the Christian Life), printed by Michael Blum of Leipzig. In March 1527 two students had been arrested by the Leipzig city council for the same reason. The fugitive printer who had fled the city was to be arrested. Hergot was interrogated at the Court of Dresden and was executed as a rebel in Leipzig on 20 May 1527, following a sentence of the Leipzig Council.

BIBLIOGRAPHY

"Hans Hergot und die Flugschrift 'Von der newen Wandlung eynes christlichen Lebens.' Leipzig, 1977. Facsimile edition with annotations. Foreword by Max Steinmetz and appendix by Helmut Claus.

Hoyer, Siegfried. "Zu den gesellschaftlichen Hintergründen der Hinrichtung Hans Hergots, 1527: Die Schrift 'Von der newen Wandlung eynes christlichen Lebens.'" *Zeitschrift für Geschichtswissenschaft* 27 (1979), 125–139.

Seibt, Ferdinand. "Johannes Hergot: The Reformation of the Poor Man." In *Profiles of Radical Reformers*, edited by H. Goertz, pp. 97–106. Scottdale, Pa., 1982.

SIGRID LOOß

Translated from German by Hans J. Hillerbrand.

HERMANN V. *See* Wied, Hermann von.

HERTEL, Franz. *See* Dávid, Francis.

HERTZ, Conrad. *See* Cordatus, Conradus.

HESS, Johann (1490–1547), the first reformer in Wrocław (Breslau), the capital of Silesia. A native of Nuremberg and son of a merchant, Hess was sent to school (1503–1506) in Zwickau, Saxony. He attended the universities of Leipzig (1506–1510), where he received the bachelor of arts degree in 1507, and Wittenberg (1510–1513), earning his master of arts in 1511. In both places Hess devoted himself to humanistic studies. As a master of arts, Hess delivered lectures, the tenor of which seems reflected by his edition (1512) of a chapter from Pliny's *Historia naturalis* (Natural History) on how to avoid drunkenness, together with a poem by a friend on how to cure the madness of love. Before Hess left for Silesia (1513), he was ordained acolyte in the March of Brandenburg, the territorial state around Berlin.

In Silesia Hess found a congenial mentor in Johannes Thurzo (1464–1520), the humanist bishop of Wrocław, to whom Hess had been recommended by Christoph Scheurl. At the bishop's court in Neisse, Hess served (1514–1516) as tutor of Prince Joachim of Münsterberg-Oels, with whom he attended the University of Prague and who, in 1546, became Lutheran bishop of Brandenburg. From 1516 to 1518 Hess was court preacher for Joachim's father, Duke Carl in Oels, who provided Hess (1518) with a canonicate in Wrocław.

Thurzo wanted to send Hess to Wittenberg for further study. Because of a challenge to his canonicate, Hess traveled to Italy, where he obtained, after studying law and theology at Bologna, a doctorate in theology at Ferrara (9 September 1519), as well as ordination as subdeacon and deacon in Bologna (18 June 1519). Hess returned from Italy to Silesia via Wittenberg, which resulted in a lifelong correspondence with Martin Luther and Philipp Melanchthon. There are about twenty extant letters from the former and about thirty from the latter.

Back in Wrocław, Hess received full holy orders shortly before Thurzo's death on 2 August 1520 and was appointed one of the preachers at the Wrocław cathedral. His public confession of Lutheranism, however, came only in early 1522 during a visit to his hometown, Nuremberg where he preached at Saint Sebald's church. "I am happy to hear that you have become a preacher of the Gospel," Luther wrote Hess on 25 March 1522.

This sermon led the city council of Wrocław to appoint Hess pastor of Saint Mary Magdalene's church in June 1523. Pope Adrian VI, King Louis II of Hungary and Bohemia (to which Silesia belonged), and the local cathedral chapter protested this usurpation of patronage. Hess defended the "divine right" of congregations to call pastors through their magistrates in a public disputation on 20–23 April 1524.

The Wrocław Disputation was probably inspired by Huldrych Zwingli's first Zurich Disputation (29 January 1523) but had a different effect. While the Zurich Disputation led to iconoclasm and the abolition of the Mass, the Wrocław Disputation started with a mass to the Holy Spirit and ended with a *Te Deum.* As in Zurich, however, the city council ordered all priests within its domain to preach the gospel and follow the example of Hess.

Hess combined evangelical preaching with Catholic worship, discontinuing only such popular devotions as Desiderius Erasmus had deemed superstitious. In 1525 Hess went on a preaching strike until the city council had provided an All Saints' hospital for the care of the sick and the homeless. Beginning in 1530 Hess gave Latin lectures on the Old Testament in order to raise a new generation of theologians. Working in an area where the overlords remained Catholic, he hoped for an eventual reconciliation. He attended the Colloquy of Regensburg (1541), received a delegation from the Moravian Brethren (1540), and was interested in dialogue with the Greek church.

Hess was married in September 1525 to Sara Jopner (d. 1531) and in 1533 to Hedwig Wahle. Six children survived. Hess's only humanist publication was *De vitanda ebrietate* (Wittenberg, 1512), and his only theological one was *Axiomata disputationis Vratislaviensis* (Wrocław, 1524).

BIBLIOGRAPHY

Bautz, Friedrich Wilhelm, ed. *Biographische-Bibliographisches Kirchenlexikon.* Hamm, 1970–. See vol. 2, p. 784.

Fleischer, Manfred P. "Humanism and Reformation in Silesia: Imprints of Italy—Celtis, Erasmus, Luther, and Melanchthon." In *The Harvest of Humanism in Central Europe,* edited by Manfred P. Fleischer, p. 63, n. 89, and p. 53, n. 68. St. Louis, 1992. For periodical literature.

Kolde, Carl Adolf Julius. *Dr. Johann Hess, der schlesische Reformator.* Breslau, 1846. The only book-length biography.

MANFRED P. FLEISCHER

HESSE. The landgraviate, or imperial principality, of the house of Brabant was united from 1479 to 1567. Early sixteenth-century Hesse comprised approximately the same territory as the contemporary federal state in Germany, except that large blocks of land, especially in the south, were held by various counts and ecclesiastical powers. Moreover, Frankfurt am Main, the largest town in the Hessian orbit and a major commercial hub, was a free imperial city. From the eighth century, the people, a varying mixture of Franks and Chatts, were known as Hessians. They spoke High German, although there was a perceptible shading into Low German as one moved northward. According to tradition, the Anglo-Saxon missionary Saint Boniface (d. 747) christianized the Hessians. Most of the area became subject to the jurisdiction of the archbishopric of Mainz. Before the Reformation, the two most important ecclesiastical centers in Hesse were Fritzlar in the north and Amöneburg in the south, both of which were seats of ecclesiastical justice. The town of Marburg was a major Hessian religious center, honoring the charitable work of Saint Elizabeth of Hungary (d. 1231), a landgravine.

The political core comprised two large sections. Lower Hesse, the historic "Land zu Hessen," was bounded on the northeast by the Werra River and included the valleys of the Fulda, Schwaim, and Eder. Kassel was its principal town. Upper Hesse contained the Lahn and Ohm river valleys, with its principal town at Marburg. The mid-fifteenth-century inheritance of the counties of Diez, Ziegenhain, and Nidda allowed the landgraves to make this core a mostly contiguous territory. Topographically, this core area was not fertile but was mostly highlands, suitable for the production of grains and sheep. The relative poverty of Hesse was caught in a folk saying: "In the land of Hesse, there are great mountains, and nothing to eat, large mugs and sour wine."

The Katzenellenbogen Inheritance (1479) comprised two counties. Upper Katzenellenbogen was centered on its principal town of Darmstadt and bordered by the Rhine on the southwest. The Rhine bordered Lower Katzenellenbogen on the west, except for its principal town of Saint Goar, which was located on the left bank. These counties were not contiguous, and they were separated from the rest of Hesse by the lands of the counts of Nassau.

As Rhenish provinces, the Katzenellenbogen counties brought Hesse into the mainstream of the commercial life and politics of the German southwest. Their rich Rhine and Main tolls greatly augmented the Hessian treasury. Hence Hesse joined the Rhenish electors in regulating and facilitating trade. Having become a rich and large Rhenish state, Hesse was a pivotal force between north and south Germany. Its central location guaranteed that it must be concerned with both areas. During the Reformation, this position undoubtedly was a factor behind Landgrave Philipp's concern for uniting north and south German Protestants.

The Katzenellenbogen inheritance involved Hesse in a struggle with the counts of Nassau, who also claimed the counties. As antagonists of a larger, prominent Hesse, Nassau gained the support of the Habsburgs, who were attempting to establish a land bridge between their Austrian and Burgundian bases. Thus, the Habsburgs seized the duchy of Württemberg in 1520. This strategy set the stage for a struggle with Hesse, because it was a large, expanding Rhenish power. In addition, the landgraves were related to the deposed duke, Ulrich, for whose welfare they felt a certain responsibility. Whatever the secular motives, once converted to Lutheranism, Philipp saw Charles V as the major threat to the evangelical movement. The protection of Protestantism was a major motive for conflict with the Habsburgs. Simultaneously, Philipp's conversion drove the Habsburgs to side with Nassau.

With the recess of the Diet of Speyer (1526), Philipp began building one of the first evangelical (after 1529, Protestant) territorial churches. The Synod of Homberg (Efze), in 1526, led by François Lambert, debated the religious issues, approved of ecclesiastical reform, and created a vast plan for rapid implementation. But instead of enacting the plan, reform was administered gradually. The building of the new church began with the appointment of preachers to key towns. A church order of 1532 fixed the new divine services. Under the influence of Martin Bucer, the Ziegenhain Discipline Order of 1538 and the Kassel Church Order of 1539 established a new Protestant confirmation and provided for stricter enforcement of discipline. These changes stemmed the Anabaptist threat in Hesse, which was the reason Bucer was invited to Hesse. The great Church Order of 1566 continued commitment to all these principles until the end of Philipp's reign.

Monastic orders were officially dissolved by a Hessian diet (1527), which promised to the nobility revenues for dowries. Much monastic property, however, was devoted to supporting pastors, schools, and the poor. The Hessian state did not compel the religious to leave their orders. They might remain for life but were compelled to end certain Catholic practices.

In the decade after Speyer, Philipp gradually restructured education, charity, and moral control. He established a public school system and the University of Marburg (1527). He developed a system of scholarships to enable the lower classes to be educated. Beginning in 1527, he introduced a common chest system, providing for the disbursement of preventive relief to those needy who had a residence but did not enjoy a source of support sufficient to meet their needs. He restructured town hospitals to provide relief for the poor who required institutionalization because of physical or mental illness or old age. He founded territorial hospitals to serve the peasantry. In keeping with Luther's advice, the police orders of 1524 and 1526 secularized discipline.

Hesse under Philipp provided an example of religious toleration and reason in a period when intolerance was the norm. Dissenters were not converted by force or executed for religious reasons. Philipp used dialogues to convert Anabaptists. He rejected the harsher recommendations of theologians for persecution of Jews in his territories. Demands for the persecution of "witches" were also rejected.

The Reformation included a system of alliances that discouraged the emperor and others from suppressing Protestantism. Hesse relied first on bilateral defensive agreements with the Lutherans and Upper German evangelicals. The Schmalkald League (1531) represented a stronger single alliance. Philipp brought non-German powers into these arrangements, including Denmark, France, and the Swiss towns. Moreover, Hesse arranged a promise of neutrality from Catholic Bavaria. Philipp's concessions to the emperor because of his bigamy weakened the league and led to defeat in the Schmalkald War. From 1547 to 1552 the emperor imprisoned Philipp and attempted to interfere in the Hessian church. After that difficult period was over, Hesse won greater security with the Peace of Augsburg (1555).

The sixteenth-century Hessian state was fairly well developed in comparison to its medieval precursor. Philipp furthered rationalization of government, a process that had already commenced by 1500. Professionalism, specialization, and esprit de corps among state servants were all achieved. The Reformation furthered these achievements by demanding lay administration of education, charity, and moral control. The burgher class, mostly patricians, dominated much of the bureaucracy, except for the gubernatorial and military posts.

Hesse had a monarchy. The landgrave was the center of administration, but a chancellery consisting of the governor, chancellor, and counselors ran the daily affairs of state. The regional administrators, who administered the four major sections of Hesse, were responsible to the chancellery. In turn, the four sections were subdivided into districts, each headed by a manager. Treasury agents also held great financial and other responsibilities on the district level. Philipp established a financial secretary's office, independent of the chancellery. The governors and the financial secretary were charged with keeping records of properties, debts, and contracts of all kinds.

Lawgiving was still practiced by the landgrave. Though not lacking, the idea of a representative diet with lawmaking authority did not progress well in Hesse. The diet had been the center of the rebellious nobility's opposition to the landgrave during Philipp's regency and early reign. Hence he reduced it to a forum for winning support for the Reformation and gaining consent for taxation. Roman law was received in 1497/98, giving Hesse a centralized judiciary, written law, and learned judges.

As Philipp commenced erecting a new church structure in 1527, he assigned central executive control to visitors (after 1531, superintendents). The superintendents were originally princely agents with extensive powers to appoint pastors and maintain uniformity. But after 1531 territorial synods, local pastors, and congregations gained considerable power over appointments, doctrines, and discipline. In 1539 elders joined the pastors in maintaining congregational order. The doctrines of the Hessian church under Philipp were based on the Augsburg Confession (1530) and the Wittenberg Concord (1536). By the end of Philipp's reign, the church strongly emphasized conforming to patristic practices.

When Philipp died (1567), Hesse was divided between his four legitimate sons, so that central state administration ended. Philipp had attempted to preserve Hesse with common institutions—territorial diet, the University of Marburg, a common purse, territorial hospitals, and a general synod. Growing confessional antagonism between the Reformed and Lutherans and differences among Philipp's sons, however, eventually led to greater separation.

[*See also* Marburg, Colloquy of; Marriage; Philipp of Hesse; *and* Schmalkald League.]

BIBLIOGRAPHY

Beck, Kurt. "Der Bruderzwist im Hause Hessen." In *Die Geschichte Hessens,* edited by Uwe Schultz, pp. 95–105. Stuttgart, 1983.

Heinemeyer, Walter. "Armen- und Krankenfürsorge in der hessischen Reformation." In *450 Jahre Psychiatrie in Hessen,* edited by Walter Heinemeyer and Tilman Pünder, pp. 1–20. Veröffentlichungen der Historischen Kommission für Hessen, vol. 47. Marburg, Germany. 1983. Clear presentation of the comprehensive system of caring for the needy established with the Reformation.

———. "Das Zeitalter der Reformation." In *Das Werden Hessens,* edited by Walter Heinemeyer, pp. 225–266. Marburg, Germany, 1986.

Moraw, Peter. "Hessen und das deutsche Königtum im späten Mittelalter." *Hessisches Jahrbuch für Landesgeschichte* 26 (1976), 43–95.

———. "Das späte Mittelalter." In *Das Werden Hessens,* edited by Walter Heinemeyer, pp. 195–224. Marburg, Germany, 1986. Provides a clear picture of Hesse before the Reformation.

Philippi, Hans. *Das Haus Hessen: Ein europäisches Fürstengeschlecht.* Kassel, Germany, 1983. Surveys the ruling family and its high points.

Press, Volker. "Hessen im Zeitalter der Landestellung, 1567–1655." In *Das Werden Hessens,* edited by Walter Heinemeyer, pp. 267–331. Marburg, Germany, 1986. Very helpful analysis of Hesse after the death of Philipp.

Siebeck, Hans. "Die landständische Verfassung Hessens im 16. Jahrhundert." *Zeitschrift des Vereins für hessische Geschichte und Landeskunde* 17 (1914). Best source on the development of the diet.

Stalnaker, John C. "Anabaptism, Martin Bucer and the Shaping of the Hessian Protestant Church." *Journal of Modern History* 48 (1976), 601–643.

Wright, William J. "Reformation Contributions to the Development of Public Welfare Policy in Hesse." *Journal of Modern History* 49 (1977), D1145-D1179.

———. "A Closer Look at House Poor Relief through the Common Chest and Indigence in Sixteenth Century Hesse." *Archiv für Reformationsgeschichte* 70 (1979), 225–238.

———. *Capitalism, the State and the Lutheran Reformation: Sixteenth-Century Hesse.* Athens, Ohio, 1988. Places the Hessian Reformation in the context of rising capitalism, state-building, demographic changes, and the crisis of feudalism.

William J. Wright

HESSHUS, Tilemann (1527–1588), German Gnesio-Lutheran theologian and confessional controversialist. He came from an influential family in Wesel on the lower Rhine. After schooling in Antwerp, he became Philipp Melanchthon's student at Wittenberg in 1546. Though favoring his mentor's concession of adiaphora matters in the Leipzig Interim, Hesshus avoided controversy while away at Oxford and Paris. After receiving his M.A. at Wittenberg in 1550, he stayed to lecture on rhetoric and dogmatics before becoming superintendent in Goslar in 1553. While in Goslar he received a doctorate from Wittenberg. There he also married Hanna von Bert (1533–1564).

Hesshus's efforts in 1556 to exercise church discipline against the son of the mayor of Goslar caused friction with the city council, and Hesshus left Goslar. He lived briefly in Magdeburg, where he had contact with the Gnesio-Lutherans Nicolaus Gallus, Johann Wigand, Matthaeus Judex, and Matthias Flacius Illyricus, assisting on Flacius's *Centuriae Magdeburgenses* (Magdeburg Centuries). That same year Hesshus joined the theology faculty of the University of Rostock. His part in a 1557 church-order revision sparked conflict with Rostock's city council because of Hesshus's opposition to Sunday weddings, and Hesshus was expelled. He moved to Heidelberg as superintendent, a call arranged by Melanchthon. The support of the Palatinate elector Frederick III for Calvinist theology drew Hesshus's criticism, and a controversy over the Lord's Supper and the nature of Christ's presence saw Hesshus aligned with the Gnesio-Lutheran camp. That brought his dismissal in 1559.

Hesshus next went to Bremen, where he served as superintendent and opposed Albert Rizaeus Hardenberg's Reformed understanding of the Lord's Supper. Although Hardenberg was forced out in 1561, the following year Mayor Daniel von Büren, won to Hardenberg's view, engineered the expulsion of Hesshus and other Lutheran pastors. From Magdeburg Hesshus attacked his opponents, insisting Christ's sacramental presence be based only on a literal view of the words "this is my body" without also arguing Christ's ubiquity as other Lutherans did. His narrow approach echoed Martin Luther's 1529 response to Huldrych Zwingli but ignored the omnipotence language found, for instance, in Luther's Large Catechism or the Great Confession of 1528. Hesshus also criticized the Reformed Heidelberg Catechism of 1563, treating John Calvin's view as little more than Zwingli revisited. As the paper war raged, pressure from Melanchthon's Philippist supporters, with their more flexible understanding of Christ's sacramental presence, caused Hesshus to leave Magdeburg. Returning to Wesel, he found a chilly welcome in a Reformed climate. At his wife's death Hesshus refused the "crypto-Calvinist" ministrations of Wesel's pastor and was ousted from the city.

His next assignment was that of court preacher and superintendent for Duke Wolfgang of Zweibrücken (Palatinate), where he led the territory in a Gnesio-Lutheran direction. In 1568 he rallied Wigand, Gallus, Martin Chemnitz, David Chytraeus, and others against Flacius's teaching that Original Sin was part of fallen human nature's substance. After Duke Wolfgang died in one of the French religious wars, Hesshus joined the faculty at the University of Jena. There he argued that, along with word and sacrament, obedience to the pastoral office marked the church's presence. He criticized Jakob Andreae's efforts at uniting Lutheran factions.

With the accession in 1573 of the Saxon elector August I, who had been influenced by crypto-Calvinism, Hesshus left to succeed Joachim Mörlin as bishop in Königsberg. Hesshus continued to criticize Reformed sacramental theology and to complain of "new Lutheran" arguments from ubiquity. Pressure from several sides brought his 1577 ouster. His last move was to Helmstedt, where Duke Julius von Braunschweig-Wolfenbüttel invited Hesshus to join Julius's new university. He died in 1588.

BIBLIOGRAPHY

Barton, Peter F. *Um Luthers Erbe: Studien und Texte zur Spätreformation.* Untersuchungen zur Kirchengeschichte, vol. 6. Witten, 1972. Although focusing especially on 1527–1559, the volume touches on Hesshus's entire life. Barton is the author of numerous articles on Hesshus. Here, he includes an extensive German-language bibliography and lists well over one hundred titles by the prolific controversialist.

Schierenberg, Kurt August. "Tileman Heshusen, 1527–1588: Kurzes Lebensbild eines lutherischen Streittheologen." *Monatshefte für evangelische Kirchengeschichte des Rheinlandes* 14 (1965), 190–204. A short sketch of Hesshus's career.

Steinmetz, David C. "Calvin and His Lutheran Critics." *Lutheran*

Quarterly n.s. 4 (1990), 179–194. A detailed examination of Hesshus's sacramental theology, arguing that Hesshus did both Calvin and Luther a disservice, misunderstanding and misrepresenting the former and making poor use of the latter.

Wilkens, Cornelius A. *Tilemann Heßhusius: Ein Streittheologe der Luther-Kirche.* Leipzig, 1860. An old, oft-cited biography.

ROBERT ROSIN

HESSUS, Eobanus (1488–1540), Neo-Latin poet from Hesse, "king" of the Erfurt humanists. Hessus studied in Erfurt, where he soon joined the circle of humanists around Conrad Mutianus Rufus in nearby Gotha. His early poetry depicts university life; his later works take up moral, religious, and nationalistic themes. Having become professor of Latin at Erfurt, Hessus set out in autumn 1518 to make his pilgrimage to Erasmus in Louvain, a journey vividly described in his *Hodoeporicon* (1519). When Erasmus subsequently asked the Erfurt humanists to attack the conservative theologian Edward Lee, Hessus responded with a volley of vituperative epigrams (1520).

During the early years of the Reformation Hessus virtually ignored Luther. Not until April 1521, after Luther stopped over at Erfurt on his way to Worms, did Hessus compose his *In evangelici Doctoris M. Lutheri laudem Elegiae* (Elegies in Praise and Defense of the Evangelical Doctor Martin Luther; 1521). In this work he hailed Luther as the heroic restorer of God's word and liberator of the church from papal tyranny. The elegiac *Ecclesiae afflicte Epistola ad Lutherum* (Letter from the Afflicted Church to Luther; 1523) continues to bear witness to Hessus's pro-Lutheran fervor; but it also reflects the troubles that the Reformation was beginning to visit upon Erfurt and its university. In later writings Hessus blamed the university's decline on the runaway monks—the same "obscure men" who had earlier attacked Johannes Reuchlin and who now, as evangelical preachers, were fomenting hatred against true learning.

In this increasingly precarious position Hessus fought hard to restore humanistic studies to their rightful place at Erfurt. To this end he published a collection of letters written to him by Luther, Melanchthon, and others concerning the need for theologians to study the ancient languages (1523); he added an appeal to the city council to help the university regain its glory. In his *Dialogi tres* (1524) he pilloried the itinerant preachers for their intolerance and ignorance.

In 1526 Hessus went to Nuremberg to teach at the new Egidien-Gymnasium, founded by Melanchthon. Among the numerous works of his Nuremberg years the *De tumultibus horum temporum Querela* (Poems Lamenting the Tumults of This Age; 1528) merits special note. The work includes an account of the Peasants' War from a Lutheran perspective. Thomas Müntzer is condemned as a "false evangelist," while the slaughter of the peasants is judged to have been as lamentable as it was justified.

After another stay at Erfurt (1533 to 1536), Hessus accepted a call to the University of Marburg. There he completed his metrical paraphrase of the *Psalms* (1537). Endorsed by Luther and Melanchthon, it was reprinted over fifty times.

Although the effects of the Reformation on humanistic studies dismayed him, Hessus never deserted Luther's cause. As a poet in the Erasmian mold, however, he was far more perturbed by the cultural barbarians of his age than by confessional differences. He eschewed zealotry and dogmatism and sought instead to maintain close ties to all his old friends, Protestant and Catholic alike, on the basis of their common humanistic creed.

BIBLIOGRAPHY

Entner, Heinz. "Helius Eobanus Hessus und die lutherische Reformation in Erfurt, 1521–1525." In *Weltwirkung der Reformation*, edited by Max Steinmetz and Gerhard Brendler, vol. 2, pp. 472–484. Berlin, 1969. Concise overview of the role of Hessus in the Reformation.

Krause, Carl. *Helius Eobanus Hessus: Sein Leben und seine Werke* (1879) 2 vols. Reprint, Nieuwkoop, Netherlands, 1963. Still the best biography of Hessus, with a full bibliography of the primary literature.

Scribner, R. W. "The Erasmians and the Beginning of the Reformation in Erfurt." *The Journal of Religious History* 9 (1976), 3–31. Thorough account of the reasons why Erasmian humanism failed to take root in Erfurt, despite the best efforts of Hessus and other humanists.

Trillitsch, Winfried. "Humanismus und Reformation: Der Erfurter Humanist und 'Dichterkönig' Helius Eobanus Hessus." *Wissenschaftliche Zeitschrift, Friedrich-Schiller-Universität Jena, Gesellschaftswissenschaftliche Reihe* 33 (1984), 343–357. Offers an encompassing picture of the life and works of Hessus in the context of humanism and the Reformation.

Vredeveld, Harry, ed. *Helius Eobanus Hessus. Dichtungen. Lateinisch und Deutsch.* Bern 1990–. Also in progress by the same editor, the correspondence of Hessus.

HARRY VREDEVELD

HEYDEN, Gaspar van der (1530–1586), Calvinist preacher in the Netherlands and the Palatinate. The son of propertied burghers in Mechelen (Malines), Heyden settled at the age of sixteen or seventeen in Antwerp as a cobbler's apprentice. After 1551 he provided leadership for the Reformed of Antwerp. As a full-time preacher, he brought them together in 1555 into a structured church organization. In 1557 he was confirmed in his office as pastor by the church in Emden.

From the beginning of his duties in Antwerp, he sought strict exclusivism according to the example of John Calvin: a radical break with the Roman church, a confession of faith, and submission to church discipline. He organized those who attended in closed circles in the greatest secrecy. Thereby he came into conflict with the second pastor, Adriaan Corneliszoon van Haemstede, who had been sent as a reinforcement from Emden in 1556. Haemstede refused to confine his ministry to the strictly defined congregation and thus endangered the security of the congregation. A celebration of the Lord's Supper on 18 June 1558 led to persecution. Heyden fled to Frankfurt am Main, where he became pastor to the Netherlandish refugee congregation, along with Peter Dathenus. After a dispute between the Lutherans and Reformed over the doctrine of the Lord's Supper, Dathenus was offered the cloister at Frankenthal (south of Worms) from Elector Frederick III of the Palatinate. Together with Dathenus, Heyden became pastor in Frankenthal.

In the summer of 1566 he returned to the Netherlands. From Antwerp, where an iconoclastic riot had broken out on 20 August, Heyden went to the northern Flemish towns of Axel and Hulst. There he preached from 24 to 29 August and organized further iconoclastic riots. In Antwerp again he joined those resisting the drift of the Reformed toward the Augsburg Confession. After the failure of the rebellion in the Netherlands, he again took up his function as pastor at Frankenthal in March 1567. Close ties were formed with Philip Marnix van Saint Aldegonde. Heyden presided over the Synod of Emden (1571), which established rules for the organization of the church (regular gatherings of consistories, classes, and synods), unity of doctrine (obligatory subscription to the Belgic Confession), and the practice of church discipline. In June 1574 Heyden presided over the provincial synod of Dordrecht.

In March 1574 he was called as pastor to recently liberated Middelburg, where he introduced the first Reformed celebration of the Lord's Supper on 18 July with three hundred communicants. He was active in the preparations for the national Synod of Dordrecht in 1578, where he functioned as assessor and contributed to the synod's decision to place itself in support of the politics of William of Orange. The same year he was called as pastor to the congregation in Antwerp. He published a Dutch version of the Heidelberg Catechism and worked on the drafting of a church ordinance. After the fall of Antwerp (17 August 1585), he retreated by way of Zeeland back to Frankenthal. Prince Elector Johann Casimir named him church inspector for Bacharach and its surrounding area.

Heyden's significance lies above all in his pastoral work, his accomplishments in church organization and church ordinances, his functioning at synods, and his work on the Heidelberg Catechism and liturgical formulations. With both words and writings he stood in strong opposition to the Anabaptists.

BIBLIOGRAPHY

Bremmer, R. H. *Reformatie en Rebellie: Willem van Oranje, de Calvinisten en het recht van opstand; Tien onstuimige jaren, 1572–1582*. Franeker, 1984. This volume deals with Gaspar van der Heyden's role in several synods.

Itterzon, G. P. van. "Heyden, Gaspar van der." In *Biografisch Lexicon voor de Geschiedenis van het Nederlandse Protestantisme*, vol. 2, pp. 240–243. Kampen, 1983.

Lennep, M. F. van. *Gaspar van der Heyden, 1530–1586*. Amsterdam, 1884.

Marnef, Guido. *Antwerpen in Reformatietijd: Ondergronds Protestantisme in een internationale handelsmetropool*. 2 vols. Doctoral diss., Katholieke Universiteit Leuven, 1991. Discusses his ministry in the early Reformed church of Antwerp.

Roosbroeck, Rob van. "Heydanus, Gaspar." In *Nationaal Biografisch Woordenboek*, vol. 5, pp. 448–453. Brussels, 1972.

JOHAN DECAVELE
Translated from Dutch by Jeff Bach

HOEN, Cornelis Henricxzoen (also Henrici, Hoon, Honius; c.1460–1524), Dutch humanist, lawyer, and lay theologian. Hoen is known in Reformation history because of his Latin treatise proposing a symbolic interpretation of the Eucharist. As a lawyer Hoen was attached to the court of Holland in The Hague, while he also formed part of a circle of reform-minded dissidents, which had its center in Delft and The Hague. Hoen was known by contemporaries as an accomplished humanist scholar. In 1523 he was arrested and eventually condemned to conditional liberty within his place of residence because of his "Lutheran" sympathies. He died during the winter of 1524/25.

Hoen's treatise on the Eucharist, published posthumously, survives in two Latin and three German editions. His writing presents a choice of arguments against the dogma of transubstantiation, which is assessed as a recent papal and satanic invention. Best known is Hoen's interpretation of the words "this *is* my body" as "this *signifies* my body"; his main argument was his appeal to *Matthew* 24:23, where, according to Hoen, Christ is said to be not locally on earth and for that reason not in the eucharistic bread either.

As sources of Hoen's ideas one should mention Erasmus's *Annotationes in Nouum Testamentum*, Luther's *De captivitate Babylonica*, the contemporary juristic concept of *traditio symbolica*, and, more unlikely, the works of the fifteenth-century theologian Wessel Gansfort. But the distinctive characteristics of his treatise Hoen derived from Wycliffite and Hussite traditions of dissent, which also existed in the fifteenth-century Low Countries.

In the Netherlands as well as elsewhere in Europe Hoen's treatise was influential. Andreas Bodenstein von Karlstadt, Johannes Oecolampadius, Huldrych Zwingli, and Martin Bucer learned of his arguments from the visits Hoen's friend Hinne Rode paid them, and were impressed, but Luther condemned Hoen's interpretation of the Eucharist.

BIBLIOGRAPHY

Huldreich Zwinglis sämtliche Werke. Leipzig, 1927. See vol. 4, pp. 512–519, for a critical edition of Hoen's treatise, *Epistola christiana admodum*.

Köhler, Walther. *Zwingli und Luther: Ihr Streit über das Abendmahl nach seinen politischen und religiösen Beziehungen*. Vol. 1. Reprint, New York and London, 1971. Shows the influence of Hoen's treatise on the sacramental controversy between the Wittenberg and Swiss reformers.

Oberman, Heiko A. *Forerunners of the Reformation: The Shape of Late Medieval Thought Illustrated by Key-Documents.* 2d ed. Philadelphia, 1981. See pp. 268–278 for an English translation of Hoen's treatise.

Pegg, Michael A. *A Catalogue of German Reformation Pamphlets, 1516–1550, in Swiss Libraries.* Baden-Baden, 1983.

Scheffer, J. G. de Hoop. *Geschiedenis der Kerkhervorming in de Nederlanden van haar Ontstaan tot 1531.* Amsterdam, 1873. Describes elaborately the circle of dissidents and Hoen's trial.

Spruyt, B. J. "*Annulus... mei amoris pignus*: Wessel Gansfort and Cornelis Hoen's *Epistola christiana.*" In *Wessel Gansfort and Northern Humanism,* edited by F. Akkerman, G. C. Huisman, and A. J. Vanderjagt, pp. 122–141. Leiden, 1993. On the alleged relationship between Wessel and Hoen.

———. "Laat-middeleeuwse ketterijen en de vroege Hervorming in de Nederlanden: Cornelis Henrisxz. Hoen en zijn *Epistola christiana* (1525)." *Doopsgezinde bijdragen* n.s. 19 (1993), 15–28. Shows the influence of Wycliffe and Hus on Hoen's thought.

———. *Cornelius Henrici Hoen (Honius) and His Epistle on the Eucharist (1525): Medieval Heresy, Erasmian Humanism and Reform in the Early Sixteenth-Century Low Countries.* Leiden, forthcoming.

Trapman, J. "Le rôle des 'sacramentaires' des origines de la Réforme jusqu'en 1530 aux Pays-Bas." *Nederlands Archief voor Kerkgeschiedenis* 63 (1983), 1–24. Sets Hoen and his treatise within the wider context of the early Dutch reformation.

Verzeichnis der im deutschen Sprachbereich erschienenen Drucke des XVI. Jahrhunderts. Vol. 9. Stuttgart, 1987.

BART JAN SPRUYT

HÖE OF HÖENEGG, Matthias (1580–1645), Lutheran theologian, polemicist, and court preacher in Dresden. The son of Leonhard Höe, he was an imperial councillor and legal expert ennobled in 1592. He was educated at home by a Flacian tutor and briefly visited the school of Saint Stephen's cathedral in Vienna. With his brother, Christian, Höe went to school in Steyr (1594), then under Philippist and Calvinist influence. In June 1597 he enrolled at Wittenberg, where he studied law and theology until October 1601.

In 1602 Höe was appointed by Elector Christian II one of his court preachers in Dresden. On 1 January 1604 he was named superintendent of Plauen and in March of the same year received his doctorate in theology at Wittenberg. His patron allowed him to go to Prague in May 1607 to work among the Lutheran community there. In 1613 he returned to Dresden as the first court preacher of Elector John George I. Immediately a conflict erupted between Höe and the second court preacher, Daniel Hänichen, which lasted until Hänichen left for Prague. When Elector Johann Sigismund of Brandenburg converted to Calvinism in 1613, Höe's already sharp attacks on Calvinism became even more bitter, and in his "99 Points" (1621) he equated Calvinists with Arians and Turks. Responding to a plea from Simon Gedicke, provost in Berlin, Höe attacked the Calvinists in Brandenburg and, in particular, Abraham Scultetus. Höe's anti-Calvinism led him, as it had his predecessor, Polycarp Leyser, to advocate a Saxon alliance with the emperor, Ferdinand II, rather than aid the Calvinist Friedrich of the Palatinate. But, after the Edict of Restitution clearly threatened the Lutherans in electoral Saxony, he advocated closer cooperation with the Protestant forces in Germany, and his anti-Jesuit critique became sharper.

After the death of the Swedish king Gustavus Adolfus in 1632, Höe returned to his previous support of cooperation with the emperor. He opposed the entry of Saxony into the Heilbron League and urged acceptance of the Peace of Prague of 1635, which led some to accuse him of having been bribed. His polemical and political activities decreased markedly prior to his death in Dresden on 4 March 1645. Höe also was instrumental in resolving the christological conflict between the Tübingen and Giessen theologians in the *decisio Saxonica* of 1623.

BIBLIOGRAPHY

Primary Sources

Höe von Höenegg, Matthias. *Eine schöne Geistliche, Geistreich Comoedi.* 1602.

———. *Evangelisches Handbüchlein wider das Papstthum.* 1603.

———. *Triumphus Calvinisticus.* 1614.

———. *Augenscheinliche Prob, wie die Calvinisten in Neun und Neuntzig Puncten mit den Arrianern und Türckern übereinstimmen.* Leipzig, 1621.

———. *Nothwendige verteidigung des heiliger Römischen reichs evangelischer churfürsten und stände augapffels, nemlich der wahren, reinen ungeenderten... hierzu verordnete theologen.* Leipzig, 1629.

Otto, Ernst. *Die Schriften des ersten kursächsischen Oberhofpredigers Höe von Höenegg.* Dresden, 1898.

Secondary Sources

Hertrakampf, Hans-Dieter. "Der kursächsische Oberhilfprediger Matthias Höe von Höenegg: Seine Theologie, Polemik und Kirchenpolitik." Diss., Universität Leipzig, 1967.

Knapp, Hans. *Höe von Höenegg und sein Eingreifen in die Politik und Publizistik des dreissigjährigen Krieges.* Hallesche Abhandlungen zur neuren Geschichte, 40. Halle, Germany, 1902.

Otto, Ernst. "Der Streit der beiden kursächsischen Hofprediger Matthias Höe von Höenegg und Mag: Daniel Hänichen, 1613–1618." *Beiträge zur Sächsische Kirchengeschichte* 21 (1908), 89–123.

DAVID P. DANIEL

HOFFMAN, Melchior (also Hofmann; 1495?-1543), sometime Lutheran, then Anabaptist, radical lay preacher and reformer in northern Europe, credited with taking Anabaptism to the Low Countries. Apocalypticist, visionary, and allegorical exegete, Hoffman exhibited virtually all the qualities of a radical save the advocacy of outright rebellion. Although charged in his own time with inspiring the violent theocracy established in the northwestern German city of Münster in 1534–1535—its leaders were guided in part by his writings—he may have disapproved of those events, for he consistently said that only magistrates should use the sword; nevertheless, his predictions of the destruction of the corrupt priesthood and other warnings of wars in the final days were put into action by this violent branch of the Melchiorites.

Hoffman is described in the sources as a Swabian, but solid information on his life is lacking until his appearance in 1523 in Livonia (present-day Estonia and Latvia) on the Baltic Sea, where as a furrier and lay preacher he was a fiery advocate of Luther's reform ideas. In the Baltic towns of Wolmar (Valmiera), Dorpat (Tartu), Riga, and Reval (Tallinn), Hoffman publicly advocated Luther's themes of justification by faith, predestination, and a warning of the near end of the age, but his call for congregational governance and the restraint of secular authorities in the enforcement of religious practices echoed the early, not the later, Luther. Other ideas contradicted Luther: he denied Christ's real presence in the Eucharist in favor of a spiritual presence; he claimed to have a gift of the Spirit that made him a prophet able to discern the spiritual meaning behind the letter of the biblical text, a view that linked him more to late medieval mysticism than to Luther; he objected to the use of images; and he affirmed a doctrine of sanctification that went beyond Luther's justification by faith.

In Dorpat Hoffman was indirectly involved in an outbreak of iconoclasm, for when town authorities attempted to arrest him a crowd charged into churches and cloisters smashing images and other holy objects. Hoffman built on the social unrest that pitted merchants and landholders against nobility, a struggle that involved the adoption of Lutheran ideas as a means of gaining freedom from the Catholic-oriented nobility. But his radical ideas of direct revelation, his view of the Eucharist, and the radical overtones of his apocalypticism brought him into conflict with both Catholics and Lutherans in Livonia until his final expulsion in 1526.

Hoffman fared little better in the fur-trading center of Stockholm. Supported by German merchants who sought ecclesiastical reform, Hoffman was allowed to preach openly and even published a book on the prophecies of Daniel. He also married, and his wife gave birth to a son. But his announcement that the end of the world was to come in 1533 and his tendency to foment mistrust between the German and Swedish populations in Stockholm convinced the authorities he was unstable; King Gustavus Vasa ordered him to leave. In 1526 Hoffman fled to Lübeck in northern Germany, where another threat of persecution forced him to flee once again.

He resettled in Schleswig-Holstein, then ruled by King Frederick I of Denmark and Norway, who granted him a license to preach in Kiel. Questions about him led Hoffman to seek Luther's approval of his work, but a visit to Wittenberg brought a warning against him from both Luther and Johannes Bugenhagen, the Wittenberg pastor.

A public disputation on Hoffman's views at the Schleswig city of Flensburg in 1529 proved to be a turning point for the lay preacher. Thinking himself an advocate of Lutheranism, he found himself abandoned by the Lutherans, including Bugenhagen, the ranking Lutheran in the debate. His apocalypticism and rejection of the real presence of Christ in the sacrament, his sometime advocacy of civil disobedience, and his spiritualist-allegorical interpretations of the Bible were unacceptable to both Catholic and Lutheran leaders, who had enough problems among themselves without the complications Hoffman brought. Two days after the disputation the king ordered all Hoffman's possessions seized and him banished. During a brief ministry in eastern Frisia in the company of the spiritualist reformer Andreas Bodenstein von Karlstadt, Hoffman allied with the Zwinglian faction, again in a setting where debate over reform was still under way.

He entered Strasbourg, which had sided with the Reformation, in June 1529, where his eucharistic views won support among both the evangelical preachers of the city and the strong sacramentarian population, the group that favored the Zwinglian view of the sacrament. Hoffman's Strasbourg stay was the second major turning point in his ministry. There he encountered Anabaptist sentiment and converted to the movement in 1530; he fell under the sway of Lienhard Jost, Ursula Jost, and Barbara Rebstock, whose vision-inspired prophecies convinced him that the last days had arrived and that he was Elijah, the first of the two witnesses predicted in *Revelation* 11:3; from the Anabaptist leader Hans Denck he gained a view of God's universal grace and human free will—a view that fitted Hoffman's spiritualism far better than did Luther's predestination—and he affirmed the possibility of sanctification through good works in the latter stages of spiritual growth in Christ; and finally, he adopted the doctrine espoused by the Silesian nobleman and spiritualist Kaspar von Schwenckfeld concerning the celestial flesh of Christ.

Using the revelations from the Strasbourg prophets, Hoffman proclaimed that the city would be the spiritual Jerusalem where Christ would establish his new kingdom. God would soon pour out the Holy Spirit upon true believers, and from them would come the 144,000 apostolic messengers of *Revelation* 14:1–5 who would be missionaries to the whole world, while the godless priests and religious leaders would be destroyed. After these events Jesus would return. Hoffman had abandoned Lutheranism for Anabaptism, but it was an Anabaptism heavily laced with apocalypticism. His activities brought an order of arrest from the Strasbourg authorities in April 1530. Although gladly accepted by the city's nonconformists, Hoffman had now been rejected by the evangelicals whose Zwinglianism he had first found to be a basis of hope for his work in Strasbourg. Meanwhile, his writings on apocalyptic themes in the scriptures and the visions of the Strasbourg prophets circulated along the middle Rhine and in the Netherlands.

Escaping Strasbourg he returned to East Frisia for his

most successful ministry. There, in an Anabaptist mode, he gathered some three hundred followers, conducted a mass baptism in the Great Church at Emden, and organized a congregation, thereby bringing Anabaptism to the Low Countries. But the public stir from these activities was so great that Hoffman left the city, naming Jan Volkerts, also called Trijpmaker, as preacher in his place.

Returning to Strasbourg he wrote and published *Die Ordonnantie Godts* (The Ordinance of God) that articulated his view of baptism. By 1531 Hoffman was in Holland, where he baptized some fifty persons in Amsterdam. However, when Trijpmaker and nine other Melchiorites were executed in The Hague, Hoffman, who had returned to Strasbourg, declared he would baptize no others for two years, that is until 1533, the announced year of the Parousia. Using his typological hermeneutics, he noted that the post-exilic rebuilding of the Jerusalem temple (*Ezr.* 4:24) was delayed two years on account of the Samaritans, a pattern now being repeated as the spiritual temple was being readied. But the Melchiorite movement grew. Two new leaders under Hoffman were Obbe Philips, important in Dutch pacificist Anabaptism and then in spiritualism, and Jan Mathijs (Matthys), a Münsterite revolutionary: the contrary careers of these two Hoffman converts well illustrate the tensions in Hoffman's thought. In 1531 and 1532, certain that he was the expected Elijah and that his predictions were true, Hoffman published yet more books and tracts on apocalyptic themes, but another order for his arrest prompted him to flee Strasbourg.

After traveling in Hesse and the Netherlands Hoffman returned to Strasbourg (his fourth and final visit) in 1533. This time he made himself more visible than before, even seeming to challenge the town council to arrest him. Upon charges brought to the town council by one Nicholas Frey, whose excommunication from the Anabaptist congregation Hoffman had arranged, the town council ordered Hoffman's arrest on the grounds that he had threatened rebellion (despite the fact that his writings counseled obedience to the authorities). Hoffman rejoiced and saw the arrest as a sign that the end of the age was near. When no convincing evidence was produced to prove he had actually advocated an uprising, the charge was dropped; the preachers remained convinced that he had seditionary plans, however. In the Strasbourg synod, convened to deal with the nonconformist question, Hoffman defended his ideas: his monophysite Christology, the universal availability of divine grace, the freedom of the human will after enlightenment, the rejection of infant baptism, and the impossibility of forgiveness for mortal sins committed after conversion. The decision of the synod was to outlaw Anabaptism in Strasbourg, and several of the group were banished. Hoffman's punishment was imprisonment.

In a series of conversations, smuggled missives, and other communications from prison, Hoffman first announced the Parousia, then said it would be delayed; he asked for more severe conditions for himself, then asked for their alleviation; and so on. In 1539, when Johannes Eisenburg and Peter Tasch, Melchiorites and members of the Strasbourg prophets, were negotiating a series of compromises that brought many of the Anabaptist brotherhood back into the evangelical church, Martin Bucer, Wolfgang Capito, and the other Strasbourg preachers attempted to get Hoffman to moderate his views. He did in fact yield on adult baptism, a step he had already taken when he stopped baptizing in 1531, and on the idea of unforgivable sin, but that was all.

Weary of Hoffman's protestations and obstinacy, the town council made his conditions more harsh. Weakened by poor diet (partly of his own choosing), isolation, and unhealthy conditions, Hoffman died toward the end of 1543—the exact date is unknown.

Hoffman published some twenty-seven works including books, pamphlets, and letters. *Das XII Capitel des propheten Danielis aussgelegt* (The Twelfth Chapter of Daniel Explained; Stockholm, 1526) is the source of his famous prediction of the end of the world in 1533. His argument for lay preachers who speak from the inspiration of the Holy Spirit alongside the trained and educated official clergy—a group he severely criticized—appears here as well as his objection to the use of force to establish religious faith. The account of the Flensburg Disputation of 1529, *Dialogus vnd gründtliche berichtung gehaltner disputation im land zu Holstein* (Dialogue and Complete Report of a Disputation Held in the Land of Holstein; Strasbourg, 1529), is the best source for his views on the Eucharist. Here he criticizes the Lutheran view of the real presence, arguing that it leads to idolatry and requires an official priesthood, thereby eliminating a lay ministry.

A series of writings on eschatology, including commentaries on *Romans* and *Revelation*, the commentary on *Daniel* 12, and the works on the Strasbourg prophecies presented his view of history. Applying categories developed by the medieval Calabrian prophet Joachim of Fiore, Hoffman saw human history as proceeding in three stages: the Old Testament period, the New Testament period, and the new age breaking around Hoffman when the Spirit would be poured forth, the godless would be destroyed, and Christ's kingdom would be established in Strasbourg. The Holy Spirit would replace the letter of scripture, fulfilling scripture's true meaning, a meaning unrecognized by the school-trained preachers but known to the Spirit-led Hoffman.

Hoffman combined themes and impulses from late medieval mysticism and spiritualism, Joachimite apocalypticism, the Lutheran and Zwinglian reformations, and the Anabaptist movement. He moved from a quasi-Lutheranism into apocalyptic spiritualism and Anabaptism as he gradually discarded themes that contradicted his main ideas. The Melchiorite movement soon faded away, the revolutionary part of it destroyed at Münster, the rest joining the

Mennonite movement. By his life and thought, Hoffman, termed by some the most influential lay preacher of the sixteenth century, represented the intertwining of medieval lay mysticism, apocalypticism, and sixteenth-century reformist ideas.

BIBLIOGRAPHY

Primary Source

Williams, George H., ed. *Spiritual and Anabaptist Writers: Documents Illustrative of the Radical Reformation.* The Library of Christian Classics, vol. 25. Philadelphia, 1957. Translates Hoffman's *Die Ordonnantie Godts* along with other radical Reformation documents.

Secondary Sources

Beachy, Alvin J. "The Grace of God in Christ as Understood by Five Major Anabaptist Writers." *Mennonite Quarterly Review* 37 (1963), 5–33, 52. Hoffman is one of the representatives in this brief study.

Cohn, Norman. *The Pursuit of the Millennium: Revolutionary Messianism in Medieval and Reformation Europe and Its Bearing on Modern Totalitarian Movements.* 3d ed. London, 1970. The standard work on the history of apocalyptic and chiliastic movements.

Deppermann, Klaus. *Melchior Hoffman: Social Unrest and Apocalyptic Visions in the Age of Reformation.* Edinburgh, 1987. The best work on Hoffman; social setting as well as biography and thought.

Kawerau, Peter. *Melchior Hoffman als religiöser Denker.* Haarlem, Netherlands, 1954. The best study of Hoffman's ideas.

Klaassen, Walter, ed. *Anabaptism in Outline: Selected Primary Sources.* Classics of the Radical Reformation, no. 3. Kitchener, Ont., and Scottdale, Pa., 1981. A collection of translations that includes several valuable selections from Hoffman.

Krahn, Cornelius. *Dutch Anabaptism: Origin, Life, and Thought, 1450–1600.* 2d ed. Scottdale, Pa., 1981. The best history of Dutch Anabaptism in English; a chapter on Hoffman.

Noll, Mark. "Luther Defends Melchior Hoffman." *Sixteenth Century Journal* 4.2 (1973), 47–60. A brief study that examines Luther's defense of Hoffman after Luther's early warnings about him.

ROLLIN S. ARMOUR, SR.

HOFMEISTER, Sebastian (Lat., Oeconomus; 1476–1532), Swiss reformer and coworker of the Zurich reformer Huldrych Zwingli.

HOFMEISTER, Sebastian (Lat., Oeconomus; 1476–1532), Swiss reformer and coworker of the Zurich reformer Huldrych Zwingli. A native of Schaffhausen, Hofmeister was a Franciscan trained in classical and biblical languages at Paris, receiving a doctorate of holy scripture in 1520. While teaching at the Franciscan convent in Zurich, he began his friendship with Zwingli. After a short stay in Constance, he moved to Lucerne, where he began preaching Reformed doctrine. Forced to leave by Hugo von Hohenlandenberg, bishop of Constance, he established himself in Schaffhausen, where he enjoyed considerable popular acclaim preaching in various churches, eventually settling at Saint John's, the city parish church. Although the Great Council supported Hofmeister, the Small Council and the guardian of the Franciscans opposed him. The influential Catholic spokesman Erasmus Ritter, brought from Bavaria to oppose Hofmeister, soon became his supporter. During this time Hofmeister was close to Balthasar Hubmaier, the reformer of Waldshut and a later Anabaptist leader.

Strong support notwithstanding, Hofmeister was required in 1525 by the opposition in Schaffhausen to obtain a statement of approval from the University of Basel for his reform activity. During his absence he was banished from the city. He returned to Zurich, where he accepted a position at the Fraumünster. After accompanying Zwingli to the Bern Disputation in 1528, Hofmeister stayed on as teacher of Hebrew and catechetics at the newly formed theological school. The Bern government sent Hofmeister to Zofingen on 6 May 1528 to serve as pastor and to establish Reformed work there. He was eminently successful. Hofmeister is best known for being a highly learned and capable participant in numerous disputations: the First Zurich Disputation, January 1523; as a president at the Second Zurich Disputation, October 1523; the Zurich Anabaptist Disputation of November 1525; the conversations in Ilanz, January 1526; the Bern Disputation, January 1528; and the Zofingen Colloquy with the Anabaptists, July 1532.

BIBLIOGRAPHY

Primary Sources

Hofmeister, Sebastian. "Ein treüwe ermanung an die Strengen, Edlen, Festen, Frommen und weißen Eidgnossen, das sy nit durch ire falschen propheten verfürt, sich wider die lere Christi setzend" (Basel, 1523). In *Flugschriften des Frühen 16. Jahrhunderts,* edited by H. J. Köhler, H. Hebenstreit, and Chr. Weismann, no. 858, fiche no. 296 and no. 1591, fiche no. 616. Zug, Switzerland, 1979 and 1981. Defense of the Swiss Reformation published by Adam Petri one month after the First Zurich Disputation of January, 1523.

———. "Antwurt uff die Ableinung doctor Eckens von Ingoldstatt, gethan uff die Widergeschrifft Huldrychs Zuinglis, uff sin Missiuen an ein lobliche Eydgnoschafft." In *Flugschriften des Frühen 16. Jahrhunderts,* edited by H. J. Köhler, H. Hebenstreit, and Chr. Weismann, no. 406, fiche no. 147. Zug, Switzerland, 1981. Defense of Zwingli against John Eck thought to have been published at the end of 1524.

———. "Acta und handlung des Gesprächs, so von allen Priesteren der Tryen Pündten im 1526: jar, uff Mentag und Zynstag nach der heyligen III. Künigen tag zuo Inlantz im Grawen Pundt ufs Ansehung der Pundtsherren geschehen" (Zurich, 1526). In *Flugschriften des Frühen 16. Jahrhunderts,* edited by H. J. Köhler, H. Hebenstreit, and Chr. Weismann, no. 1842, fiche no. 725. Zug, Switzerland, 1981. Account of the conversations in the Swiss village of Ilanz on 12–13 January 1526 between Reformed and Catholic theologians.

Secondary Sources

Schumann, A. "Hofmeister, Sebastian." In *Allgemeine Deutsche Biographie,* vol. 12, pp. 643–644. A reliable introduction to Hofmeister.

Verzeichnis der im deutschen Sprachbereich erschienenen Drucke des XVI. Jahrhunderts. Stuttgart, 1983–. See vol. 9, nos. 4305–4308.

H. WAYNE PIPKIN

HOLBEIN, Hans the Younger (1497/98–1543), painter active at the court of Henry VIII. The career of Holbein paralleled the crucial events of the Reformation. He lived to see iconoclasts destroy his father's altarpiece for Saint Moritzkirche in Augsburg. Among the juvenilia of Hans the Younger were marginalia in a copy of the most influential attack on corruption in the church, Erasmus's *Morie Encomium* (In Praise of Folly). These apt drawings in the copy of the 1515 edition belonging to the humanist scholar Oswald Myconius delighted Erasmus himself and led to Holbein's first border designs for a conventional book of piety, designed by the scholar for Pope Leo X.

Holbein's first formal commissions for paintings, in Lucerne and then in Basel, were within the mainstream of late medieval religion: a diptych of the *Man of Sorrows* and *Mater Dolorosa*; *Adorations of Shepherd and Magi* for the Carthusians at Klein Basel; the *Corpus Christi*; the *Soluthurn Madonna.* His *Last Supper*, quoting Leonardo, and his *Noli me Tangere* were probably painted after his visit to the French court at Lyon in 1524 with his patron Jacob Meyer. Holbein's last altarpiece was a *Mater Misericordia* for Meyer's castle chapel at Gross Gundeldingen.

Holbein's first portraits of Erasmus probably went to Archbishop William Warham of Canterbury, one of Erasmus's best patrons, and to Thomas More, Erasmus's old friend. In 1526 Holbein followed them to England. Armed with Erasmus's famous letter speaking of the arts freezing in Basel, Holbein entered the eminent circle of More. His masterpiece, the *More Family* group, is known only from the first sketch, from drawings of the heads, and from later sixteenth-century copies. Holbein also painted Warham, who like Erasmus and More was withdrawing as the Reformation gained impetus. These crowded months also gave Holbein his first introduction to the royal circle, with work for Greenwich Palace and portraits of intimates of Henry VIII.

He returned to Basel in 1528 in order not to forfeit citizenship and to establish in greater comfort his wife and growing family, of whom his tragic portrait describes the private griefs attendant upon fissures of the church. A pair of his prints, *Christ, Light of the World* and *The Sale of Indulgences,* with its bitter contrast between true personal repentance and scandalous traffic in indulgences, had lost him his original Catholic clientele. One small roundel of the aging Erasmus depicts the great scholar dismayed at the forces he had unleashed.

In 1532 Holbein returned to England, where his earlier patrons were in decline. He apparently attached himself to Ann Boleyn's supporters, among them John Godsalve and the rising Thomas Cromwell. Through their offices he gained the opportunity to paint Jean de Dinteville and Georges de Selve (*The Ambassadors*), briefly together in London at the behest of Francis I in April 1533 to discuss the divorce crisis. The elaborate "*memento mori*" planted in this picture could refer to Holbein's original patron, now living in cautious retirement. The gap between that landmark and the first payments to Holbein as king's painter in 1536 may only represent lacunae in the royal accounts. His title page for Miles Coverdale's Bible of 1535 casts Henry VIII in the role of the giver of the Word to the priesthood. There followed the Whitehall icon of the dynasty of Henry VIII, and after the death of Jane Seymour in 1537, commissions to paint prospective royal brides, each representing a variant in Henry VIII's Catholic or Protestant stance.

Holbein left searching likenesses of all the leading protagonists of the English Reformation. In his title page for Cranmer's Bible of 1539 the king distributing the *Verbum Dei* to priests and people almost ousts the Godhead altogether.

BIBLIOGRAPHY

Rowlands, John. *Holbein: The Paintings of Hans Holbein the Younger.* Oxford, 1985. Standard monograph.

Starkey, David, ed. *Henry VIII: A European Court in England.* Greenwich, 1991. Important examination of the artistic patronage extended by Henry VIII.

PAMELA TUDOR-CRAIG

HOLIDAYS. *See* Festivals; Liturgical Calendar.

HOLY COMMUNION. *See* Eucharist.

HOLY LEAGUE. *See* Catholic League.

HOLY ROMAN EMPIRE. At the beginning of the sixteenth century, the Holy Roman Empire of the German Nation (*Heiliges Römisches Reich deutscher Nation*) encompassed most of central Europe from the Baltic and North Seas and the Danish kingdom in the north to the Swiss Confederation and the Venetian republic in the south. On its western flank loomed the powerful French kingdom with which the empire was embroiled in ongoing border disputes and wars caused chiefly by Habsburg claims to the Burgundian inheritance at the end of the fifteenth century. To the east the empire faced the Polish and Hungarian kingdoms and the threat of the advancing Ottoman Turks, who would take Belgrade in 1521 and threaten Vienna in 1529.

Its roughly fifteen million inhabitants spoke a variety of languages and dialects, although various forms of German predominated. High German (*Hoch Deutsch*) was spoken primarily in the higher ground of central and southern "Germany." So-called Low German (*Platt Deutsch*) was favored in the lowlands of the northern part of the empire, where it was sometimes in competition with versions of Dutch, Flemish, Frisian, and Walloon. Along the western border, many spoke French. Italian was common in the south, and various Slavic and Polish dialects were spoken in eastern parts of the empire. Ethnic divisions usually followed along linguistic lines. Latin continued to be the major language of academicians, advanced students, lawyers, and theologians. Hebrew was spoken by the empire's Jewish population and a few Christian scholars, some of whom also knew Greek.

Despite the wide variety of spoken and written languages in the empire, the use of German in one form or another increased as written German became more standardized in the sixteenth century, partly as a result of the widespread printing of Reformation polemics written in New High German by Martin Luther and others and the widespread use of the similar German chancery language by the imperial government and its agents. Even with the rise of German in the sixteenth century, the advice of the Golden Bull of 1356 that the "sons" of electors should learn the "German, Italian, and Slavic tongues" remained sound.

At the start of the sixteenth century, almost all of the empire's people were nominally Roman Catholics. Some Czech-speaking Bohemians had a different understanding of the Eucharist as a result of the Hussite revolt of the fifteenth century, but for the most part almost everyone in the empire at least in principle looked to Rome for spiritual leadership. The major exception at the beginning of the century was a small number of Jews, estimated to be no more than 0.5 to 0.8 percent of the empire's population. Even a town like Vienna, with one of the largest Jewish communities in the empire, did not have more than about five hundred Jews in 1500. Although legally protected as "chamber serfs of the emperor" since the reign of Frederick II in the thirteenth century, Jews continued to be subjected to expulsions, forced conversions, and judicial murder until well into the middle of the sixteenth century. For example, Emperor Maximilian I gave the government of Nuremberg permission to expel all its Jews in 1498/99, although some of them moved only a few kilometers to nearby Fürth. His grandson, Emperor Charles V, permitted occasional persecutions of Jews during his reign despite the protestations of the imperially designated spokesman, Rabbi Josel of Rosheim, and his own humanist-influenced sympathies.

During the course of the sixteenth century, the Reformation movements ended forever the virtual monopoly of Roman Catholicism in the empire. By the end of the century, the religious complexion of the empire included large Lutheran and Reformed (Calvinist) communities as well as small pockets of Anabaptists and other Protestant sectarians. The Protestant movement had a special urban appeal as fifty of the sixty-five imperial cities in one way or another recognized the Reformation during the sixteenth century. A majority of the empire's two hundred towns with populations of at least one thousand became Protestant. Lutheranism became established in a number of principalities, including two, Brandenburg and Saxony, that were imperial electorates.

Roman Catholicism remained entrenched in large duchies such as Bavaria in the south, along most of the eastern border of the empire, and throughout the Austrian crown lands of the ruling emperors, all of whom were from the House of Habsburg in the sixteenth century. Almost all of the seventy ecclesiastical territories remained Catholic, but even among the ranks of the archbishoprics conversions to Protestantism could occur, as was the case for two successive archbishops of Cologne in 1547 and 1583. At times in the second half of the century, the Catholic majority in the imperial college of electors seemed threatened. A version of the territorial principle of "who rules, determines religion" (*cuius regio, eius religio*) had become part of imperial law as a result of the Diet of Augsburg of 1555 and thus had made Lutheranism legal in the empire. Anabaptists were not legally recognized and were under imperial ban. The Reformed were also not covered by the agreement reached at Augsburg, but they were so deeply entrenched by the end of the century that they held one of the prestigious electorates, that of the Count Palatine of the Rhine who had his capital at Heidelberg. Lutherans held two electoral votes in Brandenburg and Saxony. The Holy Roman Empire had long been a federated, supranational, multiethnic state; the Reformation made it even more variegated.

Imperial Institutions. The Holy Roman Empire in the sixteenth century continued to be a patriarchal monarchy headed by an elected emperor. From 1273 Holy Roman emperors were formally elected by a powerful group of seven princes called electors (*Kurfürsten*). Throughout the sixteenth century, the archbishops of Mainz, Trier, and Cologne, the king of Bohemia, the count Palatine of the Rhine, the duke of electoral Saxony, and the margrave of Brandenburg served as electors. Because the emperors received their crowns through election rather than inheritance, rival candidates for the imperial dignity resorted to bribery even as they had to make concessions. These so-called election agreements (*Wahlkapitulation*) became part of imperial law and tradition. They guaranteed that the governance of the empire would not be solely in the hands of the Emperor, but would be shared among competing interest groups, with the electors being in a particularly advantageous position.

Only males were allowed to rule in the empire. There were no German counterparts to Mary Tudor and Elizabeth I in England or Catherine de Médicis in France. In the sixteenth century even the wives of the Holy Roman emperors were not as influential or as visible as some had been earlier in imperial history. For example, no sixteenth-century Holy Roman empress was as powerful as Adelheide of Burgundy (wife of Otto I) or Theophano (wife of Otto II) had been in the tenth century. The Habsburg sovereigns of the sixteenth century did not share much power with their wives, though Margaret of Austria, aunt of Emperor Charles V, served as his regent in the Low Countries and did help negotiate the Treaty of Cambrai with France in 1529. Habsburg princesses were trusted as stand-ins for their male relatives. However, patriarchy prevailed at all levels throughout the empire, including the all-male imperial chancellery, privy council, and court system.

Although the emperors did have to share authority with some of their mighty subjects, they still had many privileges and responsibilities. In theory they derived their powers from God and served as his vicar on earth. Maximilian I took this notion so seriously that he at one time thought of becoming head of the Catholic church as well as emperor. While his successors did not knowingly covet the papal crown, they still had enormous influence in the religious sphere. The House of Habsburg was considered a bulwark of Roman Catholicism. Hence the near conversion of Maximilian II, the heir-presumptive to the throne, to Lutheranism in 1562 set off a major crisis.

Well into the sixteenth century, Holy Roman emperors were still hailed by some propagandists as "the last descendants of Aeneas." The German humanist Conradus Celtis (1459–1508) was among those who attempted to connect the living Emperor Maximilian I with the glories of ancient Rome. Emperors throughout the sixteenth century continued to style themselves as "Caesar" and "Augustus." They also attempted to partake of the glory of their more illustrious medieval "ancestors," such as Charlemagne, Otto I, and Frederick Barbarossa. This reflected glory was not always sufficient to keep some of the emperor's subjects from treating the living embodiment of Caesar with scorn and derision, as in 1474 when some burghers of Augsburg threw dung at Emperor Maximilian II when he could not pay his bills, or when doubts about Emperor Rudolf II's sanity echoed through the streets of Prague at the end of the sixteenth century.

Despite the efforts of the late fifteenth-century imperial reform movement to reduce the power of the emperor and shift more authority to the princes, Holy Roman emperors retained the responsibility for defending the empire from its foes—foreign and domestic. They were responsible for maintaining peace as well as presiding over the imperial diet (*Reichstag*), where issued were discussed and imperial edicts were promulgated. Although emperors from the time of Charles V's election in 1519 had to receive permission of the imperial electors to bring foreign troops into the empire or to declare war, the imperial position was still considered to be one of the most prestigious crowns in Europe. Only Holy Roman emperors were allowed to hunt with a golden eagle or to lay claim to the "legacy of the Romans."

However powerful some of the imperial majesties claimed to be, governance always had to be shared. The Imperial Council of Regency, or Governing Council (*Reichsregiment*), created at the Diet of Augsburg in 1500, consisted of twenty prominent princes presided over by the emperor or one of his appointed deputies. It was initially to consist of the seven imperial electors and thirteen others appointed by the German princes. But when the princes refused to pay for the operation of the *Reichsregiment* or give it a means to enforce its decisions, it was doomed to failure. Emperor Maximilian I also hastened the council's demise by announcing (in much the manner of a territorial prince) that he would not accept any of its decisions in his own territories. When revived in 1521 by the Diet of Worms, the *Reichsregiment* was a body dominated by the princes, not the emperor. While it put forward sensible schemes to give the empire a more professional bureaucracy and military, it soon became crippled by religious and dynastic rivalries among its member princes, not to mention its system of rational representation. By 1531 the *Reichsregiment* was defunct, a clear victim of the Reformation and the conflicting ambitions of princes and emperor.

The system of imperial circles (*Reichskreise*) was also established as a result of imperial reforms at the beginning of the sixteenth century. The circles were regional alliances for the purposes of helping the emperor maintain internal peace and external defense. Each circle had a captain and a council of delegates. By 1512 there were ten circles: the Austrian, Burgundian, Electoral Rhenish, Franconian, Bavarian, Swabian, Upper Rhenish, Lower Rhenish-Westphalian, Upper Saxon, and Lower Saxon. Bohemia, Moravia, and Silesia were not part of any imperial circle, but still parts of the empire. The circles became useful agencies for collecting taxes, the recruitment of troops, and the nomination of judges to the imperial court (*Reichskammergericht*). During the early decades of the Reformation, the Habsburgs attempted to use the *Reichskammergericht* as a tool to suppress the growing Protestant movement, albeit without success.

Reformation and Reich. The Protestant movement begun in the empire by the Saxon Martin Luther and his supporters was able to survive largely because of the structure of the Holy Roman Empire. Even though Luther himself was outlawed by the Diet of Worms in 1521, Emperor Charles V was unable to enforce the edict against him, his followers, or even his writings. Luther was protected by a series of Saxon electoral princes beginning with Frederick III, "the Wise" (1463–1525). Given Frederick's constitutional position within the empire, Charles V and his brother, Archduke Ferdinand, were unable to move imperial troops into Electoral Saxony to arrest Luther and his followers. Efforts by Ferdinand at three successive imperial diets at Nuremberg between 1522 and 1524 to enforce the Edict of Worms also met with failure.

Not only were committed Roman Catholic princes in the empire unwilling to move against one of their own whose territorial sovereignty was protected by law and tradition, but the situation was further complicated by the Habsburg need for imperial subsidies for their wars with France and the Ottoman Empire. Indeed throughout the imperial diets of the 1520s and early 1530s, the issue of aid for the war against the Ottomans always took precedence over the need to take action against the evangelicals. Complicating matters were the demands placed on Charles V's energies by his role as head of the vast Spanish empire. Not until 1546, when he had achieved peace with France (Treaty of Crépy), an armistice with the Ottomans, and an agreement with the papacy, was the emperor able to wage war in the empire against the Protestants. By then, however, the movement had become too deeply entrenched to eradicate, even though Charles's forces won all the skirmishes of the Schmalkald War (1546–1547).

Charles V soon discovered that even though a majority of the estates at the Diet of Augsburg of 1547/48 had accepted an interim religious policy until the Council of Trent had completed its work, they had no intention of allowing the emperor to pursue his centralizing goals and interfere with their territorial privileges. By 1552 the opposition against Charles led to a revolt of princes. While their number was small, their defiance—and alliance with Henry II of France—marked the breakdown of Charles's political and religious agenda. Charles was forced to allow his brother, Ferdinand, a free hand in the Peace of Augsburg in 1555, which annulled the Edict of Worms of 1521 against Luther and allowed Lutherans freedom of worship under a version of the "he who rules, his religion" formula articulated in the recess of the 1524 Diet of Nuremberg and restated at the recess of the imperial Diet of Speyer of 1526.

Charles V formally abdicated his title as Holy Roman Emperor in September 1556, but that abdication was not ratified until February 1558. Ferdinand was crowned Holy Roman emperor at Frankfurt am Main on 24 March 1558 and tried to settle the religious divisions in the empire by peaceful means. Since the 1520s Ferdinand had reinvented himself as a German rather than a Spanish prince. He arranged meetings between Protestants and Catholics at the Diet of Regensburg of 1556/57 and put pressure on the pope to permit clerical marriage and Communion in both kinds, while also supporting the efforts of the Jesuits to spark a Catholic revival. Although Ferdinand I had some hopes that Protestants and Catholics might be reconciled, he refused to allow his son, Maximilian, to become a Lutheran in 1562.

As emperor, Maximilian II (r. 1564–1576) favored a policy of religious toleration while remaining nominally a Roman Catholic. He challenged Spain's oppressive policies against Protestants in the Low Countries with no success. His cousin, King Philip II of Spain, who was recognized as head of the House of Habsburg, refused to accept his efforts at mediation. Maximilian's position as emperor was further undermined by the failure of his war against the Ottomans (1566–1568), to whom he ended up paying a humiliating tribute. Although well intentioned, Emperor Maximilian II had insufficient power to establish a policy of religious toleration that would include the growing Calvinist movement in the empire, a movement that had not been recognized by the Peace of Augsburg in 1555.

Maximilian II was succeeded by his oldest son, Rudolf, in 1576. As Holy Roman Emperor, Rudolf II hoped to produce a synthesis of the best features of Catholicism and Protestantism, which would lead to religious peace throughout the empire. Unfortunately, the irenic notion ran against the prevailing current of confessionalism, which viewed alternate religious practices and understandings with deep suspicion. He only added to his problems by his, at times, reclusive demeanor, obsession with astrology and erotica, and increasing bouts of mental illness. As the sixteenth century ended, it seemed that the Holy Roman Empire was well on its way to yet another round of religious and political crises that threatened to overshadow even the upheavals of the tumultuous sixteenth century. A number of forces, notably, of course, the Reformation, had strengthened German particularism and weakened both the central authority of the emperor and the cohesiveness of the Holy Roman Empire. No emperor was ever again to play the role of Charles V: centrifugal forces propelled the likes of Brandenburg-Prussia, Saxony, Bavaria, and Austria into the limelight. Their histories shaped the history of early modern Germany. When, finally in the early nineteenth century, a victorious Napoleon abolished the Holy Roman Empire of the German Nation, few noticed its passing.

[*See also* Augsburg, Peace of; *and* Diet.]

BIBLIOGRAPHY

Angermeier, Heinz. *Die Reichsreform, 1410–1555*. Munich, 1984. An indispensable study of the imperial reform movement.

Aulinger, Rosemarie. *Das Bild des Reichstages im 16. Jahrhundert*. Göttingen, 1980. An imaginative study of imperial diets based on visual as well as literary sources.

Brady, Thomas A., Jr. *Turning Swiss: Cities and Empire, 1450–1550*. Cambridge, 1985. A masterful examination of the relations between the south German cities and the Empire.

———. *Protestant Politics: Jacob Sturm, 1489–1553, and the German Reformation*. Atlantic Highlands, N.J., 1995. Uses the career of a leading Strasbourg politician to shed new light on the interaction between politics and religion.

Brandi, Karl. *The Emperor Charles V: The Growth and Destiny of a Man and a World Empire*. Translated by C. V. Wedgwood. Reprint, London, 1980. Although dated, it remains the best study of the emperor as he was involved with German affairs.

Evans, R. J. W. *Rudolf II and His World: A Study in Intellectual History, 1576–1612*. Reprint, Oxford, 1994. A classic study of a fascinating emperor and his intellectual milieu.

Fichtner, Paula Sutter. *Ferdinand I of Austria*. New York, 1982. The leading study in English of Ferdinand.

Headley, John. *The Emperor and His Chancellor: A Study of the Imperial Chancellery under Gattinara*. New York, 1983. A superb account of the workings of government under Charles V's chancellor.

Holborn, Hajo. *A History of Modern Germany: The Reformation*. New York, 1970. Still a valuable survey with a wealth of information.

Hughes, Michael. *Early Modern Germany, 1477–1806*. Philadelphia, 1992. A well-done and concise synthesis of recent research.

Köhler, Alfred. *Das Reich im Kampf um die Hegemonie in Europa, 1521–1648*. Munich, 1990. An important overview of the Empire's relations with its neighbors.

Neuhaus, Helmut. *Reichstag und Supplikationsausschuß: Ein Beitrag zur Reichsverfassungsgeschichte der ersten Hälfte des 16. Jahrhunderts*. Berlin, 1977. A major contribution to our understanding of the mechanics of imperial government.

Press, Volker. *Kaiser Karl V, König Ferdinand und die Entstehung der Reichsritterschaft.* 2d ed. Wiesbaden, 1980. A sophisticated look at the relations between the Habsburgs and the imperial knights.

———. "The Habsburg Lands: The Holy Roman Empire." In *Handbook of European History, 1400–1600: Late Middle Ages, Renaissance and Reformation,* edited by Thomas A. Brady, Jr., Heiko A. Oberman, and James Tracy, pp. 437–466. Leiden, 1994. A brilliant summary.

Rabe, Horst. *Reich und Glaubensspaltung: Deutschland, 1500–1600.* Munich, 1989. The most important survey to date of the empire in the sixteenth century.

Tanner, Marie. *The Last Descendant of Aeneas: The Hapsburgs and the Mythic Image of the Emperor.* New Haven, 1993. Examines imperial symbols and myths.

Wiesflecker, Hermann. *Kaiser Maximilian I: Das Reich, Östterreich und Europa an der Wende zur Neuzeit.* 5 vols. Vienna, 1971–1986. A monumental study of the emperor and his world.

Zophy, Jonathan. *An Annotated Bibliography of the Holy Roman Empire.* Westport, Conn., 1986.

———. *Patriarchal Politics and Christoph Kress, 1484–1535, of Nuremberg.* Lewiston, N.Y., 1992. Examines imperial politics from the perspective of an urban diplomat.

Zophy, Jonathan, ed. *The Holy Roman Empire: A Dictionary Handbook.* Westport, Conn., 1980. Short essays with concise bibliographies on all phases of imperial history.

JONATHAN W. ZOPHY

HOMBERG, SYNOD OF. In October 1526 at the Synod of Homberg, Landgrave Philipp of Hesse began the organization of one of the first Protestant territorial churches. This combined church synod and meeting of the Hessian estates included a religious disputation, discussion of the character of the new Hessian church, and the creation of a church ordinance for Hesse.

Philipp (through his chancellor Johann Feige) began the synod by arguing that the Diet of Speyer left the organization of the church to the princes and estates, at least until the convening of a general council. The meeting continued with a disputation. The Protestants were led by a former Franciscan, François Lambert, the Catholics by Nicolaus Ferber, guardian of the Franciscan house in Marburg. As with most disputations, the outcome at Homberg was predetermined. Lambert was given the first and last word, and Ferber left hurriedly for Cologne.

More important for Protestant theology and the Reformation was the *Homberger Kirchenordnung* (church ordinance) produced at the synod. Written essentially by Lambert, the ordinance is not remarkable for its theological positions, which followed closely those of Luther. What is surprising, especially given the active role of Philipp in the synod, were the ecclesio-political structures Lambert sought to create. The ordinance proposed a communally organized church (with local control of clerical appointments and church discipline), a division of the Christian community into two groups (the mass of nominal Christians and the elite group of "True Christians"), and the establishment of a large number of educational institutions. This notion reflects not only Lambert's particular ideas but also the continued importance of the "communal church" at this stage of the Reformation. It is also similar to legislation Martin Bucer advanced in Strasbourg in the 1540s. Above all, the ordinance showed the confidence of many evangelical leaders that "true Christian" communities could be quickly created, if only the true word of God were correctly taught and preached.

Philipp's personal opinion of the church ordinance is not known, but he was clearly skeptical enough to submit it to Luther for his recommendation. Luther responded negatively, criticizing the ordinance as overly idealistic, impractical, and perhaps dangerous, and argued strongly that it not be published. Luther recommended that Philipp first place qualified pastors and schoolteachers in the parishes, then begin to build his church. By killing the church ordinance, Luther and Philipp reinforced the traditional notion of having the church comprise all baptized persons (which was everyone) organized on a territorial basis, rather than focus on smaller conventicles of those who claimed a more serious commitment. Lambert's ordinance never went into effect in Hesse; his recommendation that Landgrave Philipp establish a university, however, led to the founding of the University of Marburg in 1527.

[*See also* Eucharist; Gnesio-Lutherans; *and* Lutheranism.]

BIBLIOGRAPHY

Friedrich, Julius. *Die Entstehung der Reformatio Ecclesiarum Hassiae von 1526: Eine Kirchenrechtliche Studie.* Giessen, 1905.

Mirbt, Carl. "Homberger Synode und Kirchenordnung von 1526." In *Realencyclopädie für protestantische Theologie und Kirche,* pp. 288–294. Leipzig, 1896–1913.

Müller, Gerhard. *Franz Lambert von Avignon und die Reformation in Hessen.* Marburg, 1958.

Wright, William J. "The Homberg Synod and Philip of Hesse's Plan for a New Church-State Settlement." *Sixteenth Century Journal* 4 (1973), 24–36.

MARC R. FORSTER

HOMILETICS. *See* Preaching and Sermons.

HOMMIUS, Festus (1576–1642), Dutch Calvinist minister and theologian; opponent of Jacobus Arminius and the Remonstrants. Born in the northern province of Friesland in the Netherlands, Hommius received his earliest theological training at the theological college in Franeker; in 1595 he moved briefly to France and then returned to Holland, where he studied with Franciscus Gomarus. He served as a Reformed minister in Dokkum (Friesland) for a short period before he was called in 1602 to the Reformed church at Leiden, where he then spent the remainder of his career. In Leiden Hommius became a vigorous critic of Arminius and the Remonstrant party, was in frequent conflict with his Remonstrant colleagues, and was one of the main spokesmen for the Contra-Remonstrant party prior to the Synod of Dordrecht (1618/19). Hommius distinguished himself as a strict Calvinist, a defender of a predestinarian theology, and a strong proponent of the right of the Reformed church to supervise its own ecclesiastical affairs, free from the influence of the civil magistrate.

In 1602 Hommius published an important Dutch translation of Zacharius Ursinus's commentary on the Heidelberg Catechism; it was a rather loose translation that frequently expressed Hommius's own theological opinions, and it became very popular in the Netherlands. In the early 1600s Hommius led the opposition to Arminius, first by opposing his appointment to the theological faculty of the University of Leiden and then by challenging Arminius's theological orthodoxy during his tenure at the university. Hommius frequently accused Arminius of heresy both from the pulpit and in writing; after Arminius's death Hommius continued the attack on Arminius's theological successors, the Remonstrants. Hommius believed that acceptance of the theological opinions contained in the Remonstrance of 1610 would separate the Dutch Reformed church from the international Reformed community, and he strongly opposed the efforts of the States of Holland to promote toleration of the Remonstrants in the Reformed church of the Netherlands. At the Hague Conference called by the States of Holland in 1611 Hommius led the opposition to the Remonstrants and was most likely the main author of the Contra-Remonstrance of 1611. In 1614 he produced a series of disputations that expressed his strong support for predestination. Hommius was also influential in swaying popular opinion against the Remonstrants through his preaching and his efforts as a pamphleteer.

In 1618, just before the Synod of Dordrecht began, Hommius published his influential *Specimen Controversiarum Belgicarum*. This work, which also appeared in a Dutch translation, drew freely on earlier Contra-Remonstrant writings and was designed to introduce the foreign delegates at the synod to the errors of the Remonstrants. Highly polemical in nature, the *Specimen* pointed out where the Remonstrants deviated from Calvinist orthodoxy, especially with regard to the teachings of the Belgic, or Netherlands, Confession.

Hommius played a leading role at the Synod of Dordrecht. He served as one of its official secretaries and also helped to write a general historical introduction for an abridged version of the acts of the Synod. He worked as one of the editors for the new translation of the Bible commissioned by the synod and was primarily responsible for the translation of the New Testament. Hommius also translated the Heidelberg Catechism into Greek for use in the Greek Orthodox church.

BIBLIOGRAPHY

Bangs, Carl. *Arminius: A Study in the Dutch Reformation.* 2d ed. Reprint, Grand Rapids, Mich., 1985. An excellent introduction to the theological controversy between Arminius and Gomarus, and Hommius's role in it.

Deursen, A. Th. van. *Bavianen en Slijkgeuzen: Kerk en Kerkvolk ten tijde van Maurits en Oldenbarnevelt.* Reprint, Franeker, 1991. Based on extensive archival research. The single best work on the development of Calvinism in the Netherlands and the significance of the Arminian controversy.

Nobbs, Douglas. *Theocracy and Toleration: A Study of Disputes in Dutch Calvinism from 1600 to 1650.* Cambridge, 1938. A detailed source of information but not readily available.

Tex, Jan den. *Oldenbarnevelt.* 2 vols. Translated by R. B. Powell. Cambridge, 1973. Excellent on the political context of the Arminian controversy.

Wijminga, P. J. *Festus Hommius.* Leiden, 1899. The only biography of Hommius.

MICHAEL A. HAKKENBERG

HONIUS, Cornelis. *See* Hoen, Cornelis Henricxzoen.

HONTER, Johannes (1498–1549), humanist, printer, city pastor, and evangelical reformer in Transylvania. He was born in Braşov (Kronstadt, Romania) and studied at the University of Vienna, where he probably received the degree master of arts. In 1529 he visited the humanist Johannes Aventinus in Regensburg and described himself as living in exile. From there he traveled to Kraków, where, in 1530, he taught briefly at the Knights' Academy and issued his first two humanist works, a Latin grammar and a textbook of astronomy and geography. Subsequently he traveled to Nuremberg, Augsburg, and Basel, where he learned the printing and wood-cutting trade. He also furthered his education as a humanist and was influenced by the theology of Johannes Oecolampadius. While in Basel (1532) he produced an astronomical map and the first map of Transylvania (*Chorographia Transylvaniae/Sybembürgen*).

Returning to his homeland in 1533, Honter quickly established himself as an influential citizen, becoming a member of the Council of One Hundred and then of the Inner Council. In the 1540s he became one of the leading advocates of ecclesiastical reform in Braşov and Transylvania. Supported by the council and assisted by Valentin Wagner, Matthias Glats, Johannes Fuchs (also a member of the council), and Jeremias Jekel (the city pastor), Honter directed his energies toward the reform of the educational and ecclesiastical system in the city. In 1543 his *Constitutio Scholae Coronensis*, a guide to educational reform, was approved by the council. He supervised the construction of a new school building, which was completed in 1544. The first evangelical service was held in Braşov in October 1542, and by the end of the year the members of the council and the local clerics carried out a visitation of the churches in the region. Honter's *Formula reformationis ecclesiae Coronensis ac Barcensis provinciae* (1543), in the preparation of which he was probably assisted by Wagner, abolished the Mass and other liturgical practices and replaced them with an evangelical service that included Communion in both kinds, Matins, and Vespers. He also prepared, in 1543, an *Apologia* in connection with the diet held at Alba Iulia (Weissenburg). However, a controversy that broke out in late 1543–early 1544 between Jekel, the three city clerics, and the municipal council led to the resignation of the clerics. Jekel seems to have begun to oppose the strong hand of the laity on the council in church affairs. On 22 April 1544, despite lack of theological preparation, Honter assumed the position of city pastor. During the next three years, he strengthened the allegiance of Sibiu to the Reformation and participated, together with Wagner and Glatz, in preparing a new church order for the Transylvanian Germans that would be approved at a synod in Sibiu in 1547 (*Reformatio Ecclesiarum Saxonicarum in Transylvania*). He also published a German translation of the church order (*Kirchenordnung aller Deutschen in Sybembürgen*) and an agenda (*Agenda für die Seelsorger und Kirchendiener in Sybembürgen*). In 1544 he prepared a compendium of civil law (*Compendium iuris civilis*), which defined the unique status of the Germans in Transylvania. He advanced the cause of the reform by means of the printing press that he had established by 1539; by the time of his death on 23 January 1549, he had been able to issue at least twenty-six such works.

Honter is a classic example of the evangelical humanist and magisterial reformer. Although not trained as a theologian, he marshaled political power, implemented structural changes, and cooperated with those more trained in theology to bring about and establish the German Reformation in Braşov.

BIBLIOGRAPHY

Primary Sources

Honter, Johannes. *Approbatio Reformationis Ecclesiae Coronensis ac totius Barcensis Provinciae a Clariss. D. Martino Luthero, Philippo Melathone et Joanne Pomerano Viteberga Cibiniensi Pastori, suae Ecclesiae reformationem petenti transmissa, ex autographo sive originali descripta.* Braşov, 1543.

———. *Reformatio ecclesiae Coronensis ac totius Barcensis povinciae* (1543). Reprint, Vienna, 1865.

———. *Compendivm Ivris Civilis in vsvm Ciuitatum ac Sedium Saxonicarum in Transsylvania collectum.* Braşov, 1544.

Netoliczka, Oskar, ed. *Johannes Honterus' Ausgewählte Schriften.* Vienna, 1898.

Secondary Sources

Bautz, Friedrich Wilhelm, ed. *Biographisch-Bibliographisches Kirchenlexikon.* Herzberg, 1990.

Binder, Ludwig. "Johannes Honterus und die Reformation im Süden Siebenbürgens mit besonderer Berücksichtigung der Schweizer und Wittenberger Einflüsse." *Zwingliana* 13 (1972), 645–687.

Klein, Karl Kurt. *Der Humanist und Reformator Johannes Honter: Untersuchungen zur siebenbürgischen Geistes- und Reformationsgeschichte.* Munich, 1935.

Myss, Walter, ed. *Lexikon der Siebenbürgischen Sachsen.* Thaur, 1993.

Reinerth, Karl. *Die Reformation der siebenbürgish-sächsischen Kirche.* Gütersloh, 1956.

Wittstock, Oskar. *Johannes Honterus, der Siebenbürger Humanist und Reformator.* Göttingen, 1970.

DAVID P. DANIEL

HOOFT, Cornelis Pieterszoon (1547–1626), Amsterdam burgomaster. He was a shipper and trader in herring, oils, and grain during the years of Amsterdam's transition from a Roman Catholic to a Protestant regime. He was self-taught, a forerunner of the movement to make the Dutch language a vehicle of literary stature. As one of the new merchant class that was becoming restive under the fiscal and religious policies of the traditional oligarchy, he participated in the revolt of the "Old Beggars" (as the initiators of Amsterdam's civil and religious change were known) against Amsterdam's Roman Catholic regime in 1566. The revolt failed at the time, and Hooft was among those forced to flee the city, suffering exile from 1569 to 1574.

From the uprising of the Sea Beggars in 1572 to the Pacification of Ghent in 1576, Amsterdam as a Roman Catholic city became increasingly isolated in the rising Protestant tide. The Protestant merchant-exiles filtered back into the city, and in May 1578 they effected the "Alteration," driving out the Roman Catholic clergy and religious, instituting a new city government, and opening the churches to Reformed worship. Hooft was among those who returned, and, although he held no office in the now Reformed church, he was soon a leader in the new city government. He was chosen as an alderman (*schepen*) in 1582, became a member of the city council (the *Vroedschap*) in 1584, and was selected by the council for ten terms as burgomaster between 1588 and 1610.

As a republican, he opposed those who wanted to make William of Orange a count or the House of Orange a monarchy. He later defended Johan van Oldenbarnevelt, the civil arm of Holland's government, in resistance to Prince Maurits van Nassau, the military leader, who aspired to such status and power.

In Amsterdam Hooft advocated religious toleration rather than dogmatic precision. He was a leader of the city authorities who supported the Amsterdam pastor Jacobus Arminius when Arminius was being attacked by the strict Calvinist clergy of the city. He also defended the rights of Amsterdam's Mennonites, among whom was his wife, Anna, daughter of the famed printer Jacob Blaeu, who, incidentally, attended the Reformed church when Arminius preached.

Hooft even sprang to the defense of a confused heretic, Goosen Michielszoon Vogelsangh, because of clergy who used the affair to try to drive from the church all who would not conform to their views. On that occasion, in 1597, he made one of several notable speeches in the council. He complained that the clergy, except for Arminius, were "foreigners" who did not understand Holland's virtues of prudence and peace but had seized control of the church and used it to interfere with the liberties of the citizens.

As the city government came under the control of supporters of Prince Maurits and Calvinism, Hooft lost his place as burgomaster. When the city government was reconstituted in 1618, he was deemed to be too old to make further trouble and was retained on the council. He lived long enough, however, to see a new generation of Arminians come into power in Amsterdam.

Hooft has been described as a "humanist libertine," more a follower of Erasmus than of Calvin. Among his children was Pieter Corneliszoon Hooft, one of the Muiden Circle pioneers of Dutch letters.

BIBLIOGRAPHY

Bangs, Carl. *Arminius: A Study in the Dutch Reformation.* Reprint, with corrections and addenda. Grand Rapids, Mich., 1985.

Brandt, Gerard. *The History of the Reformation and Other Ecclesiastical Transactions in and about the Low Countries.* 4 vols. Reprint, New York, 1979.

Elias, Johan E. *De Vroedschap van Amsterdam, 1578–1795.* Reprint, Amsterdam, 1963.

Evenhuis, R. B. *Ook Dat Was Amsterdam.* Vols. 1 and 2. Amsterdam, 1956–1957.

CARL BANGS

HOOKER, Richard (1554–1600), theorist of and polemicist for the Elizabethan Settlement. Hooker's *Of the Lawes of Ecclesiastical Politie* (published between 1593 and 1662) became the major defense of the establishment of the English church which had been adumbrated by earlier apologists, such as John Jewel (Hooker's first patron) and Archbishop John Whitgift. In addition to producing an imposing monument to conformity, Hooker improved on most of his predecessors and contemporaries by grounding his work in first principles, especially the lawful nature of God and his universe. Although parts of the work (particularly book VIII on royal power) remained unpublished until long after Hooker's death, the first four books quickly became the cornerstone of an "Anglican" position even in the early seventeenth century; by the nineteenth century, *Of the Lawes of Ecclesiastical Politie* was regarded as almost the constitutional text of Anglicanism. Without spot or blemish, Hooker was read as having intended from the first to lay down timeless principles of church order. From the middle of the twentieth century that position attracted challenges intended to map various inconsistences or incoherences in Hooker's writing. Late in the century those attacks in turn attracted criticism, which led to a majority position defending the coherence of Hooker's eight books while arguing (in opposition to the Victorian view of Hooker's unshakable serenity) that his intent was strongly polemical.

Hooker had a modest career. Educated at Corpus Christi College, Oxford (B.A., 1574; M.A., 1577), he became a full fellow of the college in 1579. There he met John Spenser, his lifelong friend and literary executor. In 1581 he gave his first sermon at Paul's Cross in London, in which he defended a doctrine that would later be central to the *Lawes*: God wished all men to be saved, but only those who responded properly to the grace he offered them would actually gain heaven. Hooker avoided spelling out the full implications of this anti-Calvinist position until the end of his life, but his claim would become one of the main tenets of Arminianism.

In 1585 Hooker was appointed master of the Temple in London, the church for members of two of the Inns of Court. At about the same time, perhaps the most important polemical battle of his career broke out with the presbyterian Walter Travers. Hooker won that round with the assistance of Whitgift, but the experience could well have had a major impact on his more settled views. In 1588 Hooker married Joan Churchman, daughter of a wealthy merchant tailor; she brought Hooker a substantial dowry. Relieved of financial concerns, Hooker acquired a few other ecclesiastical preferments, but he seems to have been content to devote himself to his writing—which Whitgift may have deliberately fostered—and pastoral duties and did not seek higher office in the church.

In 1593 the first four books of *Lawes* were published in London by John Windet, Hooker's cousin. It may have been necessary for Hooker to trade on this family connection since he had difficulty persuading a publisher to issue his book. The reservations of those who refused it for its lack of commercial appeal would appear to be borne out by its slow sales, which earned Hooker only £30. He spent the last seven years of his life working on the final books of *Lawes*; Windet published book V in 1597 (his successor, William Stansby, frequently republished the first five books in the early seventeenth century). Hooker died at Bishopsbourne in 1600.

Books VI-VIII of *Lawes* have a complicated textual history. (Opinions also differ on the care with which Windet produced the first four books.) Some of Hooker's manuscripts were apparently destroyed at his death, but Spenser preserved the corpus of books VI-VIII, which still exists, although Hooker's autographs do not. Book VII was left nearly complete, but books VI and VIII (subsequently the most popular, existing in ten manuscripts) were not finished. James Ussher had books VI and VIII published in

1648 after various misfortunes had befallen some of his manuscripts. Despite these difficulties, P. G. Stanwood, a twentieth-century editor of these books, believes all three fit coherently with the first five and that Hooker intended all eight as a whole, composing them in strict sequence.

In addition to controversy over the coherence of the whole of *Lawes*, perhaps the sharpest words have been exchanged over Hooker's intended target. Yet Hooker made himself clear on both points, especially in the preface. He insisted (preface 7.7; cf. I.I.2) on the tight structure of his work and specifically identified his opponents as believers in Calvinist church polity, Familists (members of the Family of Love), and Anabaptists (and others inclined to follow private revelation). Elsewhere Hooker added Brownists (followers of the principles of Robert Brown) and all separatists to the list, but he was perhaps a little coy in refusing to name Catholics, with whom he constantly argued but with whom he wished to minimize his differences. To all of these Hooker professed his desire "to be joined with you in bands of indissoluble love and amity" (preface 9.3).

The best way to achieve that goal was to reduce as many controversies as possible to properly understood first principles. That meant, above all, positing a universe ruled by God and by a hierarchy of laws. (The precise form of this hierarchy is one of Hooker's most creative contributions.) Closely following an Aristotelian framework, Hooker argued that everything works "according to law" and that everything has an end, a first cause, to which it is directed. Discovering these causes depended on reason, even if human reason (or discourse, as Hooker also called it) could never know all that divine reason did. In short, "let no man doubt but that everything is well done, because the world is ruled by so good a guide, as trangresseth not his own law, than which nothing could be more absolute, perfect and just" (I.2.6). What held for God, held naturally for all other creatures. On the basis of this reverence for law, Hooker constructed both a civil and an ecclesiastical polity.

The major problem, as it would be for Thomas Hobbes, was how to resolve disputes before they destroyed the body politic. Although Hooker did not emphasize the coercive force of law—given his stress on reason, coercion initially became less important for Hooker than for his so-called positivist predecessors (e.g., Marsilio of Padua)—he did stress the guiding role of divine providence. Through its workings, humans, who started only with a soul "as a book, wherein nothing is" (a curiously non-Aristotelian view), could be led to virtue through "education and instruction." The most important thing to learn was how, through the conjunction of knowledge and will, to act in the face of things indifferent. But like nearly everything else in Hooker's cosmos, the will's freedom to choose among indifferents, which he stressed strongly, turned out to depend on collective action. Thus, "a law is properly that which reason . . . defineth to be good that it must be done. And the law of reason or human nature is that which men [collectively] by discourse of natural reason have rightly found out for themselves to be all forever bound unto in their actions" (I.8.8). It was the right of every community (but only of every community) to make whatever positive laws it pleased; once in existence, the members of that society had no choice but to obey such laws. As Hooker put it in book III, "[t]he safest and unto God the most acceptable way of framing our lives therefore is, with all humility, lowliness and singleness of heart, to study which way our willing obedience both unto God and man may be yielded even to the utmost of that which is due" (III.9.3). Drawing on Cicero and Roman law, as many of his humanist predecessors had done, Hooker described a transition to civil society that made the same point.

As a good Aristotelian, Hooker did not hold humans to any particular form of polity or laws, even if he did reject some then-popular theories, including patriarchalism. Hooker insisted, like Aristotle, that any good government had to rest on consent, but from the first Hooker's definition was so elastic as almost to empty the term of meaning. For example, he argued (I.10.8) that "the act of a public society of men done five hundred years since" still binds present members of the same society "because corporations are immortal," and in his discussion of Parliament he apparently deliberately avoided discussing how it "represented" the rest of the body politic. (In fact, he almost never used the term *represent*, in strong contrast to Sir Thomas Smith's allegedly normative description of the Elizabethan Parliament.) Similarly, although Hooker repeatedly said that kings depended on consent, he gave subjects no recourse against tyrants, explicitly leaving such questions unresolved. He cited the Roman law maxim "Quod principi placuit," one of the principal mainstays of absolutism, only for its reference to the *lex regia* by which the Roman people had allegedly transferred its power to the emperor (not the usual text used to support that point), a law that Hooker claimed was reversible (also not the majority position). But aside from ambiguities like this, Hooker's position was neatly summed up in the obligatory appeal to *Romans* 13.1–5 in book VIII.

Hooker may have been so determined that controversy be suppressed that he was willing to sacrifice central tenets of the English *regnum politicale* descended from at least Sir John Fortescue. Although Hooker conceded that Catholic apologists claimed too much for papal sovereignty, he nevertheless demanded a virtually total "chiefty" or "principality" of "ecclesiastical dominion" for the English monarch. As in the case of bishops, whom Hooker excoriated for failing to consult their clergy on major decisions, the prince also had to take advice, but there was no institutional guarantee that he would. Moreover, because Hooker explicitly charged his presbyterian opponents with pandering to the people, it is uncertain what he meant by consent, although it is clear whose consent mattered most. Hooker's convoluted dispute about who took more account of the people's wishes (VII.14.10) makes the same point.

Perhaps because he de-emphasized the coercive aspect of law, Hooker maintained that even the best law still needed authority, "a constraining power," to be exercised by humans holding office, especially by the bishops. Summing up his case, he turned to the mean, the necessary concomitant of his emphasis on indifferent things, and argued in favor of "prelacy, the temperature of excesses [i. e., the mean] in all estates, the glue and solder of the public weal, the ligament which tieth and connectecth the limbs of this body politic each to other" (VII. 18.12). Hooker defended not only the bishops' preeminence and honor but also their economic power (calling them in one chapter title "receivers of God's rents" and in another long chapter attacking secular expropriation of church property). He concluded "we must needs think it a thing necessary unto the common good of the church, that great jurisdiction being granted unto bishops over others, a state of wealth proportionable should likewise be provided for them," even if this was in part a concession to "this golden age" where money counted, a nice bit of polemical sarcasm (VII.24.18).

Such a combination of relatively broad views (like the stress on consent in the abstract) with specific applications, which tended toward compulsion (like the defense of prelacy), is typical of the work, as is the movement back and forth between institutional modes of power and much less clearly defined, almost mystical sanctions (as in the case of laws, which might rule, but only if they had humans to execute them). This movement arose because Hooker's principal frame of reference was the community, not the person in the singular, or institutions, whether identified in secular or ecclesiastical terms. Such labels did not matter, as the only difference between the two kinds of society was that a good Christian church had to have proper belief. If it did, both societies—the mystical body of the church and the body politic (the church was, after all, a political society in its outward form)—were indistinguishable. This led Hooker to reject predestination and the idea of a gathered (or otherwise invisible) church and to turn instead to a heavily sacramental piety that would keep believers (all members of the visible church) in the right way to salvation; in the same manner the external marks of honor paid to bishops and other governors were at least as important to the working of the state as any precise arguments about the extent or nature of its jurisdiction. Again, Hooker's most powerful point against his "Puritan" opponents was the claim that no human community, including the political society of the church, could be deprived of the right to legislate for itself (as it would be by those who argued that an immutable standard of church polity was contained in the New Testament). Here Hooker adapted the medieval doctrine of circumstances, first developed in confessional practice, to a more general question. (As he elsewhere showed, Hooker had thorough familiarity with canon law and Roman sacramental practice.) Even tradition, one of Hooker's most important anchors, was subject to the will and the reason of the community.

Hooker might, then, have readily echoed Sir Richard Morison's famous "an order, an order must be had" in rejoinder to the Pilgrims of Grace. Like Morison, Hooker wrote in the heat of the moment. That he meant his work to be, in part, topical emerges from frequent laments of the current state of affairs (e.g., VII.18.7). Unlike Morison, Hooker could yet take time to generalize his polemical points, but again like Morison and in common with most Aristotelians, Hooker's universe of reason was strictly hierarchical.

In addition to the substance of his argument, Hooker's work is important for how he made his case and how he wrote it up. Thoroughly versed in medieval philosophy and theology, Hooker yet had the humanist education provided by Corpus Christi, one of the first Oxford colleges to embrace that "New Learning" (humanism). While the medieval Schoolmen, along with Aristotle, provided some of Hooker's strongest points, he made them not in their preferred mode of the syllogism but rather in the enthymeme, a syllogism missing one premise, which was favored by humanists and others for whom rhetoric mattered. Similarly, Hooker wrote as one capable of deploying an almost overwhelming arsenal of rhetorical turns and could be very harsh in his judgments of opponents. But the power of Hooker's rhetoric, as well as its necessity to the polemical and philosophical flexibility of *Lawes*, comes out most clearly in his treatment of sovereignty and words for political communities, especially in book VIII, where it becomes virtually impossible to determine the precise nature of concepts that others, such as Jean Bodin, had been at great pains to spell out. In this, once more, Hooker was at one with his humanist predecessors, perhaps especially Thomas Starkey. Such was also the case in Hooker's very eclectic choice of sources, from more or less orthodox fathers like Cyprian (on whom he depended heavily) to Hermes Trismegistus, the invented patron saint of magicians (about whom Hooker seemed to know quite a lot).

BIBLIOGRAPHY

Allen, J. W. *A History of Political Thought in the Sixteenth Century*. London, 1928. One of the best short treatments, bringing out some of the greatest weaknesses in Hooker's argument.

Archer, Stanley. *Richard Hooker*. Boston, 1983. Brief introduction, especially useful for students. Tends to the hagiographic.

Collins, Stephen L. *From Divine Cosmos to Sovereign State: An Intellectual History of Consciousness and the Idea of Order in Renaissance England.* New York, 1989. Argues that Hooker was an innovator, not a conservative. Can be difficult to follow.

D'Entrèves, Alexander Passerin. *The Medieval Contribution to Political Thought: Thomas Aquinas, Marsilius of Padua, Richard Hooker.* Oxford, 1939. Overdoes Hooker's medievalism, but less eccentric than other Italian studies of English political ideas.
Eccleshall, Robert. *Order and Reason in Politics: Theories of Absolute and Limited Monarchy in Early Modern England.* Oxford, 1978. Follows Munz in locating Hooker between medieval and modern, but brings out the hierarchical dimension of Hooker's thought.
Faulkner, Robert K. *Richard Hooker and the Politics of a Christian England.* Berkeley, 1981. Hooker read against Aristotle.
Hill, W. Speed, ed. *Studies in Richard Hooker: Essays Preliminary to an Edition of His Works.* Cleveland, 1972. See W. D. J. Cargill Thompson, "The Philosopher of the Politic Society: Richard Hooker as a Political Thinker"; Georges Edelen, "Hooker's Style"; and Hill's "The Evolution of Hooker's *Laws of Ecclesiastical Policy.*"
Hill, W. Speed, gen. ed. *The Folger Library Edition of the Works of Richard Hooker.* 6 vols. Cambridge, Mass., 1977–1993. Now the standard text, replacing Keble. Index yet to be published.
Kirby, W. J. Torrance. *Richard Hooker's Doctrine of the Royal Supremacy.* Leiden, 1990. Argues that all of the *Lawes*, including Hooker's defense of the royal supremacy, were rooted in his Christology.
Lake, Peter. *Anglicans and Puritans? Presbyterianism and English Conformist Thought from Whitgift to Hooker.* London, 1988. Best treatment of Hooker's anti-Calvinism; very good on his immediate intellectual context.
McGrade, Arthur S. "The Coherence of Hooker's Polity: The Books on Power." *Journal of the History of Ideas* 24 (1963), 163–182.
Munz, Peter. *The Place of Hooker in the History of Thought.* Reprint, Westport, Conn., 1971. Good on Hooker's sources, but assesses his ideas by the extrinsic categories of "medieval" and "modern." Leading exponent of the lack of coherence in Hooker's work.
Walton, Izaak. *The Life of Mr. Richard Hooker.* In *The Works of that Learned and Judicious Divine Mr. Richard Hooker*, edited by John Keble. Oxford, 1836. For help in interpreting Walton's fundamental life, see William H. Epstein, *Recognizing Biography*, Philadelphia, 1987; and Richard Wendorf, *The Elements of Life: Biography and Portrait-Painting in Stuart and Georgian England*, Oxford, 1990.

THOMAS F. MAYER

HOON, Cornelis. *See* Hoen, Cornelis Henricxzoen.

HOOPER, John (d. 1555), English Protestant reformer, bishop, and martyr. Expelled from orders as a Cistercian monk at the time of the dissolution of the monasteries, Hooper fell under the influence of writings by Zwingli and other reformers. He went into exile when passage of the Act of Six Articles (1539) imposed harshly punitive measures to restore Catholic orthodoxy at the end of Henry VIII's reign. He developed extreme Protestant ideas resulting from close association with Heinrich Bullinger, Zwingli's successor at Zurich. Hooper's earliest theological books were published there for export to England when the accession of Edward VI (r. 1547–1553) allowed for a relaxation of restrictions upon Protestant publication. King Edward's reign marked the most radical phase of the English Reformation.

Following Hooper's return from exile in May 1549, he developed a reputation as a pugnacious proponent of radical ecclesiastical reform by preaching against clerical vestments and in favor of Zwingli's view of Holy Communion as a purely commemorative service. Appointed bishop of Gloucester in 1551 and to a second bishopric at Worcester in 1552, he tried to impose Zwinglian reforms against the opposition of the local clergy. By joining the attack against the theological conservatism of the first *Book of Common Prayer* (1549), he promoted revision of the second Edwardian prayer book (1552) along more distinctively Protestant lines.

After Edward VI's death Marian authorities condemned Hooper as a heretic. The account of his burning at the stake in February 1555 is one of the more memorable martyrologies in John Foxe's *Acts and Monuments of These Latter and Perilous Days* (*The Book of Martyrs;* 1563). That account and the radical reforms that Hooper advocated by personal example and through his writings all contributed to his reputation as a hero of the English Puritan movement.

BIBLIOGRAPHY

Primary Sources

Hooper, John. *Early Writings.* Edited by Samuel Carr. Parker Society, vol. 20. Reprint, New York, 1968.
———. *Later Writings.* Edited by Charles Nevison. Parker Society, vol. 21. Reprint, New York, 1968.

Secondary Source

Foxe, John. *Acts and Monuments.* Edited by S. R. Cattley, 4th rev. and corr. ed. by J. Pratt. London, 1877. Contains a stirring account of Hooper's execution.

JOHN N. KING

HOPPERUS, Joachim (also Jochem Hoppers; 1523–1576), Frisian jurist, lecturer at the University of Louvain, councillor in the Grand Council of Mechelen, member of the Secret Council at Brussels, and member of the Junta de Flandes. The son of Sjoerd Hoppers and Rixtje Piersma, he married Christine Bertollf, and they had eight children.

Born on 11 November 1523 in Sneek, Friesland, Hopperus studied at the University of Louvain, where he was promoted to doctor of both laws in 1553. He was a student of Gabriel Mudaeus, who introduced the philological-historical method to the study of law. Hopperus published a few juridical works and contributed the map of *Antiqua Frisia* (Roman Friesland) for the atlas of Abraham Ortelius (1570). On 10 February 1561, thanks to the support of his fellow countryman and protector Viglius Zuichemius van Aytta, Hopperus was appointed a member of the Secret Council, one of the three administrative councils in the Netherlands.

Hopperus's orthodoxy was suspect to a number of ultra-Catholic observers, because of his friendship (during a stay in France in the 1540s) with the Schwenckfeldian Aggaeus van Albada and with such known Protestants as François Hotman and Franciscus Balduinus. Moreover, he continued to sympathize with the Flemish irenicist Joris Cassander. Politically, Hopperus was mistrusted by some because of the contacts he maintained with the aristocratic opposition in 1564–1565. Nonetheless, he was called to Madrid as keeper of the seal for the Low Countries affairs, and from then until his death (Madrid, 15 December 1576) he sat on the Junta de Flandes, a commission that dealt with policy toward the Low Countries problems for the Consejo de Estado.

In all probability King Philip II of Spain removed Hopperus from the Netherlands because he thought he would do less harm in Madrid. In Spain Hopperus wrote a report on the beginning of the Revolt of the Netherlands, *Recueil et mémorial des troubles des Pays Bas du Roy,* which was given to Fernando Álvarez de Toledo, duke of Alba, at his departure for the Netherlands and appeared in print for the first time only in the eighteenth century. The document must be consulted with due caution but is not to be underestimated as a source for the political history of the Netherlands from the departure of Philip II to Spain until just before the Iconoclastic Fury (1559–1566). Information on Hopperus's activity in Spain is found primarily in his letters to Aytta and to Philip II, in the session reports of the Junta for the Netherlands, and in numerous reports and memoranda.

Initially, Hopperus supported the policy of Philip II and of the duke of Alba in the Netherlands, but from the middle of 1572, he began to express criticism both to Aytta and to the king about the actions of the duke of Alba, fearing that the ever increasing opposition to Alba's government would threaten the authority of the king himself. Hopperus turned strongly against William of Orange, opposing negotiations with the enemy, but argued for conciliatory measures (a "general pardon") for those who would submit to the king. He warned against hard military action and proposed the establishment of a full-fledged council for the Netherlands in Madrid, hoping to deflect the ever stronger demand in the Netherlands to convene the States-General, which Hopperus considered humiliating for the king. He was convinced that power had to remain not with the States-General, the rebels, or the foreign soldiers but with the king—a king who acted justly and compassionately.

It is difficult to determine Hopperus's influence on the policy of Philip II. Notes by the king in the margins of Hopperus's letters and recommendations demonstrate that Philip II read everything very attentively, but at the same time, it is certain that the king himself, as well as governors Alba and Luis de Requeséns, always mistrusted him. Hopperus belonged to the loyal middle group that did not question the legal authority during the revolt against Philip II but that opposed the growing royal absolutism because of a commitment to class representation and privileges.

BIBLIOGRAPHY

Primary Sources

Hopperus, Joachim. *Ad Iustinianum de obligationibus ΠΕΙΘΑΝΩΝ libri quinque.* Louvain, 1553.

———. *De iuris arte libri tres, eiusdem iuris pontificii et civilis liber singularis.* Louvain, 1553.

———. *Paraphrasis in Psalmos Davidicos . . . , cum libello De Usu et divisione Psalmorum, et indicibus,* Antwerp, 1590.

———. *Seduardus, sive de vera iurisprudentia, ad regem, libri 12.* Antwerp, 1590. Also contains *Ferdinandus sive de institutione principis.*

———. *Epistolae ad Viglium ab Aytta Zuichemum.* Edited by C. F. de Nélis. 2d ed. Haarlem, 1802. Edition of the letters of Hopperus to Viglius.

———. "Recueil et mémorial des troubles des Pays Bas du Roy." In *Mémoires de Viglius et d'Hopperus sur le commencement des troubles des Pays Bas,* edited by Alphonse Wauters, pp. 231–374. Collection de mémoires relatives à l'histoire de Belgique, vol. 2. Brussels, 1858. Reprint, Nendeln, Liechtenstein, 1977.

———. "Doctrina y officio del rey según el consejero Hoppero (J. Hopperus)." Edited by Gustaaf Janssens. *Lias* 9 (1982), 137–155. Edition with introduction of Hopperus's commentary on Psalm 119 applied to the duty of a just king.

Secondary Sources

Janssens, Gustaaf. "Joachim Hopperus, een Fries rechtsgeleerde in dienst van Filips II." In *Recht en instellingen in de Oude Nederlanden tijdens de Middeleeuwen en de Nieuwe Tijd: Liber amicorum Jan Buntix,* edited by G. Asaert, et al., pp. 419–433. Symbolae Facultatis Litterarum et Philosophiae Lovaniensis, ser. A, vol. 10. Louvain, 1981. Biographical essay on Hopperus.

———. "Barmhartig en rechtvaardig': Visies van L. de Villavicencio en J. Hopperus op de taak van de koning." In *État et religion aux 15e et 16e siècles: Actes du colloque à Bruxelles du 9 au 12 octobre 1984.* Edited by W. P. Blockmans and H. Van Nuffel, pp. 25–42. Brussels, 1986. Hopperus's view on the king's duty.

———. *"Brabant in het Verweer": Loyale oppositie tegen Spanje's bewind in de Nederlanden van Alva tot Farnese, 1556–1578.* Standen en Landen, vol. 89. Kortrijk, Belgium, 1989. On the loyal opposition in the Netherlands, with a large interest in the activities of J. Hopperus.

Postma, Folkert. "Viglius van Aytta en Joachim Hopperus tegen over de Nederlandse opstand." *Bijdragen en Mededelingen betreffende de Geschiedenis der Nederlanden* 102 (1987), 29–43. Comparative study on the attitudes of Hopperus and Viglius during the Dutch revolt.

Waterbolk, E. H. "Aspects of the Frisian Contribution to the Culture of the Low Countries in the Early Modern Period." In *Verspreide opstellen aangeboden aan de schrijver bij zijn aftreden als hoogleraar aan de Rijksuniversiteit te Groningen,* pp. 172–188. Amsterdam, 1981.

———. "Werkelijkheid of verbeelding?" In *Freonen om ds. J. J. Kalma hinne: Stúdzjes, meast oer Fryslân, foar syn fiifensantichste Jierdei,* pp. 255–265. Leeuwarden, Netherlands, 1982. On Hopperus's *Ferdinandus sive de institutione principis.*

GUSTAAF JANSSENS

HORNER BUND. An alliance of nobility against the accession of Matthias, the Horner Bund was established in 1608 in the small town of Horn in Waldviertel, a holding of the Puchheim family, which gained significance in the history of the Reformation in the region below the river Enns. After the breakup of the traditional church (as a result of the impossibility of filling ecclesiastical positions), the Reformation succeeded in establishing itself around 1560. Apparently efforts of the nobility to determine the appointment of ministers and a "Reformation from below" went hand in hand. Under Veit Albrecht of Puchheim (d. 1584) preaching was in accord with the Lutheran theology of Matthias Flacius Illyricus. From 1581 until 1584 the provincial Protestant school that had been driven from Vienna was relocated in Horn. A church visitation took place in 1580.

In the course of the conflict following Rudolf II's partial loss of power and the recognition of Matthias as sovereign, the members of the nobility who refused to pay homage, 166 of them, gathered in Horn and signed an alliance "for the defense of their rights and their religion." Because of the religious and political activities directed from it, Horn became for a time the symbol of the rebellious estates in Lower Austria. However, the actual leadership of the noble opposition was exercised by the Upper Austrians. A "religious tax" levied on the Protestant nobility was called the "Horn assessment" (*Hornischer Anschlag*).

The formation of the alliance in 1608 brought the desired success through the so-called "resolution of surrender" (March 1609). But a renewed attempt of the Protestant nobility, undertaken after the death of Matthias, failed. There was a refusal of homage, a gathering in Horn (later in Retz), the conclusion of alliances, and the recruitment of mercenaries. Ferdinand II not only succeeded in dividing the estates (some of whom did pay homage) but was also victorious in the military conflict (skirmish at Gars and the Battle of White Mountain). The Horner Bund was ostracized, and their property confiscated.

The same fate befell the brothers Hans and Reichert von Puchheim, against whose will Horn had became the center of these activities. The Protestant preacher was expelled, and in 1621 the Catholic parish was reestablished. Except for a few who emigrated, the citizens apparently resisted the Catholicizing efforts only haphazardly. By around 1640 the city was once again Catholic.

BIBLIOGRAPHY

Petrin, Silvia. "Die niederösterreichischen Stände im 16. und 17. Jahrhundert." In *Adel im Wandel: Politik, Kultur, Konfession, 1500–1700*, edited by Herbert Knittler, p. 285. Exhibition catalog. Vienna, 1990.

Reingrabner, Gustav. "Die Reformation in Horn." *JbGPrÖ* 85 (1969).

———. "Reformation und katholische Restauration." In *Zwischen Herren und Ackersleuten. Bürgerliches Leben im Waldviertel 1500–1700*, edited by Erich Rabl. Exhibition catalog. Horn, 1990.

GUSTAV REINGRABNER

Translated from German by Susan M. Sisler

HOSIUS, Stanislaus (Pol., Stanisław Hozjusz; 1505–1579), humanist, theologian, leading bishop for Counter-Reformation initiatives in Poland, and Roman curial cardinal. Born and educated in Kraków during the flowering of humanism there, Hosius was active in the Polish circle of Erasmus's admirers in the 1520s and 1530s. Sent in 1530 by the bishop of Kraków (who was also royal vice-chancellor) to study law in Bologna and Padua, he entered royal service in 1534. Appointed bishop of Chełmno (Kulm) in 1549, then of Ermeland (Warmia) in 1551, he led the struggle against Protestant influences in Poland. He immediately secured the Polish bishops' adoption of his *Confessio fidei catholicae christiana* (1551).

This work, which appeared in over thirty editions and numerous translations, contrasted Protestant beliefs with Catholic doctrine; it also demonstrated from scripture and tradition the authenticity of Roman Catholic faith. In 1558 Hosius published *Confutatio. . . Brentii* against the Lutheran theologian Johannes Brenz and *De expresso Dei verbo* on the need for authority in the explication of the Bible. He was summoned in 1558 to advise the Roman curia, dispatched in 1560 to reconvert the imperial Habsburg heir Maximilian II from Protestantism, and created cardinal in 1561. He served as a papal legate to the Council of Trent in its difficult but productive final phase in 1562–1563 and as a president of the council in its closing year. He proved vigorous in conciliar debates over dogma and in defense of papal primacy.

In Poland again from 1564 to 1569, he secured Catholic influence there, notably by establishment of the Jesuit college in Braniew (Braunsberg). Hosius spent his last decade in Rome as a curial official and as representative of the Polish king. Through correspondence he directed reforms in Poland, Sweden, and the empire. As grand penitentiary from 1573, he oversaw important cases of penance and absolution. He died at Capranica and is buried at Rome.

BIBLIOGRAPHY

Grabka, G. "Cardinal Hosius and the Council of Trent." *Theological Studies* 7 (1946), 558–576.

"Hosius, Stanislaus." In *The Oxford Dictionary of the Christian Church*, 2d ed., edited by F. L. Cross & E. A. Livingstone, pp. 668–669. Oxford, 1983.

Jedin, Herbert. *Geschichte des Konzils von Trient.* Vols. 4.1 and 4.2. Freiburg, 1975. More authoritative and up-to-date than the Grabka article for essential details on Hosius's diplomacy and theology at Trent.

Kowalska, Halina. "Stanislaus Hosius." In *Contemporaries of Erasmus: A Biographical Register of the Renaissance and Reformation*, edited by Peter G. Bietenholz, vol. 2, pp. 206–207. Toronto, 1986. Lists original sources and recent Polish research with some emphasis on Hosius as humanist.

Verzeichnis der im deutschen Sprachbereich erschienenen Drucke des XVI. Jahrhunderts. Stuttgart, 1983–. See vol. 9, nos. 4305–4308.

JAMES MICHAEL WEISS

HOTMAN, François (1524–1590), French jurist and legal reformer. Hotman was a humanist scholar and historian and Huguenot agent and propagandist who is best known as one of the leading resistance theorists of the French Wars of Religion. Born in Paris in 1524 as the eldest son of a French *famille de robe* of Silesian descent, Hotman attended the University of Paris and the law school of the University of Orléans, from which he took his licentiate in law in 1540. He lectured on law in the *Faculté du décret*, taught liberal arts in the Academy of Lausanne, and was later professor of law at the Academy of Strasbourg and the universities of Valence and Bourges, which had become renowned as the center of the "reformed"—that is, the humanist—school of jurisprudence.

Before the age of twenty-one Hotman had turned to another sort of "reformation"—that of the evangelical religion, which had appeared in France during the 1520s in the wake of Luther. This plague of heresy had been proscribed by the French King Francis I in an edict of 1542; it was actively opposed by Hotman's own father, Pierre, who was a member of the famous court called the Chambre Ardente ("burning chamber") formed in 1547 for the "extermination" of the "so-called reformed religion." In 1548 Hotman joined other young defectors from "papist" religion, most notably his close friend Théodore de Bèze (eventually to become John Calvin's successor in Geneva), and took up exile in Geneva to cast his lot with Calvin, who became a psychological as well as pastoral father-figure to this new generation of Protestants. In Geneva Hotman served Calvin as secretary and was rewarded with academic positions in the new evangelical schools first of Lausanne and then of Strasbourg, which at that time (1555) was also a refuge for the Marian exiles from England. Here began both Hotman's lifelong service to the Calvinist "cause" and his lifelong feud with François Baudouin, his predecessor in the chair of law in Strasbourg and a rival for Calvin's affections before abandoning what he called "Calvinolatry" for an ecumenical form of religion.

Following Calvin and Bèze, Hotman rejected Baudouin's Erasmian irenicism, and while beginning to build an impressive reputation as a legal scholar, he launched at the same time into a subcareer as polemicist and champion of the *Causa Calvinista*. From the beginning Hotman's target was "tyranny"—whether that of the Roman (and Gallican) church or that of the Guise family, whose persecutions of Protestants began first in their home territory of Lorraine, especially in Metz, from which the French Protestants were expelled in 1559. This was the year, too, of the "Conspiracy of Amboise," which, in the wake of the death of Henry II and the subsequent constitutional crisis, was directed against Guise control over the young king Francis II and especially against the cardinal of Lorraine, who was brother of the duke of Guise and head of the Gallican church. In this abortive uprising Hotman took an active, if mysterious, role, if only as a messenger and apologist after the fact; it was in the context of this prewar turmoil that the major themes of Hotman's ideas of resistance were formulated.

In his anonymous *Tiger of France* (1560) Hotman, lamenting the "martyrs" of Amboise, identified the cardinal of Lorraine as the embodiment of tyranny and not only began fashioning his constitutionalist vision of the French monarchy but also hinted at tyrannicide as a possible remedy for political and religious oppression. The shooting war began two years later, and Hotman entered the service of the Huguenot leader, the prince of Condé. Hotman began extending his personalized polemic of the prewar years (focused on Baudouin as well as the cardinal) into a larger assault on the Catholic party in France and its Italianate style (associated with the rule of Catherine de Médicis). A byproduct of this was Hotman's *Antitribonian*, written in 1567, which deplored the influence of Roman law (both canon and civil) and celebrated the native, originally Germanic customs of France as the proper basis of society and legal education.

But the turning point of Hotman's life—and indeed that of the French monarchy in general—came with the Saint Bartholomew's Day Massacre in 1572, which according to Huguenot opinion was a betrayal not only of true religion but also of the French people. It was widely believed that the government itself had sanctioned the murder of Admiral Gaspard II de Coligny and encouraged the slaughter of his followers throughout France. Narrowly escaping from Bourges with his own life, Hotman denounced not only the Catholics but also the king himself, rejecting the "majesty" of one guilty of such atrocities. In his Genevan exile he wrote a general account of the massacre and a life of Coligny. Then, again following the lead of Calvin and Bèze, he published the most comprehensive statement of his ideas on the legitimacy of resistance and on the liberal and even populist traditions of the monarchy; it was based on an extraordinarily well-researched and heavily argued reading of French history as the product of pristine Germano-Celtic traditions originally free from the taint of "Roman tyranny" in both religious and institutional terms. In general, Hotman's *Francogallia* of 1573 set up a constitutional ideal analogous to the "primitive church" praised by Calvin. It invoked the notion of the originally elective character of French kingship, it honored the "Great Council"—in effect, the Estates-General—as the foundation of monarchy, and it celebrated "liberty" in its jointly Germanic, Christian, and anti-Roman forms.

In later years, when the Huguenot leader Henry of Navarre (later Henry IV) became the legitimate heir to the crown, Hotman moderated his radical views (deleting the thesis of elective kingship from later editions of the *Francogallia*), but he continued to write for the "cause." In his *Brutum Fulmen* of 1586 he attacked Sixtus V's bull of excommunication, and he continued his support or Henry of Navarre in tracts defending the Bourbon succession. Throughout his life as propagandist Hotman continued also to serve as Huguenot agent, especially to various princes in

Germany, and to publish his many scholarly studies of Roman law. In his last years Hotman moved to Basel, where he died in 1590, still in exile, still suing for the return of his property in France, and leaving a potent legacy of political radicalism for later generations.

BIBLIOGRAPHY

Franklin, Julian H., ed. *Constitutionalism and Resistance in the Sixteenth Century: Three Treatises by Hotman, Beza, and Mornay.* New York, 1969. Essential texts of resistance theory, with partial translation of the *Francogallia.*

Giesey, Ralph E. "When and Why Hotman Wrote the *Francogallia.*" *Bibliothèque d'Humanisme et Renaissance* 29 (1967), 581–611.

———. "The Monarchomach Triumvirs: Hotman, Beza, and Mornay." *Bibliothèque d'Humanisme et Renaissance* 32 (1970), 41–76. Historical, comparative study of resistance theory.

Hotman, François. *Francogallia.* Edited by Ralph E. Giesey and translated by J. H. M. Salmon. Cambridge, 1972. Variorum edition with translation and valuable introduction.

———. *La Vie de Messire Gaspar de Colligny Admiral de France* (c. 1577). Geneva, 1987. Facsimile edition with critical notes, commentary, and newer bibliography.

Kelley, Donald R. *François Hotman: A Revolutionary's Ordeal.* Princeton, 1973. Comprehensive biography, with full documentation and references.

Reynolds, Beatrice. *Proponents of Limited Monarchy in Sixteenth-Century France: Francis Hotman and Jean Bodin.* Reprint, New York, 1968. Study of the "constitutionalist" aspect of Hotman's work.

Skinner, Quentin. *The Foundations of Modern Political Thought.* 2 vols. Cambridge, 1979. The *Francogallia* in the context of sixteenth-century political theory.

Verzeichnis der im deutschen Sprachbereich erschienenen Drucke des XVI. Jahrhunderts. Stuttgart, 1983–. See vol. 9, nos. 5188–5248.

DONALD R. KELLEY

HOTTINGER, Hans (fl. 1523–c.1530), Zurich craftsman and night watchman at the Zollikon jail; active lay participant in the incipient Anabaptist movement in Zurich. Hottinger's first association with the radical reform movement occurred in the fall of 1523 when he participated in an iconoclastic raid on the Catholic church at Zollikon (canton of Zurich). In February 1525 Hottinger—along with twenty-three others—was imprisoned by Zurich authorities; at their trial on 7 February 1525 he acknowledged his baptism as an adult. (According to court testimony given later in January 1526, Hottinger apparently had been baptized by Heini Aberli during a journey to Waldshut.) He and the others were released upon payment of a surety and a promise (*Urfehde*) to refrain from further reform activities.

A short time later, however, Hottinger appeared as an outspoken defender of the Anabaptists in a debate with Zwingli supporters, claiming that Zwingli had once acknowledged the scriptural validity of rebaptism on the basis of *Acts* 19. "When he [Zwingli] says God has commanded that infants should be baptized," Hottinger reputedly argued, "he is lying like a rascal, villain, and heretic." Again he was imprisoned, but was released after he denied the charge and promised once more to cease his agitation. At the Anabaptist trial in March 1525 Hottinger appears to have reaffirmed this recantation, stating his satisfaction with Zwingli's teaching on baptism and offering a renewed vow of obedience to city magistrates. But in March 1526 Hottinger again was imprisoned, this time for his zealous defense of believers' baptism and his close association with Balthasar Hubmaier. Hubmaier mentions Hottinger favorably in his *Ein Gesprech Balthasar Hubmörs von Friedberg auf Mayster Ulrichs Zwinqlens Taufbüchlein* (A Discourse of Balthasar Hubmaier of Friedberg on Master Ulrich Zwingli's Booklet on Baptism; 1525). Little is known about Hottinger's life following his escape from prison on 21 March 1526, although there is some evidence that he fled to the Anabaptist community in Moravia.

BIBLIOGRPAHY

Geiser, Samuel. "Hottinger, Hans." In *Mennonite Encyclopedia*, pp. 819–820. Scottdale, Pa., 1956. Draws on Emil Eglis's *Aktensammlung zur Geschichte der Zürcher Reformation* for biographical details of Hottinger's life.

Harder, Leland, ed. *The Sources of Swiss Anabaptism: The Grebel Letters and Related Documents.* Scottdale, Pa., 1985. Critical edition of key documents related to the early Anabaptist movement in Zurich; includes exhaustive indexes and short profiles of the 106 individuals, including Hottinger, who appear in the documents.

JOHN D. ROTH

HOUSE OF ______. *See under family name.*

HOVIUS, Mathias (1542–1620), third archbishop of his native Mechelen (Malines), serving from 1596 to 1620. Like those of a number of bishops in the Low Countries soon after the Council of Trent, Hovius's family background was modest, his father rising to become dean of the Fullers' guild. Good work at the Standonck college for poor-to-middling boys enabled Hovius to advance to the Pope Adrian VI college at Louvain, where he graduated in theology. In his background, training, and early positions (ordination, 1566; parish priest in Mechelen, 1569; canon of the cathedral chapter, 1577) Hovius reflected the emphasis of Trent upon able clergy. As important to the development of his zeal, however, were the dramatic events through which he lived, including the Calvinist fury in Mechelen of 1580–1585, when Hovius escaped from the mob by dressing as a peasant.

While in exile in Liège, Hovius was named archdeacon of the cathedral chapter of Mechelen, a position he filled upon returning to that city in 1585. Only four years later, Hovius was made vicar-general, *sede vacante*, at the death of Jean Hauchin. It took Philip II six years to find a suitable, willing candidate for the archbishopric—although this prelate would be primate of the Low Countries, the see was also one of the worst endowed among the new bishoprics established by Philip in 1559. Laevinus Torrentius of Antwerp wavered. Cardinal William Allen died before taking possession. Almost by default, the choice finally fell upon the poorly bred vicar-general, who by 1595 had exhibited his ability to run the see.

Hovius may rightly be seen as the founder of Tridentine reform in the archdiocese and indeed as a major figure in all the Spanish Netherlands. Partly because of circumstance, partly because of disposition, it was he more than his famous predecessor, Antoine Perrenot de Granvelle, who established a definitive ecclesiastical organization, a task that involved firming up the financial footing of the diocese, reforming the ever-incorrigible chapters, dividing the more than four hundred parishes into manageable deaneries, visiting parishes and convents, finding well-trained, dutiful priests (Henri-François van der Burch and Jacob Boonen were among his protégés), establishing a seminary, reorganizing the ecclesiastical court, and calling perhaps the most important provincial synod in the Spanish Netherlands (1607). Hovius's greatest contributions to popular piety were the promotion of the famous shrine at Scherpenheuvel and working for the canonization of the martyrs of Gorcum.

In the political sphere, Hovius's role was not as great as that of his successor, Jacob Boonen, or even that of other bishops—despite the prominence of his position and his seat in the States of Brabant. In part this may have been because of the relative peace that prevailed during his episcopacy, in part because of inclination (his personality was too severe to have been effective in politics), and in part certainly because he was of non-noble background, a point that arose more than once in his relations with the archdukes Albert and Isabella, who otherwise admired the man. In the end, the picture of Hovius that emerges from the available documentation, including his intriguing journal, is of an efficient, almost unyielding proponent of Catholic reform, one whose impact in the Spanish Netherlands was both immediate and lasting.

BIBLIOGRAPHY

Claessens, P. *Histoire des archevêques de Malines.* 2 vols. Melchelen, Belgium, 1881. Contains sketches of Hovius and other archbishops of Mechelen.

Harline, Craig, and Eddy Put. "A Bishop in the Cloisters: The Visitations of Mathias Hovius, Malines, 1596–1620." *Sixteenth Century Journal* 22.4 (Winter 1991), 611–639. Treats one aspect of Hovius's reform efforts. The same authors are engaged in a full-scale study of Hovius.

Laenen, J. *Geschiedenis van het Seminarie van Mechelen.* Mechelen, Belgium, 1930. Contains much about Hovius, given his role as founder of the seminary.

Ram, P. F. X. de. *Nova et absoluta collectio synodorum... Synodicon Belgicum.* 2 vols. Mechelen, Belgium, 1828–1829. This massive publication contains all the decrees and much of the correspondence of the provincial and diocesan synods, and thus plenty of material on Hovius.

Craig Harline and Eddy F. Put

HOWARD, Thomas (1473–1554), earl of Surrey, third Howard duke of Norfolk, military commander, and politician. His first important command came in 1512 as lieutenant general to the marquess of Dorset, Thomas Grey, in Spain. The following year he was named lord admiral for Henry VIII's campaign in France but remained behind, leading the English army that beat the Scots at Flodden (September 1513). A little before that he married his second wife, Elizabeth—daughter of Edward Stafford, the last Stafford duke of Buckingham—but the symbolic significance of this event as a sign of Howard's opposition to Thomas Wolsey has been overdone. In fact, he probably cooperated in one of Wolsey's most important administrative reforms, the overhaul of the Privy Chamber in 1519. Deputy of Ireland in 1520–1521, Howard fought again in France and in the Scottish marches upon his return.

In 1525 Howard supported the Amicable Grant and helped to quell a rebellion against it in his home county of Norfolk. When Cardinal Wolsey was disgraced in 1529, Norfolk tried to lead the Privy Council and may have fostered the vaguely anticlerical campaign inspired by Wolsey's fall, but aside from helping to manage Henry's divorce from Catherine of Aragon, he enjoyed little success. Howard played a key role in suppressing the Pilgrimage of Grace in 1536. In the later 1530s he was one of Thomas Cromwell's principal enemies and arrested him in 1540. Howard tried to capitalize on Cromwell's fall by encouraging Henry to marry his niece Catherine Howard, easily the most disastrous of Henry's liaisons. Howard's military career suffered no damage, however, and he defeated the Scots again at Solway Moss (1542) before engaging in the abortive Boulogne expedition of 1544.

In the factional fighting of Henry's final years, Howard was bested by Edward Seymour and imprisoned in the Tower, where he remained throughout Edward VI's reign (1547–1553). Under Mary Tudor he was restored, but his military prowess deserted him in the face of Wyatt's Rebellion (1554), and he retired to Norfolk. Howard was a scion of the new Tudor aristocracy, who made a successful career in service to the Crown without concerning himself overmuch with religious matters, despite usually aligning himself with the conservatives.

BIBLIOGRAPHY

Mattingly, Garrett. *Catherine of Aragon.* New York, 1941; reprint, 1991. Out of date, but still a compelling characterization.

Williams, Neville. *Henry VIII and His Court.* London, 1971.

Thomas F. Mayer

HOZJUSZ, Stanisław. *See* Hosius, Stanislaus.

HUBMAIER, Balthasar (1480/85–1528), German Anabaptist leader. Hubmaier was the best theological exponent of early Anabaptism and the only Anabaptist leader grounded in scholastic theology. Born in Friedberg in Bavaria, he attended Latin school in Augsburg and matriculated at the University of Freiburg im Breisgau in 1503. During his theological education there he came under the influence of Johann Eck, one of the Roman church's most skilled and tenacious defenders against the Reformation. Hubmaier was ordained to the priesthood at Constance and was active as a preacher while at Freiburg. In 1512 he matriculated at the University of Ingolstadt, drawn by Eck, who had moved there a year and a half earlier. Within a few months Hubmaier was made a doctor of theology; he gave theological lectures until he left Ingolstadt to become cathedral preacher in Regensburg in January 1516.

Hubmaier stayed for five years as the most prominent preacher in Regensburg. His most important action during this time of the first stirrings of the German Reformation was the expulsion of the Jewish community during four days in Lent in 1519. Regensburg was an imperial city of fifteen thousand, then in a long economic decline; its Jewish community was one of the oldest and largest in Germany. With wealth based on moneylending and commerce, the Regensburg Jews had since the 1470s come under attack from the town council, but they enjoyed the protection of the Habsburg emperors. The new preacher declaimed against their practice of usury and their defamation of the Virgin Mary (especially their stiff-necked insistence that *Is.* 7:14 referred not to a "virgin" but to a "young woman"). He denounced the Jews as "idle, lecherous, and greedy" and called for their expulsion.

The imperial government tried unsuccessfully to have Hubmaier removed from his post. Instead, the interregnum following Maximilian I's death in January 1519 provided the council and Hubmaier with the long-awaited opportunity to destroy the synagogue, level the ghetto, and expel the Jewish population. On the synagogue site the Chapel of the Blessed Mary was built, and Hubmaier, who had suggested the name, was made its chaplain. It gained a reputation as a place of miracles, so that Hubmaier found himself by 1520 a pilgrimage preacher at a chapel that attracted tens of thousands of devout visitors from as far away as Hungary. He appears to have participated in this expression of traditional Catholic piety with full conviction, although he opposed the ecstatic behavior of some of the pilgrims. Heiko Oberman cautions against viewing this portion of Hubmaier's career as something that was simply left behind when he joined the Reformation. There was populist social radicalism in anti-Jewish preaching that could easily be transmuted into denunciations of the "idle, lecherous, and greedy" clergy of the old church. Marian piety, too, had a special appeal to the humble and the poor. Later as an Anabaptist Hubmaier abandoned the Mariolatry but defended the anti-Judaism.

At the beginning of 1521 Hubmaier accepted a call to the Austrian town of Waldshut on the Rhine, a place with about one thousand inhabitants. During his first two years in the new charge he remained true to Catholic observances but at the same time established connections with humanist circles in Basel and read the publications of Wittenberg theologians. A brief return to Regensburg from December 1522 through March 1523 found the former pilgrimage preacher more concerned with evangelical reform than with the Marian chapel, its processions, and its miracles. Back in Waldshut in early 1523, Hubmaier became an open partisan of the Reformation, establishing contacts with the neighboring Swiss reformers Joachim Vadian of St. Gall and Huldrych Zwingli of Zurich. In May he had a conversation with Zwingli in Zurich in which the two of them apparently agreed that "children should not be baptized before they were of age" and could be instructed in the faith. In October he was again in Zurich, endorsing through his attendance and his spoken opinions the official disputation intended to show that the Mass and images were not grounded in scripture. Waldshut's defection to the Reformation caught the attention of its ecclesiastical and temporal overlords by December 1523, when Austrian officials arrived in the town to denounce Hubmaier and demand that he be arrested and turned over to the bishop of Constance. The Waldshut council refused, saying that Hubmaier proclaimed the word of God purely and clearly, thus beginning a two-year resistance that would bring the town involvement with both the Peasants' War and Anabaptism.

Following the example of Zwingli in Zurich, Hubmaier organized a religious disputation in Waldshut in April 1524 in which he challenged the clerics of the old faith with eighteen theses. In the *Achtzehn Schlußreden* (Eighteen Theses), his first publication, Hubmaier affirmed justification by faith alone, stated that the Mass was not a sacrifice but a memorial of Christ's death, rejected all the major scholastic theologians by name, and denounced belief in purgatory and most traditional Catholic practices, including pilgrimages. The outcome of Hubmaier's support by the people and council was that the Catholic priests left Waldshut in the spring.

In the same May days in which the evangelical party asserted its dominance in Waldshut, the first precursor episodes of the Peasants' War took place in neighboring Klettgau. The rural commoners entered into armed negotiations with their lords and appeared in Waldshut as early as July. Both the Klettgau and Black Forest peasants and Waldshut threatened and felt threatened by the Austrian government. A complicated series of events took place in which peasant bands from the Black Forest and evangelical "volunteers" from Zwinglian Zurich took turns protecting Waldshut from the Austrians until the end of 1524, at which point the peasant armies became the town's main defender, which they remained until the battle of Griessen in November 1525; here, Austrian forces overwhelmed Klettgau peasants and townsmen from Waldshut. Neighboring Zurich played an ambitious but vacillating game in these Austrian territories into which it aspired ineffectually to expand territorially and to spread the Zwinglian gospel. In 1525 both the Waldshuters and Klettgauers espoused the Reformation against Catholic Austria, but according to both Torsten Bergsten and Tom Scott, who have studied the matter in most detail, theirs was an alliance of convenience created by the common threat, not a genuinely religious bond.

Meanwhile Hubmaier pursued his individual religious path. During September and October 1524 he sought temporary exile in Schaffhausen, then inclining toward a Zurich-style Reformation, in order to alleviate some of the Austrian pressure on Waldshut. Here he wrote *Von Ketzern und ihren Verbrennern* (On Heretics and Those Who Burn Them), an early Reformation plea for religious liberty, which concludes that "the burning of heretics is an invention of the devil. Truth is unkillable"—the latter motto appears on his published works throughout his career. Upon returning to Waldshut Hubmaier came into serious contact with Reformation radicals; he read Andreas Bodenstein von Karlstadt, may have met Thomas Müntzer (who spent eight weeks in neighboring Griessen in the Klettgau from November 1524 to January 1525), and, most important, among the Zurich defenders of Waldshut encountered persons dissatisfied with the slow pace of the Zurich reformation as set by Zwingli and the government. When Zurich radicals instituted believers' baptism in January 1525 they found a sympathizer in Hubmaier. The important Zurich Anabaptist leader Wilhelm Reublin established a territorial base in the Schaffhausen village of Hallau from late January 1525. He visited nearby Waldshut, conducted some adult baptisms, and sought Hubmaier's support for the Anabaptist position. Hubmaier meanwhile corresponded with Sebastian Hofmeister, the reformer of Schaffhausen, and Johannes Oecolampadius, the reformer of Basel, and thought that the three of them had established a consensus against infant baptism.

On Easter Sunday, 15 April 1525, Hubmaier and sixty others received baptism from Reublin in Waldshut, after which Hubmaier baptized about three hundred persons, thus giving an Anabaptist color to the Waldshut reformation. Stung by Zwingli's publishing campaign against the Anabaptists, Hubmaier felt challenged to respond with his first major theological treatise, *Von der christlichen Taufe der Gläubigen* (On the Christian Baptism of Believers; July 1525)—the most effective defense of believers' baptism in the Reformation era. Hubmaier clearly aspired to make believers' baptism part of the general program of the Reformation, not the distinctive teaching of nonconformist conventicles. But Zwingli's hold on his fellow humanist reformers in southwest Germany and Switzerland and his discreet distance from the Peasants' War enabled him to outmaneuver Hubmaier and to embed infant baptism within the Reformed tradition.

Hubmaier and Anabaptist leaders like Reublin at first advanced their cause in the wake of the breakdown of authority caused by the Peasants' War. Hubmaier was a major factor, if not the sole leader, in Waldshut's involvement in the Peasants' War. Because the town supported him as its reformer it was obliged to seek rebel support against its political overlord, a frequent situation when towns were drawn into the Peasants' War. It is likely, and now accepted by most scholars (against Bergsten), that Hubmaier was the author and editor of peasant programs in his region. In December 1525, when Austrian troops occupied Waldshut in the aftermath of the Peasants' War and Hubmaier fled to Zurich, Johannes Faber, vicar general of the bishop of Constance, found among Hubmaier's abandoned papers two peasant programs, the *Artikelbrief* (Letter of Articles) and the *Verfassungsentwurf* (Constitutional Draft). We know the *Verfassungsentwurf* only through Faber, but the *Artikelbrief* was used by the Black Forest peasant band and is clearly an authentic Peasants' War document. Faber states that Hubmaier edited the text of the *Verfassungsentwurf* and composed the *Artikelbrief*, which calls for a general nonviolent boycott of the peasants' opponents. It is also probable from Faber's accusations and Hubmaier's confession before his execution in Vienna in March 1528 that Hubmaier edited one of the regional versions of the *Bundesordnung* (Federal Ordinance), an organizational document in wide use among the peasant bands, which circulated together with the *Artikelbrief* in the Black Forest region. One can infer this activity from Hubmaier's admission that "I elaborated and interpreted the peasant articles that they brought to me from Höre [Upper Swabia] and led them to imagine that they could be accepted as Christian and just." Like most Reformation figures who took the side of the commoners in the Peasants' War, Hubmaier later regretted his involvement and saw a divine judgment in the suppression of the rebels. At the time, however, he must have seen himself as expounding the social meaning of the gospel and doing what was necessary to defend the Reformation in Waldshut.

Hubmaier and his wife, Elsbeth Hügline, whom he married at the beginning of 1525, sought refuge with Anabaptists in Zurich, but he was promptly imprisoned and subjected to what he later described as Zwingli's attempt to give him a theological education through torture. The first time that Hubmaier was supposed to recant publicly he affirmed the new baptism instead, but eventually he was forced to recant and was allowed to leave Zurich in April 1525. After brief stays in Constance and Augsburg Hubmaier joined Anabaptists emigrating to Moravia, where a plurality of confessions were legally tolerated. By late spring or summer of 1526 he was in Nikolsburg (now Mikulov), where he established himself and enjoyed a productive career of about one year. Here he won to Anabaptism both Martin Göschl, the coadjutor bishop of Olomouc and leading cleric in the area, and Count Leonhart von Liechtenstein, the temporal lord. He created at Nikolsburg his own version of the socially conservative, magisterially ordered Reformation that emerged in the aftermath of the Peasants' War. At Nikolsburg, he had his own printer, Simprecht Sorg, a nephew of the Zurich printer Christoph Froschauer, who followed Hubmaier from Zurich to Moravia. Sorg printed sixteen works of Hubmaier, some from manuscripts written earlier, some newly composed—the bulk of Hubmaier's published work.

The Nikolsburg writings of Hubmaier, in their focus on baptism, the Lord's Supper, the ban, free will, and the sword, combine his scholastic education with contemporary ideas drawn from Karlstadt, Luther, Zwingli, and Erasmus. Like other first-generation reformers he rejected all the extant scholastic theological systems but drew on scholastic methods when he worked most energetically to construct his own theology. He used the scholastic distinction between God's absolute power and the covenant God established with humanity to find a place for prevenient grace, human free will, and believers' baptism. A baptism of the Holy Spirit occurred following the preaching of the word of God, but it could only take effect through the person's free and uncoerced consent. Since infants could not respond freely to the moving of the Holy Spirit, external baptism with water should wait until one could affirm one's faith, confess one's sin, and place oneself under the discipline of the church. Following on the baptisms of the Holy Spirit and of water, a life of suffering Christian obedience gradually regenerated the soul. This suffering, which could sometimes end in actual martyrdom, was the baptism of blood. The Lord's Supper particularly incites to the active following of Christ's way of the cross, which the church memorializes through it; like Zwingli and Karlstadt, Hubmaier had a spiritual understanding of the Communion that separated the elements of bread and wine from the grace they signified.

The external course of Hubmaier's year in Nikolsburg was not smooth. The Anabaptists in Moravia, estimated at two thousand at that time, consisted of a settled German-speaking population as well as of refugees from south and central Germany and Switzerland. Some Anabaptist fugitives in Moravia were also fugitive veterans of the Peasants' War. When Hans Hut, the great Anabaptist apocalyptic missionary, arrived in Moravia preaching the imminence of the Lord's return, his message was far more attractive to the fugitives than was Hubmaier's ordered, magisterially protected Anabaptism. Hubmaier summoned Hut to a disputation at Nikolsburg in which he attacked Hut's apocalyptic projections. In his final tract at Nikolsburg, *Von dem Schwert* (On the Sword), he also had to take issue with the Swiss Anabaptist idea, stated in the Schleitheim Articles, that there was no place in the Christian congregation for a magistrate wielding the sword. Even in his Waldshut days Hubmaier had shown no sympathy for the notion of separation between the Christian church and the magistracy, believing that only Christians were qualified for governmental authority. The future of Moravian Anabaptism, however, lay not with Hubmaier's established church but with the amalgamation of Hut's Anabaptism and Swiss Anabaptism that gave rise to the Hutterites.

Hubmaier's Nikolsburg career ended abruptly when he was extradited to Vienna in July 1527. Ferdinand of Austria, Hubmaier's old enemy from Waldshut, had assumed the crown of Bohemia and Moravia shortly after Hubmaier came to Nikolsburg. So as not to seem to violate the religious liberties of Moravia, the charges against Hubmaier stressed his rebellion while in Waldshut. But once he was incarcerated at Kreuzenstein Castle near Vienna, he was interrogated by Faber, now risen to be bishop of Vienna, about his various heresies. Hubmaier tried to take a conciliatory theological position in the *Rechenschaft des Glaubens* (Account of Faith) addressed to King Ferdinand, but his execution was a foregone conclusion once he was in the Habsburg grasp. He died bravely, burned at the stake in Vienna, on 10 March 1528; three days later his wife, who had followed him steadfastly since Waldshut, was drowned in the Danube.

BIBLIOGRAPHY

Primary Sources

Pipkin, H. Wayne, and John H. Yoder, eds. and trans. *Balthasar Hubmaier: Theologian of Anabaptism.* Classics of the Radical Reformation, vol. 5. Scottdale, Pa., 1989. An English translation of Hubmaier's complete works, more extensive than the standard German edition by Westin and Bergsten, with a high degree of accuracy.

Westin, Gunnar, and Torsten Bergsten. *Quellen zur Geschichte der Täufer.* Balthasar Hubmaier Schriften, vol. 9. Gütersloh, 1962. The standard German edition of twenty-five writings by Hubmaier.

Secondary Sources

Armour, Rollin S. *Anabaptist Baptism: A Representative Study.* Scottdale, Pa., 1966. Hubmaier is one of four sixteenth-century Anabaptist theologians of baptism studied here. The objective efficacy of baptism, mediated through the church, and the interlocking of baptism, free will, and regeneration are presented as the substance of his teaching.

Bergsten, Torsten. *Balthasar Hubmaier: Anabaptist Theologian and Martyr.* Edited by William R. Estep. Valley Forge, Pa., 1978. Abbreviated version of Bergsten's major biography, *Balthasar Hubmaier: Seine Stellung zu Reformation and Täufertum, 1521–1528,* Kassel, 1961, without the scholarly apparatus. Bergsten places Hubmaier's Anabaptism in a Reformation context but minimizes his involvement in the Peasants' War. The study is comprehensive, without an apologetic tone.

Loserth, Johann. *Doctor Balthasar Hubmaier und die Anfänge der Wiedertaufe in Mähren.* Brünn, 1893. The ground-breaking early scholarly biography of Hubmaier, presenting him very favorably as the major early Anabaptist leader.

Moore, Walter L., Jr. "Catholic Teacher and Anabaptist Pupil: The Relationship between John Eck and Balthasar Hubmaier." *Archive for Reformation History* 72 (1981), 68–97. Argues for continuity of Hubmaier's teaching on free will from his studies with Eck to his Anabaptist period.

Oberman, Heiko A. *The Roots of Anti-Semitism in the Age of Renaissance and Reformation.* Translated by James I. Porter. Philadelphia, 1984. Points out the connection between Hubmaier's anti-Judaism and his anticlerical populism.

Stayer, James M. *Anabaptists and the Sword.* 2d ed. Lawrence, Kans., 1976. Discusses Hubmaier's unusual, legitimist affirmation of the sword of the magistrate in comparison to nonresistant and radical standpoints more typical of the Anabaptists.

———. *The German Peasants' War and Anabaptist Community of Goods.* Montreal, 1991. Makes the case for Hubmaier as the probable author of one Peasants' War program, the *Artikelbrief,* and an important editor of two others, the *Verfassungsentwurf* and a regional version of the *Bundesordnung.*

Steinmetz, David C. *Reformers in the Wings.* Philadelphia, 1971. Stresses Hubmaier's background in late medieval nominalism; see pp. 197–208.

Vedder, Henry C. *Balthasar Hubmaier: The Leader of the Anabaptists* (1905). New York, 1971. A biography that idealizes Hubmaier as the epitome of the positive qualities of early Anabaptism.

Verzeichnis der im deutschen Sprachbereich erschienenen Drucke des XVI. Jahrhunderts. Stuttgart, 1983–. See vol. 9, nos. 5634–5653.

Windhorst, Christof. *Täuferisches Taufverständnis: Balthasar Hubmaiers Lehre zwischen traditioneller und reformatorischer Theologie.* Leiden, 1976. A study of Hubmaier's baptismal theology, comparing it with Luther, Zwingli, and medieval scholasticism. By far the most thorough treatment of the topic.

———. "Balthasar Hubmaier: Professor, Preacher, Politician." In *Profiles of Radical Reformers,* edited by Hans-Jürgen Goertz, pp. 144–157. Scottdale, Pa., 1982. A brief biographical and theological assessment.

JAMES M. STAYER

HUGUENOTS. The word *Huguenot* was first used in 1560 as a pejorative name for French Calvinists, for whom the official title of "those of the so-called Reformed religion" later came into fashion. In many French towns Reformed churches grew from earlier heterodox groups influenced by Lutheranism and biblical humanism. Persecution in the 1540s and 1550s drove many Protestants to seek refuge in Geneva, where John Calvin had established his ecclesiastical discipline. From 1555, the year in which a Calvinist church was secretly established in Paris, the Genevan Compagnie des Pasteurs ("Company of Pastors") began to send trained ministers back to France. Over the next five years French Protestantism became indisputably Calvinist, but it always regarded the earlier martyrs as its own.

At flood tide in the early 1560s the movement comprised perhaps 10 percent (1.8 million) of the total population. While at first its strength lay in small merchant and artisan communities, it soon attracted urban notables and officials as well as converts from the Catholic clergy. There were many Reformed churches in Normandy and along the Loire at the beginning of the Wars of Religion, but the numerical strength of French Calvinism was in the south. Substantial numbers of Huguenot peasant communities existed in Languedoc and Guyenne, and by no means all of them had followed the lead of their seigneurs. In the five years before the first civil war of 1562 about one third of the traditional nobility became converts or supporters of the Huguenot movement. This influx drastically changed its political leadership and muted the aggressive iconoclasm of the Protestant lower classes.

The first Huguenot national synod met secretly in Paris in May 1559. It accepted a Genevan confession of faith and ecclesiastical discipline. The powers, responsibilities, and manner of selection of elders, pastors, and deacons were established, and oligarchic rule of each church reposed in a consistory composed of these officials, who were often local notables. Chaplaincies in noble households were, of course, more under control of the seigneurs. Democratic tendencies, which had earlier been common in church government, were gradually eliminated, although they continued to manifest themselves until the national Synod of La Rochelle in 1571. This synod, attended by the leaders among the high nobility as well as representative pastors and elders from the churches and from Geneva, made some minor revisions in the arrangements of 1559 and set the seal on Huguenot organization. The pattern of regional meetings in colloquies, provincial synods, and political assemblies had already been established. Under the threat of civil war in 1561, a protector system had been set up in the south with noble captains of consistories and colonels of colloquies and provinces.

Catholics often alleged that the Huguenots were republicans who sought to establish a federal state on the model of the Swiss cantons. For several years after the Saint Bartholomew's Day Massacre (1572) Huguenot republics did indeed exist in Languedoc, and the Protestant nobility had often to contend with popularly elected secular assemblies. Generally, however, the Huguenots continued to support monarchical principles, even though the monarchy their theorists defined was limited constitutionally. When their leader, Henry of Navarre, became heir to the French throne in 1584, many Huguenots adopted royalist views indistinguishable from Catholic Politiques. Such was the stance of Philippe Duplessis-Mornay, Henry's counselor who was known to English contemporaries as "the Pope of the Huguenots."

The Huguenots fought for the recognition of their religion and obtained toleration in varying degrees at the treaties marking various phases of the wars. The guiding hand of the pastor Théodore de Bèze supported their struggle. Bèze served as a chaplain in the Huguenot army, succeeded to Calvin's position in Geneva in 1564, and defended the orthodox line at the Synod of La Rochelle. Among early military leaders were the Bourbon prince, Louis I of Condé, and the Châtillon brothers, Admiral Gaspard II de Coligny and François d'Andelot, colonel-general of the infantry.

Many noblewomen converted to the Reformed faith before their husbands and played an important part in the movement—none more so than Jeanne of Navarre, mother of Henry of Navarre. Henry was the most notable Huguenot leader, although many Calvinists found it difficult to forgive his conversion to Catholicism in 1593, which assured him the crown of France as Henry IV. It was he who granted (after hard negotiations) the final edict of toleration at Nantes in 1598.

[*See also* Bèze, Théodore de; Calvinism; France; Henry IV of France; La Rochelle, Synod of; Nantes, Edict of; *and* Wars of Religion.]

BIBLIOGRAPHY

Kingdon, Robert M. *Geneva and the Consolidation of the French Protestant Movement, 1564–1572.* Geneva, 1967. Deals with Genevan attitudes to the religious wars and discusses the congregationalist movement inside French Protestantism.

Mours, Samuel. *Le protestantisme en France au 16e siècle.* Paris. 1959.

Prestwich, Menna. "Calvinism in France, 1559–1629." In *International Calvinism, 1541–1715,* edited by Menna Prestwich, pp. 71–107. Oxford, 1985.

Rothrock, George A. *The Huguenots: A Biography of a Minority.* Chicago, 1979.

Sutherland, N. M. *The Huguenot Struggle for Recognition.* New Haven, 1980. Focuses on the political aspects and analyzes the peace edicts.

J. H. M. SALMON

HUMANISM. Contemporary scholarship increasingly acknowledges the importance of humanism in the origins, development, and implementation of the Protestant and Catholic Reformations. Among the chief reasons for this acknowledgment are: a more flexible understanding of humanism based on the avowed aims and practices of the humanists in the fifteenth and sixteenth centuries; a wider recognition of the inherently religious and theological interests of many humanists in Italy and throughout Europe; the establishment of humanist schools and university curricula as part of the implementation of the major German, Swiss, English, and Netherlandish Protestant reforms as well as of many Catholic reforms, notably those of the Jesuits; and, finally, the recognition of a humanist culture as taken for granted by educated persons of whatever religious stripe by 1600.

German scholars in the early nineteenth century coined the term humanism (*Humanismus*) to denote an educational and cultural movement originating in Italy in the late 1300s that soon stimulated imitation abroad or fused with similar indigenous movements throughout Europe. The term derives from an educational curriculum known as the *studia humanitatis,* the study of rhetoric, grammar, poetry, history, and moral philosophy. The humanists found their models in the authors of Greek and Latin antiquity. One needs to remember that many humanists included among their models the early Christian fathers, notably Jerome and Augustine, as Christians skilled in the arts of language. Proponents argued that humanist studies prepared one better for the tasks of active life and public service than did the scholastic trivium and quadrivium with their emphasis on logic and dialectic. The humanists' emphasis on rhetoric signified a preoccupation with techniques of persuasive argumentation rather than a delight in style for its own sake. This "pursuit of eloquence" reflected a conviction common to many of them that a text lacked the full power to convince if it was not endowed with the rhetorical means to elicit an affective or ethical response. This conviction often bespoke a fresh understanding of what it meant to be human, one that emphasized moral, emotive, and aesthetic powers. Rhetorical technique thus also predisposed a large number of humanists to a concern with practical rather than speculative matters: they wanted to change not only minds but lives.

Humanists followed two paths. On the one hand, their recovery of classical, patristic, and biblical texts made them pioneers of philology and textual criticism. On the other hand, their practice of imitation, while sometimes instilling a drably repetitive classicism, also spurred imaginative renewals of traditional forms such as historical writing, neo-Latin poetry, and the dramatic dialogue. It could even inspire the best among them to new genres of discourse such as the *Adagia* of Erasmus or the *Essais* of Montaigne.

The diffusion of humanist interests beyond Italy began as early as the mid-1400s. While the revival of ancient literature or educational reforms enjoyed some indigenous trans-Alpine beginnings, it was Italian teachers, historians, diplomats, poets, philosophers, and textual critics who decisively accelerated and popularized humanism. The chief modes of diffusion were three. First, Italian humanists traveling or residing abroad awakened interest in the new literary movement, as, for example, the diplomat and curialist Enea Silvio Piccolomini (later Pope Pius II) when he traversed central and eastern Europe, and the historian Polydore Virgil when he settled in England. Second, many non-Italians flocked into Italy to explore new interests in depth, often returning to promote them at home. Third, above all, the advance of the printing press accelerated the diffusion of humanist modes of thought. Once humanist studies had been established in political or cultural centers, they developed autonomous local and national traditions, increasingly independent of Italian models. This article forgoes an account of the general transmission of humanism beyond Italy in order to concentrate on the more relevant topic of humanist contributions to the various reformations.

Within the wider transmission of Renaissance humanism, one may distinguish a specific current commonly called Christian humanism, which prepared the climate and even set some agendas for the major reform movements. Beginning with Italian humanists whose work included religious and theological concerns, such as the poet and historian

Francesco Petrarca (d. 1374), the statesman and biblical scholar Gianozzo Manetti (d. 1459), and the philologist and critic of church abuses Lorenzo Valla (d. 1457), Christian humanists advocated a synthesis of classical, biblical, and patristic learning as the basis for an ambitious renewal of theology, piety, and public morality. To reconstruct Christian theology, they took the motto *Ad fontes* ("to the sources"): they favored a philological sensitivity that would promote a renewed study of the Bible, guided by a deepened reading of the earliest church fathers, thereby rejecting the dialectical modes of late medieval Scholasticism as too technical for the primary functions of theology, which they usually took to be pastoral and devotional. They trusted that the path "to the sources" would lead people away from rote, venal, and superstitious forms of piety and toward simplified rituals, personal prayer, and a morally heightened fulfillment of familial and vocational duties.

Before 1520 the humanists' commitment entailed frequent attacks on corruption in the institutional church. Humanists were hardly unique in such critiques, but their satires in that vein earned them their most enduring popularity, as in *The Letters of Obscure Men,* Erasmus's *Colloquies* and *Praise of Folly,* and even Thomas More's *Utopia.* Inevitably, their religious vision comprised a vital sense of lay morality and vocation, which found expression in numerous treatises for Christian laypeople. This emphasis on the laity proved deeply compatible with later schools of Catholic spirituality, especially those of the Jesuits and of Francis de Sales's "devout humanism," and with Protestant doctrines of vocational calling and the priesthood of all believers.

In the early phases of reforms, the sophistication of the Christian humanists led them to form distinctive coteries—the German sodalities at Heidelberg and Nuremberg, the circle of Meaux around Jacques Lefèvre d'Étaples, the Italian *spirituali* around Juan de Valdés, and the like. The aristocratic or patrician tone among the earlier Christian humanists was easily derived from or reinforced by their lofty patrons: princes, nobles, and counselors of every significant court and jurisdiction, prelates of every rank, ambitious bourgeois, and the owners of prestigious printing houses. Yet as specific reform movements began in earnest, numerous humanists entered the more quotidian sphere of university and secondary education, state service, parish life, and popular writing to serve the general public.

Thus humanists before and during the Reformation did *not*—this point requires considerable emphasis in the face of perennial misunderstanding—they did *not* share philosophical or theological positions on human nature, revelation, justification, sacraments, free will, or the other questions that generated Reformation controversy. On these points, their theologies could and did differ widely, just as they differed on other matters in which their humanist background nevertheless decisively figured, such as political theory and literary taste. What they did share were methods of discourse: an insistence on the authority of ancient biblical and patristic sources over medieval scholastic authorities (a point complementary to but not identical with the theological principle *sola scriptura*); a philological sensitivity in commentary on authoritative texts; and a rhetorical construction of arguments in preaching, pedagogy, and polemics. They also favored widespread formal education, especially for the clergy, as essential to successful reform. The use of poetry and drama derived from classical models to promote Catholic and Protestant reformers' ideals and doctrines also became an enduring humanist legacy.

In order to appreciate the flexibility of the humanists' method and the diversity of their institutional settings, one might recall some polarities that found humanist advocates at either end. Some were curialists, such as the papal diplomat Girolamo Alexander; others were antipapal, such as the German satirist Ulrich von Hutten. Some were regional patriots, such as the Alsatian priest Jakob Wimpfeling; others were cosmopolitan, such as the versatile Spaniard Juan Luis Vives. Some favored interior and mystical piety, such as Marguerite d'Angoulême; others were sacramental and dogmatic, such as Cardinal Gasparo Contarini. Some became irenic, such as Philipp Melanchthon; others partisan, such as Huldrych Zwingli. Some strove for orthodoxy, such as Thomas More; others turned eclectic, such as Conrad Mutianus Rufus or covertly heretical such as Juan de Valdés.

Desiderius Erasmus of Rotterdam (c.1467–1536) ultimately epitomized Christian humanism in both its critical and its constructive purposes, not because all could agree with him but because he made substantial contributions as did no other to the comprehensive range of Christian humanist endeavors. Around 1500 he began to apply his long-standing literary interests to a programmatic renewal of Christian life and learning that he came to call the *philosophia Christi.* Fundamental to this approach was the use of humanist textual criticism in order to understand the Bible better and, along with it, the fathers of the church who had been its earliest interpreters. As conceived in his treatises on theological method (notably the *Ratio Verae Theologiae* [1518] and *Ecclesiastes* [1535]) and as exemplified in his repeatedly reissued *Paraphrases* of and his *Annotations* on the New Testament, in his other scriptural commentaries, and in the mass of polemics and apologiae that filled his later years, he proposed to base theology on philological and historical methods rather than metaphysical and logical ones. Hence Erasmus's lifelong projects were the editing of the New Testament, as well as of Augustine, Jerome, Origen, John Chrysostom, and other church fathers. He intended this methodological turn to serve his ultimate goal of church reform and widespread spiritual renewal. To those ends, he published throughout his life practical treatises: on the educations of children, youth, and the clergy; on literary style and social manners; on the spiritual practice appropriate for different callings, notably for laypersons, princes, spouses, widows, preachers, and youths. In his much-published *Colloquies*, fictional dialogues often in a playful or satirical vein, and in his *Adages*, commentaries on literally thousands of sayings culled from Greek and Latin sources, he found literary genres to popularize his philosophy and the classics while commenting on current affairs. While his still classic *The Praise of Folly* epitomizes his lifelong call for church reform, he refused, as did many humanistic reformers of his generation, to side with the Protestant reformers. Catholic and Protestant officials found him recurringly suspect, yet he exercised enduring, if elusive, influence on many in subsequent generations.

Some might say that Philipp Melanchthon (1497–1560) reflected Erasmus's breadth of scope—or even surpassed it by his institutional applications of it—but Melanchthon's professed Lutheranism limited his range of effectiveness in a way that Erasmus's somewhat ambiguous Catholicism did not. In any event, from about 1516 to the mid-1550s, virtually all the major reformers and Christian humanists had to come to terms with some aspect of Erasmus's protean legacy as they developed their own programs. Erasmus's own theology and his proposals for reform were nowhere implemented exactly as he had envisioned them, but elements derived from his teachings, methods, style, and even temperament reappeared as if refracted in the many reformations of the era. Many masters of sixteenth-century Spanish spirituality drew substantively from Erasmus. The irenic strain of Anglicanism, with its willingness to forgo debate on adiaphora, is often traced to Erasmus's wide influence in England. Johannes Sturm's model gymnasium at Strasbourg, itself the model for Calvinist academies at Geneva and internationally, incorporated elements of Erasmian pedagogy. Many radicals and Anabaptists drew their highly spiritualized notion of sacrament from premises found in Erasmus. Thus the humanist character or the Erasmian influence found in a given reformer or reform must be assessed case by case.

Bearing in mind the flexibility of humanist method and the actual variety of humanists' beliefs and teachings, one may survey the humanist elements in the various reformations. From the late 1510s, Martin Luther's enthusiasm for the classics, as well as the early support he received from influential humanists, further enhanced the status of humanist studies at the University of Wittenberg, where they had been favored since the university's founding in 1502. Similarly, Luther's closest associates at Wittenberg had been deeply versed in humanist studies before their association with him. Justus Jonas had introduced a humanist curriculum at the University of Erfurt before he became Luther's translator and his representative at diets and colloquies. Johannes Bugenhagen had been a classicist pedagogue before he became pastor of the Wittenberg parish, Luther's confessor until Luther's death, and the appointed reformer of numerous northern cities and principalities, notably Denmark.

Again, despite the sometimes serious disagreements between Luther and Melanchthon, Luther, as also the Lutheran princes and magistrates, valued that formation whereby Melanchthon imparted an enduring humanist cast to Lutheran preaching, secondary and clerical education, the ethos of the new Lutheran universities, and especially the rhetorically derived theological method of his influential *Loci Communes*. Thus, the traumatic debate between Luther and Erasmus from 1524 to 1527 on the freedom or bondage of the will, which resulted in implacable hostility between them, should not distract from the emergence of something like a Lutheran humanism. It is symptomatic of this influence that important associates of Luther maintained a respect for Erasmus at variance from Luther's abusive stance, except for Jonas, who came hesitantly to share Luther's view.

The Lutheran reform also stimulated literary production in the high classical style, as in the skillful Latin poetry of Eobanus Hessus, and the satires, polemics, and Latin dramas of Thomas Kirchmeyer. Beyond 1560, even as Melanchthon's posthumous fortunes varied in the Gnesio-Lutheran struggles, humanist education and tastes dominated the culture of the educated classes in Lutheran Europe into the seventeenth century.

To a marked degree, humanism influenced all the initial reformers of Switzerland and Strasbourg, as also their successors. Strasbourg, and Alsace more widely, had been receptive to Christian humanism since at least the 1490s. The satire and moralism of Sebastian Brant's *Ship of Fools* (1494) enjoyed wide and ongoing popularity. The pedagogical efforts of Jakob Wimpfeling at the turn of the century were a harbinger of Johannes Sapidus's and later Johannes Sturm's Reformed humanistic schools. In the Franciscan humanist Thomas Murner, Alsace produced one of the strongest polemicists and satirists against the Lutheran cause. At Strasbourg from 1523, Martin Bucer's theology, especially regarding the sacraments, was influenced equally by Erasmus and Luther, but his irenic churchmanship followed an Erasmian pattern. Bucer expanded his influence when he was called to England in 1549 as adviser to Archbishop Thomas Cranmer and as regius professor of theology at Cambridge. Wolfgang Capito, another leader of reform at Strasbourg, had advised Erasmus on points of Hebrew arising from Erasmus's 1516 edition of the New Testament. At Strasbourg Capito's establishment of public schools with carefully supervised moral education embodied humanist ideals, as his irenic abhorrence of public unrest reflected Erasmus's own. Similarly, Nikolaus Gerbel brought to his reforming and educational work the distinction he had earned in Strasbourg's humanist literary circles.

In German-speaking Switzerland, Zwingli came to his reforming work at Zurich in 1519 after long humanist studies of the classics, holy scripture, and the church fathers, as well as a deep acquaintance with Erasmus's works. He reformed devotional practices long lampooned by humanists; his theological positions, which showed parallels to Luther's, also manifest indubitable signs of humanist, even Erasmian, influence in his style and argumentation. When Johannes Oecolampadius introduced the reform at Basel in 1527, he brought to bear the convictions and skills of a distinguished humanist training that included Hebrew and Greek studies under Johannes Reuchlin, assistance to Erasmus in preparation of his 1516 New Testament, and a long friendship with Capito. Although theological and pastoral disagreements strained his relationship with Erasmus, the two avoided an open breach. On Oecolampadius's death in 1531, Oswald Myconius, Zwingli's humanist colleague, assumed leadership of the church in Basel until 1552. Even the remote St. Gall found its reformer in the humanist poet laureate and physician Joachim Vadian, active there from 1520 to his death in 1551.

The case of Geneva extends the pattern of Swiss humanist reformers, except that its representatives, Guillaume Farel, Pierre Viret, and John Calvin, had studied in France. Farel had studied at Paris under Jacques Lefèvre d'Étaples, the humanist theologian with evangelical and reformist leanings, prior to Farel's introduction of reform at Neuchâtel in 1530 and, with Viret, at Geneva in 1535. Calvin had distinguished himself as a humanist by his commentary on Seneca's treatise on mercy, *De Clementia* (1532); he participated to some degree in the humanist circles at Paris, whose agitation for reform led to their being discredited by the king and the Sorbonne in 1533–1534. Scholars agree that humanist methods, style, and even intellectual perspectives deeply influenced his theology, his masterful French and Latin prose, his sense of public morality and civic order, and his insistence on sound and universal education; they differ predictably on the specific extent of humanist influence in any given point of Calvin's theology.

Humanist elements stand out also in Calvin's legacy. When Calvin founded his internationally celebrated Genevan academy to carry on his teaching, he modeled it on Sturm's humanist gymnasium at Strasbourg. His successor as leader of the Genevan church until 1605 was Théodore de Bèze, who had composed humanist poetry as a loose-living youth and humanist history later on, and who went on to produce a critical edition of the Greek New Testament in his mature years. As with Lutheranism after Luther, so did Calvinism after Calvin often, but not always, foster humanist schools and studies as it spread beyond Geneva. Dutch Calvinist culture proved amenable to the humanist spirit in its openness to classical tastes, the arts, and incipient scientific study.

Although the English Reformation is often pictured as a series of shifting compromises, closer attention reveals a continuity of humanist, even Erasmian, influence shaping the religious ethos of the Henrician, Edwardian, and Elizabethan reforms and settlements. From the 1490s, prominent humanist reformers had generated patronage for educational innovations. John Colet, the founder of Saint Paul's School at London, John Fisher, the founder of Saint John's College at Cambridge, and Lady Margaret Beaufort, the founder of Christ's College also at Cambridge, established their respective institutions to instill ideals of piety and humanist learning among clergy, lawyers, and courtiers. Such goals were epitomized in the ascent of the great humanist Thomas More to the chancellorship of the realm (1529–1532), the first layman to hold that office. The disastrous ends of John Fisher and Thomas More should not distract attention from the Erasmian ideals of the humanists enlisted to guide Henry VIII's and Cromwell's conservative middle way between Roman allegiance and Continental Protestant "excess," a royal policy that opposed monasticism (albeit with motives of royal profit) and favored a simplification of traditional doctrine, lay piety, and ritual.

These ideals were expanded during the moderate Protestant phase (1547–1550) of Edward VI's reign, led by the dowager queen Katherine Parr, who was imbued with traditions of humanist evangelicalism and Erasmian piety. As a chief example, Erasmus's *Paraphrases* of the Gospels were required to be translated and accessible in every church of the realm. Martin Bucer and Peter Martyr Vermigli, the moderate Continental reformers called to advise and teach in England, guaranteed an Erasmian mediating influence among Protestant differences even in the more Calvinist phase of the reign (1550–1553). The Elizabethan Settlement of 1559 itself incorporated many principles of earlier Christian humanism and Erasmianism: a commitment to considering as nonessential a wide range of dogmatic issues whose theological clarification might rend the church; a full sense of lay vocation nurtured by scriptural study; education of the clergy that emphasized scripture and the church fathers; and extermination of practices and beliefs considered unscriptural or extravagant.

Whatever other influences marked the Elizabethan and later Stuart church, there are undeniably humanist strains in the Anglican *via media*. As J. K. McConica has argued, these result not from political compromise but from a constructive program in recognizable continuity with Christian humanist traditions; their humanism is furthermore of a piece with the humanist and classicizing tendency in later Tudor and Stuart English culture at large. In the Puritan experience, moreover, Margo Todd has discerned patterns of public life derived from humanist paradigms.

The enormous diversity among the so-called radical reformers—the various Anabaptists, spiritualists, evangelical rationalists, and antitrinitarians—makes it difficult to generalize about humanist elements in their work. One must proceed with the radicals virtually person by person or movement by movement, especially because in many instances one may be dealing not with direct humanist orientation or influence on a reformer but with parallels, similarities, or simultaneous developments. Moreover, since most of the radical reform movements did not have the long-term institutional stability and political support that Protestant and Catholic reforms enjoyed, they could not foster the academies and universities that elsewhere insured the reciprocity of humanist studies and official religious reform.

Despite these limitations, one may observe the relevance for some radicals of humanist methods as well as the recurrence among them of the ideals of specific prominent humanists. Thus the humanist insistence on grounding theology in philological study of the Bible in its original Greek and Hebrew did indeed promote text-critical habits that led some, such as Lelio and Fausto Sozzini, to reject classical doctrines such as the Trinity and the divinity of Christ on the grounds that they lacked clear or sufficient scriptural basis. Some tendencies suggested by Erasmus's work found more forceful, systematic statement among Anabaptists and other radicals such as Conrad Grebel, Balthasar Hubmaier, and Menno Simons, all of whom used Erasmus's edition of the New Testament with his *Annotations* and *Paraphrases*. For example, his preference for the spiritual over the physical aspect of the sacraments led some to a complete spiritualization of them; his emphasis on the exemplary, moral, and pedagogical roles of Christ could be developed into a rejection of the atonement or of the divinity of Christ; his pointed comments on the centrality of the baptismal vows were adduced to oppose infant baptism; and his advocacy of peace converged with the Christian pacifism of some radicals.

An assessment of humanism in the Roman Catholic reform requires a preliminary note. The lands that remained in communion with Rome did not pursue a unified reform, much less accept papal leadership in the matter. In the early modern period and until the mid-1800s Roman Catholicism functioned as an assemblage of national churches jealously guarding historical prerogatives and jealously guarded by the Catholic monarchs. This feature rendered Catholic monarchs and hierarchy very selective in their cooperation with Roman authority, and it fostered a diversity and national autonomy in Catholic life entirely unfamiliar to Roman Catholics of the twentieth century. Moreover, just as in Protestant Europe, the reception of humanism varied from one realm to the other among the Catholic lands.

Hence two precautions are needed about the role of humanism in the Catholic reform. First, one must specify the forms of humanist influence prevalent in a realm or region. For example, Erasmus weighed far more heavily in reforms of the Spanish church than in those of the French. Second, and paradoxically in view of the first point, some aspects of Roman Catholicism (e.g., religious orders with their schools and colleges) did impart some homogeneous international features to Catholic reform as influenced by humanism.

Those international aspects are easily summarized. It is customary to note that during its first phase (1545–1549) the Council of Trent dealt a decisive blow to the influence of humanist biblical criticism by its affirmation of the authority of the Vulgate text as sufficient for use in dogmatic pronouncements. While this decree did not forbid further critical labors or even vernacular translations, it effectively broke for Catholics the bond that Lorenzo Valla, Erasmus, and others had sought to forge between philology and dogmatic theology. Beyond that, however, humanist influences were numerous on the international Catholic landscape. The history of preaching from 1550 through 1700 shows profound humanist influence in almost every Catholic region, as in many Protestant territories. While the history of schools, colleges, and seminaries still requires detailed research, the initiatives toward Latin education for a broader range of society, toward a learned and pious laity, and toward a better-trained clergy sprang from humanist ideals, among other incentives. During the Catholic reform, for the first time religious orders were founded for the exclusive purpose of teaching youths, although again their inspiration was not humanist in all cases. Two of the great new orders, however, were decidedly humanist in their educational and even pastoral ideals, the Jesuits and the French Oratorians. Indeed, modern research discloses more deeply the humanist elements inherent in early Jesuit spirituality, theology, and pastoral care.

For Italy, it is awkward to specify the role of humanism in reforming circles, first because humanism pervaded the intellectual life of Italy as nowhere else, and second because from its earliest appearance humanism was in league with a wide range of devotional, institutional, and theological reform movements. Some specific moments and persons do stand out, however, in the period after 1520. When Paul III (r. 1534–1549) took definitive steps toward curial and clerical reform and the calling of a council, he drew into his service churchmen distinguished by their humanist learning, their humanist piety and pastoral ideals, and their administrative or diplomatic vigor, notably his cardinals Gasparo Contarini, Girolamo Aleander, Jacopo Sadoleto, Giovanni Morone, Reginald Pole, and others. These humanist prelates influenced attempts at irenic relations with Protestants, the progress of some debates at the Council of Trent, and the like, although one must specify the humanist elements of their contributions in each case.

Another notable movement in Italy from the 1520s through the 1540s was the emergence of "evangelical" and "illuminist" circles among humanistically trained aristocrats and prelates. Their link to humanism appears in an emphasis on interpretation of biblical texts in philological context, together with their humanist ideal of a conscientious and competent laity. These elites sometimes preferred inward illumination to outward sacramental acts. This "spiritualizing" tendency often involved a striking coincidence with or even direct adoption of northern Protestants' teachings, leading them to hold positions increasingly in tension with what was emerging as the official Catholic teaching.

Juan de Valdés, an accomplished Spanish humanist active in Italy from 1531 to his death in 1541, represents a forceful figure in that development. Through the patronage of influential aristocratic women like Vittoria Colonna, Giulia Gonzaga, and others, as well as through the posthumous cultivation of his teachings in the entourage of Cardinal Pole, Valdés influenced numerous higher clergy and nobles. Employing a humanist analysis of the original biblical texts, he reached, apparently on his own, views of justification by faith and of good works strikingly similar to Luther's. He also precipitated profound conversions. Some of his followers struggled secretly with the implications of their conversions; others fled from Italy to become Protestant leaders abroad, most spectacularly Peter Martyr Vermigli and Bernardino Ochino.

Other than Valdés, Erasmus also aroused both discipleship and opposition on a widespread basis in Italian reform circles. By the 1550s, the Jesuits had begun to incorporate the humanist legacy in the popular boarding schools that they instituted for the formation of pious, learned laymen throughout Italy.

Even as more vigorous reform ensued after the Council of Trent, Italian culture was marked by an ingrained humanist legacy. This legacy accounts for the humanist historiography of the apologist Cardinal Cesare Baronio; the patristic pastoral ideal and rhetorical preaching style of many bishops; and a growing papal interest in the archaeology of the pagan and early Christian eras as part of their rebuilding of Rome as the center of Christendom.

In Castile and Aragon, the kingdoms then at the heart of what later became Spain, humanism could flourish thanks to indigenous humanist currents dating from the mid-fifteenth century as well as to powerful influences borne into Spain from Italy, where the king of Aragon was king of the Two Sicilies after 1504, and from the Low Countries, where Iberian commercial interests were strong. The flowering of Iberian humanism included one offshoot initially marked by strong reforming purposes. Elio Antonio de Nebrija (1441/44–1522) typified this early phase: trained in law and humanist studies in Italy, his philological approach to the scriptures presaged, and then contributed directly to, the great reforming efforts of Cardinal Francisco Jiménez de Cisneros. In Jiménez's capacities as primate of Spain, archbishop of Toledo, grand inquisitor, chancellor of Castile, and adviser to Isabella and Ferdinand, he undertook a vigorous and enduring reform of the church from the 1490s until his death in 1517. Although not himself a humanist, Jiménez patronized humanist methods in his reform of clerical education. His shining achievement was the opening in 1508 of a new university with a humanist curriculum at Alcalá (in Latin, *Complutum*), the first anywhere to offer Latin, Greek, and Hebrew as the basis of biblical study. This foundation led to one of the crowning glories of all Christian humanism, the *Complutensian Polyglot* (6 vols., 1514–1517), an edition of the Old Testament in Hebrew, Greek, and Latin, with an additional Aramaic text of the Pentateuch and the New Testament in Greek and Latin.

At this juncture, new influences enriched Spanish humanism as the international retinue of Charles V encouraged exchanges between Flemish and Spanish humanists. Just as the Dutch Erasmus enjoyed perhaps his widest range of influence in Spain, so the two greatest Spanish humanists of the age were to spend their careers abroad, Juan Luis Vives in and near Brugge, and Juan de Valdés at Naples. Vives, a man of exceptionally versatile talents, wrote important treatises on the education of women, relief of the poor, pedagogy of children, Christian devotion, and more. Valdés's immediate field of activity was Italy, as already discussed. As in Italy, so in Spain his work nurtured ideals of quietist, purely interior religiosity among covert reform circles and the illuminists, or *Alumbrados*. Moreover, his linguistic studies of Castilian decisively affected the development of the Spanish language.

Thanks to the exhaustive scholarship of Marcel Bataillon, scholars in the twentieth century have tended to conceive of what Bataillon called *"érasmisme"* as the dominant, even sole, influence pervading all the forms of Spanish humanism, whether heretical or orthodox, from about 1520 to 1550. The extent of Erasmus's influence within Spain was indeed varied, and arguably more widespread than in any other part of Europe.

Scholars are rediscovering, however, other important currents within Spanish humanism, such as the Italian variety that Spaniards learned while studying in Bologna, a philological sensitivity open to Aristotelian philosophy that proved over time more compatible with the revival of Scholasticism that occurred in Spanish universities of the later sixteenth century. A prominent forerunner in this direction was Juan Ginés de Sepúlveda (1490–1573), the royal chronicler for Charles V and Philip II and a distinguished translator of Aristotle, who defended both the Spanish conquest of America and the criticisms of Erasmus by the Catholic Alberto Pio of Carpi. Another was Francisco de Vitoria (1483/86–1546), a Dominican professor at Salamanca who mingled humanist and scholastic methods in his Thomist theology and whose still influential teachings on the theory of a just war led him to notable criticisms of the Spanish regime in the New World.

As the Spanish Inquisition grew more vigilant from about 1530, and more vigorous after the accession of Philip II in 1556, it sidetracked the reformist tendencies of Christian humanists. In some cases the humanists met with direct persecution, as in the protracted trial and punishment that finished the career of Juan de Vergara, an outspoken defender of Erasmus and Valdés, in the mid-1530s. Other humanists turned to noncontroversial subjects, as when Juan Maldonado came to distrust Erasmian ideals and turned to historical writing. Some currents simply went underground into the still incompletely explored world of the *Alumbrados* and the *Conversos*, Christian converts from Judaism and Islam. Finally, as noted with Sepúlveda and Vitoria, some Christian humanism simply merged with the Thomist and scholastic revival that flourished in the later sixteenth century at the University of Salamanca.

In Portugal the course of Christian humanism resembled that taken in Spain, an initially enthusiastic interest invigorated by contact with Erasmian currents but safely transmuted or simply muted after midcentury. Typical of the Iberian pattern, the best Portuguese humanist, Damiao de Gois, spent much of his career abroad. He took a lively interest in church reform, although he found Luther personally disappointing after their meeting in Wittenberg. He wrote humanistic treatises calling for humane treatment of the Ethiopians and the Lapps by merchants and colonizers dealing with them. The cardinal-prince Henry of Portugal (1512–1590), the inquisitor who closed his days as king, also typifies the Iberian pattern: a generous patron of humanists in his earlier years, he grew more cautious of their reforming ideals yet did invite the Jesuits to tutor the royal heir and to establish a university at Evora (1558).

Christian humanism in France enjoyed distinguished patronage from the 1510s through about 1540. The prodigious gifts of Jacques Lefèvre d'Étaples as textual critic and humanist commentator on Aristotle, the *Psalms*, and the New Testament stood for a program of recovering biblical and patristic texts as the path to purifying theology and reforming church life. (He also took a lively interest in mathematical and hermetic writings.) In 1521 he joined the reforming efforts of Guillaume Briçonnet, bishop of Meaux. Briçonnet sponsored Lefèvre's French translation of the New Testament; he assembled a like-minded group of clerics to preach reform in his see; and he used his influence at court to promote the Meaux reform throughout France. In the early 1520s Lefèvre and the Meaux circle grew closer to Luther's or Zwingli's positions on justification, the sacraments, and the priesthood. This potential for heresy prompted harsh reactions against them. Although rehabilitated by 1530, they maintained a low profile thereafter. Their most influential affiliation was with Marguerite d'Angoulême, sister of King Francis I and wife of Henry II, king of Navarre, an exceptionally learned and pious woman, and the author of distinguished literary and religious works. Her *Mirror of a Sinful Soul* stirred controversy for its resemblance to Protestant views of faith. She defended French evangelicals as she herself moved toward eclectic, heterodox beliefs.

The continuity of reformist French Christian humanism was disrupted, however, as the penetration of Protestant propaganda from Switzerland and Germany made the royal court and the censors of the Sorbonne increasingly vigilant against innovation from 1534 forward. Although desires for religious peace deriving from humanist circles did animate the hopes of some for an irenic settlement of Huguenot-Catholic differences at the unsuccessful Colloquy of Poissy (1561), the subsequent Wars of Religion deferred until after 1594 any effective reform of the French church, and thereby any question of humanist influence in such reform. Humanism penetrated many other areas of French intellectual life during the religious wars and thereafter contributed to discrete developments within the French church, as in the spirituality of Francis de Sales known as Devout Humanism, in the Jesuit colleges, and in the great age of French pulpit oratory during the seventeenth century. Other equally prominent schools of French spirituality were not, however, distinctively humanist.

Taken as a whole, the Habsburg hereditary territories within and adjoining the Holy Roman Empire—from Swabia, the Tirol, and Austria to Hungary, Moravia, Bohemia, and Silesia—came after 1550 to represent a religious amalgam more exceptional than typical for Europe. That pattern, however, reveals an important dimension of the enduring legacy of Reformation humanism. In the interests of territorial and dynastic integrity, the Catholic Habsburgs generally tolerated the entire range of available religious positions to co-exist in their dominions, including, beside the official Catholicism of their own dynasty, most of the magisterial Protestant groups, the Bohemian Brethren, and even antitrinitarians. This *de facto* pluralism made most confessional groups recognize their need for knowledgeable members and articulate apologists trained in the humanist arts of rhetoric and history. Confessionally based humanist schools, sometimes modeled on Jesuit or Calvinist academies, frequently supplied that need. Imperial counselors from the later years of Charles V through his successors Ferdinand I (r. 1556–1564) and Maximilian II (r. 1564–1576) typically advised moderate Erasmian religious policies. Central European "late humanism," or *Späthumanismus,* under these Habsburgs, with its memorable flourishing in the cosmopolitan atmosphere of Prague under Rudolf II (r. 1576–1612), merged with this religious pluralism to favor a spirit of comprehensiveness transcending confessional divisions, best seen perhaps in the fascination of the age for hermeticism and schemes of universal knowledge.

The Habsburgs' toleration decisively changed as the Thirty Years' War drew on. The earlier Rudolfine pattern, however, points to a larger truth about humanism throughout Europe as the sixteenth century came to its close. By the end of the century, religious unity proved elusive even within major confessions as their attempts at doctrinal refinement triggered furious intra-confessional divisions. Yet whether in the bitter dogmatic polemics among late Reformation Lutherans, or in the jaded religious atmosphere of the Habsburg court, everyone had read Cicero. That is, humanism provided Europeans with the basis of a cosmopolitan culture that religion could no longer offer. Even as vernacular literatures took shape in the age of Montaigne, Cervantes, Luìz Vaz de Camões, Shakespeare, Torquato Tasso, and Hans Sachs, they did so often under impulses toward definition of genre, unity of style, consolidation of vocabulary, and regularization of syntax gleaned from classical and humanist influences.

Humanists, their interests, and their methods shaped the religious reforms in every corner of Europe, decisively overall yet diversely according to the varying doctrinal struggles, exegetical methods, and institutional or political configurations. They also contributed substantively to the other major developments of the sixteenth century, not only in the arts but also notably in secondary education and university reform, the writing of contemporary history as a means of defining and legitimating the political and religious changes of the era, and the reshaping of statutory law and of political theory. By 1600 educated Europeans could regularly assume in each other familiarity with a canon of readings, tastes, and skills imparted by a humanist curriculum, an idiom that helped them to transcend geographical and denominational divisions. By providing one basis among others for a new common culture, a recognizably European culture that would endure into the twentieth century, humanism joined together what religion had put asunder.

[*See also* Adiaphora; Antitrinitarianism; Colloquies; Jesuits; Nicodemism; Pacifism; Pelagianism; Philippists; Politiques; Renaissance; *and* Socinianism.]

BIBLIOGRAPHY

Augustijn, Cornelis. *Erasmus: His Life, Works, and Influence.* Translated by J. C. Grayson. Toronto, 1991. An excellent recent introduction to the major Christian humanist, if not as popular as Roland Bainton's *Erasmus of Christendom,* New York, 1969.

Bouwsma, William. *John Calvin: A Sixteenth-Century Portrait.* New York, 1988. Explores the profound relationship of Calvin's humanist origins to his activities as a reformer.

Chrisman, Miriam Usher. *Lay Culture, Learned Culture: Books, Men, and Ideas in Strasbourg, 1480–1599.* New Haven, 1982. Describes the civic and institutional context of one of the major meeting places of humanism and reform.

Evans, R. J. W. *The Making of the Habsburg Monarchy, 1550–1700.* Oxford, 1979. Chapters 1, 3, and 9–12 offer rich detail on intellectual and religious developments in Habsburg territories, assigning great weight to humanist interests in the later Reformation period and developing the thesis of the author's acclaimed ealier work *Rudolf II and His World,* 2d ed., Oxford, 1984.

Fenlon, Dermot. *Heresy and Obedience in Tridentine Italy: Cardinal Pole and the Counter-Reformation.* Cambridge, 1972. Although not about humanism as such, this work takes a close look at some of the humanist Italian circles influenced by Juan de Valdés.

Fleischer, Manfred P., ed. *The Harvest of Humanism in Central Europe: Essays in Honor of Lewis W. Spitz.* Saint Louis, 1992. Essays demonstrating the enduring humanist influence in German religion and culture in the later 1500s and early 1600s.

Friesen, Abraham. "Humanism and Anabaptism: A Study in Paradigmatic Similarities." In *The Harvest of Humanism in Central Europe: Essays in Honor of Lewis W. Spitz,* edited by Manfred P. Fleischer, pp. 233–262. Saint Louis, 1992. Brief overview and helpful bibliography on the relationships between humanism and the radical reformers.

Goodman, Anthony, and Angus MacKay. *The Impact of Humanism on Western Europe.* London and New York, 1990. Probably the first book a beginning student should read; twelve essays cover every facet of humanism and the regions of western Europe affected by it. Chapter 2 (on church reform) is relevant to the present entry.

Kelley, Donald R. *Renaissance Humanism.* Boston, 1991. Insightful, comprehensive, brief introduction to the many aspects of humanism, with helpful bibliography of works in English. Together with Goodman and MacKay and Kristeller, excellent for a beginner.

Kohl, Benjamin. *Renaissance Humanism, 1300–1550: A Bibliography of Materials in English.* New York, 1985. Helpful for beginning research in English. (See Rabil and Tracy for materials in other languages.)

Kristeller, Paul Oskar. "Humanism." In *The Cambridge History of Renaissance Philosophy,* edited by Charles B. Schmitt, et al., pp. 113–137. Cambridge, 1988. Kristeller reoriented scholarship so as to see humanism as a set of disciplines and intellectual methods derived from the fivefold *studia humanitatis* rather than as a specific philosophy. His view, synthesized in this article, has become definitive.

Logan, George M. "Substance and Form in Renaissance Humanism." *Journal of Medieval and Renaissance Studies* 7 (1977), 1–35. A crucial complement to Kristeller's view, this article argues that beyond the disciplines shared by humanists (as defined by Kristeller), specific substantive issues and habits of mind also shaped and united them.

Mansfield, Bruce. *Phoenix of His Age: Interpretations of Erasmus, c.1550–1750.* Toronto, 1979. Describes Erasmus's enduring role in Christian humanism and in the varieties of reform.

McConica, James Kelsey. *English Humanists and Reformation Politics under Henry VIII and Edward VI.* Oxford, 1965. Documents the centrality of Erasmian humanism in English reform even into the reign of Elizabeth I.

O'Malley, John W. *The First Jesuits: Their Ministries, Their Culture, Their Way of Proceeding, 1540–1565.* Cambridge, Mass., 1993. Shows the importance of humanism for the Jesuits, especially chapter 7.

Rabil, Albert, Jr., ed. *Renaissance Humanism: Foundations, Forms, and Legacy.* Vol. 1, *Humanism in Italy;* Vol. 2, *Humanism beyond Italy;* Vol. 3, *Humanism and the Disciplines.* Philadelphia, 1988. Encyclopedic treatment of humanism in forty-one articles by almost three-dozen specialists. Unfortunately, some important essays in vol. 2 do not move far enough into the sixteenth century. On humanism, theology, and reform, see especially the articles by Trinkaus, D'Amico, and Spitz in vol. 3.

Spitz, Lewis W. "The Course of German Humanism." In *Itinerarium Italicum: The Profile of the Italian Renaissance in the Mirror of Its European Transformations,* edited by Heiko Oberman and Thomas A Brady, Jr., pp. 371–436. Leiden, 1975. Spitz traces the relationships of humanism and Protestant, especially Lutheran, reform in greater detail than in his (also insightful) essays on the same topic in the Rabil and Goodman and MacKay volumes.

Tracy, James D. "Humanism in the Reformation." In *Reformation Europe: A Guide to Research,* edited by Steven Ozment, pp. 33–58. Saint Louis, 1982. A guide to bibliography on the entire subject.

Trinkaus, Charles. *In His Image and Likeness: Humanity and Divinity in Italian Humanist Thought.* 2 vols. Chicago, 1971. This work reoriented the understanding of Italian humanism by disclosing its widespread interest in religion and theology.

Todd, Margo. *Christian Humanism and the Puritan Social Order.* Cambridge and New York, 1987. Develops important theses about civic, religious, and Calvinist forms of humanism by exploring their relevance to Puritanism.

James Michael Weiss

HUNGARIAN COETUS. *See* Liber Bursae Wittenbergae.

HUNGARY. King Matthias Corvinus (Mátyás Hunyadi; r. 1458–1490) was dead and Hungary's "Golden Age" seemed to be drawing to a close when the sixteenth century began. Matthias, the nemesis of Frederick III, was followed on the Hungarian throne by the Polish Jagiellons—the weak Ulászló II (r. 1490–1516) and his son, Louis II, who died at the Battle of Mohács in 1526 at the age of twenty. Ferdinand I, the brother of the widowed Queen Mary, was crowned king of Hungary in 1527, but his rule of Hungary was not secure. A majority of Hungarian nobles had previously elected János Zápolya as king. Ferdinand was able to establish Habsburg rule only in western and Upper (or northern) Hungary (the Felvidék, modern Slovakia), which was inhabited by Slovaks, Magyars, Germans, Ruthenes, Poles, and Jews. Transylvania and the *Partium*, the eastern counties of Hungary along the Tisza River, were governed by Zápolya, his son János Zsigmond, and the Báthorys for the rest of the century. The Turks, under Süleyman II, established their control over central Hungary by 1541.

While the Magyar nobles bemoaned the division of Hungary, they had contributed to its decline. Most of its land was owned and administered by about twoscore magnate families. The lesser Magyar nobles resented the influence foreigners had obtained. During the fifteenth century Italian influence grew after Matthias Corvinus married Beatrix of Aragon. Germans had been invited by Louis I "the Great" to repopulate sections of Hungary ravaged by the Tatars in 1242. They prospered and contributed significantly to the cultural diversity and economic resources of Hungary. They also aroused the envy of many lesser Magyar nobles. The dissatisfaction of the peasants and mine workers grew as their financial condition deteriorated and exactions to maintain the nobles, the monarch, and the state administration increased. In 1514 a peasant force recruited for a crusade against the Turks, which rebelled under the leadership of George Dózsa, was crushed by Zápolya and his army. The *Opus Tripartitum*, the compilation of Hungarian laws prepared by István Werböczy, confirmed the exclusion of the peasantry from the political life of the nation while confirming the privileges of the nobility and of the free cities. In 1526 a Miners' Revolt in Upper Hungary, which the lesser nobles and ecclesiastical hierarchy blamed on the spread of Reformation ideas, was also suppressed. Even the relatively well-to-do citizens of the free cities and market towns began to experience economic difficulties and sought to assert their civic rights. Each group in Hungary was ready and determined to advance its own interests; no one found the political will or made the financial commitment necessary to maintain the kingdom.

The church in Hungary, as part of the political, economic, and social order, reflected and even contributed to the distress of the kingdom. The hierarchy was probably no worse than it was in other European countries; it certainly was no better. The income of the higher clergy, who frequently held multiple benefices, was substantial and stood in stark contrast to that of the lower clergy. The nobility were equally offended by and envious of the wealth, political power, nepotism, and pluralism of the higher clergy, and the foreign origin of some of the highest clerics infuriated the lesser Magyar nobles. During the reign of Matthias Corvinus two Italians held the archbishopric of Esztergom. At the end of the fifteenth century, a cousin of Queen Beatrix, Hippolyte d'Este, held the same archdiocese at the age of seven and was named a cardinal at the age of fourteen. The life of the regular and secular clergy often came under scrutiny and was criticized by many in Hungary who, as early as the end of the fifteenth century, advocated the secularization of church lands, cloisters, and schools.

At the same time, the religious and intellectual life of Hungary flourished. In Bardejov, in northeast Upper Hungary, thirteen winged altars were commissioned for the parish church between 1450 and 1510, while in nearby Levoča, in 1518, the noted sculptor Master Paul (Pavol of Levoča) completed work on the largest late-Gothic carved altars in middle Europe. Common throughout the region were religious-social lay associations, or fraternities, such as the Corpus Christi fraternity in Banská Bystrica. The preserved works of late Gothic and early Renaissance artisans bear witness to both the piety and wealth in late medieval Hungary. The *Devotio Moderna* and humanism, both in their Italian and northern forms, spread throughout the kingdom as, during the second half of the fifteenth century, nearly one thousand students from Hungary attended the University of Vienna and more than twelve hundred matriculated at Kraków. Erasmianism and Franciscan spirituality—as preached, for example, by Pelbart Temesvári and Oszvát Laskai—was a significant force throughout the region, and some of the early reformers were originally Franciscans. The scattered remnants of Hussitism also indirectly helped to prepare the way for the Reformation.

The Evangelical Phase, 1520–1548. The first reports about Martin Luther and his earliest printed works were probably brought to Hungary by merchants who regularly traveled to Poland and the empire. In 1521 Thomas Preisner of Lubica (near Kežmarok) read Luther's Ninety-five Theses from his pulpit. By 1522 the views of the Wittenberg reformer were known in the mining cities of central Upper Hungary and in Transylvania. The prior of a monastery near Dresden sent some of Luther's pamphlets to the pastor of Banská Štiavnica, while the notary of the town, Bartolomew Fankfordinus, and George Eysker, a member of the council, expressed sympathy with the reformer in their correspondence. In the same year George Baumheckel from nearby Banská Bystrica became the first of more than one thousand students from Hungary to matriculate at the University of Wittenberg. Valentin Schneider, the churchwarden, and his brother-in-law Valentine Schneider were open advocates of reform. Their attempt to call Simon Bernhard from Silesia to preach in the town precipitated a quarrel with Nicholaus of Sabinov, the city pastor, that lasted until the end of the decade. The city council, however, did invite Dominic Hoffmann from Silesia, John Kresling, and Conrad Cordatus to preach in the town for specific periods.

At the same time that Reformation theology entered northern Hungary, it also found supporters at the court in Buda: Simon Grynaeus, curator of the magnificent Corvina library; Viet Winsheim; Kresling, later the town pastor of Banská Štiavnica; and Cordatus, who served briefly as the chaplain of Queen Mary. Perhaps the most ardent advocate was George of Brandenburg-Ansbach, who was the military tutor of the young Louis II and confidant of his wife, Mary of Habsburg. Cordatus and George were criticized for their Germanic origins and religious views, and Cordatus was dismissed and imprisoned briefly. Mary herself seems to have sympathized with Erasmian views of ecclesiastical reform shared by John Henckel of Levoča, who replaced Cordatus as chaplain and served until she left for the Netherlands.

The support for the "German heresy" aroused the concern of the ecclesiastical hierarchy and the lesser Magyar nobles. In April 1523 the Hungarian Diet decreed that "all Lutherans and those favoring them . . . should have their property confiscated and themselves punished with death as heretics and foes of the most Virgin Mary." Werböczy was commended by the pope for his criticism of Luther, while Cardinal Lorenzo Campeggio, the papal legate to Hungary, urged sterner measures against the spreading heresy. In 1524 Cardinal Laszlo Szalkai, archbishop of Esztergom, sent a commission to the mining cities to search for and destroy heretical publications, and the following year the diet decreed that all Lutherans should be purged from the land.

The Miners' Revolt of 1525–1526 provided the opponents of the Reformation with arguments for even sterner antireformist measures; the disastrous Battle of Mohács (29 August 1526), however, made such measures difficult to enact and almost impossible to enforce. The battle cost the lives of King Louis II, the archbishops of Esztergom and Kalocsa, five bishops, twenty-eight magnates, hundreds of nobles, and thousands of impressed or mercenary soldiers and created conditions that fostered the further spread of the Reformation in Hungary.

While the rival kings struggled to exert their claimed royal authority and the Turks consolidated their occupation of central Hungary, bishoprics remained unoccupied or administered by nonconsecrated nominees, monastic communities dissolved, and ecclesiastical property was secularized. The Perényi and Szereny families, early staunch supporters of reform, enjoyed the substantial revenues from the bishopric of Eger from 1526 to 1545. Vacant ecclesiastical property was "administered" by the cities, by nobles, or was seized by the rival kings to finance their feud with and the expulsion of the Turks; some was in Turkish hands.

After the Battle of Mohács the number of schools increased steadily, and by the end of the sixteenth century more than 120 evangelical schools were maintained by the cities, towns, villages, and nobles. In the spirit of Johann Sturm, the rector in Strasbourg, and Philipp Melanchthon, they sought to inculcate both evangelical piety and humanist eloquence in the students, who were drawn from almost all strata of the population. Many of the graduates of these schools attended universities abroad, especially Wittenberg and other universities in Germany. These schools were important agents for the spread of the Reformation in Hungary.

As these students came home to become teachers, rectors, and pastors, they joined preachers supporting reform who had been called from or were natives of Bohemia, Silesia, and Germany. The German inhabitants in the cities of western and northern Hungary, as well as in Transylvania, identified with the Lutheran reform and were gradually joined by some of the leading noble families, who invited preachers of reform to serve in the courts and on their lands. In the Upper Hungarian cities and in Spiš county, where many of the inhabitants were German, Lutheranism was adopted during the 1530s and 1540s. In 1540 Michael Radašín became the city pastor of Bardejov and joined Leonard Stöckel, who had returned to the city as rector in 1539, to transform the city into a bastion of Lutheranism. In Spiš county George Leudischer introduced the Reformation in Kežmarok in 1531. In 1541 George Moeller, the senior of the fraternity of the pastors of the twenty-four Spiš towns, complained that it was impossible to find a Catholic priest to serve in the vacant parishes. Alexius Thurzo—the viceroy, or *locum tenes*, of Ferdinand I—became a Lutheran, as did Moeller, and the provost of Spiš county. Bartolomew Bogner from Brassó (in Transylvania) was called to implement Lutheran reforms in Levoča. By midcentury the pastoral fraternities of Spiš county, the five royal free cities of northeastern Upper Hungary, and the mining cities of central Upper Hungary were controlled by Lutheran reformers. During the 1540s the councils of the cities and nobles sympathetic to reform also appointed Slovak evangelical preachers to provide services for the largest segment of the population of Upper Hungary.There were, to be sure, individuals whose doctrines were more radical than those taught at Wittenberg. In Bardejov Wolfgang Schustel, a native of Košice who had studied at Kraków, was uncompromising in his demands for greater public piety, and his conflicts with the city council and the town pastor, Matthew Binder, ultimately led to Schustel's departure in 1531. Andreas Fischer, a Sabbatarian Anabaptist, traveled throughout Upper Hungary and Moravia and attracted a few supporters in Levoča and Švedlar before his execution in 1540.

The vast majority of early reformers in Hungary, however, were evangelical humanists inspired by, but not slavish adherents of, Luther and Desiderius Erasmus. The humanist János Sylvester, who studied at Kraków and Wittenberg and published a Hungarian translation of the New Testament in Sárvár (1541), taught on the estates of Thomas Nádasdy until he became professor of Hebrew at Vienna in 1554. Mátyás Bíro Devai, a former Franciscan and student at Kraków (1523–1526), returned from a brief stay at Wittenberg in 1529 to spread reform doctrines among the Magyar population of northern and central Hungary. His expositions of the doctrine of the Lord's Supper differed enough from Luther to arouse the concern of the Wittenberg reformer's followers in Upper Hungary. Michael Sztárai was also influenced by Luther and Melanchthon but was more concerned with practical reform of church life than with precise theological formulations. Trained in Padua and a member of the Franciscan order, he converted to the evangelical cause during the 1530s and worked in the western portions of Hungary occupied by the Turks, where he founded at least 120 congregations. Because of his conservative liturgical views and his less than precise presentation of the doctrine of the Lord's Supper Sztárai was attacked by advocates of Helvetic theology for his Lutheranism and by the Lutherans for his Sacramentarianism. The posthumously published works of István Szegedi Kis (1505–1572), who studied at Vienna, Kraków, and Wittenberg and began to work as a schoolmaster in the 1540s, manifest his affinity for the theology of Heinrich Bullinger.

As the Reformation spread throughout Hungary, evangelical pastors sought at regular synods to organize and regulate the life of the Protestant communities. These synods, however, began to reveal that reformers were not in full theological accord. While the synods of Ordea Mare and Ardud (in Transylvania) and then at Prešov (in Upper Hungary) in 1546 expressed the agreement of the pastors with the Augsburg Confession, they often differed on the exact meaning of its formulations. The differentiation of the evangelical humanist reform movement into confessional communities had begun.

The Confessional Phase, 1548–1570. The confessionalization of the Reformation in Hungary was precipitated by the Council of Trent and the attempt to revitalize Catholicism in Hungary, by the defeat of the Protestant Schmalkald League in Germany, and by the 1548 edict of the Hungarian Diet against religious innovations. The Lutheran party joined with the Roman Catholics to enact an article that decreed the expulsion of Anabaptists and Sacramentarians from the kingdom. The Lutheran cities and nobles believed that Ferdinand had tacitly recognized the Augsburg Confession and that the edict did not threaten them. The Roman Catholic hierarchy, however, interpreted it as prohibiting all religious innovations and was prepared to enforce it against all the evangelical reformers who were still under their ecclesiastical jurisdiction. They created commissions of inquiry to conduct visitations and expel reformers of whatever persuasion. In response to these internal and external threats, the reform communities in Hungary began to prepare confessional statements, to defend the orthodoxy of their faiths, to petition for toleration, and to define more precisely the content of the faiths to be tolerated.

In 1549 Bishop Stephen Bardala undertook a visitation of northeastern Hungary. Representatives of the five royal free cities of the region (Bardejov, Prešov, Košice, Sabinov, and Levoča) gathered and accepted a confession of twenty articles (*Confessio Pentapolitana*), prepared by Leonard Stöckel of Bardejov on the basis of the Augsburg Confession, which they presented to the bishop for transmission to Ferdinand. During the next decade, as Nicholas Olah sought to introduce Tridentine reforms into Hungary, called regular synods, and ordered visitations to improve pastoral discipline in the local pastoral conferences, or *contubernia*. In August 1557 he ordered the pastors of the seven mining cities of central Upper Hungary (Banská Štiavnica, Banská Bystrica, Kremnica, Ľubietová, Nová Baňa, Banská Belá, and Pukanec) to meet with him at his residence in Trnava and to respond to the articles he had sent to them the previous year. They refused to attend the meeting and in 1559, at a synod in Kremnica, adopted the *Confessio Montana* as a defense of their faith. For this, the primate excommunicated the clergy. But neither he nor Ferdinand were in a position to move against the cities. Eleven years later Bishop Paul Bornemisza ordered visitations to restore the cities and towns of Spiš county to Catholicism. They also defended their faith, this time with the *Confessio Scepusiana* of 1569, which was based on the *Confessio Montana*.

In the regions inhabited predominantly by the Magyars, the evangelical humanist reform movement began to divide into specifically Lutheran and Helvetic communities. Many Magyars studied at Wittenberg, where they organized the *Liber Bursae Wittenbergae*, a Hungarian bourse, and were particularly influenced by Philippism. The number visiting other reformed universities also increased, as did their attraction to Helvetic theology, especially that of Heinrich Bullinger, who wrote for the Hungarians a short summary of his doctrine, *Institutio Christianae fidei ad oppresas Hungariae Ecclesias*.

While Péter Bornemisza, who studied at Padua and Wittenberg, and Michael Sztárai were leading supporters of Lutheranism among the Magyars, Mártin Kálmáncsehi, and Péter Somogyi Melius, and Gáspár Károlyi, senior at Göncz and translator of the Bible into Hungarian (Vozsoly, 1590), were among the most significant Magyar supporters of Helvetic theology during the confessional phase. Kálmáncsehi worked in the region around Debrecen and in the *partium*, the lands east of the Tisza River, protected by Peter Petrovics. At synods held at Beregszáz (1552), Ovár (1554), and Ardud (1555), Philippist and Bullingerian influences were clear among the evangelical clergy. At a synod in Czenger in 1558, the formulations of the Second Helvetic Confession were reflected in the *Confessio Czengerini*, which it accepted. When the bishop of Eger, Anton Verantius, sought to restore Catholicism to the city in which he had his cathedral, the citizens adopted a confession of faith known as the *Confessio Agrovallensis*, or *Confessio Catholica* (1562). Five years later, Péter Melius convened a synod at Debrecen to deal with the growing influence of antitrinitarian doctrines in eastern Hungary. Three confessions were accepted: one in Hungarian, a longer one in Latin, and the Second Helvetic Confession.

The Consolidation of the Reformation, 1570–1608. By 1570 the Reformation had gained broad support throughout Hungary, though the process of confessionalization, which broadly differentiated the evangelical reformers in Hungary, also led to continuing theological conflict within and among reform groups. When the Lutherans in northern Hungary attempted to establish the Formula of Concord and *Book of Concord* as their doctrinal standard, nearly a quarter century of controversy followed. With the support of Gregor Stančič Horváth de Gradecz—a capable lay theologian, patron, and rector of a school at Strážky (in Spiš county)—Eliás Láni, Severín Škultéty, Albert Grawer, and others sought to have the formula accepted at several synods in the region during the last two decades of the sixteenth century. They were opposed by representatives of Philippist and crypto-Calvinist views, including Sebastian Lam, Caspar Pilcz, and Anton Platner. Only after the turn of the century was the *Book of Concord* accepted as a doctrinal standard at synods (Žilina, 1610; Spiške Podhrade, 1614), thus establishing an ecclesiastical organization for the Lutherans of Habsburg Hungary legally independent of the jurisdiction of the Roman Catholic hierarchy. At the same time, the Reformed had to contend with the influence of antitrinitarianism, especially in eastern Hungary and Transylvania, as they also wrestled with the establishment of their communities at the end of the sixteenth century and with the implementation of Calvinist orthodoxy during the early seventeenth century. The separation of the various confessional camps was also confirmed at a series of colloquies. One of the most significant was held in 1581 at Csepreg (in western Hungary) on the lands of Francis Nádasdy, where Škultéty, Stančič, and others debated the representatives of the Reformed, led by Stephen Böjthe. The colloquy made it clear that neither party was able or willing to accept the other's views.

These confessional conflicts, the Lutheran attitudes toward the state, and the loyalty of many Lutheran magnates to the Habsburg dynasty help explain their initial reluctance to support the Calvinist Stephen Bocskay from Transylvania in his armed defense of religion and noble privileges (1604–1606). The Habsburgs, the Catholic hierarchy, and the Jesuits, sporadically active in the region after 1560, were not willing to admit defeat or allow the Protestants to gain formal legal recognition and toleration. During the Fifteen Years' War with the Turks (1591–1606), the Catholics had seized the church of Saint Elizabeth in Košice from the Lutherans (1604), and the Lutheran magnate Stephen Illésházy had his lands seized and was forced to flee into exile. When the diet of 1604 demanded a discussion of religious issues, Matthias dismissed the diet and added to the twenty-one articles it had approved a twenty-second article that prohibited the discussion of religious questions by the diet. Bocskay subsequently seized much of Upper Hungary. Matthias and Rudolf II were forced to accept the Peace of Vienna of 1606, negotiated by Bishop Melchior Khlesl and George Thurzo, the staunch patron of Lutheranism and palatine (1609–1616) in Hungary. Despite the opposition of the Roman Catholic hierarchy, the provisions of the treaty establishing toleration to the reform communities in Hungary were confirmed and enlarged by the diet of 1608. The reform communities, which included the majority of the population, were finally able to establish legally independent ecclesiastical organizations in Hungary.

BIBLIOGRAPHY

Benda, Kalman. "La réforme en Hongrie." *Bulletin de la Société de l'histoire du protestantisme français* 122 (1976), 1–53. An excellent brief overview of the Reformation in Hungary.

Bucsay, Mihály. *Der Protestantismus in Ungarn, 1521–1978: Ungarns Reformationskirchen im Geschichte und Gegenwart.* Vol. 1, *Im Zeitalter der Reformation, Gegenreformation und katholischer Reform.* Vienna, 1977. The standard modern survey of Hungarian Protestantism.

Daniel, David. P. "The Lutheran Reformation in Slovakia, 1517–1618." Ph.D. diss., Pennsylvania State University, 1972. The only lengthy treatment of the Reformation in Slovakia in English.

———. "The Acceptance of the Formula of Concord in Slovakia." *Archiv für Reformationsgeschichte* 70 (1979), 260–277. Examines the conflict between Lutherans and Calvinists and within the Lutheran movement in Hungary at the end of the sixteenth century.

———. "The Fifteen Years' War and the Protestant Response to Habsburg Absolutism in Hungary." *East Central Europe/L'Europe du centre-est* 8.1 (1981), 38–51. Examines the revolt of Stephen Bocskay and the extension of toleration to the Hungarian Protestants.

———. "The Reformation and Eastern Slovakia." *Human Affairs* 1.2 (1991), 172–186. Recent survey of cultural and theological developments.

———. "Hungary." In *The Early Reformation in Europe*, edited by Andrew Pettegree, pp. 49–69. Cambridge, 1992.

Evans, R. J. W. "Calvinism in East Central Europe: Hungary and Her Neighbours." In *International Calvinism, 1541–1715*, edited by Menna Prestwich, pp. 167–196. Oxford, 1985. An excellent survey of the role of Calvinism in early modern Hungary.

Glettler, Monika. "Problem und Aspekte der Reformation in Ungarn." *Ungarn-Jahrbuch: Zeitschrift für die Kunde Ungarns und verwandter Gebiete* 10 (1979), 225–239. A review of main themes and questions of the Hungarian Reformation.

Kvačala, Ján. *Dejiny reformácie na Slovensku.* Liptovsky svaty Mikula, Slovakia, 1935. Older but still useful history of the Reformation in Upper Hungary.

Mészáros, István. *XVI századi városi iskoláink és "studia humanitatis."* Humanizmus és Reformáció, no. 11. Budapest, 1981. Education in sixteenth-century Hungary.

Nagy, Barnabas. "Geschichte und Bedeutung des Zweiten Helvetischen Bekenntnisses in den Osteuropäischen Ländern." In *Glauben und Bekennen, Vierhundert Jahre Confessio Helvetica Posterior: Beiträge zu Ihrer Geschichte und Theologie,* edited by Joachim Staedtke, pp. 109–204. Zurich, 1966. Excellent examination of the significance of Heinrich Bullinger for Hungary.

Nyikos, Lajos. "Erasmus und der böhmisch-ungarische Königshof." *Zwingliana* 7 (1937), 246–374. Brief examination of the influence of early Reformation humanism at the court of Hungary.

Saria, Balduin. "Die Reformation im südslawischen Raum." *Kirchen im Osten* 12 (1969), 58–77. Good introduction to the Reformation in Slovenia and Croatia.

Sólyom, Jenő. *Luther és Magyarország: A Reformátor kapcsolata hazákkal hálálág.* Budapest, 1924. An older, classic study of the impact of Luther on Hungary.

Székely, György. "Gesellschaft, Kultur und Nationalität in der Lutherischen Reformation in Ungarn." In *450 Jahre Reformation,* edited by Leo Stern and Max Steinmetz, pp. 201–216. Berlin, 1967. An effective, brief presentation of the social context and impact of the Reformation.

Szlávik, Matthias. *Die Reformation in Ungarn.* Halle, 1884. A useful survey of the early Reformation in Hungary.

Tóth, William. "Highlights of the Hungarian Reformation." *Church History* 9 (1940), 141–156. For English-speaking readers a most useful brief survey.

Vajcik, P. *Školstvo, študijné a školské poriadky na Slovensku v. 16. storoši.* Bratislava, 1955. An excellent presentation of the development of schools in upper Hungary (Slovakia).

Zoványi, Jenő. *A reformáczió Magyarországon 1565-ig.* Reprint, Budapest, 1922. A classic older survey of the Reformation in Hungary.

———. *Magyarországi Protestáns Egyháztörténeti Lexicon.* Budapest, 1977. An encyclopedic dictionary of the history of Protestantism in Hungary.

DAVID P. DANIEL

HUNNIUS, Aegidius (also Giles Hunnius; 1550–1603), German Lutheran theologian and controversialist representing early Lutheran orthodoxy. Hunnius studied theology under Jakob Andreae, Jakob Heerbrand, Johannes Brenz, and Erhard Schnepf at Tübingen (1565–1574), becoming a staunch adherent of Württembergian confessionalism. After earning a doctorate in theology, Hunnius taught at the University of Marburg (1576–1592), where he worked energetically to eradicate "crypto-Calvinist" theological tendencies from the region (which seemed evident in movements toward Protestant unity in Hesse). The primary issue at stake in these controversies was the doctrine of ubiquity (cf. Hunnius's, *De persona Christi,* 1585). Hunnius's activities evoked heated debate and contributed to—and Hunnius himself approved of—the 1578 split between southern (Lutheran) and northern (Reformed) Hesse.

In 1592, Frederick William of Saxony invited Hunnius to the University of Wittenberg so that, together with two members of the Wittenberg faculty, Polykarp Leyser and Leonhard Hutter, he could help assure the ascendancy of Lutheran orthodoxy's theological priorities in Saxony. To that end, Hunnius accompanied Frederick William to the diet at Regensburg (1594) and counseled the duke to reject the proposal that the *variata* be submitted alongside the unaltered Augsburg Confession. At the Colloquy of Regensburg of 1601, Hunnius uncompromisingly represented Lutheran positions and led the debates against the Jesuits (particularly Jakob Gretser and Adam Tanner). Hunnius died at Wittenberg in 1602.

As a preacher and a theologian, Hunnius played a leading role in forging a distinctively Lutheran confessional theology in the period following the publication of the *Book of Concord* (1580). Negatively, Hunnius criticized all (whether Protestant or Roman Catholic) who, in his view, deviated from the theological priorities of the Lutheran confessional writings. Positively, Hunnius helped articulate early orthodox Lutheran understandings of Christology (the two natures and ubiquity of Christ), predestination (divine election), the scriptures (the church "recognized" them as inspired by God), and ecclesiology (the church was both invisible and visible).

BIBLIOGRAPHY

Bautz, Friedrich Wilhelm. "Hunnius, Aegidius." In *Biographisch-bibliographisches Kirchenlexikon,* edited by Traugott Bautz, vol. 2, pp. 1182–1183. Herzberg, 1990. The most recent and bibliographically sophisticated sketch of Hunnius available.

Elert, Werner. *The Structure of Lutheranism.* Saint Louis, 1962. Elert's systematization of Lutheran orthodoxy makes ample reference to Hunnius.

Montgomery, John. "The Fourth Gospel Yesterday and Today: An Analysis of Two Reformation and Two Twentieth-Century Commentaries on the Gospel According to St. John." *Concordia Theological Monthly* 34 (1963), 192–222. Includes a brief analysis of Hunnius's commentary on John.

Preus, Robert D. *The Theology of Post-Reformation Lutheranism: A Study of Prolegomena.* Vol. 1. Saint Louis, 1970. Refers to Hunnius in the context of Lutheran orthodoxy.

Schurb, Ken. "Sixteenth-Century Lutheran-Calvinist Conflict on the *Protevangelium.*" *Concordia Theological Quarterly* 54 (January 1990), 25–47. An investigation of Hunnius's disagreement with Reformed theologian David Pareus over the interpretation of *Genesis* 3:15.

WILLIAM R. RUSSELL

HUS, Jan (c. 1372–1415) Czech reformer and central figure in the early Bohemian Reformation. Born in Husinec in southern Bohemia, Hus received a master of arts degree from Charles University in Prague (1396) and commenced lecturing. He became a popular preacher at Prague's non-parochial Bethlehem Chapel (1402) and came under the influence of the English heretic John Wycliffe and, more significantly, the native Czech reform tradition of Jan Milič of Kroměříž and Matěj of Janov. Hus's extant sermons are consistently orthodox in his call for moral reform, but he created controversy by denouncing popular religious superstitions in Litomyšl and Wilsnack in Brandenburg (1405) and by defending preaching without an official approbation (1408). Hus's agenda cannot be considered radical in the sense of his Prague successors, the Hussites Jakoubek of Stříbro and Jan Želivský.

When the Council of Pisa (1409) exacerbated the Great Schism by electing Alexander V as the third pontiff in Christendom, King Václav IV, along with Hus, supported the Pisan pope. Archbishop Zbyněk maintained obedience to the Roman pope, Gregory XII. The ensuing conflict disrupted the progress of reformation. Spies were regularly present in Bethlehem Chapel, and in late 1409 Alexander instructed Zbyněk to prohibit preaching in private chapels, essentially a directive against Hus. Queen Žofie, who frequently was present when Hus preached, interceded on his behalf. But Hus's dramatic public stance of defiance, backed by more than two thousand parishioners, marked the transition of the Bohemian reform movement from reformation to revolution.

The popular movement gained control of the university when King Václav issued the Decree of Kutná Hora (1409), giving control of the German dominated institution to the Czechs. The Germans seceded and left to found a university in Leipzig. Hus was elected rector the same year.

The nascent popular movement with Hus as spokesman rapidly became identified, partly in error, as Wycliffite. Wycliffe's works had been condemned in 1403 and were burned in 1410 by order of the archbishop in Hradčany Castle. Hus protested, and two days later he was censured by Zbyněk in the first of four excommunications. During this time Hus transferred his appeal from the Curia Romana to Christ. He forfeited the political backing of the palace when he denounced the sale of indulgences. His bastion of popular endorsement, however, never wavered. Street demonstrators in Prague pledged obedience to Hus and decried his ecclesiastical and political detractors; Hus continued preaching. When Prague was placed under interdict (1412), Hus voluntarily went into exile.

During two years in retirement at the castles of Kozí Hrádek and Krakovec, Hus wrote no fewer than fifteen books. Among them were his most important, the Czech tracts *The Expositions* (1412), *Concerning Simony* (1413), the Latin treatise *De ecclesia* (1413), and his *Postil* (1413). These works contain theological critiques of the ecclesiastical system, the papacy, definition of the church, circumstances of obedience to ecclesiastical authority, and the abuses of simony and indulgences, all coupled with social concerns.

In the fall of 1414 Hus accepted an invitation to appear at the Council of Constance, which had been called by emperor-elect Sigismund and Pope John XXIII to deal with the papal schism. Although Sigismund promised Hus safe-conduct, Hus was arrested and incarcerated in the dungeon of a Dominican monastery. Pierre d'Ailly, Jean Gerson, and Francesco Zabarella were involved in the Hus case. The trial consisted of repeated calls for Hus's recantation, without discussion or qualification, of the alleged Wycliffite heresies in thirty articles extracted from Hus's works. Believing that none of the charges was accurate, Hus refused to perjure himself by abjuring that which he neither taught nor held. On 6 July the council degraded Hus from the priesthood, banned his teachings, and burned him and his books. He went to the stake and died singing. The events were carefully recorded in the chronicle of Petr of Mladoňovice, an eyewitness.

Johann Loserth (*Wiclif and Hus*, translated by M. J. Evans, London, 1884) first advanced the ideas that Hussitism was Wycliffism writ large in Bohemian letters and that Hus was an unoriginal thinker who was theologically and philosophically dependent on Wycliffe. While the notion prevails, in some quarters, that there is no basis for referring to a "Hussite" system of thought, since Hus's doctrine mirrors Wycliffe's (Howard Kaminsky, *A History of the Hussite Revolution*, Los Angeles, 1967), later scholarship has disputed these assumptions. During the sixteenth century Hus was perceived as being in the vanguard of Protestantism. While Hus has frequently been regarded as a precursor or forerunner to the Protestant movements, this notion has also been called into question. Hus challenged the structure and authority of the medieval church, denounced abuses, and approved the practice of Utraquism but held the soteriological principle *fides caritate formata*, retained the eucharistic dogma of transubstantiation, and delineated his paradigm of authority in terms of scripture, conscience, and tradition, not *sola scriptura*. He neither replaced the altar with the pulpit (Calvin, Zwingli) nor preached justification by faith (Luther).

As a luminary of late medieval dissent, Luther, Thomas Müntzer, and other reformers invoked Hus's memory. He passed into the hagiography and propaganda of the sixteenth century, which either made him Protestant or presented him in the role of a forerunner (Robert W. Scribner, *For The Sake of Simple Folk*, Cambridge, 1981). Distinct from the forerunner motif, Hus and the Hussites, together with the Waldensians, are sometimes referred to as "the First Reformation." His influence on the Reformation in the Czech lands comes indirectly via the Taborites and the Bohemian Brethren (Unitas Fratrum). Indeed, by the time the reforms of Luther and Calvin reached Bohemia a reformation spanning more than 150 years had preceded them. The implications of Hus's reforms involved religious, political, and socioeconomic factors, all of which had some impact in the sixteenth century, especially on the radical Reformation. Scholarly debates persist on whether Hus was a loyal son of the Roman church or a heretic, a Wycliffite or a product of the Czech reform tradition. His importance for the sixteenth-century Reformations lies more in his attack on abuses and immorality (moral reform) than in his theology (intellectual reform).

In the final analysis, Hus is distinguished among "heretics" in his almost immediate apotheosis from parish priest to promoter of sectarian innovation. Records of Hus's *passio* were read from the first anniversary of his death, his picture was circulated, and in some instances a liturgical office for his feast was observed. He was posthumously remembered as "Saint" Jan Hus, patron of a popular movement and reformation.

BIBLIOGRAPHY

Primary Sources

Hus, Jan. *On Simony.* Translated by Matthew Spinka. In *Advocates of Reform from Wyclif to Erasmus*, pp. 196–278. The Library of Christian Classics, vol. 14. Philadelphia, 1953. The most vigorous of Hus's works identifying simony as the greatest heresy of the church. Reflects the Bohemian context in salient fashion.

———. *The Letters of John Hus.* Translated by Matthew Spinka. Manchester and Totowa, N.J., 1972. A collection of over one hundred letters spanning the period c.1404–1415. More than half are from the Dominican prison in Constance. Especially valuable for its unsophisticated presentation of Hus's faith.

———. *De ecclesia* (The Church). Translated by David S. Schaff. Reprint, New York, 1974. Hus's definitive ecclesiology and the summation of his revolt against authoritarian papal primacy. The most systematic, comprehensive statement of the early Hussite movement. Provided the basis for much of the judgment against Hus at Constance.

Spinka, Matthew. *John Hus at the Council of Constance.* New York, 1965. A translation of the *Relatio de Mag: Joannis Hus causa* by Petr of Mladoňovice. The chronicle is based upon an eyewitness account of the proceedings of the council against Hus. The record is extremely sympathetic to Hus but is a faithful, comprehensive, and reliable source.

Secondary Sources

Fudge, Thomas A. "Myth, Heresy and Propaganda in the Radical Hussite Movement, 1409–1437." Ph.D. diss., University of Cambridge, 1992. Discusses Hus as a foundation of the Hussite movement, his years in exile, and his transmutation from reformer and martyr to patron saint and demagogue of a popular revolutionary movement. Comprehensive bibliography.

Spinka, Matthew. *John Hus' Concept of the Church.* Princeton, 1966. Strong historical articulation of Hus's ecclesiology. Fully conversant with the broad scope of Hus's works, both Latin and Czech. Denies that Hus's thought changed radically after 1412. Marred by the failure to take Marxist historiography seriously. Fails to appreciate the lacuna between Hus's ideas and the development of Hussitism and ignores any possible correlation.

———. *John Hus: A Biography.* Reprint, New York, 1978. The definitive biography. Does not come to terms with the social implications of Hus's agenda.

Vooght, Paul de. *L'hérésie de Jean Huss.* 2d. ed., rev. & enl. Louvain, 1975. Sympathetic treatment from a Roman Catholic perspective free from nationalistic bias. Separates Hus's defiance of authority from doctrinal deviance. Refutes the idea that Hus was completely dependent on Wycliffe. Judges Hus to be orthodox in most areas but seems reluctant to exonerate him completely of heresy in terms of ecclesiology and papal primacy. Fails to connect Hus to the Hussites.

Werner, Ernst. *Jan Hus: Welt und Umwelt eines Prager Frühreformators.* Weimar, 1991. Marxist perspective. Places Hus in the sociocultural context of late medieval Prague and in the cleavage between tradition and innovation. Restricted to the use of printed sources and neglects some significant secondary sources.

Zeman, Jarold K. *The Hussite Movement and the Reformation in Bohemia, Moravia and Slovakia, 1350–1650: A Bibliographical Study Guide.* Ann Arbor, 1977. Lists more than 3,800 primary and secondary sources in fourteen languages. Concentrates on resources available in North America.

THOMAS A. FUDGE

HUSSITES were adherents of the first Reformation in Europe, which developed in Bohemia and Moravia between 1415 and 1620. The designation derives from the reformer Jan Hus, the leading figure of the ecclesiastical reform movement in Prague from about 1400. His doctrines were drawn from John Wycliffe and held that the "Law of God" (the holy scriptures and the doctrine of the ancient church) were the highest standard for both church, whose only head is Christ, and society. This led to the Hussite rejection of the papacy as the highest ecclesiastical authority and to criticism of lay authorities and the social fabric of the kingdom. The first Reformation was characterized by an understanding of the "Law of God" as capable of transforming not only the inner beliefs of an individual but also the active beliefs and structures of church and society. This biblicism and the Communion of the laity in both kinds in keeping with the original form of the Last Supper were considered to be necessary for salvation. From 1415 they became the criteria for identifying the Hussites.

After the condemnation and burning of Hus by the Council of Constance, the Hussite nobles and cities united to defend the reform movement. Resisting the attempts at suppression by the king and in opposition to German citizens loyal to the king and the established church, the Hussite revolution broke out in 1419 with an uprising in Prague. King Sigismund's five crusades could not defeat the movement. The Hussites, however, soon split into moderate Utraquists (including those in the nobility, university, and Prague City Union)—who wanted to preserve the social order and were on the principle loyal to the kingship while wanting the church to be reformed according to the ideas of Hus—and the radical Taborites. The latter gathered the rural population and the urban lower classes into brotherhoods under the leadership of lower clerics and nobles in order to await the thousand-year kingdom of Christ. They rejected the feudal and ecclesiastical order. Gradually they organized themselves into powerful armies as "Warriors of God" and conquered almost all of Bohemia and a part of Moravia for Hussitism, even attempting to spread it into neighboring countries. Fear of the Hussites, however, remained stronger in neighboring countries than the attraction of Hussite ideas, and as a result the first Reformation took root in and was limited to Bohemia and Moravia.

Common to all Hussites was the compromise program of the Four Articles of Prague of 1420. These articles demanded the distribution of the Eucharist in both forms to the laity; the free preaching of the gospel; the rejection by the church of worldly authority and the secularization of church goods; and the punishment of public sins, particularly those of the clergy (such as Simony). After the defeat of the last crusade (1431), the Council of Basel approved these articles, giving them, however, a Catholic interpretation (the Basel Compacts of 1433). The final treaty of peace between the council, the Hussites, and Sigismund, the king and Holy Roman Emperor, was not achieved until 1436, two years after the military defeat of the Taborites by the moderate Hussites. The result of this peace guaranteed the continued existence of the Hussite communities that practiced lay Communion in both kinds, as well as equal rights of Hussites and Catholics to hold public offices. Church goods remained secularized since even the emperor refused to return them, though in Moravia church property was retained by the bishop of Olomouc (Olmütz) and some monasteries. Rome never officially accepted the settlement, but until 1525 the Hussites repeatedly demanded papal confirmation of the compacts. In defending themselves they cited, on the one hand, the recognition of Hussitism by the Council of Basel and, on the other, the guarantees made by the emperor.

As a result of the compacts, two confessions existed alongside one another in a single Christian country, as the Hussites did not subordinate themselves to the Catholic hierarchy. In Bohemia the majority of the Czech population, part of the high nobility, the largest part of the lower nobility, and the cities (except in the German-speaking border areas) were Hussite. In Moravia a larger percentage remained Catholic, above all the German-speaking royal free cities and those living on ecclesiastical manors. Because the Hussite university master Jan Rokycana (1390/92–1471), who was elected archbishop by the estates in 1436, was accepted neither by the Council of Basel nor by the pope, the archbishopric of Prague remained vacant until 1561. The Hussites formed their own church government, with an administrator and consistory. This church of the Utraquists (Calixtines) represented the majority of the Hussites after the remaining Taborites had been defeated or gradually integrated.

The political result of the Hussite revolution was the strengthening of the estates, who in times to come freely elected the Bohemian kings, expanded their legislative rights in the diet (representing high nobles or barons, knights, and cities), occupied the highest offices of the country, and dominated the jurisdiction in the highest court. This was possible because the nobility had been economically victorious at the expense of the kingdom and the church. Until 1620 the strength of the estates also contributed to the political security of the Hussites and other non-Catholic religious communities despite the policies of the kings of the Jagiellon dynasty (1471–1526) and the Habsburgs.

The opposition of Catholic barons supported by the pope and a military campaign led by the Hungarian king Mathias Corvinus against the Hussite king George of Poděbrad (r. 1458–1471) again endangered the existence of the Hussites in the bitter second Hussite War (1465–1478). After the Peace of Olomouc (1478), however, the Religious Peace of Kuttenberg (Kutná Hora) established in 1485 not only the religious freedom of the estates and the confessional status quo of the parishes in Bohemia until 1620, but also individual religious freedoms held by citizens and subjects. In Moravia this was accomplished during the second half of the fifteenth century through sentence of the high court. This freedom, however, applied only to Catholics and Utraquists and not to the Bohemian Brethren (Unitas Fratrum), a Hussite community that adhered to the traditions of the Taborites, rejected all connection with the Catholic church, and therefore also rejected the compacts. They recognized only the holy scriptures, the life of Christ, and the life of the apostles as their standards of faith and practice. They were regarded by the Utraquists as heretics.

In the sixteenth century Hussitism developed separately in these two directions and confessions. In the first half of the century the Utraquists competed with the Bohemian Brethren, because the communities of the Bohemian Brethren spread within the Utraquist parishes under the shelter of their noble protectors despite their illegal status. The Bohemian Brethren and the Utraquists finally accepted a common Bohemian Confession (1575), influenced by Lutheranism, but this confession did not result in a common church organization until 1609, when in a Letter of Majesty (Majestätsbrief) the emperor conceded a common organization of all Protestants. The Bohemian Brethren, however, adhered to Calvinism, while the Utraquists remained under Lutheran influence. Despite the elimination of Protestants in the Bohemian lands after 1620, Hussites in many villages of eastern Moravia secretly held fast to their beliefs until they could meet again in Protestant churches after Joseph II issued his patent of toleration in 1781.

[*See also* Hus, Jan.]

BIBLIOGRAPHY

Bartoš, František Michalek. *The Hussite Revolution, 1424–1437*. East European Monographs 203. Boulder, 1986. An abridged English translation of the Czech original (*Husitská revoluce*, 2 vols., Prague, 1965–1966). The author was a highly esteemed specialist on Hussitism.

Kaminsky, Howard. *A History of the Hussite Revolution*. Berkeley, 1967. Traces the development of the revolution up to the first high point in 1421; above all an analysis of the history of ideas.

Klassen, John M. *The Nobility and the Making of the Hussite Revolution.*

New York, 1978. Investigates the motives of the nobility for its opposition to the king from 1394 to 1405 and for the genesis of the revolution.

Macek, Josef. *Jean Hus et les traditions hussites, XVe-XIXe siècles.* Paris, 1973. An undogmatic Marxist presentation of the radical and moderate wings of the revolution, of the various streams of the Hussite Reformation of the fifteenth and sixteenth centuries, and of the Hussite traditions in Czech national historical consciousness.

Molnár, Amedeo. "Der Hussitismus als christliche Reformbewegung." In *Bohemia Sacra: Das Christentum in Böhmen 973–1973*, edited by Ferdinand Seibt, pp. 92–109 and 565–566. Düsseldorf, 1974. Shows the connections and differences in the theological development of the Hussite Reformation and of Hussite groups from the fourteenth century into the seventeenth century.

Odložilík, Otakar. *The Hussite King: Bohemia in European Affairs, 1440–1471.* New Brunswick, N.J., 1965. Particularly well done on the religious contrasts.

Říčan, Rudolf. *Das Reich Gottes in den böhmischen Ländern: Geschichte des tschechischen Protestantismus.* Stuttgart, 1957. An informative survey of the confessional development of the Bohemian Reformation.

Seibt, Ferdinand. "Die Zeit der Luxemburger und der hussitischen Revolution." In *Handbuch der Geschichte der böhmischen Länder*, edited by Karl Bosl, vol. 1, pp. 351–568. Stuttgart, 1967. Classic presentation with many bibliographical references.

———. *Hussitenstudien: Personen, Ereignisse, Ideen einer frühen Revolution.* Munich, 1987. A collection of important essays on the Hussite revolution.

Šmahel, František. *La révolution hussite, une anomalie historique.* Paris, 1985. An opinionated presentation by the best specialist of the Hussite revolution.

Zeman, Jarold K. *The Hussite Movement and the Reformation in Bohemia, Moravia and Slovakia, 1350–1650: A Bibliographical Study Guide.* Ann Arbor, 1977. With particular stress on the sources available in the United States.

WINFRIED EBERHARD

Translated from German by Walter D. Morris

HUSZGEN, Johannes. *See* Oecolampadius, Johannes.

HUT, Hans (c.1490–1527), German Anabaptist leader. The founder of a mystical-spiritualist Anabaptism characterized by apocalypticism, Hut was born in Haina, probably shortly before 1500. He later lived in Bibra in the Würzburg region, working as a sexton and retailer. In the years after 1521, as an accountant operating in the area between Nuremberg and Wittenberg, he was influenced by the mystical spiritualism of Andreas Bodenstein von Karlstadt, Hans Denck, and Thomas Müntzer. In the fall of 1524 he arranged to have Müntzer's *Ausgedruckte Entblössung* published in Nuremberg. At the end of the same year Hut was expelled from Bibra for refusing to have his third child baptized. As a member of Müntzer's "Eternal Covenant," Hut participated in the Battle of Frankenhausen, managing to escape with his life and eluding arrest. After the defeat of the peasants, he found in the Anabaptists the "true" Christians, receiving baptism from Denck in Augsburg on Pentecost 1526. Subsequently he began his own missionary work in his home region and in northern Franconia.

Like Müntzer, Hut viewed Christianity as having been perverted and corrupted by the clergy and temporal government. He rejected as unchristian the social order of his time, based as it was on property, violence, and social class distinctions. He also followed Müntzer in counting on the imminent establishment of the kingdom of Christ during the time of the Peasants' War. Later, by interpreting contemporary events in light of biblical apocalypticism, he came to expect the end of times in the summer of 1528. Regarding himself as the man in *Ezekiel* 9:1–4 and the angel in *Revelation* 7:3, he did not repeat the baptism received in infancy, but rather "sealed" the elect for the end of times. This "sealing" consisted of making the sign of the cross with a wet finger on the forehead.

Although Hut pressed for a special designation for the "pious," he developed no distinctive marks for them, as others had done. Neither did he structure his congregation in any way, as he saw the end of times aproaching. Only those for whom the reversal of the order of creation had been suspended (i.e., the rule of creatures rather than the reign of God over man) were among the elect. This suspension was possible only by an inner and outer process of suffering that transforms man into an image of Christ. Hut believed that all were capable of coming to understand this concept through his "gospel of all creation" (*Mk.* 16:15 and *Col.* 3:1), according to which creation reaches its goal of serving humanity through a process of and readiness for suffering, just as people must also be ready to suffer in order to reach their goal, which is to serve God. The elect were to participate in the judgment over sinners in the summer of 1528 and complete the purification of the world.

In the face of the persecution of his followers and himself, Hut fled to Augsburg, traveled down the Danube to Moravia, and, after an encounter with Balthasar Hubmaier at Mikulov (Nikolsburg), went on to Lower and Upper Austria, Salzburg, Bavaria, and back again to Augsburg. Everywhere he went, he secretly continued his missionary work and "baptizing." He was arrested in Augsburg after the so-called Martyrs' Synod. The death sentence passed for his participation in the Peasants' War was not carried out, as Hut died on 6 December 1528 as a result of smoke poisoning contracted in an attempt to break out of jail.

Hut's Anabaptism did not long survive him. A few of his followers continued his apocalypticism with altered calculations, and others were integrated into Swiss Anabaptism or proto-Hutterite groups in Austria. Hut's published writings, which contain little of his apocalypticism, were the basis for the mystical-spiritualist tone in the Anabaptist groups influenced by Pilgram Marpeck and the Hutterites.

BIBLIOGRAPHY

Primary Source

Müller, Lydia, ed. *Glaubenszeugnisse oberdeutscher Taufgesinnter.* Quellen und Forschungen zur Reformationsgeschichte. Leipzig, 1938.

Secondary Sources

Goertz, Hans-Jürgen, and Walter Klaassen, eds. *Profiles of Radical Reformers.* Scottdale, Pa., 1982.

Packull, Werner O. *Mysticism and the Early South German-Austrian Anabaptist Movement, 1525–1531.* Studies in Anabaptist and Mennonite History, no. 19. Scottdale, Pa., 1977.

Seebass, Gottfried. "Hans Hut." In *Theologische Realenzyklopädie,* vol. 15, pp. 741–747. Berlin, 1986. Includes further bibliographical references.

GOTTFRIED SEEBASS
Translated from German by Jeff Bach

HUTTEN, Ulrich von (1488–1523), German humanist, neo-Latin poet, and political publicist in the service of the Reformation. Born into a family of imperial knights in Steckelberg castle near the town of Schlüchtern in Franconia, Hutten entered the school of the Benedictine abbey in nearby Fulda in 1499. Against the will of his parents he left that school in 1505 and spent the following six years at the universities of Mainz, Cologne, Erfurt, Frankfurt an der Oder, Leipzig, Greifswald, and Rostock, where he became part of the broad humanist circle. A dispute over financial matters with his host family in Greifswald prompted his first major humanist work, the *Querelarum libri duo* (Two Books of Complaints), a series of twenty poems, in which he elevated his personal affair to a world-historical conflict between the outdated academic establishment and the guild of young poets. On his way to Italy to study law he visited Joachim Vadian in Vienna and other humanists in the circle of Emperor Maximilian. He then turned from personal and literary interests to political matters. After studying at the universities of Pavia and Bologna and serving briefly in the army of Maximilian, Hutten returned to Germany in 1514. There he met Erasmus, who expected much of the young poet and who dedicated his epistolary biography of Thomas More to the young aristocrat. The murder of his cousin Hans von Hutten by Ulrich of Württemberg prompted the Hutten family to embark on a long feud with that powerful prince to which Hutten contributed five Latin orations and the dialogue *Phalarismus,* a general denunciation of tyrants. In the controversy between the Cologne Dominicans and the Hebraist Johannes Reuchlin, Hutten sided forcefully with the latter and authored the major part of the second edition of the *Epistolae obscurorum virorum* (The Letters of Obscure Men). During a second stay in Italy (1515–1517) he wrote a series of epigrams denouncing not only the enemies of Emperor Maximilian—the French and Venetians—but also Pope Julius II. On his return from Italy Hutten was crowned poet laureate by Maximilian and entered the service of Albert of Brandenburg, archbishop of Mainz, as councillor; in four dialogues, *Febris I* and *Febris II* (Fever I and Fever II), *Inspicientes* (The Onlookers), and *Vadiscus sive Trias Romana* (Vadiscus or the Roman Trinity; Latin, 1520; German, 1521), Hutten nonetheless castigated not only the luxury and moral excesses of the papal court and the concept of celibacy but also Rome's fiscal exploitation of the German nation. With its pointed triplets the Vadiscus contains the most comprehensive catalog of German grievances against Rome.

Despite his antipapal stance, Hutten initally viewed the controversy following Luther's posting of the Ninety-five Theses in Wittenberg as a monks' squabble and a welcome rift among his opponents. It was only after almost two years of virtually ignoring Luther, after the Leipzig Disputation of June-July 1519, that Hutten began to consider himself as an ally. He was well aware, however, of the profound difference between him and the Wittenberg monk. He explained in a letter written to Luther at the time of the Diet of Worms: "I look to men. You, who are already more perfect, entrust everything to God." Although Luther's opposition to Rome was rooted primarily in religious-theological concerns and Hutten's was prompted by political-national aspirations, the two men exercised considerable influence on one another. Luther, for instance, may have been influenced by Hutten's reform program in his treatise *To the Christian Nobility of the German Nation* and definitely used Hutten's edition of Lorenzo Valla's work on the Constantine Donation. At the same time Hutten found in Luther the theological confirmation of his own ideas.

The archbishop of Mainz at last withdrew his patronage, and in 1520 Hutten found refuge at Ebernburg castle, home of his friend Franz von Sickingen, a powerful knight and German condottiere of considerable influence. From the security of this castle Hutten embarked on a feverish literary campaign in which he challenged the emperor, the German nobility, the princes, cities, and the general reader to take up the fight against Rome, if necessary with arms. Hutten tellingly turned from Latin to German and had his previous works translated into the vernacular. Consequently, during the Diet of Worms he, next to Luther became the most prominent representative of the antipapal party in Germany.

Realizing in the wake of the diet that a general uprising would not occur, Hutten launched the so-called *Pfaffenkrieg* ("Priests' War") in the hope that it would provide the spark that would ignite the German powder-keg. In these activities Hutten enjoyed the protection of Sickingen. In the summer of 1522, however, Sickingen, took part in a disastrous military campaign against Richard von Greifenklau, archbishop of Trier, and in November Hutten fled to Basel. Leaving that city in January 1523, he found refuge first in an Augustinian monastery in Mühlhausen and finally in Zurich with

Zwingli. He died on 29 August 1523 on the island of Ufenau in Lake Zurich.

Hutten was one of the most engaged and engaging figures of his era and was for a brief time a major force in Reformation politics. In later centuries he caught the imagination of his fellow Germans as no other contemporary author except Luther. His depiction of the Germanic leader Hermann as the liberator of Germany—in *Arminius*, a dialogue published posthumously in 1529—would be echoed in more than ninety novels, plays, and operas on the subject. Frequently regarded by Lutheran reformers as being too warlike, Hutten was claimed as an ancestor by the most divergent political ideologues, to whom he was variously a tragic hero, a champion of freedom, a fighter against tyranny, and a visionary whose dream of a united Germany was not realized for another three-and-a-half centuries.

BIBLIOGRAPHY

Primary Sources

Böcking, Eduard, ed. *Ulrichi Hutteni equitis germani opera quae reperiri potuerant omnia* (1859–1870, 7 vols.). Reprint, Aalen, 1963. Hutten's Latin and German works, as well as related contemporary documents. A mine of information on Hutten and his times.

Hutten, Ulrich von, et al. *On the Eve of the Reformation: Letters of Obscure Men.* Introduction by Hajo Holborn. New York, 1964. English translation of 1909 by Francis Griffin Stokes.

Ukena, Peter, ed. *Deutsche Schriften.* Munich, 1970.

Secondary Sources

Bernstein, Eckhard. *German Humanism.* Boston, 1983. Brief essays on Hutten and *The Letters of Obscure Men* in the context of a survey of German Renaissance humanism.

———. *Ulrich von Hutten mit Selbstzeugnissen und Bilddokumenten.* Reinbek, Germany, 1988. Concise, illustrated account of Hutten's life and work.

Füssel, Stephan, ed. *Ulrich von Hutten.* Pirckheimer-Jahrbuch 1988. Munich, 1989. Six lectures delivered at the International Hutten Symposium held in July 1988 in Schlüchtern.

Holborn, Hajo. *Ulrich von Hutten and the German Reformation.* Translated by Roland Bainton. New York, 1966. The best study in English.

Laub, Peter, ed. *Ulrich von Hutten: Ritter, Humanist, Publizist.* Wiesbaden, 1988. Exhibition catalogue. Some 30 articles written by historians, art historians, and literary historians on various aspects of Hutten's life and work. Most comprehensive collection of current Hutten research.

Spitz, Lewis W. *The Religious Renaissance of the German Humanists.* Cambridge, Mass., 1963. Short, elegantly written essay on Hutten within the context of the Reformation.

Strauss, David Friedrich. *Ulrich von Hutten: His Life and Times.* Translated by C. Sturge. London, 1874. Classic study by a German liberal who saw in Hutten a fighter for German freedom.

Wheelis, Sam. *Ulrich von Hutten: Representative of Patriotic Humanism.* In *The Renaissance and Reformation in Germany,* edited by Gerhart Hoffmeister, pp. 111–127. New York, 1977.

ECKHARD BERNSTEIN

HUTTER, Jacob (1500?–1536) Anabaptist leader. Hutter was born in Moos, not far from Bruneck, in the Puster Valley of the Tirol. After a brief period of study in the local school, he left for Prague to learn the hatter's trade—hence the name "Hutter." As was the custom in those days, Hutter traveled extensively learning and plying his trade, finally settling in Carinthia. It is generally assumed that he first encountered Anabaptists and their teachings in Klagenfurt. But exactly when and through whose auspices he was converted and baptized is not known, the Hutterite Chronicle saying only that he "accepted the covenant of grace with a good conscience in Christian baptism, [promising] to lead a life of godliness in true resignation."

Like Menno Simons in the Netherlands, Hutter was not the founder of a movement, nor even the transmitter of Anabaptism to the Tirol; it was well established there when he joined shortly before 1529. Nor did he introduce the idea of community of goods into the movement; Jacob Wiedmann is usually the credited with this introduction, the original impetus sometimes ascribed to Hans Hut, a former follower of Thomas Müntzer. More probably, however, the idea derived from Desiderius Erasmus, whose notes on the famous passage in the *Acts of the Apostles* in his *Annotations* and *Paraphrases* were so well known that even Bernhard Rothmann could write:

> These . . . things they practised in all earnestness in the breaking of bread, which they had in common, as Erasmus interprets the passage in his *Annotations.* First, he presents the teaching of the Gospel; second, brotherly love, which caused them to have all things common; third. . . . This custom [community of goods] is not only found in St. Paul, but was also present in the early Church. See *Acts* 2[44], Erasmus' *Paraphrases,* Sichard on the 4th Epistle of Clement, for the kind of appearance and structure the first church had.

Whatever the case with respect to the above issue, Anabaptism itself spread into the Tirol, Austria, and Carinthia in the late 1520s. The Hutterite Chronicle credits George Blaurock and Wilhelm Reublin—two of the original Swiss Brethren—with bringing it into these regions. In 1526 Balthasar Hubmaier brought his brand of Anabaptism to Nikolsburg in Moravia, where he and his followers found sanctuary on the lands of the lords of Liechtenstein. Here the religious climate was more tolerant, Hussites and Picards having lived side by side for some time without detriment to the state. Furthermore, many nobles in the region had espoused Protestant ideas and were therefore less inclined to persecute religious nonconformists. Nor did it hurt that the resettlement of ruined towns and villages by industrious religious dissenters was to the nobles' economic advantage.

Hubmaier's brand of Anabaptism has sometimes been called "Magisterial Anabaptism" because of its close ties to the lords of Liechtenstein, with Leonhard von Liechtenstein himself accepting rebaptism. Hubmaier also accepted defensive warfare as justifiable; his followers came to be called *Schwertler* ("sword carriers"). Those adhering to the nonviolent principles of the Swiss Brethren and the Schleitheim Confession rejected this position and came to be known as *Stäbler* ("staff carriers"). By 1528 a dissenting group of *Stäbler* were either expelled from Nikolsburg by Leonhard von Liechtenstein or began to meet separately from the larger group in the village of Bergen, just outside Nikolsburg. In the spring of 1528 the group left the region entirely. Whether from the beginning, or only upon their departure from the region, the members decided to share their resources for the common good, the Hutterite Chronicle observing: "these men laid a coat on the ground before the people and everyone placed his possessions on it, with a willing spirit and without coercion, for the support of the needy in accordance with the teachings of the prophets and the apostles. *Isaiah* 23, *Acts* 2:4 & 5." The group, led by Jacob Wiedmann, does not appear to have understood their action as a temporary measure. The continuing influx of other religious refugees of varying degrees of poverty eventually necessitated its permanent institution. The group then settled in Austerlitz; a little later another group settled in Auspitz.

In 1529 Hutter succeeded Blaurock as leader of the Anabaptists in the Tirol, the latter having been executed. Having traveled widely in the Puster Valley, Hutter now became the leader of a small congregation in Welsperg. In May 1529 the government at Innsbruck ordered the arrest and seizure of Hutter and the congregational members. Some were captured, but Hutter and a few others escaped. In the persecution that followed even Hutter's sister, Agnes, was executed. Needing a sanctuary from the onslaught, the elders of the group sent emissaries to survey conditions in Moravia. Upon receiving a favorable report, Hutter appointed his coworker, Jörg Zaunring, to lead the first group of migrants to Moravia. One small group was sent after another; Hutter, however, remained behind to continue his work in the Tirol.

Troubles soon arose in the congregations just transplanted to Moravia that seriously threatened their existence. Caused by internal divisions over partial treatment, irregularities in church discipline, mismanagement of funds, the arrogance of church leaders, and sundry other problems, Hutter was repeatedly forced to travel to the region in order to correct matters. All the while refugees from Silesia, Swabia, the Palatinate, and the Tirol continued to arrive, bringing new problems. Continued—even intensified—persecution of Anabaptists in the Tirol finally forced even Hutter to leave, for the government at Innsbruck had become obsessed with his capture because he had "brought so many people of the district into the sect." Consequently, Hutter was forced to go to Moravia once more, this time to find a new home for what remained of his flock.

Hutter arrived in Auspitz on 11 August 1533, finding conditions in the congregations so bad that he was led to assert his apostolic calling in their midst. The local leaders, however—Schützinger, Philip, and Gabriel—men of limited Anabaptist vision and incapable of establishing order in the congregations, opposed him. When Schützinger became ill and was discovered to have set some money aside from the common fund for himself, the congregation chose Hutter as their shepherd. Once established, Hutter began to clean house.

Motivated by a powerful sense of God's calling, which had impressed even his opponents on his arrival in Moravia, Hutter restored order in the church. The disaffected who departed were quickly replaced by new members from the Tirol who were continuing to flee to Moravia. Hutter reestablished Anabaptist principles, his nearly autocratic manner now muted by a studied dependence on the decision making of the community in spiritual matters. He transformed what appears to have been a haphazard communalism into a full-fledged and well-structured communal organization with complete economic sharing. Separate leaders for economic affairs—called servants of temporal needs and spiritual concerns—were put in place and an overall organization was established that has lasted to the present day. What appeared to have been a temporary expedient had become a permanent organization. The needs of the refugees and the example of the apostolic church were powerful incentives. As Erasmus himself had emphasized, the goal was the existence of a true sense of "brotherly love" in a community where the normal tensions between rich and poor were nearly eliminated by intimate contact and at times desperate need.

For two years Hutter stood at the head of the congregations in Moravia, guiding them under the benevolent eyes of the local nobles, even the abbess of Brno on whose lands the Auspitz congregation lived. But the animosity of Ferdinand, archduke of Austria and king of the Romans since 1530, and the Catholic government at Innsbruck was pushed to a fever pitch by the events that transpired in Münster during 1534–1535. If persecution had been severe before, it became intolerable afterward, a fact repeatedly remarked upon by the Hutterite Chronicle. Not only did the Innsbruck authorities pursue Anabaptists with a diabolical vengeance, they also brought pressure to bear on the lords of Liechtenstein and other nobles to expel the Hutterites from their lands, Ferdinand attending the Moravian Diet in person to see that his wishes were fulfilled. Thus, despite the fact that no complaints had ever been lodged with the Moravian authorities because of them, and despite the fact that Hutter himself complained bitterly to the government about such illegal treatment, the Hutterites were turned away from their villages into a wretched existence described in vivid terms by the Hutterite Chronicle. Wherever they went they were turned away. Some eventually settled at Steinabrunn in Lower Austria; others, including Hutter, began to return to the Tirol from whence they had come.

In the Tirol the congregations reorganized themselves and renewed the work of evangelization. Soon they were again being denounced from local pulpits by the priests. In the midst of this their missionary efforts appear to have been remarkably successful. Yet the danger in which they lived was extreme. Hutter wrote: "They threaten with hangmen and bailiffs. . . . The Sodomite sea is raging madly."

Hutter himself was captured in the fall of 1535. By 1 December the authorities at Innsbruck were so informed, and on 9 December he was transferred to the seat of government under strong guard. Two days later he was cross-examined and pressured to recant. Had he done so it would have done him little good, for Ferdinand had himself decreed: "We are determined that even if Hutter should renounce his error, we will not pardon him, for he has misled too many, but we will let the penalty which he has so abundantly merited take its course." He was burned at the stake on 25 February 1536.

Aside from his major contribution to the reorganization and stabilization of Anabaptist congregations in the Tirol and Moravia that were trying to implement a communal way of life, Hutter is important for at least two other reasons. First, he was a fearless and—if one can believe Ferdinand of Austria, his worst enemy—extremely effective Anabaptist missionary. Second, he established the Hutterite colonies on the basis of the Schleitheim Confession. This can be seen not only in the transformation of early spiritualist leaders such as Peter Riedemann into eloquent spokespersons for a Swiss Brethren theological position, but also in the encounter, around 1535, of the congregations under Hutter's leadership with Hans Bot, head of a Hessian congregation at Sorga. Bot, a disciple of Melchior Rinck, proclaimed the superiority of the "inner word" to the written gospel. He was told by the Hutterian congregations, however, to cease and desist from such heresy. In response, Bot appealed to the authority of Rinck himself. The brethren refused to believe that Rinck would teach such doctrines; but if he did, they said, he too would be a "false prophet." Such teachings they charged, did not agree with "the saving teachings of our Lord Jesus Christ."

BIBLIOGRAPHY

Bergsten, Torsten. *Balthasar Hubmaier: Seine Stellung zu Reformation und Täufertum, 1521–1528.* Kassel, 1961. An abridged English translation is available: *Balthasar Hubmaier: Anabaptist Theologian and Martyr,* translated by W. R. Estep, Jr., Valley Forge, Pa., 1978.

Clasen, Claus-Peter. *Anabaptism: A Social History.* Ithaca, N.Y., 1972.

Friedmann, Robert. *Hutterite Studies: Essays by Robert Friedmann, Collected and Published in Honor of His Seventieth Anniversary.* Edited by Harold S. Bender. Goshen, Ind., 1961.

Gross, Leonard. *The Golden Years of the Hutterites.* Scottdale, Pa., 1980.

———. "Jakob Huter: Ein christlicher Kommunist." In *Profiles of Radical Reformers,* edited by Walter Klaassen, pp. 137–145. Scottdale, Pa., 1982.

Horsch, John. *The Hutterian Brethren, 1528–1931.* Reprint, Cayley, Alberta, 1985.

Loserth, Johann. *Der Anabaptismus in Tirol.* Vienna, 1892.

Mueller, Lydia. *Der Kommunismus der mährischen Wiedertäufer.* Schriften des Vereins für Reformationsgeschichte, vol. 45, no. 1. Leipzig, 1927.

Williams, George H. *The Radical Reformation.* Kirksville, Mo., 1992.

Wolkan, Rudolf, ed. *Das große Geschichtsbuch der Hutterischen Brüder.* Cayley, Alberta, 1982. An English translation is available: *The Chronical of the Hutterian Brethren,* translated and edited by the Hutterian Brethren, Rifton, N.Y., 1987.

Ziegelschmid, A. J. F., ed. *Die älteste Chronik der Hutterischen Brüder.* Ithaca, N.Y., 1943.

ABRAHAM FRIESEN

HUTTERITES. One of the three main branches of Anabaptism with continuity to the present, the Hutterites are the only Reformation-era movement based on religious communism to survive. In contrast to the other two Anabaptist branches with continuity to the present, the Swiss Brethren and the Dutch Anabaptists (sometimes called Mennonites), the Hutterites were Austrian in origin.

The movement began in and around Nikolsburg (Mikulov), Moravia, where semiautonomous Moravian lords, unlike most other European rulers, tolerated religious groups that deviated from the politically established religion. Balthasar Hubmaier had introduced Anabaptism into the area in 1526. Moravian lords were looking for craftsmen, artisans, and farmers to settle their domains and to develop their economies. These lords were also trying to wrest for themselves more political independence from the Holy Roman Empire. Allowing the Anabaptists and other groups to flourish was in itself a visible symbol of the high degree of independence these Moravian lords had indeed been able to instill within their lands.

Furthermore, the lords were part of a tradition, beginning with Jan Hus around 1400, that had needed to deal with the impulses of a religious pluralism that would extend throughout much of Bohemia and Moravia well into the sixteenth century. They were hence more open to religious minorities than were most other European political leaders.

In any case, under Hubmaier's leadership, Nikolsburg formally became an Anabaptist center, with as many as twelve thousand Anabaptists drawn to South Moravia during the years 1526 to 1528. The lord of Nikolsburg, Leonhard von Liechtenstein, himself submitted to (adult) baptism. This form of magisterial Anabaptism, which included an acceptance of defensive warfare, was later rejected by all three Anabaptist groups that survived.

Nor did all Nikolsburg Anabaptists accept the idea of magisterial Anabaptism. In 1528 a group of Anabaptists separated themselves from the main Nikolsburg community on account of this issue. The efforts of Hans Hut, an Anabaptist leader who visited Nikolsburg in 1527, helped spark this emerging group of dissenters, who became known as the *Stäbler* ("staff carriers"), in contrast to the majority in Nikolsburg, known as the *Schwertler* ("sword carriers"), who continued to follow Hubmaier's teachings. Jakob Wiedemann was leader of the *Stäbler,* a group of two hundred adults with their children. By 1528 Lord Leonhard began viewing the *Stäbler* as a separatist movement that posed a threat to political and religious unity. He issued an ultimatum to the group, expelling them from his territory.

They left accordingly, encamped at a deserted village, and immediately appointed several leaders to oversee the group's temporal affairs. *Die älteste Chronik der Hutterischen Brüder* (The Oldest Chronicle of the Hutterian Brethren) recounts this event, the birth of proto-Hutterianism, as follows: "These men then spread out a cloak in front of the people, and each one laid his possessions on it with a willing heart—without being forced—so that the needy might be supported in accordance with the teaching of the prophets and apostles" (*Is.* 23:18; *Acts* 2:44–45; 4:34–35; 5:1–11). This communal group ultimately found refuge at Austerlitz (Slavkov), assured by Lord Ulrich von Kaunitz that they would be exempt from payment of war taxes and from military service for a period of six years.

Other Anabaptist groups were also developing simultaneously in other areas of Austria, especially in the Tirol, in part through the missionary efforts of George Blaurock, a Swiss Brethren leader. Although many were executed for their faith, the movement spread rapidly. One of the many converts was Jacob Hutter, from Moos, a hamlet below Saint Lorenzen in the Puster Valley. He was soon called to be minister.

No sources state explicitly that Hutter had known Blaurock; yet Hutter's Anabaptist legacy, at least in part, may be traced directly to the Swiss Brethren, via Blaurock's short-lived yet effective ministry in the Tirol. Herein lies a second major element defining Hutterianism: the Swiss Brethren tradition. Hutter succeeded Blaurock as the major Anabaptist leader in the Tirol in 1529. That year Hutter traveled to Austerlitz and was accepted into the *Stäbler* community. Hutter returned to the Tirol, spreading the word about the union, and because of increased persecution in the Tirol, he organized a constant flow of small groups destined for tolerant Moravia.

In 1530, the *Stäbler* group experienced some problems in leadership, and the group divided, one part moving to Auspitz (Hustopeče) under the new leadership of Georg Zaunring and Wilhelm Reublin (who stemmed from the Swiss Brethren). Still living in the Tirol, Hutter aligned with this group. By 1533 divisiveness again threatened the well-being of the new movement. Backed by his Tirolean flock, Hutter responded to the threat by moving to Auspitz. Through strict disciplinary measures he effectively reorganized the small communal group living there.

The next years proved difficult for this Hutterian community. The Münster debacle of 1534/35 affected the Moravian as it did the other Anabaptist groups, and persecution dislodged the Hutterites. Ferdinand, archduke of Austria, succeeded in forcing the hand of even the tolerant Moravian lords to expel all types of Anabaptists. Month after month, forest and cave provided primitive shelter. As a major leader, Hutter's life hung in the balance, and he once again returned to the Tirol. His activities there were cut short by his capture and martyrdom at Innsbruck in 1536. In spite of intense persecution, the unity and stability that Hutter had brought to the group helped grant a communal structuring and spirit that has carried the group into its fifth century.

After 1536, persecution abated, and the Hutterites again found refuge in Moravia. The Hutterian *Chronicle* divides the rest of sixteenth-century Hutterian history into the following epochs: 1533 to 1536, "the emerging brotherhood"; 1536 to 1547, "growth despite persecution"; 1547 to 1553, "the second great persecution"; 1554 to 1564, "the good years"; 1565 to 1591, "the golden years"; and 1592–1618, "renewed persecution." The horror and devastation that came thereafter as the result of the Thirty Years' War can be grasped only by reading the *Chronicle* entries themselves for this period. That war drove the few surviving Hutterites out of Moravia into Slovakia. A remnant migrated ultimately to Transylvania (Romania), then on to the Ukraine. In the 1870s about four-hundred emigrated to North America, where numerically they now exceed their sixteenth-century population at its high point in the 1590s—in 1994, some 35,000, living in 350 *Haushaben*, or voluntary communal societies.

The Hutterites gradually developed their own culture and with it creative and innovative products and services. Best known are ceramics (highly prized by the nobility—today in leading museums in central Europe), medical services (medicines and trained physicians, known and sought after far and wide, even by royalty), group child care (innovative kindergartens—some of the first such schools in Europe), and elementary schools (where every child learned to read and write, and where many children from the outside were also taught).

The *Chronicle* lists thirty-nine distinct occupations, making the Hutterites more than simply a rural group. As artisans and manufacturers, they must be viewed as a complex, quasi-urban movement. Codes were developed for the various types of industry and services, with *Ordnung* (an ordered life, in all areas of existence) at the center, aligned with the divine "Master Builder and Establisher."

The central Hutterian idea of communal living, begun by the *Stäbler,* and set structurally by Hutter, was given further definition by Peter Riedemann in his confession of faith (1542), a volume which would become the formal Hutterian confession. In the 1560s and 1570s Leonhard Dax went on to define further how the Hutterian idea contrasts with Catholicism, Lutheranism, and Calvinism. Peter Walpot made the same contrasts vis à vis the Polish and Swiss Brethren. Finally, Andreas Ehrenpreis (1639–1662) would round out the Hutterian written tradition by organizing the whole set of *Gemeindeordnungen* ("community codes"), as well as the written sermons and hymns, all of which would continue to serve the ongoing Hutterian movement over the centuries.

Through the influence of Blaurock and Reublin, the

movement found continuity with the Swiss Brethren tradition, as expressed in the Schleitheim Articles of 1527, all seven points of which are also found in the *Chronicle.* The main additional element is community of goods, the central point of controversy between the Hutterites and the other main Upper German Anabaptist group, the Swiss Brethren. The earlier spiritualistic legacy of German (Augsburg) Anabaptism (especially Hut and Hans Denck) was thereby transformed into a more concrete manifestation of the gathered church, in line with the Swiss Brethren tradition.

The Hutterites did not discover Christian communism. By the mid-1520s the communal idea was everywhere, "in the air." Wolfgang Brandhuber of Upper Austria (d. 1528 as a martyr) was certainly an Anabaptist source for this idea, which the proto-Hutterites had turned into reality on the road to Austerlitz in 1528. Yet as an ongoing religious group, the Hutterites remain the only communal movement with continuity stretching back to the Reformation. The Hutterites fulfilled historically what many Renaissance intellectuals had only dreamed of—a utopian idea become reality.

BIBLIOGRAPHY

Friedmann, Robert. *The Theology of Anabaptism.* Scottdale, Pa., 1973. Interpretation suggesting the "existential" nature of the Anabaptist faith in general, and Hutterian faith in particular.

Gross, Leonard. *The Golden Years of the Hutterites: The Witness and Thought of the Communal Moravian Anabaptists during the Walpot Era, 1565–1578.* Scottdale, Pa., 1980. Contrasts, confessionally, the Hutterian approach to faith and theology with that of the Catholics, Lutherans, Calvinists, Polish Brethren, and Swiss Brethren.

Horsch, John. *The Hutterian Brethren, 1528–1931: A Story of Martyrdom and Loyalty.* Goshen, Ind., 1931. General history of the Hutterites through the centuries.

Hillerbrand, Hans J., ed. *Anabaptist Bibliography, 1520–1630.* 2d. ed., rev. & enl. Saint Louis, 1991. See especially the section on "Moravia [Hutterite]," pp. 22–33.

Riedemann, Peter. *Account of Our Religion, Doctrine, and Faith. . . .* 2d ed. Rifton, N.Y., 1974.

LEONARD GROSS

HYCHYNS, William. *See* Tyndale, William.

HYMNALS.

Manuscript *Hymnaria* dating from the eleventh century were anthologies of hymns proper to the festivals and seasons of the church year. From the late fifteenth century *Hymnaria* appeared in printed versions; thus, the Sarum *Hymnarium* was published in such editions as Cologne (1496), London (1496), Paris (1518), and Antwerp (1524). Although these *Hymnaria* were designed for use by clergy and choirs, they nevertheless provided a model for Lutheran collections of congregational hymns, as many of these German hymns, like the earlier Latin office hymns, were intended to be sung on Sundays and festivals of the church year.

Germany. Vernacular hymnody existed before the Reformation. Various Marian hymns and *Leisen* ("folk hymns") were common and circulated as printed broadsides. These hymns, though sometimes based on liturgical pieces, were essentially extraliturgical. It was Martin Luther's genius to bring such hymnody, together with newly created hymns, into evangelical worship. Luther was not, however, the first to create a vernacular hymnal; the Bohemian Brethren in Prague published such a hymnal as early as 1501. Similarly, Luther's provision of liturgical hymnody was anticipated by Nikolaus Decius, who as early as 1522 produced German versions of the *Gloria in Excelsis Deo* and *Agnus Dei* (*Allein Gott in der Höh sei Ehr* and *O Lamm Gottes unschuldig*). Thomas Müntzer may also have anticipated Luther in translating Latin hymns, which Müntzer included in his *Deutzsch kirchen ampt* (Eilenburg, 1523 or 1524).

By the end of 1523 Luther and his colleagues in Wittenberg were actively writing and promoting vernacular liturgical hymnody. For example, in the *Formula Missae* (Wittenberg, 1523) Luther drew attention to appropriate *Leisen* that could be sung in the evangelical Mass but registered the need for newly written liturgical hymns. During the winter of 1523/24 Luther and others wrote many metrical psalms and hymns, which were circulated as broadsides. Jobst Gutknecht of Nuremberg, an enterprising publisher, collected eight of these broadside "Wittenberg" hymns as *Etlich Cristliche Lider*, commonly known as the *Achtliederbuch* (Eight Song Book). Three different imprints came from the Nuremberg press in 1524, and another was printed in Augsburg the same year. Also in 1524 two different printers in Erfurt (Johannes Loersfeld and Mathes Maler) produced hymnals under the title *Enchiridion* with similar contents. These Erfurt *Enchiridia*, like the *Achtliederbuch*, contained hymns that had first been published as broadsides but included more hymns than their Nuremberg counterpart.

Around the same time that the Nuremberg, Augsburg, and Erfurt publications appeared, the so-called *Chorgesangbuch* (a set of partbooks for choral rather than congregational use) was published in Wittenberg, with polyphonic settings of the chorale melodies by Johann Walter and a preface by Luther (*Geystliche gesangk Buchleyn*, 1524). The *Chorgesangbuch* was reprinted in Worms (1525) and Strasbourg (1534 and 1537) and later expanded in Wittenberg editions (1544, 1550, and 1551).

The year after the "choir" partbooks were issued, a congregational hymnal was published in Wittenberg; it was revised and reissued the following year as *Enchyrydion fur die Leyen* (1525 and 1526). The hymns of this congregational book were the same as those found in the *Chorgesangbuch.* The first collection that Luther prepared specifically for congregational use in Wittenberg was the *Geistliche Lieder*, printed by Joseph Klug in 1529. Walter's collection, as well as the congregational collection based on it, had been compiled with no specific arrangement of its contents, but the

1529 Wittenberg hymnal was carefully planned and followed closely the structure of the church year. The Wittenberg hymnal was reissued in enlarged and revised forms during the remainder of Luther's life: later known editions appeared in 1533, 1535, 1543, 1544 (three times), and 1545. The beautiful edition published by Valentin Bapst, *Geystlicher Lieder* (Leipzig, 1545), was effectively a later edition of the "Wittenberg" hymnal, the last to be overseen by Luther. Hymnals published elsewhere in Germany, such as Zwickau (1525 and 1528), Nuremberg (1525 and 1527), and Leipzig (1539), owe much to these Wittenberg hymnals.

All these hymnals were in High German, the language of central Germany. In the north Low German was spoken. In 1525 a Low German hymnal compiled by the Rostock reformer Joachim Slüter (*Eyn gantz schone vnde seer nutte gesangk boek*) was published. Slüter's principal sources were Walter's *Chorgesangbuch* of 1524, hymnbooks published in Erfurt and Strasbourg in 1525, and a corpus of Low German hymns from north Germany. Issued in 1531 was a revised edition, the double hymnal, so-called because of its two main parts, the first of which was based on the 1529 Wittenberg hymnbook. This double hymnal was reissued in Magdeburg (1534, 1538, 1540, 1541, and 1543), Rostock (1543), and Lübeck (1545 and 1547/48).

Later collections—such as Johann Spangenberg's *Cantiones ecclesiasticae latinae . . . Kirchengesenge deudtsch* (Magdeburg, 1545), Lucas Lossius's *Psalmodia* (Wittenberg, 1553, 1561, and 1597), and Johannes Keuchenthal's *Kirchen Gesenge latinisch und deudsch* (Wittenberg, 1573)—were compiled to serve the specific hymnodic needs of the Lutheran macaronic liturgical tradition. Lucas Osiander's *Fünfftzig geistliche Lieder und Psalmen* (Nuremberg, 1586) established the basic four-part, "cantional" settings of the chorale melodies, which ultimately led to Johann Hermann Schein's *Cantional, oder Gesangbuch augspurgischer Confession* (Leipzig, 1627), one of the influential hymnals of the seventeenth century.

Not all hymnal publication in Germany was the result of the Lutheran Reformation. The long-standing tradition of vernacular *Leisen*, together with contemporary translations of Latin hymnody, encouraged Roman Catholics to compile their own hymnals. Michael Vehe edited *Ein New Gesanbuchlin* (Leipzig, 1537), which was followed by other Catholic collections, such as those published in Cologne (1550) and Nuremberg (1550) and especially the impressive *Geistliche Lieder und Psalmen* (Bautzen, 1567, 1573, and 1584), edited by Johann Leisentritt. Later German Catholic hymnals include those published in Prague (1581), Cologne (1582), Munich (1586), Innsbruck (1588), Constance (1600), Graz (1602), and Mainz (1605), as well as the *Außerlesene, catholische, geistliche Kirchengesäng*, published in Cologne (1623).

By the third quarter of the sixteenth century Calvinism had taken root in Germany, and Reformed churches had become numerous. To meet the specific worship needs of these congregations, Ambrosius Lobwasser translated the *Psalms* into German verse using the same meters and melodies as the French Genevan *Psalter dess Königlichen Propheten Davids* (Leipzig, 1573). The Lobwasser Psalter was extremely popular and went through numerous editions. Lutherans were impressed by these Lobwasser psalms but were suspicious of their Calvinist "errors." Cornelius Becker, therefore, produced "Lutheran" metrical psalms in *Der psalter Davids Gesangweis* (Leipzig, 1602), for which Seth Kalwitz (Calvisius; 1605) and Heinrich Schütz (1628) provided suitable musical settings.

Scandinavia. The Swedish reformer Olaus Petri, a student of Luther's in Wittenberg, produced the first collection of Swedish hymns, *Swenska Songer eller Wijsor* (Stockholm, 1526), a small collection, half of which comprised versions of German Lutheran hymns, while the remainder were Swedish originals. Several expanded editions, some edited by Olaus's brother Laurentius Petri, appeared in later years (*Svenska Psalmboken,* Stockholm, 1549, 1567, 1572, 1586, 1594, and 1601).

The influence of the Rostock reformation was also felt in Denmark and in what is now southern Sweden. Hans Mortensen's Mass book, *Dat kristelige Messeembede* (Malmø, 1528), included a small collection of Danish hymns. The following year the Rostock printer Ludwig Dietz published a Danish hymnbook, *Een hy handbog, med Psalmer or aan dalige lofsange* (Rostock, 1529), compiled by Arvid Pedersen. Around two-thirds of the book comprised Danish versions of hymns found in Slüter's 1525 Low German hymnbook; some were Danish versions of other German hymns, and eight appear to be Danish originals. A slightly expanded edition, *Malmø-Salmebogen,* probably appeared in 1531 (reprinted 1533), and the 1529 Danish hymnal was reissued in 1536 with a substantial supplement of additional hymns. Some years later Hans Tausen produced an expanded Danish hymnal, *En ny Psalmebog* (Copenhagen, 1544 and 1553, with at least three editions issued in Lübeck between 1556 and 1568), but the most influential was Hans Thomissøn's *Den danske Psalmebog* (Copenhagen, 1569), the official Danish hymnal for more than a century and a half.

Other hymnals of Nordic use include the two Icelandic collections *Ein ny psalma Bók* (Hólar, 1589) and *Graduale: Ein almeneleg messusöngs Bók* (Hólar, 1594 and 1607), both based on Danish hymnals; and the Finnish *Piae cantiones* (Griefswald, 1582), reformed versions of medieval Latin hymns compiled for use in schools.

Alsace and Switzerland. The Reformation in Strasbourg, under the leadership of Martin Bucer, maintained a distinctive style that influenced reforming movements in other areas. Editions of vernacular liturgies, including various hymns, were published under the title *Teutsch kirchen Ampt* in 1524 and 1525. Between 1524 and 1537 at least twelve new editions of the basic liturgy were published, and in each more congregational songs (notably metrical psalms) were included. The liturgy *Psalter mit aller Kirchenübung* (Strasbourg, 1539; expanded editions in 1545, 1547, and 1568) contained mostly metrical psalms by Reformed and Lutheran authors. In 1541 Bucer issued the *Gesangbuch* (Strasbourg, 1541), an impressive collection that focused on hymns rather than metrical psalms. For this hymnal Bucer wrote a significant preface that was to influence the thinking of John Calvin. An expanded version of the 1541 hymnal was published as *Das gros kirchen Gesangbuch* (Strasbourg, 1560 and 1572).

Despite Huldrych Zwingli's opposition to congregational singing, Zurich made a positive contribution to the development of hymnody through the printer and publisher Christoph Froschauer. But his hymnals were issued for use in Constance, some forty miles to the northeast, where the leading reformers were Johannes Zwick and the Blarer brothers, Ambrosius and Thomas. Under the influence of Bucer in Strasbourg, all three were involved in the compilation of these Zurich-imprint hymnals. Froschauer produced the edition of the Constance hymnal in 1533 or 1534. The earliest extant edition is the *Nüw Gesangbüchle* (Zurich, 1540), structured according to the Pauline triad of psalms, hymns, and spiritual songs. At least seven further editions appeared by the year 1561.

The all-pervasive Genevan Psalters had their origins in Strasbourg. In 1538 Bucer called Calvin as the pastor of the French-speaking congregation in Strasbourg. The following year Calvin issued a small hymnal, *Aulcuns pseaulmes et cantiques mys en chant* (Strasbourg, 1539). Most of the twenty-two items were influenced by the hymns and metrical psalms sung by the German congregations in Strasbourg and were written by Calvin and Clément Marot. Calvin returned to Geneva in 1541 and the following year published *La forme des prieres et chantz ecclesiastiques* (Geneva, 1542), which included an expanded collection of metrical psalms, mostly written by Marot.

The next edition, issued in Geneva in 1543, had an expanded version of Calvin's 1542 preface that was greatly influenced by Bucer's 1541 preface. After Marot's death Théodore de Bèze took over the work of translating the *Psalms* into French verse. The *Pseaumes octante trois de David* (music edited by Louis Bourgeois) appeared in 1551 and was followed by the complete Psalter, *Les Pseaumes mis en rime françoise* (music edited by Claude Goudimel), in 1562. This French-Genevan Psalter was widely influential throughout Europe, inspiring or creating vernacular metrical Psalters in Dutch, German, English, Polish, and other languages. Swiss Anabaptists produced their *Etliche schöne christliche Gesang* (1564), which was later incorporated into the *Aussbund* (1583), the principal hymnal of the Anabaptist and especially the Mennonite tradition.

The Low Countries. Between 1529 and 1536 a number of Dutch "martyr-songs" were written by David Joris and his followers to celebrate the lives and deaths of executed Anabaptists. Joris later issued a small collection of these songs as *Een geestelijck liedt-boecxken.* From its content some propose a publication date of about 1540; others assign a later date. In 1539 Simon Cock of Antwerp published *Een devoot ende profitelyck boecxken,* a collection of religious songs set mostly to folk-song melodies. The following year Cock issued a complete metrical Psalter, the *Souterliedekens* (Antwerp, 1540). Nine different imprints bear the same publication date of 12 June 1540, and this popular collection remained in print until the early seventeenth century. Like the 1539 collection, the *Souterliedekens* employed mostly folk-song melodies for the *Psalms.* Although there is a confessional ambiguity about the content of this Psalter, it was almost certainly Protestant rather than Catholic.

In London Jan Utenhove issued a collection of ten Dutch metrical psalms. Expanded editions were published in Emden between 1557 and 1559, and in 1560 the *Hondert Psalmen* was published in London. Utenhove's complete metrical Psalter, *De Psalmen Davidis in nederlandischer Sangs-Ryme* (London, 1566), was issued six years later. Utenhove's psalms employed an idiosyncratic approach to the Dutch language and used tunes from a variety of sources. They were thus displaced by Petrus Dathenus's *De Psalmen Davids* (Heidelberg, 1566), effectively a Dutch version of the French-Genevan Psalter. Dathenus's Psalter became the official Psalter of the Dutch Reformed church and was reprinted innumerable times. Other attempts at metrical Psalters, such as *Het Boeck der Psalmen* (Antwerp, 1580) by Philip Marnix van Saint Aldegonde, were made from time to time, but none displaced Dathenus's Psalter until the late eighteenth century.

East-Central Europe. The Bohemian Brethren published a Czech hymnal in Prague in 1501, with at least five further editions appearing by 1561. German translations of these Czech hymns, edited by Michael Weisse, were published in Bohemia as *Ein new Gesengbuchlen* (Jungbunzlau, 1531; reprinted in Ulm at least four times by 1541). A few years later Johann Horn edited *Ein Gesangbuch der Brüder inn Behemen und Werherrn* (Nuremberg, 1544), reprinted thirteen times by 1611.

The earliest known Hungarian Protestant hymnal, edited by István Gálszécsi and comprising translations of German Lutheran hymns, was published in Kraków in 1536. Although there had been earlier collections of metrical psalms, the influential Reformed Psalter, following the Genevan model, was the *Psalterium Ungaricum* (Herborn, 1607) by Albert Szenczi Molnár. A Bohemian Brethren *Cantional,* consisting of Polish translations from Czech, was published in Königsberg in 1554, and Mikołaj Gomółka's four-part settings of Polish metrical psalms were issued in Kraków in 1580.

England and Scotland. The early Reformation in England was influenced by Lutheranism. At a time when

Henry VIII was considering an alliance with the German princes, Miles Coverdale issued the first English hymnal, *Goostly Psalmes and Spirituall Songes* (London, c.1535). It contained mostly translated German hymns, primarily from north German and Danish sources. During the latter part of the reign of Henry VIII, Thomas Sternhold began writing metrical psalms, which were published during the early reign of Edward VI as *Certayne Psalmes* (London, c.1547). After Sternhold's death John Hopkins republished Sternhold's psalms—with additional texts, including a few of his own—under the title *Al Such Psalmes of David*... (London, 1549). This was reprinted at least ten times between 1549 and 1553 and became the nucleus of the later English metrical psalter. The English Protestant exiles in Germany and Switzerland during the reign of the Catholic queen Mary Tudor sang the psalms of Sternhold and Hopkins. In Wesel they were reissued with additional psalms and hymns as the *Psalmes of David in Metre* (c.1556); in Frankfurt am Main they were revised by William Whittingham and others and published as *One and Fiftie Psalmes of David in English* (Geneva, 1556). Additional psalms by Whittingham, John Pullain, and William Kethe, following Genevan models, were included in subsequent editions of the Anglo-Genevan Psalter (1558, 1559, and 1560).

On the accession of Elizabeth I in 1558, a number of different psalters were printed in London, and to a greater or lesser degree these were based on the Anglo-Genevan Psalters, though there was a tendency to avoid those psalms that were overtly based on French-Genevan models. Ultimately a complete English metrical Psalter was published as *The Whole Book of Psalmes* (London, 1562), which was reprinted numerous times in the following three centuries. The Psalter was referred to as "Sternhold and Hopkins" until the publication of Nahum Tate and Nicholas Brady's *New Version of the Psalms of David* (London, 1696), when it came to be known as the "Old Version."

In Calvinist Scotland the Psalter issued with *The Form of Prayers* (Edinburgh, 1564; subsequent editions in 1565, 1566, 1575, 1594, 1595, and 1602, with many later editions), exhibited a marked preference for English versions based on French-Genevan psalms, although it had much in common with its English counterpart. Some English Calvinists—the Separatist Puritans—moved to the Netherlands during the later Elizabethan years. For their worship a number of Middelburg editions of the Scottish and English Psalters were issued from 1594. A more consistent Calvinist English Psalter, published by Henry Ainsworth, was *The Book of Psalms* (Amsterdam, 1612 and 1618), the Psalter the Pilgrims took with them across the Atlantic in 1620.

A sequence of publications of four-part settings of the English psalm tunes was begun with the partbooks edited by William Parsons (London, 1563). It was continued by the Psalters of William Damon (London, 1579 [part 1] and 1591 [part 2]) and Thomas Este (London, 1592). This sequence culminated in *The Whole Book of Psalms, with the Hymns Evangelical, and Songs Spirituall* (London, 1621), a tune book edited by Thomas Ravenscroft and commended by the editors of the *Bay Psalm Book,* published in Cambridge, Massachusetts, in 1640.

[*See also* Hymns *and* Music.]

BIBLIOGRAPHY

Ameln, Konrad, Markus Jenny, and Walther Lipphardt, eds. *Das deutsche Kirchenlied.* 2 vols. Kassel, 1975–1980. An extremely useful bibliography listing all German-language hymnals printed before 1801; vol. 2 comprises extensive indexes. For German hymnals published without music see Wackernagel.

Chrisman, Miriam Usher. *Bibliography of Strasbourg Imprints, 1480–1599.* New Haven, 1982.

Frost, Maurice. *English and Scottish Psalm and Hymn Tunes, c.1543–1677.* Reprint, Oxford and New York, 1964. A basic bibliography and anthology of the tunes that retains its usefulness; for the results of more recent research see Leaver.

Glahn, Henrik. *Melodistudier til den lutherske salmesanges historie fra 1524 til c.1600.* 2 vols. Copenhagen, 1954. The Danish equivalent of Frost.

Höweler, C. A., and F. H. Matter, eds. *Fontes hymnodiae neerlandicae impressi 1539–1700: De melodieën van het Nederlandstalig geestelijk lied 1539–1700; Een bibliografie van de gedrukte bronnen.* Nieuwkoop, 1985. This volume is the Dutch equivalent of Ameln et al., though of a narrower time frame; for Dutch word-only hymnals and psalters see Wieder.

Jenny, Markus. *Geschichte des deutschschweizerischen evangelischen Gesangbuches im 16. Jahrhundert.* Basel, 1962. See also the supplement in *Zwingliana* 13 (1969), 132–143.

Leaver, Robin A. "*Goostly Psalmes and Spirituall Songes*": *English and Dutch Metrical Psalms from Coverdale to Utenhove, 1535–1566.* Oxford, 1991. The most recent and full discussion of English and Dutch psalmody of the period, but also covers developments in Germany, Scandinavia, and Switzerland.

Meyer, Christian. *Les mélodies des églises protestantes de langue allemande: Catalogue descriptif des sources et édition critique des mélodies.* Vol. 1, *Les mélodies à Strasbourg, 1524–1547.* Baden-Baden, 1987. Detailed bibliography and anthology of the melodies; needs to be used with Chrisman for Strasbourg hymnals and liturgical books published without music.

Müller, Joseph Theodore. *Hymnologisches Handbuch zum Gesangbuch der Brüdergemeine.* Gnadau, 1916. Reissued as *Nikolaus Ludwig von Zinzendorf Materialien und Dokumente,* edited by Erich Beyreuther et al., series 4, vol. 6, Hildesheim, 1977. The standard work on the hymnals of the Bohemian Brethren and later Moravianism.

Pidoux, Pierre. *Le psautier huguenot du XVIe siècle: Mélodies et documents.* 2 vols. Basel and Kassel, 1962. The standard work on the development of the French-Genevan Psalter.

Wackernagel, Philipp. *Bibliographie zur Geschichte des deutschen Kirchenliedes im XVI. Jahrhundert* (1885). Reprint, Hildesheim, 1961.

Wieder, F. C. *De Schriftuurlijke liedekens: De liederen der Nederlandsche Hervormden tot op het jaar 1566; Inhouds-beschrijving en bibliographie.* The Hague, 1900.

Wolkan, Rudolf. *Die Lieder der Wiedertäufer: Ein Beitrag zur Deutschen und niederländischen Literatur- und Kirchengeschichte* (1903). Reprint, Nieuwkoop, 1971. On German and Dutch Anabaptist hymnody.

Zim, Rivkah. *English Metrical Psalms: Poetry as Praise and Prayer, 1535–1601.* Cambridge, 1987. A useful overview with an annotated bibliography of sources.

Robin A. Leaver

HYMNS. The Reformation returned to the laity an active and essential role in the liturgy in the form of vernacular hymns. Historically, the term *hymn* has had many meanings, broad and narrow, from antiquity to the present. For the Reformation it has meant sacred metric poetry sung in the vernacular by the congregation in corporate worship and set to a simple, sturdy melody repeated for each of its stanzas. Because many songs of this type have been written that were not used in church until some later time, the definition is usually extended to include them as well. Hymns may be approached as literature or as music, as components of liturgy or as means of devotion. In practice hymns have not been limited to praise but have also embraced prayer, thanksgiving, proclamation, confession, teaching, exhortation, personal experience, communal memory, and so on, usually in connection with the scriptures. For example, much early Reformation hymnody takes its inspiration directly from the *Psalms*, which vividly portray these motives. The familiar term *chorale* for the hymn of the Lutheran tradition derives from the German word for Latin chant and only gradually came to be used for the hymn, for like chant it was originally an unaccompanied, unison liturgical song. The other principal branch of Protestant hymnody was established in the Reformed church by John Calvin, who restricted it almost exclusively to metrical paraphrases of the *Psalms*.

Pre-Reformation Antecedents. Although Martin Luther initiated the reception of congregational song in Protestant worship, his enthusiasm for vernacular hymns was not new. For centuries the people had been permitted to sing in paraliturgical and devotional situations, and a huge repertory of simple Latin and vernacular texts and melodies had become their property as a form of folk song, especially in German-speaking lands. They were sung in processions, on pilgrimages, at votive services, and in rare cases in the liturgy at high festivals. Their beginnings can be traced to refrain-like acclamations in Latin litanies, psalms, and hymns. The interaction between the leader (precentor) and the people in these *Rufe* resulted in longer sections and increased popular participation. The most important type were the *Leisen*, vernacular stanzas that evolved from refrains added to the festival sequences (hymnic chants following the Alleluia in the Mass), to which the people joined their "Alleluia" or more often, "Kyrieleis." The *cantio* was another source of semiliturgical religious song. Originally in Latin, many exist in vernacular or Latin-vernacular (macaronic) versions, and with their tuneful, sometimes dancelike character, they became extremely popular.

Most of these songs were produced by monks, clerics, and other members of the educated classes and then passed on to the people, who learned them in various devotional contexts. It is not always clear how and to what extent the people actually sang these songs and how much was sung by the leader, to whom they responded. Although church authorities continued to prohibit vernacular congregational singing in the Latin liturgy with rare exceptions, pastoral concerns induced sympathetic clergy to encourage the laity to sing not only at extraliturgical devotions but also before and after the sermon, usually in a service apart from the Mass. The legacy of Jan Hus carried on by the Czech and German Bohemian Brethren provided the most impressive example of pre-Reformation congregational participation in the Mass. In the century before Luther their worship, beginning with Hus, drew from a treasury of vernacular liturgical chants, hymns, and sacred songs preserved in their remarkable collections called *Kantionals*.

The Wittenberg Tradition. Early in 1523 Luther published a brief tract on worship with no mention of congregational singing, but in the same year the controversial Thomas Müntzer published his *Deutsch kirchen Ampt*, which included psalms, responsories, and eleven hymns of the Divine Office in German versions set to their Latin chants. Although Luther sharply criticized this work, it is quite unlikely that Müntzer meant his congregation to sing these complex chants or those of his Mass of 1524. On the other hand, by this time Luther must have seen the Low German hymn versions of the *Gloria*, *Sanctus*, and *Agnus Dei* chants of the Mass by Nikolaus Decius. The first and third of these are among the most beloved of chorales and may well count as the first Lutheran hymns.

Luther's first liturgical directive was basically conservative in that it assumed traditional Latin liturgical forms; its central theme, however, was the preaching of the word, without which he held reading and singing to be useless, especially the chants of the canonical hours. Near the end of 1523 he published the highly influential *Formula missae et communionis* (Order of the Mass), which specified German hymns in the Latin liturgy. In a well-known letter to Georg Spalatin Luther described the plan to acquire versified psalms in the vernacular, "that is, spiritual songs, so that the Word of God may be among the people also in the form of music." He assigned some of the *Seven Penitential Psalms* to two friends and, having done Psalm 130 already, suggested Psalm 6 or 143 as Spalatin's contribution. He urged him to use plain language, avoiding new words or sophisticated courtly expressions.

Luther was unconcerned with innovation or originality. On the contrary, his work was extraordinarily conservative, borrowing from the past and adapting it to the present. He knew from experience that vigorous metrical poetry and simple, rhythmic melody were essential for a congregation to sing together "by heart" with confidence, unity, and understanding. Consequently, Luther appropriated and adapted familiar tunes and one or more stanzas of medieval songs such as the old *Leisen*. In about one year Luther produced twenty-four chorales, two-thirds of his known output.

Skillfully derived from popular traditions, they provided the people with the biblical message set to singable melodies. He forged six of his seven psalm chorales at this time, becoming the inventor of the vernacular metrical psalm. He translated and paraphrased Latin hymns, antiphons, canticles, and parts of the Mass, transforming them into vigorous, idiomatic German poetry. Several more are based on pre-Reformation sacred songs, which he revised and supplied with stanzas of his own. A few of his poems are essentially his own creation, but most have some formal relationship to earlier models. Yet, for all the variety in styles and types of the originals, Luther's hymns bear his personal stamp—vivid, forceful expressions of biblical faith, carved out in high relief for the people to sing in their own language. Luther's poetry is sometimes rough-hewn, seemingly naive in its directness and simplicity, but he knew precisely what he was doing. With his sensitivity to language and its relationship to music, he established the vernacular hymn as a powerful weapon of the Reformation.

Dissemination in print. The popular response to the chorales was immediate and enthusiastic. Thanks to printing and oral transmission, they circulated through much of Germany with unprecedented speed. This remarkable situation was apparently initiated by Luther's first attempt at song, a narrative ballad on the martyrdom of two fellow Augustinians in Brussels in July 1523. Although not a hymn, the song, *Ein neues Lied wir heben an* (A New Song We Now Begin), awakened Luther's lyric talent, and, printed on a broadsheet, whose popularity must have been considerable, it began a wave of hymn writing. By the beginning of 1524 several chorales of Luther and his associates had been printed in this form, and eight of them reached Nuremberg, where they were issued in a booklet entitled *Etlich Cristlich lider, Lobgesang unn Psalm* . . . (Some Christian Songs, Hymns, and Psalms . . . ; the so-called *Achtliederbuch*). It contained Luther's *Nun freut euch* and his Psalms 12, 14, and 130, three chorales by Paul Speratus, and one anonymous, but only four tunes. The appearance of the two small Erfurt hymnals (*Enchiridion*, "handbook") some months later shows how swiftly the chorales were being written, circulated, and printed. The two are nearly identical, and, though unauthorized by Wittenberg, each included eighteen hymns of Luther, the three of Speratus, and one each by four others, altogether twenty-five chorales and sixteen tunes.

Luther's authorized hymnals. For whatever reason, Luther waited about five years before publicly authorizing a hymnal, while in the meantime several dozen publications of evangelical hymns came off presses in Wittenberg, Erfurt, and Zwickau and from as far as Nuremberg, Augsburg, Strasbourg, Breslau, and Königsberg. An unusual initiative, however, came from Johann Walter (1496–1570), a young singer and composer in Elector Frederick's musical establishment in Torgau. In an astonishingly brief time Walter had acquired all twenty-four of Luther's first hymns, either with Luther's tunes or others, adapting them and composing some himself. Adding eight chorales of other authors, he made effective polyphonic settings of all of them and had them set in type for printing by late summer of 1524 along with five Latin motets. Luther supplied the preface. The collection was thus not a true hymnal, but within two years the Wittenberg printer Hans Lufft increased the practical value of Walter's work by publishing its chorales with their melodies in hymnbook form. This, or a lost edition of 1525, was the first Wittenberg hymnal. Luther finally prepared an authorized version, which was printed in Wittenberg in 1529 by Joseph Klug. By the edition of 1543/44 it had established the core of the Lutheran chorale tradition for at least two centuries.

The format of Luther's hymnal not only identified his hymns and the authors of many others, but it also lent to the whole collection a representative character that in retrospect appears conciliatory and ecumenical. Luther's work gained wide acceptance. Like his preaching, he offered the people at large songs they could easily grasp and make their own. Not only his language but also his melodies were carefully designed for them. Over 40 percent of them are in the AAB form of *Minnelied* and *Meistergesang*, an aid to learning. Although in many instances we do not know which tunes are Luther's and which are Walter's, they were shaped effectively for singing. The adaptations of earlier melodies are especially instructive. If one compares his *Komm, Gott, Schöpfer* and *Nun komm der heiden Heiland* with the chants of *Veni creator* and *Veni redemptor* in either the Latin or the version of Müntzer, one can see how their subtle flow has been replaced by sturdy, solid tunes.

Luther's success with the common people held a hidden danger. Although he believed that the gospel would speak equally to all levels of society, his own love of Latin chant and polyphony should have warned him that these rugged hymns and the liturgy associated with them might in time fail to satisfy the more sophisticated and widen the gap between the upper and lower classes. The hymnal preserves his splendid chorales, but at the same time it signaled the fixing of the people's music and the eventual reemphasis on the choir at their expense.

Continuing the Tradition. The movement begun by Luther was continued by others in German-speaking territories. Among those close to him were Paul Speratus (1484–1551) with *Es ist das Heil uns kommen her* (EKG 242); Justus Jonas (1493–1555) with Psalm 124, *Wo Gott der Herr nicht bei uns hält*; Johann Walter (1496–1570), who, besides his work on the melodies of 1524, late in life wrote some sacred songs and tunes, for example, *Wach auf, du deutsches Land* and *Herzlich tut mich erfreuen*; Philipp Melanchthon (1497–1560), whose Latin hymns were translated into German by others; Elisabeth Creutziger (c.1504–1535) with *Herr Christ,* *der einig Gotts Sohn*; Erasmus Alber (1500?–1553); Johann Gramman (1487–1541); Erhart Hegenwald; Johann Agricola (1492?–1566); and Paul Eber (1511–1569), a devoted colleague of Luther and Melanchthon whose fine hymns date from about 1560.

The publication in Leipzig in 1545 of the so-called *Babst Gesangbuch* proved uniquely significant. Beautifully printed by Valentin Babst, it was Luther's final and most authoritative hymnal. Although he wrote the new preface, all indications are that Luther saw and approved only the first part, which was essentially the 1543 Klug edition and a modified reprint of the Latin and German burial songs of 1542. The third and last section, however, has the appearance of an entirely separate publication, with its own title page, signatures, and index; but its elaborate graphic design, lacking only the woodcuts, is identical to the rest, indicating that Babst intended to include it from the start. These "Psalms and Spiritual Songs Composed by Pious Christians" clearly represent an important step in extending the repertory of chorales for Lutheran use without Luther's express consent. With Luther's death in the following year, tension between Luther's authority and the desire for change was bound to increase. In effect, the belief that the reformer had approved Babst's book *in toto* opened the floodgates to new hymn writing, more Brethren hymns, and eventually the adoption and imitation of Genevan melodies as well.

The Strasbourg-Constance Tradition. While the Wittenberg tradition dominated much of northern Germany, the Reformation in the south emanated primarily from Zurich, Constance, and Strasbourg. Even before Calvin came on the scene, the liturgy and music showed signs of Zwingli's influence. Huldrych Zwingli (1484–1531) was the most musically accomplished of the reformers. As the leading reformer of Zurich and much of German-speaking Switzerland, he radically simplified the liturgy, introduced the vernacular, and with cogent theological arguments succeeded in abolishing all music from public worship in the city, a ban not lifted until 1598. He was, however, the composer of at least three sacred songs, one of which made its way into Protestant collections across Germany as far away as Königsberg. His earnest theological and psychological stance initiated serious examination of the nature of music and its uses and abuses in the church.

The significance of Strasbourg for liturgical change, congregational singing, and hymnody was extraordinary. Its influence extended northward to Hesse and south and east to parts of Switzerland and southern Germany, but its local situation was different from either Wittenberg or Nuremberg. With a cathedral and its Catholic bishop still in place (though not resident in the city), several collegiate churches and clergy hostile to reform, and a patrician council willing to permit reform while allowing old practices to continue for the first critical years, radical change was cautiously tolerated. Austere simplicity, the active role of the congregation, exclusive use of the vernacular, and the centrality of preaching marked the early Strasbourg liturgies. In one critical respect, however, they did not follow Zwingli. Although they completely rejected all elaborate ceremonial music, they could not do without congregational singing. In his *Grund und Ursach* (1524) Martin Bucer declared that the injunctions of *Ephesians* 5 and *Colossians* 3 required the word of God and his praises to be sung by all the people to nourish the community of faith. Strasbourg chose to follow Luther's example.

Strasbourg printed its own booklets of Reformation liturgies and hymns then in use. The first ones included liturgical orders with prose chants for some of the traditional parts of the Mass and the Divine Office. More important are the hymns, few at first, but a 1524 edition of *Teutsch kirchen ampt* contains nine, of which five are Luther's. One of the nine is a metrical Magnificat and five are metrical psalms. By 1533 the number of hymns in the *Psalmen, Gebett, und kirchen Übung* had grown to forty-five with at least thirty metrical psalms, almost all of the rest consisting of versified biblical and liturgical hymns. Many texts and melodies of these hymnals were contributed by Strasbourg musician-poets, two of the most important being Matthias Greiter (c.1495–1550) and Wolfgang Dachstein (c.1487–1553). Although Luther's hymns continued to be printed and sung in Strasbourg, six of the twelve in this collection are psalms. Strasbourg evidently leaned more toward Zwingli's biblicism, espoused by Bucer, than the freer and more christological hymnody of Wittenberg.

At the end of the 1530s, complete series of psalms were available in Strasbourg and Augsburg. In the meantime Strasbourg turned toward a larger and broader representation of hymns including those of Wittenberg, likely in response to developments in Constance. Johannes Zwick and the brothers Ambrosius and Thomas Blarer prepared a new hymnal, which by its third edition (1540) contained over sixty psalm-hymns. In his original preface, Zwick, taking his cue from Bucer, forcefully defended congregational singing with a point-by-point refutation of Zwingli's argument against music. But he also questioned the need to limit the music to psalms and texts taken literally from the Bible. Armed with this preface, the new anthology, with hymns not only from Constance, Wittenberg, and Strasbourg but also Augsburg, Basel, and Nuremberg, is credited with bringing hymn singing to many areas for the first time. It was also seen as a means of unifying diverse Protestant groups, a point not missed by Bucer, who, to further his conciliatory efforts, may have encouraged the printing of a few hymnals on this Constance model.

By 1540 the political situation had increased the vulnerability of the Protestant cities of the empire. Bucer, like Luther, recognized that the proliferation of hymnals worked against evangelical unity, that the poor quality of many hymns made them unfit for worship, and that the questionable, even offensive character of some hymns intensified hostility to the movement. Symbolic of this realization was the extraordinary first edition in 1541 of a large folio choralebook "of all the foremost and best psalms, spiritual songs and chants assembled from the hymnals of Wittenberg, Strasbourg, and other churches," printed in Strasbourg with a lengthy foreword by Bucer. Extolling music in worship but warning of its power for evil as well as good, particularly for the young, he goes on to explain that he designed this new hymnal specifically to serve many different churches because they lacked a common repertory of hymns. In it, however, each would find songs it was accustomed to sing. Especially significant, moreover, is Bucer's fulsome praise of Luther, his hymns, and his hymnal. The book reduced by about half the number of hymns in the Strasbourg hymnals of the 1530s, and as much as anything its purpose was to promote trained student choirs to lead and support the singing of a limited number of hymns for the liturgy. Ironically, it was also prophetic of the theological, liturgical, and musical direction Strasbourg would take later in the century.

The Catholic Response. Not since the early church did congregational song in the vernacular or Latin have any essential liturgical function in Catholic worship, but with the Reformation and the success of Luther's hymns, concerned leaders of the old faith acknowledged the need for a comparable religious musical expression for the laity. The foremost of these was Georg Witzel (1501–1573), who as an Erasmian humanist, one-time Lutheran pastor, and reconverted Catholic had become particularly sensitive to this problem. Knowing firsthand the value of lay participation, Witzel hoped to see the eventual introduction of vernacular hymns in the Mass as a step toward restoring the church.

His concerns were shared by Michael Vehe (c.1480–1539), the Dominican provost of the new abbey church in Halle, who with Kaspar Querhamer prepared the first Catholic hymnal in German printed with music. Published in Leipzig in 1537, it contained fifty-two hymns and forty-six melodies. Although about half were of recent origin, five by Witzel and many by Querhamer, others were pre-Reformation songs based in several instances on Lutheran versions of texts and melodies. As earlier, they were to be sung by the people before and after the sermon, in processions, and perhaps at low Mass. Although Witzel also published *Odae Christianae* (1541) and *Psaltes Ecclesiasticus* (1550), collections of hymns, prayers, sacred songs, and liturgical texts in translation, including the Mass, they contained no music.

Apart from a few pamphlets, nothing comparable to Vehe's hymnal appeared until its second edition in 1567, the same year as Johann Leisentrit's huge *Geistliche Lieder und Psalmen der alten Apostolischer recht und warglaubiger Christlicher Kirchen* (1567). Leisentrit, a priest and a papal administrator of a Bohemian crown territory, was a firm but conciliatory Catholic influenced by Witzel. Drawing on most of Vehe's book, he expanded his hymnal, beautifully produced in the style of Babst, to include 250 hymns with nearly 180 melodies. It covers a broader range than Vehe's, but it also adapts a great many Lutheran sources, for which his colleagues criticized him.

It is doubtful that congregational singing in the liturgy was widespread. In its next phase, however, the Catholic Reformation found another approach to vernacular song for the people.

Calvinist Metrical Psalmody. Although metrical versions of Psalms date back as early as the fourth century and were used for private devotion in the Middle Ages, their composition and use by the congregation at worship was an innovation of the Reformation. Luther may well have been the first to offer them as liturgical hymns in the vernacular, but Strasbourg took the lead, followed among others by Augsburg and Basel, the first reformed Swiss city to permit any congregational singing. By 1538 a complete psalter had been printed in Strasbourg and another in Augsburg. These collections, however, contain psalm versions in a variety of styles and forms, including some of Luther's, as well as several hymns that are not derived from psalms. It remained for John Calvin (1509–1564) to conceive the gradual creation of a complete metrical psalter of uniform poetic and musical character intended for the people at worship. His Genevan psalm tradition was an achievement in its own way as remarkable and influential as the hymnody of Luther.

Franco-Genevan psalmody. Calvin showed no serious interest in music until he first assumed responsibility for worship for Geneva in 1536/37. From near indifference his theological and psychological understanding of music evolved over a period of about six years to a level of some precision and sophistication. His initial comments date from the first edition (1535/36) of his *Institutes of the Christian Religion* and refer primarily to inward speech and singing "from the heart," echoing Zwingli, but going slightly beyond him in approving publicly sung praise and thanksgiving. In January 1537 Calvin submitted to the Genevan city council his *Articles* on the church and its worship, in which he strongly recommended the singing of psalms in public worship as an effective means of arousing a more intense and ardent devotion in place of the cold prayers then in use.

His expulsion from Geneva in 1538 and subsequent move to Strasbourg was the critical next step. Invited by Bucer to serve as pastor to the French refugee congregation in the city, the two soon became close friends, and Calvin was undoubtedly influenced by the musical thought of the reformer, who shared Luther's enthusiasm for congregational singing. Profoundly moved by the metrical psalm singing in the churches, Calvin desired to have a collection of metrical psalms in French for his people. He had earlier met Clément Marot in Ferrara and knew his work. When copies of several of the poet's metrical psalms came into his hands, Calvin hoped to publish them for his congregation in the relative safety of Strasbourg. But first he tried his hand at six more in Marot's manner, adding versions of The Song of Simeon, the Decalogue, and the Apostles' Creed. While he modeled all but one of his own poems to fit familiar melodies by Strasbourg composers Greiter and Dachstein, he in all likelihood called on them to compose unique tunes for the thirteen Marot psalms. Thus, with *Aucuns pseaulmes et cantiques mys en chant* printed in 1539, the evolution of the Genevan (also known as the Huguenot) Psalter began.

The Genevan Psalter. The complex history of the Psalter continued over the next two decades, an extraordinary achievement guided at each formative stage by Calvin himself. Recalled to Geneva in 1541, he lost no time in issuing in 1542 the Genevan church order *La forme des prieres et chantz ecclesiastiques*, which specified the musical participation of the congregation and included, along with a forceful statement on worship and music, thirty psalms of Marot, five of Calvin, and four other sacred pieces. During Marot's brief stay in Geneva in 1543, nineteen more psalms were added, requiring another edition that year but with an important addition to its preface and the replacement of Calvin's psalms by versions of Marot. After Marot's death in 1544 Calvin persuaded Théodore de Bèze to supply the remaining psalms in stages from about 1548 to 1562, when the complete Psalter was published in Geneva, Paris, Lyon, and elsewhere.

With the same purism that permitted only faithful paraphrases of psalms and a few other biblical songs to be sung in public worship, and these only in unison and unaccompanied, Calvin insisted on a distinctively *sacred* musical style as the only appropriate and worthy vehicle for the divinely inspired texts. The polished French poetry, in contrast to most other hymn traditions, consisted of 110 different metric forms, requiring at least that many different tunes (there are 125), and Calvin stipulated that the style be suited to the content of the text, suggesting gravity, majesty, moderation, and modesty, distinct from secular music and lacking any hint of sensuality. Although indebtedness to Strasbourg melodies is clear, although traces of secular *chansons* can be found, and although some derivations from plainchant are also identifiable, the style on the whole is somehow unique. Only two note values, the long and the short of classical poetry, are used; none of the melodies uses triple meter, typically suggestive of the dance; and dotted rhythms are scrupulously avoided. Only one Strasbourg melody was retained in the final version, and of the three or so composers responsible for all the rest, Louis Bourgeois was the most gifted, even though some of his fine melodies did not survive scrutiny in the end. Granted some unevenness in the 125 melodies, as a whole their singability, their stylistic consistency, their union with the poetry, and their durability for generations were the realization of Calvin's vision. Calvin did not live to see the outcome, but the dedication to the Psalter was no less in France than in Geneva, and in the Huguenots' trials psalm singing took on added meaning as an openly militant and courageous affirmation of faith.

Metrical Psalmody in the Low Countries and Germany. Protestantism was unable to take hold in the southern provinces of the Low Countries, where Catholicism under Spanish rule was never seriously threatened. In the north, however, it eventually succeeded and brought with it the Genevan Psalter. Yet, even before Calvinism had made headway, the *Souterliedekens*, a collection of rhymed psalms in Dutch, was published in Antwerp in 1540 with melodies drawn from chant, French *chansons*, and German and Dutch folk songs. Although the author evidently did not intend them for church use, he apparently had Protestant sympathies, and the psalms were sung in Calvinist services. In the next decades a few composers published them in polyphonic versions, but no Calvinist psalters in Dutch were printed in the Netherlands until those of Lucas de Herre (1565) and Petrus Dathenus (1566). In 1568 Dathenus's work, carefully modeled after the Genevan texts and melodies, became the official Calvinist songbook for the next two centuries. In the meantime, religious persecution on both sides of the English Channel led to another episode in the history of the psalter. Dutch refugees in England and Germany acquired their own psalmbooks, thanks to the efforts of Jan Utenhove from 1551 to 1566, while English refugees on the Continent were exposed to Dutch, German, and Genevan psalmody, circumstances fateful for the development of metrical psalms in England and Scotland.

The Genevan model and its success soon attracted not only German Calvinists but Lutherans as well. Ambrosius Lobwasser (1515–1585), Lutheran cosmopolite, humanist, and law scholar in Königsberg, translated the whole Genevan set in 1565 for his patron, Duke Albert of Prussia, observing the verse forms of the originals so precisely that they could be sung to their proper tunes. He published them in Leipzig in 1573 (possibly already in Danzig in 1572), not only with their melodies but also with Claude Goudimel's simple four-voice settings of 1565. In Germany the Lobwasser versions were probably first officially adopted in the Reformed Palatinate, where the elector insisted on strict adherence to unaccompanied unison singing. Elsewhere they were sung with the Goudimel harmonizations in Lutheran churches and even in some Reformed areas where Calvin's principles were less stringently observed. So successful was Lobwasser's work that it was widely imitated well into the seventeenth century. Several of its Genevan melodies became favorite chorale tunes, and their style influenced a new generation of Lutheran composers.

Congregational Psalmody in England. Psalms in verse had been used for private devotion before the Reformation, but the news of congregational singing among Lutherans on the Continent stirred the imagination of many in England. The most striking document is Miles Coverdale's *Goostly psalmes and spirituall songes*, a collection of English versifications with music, most of which are easily identifiable as Lutheran texts and tunes. It contains fifteen metrical psalms and twenty-six hymns, including Luther's seven psalms and eleven of his chorales. Undated but now believed to have been printed as early as 1535, it was burned in 1546 along with other prohibited books (Leaver, 1991, pp. 65–66). The book was restricted to private use and was once thought to have had little influence on psalmody in England. But it introduced Luther's hymns and his view of music in worship, ardently championed by Coverdale.

With the accession of Edward VI, growing Puritan sentiment followed the Reformed churches on the Continent in attempting to eliminate all vestiges of Catholic musical practice in favor of congregational singing. As early as 1550 the English received a convincing demonstration of the value of psalmody in the French, Dutch, German, and Italian refugee churches established in London and elsewhere by Jan Łaski, with the support of Archbishop Thomas Cranmer. Their simple order of worship with metrical psalms set a pattern for music in English parish churches for well over a century. As yet, however, the English did not have their own versified psalter with music suitable for congregational use. About this time it was becoming fashionable to base poetry on the *Psalms*, but the only psalter of lasting importance was begun by Thomas Sternhold, a court poet, whose small collection came out around 1549, the year of his death. At the end of the same year an expanded set was printed with thirty-seven of his psalms, augmented by seven by John Hopkins. It contained no music, but it became the core of what was to be the *Whole Booke of Psalmes*, printed in London in 1562, the Psalter that for all practical purposes stood as the authorized version for the next century. Although in its final version the work of Hopkins dominates, its complex history owes much to the exiles on the Continent.

When in 1553 the English Protestant leaders as well as the "stranger churches" were driven to seek refuge across the English Channel, they were able to found "alien churches" in Frankfurt am Main, Strasbourg, Emden, Wesel, and Geneva. Failing in their attempt to resolve their differences with the supporters of the 1552 *Book of Common Prayer*, the Genevan group presented its own liturgical order to Calvin and won his approval. Printed in Geneva as *The forme of prayers and Ministrations of the Sacraments* . . . (1556), it contained the Anglo-Genevan Psalter, the first of the series to include music. Other editions followed, significant for the addition of some fine Genevan tunes and several new psalm versions.

With the coronation of Elizabeth I in 1559, the exiles returned home, and together with the original psalms of Sternhold and many more by Hopkins, the contributions of both the Genevan and Anglican groups were finally sifted and combined to form the *Whole Booke of Psalmes* printed by John Daye. The process resulted in a collection including the complete metrical Psalter, some hymns and canticles, mostly in the simple and familiar "double common meter" (8 lines in couplets of 8 and 6 syllables), some good tunes easy to learn, and a selection of liturgical pieces. A few traces of German influence survived, hardly recognized by the English, the most curious instance being *Preserve us, Lord by thy dear Word*, Robert Wisdome's version to the original tune of Luther's *Erhalt uns, Herr, bei deinem Wort*.

In spite of conservative resistance to the veritable explosion of psalm singing at her accession, Queen Elizabeth referred to church music in one of the Royal Injunctions (1559) in sufficiently ambiguous terms to permit both congregational psalms and polyphonic anthems under some conditions. In parish churches, however, with rare exceptions the only music sung was the psalmody of the people. In the cathedrals, collegiate churches, and colleges with endowed foundations, the singing in the daily and festival liturgies was exclusively choral, although in some cathedrals congregational song was permitted in connection with the sermon, usually after Morning Prayer. In contrast to the Presbyterian church of Scotland, the Anglican *Book of Common Prayer* made no explicit provision for congregational hymnody before the twentieth century.

The Hymn in Worship. The liturgies of the Reformation assumed many different forms, especially in Germany, where they were not under the control of a single centralized authority.

Liturgical function. The use and extent of congregational singing varied from place to place in accordance with Luther's principle of freedom in external ceremonies. For him, however, the role of the congregation was essentially liturgical, not incidental. His two published Mass liturgies, the *Formula missae* and the *Deutsche Messe*, constitute polar examples of these principles within the traditional framework. The former was outwardly a Latin mass, and the latter a somewhat freer structure entirely in German. Both provided for the use of hymns sung by the people. Luther's earlier *Formula* illustrates two methods. In it he suggests adding a hymn after the Latin Gradual and after the *Sanctus*, an *additive* method by which the hymn duplicates the function of the preceding choral section. Luther also hinted at the *substitutive* approach: on alternate Sundays, for example, congregational hymns might replace one or more of the prescribed Latin chants. By contrast, in the *Deutsche Messe* Luther applies the second method, for he suggests chorales, and in some cases assigns specific ones, to replace traditional parts of the liturgy (e.g., the Introit, Gradual, *Credo*, *Sanctus*, and *Agnus Dei*).

Although local and regional church orders varied widely in their liturgical practices, wherever Luther's influence was strong they employed the hymn in one of these two ways or a combination of both. In small parishes without Latin schools, especially in rural areas, German chorales supplied the music for the liturgy. In larger communities with Latin schools and competent choirs, some substitution was used, but addition by duplication was also common. Typically on high festivals, Latin chant or polyphony was followed by, or alternated stanza by stanza with, corresponding hymns for the congregation. Cities under conservative patrician rule such as Nuremberg, as well as academic communities such as Wittenberg and Leipzig, favored Latin chant and polyphony for much of the liturgy, reserving most vernacular hymns to be sung before and after the sermon.

Other areas in Germany less influenced by Luther placed greater emphasis on preaching services and preferred simpler orders to the traditional form of the Lord's Supper. Strasbourg was again highly influential, having embraced the vernacular and congregational singing even more enthusiastically than Wittenberg. Most of the chanted parts of the Mass were either omitted or replaced by hymns and metrical psalms. Sunday Vespers naturally relied heavily on metrical psalmody, but increasingly important were the many sermon services. In these, typically three times daily, the people sang metrical psalms before and after the sermon, and the regular catechetical services for the children made use of them as well.

The debt to Bucer and to Strasbourg is apparent in the orders prepared for Geneva by Calvin. Parallels can be seen in the music for the congregation. In its developed form the service without Communion included an entrance psalm, psalms before and after the sermon, and a concluding psalm before the Benediction. The less frequent full service with Communion also included the Decalogue, Psalm 138, and the metrical Song of Simeon.

In spite of the influence of Luther, Bucer, and Calvin in England *The Book of Common Prayer* ignored congregational singing. Many English parish churches nevertheless inserted and substituted metrical psalms in the prayer book services, in accord with the ideals of the reformers.

Practical problems. Congregational singing then as now required leadership. In Luther's day at least one person assumed this responsibility, usually a singer, clerical or lay (precentor, cantor, *Vorsinger*), who was often assisted by a vocal ensemble or choir. In contrast to later practice, the organ if used was at first a participant, neither leading nor accompanying. The primary function of the leader was to introduce, begin, and lead the singing. Where Lutheran hymnody became firmly established, elaborate patterns of alternation of congregation, choir, and organ enriched the liturgical music, especially at princely courts and communities with school choirs or other choral groups (*Kantoreien*). This depended, of course, on the people's having learned the songs. Even where literacy was adequate, hymnbooks were rarely used by the congregation, for Luther advocated singing hymns from memory; consequently, the number of hymns for public worship was at first small. In Strasbourg, however, and other areas influenced by Reformed thought and its metrical psalmody, hymnals were in the hands of the people, and the number board appeared about midcentury. Nevertheless, in either case teaching the songs to the people was taken seriously.

Many approaches were tried. A leader or pastor might teach a hymn by singing it to the congregation at a sermon service until the congregation could sing along. Choirs were instructed to sing clearly so that people might learn by listening. Children sang chorales in school and taught them to the family at home, sometimes with limited success, for Luther scolded lazy parents who failed to learn from the students. Bucer urged school choirs to support the diffident singing of the people, and Calvin, following Strasbourg, appointed the school choirs to teach the many complex metrical psalms to the congregation and for that purpose called for an hour of music study four days a week. In Lutheran circles artistic polyphonic settings of chorales were sung and played in church, practiced in schools, and performed as chamber music in the homes of the educated—all for worship, musical training, and wholesome pleasure that internalized the tradition. Although rarely admitted in church, a similar type of music making found its way into Calvinist schools and homes. These and other methods succeeded within a few decades in restoring the congregation, at least potentially, to full and active participation in public worship.

Advancing the Reformation. Although the life of faith envisioned by the reformers was nurtured primarily in the worship life of the community, many of the same hymns were also taught, read, and sung in school and at home. At first little distinction was made between hymns for worship and those for teaching; even those assigned for catechetical exercise were liturgical or at least biblical. Soon, however, didactic songs spreading Reformation ideas began to multiply, and hymns new and old conveyed the message in still other ways. They were sung at work, on the battlefield, and in the marketplace and town square. Like reading aloud the news of events to a largely illiterate crowd, broadsheet peddlers sang to enthusiastic audiences the new Lutheran hymns circulating widely as objects of popular culture. Furthermore, group street singing provided a common outlet for public expressions of social comment, political opinion, and discontent, often in satirical or protest poems set to familiar tunes.

The contribution of hymns. Whether the Reformation was ultimately a magisterial or a popular movement, the new hymn contributed mightily to its spread. In part, at least, its effectiveness lay in its broad appeal. For Luther and most of the reformers the hymn was a bearer of the word of God without class distinction; as he put it, hymns were a Bible for children and for the learned as well. They celebrated salvation history in the feasts of the liturgical year, joining individual experience to that of the community. They turned many of the traditional chants of the Mass and Divine Office into songs of the people. They transformed the *Psalms* into personal responses to the divine-human encounter in straightforward songs of prayer, praise, penitence, and proclamation. In sum, they added a new sacramental dimension to the offering of thanksgiving for the gospel of grace and forgiveness.

The appeal of translated Lutheran hymnody probably facilitated the relatively early acceptance of the Reformation in Scandinavia. In Denmark, for example, the first chorales in Danish were printed in 1528, eight years before the new church was officially established. Norway and Iceland, both under Danish rule, followed soon after. The Swedish reformer Olaus Petri, like Gissar Einarsson of Iceland and Michael Agricola of Finland, had studied with Luther. In 1526 Petri published a small collection of Lutheran hymns in Swedish, and in the following year Sweden broke with Rome. Finland, although Lutheran, resisted the German chorale for decades. A late witness to Finnish devotion to medieval song was the *Piae cantiones* (1582), a remarkable Latin collection prepared by Jacob Finno and printed in Greifswald by his student, Theodoric Petri Rutha.

The Czechs and Slovaks, with their long tradition of vernacular sacred music stemming from the Hussites, were readily attracted to the Reformation, but they relied on the rich Czech sources of the Bohemian Brethren in the absence of translated Lutheran hymns. Similarly, Polish Protestants turned to pre-Reformation hymns but also found models in German Lutheran and Czech Brethren hymnody; not surprisingly, Reformed congregations used psalm paraphrases, even adopting French melodies late in the century. In Hungary, where the Reformed were strong, Lutherans tended to prefer traditional liturgical song, although the hymns of the two confessions had much in common.

Reformed metrical psalmody. The phenomenal success of Calvinist psalmody deserves further comment. On the one hand it restricted creativity and precluded any new response to changing circumstances, and on the other it was uniquely concentrated, sophisticated poetry and music. It was also much more. For the faithful it was God's word they were privileged to sing, and it spoke to their most profound human needs and aspirations. The psalms became their badge of identity, the banner of the people of God struggling for power or survival in France, the Low Countries, much of Germany, and elsewhere. Their refined power was the envy of cultivated Lutherans, as a Nuremberg pastor had to admit in defending himself against the charge of crypto-Calvinism. In England, however, the metrical psalms were scorned by the aristocracy while beloved by the less privileged classes. As the voice of the Puritan party, however, the popular Psalter helped keep the Reformation in a lively tension with the traditionalism of the Church of England. In Scotland the sole use of metrical psalmody was the norm.

The radical Reformation. Besides Müntzer, many of the groups of the left wing produced their own hymns and spiritual songs. Spiritualists known for their songs included David Joris and Sebastian Franck. A number of the followers of Kaspar von Schwenckfeld were also active poets, one of whom was Adam Reusner, whose Psalm 31 is still in use, and another, Daniel Sudermann, who wrote over two hundred hymn texts.

Hymns have been extremely important among the Anabaptists. Their hymns were printed in hymnbooks, the most long-lived of which is usually referred to by the short title *Ausbund*, which survives in numerous editions. The early books contained no melodies, but one or more tunes were indicated for each hymn. These were from well-known sacred and secular songs, pre-Reformation and contemporary, many from Bohemian Brethren and Lutheran sources. The extraordinary sense of community and mutual caring and the irenic spirit of much Anabaptist hymnody is especially moving, in view of the hatred and deadly persecution they endured. Understandably, their songs frequently memorialized an actual martyrdom and testified to their trust in the redemptive value of suffering.

The post-Tridentine reform. Although the Council of Trent made no pronouncements on vernacular song in the liturgy and its few decrees on music were relatively mild, it rejected proposals of men like Witzel and affirmed the exclusive use of Latin, in effect denying the laity active participation in the Mass. At the same time, however, its concern for ministry and religious education lent support to the use of music as a tool of the Catholic revival in German-speaking territories. The earlier approaches had emulated the Lutherans, but except for emphasis on the home and the school, the new tactics stressed the differences between the confessions by reaffirming Catholic traditions. Nonliturgical activities for lay participation were revived and expanded, especially devotions venerating Mary and the saints. The authorities fostered the use of medieval sacred songs, which were still very much alive in Catholic folk culture, while they prohibited the use of Lutheran songs and interdicted access to their hymnbooks. The Jesuit Peter Canisius induced fellow Jesuits and others to publish hymns that were appropriate for catechetical exercise and devotional use. One such example was the songbook of Canisius's associate Adam Walasser (1574), whose second edition in 1577 contained several *Rufe*, one of the simplest and most popular types of medieval sacred song. They were soon imitated and spread in broadsheets and pamphlets. Dealing mainly with saints' legends and miracles, they were ideal for the revived Litany, processions, and pilgrimages. The old *Leisen* for high feasts were also approved in connection with the sermon. A notable exception to the avoidance of Protestant models was the highly prized complete metrical Psalter of Caspar Ulenberg (1582), who composed eighty-one new tunes for it in the Genevan manner. As this and the successes of the Jesuits in the next century demonstrated, the vernacular hymn did for the Catholic cause what it had earlier achieved for the Protestants.

Lutheran Hymnody after Luther. After Luther's death theological controversy worsened among Lutherans, Catholics, and various splinter groups. Beginning with the Augsburg Interim (1548) and the ensuing adiaphoristic controversy, Protestant songs not only attacked the pope, Catholic clergy, dogma, and abuses; they also voiced the angry mutual hostility among Gnesio-Lutherans, Philippists, and other partisans. When a settlement was finally achieved in the Formula of Concord (1577), Lutherans targeted the increasingly aggressive Calvinists and other "enemies of the gospel." Few of these songs in hymn form can qualify as hymns, but as the battle songs of "pure doctrine" they have overshadowed the authentic sacred lyrics that did emerge, many of which were directed at the young and were not candidates for inclusion in the accepted canon. Confessional motives inspired these songs as well; for example, they caused renewed concern for biblical literacy among Lutherans, who had stoutly proclaimed the Bible the sole rule of faith. Lutherans had also insisted on the centrality of preaching, and for that reason the Joachimsthal cantor Nikolaus Herman (c.1480–1561) hoped to enhance its effectiveness with songs based on the usual sermon texts. Believing that preaching accomplished more if the listener was thoroughly familiar with the text beforehand, he published his rhymed *Sontags Evangelia uber das gantze Jar, In Gesenge verfasset* (The Gospels for All the Sundays [and festivals] of the Year; 1560), 101 songs to fit at least one of seventeen tunes, to be taught, learned, and sung "not in church" but by everyone at home. (At least nine more editions appeared by 1607.)

Similarly, anxiety over doctrinal purity made the preservation of the core of Lutheran hymns in worship all the more urgent. The accepted canon of the Babst hymnal of 1545 had been observed in many areas—even Bucer advocated it—but now there was all the more reason to hold to it while expanding the canon to include appropriate chorales for the whole calendar, not just the principal feasts. Citing Luther's warning against "false hymns," Nicholas Selnecker published the first known attempt at such an ordering in the preface to his *Christliche Psalmen* . . . (1587), in which he listed the chorales sung in Leipzig for every Sunday and holy day of the entire liturgical year. These became in effect *Graduallieder*, the *de tempore* hymns, which in association with Gospel pericopes provided another link to scripture for the laity.

Unfortunately, as Paul Eber lamented in his preface to Herman's Gospels, "People have become weary of preaching of the word, and the sacred songs have likewise fallen from favor." Herman, Eber, and Selnecker each insisted that hymns, especially Luther's, were powerful tools of the gospel, but that the times were against them. Selnecker had claimed earlier, in his 1569 sermons on *Psalms*, that hymns were often more effective than preaching, but he admitted that he had prepared his 1587 hymnal "to honor God and support his churches, which now more than ever are everywhere in ruin." In an effort to revive appreciation for Luther's theology and hymns, Cyriakus Spangenberg published *Cithara Lutheri* (Luther's Lyre; 1581), which consists of one or more sermons on each of Luther's chorales for use in the homes of the faithful, the only hope, he thought, of preserving the gospel in some areas.

The classic repertory of Lutheran chorales, between fifty and seventy at the end of the century, remained at the heart of Lutheran worship, but the bitter theological disputes, war, plague, inflation, the successes of the Catholic reform, and the fading of initial Reformation optimism profoundly influenced the tenor of popular religious life. The frozen core of hymns in regular use was not sufficient to meet the needs of the post-Luther generation. As a result the participation of the congregation reportedly gave way to apathy. In many churches the choir assumed ever-greater responsibility in the liturgy, turning to polyphony and Latin chant, in part as a symbol of Lutheran orthodoxy over against Calvinism. In any case, the character of sacred lyricism began to change, placing increasing emphasis on songs for private devotion. Reflecting a hunger for a deepening of spiritual experience, the poetic tone of the new hymns grew markedly subjective and personal. The burden of expression became primarily the needs of the individual believer, the dominant themes being *Trost* ("solace, consolation"), the cross, and preparation for death. By 1600 the shift assumed aspects of a renewed medieval mysticism. The hymns of Martin Behm, the translations and lyrics of Martin Moller, and the "bridal" motif, "Jesus piety," and visionary imagery of Philipp Nicolai mark the transition to the devotional mode of the next century.

These examples suggest that Luther's influence on hymnody had broader consequences for the future than the obvious, for his espousal of free hymnic poetry in contrast to the nearly exclusive use of the Psalter by the Reformed churches led to the proliferation of sacred lyrics responding to historical changes in each succeeding generation. They in turn served to shape that generation's religious thought, feeling, and expression. Although Luther warned of the danger, his example opened the way for conflict, progress, decline, and potential regeneration.

[*See also* Devotional Practices; Hymnals; *and* Music.]

BIBLIOGRAPHY

Ameln, Konrad. *The Roots of German Hymnody of the Reformation Era.* Church Music Pamphlet Series, Hymnology, no. 1. Saint Louis, 1964. A brief but scholarly account with many examples from pre-Reformation sources.

Ameln, Konrad, et al., eds. *Jahrbuch für Liturgik und Hymnologie.* Kassel and Hannover, 1955–. Essential resource for hymnody and its music. Includes copious annotated international bibliographies of current publications.

Blume, Friedrich, ed. *Die Musik in Geschichte und Gegenwart.* 16 vols. and index. Kassel, Basel, and London, 1949–1979. Standard reference for music history, with generous bibliographies and comprehensive articles on hymnody. See vol. 8, 'Lied,' section C, "Kirchenlied" and congregational song, vol. 4, "Gemeindegesang".

Blume, Friedrich, et al. *Protestant Church Music: A History.* New York,

1974. The one major comprehensive and authoritative book in English on music from the Reformation to the twentieth century, a translation (with three new chapters) of *Geschichte der evangelischen Kirchenmusik*, Kassel, 1964; extensive classified bibliography.

Buszin, Walter E. "Luther on Music." *Musical Quarterly* 32 (1946), 80–97. Luther's views on music, largely in his own words.

Butler, Bartlett R. "Liturgical Music in Sixteenth-Century Nürnberg: A Socio-Musical Study." 2 vols. Ph.D. diss., University of Illinois at Urbana-Champaign, 1970. Shows the important but limited role of congregational singing in the highly conservative liturgy of Lutheran Nuremberg.

Dolan, John P. "Liturgical Reform among the Irenicists." In *Sixteenth-Century Essays and Studies*, edited by Carl S. Meyer, vol. 2, pp. 72–94. Saint Louis, 1971. Includes Georg Witzel's efforts to increase lay participation in worship.

Fellerer, Karl Gustav, ed. *Geschichte der katholischen Kirchenmusik.* Vol. 1, *Von den Anfängen bis zum Tridentinum*; vol. 2, *Vom Tridentinum bis zur Gegenwart.* Kassel, Basel, Tours, and London, 1972–1976. A detailed survey including sections on medieval sacred vernacular songs and their use, the impact of the Reformation, and Counter-Reformation developments after Trent.

Frost, Maurice, ed. *Historical Companion to Hymns Ancient and Modern.* London, 1962. Important for the Calvinist influence on English metrical psalms.

Garside, Charles. "The Origins of Calvin's Theology of Music, 1536–1543." *Transactions of the American Philosophical Society* 69 pt. 4 (1979), 1–36. Traces the evolution of Calvin's rationale for music in worship and social life.

Jenny, Markus. *Luther, Zwingli, Calvin in ihren Liedern.* Zurich, 1983. Edition of their hymns with melodies, historical introductions, and commentaries. For the general reader. Anticipates his *Luthers geistliche Lieder und Kirchengesänge*, Cologne, 1985.

Julian, John, ed. *Dictionary of Hymnology: Setting Forth the Origin and History of Christian Hymns of All Ages and Nations*, (1908). Rev. ed. with new supplement. Reprint in 2 vols., New York and Grand Rapids, Mich., 1957 and 1985. Though outdated and superseded in many details, this remarkable hymnological tool is still highly useful and has yet to be replaced.

Leaver, Robin A. *'Goostly Psalmes and Spirituall Songes': English and Dutch Metrical Psalms from Coverdale to Utenhove, 1535–1566.* Oxford, 1991. Perhaps the most impressive recent contribution in English to the historical hymnology of the Reformation in Britain and on the Continent.

Le Huray, Peter. *Music and the Reformation in England, 1549–1660.* Rev. ed. Cambridge, 1989. Concerned primarily with the music of cathedrals, collegiate churches, and aristocratic chapels, but traces its initial decline and the Puritan pressure for congregational singing. Chapter 11 takes up the metrical psalm.

Luther, Martin. *Luther Works.* Vol. 53, *Liturgy and Hymns.* Edited by Ulrich S. Leupold. Philadelphia, 1965. English translations of the liturgical writings, hymns, and chants with melodies, and other related texts, with introductions and commentary.

Müller, Karl Ferdinand, and Walter Blankenburg, eds. *Die Musik des evangelischen Gottesdienstes.* Vol. 4, *Leiturgia: Handbuch des evangelischen Gottesdienstes.* Kassel, 1961. Thorough and well-documented essays on various aspects of liturgical music, including a lengthy article by Blankenburg on congregational hymnody.

Pidoux, Pierre. *Le psautier huguenot du XVIe siècle: Mélodies et documents.* 2 vols. Basel, 1962. The standard recent work.

Pratt, Waldo Selden. *The Music of the French Psalter of 1562: A Historical Survey and Analysis with the Music in Modern Notation.* Columbia University Studies in Musicology, 3. Reprint, New York, 1977. The basic study in English.

Reid, Stanford W. "The Battle Hymns of the Lord: Calvinist Psalmody of the Sixteenth Century." In *Sixteenth-Century Essays and Studies*, edited by Carl S. Meyer, vol. 2, pp. 36–54. Saint Louis, 1971. Illustrates the vital role of metrical psalms in the confessional and political struggles in France, the Low Countries, and elsewhere.

Riedel, Johannes. *The Lutheran Chorale: Its Basic Traditions.* Minneapolis, 1967. An introductory survey from its medieval precursors to the mid-eighteenth century, with emphasis on liturgical background and musical characteristics.

Sadie, Stanley, ed. *The New Grove Dictionary of Music and Musicians.* 20 vols. London, 1980. Authoritative, compact articles on Calvin, Luther (and Lutheran music), and Zwingli; chorale, psalms (metrical), and psalmody (though here referring to the seventeenth century and later). The article on hymn omits the Reformation, citing instead the above entries. Scholarly bibliographies.

Schalk, Carl, ed. *Key Words in Church Music: Definition Essays on Concepts, Practices, and Movements of Thought in Church Music.* Saint Louis, 1978. Useful compendium, alphabetically arranged, of generally accurate historical and practical information, with fair treatment of the principal traditions. Selected readings for further study.

Stulken, Marilyn Kay. *Hymnal Companion to the Lutheran Book of Worship.* Philadelphia, 1981. One of several modern hymnal companions, it provides the customary background to each hymn and tune; also includes eleven national historical essays.

Temperley, Nicholas. *The Music of the English Parish Church.* 2 vols. Cambridge, 1979. A masterly study of a neglected topic. Its first three chapters cover the Reformation to the early seventeenth century, including the metrical psalm; exhaustive bibliography of primary and secondary sources.

Wackernagel, Philipp. *Bibliographie zur Geschichte des deutschen Kirchenliedes im XVI. Jahrhundert* (1855). Reprint, Hildesheim, 1961. Indispensable tool. Also valuable for its many prefaces and dedications in German and Dutch hymnbooks of the sixteenth century.

BARTLETT R. BUTLER

HYPERIUS, Andreas (1511–1564), Dutch Protestant theologian. Andreas Gerhard, named Hyperius after the city of his birth, Ypern, in West Flanders, had a humanist education typical for his time, in the form of a wandering scholar: Wästen, Lille, Tournai, Paris (1528), Löwen (1535), plus important stays in upper Italy, the Rhineland, and, particularly important, England for four years. His advanced studies were in theology, canon law, and medicine. He became friendly with Johann Sturm, probably learned about reform thought through him, and possibly became aware of Martin Bucer through English friends. On the way to Strasbourg to visit Bucer, he was urged in 1541 to remain in Marburg as a substitute for the theologian Gerhard Geldenhauer, and he became his successor a year later after Geldenhauer's death. In 1553 he became a doctor of theology. Until his own death in 1564 he lectured on historical, systematic, and practical theology.

Hyperius took an intermediate position between the various wings of reform. On the one hand, like Luther, he placed the sermon in the center of pastoral responsibilities. It is not by chance that the theological-historical significance of Hyperius comes from his homiletic, the first Protestant homiletic (*De formandis concionibus sacris*, 1553). The central role of the Bible in the practice of domestic piety is reminiscent of Luther (*De s. scripturae lectione ac meditatione quotidiana*, 1561). On the other hand, his high appreciation of the doctrine of predestination puts him close to Calvin, as does his stronger connection of theological to legal thought. Above all, because of his dogmatic method, he must be classified with early Reformed orthodoxy. He used the so-called synthetic method that starts with "first principles"—in contrast to the analytical one, with the help of which entelechies are abstracted empirically.

Hyperius considered the God-made harmony to be an essential principle: the church is like the vehicle through which the harmonic creation of the world takes shape. Such an ecclesiology would not be thinkable without the strong influence of humanism: as with Desiderius Erasmus, *reformatio* can be interpreted as the *restitutio* of the church's ideal original state.

For Hesse (Marburg), Hyperius became something like a reforming church father. In the irenic-ecumenical university atmosphere of Marburg his supraconfessional humanistic point of view was confirmed and strengthened. Above all, his interest in sanctification was quite significant for the training of preachers, as seen in *De recte formando Theologiae studio* (1556) and the Marburg University reform from 1558. This interest in a new order of the church according to eternal principles therefore benefited Hesse.

Without returning to a Roman Catholic sacramental or institutional way of thinking, Hyperius placed neither Christ nor the word, but the church in the center of his theology. Salvation through belief in Christ is seen in the new obedience, from which a new, pure church grows directly, one that corresponds to God's purpose in creation. With this basis, Hyperius sought to consolidate reform perceptions by weakening anti-institutional elements.

Hyperius's great significance for the history of practical theology is undisputed, all the more so since he made important contributions to ministerial training, to preaching, to church administration, and to Bible study. He also claimed that the care of the poor was a model in accordance with the creation. Here, however, he wanted to engage the Christian authorities (*De publica in pauperes beneficentia*, 1570 [published posthumously]).

Hyperius is important for the relation of the German Reformed churches to the west European churches and their more Calvinist tradition. His supraconfessional point of view was productive in the consolidation of new forms of Christian life and fellowship, particularly under the leading idea of a public peace. But Hyperius's writings are also significant for the so-called noncreative periods of church history, because in them new ideas that had already been accepted were transformed into individual and collective public behavior. Thus in Hyperius there appeared a further developed Lutheran, a Reformed, and not least of all, an Erasmian ecclesiology.

BIBLIOGRAPHY

Primary Sources

Hyperius, Andreas. *De Formandis Concionibus sacris libri 2*. Edited by Heinrich Balthasar Wagnitz. Halle, 1781.

———. *Elementa christianae religionis*. Edited by Walter Caspari. Erlangen, 1901.

Secondary Sources

Achelis, Ernst Christian, and Eugen Sachsse. *Die Homiletik und die Katechetik des Andreas Hyperius*. Translated into German with an introduction. Berlin, 1901.

Krause, Gerhard. *Andreas Gerhard Hyperius: Leben, Bilder, Schriften*. Beiträge zur Historischen Theologie, vol. 56. Tübingen, 1977. A bibliography appears on pp. 125–167.

GERHARD RAU

Translated from German by Walter D. Morris

I

ICELAND. An island in the North Atlantic with an area of 102,973 square kilometers, Iceland is the second largest island in Europe, after Great Britain. The climate is oceanic, with cool summers and rather mild winters. Iceland has a homogeneous population of about 260,000; there are no ethnic minorities. The language is Icelandic, a Germanic language. Iceland's parliament, founded in A.D. 930, is the oldest in the world; the country became an independent republic in 1944. Over 93 percent of the population belongs to the state church, which is Lutheran.

In the sixteenth century Iceland was ruled by Denmark. The two last pre-Reformation Catholic bishops, Ögmundur Palsson in Skalholt and Jon Arason in Holar, were the most powerful leaders in the country. People had confidence in the church; all criticisms of it were secular and political, not religious. Many felt, for instance, that the church had become too strong; at that time, indeed, it possessed about half of all the real estate in the country. But generally speaking, the Icelanders were unprepared for the Reformation.

The Reformation in Iceland occurred in three phases. The first was centered in the diocese of Skalholt. German merchants from Hamburg held the first evangelical services in Iceland. Around the same time, two young Icelanders studying abroad were converted to Lutheranism: Gizur Einarsson, later the first Lutheran bishop in Skalholt, and Oddur Gottskálksson, son of a Roman Catholic bishop in Holar. They both came to live in Skalholt as assistants to Bishop Palsson, who was old and almost blind. In Skalholt a group of young men started to study the evangelical doctrines under their leadership; and, without the knowledge of the old bishop, Gottskálksson began to translate the New Testament into Icelandic. His translation was printed in Denmark in 1540—the oldest known book printed in Icelandic.

When Denmark became Lutheran, the king tried to enforce a new evangelical church ordinance in Iceland, but this was met with resistance. The king's men seized the richest Icelandic monastery, but later some of them were killed. In 1539 the old Bishop Palsson got Einarsson elected as his successor. Einarsson was appointed bishop by the king; but he was not ordained, perhaps because he was young and inexperienced. Einarsson did not succeed in getting the church ordinance adopted as he had promised, so the king found it necessary to send an army to Iceland in 1541 to strengthen his position there. Shortly thereafter, the diocese of Skalholt adopted the new ordinance; Bishop Palsson was captured and his property confiscated. He died in captivity on the way to Denmark.

In 1542 Einarsson was ordained bishop and some peaceful years followed. Bishop Einarsson tried to further the cause of the evangelical church in his diocese but encountered severe difficulties. He died, only forty years old, in 1548.

His successors were not of the same stamp as he and were unable to withstand the growing power of the king. The king had promised Einarsson the use of monastic properties in Iceland for the purpose of building schools; but after Einarsson's death, this promise was not fulfilled.

Einarsson's death initiated the second phase of the Icelandic Reformation. Jon Arason, the Catholic bishop in Holar, tried to seize Skalholt by force, but failed. The clergy of the diocese of Skalholt could not agree who should become a new bishop. The majority voted for a Catholic, while the minority supported a Lutheran, Marteinn Einarsson, who subsequently became bishop.

Shortly after Marteinn Einarsson returned to Iceland from abroad, he was captured by Arason, whose power within the country seemed unrivaled. When Arason tried to capture the last of his enemies, a brother-in-law of Marteinn Einarsson, he overestimated the strength of his position and took only a few men with him. He was then captured himself; and, as nobody dared to try to keep him in captivity during the winter, he and two of his sons were beheaded in November 1550. With his death, all resistance to the Reformation came to an end.

The third phase of the Icelandic Reformation began when Bishop Guðbrandur Thorláksson in Holar got hold of a small printing press, which Bishop Arason had purchased. Thorláksson produced the many books necessary for the evangelical church. The Icelandic Bible was published in 1584. This edition incorporated the New Testament translation of Oddur Gottskálksson, but Thorláksson himself had to translate many of the Old Testament books. A hymnal appeared in 1589 and a ritual book, *Grallarinn*, in 1594. Bishop Thorláksson's great publishing work firmly established the evangelical church in Iceland.

The general effect of the Reformation in Iceland was similar to its effect in most other European countries. The influence and power of the Danish king was greatly strengthened, and Iceland was increasingly exploited, both financially and culturally. Royal power was increasing all over Europe in those years with support from the growing bourgeoisie, which demanded the peace and stability that only strong central power could guarantee. Indisputably, the Reformation provided many European kings with the opportunity to expand their power at the cost of the Catholic church; and in this, Iceland was no exception.

BIBLIOGRAPHY

Einarsson, Stefán. "The Reformation." In *A History of Icelandic Literature*, pp. 170–178. New York, 1957.

Hannesson, Jóhann. "Iceland." In *The Encyclopedia of the Lutheran Church*, edited by Julius Bodensieck, vol. 2, pp. 1103–1110. Minneapolis, 1965.

Helgason, Jón. "Die Kirche in Island." In *Ekklesia*, edited by Friedrich Siegmund-Schultze, vol. 2., pp. 7–35. Gotha, 1934.

Hood, John C. *Icelandic Church Saga*. Reprint, Westport, Conn., 1981.

Thordarson, Thorir Kr. "The Church." In *Iceland 1986*, edited by Jóhannes. Reykjavík, 1987.

JÓNAS GÍSLASON

ICKELSHAMER, Valentin

ICKELSHAMER, Valentin (also Ickelsamer; 1500?–1547), German teacher in Rothenburg ob der Tauber, Erfurt, and Augsburg, and follower of radical reform. The first confirmed biographical data on Ickelshamer is a notice in the records of the University of Erfurt from the fall of 1518. Ickelshamer is listed as a native of Rothenburg and was probably born around 1500. He received his bachelor's degree in 1520. Until 1524 he pursued further studies in Wittenberg with Martin Luther, Philipp Melanchthon, Johannes Bugenhagen, and Andreas Bodenstein von Karlstadt. In 1524 he became a schoolmaster at a German school he founded in Rothenburg. His religious ideas were not unlike those of Karlstadt, characterized by simplicity of life, rigorous practice of charity, suffering for the sake of faith, and the renunciation of worldly vanity coupled with the notion of a solid education for everyone. In his tract *Clag etlicher brüder* . . . (Complaint of Several Brethren . . .) of March 1525, Ickelshamer defended Karlstadt against Luther. Toward the end of March he was elected to a committee representing the guilds of the town that were opposed to the patrician city council. On 14 May 1525 this committee facilitated an alliance with the rebellious peasants. Fearing the reprisal of the Swabian League, which had been victorious over the peasants, Ickelshamer fled to Erfurt, where he once again assumed a teaching position and where, as earlier in Rothenburg, he wrote several dialogues as pedagogical texts for children. In 1529 or early 1530 he was forced to leave Erfurt. Between 1530 and 1547 he lived in Augsburg, where he worked as a private tutor and taught in an elementary school. In 1534 his major work appeared, *Ain Teutsche Grammatica* . . . (A German Grammar . . .), published in Augsburg. It was reprinted numerous times. During this period Ickelshamer befriended Kaspar von Schwenckfeld, who wrote the Letter of Consolation in 1537. He probably also was acquainted with Sebastian Franck.

His relationship to the Anabaptist Pilgram Marpeck was controversial. He had contacts with the Italian reformer and theologian Bernardino Ochino. In all probability Ickelshamer expanded Sebastian Franck's poem "Die Gelehrten, die Verkehrten" (The Learned, the Mistaken). The marginal notes of Ickelshamer's version express his repudiation of the Anabaptist kingdom in Münster and of the Schmalkald War. Nothing further is known about him. He died sometime in Augsburg during the second half of 1547.

BIBLIOGRAPHY

Looß, Sigrid. "Der Rothenburger Schulmeister Valentin Ickelshamer: Position und Leistung." *Zeitschrift für bayrische Kirchengeschichte* 60 (1991) 1–20. Provides a critical summary of the research to date and new sources on Ickelshamer's biography and works.

Verzeichnis der im deutschen Sprachbereich erschienenen Drucke des XVI. Jahrhunderts. Stuttgart, 1983–. See vol. 9, nos. 24–35.

SIGRID LOOß

Translated from German by Wolfgang Katenz

ICONOCLASM

ICONOCLASM. The term *iconoclasm* can be understood on two levels, abstractly or concretely. In a figurative or abstract sense, an iconoclast (Greek *eikon* [image] plus *klastes* [breaker]) is anyone who challenges cherished beliefs and institutions. Abstract iconoclasm of this sort, broadly conceived, was an integral element of the whole Reformation. In a narrower more concrete sense, an iconoclast is also someone who rejects the symbolic, transcendent meaning of religious works of art, or of sacred objects, and seeks to destroy them. This literal iconoclasm was an integral part of the expansion of the Reformation, from 1520 to 1648, but in a limited way, varying in intensity and magnitude from place to place. Iconoclastic violence often followed in the wake of Reformed Protestantism—in northern Switzerland, southwest Germany, France, the Netherlands, Scotland, and England—but was by no means limited to Reformed Protestants or to these regions. Even staunchly Catholic Italy and Spain experienced isolated incidents. Religious works of art were not the only sacred objects to be menaced. Relics, altars, consecrated hosts, chalices, vestments, missals, lamps, organs, windows, and holy water fonts also fell victim to iconoclastic ruin.

History. The Protestant war against idolatry began with Andreas Bodenstein von Karlstadt, a colleague of Martin Luther at the University of Wittenberg. Well versed in the scriptures, Bodenstein was also an avid reader of Desiderius Erasmus, a humanist who had popularized in learned circles a negative attitude toward much of medieval Catholic piety, especially the cult of saints, images, and relics. In 1518 Bodenstein began to condemn the use of holy water; by 1521 he was attacking the veneration of images and denying the sacrificial dimension of the Eucharist. In December 1521, during Luther's absence from Wittenberg, Bodenstein spearheaded the first iconoclastic riots of the Reformation. In January 1522, as a response to these riots, the Wittenberg magistracy enacted the first municipal Reformation ordinance, calling for the abolition of the Mass and the removal of all religious imagery. At the same time, Bodenstein published a treatise entitled *Von Abtuhung der Bylder und das keyn Betdler vnter den Christen seyn sol* (On the Abolition of Images, and That There Should Be No Beggars among Christians). In this influential manifesto Bodenstein argued that the veneration of images polluted the Christian community and angered God. Two central points of this work would become the foundation of all subsequent iconoclastic theology: (1) All Christians should observe the commandment against images in the Decalogue; (2) the spiritual realm cannot be approached through the mediation of the material world, as assumed in Catholic sacramental theology and piety, for infinitude cannot be conveyed by anything finite (*finitum non est capax infiniti*).

As the Wittenberg magistrates delayed in removing the images, Bodenstein incited yet another iconoclastic riot in February 1522. Luther hurried back from hiding at Wartburg Castle and preached against Bodenstein's tactics, forcing him out of Wittenberg. Undaunted, Bodenstein continued developing a revolutionary iconoclastic theology. In *Ob man gemach faren vnd des ergernüssen der schwachen verschonen soll in sachen so gottis willen angehn* (Whether One Ought to Behave Peacefully and Spare the Feelings of the Simple; 1524), Bodenstein proposed an insurrectionist policy against idolatry: whenever the idols are not removed by law, he argued, God requires all true Christians to destroy them by force.

Luther's disagreement with Bodenstein marks the first major parting of ways in the Reformation. Since he was not concerned with the metaphysical issue of matter versus spirit but rather with the soteriological question of law versus gospel, Luther saw Bodenstein's iconoclastic theology as a legalistic return to "works righteousness." Luther and his followers would remain indifferent to images, arguing that it was better to remove them from the hearts of Christians than from the walls of churches. Consequently, the Lutheran church developed a cautious rather than hostile attitude to religious imagery and generally shied away from iconoclasm.

The legacy of Bodenstein came to full fruition in Switzerland among those who came to be known as Reformed Protestants—and among the Anabaptists—though the actual extent of his influence there remains uncertain. As early as 1520, isolated acts of iconoclasm had already begun to occur around Zurich. At that time another young Erasmian, Huldrych Zwingli, had already been preaching against the cult of saints and images in Zurich for a year. Sporadic, isolated attacks on religious images of the kind recommended by Bodenstein began to take place in and around Zurich in 1523, as Zwingli and other pastors intensified their attack against images and the Mass. A series of public disputations on worship held at Zurich in 1523–1524 resulted in a victory for the iconophobes. On 15 June 1524 the Zurich magistracy called for the abolition of the Mass and the orderly removal of all religious imagery. During a two-week period, all of Zurich's churches were carefully "cleansed" of their religious images by teams of craftsmen behind closed doors. The following year, 1525, Zwingli wrote and published his two most complete statements on the image question, *Ein Antwurt Valentino Compar gegeben* (An Answer to Valentin Compar), and *De vera et falsa religiune commentarius* (Commentary on the True and False Religion), which contain the marrow of Reformed Protestant iconoclastic theology.

Zurich established a pattern. Image destruction spread in waves to smaller towns under its jurisdiction, and, in turn, to other Swiss cities and their territories, where it was often employed as a means of challenging the status quo and of ushering in the Reformation: Bern and St. Gall (1528), Basel and Schaffhausen (1529), Neuchâtel (1530), Geneva and Lausanne (1535). Some cities in southwest Germany (1530–1531) also did away with images, most notably Strasbourg, Nuremberg, and Ulm; and the Strasbourg Reformer Martin Bucer (1491–1551) further propagated iconoclastic theology in his treatise *Das einigerlei Bild bei den Gotglaeubigen an orten da sie verehrt nit moegen geduldet werden* (That Any Kind of Images May Not Be Permitted; 1530). Uncharacteristically, some Lutheran cities in the Baltic region also turned iconophobic: Danzig, Königsberg, Riga, Stockholm, Stralsund, Stettin, Pernau, Braunschweig, and Malmö all experienced iconoclasm (1524–1529). The Anabaptists, too, became vehement iconophobes, but their pacifism and their separatist beliefs prevented the majority from becoming iconoclasts. Only those radicals who advocated revolutionary violence actually engaged in iconoclasm, particularly during the Peasants' War (1524–1525) and in the uprising at Münster (1534–1535).

After 1536 the intellectual and moral leadership of iconoclasm shifted to Geneva and its reformer, John Calvin (1509–1564). Though he never engaged in image destruction and always publicly condemned illegal acts, Calvin further intensified Reformed Protestant animosity toward idolatry in his magisterial *Institutes* (four Latin editions, 1536–1559), and in numerous treatises, letters, and sermons. In Calvin's native France, sporadic acts of image destruction and desecration had been occurring since the early 1520s, but not until 1560 did the Calvinists, known as Huguenots, dare to launch a full-scale attack on idolatry. Rouen and La Rochelle were the first cities to experience iconoclastic riots. Over the next two years, the rioting spread to other cities, including Paris, Le Mans, Nîmes, Pontoise, Auxerre, Bourges, Lyon, Marseille, Meaux, Orléans, Sens, and

Tours. This violence presaged the Wars of Religion (1562–1598), during which iconoclasm became the external earmark of the Calvinist Huguenot movement.

In the Low Countries, Calvinists precipitated the most dramatic iconoclastic outbreak of the Reformation. In August 1566 churches throughout the seventeen provinces were ransacked by frenzied but well organized mobs of iconoclasts, some numbering in the thousands. King Philip II (1527–1598), the Spanish Catholic ruler of the Netherlands, responded by sending an army to quell the rioting and to punish the iconoclasts, a move that pushed the Netherlands into open rebellion and war against Spain, starting a prolonged military conflict (1566–1609, 1621–1648) in which iconoclasm became a routine expression of religious violence.

Calvinism made further inroads and caused further iconoclasm in Germany during the so-called Second Reformation (1570–1618), most notably in Oberpfalz (1581–1589), Danzig (1590), Marburg (1605), and Berlin (1615). As Calvinism gained strength in Poland-Lithuania in the early 1600s, many cities there, too, began to experience iconoclasm.

British iconoclasm has a complex and protracted history. Though Calvinist Scotland did away with its images quickly and thoroughly in 1559, England drew out its iconoclasm over more than a century. King Henry VIII (1491–1547) had decreed the abolition of "abused" images, giving rise to unsystematic and relatively moderate attacks on idolatry. This equivocal policy was followed by all of Henry's Protestant successors and became a focus of discontent among the growing number of Calvinist Puritans in the late sixteenth and early seventeenth century. When these Puritans finally came to power in 1640, England was being ravaged by intense iconoclasm. This iconoclastic fury even spilled over into Ireland in 1641, with Oliver Cromwell's (1599–1658) repression of the Catholic insurrection.

Morphology. Animosity toward the symbolic structure of medieval Catholicism was an inevitable effect of the Reformation, for the rejection of external forms and the creation of an inner/outer dialectic are necessary components of virtually all attempts at religious reform. Moreover, the prohibition of religious imagery found in *Exodus* 20:4–6, *Leviticus* 5:8–10, and numerous other biblical texts made it difficult for scripturally centered Protestants to skirt the issue of idolatry. These same texts had made iconoclastic tendencies endemic to Christianity. Before the Reformation, iconophobia had surfaced among the Byzantines in the eastern Mediterranean (725–842), and among some reforming movements in the medieval West, most notably the Cathars and Waldenses in parts of France, Italy, and Catalonia (twelfth–thirteenth centuries), the Lollards in England (fourteenth–fifteenth centuries), and the Hussites in Bohemia (fifteenth century).

Though always violent and revolutionary to some degree, iconoclasm manifested itself in many different ways. First, one can distinguish between two basic categories of iconoclasm—unlawful and lawful—and also among various subtypes in each of these categories.

Throughout Europe before the Reformation, the destruction of sacred objects was prohibited by law and was punishable as blasphemy or sacrilege. Illegal or unlawful iconoclastic acts were those committed against these established laws. Such acts were sometimes committed by individuals who acted alone and furtively, but most frequently they involved groups of iconoclasts who wished to call public attention to their acts of desecration. Unlawful iconoclasm aimed not only to destroy specific objects but also to call the legality of sacred objects into question. Group attacks could be isolated incidents, as in Zurich in early 1523; or systematic and persistent, as in Schaffhausen in 1525; or final and decisive, culminating in urban riots, as in Basel in 1528, or even in nationwide revolt, as in the Netherlands in 1566. Illegal iconoclasm could also be carried out by soldiers engaged in religious warfare, as in France, 1562–1598.

Iconoclasm could also be effected lawfully, after a local or national government had withdrawn its protection from sacred objects (usually after repeated illegal iconoclastic acts had challenged the law). At one extreme of the political spectrum, such decisions could be reached by democratic consensus (Switzerland, 1524–1536); or instead, at the other extreme, imposed by fiat from above (Oberpfalz, 1570–1618). This legal iconoclasm could be orderly, as in the case of Zurich in 1524; or disorderly, as in Bern in 1528, when a mob refused to wait for the appointed officials to clear out the images from the cathedral; or a combination of the two, as in Scotland in 1559 and France in 1561–1562.

Since iconoclasm was an expression of discontent and was most often carried out by the laity, it was not only the most visible change brought about by the religious crisis of the early modern age but also one of the most radical and democratic, advancing the Reformation tangibly at street level and allowing for popular participation in the political process. Though it is possible to identify social, political, and economic grievances that contributed to the development of iconoclasm, it would be wrong to isolate them, or, even worse, to distinguish them from religion as more pressing motives. If symbols function on multiple levels of meaning, so do the actions taken against them.

On an intellectual and spiritual level, iconoclasm was a means of proving the falsehood of Roman Catholicism and of desacralizing its symbolic structure. It was often not enough simply to destroy the images: public acts of defilement ensured that they would be discredited as well as destroyed and that the community would know it had been ritually cleansed from its "idolatrous" pollution. Protestants routinely put sacred objects to the test. For instance, at Wesen, Switzerland, in the late 1520s the images were piled up in a public place, ritually mocked, and asked to protect themselves from the flames as they were set afire; in Saint-Jacques, France, in 1566 a Christ figure was scourged with tree branches and taunted: "If you are God, speak!" Similarly, soldiers at Le Mans, France, in 1562, and at Saffron Walden, England, in 1640, proved images powerless by using them to cook their meals. Images were thrown into rivers and lakes (Warendorf, 1533; Berlin, 1615), stuck with pikes and shot at (Nîmes, 1561), buried in mass graves (Straslund, 1525), and thrown into charnel houses (Oberpfalz, 1598). Debasement and destruction could go hand in hand. Images were thrown into latrines, ditches, and sewers (Geneva, 1535); used as construction materials for town walls and barricades (Münster, 1534–35); and given as toys to children (Cologne, 1536). Consecrated hosts were fed to animals (Geneva, 1535). Total destruction was not necessary: disfigurement and ridicule served the same purpose. In Perth, Scotland, a statue of Francis was desecrated in 1544 by having a ram's horns nailed to its head and a cow's tail to its rear before it was hung from the gallows. In Poland, near Lublin, in 1628, a young man fashioned a carnival mask for himself by slicing off Mary's face from a painting and cutting out its eyes and mouth. On many occasions, hurried iconoclasts saved time by merely lopping off heads and limbs or, more frequently, by gouging out the eyes from images.

Iconoclasm was often also linked to social and economic issues. All the wealth lavished on church decorations in medieval times seemed a waste to iconoclasts, who saw it as a squandering of resources that could have been spent on the poor and needy. As Martin Bucer summarized it in one of his sermons, idolatry was "against both faith and love." Throughout Switzerland in the late 1520s, ravaged wooden images were routinely given to the poor as firewood, and precious metals were redeemed for charitable or civic purposes. In the Netherlands (1566) many works of art were sold abroad rather than destroyed, and the proceeds were used for civic and charitable purposes. Since images, altars, and other devotional objects could be donated only by those who had sufficient wealth—nobles, successful artisans and merchants, guilds, and confraternities—iconoclasm could also be an expression of class hostility: many eyewitnesses later blamed the destruction on the lowest elements in society. In addition, one cannot discount youthful unrest, for adolescents and children were also often credited with the bulk of the violence. Nonetheless, one should not assume that all iconoclasts were poor or young, for examples are also numerous of mature, wealthy, and powerful iconoclasts throughout the entire Reformation period. In France, particularly, the nobility often cooperated with the poorer folk in the sacking of churches. Respect for property rights could vary wildly according to location. Whereas in some German and Netherlandish cities (1530–1531 and 1566) donors were allowed to rescue and conceal their sacred objects, in Nîmes (1561) priests were apparently tortured so they would reveal the location of hidden "idols."

Protestant iconoclasm derived mainly from the Hebraic biblical condemnation of idolatry, or false worship, and it aimed not only to destroy the physical idols and their ritual objects but also to abolish a complex symbolic system and to remove the clerics who sustained it. Images, relics, and sacramental objects were a crucial part of the restricted code of medieval Christian society, the very embodiment of the social myth that gave shape and form to accepted values and enabled them to be transmitted and enforced.

Reformation iconoclasm was revolutionary on two fronts. First, it was a theological upheaval, a redefining of the sacred. Forsaking much of medieval Christian metaphysics and epistemology, Reformation iconoclasts denied some correlations between body and soul, or heaven and earth, and transfigured the meaning of prayer and sacrament. Iconoclasm was also revolutionary in a practical sense, for it was an act of violence against the accepted symbolic code and its guardians, a fact that may have given rise to the rare cooperation of rich and poor in some places, and that may have been inchoately grasped by the young iconoclasts in Geneva who burst forth from the cathedral in May 1536, carrying fragments of the images they had just shattered, roaring: "Here we have the gods of the priests; would you like some?"

BIBLIOGRAPHY

Aston, Margaret. *England's Iconoclasts.* Vol. 1, *Laws Against Images.* Oxford, 1988. An insightful and detailed survey.

Christensen, Carl C. *Art and the Reformation in Germany.* Athens, Ohio, 1979. Excellent narrative and analysis of early Reformation iconoclasm with an emphasis on its cultural impact.

Christin, Olivier. *Une révolution symbolique: L'iconoclasme Huguenot et la réconstruction Catholique.* Paris, 1991. Analyzes French iconoclasm and the Catholic response.

Crew, Phyllis Mack. *Calvinist Preaching and Iconoclasm in the Netherlands, 1544–1569.* Cambridge, 1978. Deftly traces the repercussions of iconoclastic theology.

Davidson, Clifford, and Ann Eljenholm Nichols, eds. *Iconoclasm vs. Art and Drama.* Kalamazoo, 1989. A collection of essays, mostly on English developments.

Davis, Natalie Zemon. "The Rites of Violence: Religious Riot in Sixteenth-Century France." *Past and Present* 59 (1973). Indispensable reading.

Deyon, Solange, and Alain Lottin. *Les "casseurs" de l'été 1566: L'iconoclasme dans le nord de la France.* Reprint, Lille, 1986. Excellent analysis of iconoclasm in one small region with a focus on its sociopolitical dimensions.

Eire, Carlos M. N. *War Against the Idols: The Reformation of Worship from Erasmus to Calvin.* Cambridge, 1986. Traces the development of iconoclastic ideology beyond the image question.

Freedberg, David. *Iconoclasm and Painting in the Revolt of the Netherlands.* New York, 1988. Emphasizes the cultural impact.

Garside, Charles. *Zwingli and the Arts.* Reprint, New York, 1981. An eloquent and seminal study.

Michalski, Sergiusz. *The Reformation and the Visual Arts.* London, 1993.

Phillips, John. *The Reformation of Images: Destruction of Art in England,*

1535–1660. Los Angeles, 1973. A good survey, now superseded by Aston.

Scribner, Robert, ed. *Bilder und Bildersturm im Spätmittelalter und in der frühen Neuzeit*. Wolfenbüttel, 1990. A collection of essays on a wide variety of topics.

Wandel, Lee Palmer. *Always Among Us: Images of the Poor in Zwingli's Zurich*. Cambridge, 1990. Analyzes the cultural and sociopolitical dimensions of the image question in relation to the issue of poor relief.

Warnke, Martin, ed. *Bildersturm: Die Zerstörung des Kunstwerks*. Reprint, Frankfurt a.M., 1988. Includes several seminal essays.

CARLOS M. N. EIRE

ICONOGRAPHY. The debate by Reformation leaders concerning religious images centered on two key issues: their misuse as objects of veneration and their role as symbols of the Roman church. Whereas Huldrych Zwingli (1484–1531) and Andreas Bodenstein Karlstadt (1486–1541), for example, advocated iconoclasm, or the destruction and abolition of all devotional artworks, Martin Luther gradually recognized their potential effectiveness as instructive tools. In his treatise *Wider die Himmlischen Propheten, von den Bilderen und Sakrament* (Against the Heavenly Prophets; 1525), he agreed that images should not be worshiped, but he endorsed their limited use as supplementary teaching tools, especially among the young and illiterate. Indeed, the emergence and prevalence of prints during this period reflected his insistence on the primary importance of the scriptural word and of his teachings on morality.

Rejected by Luther were iconic representations of figures in favor of narrative scenes. Appropriated and promoted were those representations of biblical stories illustrating individual faith and salvation through divine grace. The predominance of themes from the New Testament was typical of the iconography of the Reformation. Thus, the Crucifixion continued to be a popular subject of various graphic media as well as of altarpieces. It was often interpreted as a highly populated drama. The 1517 engraving by the Dutch painter Lucas van Leyden, for example, features not only the figure of Christ on the cross between those of the two thieves as well as the figures of his grieving followers and of the Roman soldiers, but also figures of many other curious spectators who are shown engaged in diverse activities. More important, the panoramic engraving relegates the Calvary group to the background and to the left side; it brings to the fore the secondary figures of the townspeople, whose indifference seems to become the focus of the work.

Also retained were other New Testament stories of the life and passion of Christ such as the Nativity, Agony in the Garden, Resurrection, and Ascension. One of the subjects that gained special popularity was that of Christ and the adulteress. Luther's close friend in Wittenberg, the German painter Lucas Cranach the Elder, depicted this theme in 1523. Luther objected to medieval portrayals because they had presented Christ as a harsh judge; Cranach conceived of an image that is compassionate and forgiving. He displayed Christ tenderly holding the adulteress's arm while admonishing the men who were intent on stoning her. The implication is that although the adulteress is a sinner under the old law, she is not condemned, but saved through the merciful grace of God.

The parable of the prodigal son, also from the New Testament and also depicted before the advent of Luther, was frequently mentioned by him as an expression of faith and divine mercy. Nevertheless, rather than continuing to serve as an analogy for the relationship between Jews and Christians, it now exemplified the difference between Catholics and Protestants. Luther identified the elder brother in the parable with the Catholics and their insistence on good works, and the younger, prodigal son as one who was saved through faith. The 1540 woodcut by the Dutch artist Cornelis Anthoniszoon, the last in a series of six on the subject, is an example in point. It displays the principal scene of the prodigal son being welcomed by his father and two background scenes of the two Lutheran sacraments, baptism and Communion. One should note that several other representations of the parable include secondary scenes of debauchery as a moral warning against improper behavior.

Christ blessing the children is one of the subjects that emerged almost exclusively in the art of the Protestant areas of Germany and the Low Countries. Rarely appearing in Europe before the Reformation, it was now used to promote the importance of simple faith, on the one hand, and to attack both the Catholic hierarchy and its sumptuous paraphernalia, on the other. According to Christine O. Kibish ("Lucas Cranach's 'Christ Blessing the Little Children': A Problem of Lutheran Iconography," *Art Bulletin* 37.3 [1955], 196–203), the theme of Christ blessing the children may have also served to support the Lutheran retention of infant baptism. Appearing more frequently during Lutheran debates with Anabaptists (1536–1566), it may have also helped defeat the Anabaptists. Once infant baptism was no longer an issue, the image of the baptism of Christ seems to have gradually taken the place of that of Christ blessing the children. Artists probably chose this New Testament image to stress Luther's acceptance of baptism as one of two true sacraments instead of the seven sanctioned by the Catholic church.

The Last Supper, an appropriate subject for altarpieces according to Luther's treatise *Der 111. Psalm Ausgelegt* (Commentary on Psalm 111; 1530), served to promote the sacrament of Communion. In Catholic art the story had been primarily presented as one of the scenes of the passion of Christ. In the Reformation it stood for Christ's sacrifice and Christ's direct administration of the church. In order to help propagate the reinstatement of Communion in both kinds for all, and not just for the clergy, portrayals of the Last Supper often included the image of the chalice. They also often featured the figures of various reformers around the table so as to emphasize their inclusion in Christ's community.

The supremacy of the New Testament over the Old Testament seems to have found its fullest expression in innovative compositions entitled either *The Law and the Gospel* or *The Fall and Redemption of Man.* Cranach the Elder's 1529 panel painting of this unprecedented subject (Schlossmuseum, Gotha) is an early example. Divided in the center by the Tree of Knowledge, this work presents scenes from the Bible that symbolize condemnation, on the left, and scenes from the gospel that symbolize redemption, on the right. Even as one part depicts in the foreground the prophets, including Moses, next to the devil and a personification of death, its counterpart displays John the Baptist. Likewise, even as the former features in the background the temptation of Adam and Eve, the latter exhibits the crucified Christ.

Although Luther rejected iconic representations venerated by the Roman church, some of his own portraits became venerable icons. As Robert Scribner ("Incombustible Luther: The Image of the Reformer in Early Modern Germany," *Past and Present* 110 [1986], 38–68) demonstrates, this adaptation of "the Catholic cult of saints" originated in documented as well as mythical reports of the miraculous survival of some of Luther's pictures and lasted from 1520 to circa 1800.

The reproductivity of the woodcut print lent itself to anti-Catholic propaganda, and broadsheets containing both words and images were used in the 1550s to attack the pope and his clergy. Among them were *The Fall of the Papacy* and *The Roman Clergy's Procession into Hell* by the Nuremberg artist Sebald Beham, *The Sale of Indulgences* by the Basel artist Hans Holbein the Younger, and *The Confrontation of the True and False Church* by the Wittenberg artist Lucas Cranach the Younger. Often reflecting the apocalyptic beliefs of Lutherans, Anabaptists, and other Protestant groups, these images represented the demise of the Roman church and the pope, symbolized by Babylon and the Antichrist respectively, and the rise of a new kingdom of true believers in Christ. Other broadsheets, reflecting the kind of morality espoused by Reformation leaders, served other didactic and social purposes. Some, promoting proper conduct for wives, that of submission to their husbands, conveyed Luther's conviction that marriage was a model for the state.

Although misogynist images were not exclusively a Protestant genre, Allison P. Coudert ("The Myth of the Improved Status of Protestant Women: The Case of the Witchcraze," in *The Politics of Gender in Early Modern Europe*, edited by J. R. Brink, A. P. Coudert, and M. C. Horowitz, pp. 61–68, Kirksville, Mo., 1989) states that the sheer number of broadsheets displaying the downright dangerous nature of women in sixteenth- and seventeenth-century Germany was unprecedented. These included engravings and woodcuts of Adam and Eve; Samson and Delilah; Hercules and Omphale; David and Bathsheba; Solomon and his wives; and Aristotle and Phyllis, which represented the common motif of the dreaded woman on top. They also included depictions of witches, such as the painting *Weather Witches* (1523, Stadelsches Kunstinstitut, Frankfurt am Main) and the woodcut *The Bewitched Groom* (1544) by the Strasbourg artist Hans Baldung, typical of the iconography of northern rather than southern Europe. Even though witchcraft had already been a popular subject in late fifteenth-century German art, Luther's juxtaposition of the witch and the ideal wife in a 1523 sermon popularized it even further. That the iconoclasm accompanying the Reformation was, in Coudert's view, especially directed toward images of Mary and female saints indeed attests to the continuation of the patriarchal and misogynist views that already characterized the Roman church.

[*See also* Art.]

BIBLIOGRAPHY

Christensen, Carl C. *Art and the Reformation in Germany.* Athens, Ohio, 1979.

Halewood, William H. *Six Subjects of Reformation Art: A Preface to Rembrandt.* Toronto, 1982.

Harbison, Craig. *The Last Judgment in Sixteenth Century Northern Europe: A Study of the Relation Between Art and the Reformation.* New York and London, 1976.

Hults, Linda C. "Baldung and the Reformation." In *Hans Baldung Grien: Prints and Drawings Exhibition*, edited by James H. Harrow and Alan Shestak, pp. 38–59. New Haven, 1981.

Moxey, Keith. *Peasants, Warriors and Wives: Popular Imagery in the Reformation.* Chicago and London, 1989.

Panofsky, Erwin. "Comments on Art and Reformation." In *Symbols in Transformation: Iconographic Themes at the Time of the Reformation*, edited by Craig Harbison, pp.9–14. Princeton, 1969.

Parshall, Linda B., and Peter W. Parshall. *Art and the Reformation: An Annotated Bibliography.* Boston, 1986.

Schade, Werner. *Cranach: A Family of Master Painters.* Translated by Helen Sebba. New York, 1980. Originally published as *Die Malerfamilie Cranach*, Dresden, 1974.

Schiller, Gertrud. *Iconography of Christian Art.* Translated by Janet Zeligman. 2 vols. Greenwich, 1972. Originally published as *Ikonographie der christlichen Kunst*, Gütersloh, 1968.

Stechow, Wolfgang, ed. *Northern Renaissance Art 1400–1600: Sources and Documents.* Reprint, Evanston, Ill., 1989.

YAEL EVEN AND PATRICIA VETTEL TOM

IGNATIUS LOYOLA (1491?–1556), founder of the Society of Jesus and Roman Catholic saint. Born into a noble family in the Basque territory of northern Spain, he was baptized Iñigo, but beginning about 1537 he also used Ignatius, particularly in official documents. He had the chivalric and academically sparse education of his class. His brief military career ended in 1521 when he was wounded at the siege of Pamplona. While convalescing at Loyola, he underwent a profound religious conversion, during which he became aware of the importance of attending to his feelings of "consolation" and "desolation," which would become a consistent point of reference in his religious teaching.

He spent a year in prayer and mortification at Manresa (1522–1523), near Barcelona, where he experienced temptations and aridity of spirit but also deep and refreshing mystical insights. He conversed with others about "the things of God," the modest beginning of the dedication to ministry characteristic of him and his future disciples. He began to put reflections about his experience on paper, and they formed the substance of his *Ejercicios Espirituales* (Spiritual Exercises), which he continued to amplify and revise for the next twenty-five years.

After a pilgrimage to Jerusalem, he decided to pursue a university education in order better "to help souls," his characteristic expression for ministry. He studied in several cities of Spain (1524–1528), where he also taught catechism, guided persons in his *Exercises,* and collected a few companions. In both Alcalá de Henares and Salamanca, his teaching fell under suspicion of the heresy of the Alumbrados, members of a Spanish mystical movement of the times. He was vindicated, but similar charges against his *Exercises* would be made for decades. He then studied at the University of Paris for seven years (1528–1535), where in 1533 he received his licentiate in philosophy, after which he devoted a year and a half to theology without taking a degree.

In Paris he gathered a new group of six students, whom he guided in the full course of the *Exercises.* They were the nucleus of the future Society of Jesus and included Francis Xavier, the great missionary to India and Japan, and Diego Laínez, theologian at the future Council of Trent and Ignatius's successor as head of the order. In 1534 they bound themselves to go to Jerusalem to work among the Muslims or, if they could not secure passage, to offer themselves to the pope to do ministry wherever he saw fit. They traveled to Venice, where practically all of them, including Ignatius, were ordained as priests in 1537.

Since war prevented going to Jerusalem, they offered themselves to Pope Paul III, and then in 1539 they decided to found a new order, which Paul III approved on 27 September 1540. The founding was formally a corporate venture, the work of the now ten members of the group. Some of the original number would later challenge the claim that Ignatius was the sole founder, but he was no doubt the center and guiding spirit from the beginning, as his unanimous election in 1541 as superior general for life testified. During the next fifteen years, moreover, he continued to shape the new institution in ways that for the most part would be definitive.

With headquarters established in Rome, he set about governing the rapidly growing and geographically sprawling organization coming into shape before his eyes, as from a handful of members it grew by the time of his death to a thousand, located in most countries of western Europe and in India, Japan, Brazil, and elsewhere overseas. A number of colleagues aided in this task, none more important than Juan Alonso de Polanco, his secretary from 1547, and Jerónimo Nadal, whom from 1552 he several times invested with plenipotentiary powers and sent to almost every Jesuit community in Europe.

During these years he composed with Polanco's help the *Constitutions* of the society and wrote almost seven thousand letters, the largest extant correspondence of any sixteenth-century figure. From 1548 he enthusiastically promoted the running of schools as a primary ministry of the society, an important change from an earlier emphasis on itinerant ministry of preaching, lecturing, teaching catechism, hearing confessions, and fostering spiritual and corporal works of mercy. Following a crisis in leadership and authority in Portugal (1552–1553), he shifted his emphasis from poverty to obedience. By 1550 he had come to see combating the Reformation as a primary objective for the society.

He was more interested in religious experience than ideas. Opposed in principle to the Reformation, he never attempted to deal directly with the contested doctrinal issues. Having only late in life begun an education that included the Latin classics and scholastic philosophy and theology, he developed an appreciation for them but showed no desire to become a practitioner of their skills.

Despite his large correspondence, the man behind the words remains somewhat elusive. In this aspect, he resembles Calvin more than Luther, with whom he is often compared. Nonetheless, during his lifetime he won the admiration of his colleagues for his courage and perseverance in difficult undertakings, for his prudent and generally flexible advice, for his ability to help individuals achieve peace of conscience, and for what seemed to be an abiding, even mystical, awareness of God's presence in his life. The success of the society was largely secured by his ability to choose capable assistants.

The *Spiritual Exercises.* The *Exercises* is without doubt Ignatius's most important and characteristic writing. It was virtually complete by 1540, and only minor changes were made thereafter until its first printing in Rome in 1548. Intended as a manual for the person guiding others through the program it outlines and basically structured into four "weeks" or major parts, the book is not laid out in continuous discourse and lacks literary grace. It consists of interspersed pieces from different literary genres—meditations, prayers, declarations, procedures, sage observations and rules. Points critical for understanding it sometimes appear in seemingly subordinate or supplementary locations.

The *Exercises* are not an exposition of doctrine but a detailed program, in outline form, for a month of prayer and reflection on one's life and on the central mysteries of Christianity. It has been called with some accuracy "a recipe for conversion." It gave the first effective codification to what came to be known as the religious retreat. Although the text is structured for the ideal situation of a month of seclusion, it allows a great deal of flexibility about the length of time one might spend in the *Exercises* and about the circumstances in which one might do them.

In its concepts, images, and directives the book stands squarely within the late medieval tradition, so that the search for its sources has consistently been frustrated by the commonplace nature of its ideas. In a general way it reflects some aspects of the *devotio moderna,* with which Ignatius was surely familiar. The only specific source identified as definitive for some key elements is the *Vita Jesu Christi* by Ludolf of Saxony (1300?–1378), which Ignatius read in Spanish in 1521 during his convalescence at Loyola. But the structure and orientation of the *Exercises,* as well as the development and emphasis that Ignatius gives to certain ideas, make the book original.

The rules "for the discernment of spirits," although located in a quasi-appendix, provide a key for understanding the entire text, which is based on the presupposition that God speaks directly to the person in ways registered through motions of consolation and desolation experienced within. Perhaps the best-known section of the *Exercises* is another quasi-appendix, the rules "for thinking with the church," the last section of any substance added to the text, between 1535 and 1540. Important for what these rules reveal about Ignatius's attitude on certain religious issues of the day, they relate only indirectly to the rest of the book and were never seen by Ignatius or Jesuit commentators as its culmination, as some critics assume.

The *Constitutiones.* Among the many tasks facing Ignatius in 1541, few were more important than the construction of constitutions. Ignatius made notes and drafted important statements but did not set about it in a fully systematic way until 1547, after he had secured Polanco as his secretary. Although the traditional interpretation that Ignatius was the principal inspiration behind the *Constitutiones* still stands, much of the wording and arrangement, many of the details, and the substance of certain sections must be attributed to the secretary.

By 1550 Ignatius had a first draft reviewed by a few leading Jesuits and two years later sent Nadal to Sicily and then to Portugal and Spain to propagate them. He continued to revise them until his death, after which they were formally approved by the first general congregation in 1558. Many of their stipulations were abrogated by subsequent congregations, but they remain the instrument of government of the order.

The *Constitutiones* were a strikingly original document, quite unlike almost all their religious or secular counterparts. Whereas the constitutions of other orders are simply collections of ordinances, the Jesuit *Constitutiones* has a formal design based on a developmental principle of spiritual growth from time of entrance until full profession in the order. Providing further cohesion, for instance, are certain theological assumptions, of which the most important is that grace perfects nature. They also contain Ignatius's most characteristic ideas, such as the ideal of pastoral adaptation to circumstances, of the moral and ascetic mean between extremes, and of the deepest inner appropriation of religious values.

Other Writings. Between 1553 and 1555 Ignatius dictated in three relatively short periods of time an account of his life from 1521 up to his arrival in Rome in 1538. Polanco and Nadal importuned the narration from him as a testament that would show members of the order how and to what God had called him. Although Ignatius told of the external circumstances of his life, he was more concerned to reveal how he was "taught by God" and learned how to discern between divinely and diabolically inspired impulses.

Despite the critical problems endemic to any such personal memoir, it remains the most reliable source for the early life of "the pilgrim," as he consistently referred to himself. Since Nadal utilized it in his encounters with other Jesuits as providing a living incarnation of the meaning of the society that could be held up for emulation and appropriation, it had an impact within the order. The original account lacks a title, but it is generally referred to as the "autobiography" or something equivalent.

Of the almost seven thousand letters that have survived, all but about 175 date from after Polanco's appointment as secretary, and a large number were explicitly written by him "on commission" from Ignatius. Much of the correspondence has, therefore, the same problems of attribution as the *Constitutiones.* Many of the letters concern details of government within the order and practical matters of business such as the financing of the schools and the establishment of communities. But a few to Jesuits address general issues, like the stipulation of obedience as characteristic of the Jesuit (no. 3304); the warning, with an instruction, about being taken in by apocalyptic speculations (no. 790); and the principles for ministry in beginning a new school (no. 1899). A large number are addressed to lay magnates about matters of mutual concern, and a number are to women. The correspondence is a rich but practically unexplored resource for understanding the religious culture of the mid-sixteenth century.

Ignatius composed a few sets of rules for the domestic discipline of the principal house in Rome and for other circumstances that with modification became normative in the society, along with similar directives and job descriptions composed by others, especially Nadal. Only some fifty pages of his personal journal, from 1544/45, escaped the destruction he effected for the rest. They reveal that the spiritual and mystical visitations described in his autobiographical account continued, as did his careful attention to them for providing guidance.

Reform and the Reformation. In his autobiography Ignatius mentioned the Reformation in only the most incidental and generic way, although he surely had no sympathy with it even during his "pilgrim years." When he and his companions drew up their plans for the new order in Rome in 1539, they primarily wanted to establish for themselves an association that would more closely imitate the lifestyle and especially the ministries of the early disciples of Jesus as they understood them, even though they had begun to take account of Protestantism as in some way pertaining to their mission.

During the 1540s Ignatius urged or permitted a few Jesuits to accept invitations to work in Germany, but he gave no specific instructions regarding their destination. When in early 1546 he sent a letter of instruction to the three Jesuits invited as theologians to the Council of Trent, he still had no specific recommendations for them about reform of the Catholic church or about how to deal with the Reformation (no. 123). The letter reveals Ignatius's interests and priorities by speaking principally about the ministries the Jesuits were to perform at Trent.

In the last six years of his life, he increasingly saw the society as called to oppose the Reformation and especially to provide for Catholics in areas where Protestantism was strong. After he sent Peter Canisius back to Germany in 1549, he continued to encourage him as he emerged as a key figure in the confessional struggle. In 1554, on the eve of the Peace of Augsburg, when it was clear that the program of Charles V for the restoration of Catholicism was collapsing, he answered Canisius's plea for advice for Ferdinand by recommending strongly repressive measures (no. 4709). He urged Jesuits to write against "the errors of the heretics" but wanted them to avoid polemics in the pulpit by simply presenting Catholic teaching in a positive way.

Almost nothing he ever said suggests that he thought reform of the Catholic church was his task or the responsibility of the Society of Jesus. He was a religious enthusiast intent on "the help of souls" through a pattern of ministry that in its intensity and single-mindedness imitated the ministry of the apostles. He was thus intent on evangelization of the newly discovered peoples but also on fostering a deeper inwardness, devotion, and religious conversion in those who called themselves Christians. He founded an organization that would pursue these ends, which, for all the distinctiveness that the Jesuits did bring to them, were much in concert with the epoch and, as put in motion by Ignatius and his early companions, were rarely explicitly related to reform of the Roman Catholic church.

No one has yet written a fully satisfactory biography of Ignatius. He died on 31 July 1556 and was canonized in 1622. His feast day is 31 July.

BIBLIOGRAPHY

Primary Sources

Begheyn, Paul, and Kenneth Bogart. "A Bibliography on St. Ignatius's *Spiritual Exercises*." Studies in the Spirituality of Jesuits, vol. 23, fasc. 3. Saint Louis, 1991. A listing of 750 entries, some annotated, of which a relatively small percentage is by professional historians.

Ignatius Loyola. *Saint Ignatius Loyola: Letters to Women.* Edited by Hugo Rahner, translated by Kathleen Pond and S. A. H. Weetman. Edinburgh and London, 1960. Rahner's extensive introductions make the book especially valuable; perhaps the best introduction to the correspondence.

———. *The Constitutions of the Society of Jesus.* Translated and annotated by George E. Ganss. Saint Louis, 1970. Ganss's notes and commentary make this the most informative and useful edition in any language.

Secondary Sources

Aldama, Antonio M. de. *An Introductory Commentary on the Constitutions.* Translated by Aloysius J. Owen. Saint Louis, 1989. Succinct and authoritative account by a careful historian.

Bertrand, Dominique. *La politique de s. Ignace de Loyola: L'analyse sociale.* Paris, 1985. Only lengthy attempt to analyse Ignatius's correspondence.

Dalmases, Cándido de. *Ignatius of Loyola, Founder of the Jesuits: His Life and Work.* Translated by Jerome Aixalá. Saint Louis, 1985. Succinct and factually reliable.

Garcia-Villoslada, Ricardo. *San Ignacio de Loyola: Nueva Biografía. Madrid,* 1986. The most compendious biography, valuable for the information it provides and summarizes.

Leturia, Pedro de. *Estudios ignacianos.* Edited by Ignacio Iparraguirre. Rome, 1957. Still the single most important and fundamental collection of studies about Ignatius and his background.

Meissner, William W. *Ignatius of Loyola: The Psychology of a Saint.* New Haven, 1992. Ambitious psycho-biography.

O'Malley, John W. "Was Ignatius Loyola a Church Reformer? How to Look at Early Modern Catholicism." *The Catholic Historical Review* 77 (1991), 177–195. Raises the question of how to categorize Ignatius and his institution.

———. *The First Jesuits.* Cambridge, Mass., 1993. Especially valuable for relating Ignatius to the general context of the early Society of Jesus.

Ravier, André. *Ignatius of Loyola and the Founding of the Society of Jesus.* Translated by Joan Maura and Carson Daly. San Francisco, 1987. Thoughtful study of Ignatius's government of the Society of Jesus.

JOHN W. O'MALLEY

ILLEGITIMACY. Children born outside of marriage were considered illegitimate in early modern European society. Pre-Reformation Christian doctrine, no less than that of Protestants and reformed Catholics, construed illegitimate children as products of illicit sexuality, universally condemned because it occurred outside of marriage. Illegitimate children were thus the products of either premarital sexual relations (fornication) or extramarital relations (adultery). Condemnation of the former sprang not only from religious concerns but from social and political ones as well. Reformers and secular authorities alike feared unrestrained fornication would lead to a generation of poor bastards, by definition outside the orderly confines of the patriarchal family. Such children would contribute to the pressing social problem of poverty and vagabondage, which were visibly on the rise everywhere in Europe in the sixteenth century.

Adultery was even more worrisome (and a capital offense

in France, for example), not only because it explicitly violated Mosaic law but also because it struck at the patrimony of the patriarchal family (considered the bedrock of social and political order). Adultery could produce undetected illegitimate offspring who would then obscure the legitimate lines of inheritance and, in effect, steal part of the patrimony from the rightful heirs. For these reasons prenuptial chastity and marital fidelity were the unbending rules of reformers, as well as secular authorities, throughout Europe during the sixteenth and seventeenth centuries. Indeed, in some places, such as German cities, illegitimacy excluded one from guild membership and thus from civil and political status.

Illegitimacy, moreover, was apparently repudiated among the popular classes, as evidenced, for example, by popular proverbs and slanders. In both, female sexual behavior was disapproved only if no marriage was intended. If marriage was intended and especially if the couple was betrothed, then there are clear indications (in legal testimony arising from litigation over broken marriage promises, for instance) that sexual relations were an accepted part of courting in the popular classes.

So great was the concern of religious and secular authorities for illegitimacy that it may be surprising that the illegitimacy rates (baptisms per 100 live births out of wedlock) were quite low by modern standards. Such rates are based on parish registers, unfortunately few of which are extant from the sixteenth century, especially in cities. Current findings nonetheless reveal that in rural France in the sixteenth century the illegitimacy rate likely hovered around 3 percent, dropping to less than 1 percent in the seventeenth century. In England the rates rose to a peak of 3 percent around 1600, then declined to 2 percent in the 1630s and to 1.5 percent in the late seventeenth century. These rates mirror western and northern Europe as a whole: rates in rural areas averaged below 2 percent before the eighteenth century, while in most countries they seldom rose to as high as 5 percent. Urban rates have been much more difficult for historical demographers to determine because of the difficulty of doing demographic analysis in the urban environment. The limited information available suggests that, though higher than rural rates (pregnant women often came from the countryside to the city to give birth in anonymity), the urban rates were still low enough not to become a substantial element in overall fertility, although they rose sharply in the eighteenth century throughout Europe.

Some historians have suggested that the low and declining illegitimacy rates reflect the impact of ascetic teachings of reformed Protestantism and Catholicism. Others have cautioned against such a conclusion, suggesting that illegitimacy rates are an inaccurate indicator of premarital and extramarital sexual relations and thus challenging the supposed impact of asceticism. The rates quite possibly underestimate illegitimacy and overemphasize prenuptial chastity. (Indeed, it is known that about 20 percent of all brides in sixteenth-century England, for example, were pregnant at their weddings.) Many illegitimate children undoubtedly were never baptized, and the practice of infanticide (which, according to some studies, may have been more frequently practiced than historians have traditionally assumed) would reduce the record of illegitimate births but not necessarily reflect their incidence. Moreover, abortion (also probably more widely attempted than historians have thought) and contraception (how widely it was practiced has been hotly debated) would further obscure the reliability of illegitimacy rates as reflections of illicit sexual relations. Finally, low levels of fertility (it has been suggested that there was less than a one in fifty chance that a single act of sexual intercourse would result in pregnancy) point to the same conclusion: recorded illegitimate births were only a small (though ultimately unknowable) fraction of pre- and extramarital sexual relations.

BIBLIOGRAPHY

Dupâquier, Jacques, et al. *Histoire de la population française.* Vol. 2, *De la Renaissance à 1789.* Paris, 1988. Combines the most recent demographic scholarship on early modern France.

Flandrin, Jean-Louis. *Les amours paysannes, XVIe-XIXe siècle.* Paris, 1975. Collection of documents with interspersed commentary on popular sexuality in general and much useful information concerning attitudes about illegitimacy.

Flinn, Michael W. *The European Demographic System, 1500–1820.* Baltimore, 1981. The best overview available; contains useful material on illegitimacy.

Laslett, Peter, Karla Oosterveen, and Richard M. Smith, eds. *Bastardy and Its Comparative History: Studies in the History of Illegitimacy and Marital Nonconformism in Britain, France, Germany, Sweden, North America, Jamaica, and Japan.* Cambridge, Mass., 1980. The best and most complete study of this subject available.

JAMES R. FARR

ILLUMINISM. This term refers to the doctrine of the Illuminated—Spanish, *Alumbrados*—a group of sixteenth-century religious dissenters whose homeland and activities were located in the region of New Castile, with a particular concentration in the provinces of Toledo and Guadalajara. Many were of Jewish ancestry, and at least some enjoyed both the protection and the sympathy of some of the region's most prominent noble houses. The reason for this protection is not quite clear, but it seems probable that it was because many of those noblemen were also of Jewish ancestry. Thus, by employing and protecting them, the nobles were surrounding themselves with people of similar politico-religious leanings.

The *Alumbrados* belonged to the urban lower-middle class; most lacked higher education, but many were self-taught, and they had a well-established reputation as honest, hardworking people. They were part of the early generation of *Conversos* who, under pressure, had adopted Christianity and repudiated their ancestors' religion. Social ferment had begun to create a class distinction based primarily on religion but also on race: "Old Christians," or *Castizos*, who had no Jewish blood; and "New Christians," or *Conversos*, who, although practicing Christians, or claiming to be so, were of Jewish origin. A third caste was made up of those converted to Christianity but of Islamic ancestry, known as *Moriscos* and sometimes as *Conversos*. While the Jewish population was urban, the Muslim population was primarily rural. The *Moriscos* did not play a role in the *Alumbrados's* incipient sectarian movement, which was confined rather to *Conversos* of Jewish origin. This is not, however, to suggest that the *Alumbrados* were Christians only in appearance. There are no instances of charges by the Inquisition of their secretly practicing Judaism. The *Alumbrados* were sincere Christians, deeply committed to the Christian faith, which they sought to purify and interpret according to basic New Testament concepts. Although the *Alumbrados* were themselves the great-grandchildren of the Cabbalist Spanish masters and had perhaps been exposed to some of their ideas, they showed no evidence of Cabbalist thought. Whatever they might have learned through their Jewish tradition had eventually been transformed or forgotten. Christianity took the place of their Jewish religious concern and practice. They sought in their new religion the God of the Old and New Testaments as the God of Jesus Christ, the Redeemer and Savior.

The two prominent figures of the heretical *Alumbrados dexados* ("abandoned"), Isabel de la Cruz and Pedro Ruiz de Alcaraz, were typical of the *Alumbrados* in social status. He was an accountant and secretary by profession. Alcaraz served first the powerful and noble Mendoza family in their palace in Guadalajara and later the no less noble and powerful family of the marquis of Villena in Escalona in Toledo. Alcaraz was a "lay preacher" to the marquis. Isabel was also of a *Converso* family and had entered the Franciscan tertiary order of laywomen; she lived outside the religious community, loosely maintaining ties with the Franciscans. No personal documents of her literary expression exist. Her "confessions," or depositions, before the Inquisition are not in her own handwriting. There is, however, some indication that she was writing or planning to write a book on "new doctrines." Like the later Teresa of Ávila, Isabel was both of the urban middle-class and of Jewish ancestry, and the two had in their femininity that restlessness of spirit that has given the former a prominent place among the *Alumbrados* and the latter a prominent place as leader of the Carmelite reform and an original writer and mystic.

The heretical *Alumbrados*'s basic claim was that God, through the holy scriptures and without the need of any other authority, reveals in the heart and mind of the believer the right interpretation of the scriptures. This claim appears often both in the "confessions" of Isabel and in the two letters of Alcaraz. In its uncompromising form, this claim threatened the established institutional church and explains why personalities of different religious conceptions, such as Ignatius Loyola, Juan de Vergara, Bartolomé Carranza, John of the Cross, and Teresa of Ávila, were accused of being *Alumbrados*. The accusers, rightly or wrongly, saw in them this dependence on the spirit that threatened the institution. The accused, however, remained within the institutional church. This also applies to the apocalyptic-ecstatic Franciscan *Alumbrados* reformers such as Francisco de Ocaña and Juan de Olmillos, while the *Alumbrados dexados* were charged as heretics for proclaiming "new doctrines."

The *Alumbrados*, as a pre-Reformation phenomenon, belong to the cultural milieu of the Cisnerian Catholic reformation. The interest of Cardinal Francisco Jiménez de Cisneros in the translations of Christian spiritual classics into the vernacular made available to the people a treasure of spirituality. To this one must add the availability of extensive portions of the Bible and the Gospels in translation. If the origins of the *Alumbrados* go as far back as 1509–1510, their final days must be dated to April 1524, when Alcaraz was seized by the Inquisition at the church of Santa Clara in Toledo. The *Alumbrados* edict of 1525, almost a year and a half after Alcaraz's arrest, is, in fact, the legal certification of the *Alumbrados*'s death. The trial of Alcaraz, however, continued until 22 July 1529, when he was formally charged with the heresy of the *Alumbrados*.

The heretical *Alumbrados dexados* based their doctrines on the vernacular reading of the scriptures without allegorical interpretation. They developed organizational forms of religious meetings and missionary activities encompassing the surrounding towns. Juan de Valdés's earliest recorded historical activities show him attending these religious meetings headed by Alcaraz. These *Alumbrados* rejected ceremonies, almsgiving, and indulgences as worthless for salvation. With some criticism they kept the sacraments of baptism and Communion but rejected the rest. They also rejected the veneration of the Virgin, the saints, and the rosary. They criticized the ecclesiastical hierarchy on doctrinal rather than on moral issues. They were neither quietists nor mystically oriented. Their name, *dexados*, or "abandoned" (to the love of God), expresses their repudiation of freedom of the will as a means of cooperation with God's grace for salvation. Rather, they trusted God's love and his "benefits" for their forgiveness. They never made use of the formula of "justification by faith."

BIBLIOGRAPHY

Andrés, Melquiades. "Alumbrados, Erasmians, 'Lutherans,' and Mystics: The Risk of a More 'Intimate' Spirituality." In *The Spanish Inquisition and the Inquisitorial Mind*, edited by Angel Alcalá, pp. 457–494. New York, 1987.

Bataillon, Marcel. *Érasme et l'Espagne.* 3 vols. 2d enl. ed. Geneva, 1991.

Beltrán de Heredia, Vicente. "El edicto contra los alumbrados del Reino de Toledo (23 de septiembre de 1525)." *Revista Española de Teología* 1 (1950), 105–130.

Huerga, Alvaro. "Erasmismo y alumbradismo." In *El erasmismo en Es-*

paña, edited by Manuel Revuelta Sañudo, pp. 339–356. Santander, Spain, 1986.
Longhurst, John E. "The Alumbrados of Toledo: Juan del Castillo and The Lucena." In *Archive for Reformation History* 45 (1954), 233–253.
———. "La beata Isabel de la Cruz ante la inquisición." *Cuadernos de Historia de España* 25–26 (1957), 279–303.
———. *Luther's Ghost in Spain, 1517–1546*. Lawrence, Kans., 1969.
Márquez, Antonio. *Los alumbrados*. 2d enl. ed. Madrid, 1980.
Nieto, José C. *Juan de Valdés and the Origins of the Spanish and Italian Reformation*. Geneva, 1970. Also available in Spanish, revised and enlarged edition, Madrid, 1979.
———. "En torno al problema de los alumbrados de Toledo." *Revista Española de Teología* 35 (1975), 77–93.
———. "The Franciscan Alumbrados and the Prophetic-Apocalyptic Tradition." *Sixteenth Century Journal* 8 (1977), 3–16.
———. "The Heretical Alumbrados Dexados: Isabel de la Cruz and Pedro Ruiz de Alcaraz." *Revue de littérature comparée* 52 (1978), 292–313.
———. "Valdesianism, The Viterbo *Spirituali* and the 'Beneficio di Cristo.'" *Proceedings of the Unitarian Universalist Historical Society* 20.2 (1985–1986), 1–10.
———. "L'Hérésie des Alumbrados." *Revue d'histoire et de philosophie religieuses* 66 (1986), 403–418.
———. "The Nonmystical Nature of the Sixteenth-Century Alumbrados of Toledo." In *The Spanish Inquisition and the Inquisitorial Mind*, edited by Angel Alcalá, pp. 431–456. New York, 1987.
Pérez, Joseph. "El erasmismo y las corrientes espirituales afines." In *El erasmismo en España*, edited by Manuel Revuelta Sañudo, pp. 323–338. Santander, Spain, 1986.
Redondo, Augustin. "Les premiers 'Illuminés' Castillans et Luther." In *Aspects du libertinisme au XVI siècle*, edited by Marcel Bataillon, pp. 85–91. Paris, 1974.
Selke, Angela. "Algunos datos nuevos sobre los primeros alumbrados: El edicto de 1525 y su relación con el proceso de Alcaraz." *Bullentin Hispanique* 54 (1952), 125–152.
———. "El iluminismo de los conversos y la Inquisición: Cristianismo interior de los alumbrados, resentimiento y sublimación." In *La Inquisición española: Nueva visión, nuevos horizontes*, edited by Joaquin Pérez Villanueva, pp. 617–636. Madrid, Spain, 1980.
Serrano y Sanz, Manuel. "Pedro Ruiz de Alcaraz, iluminado alcarreño del siglo XVI." *Revista de Archivos, Bibliotecas y Museos* 7 (1903), 1–16, 126–139.

JOSÉ C. NIETO

IMAGES. *See* Art; Iconography; Iconoclasm; Saints, *article on* Cult of Saints.

INDEX OF PROHIBITED BOOKS Neither state nor church in the Reformation era believed in complete freedom of expression. Nevertheless, religious discussion was remarkably free and open in the century before the Reformation because little heresy existed. This freedom continued through the first three decades of the Protestant Reformation because the papacy held off from drafting an index until all hope of reunion with Protestants was gone. By the middle of the sixteenth century Catholic ecclesiastical and civil authorities concluded that only coordinated press censorship would prevent the further spread of heresy. They saw the need for a catalog identifying heretical books, authors, and ideas. With such a list, governments might impose prepublication censorship to prevent the printing of heretical books and to block the importation of heretical books from abroad.

At first individual Catholic states tried to censor the press by means of local indexes. After these efforts failed, the papacy took the matter in hand. Pope Paul IV promulgated an *Index librorum Prohibitorum* (Index of Prohibited Books) in early 1559. For the first time, the supreme spiritual authority of Catholicism defined for Catholics which books and authors could not be printed or read. The so-called Pauline index was very restrictive: it prohibited the *opera omnia* of about 550 authors as well as individual titles, the vast majority of them Protestant religious works. It went beyond heresy to ban some anticlerical and lascivious works. Machiavelli's works, with their allegedly immoral principles of statecraft, were prohibited. Most important for learning, it banned the *opera omnia* of a long list of northern Protestant scholars, the bulk of whose writing dealt with nonreligious topics, even though they had usually written one or more anti-Catholic titles. According to the Pauline Index, the heretical convictions of an author contaminated all that author's writing. This Index also promulgated sweeping rules designed to control the distribution of books.

The Pauline Index was widely criticized within Catholic circles. After a tenacious struggle among Italian printers, governments, and the papacy, during which thousands of books were destroyed but compliance was grudging, Paul IV died on 18 August 1559. Enforcement stopped, and Pius IV announced his intention to moderate the Pauline Index. It had lasted less than a year. The common assumption of twentieth-century scholars that the Index of 1559 was the definitive statement of catholic censorship is inaccurate. Instead, the Pauline Index signaled a decisive turn in papal policy, which could be modified but not repudiated.

The Council of Trent discussed an index in January 1562, then appointed a commission to draft one. When the Council of Trent ended in November 1563 before the index commission could complete its work, the task was turned over to the papacy. Pius IV promulgated the Tridentine Index in the spring of 1564, employing that title because the Index had been authorized by the Council of Trent. Unlike its predecessor, it won immediate and widespread, but not total, acceptance in Catholic lands. The Tridentine Index repeated ninety-nine percent of the condemnations of authors and titles of the Pauline Index. It also promulgated guidelines for prepublication censorship, the enforcement of the Index, and the regulation of the printing industry. But the changes from 1559 were significant; they moderated some of the most criticized features of the previous Index. For example, the Tridentine Index banned only six titles of Erasmus, leaving the enormous bulk of his original works and numerous editions of classical and patristic authors and the

New Testament to be expurgated. Heretical and overly critical comments about the church and churchmen were to be excised but the rest of the text left unchanged. Other authors were also to be expurgated.

The Tridentine Index reflected an unresolved conflict between total hostility against any book tainted, however slightly, by heresy, and the continuing belief of Renaissance humanism that one could find truth amid error in one's reading. The humanists had followed the latter approach in their study of the pagan classics of the ancient world. The prohibitions and rules of the Tridentine Index were generally sweeping and harsh, but a few offered concessions. Books containing some error but "whose chief matter" was "good" might be held in expurgated form. Texts accompanied by scholarly apparatus prepared by heretics might be held after expurgation. These moderations signified a grudging awareness that Catholics and Protestants inhabited a common scholarly world based on Christian and pagan antiquity. Expurgation was the compromise decreed by the Tridentine Index for those who wished to read nonreligious books written by Protestants. Numerous surviving copies of sixteenth-century volumes with passages inked out by hand, or pages cut out or glued together, document the practice of expurgation. By the end of the sixteenth century, reprinted texts with offending passages expurgated by omission were common.

The Tridentine Index, with its prohibitions and rules for enforcement, provided the approach and structure for Catholic censorship. Governments implemented prepublication censorship and regulated the book trade on the local level usually through enforcement bodies composed of civil and ecclesiastical representatives supported by the police power of the state. The French and Spanish monarchies asserted their traditional claims of jurisdictional autonomy from Rome by assuming power over censorship without reference to the papacy. For example, Spain issued its own *Indices librorum prohibitorum.* But they were modeled on the Tridentine Index, and the prohibitions were much the same.

Press censorship was a typical measure at a time of religious strife. Protestant states also attempted to censor the press, but, lacking religious unity, they did not issue indexes and found it difficult to censor beyond local political boundaries. The extent and effectiveness of press censorship in both Catholic and Protestant Europe varied from state to state and according to the political and religious climate. Catholic prepublication censorship was generally effective; few banned books were printed in Catholic lands. But state and church authorities never completely halted the entry and circulation of heretical books from abroad.

The papacy issued a revised version of the Tridentine Index with new prohibitions in 1596 and periodically revised the Index over the next three-and-one-half centuries. It was formally abolished in 1966.

BIBLIOGRAPHY

Bujanda, J. M. de, et al, eds. *Index des Livres Interdits.* Sherbrooke, Qué., and Geneva, 1984–. Publication of all sixteenth-century indexes. Each volume has a historical introduction, analysis of the contents of the index, identifications of all prohibited books, photographic reproduction of the original printing of the index, and discussion of the relationship between indexes. The basic source.

Grendler, Marcella T., and Paul F. Grendler. "The Survival of Erasmus in Italy." *Erasmus in English* 8 (1976), 2–22. Studies the growing hostility to Erasmus's books in Italy and in the indexes.

Grendler, Paul F. *The Roman Inquisition and the Venetian Press, 1540–1605.* Princeton, 1977. A detailed study of the Index in the context of the Venetian press and papal-Venetian relations.

———. "Printing and Censorship." In *The Cambridge History of Renaissance Philosophy,* edited by Charles B. Schmitt et al., chap. 2, pp. 25–53. Cambridge, 1988. Surveys printing and both Catholic and Protestant censorship.

Higman, Francis N. *Censorship and the Sorbonne: A Bibliographical Study of Books in French Censured by the Faculty of Theology of the University of Paris, 1520–1551.* Geneva, 1979. Deals with French-language books only.

Hirsch, Rudolf. "Pre-Reformation Censorship of Printed Books." *Library Chronicle* 21 (1955), 100–105. Describes incidents of censorship in Germany, 1475–1500.

———. "Bulla super impressione librorum, 1515." *Gutenberg Jahrbuch* 48 (1973), 248–251. Discusses papal bull of 1515, which decreed universal press censorship. It had no effect.

PAUL F. GRENDLER

INDULGENCES. According to a doctrine established in the thirteenth century, an indulgence is the complete or partial remission by the church of temporal punishment (as opposed to the eternal punishment of hell) for sins that have already been forgiven, provided that certain conditions (for example, going on a pilgrimage, going on or supporting a crusade, almsgiving, making a contribution toward the building of a church or of a hospital) have been fulfilled. The debt of punishment is paid off from the treasury of merit that has been acquired by Christ, the Blessed Virgin, and the saints. The practice presupposed the high medieval regime of sacramental penance, in which the priest-confessor absolved the truly contrite penitent from the guilt (*culpa*) of sins but stipulated an appropriate penance or punishment (*poena*). If the penitent died before completing the penance, or if the stipulated penance was for some reason insufficient, the remainder could be fulfilled in purgatory. In effect, therefore, an indulgence offered remission from purgatory to a person who made a good confession and fulfilled the stipulated conditions. The power of giving indulgences was vested primarily in the pope, who alone could grant remission from *all* temporal punishment (plenary indulgence). The merits acquired from a plenary indulgence might also be applied for the benefit of souls who were already in purgatory. The practice and the doctrine were the product of a complicated historical process reaching back to the third century.

The practice became progressively inflated during the high and late Middle Ages, and it was prone to abuse and to fraud. Although attempts were made to limit it and to obviate abuses (for example, at the Fourth Lateran Council of 1215 and at the Council of Trent), indulgences became devalued in the minds of the faithful. Some who professionally preached and distributed indulgences (including the Dominican friar Johann Tetzel, whose preaching provoked Luther's objections) obscured important distinctions and insinuated that indulgences were a means to salvation. The popes themselves encouraged this impression by declaring that plenary indulgences gave remission from guilt as well as from punishment (*indulgentia a culpa et poena*).

When Luther began to raise doubts about indulgences, he regarded the practice as symptomatic of a profound sickness within the church but had no desire to part with the Roman hierarchy. His Ninety-five Theses of October 1517 soon circulated widely, but they were written in Latin and were intended as the subject of an academic disputation on indulgences. Luther's alienation from the Roman church was made clear to him when he was interrogated by Cardinal Cajetan at Augsburg in 1518. Although the posting of the Ninety-five Theses is justly regarded as the dawn of the Reformation, little in them was novel. At various times over the previous two centuries, scholastic theologians had raised Luther's chief objections.

Luther objected to the avarice and money-grubbing associated with indulgences (thesis 28) and to the tendency to suppose that one could buy one's own salvation or the release of deceased persons from purgatory. Thus he emphasized the need for true contrition (thesis 40). His chief objection, however, was to the principle and not to the abuse of the practice. The crux of the Ninety-five Theses was the premise that the church can remit only penances imposed by itself, and that this jurisdiction does not extend to the dead (theses 5, 8, 10–11, 13, 20–22, 34). The only influence the pope has over souls in the next world, therefore, is the ordinary one of intercession (thesis 26). Luther's line of argument had devastating implications for the doctrine of purgatory and for the authority of the papacy and of the councils and cast doubt on the penitential regime itself (cf. theses 1–3), but it was not new. The scholastic theologian Bonaventure (d. 1274) noted the opinion of "certain persons" (*quidam*) that any relaxation of penance is effective only as far as the church is concerned (*quantum ad forum ecclesiae*), not as far as God's judgment is concerned (*quantum ad forum Dei*). Bonaventure objected that if this view were true, relaxation of penance by the church would be a cruel deception (commentary on book IV of Peter Lombard's *Sententiae*, dist. 20, pars 2, quaest. 2). Luther was characteristically willing to tolerate the immense gulf that his doctrine opened up between ecclesiastical and divine judgment.

[*See also* Penance.]

BIBLIOGRAPHY

Primary Sources

Enchiridion Indulgentiarum. 3d ed. Rome, 1968.

Mirbt, Carl. *Quellen zur Geschichte des Papsttums und des römischen Katholizismus*. 6th ed. Tübingen, 1967–1972.

Secondary Sources

Benrath, Gustav A. "Ablaß." In *Theologische Realenzyklopädie*, vol. 1, pp. 347–364. Berlin and New York, 1985.

Campbell, J. E. *Indulgences*. Ottawa, 1953.

Journet, Charles. *Teologia delle indulgenze*. Rome, 1966.

Oberman, Heiko A. *Luther: Man Between God and the Devil*. Translated by E. Walliser-Schwarzbart. New Haven and London, 1989. See especially pp. 16–18, 67–77, and 187–197, in which Oberman sets Luther's critique of indulgences in the context both of his personal development and of contemporary ecclesiastical and political affairs.

Palmer, B. F. "Indulgences." In *New Catholic Encyclopedia*, edited by William J. McDonald, vol. 7, pp. 482–484. New York, 1967. Summarizes the history of indulgences from the third century to the Council of Trent.

Paulus, Nikolaus. *Indulgences as a Social Factor in the Middle Ages*. Translated by J. Elliot Ross. New York, 1922.

———. *Geschichte des Ablasses im Mittelalter, vom Ursprunge bis zur Mitte des 14. Jahrhunderts*. 3 vols. Paderborn, Germany, 1922–23. Standard treatment of the evolution of indulgences, still not superseded.

Pelikan, Jaroslav. *The Christian Tradition*. Vol. 4. *Reformation of Church and Dogma, 1300–1700*. Chicago and London, 1984. See pp. 128–138, in which Pelikan examines the development of Luther's thought on confession, contrition, and divine justice.

Southern, R. W. *Western Society and the Church in the Middle Ages*. Reprint, Harmondsworth, England, 1970. See pp. 136–143 on the inflation of indulgences in the high Middle Ages and on indulgences as an instrument of the papacy.

Vodola, Elisabeth. "Indulgences." In *Dictionary of the Middle Ages*, edited by Joseph R. Strayer, vol. 6, pp. 446–450. New York, 1985. Includes a detailed account of the development of the high medieval doctrine.

PHILIP LYNDON REYNOLDS

INFLATION. *See* Capitalism.

INGOLSTADT.

Founded in 1472, the University of Ingolstadt took pride in the fact that it was the heart of the Counter-Reformation. The humanist movement at the university was connected with the names Johann Tolhopf, Karoch de Monte Rutilo (the Heidelberg humanist Samuel Karoch von Lichtenberg), Ventimontanus Aeolodis, and Conradus Celtis. In his inaugural address on 26 June 1472, Martin Mair, counselor to Duke Ludwig of Bavaria, stressed the humanist character of education and the liberal arts curriculum at the university. He asserted that education raised humanity to the divine sphere.

The first humanist to be inscribed in the university register in 1472 was Tolhopf, who had obtained his liberal arts education at the University of Leipzig. In a letter to Celtis, the German archhumanist, he considered himself to have an understanding of antiquity superior to that of the theologians. Tolhopf simultaneously held collegiate canonries at Ingolstadt and the Leipzig Collegium Maius, though he did not reside in either of the two towns after 1480, when he became court astrologer for King Matthias Corvinus of Hungary. As such he exercised the same practice of absenteeism as did other prelates of the Roman church, who sent poorly paid vicars to their churches, which they themselves never looked after and for which they were well paid. This explains in part the widespread identification of the humanists with the Reformation. In the case of Tolhopf there was protest against his accumulation of canonries. After 1482 he was in Ingolstadt again, but the liberal arts faculty protested against his reclaiming the collegiate canonry. Although a humanist, Tolhopf represented as dean of liberal arts the *via antiqua* in theology. As the theology faculty adopted the *via moderna,* it was in theology that a major difference arose between the humanists and the theologians at Ingolstadt. With regard to this difference, humanism can be seen as a forerunner of the Reformation, in spite of the fact that Martin Luther and many other reformers came from the *via moderna.*

Another early humanist in Ingolstadt was Peter Schwarz. On 2 January 1476 he was promoted to doctor of theology at Ingolstadt. Schwarz introduced Hebrew studies in order to prepare for disputations with Jews. In 1475 he published a guideline for converting Jews. In a way Schwarz was the predecessor of both Johannes Pfefferkorn and Johannes Reuchlin. He also was Luther's predecessor in his attempt to convert Jews.

A third humanist was Erhard Windsperger (Ventimontanus), who asked Duke Ludwig of Bavaria for a raise in his yearly income of sixty gold guilders in light of his humanist lectures. The duke responded favorably.

In 1480 Ventimontanus dedicated to the senate and the people of Nuremberg an exhortation that Christian princes should be united against the Turks, not unlike Luther's call for Christian unity against the Turks. After 1486 he served as physician to Duke Albert of Saxony and joined him in Frankfurt am Main to participate in Emperor Maximilian's coronation. He became a friend of Reuchlin and received a knighthood from Emperor Maximilian, who tipped him on the shoulder with the sword of Charlemagne.

Conradus Celtis entered the University of Ingolstadt in 1492 and the humanist period, anticipating the appeal of the Reformation to the patriotic sentiment of the people, came into full bloom. By exercising humanist patriotism, Celtis set an example for the Reformation. Luther inherited from Celtis the concern for Germany (*Germania mea*). In contrast to humanism, which sought to renew the strength of the empire and the knights as its foremost pillars, northern Europe, which had fought Rome as early as A.D. 9, tried to liberate the church from the Roman yoke.

Although Celtis remained in Ingolstadt only five years, the city during this time became so reform oriented that Johann Eck, who had taught in Ingolstadt since 1510, felt it necessary to direct his energy against the results of reform humanism. The importance of humanism as a precursor of the Reformation subsequently ended in Ingolstadt because of the impact of Eck, who dominated not only the theology faculty but also the entire university. Even before Eck encountered Luther in the Leipzig Disputation of 1519, he frequently participated in disputations outside Ingolstadt and made the university known as an adversary of the Reformation. In Eck's fight against all reform tendencies, he subdued humanism at the university. As deputy chancellor of the university and, at the same time, as papal protonotary, Eck censured Luther's books and organized their burning. He called on Bavaria to incarcerate religious dissidents and forced reform-oriented believers to emigrate. Eck's enormous influence can be understood only in the context of the territory's struggle against heresy. Bavaria stood in the forefront of the Counter-Reformation, and the case of Ingolstadt shows that Eck's literary polemics led directly to the period in which the Jesuits were the vanguard of the Counter-Reformation and in which Bavaria became the stronghold of Catholicism in Germany.

The basis of Eck's anti-Reformation activities was his position, on the one hand, as deputy chancellor of the university and, on the other, as papal protonotary, which gave him the status of an inquisitor along with the right of the theology faculties to judge the teaching of colleagues. This right can be traced back to the Sorbonne, which had demanded it in 1207. With papal approval the Sorbonne acquired the right to decide theology matters for all theological faculties. In 1441 the Council of Basel endorsed this right, and Pope Nicholas V confirmed it on 28 March 1452 by adding the task of fighting heretical teaching.

On 17 October 1520 Eck asked the university to publish the bull *Exurge Domine,* in which forty-one articles of Luther's teaching were banned, to all its members and to defend it in lectures and disputations. A commission was to inspect all bookstores. Eck threatened the university that if it did not go along with his directives, it was in danger of losing the right to confer academic degrees. As a result of Eck's measures, many books were handed over to the rector of the university for the purpose of an auto-da-fe. Under Eck's influence the professor of theology Georg Hauer von Tirschenreuth wrote *Acta contra hereticos Lutheranos,* which described the measures taken by the university against Reformation theology. With this action of his co-worker, Eck established himself as the undisputed theological authority of Ingolstadt, and through him the university became known throughout Christendom. Eck's authority superseded the Bavarian courts' original tolerance of the Reformation. Together with Hauer and Franz Burkhardt, Eck asked the ducal court to issue the first religious mandate of Bavaria. When this occurred on 5 March 1522, Eck effectively turned Bavaria against the Reformation. The university ordered a second inspection of all bookshops in order to confiscate Luther's writings.

In September 1523 the university censured the writings of the humanist Brassican, who was suspected of Lutheran tendencies. This action makes it clear that Eck and his followers saw reform humanism as a forerunner of the Reformation. The student of theology Georg Schack was fined for expounding Luther's theology in his sermons. During the winter semester of 1522/23 Arsatius Seehofer transferred from Wittenberg to Ingolstadt and expounded views of Luther and Philipp Melanchthon. Seehofer was forced to recant seventeen articles that were pronounced heretical, particularly the thesis on justification by faith alone. In November 1523 the senate of the university ruled that all non-Bavarian students must promise not to represent Lutheran views. As a result of this decision, Ingolstadt became known as the capital of the anti-Reformation party. Luther wrote a tract against the practices at Ingolstadt.

In connection with the case of Seehofer, the university organized a disputation on 11 April 1524 concerning Christian freedom, faith, hope, and love, in which Eck, Hauer, and Burkhardt planned to crush all representatives of Lutheranism. Their plan failed because the followers of the Reformation in Ingolstadt did not attend, fearing that they would be taken into custody for proclaiming Reformation views.

After 6 July 1524 Bavarians were forbidden to study in Wittenberg. A second religious mandate of Bavaria, published at the University of Ingolstadt on 14 November 1524, reinforced the decisions of the imperial regiment at Regensburg. That Eck's Counter-Reformation in Ingolstadt gained a spiritual supremacy in south Germany can be proven by the case of Master Job from Ochsenfurt and Karl Münch from Würzburg, who were forced by Eck to renounce their Lutheran leanings.

In 1527 Eck was asked by the bishop Ernst von Passau for advice in dealing with the vicar Leonhard Kaiser, who represented Luther's teaching in his sermons at Waitzenkirchen. When Kaiser was denounced by his priest, he went to Wittenberg, although that was forbidden by ducal order. When he returned to his dying father, he was again denounced by provost Petrus Doerff von Suben at Schärding and imprisoned at Feste Oberhaus at Passau. Kaiser was interrogated by Eck and was handed over to the ecclesiastical court on 18 July 1527. Luther sent him a letter of consolation. He was later turned over to the secular court and sentenced to be burned at the stake on 16 August 1527. Soon after his death a Reformation tract called Kaiser a martyr of the evangelical truth. Eck responded with the tract *Warhafftige handlung, wie es mit herr Lenhart Käser, zu Schärding verbren ergangen ist.*

In 1531 the third Bavarian religious mandate was issued, and a man named Mittermüller was thrown into the city prison because he did not want to take the sacrament of confession more than once a year. In November 1531 all writings of Luther and Melanchthon were again banned by the university.

After the Diet of Augsburg the Reformation, although still illegal according to imperial law, had become established in several German territories. It took twenty-two years for the Lutheran Reformation to become an established faith in the empire, but by 1530 the epoch of confessionalization had begun, diminishing the importance of Eck. When he died in 1543, it became obvious that the academic senate had become more lax in the persecution of nonorthodox religious views. In 1548 the reading of Lutheran books was no longer punished in Ingolstadt, and the Reformation seemed to gain ground. But that year was only an interlude before the ultimate defeat. When the Jesuits arrived in Ingolstadt in 1549, they started where Eck had left off. Peter Canisius, the first German Jesuit, became rector of the Jesuit college at Ingolstadt in October 1550. He proved to be a competent successor of Eck in his Counter-Reformation orientation. In December he ordered the compilation of an index of Reformation literature. Six years later the first Munich index for all Bavaria was published. This avant-garde in Counter-Reformation practices shows superbly Ingolstadt's role as a leading opponent of the Reformation.

BIBLIOGRAPHY

Bauch, G. *Die Anfänge des Humanismus in Ingolstadt.* Munich, 1901.

Betzold, F. v. "Konrad Celtis, Der deutsche Erzhumanist." *Historische Zeitschrift,* n.s. 13 (1883), 1–45.

Druffel, A. von. *Die bairische Politik im Beginne der Reformationszeit, 1519–1524.* Munich, 1886.

Ekkert, A. "Leonhard Keysser (Käser) in neuer Betrachtung." *Ostbairische Grenzmarken* 7 (1965), 304–309.

Hartfelder, K. "Conrad Celtis und Sixtus Tucher." *Zeitschrift für vergleichende Litteraturgeschichte,* n.s. 3 (1890), 331–349.

Leeb, Friedrich, and Friedrich Zoepfl. *Leonhard Käser: Ein Beitrag zur bayrischen Reformationsgeschichte.* Münster, 1928.

Muther, Theodor. *Aus dem Universitäts- und Gelehrtenleben im Zeitalter der Reformation* (1866). Reprint, Amsterdam, 1966.

Prantl, Carl. *Geschichte der Ludwig-Maximilians-Universität in Ingolstadt* (1872). 2 vols. Reprint, Aalen, 1968.

Wattenbach, W. "Samuel Karoch von Lichtenberg, ein Heidelberger Humanist." *Zeitschrift für die Geschichte des Oberrhein* 28 (1876), 38–50.

Winter, Vitus Anton. *Geschichte der Schicksale der evangelischen Lehre in und durch Baiern bewirkt.* 2 vols. Munich, 1809–1810.

ULRICH MICHAEL KREMER

INQUISITION. Although existing in Europe since the thirteenth century, the Inquisition acquired renewed importance during the age of the Reformation. The rise of Protestantism intersected with the history of the Inquisition in various ways. If the old system had been able to control heretics in the Germanic lands, Martin Luther might never have become famous. Without Luther, however, no new Inquisition would have been created in the Low Countries, nor would a permanent tribunal have been established at Rome itself. Some kingdoms, such as England, had many Protestants but no viable Inquisitorial apparatus; others, such as Spain, had state-run Inquisitions but no significant Protestant movement. Protestantism played no role whatsoever in the creation of a national Inquisition in Portugal in the 1530s and remained only a marginal concern of the Spanish Holy Office until the late 1550s. Protestants, however, made fear and loathing of the Spanish Inquisition into a potent propaganda weapon during the age of religious warfare.

The older system of papally commissioned inquisitors survived into the sixteenth century in the Holy Roman Empire, though by this time its prestige had been fatally impaired by the Reuchlin-Pfefferkorn quarrel over the prohibition of Hebrew; the *Epistolae Obscurum Vitorum* (Letters of Obscure Men), a vitriolic humanist satire, ridiculed Inquisitor Pfefferkorn's attempts at censorship. Luther's successful defiance of the papacy was undoubtedly abetted by the absence of any Inquisitorial authority in the empire capable of imposing effective sanctions. Charles V recognized this problem by establishing a vigorous Inquisition in the Netherlands as early as 1522 in order to combat the new heresy of Lutheranism. Other monarchs bothered by the new heresy but suspicious of the papacy—Henry VIII in England and Francis I in France—generally preferred to have "Lutherans" tried by secular courts.

The new Netherlands Inquisition created Europe's first Lutheran martyrs when it ordered the burning of two Augustinians at Brussels in 1523; it remained the most active Inquisition north of the Alps until the outbreak of the Revolt of the Netherlands, despite obstruction from secular authorities objecting to its claims to the property of convicted heretics. In the province of Flanders, where an unusually dedicated inquisitor named Pieter Titelmans worked for almost twenty years, this Inquisition tried more than 2,300 suspected Protestants before 1566 and executed 264 of them, mostly Anabaptists.

Before Luther was born, a new variety of state-run Inquisition had already been developed in Spain in 1478 in order to deal with Judaizing behavior by converted Jews. (Portugal, after much lobbying in Rome, founded a similar national Holy Office in the late 1530s for the identical reason). The papacy itself, attempting to bring the Protestant movement in Italy under control, adapted some features of these national models when it created the Roman Inquisition in 1542. Mediterranean Europe, therefore, contained three permanent, official state Inquisitions into "heretical pravity," each with different priorities.

The Roman Inquisition, run by a standing committee of six cardinals meeting once a week with the pope presiding, was the most prestigious, if not necessarily the most effective, of these institutions. Two future popes sat among its first six appointees in 1542. One of them, Cardinal Gian Pietro Carafa, was responsible for gross miscarriages of justice, such as the trial of Cardinal Giovanni Morone, during the time he was its dominant member and subsequently as Pope Paul IV. In general, however, the Roman Holy Office operated with meticulous care and maintained a high reputation for impartiality. When the papal court was reorganized in 1588, it was ranked first among fifteen congregations. Although the Roman Inquisition could function without hindrance in the Papal States, it had to negotiate its privileges, such as extradition of important heretics, with other Italian governments. In Venetian territory it could do nothing unless representatives of the Most Serene Republic were present.

Like its Spanish counterpart, the Roman Inquisition was famous for the secrecy of its proceedings—a secrecy, in fact, that still persists: its official archive in the Pallazzo dello Santo Uffizio ("palace of the Holy Office"), built in 1566, has remained generally inaccessible to scholars. Because of the dispersal, loss, and unavailability of so many of its records, it is impossible to measure its anti-Protestant activities during the sixteenth century with much accuracy. Probably fewer than a hundred heretics died at Rome (where the most serious cases were usually extradited) before 1600, with perhaps another hundred executed elsewhere in Italy by order of the Roman Inquisition. Its best-known prisoners included a few foreign prelates, such as the Spanish archbishop of Toledo, Bartolomé de Carranza, transferred to papal jurisdiction in 1566; heliocentrists either with or without Protestant connections (Giordano Bruno and Tommaso Campanella); and, of course, Galileo. Records of these trials have been made available, but it is perhaps through its investigation of an obscure and stubborn freethinker like Domenico Scandella (alias Menocchio), finally executed in the Friuli as a relapsed heretic in 1600, that one can best understand its methods.

The Spanish Inquisition had restrained its campaign of terrorism against converted Jews before it ever heard of Luther. It encountered far fewer native Protestants than its Roman counterpart but executed more people for "Lutheranism." As late as 1558 Inquisitor General Valdés could boast to Paul IV that "the province which by God's grace has been freest of the stain [of Protestantism] has been the very heart of Spain, thanks to the great care and vigilance of the Holy Office of the Inquisition." When Protestant groups were discovered at Seville and Valladolid, it moved rapidly and effectively to crush the nascent movement, executing more than eighty suspects within five years. Henry Charles Lea exaggerated only slightly when he described Spanish Protestantism as a "mere episode, of no practical moment save as its repression fortified the Inquisition." Except for the decade after 1558, the Spanish Inquisition usually worried more about converted Muslims, or Moriscos, than about Protestants: between 1560 and 1614 it tried four times as many people for Islam as for "Lutheranism" (8,911 vs. 2,233).

The Spanish Inquisition, however, also persecuted foreign Protestants. From 1539, when a Fleming died at Bilbao, until 1640, when a Frenchman died at Palermo, it executed about one hundred fifty foreigners (two-thirds of them French) and about one hundred Spaniards for "Lutheranism." Even in Italy the Spanish Inquisition was more severe than the Papal Inquisition; Sicily, which belonged to the Spanish system, executed more Italians for Protestantism than did cosmopolitan Venice. (The Portuguese Inquisition never displayed sufficient concern over Protestants, whether domestic or foreign, to put them in its *autos-de-fe*).

Trying to explain the appearance of Protestants in 1558, the Spanish Inquisition argued that heretical books "have been the principal cause of this damage." Both the Spanish and Papal Inquisitions made strenuous efforts to enforce the various prohibitions and expurgations of Protestant literature, though never with complete success. The Spanish Inquisition made its own Index of prohibited and expurgated books, while the papacy created a separate congregation to manage its Index. At a major publishing center like Venice, the Roman Inquisition was never quite able to stop the importation of prohibited works or even to prevent the printing of unexpurgated editions of suspect authors. Large libraries in both countries sometimes contained hundreds of illicit books. Nevertheless, Inquisitorial censorship worked well enough to inhibit responsible Mediterranean authors and publishers from producing innovative or controversial works; Galileo's trial is merely one of the final episodes in a long, futile, and poorly known quest for confessional purity after the Council of Trent. (The archives of the Congregation of the Index housed within the palace of the Roman Inquisition have also remained closed to scholars.)

While the great Mediterranean Inquisitions investigated thousands of suspected Protestants and executed hundreds of them during the sixteenth century, their reputation was further enhanced by alarmist Protestant literature that exaggerated their cruelty and distorted their procedures. Nowhere was this process more significant than in the Netherlands, where a well-organized campaign of disinformation had created a hysterical fear of the Spanish Inquisition by the late 1560s. A clever blend of fact and fiction written by a Spanish Protestant refugee closely related to an inquisitor, printed in 1567, preceded several outright forgeries in the 1570s, many of which were soon translated into English. Philip II was correct in his well-known remark that the Netherlands Inquisition was "much less merciful" than its Spanish counterpart, but fears that an Inquisition "in the Spanish manner" would be imported stiffened the resolve of the Dutch rebels; the famous *Apologie de Guillaume IX, Prince d'Orange, contre la Proscription de Philippe II, Roy d'Espagne* (Apology of Prince William of Orange against the Proclamation of the King of Spain; 1581) emphasized how William had warned against any attempt to "set up the cruell inquisition of Spayne." Of course, Catholics could also be stirred up against the Spanish Holy Office: serious rioting broke out twice at Naples, in 1509 and 1547, when it was to be introduced, and Gallican propaganda used it in the 1550s to prevent the creation of a national Inquisition in France. Inquisitorial secrecy encouraged myths about these institutions.

BIBLIOGRAPHY

Ginzburg, Carlo. *The Cheese and the Worms.* Baltimore, 1980.

Grendler, Paul F. *The Roman Inquisition and the Venetian Press, 1540–1605.* Princeton, 1977.

Henningsen, Gustav, and John Tedeschi, eds. *The Inquisition in Early Modern Europe: Studies on Sources and Methods.* DeKalb, Ill., 1986.

Kamen, Henry. *Inquisition and Society in Spain in the Sixteenth and Seventeenth Centuries.* Bloomington, Ind., 1985.

Monter, William. *Frontiers of Heresy: The Spanish Inquisition from the Basque Lands to Sicily.* Cambridge, 1990.

Peters, Edward. *Inquisition.* Berkeley, 1988.

Tedeschi, John. *The Prosecution of Heresy: Collected Studies on the Inquisition in Early Modern Italy.* Binghamton, N.Y., 1991.

E. WILLIAM MONTER

INTERIMS. Charles V's decisive victory in the Schmalkald War opened up new possibilities for him to resolve finally the religious question in line with his own thinking. The failure of the religious colloquies at Worms and Regensburg had brought about the war against the Protestant territories of the empire that had joined in the Schmalkald League. But, the situation in the empire—the commitments made to allies who were Protestant, such as Duke Moritz of Saxony, as well as his deteriorating relations with the pope—did not allow the emperor simply to restore the late medieval church. Charles was convinced he could resolve the conflict over religion by having the estates of the empire attend a general council. Until then the estates were to live "in divine blessedness and in good and friendly manner" with one another. For this purpose Charles V drafted a transitional and intermediate solution, which would be in force until the successful conclusion of a council. This imperial law on religion is known as the Augsburg Interim. Through its adoption into the recess of the imperial diet on 30 June 1548 it acquired binding legal force in the empire. The controversy over the interim did not remain a dispute over the true faith. The religious question once again intersected with the dispute between the imperial desire for hegemony and centralization and the princes' concern for influence and liberty. In turn, France and England were opposed to the dominance of the Habsburgs. It is against the backdrop of this tension that one must understand the relations between the emperor and the pope. Pope Paul III did not concede any decision-making authority in the religious question to the emperor, thus weakening Charles V's position.

The emperor determinedly pursued his plans for an interim, utilizing briefs prepared by Julius Pflug, Johannes Gropper and Michael Helding in 1545–1546. A first draft of December 1547 uncompromisingly affirmed the basic positions of the old faith, but it was not published. When the official committee of the diet dealing with the Interim was unable to reach an agreement in February 1548, Pflug, Helding, and Johann Agricola, the Protestant preacher at the court of Joachim II of Brandenburg, consulted about a compromise proposal. After further talks, a new draft came into being in March 1548. It remained the basis for the subsequent negotiations. After several modifications, particularly in response to the wishes of Catholic estates of the empire, the draft was published on 15 May 1548. The determined efforts of the emperor, King Ferdinand, and several electors to obtain Moritz's acceptance proved most difficult. Despite threats and intense pressure, Moritz held to his reservation that he could not give his assent without consulting the estates of his territory. Although he accepted the official reading, he filed a protest with the emperor on 18 May over the limitation of the Interim to Protestants, committed himself to consulting his subjects, and left Augsburg. In even more explicit terms Margrave John of Brandenburg informed the emperor that he could in no way agree to the Interim. This resistance against the imperial mandate on religion became the starting point for the subsequent political opposition in the empire and formed a common basis for action by John and Moritz, which, however, broke down in 1551 due to Moritz's alliance with France. That the Interim focused in the end only on the evangelical estates of the empire further hampered Charles V's reform efforts. The ecclesiastical electors had insisted on separating the Interim and reform. Consequently the emperor issued a *formula reformationis* ("formula for reform") on 14 June 1548 that detailed a program for the reform of the clergy and the monasteries, for visitations, and for convening provincial synods. These directives against abuses and scandals were hardly observed.

The Augsburg Interim deals in its twenty-six articles with various questions of doctrine: articles 1–2, man before and after the Fall; 3, redemption; 4–6, justification; 7–8, faith and works; 9–13, church; 14–21, sacraments; 22, sacrifice of the Mass; 23, veneration of the saints; 24, masses for the dead; 25–26, church practice.

The articles on justification were worded with particular care. A twofold justification (*duplex iustificatio*) encompassing the merits of Christ (*iustitia Christi*) and righteousness infused by the Spirit (*iustitia inhaerens*) is the basis. The gift of love renews one and enables one to perform works of love. Thus Reformation views were not ruled out. The other articles represented views of the old faith throughout, as in the doctrine of the church and papal primacy, the seven sacraments, or holidays and ceremonies. The implementation of the emperor's mandate would have led to a complete return to the late medieval church. The concessions to the Protestants were limited to clerical marriage and the cup to the laity, both, however, only until a decision by a general council.

The subsequent controversy over the Interim played out on political and theological levels. As an attempt to implement his provisions, the emperor succeeded for a short time but only where imperial troops were stationed (Württemberg and imperial cities in southern Germany), and the electors of Brandenburg and the Palatinate officially promulgated the text but did not enforce its observance. Thus, the political center of the empire was weakened as a result. The controversy over the Interim also developed as a feud between the adiaphorists and the interimists into one of the greatest crises in Lutheran theology after 1546.

Moritz of Saxony played a central role in the controversy. The support for his policy by the Wittenberg theologians in Philipp Melanchthon's circle led to harsh disputes that have affected Melanchthon's image to the present day. However, it was not so much the emperor's religious policy itself as the politically motivated attempts of Saxony to obstruct and delay the Interim that led to the profundity of the crisis. Despite pressure from the emperor, Moritz was not swayed from his independent position.

After failing to reach an agreement over the doctrine of justification with Pflug and Johann von Maltitz of Meissen, the Dresden court counselors, with help from Brandenburg, tried to get the Wittenberg theologians to accept a modified form of the Interim and thus counter the emperor by introducing their own version. This text came before the Diet of Leipzig by the end of 1548. The estates, however, rejected it since the Wittenberg theologians accepted these counselors' articles as a basis for negotiations only with great reservations, while Pflug and Maltitz rejected them outright. Matthias Flacius Illyricus published the text as the "Leipzig Interim" and thus exacerbated the controversy.

Early in July 1549, with the collaboration of Melanchthon, an "excerpt" (the "little Interim") from the Leipzig articles appeared that provided for the introduction of *adiaphora* (ceremonies, feast days, surplice), which was likewise not implemented. The "Leipzig Articles" and the "excerpt" were intended to provide Moritz with leeway for his political activities. There was probably never any thought of introducing the Interim in Saxony in its Augsburg version. The intended effect of the Leipzig articles never materialized, although they retained the fundamental theological convictions of the reformers. The catalyst was the proposed reintroduction of rites that had already been abolished (*adiaphora*). For Flacius Illyricus, even "middle things" could invoke a *status confessionis*: in matters of confession there is no *adiaphoron*. The return to medieval forms of spirituality must have appeared as a restoration of the papal church, despite the attempts to interpret it evangelically. This separation between doctrine and externals was not convincing since Saxon policy between 1548 and 1552 seemed to be more loyal to the emperor than evangelical. As a matter of fact, as regards the Interim Moritz subordinated questions of faith to politics. He put the Wittenberg theologians into a difficult situation that caused them to be accused of fearfulness and lack of faith. Nikolaus von Amsdorf supported Flacius Illyricus. In Magdeburg resistance against the emperor was related to opposition to the Interim. Resolute resistance also occurred in Lübeck, Hamburg (Johannes Aepinus), Bremen, and Braunschweig-Kalenberg (Antonius Corvinus).

Although the Treaty of Passau (August 1552) and the Peace of Augsburg formally superseded the Interim, the emperor's unsuccessful mandate on religion signaled a new phase in the history of the religious controversy. The Interim marked the end of the religious colloquies between Catholics and Protestants and furthered the emergence of confessions. Lutheran theology became divided. The Gnesio-Lutherans around Flacius Illyricus, Nikolaus von Amsdorf, Nikolaus Gallus, Johann Wigand, and others were opposed by the Philippists, who included, besides Melanchthon, Georg Major, Justus Menius, Johannes Pfeffinger, and Caspar Cruciger the elder. Although internal disagreements arose in both factions, only the Formula of Concord overcame the division that had erupted in 1548/49.

[*See also* Augsburg; Charles V; Flacius Illyricus, Matthias; Gnesio-Lutherans; Leipzig; Lutheranism; *and* Philippists.]

BIBLIOGRAPHY

Hermann, Johann, and Günther Wartenberg, eds. *Politische Korrespondenz des Herzogs und Kurfürsten Moritz von Sachsen*. Berlin, 1978–1992. See vols. 3 and 4.

Lohse, Bernhard. "Dogma und Bekenntnis in der Reformationszeit; von Luther bis zum Konkordienbuch." In *Handbuch der Dogmen- und Theologiegeschichte*, edited by Carl Andresen, vol. 2, pp. 102–113. Göttingen, 1980.

Mehlhausen, Joachim. "Interim." In *Theologische Realenzyklopädie*, vol. 16, pp. 230–237. Berlin and New York, 1987. Extensive bibliography.

Mehlhausen, Joachim, ed. *Das Augsburger Interim von 1548*. Neukirche-Vluyn, 1970. The relevant sources.

Wartenberg, Günther. "Philipp Melanchthon und die sächsisch-albertinische Interimspolitik." *Lutherjahrbuch* 55 (1982), 60–82.

GÜNTHER WARTENBERG

Translated from German by Robert E. Shillen

IRELAND. In the context of the European Reformation, Tudor Ireland and the Spanish Netherlands stand out as exceptions to the usual pattern of development. In most regions the eventual outcome was determined by the attitude of the prince. In Ireland and the Netherlands the political mishandling of the local magistrates by a centralizing state sparked off waves of unrest and rebellion in which religion was a key issue. And religious differences and consequent political instability were a major reason for the partition of the two territories, albeit much later in Ireland, and the emergence of new states.

In other respects, however, the problems faced by the Reformation in Ireland had much in common with those encountered in other outlying Tudor territories. Tudor Ireland was distant from the center of royal power in London; it was politically decentralized and, like Wales, also culturally divided between English settlers and Celtic-speaking natives; and it was, like the far north of England, a predominantly pastoral region of large, poor parishes and scattered settlement, with a turbulent frontier separating the English and Gaelic parts. Not surprisingly, therefore, traditional explanations for the failure of the Tudor Reformation in Ireland—in contrast with its rapid progress in the Home Counties—have centered on the differing conditions encountered in the two regions: for instance, a movement which sought to reform Christianity by replacing a predominantly visual presentation of religion with one based on Bibles, sermons, and services in English was at a serious disadvantage in a predominantly non-literate, Gaelic-speaking society like Ireland. Yet, if it were just a question of the preconditions for reform, one should expect to find that, as elsewhere, the Reformation's main impact was largely delayed into the seventeenth century, with Protestantism eventually spreading from the prosperous English Pale and the towns into the surrounding countryside. In practice, it was the Counter-Reformation that first became established in these English parts of Ireland, and by the end of the Tudor period the Church of Ireland was increasingly seen as a colonial church of the recent New English settlers, with little indigenous support from the traditional Gaelic and Old English communities.

Despite its eventual failure, however, there were few signs before the mid-1570s that the outcome of the Tudor Reformation in Ireland would be so different from that in other "dark corners of the land." Under Henry VIII there was no Irish equivalent of the Pilgrimage of Grace, and resistance in English Ireland was largely confined to individual acts of disobedience and secret obstruction. Moreover, those Gaelic chiefs who in the 1540s accepted "surrender and regrant" (the strategy for securing Gaelic recognition of Tudor sovereignty by issuing to individual chiefs feudal charters for native lordships) also recognised Henry VIII as supreme head of the Church of Ireland. Altogether Henry eventually secured some recognition in 24 of Ireland's 32 dioceses, and by 1547, 55 percent of the 140 or so monasteries and 40 percent of some 200 mendicant communities had been dissolved. Yet for two reasons opposition to the Reformation became much more strenuous after mid-century.

In the first place, the establishment of an unambiguously

Protestant religious settlement centering on *The Book of Common Prayer,* briefly under Edward VI and permanently under Elizabeth I, marked a far more radical departure from pre-Reformation Christianity than the piecemeal, humanist-inspired reforms of Henry VIII's reign. The enforcement of the new settlement demanded a vigorous campaign of instruction and preaching, which the Dublin goverment lacked the resources to mount. Despite proposals to import preaching ministers from England and Gaelic-speaking ministers from Scotland in order to spearhead the campaign, few were willing to take up the challenge in war-torn Ireland. Moreover, partly because Gaelic culture was identified with political subversion, the government was slow to exploit the Gaelic language as a reform medium. A Gaelic catechism was published in 1571, but the Gaelic New Testament did not appear until 1603, and the Gaelic *Prayer Book* not until 1608—forty years after the publication of these works in Welsh. Thus the central message of the reformers was very imperfectly understood, particularly in Gaelic Ireland.

Second, the government's campaign—such as it was—coincided with an ambitious political campaign to assimilate Gaelic Ireland into the Tudor state. Commencing with the erection of Ireland into a kingdom in 1541 and the extension of English law and government into the Gaelic lordships through "surrender and regrant," this effort continued sporadically until 1603. It was finally completed when Hugh O'Neill, earl of Tyrone, surrendered to Elizabeth's last viceroy, Lord Mountjoy, at Mellifont six days after her death. Initially, the terms offered to persuade the Gaelic chiefs to become English subjects had been favorable enough, and the opposition had been muted. Yet opposition mounted after 1547, when the size of the garrison was tripled in a bid to force the pace and the government began to confiscate Gaelic land for plantation by New English adventurers. Moreover, although the unrest and "rebellion" was originally centered on the midland Irish and Shane O'Neill's lordship of Tyrone—the earliest victims of Tudor expansion—by 1568–1569 it had spread to the Englishry (the English community in Ireland), where uprisings were led by relatives of the earls of Ormond and Desmond. Unrest in English Ireland reflected the declining status of the traditional ruling elite there under the impact of the government's new policies. Conquest and colonization provided offices and land for a new class of soldiers and administrators from England, but the costs of this policy, in terms of military taxation and the quartering of troops on the local community for "defence," were borne chiefly by the Englishry. Although the separate grievances of the Englishry and Irishry usually kept them from combining effectively against the government, by the 1580s religious dissenters and political dissidents within each of the two communities were nevertheless beginning to make common cause. And by then, too, Philip II was beginning to repay Elizabeth for her interventions in the Spanish Netherlands by encouraging opposition to English rule in Ireland. These developments set the scene for the bloody and ruthless campaigns of the Nine Years' War (1594–1603), the final phase of the Tudor conquest, which cost Elizabeth some £2 million and left large areas of the country devastated and depopulated.

With growing unrest and rebellion the reform of religion was increasingly neglected under Elizabeth. Yet the challenge mounted by the Counter-Reformation was also slow to develop. The Irish Act of Uniformity (1560) permitted ministers ignorant of English to use the more conservative Latin version of the *Prayer Book,* with its provision for the reservation of Holy Communion and for a Requiem Eucharist. Thus, since no articles of religion were authorized and since the authorities were anyway very lax in enforcing strict uniformity, conservative priests had considerable liberty to "counterfeit the Mass" and to conceal from their congregations the full extent of the changes. In opting to remain within the Irish church, priests and people followed the lead of their bishops: in English areas a majority of the bishops took the oath of supremacy and agreed to serve in the Elizabethan church, by contrast with the principled stand of the Marian bishops in England. This suggests that religious attitudes were less polarized than in England, and for many years the usual popular response to the changes was reluctant conformity rather than rigid recusancy. Until approximately 1580 services were usually well attended.

Yet already in the mid-1560s the Pale aristocracy was evading the settlement by maintaining Catholic priests as chaplains, and in Waterford disaffected parish clergy were financing clerical students at Louvain. Within ten years these newly trained seminary priests were beginning to return to Ireland. Concurrently, the number of Old English merchants' sons attending continental universities greatly increased, while those going to Oxford declined. Although native-born clergy probably still formed a majority in the Irish church into the seventeenth century—the Jesuit mission to Ireland, for instance, had hardly started by 1603—these developments suggest that the Reformation was losing in the battle for the hearts and minds of the Old English youths. Beginning in the Pale in the mid-1570s, but not until the 1590s in outlying towns, religious opinion polarized: conservative conformists increasingly opted for recusancy, although a significant minority became enthusiastic Protestants. Moreover, in many parts of Gaelic Ireland the established church simply lacked an effective presence. How the increasing numbers of recusant priests were supported is not yet fully established; but with the political alienation from government of the wealthy merchants and gentry from the towns and the Pale, funds that in England would have been provided to endow Puritan lectureships and grammar schools were apparently diverted to support the Counter-Reformation. One such religious foundation was the chantries, whose property was not confiscated by statute, as in England in 1547. In response the authorities recruited ministers from England to fill the more important ecclesiastical benefices, but by so reinforcing the church's increasingly colonial appearance they further reduced its appeal to the indigenous communities. Thus, although popular religion remained in many regions largely unaffected by either reform movement until well into the seventeenth century, the fact that by 1603 the attitudes of the leading Old English and Gaelic Irish were overwhelmingly fixed in recusancy was surely decisive for the failure of the Reformation.

BIBLIOGRAPHY

Bradshaw, Brendan. *The Dissolution of the Religious Orders in Ireland under Henry VIII.* Cambridge, 1974. Model study, with general observations.

———. "Sword, Word and Strategy in the Reformation in Ireland." *Historical Journal* 21.3 (1978), 475–502. Explores tensions in reform circles during the Tudor campaign.

Brady, Ciaran. "Conservative Subversives: The Community of the Pale and the Dublin Administration, 1556–1558." In *Radicals, Rebels and Establishments: Historical Studies,* edited by Patrick J. Corish, pp. 11–32. Historical Studies (Irish Conference of Historians), vol. 15. Belfast, 1985. Addresses the relationship between political and religious dissent in the English Pale.

Canny, Nicholas. "Why the Reformation Failed in Ireland: Une question mal posée." *Journal of Ecclesiastical History* 30.4 (1979), 423–50. Critique of Bradshaw's work on the progress of the Reformation.

Edwards, R. Dudley. *Church and State in Tudor Ireland: A History of Penal Laws against Irish Catholics, 1534–1603.* Dublin, 1935. Traditional Catholic perspective, concentrating on statutes, injunctions, and resistance.

Ellis, Steven G. *Tudor Ireland: Crown, Community and the Conflict of Cultures, 1470–1603.* London and New York, 1985. Standard survey, with a chapter on religion.

———. "Economic Problems of the Church: Why the Reformation Failed in Ireland." *Journal of Ecclesiastical History* 41.2 (1990), 239–265. Uses the recently rediscovered Irish *Valor Ecclesiasticus* to demonstrate the poverty of church livings.

Ford, Alan. *The Protestant Reformation in Ireland, 1590–1641.* Frankfurt a.M., 1985. Mainly emphasizes the post-conquest reconstruction, but also addresses the problems of the Elizabethan church.

Jefferies, Henry A. "The Irish Parliament of 1560: The Anglican Reforms Authorised." *Irish Historical Studies* 26.102 (1988), 128–141. Indicates that the Elizabethan settlement attracted less opposition than had been thought.

Lennon, Colm. *The Lords of Dublin in the Age of Reformation.* Blackrock, Ireland, 1989. Includes two important chapters on religion in the city.

STEVEN G. ELLIS

ISLAM. *See* Ottoman Empire.

ISRAEL, George (1508?–1588), bishop of the Bohemian Brethren (Unity of Brethren) as well as organizer and senior of its congregations in the first Polish exile after 1547. He was born in Uherský Brod (South Moravia) and studied at a school of the brethren in Mladá Boleslav. He served as assistant to Bishop Ján Augusta in Litomyšl and accompanied Augusta to Wittenberg. He became a deacon in Brandýs nad Orlicí (1531) and a priest in Mladá Boleslav (1540). For his energies and endurance the brethren gave him the name Israel.

After the Schmalkald War (1547) a number of brethren left for Prussia and Poland, and in May 1548 Israel was arrested and jailed at Prague castle. Two months later he escaped and fled to Poland, where he served the Bohemian Brethren in exile. In 1548 he and his co-workers Matěj Vorel and Urban Hermon defended the teachings of the brethren against Lutherans in Königsberg. He was then in Kwidzyń (Marienwerder, Prussia) and in 1550 in Poznań. He attempted to strengthen the Reformation and extend the Bohemian Brethren in Poland. He converted Jacob of Ostrorog, a nobleman of Great Poland.

In 1553 Israel settled in Ostrorog and remained there until the end of his stay in Poland (1579). There he founded a seminary to prepare pastors and a school. After the death of Bishop Mach Sionský in 1551, Israel became the actual head of the brethren in Poland, although not until 1557 was he elected a bishop at a synod in Sležany near Kroměříž (Moravia), which also elected Jan Blahoslav. Israel engaged in talks with Polish Protestants of different orientations and in 1555, with Jan Černý, Jan Lorenc, and Jan Rokyta, took part in the Great Protestant Synod in Kozminek. He was sent with Jan Rokyta to the Protestants in Minor Poland to acquaint them with the brethren. He participated in important confessional dialogues in Poland, including the disputation of the Reformed church with the antitrinitarians in Kraków in 1563. In Poznań and Toruń dissension between the brethren and the Lutherans developed, and Israel sought help from Caspar Peucer and Johannes Maier in Wittenberg. He frequently traveled to Bohemia and Moravia to participate in sessions of the elders. In 1571, when Augusta was removed, Blahoslav and Israel substituted for him.

Israel left Poland for Moravia in 1579. He may not have agreed with novelties in the order of brethren, including the abandonment of clerical celibacy. He sought cordial relations with the Lutherans as well as the Reformed, but, like Blahoslav, insisted on the independence of the brethren.

Although he did not receive higher education, he had a good knowledge of Latin and Polish. None of his works have been preserved, but his reports have been preserved in volume 10 of the Acts of the Unity of Brethren. He was a coauthor and coeditor (with Lorenc and Rokyta) of *Stručné a upřímné odpovědi na výtky velkopolských luteránů* (The Brief and Plain Responses to the Reproaches of the Lutherans of Great Poland), written in 1567, which stressed the necessity of independence for the brethren. Jan Komenský called Israel the "Ecclasiae Majoris Poloniae apostolus," and though Israel was not a leading theologian, he organized the Bohemian Brethren in Poland during the initial stage of their existence.

BIBLIOGRAPHY

Bečková, Marta. "Jiří Israel a Jan Blahoslav." In *Jan Blahoslav, předchůdce J.A. Komenského 1571–1971,* edited by S. Bimka and P. Floss, pp. 64–72. Uherský Brod, Czechoslovakia, 1974.

Bidlo, Jaroslav. *Jednota bratrská v prvním vyhnanství.* 3 vols. Prague, 1900–1909.

Hrejsa, Ferdinand. *Dějiny křesťánství v Československu.* Prague, 1948–1950.

Kuske, R. *Georg Israel, erster Senior und Pastor der Unität in Großpolen.* Breslau (Wrocław), 1894.

Lochner, G. W. *Entstehung und die ersten Schicksale der Brüdergemeinde in Böhmen und Mähren und Leben des Georg Israel ersten Ältesten der Brüdergemeinde in Groß-Polen.* Nuremberg, 1832.

JAN BLAHOSLAV LÁŠEK

ITALY. A peninsula that juts into the center of the Mediterranean, Italy is bordered on the north by Switzerland, on the west by France, and on the east by Austria and Slovenia. Within the confines of the peninsula are two tiny independent states—San Marino and Vatican City—the borders of which were defined by the Lateran Treaty of 1929 between Italy and the Holy See. Italy has considerable diversity in geography, climate, economy, and culture, so much so that during the wars for independence in the 1800s Prince Metternich said scornfully that Italy was merely a geographic expression.

The liberal philosopher Benedetto Croce, the true critical conscience of twentiety-century Italian antifascism, recognized as a historic contribution of the Catholic church the fact that it had preserved during the Reformation period the religious unity of the country. Thus, it prevented a division between "a Protestant north and a Catholic south" from being added to the other divisions of Italy. Croce—while refuting the Fascists' praise of the Catholic Counter-Reformation and corroborating the historical judgment that characterized the Protestant Reformation and the Renaissance as expressions of universal demands of humanity—maintained that "even today the work of the Counter-Reformation is bearing fruit of social utility."

This observation of Croce's summed up and revised a long debate among historians over the question of why the Protestant Reformation was unsuccessful in Italy. The question itself arose in the study of the religious martyrs of the 1500s. The Calvinist exile Francesco Negri recounted in a small published work the execution of Fanino Fanini of Faenza, which took place in Ferrara on 22 August 1550 by order of the Roman Inquisition (*De Fanini Faventini ac Dominici Bassanensis morte, qui nuper in Italia Rom. Pon. iussu impie occisi sunt, brevis historia* [Brief Account of the Death of Fanino Fanini and Domenico Bassanese, Who Were Recently Killed Unjustly by Order of the Roman Pontiff]; Clavennae, 1550). The *Livre des martyrs* of Jean Crespin and the Protestant martyrologies of John Foxe and Ludwig Rabus narrated edifying accounts of martyrs of the papist persecution while offering as food for thought the story of Francesco Spiera, who died in despair because he had abjured the evangelical faith when brought before the Inquisition. From these incidents two different conclusions were drawn: first, that even in Italy the evangelical truth could be known and could bear fruit despite the strength and cruelty of its enemies; and, second, that in Italy it was impossible to live in a Christian manner. Later the history of the martyrs for the gospel in Italy offered a new track for historical literature on the Reformation, from the work of the Dutchman Daniel Gerdes (*Specimen Italiae reformatae,* [A Model of Reformed Italy]; edited posthumously in 1765) to that of the Scotsman Thomas MacCrie on the advances and extinction of the Reformation in Italy (1827), which intended to recount the history of the Reformation as a story of the spread of evangelical "truth" (according to Martin Luther, Huldrych Zwingli, or John Calvin). The features of these histories of the martyrs were those of apologetic literature and anti-Catholic polemics, which paralleled and countered similar historical literature on the Catholic side. The basic thesis of these studies is that only the violence (burnings at the stake and torture) employed by the tribunals of the Inquisition could have prevented the spread and triumph of the Reformation in Italy. The story of the many cases of followers of Reformation ideas who were imprisoned and put to death was reconstructed by these scholars to show the breadth and importance of the conquests made in Italy by the preaching of the reformers. An exception to this trend was the historiography of the Unitarian church and of the Socinian movement, which, in contrast to those of the Lutheran, Calvinist, and Zwinglian reformations, preserved the memory of heretical tendencies (spiritualist, Anabaptist, and antitrinitarian) that were widespread in Italy at the beginning of the 1500s.

Things changed with the unification of Italy. The liberal pro-Protestant historiography that attended the movement for national unification in the 1800s (*Risorgimento*) also emphasized that the political process should be accompanied by a process of moral renewal among the Italian people. The papacy's opposition to the reunification of Italy had dug a trench between Catholics and liberals. Therefore, rather than the history of the spread of the German Reformation into Italy, it was that of the native reform tendencies that stirred interest. The question of the Reformation in Italy was transformed into a question of the existence or nonexistence of an Italian Reformation, which, though a national variant, was original and independent of the overall European Reformation movement. Once national unity was won, the profound differences that existed among the old Italian states and the disillusions caused by the annexation to Piedmont made the new state structure seem fragile. The deep roots of the present weaknesses and deficiencies were identified with the fact that, in contrast to the more evolved European countries, Italy had not undergone a religious Reformation at the beginning of the modern age. The failed (Protestant) Reformation was identified as the cause of all the ills that afflicted the Italian nation. Defects perceived as typical of Italians included the lack of moral seriousness, of entrepreneurial spirit, and of responsibility and efficiency of individuals and institutions. The historian and statesman Francesco De Sanctis—in a history of how the Italian civic consciousness formed over the centuries—accused the church of the Counter-Reformation of having enfeebled the character of Italians and having accustomed them to superficial devotion and feigned morality. Luther's Reformation was considered to be the birth of the modern age, but nineteenth-century historians also proposed another genesis of the modern age, crediting the Renaissance with having freed the individual from the chains that bound people during the Middle Ages. In particular, the culture of the Italian city-states between 1300 and 1500 then appeared as the embodiment of the Renaissance. This conflict in assessments and judgments—on the one hand, Italy as the cradle of modern civilization marked by individualism, and, on the other hand, the Italian Counter-Reformation as the denial of the freedom of conscience, the age of the Inquisition, and burnings at the stake, with the resulting separation from the German and Anglo-Saxon world, which was destined to bring about the most profound social and economic transformation of Europe—is what gave rise to the singular historical question concerning the failed Reformation in Italy. It is a history of "what if": in examining the features of the reform movement in sixteenth-century Italy, one continually faces the image of what might have been the desired direction of development if the Reformation had also triumphed in Italy. At the same time, when nationalism filtered into historiography, this led to an emphasis on the original elements of the Italian contribution to the European Reformation. With a famous quote, De Sanctis wrote that "the Italian Luther was Niccolò Machiavelli," meaning by this that Italian culture of the sixteenth century had made greater progress than that of other nations on the road to modernity, since with Machiavelli it had already overcome the medieval religious wrappings in which Luther still covered the aspirations of modern man.

This greater Italian modernity was the subject of liberal and pro-Protestant historians. Thus, a series of studies arose on the "martyrs of freethinking"—that is, on those victims of ecclesiastical intolerance who had been persecuted not as followers of the Protestant Reformation but on account of the boldness of their thinking. The interest of these historians focused especially on the philosophers and scientists in whose ideas science and modern philosophy saw their precursors: the triad of Giordano Bruno, Tommaso Campanella, and Galileo Galilei were placed at the center of Italian liberal historical studies between 1800 and 1900. With B. Spaventa, B. Croce, and G. Gentile, the question of the circulation of Italian thought in Europe was at the center of a series of studies that also touched upon the history of the Italian Protestant movement in the sixteenth century. This movement, in turn, was the subject of historical interest on the part of Anglican, Lutheran, and Waldensian scholars. Significant progress was made in this area, with the discovery of unknown documents and pieces of evidence that were thought to have been lost forever. For example, one may note the discovery made by Churchill Babington of a copy of the *Beneficio della morte di Cristo* (The Benefit of Christ's Death; London, 1855), as well as the research of Karl Benrath and Giovanni Jalla in the archives of the Inquisition in Venice, which had been made accessible to scholars thanks to the Italian state's policy of suppressing ecclesiastical agencies and confiscating their assets. On the Catholic side, the research of C. Cantù and other scholars attempted to demonstrate that the harshness of the Inquisition was the result of spreading "heretical" ideas and the danger they represented for ecclesiastical institutions. Catholic historiography has always insisted on the fact that the acceptance of Luther's and Calvin's ideas was a phenomenon restricted to small groups of restless spirits and intellectuals, while the masses were said always to have remained faithful to the traditional religion. From Ludwig von Pastor to P. Tacchi Venturi and H. Jedin, the thesis of Catholic historians has been that the true Italian Reformation was the Catholic Reformation.

In the twentieth century, research on the history of the Italian religious movements of the sixteenth century has generally taken the tack of the "Italian Reformation" rather than that of the "Reformation in Italy." As Frederic C. Church wrote, "the Italian Reformation is not really the history of the penetration of Lutheran, Calvinist and Zwinglian ideas into Italy. . . the Italian Reformation should be considered the solution of the problem of religion in the Renaissance period" (*The Italian Reformers, 1534–1564*, 1932). Thus, there has been historical research on the circulation of religious ideas and attitudes seen as an expression of Italian problems and traditions. Particularly significant in this sense have been the studies of Delio Cantimori. Starting from philosophical premises—G. Gentile's interest in Bruno and in the contribution of Renaissance Italian thought to European culture—Cantimori devoted himself to historical research on Italian religious ideas in the sixteenth century. Cantimori's most important work was devoted to the *Eretici italiani del Cinquecento* (Italian Heretics of the 1500s; 1939 and 1992), in other words to those men of the sixteenth century who were in revolt against all forms of ecclesiastical institutions and who were consequently judged as heretics by all the Christian confessions of the time. In the ideas of men like Celio Secondo Curione, Lelio and Fausto Sozzini, Giorgio Siculo, Francesco Pucci, and many others, Cantimori showed the resurfacing of profound currents of Italian humanism: a radical critique of dogmas; an insistence on the imitation of Christ and on Christianity as morality rather than as a dogma; free will; and indifference to religious practices and rites. Through the various fortunes of these groups and the history of their attitudes and strategies, the underground world of Nicodemism was examined, in other words the similarity and dissimilarity in doctrine and practice by groups combated by all the churches.

The Italian heretics were just one current among the religious trends within the Italian reform movement of the sixteenth century. Within this group there were also the followers of Luther, Zwingli, and Calvin, but the complex situation created in Italy by the presence of the papacy as one of the strongest Italian states and as an authority on which many princes and lesser states depended is also manifest in the way the reform movement had to mask its purposes. That is what occurred in the most famous text of the "Italian Reformation," the *Trattato utilissimo del beneficio di Cristo.* The thesis of the originality of the Italian reform movement suffered a serious blow when the scholar T. Bozza discovered that this text is studded with quotes from Calvin's *Institutio christianae religionis.* Something similar happened when Carlos Gilly found a large number of quotes from Luther in the *Diálogo de doctrina cristiana* of Juan de Valdés. On other crucial points of the so-called Italian Reformation, the debate is still open—for example, on the religious convictions of an important group of prelates who gathered around Gasparo Contarini and Reginald Pole. Over them hangs the accusation of heresy that Pope Paul IV made in opening a series of investigations of the survivors of that group, and in particular of Cardinal Giovanni Morone. In general, historians have interpreted their attitude as one of mediation and their search for an accord with the Lutherans as an orientation motivated by Erasmian tolerance. H. Jedin has discovered that the young Contarini had in 1511 gone through a grave spiritual crisis, which concluded, as did Luther's *Turmerlebnis* ("tower experience"), with the Augustinian choice of justification by faith, though without the Lutheran denial of works. One edition of the Inquisition trial against Cardinal Morone, edited by M. Firpo and D. Marcatto, has shown how much can be learned about the ideas of this important group of prominent prelates (who were on the frontier between the Reformation and the Counter-Reformation) from the archives of the Inquisition, which have been studied only in part (also because the central archives of the Congregation of the Holy Office have been closed to scholars). S. Seidel Menchi has made a systematic study of the heresy trials conducted by the Roman Inquisition that are accessible to scholars and with this research (*Erasmo in Italia, 1520–1580,* 1987) has shown the breadth and depth that the circulation of Reformation ideas had attained in Italy. These ideas affected not only limited circles of highly educated men but also broad masses of people and were stamped out only through an extremely harsh persecution.

The history of the sixteenth-century reform movement in the Italian states, although having a wide variety of internal differences and local characteristics, exhibits certain common traits. The most basic is attention to and reflection on the ideas of such reformers as Luther, Zwingli, Martin Bucer, Calvin, and Philipp Melanchthon. It was precisely the seriousness of the break opened up by the leaders of the Reformation that had such a profound impact on dynamic religious trends in Italy, from the medieval heretical currents (Cathars, "fraticelli", and Waldensians) to the new humanist ideas of Valla and Ficino and from the ferment caused by the *Devotio moderna* to the preaching of religious leaders such as Girolamo Savonarola (a Dominican friar from Ferrara). From the very first news of Luther's preaching, there was intense curiosity and keen interest in the most diverse quarters of Italian society. The relative freedom to circulate books and ideas that was enjoyed up to the institution of the Holy Office (1542) allowed for the birth of a lively and widespread movement. Its history can be divided into three periods. The initial phase lasted from the earliest dissemination of writings and news of Luther up to the institution of the Sacred Congregation of the Holy Office (1542). In the second, lasting from about 1542 to 1580, the history of repression by the Inquisition moves forward with sudden eruptions followed by periods of lesser intensity. During this period the organized presence of groups and communities that followed non-Catholic confessions was stamped out (Waldensians in Calabria and Apulia [Puglia] and Venetian Anabaptists), and small groups and single individuals were persecuted. In the last period, beginning after 1580, the repressive and vigilant work of the Counter-Reformation no longer had to deal with either a reform movement or with organized groups of followers of the Reformation. Instead, the "missionary" counteroffensive was expanded to countries where the Reformation had won out. The phenomenon of heretics (in the sense used by Cantimori) ebbed. Henceforth the dissemination of the Reformation depended on the work of exiles like Jean Diodati and on the printed word.

During the first period there was an intense circulation of books and ideas between Italy and the centers of the Reformation elsewhere in Europe. The hegemony of Italian culture over Europe between 1400 and 1500 and the presence of the papacy in Italy drew the attention of the reformers toward Italy. Moreover, in the consciousness of Italians there was a vivid perception of Luther's importance, and the special significance they gleaned from his work was a moral protest against the Curia Romana and the corrupt clergy. The political and military crisis of the Italian states after the death of Lorenzo de' Medici and the occupation of the peninsula by the army of the French king, Charles VIII (1494)—along with the rise of the Roman papacy, thanks to the unscrupulous policy of ambitious and simoniac popes, such as Alexander VI—had caused a widespread moral protest to grow along with the hope for change. Savonarola—in the impassioned sermons, marked by a prophetic and visionary character, that he preached in Florence starting in 1494—became the most famous representative of this current. After Savonarola's execution (1498), a movement inspired by him remained alive, especially in Florence, although it was harassed by the Medici popes Leo X and Clement VII. Yet all of Italy was alive with the protest of popular prophets, such as Brandano da Pretoio and Matteo da Bascio, who, with their fiery rebukes and warnings of imminent divine retribution, fueled a widespread social religious anxiety.

The social and political situation of the Italian states during the first thirty years of the 1500s had been made difficult by the wars between France and Spain for dominance over the peninsula. Up to the Sack of Rome (1527) and the fall of the Savonarolan republic in Florence, expectations for the reform of the church were coupled with the hope for peace. In this context anti-Curia and anticlerical protest found wide approval. The result was an interpretation of the Reformation as a moral renewal and condemnation of ecclesiastical abuses. Although Luther's books were quickly circulated (thanks to the bookseller Francesco Calvo, among others), this did not prevent Bartolomeo Cerretani, a Florentine follower of Savonarola, from thinking of Luther as a continuer of the work of Savonarola. Soon the Inquisition also began proceedings against those suspected of sympathies for Luther. One of the first instances was the case brought by the patriarch of Venice against the professor Francesco da Casteldurante, accused of reading books by Luther (1526). With the advent of trials, there also arose the need for people to go into hiding and to conceal their own ideas. Another "humanist" (i.e., professor of Latin), Fulvio Pellegrino Moretto, or Morato, published a harsh attack against Luther in which he played on the Latin word *lutum* to describe Luther as a piece of mud; however, Moretto was, in fact, very attracted to the ideas of the Reformation. More than Luther and his monastic theology, the ideas of Desiderius Erasmus, Zwingli, and Bucer and later those of Calvin aroused interest in humanist circles. Often under the cover of Erasmus's name, Luther's writings and ideas circulated; interest was keen, and the desire to find out more prompted many young enthusiasts to move outside of Italy, thus reversing the trend that had brought men of letters to Italy from all over Europe. Typical is the case of two students from the University of Bologna, Giovanni Angelo Odoni and Fileno Lunardi, who went to Freiburg to meet Erasmus and from there to Strasbourg, where they lived for two years (1534–1536) as boarders in Bucer's house.

Still there was a lack of any political protection for the emerging reform movement. Only in the court of Renée of France, duchess of Ferrara, did some followers of the ideas of the Reformation find refuge and protection, among them Calvin himself. For this reason Paul III noted with alarm the advance of "heresy" on Italian territory. During this period, however, it was within religious orders—for example, the Carmelites, Franciscans, Augustinians, and Capuchins—that doctrinal dissent found the most fertile ground, but the opinions that the Roman church considered suspect or heretical and that were being spread at that time through sermons and books were not just those of the Reformation. While the Augustinians were among the most important supporters of the ideas of the Reformation (with men like Giulio of Milan, Agostino Mainardi, Ambrogio Cavalli, and many others), there were also mystical and prophetic figures—such as the Benedictines Luciano degli Ottoni and Benedetto da Mantova but also the Dominican Battista di Crema—who countered the Augustinianism of the reformers with positions that were Pelagian in nature. The most famous case was that of the great Capuchin preacher Bernardino Ochino, sought after in every city of Italy on account of the extraordinary popular appeal that his preaching had. Finally, he even preached before Emperor Charles V in Naples in 1536, and it was in Naples that he drew close to the circle that was gathering around Valdés and that included Giulia Gonzaga, Pietro Carnesecchi, Marcantonio Flaminio, and several others.

As to the ideas spread by Valdés in his conversations and in his writings, the debate among historians is still open. What is certain is that the fates of the members of the group varied. The Roman church considered this group the most insidious cenacle of heretics that existed in Italy at that time. Persecution against them was launched soon after the death of Valdés (1541), and one of the first victims chosen by the Inquisition was Ochino. When in 1542 he received a summons in Verona to appear before the Roman tribunal of the Holy Office, Ochino decided to flee from Italy so that he no longer had to preach Christ "with a mask." With Ochino's flight and the death of Contarini at about the same time, there was a grave crisis in the "spiritualist" group of prelates who were favorable to reaching an understanding with the Reformation. In Rome it was the Counter-Reformation that prevailed: the council that had convened at Trent had been adjourned, and in turn a policy of "spiritual warfare" against heretical dissent was initiated. The beginning of the activity of the Sacred Congregation of the Holy Office was felt even in Lucca and Modena, the cities where the dissemination of Reformation ideas was strongest. In Modena the men of letters who constituted the city academy were forced to sign a profession of faith; in Lucca the threat of arrests and prosecution forced the Augustinians Peter Martyr Vermigli, Emanuele Tremellio, and Paolo Lazise to emigrate, and the humanist Celio Secondo Curione also followed their example.

From 1542 the repression by the Inquisition was not particularly effective or harsh. There were political reasons that caused periods of relative tranquillity for those Italians the church considered heretics (Protestants and Anabaptists). The Council of Trent was starting up, and Charles V was determined to force the papacy to reform the church and to come to an accord with the Protestants. Moreover, the structure of the Inquisition was not yet effective. It was only with the pontificate of Paul IV (1555–1559) of the Carafa family that the Inquisition took a harsher course. During these years the Calvinists had put down roots in several Italian cities; in Cremona there was even an actual Calvinist church that met to celebrate the Lord's Supper. For political reasons some Italian states maintained tolerant attitudes toward the Protestants. In Ferrara Renée of France continued to use her power to protect those who shared her religious persuasion, despite the increasingly aggressive stance of the papacy and the Jesuits. In Venice, for a number of reasons (including the anti-Spanish policy of that state and the presence of a large German community), the Protestants hoped to make "la Serenissima" the first Italian state to be won for the Reformation. Nevertheless, it became ever clearer that Italian followers of the ideas of the Reformation were to be faced with the difficult choice between exile and martyrdom. In 1547 Venice allowed the Roman Inquisition to be introduced, although it was somewhat tempered by the presence of lay delegates. The first individuals put on trial often chose the path of abjuration, but in 1548 Francesco Spiera, a Paduan jurisconsult, died in despair because he was convinced he merited eternal damnation for having abjured his faith. His death touched off a battle of pamphlets. Pier Paolo Vergerio, bishop of Capodistria, who had gone over to the Reformation, became convinced that he had to leave Italy to practice the evangelical faith. The ex-Benedictine Giorgio Siculo, on the other hand, maintained that it was the Calvinist doctrine of predestination that led men to despair. Thus, there was no need to flee; one merely had to adapt to the rites of the place while concealing that which could not be revealed. Against these Nicodemites Calvin himself went into battle. In the meantime, the exiles increased in number and came to form whole new communities in the cities open to emigrants for religious reasons. A notable sensation was caused by the flight to Geneva of a noble Neapolitan, Galeazzo Caracciola, marquis of Vico. He had ordered a mausoleum built for himself and his wife in the family chapel in 1544, but in 1551, when he was converted to the new ideas by the preaching of Vermigli, he left his wife and children and moved to Geneva.

There were both escapes by individuals and collective migrations. The deeper the roots put down by the Reformation movement, the more numerous were the groups who chose the path of emigration. Thus, from the city of Lucca, many families moved to Geneva to escape the threat of the Inquisition. On the other hand, it was to eastern Europe—Poland, Moravia, and Transylvania—that Anabaptists and antitrinitarians emigrated. It was in those lands that the most original current of the Italian Reformation, that which was truly and properly heretical (Anabaptist and antitrinitarian), took root. Against these groups even the Italians adhering to the Lutheran and Calvinist confessions waged a merciless battle. The Nicodemite Giorgio Siculo, who had managed to elude the suspicions of the Catholic inquisitors, was denounced to the Inquisition and ordered put to death by Vergerio, who was thus the first to implement a policy of police cooperation among the churches, which was to be seen subsequently in the case of the Spanish heretic Michael Servetus. The crisis generated by the execution of Servetus in Geneva caused many Italians, among them Lelio Sozzini, to seek elsewhere the freedom to practice their faith. As mentioned above, it was to eastern Europe that this migration turned; emigrations became even more numerous after an extensive Anabaptist church was uncovered operating principally in Venice.

In that year (1551) the denunciation of a traitor, the Anabaptist bishop Pietro Manelfi, placed into the hands of the Inquisition a long list of heretics of every kind, from Lutherans to Anabaptists and antitrinitarians. Thanks to this information, Pope Julius III was able to convince Venice of the political danger represented by such a vast underground network of Anabaptists. Thus, an extremely harsh repression ensued. Just as harsh and violent was the repression carried out against smaller communities where the Reformation had gained significant support. This was the case of Faenza, where a large part of the city council was put on trial and subjected to harsh sentences. Secret accusations, the careful gathering of circumstantial evidence, and help from political authorities all made it possible for the ecclesiastical tribunals to identify and strike out against heretics.

There were even actual military campaigns to eliminate entire communities that had gone over to the Reformation; such was the fate of the Waldensians. In the course of the 1560s, both the Waldensians of Calabria and Apulia and those living in the valleys of the Alps were attacked by military expeditionary forces accompanied by preachers and inquisitors. In Calabria and Apulia the Spanish king succeeded in completely exterminating the Waldensians, while the duke of Savoy Emmanuel Philibert's campaign against the Waldensian communities of the Alpine valleys did not completely succeed in its intent. It is a fact, however, that during the years of the pontificate of Pius V, when the grand inquisitor was the friar Michele Ghislieri, the threat of heretical subversion completely disappeared from the Italian states.

BIBLIOGRAPHY

Bainton, Roland H., and Eric W. Gritsch, eds. *Bibliography of the Continental Reformation: Materials Available in English.* 2d ed. Hamden, Conn., 1972.

Cantimori, Delio. *Eretici italiani del Cinquecento.* 3d rev. ed. Edited by Adriano Prosperi. Turin, 1992. Earlier edition available in English: *Italian Heretics of the Sixteenth Century*, Cambridge, Mass., 1979.

Caponetto, Salvatore. *La Riforma protestante nell'Italia del Cinquecento.* Turin, 1992.

Church, Frederic C. *The Italian Reformers, 1534–1564.* Reprint, New York, 1974.

Dickens, A. G., and John Tonkin, eds. *The Reformation in Historical Thought.* Cambridge, Mass., 1985.

Fenlon, E. *Heresy and Obedience in Tridentine Italy: Cardinal Pole and the Counter Reformation.* Cambridge, 1972.

Firpo, Massimo. *Riforma protestante ed eresie hell'Italia del cinquecento.* Bari, 1993.

Ginzburg, Carlo. *I costituti di don Pietro Manelfi.* Florence and Chicago, 1970.

MacNair, Philip. *Peter Martyr in Italy.* Oxford, 1967.

Martin, John. *Venice's Hidden Enemies: Italian Heretics in a Renaissance City.* Berkeley, 1993.

Ozment, Steven, ed. *Reformation Europe: A Guide to Research.* Saint Louis, 1982.

Perrone, Lorenzo, ed. *Lutero in Italia.* Casale Monferrato, 1983.

Rotondò, Antonio. *Studi e ricerche di storia ereticale italiana del Cinquecento.* Turin, 1974.

Seidel Menchi, Silvana. *Erasmo in Italia, 1520–1580.* Turin, 1987.

Tedeschi, John A., ed. *Italian Reformation Studies in Honor of Laelius Socinus.* Florence, 1965.

ADRIANO PROSPERI

Translated from Italian by Robert E. Shillenn

IZRAEL, George. *See* Israel, George.

J

JÄGER, Johann. *See* Crotus Rubeanus.

JAGER, Venator de. *See* Venator, Adolphus Tectander.

JÁNOS II. *See* Zápolya, János Zsigmond.

JANSENISM. This term is applied to an international movement that derived its name from Cornelius Jansenius (Cornelis Otto Jansen, 1585–1638), bishop of Ieper (Ypres; 1636–1638) in the Spanish Netherlands. The Catholic church judged as heretical a number of propositions supposedly extracted from his book *Augustinus*. Defenders of Jansenius's theology became known as Jansenists in derision. They considered themselves orthodox Catholics who reminded the church of truths expounded by the church father Augustine.

Born of a Catholic family in Accoi, near Leerdam, Holland, Jansen studied at Utrecht and Louvain (from 1602), where he Latinized his name and encountered the ideas of a former professor, Michael Baius (Michel de Bay, 1513–1589), whose interpretation of Augustine had been declared heretical. In 1609 he went to Paris. He joined a fellow Louvain student from France, Jean Du Vergier de Hauranne (1581–1643), near Bayonne, where Jansenius became principal of a *collège*. The two men studied together. Jansenius was ordained a priest (1614), returned to Holland, continued contact with Du Vergier, became director of the Collège of Sainte-Pulchérie at Louvain, received a doctorate (1619), and died of the plague before the *Augustinus* could be published in 1640.

The *Augustinus* conflicted with the theology of the Spanish Jesuit Luis de Molina (1536–1609). Jansenist supporters of the *Augustinus* considered "Molinism" a semi-Pelagian erosion of Augustine's understanding of predestination, sin, and grace. Molinism minimized the consequences of Adam's fall and considered humans able to do good works and to merit eternal life with the help of God's sufficient grace.

Jesuits and the papacy were suspicious of Jansenist beliefs, which seemed, like Protestantism, to limit free will and the ability to choose to do good or evil. Jansenists were accused of being crypto-Calvinists, despite their ardent pro-Catholic stance and differences with Calvinists, who believed in justification by faith, not works. Calvinists believed in the perseverance of the saints to eternal life and ennobled secular callings as Christian vocations, whereas Jansenists believed that one could fall from a state of grace and tended toward ascetic retreat from the world.

Jansenius's friend, Du Vergier (ordained in 1618), became abbot of the Benedictine monastery of Saint-Cyran (1620) and spiritual director of Port-Royal (1636), a convent where Antoine Le Maistre (1608–1658) became the first of the *solitaires* (1637). Saint-Cyran, as Du Vergier came to be called, offended Cardinal Richelieu (Armand-Jean du Plessis; cardinal, 1622–1642), chief minister of Louis XIII (r. 1610–1643), by objecting to French foreign policy: cooperation with Protestants in the Thirty Years' War (1618–1648) and war with Catholic Spain (1635–1659). Richelieu imprisoned him in 1638 on charges of holding a penitential theology contrary to the Council of Trent. Saint-Cyran commended his young pupils to the *solitaires*, who gathered them into "Little Schools" attended by individuals such as the writer Jean Racine (1639–1699).

The charge of heresy was unfounded. Saint-Cyran's letters from prison established the Jansenist position on penitential discipline: true contrition (sorrow for sin and desire for amendment of life based on love of God) as opposed to attrition (regret caused by fear of God's punishment). Jansenists also espoused abstinence from the Eucharist either to move sinners to repentance or as public penance.

After Richelieu died, Saint-Cyran was released (1643), though he died within the year. By then he had won adherents among important Parisian families, nobility of the robe, and members of the French courts of justice (the parlements). He had also befriended Pierre de Bérulle (1575–1629), cardinal and founder of the French Oratory (1611) for secular priests, some of whom became Jansenist.

Nicolas Cornet (1572–1663), syndic of the Faculty of Theology of Paris, identified as heretical several propositions attributed to the *Augustinus*, five of which Pope Innocent X (r. 1644–1655) condemned in 1653. The next year the Jansenist Antoine Arnauld (1612–1694) denied that the propositions were in the *Augustinus*. In 1655 Innocent declared they were but did so under pressure from Cardinal

Jules Mazarin (r. 1641–1661), successor to Richelieu. Mazarin opposed the Jansenists, who had associated with leaders of the Fronde, an aristocratic rebellion against royal authority (1648–1652).

In 1655 Arnauld defended a duke whom a Molinist priest threatened with refusal of the sacraments because of Jansenist sympathies. Arnauld lost his post at the Faculty of Theology (1656) despite the *Lettres provinciales* (1656–1657) of Blaise Pascal (1623–1662), which defended Jansenism against the Jesuits. The Assembly of Clergy in 1657 and Pope Alexander VII (r. 1655–1667) in 1665 imposed signature on clergy of formulas condemning Jansenism; some refused. Mazarin closed the "Little Schools" in 1659.

The Peace of the Church under Clement X (1670–1676) brought respite, though persecution recommenced in 1679. Arnauld went into exile in Brussels. In 1709 Louis XIV (1638–1715) dispersed the nuns and razed Port-Royal, exhuming the bones of those buried there. In 1713 Pope Clement XI's bull *Unigenitus* condemned the 101 propositions from *Réflexions morales* (Moral Reflections; 1695) by Arnauld's friend the Oratorian Pasquier Quesnel (1634–1719). In the Netherlands a Jansenist church grew up around the exiled Arnauld and Quesnel. Jansenism broadened to include diverse persons opposed to the Jesuits and contributed to the condemnation of the Jesuits by the Parlement of Paris (1762) and their expulsion from France.

BIBLIOGRAPHY

Primary Sources

Du Vergier de Hauranne, Jean. *Lettres inédites de Jean Du Vergier de Hauranne, Abbé de Saint-Cyran: Le manuscrit de Munich (Cod. Gall. 691) et La vie d'Abraham, édités avec notes et commentaires.* Edited by Anne Barnes. Les origines du jansénisme, vol. 4. Paris, 1962. The correspondence of Jean Du Vergier de Hauranne, the abbot of Saint-Cyran, friend of Jansenius and leader of the movement in France.

Jansenius, Cornelius. *Cornelii Iansenii Episcopi Iprensis Augustinus cum duplici indice Rerum et S. Scriptura.* Louvain, 1640; reprint, Frankfurt a.M., 1964. A facsimile edition of Jansenius's great posthumous work on Augustine and Pelagian errors. Three vols. in one.

Pascal, Blaise. *Pascal: The Provincial Letters.* Translated by A. J. Krailsheimer. Baltimore, 1967. A translation of Pascal's letters in defense of Antoine Arnauld and Jansenism.

Secondary Sources

Arnauld d'Andilly, Robert. *Arnauld d'Andilly, Défenseur de Port-Royal, 1654–1659: Sa correspondance inédite avec la Cour conservée dans les Archives du Ministère des affaires étrangères.* Edited by P. Jansen. Paris, 1973. The correspondence of the Jansenist Robert Arnauld d'Andilly, brother of Antoine and Angelique Arnauld, with the court, some of it with Cardinal Mazarin.

Ceyssens, Lucianus. *Jansenistica.* Vols. 1–2, *Studiën in verband met de Geschiedenis van het Jansenisme.* Vols. 3–4. *Études relatives à l'histoire du jansénisme.* Mechelen, Belgium, 1962.

———. *Jansenistica Minora.* 13 vols. Mechelen, Belgium, 1951–1979. Extracts and articles on Jansenism.

Orcibal, Jean. *Les origines du jansénisme.* Vol. 1, *Correspondance de Jansénius.* Louvain, 1947. Jansenius's correspondence.

———. *Les origines du jansénisme.* Vols. 2–3, *Jean Du Vergier de Hauranne, Abbé de Saint-Cyran et son temps, 1581–1638.* Louvain, 1947–1948. Biography of Jean Du Vergier de Hauranne, Abbot of Saint-Cyran.

———. *Jansénius d'Ypres, 1585–1638.* Paris, 1989. Biography of Jansenius in French.

Parish, Richard. *Pascal's Lettres Provinciales: A Study in Polemic.* Oxford, 1989. An analysis of the lines of argument in Pascal's *Provincial Letters.*

Sedgwick, Alexander. *Jansenism in Seventeenth-Century France: Voices from the Wilderness.* Charlottesville, Va., 1977. A clear, sympathetic description of early French Jansenism with particular attention to the contribution of Port Royal, the Abbot of Saint-Cyran, the Arnauld family, and the *solitaires.*

Van Kley, Dale. *The Jansenists and the Expulsion of the Jesuits from France, 1757–1765.* New Haven, 1975. Chapter one is an excellent introduction to Jansenism.

Jeannine E. Olson

JEANNE OF NAVARRE (Fr., Jeanne d'Albret; 1528–1572), queen of Navarre. Her ancestry largely determined her character and career. Her father, Henry d'Albret, inherited the rump of the medieval kingdom of Navarre left on the northern side of the Pyrenees after the conquest of the southern part by Ferdinand of Aragon in 1512. The reconquest of the lost part was d'Albret's lifelong obsession. He insisted on the imaginary title "king of Navarre"—his real possessions being the remnant, Basse-Navarre, and the *vicomté* of Béarn. This all-consuming ambition caused acute friction with Francis I, who did not consider the settlement of the "Navarre question" advantageous for French foreign policy. D'Albret's marriage to the king's sister, Marguerite d'Angoulême, admired patroness of humanist reformers throughout Europe, was ill-starred from the start. Repeatedly victimized by both men, she always supported her adored brother in the end.

The only child of this mismatch, Jeanne had infrequent and strictly formal contacts with both parents during childhood, which she spent in Normandy with a governess. While sources are scarce, the few known facts shed light on her later life and her place in history: her health was poor (she died of tuberculosis at forty-four), and she was educated by an undistinguished humanist, Nicolas Bourbon, whose unorthodox religious ideas probably stemmed from several years in the service of Anne Boleyn. She displayed an intransigent, imperious temperament in every relationship from infancy, manifested most conspicuously in a passion for independence for herself and also—like her father—for her kingdom.

In 1540 Jeanne became a pawn in international diplomacy. Francis I's insistence on marrying her to the duke of Cleves to reinforce his anti-Habsburg policy in the Rhine Valley was unalterably opposed by her father, initially with Marguerite's cooperation until she caved in under the king's pressure. Jeanne protested against the alliance from start to finish (1542–1546), sometimes in the face of life-threatening intimidation. The twelve-year-old defied her omnipotent uncle as no other subject ever did, and survived only when a shift in his foreign policy allowed her to escape. What politics can do, politics can undo. For the rest of her life Jeanne's actions were in large part motivated by "accounts to settle" with the Crown, with the pope, with her unreliable husband, and ultimately with her rebellious subjects.

In 1548 she married Antoine of Bourbon, with whom she was infatuated, over strenuous objections by parents and uncle. Antoine had one indisputable asset: his status as first prince of the blood, in line for the French throne after the reigning Valois. This advantage was soon cancelled out, however, by his slippery, opportunistic character. His only consistency lay in the pursuit of the Navarre fantasy—imitating his father-in-law.

When the French Reformation was taking shape (1555–1560), Antoine was the despair of both the emerging Protestant movement and the pope and Philip II of Spain, who exploited his vanity and ambition in order to keep him in the Catholic fold. He was not successful in attempting to play them off against each other, for instance by attending both Mass and Calvinist services on Sundays. He was eventually captured by the Catholic camp (January 1562) and led the Catholic armies until his death later in the year.

By contrast, Jeanne made a public announcement of her conversion in December 1560 and remained a resolute Calvinist until her death. She imposed the reform on their young son, Henry of Navarre (later Henry IV), and established a Calvinist settlement in Béarn, in the Erastian style, calling herself *Dame souveraine* and recognizing no superior power but God's. This policy brought excommunication by the pope and her defense by the French Crown (1563) in the name of the Gallican Liberties, according to which the pope's authority in France was confined to doctrinal matters—such as interpretation of the sacraments—with all administrative matters in the hands of French authorities. Kings naturally claimed these powers, but there was great support for "episcopal" Gallicanism among French bishops and other influential bodies such as the parlements. Jeanne's conversion to the reform also provoked a rebellion of her Catholic subjects, a rebellion that was supported by the Crown in the Third War of Religion (1569–1570). For the first time the Protestants obtained a relatively favorable settlement (Peace of Saint-Germain), and as a consequence Jeanne in her last two years was able to share the leadership with Gaspard II de Coligny and Odet de Coligny, cardinal of Châtillon. Gaspard was commander in chief, Jeanne the political leader in the Huguenot stronghold and port city of La Rochelle, while the cardinal negotiated some support from Queen Elizabeth I until his death in 1571.

Jeanne's driving ambition was to secure the succession to the French throne for her son. Though a charismatic Huguenot leader, Henry was only nineteen years old and the target of every possible pressure and strategy to convert to Catholicism. Jeanne's greatest gamble was in abandoning her deep-seated opposition to his marriage to Marguerite of Valois, daughter of Henry II and Catherine de Médicis, *de facto* ruler of France for her weak son, Charles IX (1560–1574). Months of bitter confrontation between the two queens ended with Jeanne's acceptance in May 1572. She died a few weeks later, terminally ill and worn out. She was therefore spared the humiliation of the wedding and the tragedy of the Saint Bartholomew's Day Massacre, four days later (24 August 1572). Her worst fear—Henry's defection to Catholicism—was later realized (July 1593) when France was threatened with Spanish domination and his Catholic subjects would not accept him despite his indisputable legal claim. Jeanne's secular goal, the succession of the Bourbon line, was nevertheless attained, and every subsequent king of France has been her descendant. Despite the failure of the reform to prevail, Jeanne has a place in Reformation history because she was "queen of Huguenot France" in the years of its greatest power and influence.

BIBLIOGRAPHY

Bordenave, Nicolas de. *Histoire de Béarn et Navarre.* Edited by Pierre Raymond. Paris, 1873. Valuable because written by a person in Jeanne's employ; bears the marks of her style.

Dartigue, Charles. *Jean d'Albret et le Béarn.* Mont de Marsan, France, 1934. A major source of Jeanne's policies and administration.

Kingdon, Robert M. *Geneva and the Coming of the Wars of Religion in France.* Geneva, 1956.

———. *Geneva and the Consolidation of the French Protestant Movement.* Geneva, 1967.

Roelker, Nancy Lyman. *Queen of Navarre, Jeanne d'Albret, 1528–1572.* Cambridge, Mass., 1968. The only twentieth-century study; aims to give a balanced account of both historical role and life. Sources fall into three main areas: Jeanne's religious-political career on the national level, her role as administrator and ruler of Béarn and many fiefs held by the Crown, and her personal story.

———. "The Role of Noblewomen in the French Reformation." *Archive for Reformation History* 63 (1972), 168–195.

———. "The Appeal of Calvinism to French Noblewomen in the Sixteenth Century." *Journal of Interdisciplinary History* 2 (Spring 1972), 391–418.

Ruble, Alphonse de, ed. *Mémories et poésies de Jeanne d'Albret.* Paris, 1893.

Salefranque, Pierre de. "Histoire de l'Hérésie en Béarn et Navarre." *Bulletin de la societé des sciences, lettres et arts de Pau* (1921–1922).

Sutherland, N. M. *The Massacre of St. Bartholomew and the European Conflict, 1559–1572.* London, 1973. Major treatment of the diplomatic context.

———. *The Huguenot Struggle for Recognition.* New Haven, 1980. Valuable for establishing for the first time the texts and chronology of the Edicts of Pacification, previously confused and often contradictory.

NANCY LYMAN ROELKER

JESUITS. The Society of Jesus, a religious order of the Roman Catholic church founded by Ignatius Loyola and his companions, was officially inaugurated by the bull of Pope Paul III *Regimini militantis ecclesiae,* 27 September 1540.

While studying at the University of Paris (1528–1535), Ignatius had attracted six other students, who with him in 1534 pronounced vows of poverty and chastity and determined to travel to Palestine to convert the Muslims or, if they could not secure passage, to offer themselves to the pope for ministry wherever he saw fit.

In the environs of Venice as they later awaited passage, the companions (now ten) were ordained as priests and began to call their band *Compagnia di Gesù* (Lat., *Societas Jesu*) because they had no superior but Jesus. Since war continued to prevent their travel to Jerusalem, in 1539 they decided in Rome to found a new religious order dedicated "to the progress of souls in Christian life and doctrine and to the propagation of the faith," as the papal bull stated. They would accomplish these goals through ministries like preaching, guiding persons in Ignatius's *Ejercicios Espirituales* (Spiritual Exercises), teaching catechism, hearing confessions, and performing the spiritual and corporal works of mercy.

They envisaged an order dedicated largely to itinerant ministry after the model of Jesus' disciples and the evangelizing Paul. This vision induced them to preclude for their membership the recitation or chanting of the canonical hours in common, a practice many of their contemporaries considered the very essence of a religious order, and to stipulate for their members a special vow to obey the pope "concerning missions" because he presumably knew where the greatest pastoral need might be. Two reasons often alleged for the founding of the society—confuting Protestants and working for the reform of the Catholic church—were only incidental to its scope at this time.

From the beginning the Jesuits' pursuit of ministries, which in many ways was almost indistinguishable from the mendicant friars', was special because of the influence on them of Ignatius's *Exercises*. That book created for them in effect the new ministry of the "retreat," days or weeks spent apart in prayer, but it also imbued their other ministries with certain emphases, like the fostering of greater inwardness that paradoxically issued in a commitment to greater service in the world.

In 1548 the Jesuits entered a dramatically new phase when they opened their first school in Messina, Sicily. Until that time they had avoided permanent teaching assignments; but, with the success of Messina and other schools like it run in the humanistic mode, by 1560 they recognized such institutions as their primary ministry. They thus became the first teaching order in the Catholic church. Two decades later they operated some 150 schools, about 370 by 1615, and by the time the society was suppressed by papal edict in 1773 more than 800 around the globe.

Growth, Membership, Organization. In early 1541 the original companions elected Ignatius superior general for life. Unlike most other orders of men founded in the sixteenth century, the society expanded rapidly. When Ignatius died in 1556, it numbered about 1,000, about 3,500 ten years later, 5,000 by 1580, and 13,000 by 1615.

In the first decade the Jesuits drew their largest membership in Portugal and flourished there, mainly because of the unswerving friendship of King John III, the monarch also responsible for proposing to them their first evangelizing efforts outside Europe—the missions to India led by Francis Xavier, who arrived there in 1542, and to Brazil in 1549 led by Manuel de Nóbrega. They then recruited large numbers from other areas of Europe where they were active. Toward the end of the century, they began, under the influence of the farsighted Alessandro Valignano, to accept Japanese Christians into the society, but for the most part they refused entry to other non-Europeans in Brazil, India, and elsewhere overseas.

Although most of the members were priests or destined for the priesthood, laymen, known as "temporal coadjutors," constituted about twenty-five percent of the total membership. They were generally drawn from the artisan and landowning peasant classes and helped the organization as cooks, gardeners, masons, carpenters, and in other "temporalities."

Like the mendicant orders, the Society of Jesus was divided into administrative units called provinces. Twelve provinces had already formed when Ignatius died in 1556—Italy, Sicily, Upper Germany, Lower Germany, France, Aragon, Castile, Andalusia, Portugal, Brazil, India, and Ethiopia—but the last existed only on paper. Many more were to come. The distribution of manpower among the provinces was always uneven, with the heaviest concentrations in the Iberian and Italian peninsulas. Rome claimed disproportionately large numbers—close to ten percent in 1565—because it early became a training center for the order and was where some of the society's most characteristic institutions began and flourished.

The Jesuits departed from the mendicant tradition of governance by eliminating chapters held at regular and frequent intervals. Although broad policy was determined in the society by so-called general congregations, other decisions were made by superiors who, except for the superior general, were themselves appointed, not elected. The superior general was elected for life by a general congregation and was the executor of its policies and decrees.

The *Constitutionales* (Constitutions), a remarkably flexible instrument written by Ignatius and his secretary Juan Alonso de Polanco (1516–1576), were ratified by the first general congregation in 1558. To explain them to the already far-flung members of the society, in 1552–1553 Ignatius chose Jerónimo Nadal, whom he at the same time invested with almost plenipotentiary powers for these and subsequent journeys throughout Europe, a concession repeated for him by the next two generals—Diego Laínez (1558–1565) and Francis Borgia (1565–1572). Next to Ignatius,

Nadal was the person most responsible for how the Jesuits of the era understood their call and their mission.

Other regulatory documents received definitive formulation under Claudio Acquaviva, the fifth general (1581–1615). Particularly important was the *Ratio Studiorum* (1599), which codified many aspects of the Jesuits' educational enterprises. Ignatius's insistence on frequent correspondence between superiors and subjects also established a tradition that helped the Jesuits achieve a certain coherence of outlook, and it provided an immense and invaluable resource for future historians of the era. Much of it is now published in the approximately 125 volumes of the *Monumenta Historica Societatis Jesu* and in some other collections.

The society nonetheless experienced serious internal crises. After the death of Ignatius, Nicolás de Bobadilla, one of the original companions from Paris, challenged the direction Ignatius had given the society. Although Bobadilla was supported by Pope Paul IV (r. 1555–1559), his efforts did not succeed. More protracted was the challenge to Acquaviva from a well-organized faction of Spanish Jesuits, which was finally resolved in Acquaviva's favor by the fifth general congregation in 1593.

Religious and Theological Culture. Indisputably basic to the Jesuits' religious self-understanding was Ignatius's book of *Spiritual Exercises,* which every member had to make in its thirty-day entirety shortly after entrance and which by 1570 most Jesuits repeated in abbreviated form every year. From the first years of the society, the Jesuits also guided in the *Exercises* women and men from almost every social strata, who undertook them in a variety of forms and with varying degrees of intensity.

The Jesuits were assiduous preachers who prided themselves on preaching as often in the open air as in church. Taking their example from Ignatius, who taught catechism as early as 1525 in Alcalá de Henares, the Jesuits assigned catechization a high priority for themselves and developed techniques of putting it to tunes and of having children teach other children. They were from the beginning proponents of frequent reception of the Eucharist (about once a week), because they thought it was the practice of the early church.

Among the sacraments they gave special attention to penance. Thus they began to lecture on "cases of conscience" for clerical and lay audiences. By 1563 they made the cases into a regular course in the theological curriculum at their Collegio Romano, a significant step in the development of casuistry as well as of a more pastoral orientation for the traditional theological program. By the end of the century the Jesuits were well on the way to widespread adoption of the system of moral reasoning known as probabilism, satirized by Blaise Pascal in his *Lettres provinciales* (Provincial Letters; 1656–1667).

Under the inspiration of the spiritual and corporal works of mercy that they inculcated in their catechism, the Jesuits founded or inspired a number of works of social assistance, such as orphanages and women's asylums. Almost all these institutions were turned over to lay confraternities for their management and governance. Particularly innovative was the Casa santa Marta founded in Rome in 1543 to provide prostitutes a way out of their profession through entrance into a convent, into service as a domestic, or, most frequently, through marriage. In 1563 at the Collegio Romano, the Jesuits founded a confraternity for their students that developed into their influential Marian congregations around the world.

The decision after 1548 to undertake education on a large scale had an immense impact on how the Jesuits conceived of themselves and operated. It meant, most obviously, that their earlier ideal of being itinerant preachers had to coexist with the reality of being resident schoolmasters. But it also meant a new relationship to culture, for they now had to learn many basically secular subjects so as to become skilled professionals in teaching them. This development largely explains why and how the society began to earn its reputation for learning. Other orders had teachers and erudite members, but in the Jesuits learning became systemic in ways and to a degree different from the others.

Because of their schools the Jesuits were deeply affected by humanism, more perhaps in its literary and rhetorical aspects than in historico-critical aspects. The training of the original companions at Paris virtually assured that Scholasticism would play a major role in the theological education they provided for their own members and others, even though they were critical of it for being too cerebral. During the lifetime of Ignatius they adopted Thomas Aquinas as their official master in theology.

That choice confirmed and promoted their penchant for seeing grace as perfecting nature and oriented them toward opposing more Augustinian viewpoints. Although the Jesuits did not in their early decades have any doctrines that they professedly called their own, this one in effect pervaded their approach to almost all practical and theoretical issues and was implicit and explicit in their *Constitutions.* In Louvain as early as 1570, for instance, both Leonard Lessius and Roberto Bellarmino found themselves at odds with the teaching of Michel de Bay, the forerunner of Jansenism.

By the later decades of the century, the Jesuits had eclipsed the other orders in producing leading Catholic theologians—men like Roberto Bellarmino, Francisco de Toledo, Luis de Molina, and Francisco Suárez. Jesuits also published important works in other areas of learning, like José de Acosta's *Historia natural y moral de las Indias* (1590) and Juan de Mariana's *Historia general de España* (1601) and his controversial *De rege et regis institutione* (1599). They established in their schools a strong tradition in drama and music and a similarly strong tradition in mathematics and the sciences through persons like Cristoph Clavius, who helped design the Gregorian calendar (1582).

Reformation and Reform. In 1550 the Jesuits officially added "defense of the faith" to the stated purposes of their order, an indication of their growing commitment to opposing the Reformation and perhaps especially to strengthening wavering Catholics. In Spain, Portugal, and Italy they supported the many ecclesiastical tribunals dealing with persons accused of heresy, although in principle they preferred to use directly pastoral means whenever possible.

In the 1550s and 1560s their most concerted efforts to deal with the impact of Protestantism took place in German-speaking lands, where they were warmly supported by rulers like Emperor Ferdinand I (r. 1558–1564) and Duke Albert V of Bavaria (r. 1550–1579). Leading the Jesuits in these territories was Peter Canisius, to whom was due in considerable measure Catholic success in south German lands.

By 1555 there were about fifty Jesuits in the empire—some fifteen in Cologne and practically all the rest in Vienna. By the turn of the century, there were about seventeen hundred. In efforts to stabilize or win back Catholics, they employed the same ministries as elsewhere but gave them a more apologetic and polemical orientation. A few Jesuits used their role as confessor to monarchs to influence politics, as did Wilhelm Lamormaini with Ferdinand II. The backbone of their efforts, however, was formal education.

In 1552 at Vienna they established their first school in German lands, where by 1600 the number of schools had grown to forty. The enrollments in these basically secondary institutions were often large (700–1,000 students). Besides teaching in their own institutions, Jesuits soon came to hold positions on theological faculties of universities like Cologne, Trier, and Mainz. By the later part of the century, the Collegio Germanico, which Ignatius established in Rome in 1552 for the training of diocesan clergy for northern Europe, began to bear fruit, and from the alumni came a number of especially well-trained pastors and theologians. In 1555 at the Collegio Romano they initiated a course in controversialist theology for precisely these students.

In 1556 the Jesuits opened their school in Prague, where they accepted a significant number of Hussite and Lutheran students. In the 1570s and 1580s Antonio Possevino led bold, important, but ultimately unsuccessful ventures in high-level conversion in Sweden and Russia.

The Jesuits entered the Polish-Lithuanian commonwealth in 1564 at a critical moment in the religious struggle there. Within ten years they were operating five schools and were able to establish a province, in which many of the most effective Jesuits came from Protestant families. Piotr Skarga's *Żywoty Świętych, starego i nowego Zakonu* (Lives of the Saints from the Old and New Testaments; 1579) and Jakób Wujek z Wagrowca's translation of the Bible (1593–1599) were powerful instruments for the Catholic cause that became classics of Polish literature.

In 1580 Robert Parsons and Edmund Campion entered England. The latter was hanged, drawn, and quartered within a year. The English mission became embroiled in tactical and political disputes with other Catholics, one of which evolved in the early seventeenth century into the theological controversy between Bellarmino and King James I on the divine right of kings. Parsons perhaps contributed most effectively to the Catholic cause by founding at the end of the century the college Saint-Omer in Flanders for the sons of recusants. In 1623 the English province was established with 213 members.

Jesuits tried to answer Protestantism on an intellectual level; some of them, like Canisius, Laínez, and especially Alfonso Salmerón, had precise and wide-ranging knowledge of Protestant authors. They read them, however, with polemical intent. As they attempted to refute the Protestants, they perforce gave an emphasis to certain Catholic teachings—for example, the real presence and papal primacy—that contributed to the imbalance in confessional statements of faith typical of the era.

They also began to reinterpret elements in their own origins so as to make them into apologetic or anti-Protestant statements, like their promotion of more frequent Communion or their vow to obey the pope concerning missions. In his travels around Europe after Ignatius died, Nadal loved to contrast Ignatius with Luther, originating a diptych that became standard for historians of every persuasion.

Laínez and Salmerón were active at the Council of Trent in all three of its phases (1545–1563), where they and a few Jesuit colleagues made substantial and occasionally controversial contributions. When the council ended, Canisius carried its decrees to the German bishops, and Jesuits elsewhere in Europe tried to aid bishops in their efforts to reform their dioceses and implement Trent.

Important though these activities were in some cases, the Jesuits correctly saw the reforming decrees of Trent as dealing almost exclusively with the duties and powers of bishops and pastors, offices that their *Constitutions* forbade to them. The Jesuits' great impact on early modern Catholicism came, therefore, through their working with the Catholic population in institutions and activities outside the parish structure and in their missions outside Europe, which were matters of little interest at Trent. It is thus perhaps misleading to call them reformers, for they did not directly engage in efforts to change canonical discipline or the mode of operation of ecclesiastical offices.

Their schools inaugurated, however, a new era in how the church related to formal education, and they thereby set a pattern that a large number of orders of men and women would follow. Their emphasis on frequent confession and Communion helped change patterns of piety in many places. Their practice of guiding others in the *Exercises* helped move the practice of spiritual counseling to a new level. Their adamant refusal to accept any direct recompense for the ministries, especially for hearing confessions, was a silent but powerful word to other clergy against exacting fees for their ministrations. They gave to the clergy an example of energetic, imaginative, learned ministry.

Ignatius instructed the Jesuits many times to avoid controversy with fellow Catholics, but, given the contentiousness of the age and the roles Jesuits played, they could hardly achieve that ideal. Moreover, aspects of the Jesuits' way of life itself offended some Catholics and made them suspicious—for instance, not chanting the hours, reliance on inner inspiration through "discernment of spirits," a special vow to obey the pope, and a policy in Spain and Portugal of receiving into the society persons of Jewish ancestry.

In 1554 the Faculty of Theology of Paris condemned the society as "a danger to the faith, a disturber of the peace of the church, destructive of monastic life, and destined to cause havoc rather than edification." Juan Martínez Guijeño (known as Silíceo), archbishop of Toledo and primate of Spain, saw to the condemnation of parts of the *Exercises* as heretical in 1553. Melchior Cano, a Dominican theologian, raged against the Jesuits as barely distinguishable from the Alumbrados and Lutherans. The antagonism between Spanish Jesuits and Dominicans erupted on the theological level later in the bitter controversy over grace (the so-called Molinists [Jesuits] and Banesians [Dominicans]).

The Jesuits continued to send large numbers to overseas missions, where they gradually developed policies of evangelization that distinguished them from the mendicants and led to conflict with them. This distinction was most evident in the program of accommodation to Chinese customs, rites, and mentality initiated in 1583 by Matteo Ricci and his colleagues that won them access to the Chinese elite until the experiment was condemned by the Holy See in a series of documents (1704–1742).

Jesuit Accomplishments. The Jesuits gave across-the-board evidence of greater vigor and accomplishment than any other order, old or new, in the sixteenth century. Their accomplishments resulted from a convergence of many factors. The society was, for instance, an international body from the beginning, desirous of growth and eager to be on the move. The original members had excellent educations and wished to continue this tradition for new recruits. In the *Exercises* and the *Constitutions,* the Jesuits had unique means for fostering a cohesion that still prized flexibility. The schools were a dazzlingly new instrument of ministry that gave Jesuits entry into families and civic life in ways that churches did not and helped them attract intellectually gifted novices. The Jesuits were quite modern in their use of edifying letters, especially from missionaries like Xavier, as means of advertising their goals, activities, and successes. In Ignatius they had a cool-headed leader who lived long enough after the founding to provide continuity and stability. He also chose good lieutenants and then delegated authority with an open hand.

[*See also* Ignatius Loyola *and* Laínez, Diego.]

BIBLIOGRAPHY

Aldama, Antonio M. de. *The Formula of the Institute: Notes for a Commentary.* Translated by Ignacio Echániz. Saint Louis, 1990. Brief, lucid, authoritative commentary on the two papal bulls approving the order, 1540 and 1550; essential reading.

Bangert, William V. *A History of the Society of Jesus.* 2d ed., rev. & corr. Saint Louis, 1986. Comprehensive and factually reliable.

Bireley, Robert. *Religion and Politics in the Age of the Counterreformation: Emperor Ferdinand II, William Lamormaini, S.J., and the Formation of Imperial Policy.* Chapel Hill, N.C., 1981. Study of the political impact of Lamormaini, one of the most famous Jesuit confessors.

Brodrick, James. *Saint Peter Canisius* (1935). Reprint Chicago, 1962. Still the standard study.

Châtellier, Louis. *The Europe of the Devout: The Catholic Reformation and the Formation of a New Society.* Translated by Jean Birrell. Cambridge, 1989. Best study of the Jesuits' "Marian Congregations."

Codina Mir, Gabriel. *Aux sources de la pédagogie des jésuites: Le "Modus parisiensis."* Rome, 1968. Fundamental for the origins and development of the Jesuits's educational style.

Duhr, Bernhard. *Geschichte der Jesuiten in den Ländern deutscher Zunge.* 4 vols. Freiburg and Regensburg, 1907–1928. Outdated but comprehensive and basic.

Guibert, Joseph de. *The Jesuits, Their Spiritual Doctrine and Practice: A Historical Study.* Translated by William J. Young. Reprint, Chicago, 1972. Narrow in methodology but useful as a repertoire of issues, authors, and works.

Harris, Steven J. "Transposing the Merton Thesis: Apostolic Spirituality and the establishment of the Jesuit Scientific Tradition." *Science in Context* 3 (1989), 29–65. Best overview, with prosopography and bibliography.

Hengst, Karl. *Jesuiten an Universitäten und Jesuitenuniversitäten: Zur Geschichte der Universitäten in der Oberdeutschen und Rheinischen Provinz der Gesellschaft Jesu im Zeitalter der konfessionellen Auseinandersetzung.* Paderborn, 1981. Study of an aspect of Jesuit activity generally ignored by scholars.

Martin, A. Lynn. *The Jesuit Mind: The Mentality of an Elite in Early Modern France.* Ithaca, N.Y., 1988. Study of Jesuit attitudes on a variety of issues as reflected in their correspondence.

Martín, Luis. *The Intellectual Conquest of Peru: The Jesuit College of San Pablo, 1568–1768.* New York, 1968. Case-study of Jesuit missionary and educational methods.

O'Malley, John W. *The First Jesuits.* Cambridge, Mass., 1993. Treats practically every aspect of Jesuit activity in the period 1540–65, with extensive bibliographical citations.

Polgár, László, ed. *Bibliographie sur l'histoire de la Compagnie de Jésus, 1901–1980.* 3 vols. Rome, 1981–1990. Indispensable guide to secondary literature, whose continuation since 1980 can regularly be found in the *Archivum Historicum Societatis Jesu.*

Scaduto, Mario. *L'epoca di Giacomo Laínez, 1556–1565.* 2 vols. Rome, 1964–1974. Exhaustive study of the Jesuits in Italy under the successor of Ignatius as general.

Scaglione, Aldo. *The Liberal Arts and the Jesuit College System.* Amsterdam and Philadelphia, 1986. Short but broad presentation of important aspects of Jesuit schools in France and Italy.

Schütte, Josef Franz. *Valignano's Mission Principles for Japan.* 2 vols. Translated by John J. Coyne. Saint Louis, 1980–85. Essential for understanding Jesuit evangelization in Japan and China.

Sommervogel, Carlos, et al., eds. *Bibliothèque de la Compagnie de Jésus.* 12 vols., 2d ed. Brussels, 1890–1960. Standard listing of works written by Jesuits.

Valentin, Jean-Marie. *Le Théâtre des Jésuites dans les pays de langue allemand, 1554–1680: Salut des âmes et ordres des cités.* 3 vols. Bern,

Frankfurt, and Las Vegas, 1978. Study of the theater that reveals deeper religious and cultural attitudes.

Wittkower, Rudolf, and Irma Jaffe, eds. *Baroque Art: The Jesuit Contribution.* New York, 1972. General, but a good introduction to the issues.

JOHN W. O'MALLEY

JEWEL, John (1522–1571), English prelate, intellectually the most powerful of the original bishops and founding fathers of the reformed Church of England as settled by Elizabeth I. With his fellow Devonian Richard Hooker, whose early career he launched, he is considered one of its two principal apologists.

Jewel was reared in a substantial farmhouse on the North Devon coast, whence he was recruited to Oxford, first to Merton College and then to Corpus Christi. At Merton he formed one of the great friendships of his life with John Parkhurst, an older man and destined to be an episcopal colleague but no match for Jewel intellectually or managerially. Corpus Christi was a leading center of English humanism, and Jewel developed as an accomplished humanist and rhetorician, a master of the art of memory and of irony: witness a juvenile *Oratio contra Rhetoricam* in the style of Desiderius Erasmus and Thomas More. In the reign of Edward VI, the second great influence on Jewel's life arrived in Oxford in the person of Peter Martyr Vermigli, who gathered around him a small circle of devotees in a university still firmly attached to the old ways in religion.

With Mary Tudor's accession, Jewel was deprived of his fellowship but at first remained in Oxford, where he acted as a notary at the trial of Thomas Cranmer and Nicholas Ridley and, to his shame, subscribed to Catholic articles. He left for the Continent only after a visit to Parkhurst's country rectory found the rector no longer at home. Jewel settled first in Strasbourg, in the company of Vermigli, but was involved, together with other leading Strasbourg cadres, in the troubles of the congregation at Frankfurt. When the hardline Lutheranism of Strasbourg drove Vermigli to Zurich, Jewel followed him. It is possible, but by no means certain, that at some point in his exile he spent a year at Padua. With Mary's death, the Strasburghers hurried home, but the more scholarly and detached Zurich group took their time.

Back in England, Jewel's letters to Vermigli and other Continental friends report on the uncertain beginnings of the new Protestant dispensation under the so far untried Elizabeth: the parliamentary settlement, the Westminster Disputation with the Catholics, the Royal Visitation of 1559 (which found Jewel back in the West Country), the confrontation between the new episcopate and a queen too much addicted to Catholic imagery. Jewel was appointed bishop of Salisbury, where he would prove an exemplary, almost permanently resident diocesan who kept regular visitations. He lived in style, as we learn from the young Swiss tourist Christopher Froschover, who enjoyed the bishop's hospitality, hunted his deer, and was taken to see Stonehenge.

But before reaching his diocese, Jewel became involved in controversies that were the principal labor of the last ten years of his life and may even have precipitated his premature demise. On 26 November 1559 he preached a sermon at Paul's Cross, later repeated at Court, in which he challenged the Catholics to prove that various doctrines and practices, and in particular five principal points of Catholicism, had been known in the first six Christian centuries. It was a clever tactic to shift the onus of proof from antiquity to the Catholic side of the argument, one that placed Jewel, a learned patristic scholar, in an advantageous position. In 1562 Jewel published a semiofficial *Apologia Ecclesiae Anglicanae,* which was at once translated into excellent English by the mother of Francis Bacon. After some preliminary skirmishes, Jewel's challenge evoked a worthy *Answer* in 1564 from Thomas Harding, Jewel's Oxford contemporary and a canon of his cathedral in Salisbury, who had withdrawn into exile in Louvain. Jewel wrote a massive *Replie unto M. Hardinges answer* (1565). But by now Harding had published his *Confutation* of Jewel's *Apologia.* Jewel's voluminous *Defence of the apologie* (1567) was called by R. W. Dixon "one of the most complete pieces of controversy in the world," and these exchanges in their entirety have been called the "Great Controversy." Two of the concluding sentences of Jewel's *Defence* can stand for the whole as examples of the polite, if wounding, urbanity of Jewel's controversial decorum: "If ye shall happen to write hereafter, send us fewer words and more learning. . . . Will ye, nill ye, the truth will conquer."

Jewel's anti-Catholic polemic was sufficient for its time, although by the later sixteenth century the intensification of the Counter-Reformation and the appearance of more formidable antagonists, such as Cardinal Roberto Bellarmino, would require the Church of England and its universities to respond with a fortified controversial athleticism. But this was not the only enemy. In the last year of Jewel's life, the Puritan attack on the Elizabethan Settlement began to touch fundamentals. It is often suggested that if the bishop of Salisbury had not died in September 1571, he rather than John Whitgift might have written another series of answers and defenses, this time to the presbyterian *Admonition to the Parliament* (1572), perhaps making a difference to history.

The title of Jewel's *Apologia Ecclesiae Anglicanae* was rendered into English by Lady Ann Bacon as *An apologie or answer in defence of the Church of England*; and that is what it was. But the phrase can also be understood as an apology of (or by) the Church of England on behalf of a faith that could be described as Protestant or Catholic (claiming antiquity and universality) but not "Anglican." Only at the risk of anachronism can Jewel be called an Anglican, constructing a defense of something called "Anglicanism." This anachronistic error confuses our view not only of Jewel's position on the confessional spectrum but of the early Elizabethan church establishment more widely. A lengthy Latin biography by his contemporary Laurence Humphrey, abbreviated in English in the early seventeenth century by Daniel Featley, did not misrepresent Jewel as a Protestant churchman. This *Vita* (1573), together with the publication in 1609 of the *Works*, was a major source of inspiration for the evangelical episcopate of the Jacobean church.

BIBLIOGRAPHY

Primary Sources

Ayre, J., ed. *Works of John Jewel, Bishop of Salisbury*. 4 vols. Parker Society. Cambridge, 1850. Contains the entire works, together with letters and miscellaneous pieces.

Booty, John E., ed. *An Apology of the Church of England by John Jewel.* Folger Documents of Tudor and Stuart Civilization. Ithaca, N.Y., 1963.

Secondary Sources

Booty, John E. *John Jewel as Apologist for the Church of England.* London, 1963. Jewel seen from the point of view of a leading scholar of the Protestant Episcopal church as the author of an admirable and watertight defense of the Anglican church.

Creighton, Mandell. "John Jewel." In *Dictionary of National Biography*. London, 1892. An admirable and only slightly dated account by a major church historian and bishop.

Cross, Claire. *The Royal Supremacy in the Elizabethan Church.* London, 1969. Includes a valuable collection of texts and documents, including passages from Jewel.

Dixon, R. W. *History of the Church of England from the Abolition of the Roman Jurisdiction* (1884–1902). 6 vols. Reprint, Farnborough, 1970. Vols. 5 and 6 cover the Elizabethan church to 1570. A monument of impeccable Victorian scholarship.

Fincham, Kenneth. *Prelate as Pastor: The Episcopate of James I.* Oxford, 1990. Jewel's legacy.

Haugaard, William P. *Elizabeth and the English Reformation.* Cambridge, 1968. A modern, scholarly account of the laying of the foundations of the Elizabethan church.

Southgate, W. M. *John Jewel and the Problem of Doctrinal Authority.* Cambridge, Mass., 1962. A learned and elegant if overly "Anglican" account of Jewel and his apologetics.

PATRICK COLLINSON

JEWS.

On the eve of the Reformation, Jews in Christian Europe were divided into two main groups—the Spanish-speaking Sephardim in the Mediterranean world and the German-speaking Ashkenazim, mainly in northern Europe. The expulsion of Jews from Spain in 1492 was a crucial event because it dispersed the largest Jewish community in Christian Europe throughout the Mediterranean. Sephardic Jews resettled in Portugal, north Africa, central and southern Italy, Greece, Asia Minor, and Palestine. A similar migration, albeit on a much smaller scale, was taking place among the Ashkenazim as rising persecutions in the Holy Roman Empire during the last decades of the fifteenth century drove many Jews to seek refuge in northern Italy and east-central Europe.

Although European Jews spoke different languages in daily life and observed slightly different liturgies in their communities, they were unified internally through adherence to their ancestral religion, Judaism, and its language, Hebrew. The common experience of persecution and the hope for messianic deliverance further strengthened the consciousness of being the chosen people. A vernacular popular culture, represented by festivals and secular texts (including translations from Christian vernacular literature), existed alongside the Hebrew religious culture of the rabbis.

In the generations before the Reformation, the Jewish communities of Europe experienced a renewed wave of persecutions, owing largely to a heightened sense of Christian piety coupled with a new anxiety about the threat of the Muslim Ottoman Turks. Between the 1390s and their expulsion in 1492, Spanish Jews suffered campaigns of forced conversion, sporadic violence, and everyday discrimination. Even Jewish converts, labeled *Conversos*, or New Christians, could not escape the vigilance of their neighbors and the Spanish church. Many were prosecuted for real or alleged relapses into Judaism, punishable in extreme cases with the death sentence. A similar intolerance characterized the relationship between Christians and Jews in German-speaking central Europe. Raised again and again were the long-standing accusations that the Jews practiced usury (lending money to Christians at exorbitant rates), desecrated the Host (the body of Christ), blasphemed against Jesus and the Virgin Mary in their liturgies, and kidnapped and murdered Christian children for Passover.

The accusation of usury was based on the economic exclusion of Jews from all Christian professions, which included all manners of handicraft and most of commerce. The permission to charge higher interest rates, granted readily by many Christian princes to Jews, actually disguised a hidden tax, since Jewish communities were obliged to pay considerable sums for protection and toleration. Jewish credit often took the form of pawnbroking, in which a commodity was deposited as a pledge for the loan. Usury, therefore, operated in a real sense as retail trade. Jewish moneylenders usually doubled as traders, offering various consumer wares at discounted prices to Christian buyers. Their competition aroused the hatred of Christian artisans, whose anti-Jewish rhetoric used the language of religious difference to express an underlying economic and social resentment. Translated into religious terms (with reference to the prohibition of usury in the Bible and in canon law), the polemic against usury inflamed anti-Jewish hatred on the eve of the Reformation; it also became commonplace in the early Reformation rhetoric against monopolies and moneylending. That the rhetoric against Jewish usury represented a theme that ran through the years before and during the Reformation movement is perhaps best reflected in the reformer Balthasar Hubmaier (1480/85–1528), as discussed below.

A far more pernicious charge against the Jews was the accusation of Host desecration. Stories of eucharistic abuse multiplied after the thirteenth century, when the church affirmed the doctrine of transubstantiation. Jews, along with women and occasionally clerics, were represented as perpetrators of this sacrilege. The later Middle Ages witnessed the height of Host-desecration accusations against Jews, although several Jews in Brandenburg were convicted and executed on a similar charge as late as 1510. With the coming of the Reformation, Host desecrations attributed to Jews effectively disappeared in Christian Europe: not only was this anti-Jewish belief replaced by the bitter controversies among Christians over the nature of the Eucharist, but Catholic polemicists turned their hatred instead to Calvinists as desecraters of the Host.

Yet another accusation against the Jews was the blood libel. The belief that Jews kidnapped and killed Christian children for their blood during Passover dated from the twelfth century. From time to time during the late Middle Ages, Jewish communities came under the suspicion of ritual murder, a widespread Christian belief that arose out of a mixture of religious ignorance, fear of Jewish magic, and anxiety about child murders. In the two generations leading up to the Reformation, ritual-murder accusations reached a new crescendo. The most notorious ritual-murder trial took place in 1475 in Trent, an episcopal city in northern Italy with an important German minority. Discovery of the body of a missing Christian boy, Simon, led to the summary arrest, torture, and execution of most men of the Jewish community. The subsequent campaign to win papal recognition of sainthood for the alleged boy martyr spread the news of this imagined Jewish atrocity to many parts of Europe. In the intense debates about Jewish conversion during the early years of the Reformation, the subject of ritual murder featured prominently, with some reformers, such as Martin Luther, affirming its historical veracity, while others, such as the Nuremberg reformer Andreas Osiander, condemning the blood libel and past persecutions of Jews.

The half century leading up to the Reformation brought important changes in Jewish-Christian relations. Whereas the medieval church had long been opposed to the synagogue, the second half of the fifteenth century witnessed a new Christian interest in Hebrew learning. There were three major reasons for the rise of Christian Hebraica, which can be summarized by the words conversion, mysticism, and biblicism. Conversion referred to the renewed Christian missionary efforts during the late fifteenth century to convert Jews, a movement spearheaded by the mendicant orders and a small number of Jewish converts. Mysticism reflected the Christian fascination with the Cabbala (or *Kabalah*, a word meaning "tradition"), an intellectual and interpretive tradition in medieval Judaism combining numerological and allegorical readings of Hebrew sacred texts. Biblicism developed in the context of the humanist revival of ancient texts, which led to efforts to emend the Latin Vulgate Bible with the aid of the original Hebrew, Aramaic, and Greek texts. These three themes in Christian Hebraica shaped Christian-Jewish relationships from the late Middle Ages to the Reformation; they represented a historical continuity unbroken by the division within Christianity as a result of the Reformation.

In central Europe, the heartland of the Reformation, Christian missions among Jews intensified during the last decades of the fifteenth century. The most prominent missionary was the German Dominican Peter Schwarz (Niger), who studied Hebrew in Spain and in 1474 engaged the leading rabbis of the Regensburg community in a religious disputation. His written account of the disputation, first printed in 1475 under the title *Tractatus contra perfidos Judaeos de conditionibus veri Messie* (A Treatise against the Perfidious Jews Concerning the Conditions of the True Messiah), was reprinted in Latin in 1495 and 1518; a German translation, *Der Stern des Meschiah* (The Star of the Messiah), was published in 1477. Another influential anti-Judaic polemic was the treatise by Pedro Alfonso, alias Moses Sephardi, an eleventh-century Aragonese Jewish convert to Christianity. At least five Latin editions of this treatise, which argued for the true messiahship of Jesus, appeared in the Holy Roman Empire between 1485 and 1536. In 1524 Ludwig Hätzer, who would become an early Anabaptist leader, translated the work into German under the title *Ain beweysung das der war Messias komen sey* (A Demonstration That the True Messiah Has Come).

Jewish converts themselves participated in the anti-Judaic missions. The two best-known figures on the eve of the Reformation were Johannes Pfefferkorn, the nemesis of the Christian humanist and Hebrew scholar Johannes Reuchlin, and Anton Margaritha, the son of Rabbi Jacob Margolis of Regensburg and author of the 1530 book *Der Gantz Jüdisch Glaub* (The Entire Jewish Faith), a work that would exert a significant influence on Luther's and the Lutheran church's views of Jews. *Der Gantz Jüdisch Glaub* describes in great detail the celebration of Passover; the feasts of the New Moon and Sucos; the rites of passage, circumcision, marriage, and death; and Jewish magical and Cabbalistic beliefs. There are also long passages describing the organization and inner workings of Jewish communities. By far the most comprehensive description of Jewish rituals and community life available to Christians, the book enjoyed a long history of reception because of its skillful integration of ethnography and religion. It was reprinted as late as 1713 in Leipzig and became a standard text on Judaism for many generations of Lutheran pastors.

Remembered for their anti-Judaic polemics, Pfefferkorn

and Margaritha were just two of the many German-speaking Jewish converts who appeared in print during the Reformation. A partial list includes the following polemicists (with their dates and places of conversion): the Cologne priest Victor von Carben (1507?); Paul Riccius, physician to Emperor Maximilian I; Paul Staffelstein of Nuremberg (1530s?), an early convert to the evangelical movement; Johann Isaac (1546, Marburg); Paul Emil (1548, Rome); Philip Wolff (1554, Gdańsk); Paul of Prague (1556, Nuremberg?); Paul Weidner (1558, Vienna); Philipp Auerbacher of Niklasburg (1597, Carinthia); and Johann Adrian of Emden (1607, Frankfurt am Main).

Although Jewish converts constituted a very small minority, the issue of conversion featured prominently in the evangelical movement. In the millenarian enthusiasm of the 1520s and 1530s, many reformers expected an imminent and massive conversion of the Jewish people in anticipation of the second coming of Christ and in fulfillment of biblical prophecy. Luther himself was the best example. In his 1521 treatise *Dass Jesu Christus ein geborner Jude sei* (That Jesus Christ Was Born a Jew), Luther excoriated the Roman church for persecuting Jews and enjoined the latter to recognize the truth of the gospel and adhere to the evangelical cause. Although Luther was to change his views on Jews, a theme discussed below, other reformers—notably the Strasbourg Hebrew scholar Wolfgang Capito, the Nuremberg reformer Andraes Osiander, and the Braunschweig reformer Urbanus Rhegius—argued that toleration would remain the best hope for Jewish conversion in the long run.

An important current in medieval Jewish mysticism, the Cabbala exercised a considerable influence on Christian thought, thanks to its occult appeal and its interpretive strategy of locating hidden meanings in sacred texts and in the language of the Hebrew scriptures. Although the Cabbala was known to Christian scholars in medieval Spain, it was actually in the fifteenth century that Jewish mysticism became influential for Christian thinkers in Italy and central Europe. The Italian humanist Pico della Mirandola (1463–1594) dabbled in the Cabbala, but the first significant Christian attempt to appropriate Jewish mysticism for Christian theology was undertaken by Johannes Reuchlin, a legal humanist and the leading Hebraist in the Holy Roman Empire. In *De verbo mirifico* (On the Wonder-Working Word), published in 1494 and presented as a dialogue between a Jew, a Christian, and an Epicurean, Reuchlin used the Cabbalistic method to identify the true messiah, whose "wondermaking name" was the Pentagrammaton (YHSVH, from the Hebrew for the name of Jesus). In a second and more voluminous work of 1516, *De Arte Cabalistica* (On the Cabbalistic Art), Reuchlin explained for the Christian reader the tenets of *Zohar,* the classic text in Jewish mysticism, and expounded on his idea of the true messiahship of Christ.

Aside from Reuchlin, the leading Christian expert on the Cabbala during the Reformation was Paul Riccius. Like his fellow convert Anton Margaritha, Riccius used his knowledge of Hebrew texts to introduce Judaism to Christian readers. He was the author of two treatises on the Cabbala, the best known being *Portae Lucis* (The Gates of Light), which was published in 1516 in Augsburg. The title of his treatise, as Riccius explains to the reader, refers to the nature of the Cabbalistic art, which enables its practitioner to regain access to the macrocosm of God and the spiritual universe through the study of written texts and laws and through understanding their hidden, allegorical meaning.

The humanists' fascination with the Cabbala, however, was not shared by Protestant reformers. Luther attacked the Cabbala as mere superstition. In his 1543 work *Vom Schem Hamphoras* (On the Ineffable Name), Luther condemned the Cabbala as Jewish word magic: "A Jew fabricates as much idolatry and magic as the hair on nine cows, that is, countless and infinite." He further compared the Cabbala to Catholic rituals: "The pope and his whole church has filled the entire world with swindle, magic, idolatry, for he has his special *Schem Hamphoras*. . . enchants water with wanton, mere meaningless letters, says it is holy water which washes away sins, chases away the devil, and has many virtues." Although Christian Cabbala lost its appeal amidst the harshness of confessional polemics, Hebrew biblical exegesis and the Hebrew scriptures would have a lasting influence on Protestant theology and identification.

Medieval Christian biblical exegesis largely rejected Hebrew glosses. The most influential exegete, the Franciscan friar Nicholas of Lyra (1270–1349), referred occasionally to Hebrew texts and commentaries for philological elucidation, but rabbinic glosses were summarily condemned. With humanism the desire to emend the Latin Vulgate Bible with reference to the original scriptural languages led to a more positive attitude toward Jewish biblical scholarship. The Complutensian Polyglot, published in 1514–1517 under the patronage of the Spanish cardinal Garcia Jiménez de Cisneros at Alcalá de Henares, with parallel Greek, Latin, and Hebrew texts, represented a landmark in biblical scholarship. In addition to the study of the Hebrew Bible, rabbinic glosses were selectively introduced by Christian scholars. Among the pioneers of this effort in the Holy Roman Empire was Johannes Böchenstein, author of *Rudimenta Hebraica Mosche Kimchi* (1520), in which he introduced the exegesis of the great medieval rabbi David Kimchi. Böchenstein taught Hebrew at various universities—Ingolstadt in 1505, Augsburg in 1513, and Wittenberg in 1518. His students included Sebastian Münster, well known for his publications in Hebraica and cosmography, and Philipp Melanchthon, Luther's younger colleague and close collaborator at the University of Wittenberg. For his adherence to the cause of reform, Böchenstein was stigmatized as a Jewish convert, although he denied any Jewish ancestry in a published apology. He died in 1532 at the age of sixty.

Another pioneer in Christian Hebraica was Konrad Pellikan, born in 1478 in Ruffbach, Alsace. He became a Cordelier monk in 1493, learned Hebrew on his own from the works of Nicholas of Lyra, and in 1503 published *De Modo legendi et intelligendi Hebraea* (How to Read and Understand Hebrew), a work that established his scholarly reputation. He was appointed professor at Basel (1523–1526); in 1526 he went to Zurich at the invitation of Huldrych Zwingli and died there in 1556. Münster was his successor at the University of Basel. Other Christian Hebraists included Johannes Oecolampadius, a student of Reuchlin and reformer in Basel, who published a lengthy commentary on the book of Isaiah (1524), in which he made use of the Targum and quoted Rabbi Kimchi; and Sebastian Hofmeister, a Franciscian friar, doctor of theology from the Faculty of Theology of Paris, and reformer in Lucerne and Schaffhausen in 1523.

As already discussed, the evangelical movement of the 1520s and 1530s carried the hope of Jewish conversion to many reformers, some of whom cited past persecutions of Jews as evidence of corruption in the Roman church. Not surprisingly, early Catholic polemicists reacted by labeling their opponents Judaizers. Johann Eck, a staunch defender of the old church, whipped up traditional antisemitic feelings while attacking a pamphlet, published anonymously by Osiander in 1539, that defended several Jews against the charge of ritual murder. In addition to listing a litany of "Jewish crimes" against Christianity, Eck accused Jews of instigating the schism and cursed the author (whose identity he probably knew) as *Judenvater* ("father of Jews"). When Protestants criticized Catholic sacraments and the cult of saints, their arguments often echoed traditional Jewish polemics against Christianity, at least so it seemed to defenders of the old faith. An associate of Osiander, the preacher Johann Böschenstain, was forced to defend his ancestry in print because he had preached sermons against icons and statues. In Böschenstain's words, "It happened that a member of the clergy said that I was a baptized Jew and that my father was a learned rabbi, and therefore I was against icons and statues." Affirming that faith, not descent, was what mattered, Böschenstain nonetheless emphatically denied he was Jewish in order to clear his name and to protect his descendants from persecution.

From 1536 to 1546 the accusation of Judaizing and the issue of conversion compelled the evangelical movement to clarify its relationship to Jews and Judaism. In addition to Catholic charges that all Protestants were Judaizers, the challenge from Anabaptists and sectarians further complicated the issue. By claiming their community as the "true Israel," the Münster Anabaptists, for example, modeled their regime (1534–1535) after the Old Testament, instituting patriarchy, polygyny, and messianic kingship. For Lutherans, refuting the radical Reformation became synonymous with rejecting Judaizing tendencies. In 1536 the Braunschweig reformer Urbanus Rhegius published a treatise refuting the doctrines of the Münster Anabaptist kingdom. Entitled *De restitutione regni Israelitici* (On the Restitution of the Kingdom of Israel), Rhegius directed his polemic against "all millenarians, particularly against the millenarians of Münster." Rhegius argued that Christ's kingdom was spiritual, not temporal, and in addition to attacking the Anabaptists, he also criticized the Jews for persisting in their belief of a worldly messianic kingdom. Luther himself began to lump together all Anabaptists, sectarians, Jews, and Catholics in his polemics: he admonished reformers to beware of Sabbatarians and of the seductions of Jews. His polemic against Jews grew more embittered toward the end of his life. In *Von den Juden und ihren Lügen* (On the Jews and Their Lies) and *Vom Schem Hamphoras* (On the Ineffable Name of God), both published in 1543, Luther turned the earlier Catholic charge of evangelical Judaizing on its head: in these treatises it was the Jews and papists who performed magic with their empty letters, formulas, and ceremonies, killing the living faith of the spirit with the dead tradition of superstition. To quote Luther: "I do not wonder, neither about the Turks nor the Jews, about their blindness, hardness, wickedness, because I see them in the most holy fathers of the church, in the popes, cardinals, and bishops."

Luther was not alone in his hostility toward the Jews. Despite the sympathetic statements of several prominent reformers, many leaders of the evangelical movement, particularly those with strong ties to urban communes, harbored strong anti-Jewish feelings. As corporations that enjoyed a high degree of self-rule, urban communities in the Holy Roman Empire were intolerant of those who stood outside the body politic, be they clerics, vagrants, or Jews. Legally serfs of the emperor, Jews stood under imperial protection and hence were resented by the burghers as an alien privileged minority. It was therefore a natural outgrowth that the Reformation movement, with deep roots in the communal tradition of the South German imperial cities, was hostile to the Jews. Anti-Judaism was implicit in the religious renewal of the south German cities. The examples of Martin Bucer and Balthasar Hubmaier are instructive.

Bucer was the leading reformer in Strasbourg, an imperial city that had refused to tolerate Jewish residents for more than a century before the Reformation. In 1539, under Bucer's leadership, a group of evangelical preachers petitioned Philipp of Hesse to restrict his protection for Hessian Jews. They argued that Christian magistrates should foster unity and true religion; nobody in a city or community should be allowed to worship a false god. Although Jews could be tolerated under Christian charity, they must be made to serve Christians and not the other way round. Bucer further condemned usury and urged that all Jews be made to work with their hands and listen to the gospel. The provisions in the memorandum, however, were not accepted by Philipp of Hesse.

The theme of usury, a prominent trope in anti-Jewish polemic, transcended confessional divides. Before joining the evangelical movement, Hubmaier, the cathedral preacher in Regensburg in 1519, stirred up his audience by attacking the injurious effect of Jewish usury. With one of the largest Jewish communities in the empire (some six hundred adults and children), this imperial city had tried unsuccessfully to expel the Jews by staging a ritual-murder investigation from 1476 to 1480. Hubmaier's sermons added fuel to the fire of popular antisemitism; his anti-Jewish rhetoric echoed the grievances of the guilds, who bitterly resented economic competition from Jews. Emboldened by Hubmaier, the Christian population refused transactions with Jews, and the town fathers took advantage of the death of Emperor Maximilian in 1519 to expel the entire community. Shortly thereafter Hubmaier went over to the evangelical movement, and in 1527 he was beheaded as an Anabaptist preacher in Vienna.

Not all voices condemned the Jews. A few reformers continued to argue for Christian charity, patience, and toleration. For example, in 1540 Rhegius, who served as superintendent of the evangelical church in Celle, wrote to the Protestant clergy of Braunschweig, urging his fellow pastors to tolerate Jews. He reminded his readers that, although the Jews were in exile, they would one day be reconciled with God in Christ.

In spite of this minority philosemitic position within the evangelical church, the dominant position, as it was shaped during the 1540s by Luther, Bucer, and other reformers, represented a harsh anti-Jewish view. Three themes in particular are essential in this discourse. First, economic and theological motives were intrinsically related in Protestant anti-Judaism. To paraphrase Bucer, because Jews were allowed to practice usury and run pawnshops, they considered themselves better than Christians and, hence, refused to convert. Similarly, Luther opposed "honest Christian manual work" to "dishonest Jewish indolence." This specific anti-Jewish rhetoric was embedded in a larger context during the early decades of the evangelical movement: the reformers considered monopolies, merchant companies, and the charging of interest among both Jews and Christians as unchristian.

The second characteristic in the anti-Jewish polemic of midcentury was its function as propaganda: these pamphlets and publications were intended to shape public opinion and mobilize political opposition to Jewish communities. Although Bucer's memorandum failed to persuade Philipp of Hesse, Luther's anti-Jewish treatises mobilized strong opposition to Jews in the Saxon territories and provoked anti-Jewish riots in Braunschweig. Crucial to their active political role was the Protestant clergy's self-image as prophets to godly rulers, who might deviate from God's path, as did the kings of ancient Israel.

The third and final characteristic was one of identity. Echoing Paul, Bucer claimed that Jews were not the true Israel, the sons of Isaac, but rather the sons of Hagar Ismahel; therefore, they hated Christians, the true Israel. The opposition of old Israel to new, false religion to true, and lifeless letters to the living spirit of the word thus furnished material for the construction of parallel and opposite identities for the new Lutheran church and Judaism, an opposition based not only on theology but also on genealogical differences.

Owing to Luther's powerful legacy and in part to the sharpened polemics among the Christian confessions, hostility to Judaism and Jews became entrenched among the Lutheran clergy during the second half of the sixteenth century. Georg Schwarz (1530–1602), a theologian at the University of Giessen, invoked a long line of anti-Jewish polemicists from the church fathers to his own day, though he claimed that "nobody has written as mightily, seriously, and thoroughly against [the Jews] in German as Martin Luther of blessed memory." For Schwarz, Catholics and Jews were common enemies, for they both attacked Luther's good name. After accusing Jews of the usual offenses—blasphemies, usury, Host desecration, and ritual murder—Schwarz called upon Christian rulers to expel all Jews because tolerating Jews, in his words, "meant warming snakes in one's bosom and raising wolves in one's house." Unfortunately, according to Schwarz, there were rulers and city magistrates who allowed all confessions and religions to coexist, a deplorable regime that led to uprisings, treason, and civil war. For those who said Christians should love all equally, Schwarz reserved his most sarcastic remarks: he did not know there was still so much love in the world. Let these people tolerate Jews, Catholics, Turks, Anabaptists, and heretics, he said, let them tolerate witches, blasphemers, murderers, adulterers, thieves, and robbers; he himself must go to school again to learn anew the meaning of Christian love when it required loving Jews and doing harm to Christians.

Unlike the Lutheran church, the Reformed tradition had a more positive view of Jews and Judaism. Together with Capito and Pellikan, later professor of Hebrew at Basel University, Zwingli himself studied Hebrew with Thomas Wyttenbach. Based on his acceptance of the Bible as the supreme guide for Christian life, Zwingli emphasized the importance of studying Hebrew. In the preface to the exegesis of *Isaiah,* he writes:

> The ignorance of Hebrew forms of expression has led to an erroneous interpretation of many passages of Scripture. . . . Translators and commentators have given us the Hebrew forms of expression without breaking down and reducing the figures they contain, which are untranslatable into any foreign languages whatsoever. . . . Thus we have translations in which the words indeed are counted, but the thoughts carelessly and dubiously expressed.

With the proper study of Hebrew, Zwingli continued:

> Then we should have penetrated into the knowledge of the ideas

> and tropes, the images and figures of speech which meet us at every turn in the books of Scripture, so that there is scarcely a single sentence of the Bible that can be opened by any other keys but such as these; then we should have clearly known the thoughts of inspiration, and not rashly substituted our own for the thoughts of Scripture; then long ago, all uncertainty would have disappeared.

Between 1517 and 1519 Zwingli obtained a copy of Reuchlin's *Rudimenta Hebraica* to help him read *Psalms* in the original. He relied on the Septuagint and rejected the Vulgate Bible. In 1522 Zwingli got Jacob Ceporinus (Wisendanger), a student of Reuchlin, appointed Hebrew teacher in Zurich. In his translations and commentaries on books of the Old Testament, Zwingli consulted extensively rabbinic exegesis, particularly those of David Kimchi. Zwingli's positive assessment of the Hebrew language extended in part to the Jewish people: "The same covenant which [God] entered into with Israel he has in these latter days entered into with us, that we may be one people with them, one church, and may have also one covenant. I suppose that some one will vainly cry out: See how that fellow would make Jews of us, though we have always been told of two peoples, two churches, and two covenants." Indeed, Zwingli, like other reformers, had to defend himself against the accusation of Judaizing. In 1524 Zwingli published a pamphlet, *Ein flyssige und kurze underrichtung wie man sich vor luegen (dero dise zyt nit on gefaerd volloufend) hueten und bewaren soll.* In it he defended himself against the rumor that "certain monks, supported by certain prominent people, are saying that we have learned at Zurich all our knowledge of the Divine Word from the Jews. . . . It has been said that the Jew, Moses of Winterthur, has openly boasted that he comes to us and teaches us, and that we have repeatedly gone to him in secret." Zwingli denied any association with Moses except a dispute with the rabbi over the nature of messianic prophecies.

Among the first generations of reformers, Paul Fagius, Capito's successor in Strasbourg, was a noted Hebraist who used his linguistic skills to clarify Christian dogma. By explaining the Lord's Supper in the context of the seder and by comparing the ethics of the Pharisees and the apostolic community, Fagius gave a historical reading to the New Testament that stood him in danger of being labeled a Judaizer.

For the radical Reformation there was no single view of Jews and Judaism. As discussed, Anabaptists such as Hätzer, Hans Denck, and Hubmaier showed various degrees of interest in Judaism, a reflection of their millenarian and prophetic concerns. But the one person who was most indebted to Judaism was the Spanish physician Michael Servetus. Unlike Calvin, Zwingli, and other magisterial reformers, Servetus was not content to inform himself about Jewish opinions through the guidebooks issued by earlier Christian Hebraists, such as Reuchlin and Münster, through whom the commentaries of medieval rabbis had been made available to Christians. Severtus went directly to the sources—Maimonides (Moses ben Maimon), Rashi (Shlomo Yitzhaqui), Abraham ben Meir Ibn Ezra, Abraham Saba, David Kimchi, Isaac Arama, and Lipmann of Mühlhausen. He followed rabbinic commentary in interpreting the messianic passages in the Old Testament as referring to King David and not Christ. His study of Judaism led to the rejection of the doctrine of the Trinity and to his death in Geneva.

Initially unsure about the reform movement, the Jews of the Holy Roman Empire by the 1540s perceived the Reformation as a hostile force. During the Schmalkald War (1547) Jewish communities under the leadership of Joselmann of Rosheim contributed money to the war coffers of Charles V and prayed for imperial victory on the battlefield. On Jewish responses to the Reformation, there are direct Jewish sources and reactions gleaned from Christian testimonies, as, for example, Luther's *Tischreden* (Table Talk), which mentioned the visits of rabbis. In the Hebrew chronicle *Tzemah David,* written by the Prague Jew David Gans (1541–1613), the major impression is one of an underlying millenarianism in the midst of Christian schism. Although Gans could not read Latin, he was well informed of Christian attitudes toward Jews, and he was optimistic of the protection offered by the emperor and princes. Unlike earlier Hebrew chroniclers, Gans did not elaborate on the persecutions of Jews. Instead, describing the Reformation years, he wrote: "At a time when Christians are fighting among themselves and more than a million Christians have been killed and slaughtered in our time during the past fifty years, the children of Israel have remained unscathed and blessed be the Lord who has bestowed his loving kindness upon us." Gans made the history of Christian martyrology and the discord within Christianity two of the major themes of his work.

[*See also* Antisemitism *and* Reuchlin, Johannes.]

BIBLIOGRAPHY

Bebb, Phillip N. "Jewish Policy in Sixteenth Century Nürnberg." In *Occasional Papers of the American Society for Reformation Research,* edited by Robert C. Walton, pp. 125–136. Saint Louis, 1977.

Ben-Sasson, Haim Hillel, ed. *A History of the Jewish People.* Cambridge, Mass., 1976. A reliable introduction to Jewish history incorporating recent scholarship.

Breuer, Mordechai. "Modernism and Traditionalism in Sixteenth-Century Jewish Historiography: A Study of David Gans' *Tzemah David.*" In *Jewish Thought in the Sixteenth Century,* edited by Bernard Dov Cooperman, pp. 49–88. Cambridge, Mass., 1983.

Cohen, Jeremy. *The Friars and the Jews: The Evolution of Medieval Anti-Judaism.* Ithaca, N.Y., 1982. Essential reading for understanding the scholastic background to later theological disputes about Jews.

Edwards, Mark U. *Luther's Last Battles: Politics and Polemics, 1531–46.* Ithaca, N.Y., 1983. A succinct analysis of Luther's anti-Jewish polemics.

Freimann, Aron, and Isidor Kracauer. *Frankfurt.* Translated by Bertha S. Levin. Jewish Community Series. Philadelphia, 1929. Contains the highlights of Kracauer's standard two-volume German history of the Frankfurt Jewish community, one of the two most important communities in central Europe.

Friedman, Jerome. "Luther, Forster, and the Curious Nature of Wittenberg Hebraica." *Bibliothèque d'humanisme et Renaissance* 42 (1980), 611–619.

———. "Sixteenth-Century Christian-Hebraica: Scripture and the Renaissance Myth of the Past." *Sixteenth Century Journal* 11 (1980), 67–85.

Hobbs, R. Gerald. "Hebraica Veritas and Traditio Apostolica: Saint Paul and the Interpretation of the Psalms in the Sixteenth Century." In *The Bible in the Sixteenth Century*, edited by David C. Steinmetz, pp. 83–99. Durham, N.C., 1990.

Hsia, R. Po-chia. *The Myth of Ritual Murder: Jews and Magic in Reformation Germany*. New Haven, 1988. Traces the debates and decline of ritual murder trials in pre-Reformation and Reformation Germany.

———. *Trent, 1475: Stories of a Ritual Murder Trial*. New Haven, 1992. A detailed narrative of the most notorious ritual murder trial on the eve of the Reformation.

Hsia, R. Po-chia, and Hartmut Lehmann, eds. *In and Out of the Ghetto: Gentile-Jewish Relations in Late Medieval and Early Modern Germany*. New York and Cambridge, 1995. Collection of conference papers from German, Israeli, and North American scholars representing the recent research.

Kirn, Hans-Martin. *Das Bild vom Juden im Deutschland des frühen 16. Jahrhunderts*. Tübingen, 1989. A thorough investigation of the writings of the convert Pfefferkorn set in the context of the time.

Kisch, Guido. *Zasius und Reuchlin: Eine rechtsgeschichtlich-vergleichende Studie zum Toleranzproblem im 16. Jahrhundert*. Stuttgart, 1961. An important study of the attitudes toward Jews of two legal humanists in the Holy Roman Empire.

Newman, Louis Israel. *Jewish Influence on Christian Reform Movements* (1925). Reprint, New York, 1966. An older but still indispensable study of the early Christian Hebrew scholars and the relationship between Hebrew scholarship and the early reformers.

Oberman, Heiko A. *The Roots of Anti-Semitism in the Age of Renaissance and Reformation*. Philadelphia, 1984. A brilliant interpretation of the polemics against Jews in the generation leading up to Luther.

Scholem, Gershom G., ed. *Zohar: The Book of Splendor; Basic Readings from the Kabbalah*. Reprint, London, 1977. English translations from the fundamental text of medieval Jewish mysticism by its greatest scholar.

———. *Major Trends in Jewish Mysticism*. Reprint, New York, 1988. A classic.

Stern, Selma. *Josel of Rosheim: Commander of Jewry in the Holy Roman Empire of the German Nation*. Translated by Gertrude Hirschler. Philadelphia, 1965. Authoritative biography of the leading rabbi in Reformation Germany.

Straus, Raphael. *Regensburg and Augsburg*. Translated by Felix Gerson. Jewish Community Series. Philadelphia, 1939. This book is by one of the leading German-Jewish historians of his time.

Trachtenberg, Joshua. *The Devil and the Jews: The Medieval Conception of the Jew and Its Relations to Modern Antisemitism*. Reprint, New Haven, 1966. Still an indispensable classic.

———. *Jewish Magic and Superstition: A Study in Folk Religion*. Reprint, New York, 1987. Interesting study on Jewish popular religion based on Yiddish books.

R. Po-chia Hsia

JIMÉNEZ DE CISNEROS, Francisco (also Ximénez; 1436–1517), Spanish cardinal, reformer, and statesman. Perhaps the greatest of Spanish church reformers, Cisneros, as he is known in Spain, was born Gonzalo Jiménez de Cisneros at Torrelaguna. His father was a hidalgo who supported himself in part as a tax collector. After taking holy orders and studying at the University of Salamanca, Jiménez spent the years 1459 to 1466 in Rome, where he became acquainted with humanist scholarship. He returned to Spain with a letter from Pope Paul II nominating him to the first vacant benefice in the archdiocese of Toledo, but Archbishop Alonso de Carrillo refused to honor the appointment and eventually imprisoned him when he persisted in his claims to a position. In a display of the iron will for which he would later become famous, Jiménez chose to remain in jail for six years rather than abandon what he saw as his rights. He was released in 1479 after Carrillo sided with the Portuguese in opposing the accession of Ferdinand and Isabella.

His struggle with Carrillo brought him to the attention of Cardinal Pedro González de Mendoza, a powerful supporter of Isabella. When Mendoza became archbishop of Toledo in 1482, he appointed Jiménez vicar-general of the diocese of Sigüenza, but in 1484 Jiménez abandoned his career as a secular priest and entered the Franciscan convent of San Juan de Los Reyes at Toledo. It was at this point that he changed his name to Francisco.

Though noted for piety and asceticism, Jiménez maintained his contacts with the court, and in 1492 Isabella appointed him her confessor at Mendoza's suggestion. Three years later he succeeded his mentor as archbishop of Toledo and primate of the Spanish church. He was nearly sixty, but his career as a reformer had just begun.

Like the queen, Jiménez was acutely sensitive to demands for ecclesiastical reform. In 1491 the Crown had secured authorization from Pope Alexander VI to reform the monastic orders, and Jiménez began by enforcing obedience to the rule among his own Franciscans. Resistance was ruthlessly suppressed, and appeals to the pope were ignored. He soon extended the process to Benedictines, Dominicans, and Jeronymites, but the work required years because it was necessary to reform individual houses one by one. When he died in 1517 Spanish monasteries, though far from perfect, were among the best in Europe.

In 1499 he turned his energy and uncompromising devotion to the faith against the Muslims of Granada. Hernando de Talavera, the bishop of Granada, favored a gradual approach to the conversion of newly acquired Muslim subjects, and those who converted were granted forty years' exemption from Inquisitorial prosecution. Jiménez would have none of this. With the full backing of the queen, he insisted that all Muslims within the kingdom of Castile convert or leave. The new policy provoked rebellion and led to the expulsion of 1502, but it failed to resolve the issue. Like the Jews before them, thousands of Muslims converted without truly abandoning their faith or their grievances, thereby laying the groundwork for the Morisco revolts of the sixteenth century.

Though Ferdinand of Aragon had opposed the extension of these policies to the Muslims of his own kingdom, he continued to support Jiménez after Isabella's death in 1504. The archbishop favored a crusade to conquer all of North Africa and partially funded the campaigns of 1505–1510 with his own revenues, but the king lost interest in the project after securing Oran and other strategic ports. In spite of this he made Jiménez regent of Castile in 1506 and inquisitor general in 1507. The archbishop received a cardinal's hat in the same year.

In 1508 the cardinal formally established a university at Alcalá de Henares, not far from his birthplace. Jiménez had long been concerned with the educational level of the Spanish clergy and hoped that the new foundation would stimulate an intellectual revival. Though not himself a humanist, he thought that philology and textual criticism could be put to the service of religion. The scholars he attracted to Alcalá are perhaps best known for their work on the Complutensian Polyglot Bible, in which Greek, Latin, and Hebrew texts were printed in facing columns. He also hoped to broaden the theological curriculum. Scotism and Ockhamism were to be taught along with the Thomism that had long been dominant at Salamanca.

The cardinal's last months were troubled. His first regency had been short-lived, but he was recalled when Ferdinand died in 1516. Castile was by this time at the edge of anarchy. Jiménez maintained order by establishing a volunteer militia of thirty thousand men known as the *gente de ordenanza*, but his authoritarianism earned him a host of enemies. When the new king, Charles of Ghent (from 1519 Holy Roman Emperor Charles V), arrived in 1517, he abruptly dismissed the aging regent, but Jiménez never saw the letter. He died near Valladolid on 8 November 1517.

The reforms undertaken by Jiménez de Cisneros are sometimes credited with blocking the extension of the Reformation to Spain. His attack on clerical abuses no doubt diluted an important cause of religious discontent, but the Spanish monarchy, by securing control of its own ecclesiastical appointments after 1482, had already eliminated a more important source of friction with the papacy. At the same time, his approach to reform, heavily influenced by Franciscan observant models and by humanism, introduced ideas that the Inquisition would later find unacceptable. His own simplicity, moralism, and belief in systematic mental prayer are thought to have paved the way for the *alumbrados* of the 1520s, while his encouragement of the humanists and of scripturalism, however orthodox its intent, led directly to the tragedy of the Erasmians.

The cardinal may best be regarded as one who in attempting to reform the Spanish church introduced it to the broader currents of European thought. That those ideas would one day be found suspect, if not openly heretical, is no more ironic than the fact that as inquisitor general Jiménez greatly increased the power and effectiveness of the institution that would in time devour his intellectual children.

BIBLIOGRAPHY

Azcona, Tarsicio de. *La elección y reforma del episcopado español en tiempo de los Reyes Católicos*. Madrid, 1960.

WILLIAM S. MALTBY

JIMÉNEZ DE CISNEROS, García (1455/56–1510), Spanish reforming abbot of Montserrat. Born in Cisneros, he was the only son of a hidalgo family. Although heir to its entailed estate, he instead entered monastic life in 1475 at the austere Benedictine monastery of San Benito of Valladolid, which was promoting strict observance in Castile and extending its control over other Benedictine houses.

Ferdinand and Isabella, as proponents of monastic reform, in 1493 obtained a papal bull that subjected the abbey of Montserrat, the great pilgrimage site in Ferdinand's territory of Catalonia, to San Benito of Valladolid in Castile. Cisneros, cousin of Queen Isabella's new confessor, was entrusted with the responsibility of reforming Montserrat. He was among fourteen monks who went from Valladolid to Montserrat, far outnumbering survivors from the abbey's old regime.

As abbot Cisneros emphasized a contemplative life based on methodical silent prayer. Bringing a press to Montserrat, he printed not only liturgical volumes but also Gerard Zerbolt's *De spiritualibus ascensionibus*, representing the *devotio moderna*, and his own *Exercitatorio de la vida spiritual*, which may later have influenced Ignatius of Loyola. Deviating from Benedict's rules, Cisneros allocated only fifteen minutes daily to manual labor, insisted that monks have individual cells, and encouraged private meditation even during the canonical services.

Montserrat flourished under Cisneros. Efforts to spread reform in Catalonia and Aragon, however, proved futile, even after Cisneros became one of the three reformers-general for all Spain in 1505. In Castile Cisneros participated in the general chapters of the Congregation of San Benito of Valladolid until the domineering Valladolid reformers, who enjoyed consistent support from the Crown, were attacked by Pope Julius II in 1509. Montserrat's predicament was summarized as "los de Castella han fet lo mal y nosaltres lo havem de pagar" (those of Castile have committed the fault, and we have to pay for it). Cisneros's last recorded act was to disassociate Montserrat from Valladolid, withdrawing obedience to its excommunicated abbot on 10 October 1510.

BIBLIOGRAPHY

Colombás, García M. *Un reformador benedictino en tiempo de los reyes católicos: García Jiménez de Cisneros, Abad de Montserrat.* Montserrat, Spain, 1955. A thorough study of Cisneros' activity and writings by a monk at Montserrat. Colombás emphasizes the Benedictine reform of the Congregation of San Benito of Valladolid as well as Cisneros's reforms at Montserrat.

Jiménez de Cisneros, García. *Book of Exercises for the Spiritual Life.* Translated by E. Allison Peers. Montserrat, 1929. His main work in English translation.

CONSTANCE J. MATHERS

JOHANN CASIMIR (1543–1592), count Palatine and regent of the Electoral Palatinate. Johann Casimir's youth was incisively influenced by the conversion of his father (Elector Frederick III of the Palatinate) to Calvinism, a decision that Johann Casimir embraced as well. Extensive travels to France (Paris, Nancy, etc.) exposed him to French language and culture. These travels acquainted him with the problems of the Reformation in France. In 1567, and again nine years later, he supplied an auxiliary force in support of the French Huguenots. Both ventures provided the basis for Johann Casimir's reputation as a soldier and military ruler.

Johann Casimir pursued a pointedly anti-Catholic policy in Germany and at the same time was a staunch supporter of European Calvinism and European Protestantism. In 1576 he succeeded his father as ruler of Pfalz-Lautern, an area consisting of most of the present-day Palatinate (Neustadt, Kaiserslautern, Böckelheim). Religious and confessional tensions with his older brother Ludwig VI, who had succeeded his father as Elector Palatine, overshadowed the next years. In 1583, on Ludwig's death, Johann Casimir became regent for his minor nephew.

Johann Casimir not only showed himself responsive to diplomatic entreaties from Elizabeth I of England and Henry of Navarre for support, but also became the heart and soul of political Protestantism in Germany. At issue were ties with Protestant forces in western Europe in order to strengthen the domestic efforts against the Counter-Reformation. While initially he had great support, including that of the new Saxon elector Christian in 1586, Lutheran confessional considerations that precluded ties with Calvinists and aversion to risk reduced his ranks of supporters. Still, Johann Casimir used English and Danish funds to hire mercenaries, whom he led to France in 1587 to support the French Huguenots.

In 1590 Johann Casimir was the motor behind the notion of a European alliance of Protestants. He persuaded Elector Christian to inform the emperor of Protestant grievances and to agree to a meeting with Protestant princes. In 1591 the Protestant princes agreed at Torgau on mutual assistance and alliance, which resulted in the League of Torgau.

Johann Casimir opposed a rigid Calvinism; his primary concerns were political considerations in the empire and beyond. He was the heart and soul of several political adventures, none of which proved successful. All were characterized by tensions between his far-reaching political ambitions and his modest political base as ruler of Pfalz-Lautern.

His goal was to effect a conciliation between Calvinists and Lutherans, but at the same time to give the Calvinists a more important role in Pfalz-Lautern. Since most of his clergy were decidedly Calvinist, his ideal of amicable coexistence was not viable. Johann Casimir's support made the University of Heidelberg one of the foremost Calvinist universities in Europe.

Johann Casimir's backing of the French Huguenots continued until the end of his life. In 1587 he undertook another venture in their support, aided by Elector Christian of Saxony, who himself leaned toward crypto-Calvinist views. At the end of his life resignation over his numerous unsuccessful ventures befell him. He died at age 49, having been paralyzed by a stroke.

BIBLIOGRAPHY

Baumann, K. "Pfalzgraf Johann Casimir als Politiker und Landesherr." In *Kaiserslautern, 1276–1951.* Kaiserslautern, 1951.

Kuhn, Manfred. *Pfalzgraf Johann Casimir von Pfalz-Lautern, 1576–1583.* Otterbach-Kaiserslautern, 1961.

Press, Volker. "Johann Casimir." In *Neue Deutsche Biographie,* vol. 10, pp. 510–513. Berlin, 1953–.

———. *Calvinismus und Territorialstaat: Regierung und Zentralbehörden der Kurpfalz, 1559–1619.* Stuttgart, 1970.

HANS J. HILLERBRAND

JOHN III OF SWEDEN (1537–1592; r. 1568–1592), king who pursued policies of liturgical enrichment and ecumenical rapprochement. The second son of King Gustavus Vasa, John came to the throne of Sweden in 1568 when a coup d'état of the nobles toppled his brother, Erik XIV, who had shown signs of insanity. Concerned to secure Sweden's commerce in the Baltic against Danish, Hanseatic, and Russian interference, he acquired Estonia and strongholds in Livonia (Latvia) and formed closer ties with Poland. In 1562, while duke of Finland, he had married Catherine Jagiellon, the sister of King Sigismund II Augustus of Poland, the daughter of the fabulously wealthy Bona Sforza of Naples, and a Catholic. The Roman Catholic marriage played a role in his church policy, since John tirelessly negotiated with the papacy, not only in the interest of gaining the Vatican's intervention in the release of his wife's fortune, frozen in Naples, but also in the cause of reconciliation between the church of Rome and the church of Sweden.

John III was probably the most capable theologian ever to sit on the throne of Sweden. A humanist scholar, he appreciated the Philippist tendencies of Archbishop Laurentius Petri, the primate of Sweden, and of his private secretary, Petrus Fecht, both of whom had studied with Melanchthon at Wittenberg. One of John's first ecclesiastical acts was to promulgate, under royal authority, the church order of Archbishop Petri (1571). This weighty piece of doctrinal articulation and ecclesiastical legislation officially aligned the church of Sweden with German Lutheranism and was subscribed to by the clergy at a synod at Uppsala in 1572.

The old archbishop died in 1573, and thereafter John III's ecclesiastical policies were more inspired by the mediating theology of the Roman Catholic Joris Cassander, as expressed in his *De articulis religionis inter catholicos et protestantes controversis consultatio.* Fecht also convinced John of the humanist ideal of reconciliation between the Reformation and Catholicism on the basis of the "consensus of the first five centuries" (*consensus quinquasaecularis*).

John III's first personal contribution to church renewal along these lines were ten articles placed before a church council held in Uppsala in 1574. These were designed to inject greater reverence into the conduct of church services. In 1575 he laid before the clergy his *Nova ordinantia ecclesiastica* (New Church Order), which purported to be a commentary on the church order of Laurentius Petri but was in fact a new piece of legislation, wrapped up in weighty theological argumentation. Many of its practical provisions were in accordance with strict Lutheranism, but its doctrinal treatment was patristic and, in many instances, Cassander was quoted verbatim. Its ritual tendencies became clear when John required the new archbishop, Laurentius Petri Gothus, to assume crook and mitre and submit to unction at his consecration.

Many of the clergy were wary of the "papistic" directions indicated by *Nova ordinantia.* Their fears were fanned the next year when John promulgated a new liturgy, *Liturgia svecanae ecclesiae catholicae et orthodox conformis* (1576). Called the "Red Book" because of the color of its binding, it was printed in Latin and Swedish parallel columns with copious Latin commentaries in the margins. The preface, penned by Archbishop Gothus, professed that the liturgy was combating both *superstitio* and *profanitas*, but asserted that of the two the latter was the more dangerous at the moment. Analysis shows that the liturgy drew upon texts from medieval Swedish missals, Reformation church orders, patristic liturgies, and even *The Book of Common Prayer.* (John had been in England in 1559.) It included vesting prayers, offertory prayers, and a full eucharistic prayer not found in Reformation-era Lutheran Mass orders. The liturgy was accepted by the estates in 1577, albeit only reluctantly by the clergy, and with John taking steps to ensure that some of the opposition was not in attendance. Its use was enforced on pain of being fined, jailed, or deprived of one's appointment (the first instances of religious persecution during the Swedish Reformation).

It did not help John's cause with the vocal antiliturgists that at this time he was negotiating with Pope Gregory XIII; that the queen had Catholic chaplains attending her; that Crown Prince Sigismund was being raised as a Roman Catholic, in accordance with the marriage contract; and that the Jesuits had undertaken a secret mission to establish the Counter-Reformation in Sweden. Pope Gregory XIII had dispatched the Jesuit Laurentius Norvegus to Sweden, where he won the confidence of the king and the archbishop, and, under the guise of being a Lutheran patristics scholar, was appointed rector of the new theological college established in the old Franciscan priory in Stockholm (hence his nickname "Klosterlasse"). In response to these developments, Pope Gregory dispatched the former Jesuit secretary-general, Antonio Possevino to Sweden. Possevino convinced John of the possibility of reconciliation, and the king stopped receiving Lutheran Communion in 1578 and received Communion from Possevino according to the Latin rite. But Possevino was not able to secure John III's three minimal demands from the Curia Romana: the cup for the laity, the marriage of priests, and the Mass in Swedish. The pope also told John that he could listen to Lutheran sermons if he had to; but under no circumstance was he to attend a Lutheran Mass. Since the official Lutheran Mass in Sweden was the Red Book, John's liturgy was implicitly condemned as heretical. The king was furious, and in July 1579 he again received Lutheran Communion. In reaction, Possevino tried to force John's hand by blowing the whistle on the Jesuit mission. The move backfired; and amid much popular uproar John sent the Jesuits packing.

In 1583 Queen Catherine died, and John had no further temptation to negotiate with Rome (although his ecumenical interest then shifted to the patriarch of Constantinople). He took the occasion of the consecration of Anders Lars Björnram as archbishop of Uppsala to get the bishops to agree to wear the cope, use unction, make greater use of music in the church services, and preach sermons based on the Fathers. It was the high point of John's church program. But general acceptance was marred by a strident antiliturgist faction, whose members included the leading theologians of the realm, and by the resistance of John's brother, Duke Charles of Södermanland, to his whole church policy. After John's death a national assembly of the Church of Sweden abolished the Red Book and restored the church order of Laurentius Petri.

BIBLIOGRAPHY

Bergendoff, Conrad. "The Unique Character of the Reformation in Sweden." In *Symposium on 17th Century Lutheranism.* Concordia Historical Society. Saint Louis, 1962. Contains a description and translation of some passages in Archbishop Petri's church order.

Brilioth, Yngve. *Eucharistic Faith and Practice, Evangelical and Catholic.* Translated by A. G. Hebert. London, 1965. Originally published in Swedish (*Nattvarden in Evangeliskt Gudstjänstliv*, 1926); the English translation abridges the final chapter on the Swedish Eucharist, but it has a discussion of "King John III and the Liturgical Controversy" (pp. 254–260). Bishop Brilioth's assessment is that John would have gained much if he had stopped with *Nova Ordinantia* and not promulgated the liturgy.

Garstein, Oskar. *Rome and the Counter-Reformation in Scandinavia.* New York and Leiden, 1963–1992. See vol. 1. The fullest study of the Jesuit *Missio suetico* based on a wide-ranging collection of sources. Its major weakness is a disinclination to accept the tenacity with which John III held his personal religious convictions, even during the time in which he received Communion from Roman Catholic priests. His concern was that the Church of Sweden should be catholic, not necessarily Roman Catholic.

Harjunpaa, Toivo. "Liturgical Developments in Sweden and Finland in the Era of Lutheran Orthodoxy." *Church History* 37.1 (1968), 15–35. Good overview of the liturgical controversy and its settlement at the Uppsala Assembly of 1593.

Kroon, J., ed. *Liturgia svecanae ecclesiae catholicae et orthodoxae conformis, 1576.* Malmö, 1953. A facsimile of the Red Book with an afterword by the editor, available in some university and Lutheran or Episcopal seminary libraries.

Persson, Roland. *Johan III och Nova Ordinantia.* Lund, 1973. A detailed analysis of the background and sources of *Nova Ordinantia,* which views this church order as a typical compromise between John and the bishops; German summary pp. 163–173.

Robert, Michael. *The Early Vasas: A History of Sweden, 1523–1611.* Reprint, Cambridge, 1985. The most detailed and readable history of Reformation-era Sweden available in English, with a sympathetic treatment of John III and his church policies.

Senn, Frank C. *Liturgia svecanae ecclesiae catholicae et orthodoxae conformis: An Attempt at Eucharistic Restoration during the Swedish Reformation.* Notre Dame, 1979. A dissertation dealing with the Red Book Liturgy, its sources and place within the evolution of Swedish Reformation liturgy, with a detailed analysis of its eucharistic prayer and theology.

Serenius, Sigtrygg. *Liturgia svecanae ecclesiae catholicae et orthodoxae conformis: En liturgie-historisk undersökning med särskild hänsyn till strukture och förlagor.* Turku, 1966. A detailed study of the Red Book with special attention to its structure and sources. Serenius has demonstrated John's reliance on Swedish medieval missal traditions more than on the post-Tridentine missal, as well as on Reformation church orders.

Yelverton, Eric E. *The Mass in Sweden: Its Development from the Latin Rite from 1531 to 1917.* Henry Bradshaw Society, vol. 57. London, 1920. An introduction, the Latin-Swedish text, and an English translation of the Mass of John III. It lacks the preface of Archbishop Gothus and the propers.

Wordsworth, John. *The National Church of Sweden.* London and Milwaukee, 1911. An appreciative, if somewhat idealistic, assessment of the Church of Sweden from an Anglican point of view. Pages 231ff. deal with the church crisis during the reign of John III.

FRANK C. SENN

JOHN OF AUSTRIA

JOHN OF AUSTRIA (Span., Don Juan; 1547–1578), captain general of the Mediterranean Sea and governor general of the Netherlands. Illegitmate son of Emperor Charles V, John was born in Regensburg, raised in Spain, and recognized in 1559 by his half brother, King Philip II. His career was spent in war, diplomacy, and government. A pious Catholic and bold leader, he was diligent but sometimes impatient with routine. Success came early when, guided by veteran counselors, he subdued the Morisco rebellion in Granada (1568–1570) and defeated the Turks at the Battle of Lepanto (1571). Pope Pius V exclaimed, "There was a man sent from God, and his name was John" (*Jn.* 1:6). But in 1574, lacking sufficient forces because of Philip's financial straits, he lost Tunis.

He directly encountered the Reformation in 1576 when appointed governor general of the rebellious Netherlands, where it was hoped he would enjoy Charles V's popularity and restore peace. But he saw another destiny when English Catholic exiles and Rome urged him to use the Netherlands to invade England, put Mary Stuart on the throne, and marry her. He wasted six crucial months by detouring via Spain to persuade Philip to support the project.

Ordered to pacify the Netherlands first, he arrived there in November to find that his army had mutinied. The States-General, armed and dominated by William of Orange, denied his authority until he accepted their demands, which included limited religious toleration. He and Philip opposed toleration, so he temporized and, by disbanding his army and thus postponing his design on England, gained acceptance of his government in May 1577.

Without accommodation on religion, further negotiations failed. Fearing assassination, he sent his secretary Juan de Escobedo to Spain to recall the army. Philip agreed reluctantly and in 1578 John commenced the reconquest of the Netherlands. In Madrid Escobedo was murdered, reportedly with Philip's approval. Despairing of Philip's confidence, John campaigned through the summer but, falling ill, died on 1 October, leaving the task to his successor Alesandro Farnese, duke of Parma.

BIBLIOGRAPHY

Stirling Maxwell, William. *Don John of Austria.* 2 vols. London, 1883. Old-fashioned but thorough and still the best study, as the romantic hero quality seen in G. K. Chesterton's poem *Lepanto* (1911) tends to confound biographers.

Törne, Per Olaf von. *Don Juan d'Autriche et les projets de conquête de l'Angleterre.* 2 vols. Helsinki, 1915–1928.

PETER O'M. PIERSON

JOHN OF ÁVILA

JOHN OF ÁVILA (1499?–1569), Spanish Erasmian, clerical reformer, and spiritual writer; Roman Catholic saint, known as "el Maestro de Ávila" and "the apostle of Andalucía." A "New Christian" of Jewish lineage, John studied at the Universities of Salamanca and Alcalá. Ordained in 1526, he requested assignment as a missionary to the New World but was barred by the bishop of Seville, Alonso Manrique, possibly because of Spain's "purity of blood" statutes.

Like so many who studied at Alcalá in the 1520s and became Erasmians, John blamed the clergy for the decline of Christian faith and morals and thought that the priesthood had been corrupted by insincere, uneducated men of privilege, especially through the abuse of benefices. John aimed some of his sharpest criticism against chaplaincies, for he thought they tied down the clergy to a single duty and prevented them from ministering in other important ways to the faithful. "In many places," he charged, "there is a sufficient number of masses and extreme want among the poor" (*Obras* 1.47). In 1531 he was denounced to the Inquisition as a heretical revolutionary, but he earned an acquittal two years later, despite the power and influence of his accusers.

Vindicated by this ordeal, which cleared him of any association with Protestantism, John dedicated himself to the betterment of the Roman Catholic church in his native land, particularly through the improvement of clerical education, establishing numerous schools and seminaries throughout Spain. When the Council of Trent tackled the issue of clerical reform it relied heavily on John's *Tratado de la reformación del estado eclesiástico*. A prolific writer of spiritual literature and a tireless advocate of reform, John became one of the leading lights of the Spanish church in his own day. His reform ideals and his spirituality—particularly his accent on mental prayer and inward piety (*recogimiento*)—had a profound influence on Ignatius Loyola, founder of the Jesuits, and on Teresa of Ávila, leader of the Discalced Carmelite reform. He was beatified in 1894, named the patron of the Spanish secular clergy in 1946, and canonized by Pope Paul VI on 6 May 1970.

BIBLIOGRAPHY

Abellán, Jose Luis. *El Erasmismo Español*. Reprint, Madrid, 1982. See especially pp. 229–236.

Bataillon, Marcel. "Jean d'Avila retrouvé." *Bulletin Hispanique* 57 (1955), 5–44.

Bilinkoff, Jodi. *The Ávila of Saint Teresa: Religious Reform in a Sixteenth Century City*. Ithaca, N.Y., 1989. Traces the influence of John of Ávila on other reform movements in Spain; see pp. 80–87.

Jedin, Hubert. "Juan de Ávila als Kirchenreformer." *Zeitschrift für Askese und Mystik* 11 (1936), 124–138.

Peers, E. Allison. *Studies in the Spanish Mystics*. 2 vols., 2d ed. London, 1951. Includes a brief and perceptive study of John of Ávila; see vol. 2, pp. 121–148.

Sala Balust, Luis, ed. *Obras completas del Santo Maestro Juan de Ávila*. 6 vols. Madrid, 1970–1971. See especially Sala Balust's "Vida," vol. 1, pp. 2–392, the most recent and complete biography available.

Sanchez Bella, Florencio. *La reforma del clero en San Juan de Ávila*. Madrid, 1981.

CARLOS M. N. EIRE

JOHN OF HUNGARY. *See* Zapolya, János.

JOHN OF LASCO. *See* Łaski, Jan.

JOHN OF LEIDEN (Dutch, Jan van Leyden; 1509–1536), prophetic ruler and then king of Anabaptist Münster, April 1534–June 1535. John is also known by his patronymic as John Bokelson. His father was mayor of a village outside Leiden; his mother was a maid from the vicinity of Münster. As a journeyman tailor John spent four years in England. In Leiden he married the widow of a shipper and traveled as far as Lisbon and Lübeck. Unsuccessful in trade, he became an innkeeper in Leiden and participated in the amateur theatrical societies called chambers of rhetoric.

The Reformation attracted John's attention. In the summer of 1533 he insisted on a visit to Münster against his wife's wishes because he had heard "that the word of God was preached there best and most forcefully." John was likely already initiated into the apocalyptic teachings of the Melchiorites, which the leading pastor in Münster, Bernhard Rothmann, was then championing. If he was not already a Melchiorite before his visit to Münster, however, the visit there clearly turned him into one. During that trip he also made contact with the Westphalian noble Heinrich Krechting, who was soon to join him in the leadership of Münster Anabaptism. Baptism of adult believers had earlier been suspended among the Melchiorites, but it was reintroduced sometime in 1533 by the charismatic baker Jan Matthijs from Haarlem. Matthijs spent two weeks in Leiden at John's home, around November 1533. Their extensive discussion of the true baptism eventuated in John's receiving both baptism and the commission of an evangelistic "apostle." He was sent to Amsterdam and other cities in Holland and then in mid-January 1534 to Münster, where other emissaries of Matthijs had already baptized the leading pastors.

John witnessed and participated in the political "miracle" that resulted in the election of an Anabaptist town council in Münster in late February. In the weeks leading up to Easter (5 April 1534), for which Matthijs had predicted the end of the world, John acted as the dutiful lieutenant of the senior prophet. During this time the city came under siege, community of goods was introduced, 2,000 non-Anabaptists were expelled from Münster, and about 2,500 Anabaptists immigrated from surrounding lands. Münster had established its reputation as the Jerusalem that God had provided for his persecuted flock. Because of their astonishing rise to power in Münster, Anabaptist predictions of the end of the world were widely believed, and the Melchiorites in the Netherlands mushroomed from a sect into a mass movement. But Matthijs's credibility hinged largely on the world ending on 5 April 1534. His world ended that day in a suicidal attack on the besiegers, and the sorcerer's apprentice, the twenty-five-year-old John of Leiden, found himself in charge of Anabaptist Münster.

Lacking the senior prophet's authority, John contrived a governmental structure that carefully balanced the immigrants from Westphalia and the Netherlands with natives of Münster, particularly those Münster notables who had rallied to Anabaptism in early 1534. This government was ornamented with Old Testament pageantry: from April to

September 1534 the rulers were called the Twelve Elders of Israel, and from September to the fall of the city John made himself a new warlike King David, with messianic pretensions to ruling the world in preparation for the return of Christ, "the peaceful Solomon." This structure, in practice, blunted the aspirations of Matthijs and Rothmann for community of goods. The immovable property of the Münster notables was not redistributed among the population, and the royal court enjoyed a luxury that mocked the suffering of the general population in the final days of the siege.

The king's individual hand was most apparent in the introduction of polygamy in July. He took a week to convince the preachers of his interpretation of the Old Testament commandment in *Genesis* 1:28 to be fruitful and multiply, and the resulting citizens' rebellion came close to putting a quick end to Anabaptist power in the city. A reasonable estimate is that 70 percent of the adult population of Anabaptist Münster were women; to control them and use them to support the various measures of defense were the practical objectives of Münsterite polygamy. Nontheless, the traditional view that John of Leiden lusted after Divara, the widow of the slain prophet Matthijs, whom he made his chief spouse and queen, and that having sixteen wives was an agreeable accompaniment to the young man's fantasies of world dominion, is hard to dismiss totally. King John promised the deliverance of Münster by Easter 1535, and when this did not happen he lost much credit as a prophet among the Melchiorites in the Netherlands. The militants turned to Jan van Batenburg as their "new David," and a tract attributed to Menno Simons insisted that Christ was the only promised David.

When Münster was finally conquered on 25 June 1535, John was taken alive. The bishop of Münster, Franz von Waldeck, kept him on display for a few months, during which time his interrogations and interviews considerably expanded historical knowledge about him. Finally, on 22 January 1536, he was publicly and gruesomely tortured to death in Münster. His corpse and those of two associates executed with him were long displayed in cages hanging from the tower of Saint Lambert's Church, a barbaric civic symbol of Counter-Reformation Münster.

BIBLIOGRAPHY

Bax, E. Belfort. *Rise and Fall of the Anabaptists.* Reprint, New York, 1970. Old fashioned, socialist-oriented narrative with heavy emphasis on revolutionary followers of Melchior Hoffman and the Münster kingdom.

Cornelius, C. A. "Bokelson." In *Allgemeine Deutsche Biographie* (1876). Reprint, Berlin, 1967. A sober, concise assessment by the preeminent nineteenth-century historian of Münster Anabaptism.

Cornelius, C. A., ed. *Berichte der Augenzeugen über das münsterische Wiedertäuferreich.* Die Geschichtsquellen des Bisthums Münster, vol. 2. Reprint, Münster, 1983. Contains Heinrich Gresbeck's eyewitness narrative as well as protocols of interrogations of John of Leiden.

Detmer, Heinrich. *Bilder aus den religiösen und sozialen Unruhen in Münster während des 16. Jahrhunderts: 1. Johann von Leiden; Seine Persönlichkeit und seine Stellung im Münsterschen Reiche.* Münster, 1903. Most extensive biography, reliable and scholarly but moralizing.

Kirchhoff, Karl-Heinz. *Die Täufer in Münster, 1534–1535.* Münster, 1973. A prosopographical study that establishes the prominent role of Münster notables during the period of Anabaptist rule.

Rammstedt, Otthein. *Sekte und soziale Bewegung. Soziologische Analyse der Täufer in Münster.* Cologne, 1966. A provocative interpretation of John of Leiden's rule of Münster in succession to John Matthijs as the "institutionalization of charisma."

Stayer, James M. *Anabaptists and the Sword.* 2d ed. Lawrence, Kans., 1976. Contains the most extensive English language narrative treatment of Münster Anabaptism in recent academic literature.

JAMES M. STAYER

JOHN OF THE CROSS (Span., Juan de la Cruz, Juan de Yepes y Álvarez; 1542–1591), Christian mystic. He was born Juan de Yepes in the village of Fontiveros, in central Castile. His father died when he was only a few months old, and his mother, struggling to support three sons alone, was often reduced to begging along the roads. Álvarez would later embrace the poverty and suffering he endured as everyday experience and transform them into spiritual principles of the highest order.

His family finally settled in Medina del Campo. There clerical authorities, impressed by his intelligence and piety, accepted him as a charity student, grooming him for a career as a priest. But the young man longed for a life of solitude and contemplation. In 1563 he entered the city's Carmelite monastery. After completing his studies at the University of Salamanca he received ordination and returned to Medina in 1567.

There he met the nun Teresa of Ávila, an encounter that would dramatically alter his life. Teresa was then establishing the second of her reformed Carmelite houses for women. Álvarez, who had found his order disappointingly lax, was instantly drawn to the charismatic Teresa and her vision of an ascetic and prayerful life in accordance with the primitive Carmelite rule. Along with two others from the Medina house, he became the first of the Discalced (or reformed) Carmelite friars.

He dedicated the remaining twenty-four years of his life to the reform movement, despite the opposition of his Carmelite superiors, who had him imprisoned and beaten. It was while a prisoner in Toledo in 1577–1578 that he began an extraordinary corpus of poetry that would come to include such masterpieces as "The Spiritual Canticle," "The Living Flame of Love," "The Ascent of Mount Carmel," and "The Dark Night of the Soul." Álvarez distinguished himself as a monastic administrator, spiritual director, and theologian. But it is his exquisite poetry, shocking at times with erotic intensity, that continues to endear him to millions, Catholic and non-Catholic alike. He died in 1591, was beatified in 1675, and was canonized in 1726.

BIBLIOGRAPHY

Brenan, Gerald. *St John of the Cross: His Life and Poetry.* Cambridge, 1973. A highly readable and engaging biography, although not always reliable on historical details.

The Collected Works of St. John of the Cross. Rev. ed. Translated by Kieran Kavanaugh and Otilio Rodríguez. Washington, D.C., 1991. The most up-to-date English translation of John's works, with useful historical introduction.

Crisógono de Jesús Sacramentado. *Vida de San Juan de la Cruz.* 11th rev. ed. Madrid, 1982. This remains the definitive biography of John of the Cross, revised periodically since its original publication in 1946. There does exist an English translation of an earlier, somewhat less reliable edition: *The Life of St. John of the Cross,* translated by Kathleen Pond, London, 1958.

God Speaks in the Night: The Life, Times, and Teaching of St. John of the Cross. Translated by Kieran Kavanaugh. Washington, D.C., 1991. This volume, the collaborative effort of top Carmelite scholars from several countries, was compiled to commemorate the fourth centenary of the death of John of the Cross in 1991. Available also in Spanish and Italian.

Juan de la Cruz. *Obras Completas.* 3d ed. Edited by José Vicente Rodriguez. Madrid, 1988.

JODI BILINKOFF

JOHN THE YOUNGER. *See* Łaski, Jan.

JON, François du. *See* Junius, Franciscus.

JONAS, Justus (also Jodocus or Jobst Koch; 1493–1555), German humanist and co-worker and friend of Martin Luther. Born Jodocus Koch in Nordhausen, an imperial city northwest of Erfurt, Jonas adopted the Christian name of his father, a city councilman, as his surname during university studies. Jonas matriculated at Erfurt for the summer semester of 1506 and received his B.A. and M.A. in 1507 and 1510 respectively, setting the stage for advanced work in law. During those years Jonas began a lifelong friendship with Eobanus Hessus, who encouraged Jonas's interest in humanism. In 1511 Jonas moved to Wittenberg, to follow his law teacher Henning Göde.

Three years and a law baccalaureate later, Jonas returned to Erfurt, where humanist notions advocated by the Augustinian canon Konrad Mutian at nearby Gotha were gaining strength. Through the Gotha sodality's activities, Jonas became interested in theology and in 1516 was ordained a priest. By 1518 he was promoted to doctor in both theology and law and received a prebend at Saint Severus (next to the Erfurt cathedral), a position that also made Jonas a university licentiate in law. His admiration for Desiderius Erasmus steered Jonas into Greek and biblical studies. In 1519, while Jonas was visiting Erasmus in the Netherlands, the Erfurt faculty moved to include Greek and Hebrew in its regular university curriculum and initiated other philosophy and theology course reforms. It also elected Jonas rector, a boost for humanism's "new learning" in academic circles.

Initially Jonas favored Erasmus's approach to reform of faith and piety, but after Luther's clash with Johann Eck at the 1519 Leipzig Disputation, Jonas was drawn toward Wittenberg, despite Erasmus's efforts to prevent the shift. In June 1520 Johannes Lang relayed Luther's offer of friendship, and Jonas traveled with Luther to the 1521 Diet of Worms. His old Wittenberg teacher Göde had died in January 1521, and Jonas had been recommended as a replacement, so while in Worms Jonas was named professor of canon law by Elector Frederick III of Saxony. He also became provost of Wittenberg's castle church.

Afterward, with Luther in Wartburg castle, Jonas promoted Wittenberg's reforms with preaching and polemics. From 1523 to 1533 he was dean of the theology faculty and lectured on both the Old and the New Testaments, including *Romans, Acts of the Apostles,* and *Psalms.* As time passed he moved from the classroom to literary activities and proved especially valuable as a translator, frequently putting the treaties of Luther and Philipp Melanchthon into Latin or German. He translated such writings as Luther's *De servo arbitrio* and Melanchthon's *Loci communes* into the vernacular for a wider audience.

For more than two decades Jonas worked to reform theology and church structure. He represented Wittenberg at such gatherings as the 1529 Marburg Colloquy and the 1530 Diet of Augsburg. His counsel was sought on reforming theology and restructuring church administration. Thus, he advised the neighboring territory of Anhalt in 1532 and was the author of a new church ordinance for Zerbst in 1538. He helped introduce reform in ducal Saxony in 1539, working on its new evangelical church order. In 1541 Halle city officials invited Jonas to teach the evangelical faith to the city. Protected by Frederick's technical though rarely observed administrative tie to Halle, Jonas began preaching in 1541, became superintendent in 1542, and rewrote Halle's church order in 1543. Administration filled his schedule, leaving little time for writing and translating.

In February 1546 Jonas stood by Luther's deathbed in Eisleben and later preached the funeral sermon. That year he lost his ecclesiastical position as a casualty of the Schmalkald War. As hostilities erupted, Jonas sharply criticized Emperor Charles V and Elector Moritz of Saxony. When Moritz captured Halle in November 1546, Jonas fled. He returned in January 1547, taking the opportunity to force out monks, nuns, and the last vestiges of Roman Catholic ritual. After Halle fell a second time, Jonas left again, traveling and preaching in Mansfeld, Nordhausen, and Hildesheim. He weighed in against Andreas Osiander in the inter-Lutheran Osiandrian controversy that lay behind article 3 of the 1577 Formula of Concord.

The war took its toll on Jonas physically, personally, and professionally. Through the intervention of friends he was allowed back in Halle, but the city council balked at relying on a man aged and worn and also no friend of Elector Moritz. Barred from the pulpit, Jonas was confined to teaching Latin. In 1550 he moved to Coburg as court preacher. His long relationship with Melanchthon soured when Jonas opposed the Leipzig Interim, which was partly written by his former colleague. In reply Melanchthon characterized Jonas as an old man not up to the rigors of the pastoral office. In 1553 Jonas became superintendent in Eisfeld, resuming translation work in his last years. His importance to the Lutheran Reformation rested not so much in original theological contributions as in his administrative and especially translation abilities, thereby multiplying the effects of his talented colleagues.

BIBLIOGRAPHY

Primary Source

Kawerau, Gustav. *Der Briefwechsel des Justus Jonas.* 2 vols. Halle, 1884–1885.

Secondary Sources

Delius, Walter. *Lehre und Leben Justus Jonas, 1493–1555.* Gütersloh, 1952. A brief but useful biography.

Groll, Karin. "Jonas, Justus." In *Biographisch-Bibliographisches Kirchenlexikon,* vol. 3, pp. 636–637. Herzberg, 1992.

Leder, Hans-Günter. "Luthers Beziehungen zu seinen Wittenberger Freunden." In *Leben und Werk Martin Luthers von 1526 bis 1546,* edited by Helmar Junghans. Göttingen, 1983. Pp. 433–436 detail the relationship of Luther with his co-worker and translator.

Lehmann, Martin. "Justus Jonas: A Collaborator with Luther." *Lutheran Quarterly* 2 (1950), 189–200. Quick overview of Jonas's career.

———. *Justus Jonas: Loyal Reformer.* Minneapolis, 1963. Detailed treatment of Jonas's life and work. Lehmann seeks to give Jonas his due for his contribution to Wittenberg's reform.

Pressel, Theodor. *Justus Jonas.* Elberfeld, 1862. Old biography is part of Pressel's series on the secondary and late reformers including Caspar Cruciger, Paul Speratus, Lazarus Spengler, Nilolaus von Amsdorf, Paul Eber, Martin Chemnitz, and David Chytraeus.

ROBERT ROSIN

JÖRGER FAMILY, an aristocratic family of Upper Austria that rose to the ranks of the nobility in the sixteenth century and was connected to the Reformation in Austria. Christoph Jörger, selected by his father for a position at the royal Albertine court, experienced a conversion while reading Luther's September Testament. He initiated contact with the reformer and asked Luther to send a minister. Michael Stifel served as court preacher in Tollet, the residence of the family, and gathered a circle of reform-minded people around him. Measures taken by Ferdinand I after the Colloquy of Regensburg (1524), together with the departure of Stifel (1527), led to the dispersion of this circle.

The connections of the family to Luther did not end. They resulted in correspondence, and in the study of two young family members in Wittenberg, as well as that of another one at the court of Johann of Saxony. In her will of 1533 Dorothea Jörger made one of the first unequivocal testimonies for the Protestant faith among the Austrian nobility. Her son Christoph suffered because of the conflict between his personal convictions and the official prohibition of the Reformation. For that reason he renounced his post in the government and established relations with the Protestant clergy in Regensburg.

The religious concession of 1568 solved these problems for the time being. With the next generation (Helmhard IX) the family attained a leading role within the estates and in religious policy. As president of the court cabinet, Helmhard could support Protestant churches. Gradually the family obtained possessions in Lower Austria and established in Hernals (near Vienna) an especially important foothold for Viennese Protestants. The Jörgers, who held ecclesiastical church patronage rights, gradually secured the leadership of the provincial ministry.

Efforts to create new possibilities for the Reformation led to numerous conflicts among the landed gentry, especially during the Counter-Reformation. Hans and Wolfgang Jörger in Linz numbered among the leaders of the Protestant party of the nobility, which in 1609 temporarily obtained a resolution of issues. They also became embroiled in the catastrophic revolt of the nobility (1618–1620) and were forced to forfeit their position and their fortune. A small number managed to regain their possessions after conversion to Catholicism. The family died out in 1772.

BIBLIOGRAPHY

Westmüller, Liselotte. "Helmhard Jörger und die protestantische Gemeinde zu Hernals." *Jahrbuch zur Geschichte des Protestantismus in Österreich* 81 (1965), 151.

Wurm, Heinrich. "Die Jörger von Tollet." Forsch.z.Gesch.OÖs. 4. Linz, 1955.

GUSTAV REINGRABNER

Translated from German by Susan M. Sisler

JORIS, David (c.1501–1556), Dutch glass painter and lay reformer, Anabaptist, and spiritualist in the Low Countries. Around 1524 Joris became attracted to the writings of Luther, and in 1528 he was arrested in his home city, Delft, for distributing an anticlerical broadsheet. The resulting torture and three-year banishment made him more cautious in promoting religious reform. While in refuge in East Frisia, he became aware of the apocalyptic Anabaptist message proclaimed by the south German lay preacher Melchior Hoffman. Not until the winter of 1534/35, however, was Joris baptized and shortly thereafter ordained an Anabaptist teacher by the Melchiorite Obbe Philips and the Münsterite Damas van Hoorn. At an Anabaptist meeting in the winter of 1534/35 in the Waterland district of Holland, Joris advocated a cautious, nonviolent position and warned against full support for Anabaptist Münster. With the fall of Münster in June 1535, Joris's stature as a leader increased, and in late August 1536 he mediated a compromise settlement between militant and nonviolent Anabaptists at a meeting in Bocholt, Westphalia. Joris's accord promoted agreement on basic issues such as believer's baptism, while on the controversial question of violence, Joris proposed that vengeance on the godless was to be carried out by angels, without defining them as either human or divine agents. Joris's compromise, however, provided only a temporary reprieve from the serious rifts in the movement.

In December 1536 Joris experienced some visions depicting the apocalyptic third David who, with the power of the second David, Jesus Christ, would usher in the new spiritual kingdom and restore the "children of God" to their rightful glory. Thus inspired, Joris set out to reunite the divided Anabaptist groups under his charismatic leadership. In 1538 he stepped up his writing campaign and participated in conferences with the remnant Münsterites at Oldenburg, Westphalia, and with the refugee Melchiorites in Strasbourg. Joris spiritualized key elements of the Münsterite program: eradication of the godless would occur only after an undetermined period of inner purification on the part of believers, and Münsterite polygamy, while imprudent, was not strictly forbidden. For pacifists, Joris's teachings were in most respects faithful to those of Hoffman. Joris also prudently allowed his followers to adopt a Nicodemite procedure by hiding their true beliefs while outwardly conforming to approved religion, a safer approach to religious dissent within an urban environment. As a result of these ideas, Joris was able to win followers from the militant Anabaptists (Münsterites and the terrorist gangs of Jan van Batenburg), as well as from the peaceful Melchiorites. Joris clearly became the most important Anabaptist leader in the Netherlands from after the fall of Münster until the early 1540s.

Under the pressure of a terrible persecution in which over one hundred of his followers were executed in 1539, Joris moved that summer to Antwerp, where he gained the patronage of the noble van Berchem family. In this refuge Joris more thoroughly spiritualized his ideas, evident in his major work, *Twonder Boeck* (The Wonder Book; 1542/43). He also engaged in a heated debate with Menno Simons over Joris's leadership claims and unique teachings. Joris's case, presented in a fairly dignified manner by letters and by lieutenants such as Nicolaas Meyndertsz van Blesdijk, won to his side many Mennonites. In the summer of 1544, however, Joris assumed the pseudonym Johan van Brugge and moved with his wealthy entourage to Basel, Switzerland, where the refugees conformed to Basel society and were accorded full citizenship. Joris was now able to live in comfort and continue to write to his supporters. But Blesdijk's doubts about Joris's luxurious life and self-conception resulted in a major rift among the Davidites by 1556. Joris died in the midst of this conflict, but not until 1559 did Basel's magistrates acknowledge that the prosperous Netherlander had been a notorious heretic; they then burned Joris's disinterred corpse at the stake.

At the heart of Joris's approach was an ascetic "cross mysticism" similar to late medieval mystical forms. Salvation meant taking up the cross in a personal appropriation of Christ's self-denial and suffering with the goal of inner purification. Joris's increasing separation between the flesh and the spirit led him to affirm that whatever was committed in the flesh was inconsequential, as were all religious ceremonies, such as baptism and marriage. What truly mattered was a progressive, inner asceticism that involved mortification to sinful attitudes accompanied by a spiritual rebirth, resulting in inward purity, humility, obedience to the Spirit's teaching, and fraternal love. Joris was also preoccupied with freedom from sexual shame, achieved in part by public confession of sins that involved believers confessing their lusts before the fellowship. Furthermore, spiritual knowledge was gained by the anointed prophet through direct communication with the Holy Spirit. Joris's spiritualistic perspective also led him to reject the corporeal existence of the devil, reducing it to an evil inclination within unredeemed humanity. Although Joris was remarkably well versed in the scriptures, he based his biblical interpretation on personal, divine inspiration. The literal text of the scriptures was used to support the spirit's message when dealing with nonbelievers.

After his move to Basel, Joris reduced references to the third David, who became less an eschatological figure of judgment than an inspired teacher of esoteric knowledge. His writings also begin to reflect limited influence from humanist associates, such as the physician Jean Bauhin and the professor Sébastien Castellion, as well as some interest in the occult sciences. Joris still promoted the Netherlands as the site of the forthcoming kingdom of God—with Dutch as its language—in which would reign peace, love of neighbor, and freedom from religious persecution. Joris's writings continued to be popular after his death, evidenced by their republication in the 1580s and then again in the first decades of the seventeenth century. In all, over 240 published works have survived, as well as a large number of manuscript items and several artistic representations of his ideas. His writings, including a volume of songs and *The Wonder Book,* achieved a wide audience among those Netherlanders dissatisfied with formal orthodoxy, whether Catholic or Reformed, and who wished to promote a religion based on the inner word, personal spiritual perfection, and religious liberty.

BIBLIOGRAPHY

Primary Source

Waite, Gary K., ed. and trans. *The Anabaptist Writings of David Joris, 1535–1543*. Classics of the Radical Reformation, vol. 7. Waterloo, Ont., 1994. A selection of Joris' Anabaptist writings in English translation, including an early (auto)biography. The first modern, book-length edition of Joris's works.

Secondary Sources

Boon, K. G. "De glasschilder David Joris, een exponent van het doperse geloof: Zijn kunst en zijn invloed op Dirck Crabeth." *Academiae Analecta* (1988), 115–137. The best study of Joris's artistic abilities and influence.

Stayer, James M. "David Joris: A Prolegomenon to Further Research." *Mennonite Quarterly Review* 59 (1985), 350–61. An excellent introduction to the scholarly debate surrounding Joris.

———. "Davidite vs. Mennonite." In *The Dutch Dissenters,* edited by Irvin B. Horst, pp. 143–159. Leiden, 1986. Argues that although Menno Simons and Joris emphasized distinct elements of their common Melchiorite heritage, their theological differences have been overstated.

Valkema Blouw, Paul. "Printers to the 'arch-heretic' David Joris: Prolegomena to a Bibliography of His Works." *Quærendo* 21 (1991), 163–209. Most up-to-date discussion of Joris's printers and literary corpus.

Waite, Gary K. *David Joris and Dutch Anabaptism. 1524–1543.* Waterloo, Ont., 1990. The only monograph on Joris in English; examines his Anabaptist career, ideas, and following in their historical context, arguing that Joris's approach was particularly suited to urban Anabaptists.

———. "The Longevity of Spiritualistic Anabaptism: The Literary Legacy of David Joris." *Canadian Journal of History/ Annales Canadiennes d'Histoire* 26 (1991), 177–198. Argues from the evidence of the later publication of Joris's writings that many late sixteenth- and early seventeenth-century Netherlanders found his spiritualistic ideas attractive.

———. "The Dutch Nobility and Anabaptism, 1535–1545." *Sixteenth Century Journal* 23 (1992), 458–485. A discussion of the motives behind Netherlandish noble support of Joris.

———. "The Holy Spirit Speaks Dutch: David Joris and the Promotion of the Dutch Language, 1539–1545." *Church History* (1992), 47–59. An interesting study of Joris's writings promoting the spiritual superiority of the Netherlands and the Dutch language.

Zijlstra, Samme. *Nicolaas Meyndertsz. van Blesdiik. Een bijdrage tot de geschiedenis van het Davidjorisme.* Assen, Netherlands, 1983. The best study of Blesdijk, Joris's most important lieutenant. Argues also that Joris was the most important Dutch Anabaptist leader between the fall of Münster and his move to Antwerp.

———. "Menno Simons and David Joris." *Mennonite Quarterly Review* 62 (1988), 249–256. Explains how Blesdijk was able to convince many Mennonites to join Joris's group, in spite of Menno's hostility to some of Joris's ideas.

———. "De bestrijding van de davidjoristen aan het eind van de zestiende eeuw." *Doopsgezinde Bijdragen* 18 (1992), 11–37. An excellent survey of the controversy concerning Joris in the late-sixteenth- and early-seventeenth-century Netherlands.

GARY K. WAITE

JOSELMANN OF ROSHEIM (Hebr., Joseph Ben Gershom; 1478–1554), the leading representative of imperial Jewry during the first half of the sixteenth century. His family originated in Louhans, France, but moved to Alsace before Joselmann's birth. He was orphaned in 1484 and raised by his mother's family. As an adult, he settled in Mittelbergheim near Strasbourg and made his living from commerce. In 1507 he successfully appealed an order expelling Jews from Obernai, and in 1510 he was elected one of two leaders of the Alsatian Jewish community. Thereafter, he devoted his life to interceding with provincial and imperial authorities on behalf of Jewish communities facing expulsion, charges of Host desecration, and ritual murder, the accusation that Jews murdered Christian children to use their blood for Passover bread. Joselmann's calm and pragmatic skills earned the respect of Jew and Christian alike, and he was appointed *Befehlshaber der ganzer Judenschaft* ("commander of all Jewry") by the emperor Maximilian I.

At Charles V's coronation at Aachen in 1520, the new emperor granted Joselmann a liberal charter enumerating German-Jewish residential and commercial rights and privileges. Subsequently, Joselmann successfully represented many Jewish communities facing expulsion, including Rosheim (1525), Hagenau (1527), Poesing in Hungary (1529), and Silesia (1535). Reformation tensions aggravated Jewish-Christian relations, however, often catching Jews between Catholics and Protestants. At the meeting of the imperial diet in 1530 Charles demanded that Joselmann debate the virtues of Judaism and Christianity against Anton Margaritha, Luther's protégé and a Jewish convert to Lutheranism. Though he considerd himself an ally of Charles V, Joselmann also appealed to Protestant rulers on behalf of local Jewish communities facing expulsion, including Elector John Frederick in Saxony in 1536. Joselmann also appeared before the Protestant convention in Frankfurt in 1539 on behalf of the Jews of Brandenburg. Then in 1543 Joselmann received from Strasbourg municipal authorities a ban on the publication of Luther's anti-Jewish writings.

During the Schmalkald War Jews were often persecuted by armies of both religions, and Joselmann interceded with Charles on behalf of Alsatian Jews in 1548 and 1549. Again, in 1551, at the meeting of the imperial diet of Augsburg, Joselmann intervened on behalf of Jewish commmunities in Colmar, Württemberg, and Bavaria. His greatest accomplishment, however, was the certificate of rights for German Jewry that Charles V presented to him in 1544. This charter was the most tolerant document ever granted a community of medieval German Jews.

Joselmann wrote several short works describing his encounters with provincial and imperial agencies. These include a pamphlet against the blood libel (1530), a short *Iggeret Nehama* (Letter of Consolation; 1537) against Martin Bucer's anti-Jewish attacks, the homiletical *Derech Emunah* (The Way of Faith), and the *Derech ha-Kodesh* (The Way of Sanctification; 1531) concerning questions of ethics and martyrdom. His most important work was *Sefer ha-mikne,* his memoirs of 1541 to 1547.

BIBLIOGRAPHY

Primary Source

Fraenkel-Goldsmith, Havah, ed. *Rabbi Yosef Ish Rosheim, Sefer ha-Mikne.* Jerusalem, 1970. Only edition of Joselmann's important memoirs.

Secondary Sources

Fellchenfeld, Ludwig. *Rabbl Josel von Rosheim.* Strasbourg, 1898. Though old, this volume is still useful in understanding Joselmann's importance in terms of the Reformation.

Stern, Selma. *Josel of Rosheim.* Translated by Gertrude Hirschler. Philadelphia, 1965. Most recent and best work about Joselmann.

JEROME FRIEDMAN

JUAN DE ÁVILA. *See* John of Ávila.

JUAN DE LE CRUZ. *See* John of the Cross.

JUD, Leo (also Judä; 1482–1542), Protestant reformer, Zwingli's associate at Zurich, translator, and scholar. He was born in Alsace, at Gemar, southwest of Strasbourg. His father, Johannes Jud, was a local priest; his mother was Elsa Hochsang, from Solothurn. He had one sister, Clara. Though the family name might suggest a Jewish ancestry, Jud himself said that he did not know whether this was true. He attended Latin school with Martin Bucer at Schlettstadt and in 1499 matriculated at the University of Basel, where he met and became close friends with Zwingli. He intended to study medicine there, but soon turned to theology under the influence of Thomas Wyttenbach.

Jud was ordained to the priesthood in Rome in 1507. From 1507 to 1512 he was deacon at Saint Theodore at Basel, and from 1512 to 1518, preacher at Saint Hippolyte in Alsace. In 1519 he became Zwingli's successor at Einsiedeln, in Schwyz, where his reforming proclivities became clear. In June 1522 he was chosen, on Zwingli's recommendation, to become pastor of Saint Peter's in Zurich. He took up his duties there on 2 February 1523, just four days after the first disputation. Henceforth, Jud was Zwingli's closest associate and supporter.

As a result of his prodding, many nuns and monks left their monasteries and convents, and several priests acknowledged their marital ties and had public weddings. Jud himself married a former nun in autumn 1523. In September, iconoclastic disturbances followed his call for the removal of "idols." He was at Zwingli's side during the Second Zurich Disputation (26–28 October 1523) and during the confrontation with the radical Anabaptists in 1525. He was a judge, one of two clergymen along with four laymen, of the marriage court (*Ehegericht*) in Zurich from its inception in 1525. He also regularly participated in the *Prophezei* that Zwingli inaugurated in 1525.

Jud had great talent as a translator. He was responsible for the new modified baptismal service in German in 1523. He was a member of the team, along with Konrad Pellikan and Theodor Bibliander, that produced the Zurich Bible in the local German dialect between 1525 and 1529. He translated works of Augustine, Thomas à Kempis, Erasmus, Luther, Zwingli, Calvin, and Bullinger. He, along with others, edited and published Zwingli's exegeses of Old Testament books.

Jud met Heinrich Bullinger for the first time in 1523. After the defeat of Zurich and the death of Zwingli at Kappel, it was Jud who nominated Bullinger, in December 1531, as Zwingli's replacement as leader of the Zurich church. Then, in March 1532, in the aftermath of Kappel, Jud challenged the entire structure of Reformed society in Zurich. Initially influenced by Johannes Oecolampadius, and then clearly under the spell of Kaspar von Schwenckfeld, Jud advocated separating civil and ecclesiastical discipline and rejected the late medieval idea that the civil and ecclesiastical jurisdictions and communities were conterminous. For the next twenty months Jud corresponded with Schwenckfeld, Bullinger, and Bucer about these matters, eventually breaking with Schwenckfeld in late December 1533 and making his peace with Bullinger.

During the final nine years of his life, Jud worked closely with Bullinger. He was among the group that drew up the First Helvetic (Second Basel) Confession in 1536, and his German translation of the Latin original became the accepted text. He published a larger and smaller catechism in German in 1534, and a Latin catechism in 1538. In 1539 he published Zwingli's New Testament exegeses. When he died on 19 June 1542, Jud left behind a nearly finished translation into Latin of the Hebrew Old Testament. Completed by Bibliander, this Latin Old Testament was published in 1543 along with a revised version of Erasmus's Latin New Testament to form the first edition of the Zurich Latin Bible.

BIBLIOGRAPHY

Baker, J. Wayne. "Church, State, and Dissent: The Crisis of the Swiss Reformation, 1531–1536." *Church History* 57 (1988), 135–152. Places Jud's challenge of the Reformed structure in Zurich in 1532 and 1533 in its larger context.

Herding, Otto. "Die deutsche Gestalt der Institutio Principis Christiani des Erasmus: Leo Jud und Spalatin." In *Adel und Kirche. Gerd Tellenbach zum 65. Geburtstag dargebracht von Freunden und Schülern,* edited by Josef Fleckenstein and Karl Schmid, pp. 534–551. Freiburg, Basel, and Vienna, 1968. Comparative study of the two translations, by Jud and Spalatin, of Erasmus' *Institutio Principis Christiani.*

Pestalozzi, Carl. *Leo Judä: Nach handschriftlichen und gleichzeitigen Quellen.* Elberfeld, 1860. Only complete scholarly biography.

Verzeichnis der im deutschen Sprachbereich erschienenen Drucke des XVI. Jahrhunderts. Stuttgart, 1983–. See vol. 10, nos. 997–1023.

Weisz, Leo. *Leo Jud, Ulrich Zwinglis Kampfgenosse, 1482–1542.* Zurich, 1942. Popular, uncritical, short biography.

Wyss, Karl-Heinz. *Leo Jud, Seine Entwicklung zum Reformator, 1519–1523.* Bern and Frankfurt, 1976. Excellent coverage of Jud's life up to the beginning of his work in Zurich. Includes a bibliography of Jud's own works and another of works about Jud, as well as a list of all extant letters from and to Jud.

J. WAYNE BAKER

JUDAIZERS. The term *Judaizer* refers to someone who forsakes Christian doctrine in favor of the doctrines of Judaism. In biblical writings it refers specifically to a group of Jewish Christians who expected that Jewish dietary laws and circumcision would remain binding for both Jewish and gentile Christians. Many scholars have assumed that much of Pauline theology, so influential during the Reformation, was formed in conscious opposition to this group. It is unsurprising that during the Reformation era *Judaizer* was a commonly used invective hurled repeatedly at theological opponents.

The meaning of the term in actual practice was very fluid and could be used on both sides of any given debate. It depended for its polemical weight on the widespread societal assumption that Judaism was a false and decadent religion, superseded entirely by Christianity. Therefore, any increased influence of Judaism on Christian doctrine could only be the result of a lapse or falling away from truth. Only rarely was this assumption itself ever challenged. The common defense used against the charge of Judaizing was to attempt to prove that it was actually the opponent who was the true Judaizer.

Reformation theology passed on and even intensified the poison of Christian anti-Judaism. Yet such a keen observer as the spiritualist Valentine Krautwald saw already in the early Reformation period that Protestant theology represented a "Judaizing" of Christianity. The very roots of Christianity are in Judaism, yet this was obscured so long as Neoplatonism, Aristotelianism, and a Latin biblical text were the major vehicles for transmission of Christian doctrine. The Reformation brought renewed interest in looking at the original texts, and many reformers sought out rabbinic sources to learn the ancient Hebrew. Even Martin Luther was early on convinced that his theology would be readily accepted by Jews and wrote treatises emphasizing the Jewishness of Jesus Christ.

Jewish or Hebraic elements can also be seen in the Protestant affirmation of the secular life, renewed interest in eschatology, emphasis on the word of God, theocratic government, and justifications given for "holy warfare." These are but a few of the most obvious examples, seen particularly in Huldrych Zwingli's Zurich, Martin Bucer's Strasbourg, John Calvin's Geneva, and later in English Puritanism.

Because the term *Judaizer* was a polemical invective, it must be discounted by serious historians as a source for understanding the thought of persons or groups. Although Hebraic influences resulted from increased attention to the Hebrew Bible, none of the dominant Reformation theologians or groups sincerely looked to Judaism as a source for Christian theology. Only on the fringes of the Reformation do we find a studied "Judaizing" occurring. An important source of Judaization originated from Spanish Marranos and New Christians in Italy. Servetus, Valdez, and Spanish Judaizers might be mentioned. Another example was the small group of Anabaptists in Moravia and Silesia, led by Oswald Glaidt and Andreas Fischer. Glaidt was the originator of a Sabbatarian form of Anabaptism, which Kaspar von Schwenckfeld called an "Ebionite heresy," a term equivalent to Judaizer. Glaidt later abandoned this teaching, but Fischer continued and elaborated on it. Fischer developed a theology based on the continuity between the Old and New Covenants. This led him to reinstitute the biblical sabbath (Saturday) as the day of Christian worship. When charged with Judaizing, Fischer accepted the term without argument, pointing out simply that Jews and Christians worship the same God and that salvation has come through the Jews. He insisted that the Sunday sabbath was a violation of the Decalogue and implied that the separation of church from synagogue was the point of "fall" of the church from faithfulness. There is some evidence that Fischer also instituted circumcision among his followers. Even Fischer, however, stated clearly that "we are not Jews."

Late in the century a group of radical antitrinitarians in Transylvania went even further in their acceptance of Judaism. These Sabbatarians incorporated postbiblical Jewish sources into their worship and used a translated Jewish prayer book. Although they spent more than two centuries worshiping in secret—outwardly remaining members of various recognized religions in the territory—the descendants of this group eventually converted to Judaism. Therefore, if the term *Judaizer* is to have any scholarly value at all, it can only be as applied to the Spanish Judaizers and Sabbatarians in east central Europe.

[*See also* Antisemitism; Christian Hebraica; *and* Jews.]

BIBLIOGRAPHY

Dán, Róbert. "Judaizare - The Career of a Term." In *Antitrinitarianism in the Second Half of the Sixteenth Century*, edited by Róbert Dán, no. 5. Budapest, 1982. Especially helpful for the polemical use of this term as applied to Unitarians in east central Europe.

Kohn, Samuel. *A Szombatosok: Törtḗnetük, Doamátikaiuk ḗs Irodalmuk.* Budapest, 1889. Definitive secondary source for the Transylvanian Sabbatarians.

Liechty, Daniel. *Andreas Fischer and the Sabbatarian Anabaptists.* Scottdale, Pa., 1988. Best source, extensively documented, for Sabbatarian Anabaptism.

———. *Sabbatarianism in the Sixteenth Century.* Berrien Springs, Mich., 1993. Best English language source for Transylvanian Sabbatarianism.

DANIEL LIECHTY

JÜLICH-CLEVE. United in 1521 and today a part of North Rhine-Westphalia, these two duchies occupy a special place in the history of the Reformation. Here it was not a case of the sovereign prince deciding the course of reform. Before the Reformation, reform Catholicism from the Netherlands, manifested in the *devotia moderna*, had influenced the lower Rhine region. The court of Duke John III (r. 1521–

1539) and Latin grammar schools had embraced the humanism of Desiderius Erasmus of Rotterdam (1469–1536).

In 1525 Duke John enforced the Edict of Worms against the followers of Luther. Adolph Clarenbach, the deputy headmaster of the school of Saint Willibrordi in Wesel, publicly advocated Lutheran theology. In the same year, John issued a decree of *Ordnung und Besserung* ("order and improvement") for the churches of his territory. Criticism of the church grew, however, particularly among the burghers of the cities. Members of religious orders, individual clergy, teachers, and students spread the Protestant teachings. The growing Protestant movement was supported by the trade relations of the cities of the lower Rhine and by book circulation. In order to protect the unity of the church, the duke and his councils issued a typically humanist church order in 1532/33 and undertook church visitations. The duke tried to solve the ecclesiastical questions in a practical, pastoral manner. His principle that nothing should happen against God's word encouraged the Protestant forces as well.

Duke John III participated in the suppression of the Anabaptist uprising in Münster in 1534/35. The so-called Wassenberg preachers had joined the Anabaptists from Jülich. In Wesel, a ducal town, ten Anabaptists unwilling to recant their beliefs were executed. John III was succeeded by his son William V, "the Rich" (1539–1592), whose sister Sybilla was married to Elector John Frederick of Saxony, Luther's protector. In 1540 William's sister Anne became the wife of King Henry VIII of England. Prompted by the Colloquy of Regensburg of 1541, William attempted to solve the ecclesiastical questions in cooperation with Hermann von Wied, archbishop of Cologne and imperial elector.

Hermann was advised by the Protestant theologians Martin Bucer and Philipp Melanchthon. In the dispute over the succession in the duchy of Geldern, however, William had to yield to the power of the Catholic emperor, and in the 1543 Treaty of Venlo he was forced to refrain from all ecclesiastical change. When Hermann von Wied was forced to abdicate by the Cologne cathedral chapter in 1547, the introduction of the Reformation in northwestern Germany had been effectively thwarted by the territorial rulers.

In the two duchies of Jülich-Cleve the Protestant movement was not thwarted by the changed political situation. After the death of the Catholic priest in the city, the city council of the Hanseatic town of Wesel ordered the acceptance of the Reformation in 1540 with a celebration of the new evangelical Communion by its citizens, although without explicitly taking confessional sides. Alongside the Protestant church, the first Calvinist parish of the Rhineland was established in Wesel in 1545 by Walloon refugees. Catholics became the minority in the town. In 1548 the reform of Jülich-Cleve came to a standstill because of the Interim adopted by the imperial diet, though a new phase of expansion and consolidation occurred after the recognition of Lutheranism in the Peace of Augsburg. At the same time, a conflict arose among Protestants on the lower Rhine concerning the correct understanding of the Lord's Supper. From then on, congregations developed with a pronounced Lutheran or Calvinist confession.

Against the will of the duke, the city council of Wesel introduced a Lutheran confession in 1561. Two of the town's preachers, Calvinist in orientation, expressed reservations. Even the Walloon French-speaking refugee congregation put up resistance, strengthened by Calvin from Geneva.

Duke William stood firmly by his plans. In 1567 the long-announced church order was completed that again balanced Catholicism and Protestantism. But the problem of confessionalization was intensified by the adjournment of the Council of Trent. When the duke suffered a stroke, the order was not enacted. Beyond a schism in the church, a "third way," embraced only in the united duchies, was not practicable. The Catholic church had stood its ground; the Protestant confession had taken root.

The collapse of the Dutch rebellion against Philip II of Spain in 1567 and the threat against the duchies by the Spanish governor, Fernando Ávarez de Toledo, duke of Alba, caused the court to turn again completely to Catholicism. But the beginning of a mass exodus of Dutch refugees into the Rhine territories supported the continued existence of Calvinist congregations, the "churches under the cross" during the time of the Counter-Reformation, as did the existing Lutheran congregations.

The confessional development of the Protestant congregations scattered throughout the two duchies proceeded without a notable reformer as leader and was molded instead by town pastors or with the help of supporters from the nobility. For large parts of the two duchies no clarity exists concerning this development, except for the Calvinists. Well documented is the gradual transition of the city of Wesel, from 1561 officially Lutheran, to Calvinism and the subsequent emergence of this urban congregation as a stronghold of Calvinism in northwest Germany. In 1568 the Convent of Wesel, attended by refugees on ducal territory, decided on the principles for the structure of a Dutch Reformed church. In 1571 the refugee parishes in Emden drew up a presbyterial-synodal church order. In this way the Calvinist classis of Jülich and Wesel had their beginnings. At the same time nonrefugees belonged to these congregations in Jülich as well, and by 1570 Calvinist synods had convened there. The Wesel classis met for the first time in 1572. After 1578 the eventual merger of the Wesel magistrate church with the Calvinist synodal association appeared in outline form. The Calvinist church order, with its practice of welfare, social work, and church discipline, had exemplary effects.

After the death of John William (1592–1609), the last duke, his patriarchy on the Rhine was jointly secured by the elector John Sigismund of Brandenburg, at that time a Lutheran but after 1613 a Calvinist, and Wolfgang of Pfalz-

Neuburg, likewise first a Lutheran and after 1614 a Catholic. These "possessors," as they were called, committed themselves in 1609 to accepting the existing confessions; that is, alongside the traditional Catholic churches, the Lutheran and Calvinist congregations.

Afterward, because of this confessional latitude, secretively or openly established congregations united according to confessional standards. In 1610 a Calvinist general synod was established in Duisburg. In 1612 the Lutherans also united in synods: those of Jülich in Düren and those of Cleve in Dinslaken. The duchies permanently became confessionally mixed areas. The legal principle of the empire—*cuius regio, eius religio*—was abandoned in the case of Jülich-Cleve.

BIBLIOGRAPHY

Booma, Jan Gerhard Jakob van, and Jacobus Leonardus van der Gouw. *Communio et mater fidelium: Acta des Konsistoriums der niederländischen reformierten Flüchtlingsgemeinde in Wesel, 1573–1582*. Schriftenreihe des Vereins für Rheinische Kirchengeschichte 103. Cologne, 1991. Documents church life and the organizations of the important refugee congregation and its merger with the local church in Wesel.

Faulenbach, Heiner. *Quellen zur rheinischen Kirchengeschichte*. Vol. 1, *Das 16. Jahrhundert*. Düsseldorf, 1991. Covers the area of the present-day evangelical church in the Rhine area.

Goeters, J. F. Gerhard. "Die konfessionelle Entwicklung innerhalb des Protestantismus im Herzogtum Kleve." In *Der Niederrhein zwischen Mittelalter und Neuzeit*, edited by J. F. Gerhard Goeters and Jutta Prieur, pp. 64–113. Studien und Quellen zur Geschichte von Wesel 8. Wesel, 1986. State of current research and questions for further study.

Janssen, Wilhelm. "Kleve-Mark-Jülich-Berg-Ravensberg 1400–1600." In *Land im Mittelpunkt der Mächte. Die Herzogtümer Jülich-Kleve-Berg*, pp. 17–40. Exhibition catalog. Kleve, Germany, 1984.

Petri, Franz. "Im Zeitalter der Glaubenskämpfe, 1500–1648." In *Rheinische Geschichte*, edited by Franz Petri and Georg Droege, vol. 2, pp. 1–217. Düsseldorf, 1976. Church history in the context of secular history. Contains bibliography.

Stempel, Walter. "Die Reformation in der Stadt Wesel." In . . . *vnnder beider gestalt . . . Die Reformation in der Stadt Wesel*, edited by Werner Arand, pp. 9–73. Weseler Museumsschriften 26. Cologne, 1990. History of the reformation of Wesel, the most important town in the duchy of Cleve during the sixteenth century, against the background of the policies of the dukes and the empire.

WALTER STEMPEL

Translated from German by Susan M. Sisler

JULIUS II (Ital., Giuliano della Rovere; 1445?–1513), pope (1503–1513). Nephew of Francesco della Rovere, Pope Sixtus IV (1471–1484), Giuliano was made a cardinal by his uncle in 1471. His forceful character made him a powerful figure in the college of cardinals; self-imposed exile from Rome from 1494 to 1503, because of his distrust of Alexander VI, did not diminish his influence.

As pope most of his energies were devoted to military campaigns: to consolidate papal authority in the Papal States, to recover lands that had been lost to Venice, and, once that had been accomplished largely thanks to French military power, to drive the French from Italy. He did not shrink from personally supervising military operations.

The war he waged against the French from 1510 to 1512 brought the threat of schism, when the French king, Louis XII, backed a group of cardinals who declared a general council of the church that opened in Pisa in 1511. This council declared Julius to be deposed but won scant support except from the French. It did, however, prompt Julius to summon the Fifth Lateran Council, although it was generally recognized that his motives in summoning it were as political as Louis's had been in supporting the Pisan council.

To scandalized observers such as Erasmus, Julius was a travesty of what the vicar of Christ should be, but Julius, who as a cardinal had been known as a stalwart defender of the rights and property of the church, sincerely believed he was fighting for the honor and security of the Holy See. Ironically, his project to rebuild Saint Peter's may have caused more trouble for the papacy in the end because of the scandals that arose out of the sale of indulgences to pay for its construction under his successor, Leo X.

BIBLIOGRAPHY

Partridge, Loren, and Randolph Starn. *A Renaissance Likeness: Art and Culture in Raphael's "Julius II."* Berkeley, 1980. An interesting discussion on Julius's image as pope.

Shaw, Christine. *Julius II: The Warrior Pope*. Oxford, 1993. The only biography of Julius II in English.

Sowards, J. Kelley, ed. *The "Julius Exclusus" of Erasmus*. Bloomington, Ind., 1968. Erasmus's lively satire depicting Julius, at the head of his army, being turned back from the gates of heaven by Saint Peter.

CHRISTINE SHAW

JULIUS III (born Giovan Maria de' Ciocchi del Monte; 1487–1555), pope from 1550 to 1555. A canon lawyer by training, Monte began his ecclesiastical career under the patronage of Julius II (1503–1513), served the sees of Siponto and Pavia, and even preached at the opening of a session at the Fifth Lateran Council in 1513. He held various papal legations and opened the Council of Trent along with his co-legates Marcello Cervini (later Pope Marcellus II) and Reginald Pole. He emerged as pope from a long, bitter conclave, which nearly elected Pole as a compromise choice.

His efforts at ecclesiastical reform were inconsistent. Hard work on a bull by his reform commission in 1550 suggests that Julius had committed himself to the enterprise, but the document remained unpublished during his pontificate. He prized the initiatives of the fledgling Society of Jesus, confirmed its constitutions, and helped to establish its Collegium Germanicum (1552). He presided over the Catholic church during a period of intense development, especially through missionary activity in the New World, but was personally responsible for little of it. His love of pomp, festivals, and gift giving strained papal finances, and he promoted family members shamelessly. His most notorious appointment was raising an adopted nephew, Innocenzio del Monte (1532–1577)—who was later imprisoned for homicide—to the cardinalate. He possessed a well-deserved reputation for indecisive, moody behavior—even the defenders of his work as a reformer indicate that he was prone to vacillation.

Lacking independence in political matters, he was controlled instead by stronger personalties and by such agreements as his election capitulation, according to which he bestowed the north-central Italian city of Parma upon Ottavo Farnese, the grandson of his predecessor. His efforts from 1553 to 1555 and those of his legate, Pole, secured a short-lived restoration of papal supremacy in England.

BIBLIOGRAPHY

Erulei, R. *La villa di Giulio, suoi usi e destinazioni: Nuova antologia.* Rome, 1890. A study of the Villa Giulia he constructed as pope at Porta del Popolo in Rome.

Pastor, Ludwig. *The History of the Popes from the Close of the Middle Ages.* 3d ed., 40 vols. Saint Louis, 1938–1953. Vol. 13 still constitutes the best extended study of Julius III, and the only one in English. The work was originally published by Pastor as *Geschichte der Päpste seit dem Ausganq des Mittelalters,* 21 vols., Freiburg im Breisgau, 1866–1938.

Schweitzer, V. *Zur Geschichte der Reform unter Julius III: Funf Vorträge der Paderborner Generalversammlung der Görres-Gesellschaft.* Cologne, 1907. A study of his reform activities and bull, sponsored by the Görres-Gesellschaft, which similarly sponsored publication of the correspondence, diaries, debates, and acts associated with the Council of Trent.

WILLIAM V. HUDON

JUNIUS, Franciscus

JUNIUS, Franciscus (Fr., François du Jon; 1545–1602), reformed preacher, theology professor at Leiden, and Bible translator. Born in Bourges, then a center of humanist legal studies, Junius received a strong education in languages. He studied law in Bourges, and theology and Hebrew in Geneva. He later said his reading of Cicero made him an atheist (perhaps a reference to the legendary dream of Jerome), but that reading *John* 1 saved him. After his father's violent death during religious demonstrations, he became a preacher. In May 1565 he began his career as pastor in Antwerp, where he was also active as a pamphleteer and perhaps wrote the anonymous "Letter to Philip II" in favor of tolerance. He also helped compose a confession for the Reformed in Antwerp. Forced to leave the Low Countries in 1567, he became pastor of the refugee church in Schonau near Heidelberg but also served as army chaplain in France and the Low Countries and composed a French grammar. From 1573 to 1579 he translated, with Immanuel Tremellius, the Old Testament into Latin. In 1578 he was appointed professor of theology and Hebrew at Duke Johann Casimir's new academy in Neustadt. He was soon invited to come to Leiden but resisted that call until 1592.

He is most famous for the *Eirenicum de pace ecclesiae catholicae,* which he wrote for Henry IV, favoring peaceful coexistence among all those who base their faith on the acceptance of scripture and the centrality of Christ's redemptive death. Thus he opposed antitrinitarianism, but he thought "ubiquity," a major difference between Lutherans and Reformed, of only secondary importance. The extensive catalog of his (Calvinist) theological writings and the theses defended by his students show his importance in the formation of Dutch Reformed theology. Although ambivalent about Arminius, he almost certainly did not, contrary to later accounts, while dying, warn Franciscus Gomarus against Arminius.

BIBLIOGRAPHY

Jonge, Christiaan de. *De Irenische Ecclesiologie van Franciscus Junius, 1545–1602.* Nieuwkoop, 1980. With an extensive bibliography; lists of surviving letters; and theses defended under Junius, with an English summary. Also discusses Junius's theology and views of the church.

Muller, Richard A. *God, Creation and Providence in the Thought of Jacob Arminius: Sources and Directions of Scholastic Protestantism in the Era of Early Orthodoxy.* Grand Rapids, Mich., 1991. Excellent on the context of Dutch Reformed theology and the only modern study in English.

Verzeichnis der im deutschen Sprachbereich erschienenen Drucke des XVI. Jahrhunderts. Stuttgart, 1983–. See vol. 5, nos. 2876–2906.

DERK VISSER

JUSTIFICATION

JUSTIFICATION. The issue of justification played a decisive role in the origination and propagation of the Reformation. It is not entirely correct to suggest that it was the single issue over which the Reformation began, and still less that it was the central focus of the entire Reformation movement during the first phase of its development. Nevertheless, the debates that centered on this issue proved to be determinative for the self-definition of the early Reformation, as it centered on the figure of Martin Luther.

The term *justification* is complex and requires discussion before it is possible to proceed further. The term, along with a range of cognates (especially the verb *to justify* and the related concept of "the righteousness of God") occurs to a significant extent within the Pauline writings of the New Testament, especially *Romans* and *Galatians.* It represents one soteriological metaphor among others (including "salvation," "redemption," and "reconciliation") used to express the "benefits of Christ" (Philipp Melanchthon) that accrue to the believer as a result of Christ's death and resurrection. One of the most distinctive features of the Reformation discussion of the issue—whether within Lutheran, Reformed, or Roman Catholic contexts—is the unprecedented priority assigned to this concept. The conceptualities and vocabulary of justification come to assume a controlling influence over sixteenth-century discussions of how sinful human beings are able to find acceptance in the sight of a righteous and holy God. One may regard Luther's cry *Wie kriege ich einen gnädigen Gott?* ("How may I find a gracious God?") as setting the issue that the doctrine of justification addressed.

One may view the Reformation debates over justification as centering on the meanings of three Latin terms, each of which represents an integral aspect of the doctrine: *iustificatio* ("justification"), *iustificare* ("to justify"), and *iustitia Dei* ("the righteousness of God" or "the justice of God"—the Latin term *iustitia* bears both English meanings). In order more fully to explore these debates on justification, it is necessary to set the context in which they occurred.

Justification on the Eve of the Reformation. The general issues that related to the doctrine of justification were the subject of continuing discussion within late medieval thought. Recent scholarship has stressed the widespread degree of doctrinal pluralism and uncertainty relating to this specific doctrine on the eve of the Reformation. The issues had been thoroughly debated during the Pelagian controversy of the early fifth century. Augustine's insistence that human nature was radically compromised and weakened through sin gained the ascendancy over Pelagius's assertion of an unfettered human autonomy. The Council of Carthage (418) gave definitive expression to a series of characteristically Augustinian themes on the priority and necessity of divine grace. This was supplemented by the Second Council of Orange (529). For reasons that remain unclear, the decisions of this latter council were unknown throughout most of the Middle Ages; they first resurface in theological discussion in 1546, too late to exercise influence over the early Reformation debates on the issue. The general rediscovery and reappropriation of an Augustinian theology of grace, assisted to some degree through the publication of the Amerbach edition of the *Opera Omnia Augustini* (1506), contributed in no small way to the forging of Luther's reforming theology. As noted below, however, Luther's theology of justification appears to consist of a substructure of a more or less authentically Augustinian theology of grace, on which Luther erected a specific understanding of justification that departs significantly from Augustine at two points of major importance—the notion of justifying righteousness as alien (rather than inherent) to the believer, and a tendency to treat justification as involving two notionally distinct elements. This latter trend eventually led to the development of forensic notions of justification in the writings of Melanchthon and others.

A further point to note in this context is that the rise of subjectivism, which appears to be linked with the development of Renaissance humanism (although the nature and extent of this link remain controverted), led to a new emphasis on the subjective consciousness of the individual, in contrast to the more corporate conceptions of Christian living generally associated with the earlier Middle Ages. One may regard the new emphasis on the doctrine of justification as both reflecting and addressing this development. It is significant that Luther's doctrine of justification appears to have appealed most to individuals (such as Gasparo Contarini) who were anxious concerning their sin or lack of assurance of salvation.

But perhaps the most important aspect of the late medieval context, against which one may set the emergence of the sixteenth-century theologies of justification, is the characteristic approach of the writers of the *via moderna*, especially the noted Tübingen theologian Gabriel Biel. Biel's theology of justification may define the broad context within which Luther's early reflections on the justification of humanity before God were located (McGrath), although some scholars have suggested that any such similarities between Biel and Luther should be regarded as verbal rather than substantial (Karl Holl, Jared Wicks, and Leif Grane).

The basic features of the broad approach to justification associated with the *via moderna* are as follows. The justification of the sinner is to be set within the context of a covenant (*pactum*) between God and humanity. This covenant was established unilaterally by God and defines the conditions under which justification takes place. The individual sinner is required to meet a minimal precondition, in response to which God is under a self-imposed obligation to justify that individual. John of Paltz defines this precondition in general terms as "doing one's best" (*facere quod in se est*), and clarifies this in terms of moving toward good and away from evil. Biel has a more nuanced approach to the question, set within what is recognizably the same general framework.

Despite its potentially Pelagian overtones, Biel's approach evades the most distinctive features of Pelagianism. Biel does not regard humanity as taking the initiative in the process of justification, in that he sees the establishment of the covenant itself as initiating that process. Nor does he see human works, such as "doing one's best," as having a purchasing ability or meritorious nature *de condigno*, placing God under an obligation to reward humanity with justification in consequence. Biel stresses that God's resolve to justify such individuals is a consequence of a decision, grounded in the divine *liberalitas*, to treat such human actions in such a generous manner. Biel stresses that the intrinsic value of such human actions is quite inadequate to merit so great a treasure as justification; that they are able to lead to the justification of the sinner is due to God's prior decision to treat such actions as if they were considerably more valuable. This point is expressed in terms of a distinction between the *valor inhaerens* and the *valor impositus*, a distinction familiar from contemporary economic theory.

Nevertheless, many writers of the late medieval period regarded with considerable suspicion the general position associated with the *via moderna*. A medieval Augustinian tradition, now often referred to as the *schola Augustiniana moderna*, associated with writers such as Gregory of Rimini and Hugolino of Orvieto, stressed the total priority of grace over human actions, rejecting the general theological framework within which Biel's soteriology was set. Although much of the evidence suggests strongly that the views of the *via moderna* enjoyed considerably greater currency than such more radically Augustinian views, some evidence suggests that other late medieval writers may have been more sympathetic to Augustinian perspectives. Johannes von Staupitz is an instance of a writer who appears to swim against the more general soteriological current of the time. Such observations have naturally led scholars to reflect on whether Luther's appropriation of more Augustinian insights could be linked to the discovery of, or alignment with, such an Augustinian tradition. This question remains controverted; although there are reasons for suspecting that Luther may have had access to such currents, decisive evidence that he knew of, or appropriated, them before 1518 remains to be uncovered.

Luther's Discovery of the Righteousness of God. Intense scholarly activity has centered on the question of the nature and date of Luther's "discovery" of the doctrine of justification by faith. The framework for this discussion is generally set by the "autobiographical fragment" of 1545, in which Luther recalls his early theological difficulties. He states that these focused on the meaning of the term *iustitia Dei*, especially as it occurs at *Romans* 1:16–17.

> I had certainly wanted to understand Paul in his letter to the Romans. But what prevented me from doing so was not so much cold feet as that one phrase in the first chapter: "the righteousness of God is revealed in it" (*Rom.* 1:17). For I hated that phrase, "the righteousness of God," which I had been taught to understand as the righteousness by which God is righteous, and punishes unrighteous sinners.
>
> Although I lived a blameless life as a monk, I felt that I was a sinner with an uneasy conscience before God. I also could not believe that I had pleased him with my works. Far from loving that righteous God who punished sinners, I actually hated him. . . . I was in desperation to know what Paul meant in this passage.
>
> At last, as I meditated day and night on the relation of the words "the righteousness of God is revealed in it, as it is written, the righteous person shall live by faith," I began to understand that "righteousness of God" as that by which the righteous person lives by the gift of God (faith); and this sentence, "the righteousness of God is revealed," to refer to a passive righteousness, by which the merciful God justifies us by faith, as it is written, "the righteous person lives by faith." This immediately made me feel as though I had been born again, and as though I had entered through open gates into paradise itself. From that moment, I saw the whole face of scripture in a new light. . . . And now, where I had once hated the phrase, "the righteousness of God," I began to love and extol it as the sweetest of phrases, so that this passage in Paul became the very gate of paradise to me.

For Luther, the idea of a "righteous God" is simply not good news for sinners. A righteous God could only punish sinners; how could that be good news? Luther affirms that he learned this understanding of the term from those who taught him; indeed, one may note affinities between this idea of the "righteousness of God" and that associated with writers of the late *via moderna*, such as Gabriel Biel. For such writers, this righteousness refers to God's covenant faithfulness, by which those who do *quod in se est* are justified, and those who do not are condemned. Luther's own awareness of his personal sinfulness and unworthiness, a recurring feature of some of his early recollections, appears to have persuaded him that he was unable to make the response required in order to ensure his acceptance in the sight of God.

Luther then relates how these difficulties were resolved through his discovery of the "true" meaning of the "righteousness of God." One is not to regard this righteousness as one that belongs to God but as a righteousness that God bestows on sinners. It is not to be conceived as a personal attribute of God—that is, the righteousness by which God is righteous *in se*—but as a justifying righteousness, by which God justifies sinners. This insight, Luther declares, caused him to read scripture in a new light. He also notes that he later read Augustine's *De spiritu et littera* and found the same basic meaning of the "righteousness of God" developed there.

An examination of Luther's writings over the period 1513–1519 indicates that there is indeed evidence for such a development in Luther's thought over this period, although the rate of development is perhaps less rapid than Luther's compressed account of 1545 suggests. There are reasons for suspecting that Luther may have unconsciously modeled his later account of his theological breakthrough on Augustine's description of his conversion experience in the garden at Milan, with the result that the account may contract a series of insights gained over an extended period of time into an apparently momentous flash of illumination. Before 1515 Luther's doctrine of justification shows strong affinities with that of the *via moderna*, including the following features of decisive importance. (1) Justification is declared to take place within the context of the *pactum* between God and humanity. (2) The relation between faith and justification is conceived in terms of a covenantal, rather than an ontological, understanding of causality. Nothing is inherent to faith that relates it to justification; that relation results from the covenantal decision of God that they shall be related in this manner. (3) The assertion is made that God is just and equitable, rewarding individuals according to what they deserve. Justification thus takes place on the basis of the human response to God's initiative in the *pactum*. (4) The specification of *quod in se est* is expressed in terms of humility. Luther stipulates that true humility is the precondition for justification within the terms of the *pactum* between God and humanity and clearly implies that such humility is a genuine possibility for humanity.

But Luther moves away from this position over the period 1515–1519. The debate over the precise dating of his theological breakthrough is largely a matter of definition, in that the dating depends on which element in a series of such elements one regards as being of decisive importance. An apparent majority of scholars place this breakthrough at some point in 1515, noting the radical new emphasis on the need for grace and the inability of humanity to do *quod in se est* in the *Romans* lectures of 1515–1516. Furthermore, Luther first appears to begin citing Augustine's *De spiritu et littera* in this writing, suggesting (if one trusts the recollections of 1545) that his discovery of the true meaning of the "righteousness of God" dates from before his reading of this work. Nevertheless, a significant minority of scholars argue for a later date, such as 1518–1519, noting that Luther retains a traditional Augustinian understanding of justification as a process of healing and of faith as humility up to this point. The most realistic approach to this conundrum would seem to be that Luther's initial theological insights date from around 1515, but that the process of following through on their implications, with the attendant reworking of the remainder of his theology, took place over several years, reaching completion around 1519. One may regard Luther's distinctive insights into justification as laying the foundations for the distinctively Lutheran approach to the doctrine, which marks a decisive break with the Western theological tradition up to this point.

The Emergence of the Lutheran Doctrine of Justification. The basic features of Luther's distinctive doctrine of justification were in place by 1520 and may be seen in his *Freiheit einer Christenmensch* (Liberty of a Christian), among other writings. One may summarize those features as follows. First, he understands justification to take place on the basis of faith alone (*sola fides*). This does not mean that an individual is justified on the basis of correct belief (i.e., faith as creedal orthodoxy) or on the basis of the human achievement of trusting in God (i.e., faith as a human work). Rather, justification takes place on the basis of faith as a divine gift to humanity. Luther stresses that justification occurs on the basis of Christ's work on the cross, and is appropriated by faith, understood as a gracious gift of God. This view later finds its expression in the declaration of the Apology for the Augsburg Confession (1530), to the effect that justification is *per fidem, propter Christum.*

Second, Luther redefines faith itself. Justifying faith is not intellectual assent to revealed truth (here Luther departs from Augustine); rather, it is trust (*fiducia*) in the promises of God, supremely the promise of forgiveness, coupled with the resulting union of the believer with Christ. Luther later defines this as a "grasping faith" (*fides apprehensiva*), which takes hold of and receives Christ. In the *Freiheit einer Christenmensch,* Luther deploys the analogy of a human marriage to make the point that faith unites the believer to Christ and thus to his benefits.

> Faith unites the soul with Christ as a bride is united with her bridegroom. As Paul teaches us, Christ and the soul become one flesh by this mystery (*Eph.* 5:31–32). And if they are one flesh, and if the marriage is for real—indeed, it is the most perfect of all marriages, and human marriages are poor examples of this one true marriage—then it follows that everything that they have is held in common, whether good or evil. So the believer can boast of and glory of whatever Christ possesses, as though it were his or her own; and whatever the believer has, Christ claims as his own. Let us see how this works out, and see how it benefits us. Christ is full of grace, life, and salvation. The human soul is full of sin, death, and damnation. Now let faith come between them. Sin, death, and damnation will be Christ's. And grace, life, and salvation will be the believer's.

Third, sinners are justified on the basis of the righteousness of God, which is God's gracious gift to sinful humanity. Although Augustine had conceived this righteousness as imparted to sinners and intrinsic to their persons, Luther insists that it is an extrinsic righteousness, imputed to believers. This "alien righteousness of Christ," on the basis of which justification takes place, is perhaps best conceived as a protective righteousness, shielding believers while their own righteousness develops through the process of renewal through the Holy Spirit. Commenting on *Romans* 4:7, Luther declares that

> the saints are always aware of their sin and seek righteousness from God in accordance with his mercy. And for this very reason, they are regarded as righteous by God. Thus in their own eyes (and in reality!) they are sinners—but in the eyes of God they are righteous, because he reckons them as such on account of their confession of their sin. In reality they are sinners; but they are righteous by the imputation of a merciful God. They are unknowingly righteous, and knowingly sinners. They are sinners in fact, but righteous in hope.

Fourth, as a result, one cannot say that justification causes believers to become righteous (a characteristically Augustinian idea, based on the analysis of *iustificari* as *iustum facere*). The believer is righteous *in spe sed non in re,* in that there is an eschatological tension between the imputed status of righteousness (which is a proleptic anticipation of the final renewal of the sinner on the last day) and the present sinful nature of that same believer.

> It is just like someone who is sick, and who believes the doctor who promises his full recovery. . . . Now is this sick person well? In fact, he is both sick and well at the same time. He is sick in reality—but he is well on account of the sure promise of the doctor, whom he trusts, and who reckons him as already being cured.

Luther gives expression to this tension in the phrase *simul iustus et peccator.* By this phrase, he does not mean that believers are partly sinful and partly righteous; rather, that they are totally sinners and totally righteous, depending on the point of view taken.

Fifth, Luther's emphasis on the graciousness of justification leads him to draw a sharp distinction between law and gospel. One is to avoid the simplistic identification of "law" with Old Testament or "gospel" with New Testament; Luther's point is to contrast two radically differing outlooks, one based on human achievement and the other on divine grace. Nevertheless, most commentators feel that Luther's radical distinction at this point inevitably leads to a devaluation of the Old Testament in regard to the New, with a minimization of the continuities between them. This is perhaps one of the most significant contrasts between Luther and Calvin in relation to the doctrine of justification.

Sixth, Luther insists that the gracious justification of sinners in no way leads to a devaluation of the role of good works in the Christian life. Good works are to be seen as the fruit and consequence, not the cause or precondition, of justification. Nevertheless, Luther's sometimes ferocious defense of the graciousness of justification leads him to occasional careless statements, especially in the early 1520s, in which the role of good works in the Christian life is apparently minimized. This point is of importance in understanding the negative evaluation of Luther's doctrine of justification that came to prevail within Swiss reforming circles at this time. It also allows one to understand more readily the development of the antinomian controversy, centered on the views of Johann Agricola, minimizing the role of the law.

Seventh, as justification is a work of God, rather than a human achievement, the believer may have assurance of salvation. This assurance is grounded in the absence of the need for a specific or quantifiable human response to God's grace, which would, in Luther's eyes, lead to uncertainty as to whether the necessary response had been made with sufficient intensity. One can see the basic features of this approach to justification developed in the writings of early Lutheranism, especially those of Melanchthon and Johannes Bugenhagen.

Perhaps the most distinctive element of Melanchthon's restatement of Luther's position is the notion of forensic justification. Using the analogy of the people of Rome declaring Scipio to be a free person, Melanchthon argues that justification is to be understood as a "forensic declaration of righteousness," rather than "a making righteous." He thus draws a significant notional distinction between the event of justification, as the work of God outside believers, and the process of sanctification or regeneration, as the work of God within believers. Believers are declared to be righteous in justification, and made to be righteous in sanctification. Whereas Augustine teaches that the sinner is made righteous in justification, Melanchthon teaches that he or she is counted as righteous or pronounced to be righteous. For Augustine, "justifying righteousness" is imparted; for Melanchthon, it is imputed. Melanchthon draws a sharp distinction between the event of being declared righteous and the process of being made righteous, designating the former "justification" and the latter "sanctification" or "regeneration." For Augustine, both are simply different aspects of the same thing. According to Melanchthon, God pronounces his verdict—that the sinner is righteous—in the heavenly court (*in foro divino*). This legal approach to justification gives rise to the term "forensic justification," from Latin *forum* ("market place" or "courtyard")—the place traditionally associated with the dispensing of justice in classical Rome.

The importance of this development lies in the fact that it marks a complete break with the teaching of the church up to that point. From the time of Augustine onward, justification had been understood to refer to both the event of being declared righteous and the process of being made righteous. Melanchthon's concept of forensic justification diverged radically from this understanding. As it was taken up by virtually all the major reformers subsequently, it came to represent a standard difference between Protestant and Roman Catholic theology. In addition to their differences on how the sinner was justified, they now had an additional disagreement on what the word *justification* designated in the first place. As we shall see, the Council of Trent, the Roman Catholic church's definitive response to the Protestant challenge, reaffirmed the views of Augustine on the nature of justification and censured the views of Melanchthon.

By this stage, however, the Lutheran commitment to a forensic approach to justification had become further intensified as a result of the controversy surrounding Andreas Osiander. Reacting against a forensic notion of justification, Osiander argued that believers were justified on the basis of Christ's inherent righteousness. This view was widely regarded as a form either of Catholicism or of Platonism. The controversy led to a hardening of attitudes within Protestantism as a whole against any notion of justification by an internal righteousness, and consolidated the notion of forensic justification.

The Reformed Doctrine of Justification. One may largely trace the origins of the Reformed church to the humanist sodalities of eastern Switzerland. These sodalities defined the intellectual and cultural environment within which the reforming programs of writers such as Huldrych Zwingli and Joachim Vadian would emerge. The program of reform generally associated with such writers was primarily a reform of the life and morals of the church. Whereas Luther came to regard a critical program of doctrinal reassessment as an integral aspect of his conception of reform, the more humanist-inclined reformers of eastern Switzerland were more concerned with the moral and spiritual renewal of the church and of individual Christians. If anything, Luther's doctrine of justification was seen as something of a hindrance to this process; it appeared, at least from a distance, to remove the necessity of good works from the Christian life.

Zwingli shows little, if any, interest in the doctrine in his early phase as a reformer. While occasional references to the doctrine are scattered throughout his early writings, it is evident that the doctrine has nothing like the programmatic function it has with Luther. A related observation may be noted at this point: during the 1510s and early 1520s, Zwingli has relatively little interest in the writings of Augustine, from which Luther gained encouragement and inspiration for his understandings of grace and justification. If anything, Zwingli shows a tendency to make justification dependent on prior moral renewal. Again, while Luther regards scripture as containing the promises of God, especially the promises of forgiveness, for Zwingli it often appears as a repository of divine ethical commands and precepts. Other writers of the region, including Vadian in St. Gall, express similar views.

Such ideas were developed further in the writings of Heinrich Bullinger, Zwingli's successor at Zurich. One may regard Bullinger's most important contribution to the Reformed discussion of justification as the forging of a strongly covenantal foundation to justification, allowing the moral emphasis of the early Swiss reformers to be retained, while maintaining Luther's concern to defend the graciousness of justification. At Strasbourg Martin Bucer developed a similar approach, insisting that the possibility of an individual being justified without being morally renewed should be eliminated. To this end, Bucer developed a theology of double justification, in which the "justification of the godly by faith" is followed immediately by the "justification of the godly through works." The justification of an individual by faith has to be publicly demonstrated before the world through good works. In this way, Bucer brings together the seemingly irreconcilable views of Paul and James in the New Testament. Such approaches would be increasingly adopted in the early 1540s, as pressure to reconcile Protestant and Roman Catholic views on justification increased.

The definitive statement of the Reformed doctrine of justification is by John Calvin. Calvin opens his discussion of the appropriation of the benefits of Christ, leading up to justification, by noting that they remain external to humans unless something happens by which they can be internalized. So long as humans are separated from Christ, all that he achieved on the cross is of no importance. It is by faith that the believer appropriates these benefits. The value of faith, however, lies in what it mediates, rather than what it is in itself. Faith is a means, rather than an end, that gives rise to the presence of the real and living Christ within the believer. Through faith, Christ "ingrafts us into his body, and makes us not only partakers of all his benefits, but also of himself." It is not merely some abstract qualities or some impersonal characteristics of Jesus Christ that become the believer's through faith; it is a personal relationship with the living Christ himself. (In making this assertion, Calvin is obliged to distinguish his understanding of the nature of this relationship from that of Andreas Osiander, which he regards as little more than a crass confusion of Christ with human nature.)

The promises on which faith depends, and which it gratefully appropriates, offer the believer more than sight or knowledge of Christ; they offer a communication in his person. Faith thus channels the presence of Jesus Christ into the life of the believer, transforming it. "We receive and possess Jesus Christ, as he is given to us by the benevolence of God, and by participation in him we have a double grace. First, we are reconciled to God by his innocence. . . . Second, we are sanctified by his Spirit." With this statement, Calvin moves to identifying the consequences of union with Christ through faith, and moves the discussion on to consider the doctrines of justification and sanctification.

Although Calvin refers to justification by faith as "the principal article of the Christian religion," it seems that he is acknowledging its importance to an earlier generation, rather that stating its importance to his own theological position. Justification is not demonstrably of central importance to Calvin's conception of the Christian faith. Nevertheless, the issues raised by the doctrine of justification remained active, even in Calvin's day. Two issues stood out as particularly important.

The first issue concerns the manner in which Jesus Christ is involved in justification. As already noted, Melanchthon had developed the concept of forensic justification, by which justification was understood as "declaring right through the imputation of the righteousness of Christ." Although this development achieved a significant degree of terminological clarification in relation to Luther's ideas, it was at the price of involving Christ in a purely extrinsic and impersonal manner in justification. For Melanchthon, justification involves the imputation of an attribute of Christ, or quality or benefit deriving from him, to the believer—but not a personal encounter of Christ and the believer, a central element of Luther's conception of justification.

The second issue concerns the relation of God's initiative and the human response. How can one reconcile the utterly gratuitous justification of the sinner before God with the demands of obedience subsequently laid on him or her? Luther seems to suggest that works have no place in the Christian life, on account of the utter unconditionality of God's gift of grace—an incorrect perception, as it happened, but an understandable interpretation of his stress on the gratuity of justification. Zwingli resolves this problem by making justification dependent on moral regeneration; in justification, Zwingli appears to suggest that God confirms or seals a prior process of moral or spiritual regeneration. Luther seems to deny any place to obedience in the Christian life; Zwingli makes the Christian life dependent on such obedience. Clarification was clearly necessary.

To Calvin's credit, he resolves both these difficulties. He resolves the first through his conception of the "insertion of the believer in Christ" (*insitio in Christum*). Through faith, believers are united with Jesus Christ in a spiritual union in such a way that they are "not only partakers of all his benefits, but also of himself." All that Christ is becomes the believer's through faith. Through participating in him, the believer shares in his benefits. In this view, Calvin appears to be reappropriating a central aspect of Luther's views on the real presence of Christ within believers, neglected or deliberately minimized by Melanchthon, which is shown to be consistent with the sharing of Christ's benefits, such as his righteousness. For Luther, the believer is united with Christ and exchanges properties with him. Calvin restores this insight to the Protestant tradition, while retaining Melanchthon's emphasis on the forensic nature of justification. It is not, Calvin demonstrates, necessary to separate a forensic conception of justification from an emphasis on the real personal presence of Christ in the believer.

The second point follows from the first immediately. Acceptance in the sight of God (justification) does not depend on moral improvement or regeneration (sanctification); nor does justification render sanctification superfluous. For Calvin, both justification and sanctification are direct consequences of the believer's incorporation into Christ. If the believer has been united with Christ through faith, he or she is at one and the same time made acceptable in the sight of God (justification) and launched on the path to moral improvement (sanctification). By treating these two elements, which had hitherto been regarded as independent entities requiring correlation, as subordinate to the believer's union with Christ, Calvin is able to uphold both the total gratuitousness of believer's acceptance before God and the subsequent demands of obedience placed on believers.

The Radical Reformation on Justification. It has been noted that justification was one of a number of images used within the New Testament and the Christian tradition to denote the acceptance of the sinner in the sight of God through grace. Several radical reformers did not regard justification as the most appropriate way of dealing with issues relating to salvation, preferring to use images such as "divinization" in their discussion of such issues. The radical discussion of the doctrine of grace often took on a significantly different complexion from that associated with the magisterial Reformation, partly as a result of the insistence by a number of radicals that the traditional notion of original sin (central to an Augustinian soteriology) was misguided and unbiblical. One must stress that this rejection of such a notion was not universal; Balthasar Hubmaier and Menno Simons are examples of radical writers who retained both the term and the theological notion it expressed.

Nevertheless, Simons regarded the Lutheran approach to justification by faith as morally lightweight, and he supplemented the notion of salvation by grace with an insistence on the importance of "discipleship" (*Nachfolge*). Similarly, Hubmaier wrote scathingly of "mouth-Christians and ear-Christians," whose faith never passed into action. "Mere faith does not deserve to be called faith, for a true faith can never exist without deeds of love."

The Catholic Reformation on Justification. The early Catholic reaction to Luther was confused and misguided, often resting on the elementary misunderstanding that "justification by faith" implied "justification by a human achievement, namely faith." By the late 1530s, however, Luther's ideas were receiving an increasingly sympathetic hearing within many quarters of Catholic Europe, including parts of Germany and Italy. Convinced that Luther was basically right in his theology of justification, however incautious and provocative he may have been in its statement, a number of Catholic writers began to explore ways in which they could reconcile Luther's doctrine with more traditional Catholic approaches.

The most significant such approach came to be known as "double justification," associated with writers such as Albertus Pighius and Johannes Gropper. Two rival approaches to the question of the nature of justifying righteousness were mentioned earlier: that of Luther, which declared that justifying righteousness was extrinsic to the believer, and that of Augustine, which held it to be inherent. Gropper and others argued that there were two "formal causes" of justification: imputed and imparted (or inherent) righteousness. This mediating approach captured the imagination of a number of theologians on both sides of the Protestant-Catholic divide, including Martin Bucer and Gasparo Contarini. It was adopted as a potential basis at the abortive Colloquy of Regensberg (Ratisbon) in 1541, but its almost immediate repudiation by church authorities on both sides ensured that it never achieved widespread acceptance.

Trent on Justification. The sixth session of the Council of Trent ended on 13 January 1547. The Tridentine Decree on Justification sets out the Roman Catholic teaching on justification with considerable clarity. One can break down Trent's critique of Luther's doctrine of justification into four main sections: the nature of justification, the nature of justifying righteousness, the nature of justifying faith, and the assurance of salvation.

The nature of justification. Trent strongly opposed any forensic view of justification and vigorously defended the idea, originally associated with Augustine, that justification is the process of regeneration and renewal within human nature, which brings about a change in both the outer status and the inner nature of the sinner. Its fourth chapter provides the following precise definition of justification:

The justification of the sinner may be briefly defined as a trans-

> lation from that state in which a human being is born a child of the first Adam, to the state of grace and of the adoption of the sons of God through the second Adam, Jesus Christ our Savior. According to the gospel, this translation cannot come about except through the cleansing of regeneration, or a desire for this, as it is written, "Unless someone is born again of water and the Holy Spirit, he or she cannot enter into the Kingdom of God" (*Jn.* 3:5).

Justification thus includes the idea of regeneration. This brief statement is amplified in chapter 7, which stresses that justification "is not only a remission of sins but also the sanctification and renewal of the inner person through the voluntary reception of the grace and gifts by which an unrighteous person becomes a righteous person." Canon 11 gave this point further emphasis, condemning anyone who taught that justification takes place "either by the sole imputation of the righteousness of Christ or by the sole remission of sins, to the exclusion of grace and charity . . . or that the grace by which we are justified is only the goodwill of God."

Justification is closely linked with the sacraments of baptism and penance. The sinner is initially justified through baptism; on account of sin, however, one may forfeit that justification. But one can renew it by penance, as chapter 14 makes clear.

> Those who through sin have forfeited the received grace of justification can be justified again when, moved by God, they exert themselves to obtain through the sacrament of penance the recovery, by the merits of Christ, of the grace that was lost. Now this manner of justification is restoration for those who have lapsed into sin. The holy fathers have properly called this a "second plank after the shipwreck of lost grace." For Christ Jesus instituted the sacrament of penance, on behalf of those who lapse into sin after baptism. . . . The repentance of a Christian after a lapse into sin is thus very different from that at baptism.

In brief, then, Trent maintains the medieval tradition, stretching back to Augustine, which saw justification as comprising both an event and a process—the event of being declared to be righteous through the work of Christ, and the process of being made righteous through the internal work of the Holy Spirit. Reformers such as Melanchthon and Calvin distinguished these two matters, treating the word *justification* as referring only to the process of being declared to be righteous; the accompanying process of internal renewal, which they termed *sanctification* or *regeneration*, they regarded as theologically distinct.

Serious confusion thus resulted: both Roman Catholics and Protestants used the same word *justification* to mean very different things. Trent used the term *justification* to mean what, to Protestants, was *both* justification *and* sanctification.

The nature of justifying righteousness. Trent strongly defended the Augustinian idea of justification on the basis of an internal righteousness. Chapter 7 makes this point clear:

> The single formal cause [of justification] is the righteousness of God—not the righteousness by which he himself is righteous, but the righteousness by which he makes us righteous, so that, when we are endowed with it, we are "renewed in the spirit of our mind" (*Eph.* 4:23), and are not only counted as righteous, but are called, and are in reality, righteous. . . . Nobody can be righteous except God communicates the merits of the passion of our Lord Jesus Christ to him or her, and this takes place in the justification of the sinner.

The phrase "single formal cause" needs explanation. A "formal" cause is the direct, or most immediate, cause of something. Trent thus states that the direct cause of justification is the righteousness that God graciously imparts to us—as opposed to more distant causes of justification, such as the "efficient cause" (God), or the "meritorious cause" (Jesus Christ). But one should also note the use of the word *single*. One proposal for reaching agreement between Roman Catholic and Protestant, which gained especial prominence at the Colloquy of Regensburg in 1541, has already been noted: the doctrine of "double justification," associated with Pighius and Gropper, and subsequently at Trent by Girolamo Seripando. Seripando appears to have argued that one should recognize *two* causes of justification—an extrinsic righteousness (corresponding broadly to the Protestant position) and an intrinsic righteousness (the Roman Catholic position). Trent had no time for this compromise. The use of the word *single* in this context was thus deliberate and weighed, intended to preclude totally the idea that there could be more than one such cause. The only direct or formal cause of justification was the gift of intrinsic justifying righteousness.

The nature of justifying faith. Luther's doctrine of justification by faith alone came in for severe criticism at Trent on account of its apparent neglect of the role of works in justification. Canon 12 condemns a central aspect of Luther's notion of justifying faith in rejecting the idea that "justifying faith is nothing other than confidence in the mercy of God, which remits sin for the sake of Christ." In part, this rejection of Luther's doctrine of justification reflects ambiguity concerning the meaning of the term *justification*. Trent was alarmed that anyone should believe that one could be justified—in the Tridentine sense of the term—by faith, without any need for obedience or spiritual renewal. Interpreting "justification" to mean both the beginning of the Christian life and its continuation and growth, Trent believed that Luther was suggesting that simply trusting in God (without any requirement that the sinner be changed and renewed by God) was the basis of the entire Christian life.

But Luther meant nothing of the sort. He was affirming that the Christian life was begun through faith, and faith alone; good works followed justification and did not cause that justification in the first place. Trent itself was prepared to concede that the Christian life was begun through faith, thus coming close indeed to Luther's position. As chapter 8 of the Decree on Justification declares, "we are said to be justified by faith, because faith is the beginning of human salvation, the foundation and root of all justification, without which is it impossible to please God." This is perhaps a classic case of a theological misunderstanding, resting on the disputed meaning of a major theological term.

The assurance of salvation. For Luther, as for the reformers in general, one could rest assured of one's salvation. Salvation was grounded on the faithfulness of God to his promises of mercy; to fail to have confidence in salvation was, in effect, to doubt the reliability and trustworthiness of God. The Council of Trent regarded this doctrine of assurance with considerable skepticism. Chapter 9 of the Decree on Justification, entitled "Against the Vain Confidence of Heretics," criticized the "ungodly confidence" of the reformers. While no one should doubt God's goodness and generosity, the reformers erred seriously when they taught that "nobody is absolved from sins and justified, unless they believe with certainty that they are absolved and justified, and that absolution and justification are effected by this faith alone." Trent insisted that "nobody can know with a certainty of faith which is not subject to error, whether they have obtained the grace of God."

Trent's criticism appears to have been directed against any understanding of justification that made human confidence or boldness the grounds of justification. This view, it argued, would make justification rest on a fallible human conviction, rather than on the grace of God. The reformers, however, saw themselves as stressing that justification rested on the promises of God; a failure to believe boldly in such promises was tantamount to calling the reliability of God into question.

Conclusion. Justification by faith was of central importance to the first phase of the Reformation and continued to exercise considerable influence during its later phases. The doctrine proved to have a potent appeal to many individuals during the period, apparently offering liberation from many of the more oppressive trends within contemporary Catholic spirituality and satisfying a deep need for reassurance of individual salvation. The extensive length and unusual structure of the Tridentine Decree on Justification is itself testimony to the importance of the doctrine at the time. Whereas earlier councils had merely listed the errors of heretics, Trent was obliged to give an extended presentation of Catholic teaching on the subject, stretching to sixteen chapters, before condemning the errors of others. However difficult it may be for the modern secular historian to understand the religious concerns lying behind the Reformation debates on justification, the fact remains that they were seen as of central importance to the Reformation by those who were involved, on whatever side, in the tumult of that movement.

[*See also* Faith; Free Will; Good Works; Grace; *and* Sin.]

BIBLIOGRAPHY

Beachy, Alvin J. *The Concept of Grace in the Radical Reformation.* Nieuwkoop, 1977. Best overview of this complex subject, demonstrating the diversity of opinions within the movement.

Grane, Leif. *Contra Gabrielem: Luthers Auseinandersetzung mit Gabriel Biel in der Disputatio contra scholasticam theologiam 1517.* Gyldendal, Denmark, 1962.

Greschat, Martin. *Melanchthon neben Luther: Studien zur Gestalt der Rechtfertigungslehre zwischen 1528 und 1537.* Witten, 1965.

Hefner, Joseph. *Die Entstehungsgeschichte des Trienter Rechtfertigungsdekretes.* Paderborn, 1909.

Holfelder, Hans Hermann. *Solus Christus: Die Ausbildung von Bugenhagens Rechtfertigungslehre in der Paulus Auslegung.* Tübingen, 1981.

Knox, D. Broughton. *The Doctrine of Faith in the Reign of Henry VIII.* London, 1961. Useful survey of views on justification during the early English Reformation.

Kolb, Robert. *Nikolaus von Amsdorf: Popular Polemics in the Preservation of Luther's Legacy.* Nieuwkoop, 1978. Excellent analysis of aspects of early Lutheran controversies, including the antinomian debate.

McGrath, Alister E. *Luther's Theology of the Cross: Martin Luther's Theological Breakthrough.* Reprint, Oxford, 1990. Explores the development of Luther's doctrine of justification, 1513–1519, against its late medieval backdrop.

———. *Iustitia Dei: A History of the Christian Doctrine of Justification.* 2 vols. Reprint, Cambridge, 1993. Follows the development of the doctrine of justification from its biblical origins through to the modern period.

Oberman, Heiko A. *The Harvest of Medieval Theology.* Reprint, Durham, N.C., 1983. Valuable study of the theology of Gabriel Biel, including his doctrine of justification.

Pfnür, Vinzenz. *Einig in der Rechtfertigungslehre? Die Rechtfertigungslehre der Confessio Augustana (1530) und die Stellungsnahme der katholischen Kontroverstheologie zwischen 1530 und 1535.* Wiesbaden, 1970. Valuable survey of early Roman Catholic critiques of Luther, highlighting contemporary misunderstandings of the doctrine of justification.

Stadtland, T. *Rechtfertigung und Heiligung bei Calvin.* Neukirchen, 1972.

Wolf, Ernst. "Die Rechtfertigungslehre als Mitte und Grenze reformatorischer Theologie." In *Peregrinatio.* Vol. 2, *Studien zur reformatorischen Theologie zum Kirchenrecht und zur Sozialethik.* Munich, 1965. See pp. 11–21.

Yarnold, Edward. "*Duplex Iustitia*: The Sixteenth Century and the Twentieth." In *Christian Authority,* edited by Gillian R. Evans, pp. 204–223. Oxford, 1988. Detailed analysis of the doctrine of "double justification."

Zimmermann, Gunter. "Calvins Auseinandersetzung mit Osianders Rechtfertigungslehre." *Kerygma und Dogma* 35 (1989): 236–256. Excellent analysis of the points at issue in Calvin's critique of Osiander's views on justification.

ALISTER E. MCGRATH

JUUSTEN, Paavali (Lat., Paulus; c.1516–1575), Finnish bishop and reformer. He was born in Viipuri (Vyborg), a town located near the eastern end of the Gulf of Finland, and one to which news of humanism and Luther's reforms spread quickly thanks to its trade connections with the Baltic ports. Lutheran church services were probably introduced before 1530; by then Juusten had begun his education in his hometown school whose teaching was already influenced by the new movements. In 1536–1538, after his parents' death, he continued his education at the cathedral school in Turku

(Åbo) where he had a position as reader in Bishop Martin Skytte's household, and later as assistant teacher at the cathedral school itself. He became an ordained priest in 1541 and, after a teaching assignment in Viipuri, was sent to Wittenberg to complete his education.

In November 1543 Juusten began his studies under Philipp Melanchthon and other "Philippists," including Caspar Cruciger and Georg Major, and he also heard Luther's lectures and sermons; the two great reformers had a lifelong influence on him. A quote from "Master Philipps'" testimonial to Juusten reads: "He has grasped the consensus of the Catholic Church of Christ, which also our Academy unanimously follows and confesses.... In his virtues he came close to his name [Justus]."

After Luther's death and the outbreak of the Schmalkald War in 1546 the university was closed, and Juusten may have continued his studies in Rostock and at the new University of Königsberg. In the autumn of 1547 he returned to Turku, and early the next year the king appointed him headmaster of the cathedral school and secretary of the cathedral chapter.

Skytte, the first Finnish bishop of the royally controlled state church, died in 1550. In 1554 the king summoned Michael Agricola and Juusten to Sweden and announced his decision to divide the Finnish church into two dioceses, appointing Agricola to the western diocese of Turku and Juusten to the eastern diocese of Viipuri. The king did not call them bishops, using instead the title *ordinarius*; however, upon swearing an oath of loyalty to the king and being consecrated by Bishop Botvid of Strängnäs, the two men regarded themselves as true bishops.

Very little is known about Juusten's nine years as bishop of Viipuri, a good deal more about his later years as bishop of Turku. Organizational tasks and parish visitations in the eastern diocese were hampered by the war, which had caused much suffering and loss of life among the civilian population and destroyed some churches and parsonages. Poverty, moral corruption, and a poor knowledge of Christianity were widespread. Pagan superstitions and magic still held people in their grip. Few parish pastors knew how to preach good scriptural sermons, as ordered by the king.

When Bishop Follingius, Agricola's Swedish successor in Turku, was removed from office in 1563, Gustavus Vasa's son King Eric appointed Juusten to the see of Turku, which he occupied until his death twelve years later. Here the conditions were somewhat more favorable, though there was much room for improvement, as his pastoral letters reveal.

The years in Wittenberg had awakened in Juusten a genuine interest in church history. In Turku he had an excellent opportunity to study the medieval church archives, including a brief manuscript history of the bishops of Finland through the 1480s. Sufficient material was available also for the later years, and Juusten himself wrote brief accounts of the lives of the twenty-third and last medieval bishop, Arvid Kurki (1510–1521), and of bishops Skytte, Agricola, and Follingius; in doing so he revealed his sense of the unbroken succession of the episcopate of Finland, beginning with the English-born bishop and martyr Henry and continuing despite the break with Rome. (Juusten's concluding three-page autobiographical sketch is incomplete, ending with his years in Germany). Originally circulated in manuscript form and first printed in 1728, the work, entitled *Catalogus et ordinaria successio episcoporum Finlandensium*, has given Juusten the honor of being the first Finnish historian known by name.

In 1569 King John appointed Juusten to lead a diplomatic mission to Czar Ivan IV ("the Terrible") in the hope of removing the threat of new war between the two countries. The delegation was kept in Russia for nearly three years, in humiliating and harsh imprisonment, a period during which Juusten was nonetheless able to write a volume of sermons in Latin for all Sundays and festivals as well as a Finnish catechism. Of the former, which circulated in manuscript, only the preface has survived; it gives a clear picture of Juusten's commitment to the principles of the Lutheran Reformation. The latter, printed in Stockholm in 1574, has been lost.

Upon his return to Turku Juusten wrote his Finnish Communion rite, *Se Pyhä Messu* (The Holy Mass), published in Stockholm in 1575, which includes the lectionary and the Collect prayers for the church year. Thus it is rather a missal, and as such the first of its kind in Sweden-Finland. It provides evidence of Juusten's cautious sympathy for King John's ecumenical-Catholic reform of the Swedish Mass, which was authorized for use in 1576 against widespread resistance among the clergy. In addition, *Capita Rerum Synodicarum*, a document in Latin that Juusten prepared on the occasion of a diocesan synod held in Turku in 1573—the first of its kind in Finland since the medieval era—was used as a basis for discussion of sixteen topics dealing with important practical questions relating to the clergy and parish life. With his many accomplishments and important publications, then, Juusten stands second only to Michael Agricola in the history of the Finnish Reformation.

BIBLIOGRAPHY

Primary Sources

Juusten, Paulus. *Catalogus et ordinaria successio episcoporum Finlandensium*. Edited by Simo Heininen. Helsinki, 1988. Critical edition of Juusten's unpublished history of Finnish bishops, based on the study of several manuscripts and preceded by a valuable introduction in German by the editor.

Juusten, Paulus Åboensis. *Se Pyhä Messu Somen kielen . . . visusta Somen Turus coottu* (1575). Edited and postscript by Martti Parvio. Facsimile ed. Helsinki, 1978.

Secondary Sources

Heininen, Simo. *Die finnischen Studenten in Wittenberg, 1531–1552*. Helsinki, 1980.

———. *Suomalaisen historiankirjoituksen synty.* Helsinki, 1989. Companion volume to the author's 1988 edition of Juusten's *Catalogus.*

Jutikkala, Eino, and Kauko Pirinen. *A History of Finland.* Rev. ed. New York, 1988. A reliable one-volume history. Provides a helpful account of influential events and circumstances in the lifetime of Pavali Juusten.

Paarma, Jukka. *Hiippakuntahallinto Suomessa 1554–1604.* Diss., Helsinki Yliopisot, 1980. The most recent and comprehensive (515 pp.) study by the present dean of the cathedral in Turku. An indispensable source regarding Juusten's episcopate.

Parvio, Martti. *Paavali Juusten ja hänen messunsa.* Helsinki, 1978. A detailed study of the sources of Juusten's Finnish Mass; English summary.

Pirinen, Kauko. *Turun tuomiokapituli uskonpuhdistuksen murroksessa.* Helsinki, 1962. Closely related in its subject matter to Paarma's work. Pirinen covers masterfully the eventful story of the cathedral chapter in Turku from the early 1520s to the middle of the 1550s. Important respecting Juusten's earlier years in Turku.

Schmidt, Wolfgang. *Paul Juusten och Finlands gamla biskopkronika.* Turku, 1942. A brief biography of Juusten and the Swedish translation of his chronicle of Finnish bishops.

Toivo Harjunpaa

K

KABBALAH. *See* Cabbala, Christian; Christian Hebraica; Mysticism.

KAISER, Leonhard (also Kaser, Kayser, Keyser; c.1480–1527), Lutheran pastor executed by Archbishop Ernst of Passau as a heretic. Born in Raab, near Scharding, Upper Austria, to a middle class family, Kaiser matriculated at the University of Leipzig (B.A., 1502). In 1524, while a vicar in Weitzenkirchen, near Raab, he was forced to recant Lutheran views by episcopal authorities. He began study at the University of Wittenberg in 1525. From Wittenberg he worked for the spread of Luther's message in his homeland through letters and books that he sent to acquaintances.

After returning to Raab to visit his dying father, he was arrested in March 1527, imprisoned, and finally interrogated. Charges against him included teaching justification through faith alone, contempt for good works, and heresy on several other issues, such as the Mass and its canon, confession and satisfaction, the other sacraments, freedom of the will, purgatory, invocation of the saints, and the power of the papacy. He was burned for his Lutheran beliefs on 16 August 1527. Entreaties on his behalf from Elector John of Saxony (r. 1525–1532) and Margrave Casimir of Brandenburg availed not at all. Luther wrote him a letter of consolation during his imprisonment. His death occasioned a propaganda exchange. Nine editions of an anonymous description of his execution elicited defenses of their respective positions from his instructor, Martin Luther, at the instigation of Kaiser's student friend, Michael Stifel, and from one of his inquisitors, Johann Eck of Ingolstadt. Ludwig Rabus included Kaiser's story in his martyrology.

BIBLIOGRAPHY

Leeb, Friedrich, and Friedrich Zoepfl. *Leonhard Kaiser, ein Beitrag zur bayerischen Reformationsgeschichte.* Münster, 1928.

Roth, Friedrich. *Leonhard Kaiser, ein evangelischer Märtyrer aus dem Innviertel.* Halle, 1900. Brief biographical overview based on available sources.

ROBERT KOLB

KÁLMÁNCSEHI, Márton (also Kálmáncsehi Sánta; c.1500–1557), first Reformed cleric elected superintendent (bishop) of a Protestant church district in Hungary. He enrolled at the University of Kraków in 1523 and, two years later, became the senior of the Hungarian bourse there. He may have also studied in Germany and returned to Hungary with a master's degree in theology. He became a canon of the chapter in Alba Iulia (Gyulafehérvár, Romania) and, in 1538, the rector of its school. In the same year, he served as one of the arbitrators of the religious colloquy at Sighişoara (Segesvár, Romania) called by János Zápolya. According to a report by Caspar Heltai, he secretly expressed to the king his decision against the Roman Catholic position.

The date of his conversion to Protestantism is unknown. It is supposed that it was fostered by the spiritual climate of the chapter, an important center of humanist sympathies that produced a significant number of reformers. Upon leaving the chapter, Kálmáncsehi was a teacher at Mezőtúr (Túr) where, to cite Máté Skaricza (d. 1591), he established "the true inclination of the people towards the Word of God." In 1547 he was the parish pastor at Sártoraljúajhely, in the region of the country where Protestantism among the Hungarian-speaking people originated. By 1551 he was listed among the Reformed clerics in Debrecen and remained there, intermittently, until his death. He did spend some time as a pastor in northeastern Hungary and visited Cluj-Napoca (Kolozsvár, or Klausenburg, Romania) several times. Scholarly opinion is divided concerning the question of whether Kálmáncsehi's changes of residence during the 1550s were caused by political or religious persecution. He was elected superintendent, or bishop, for the church district of Debrecen and Oradea (Nagyvárad, Romania) around 1556. This later became the Tiszántul diocese of the Hungarian Reformed Church. In the same year he participated in a controversy, carried on in print, with the Lutheran clergy of Cluj-Napoca.

The writings of Kálmáncsehi, save for a few in translation, have perished. Most of what is known about his theological position is from preserved records that were hostile to him. Immediately after leaving the chapter, it seems his views did not differ substantially from those of the Lutherans of that era in Hungary. During the 1550s, however, he was considered a protagonist of the Swiss Reformation. He was most frequently called a Zwinglian or Sacramentarian and was even accused of baptizing children in a trough to demonstrate his indifference toward this sacrament. There was a rumor that he regarded prayer as insignificant since "God doesn't listen to it."

Despite the inconclusive evidence concerning the possible Anabaptist sympathies of Kálmáncsehi, it is clear that he was considered a founder of the Hungarian Reformed church. As such, he was regularly condemned by the Lutherans in Hungary after the first mutual excommunication of the Lutherans and the Sacramentarians took place in 1551–1552.

The only work preserved that clearly bears the imprint of Kálmáncsehi is the hymnal *Reggeli éneklések* (Morning Songs). Little was known about this work until 1970, when a 1560 edition of the Debrecen hymnal of Gál Huszár was found that included not only songs and prayers, organized to serve morning church services for seven days, but also the translations of *Psalms* by Kálmáncsehi. The construction of *Reggeli éneklések* is unique in Hungary, and the content of the texts is distinctly Protestant. While it did not appear in any further editions, the hymnal had an impact through manuscript copies made of many of its hymns.

Kálmáncsehi was a mentally adept and powerful personality. His byname, Sánta ("limping"), may mean he had a physical disorder.

BIBLIOGRAPHY

Primary Source

Kálmáncsehi, Márton. *A Keresztyéni gyülekezetben való isteni disceretik: Huszár Gál; Reggeí énekiések, 1560–1561.* Bibliotheca Hungarica Antiqua, 12. Budapest, 1983. Fascimile edition with an introductory study by Gedeon Bersa.

Secondary Source

Papp, Gusztáv. *Kálmáncsehi Sánta Márton.* Budapest, 1935. The only biography of Kálmáncsehi; more significant information about his life and work is often found in the general histories of Hungarian Protestantism.

KATALIN PÉTER

KALMAR UNION. The royal union of Denmark, Norway, and Sweden lasted from 1397 to 1523. In 1363 Haakon VI of Norway married Margaret, princess of Denmark. Margaret got their son Olaf elected heir to Denmark. After Haakon's death, Olaf IV, at Margaret's advice, called himself king of Sweden, aiming toward union. After Olaf's death, Margaret was chosen regent for her grandnephew Erik of Pomerania, nearest acceptable heir to the throne. In 1389 Sweden submitted to Margaret as another step toward the royal union of the three lands.

In 1397 Margaret called the councils of all three nations to meet at Kalmar, in southeast Sweden. They crowned Erik king and drafted a union charter: to have one king "forever," but internally for each land to retain its own laws and administration. This official union of the three lands lasted 126 years (and for Denmark and Norway until 1814).

Margaret ruled through Erik until she died in 1412. Lacking her prestige and tact, he was dethroned in 1439. To have officials responsible only to them, Margaret and Erik preferred Danes for administrative positions and manipulated popes to appoint Danes to bishoprics in all three lands. After Margaret and Erik the union suffered several breaches by Sweden, led by Swedish nobility. Christian II attempted to wipe out Swedish rebellions by his Stockholm Bloodbath (1520), beheading eighty-two nobles. That effort left hatred; surviving nobles elected Gustavus Vasa king in 1523, ending the union.

The union shaped the Reformation's introduction to all three lands: union kings selected bishops, creating a church hierarchy concerned mostly with political power. Hence the populace did not resist Reformation changes. Swedish Archbishop Gustav Trolle authorized the Stockholm Bloodbath, precipitating Vasa's takeover. Norway's Archbishop Olav Engelbrektsson fought for Norwegian independence; with his military defeat went also the last strength of the Catholic church there. In Denmark the populace listened to Reformation preachers, and union kings retained Schleswig, whence came Christian III, who in 1536/37 decreed the Reformation.

BIBLIOGRAPHY

Derry, T. K. *A History of Scandinavia: Norway, Sweden, Denmark, Finland and Iceland.* Minneapolis, 1979. Balanced short history of all Scandinavian lands by a respected British historian, expert in the subject.

Imsen, Steinar, and Jørn Sandnes. *Avfolkning og union.* Norges historie, vol. 4, edited by Knut Mykland. Oslo, 1977. Many insightful observations into the Kalmar Union; strong on societal factors in its rise and fall.

Koht, Halvdan. *Dronning Margaret a og Kalmarunionen.* Oslo, 1956. Complete and definitive work on Margaret and the Kalmar Union by Norway's eminent historian of this century.

———. "The Scandinavian Kingdoms during the Fourteenth and Fifteenth Centuries." In *The Cambridge Medieval History,* edited by C. W. Previté-Orton and Z. N. Brooke, vol. 8, pp. 533–555. Cambridge, 1959. Concise yet thorough; perceptive in portraying the role of socioeconomic factors in the decline of the Kalmar Union.

Scott, Franklin D. *Sweden: The Nation's History.* Enl. ed. Carbondale, Ill., 1988. Especially strong on the Swedish history of the break-up of the Kalmar Union.

KENNETH E. CHRISTOPHERSON

KANIJS, Peter. *See* Canisius, Peter.

KAPPEL, PEACE OF. A treaty accepted by Zurich on 16 November 1531 and by Bern eight days later, the Second Peace of Kappel ended the Second Kappel War, which had resulted from the confessional split that began in

1524–1525 with the Reformation in Zurich. Five of the thirteen states of the Swiss Confederation—Bern, Basel, Schaffhausen, and Apenzell, in addition to Zurich—embraced the Reformed faith. The Reformation penetrated Glarus, and the city of St. Gall also became Protestant. Seven states—Fribourg and Solothurn, plus the forest states of Uri, Schwyz, Unterwalden, Zug, and Lucerne—never wavered from Catholicism.

In 1529 the Protestants formed a federation, the Christian Civic Union (*Christliche Burgrecht*), which also included Constance and Strasbourg. It soon was matched by a Catholic alliance, the Christian Union (*Christliche Vereinigung*), which had a special relationship with Austria. The tensions nearly resulted in hostilities at Kappel in 1529, but actual war was averted when the Catholics accepted the First Peace of Kappel. Then, in May 1531, Zurich and Bern imposed an economic blockade on the forest states by which they hoped to force them to abide by the terms of the 1529 treaty. They declared war on Zurich on 11 October 1531 and won a decisive victory at Kappel, leaving more than five hundred Zurichers dead, including Zwingli.

The Peace of Kappel restored the political and legal situation as it had existed in the confederation prior to the hostilities. All of the old agreements and alliances were reaffirmed. The Protestant states thus retained all the legal privileges they had possessed within the confederation prior to the Reformation. The First Peace of Kappel was abrogated, and all alliances contracted outside of the confederation were canceled.

In terms of religion, the treaty specified that each of the thirteen states within the confederation would choose either the new Reformed faith or the old Catholic religion (an early example of *cuius regio eius religio*). Communities in the Common Territories (*Gemeine Herrschaften*), jointly ruled by the states of the confederation, were treated differently. Communities that had fully accepted the Reformed faith were allowed to retain it. If there was simply a Reformed majority in a community, the Catholic minority was guaranteed freedom of worship and a proportionate share of the church property. Thus began the principle of parity in the Swiss Confederation. However, wherever there was a Catholic majority, there was no parity, and Protestants were not tolerated. Nor was there any toleration of Protestants in any of the Common Territories that were ruled exclusively by Catholic states. The same was true in the Independent Districts (*Freie Ämter*) in the Aargau, a small stretch of land between Zurich and Bern, traditionally jointly ruled by Zurich, Lucerne, Zug, Glarus, Unterwalden, and Schwyz. During the war, the Independent Districts had been occupied by Catholic forces, and the treaty specified that the entire area be re-Catholicized.

The prince abbot of St. Gall, an ally of the confederation, was restored to his territory, most of which had earlier been appropriated by Zurich. His alliance with Glarus and Schwyz was reaffirmed, and Catholicism was reimposed on all his territories except for Toggenburg, where the principle of parity was accepted. The city of St. Gall retained its independence and remained Reformed. The principle of parity applied to Glarus and Appenzell, where the two faiths coexisted. Though the Peace of Kappel did not resolve the confessional split, it did, through the principle of parity, assure the future existence of the Swiss Confederation.

[*See also* Bern; Switzerland; Zurich; *and* Zwingli, Huldrych.]

BIBLIOGRAPHY

Guggisberg, Hans Rudolf. "Parität, Neutralität und Toleranz." *Zwingliana* 15.8 (1982), 632–649. Treatment of the origins of the principle of parity with the Second Peace of Kappel and its connection with the origins of the concepts of neutrality and toleration among the Swiss in the sixteenth century.

———. "The Problem of 'Failure' in the Swiss Reformation." In *Politics and Society in Reformation Europe: Essays for Sir Geoffrey Elton on His Sixty-Fifth Birthday,* edited by E. I. Kouri and Tom Scott, pp. 189–209. New York, 1987. Discusses the Second Peace of Kappel and the principle of parity within the framework of the concept of "failure."

Locher, Gottfried W. *Die Zwinglische Reformation im Rahmen der europäischen Kirchengeschichte.* Göttingen and Zurich, 1979. Brief treatment (pp. 502–553) of the background, the war, and the peace.

Meyer, Helmut. *Der Zweite Kappeler Krieg: Die Krise der Schweizerischen Reformation.* Zurich, 1976. Standard work on the war, the peace, and its aftermath.

Potter, G. R. *Zwingli.* Cambridge, 1976; reprint, 1981. Good treatment (pp. 343–417), in English, of the background, the war, and the peace.

J. WAYNE BAKER

KARL IX. *See* Charles IX of Sweden.

KARLSTADT, Andreas. *See* Bodenstein von Karlstadt, Andreas.

KÁROLYI, Gáspár (also Caspar Radics; c.1530–1591) Reformed senior and translator of the full Bible. Of Slav origins, Károlyi was born in the fairly important market town Károly (Carei, Romania). It is likely that among others he attended, from 1549 on, the school established by John Honter in Brassó (Braşov, Romania). Károlyi subsequently went abroad and matriculated at Wittenberg in 1556. From there he went to France and Switzerland. On returning home Károlyi came into contact with the royal officer Domokos Dobó, who in 1563 invited Károlyi to officiate as preacher at Gönc, a market town on his estates. Károlyi remained there, except for a short stay in nearby Tállya in 1584–1587, for the remainder of his life.

Károlyi returned home from his studies an adherent to the Swiss Reformation and became, from 1564 on, the first senior of this persuasion of the Abauj church district. He and his successors exercised authority similar to that of bishops. Károlyi took part in the struggle of the Reformed against antitrinitarianism. In 1564 he was on the losing side at the Várad Dispute, where John II Sigismund declared that he himself had adopted antitrinitarianism. Against Lukács Egri, the eminent antitrinitarian in his own *senioratus*, Károlyi led, from 1565 on, a long and in the end successful struggle. To achieve that, he joined forces with the secular authorities. Otherwise, Károlyi was most critical toward those in high places. In 1563 he published the *Két könyv* (Two Books), a work that expressed perhaps the sharpest censure of the "princes" during the entire century. Károlyi depicted in it the signs proclaiming the advent of the last days. In doing this he was influenced by Wittenberg chiliasm. The descriptions of Hungarian circumstances, however, were absolutely Károlyi's own.

He started work on a translation of the Bible in 1568, and the result might have been published as early as 1590. Károlyi had three sources of guidance in the work. He used the Vulgate, the Septuagint, and the renderings of Desiderius Erasmus and some other sixteenth-century foreign scholars. The connection between his and the former Hungarian translations has not yet been elucidated. Károlyi's edition—called the *Vizsolyi Biblia* after the village of Vizsoly, where the press for it had been established by some magnates—was of folio size. It also contained the Apocrypha, which was omitted in later issues. Károlyi's intention was to prepare a Hungarian text of the full Bible; in this he succeeded. His magnum opus, with minor alterations, has since gone through many editions. It has influenced Hungarian language, poetry, and literature more than any other work.

Károlyi was successful in other areas of life. Besides being one of the leading ecclesiastical personalities of his age, he had a notable farm and produced wine in quantity. He lost two wives and each time married into a richer family. He lost three children but had a daughter after he was fifty-seven. Károlyi did not exhibit uncertainty in matters of conscience and stated his views with conviction.

BIBLIOGRAPHY

Primary Sources

Káedyi, Gásoée. *Szent Biblia* (The Holy Bible; Vizsoly, 1590). Facsimile ed. Budapest, 1993.

———. *Két könyv minden országoknak és királyoknak jó és gonosz szerencséjeknek okairul* (Two Books on the Good and Bad Luck of All Countries and Kings; Debrecen, 1593). Edited by András Szabó. Budapest, 1984.

Secondary Source

Szabó, András. *Károlyi Gáspár, 1530–1591*. Budapest, 1984.

KATALIN PÉTER

KASER, Leonhard. *See* Kaiser, Leonhard.

KEPLER, Johannes (1571–1630), German astronomer and imperial mathematician to emperors Rudolf II, Matthias, and Ferdinand II. He grew up in Württemberg, where the dukes had introduced Latin schools throughout the duchy to provide an educated clergy and civil service and where they bore the cost of educating poor talented students like Kepler. After his seminary education Kepler entered the University of Tübingen in 1589 to prepare for the Lutheran ministry. There he learned mathematics and astronomy from Michael Mästlin (1550–1631), who introduced him to the Copernican system. Before Kepler finished his theology degree, he was sent to teach mathematics in the Protestant seminary in Graz. He was also district mathematician, requiring that he write yearly calendars for which he predicted the weather and upcoming events through astrology. He correctly forecast a bitter cold and a Turkish invasion in his first calendar for 1596. Kepler was always ambivalent about astrology; nevertheless, his success gave him a privileged position in a Catholic stronghold.

In Graz Kepler wrote his first book, *Mysterium cosmographicum* (The Secret of the Universe), in which he postulated that the distances between the planets in the Copernican system were proportional to the five regular solids. This book established his reputation as an astronomer, and he was invited to work with the Danish astronomical observer Tycho Brahe (1546–1601). Significantly, Kepler's task was to chart the orbit of Mars, the most eccentric and therefore vexatious of the planetary orbits. When he returned to Graz, he found that the duke of Styria, the future Ferdinand II (r. 1619–1637), had redoubled efforts to enforce measures against Protestants. Although Kepler had enjoyed special protection because of his contacts with Catholic notables, he, too, had to leave, and in 1600 he again joined Tycho, who was now imperial mathematician at the court of Rudolf II (r. 1576–1612). Tycho died a year later, and Kepler became imperial mathematician, a title he held until his death. Continuing his work on Mars, Kepler discovered his first two laws of planetary motion—the planetary orbit is an ellipse with the Sun as one of the foci, and the radius vector drawn from the Sun describes equal areas in equal times—which he published in *Astronomia nova* (The New Astronomy). He also did work in optics, and in *Astronomiae pars optica* (The Optical Part of Astronomy) he described the process of vision and disclosed his inverse square law of refraction. He elaborated how the telescope works in *Dissertatio cum nuncio siderio* (Conversation with the Sidereal Messenger) and *Dioptrice* (Dioptrics). A Christmas gift to a friend, *Strena seu de nive sexangula* (The Six-Cornered Snowflake) was a pioneering study of crystallography.

Kepler left Prague in 1612 after Rudolf's fall from power because he feared persecutions of Protestants would resume. He had been hoping for a position at Tübingen, but his support of the Reformed doctrine of the Eucharist closed doors there. He landed a position as district mathematician in Linz, where he was refused Communion by the local Lutheran minister because of his views on the Sacrament. Further dislocation resulted when his mother was accused of being a witch, but his contacts with Tübingen at least prevented her being tortured during the investigation.

On the other hand, musings on the quantity of wine his barrels held resulted in *Stereometria dolorium vinariorum* (Stereometrics of Wine Casks), an important study of infinitesimals. He wrote *Harmonice mundi* (Harmonics of the Universe), a work on mathematics, music, astrology, and astronomy, in which he divulged his third law of planetary motion—the squares of the periodic times of any two planets are proportional to the cubes of the mean distances from the Sun. His *Epitome astronomiae Copernicanae* (Epitome of Copernican Astronomy) became a major textbook and the means of disseminating his findings, although it was at first placed on the Index of Prohibited Books in Italy in 1619 as a result of the Galilean controversy. He began composing the *Tabulae Rudophinae* (Rudolphine Tables), his primary task as imperial mathematician, but the pressures of the Thirty Years' War forced him to leave Linz, especially after the press was destroyed by fire in 1626.

Although he finally managed to bring out the tables, the last years of his life were unsettled. As he searched for a patron, he worked briefly at the court of Count Albert of Wallenstein (1583–1634), who wanted to exploit Kepler's expertise in astrology, but the association was unhappy for Kepler. Hoping to get back salary owed him, Kepler traveled to meet the emperor, but he died on the way. His *Somnium* (The Dream), a quasi-science-fiction work that describes how the solar system would appear to a person who took a trip to the moon, was published posthumously.

BIBLIOGRAPHY

Primary Sources

Kepler, Johannes. *Gesammelte Werke.* Edited by Max Caspar et al. Munich, 1937–.

———. *Epitome of Copernican Astronomy: Books IV and V. The Harmonies of the World: Book V.* Translated by Charles Glenn Willis. Reprint, New York, 1969.

———. *The Secret of the Universe.* Translated by A. M. Duncan. New York. 1981.

———. *Somnium, The Dream.* Translated and edited by Edward Rosen. Reprint, Madison, Wis., 1987.

———. *New Astronomy.* Translated by William H. Donahue. Cambridge and New York, 1992.

———. *The Harmony of the World.* Translated by E. J. Aiton, A. M. Duncan, and J. V. Field. Philadelphia, 1994.

Secondary Sources

Baumgardt, Carola. *Johannes Kepler: Life and Letters.* New York, 1951.

Caspar, Max. *Kepler.* Translated and edited by C. Doris Hellman. Reprint, New York, 1993.

Gingerich, Owen. "Kepler." In *Dictionary of Scientific Biography,* vol. 7, pp. 289–312. New York, 1974.

SHEILA J. RABIN

KESSLER, Johann (1502–1574), Swiss schoolmaster and Protestant leader in St. Gall. Kessler was destined by his family to become a priest but his education was cut short by poverty. After attending the Latin school in St. Gall, he appeared briefly in 1521 as an unmatriculated student in Basel. For the next two years he was registered as a student at Wittenberg, where he was strongly influenced by Melanchthon's lectures but did not earn a degree.

Late in 1523 he returned to St. Gall, a Protestant by conviction with no future in the traditional church. He began training as a harness maker, a craft he pursued for more than a decade. But a small group of laymen asked him to lead them in Bible study. Over the next two years an ever-larger following gathered in craft guild houses to hear his scriptural exegesis until complaints by the abbot of the monastic house in St. Gall embroiled the diet of the Swiss Confederation and the city council in a debate about religious policy.

Kessler worked as a craftsman until he was appointed city schoolmaster in 1537. In the interim he read contemporary publications and became an admirer and confidant of Joachim Vadian, the reformer of St. Gall. Later Kessler was named to the city marriage court and served as secretary of the assembly of pastors (synod) of St. Gall. After Vadian's death in 1551, Kessler was named custodian of his extensive personal library. Although he called himself a simple craftsman, not a learned theologian, he became an intellectual and pastoral leader of St. Gall, as evidenced by his appointment in 1571 as chief pastor of the city and leader of the synod.

In his chronicle, *Sabbata,* he described how the faithful were led out of medieval darkness by the light of the true gospel. Vividly narrated, it is a valuable source for the history of the Reformation in St. Gall, the eruption of the Peasants' War, and the emergence of Anabaptist congregations in the environs. Although faithful to the teachings of the Reformed church, Kessler wrote with compassion when he described dissidents such as Anabaptists.

BIBLIOGRAPHY

Primary Source

Egli, Emil, and Rudolf Schoch, eds. *Johannes Kesslers Sabbata mit kleineren Schriften und Briefen.* St. Gall, Switzerland, 1902. Published text of the *Sabbata* with a thorough biography.

Secondary Sources

Näf, Werner. *Vadian und seine Stadt St. Gallen.* 2 vols. St. Gall, Switzerland, 1944 and 1957. Places Kessler in the context of the Reformation in St. Gall.

Rüsch, Ernst G. "Johannes Kessler: Die Rede der Klosterbibliothek zu St. Gallen an den Herrn Bürgermeister Joachim von Watt 1531." In

Vadian 1484–1984: Drei Beiträge, Vadian-Studien, Untersuchungen und Texte no. 12, pp. 7–76. St. Gall, Switzerland, 1985. Kessler's letter emphasizes the importance of learning in reformed St. Gall; also recent bibliography.

Wissman, Ingeborg. *Die St. Galler Reformationschronik des Johannes Kessler, 1503–1574.* Stuttgart, 1972. Analyzes Kessler's theology in the context of the Reformation in St. Gall.

PAUL L. NYHUS

KETTENBACH, Heinrich von (d. 1524?), Franciscan friar and forerunner of the Reformation in Ulm. Nothing is certain about Kettenbach's origins or the circumstances of his death. Kettenbach was preaching in Ulm by 1521 and was one of a handful of local clerics openly critical of church abuses. A fiery and sometimes vituperative speaker, Kettenbach generated controversy in Ulm through such sermons as *Von der christlichen Kirchen, Vom Fasten und Feyren,* and *Sermon wider des Pabsts Kuchenprediger zu Ulm.* This latter sermon, targeted against his Dominican rival Peter Hütz (Nestler), resulted in a disputation between the two clerics in 1522. Local Catholic opposition to the Franciscan mounted thereafter, and although the city council refused to take action against him, Kettenbach, claiming that he feared for his life (possibly at the hands of the Dominicans), left Ulm later that year.

There is but fragmentary information about Kettenbach's whereabouts after 1523. One source hints that he spent time in a Nuremberg monastery; his publications suggest that he might also have sojourned in Augsburg, Strasbourg, and Erfurt. In 1523 and 1524 Kettenbach produced a flurry of popular works, including *Ein neu apologia und verantwortung Martini Luthers wider der papisten mordgeschrei, Eyn gesprech . . . mit aim frömen altmüterlin von Ulm,* and his wrathful though undelivered farewell sermon to Ulm. After 1524, however, all is silence. One can only surmise from his now silent pen that Kettenbach died sometime in the late 1520s, but his popularity and notoriety lived on: among those opponents of the Catholic faith cited by Johann Eck at the 1530 Diet of Augsburg, there appears the name of Heinrich von Kettenbach.

BIBLIOGRAPHY

Brecht, Martin. "Ulm, 1530–1547: Entstehung, Ordnung, Leben und Probleme einer Reformationskirche." In *Die Einführung der Reformation in Ulm: Geschichte eines Bürgerentscheids,* edited by Hans Eugen Specker and Gebhard Weig, pp. 12–28. Stuttgart, 1981. Offers a brief overview of Ulm in the 1520s.

Clemen, Otto, ed. *Die Schriften Heinrichs von Kettenbach.* Halle, 1907. Kettenbach's writings, with a useful introduction.

Keim, C. Theodor. *Die Reformation der Reichsstadt Ulm.* Stuttgart, 1851. Still valuable on pre-Reformation Ulm.

Sehling, Emil, ed. *Die evangelischen Kirchenordnungen des XVI. Jahrhunderts.* Vol. 12, pt. 3. Tübingen, 1963. Primary documents and a synopsis of the Reformation in Ulm.

EILEEN T. DUGAN

KEYSER, Leonhard. *See* Kaiser, Leonhard.

KHEVENHÜLLER FAMILY. A noble family originating from Villach in Carinthia (a number of whom resided in Upper Austria), the Khevenhüllers became prominent during the fifteenth and sixteenth centuries and contributed in various ways to the Reformation and to the political history of the Carinthian and Habsburg territories. Elevated to the gentry in 1566, they were made counts in 1593. Although mostly Protestant, the family included Catholics as well. Protestant members included Georg (d. 1587), the builder of the fortress Hochosterwitz, and his cousin Bartholomäus (d. 1613), who belonged to the so-called Frankenburg line and who, as head of the provincial government, was leader of the Protestant estates; Bartholomäus's brother Johann, who died in 1606 while imperial ambassador to Spain, and son Franz Christoph (d. 1650), also an imperial diplomat, were Catholic.

In Carinthia the Khevenhüllers sponsored the production of remarkable works of art and architecture (including the fortress Hochosterwitz, the castle Wernberg, and the chapel and tombs in Saint Jakob of Villach). They supported scientific activities (including those of Hieronymus Megiser and Gotthard Christalnigkh) and themselves produced important historical works (for example, the *Annales Ferdinandei* of Franz Christoph).

The decline in the family's influence, which had begun when Villach was restored to Catholicism, became more obvious as Martin Brenner carried out the Counter-Reformation in Carinthia. Georg's grandson Paul and Bartholomäus's younger son Hanns left Carinthia with their families, moving at first to Nuremberg and then entering the Swedish military service. Hanns, having obtained the rank of lieutenant colonel, died on 4 August 1632 of wounds received outside Nuremberg; Paul later resigned his position in the military, took up residence in Sweden, and engaged in numerous diplomatic missions until his death in 1655. After a short stay in *Stadtschlaining* (West Hungary), his cousin Sigmund lived in exile in Nuremberg. Sigmund's son and his family converted to Catholicism in 1666. The Hochosterwitz line of the family, to which they belonged, still exists; the Frankenburg line continued through the children of Franz Christoph. During the Reformation the family was significant for its influence on local conditions and for its advocacy of Protestant interests in provincial politics.

BIBLIOGRAPHY

Czerwenka, Bernhard Franz. *Die Khevenhüller: Geschichte des Geschlechtes mit besonderer Berücksichtigung des XVII. Jahrhunderts.* Vienna, 1867.

Dinklage, Karl. *Kärnten um 1620: Die Bilder der Khevenhüller-Chronik.* Vienna, 1980.

Khevenhüller-Metsch, Georg, ed. *Hans Khevenhüller, kaiserlicher Botschafter bei Philipp II: Geheimes Tagebuch 1548–1605*. Graz, 1971.

Neumann, Wilhelm. "Zur Frühgeschichte der Khevenhüller." In *Bausteine zur Geschichte Kärntens*, pp. 120ff. Das Kärntner Landesarchiv 12. Klagenfurt, 1985.

GUSTAV REINGRABNER

Translated from German by Susan M. Sisler

KING'S BOOK. This name was commonly and significantly given to the final full formulary of the faith under King Henry VIII, officially entitled, *A Necessary Doctrine and Erudition for Any Christian Man.* The volume was the culmination of a twenty-year debate in England between proponents of a generally Lutheran Protestantism and those engaged in defending traditional Catholic theology. Bishops, universities and theologians, Convocation, Parliament, an increasingly literate and articulate laity and parish clergy, and not least King Henry himself had offered a wide variety of opinions on topics of theology, polity, and worship. Echoes of major controversies of the 1520s and 1530s—notably some parts of the king's defense of the seven sacraments against Martin Luther (*Assertio septem sacramentorum,* 1521) and his later legal and theological assertions of the royal supremacy—can still be heard prominently in the *King's Book.* But its purpose was not to be just another contribution to the debate. Rather, it was meant to end all dubious speculation and clearly state the faith of the church for England.

To that end, this volume was a reformulation of and, to some extent, a reaction to a prior attempt at doctrinal exposition, the so-called *Bishops' Book* (1537). The latter, issued after only a perfunctory reading by the king and never endorsed by him, represented an interpretation of some religious matters more Protestant than Henry could accept. A commission of mostly moderate to conservative bishops and other divines was appointed by Henry to study and revise the 1537 book. Led to some extent by the conservative bishop of Winchester, Stephen Gardiner, who contended all along with the more Protestant Archbishop Thomas Cranmer, a draft was prepared by early 1543 and presented to the king, who made significant comments and amendments. A revised version was approved by Convocation in April and by a gathering of the nobility in May. It was published on 29 May 1543.

Perhaps most important of all, the *King's Book* was then enacted into law as the official standard of religious belief and practice for the country. Parliament imposed penalties for contravening any of its provisions and reinstated significant restrictions on reading the Bible and other religious books. Until its repeal in 1548, this legal authority was widely cited to justify heresy trails, book burnings, and general control of more extreme Protestant advocates.

In formal structure, the *King's Book* opens with a preface by Henry VIII, a "Declaration of Faith," followed by expositions of the Apostles' Creed, the seven sacraments, the Ten Commandments, the Lord's Prayer (called the "Paternoster"), and the "Salutation of the Angel" (Ave Maria); articles on free will, justification, and good works; and a consideration of "Prayers for Souls departed." Although various authorial hands can be detected, the king's thinking is paramount.

Doctrinally both contemporaries and modern commentators agree that, while the *King's Book* is clearly more Catholic than its predecessor, it is not simply and univocally so. To some it seems confused. To others it represents an impressive statement of nonpapal English Catholic theology. For a number of reasons it did not play an important role in the development of later Protestant, Anglican, or Roman Catholic theology, but one should not undervalue its importance for the mid-sixteenth century.

The most significant doctrinal issue was justification by faith. Despite Cranmer's efforts to defend it, Henry was adamant that this essential Protestant belief must be denied explicitly. He reasserted the importance for salvation of obedience and meritorious works and presented more Catholic interpretations of transubstantiation, images and ceremonies, and free will. Purgatory was defended, but some doubts were raised about the efficacy of prayers for the dead. The role and importance of holy scripture was reduced. But on such topics as the history and theology of holy orders (both priesthood and episcopacy), the claim that the requirement for auricular confession was established by the law of God, and, of course, the question of papal authority, the king opposed much in current Catholic orthodoxy. On the whole and in particulars, Henry and his bishops, in their discussions and in the *King's Book* itself, remained conflicted and somewhat confused in their sacramental theology. In general, the book was stronger in its negative theology concerning the errors of Luther's innovations than in its attempts at constructing reformulations and modifications of late medieval Catholic teachings in a new language and context.

In 1544 a translation and paraphrase of the *King's Book* into Latin, *Pia et Catholica Christiani Hominis Institutio,* was published. In 1555 Bishop Edmund Bonner supervised the preparation of a revised and expanded version of the *King's Book* under the title *A Profitable and Necessary Doctrine.*

BIBLIOGRAPHY

Primary Sources

The King's Book. Introduction by T. A. Lacey. London, 1932. Text based on C. Lloyd's edition in *Formularies of Faith put Forth by Authority during the Reign of Henry VIII,* Oxford, 1825. Henry's "corrections."

A Necessary Doctrine and Erudition for Any Christian Man: Set Forth by the King's Majesty of England. London, 1543.

Secondary Sources

Haigh, Christopher. *English Reformation.* Oxford, 1993.

Hughes, Philip. *The Reformation in England.* Rev. ed. London. 1963.

Lytle, Guy Fitch. "Prelude to the Condemnations of Latimer, Ridley, and Cranmer." In *This Sacred History: Anglican Reflections for John Booty,* edited by Don S. Armentrout, pp. 222–242. Cambridge, Mass., 1990.

Muller, J. A. *Stephen Gardiner and the Tudor Reaction* (1926). Reprint, New York, 1970.

Redworth, Glyn. *In Defense of the Church Catholic: The Life of Stephen Gardiner.* Oxford, 1990.

Scarisbrick, J. J. *Henry VIII.* Berkeley, 1970.

GUY FITCH LYTLE III

KIRCHMEYER, Thomas, (also Naogeorgus; 1508–1563), Calvinist-oriented theologian, as well as polemic dramatist of a pointedly antipapal but also anti-Lutheran orientation. Born in Straubing (Bavaria) and educated along strict Catholic lines, Kirchmeyer chose the monastic profession, as did his brothers. Between 1523 and 1526 he resided in a Dominican monastery in Regensburg. In January 1526 at Nuremberg he encountered support for the Reformation. Upon leaving his monastic order, he acquired between 1526 and 1533 (at one or more unknown universities) a humanist education and obtained a master of arts degree. Subsequently he became a Protestant minister in Mühltroff (1533), Sulza (1535), and Kahla (1541/42). After 1537 his intellectual independence vis à vis Protestantism became evident. His literary works were well received at territorial courts in Saxony (Elector John Frederick and Duke John Ernst of Saxony), a fact that afforded him support against attacks from the camp of the reformers.

His controversy with the Wittenberg theologians, initially (after 1537) moderate, became fundamental after 1546 because of his position that the elect do not lose the Holy Spirit despite sins and because of his Zwinglian view of Communion. In 1546 Kirchmeyer fled to crypto-Calvinist friends in Augsburg. He then became the minister in the south German towns of Kaufbeuren (October 1546) and Kempten (August 1548). He left these towns, both of which accepted the Interim. Aided by a Fugger stipend, he studied law in Basel between March and October 1551. In November 1551 Duke Christoph of Württemberg called him to Stuttgart, where he stayed until 1560. He resigned this position because of his crypto-Calvinist leanings and became minister in Backnang (1560) and then Esslingen (May 1560–January 1563), where he became superintendent, but he was dismissed, among other reasons, because of his support of witch hunts in the city. Eventually Kirchmeyer found a welcome from the Calvinist Elector Frederick III of the Palatinate. He died on 28 December 1563 while a minister at Wiesloch near Heidelberg.

Kirchmeyer's historical significance is based on three antipapal plays—*Pammachius* (1538), *Mercator* (1540), and *Incendia* (1541)—as well as the three biblical plays—*Hamanus* (1543), *Hieremias* (1551), and *Judas* (1553). His notions of pastoral theology found expression in *Agriculturae sacrae libri quinque* (1550). A polemical work was *Regnum Papisticum* (1553). His *Satyrarum libri quinque* (which he started before 1541 and completed in 1555) signified his independence from Protestantism. In addition to his theological works, Kirchmeyer published philological studies, as well as translations of antique writers from Greek and Latin. Pedagogically, he was an optimist and, dependent on the notion of German humanism, emphasized education as the primary method to lead to piety.

BIBLIOGRAPHY

Primary Sources

Bolte, Johannes, ed. *Thomas Naogeorgus. Mercator (1540). Drei Schauspiele vom sterbenden Menschen.* Leipzig, 1927. See pp. 161–319.

Roloff, Hans-Gert, ed. *Thomas Naogeorg: Sämtliche Werke.* Berlin and New York, 1975–.

Secondary Sources

Diehl, Paul Heinrich. *Die Dramen des Thomas Naogeorgus in ihrem Verhältnis zur Bibel und zu Luther.* D.Phil. diss., Ludwig-Maximilians-Universität München, 1915.

Roloff, Hans-Gert. "Naogeorg." In *Literatur Lexikon,* edited by Walther Killy, vol. 8, pp. 330–332. Munich, 1990. The best account of Kirchmeyer's life and thought.

Verzeichnis der im deutschen Sprachbereich erschienenen Drucke des XVI. Jahrhunderts. Stuttgart, 1983–. See vol. 10, nos. 966–1012.

Weber, Wolfgang. "Kirchmeyer, Thomas." In *Biografisch-bibliographisches Kirchenlexikon,* vol. 3, pp. 1519–1521. Herzberg, Germany, 1992.

DIETER FAUTH

Translated from German by Hans J. Hillerbrand

KNIGHTS' REVOLT. In 1522–1523 free imperial knights, chiefly from Franconia and Swabia, revolted against the princes of the west central empire. The revolt's deep causes lay in the conjuncture between the lesser nobles' impoverishment during the agrarian depression of 1350–1470 and the political pressure placed on them by the growth of the territorial principalities. This double movement marginalized the imperial knights (i.e., those who had no lord but the emperor); the inflation of prices and advancing commercialization of agriculture rewarded management skills they rarely possessed; and the military changes under Emperor Maximilian I (r. 1493–1519) devalued their role as heavy cavalry in favor of mercenary infantry and cannon. The regions most affected were Swabia, Franconia, and the entire zone west of the Rhine.

The undisputed head of the revolt was Franz von Sickingen (1481–1523). A gifted commander of mercenaries, he had grown prominent in Palatine service, and his family had holdings in Alsace and the lands northward into the Moselle basin. He had help in the way of propaganda from Ulrich von Hutten (1488–1523), a Franconian of unusually broad university education and some standing as a poet. More important, Sickingen's revolt drew momentary strength from Luther's movement, which Hutten espoused in print and Sickingen introduced into the parishes of his lands. In Hutten's eyes, the nobles' degraded position was the clearest proof of the need for reform.

The revolt's provocation was doubtless the imperial public peace, renewed in 1521, which made it criminal for a nobleman to declare feud against a noble, a burgher, a city, or a prince and limited the use of force to urban regimes and territorial rulers. The program of the "fraternal association," which formed under Sickingen's leadership at Landau, expected an empire-wide rising of the lesser nobles, which proved to be not a total illusion. Free knights from Swabia and Franconia supported it, as did some territorial nobles in northern parts of the Empire: the Franconians mobilized against the bishops of Bamberg and Würzburg, while agents moved through Jülich-Cleves, Cologne, Brunswick, and Lüneburg.

The princes' reactions, however, were swift and merciless: mere threats of loss of fiefs sufficed to pacify Jülich-Cleves and Cologne, while the Brunswickers were caught on the march through Hesse and made to join the army of Landgrave Philipp of Hesse. Meanwhile, the army of the Swabian League marched across Franconia, burning castles as it went. The league destroyed twenty-five castles in Franconia, while the princes razed another twenty-seven west of the Rhine.

Only one incident, Sickingen's attack on Trier, raises the Knights' Revolt above the level of a group of minor disturbances. In August 1522 he declared feud against the elector of Trier, Archbishop Richard von Greiffenklau (r. 1512–1531), whom Sickingen purported to attack "for God and His Imperial Majesty." By the beginning of September his army had surrounded the city of Trier, but an able defense and the oncoming armies of Landgrave Philipp and Elector Louis of the Palatinate forced Sickingen to break off the siege. He retreated to Castle Landstuhl, which the princes' artillery pounded into surrender at the end of April 1523. Mortally wounded, Sickingen died in the ruins in the presence of his victors. His death brought the revolt's collapse.

It is traditional to see in the Knights' Revolt of 1522–1523 a last reflex action of an obsolete social group, temporarily revitalized by Luther's movement. It is commonly alleged that Sickingen and the others misunderstood Luther, but the reforms Sickingen sponsored, and the clergy he patronized—among them Martin Bucer—show that he understood well enough some of what was at stake, even if not in Luther's sense. His Knights' Revolt was doomed, however, by the rise of the territorial principalities, which intensified the structure of law and order to such a degree that leagues of lesser imperial estates—including free cities—no longer could play independent roles in imperial politics.

[*See also* Holy Roman Empire *and* Hutten, Ulrich von.]

BIBLIOGRAPHY

Hitchcock, William R. *The Background of the Knights' Revolt, 1522–1523*. Berkeley and Los Angeles, 1958. Reprint, Millwood, N.Y., 1980.

Holborn, Hajo. *Ulrich von Hutten and the German Reformation.* Translated by Roland H. Bainton. Reprint, Westport, Conn., 1978.

Kehrer, Helmut. "The Von Sickingen and the German Princes, 1262–1523." Unpubl. Ph.D. diss., Boston University, 1977.

Le Gates, Marlene. "The Knights and the State in Sixteenth-Century Germany." Unpubl. Ph.D. diss., Yale University, 1970.

———. "The Knights and the Problems of Political Organizing in Sixteenth-Century Germany." *Central European History* 7 (1974), 99–136.

Redlich, Fritz. *The German Military Enterpriser and His Work Force: A Study in European Economic and Social History.* 2 pts. Wiesbaden, 1964–1965.

THOMAS A. BRADY, JR.

KNIPPERDOLLING, Berndt (also Bernd, Bernhard; 1490?–1536), Protestant merchant in Münster who occupied a leading position in the Anabaptist kingdom of 1534/1535. Born around 1490 as the third son of the merchant Johann Knipperdolling, Berndt married the wealthy widow of the merchant Matthias Hangesbecke. In the house at "Prinzipalmarkt" (today no. 41) Knipperdolling carried on a lucrative cloth trade, and his connections reached as far as Antwerp and Lübeck. In 1528 he was part of the anticlerical opposition in Münster, and in February of the following year he was seized in Vechta by officers of the bishop, interrogated under torture, and held in strict confinement. Only upon payment of a heavy fine was he released. In May 1530 he brought charges against the town of Münster at the imperial high court of justice for having been detained unjustly. The town was summoned to court, but the trial did not produce a decision until 1534.

Around 1531 Knipperdolling joined the Protestant followers of Bernhard Rothmann. In a list of Protestants compiled by informants in the summer of 1532, Knipperdolling, referred to as "spokesman," was the tenth name mentioned. He arranged Rothmann's written correspondence with the council. In March 1533 he and other citizens elected a new council in which Protestants formed the majority. Followed by a segment of Rothmann's community, he turned to the Melchiorites and in January 1534, to the apostles of Jan Matthijs. John of Leiden (Jan Beuckelson) lived in Knipperdolling's house; his servant brought Matthijs from Amsterdam to Münster. On 24 February Knipperdolling was elected mayor. His house served as Matthijs's headquarters, and here men and women were baptized, communal property was established, and the expulsion of the heathens were decided. In the basement, Rothmann's texts were printed. When Leiden issued the order of the twelve elders, he conferred on Knipperdolling the office of "sword-bearer," responsible for law and order, as well as executions. He was released from this office only after Leiden's coronation. Within the new Anabaptist kingdom Knipperdolling held a high rank as "governor," though numerous accounts suggest he felt unjustly neglected by the king. Following the downfall of the kingdom, Knipperdolling was executed, along with the king, on 22 January 1536.

Through his leading position in the civil opposition of Münster, Knipperdolling furthered the development of Anabaptism and actively supported the rule of the king. His confessions show that he was true to his faith and that he refused to retract.

BIBLIOGRAPHY

Cornelius, Carl Adolf. *Berichte der Augenzeugen über das münsterische Wiedertäuferreich* (1853). Reprint, Münster, 1983. Contains the original texts of Knipperdolling's three confessions on pp. 376, 403, and 407, as well as translations into High German.

———. "Knipperdolling." In *Allgemeine deutsche Biographie*, vol. 16, pp. 293–295. Leipzig 1882.

Dülmen, Richard van, ed. *Das Täuferreich zu Münster, 1534–1535: Berichte und Dokumente.* Munich, 1974. All documents have been translated into High German; for Knipperdolling's three confessions see pp. 269, 277, and 278.

Prinz, Joseph. "Bernd Knipperdollinck und seine Sippe." *Westfalen* 40 (1962), 96–116. A genealogical survey of Knipperdolling's family.

Stupperich, Robert. "Zwei bisher unveröffentlichte eigenhändige Briefe Bernd Knypperdollyncks." *Jahrbuch für Westfällische Kirchengeschichte* 77 (1984), 41–58. One letter is dated from the time of the occupation, the other from his time in prison in Horstmar; the latter contains the answer to theological questions about which Antonius Corvinus had queried him.

KARL-HEINZ KIRCHHOFF

Translated from German by Wolfgang Katenz

KNOX, John (1513–1572), Scottish reformer. The Scottish Reformation and John Knox have come to be almost synonymous. He is the great reformer of whom everyone has heard, while his probably even more influential successor, Andrew Melville, educational reformer, leading Presbyterian, worthy opponent of a worthy king, James VI, has an infinitely less secure place in popular memory. Yet Knox had distinct limitations. When, in 1559, for example, the reformers seized the political moment offered by the death of the Catholic Mary Tudor and accession of the (presumably) Protestant Elizabeth to break out of the stalemate in which they had been kept by the regent, Mary of Guise, throughout the 1550s, their need for English support was crucial. One major difficulty was Elizabeth's determined refusal to forgive Knox for his unfortunately timed *First Blast of the Trumpet against the Monstrous Regiment of Women,* written in the autumn of 1557 not against her, but against Mary Tudor and Mary of Guise; yet none of his appeals to Elizabeth moved her, and his role had to be played down. Nor was his role with his own queen, Mary Stuart, quite so prominent as the famous interviews between them might suggest. In 1561 he emphatically asserted the right of subjects to resist their ruler, while equally emphatically denying the right of a ruler to impose a religious position on his/her subjects; and in 1563 his bullying on the subject of her marriage reduced her to such "howling" that a page had to rush for napkins to mop up the torrent of tears. But these accounts are found only in Knox's own work, his *History of the Reformation*; and while Mary had problems enough with her religious policy, there is no independent evidence that Knox was the greatest of these problems.

His relentless and single-minded zeal had earlier proved a considerable headache for the Protestant party in Scotland. The *First Blast* had in fact been written in a fit of pique and outraged frustration when he was returning to Scotland from Geneva to advance what he saw as the cause of God and arrived at Dieppe only to find letters from the Scottish nobles telling him that the time was not ripe for him to come. Frustration also produced the diatribes of 1558, the *Appellation to the Nobility and Estates of Scotland* and the *Letter Addressed to the Commonalty of Scotland.* The first appealed to the nobility to "hear the voice of the Eternal, your God," and overthrow the tyranny of Catholic rule. It was tremendous stuff, but hardly the right appeal to Protestant magnates wrestling with the realities of a political situation in which Scotland was ruled by a Catholic French regent whose main and successful policy was to bind it more firmly to Catholic France through the marriage of her daughter Mary Stuart to the Dauphin Francis, a marriage that took place in April 1558. The second diatribe was simply terrifying: resistance theory at its most radical, for it looked beyond the nobility, if they failed, to the commonalty; only Christopher Goodman, in his *Superior Powers Ought to be Obeyed,* came anywhere close to Knox in advancing such theory. Neither letter gave the Scottish Protestant party any reason to think of Knox as other than too dangerous to be allowed a part in the groping movement towards reform; indeed, he did not return to Scotland until May 1559, when Scottish Protestants had already themselves turned to open defiance and taken up arms against the regent.

The greatest irony of all, in view of Knox's abiding image, is that he was in fact deeply reluctant to come to Scotland—something that no doubt added to his fury in 1557 when he was prepared to make an effort that was rejected. He had earlier identified himself with the emerging Scottish Protestant party of the 1540s. We do not know much about him before that, except that he was born in Haddington, in East Lothian, was educated at the University of Saint Andrews, was a minor country lawyer, and—most remarkably—was ordained a priest in 1536. His road to conversion is not clear, but it was probably George Wishart who set him onto it; he was certainly part of Wishart's circle, and during the years of his ministry was teaching the sons of Protestant lairds.

What brought him to real prominence was his move to Saint Andrews in 1547, where David Beaton's murderers still lived in the haven of the castle; there, at Easter, despite initial reluctance, he preached his first sermon, a dramatic and sensational attack on the church of Rome, in which he identified the Antichrist not just with the pope but with the whole papacy. Yet again, his timing was unfortunate. In July the French took the castle, and Knox was imprisoned and sent to the galleys, where he remained for two years. On his release he turned not to Scotland, but to the Protestant England of Edward VI, where he became a preacher at Berwick and Newcastle and rose to become a royal chaplain. The accession of Mary Tudor continued his identification with English Protestantism, when he scurried abroad as one of the Marian exiles, and from there in 1554 launched a *Letter to the Faithful in London, Berwick and Newcastle*, a *Faithful Admonition unto the Professors of God's Truth in England*, and two further letters to his afflicted brethren of England. His interest in Scotland, despite his appearance there in 1555, seems to have taken second place; presumably he would have returned with the Marian exiles to England had Elizabeth allowed it.

By default, therefore, Knox found himself in Scotland, an uncomfortable ally of the Scottish Protestants, who achieved at least the beginning of their aims in the Reformation Parliament of the summer of 1560, made possible by the death of Mary of Guise in June, the reluctance of Mary Stuart to bother with her kingdom or even to come there, English intervention, and the withdrawal of French troops. Yet it would be wholly unfair to Knox to see him as a reluctant reformer. He was already preaching sermons at Perth in May 1559 so inflammatory that they provoked an outburst of iconoclasm that made him revise his ideas of the godly commonalty. He alternatively harangued and sought to woo the regent.

In 1560 he was one of the six authors of the remarkable and moving blueprint for the new church, *The First Book of Discipline,* as well as minister at Saint Giles, Edinburgh, and leading preacher. The Reformation Parliament was held to the accompaniment of his sermons on the prophet Haggai who had told his people to build the house of the Lord, who would "shake the heavens and the earth... and... overthrow the throne of kingdoms." This is surely the clue to Knox, the reason why, despite the sometimes patchy and problematic reality, he can justifiably be seen as one of the greatest figures of the Scottish Reformation. It was said of his first sermon, in 1547, that "others lop at the branches of papistry, but he strikes at the root, to destroy the whole." There can be no doubt that he was seen as a man of unusual commitment, even in this committed age, and unusual power. The English diplomat Thomas Randolph wrote of how he was "able in one hour to put more life in us than five hundred trumpets continually blustering in our ears," and, in August 1561, a week after Mary's belated and reluctant return to Scotland, described how "he thundereth out of the pulpit; he ruleth the roast, and of him all men stand in fear."

His *History of the Reformation* shows something of that power. It has been pointed out that the work itself was excellent self-propaganda, for Knox plays a prominent part in it. But if this is so, then one has to say that Knox was a reluctant self-propagandist. He began the book in 1559 and was still extending and revising it in 1571–1572, showing far less enthusiasm than with his earlier writings to let it go before the public. Yet of all his writings, it is the most masterly and inspired: bitter, vitriolic against his enemies, sometimes painful to read for that reason, but always shot through with the passion of service to his God. It is not in any normal sense a spiritual odyssey, but it is the odyssey of the people of God. Highly emotional, bad-tempered, often intolerant, quarrelsome, with a gun-barrel inspiration, and yet sometimes surprisingly tender and patient, as he was with the endless doubts of his mother-in-law about her salvation, Knox appears in the *History* a man who would have dominated reform in any society. It happened to be Scotland.

BIBLIOGRAPHY

Cameron, James, ed. *The First Book of Discipline.* Edinburgh, 1972. Text, along with an introduction which is essential reading for Reformation thought.

Donaldson, Gordon. *The Scottish Reformation.* Cambridge, 1960. A classic: the book that departed from a long tradition of Protestant-biased writing and looked at the Scottish Reformation as a historical event.

Kirk, James, ed. *The Second Book of Discipline.* Edinburgh, 1980. The follow-up to Cameron; again, essential.

———. *Patterns of Reform.* Edinburgh, 1989. A splendid collection of essays which throw a great deal of light on the problems and successes of the Kirk, including in the Highlands.

Knox, John. *History of the Reformation in Scotland.* Edited by W.C. Dickinson. 2 vols. Edinburgh, 1949. A masterly introduction to a great book.

Mason, Roger A. "Knox, Resistance and the Moral Imperative." *History of Political Thought* 1 (1980), 411–436. Subtle and satisfying analysis of Knox's resistance theory.

Percy, Eustace. *John Knox.* Reprint, Richmond, Va., 1965. An outdated but lively work, still worth reading.

Reid, W. Stanford. *Trumpeter of God.* Reprint, Grand Rapids, Mich., 1982. Forceful, but with hints of a return to the "biased" tradition.

Ridley, Jasper. *John Knox.* Oxford, 1968. Not a good guide to sixteenth-century Scotland, but informative on Knox and his writings.

Wormald, Jenny. "Princes and the Regions in the Scottish Reformation." In *Church, Politics and Society: Scotland, 1408–1929*, edited by Norman Macdougall, pp. 65–84. Edinburgh, 1983. A discussion of the problems posed for politicians by Knox's demand for total religious commitment.

Jenny Wormald

KOCH, Konrad. *See* Wimpina, Konrad.

KOCHHAFE, Nathan. *See* Chytraeus, Nathan.

KÖNIG, Urban. *See* Rhegius, Urbanus.

KRAFFT, Adam (Eng., Adam of Fulda; Lat., Fuldanus/Fuldensis, Crato, Vegetius; 1493–1558), German Lutheran church reformer, theologian, and administrator in Hesse. Krafft's father, Hans, was a burgomaster at Fulda, an abbey town east of Hesse. With a good Latin education, Krafft earned a B.A. (1514) and M.A. (1519) at the University of Erfurt. At Erfurt he became an enthusiast for humanistic studies, including the work of Erasmus, and associated with the humanist circle of Mutian.

After attending the Leipzig Disputation (1519), Krafft began preaching Lutheranism. In 1525, during the Peasant's War, he met Philipp of Hesse and won an appointment as a court preacher and visitor (after 1532, superintendent). At the Synod of Homberg (1526), which established the principles of Hessian reform, Krafft played a secondary role to François Lambert. Beginning in 1527, as a preacher and visitor, Krafft became the major force in administering the Hessian reformation, including the establishment and restructuring of schools, common chests, and hospitals. That same year, Philipp appointed Krafft professor of theology at the new University of Marburg.

Some scholars believe Krafft's influence on the landgrave was diminished as the latter became associated, in 1529, with the Zurich reformer Zwingli. In this view, Philipp came to prefer the Zwinglian teaching regarding the Lord's Supper, while Krafft remained a staunch Lutheran. It would be wrong to exaggerate this view, however, for Krafft retained his offices and remained close to the landgrave. Moreover Martin Bucer did not displace Krafft, even though during the 1530s, Bucer was closer to Philipp than any other theologian. In fact, Krafft's views were similar to Philipp's. He accepted the Augsburg Confession and the Wittenberg Concord as major theological statements. Krafft approved the changes that Bucer introduced into the Hessian church (1538/39). Moreover, Krafft defended Philipp's church against the Augsburg Interim and consoled Philipp in his imprisonment (1547–1552).

BIBLIOGRAPHY

Franz, Günther, ed. *Urkundliche Quellen zur hessischen Reformationsgeschichte.* Vols. 2–4. Marburg, 1951–1554. A collection of documents that is a must for the serious student of Krafft's life and significance.

Schäfer, Friedrich Wilhelm. *Adam Krafft, der Reformator Hessens.* Beiträge zur hessischen Kirchengeschichte, vol. 5. Darmstadt, 1913. Remains a sound treatment of the reformer.

Schäfer, Walter. *Adam Krafft: Landgräfliche Ordnung und bischöfliches Amt.* Monographia Hassiae, vol. 4. Kassel, Germany, 1976. Emphasizes Krafft's role in the church and his difficult service to Philipp of Hesse.

Zeller, Winfried. "Krafft." In *Neue Deutsche Biographie,* vol. 12, pp. 646–647. Berlin, 1953.

William J. Wright

KURSCHNER, Konrad. *See* Pellikan, Konrad.

L

LA FAYE, Antoine de (1540–1615), successor to Théodore de Bèze as supreme doctor of theology in Geneva. Born in Châteaudun in 1540, La Faye was regent at the College of Geneva from 1561 to 1574. He went to Italy in 1574 to obtain his doctorate in medicine, and upon his return in October 1575 he was appointed principal of the college, a post he held until 1579. From 1576 to 1580 he was an assistant professor of arts at the academy of Geneva. In 1589 he was appointed pastor, whereupon he gave up teaching philosophy. That same year he was elected rector of the academy. La Faye's ambition led him to seek to teach theology. He achieved his goal when Lambert Daneau left Geneva to go to Leiden in 1581, but he only obtained a post as a substitute instructor.

In 1586 La Faye accompanied Théodore de Bèze to the Colloquy of Montbéliard, where they confronted the Lutheran Jakob Andreae over the problem of the Lord's Supper, the person of Christ, predestination, and baptism. In 1588 he went with Bèze to Bern to defend the Calvinist idea of predestination against Samuel Huber. That year he also took part in writing the preface to the *Bible des pasteurs et professeurs de Genève*. Although he was incapable of defending Reformed theology against the attacks of the Capuchin fathers, who began attempts to re-Catholicise the Chablais region in 1598, La Faye managed to replace Bèze in 1600 and had himself named supreme doctor of theology in Geneva. His mediocrity, however, contributed to the decline in the teaching of theology in Geneva at the beginning of the seventeenth century. In 1606 he wrote a biography of Bèze intended to show that he was as worthy as Bèze to occupy the first place in the church of Geneva. The council forced him to modify certain passages in his book.

BIBLIOGRAPHY

Primary Sources

La Faye, Antoine de. *Theses theologicae in schola genevensi ab aliquot sacrarum litterarum studiosis sub D. D. Theod. Bez et Antonio Fayo Theologiae professoribus propositae et disputatae*. Geneva, 1586.

———. *De vita et obitu clariss. viri. D. Theodori Beze Vezelii*. Geneva, 1605.

———. *Enchiridion theologicum aphoristica methodo compositum ex disputationibus Antonii Fayi Ecclesiastae et sacrarum litterarum Professoris Genevae*. Geneva, 1695.

———. *Registres de la compagnie des pasteurs de Genève*. Geneva, 1969–1986. See vols. 3–8.

Secondary Sources

Borgeaud, Charles. *Histoire de l'Université de Geneve*. Geneva, 1900. See vol. 1, "L'Académie de Calvin."

Geisendorf, Paul-F. *Théodore de Bèze*. Geneva, 1949.

OLIVER FATIO

Translated from French by Robert E. Shillenn

LAÍNEZ, Diego (Eng., James Laynez, Laines; 1512–1565), preacher, theologian, and second general of the Society of Jesus (1558–1565). Born of Jewish-Christian ancestry at Amazan, Spain, Laínez received a humanist education at Soria and Sigüenza before studying philosophy and theology at Alcalá de Henares (1528–1533). There he heard about Ignatius Loyola and became friends with Alfonso Salmeron; together they sought out Loyola at the University of Paris, where they continued their theological studies. Along with Loyola and four other companions they took a vow in 1534 to go to Palestine as missionaries. In 1547 the companions gathered in Venice, where Laínez was ordained; when war between Venice and the Turks prevented their journey, the seven companions put themselves at the pope's disposal, who sent them to preach in various Italian cities. Laínez worked in Venice and Vicenza before Paul III assigned him to teach theology at the University of Rome "La Sapienza" during 1538 and 1539. The companions gradually decided to found a religious order, the Society of Jesus, or Jesuits, which Paul III approved in 1540.

From 1539 to 1544 Laínez resumed his preaching with great success and worked to reform monasteries and convents in Parma, Piacenza, Lucca, Venice, and Brescia. The high point of his preaching career was the sermons he gave in the convents and cathedral of Florence in 1547; some of his sermons on feast days drew about nine thousand people. Later he preached in many other Italian cities, notably Naples, Palermo, Rome, and Genoa. The goodwill he won contributed to the later founding of Jesuit colleges. In 1550 he served as a chaplain to an expedition against Muslim pirates that captured Tripoli in Africa.

Laínez was the most gifted scholar and theologian among Loyola's first followers; he and Salmeron were among the few theologians to participate in all three phases of the Council of Trent, 1545–1547, 1551–1552, and 1562–1563.

There his strongly anti-Protestant views carried considerable weight. During the first phase Laínez helped persuade the council to reject the theory of twofold justification advocated by Johannes Gropper and Girolamo Seripando. In the second phase he contributed to decrees on Christ's real presence in the Eucharist and the sacrificial character of the Mass. In the third phase, as general of the Jesuits, Laínez voted with the bishops rather than merely advising as a theologian; he successfully opposed Communion under both bread and wine and fought for episcopal reform. At Trent he helped secure the council's approval of the Jesuits.

Laínez also attended the Colloquy of Poissy in 1561, where he vehemently opposed Théodore de Bèze and Peter Martyr Vermigli on the Eucharist. While in France he had the satisfaction of seeing the official recognition of the French Jesuits, long opposed by the Parlement of Paris, under the title of Société du Collège de Clermont. He returned to Trent via Brussels, Louvain, Trier, and Munich, encouraging Jesuits and conferring with local leaders.

Laínez was provincial superior of the Jesuits in Italy from 1552 to 1556. When Loyola died in 1556, the leading Jesuits at Rome met and agreed that Laínez should serve as vicar general of the Jesuits until a new general could be elected. Laínez had to continue as vicar general from 1556 to 1558 because a war between Philip II and Paul IV prevented the Jesuits from holding a general congregation to elect a new general. This congregation finally met in 1558, approved of Loyola's *Constitutions*, and elected Laínez the order's second superior general. Under his leadership (1558–1565) the Jesuits grew rapidly, from 12 provinces to 18, from 72 houses to 130, from 1000 men to 3,500. Although enthusiastically pro-papal, Laínez found himself at odds with the headstrong Paul IV, who ordered the Jesuits to sing the divine office and to elect their generals every three years. After Paul died in 1559 and Laínez had consulted five canon lawyers, the Jesuits dropped these oral commands of Paul IV and returned to their earlier practice, which papal bulls had officially sanctioned. In 1559 he was forced to expel his gifted but unstable brother Christopher from the Jesuits.

Administrative duties prevented Laínez from publishing much during his lifetime, although in 1552 he began to write a compendium of theology. In any case, he preferred preaching to writing. Partly because of his wretched handwriting, most of his writings had to wait until the twentieth century for publication. His treatises, sermons, letters, and memos fill eight large volumes.

BIBLIOGRAPHY

Primary Source

Laínez, Diego. *Epistulae et acta Patris Jacobi Laini.* Madrid, 1912–1919. Eight large volumes of Laínez's papers, part of the series *Monumenta historica Societatis Iesu.*

Secondary Sources

Brodrick, James. *The Progress of the Jesuits, 1556–1575.* Reprint, Chicago, 1986. Popular account of Jesuit history in the two decades after the death of Ignatius Loyola.

Cereceda, Feliciano. *Diego Laínez en la Europa religiosa de su tiempo, 1512–1565.* Madrid, 1945–1946. Definitive study in two volumes, 1252 pages.

Fichter, Joseph H. *James Laynez, Jesuit.* St. Louis, 1944. The only full biography in English.

Ravier, Andre. *Ignatius Loyola and the Founding of the Jesuits.* San Francisco, 1987. Treats Laínez as Vicar General, pp. 275–317.

Scaduto, Mario. *L'epocha di Giocomo Laines, 1556–1565.* Rome, 1964 and 1974. Two large volumes that examine the Italian Jesuits under Laínez.

JOHN PATRICK DONNELLY

LAITY. New ideas about the laity—the ordinary believers outside the clergy—fueled Reformation debates and characterized Reformation thought. The medieval church used ordination to elevate a minority of men from the lay estate, creating priests who were part of a privileged spiritual estate claiming exclusive rights to preach, define doctrine, and administer the sacraments. Through the prerogatives of confession and excommunication, the priests exercised extensive spiritual and moral discipline over the laity. Vows of chastity linked priests to the monks, friars, and nuns who shared their immunity from lay rulers' legal jurisdiction and taxation. These men and women were seen as following a way of life more pleasing to God than that of the laity and as possessing a superior understanding of the Christian religion as well. This medieval superiority was challenged in the early sixteenth century by humanists and evangelicals who developed the concept of the priesthood of all believers. While these battles helped separate adherents of the new Protestant churches from traditionalists, the realities of lay responses to the reformers' new notion sparked a second round of controversy among Protestants, with the lines drawn more between clergy and laity than between confessions.

The initial rethinking of the laity's position in the church began well before the Reformation. The great heresiarchs of the late Middle Ages, John Wycliffe and Jan Hus, both encouraged lay people to study scripture on their own, favoring vernacular translations of the Bible as the foundation of lay theological independence. Defenders of clerical privilege, such as the Strasbourg cathedral preacher Geiler von Keysersberg, opposed such innovations because they feared the deceptive clarity of scripture would lure untutored minds into heresy. Christian humanist scholars, however, pinned their hope for religious renewal on the sound judgment of scripture-reading laity. Thus Erasmus argued that divine inspiration would guide Bible readers, and in the preface to his 1516 Latin edition of the New Testament he claimed that all people could become theologians.

Four years later, Martin Luther gave these ideas a wider audience in his much-reprinted vernacular pamphlet *An den christlichen Adel deutscher Nation* (To the Christian Nobility of the German Nation). Luther argued that baptism gave every Christian membership in a single spiritual estate, where all were priests, although only some were called to exercise their priesthood by preaching and administering the sacraments. According to Luther, this notion of the universal priesthood empowered Germany's rulers to defy the pope and summon a general council of the church to begin the process of reform; secular authorities could exercise emergency powers over ecclesiastical affairs until true religion was reestablished. Luther's invitation was quickly enlarged by reformers throughout Germany and Switzerland, who asked town governments to judge the doctrines and behavior of clergy in their territories. In the 1520s reformers also addressed themselves to people without political office, populating their propaganda with fictional "evangelical townsmen" and "evangelical peasants." They conjured up these altruistic, pious, scripture-quoting lay men (women rarely figured in these pamphlets) to correct the self-serving, un-Christian, and ignorant priests of the unreformed church. By deploying these virtuous characters, the preachers and pamphleteers hoped to mobilize lay followers to purge the churches of bad priests, leaving the way clear for evangelical clergymen to inaugurate pure religion.

Confident of their biblical expertise, lay people readily entered the Reformation debates, taking more autonomous stances than either humanists or the evangelical clergy had expected. University-educated men, heedless of the medieval ban on lay preaching, delivered sermons, as did craftsmen innocent of Latin, and even a few women who defied Saint Paul's prohibition on women's speaking publicly about religion. The religious tracts pouring out of the print shops in the early 1520s usually derived from clerical pens, but a significant proportion were by lay authors: minor aristocrats such as Franz von Sickingen and Hartmut von Cronberg, artisans such as Hans Sachs, Niklaus Manuel, and Sebastian Lotzer, and a sprinkling of women, such as Ursula Weyda, a Saxon tax collector's wife. In explicating their ideas, the laity did not simply echo clerical leads; they worked out their own positions, buttressing their arguments by direct reference to the Bible, truly acting as their own theologians. For all his respect for Martin Luther, Hans Sachs distanced himself from Luther's Nuremberg followers' deviations from evangelical truth as Sachs saw it. Anabaptist laymen and women rejected both the Saxon and the Swiss versions of the Reformation and tried to re-create apostolic society in gathered communities, where church and state merged. Spiritualists, like the followers of the Silesian aristocrat Kaspar von Schwenckfeld, centered their religious lives not on membership in a visible church but on personal union with God. When territorial rulers intervened in religious matters, it was to establish state churches guaranteeing lay rulers unprecedented control over the clergy, as well as over the religious lives and morals of their lay subjects. Codified in church ordinances in Lutheran and Zwinglian cities and territories from the late 1520s on, and among Calvinists after the Genevan *Ordonnances ecclésiastiques* (Ecclesiastical Ordinances) of 1541, the lay-controlled territorial church also became the organizational framework for English Protestantism through the Elizabethan Settlement of 1559.

The reformers' idea that baptism enrolled all Christians in a single spiritual estate allowed a minority of lay people to move into clerical roles by producing theology and becoming church superintendents. It also held up lay ways of life as models for all Christians. For example, both clerical and lay critics of the old church belittled the notion that monks, friars, and nuns led lives particularly pleasing to God; they demanded that members of the regular orders return to the world and do "useful" work. Outraged by the alleged fornications, adulteries, and concubinages of the professionals in religion, evangelicals endorsed marriage over "impossible" vows of chastity, holding up monogamous lay marital partners as exemplars of Christian sexual morality for the priests and members of religious orders to emulate. Reformers stressed the need for parish priests in particular to marry and run households like those presided over by master craftsmen. This domestication of the priests was also a sacralization of husbandhood, making all male heads of households members of a domestic priesthood responsible for the moral education and discipline of women and children, and reinforcing the existing superiority of married men over bachelors.

Catholics rejected the new theory of the laity. The mid-century Council of Trent reasserted the exclusive control of the Roman Catholic church by the spiritual estate, the value of monasticism, and the necessity for clerical celibacy. Meanwhile, the pastors of the newly established Protestant churches, disappointed by the attitudes and comportments of their parishioners, struggled to defend the authority of orthodox and duly appointed clergymen. Their initially flattering descriptions of the evangelical laity had reflected not just their urgent need to recruit allies against the Catholic establishment, but also their assumption that truly Christian lay people would accept doctrinal direction and moral correction from their new preachers. While a few radicals like Andreas Bodenstein von Karlstadt and Thomas Müntzer allowed the laity wide autonomy, most reformers began to differentiate disobedient reprobates of doubtful commitment to Christianity from the true evangelical laity, creating a gallery of the deaf, the slow, and the perverse, who were impeding the progress of reform.

Luther discovered that the majority of the German nobility would not listen to his message, while English-language reformers had similarly unhappy experiences of their own. William Tyndale, the great Bible translator, went to his execution in 1536 loyally but ineffectually praying for the conversion of King Henry VIII; John Knox raged at both Mary Tudor and Mary Stuart, while the more radical of Elizabeth I's clergymen denounced her church settlement as but half a reformation. Outside the ruling classes as well, many laity refused to make wholehearted conversions, including the epicureans and libertines Calvin condemned for their devotion to the temporal world. In the introduction to his *Enchiridion: Der Kleyne Catechismi* (Small Catechism), Luther pointed to the slow who, "like pigs and irrational beasts," failed to master the rudiments of their faith; other magisterial clergymen interrogating suspected sectarian heretics distinguished the "simple and deluded" followers from the "stiff-necked" leaders. The latter were among the perverters of scripture, most notorious of whom were the "murdering, robbing hordes of peasants" Luther accused of abusing Christian liberty to attack their feudal lords in the Peasants' War of 1524–1525, and the "demonic" artisans, Melchior Hoffman, Jan Matthijs, and John of Leiden, who inspired and led the revolutionary Anabaptists at Münster in northwestern Germany a decade later. Not notorious, but certainly subversive, were uppity women, like the Schwenckfelder Katharina Zell, who spoke out in public on religious affairs, in defiance of Pauline propriety.

What united these "bad" lay figures in Protestant theology and polemic was their independence: all refused to accept without reservation the authority of the new preachers. Although more liberal in their definition of the laity's place in Christian society than were the Catholics, the Protestant clergy never intended spiritual authority to pass entirely from trained and ordained professionals to amateurs in religion.

BIBLIOGRAPHY

Abray, Lorna Jane. *The People's Reformation: Magistrates, Clergy and Commons in Strasbourg, 1500–1598.* Ithaca, N.Y., 1985. Traces the lay understanding of reformation and lay-clerical rivalry for control of the church in a German city.

Chrisman, Miriam Usher. *Lay Culture, Learned Culture: Books and Social Change in Strasbourg.* New Haven, 1982. Ground-breaking study of sixteenth-century lay values based on the output of the printing industry in a major Reformation printing center.

Cross, Claire. *Church and People, 1450–1660: The Triumph of the Laity in the English Church.* London, 1976. History of early English Protestantism emphasizing the growth of lay power.

Estes, James Martin. *Christian Magistrate and State Church: The Reforming Career of Johannes Brenz.* Toronto, 1982. The emergence of the lay-controlled territorial church in Lutheranism.

Haendler, Gert. *Luther on Ministerial Office and Congregational Function.* Translated by Ruth C. Gritsch and edited by Eric W. Gritsch. Philadelphia, 1981. Tensions in Luther's theology between the powers of the laity to appoint or dismiss pastors and the ministerial authority of the clergy.

Höpfl, Harro. *The Christian Polity of John Calvin.* Cambridge, 1982. Analyzes key texts to reconstruct Calvin's views on lay roles in church and state.

Hoyer, Siegfried. "Lay Preaching and Radicalism in the Early Reformation." In *Radical Tendencies in the Reformation: Divergent Perspectives,* edited by Hans J. Hillerbrand, pp. 85–97. Kirksville, Mo., 1988.

Hsia, R. Po-Chia, ed. *The German People and the Reformation.* Ithaca, N.Y., 1988. Despite the limitation to Germany, an excellent introduction to recent scholarly approaches to the laity in the Reformation.

Monter, E. William. *Calvin's Geneva.* Reprint, Hungtingon, N.Y., 1975. Despite the title, the focus is on lay people.

Ozment, Steven E. *The Reformation in the Cities.* New Haven, 1975. Argues that reforming preachers in Germany and Switzerland won support by flattering the laity and offering release from psychological burdens imposed by the medieval church.

———. *When Fathers Ruled: Family Life in Reformation Europe.* Cambridge, Mass., 1983. Argues that Protestant marital theology enhanced the prestige of the laity and improved the status of women. Compare Lyndal Roper.

Roper, Lyndal. *The Holy Household: Women and Morals in Reformation Augsburg.* Oxford, 1989. Argues that marital theology restricting women to the household and emphasizing their submission to their husbands was a major element in the appeal of Protestantism to men. Compare Steven E. Ozment, *When Fathers Ruled.*

Russell, Paul A. *Lay Theology in the Reformation: Popular Pamphleteers in Southwest Germany, 1521–1525.* Cambridge, 1986. Detailed and original analysis of pamphlets by five men and three women who supported the evangelical cause. Often technical, but also well-illustrated with contemporary images showing lay activists at work.

Scribner, Robert W. *For the Sake of Simple Folk: Popular Propaganda for the German Reformation.* Cambridge, 1981. Provocative and fascinating examination of the use of woodcuts to mobilize the illiterate or poorly literate among the laity for the evangelical cause. Abundantly illustrated.

Strauss, Gerald. *Luther's House of Learning: Indoctrination of the Young in the German Reformation.* Baltimore, 1978. Controversial study using Lutheran examples to argue for the slow and imperfect acceptance by the laity of clerical orthodoxy. Focus is on the countryside.

LORNA JANE ABRAY

LAM, Sebastian (Lat., Ambrosius; 1544–1600), theologian and author attacked for his crypto-Calvinism by Lutherans in Upper Hungary (Slovakia). Born in Kežmarok, a city in northern Hungary that, under the Tököly's, became the leading center for Crypto-Calvinism, Lam studied first at the local Latin school and then served as a teacher in Spišská Bela and Spišská Sobota. He subsequently attended the University of Wittenberg (1575–1577) and, upon his return to Hungary, became the rector of the city school in his hometown (1577–1580). For three years (1580–1583) he was pastor of the Lutheran community in Prešov in Šariš county and returned to Kežmarok as pastor in 1583.

In 1591 Lam openly espoused a Calvinist interpretation of the Lord's Supper and urged the removal of paintings and statues from the churches of the Protestants in Upper Hungary, which led to nearly a decade of theological controversy in eastern Slovakia. Lam's theological stance was opposed in a series of treatises published by Gregor Stanšič Horváth de Gradecz, Eliáš Láni, and Albert Grawer, members of the faculty of Stanšič Horváth's school in Štražky, and other orthodox Lutherans in Hungary (e.g., Severin Šcultéty), all of whom advocated the acceptance of the *Book of Concord* as the doctrinal standard for Lutherans. These antagonists met face to face during two colloquies held in Kežmarok (5 December 1595 and 29 January 1596), and a printed summary of the discussions was widely circulated throughout Protestant Europe. Lam persisted in his views and was again criticized for his crypto-Calvinism at synods in Levoča (1595) and Prešov (1597), while, in 1599, a synod at Sabinov condemned him as a false prophet and Calvinist. He published a number of polemical works as well as hymns, occasional Latin verse, and funeral orations.

BIBLIOGRAPHY

Primary Sources

Ambrosius [Lam], Sebastian. *Achtundzwanzig geistliche Lieder.* Wittenberg, 1588.

———. *Metaphrasis graeca psalmi primi.* Wittenberg, 1588.

———. *Vierzehn geistliche Lieder.* Görlitz, 1588.

———. *Antithesis ubiquitatis et orthodoxae doctrinae de persona Christi.* Zerbst, 1591.

———. *Defensio orthodoxae doctrinae . . . a Sebatiano Ambrosio, servo Christi in Ecclesia Keimarcensi.* Viszoly, 1592.

———. *Kurze Wiederholung der reinen und gesunden Lehr . . . der Stadt Keizmarck.* Zerbst, 1598.

———. *Declaratio cirumstantiarum gemini colloquii . . . in arce Kesmarcensi habitis.* Zerbst, 1598.

Secondary Sources

Daniel, David P. "The Acceptance of the Formula of Concord in Slovakia." *Archiv für Reformationsgeschichte* 70 (1979), 260–277.

———. "The Reformation and Eastern Slovakia." *Human Affairs* 1.2 (1991), 172–186.

Ráth, György. "Gradeczi Horváth Gergely és Lám (Ambrosius) Sebestyén Hitvitája." *Irodalomtörténete Közlemenyek* 4 (1894), 150–167, 229–319, 412–427.

David P. Daniel

LAMBERT, François (also Lambert of Avignon; 1487–1530), evangelical reformer and theologian. Lambert lost his father, a secretary at the papal palace, early and joined the Franciscan community at age fifteen. The order bestowed the privileges of "apostolic preacher" on him (1517). In 1522 he became interested in Luther's writings, left his order, and went incognito to Wittenberg, where Luther received him. While learning and lecturing at Wittenberg, Lambert married.

His greater need for income and a desire to reform France, caused Lambert to move to Strasbourg (1524). When his work angered the humanists, he gladly accepted an invitation to serve Landgrave Philipp of Hesse as a reformer and theologian. He held a chair in theology at Marburg from 1527 until his death.

Lambert played a significant role in Hesse by helping Philipp establish biblically based principles for a Protestant church, in which the prince enjoyed a large role. He led the famous Synod of Homberg in 1526. His *Paradoxa,* which set forth the basic biblical principles for a new territorial church, served as theses for disputation. Lambert led the debate against the Roman Catholic opposition, and, with Philipp's support, his principles were accepted. Lambert, then, with other members of a commission, wrote a plan for their implementation called the *Reformatio ecclesiarum Hassiae.*

Lambert's greatest significance was as a theological writer. He wrote nineteen books of considerable length after his conversion to Protestantism, mostly Bible commentaries and polemical works. Translations of his Latin works also appeared, a surprising number of them in English. In his own day, Lambert's Bible commentaries did not find great favor. The *Commentarii de prophetia* minimized lingual erudition in favor of allowing the Holy Spirit to interpret the scriptures. Hence humanists came to distrust Lambert. Seventeenth-century Pietists, however, appreciated his spiritual reading of the scriptures.

Based on his sacramental views, some have classified Lambert as Lutheran from 1523 to 1529, Zwinglian thereafter. Attendance at the Colloquy of Marburg (1529) led him to adopt Zwingli's symbolic view of the Sacrament. It is difficult to place Lambert in any of the confessional camps, however; he tended to pursue new ideas. Moreover, his untimely death prevented him from maturing his theology. Indeed, Lambert did not complete *De regno, civitate et domo Dei,* an attempt at a comprehensive theology. Perhaps Lambert's most important work, it was posthumously published.

BIBLIOGRAPHY

Fraenkel, Pierre, ed. *Pour retrouver François Lambert: Bio-bigraphie et études.* Baden-Baden, 1987. A valuable new documentary source, including valuable essays on aspects of Lambert's work by Fraenkel, Rainer Haas, and R. Gerald Hobbs.

Haas, Rainer. *Franz Lambert und Patrick Hamilton in ihrer Bedeutung für die evangelische Bewegung auf den Britischen Inseln.* Marburg, 1973. Reveals Lambert's wider importance.

Hobbs, R. Gerald. "François Lambert sur les langues et la prophétie." In *Pour retrouver François Lambert: Bio-biographie et études,* edited by Pierre Fraenkel, pp. 273–290. Baden-Baden, 1987.

Maurer, Wilhelm. "Franz Lambert von Avignon und das Verfassungsideal der Reformatio ecclesiarum Hassiae von 1526." *Zeitschrift für Kirchengeschichte* 11 (1929), 209–260. Remains an important source for assessing Lambert's place in the Protestant Reformation.

Müller, Gerhard. *Franz Lambert von Avignon und die Reformation in Hessen.* Veröffentlichungen der Historische Kommission für Hesse und Waldeck, vol. 24. Marburg, 1958. A thorough study of Lambert's role in the Hessian Reformation.

Verzeichnis der im deutschen Sprachbereich erschienenen Drucke des XVI. Jahrhunderts. Stuttgart, 1983–. See vol. 11, nos. 133–159.

Winters, Roy Lutz. *Francis Lambert of Avignon, 1487–1530: A Study in Reformation Origins.* Philadelphia, 1938.

Wright, William J. "The Homberg Synod and Phillip of Hesse's Plan for a New Church-State Settlement." *Sixteenth Century Journal* 4 (1973), 23–46. Emphasizes Lambert's accommodations to Philipp of Hesse's political plans and the incorporation of most of his ideas into the Hessian church.

William J. Wright

LANG, Johannes (1488–1548), German reformer in Erfurt and the Thuringian county of Schwarzburg-Blankenburg. Born into a simple middle-class family in Erfurt, he entered the University of Erfurt in the fall of 1500, where he received his bachelor's degree in the spring of 1503. His concentration in humanist studies brought him into close contact with the publisher Nikolaus Marschalk, the poet Eobanus Hessus, and other humanists. He entered the Augustinian convent in Erfurt no later than 1506, where he influenced his friend Martin Luther in the humanist spirit. In 1508 Lang was ordained a priest. As a result of a dispute within the order over governance of the observants, Lang and Luther were both transferred in August 1511 to the monastery of the Augustinian friars in Wittenberg and matriculated at the university there.

Lang obtained his master of arts at Wittenberg and continued to give lectures on ethics until 1516. At the same time he served as subregent for the courses of study of the religious order and began the study of theology in 1515 that he concluded in 1519 in Erfurt with a doctoral degree. In the same year, he participated prominently in humanist university reforms. As prior of the Augustinian convent in Erfurt (1516–1518) and as district curate (1518–1520), he promoted Luther's reform message and belonged to a group of his first and most staunch supporters. His translation of Matthew's gospel (June 1521) brought him publishing success.

After Lang had left the monastery in January 1522 and had been expelled from the theology faculty, he found himself at the head of a small reformist pressure group. During the Peasants' War (April-May 1525), he pursued, with the city council, the reorganization of the church. He was appointed pastor and *Nonarius* ("nine o'clock preacher") of the Michaeliskirche. As superintendent of the Protestant clergy in Erfurt, he signed the Schmalkald Articles in February 1537.

In 1533 and 1539 he lead the visitation of the church in Schwarzburg-Blankenburg. His published contribution to the debates over clandestine marriages met with little response. Lang's obvious weakness as a leader is characteristic of the course that the Reformation took in Erfurt.

BIBLIOGRAPHY

Burgdorf, Martin. *Johann Lange, der Reformator Erfurts.* Kassel, 1911.

Kleineidam, Erich. *Universitas Studii Erffordensis: Überblick über die Geschichte der Universität Erfurt.* Pt. 2, "Spätscholastik, Humanismus und Reformation, 1461–1521." 2d ed. Leipzig, 1992. See pp. 304–306.

Weiß, Ulman. *Die frommen Bürger von Erfurt: Die Stadt und ihre Kirche im Spätmittelalter und in der Reformationszeit.* Weimar, 1988. See pp. 320–321.

ULMAN WEIß

Translated from German by Susan M. Sisler

LANGUEDOC. One of the largest and richest provinces of ancien régime France, Languedoc took its name from the language of the inhabitants—Occitan, or *langue d'oc, oc* being the word for "yes," which was used instead of the northern French *oïl* (modern *oui*). The language, however, was not limited to the province. Throughout southern France, an area also known as the Midi, most people spoke Occitan. Languedoc, also known as *Occitania,* dated in a territorial and administrative sense from the thirteenth century. The province offered little geographical or geological unity. Bounded on the east by the Rhône river, which separated it from Provence, it stretched westward to Gascony. The Mediterranean and the Pyrenees marked its southern boundary, while Auvergne and Forez delimited the northern reaches. Within these confines, three major regions are discernible: a dry Mediterranean coastal plain, the arid but cooler Cévennes mountains behind the coastland and, in the west, a portion of the Aquitanian wedge with its damper Atlantic climate.

The region was home to an early, lively, and enduring Protestant population. Humanists, many of them inspired by Erasmian ideals, voiced some of the first demands for religious reform. Their strong interest in scripture lent the movement an evangelical flavor. By 1532, however, the conservative judges of the Parlement of Toulouse had effectively quashed this small group of scholars and writers. The growing influx of books and similar printed materials by Luther, Zwingli, and others was not so readily stoppable, despite considerable effort by secular and religious authorities. Persons attracted to the ideas of these early reformers were frequently labeled "Lutherans," though in truth they held a wide variety of views. Moreover, notions of religious reform resonated sympathetically within a popular, if sometimes ill-informed, tradition of anticlericalism. Only gradually, during the 1540s and 1550s, did these various strains—Humanist, "Lutheran," and popular—transform what was often a disjointed and poorly focused heterodoxy into a coherent, well-organized, and broadly based movement.

By the early 1560s and the outbreak of the Wars of Religion, the Reformation in Languedoc, as elsewhere in France, coalesced under the leadership of John Calvin and his followers. The Calvinists established churches in most of the province's principal cities—Castres, Montauban, Montpellier, and Nîmes—as well as in numerous smaller towns and villages. One of the remarkable features of the Reformation in Languedoc is the manner whereby it penetrated deeply into the rural world, especially the remote hinterland of the Cévennes mountains. Altogether, Languedoc possessed a lively and dense network of Reformed communities wherein over half of all French Protestants lived by the end of the sixteenth century.

Quite apart from issues of confessional discontent and personal conversion, Protestantism in the region's many towns benefited from a lengthy medieval heritage of municipal privilege. The establishment of Reformed churches and Huguenot political regimes reinforced established mechanisms of municipal self-governance and strengthened the local elite's control over its own affairs. In many instances, civic authorities and royal officers, acting in concert with Protestant church officials, filled the vacuum left by the absence of traditional ecclesiastical and feudal powers. Numerous bishops, for instance, had long been nonresident. Many of these same towns eventually became *places de sûreté* where Protestants could freely worship. As guarantee of this prerogative, the towns were garrisoned by Huguenot troops paid by the king under a system initiated during the 1570s and subsequently confirmed and extended under the terms of the Edict of Nantes in 1598. The Huguenots also had their own sovereign court, the *chambre de l'Edit* of Languedoc, seated at Castres. Theoretically a part of the Parlement of Toulouse, this royal tribunal was established specifically to provide equitable justice for Protestants.

In a related development, a substantial number of Huguenot political assemblies met in Languedoc during the Wars of Religion. These highly independent representative assemblies occupy an important niche in the history of political resistance and, as such, offered an unusual opportunity for the exercise of legislative power by the various delegates, especially those from strongly Calvinist towns like Montauban, Nîmes, and Castres. The development has prompted some modern historians to dub the Huguenot system a "United Provinces of the Midi."

The Reformation conflict was bitter everywhere in Languedoc. Warfare first broke out during the early 1560s and continued until the late 1590s, only to erupt anew in the 1620s. Confessional violence was not limited, of course, to soldiers fighting on the battlefield. A succession of urban massacres punctuated the age. Catholics savaged Protestants at Toulouse during the first weeks of the religious wars in 1562. The slaughter was repeated there ten years later in the provincial aftermath of the Saint Bartholomew's Day Massacre. For their part, Protestants killed a hundred or so Catholics at Nîmes during the so-called *Michelade* of September 1567. Some towns felt the wrath of both sides. At Gaillac, for example, Catholics murdered Protestants in 1562, and when an opportunity presented itself a half dozen years later, Protestants did the same to Catholics.

In Languedoc, as throughout France, the individual Reformed church and its consistory were the foundation of an elaborate ecclesiastical organization. Every local church had a consistory composed of one or more pastors and a dozen or so lay persons serving as elders and deacons. In their weekly meetings, the consistory officers supervised the religious life of the community and exercised responsibility for ecclesiastical administration, social welfare, and morals control. Elders and deacons routinely distributed money and food to assist persons in distress. They also had the power to summon and punish those who committed adultery, got drunk, quarreled with their neighbors, and so forth. The arrangement vested considerable authority and independence of action in the local churches while maintaining an elaborate presbyterian-synodal organization. For its part, Languedoc was divided into four ecclesiastical provinces: Upper Languedoc, Lower Languedoc, the Cévennes, and, finally, Vivarais, Forez, and Velay. Each had its own synod whose delegates—mostly pastors and elders—met on an annual basis. The provinces were typically subdivided into three or more colloquies that assembled biannually. In the end, the Reformed churches of Languedoc possessed the distinctive tones of a federation.

BIBLIOGRAPHY

Garrisson-Estèbe, Janine. *Protestants du Midi, 1559–1598.* Toulouse, 1980. Most complete study of the Reformation in Languedoc.

Greengrass, Mark. "The Anatomy of a Religious Riot in Toulouse in May 1562." *Journal of Ecclesiastical History* 34 (1983), 367–391. Examines religious violence at the beginning of the Wars of Religion.

Le Roy Ladurie, Emmanuel. *The Peasants of Languedoc.* Translated by John Day. Urbana, Ill., 1974. Important economic and social study of the province.

Mentzer, Raymond A., Jr. *Heresy Proceedings in Languedoc, 1500–1560.* Philadelphia, 1984. Examines the early reform and the attempts to suppress it.

———. "*Disciplina nervus ecclesiae:* The Calvinist Reform of Morals at Nîmes." *Sixteenth Century Journal* 18 (1987), 89–115. Discussion of an important Protestant stronghold.

RAYMOND A. MENTZER, JR.

LANGUET, Hubert (1518–81), French Protestant, ambassador for the elector of Saxony, and possible sole author of, or collaborator on, the *Vindiciae contra tyrannos* of 1579, a work justifying resistance to government. Born in Vitteaux in Burgundy, Hubert was the second son of Germain Languet and Jeanne Devoyot. He studied under a distinguished Hellenist, Jean Perelle, acquired a masterful Latin style, and attended the universities of Poitiers, Bologna, and Padua. He studied law and in 1548 earned a doctorate. After reading Philipp Melanchthon's *Loci communes* (Common Places of Theology), he went to Wittenberg and became a Protestant. He stayed in Wittenberg, except for trips around Europe, until Melanchthon's death.

Languet never married and became a career diplomat, traveling extensively. He refused the offer of the Swedish king Gustavus Vasa to head a northern expedition but became ambassador for Augustus, elector of Saxony, who sent him to Paris in 1561. He served as intermediary, in effect, between the German rulers and Huguenot leaders, defending the Protestants in 1570 before Charles IX, king of France. Languet narrowly escaped death in Paris during the Saint Bartholomew's Day Massacre. Leaving France, he served Saxony at the imperial court, principally in Vienna from 1573 to 1577. He retired from diplomatic service because of health reasons to pursue his inheritance from his father or because of disgust with the Eucharistic quarrels among the Protestants. Pensioned by the elector, Languet accompanied Johann Casimir to England in 1579 and spent his last years advising William of Orange.

A master of Latin prose, Languet's literary fame rests on his letters. He was Philip Sidney's correspondent, for instance, and friend of Philippe Duplessis-Mornay, whose wife, Charlotte Arbaleste, tended his deathbed. Languet may have collaborated with Duplessis-Mornay on the *Vindiciae contra tyrannos.* Some, such as Pierre Bayle, attributed the work entirely to Languet. Bayle fixed the publication date at 1581. Others attributed it to Duplessis-Mornay alone.

BIBLIOGRAPHY

Primary Sources

A Defense of Liberty against Tyrants: A Translation of the Vindiciae contra tyrannos by Junius Brutus with an Historical Introduction by Harold J. Laski (1923). Reprint, New York, 1972. An English translation of this major text of sixteenth-century Protestant resistance theory. In a discussion of authorship, Laski points out that Pierre Bayle attributes it to Hubert Languet, but, more commonly, other scholars attribute it to Philippe Duplessis-Mornay.

Brutus, Etienne Junius. *Vindiciae contra tyrannos: Traduction française de 1581.* Edited by Arlette Jouanna, J. Perrin, M. Soulié, André Tournon, and Henri Weber. Geneva, 1979. This modern facsimile edition of the 1581 French translation has an introduction, notes, and an index. The editors attribute the original Latin text to Languet.

Franklin, Julian H., trans. and ed. *Constitutionalism and Resistance in the Sixteenth Century: Three Treatises by Hotman, Beza, and Mornay.* New York, 1969. An English translation of the *Francogallia,* the *Right of Magistrates,* and *Vindiciae contra tyrannos.* In an editor's note on the latter, Franklin looks upon Duplessis-Mornay as the author but does not rule out collaboration.

Sidney, Philip. *The Correspondence of Sir Philip Sidney and Hubert Languet Now First Collected and Translated from the Latin with Notes and a Memoir of Sidney* (1845). Translated by Steuart Pears. Reprint, Westmead, England, 1971. An English translation of a collection of letters between Hubert Languet and Sidney. Published collections exist elsewhere of Languet's correspondence with Joachim Camerarius and with Augustus, duke of Saxony, and his minister, Ulrich Mordeisen.

Secondary Sources

Chevreul, Henri. *Étude sur le seizième siècle: Hubert Languet* (1852). Reprint, Nieuwkoop, 1967. Biography of Languet more readily available than others because of the recent reprint. Attributes the *Vindiciae contra tyrannos* to Languet.

"Languet, Hubert." In *Biographisch-bibliographisches kirchenlexikon,* edited by Friedrich Wilhelm Bautz, vol. 4, nos. 1130–1132. Hamm, Germany, 1970–.

"Languet, Hubert." In *Verzeichnis der im deutschen Sprachbereich erschienenen Drucke des XVI. Jahrhunderts,* vol. 16.2, nos. 421–427. Stuttgart, 1983–.

JEANNINE E. OLSON

LÁNI, Eliáš (Hung., Lányi; Lat., Petrus Petschius; 1575–1618), theologian and ecclesiastical administrator in Upper Hungary (Slovakia). Born in Slovenské Pravno near Martin in Upper Hungary, Láni, a Slovak, emerged as one of the leading theologians and organizers of the Lutheran movement in Slovakia at the end of the sixteenth century. He received all his education in Upper Hungary, first in Turiec county and then at the school established by Gregor Stanšič Horváth de Gradecz in Stražky in Špiš county. He was ordained in Brieg (Brzeg) in Silesia and taught at Stanšič's academy in 1595. In 1597 he became preacher in Mošovice near Martin and served as senior of the Lutherans in Turiec county from 1602 until 1608, when he became court chaplain in Bytča near Žilina and senior of Trenčin as well as a counselor to the palatine of Hungary, George Thurzo. At the Synod of Žilina (1610) he was elected superintendent for the Lutherans in Orava, Liptov, and Trenčin counties. In 1609 he and his brother, Daniel, were granted lesser noble status.

While still at Stražky, Láni emerged as an ardent advocate for the acceptance of the Formula of Concord and *Book of Concord* in Slovakia and a leading representative of orthodox Lutheranism among the Slovaks. Despite his youth, he took part in the twin colloquies in Kežmarok (5 December 1595 and 29 January 1596), at which Sebastian Lam was criticized because of his Calvinist theological orientation. Láni's first major theological publications, directed against the iconoclasm of Thomas Fabricius Tolnai and Lam was his defense of the didactic use of images by Christians in worship on the basis of Christian freedom (*Scutum libertatis christianae in usu ceremoniarum . . . ,* 1595; *Defensio libertatis christianae in usu imaginum historico,* 1598). He also defended the actions of the Synod of Žilina against attacks by the archbishop of Esztergom, Francis Forgáč (*Apologia pro Synodo Solnensi,* 1610) and the Jesuit Péter Pázmány (*Malleus peniculi papistici . . . ,* 1612). Láni also authored hymns and helped to prepare for publication the Slovak translation of Luther's small catechism printed in Bardejov in 1612.

As an ecclesiastical administrator, Láni worked to establish the confessional and legal identity of Lutheranism in Upper Hungary. In 1602, together with Matej Lochmann, he prepared articles to govern the Turiec *contubernia,* or pastoral fraternity, that he presented to the magnate Peter Revay. In 1608, at a synod in Martin, the fraternity accepted the Formula of Concord and *Book of Concord.* He was, together with Palatine Thurzo, the co-initiator of the Synod of Žilina, where the *Book of Concord* was established as the doctrinal standard for the Lutheran clergy in ten of the counties of Upper Hungary. Láni, Samuel Melik, and Izak Abrahamides were elected superintendents of the Slovak congregations in these counties. Two seniors were also elected for the German-speaking congregations in the region and one for those in which Hungarian was the primary language. Láni's career was brief and all the more remarkable since, unlike many of the other leaders of the Lutheran movement in sixteenth-century Hungary, he did not attend Wittenberg or any other foreign university.

BIBLIOGRAPHY

Kvačala, Ján. "E. Láni a víťazstvo lutherského smeru na Slovensku." *Viera a veda* 1 (1930), 153–165.

Mocko, Ján. *Eliáš Láni, prvý superintendent cirkvi ev. a. v. a jeho doba.* Liptovský sv. Mikuláš, 1902.

DAVID P. DANIEL

LA NOUE, François de (1531–1591), French diplomat and writer. He distinguished himself as a brave Huguenot captain in the major battles of the Wars of Religion, from the capture of Orléans in 1562 to the siege in 1591 of Lamballe near Saint-Brieuc, where he was mortally wounded. His role as a diplomat was played on center stage in 1572, when he negotiated the surrender of La Rochelle at the request of Charles IX. Through his activity as a mediator, he was numbered among the *politiques* from 1573 and became the main counselor of Francis, duke of Alençon, the king's brother. Appointed in 1578 Grand Maréchal du Camp and then general in chief in the United Provinces, he was captured by the Spanish and imprisoned in the castle of Limbourg until 1585. During these years of captivity he composed his *Discours politiques et militaires* (published in 1587), a series of twenty-six treaties; the twentieth through the twenty-third are devoted to the political principles of a Christian prince, and the last is devoted to his memoirs from the years 1562–1570 (also published separately under the title *Observations sur plusieurs choses advenus aux trois premier troubles*).

In 1588 he settled in Geneva and at the same time resumed his activity as a captain. He justified the resumption of the war in his *Déclaration pour la prise d'armes et la défense de Sedan et Jamets.* After serving Henry III in the last years of his reign, he went into the service of Henry IV, whom he encouraged to convert to Catholicism. In addition to the thoughts in his *Discours,* he offered some reflections on the art of governing in *Observations politiques et morales sur l'Histoire de Guicciardini* (published in 1593 as a footnote to the translation of the *Discours*). He is the probable author of the *Vive description de la tyrannie et des tyrans* (1577). His *Correspondance* was edited in 1854 (reprinted in 1971).

Although the subject is much debated, La Noue played a significant role in the history of the Reformation in France, particularly as a peacemaker. He himself gives the explanation for this in the second treatise of his *Discours* where he presents himself as a committed defender of the reasonableness of concord as the necessary prerequisite to civil progress. In the fourth treatise he proposes the "use of moderate means" for the reconciliation of opposing parties, suggesting reciprocal concessions to be discussed in "a frank and free council."

BIBLIOGRAPHY

Primary Sources

La Noue, François de. *Discours politiques et militaires* (1587). Edited by F. E. Sutcliffe. Geneva, 1967.

———. *Correspondance de François de La Noue.* Ghent, 1854.

———. *Mémoires.* Paris, 1854.

Secondary Sources

Amyraut, Moïse. *La vie de François, seigneur de La Noue, dit Bras-de-Fer, où sont contenues . . . jusqves à l'an 1581.* Leyde, 1661.

Bourgeon, Jean-Louis. "De Mons à La Rochelle via Paris, ou les paradoxes de monsieur de La Noue." *Bulletin de la Société de l'histoire du protestantisme français* 138 (1992), 5–18.

Hauser, Henri. *François de La Noue, 1531–1591* (1892). Reprint, Geneva, 1970.

"La Noue, François de." In *Verzeichnis der im deutschen Sprachbereich erschienenen Drucke des XVI. Jahrhunderts,* vol. 16.2, nos. 428–434. Stuttgart, 1983–.

Supple, J. J. "The Role of François de La Noue in the Siege of La Rochelle and the Protestant Alliance with the Mécontants." *Bibliothèque d'humanisme et Renaissance* 43 (1981), 107–122.

Huseman, W. H. "'Bayard Huguenot' ou 'le plus ingrat gentilhomme que iamais naquist en France'? Un réexamen de la carrière de François de La Noue." *Bulletin de la Société de l'histoire du protestantisme français* 130 (1984), 137–173.

———. "François de La Noue au service du libéralisme du XIXe siècle." *Renaissance and Reformation* 9 (1985), 189–208.

MARIO TURCHETTI

Translated from French by Robert E. Shillenn

LA RENAUDIE, Jean du Barry (1520?–1560), French gentleman and conspirator. Called "La Forest," he distinguished himself by his military exploits in 1562 in the service of François de Guise, who was then count of Aumale. Along with his brother Geoffroy, he had to endure a long trial (1538–1546) at the hands of the du Tillet family, represented by Louis (a friend of John Calvin's) and the powerful Jean du Tillet, first clerk of the Parlement of Paris, concerning certain ecclesiastical benefices. The du Barrys were condemned (Jean to imprisonment and Geoffroy to permanent banishment); subsequently, Jean managed to escape, perhaps with the help of François de Guise. La Renaudie withdrew to Geneva, where he met Calvin, and then to Lausanne, where in 1533 he married Guillemette de Louvain, the sister-in-law of Gaspard de Hue, seigneur de Buy. On 14 July he was made a burgher of Bern, and at various times he asked the city authorities to intervene with the king of France to obtain a mitigation of his sentence. It was not until 1558—through the intervention of François de Guise and François's brother Charles, cardinal of Lorraine—that he obtained a lifting of the ban.

After returning to France, La Renaudie entered the service of Antoine, king of Navarre, to whom he delivered Calvin's letters. He took part in the negotiations between the king of Navarre and the German princes through the intermediary of his brother-in-law, Gaspard de Hue. During the summer Gaspard de Hue was imprisoned and tortured to death, perhaps at the instigation of the Guises. From this time on, it seems, La Renaudie began to plot his revenge against the Guises and the du Tillet family, all the more because he had become interested in the Reformed cause.

He prepared to take bold action. A first plan aimed to free the king (whom he believed was under Guisan control), to capture the Guises and have them tried, and, if they resisted, to exterminate them. In 1559, as the representative of Louis I, prince of Condé, La Renaudie went to Geneva, where he met with Calvin (who tried to dissuade him) and Théodore de Bèze (who may have encouraged him). After a short stay in Bern, La Renaudie organized his plot in the course of three successive meetings that were held in January 1560 at Aubonne and Lyon and then in Nantes on 1 February. The plan, which was to be carried out on 6 March, called for the capture of the Guises on that date and the seizure of the Blois castle, the residence of the court. La Renaudie then went to England to seek aid from Protestant sympathizers, and, upon his return to France, informed Condé, who secretly approved the plan.

The secret, however, began to leak out on 12 February, when the Parisian attorney Pierre des Avenelles (at whose house La Renaudie was staying) alerted the cardinal of Lorraine, who in turn informed Mathieu Coignet, the French ambassador in the Swiss cantons. In the meantime, for reasons that had nothing to do with what was being plotted, the court moved to Amboise. La Renaudie reworked his plan and set 16 March as the date for its execution. With the exposure and defeat of the conspiracy, many of the conspirators were summarily executed as criminals for high treason. La Renaudie was shot and killed by a harquebus bullet on 18 March. His body was transported to Amboise, where it was drawn and quartered. His head was exposed on a stake.

BIBLIOGRAPHY

Naef, Henri. *La conjuration d'Amboise et Genève*. Geneva, 1922.

Romier, Lucien. *La conjuration d'Amboise: L'aurore sanglante de la liberté de conscience*. Paris, 1923.

MARIO TURCHETTI

Translated from French by Robert E. Shillenn

LA RIVIÈRE (pseudonym of Jean Le Maçon, sieur de Launay; 1532?–?), first minister of the Reformed Church of Paris. The son of a *procureur du roi* in Angers, Jean Le Maçon was converted to Protestantism during visits to Geneva and Lausanne. He was about twenty-three years old when, in September 1555, a clandestine group of Protestant converts in Paris selected him as their pastor and formed a church on the Genevan model. The Reformed church of Paris grew rapidly, and additional ministers were soon borrowed from Geneva or recruited from the informal seminary set up in Paris in 1556. The task of preaching in Paris was made difficult by the need for secrecy and the danger of persecution. The ministers moved from place to place, preaching to small groups and frequently changing the location of their meetings. Early in 1557 La Rivière requested two years' leave to go to Geneva to study theology with Calvin, but the Paris church denied his request, claiming that it had too great need of him to allow him to depart. He did visit Geneva in October 1558, but his visit was brief. He was back in Paris within a year.

La Rivière was still serving the Paris church at the time of the Massacre of Wassy (March 1562), when he wrote to neighboring churches to encourage them to send delegations to court to protest against the cruelty of the François, duke of Guise. Like most of the Parisian pastors, La Riviére took refuge in Orléans and served as minister there during the first War of Religion. He appears not to have returned to Paris after the Peace of Amboise (March 1563). Fearing that he was too recognizable a figure to continue to serve as minister to the Parisian church, he returned to his native Anjou; little is known of his life afterwards.

BIBLIOGRAPHY

Bernus, A. "Le ministre Antoine de Chandieu d'après son journal autographe inédite 1534–1591." *Bulletin de la Société de l'histoire du protestantisme français* 37 (1888), 2–13, 57–69, 124–136. A good discussion of the Reformed church of Paris before 1572.

Diefendorf, Barbara B. *Beneath the Cross: Catholics and Huguenots in Sixteenth-Century Paris*. New York and Oxford, 1991. See especially chapter 7 on the Reformed church of Paris from its founding to 1572.

BARBARA B. DIEFENDORF

LA ROCHE-CHANDIEU, Antoine de. *See* Chandieu, Antoine de la Roche.

LA ROCHELLE. An important commercial center and politically privileged city on the west-central coast of France, La Rochelle achieved prominence in the late sixteenth and early seventeenth century as a major bastion of French Protestantism. It was one of the few French cities where a majority of the population became Protestant and remained so well into the seventeenth century. It played a leading role during the Wars of Religion: in 1568 the city actively declared for Louis I, prince of Condé, leader of the Protestant cause. Thereafter the city became an important political and military center for the national Protestant movement. It remained a principal Protestant stronghold until 1628, when it was virtually destroyed by Armand-Jean du Plessis, duke of Richelieu, after a devastating year-long siege.

Prior to the Reformation, La Rochelle was distinguished for its acquisition of considerable municipal and commercial independence. It had received the valuable *droit de commune*, or right of municipal self-government, sometime between 1169 and 1178. The city was governed by the *corps de ville*, a powerful body of one hundred magistrates headed by an annually elected mayor. In 1373 Charles V of France emancipated La Rochelle from every seigneurial overlord except the king of France. The city's relative freedom from most forms of taxation allowed Rochelais merchants to dominate the regional wine and salt trade and strengthened its independence.

The city also had some independence from ecclesiastical authority. Subject to the bishop of Saintes, who resided thirty miles away, the Rochelais were free from the powerful control often exercised by resident prelates. After 1401 Rochelais clergy were barred from active participation in municipal government. By the early fifteenth century the city supervised clerical management of municipal almshouses.

Traditionally the beginning of the Reformation in La Rochelle is traced to 1534, when a servant girl, Marie Becaudelle, was burned in her native Poitou for heretical opinions learned at her master's house in La Rochelle. There was little other evidence of "Protestant" activity before 1540.

In the 1540s and 1550s, according to *officialité* (ecclesiastical court) and other records, there was growing dissatisfaction with the Rochelais clergy, as well as more heresy charges against Rochelais. The clergy were charged with failure to perform clerical functions and with scandalous living. Repeatedly the Rochelais dissidents attacked devotion to the Virgin and the saints, feast days, and the sacraments, particularly the Mass. In July 1550 several booksellers were accused of selling books prohibited by the king, such as Desiderius Erasmus's *Colloquies*. In the same month six teachers in Rochelais schools were accused of conducting secret schools and teaching "a separate and unaccustomed doctrine."

Only in the late 1550s did Protestantism assume a clear-cut form in La Rochelle. The ministers who finally established a Protestant community were trained in Geneva, and both the confession of faith and the ecclesiastical discipline adopted by the Rochelais Protestants were Calvinist. In La Rochelle in the 1560s the Protestant printer Barthélémy Berton published several Calvinist works, including a book of John Calvin's sermons (May 1565) and Yves Rouspeau's popular *Traitté de la préparation à la sainte Cène* (1563).

The organization of the Reformed church in La Rochelle began in 1557, when an itinerant preacher, Charles Clermont (known as La Fontaine), arrived in the city and assembled a small group of roughly fifty people interested in the reform of the church. In 1558 Pierre Richer—a former Carmelite and doctor of theology who had been converted to Protestantism and had trained under Calvin in Geneva—arrived in La Rochelle as minister to the small group. Under his leadership the Protestant community grew rapidly. By November 1558 he had established a consistory, the hallmark of Genevan ecclesiastical discipline. By 1563 the number of Geneva-trained ministers in La Rochelle had grown from one to four. The Reformed church in La Rochelle was represented at all national synod meetings from 1561, and national synod meetings were held at La Rochelle in 1571, 1581, and 1607. The Confession of La Rochelle, adopted at the synod of 1571, confirmed the confession of faith from the synod of 1559.

Initially the Rochelais Protestants met secretly, but they feared royal repression rather than local Catholic opposition. The five parish churches, five monasteries, and three convents in the city offered little resistance to the new religion. The monasteries were almost empty by 1560, and the Catholic clergy were inadequately trained to debate theological issues with the Protestant ministers.

A majority of La Rochelle's estimated twenty thousand inhabitants had probably been won to the new faith by the early 1560s. The Protestant community seems to have continued to grow into the 1580s. As in other French towns, Protestantism's greatest appeal in La Rochelle was to merchants, artisans, and municipal and royal officials.

Tensions increased considerably after the outbreak of civil war in March 1562. The *corps de ville* was divided between two groups of Protestants: the moderates, who favored political loyalty to the Crown, and the radicals, who advocated commitment to the national Protestant cause. In May 1562, after a public celebration of the Lord's Supper, a Rochelais mob went on a destructive rampage against the city's Catholic churches and struck down images, statues, and altars. In September 1562 and February 1563 unsuccessful efforts were made to capture the city for the national Protestant movement.

La Rochelle's commitment to the national Protestant cause was forced upon the city by its radical mayor, François Pontard, in January 1568, when during the second civil war, he seized the city for Condé. Under his leadership the Catholic churches were virtually destroyed, ecclesiastical assets were appropriated, and several priests were murdered. In September 1568, after the third civil war began, the *corps de ville*, fearing the arrival of a royal garrison, entered into a formal treaty with the national Protestant forces. Thereafter the city served as a major political and military headquarters of the Protestant party, with Condé and other leading Protestants in residence.

After the Saint Bartholomew's Day Massacre in August 1572, the Rochelais were besieged by the king's forces from December 1572 until June 1573, when a peace treaty favorable to the Rochelais was concluded. The city remained a

Protestant bastion until its capitulation to Richelieu in October 1628. Though the Rochelais were allowed liberty of conscience, their political and military independence was destroyed: their municipal government was suppressed, and their fortifications were razed.

[*See also* Condé, Henri I; Huguenots; La Rochelle, Synod of; *and* Wars of Religion.

BIBLIOGRAPHY

Arcère, Louis-Etienne. *Histoire de la ville de La Rochelle et du pays d'Aunis.* 2 vols. La Rochelle, France, 1756–1757. A detailed older history of La Rochelle.

Barbot, Amos. "Histoire de La Rochelle." Edited by Denys d'Aussy. *Archives historiques de la Saintonqe et de l'Aunis,* vols. 14, 17, and 18. N.p., 1886, 1889, 1890. An important general history of La Rochelle, up to 1574, written by a prominent sixteenth-century Rochelais Protestant. Especially useful for the political and religious history of the sixteenth century.

Delafosse, Marcel, et al. *Histoire de La Rochelle.* Toulouse, France, 1985. An excellent recent history with a good bibliography.

Meyer, Judith P. "Reformation in La Rochelle: Religious Change, Social Stability, and Political Crisis, 1500–1568." Ph.D. diss., University of Iowa, 1977. Analyzes the appeal of Protestantism and the process of reformation in La Rochelle. Considers the religious, political, social, and economic context.

———. "La Rochelle and the Failure of the French Reformation." *Sixteenth Century Journal* 15.2 (1984), 169–183. Analyzes the importance of religion and politics at the local level. Suggests possible reasons for Protestantism's eventual failure in France.

———. "The Success of the French Reformation: The Case of La Rochelle." *Archiv für Reformationsgeschichte* 84 (1993), 242–275. Analyzes the social, economic, and religious context within which the Rochelais Reformation occurred and the reasons for the Reformation's provisional success.

Parker, David. *La Rochelle and the French Monarchy: Conflict and Order in Seventeenth-Century France.* London, 1980. Places local events of the early 1600s and especially the siege of 1627–1628 in a national political context.

Robbins, Kevin C. "The Families and Politics of La Rochelle, 1550–1650." Ph.D. diss., Johns Hopkins University, 1991. Analyzes Rochelais municipal government from 1550–1650 and emphasizes influence of kinship ties among ruling elites, both Protestant and Catholic.

Trocmé, Etienne. "La Rochelle de 1560 à 1628: Tableau d'une société réformée au temps des guerres de religion." Bach. en Théol. thesis, Faculté Libre de Théologie Protestante. Paris, 1950. An essential source for Protestant La Rochelle.

———. "L'Église réformée de La Rochelle jusqu'en 1628." *Bulletin de la Société de l'histoire du protestantisme français,* 99 (July-September 1952), 133–199. A study of the Reformed church in La Rochelle up to 1628, with good biographical information on Rochelais Protestant ministers.

Trocmé, Etienne, and Marcel Delafosse. *Le commerce rochelais de la fin du 15e siècle au début du 17e.* Paris, 1952. Analyzes patterns of Rochelais commerce and economic life from the late fifteenth to the early seventeenth century.

JUDITH P. MEYER

LA ROCHELLE, SYNOD OF. The seventh national synod of the French Reformed churches was held in 1571. The Synod of La Rochelle was in many ways the most important of the national synods of the French Reformed churches. The first national synod to be held with the permission of the royal government, it was attended by virtually all the political leaders of French Protestantism, including Jeanne d'Albret (queen of Navarre), Henry of Navarre (the future Henry IV), Henry of Bourbon (the prince of Condé), Count Louis of Nassau (the younger brother of William of Orange), Admiral Gaspard II de Coligny, and, to quote the acts of the synod, "diverse lords and gentlemen." Though the work of the synod was conducted largely by the representatives of the churches of the kingdom, these lay notables also participated in the synod's deliberations.

The synod's moderator was Théodore de Bèze, come from Geneva specifically to attend the synod. Bèze's moderatorship would prove to be controversial, since it raised suspicions at the royal court that some political intrigue was in the works between Geneva and the Protestant leaders of the kingdom. Further, Bèze's role in the synod would be used to argue that the French Reformed churches were under the direction of a foreign power, since, although Bèze was a French nobleman, he was also a pastor (and therefore an employee) of the city of Geneva.

In addition to its political significance, the Synod of La Rochelle also performed some important ecclesiastical tasks, notably by preparing fresh editions of the Gallic Confession and the *Discipline ecclésiastique,* the French Reformed churches' equivalent to the Presbyterian *Book of Order.* The Gallic Confession had been circulating in various forms; the Synod of La Rochelle thus decided to prepare a definitive text and deposit copies in Geneva, La Rochelle, and Béarn. Though the synod itself introduced relatively few modifications to the text, the confession subsequently became widely known as the Confession of La Rochelle, an indication of the synod's significance in contemporary eyes.

The new edition of the *Discipline* was also largely a matter of redaction rather than innovation, though this process introduced more substantive changes into the *Discipline* than had been introduced into the confession. The most important element of the new edition was the organization of the *Discipline* into chapters, giving the text the basic structure it would retain throughout the early modern period.

Some actions of the synod raised difficulties for the Reformed churches of France. The synod took implicit action against Jean Morély's reform program, stirring up his faction for a new round of controversy. To put political pressure on the French Reformed churches, the Morély party informed Heinrich Bullinger of a number of specific actions taken by the synod, including its condemnations of those who rejected the use of excommunication by the church, who held that the church was subordinate to the state, and who refused to use the word *substance* in connection with Christ's presence in the Eucharist. These decisions upset Bullinger tremendously, forcing both Bèze and the National Synod of Nîmes (1572) to take prompt action to try to smooth over relations with Zurich.

BIBLIOGRAPHY

Primary Sources

Aymon, Jean. *Tous les synodes nationaux des Églises Réformées de France.* 2 vols. The Hague, 1710. Also available on microfiche: Inter Documentation Company, Reformed Protestantism: Sources of the sixteenth and seventeenth centuries on microfiche 2b (France), KPRS 109. The only French edition of the Acts of the National Synods, including La Rochelle; generally inferior to the English translation by Quick.

Quick, John. *Synodicon in Gallia Reformata; Or, The Acts, Decisions, Decrees, and Canons of Those Famous National Councils of the Reformed Churches in France.* 2 vols. London, 1692. Also available on microfilm: UMI, Early English Books 1641–1700 selected from Donald Wing's Short Title Catalogue, reel 473 (Wing Q209). The best published text of the Acts of the National Synods, including La Rochelle.

Sunshine, Glenn S. "French Protestantism on the Eve of St-Bartholomew: The Ecclesiastical Discipline of the French Reformed Churches, 1571–1572." *French History* 4 (1990), 340–377. Includes an annotated text of the *Discipline* of 1571/1572 and an introductory essay setting this text into the context of the ecclesiastical development of the French Reformed churches.

Secondary Source

Kingdon, Robert M. *Geneva and the Consolidation of French Protestantism, 1564–1572: A Contribution to the History of Congregationalism, Presbyterianism, and Calvinist Resistance Theory.* Madison, Wis., 1967. The best available discussion of the ecclesiastical debates sparked by Morély, including an account of the Synod of La Rochelle.

GLENN S. SUNSHINE

LAS CASAS, Bartolomé de (1484–1566), Spanish historian, theologian, and defender of the Indians in the New World. Born in Seville into a merchant's family, Las Casas, at eighteen, came to Hispaniola in 1502 to assist his father, who had accompanied Columbus on his second voyage and received a grant of land and Indians on the island. In 1506 he went back to Spain, was ordained a priest during a visit to Rome in 1507, and then returned to Spain to finish his studies for the degree of bachelor of canon law at the University of Salamanca. Returning to Hispaniola, he combined various business activities with the office of *doctrinero*, or parish priest to the Indians. In 1510 a group of Dominican friars, led by Father Antonio Montesino, arrived on the island and mounted a protest against the barbarous treatment of the Taino Indians by the Spanish settlers. Although Las Casas treated his own Indian laborers kindly and sympathized with the Dominican complaints, he rejected their denunciation of the *encomienda* system of forced Indian labor as a mortal sin. He even served as military chaplain in the conquest of Cuba (1512–1514), though he vainly tried to prevent the atrocities that marked that campaign. He was rewarded for his services with a large *encomienda*, or grant of Indians.

In 1514, however, he experienced a conversion or spiritual awakening, renounced his own grant of Indians, and henceforth dedicated his life to the ideological and political struggle against Indian enslavement. Las Casas argued that the papal grant of America to the Crown of Castile had been made solely for the purpose of conversion and gave the Spanish Crown no temporal power or possession in the Indies. The Indians had rightful possession of their lands by natural law and the law of nations. Consequently, all Spanish conquests and wars in the New World were illegal, and Spaniards were morally obligated to make restitution of all that they had taken from the Indians. Spain must bring Christianity to the Indians by the only method "that is proper and natural to men. . . namely, love and gentleness and kindness."

Replying to Juan Ginés de Sepúlveda—a translator of Aristotle who claimed that the Indians were barbarians, slaves by nature according to Aristotle's definition of barbarian and, therefore, justly ruled by the superior Spaniards—La Casas wrote his *Apologética historia sumaria* (not published until 1909), an immense accumulation of ethnographic data designed to prove that the Indians fully met the requirements laid down by Aristotle for the good life. In the same work Las Casas offered an environmentalist explanation of cultural differences, treated with scientific detachment such deviations from European standards as Indian human sacrifices and ritual cannibalism, and subjected the term "barbarian" to a careful semantic analysis that robbed it (as applied to advanced Indian cultures like the Aztec or the Inca) of most of its sting. He may justly be regarded as a pioneer of modern cultural relativism.

Experience progressively radicalized Las Casas's tactics, as well as his program for Indian liberation. At first he hoped for a peaceful colonization of the New World by Spanish farmers who would live side by side with the Indians, teach them to farm and live in the European way, and gradually bring into being an ideal Christian community. A series of disillusioning experiences—including the destruction of an experiment along those lines on the coast of Venezuela (1521) by Indians who had suffered from the raids of Spanish slave hunters—turned Las Casas toward more radical solutions. His final program called for the suppression of all *encomiendas*, liberation of the Indians from all servitude (except a small voluntary tribute to the Crown in recompense for its gift of Christianity), and the restoration of the ancient Indian states and rulers, the rightful owners of those lands. Over these states the Spanish king would preside as "emperor over many kings" in order to fulfill his mission of bringing the Indians to the Catholic faith and the Christian way of life. The instruments of that mission would be friars, who would enjoy special jurisdiction over the Indians and protect them from the corrupting influence of lay Spaniards. Despite the seeming radicalism of Las Casas's proposals, they in fact served the royal aim of curbing the power of the conquistadors and preventing the rise of a powerful colonial feudalism in the New World.

Several ideological strands united in Las Casas's thought. He was an authentic figure of the Catholic pre-Reformation, proposing reforms later adopted by the Council of Trent. He was a spiritual son of Thomas Aquinas, the church fathers, and Aristotle, although he once referred to the latter as "a gentile burning in hell whose doctrine should be accepted only so far as it conforms to Christian thought." But he was also a child of the Renaissance, a Spanish representative of a Renaissance humanist type (exemplified by the Englishman Thomas More and the Fleming Desiderius Erasmus) who was much concerned with the problems of war, poverty, and social injustices.

Las Casas was a prolific writer. In addition to the *Apologética historia sumaria*, he wrote a great *Historia de las Indias* (not published until 1875) that is our principal source for the early history of the Spanish conquest. His *De Regia Potestate* (Frankfurt, 1571), challenging the right of the Spanish king to dispose of his Indian subjects, argues that all power derives from the people and therefore all important government acts require popular consultation and approval; a modern editor, Luciano Pereña, calls it "one of the most sensational books of political philosophy published in the sixteenth century." His influential work on mission theory and practice, *De unico vocationis modo*, which denounced war as a means of conversion, published in English in 1992 as *The Only Way*, was translated by Francis P. Sullivan, with an introduction by Helen Rand Parish. Las Casas's most widely distributed and popular writing, however, is his *Brevísima relación de la destruición de las Indias* (1552), a chilling account of the devestation wrought in the Caribbean area by the Spanish conquest, published in many languages and editions. Inadvertently, it helped to promote the so-called Black Legend of Spanish cruelty in the conquest of America.

BIBLIOGRAPHY

Friede, Juan, and Benjamin Keen, eds. *Bartolomé de Las Casas in History: Toward an Understanding of the Man and His Work.* DeKalb, Ill. 1971.

Hanke, Lewis. *The Spanish Struggle for Justice.* Philadelphia, 1949.

Wagner, Henry R., and Helen Rand Parish. *The Life and Writings of Bartolomé de las Casas.* Albuquerque, 1957.

Benjamin Keen

ŁASKI, Jan (Eng., John of Lasco, John the Younger; Fr., Johannes à Lasko; 1499–1560), Polish Calvinist reformer. Łaski was the son of Yaroslav, a fairly well-to-do nobleman of central Poland, who became the *voivode* ("governor") of Sieradz province. Jan also was the nephew of the eminent Polish primate and archbishop of Gniezno, Jan Łaski the Elder. His brothers, Jerome, a mercenary, and Stanislas, a writer, also had distinguished careers.

Jan studied primarily in Italy, where he learned Latin, German, Italian, Greek, and a smattering of Hebrew. After 1517, thanks to his paternal uncle, he obtained a series of church posts. He returned to Poland in 1519 and became the dean of Gniezno and one of the canons of Kraków, taking holy orders in 1521. In 1524–1525 he visited France and became personally acquainted with Erasmus, whose library he would later buy. Being at that time a humanist, he made contact with such reformers as Huldrych Zwingli and Johannes Oecolampadius in Basel. As a rich prelate he was the patron, among others, to a Frenchman, Anianus Burgonius, and to an Englishman, Leonard Coxe. But his attitude toward the Lutheran Reformation was reserved.

He became the titular bishop of Veszprém. In the 1530s he held church posts as pastor of Gniezno and archdeacon of Warsaw but never managed to obtain the Poznan bishopric. His uncle's death and his brother Jerome's failure brought a crisis to Jan's life. At this time he came into contact with Philipp Melanchthon.

In 1539 he left Poland for the Netherlands and there, one year later, he married Barbara, the daughter of a Louvain weaver. In 1540 he renounced Catholicism and lost his benefices. In February 1541 he renounced Protestantism, although this recantation turned out to be only temporary. He settled in East Frisia and in 1543 became the head of the local church, which he steered toward Calvinism while retaining his tolerance of other Protestants.

In 1544 he began to publish his Reformation works. As a friend of both Heinrich Bullinger and Martin Bucer he made his way in 1548 to England because of Lutheran animosity toward him. On arriving in London, he was appointed superintendent of the Protestant congregation of foreign exiles by Edward VI. Łaski worked with a Dutchman, Jan Utenhove, and was active as a writer. He married a second time, but in 1553 he had to flee England because of the accession of Mary Tudor. He returnd to East Frisia and Frankfurt am Main, where he defended Calvinist teachings on the sacraments against the Lutherans.

In 1556 he returned to Poland, where the Reformation movement had been making headway since 1548. In 1557 he met King Sigismund II Augustus in Vilnius and tried to induce the king to establish a national church. When this effort failed, he began to organize the Calvinist church himself among the Minor Poland Protestant nobility while opposing the Bohemian Bretheren, who were seeking influence in that region. Despite these quarrels, he regarded all Protestant churches as connected by a common factor. In 1558 he became seriously ill and died on 8 January 1560 while involved in a controversary over the heresy of Francis Stancarus. Łaski was buried in Pińczów, the center of Protestantism in Minor Poland.

Łaski was the only Pole whose work was widely recognized in the history of European Protestantism and was popular among Polish Protestants as well. Abraham Kuyper published his works in two volumes as *Joannis a Lasco Opera tam edita quam inedita* (Amsterdam and The Hague, 1866).

BIBLIOGRAPHY

Bartel, Oskar. *Jan Łaski.* Pt 1. *1499–1556.* Warsaw, 1964. Also available in German translation, Berlin, 1964.

Bouwmeester, G. *Johannes a Lasco: Een hitverkoren instrument Gods.* The Hague, 1956.

Dalton, Hermann. *Johannes A. Lasco: Beitrag zur Reformationsgeschichte Polens, Deutschlands und Englands.* Gotha, 1881. Also available in English translation as *John à Lasco: His Earlier Life and Labours,* 1886.

Hall, Basil. *John à Lasco, 1499–1560: A Pole in Reformation England.* London, 1971.

Kowalska, Halina. *Dzialalnosc reformatorska Jana Łaskiego w Polsce.* Wrocław, 1969.

WACŁAW URBAN

LASSO, Orlando di

LASSO, Orlando di (originally Orlande, or Rolande, de Lassus; 1530/32–1594), one of the greatest and in his day certainly the most famous of sixteenth-century composers. Born in Mons, Hainaut, Lasso was French in native culture. He went to Italy as a young adolescent; his Italianized name is an indication of the importance to him of the ten years he spent in Mantua, Naples, and Rome. By the age of twenty he was well known as a singer and composer. (In 1553 he headed the chapel at San Giovanni Laterano in Rome.) Having returned to the north, Lasso published his first collection, said to be written "in the new style of Italian musicians," in Antwerp in 1555; the following year he accepted an invitation to join the court of Albert V, duke of Bavaria. He remained in the ducal chapel in Munich, serving as its head from some time in the 1560s until his death.

Lasso began his compositional career in progressive vein, adopting aspects of Venetian and Roman style current in his youth. His music, especially in the domain of the sacred motet, was acclaimed for its vivid rhetoric and affective power, its ability in the words of a contemporary "to describe an object almost as if it were before one's own eyes." As he grew older Lasso's style developed in a largely internal way, avoiding fashionable trends in later sixteenth-century music; his work gained in refinement and economy as it came gradually to be perceived as classic, even conservative in nature.

A prolific composer of secular music, Lasso wrote madrigals, chansons, and lieder for the entertainment of the Bavarian court. But his central task as director of the court chapel was to train and conduct singers and to supply the chapel with liturgical and devotional polyphony. He wrote more than sixty masses, a hundred magnificat settings, a number of smaller liturgical pieces, and some five hundred motets.

Before Lasso's arrival in Munich there had been signs of sympathy toward Lutheranism in the ducal court. The composer's immediate predecessor, Ludwig Daser, was Protestant, and Luther himself had praised the performance of the duke's musicians under Ludwig Senfl. Albert V sent a representative to the Council of Trent, however; Bavaria remained Catholic, Jesuit educational enterprises were favored, and Albert and his successor, William V, came to adopt attitudes of Counter-Reformation piety. Lasso's settings of the Penitential Psalms and the Lamentations show his official conformity with ducal policy. He seems to have been personally committed as well. This can be seen from events in his life (a pilgrimage to Loreto, for example), from the sober conservatism of his late music, and above all from his choice of Luigi Tansillo's *Lagrime di San Pietro,* a typical Counter-Reformation poetic cycle, for his final work, a magnificent set of spiritual madrigals.

BIBLIOGRAPHY

Boetticher, Wolfgang. *Orlando di Lasso und seine Zeit, 1532–1594.* Kassel, 1958.

Haar, James. "Orlande de Lassus." In *The New Grove Dictionary of Music and Musicians,* edited by Stanley Sadie, vol. 10, pp. 480–502. London, 1980.

———. "Munich at the Time of Orlande de Lassus." In *The Renaissance: Man and Music,* edited by Iain Fenlon, pp. 243–262. Englewood Cliffs, N.J., 1989.

Leuchtmann, Horst. *Die musikalische Wortausdeutungen in den Motetten des Magnum opus musicum von Orlando di Lasso.* Reprint, Baden-Baden, 1972.

———. *Orlando di Lasso.* 2 vols. Wiesbaden, 1976–77. The most up-to-date biography of the composer; also contains an edition of Lasso's letters.

JAMES HAAR

LATERAN COUNCIL, FIFTH

LATERAN COUNCIL, FIFTH. Held from 1512 to 1517, this general council was convened to solve the church's problems on the eve of the Reformation. It was called by Pope Julius II on 18 July 1511 to defeat the schismatic Council of Pisa-Milan-Asti-Lyon (1511–1512), which was supported by Louis XII of France, Emperor Maximilian I, and several rebellious cardinals. Controlled by the pope and meeting in the Lateran Basilica in Rome, the Fifth Lateran Council was assigned the goals of restoring church unity and peace among Christians, organizing a crusade, defending the faith, and reforming the church. The opening ceremonies on 3 May 1512 were followed by twelve formal sessions stretching over almost five years and attended by over 430 named persons, of whom at least 280 held episcopal or higher rank, with an average attendance of about 116 miters (bishops, mitered abbots, cardinals, etc.) at each session. While almost all of the significant lands of Latin Christendom were represented either by the formal adhesion of their rulers and/or by bishops or procurators from some of their dioceses, the areas best represented were the Italian and Spanish lands, which sent the most bishops and the only known reform proposals. The Spanish bishops and King Ferdinand urged among other things the appointment of qualified persons to church office, an end to simony and papal expectatives and reservations, the abrogation of the Council of Basel's decree *Sacrosancta* on the superiority of the councils, and the frequent celebration of synods and councils. The proposals from Italian clerics and humanists (e.g., the Camaldolese Tommaso [Paolo] Giustiniani and Vincenzo [Pietro] Querini, the prelate Stefano Taleazzi, the court humanist Raffaelle Brandolini, and the humanist-prince Gianfrancesco Pico della Mirandola) were addressed to Leo X and urged such things as a reform of clerical morals and curial practices, the ordination and promotion of learned and upright clerics, the enforcement of existing church law, the holding of councils, and the promotion of peace among Christian princes. The bishops at the Fifth Lateran Council pushed for a restoration of their dignity and authority, an end to clerical exemptions from their jurisdiction, and the establishment of a permanent episcopal college in Rome.

The first five sessions meeting under Julius II made little substantive progress on the council's goals. Most attention was given to organizational questions and to condemning the rival Council of Pisa. The council, however, also reaffirmed the earlier curial reform decree of 30 March 1512 and the bull of 14 January 1506 against simony in papal elections, promulgated on 25 October 1510.

Following a reorganization of its committees soon after the election of Leo X, the council convened its eighth session on 19 December 1513. This session—in addition to registering the demise of the Council of Pisa in the adherence of Louis XII to the Fifth Lateran Council—enacted decrees ordering a reform of curial practices and fees (reaffirming the decree *Pastoralis officii* of six days earlier), approving Leo X's efforts to establish peace among Christian princes and reconcile the Hussites, and condemning teachings on the mortality of the individual human soul and on the possibility of contradictory truths.

Leo decided to continue the council in the hope of still securing an abrogation of the Pragmatic Sanction of Bourges, but in the meantime the bishops aggressively pushed their own agenda. At the ninth session (5 May 1514) the council approved the Great Reform Bull, which called for, among others, a reform of the cardinals' households (e.g., bishops were no longer to serve in menial positions there), a better screening of candidates for the episcopal office, restriction on pluralism, and a general reform of morals. The tenth session (4 May 1516) approved the *montes pietatis* (charitable institutions that lent money, often for a fee), gave ordinaries authority to censure a book before it was printed, and placed restraints on clerical exemptions. The eleventh session (19 December 1516) brought great joy to Leo X (*Multum placet et perplacet*) with the approval of his Concordat of Bologna, earlier negotiated with Francis I, and with the revocation of the Pragmatic Sanction of Bourges; however, it gave only limited satisfaction to the bishops, who had to drop their demand for an episcopal college to obtain even minimal restrictions on the privileges of the mendicants. Both the pope and bishops were pleased with the greater controls placed on preaching and prophesying. At this session three ambassadors from the Maronite patriarch paid their obeisance to the pope. Determined to close the council, Leo left unfinished work on a number of decrees, and at the twelfth and final session (16 March 1517) he secured approval of a condemnation of plundering cardinals' households during a conclave, the imposition of a crusade tax, and, by the barest margin of votes, the dissolution of the council.

The conciliar decrees were only partially implemented. They were issued as papal bulls that enjoyed the council's approval, were copied into papal registers, promulgated in Rome in the traditional fashion, printed individually soon after and then as part of the official conciliar *acta* edited by Cardinal Antonio del Monte on orders from Leo X in 1520, and left to the local ordinaries to implement. Although there were some initial attempts at enforcement in Rome, parts of Italy and Spain, and elsewhere, the decrees' reception and implementation were so poor that Desiderius Erasmus claimed in 1522 that perhaps the Fifth Lateran Council did not merit to be considered a general council, and even Cajetan in 1523 wondered aloud if its decrees were still binding.

Various Lateran decrees were singled out for criticism or seen as particularly significant. Luther denounced the decree on the soul's immortality for using philosophical categories and that on clerical attire for dealing in trivial details. He was most critical of the bull *Pastor Aeternus*—which abrogated the Pragmatic Sanction of Bourges and nullified what was decreed at Basel after that council was transferred to Ferrara—because the bull went on to state that "whenever there is a single Roman pontiff existing at a time, as one having full authority over all councils, he has the full right and authority to call, transfer, and dissolve councils." Luther saw this statement as contradicting the decrees *Haec Sancta* of Constance and *Sacrosancta* of Basel and thus demonstrating that councils have erred and only scripture can be a safe guide to truth. *Pastor Aeternus* and its companion Concordat of Bologna, approved by the Fifth Lateran Council, encountered initial fierce resistance by the Parlement of Paris and prolonged opposition from the University of Paris. Nonetheless, these decrees were major factors in retaining the loyalty of the French kings to Rome despite pressures from Protestants. The Lateran decree, however, that had the potential for stirring up the most opposition was that on the preventive censorship of the press. Rome urged its implementation as an antidote to Protestant propaganda, and the Council of Trent reiterated its provisions at the fourth session (1546).

The influence of the Fifth Lateran Council on the Council of Trent has yet to be systematically explored. The reluctance of Clement VII, of Paul III for awhile, and of Paul IV throughout his pontificate to call the general council demanded by the Protestants was probably in part the result of their witnessing at the Fifth Lateran Council the difficulties Leo X had in trying to control even a council meeting in Rome and composed in good part of numerous curialists and bishops from Italian lands. When the Council of Trent did meet, its early procedures and decrees were influenced by the Fifth Lateran Council—not surprisingly since its president was Giovan Maria de' Ciocci del Monte (later elected Julius III), who had attended this earlier council and whose uncle Antonio had edited its *acta*.

[*See also* Julius II; Leo X; *and* Trent, Council of.]

BIBLIOGRAPHY

Primary Sources

Concilium Lateranense V. Generale novissimum sub Julio II. et Leone X. celebratum. Edited by Antonio del Monte. Rome, 1520. Reprinted in *Sacrorum Conciliorum nova et amplissima collectio*, edited by Giovanni Domenico Mansi et al., vol. 32, cols. 649–999, Paris, 1902.

Grassi, Paride de. "Le cinquième Concile du Latran d'après le Diaire de Paris de Grassi." Edited by Marc Dykmans. *Annuarium Historiae Conciliorum* 14.2 (1982), 271–369. A firsthand account of the proceedings of the council that concentrates on ceremonial issues and anecdotes.

Secondary Sources

Bilaniuk, Petro B. T. *The Fifth Lateran Council (1512–1517) and the Eastern Churches.* Toronto, 1975. Useful for its review in English of the Latin church's relations at this time with the Eastern churches: Ukrainians (Ruthenians), Maronites, and Ethiopians.

Brosse, Olivier de la, et al. "Latran V." In *Latran V et Trente*, edited by Brosse, Joseph Lecler, Henri Holstein, and Charles Lefebvre, pt. 1, pp. 11–114. Histoire des conciles oecuméniques, no. 10. Paris, 1975. The best modern overview of this council.

Headley, John. "Luther and the Fifth Lateran Council." *Archiv für Reformationsgeschichte* 64 (1973), 55–78. Examines the reasons for Luther's criticisms of this council.

Hergenröther, Joseph. *Conciliengeschichte nach den Quellen bearbeitet.* Vol. 8. Freiburg, 1887. This continuation of Carl Joseph Hefele's *Konziliengeschichte* is the most thorough account of this council, it also contains appendixes of the council's few surviving working papers.

Minnich, Nelson H. "Prophecy at the Fifth Lateran Council." In *Prophetic Rome in the High Renaissance Period*, edited by Marjorie Reeves, pp. 63–87. Oxford, 1992. A study of the historical context, formulators, and contents of the Lateran decree regulating prophetic preaching.

———. *The Catholic Reformation: Council, Churchmen, and Controversies.* Variorum Collected Studies Series, no. CS 403. Aldershot, England, 1993. A collection containing seven essays that deal with Camaldolese support for the council, its ceremonies, its relations with the Eastern churches, the style of its decrees, attempts to enforce them at Rome, and why the council was rejected by Erasmus.

———. *The Fifth Lateran Council, 1512–17: Studies on its Membership, Diplomacy, and Proposals for Reform.* Variorum Collected Studies Series, no. CS 392. Aldershot, England, 1993. A collection of five articles that examine who attended the council, how the Pisan schism was healed, the "speech" of the imperial ambassador, and the various proposals for reform.

Oakley, Francis A. "Conciliarism at the Fifth Lateran Council?" *Church History* 41 (1972), 452–463. Attempts to show how Lateran V's statement on the pope's authority over councils can be reconciled with the decree *Haec sancta* of the Council of Constance, reiterated at Basel as *Sacrosancta.*

NELSON H. MINNICH

LATIMER, Hugh (c.1485–1555), the most notable preacher and one of the leading spokesmen for the "commonwealth" school of moral and social thinking in sixteenth-century England. The two principal objects of his pulpit onslaughts were idolatry and covetousness. He derived his inspiration partly from Martin Luther and partly from the indigenous Lollard tradition of John Wycliffe. His most famous sermons were preached at court in the presence of King Edward VI; in them he vigorously attacked not only the remnants of conservative and Catholic practices but also the plunder of the church by the Protestant government and the disposession of tenant farmers by enclosing landlords. His object was to restore the Christian stewardship of wealth, which he believed had been practiced in the past but displaced by a selfish individualism in his own day. His performances had an exceptionally high profile and were much admired by his fellow reformers but had little influence upon the council or aristocracry to whom they were addressed. When Mary Tudor came to the throne and restored Catholicism, he refused to take refuge in exile and instead courted arrest. He declined to dispute in public on the grounds of his age and inablility and played only a small part in the writing of Protestant polemic, but his complete intransigence made his eventual death inevitable. As a younger man he had several times yielded to pressure over his doctrinal position, but in 1554 and 1555 he seems deliberately to have courted martyrdom, having decided that such testimony was the best way in which he could serve his faith. He was burned at the stake in 1555.

Latimer was born in about 1485 at Thurcaston, Leicestershire, and was thus one of the oldest of the first generation of English reformers. His father was a yeoman farmer of the same name, and his boyhood experiences featured largely in his later sermons. He entered Clare Hall, Cambridge, in 1506 at the mature age of nineteen, graduated with a B.A. in 1510, and became a fellow in the same year. He completed his M.A. in 1514 and soon after took priest's orders at Lincoln. Thereafter he continued preaching and teaching in the university and as late as 1524 was still a notable defender of Catholic orthodoxy. Soon after that he began his conversion to reforming doctrine, a process that he later ascribed to the influence of Thomas Bilney. Latimer was soon in trouble for his outspokenness but succeeded in clearing himself late in 1525, when he was denounced to Thomas Wolsey as a Lutheran. In 1530 he received his first benefice at West Kington in Wiltshire and his first opportunity to preach at court. By 1535 he was high in favor, partly because of his wholehearted support of the king's matrimonial position, and was promoted to the bishopric of Worcester. The fall of Anne Boleyn and the conservative reaction of 1539 forced him to resign his see, and he was briefly imprisoned after Thomas Cromwell's fall.

Latimer's doctrinal position continued to evolve until about 1549. He denied that he had ever been a Lutheran, but he accepted Luther's views on justificaiton and on the nature of the eucharistic presence. In about 1548, after conversations with Bartholomew Traheron and others, he came to accept the Reformed view of the purpose of the Eucharist, having long since rejected the sacrifice of the Mass as idolatrous. It is likely that the execution of his mentor Thomas Bilney in 1532 had a profound effect upon his thinking, causing him to see persecution as one of the hallmarks of the true church. This was a position to which he returned with some enthusiasm under Mary Tudor and may help to explain his apparent eagerness to court martyrdom.

BIBLIOGRAPHY

Beer, Barrett L. and Ronald J. Nash. "Hugh Latimer and the Lusty Knave of Kent: The Commonwealth Movement in 1549." *Bulletin of the Institute for Historical Research* 52 (1979), 175–178.

Chester, A. G. *Hugh Latimer.* Reprint, New York, 1978.

Cricco, P. "Hugh Latimer and Witness." *Sixteenth Century Journal* 10.1 (1979), 21–34.

Gorrie, G. E., ed. *The Works of Hugh Latimer* (1844–1845). Reprint, New York, 1968.

Loades, David. *The Oxford Martyrs.* London, 1970.

DAVID LOADES

LATIN LANGUAGE.

In 1500 Latin was widely spoken as well as written and read by scholars and clerics all over Europe. It was the language of instruction in grammar schools and universities, the language of diplomacy; it was also the official language of the church. The Mass and the rest of the liturgy was recited or sung in Latin. The official version of the Bible was the so-called Vulgate, the translation into Latin attributed to Saint Jerome. Latin was also used in the ordinary business of church administration—papal letters, episcopal visitations, provincial synods, ecclesiastical courts, and so on. The preaching of sermons and the circulation of translations of the Bible in various European vernaculars in the later Middle Ages modified but did not undermine this preponderance of Latin in the ecclesiastical domain.

Criticisms of this preponderance were voiced in the fourteenth and fifteenth centuries, notably by the Waldensians and the Wycliffites. Such critics denounced Latin as a means for the clergy to preserve their position as mediators between God and the main body of the faithful. These criticisms were made still more vigorously in the early sixteenth century, and not only by heretics. Writing to Pope Leo X in 1513, the Venetian hermits Tommaso Giustiniani and Vincenzo Querini noted the general clerical ignorance of Latin, denied the superiority of that language, supported the translation of the Bible into modern languages and recommended a vernacular liturgy. Three years later, Erasmus made his famous appeal—in Latin—for the translation of the Bible into the vernacular so that plowmen, weavers, and "the lowliest women" would be able to read it.

Luther's use of German in his polemical pamphlets, in his translation of the Bible, and in the liturgy of what became the Lutheran church is one of the best-known features of the Reformation. All the same, Luther did not abandon Latin altogether as a medium of religious communication. He continued to write in Latin when he wanted to reach the European learned world. Even his German Mass of 1526 was intended for use on Sundays only, with a Latin liturgy for weekdays. As his *Table Talk* shows, the lack of equivalents in German—as in most European vernaculars of the time—for such philosophical or theological terms as *accidentia, substantia, causa, dialectica,* and *doctrina* often forced Luther to switch from German to Latin in the course of an informal conversation. Given the Latin-vernacular bilingualism common among educated men of the time, especially in central Europe, such code-switching was seldom a problem for the speaker or his listeners.

If the greatest blow given to the dominance of Latin was the multiplication of vernacular translations of the Bible in the Protestant world, the second blow was the development of vernacular liturgies. In Zurich a German liturgy was introduced on Maundy Thursday 1525, with Zwingli's approval (although he had accepted Latin prayers as recently as 1523). Another German liturgy, the Strasbourg *Psalter* of 1539, was the model for the *Forme des prières,* which Calvin, who mocked the idea of praying to God in a language one does not understand, drew up for Geneva. The French of Calvin in the liturgy, his sermons, and his *Institutes of the Christian Religion* (1541) was vigorous and clear, like Luther's German and Cranmer's English, and helped form the literary language. Yet more than half of Calvin's publications were in Latin, including the first two editions of the *Institutes* itself (1536, 1539). In Geneva in his day, people called before the consistory and asked about their religious beliefs not infrequently answered by reciting the *Pater noster,* the *Ave Maria,* and the *Credo,* all in Latin.

In the case of the Catholic church, the challenge of Erasmus and Luther could not be ignored. The language question came up for discussion at the conference in Regensburg in 1541, and again at the Council of Trent. One prelate, Friedrich Nausea, pointed out the disadvantages of the publication in Latin of the conclusions of the council itself and of other church organizations on the grounds that mistranslations were all too frequent, but his advice was not heeded. In similar fashion, and doubtless for similar reasons, a decree of 8 April 1546 forbade vernacular translations of the Bible, despite pleas by Cardinal Cristoforo Madruzzo and others. Pope Paul IV's *Index* of 1559 prohibited the printing and even the possession of vernacular Bibles without a special license from the Inquisition. A motion to abandon the Vulgate and to retranslate the Bible from Hebrew and Greek into Latin, as the humanists had recommended, was also defeated.

In 1551, when the Council of Trent reconvened, a proposal for a vernacular liturgy was put forward by the cardinal of Lorraine and the French bishops, primarily as a means to attract French Calvinists back into the church. Some prelates were in favor of introducing such a liturgy when the time was ripe, but the proposal failed to win sufficient support. The need for the Mass in Latin was reaffirmed in the canon of 5 September 1562, for which even Madruzzo and Lorraine voted. Some of the fathers argued that Latin kept the sacraments sacred, and others that it was necessary to follow the "ancient rite" (*ritus antiquus*). However, it is likely that a majority of Catholic prelates supported Latin because the vernacular had by now become firmly associated with Protestantism.

The faithful of the year 1600 were reciting the catechism in their own tongues and, compared with their ancestors of a hundred years before, were hearing more sermons in the vernacular. All the same, Latin retained a predominance in the Catholic world that would not be seriously challenged until the later twentieth century. After an initial period of uncertainty, Protestant and Catholic clergy alike had made up their minds about the vernacular, the former in its favor, the latter against it.

BIBLIOGRAPHY

Backvis, Claude. *Quelques remarques sur la bilinguisme latino polonais dans la Pologne du 16e siècle.* Brussels, 1958.

Burke, Peter. "Heu Domine, adsunt Turcae: A Sketch for a Social History of Post-Medieval Latin." In *Language, Self and Society*, edited by Peter Burke and Roy Porter, pp. 23–50. Cambridge, 1991. Distinguishes four domains of written and spoken Latin, including the ecclesiastical.

Coletti, Vittorio. *Parole dal pulpito: chiesa e movimenti religiosi tra latino e volgare nell'Italia del Medioevo e del Rinascimento.* Casale, 1983. Essays on various topics, including the vernacular in preaching and at Trent.

d'Agostino, Mari. *La Piazza e l'altare: Momenti della politica linguistica della chiesa siciliana.* Palermo, 1988. Includes an introductory chapter on the debates at Trent.

Lentner, Leo. *Volksprache und Sakralsprache: Geschichte einer Lebensfrage bis zum Ende des Konzils von Trient.* Vienna, 1964. Survey from early Christian times onward, with a chapter on the sixteenth century.

Schmidt, Herman A. P. *Liturgie et langue vulgaire.* Rome, 1950. Discusses the Reformation and Trent.

Stolt, Birgit. *Die Sprachmischung in Luthers Tischreden.* Stockholm, 1964. Technical study by a linguist.

PETER BURKE

LATVIA. The decisive events of the Reformation period in Latvia occurred in Riga, a city in the southern part of Livonia (which included present-day Estonia as well), and only subsequently spilled over into Kurland (Courland). The Roman Catholic archbishop of Livonia, Johannes Blankenfeld, could look back on a relatively successful religious life in his territory, even an intensification of religious life at the end of the fifteenth century, notably in regard to Marian devotion. There were no exceptional signs of corruption, except for the general reluctance of priests to serve outside the cities and to give up their concubines.

The Reformation came to Riga in 1521 through the efforts of Andres Knopcken (1468–1439), who was born in Küstrin (Kostrzyn), Germany. After patristic and humanist studies, he became an assistant to Johannes Bugenhagen in the city school of Treptow, Pomerania. Having written three letters to Desiderius Erasmus, whom he admired, Knopcken received a reply in 1520, from which one can gather that Knopcken, reflecting on his service in Riga from 1517 to 1519, had characterized the Livonians as "more interested . . . in their bellies than their books" and as living near "uncouth and shaggy" neighbors. Erasmus encouraged him "to press on manfully" in humanist studies and even to "risk" returning to the Roman Catholic church.

In the meantime, under the influence of Bugenhagen and Andreas Bodenstein von Karlstadt and of Martin Luther's *Die captivitate Babylonica ecclesiae praeludium* (On the Babylonian Captivity of the Church; 1520), Knopcken, supplied with a letter of recommendation from Philipp Melanchthon, returned to his post as chaplain at Saint Peter's church. There he preached on justification by grace through faith alone, accented sanctification more than justification, and exhibited radical tendencies. He also held lectures on Paul's letter to the Romans (published and then reprinted three times in 1524 and 1525 with Melanchthon's support). On 12 June 1522 Knopcken held a disputation, outlining his position in twenty-four theses. Here the emphasis was on justification by grace through faith alone and on an outspoken rejection of various medieval forms of piety, such as images, fasting, and indulgences. In September 1522 Sylvester Tegetmeyer arrived in Riga from Rostow, Germany. He was a former priest and a zealous, even fanatical, follower of Luther. The city council appointed Knopcken to Saint Peter's and Tegetmeyer to Saint Jacob's church.

Still distinctly a minority movement, the Reformation experienced no persecution. Despite the demands by Roman Catholic prelates in 1521 for the suppression of the reformation movement, at the regional diet in Valmiera (Wolmar) in 1522, the request was refused. In the meantime, Wolter von Plettenberg, the master of the Livonian branch of the Teutonic Order, while not joining the Reformation, did not suppress it. In such a relatively tolerant atmosphere, the movement grew rapidly. Of great importance were the aggressive steps taken by Johannes Lohmüller, the city clerk. He wrote to Luther on 20 August 1522 and again in 1523, and Luther replied in September 1523. The response arrived in Riga on 11 November and was entitled *Den Auszerwelten lieben Freunden gottis, allen Christen zu Righe, Revell und Tarbthe ynn Liefland, meynen lieben herren und brudern ynn Christo* (To the Christians in Riga, Reval, and Dorpat). The reply by Riga's burgomaster, Konrad Durkop, was written on the very same day. Subsequently, Luther sent to Riga his *Der hundert und sieben und zwentzigst Psalm ausgelegt an die Christen zu Rigen ynn Liffland* (Exposition of Psalm 127, For the Christians of Riga in Livonia) and *Eyne Christliche vormanung von eusserlichem Gottis dienste unde eyntrcht, an die in Liefland* (A Christian Exhortation to the Livonians Concerning Public Worship and Concord; 17 June 1525). The radicalization of the Reformation movement that soon followed may be explained in part by the arrival of Melchior Hoffman in 1521 or 1522. During his two years in Riga, Hoffman was befriended by Knopcken and Tegetmeyer. Hoffman's social concerns, eschatological hopes, and liturgical radicalism left an imprint, especially in Valmiera, where he briefly stayed in 1523. Subsequently moving farther north (into what is now Estonia), Hoffman was expelled in 1526.

On 10 March 1524 members of the *Schwarzhäupter* ("Blackhead") merchant brotherhood undertook an iconoclastic attack in Saint Peter's, limiting destruction to the altar of their own brotherhood. On 26 March led by Tegetmeyer, another iconoclastic attack followed in Saint Mary's cathedral. As the work of the Reformation continued, two further events merit note. Burkard Waldis, a humanist and a Franciscan monk, became a Lutheran and composed a Mardi Gras play, *De parabell vam verlorn Szon* (Of the Prodigal Son), first performed on 17 February 1527. Also, Johann Briessmann (1488–1549), who had successfully introduced the Reformation in Königsberg, was invited to serve as pastor of the cathedral, and in effect as bishop, from 1527 to 1531, in this way ensuring the stabilization of the Reformation. In this capacity he prepared a Low German *Kurtz Ordnung des Kirchendiensts* (Brief Order of Church Service), along with a statement on ceremonies, all patterned after Königsberg liturgy but including several items from Riga's Catholic past. In this way a direction was set for the future. Latvian Lutheranism continued to be both tolerant and conservative, evangelical yet retaining a measure of its Catholic past.

Only since 1918 have historians begun to devote attention to the Latvian population of Livonia and Kurland, which were distinct in language and culture from the German ruling class. Marxist historians have indicated that the difference between "German" and "Latvian" was not nationality but social class. In any event, in 1524 a strong Latvian congregation under the leadership of Nicolaus Ramm was established at Saint Jacob's. Ramm is noted for writing in Latvian the hymn "Ten Commandments," which was subsequently in use for 150 years.

Slowly but certainly the Reformation also embraced the countryside. In Kurland this was hastened through the efforts of Gotthard Kettler. In 1561 Kettler resigned as master of the Livonian branch of the Teutonic Order and became a feudal duke of Sigismund II Augustus, king of Poland. In 1567 Kettler ordered the establishment of seventy Lutheran congregations. By the end of the century the establishment of Lutheranism in Latvia can be seen as completed.

BIBLIOGRAPHY

Adamovičs, L. "Dzimtenes baznīcas vēsture." In *Latviešu konversācijas vārdnīca*, edited by A. vābe, A. Būmanis, and K. Dilers, vol. 11, pp. 21519–21611. Riga, 1934–1935.

Arbusow, Leonid, Jr. *Die Einführung der Reformation in Liv-, Est-, und Kurland* (1921). Reprint, Aalen, 1964.

Depperman, Klaus. *Melchior Hoffman: Social Unrest and Apocalyptic Visions in the Age of Reformation.* Translated by Malcolm Wren. Edinburgh, 1987.

Dunsdorfs, Edgars, and Arnolds Spekke. *Latvijas vēsture, 1500–1600.* Stockholm, 1964.

Grislis, Egil. "Recent Trends in the Study of the Reformation in the City of Riga, Livonia." *Journal of Baltic Studies* 7.2 (1976), 145–169.

Hoerschelmann, D. F. *Andreas Knopken, der Reformator Rigas: Ein Beitrag zur Kirchengeschichte Livlands.* Leipzig, 1896.

Packull, Werner O. "Melchior Hoffman's Experience in the Livonian Reformation: The Dynamics of Sect Formation." *Mennonite Quarterly Review* 59.2 (1985), 130–146.

———. "Sylvester Tegetmeier, Father of Livonian Reformation: A Fragment of His Diary." *Journal of Baltic Studies* 16 (1986), 343–356.

———. "Melchior Hoffman's First Two Letters." *Mennonite Quarterly Review* 64.2 (1990), 146–159.

Pater, Calvin A. *Karlstadt as the Father of the Baptist Movements: The Emergence of Lay Protestantism.* Toronto and London, 1984.

Spekke, Arnolds. *History of Latvia: An Outline.* Stockholm, 1951.

Wittram, Reinhard, ed. *Baltische Kirchengeschichte.* Göttingen, 1956.

EGIL GRISLIS

LAURENTSEN, Peder (also Peter; c.1485/90–1552), Danish reformer and lecturer. About his youth it is known only that in 1519 as a Carmelite monk he obtained a residence in the order's college in Copenhagen, which was led by the leading reform Catholic, Paul Helie. In 1529, after a stay in the monastery in Assens (Funen), he went to Malmö, the most important market town in eastern Denmark.

Laurentsen's contribution to the Reformation can be divided into three main areas. (1) His pedagogical work began as early as when he taught young colleagues in the Carmelite college. Influenced by Helie's church-critical, reform-Catholic position, which was probably supplemented by his own independent studies, Laurentsen joined the evangelical movement and became a lecturer in Malmö at a school for ministers, which was established in 1529. Here good use was made of his knowledge of the scriptures, classical literature, the church fathers, and canon law. He was a member of the commission that wrote the church ordinance (1537); when the University of Copenhagen was established (1537), however, the ministers' school was dissolved, and he became a lecturer at Lund's cathedral chapter. At the same time, he became a parish priest at Oxie church in Skåne. (2) His contribution as an author of reports on church history is of inestimable significance; his *Malmø-bogen* (Malmö Book; 1530) is one of the most important documents in the history of the Danish Reformation. Laurensten explains the new church service, church activities, social work, the ministers' school, and the Latin school. Just as significant is his *Malmøberetning* (Malmö Report; 1530) which is the main source on the ministers' *Confessio Hafniensis*, where in forty-three articles they present their theology and demand for reform. Documents on the debate of the two confessions (1530) are also found here. (3) Finally, Laurentsen played an important role as the author of polemical and theological literature, including the publication of Oluf Chrysostomus's *Lamentatio Ecclesiæ* (1529), *En stakket Undervisning... imod pavens bisper* (A Short Lecture... against the Pope's Bishops; 1533), *Expostulatio Petri Laurentii ad canonicos Lundenses* (1533), and *En... undervisning om præsteembedet* (A Lecture on the Priest's Office; 1533).

Theologically Laurentsen seems to be in accord with many other early Danish reformers who belonged to the humanist type of reform found in southern Germany and in the northern German market towns, with which Malmö and other Danish market towns carried on a lively trade. In his ideas on the Bible, salvation, church offices, and religious services he often seems to diverge from the Wittenberg-Lutheran persuasion. The same holds true of his idea of the authority of the Bible on social issues. On the other hand, he seems to come close to Martin Luther's views on the question of the Eucharist and to his idea of the relationship between the secular and spiritual authorities. Laurentsen represents a transitional period between evangelical biblical humanism and the Lutheran idea of Christianity. He himself felt that he was a good Lutheran.

BIBLIOGRAPHY

Andersen, Niels Kund. *Confessio Hafniensis: Den københavnske bekendelse af 1530*. Copenhagen, 1954.

Gierow, Kr., ed. *Malmø-Bogen 1530*. Facsimile ed. Malmö, 1979.

Grell, Ole Peter. "The City of Malmø and the Danish Reformation." *Archiv für Reformationsgeschichte* 79 (1988), 311–339.

Lausten, Martin Schwarz. *Reformationen i Danmark*. 2d ed. Copenhagen, 1992.

Rørdam, Holger Fr., ed. *Skrifter fra Reformations tiden*. Copenhagen, 1885–1890.

MARTIN SCHWARZ LAUSTEN

LAUSANNE. The Gallo-Roman port of Losanna or Lausonna became the center of a large diocese in the sixth century. During its most flourishing period (from the thirteenth to the sixteenth centuries) the bishop was responsible for the religious life of the present Swiss cantons of Vaud, Neuchâtel, Fribourg, Soleure, and half of Bern; an inventory of 1228 listed 308 parishes in the diocese. The bishop also had civil jurisdiction in the canton of Vaud. The present cathedral was built in the thirteenth century on the foundations of a sixth-century edifice. The late Middle Ages were characterized, as in Geneva, by a (markedly unspiritual) triangular struggle for power between the bishops of Lausanne, the dukes of Savoy, and the citizens of Lausanne. In 1525 the city signed a mutual defense treaty (*combourgeoisie*) with the Swiss cantons of Bern and Fribourg, in the face of opposition from both the bishop and the duke.

One does not advisedly invite a bear (the symbol of Bern) into one's living room. Bernese expansionist ambitions intensified when that city adopted the Reformation in 1528. When, in January 1536, Charles III, duke of Savoy, besieged Geneva and the Genevan magistrates appealed to Bern for military aid, the powerful canton sent an army that annexed the canton of Vaud and its capital, Lausanne; it also acquired the districts surrounding Geneva and the Savoy territories south of Lake Geneva (which it shared with the canton of Valais). Lausanne thus became a Bernese "colony," and the bishop went into exile. Bern was not slow in arranging for the official religion of its new territories to conform to that of the new rulers. As had been done in Zurich, Bern itself, and Geneva, the change was effected by a disputation according to rules laid down by the government: all debate must take place in the local modern language (German in Zurich and Bern, French in Lausanne), and the only admissible proofs were those based on the Bible (no appeals to papal or conciliar authorities were valid). The main orators on the Reformed side were Guillaume Farel and Pierre Viret, with contributions from Christophe Fabri, Pierre Caroli, and the young John Calvin. The Roman Catholic clergy was ordered by the government to attend *en masse*; 174 out of 337 came. The clergy attending were ordered (probably by the bishop) to remain silent; the debate was consequently very one-sided. After eight days of debate (1–8 October 1536), of the ten theses (or "conclusions," as they were called), the Bernese presidents were satisfied that the Reformed cause had triumphed, and—without risking a popular vote as elsewhere in French-speaking Switzerland—they issued an edict on 19 October 1536 abolishing the Mass and instituting Reformed preaching and forms of worship. Pierre Caroli was installed as first pastor of Lausanne, with Pierre Viret as his deputy. When Caroli was dismissed in 1537, Viret became the chief pastor.

If the 337 priests summoned to the disputation were now to be replaced, the Bernese authorities had a new problem: there were only fourteen preachers for the whole of the huge territory of the canton of Vaud. The urgent need to train pastors led to the founding, in 1537, of the academy of Lausanne. This rapidly became the most important French-language center of higher education, with a team of brilliant professors, including Mathurin Cordier, Pierre Viret, Conrad Gessner, Théodore de Bèze, and François Hotman. However, in 1558, a conflict between the pastorate of Lausanne and the Bern government on the subject of church-state relations led to the wholesale resignation of the teachers from the academy and their departure to Geneva, which inherited the leading educational role from Lausanne. The academy of Lausanne continued to exist, much diminished; in the nineteenth century its stature was revived under the influence of eminent teachers such as Alexandre Vinet and Sainte-Beuve (who gave his celebrated lectures on Port-Royal at Lausanne); it became the University of Lausanne in 1890.

Theologically Lausanne tended always to be in the shadow of Geneva. Its printing industry developed very late, and Viret and Bèze had their works printed in Geneva; and, although recent research suggests that Viret may have disagreed with Calvin on certain points of church organization and discipline (Viret would have given more authority to the congregation than did Calvin, as Jean Morély argued), Viret's tactic was silence rather than contradiction.

Unlike the National Protestant Church of Geneva, the Reformed Church of the Canton of Vaud has remained a state church. There remains an unformulated sense that, whereas Geneva made its own decision to opt for the Reformation, Protestantism was imposed on Lausanne and its canton by a foreign, colonizing power.

[*See also* Bern; Geneva; *and* Switzerland.]

BIBLIOGRAPHY

Gilliard, Charles. *La conquête du Pays de Vaud par les bernois*. 2d ed. Lausanne, Switzerland, 1985.

Junod, Eric, ed. *La dispute de Lausanne, 1536: La théologie réformée après Zwingli et avant Calvin*. Lausanne, Switzerland, 1988.

Piaget, Arthur, ed. *Les actes de la dispute de Lausanne, 1536*. Neuchâtel, 1928.

Vuilleumier, Henri. *Histoire de l'église réformée du Pays de Vaud sous le régime bernois*. 4 vols. Lausanne, Switzerland, 1927–1933.

FRANCIS HIGMAN

LAW. [*To describe the role and use of law and its evolution during the sixteenth century, this entry comprises three articles:*

Theological Understanding of Law
Roman Law
Canon Law

The first considers the reflections of the early reformers on the law/gospel distinction and the controversies that arose over the concept of justification by faith alone; the second discusses the process whereby Roman law, understood as common law, gradually replaced customary local laws and statutes across Europe during the course of the sixteenth century; the third examines the destructive effects of the Reformation on traditional canon law and investigates the ways in which canon law served, nevertheless, as the basis for reformed ecclesiastical regulations.]

Theological Understanding of Law

In contrast to the Augustinian-scholastic distinction between law and gospel whereby the gospel is understood as "nova lex" ("the new law"), that is, as a power that is granted by grace to fulfill the law, Luther worked out the essential difference between law and gospel with a view to salvation. Thus for Luther salvation absolutely depends on the certain divine promise of the gospel, which at the same time reveals the end of the law as a way to salvation. Accordingly, the capacity to properly distinguish between law and gospel is what makes a theologian. "He who knows how to properly distinguish the gospel from law, let him thank God, and he may rightly know that he is a theologian." The gospel consists of the utterance of the forgiveness of sins spoken by Christ and his righteousness alone. He is the word of grace, consolation, and joy. As such this word is to be strictly differentiated from the law. Thus the distinction between law and gospel is a matter of two kinds of word or preaching ("tzweyerley wort oder predigt"). Therefore law and gospel are to be distinguished in such a way "that you place the gospel in heaven and the law on earth, so that you call the righteousness of the gospel heavenly and divine, and that of the law earthly and human. . . ." Accordingly, the gospel places the law in its limits and grants salvation in Jesus Christ alone. Correspondingly, the distinction between law and gospel contains "summ[a] totius Christianae doctrinae." While this distinction is theoretically easy to describe, it is existentially difficult to manage wherever it is challenged. "Moreover the gospel is an infrequent guest, while in contrast the law is one that is often present." Consequently in the distinction between law and gospel it is a matter of man's self-understanding before God. It is certainly true, as Paul asserts, that the law leads to the recognition of the reality of sin, but it is to an even greater extent true that it is impossible to recognize from the standpoint of the law that the law is at the same time a disciplinarian that points to Christ, in whom the law is fulfilled. This theological function of the law can only be understood from the perspective of the gospel. "Evangelium facit ex lege paedagogum in Christum, non fit ab ipsa lege per sese" (the gospel makes the law a pedagogue leading to Christ; this does not happen through the law by itself). Here the gospel fulfills a twofold function: On the one hand it interprets the law spiritually ("interpretatio legis"), that is, it makes evident the death-bringing character of the law and its character as pointing to grace. On the other hand the gospel proclaims to man's conscience, which has been plunged into despair under the law, the grace and mercy of God. This understanding of the distinction between law and gospel led Luther to the doctrine of the "duplex usus legis" (the twofold function of law). The "usus civilis," or "usus primus legis," serves to punish the evil deeds of men and to outwardly limit the power of the devil in the world. It is from the perspective of this "primus usus" that Luther interprets the power of magistrates, elders, and teachers as well as all "ordinationes" that place external limits on evil in the world. This function is necessary to prevent revolts and tumults in the world, to assure external peace, and to further the progress of the gospel. This "usus civilis" must be distinguished from the "usus theologicus seu spiritualis," which is the second function of the law. It is the main and proper function of the law ("principalis et proprius usus legis") to demonstrate to man that he is essentially a sinner and at the same time to move him in the distress of his conscience toward the grace of Christ. This function of the law cannot be gleaned from the law itself, but can be discovered and taught from the perspective of the gospel. "Hunc usum legis solus Spiritus sanctus quaerit et Evangelium docet, quia solum Evangelium dicit Deum adesse contritis corde" (This function of the law is sought by the Holy Spirit alone and is taught by the gospel, for only the gospel states that God is present to the contrite of heart). Thus, as to the effect of the word of God the sequence "law then gospel" obtains, while noetically the sequence "gospel then law" obtains, because the best and most perfect function of the law (optimus ac perfectissimus usus legis) can be recognized only from the perspective of the gospel. A third function of the law that followed upon this twofold function—as an instruction on living for believers or those who have been reborn—was rejected by Luther, because living faith spontaneously fulfills the demands of divine law which coincides with the "usus civilis legis" as to its content. In this way the law is the eternal will of God, which has been written upon the heart of man, but which has been obscured by sin, and which therefore had to be newly established through Moses, and even through Christ. The Decalogue corresponds to the law that has been written on our heart, that which finds its concrete expression in the golden rule. But because sin has obscured the law of God, man must be reminded of the law by external commands, and the law must be preached not only in its theological function but also in terms of its content, since "der teuffel die hertzen so verblend und besitzt, daß sie solch (natürlich) gesetz nicht allzeyt fulen, drumb mus man sie schreyben und predigen, bis Gott mit wircke und sie erleuchte, daß sie es ym hertzen fulen, wie es im wort lauttet" (the devil so blinds and possesses hearts that they do not naturally fulfill the law at all times, until God acts and enlightens them so that they fulfill it in their hearts, as it stands in the word). Since the reality of "simul iustus et peccator" holds true for them, Christians are no longer under the law, and yet at the same time they are still under the law. As justified persons they are free from the law, while as sinners they constantly need the preaching of the law in the "usus theologicus legis." Luther asserted this position especially in his arguments against the antinomians, who negated the law in its "secundus usus" and wanted to limit the law to its "primus usus" in the town hall.

Melanchthon. In his *Loci communes* of 1523 Melanchthon took up the Lutheran distinction between law and gospel. Both derived the basic elements from scripture. "Lex peccatum ostendit, evangelium gratiam" (the law revealed sin, the gospel grace). With this formulation Melanchthon pursued the "usus theologicus" of the law. The law accuses while the gospel is understood as a promise of the forgiveness of sins and justification on account of Christ. Like Luther's, Melanchthon's theology is centered on the gospel, but Melanchthon broadens the concept of law by grounding it more firmly in natural law than does Luther. For Melanchthon it is in the law that is founded on the natural law that the political function of the law is also grounded. Following the thought expressed in *Romans* 13:1f., Melanchthon therefore also understands the courts as a "praecipua pars legis." The law subjects the physical life of "iustitia civilis" and correspondingly grounds secular power. Melanchthon insists that law has a theological as well as a political function, and he sees this theological component as the highest function of the law. The law strikes fear into consciences; it leads to repentance and awakens the longing for the gospel. Beyond this twofold function of the law, from 1535 on Melanchthon also broadened the law in terms of its third function: as a permanent instruction for living even to those who have been reborn, namely believers. There is already a hint of this tendency in the *Loci communes* of 1521, when Melanchthon concludes that the law of God was given so that the spirit may kill the flesh. His visitations in Saxony had shown Melanchthon that the spontaneity of faith to do good works was not as effective as Luther had expected. Accordingly, Melanchthon argued that, in the interest of ethics, the law should also be taught to those who have been reborn. Whereas for Luther the indicative and the imperative of the law were contained within one another, Melanchthon came to see them as divergent, for reason unguided by the word of God stood in danger of going astray. In a humanistic spirit Melanchthon more strongly stressed the pedagogical function of the law in terms of ethics, even though he also strictly held fast with Luther to the idea that the law as a way of salvation is abolished and that salvation springs exclusively from the promise of justification on account of Christ that gives consolation to consciences.

Zwingli and Calvin. Zwingli also held for a strict distinction between law and gospel in view of obtaining salvation. Thus the primary function of law is to confront men with the reality of sin. Through the law "the weakness (stemming from original sin) must be recognized before the medication is taken" (mueß der präst erkennt werden, ee einer die artzny anneme). However, Zwingli is more interested from a humanistic and pedagogical standpoint in stressing the unity between gospel and law. "Daß gesatzt ist dem gotshulder ein euangelium" (the law is a gospel for one who fears God). For the gospel that forgives sin at the same time empowers the law to fulfill the inalterable will of God. For "das Gsatzt heißt nüt anderst, dann daß ewigklich recht und guot ist; denn das Gsatzt ist guot, grecht und helig" (the law is nothing other than what is eternally right and good; for the law is good, just and holy). "Do you want to know why? Because it is nothing other than an opening and indication of the will of God, that we see in the word of the commandment what God wills and demands. Therefore a law could again be called a proper gospel. For who would not rejoice, living in human darkness and uncertainty, if God were to make known his will to him? Would that not be in itself good tidings, if the will of God were to be announced to man?" Accordingly, in their freedom from the law Christians stand on the side of the law. He who is filled by divine love at the same time rejoices in the law as an ethical reminder and is ready to fulfill the law. Thus Zwingli understands the law as an ethical reminder and at the same time as the other side of the gospel. As for the love that fulfills the law, the natural law that is written on man's heart already points to it. Here Christ turns out to be the divine lawgiver in the inner man. For Zwingli that natural law is also reflected in the Decalogue, that is, the moral law of the Old Testament. This furthermore has binding force for Christian ethics. In contrast, the Old Testament ceremonial and judicial law is revoked through Christ. In the last analysis the law is the inalterable will of God for man. According to Zwingli the civil community also orients itself by the law of the Christian community. Thus Zwingli understands the Christian community and the civil community as working together in one "corpus christianum."

In terms of obtaining salvation Calvin also proceeds from a strict distinction between law and gospel, and like Zwingli he is oriented especially along the lines of the ethical function of the law. On the whole Calvin places the law within the Old Testament covenant of grace. The law is thus an integrating part of the covenant with Abraham. While this law is at first directed to Israel, from the standpoint of salvation history it is also established in view of Christ. While Old Testament ceremonial and judicial law only indirectly point to Christ, the moral law of the Old Testament points directly to Christ. Following Melanchthon, Calvin also distinguishes a threefold function of the law.

The first function of the law is its "usus pedagogicus," in which the law serves as a mirror of sin for mankind. "The first part is that it shows us God's righteousness, i.e., what is pleasing before God, and thus it shows each individual his own unrighteousness, making him certain of this fact, and finally convicts and condemns him. . . . The law is like a mirror in which we first see our weakness, then the unrighteousness that originates from it, finally we glimpse the condemnation that stems from these two realities, just as we observe the blemishes on our face in a mirror."

The second function of the law is its "usus politicus" and consists in preventing the godless, who yield only to fear, from doing evil. The "coerced righteousness" that is the product of the law is necessary for the human community; "for our Lord provides for their peace when he keeps all things from falling into disarray; for this is what would happen, if everything were permitted to everyone."

The third function of the law (tertius usus legis) is the most important for Calvin and concerns only believers. "Although the law is written in the heart [of believers] by the finger of God, i.e., inwardly they are inclined through the leading of the Holy Spirit such that would gladly obey God, nonetheless they derive a twofold benefit from the law. For the law is a very positive means for them to come to know ever better and with greater certainty from day to day what God's will is, which is what they indeed long for, and through the law they are strengthened in recognizing it. . . . And what is more, because we are in need not only of teaching but also of admonition, a servant of God will also derive benefit from the law in that he will be driven toward obedience to God through frequent reflection on the law, he will be strengthened and drawn away from his sins." The law has this function "because the spiritual man is not yet delivered from the burden of his flesh." With this "tertius usus legis" Calvin especially emphasizes sanctification in the life of Christians. While it is true that Christ has freed us from the curse of the law, the demands of the law remain even for one who is reborn, so that he may achieve the sanctification that emerges from justification. According to Calvin the natural moral law also corresponds to the Decalogue that is anchored in the covenant of grace of the Old Testament, as it is attested in the heart or conscience of man. Yet the natural law is so obscured in the heart of man that he only dimly recognizes the first table of the Decalogue. In contrast, the legal demands of the second table of the Decalogue are more evident to natural man. The reflection on the correspondence between the Decalogue and the natural moral law in Calvin has primarily the function of showing that all men have knowledge of the will of God and are thereby inexcusable before God. Calvin's intense interest in the "tertius usus legis" lends a certain measure of legalism to Calvinism, but without detracting from the Christian freedom that springs from the gospel. For man's conscience is pointed toward Christ over and beyond the law and has its freedom in him alone. Yet according to Calvin the Christian still needs the help of the law for ethical knowledge and for the sake of fostering corresponding good works. Calvin's notion of Christian freedom is also evident in his recommendation against troubling one's conscience over merely external matters. Thus any Puritanical narrowing of the notion of sanctification has scarcely any justification in Calvin.

Controversy over the Validity of the Law. Although the antinomian controversy between Luther and Melanchthon on the one hand and Johann Agricola on the other had been settled by Luther in 1527, controversy broke out anew in the years 1537–1540 over the identical issue of the enduring validity of the law for Christians and non-Christians.

The Antinomian Controversy. In his tract on freedom Luther had defined Christian freedom to the effect that the justified Christian no longer needed any law, but rather that in the creative spontaneity of faith he did good works of himself and as a matter of course without any demand of the law. However, this did not mean that Luther utterly rejected the law, but rather that he retained it both in its "usus civilis" and in its "usus theologicus." Particularly in its "usus theologicus" the law has the function of leading both Christians and non-Christians to the recognition of sin and to repentance, so that they will truly open themselves to the gospel's liberating proclamation of grace and at the same time will allow repentance to become the fruit of faith. In contrast, Agricola had asserted that repentance is only a fruit of the preaching of the gospel. It is first the recognition of the greatness of God's mercy that truly leads to the acknowledgment of sin, not the law. Rather, the law is abolished in every respect and no longer belongs in the pulpit, but henceforth only in the town hall. In 1537 Luther revived the argument by formulating six series of theses into a scientific disputation—the so-called Antinomian Theses—and sharply defined his position against that of Agricola, holding for the enduring validity of the law both in its "usus civilis" and in its "usus theologicus" for Christians and non-Christians. According to Agricola, "poenitentia docenda est non ex decalogo aut ulla lege Mosis, sed . . . per evangelium" ("repentance should not be taught from the decalogue or any law of Moses, but . . . through the gospel"; see Tschackert, p. 481); now Luther argued that the law makes known the sinful alienation of man from God and that without this the consoling power of the gospel cannot be accepted. Thus for Luther the law leads man to repentance and orients him toward Christ, even though this theological function of the law can only be truly recognized from the perspective of the gospel. If, however, one disputes along with Agricola the "usus theologicus" of the law, then by the same token, according to Luther, one disputes the consoling power of the gospel.

The controversy over the "tertius usus legis." At issue in the controversy that broke out in 1556 over the "tertius usus legis" was whether the Lutheran legacy was to be passed on in Melanchthonian form. At a synod in Eisenach it was determined that although good works cannot be designated as necessary for salvation with respect to justification, they can be necessary "abstractive et idea in doctrina legis" (in an abstract sense and as a notion in the teaching of the law). Andreas Poach (1515–1585) and A. Otho (1505–1583), two of Luther's disciples, took the opposing view that the law should be excluded from justification, and that in fact it was not useful or necessary for any good work. In objective terms, at issue was the distinction between the ethical necessity of good works and their soteriological necessity. For the former, the "usus civilis legis" was sufficient, apart from the fact that Christians already abundantly fulfill the law from the creative love that springs from faith, and thus a "tertius usus legis" is unnecessary for Christians. Accordingly, Poach and others held for the twofold—political and theological—function of the law. The gospel was on another and higher level than the demands of a legal system of laws. A man who fulfilled the law would still have no claim to salvation. Therefore the gospel should not be viewed nomologically as based on natural law, as Melanchthon would have it, but rather should be safeguarded in its freedom, which is the foundation of salvation.

The Formula of Concord. In effect a continuation of these disputes over the validity of the law, the Formula of Concord of 1577 held fast to the distinction between law and gospel, which is to be considered as a "particularly glorious light." However the formula concedes that the word *gospel* can also be used in a wider sense and, as the teaching of Christ, can encompass law as well as gospel. But in its actual sense the gospel is exclusively the preaching of God's grace, to which is necessarily added the preaching of the law that leads to the recognition of sin. Therefore "Christ takes the law into his hands and interprets it spiritually" (*Mt.* 5; *Rom.* 7). And "thus from heaven God's wrath is revealed on all sinners." However, this preaching of the law is an "alien 'work of Christ' through which he comes to his proper office, which is to preach grace, to console, and to bring to life, which is properly the preaching of the gospel." Just as Christ taught the law in this way, so too law and gospel belong together in the preaching of the church; however, at the same time the distinction between the two must constantly be observed: the law remains the disciplinarian that points to Christ, while only grace and Christ as the end of the law are proclaimed in the gospel. Accordingly, the formula also retains the "usus civilis" and the "usus theologicus legis"; moreover, it takes up the concept of the "tertius usus legis," although it is at pains to give it a Lutheran orientation. The "tertius usus legis" concerns believers only "quatenus adhuc carnales sunt" (inasmuch as they are still fleshly); in contrast, "quatenus renati sunt" (inasmuch as they have been reborn), they give free uncoerced obedience. Thus it seemed as though the controversy over the validity of the law had been settled; nevertheless the Lutheran antithesis between law and gospel risked becoming blurred in later times.

The Council of Trent. The Council of Trent (1545–1563), the great council of the Counter-Reformation, finally refused the Lutheran conception of law and gospel. As documented by the various drafts of the council's decree on justification, Girolamo Seripando, general of the Augustinian Hermits, fought tenaciously for this conception on the basis of his own studies of Paul and Augustine. Seripando stressed the "differentia maxima" between Christ and Moses but was unable to prevent the adoption of the designation of Christ as "legislator." In its final form, the decree on justification declared, "If anyone asserts that a justified and thereby perfect man is not held to the observance of the commandments of God and of the church, but only to faith, as though the gospel were the pure and unconditioned promise of eternal life without the condition of observing the commandments, let him be anathema. . . . If anyone asserts that Christ Jesus is given to mankind as a Redeemer for them to trust in him, but not as a lawgiver for them to obey, let him be anathema." Accordingly, the Council of Trent held that good works are the material condition for the justification of man, which is effected through grace, and rejected the Lutheran distinction between gospel and law.

[*See also* Justification *and* Two Kingdoms.]

BIBLIOGRAPHY

Primary Sources

Calvin, John. *Opera quae supersunt omnia.* Edited by G. Baum, E. Cunitz, and E. Reuss. Corpus Reformatorum, 29–87. Braunschweig, 1863–1900.

Denzinger, Henrici. *Enchiridion symbolorum, definitionum et declaratisnum de rebus fidei ett morum.* Freiburg, 1957.

Luther, Martin. *Werk.* 1883ff. (WA lff.)

Melanchthon, Philipp. *Opera quae supersunt omnia.* Corpus Reformatorum, 1028. Halle, 1834–1860.

———. *Werke in Auswahl.* Edited by Robert Stupperich. Gütersloh, 1951-.

———. *Huldrych Zwinglis Werke.* Edited by M. Schuler and J. Schulthess. 8 vols. 1828–1842.

———. *Werke.* Zurich, 1905–.

Secondary Sources

Althaus, Paul. *Gebot und Gesetz: Zum Thema "Gesetz und Evangelium."* Gütersloh, 1952.

Baur, Jürgen. *Gott, Recht und weltliches Regiment im Werke Calvins.* Bonn, 1965.

Bayer, Oswald. *Gesetz und Evangelium: Bekenntnis und Einheit der Kirche; Studien zum Konkordienbuch.* Edited by Martin Brecht and Reinhard Schwarz. Stuttgart, 1980. See pp. 155–173.

Bring, Ragnar. *"Gesetz und Evangelium" und der dritte Gebrauch des Gesetzes in der lutherischen Theologie.* 1943.

Ebeling, Gerhard. "Zur Lehre vom triplex usus legis in der reformatorischen Theologie." *Theologische Literaturzeitung* 75 (1950), 235–246.

Eisinger, Walther. "Gesetz und Evangelium bei Huldrych Zwingli." Diss., Ruprecht-Karls-Universität Heidelberg, 1957.

Forster, Anselm. *Gesetz und Evangelium bei Girolamo Seripando.* Paderborn, 1963.

Greschat, Martin. *Melanchthon neben Luther: Studien zur Gestalt der Rechtfertigungslehre zwischen 1528 und 1537.* Witten, 1965.

Hägglund, Bengt. *Gesetz und Evangelium im Antinomerstreit: Luther und die Theologie der Gegenwart.* Göttingen, 1980. See pp. 156–164.

Haikola, Lauri. *Usus legis.* Uppsala, 1958.

Heintze, Gerhard. *Luthers Predigt von Gesetz und Evangelium.* Munich, 1958.

Hesselink, I. John. *Calvin's Concept and Use of the Law.* Basel, 1961.

Huschke, Rolf B. *Melanchthons Lehre vom "ordo politicus": Ein Beitrag zum Verständnis von Glauben und Politischem Handeln bei Melanchthon.* Gütersloh, 1968.

Joest, Wilfried. *Gesetz und Freiheit: Das Problem des 'tertius usus legis' bei Luther und in der neutestamentlichen Paranese.* Reprint, Göttingen, 1968.

Locher, Gottfried Wilhelm. *Huldrych Zwingli in neuer Sicht.* Zurich, 1969. See pp. 199–201, 233–239.

Mau, Rudolf. "Gesetz V: Reformationszeit." In *Theologische Realenzyklopädie*, vol. 13, p. 82–90. Berlin and New York, 1977–. Bibliography.

Maurer, Wilhelm. *Melanchthon-Studien.* Gütersloh, 1964. See pp. 103–136.

Morhaupt, Lutz. *Gesetz und Evangelium nach Art. V der Konkordienformel: Studien zur Konkordienformel der lutherischen Reformation.* Edited by Wenzel Lohff. Stuttgart, 1977. See pp. 197–222.

Neuser, H. *Der Ansatz der Theologie Philipp Melanchthons.* Neukirchen, 1957.

Räcke, G. "Gesetz und Evangelium bei Calvin." Diss., Johannes Gutenberg-Universität Mainz, 1953.

Schloemann, Martin. *Natürliches undgepredigtes Gesetz bei Luther.* Berlin, 1961.

Stakemeier, Eduard. *Der Kampf um Augustin auf dem Tridentinum.* Paderborn, 1937.

Tschackert, Paul. *Die Entstehung der lutherischen und der reformierten Kirchenlehre samt ihren innerprotestantischen Gegensätzen* (1910). Reprint, Göttingen, 1979.

Wendel, François. *Calvin: Ursprung und Entwicklung seiner Theologie.* Translated by Walter Kickel. Neukirchen-Vluyn, 1968. See pp. 159–211. Also available in English translation.

Karl-Heinz zur Mühlen

Translated from German by Robert E. Shillenn

Roman Law

The process by which Roman law replaced traditional law in much of Europe was already well underway when the Reformation crisis began. From the point of view of law, the Reformation was little more than an incident in a continuous process by which the modern European state emerged. Throughout Europe outside England, Wales, and Ireland, Roman law was understood as the *ius commune* ("common law"), structuring, modifying, and supplementing customary law and statute. In Italy and Germany, where Roman law was "received," substantive Roman law actually replaced existing private law. In the region dominated by English common law, civilians (experts at Roman law) played a major role in prerogative courts (chancery, admiralty, Star Chamber) and were perceived as a perennial threat to common law courts until the English Civil War.

The study of Roman law, revived at law schools in Pavia and Bologna in the eleventh century, achieved parity with the study of canon law only in the fifteenth century, but it had achieved supremacy in the law faculties on the eve of the Reformation. The medieval tradition of legal studies reached its classic form with the works of Bartolus of Saxoferrato (1314–1357) and Baldus de Ubaldis (1327–1400), whose commentaries applied the scholastic method to a body of legal texts including Justinian's *Corpus iuris civilis* supplemented by more recent works, such as the Lombard *libri feudorum* for feudal tenures. Because of the reliance of the municipal judge (*podestà*) on learned legal opinions (*consilia*) in complex cases for protection from censure by the syndics, who could review judgments at the end of a judge's contracted term, academic doctrine became the foundation for practical jurisprudence in Italy. This traditional method of teaching and jurisprudence came to be called the "Italian method" (*mos italicus*), and it would dominate both teaching and jurisprudence in Italy and Germany in the sixteenth century. The *mos italicus* used principles for reaching conclusions that proved unacceptable for humanistically oriented scholars, though Alberico Gentili, among others, defended it against humanist attack on account of its practicality in day-to-day jurisprudence. Some jurists regarded as humanists for their personal cultural styles, such as Ulrich Zasius (1461–1535), did not break dramatically with the *mos italicus* as jurists. At the end of the sixteenth century, some humanist methods were integrated with the *mos italicus* to create the "modern usage" (*usus modernus*), which would be the practical method used by both teachers and jurists in central Europe until the French Revolution.

In contrast to the *mos italicus*, the humanist scholarly method of applying philology to original sources and rejecting the medieval commentators became known as the *mos gallicus* ("the French method"). Originating in the scathing critique of medieval jurisprudence by Lorenzo Valla and achieving maturity in the writings of Guillaume Budé and Andrea Alciato (an Italian who began his teaching career at Bourges), the *mos gallicus* came to dominate legal studies in France, the Netherlands, and Calvinist central Europe. Even where the new method failed to supplant the *mos italicus* in jurisprudence, it stimulated the development of comparative law and the historical method. In the last quarter of the sixteenth century, the pedagogical and logical methods of Petrus Ramus had considerable impact on the teaching of law, particularly as a result of the efforts of the juristic pedagogue and publicist Johann Thomas Freigius. Ramism became a particularly important tradition in Calvinist schools. Some classically trained jurists, most notably the French Protestant François Hotman, argued in favor of "native" systems and against the form of Roman law found in Justinian's *Corpus iuris civilis.*

The introduction of Roman law in the Reformation era was an aspect of the revolutionary displacement of traditional elites in courts and chanceries by academically trained jurists that had begun in the later Middle Ages. The use of Latin or a Latinate jargon helped to exclude those who had learned their law in traditional courts. The sudden collapse of canon law institutions with the Reformation crisis opened broad new areas to state courts in both Catholic and Protestant Europe. In dealing with threatening dissident groups such as the Anabaptists, the Roman law on heresy had neither the flexibility nor the popular legitimacy that Inquisition courts had acquired over time. The result was that courts often hesitated to apply harsh retributive justice against all Anabaptists, particularly when simple persons confessed their error and promised amendment. Religious dissidence might be equated with treason (a step canon law had already taken under Innocent III), but limited civil rights came eventually to be extended to at least some dissident Christians in Germany as a result of the settlements of the mid-sixteenth century. In arguing against the planned seizure and destruction of the Talmud in 1510, the jurist Johannes Reuchlin asserted that even Jews possessed minimal rights as citizens in the empire under Roman law, despite the failure of Jews to honor Christ. The weakening of the institutional church in the Reformation opened the way to a notion of the state as an institution that was above all confessions, even openly secular.

In trials formal, oral, public, adversarial procedure vanished or became vestigial with the rise of informal written procedure, with courts frequently functioning in secret. In German criminal law, for example, the *Constitutio criminalis Carolina* (1527) reduced the Germanic adversarial trial to a mere promulgation ceremony at the end of a trial held according to inquisitorial principles. Even where codification sought to save regional or local laws, the result was "Romanized" in the process, either by the reception of substantive Roman law or by organizing existing rules according to Romanist principles.

In Germany the establishment of the Imperial Chamber Court (*Reichskammergericht*) in 1495, which was required by its statute to use "written law" (i.e., Roman law), marked a new era in the process of reception in central Europe. Although the Chamber Court was perennially stymied by shaky finances, confessional strife, exemption of territories through the privilege against appeals (*privilegium de non appellando*), and the establishment of an alternative supreme court, the Imperial Aulic Council (*Reichshofrat*), it remained the model for the application of Roman law. In the course of the Reformation crisis, the Chamber Court came to be the favored supreme court for Protestants, since it included Protestant jurists. In contrast, the Aulic Council remained wholly Catholic.

In Spain the robust revival of scholastic philosophy and theology in the sixteenth century (the "second scholastic") influenced the development of Roman legal doctrine as well, stressing the concept of a preeminent natural law largely in Roman legal terms. The political and economic importance of Spain in the sixteenth and early seventeenth centuries meant that legal institutions created there were adopted throughout Europe, most significantly the Spanish form of entail, the *fideicommissa.*

Both the population at large and elites displaced by the reception of learned jurisprudence viewed Roman law with hostility, though it was grudgingly accepted as an inevitable aspect of modernization. Courts and members of the juristic class sought to mute the arbitrary exercise of state power through judicial rulings or *consilia* imposing "constitutional" limits on rulers. Estate assemblies also tried, rather less successfully, to apply brakes to state ambitions.

Although hostility to Roman law was proverbial in the early Reformation (*Juristen böse Christen,* "Jurists are bad Christians"), no solid alternative was developed in continental Europe, and English common law would triumph definitively over the civilians only in the seventeenth century. Luther and his colleagues at Wittenberg ended up making their peace with Roman law, even conceding the revival of some elements of medieval canon law to rule the new state churches. The introduction of divorce in Lutheran communities meant that Roman laws on the dissolution of marriage became relevant again. Calvin, a jurist by training, promoted Roman law as a substitute for the legislation of the bishop of Geneva, and he injected Roman legal patterns of reasoning into his own theology (most notably in *Institutes of the Christian Religion*).

Legal education in civil law faculties became the ordinary course for members of the political classes in the sixteenth century, even for a proportion of the future clergy. Schools had multiplied in the fifteenth century, and new ones were added after the first phase of the Reformation crisis was past, since law faculties were often integrated into state bureaucracies as courts of cassation. The drafting of laws, even whole law codes, became the province of law professors and other trained jurists.

Despite some confessionally based differences within the legal profession, the Reformation did not break the unity of the Roman legal community. Germany in particular became a fragmented country with a united legal profession, and Protestant civilians routinely argued prize cases on behalf of the king of Spain before admiralty courts in London. Those who sought to transcend conflicts among faiths in the later sixteenth and seventeenth centuries often sought to use Roman law or a Romanized international law as a new common ground for all peoples (Alberico Gentili, Hugo Grotius, Arthur Duck).

BIBLIOGRAPHY

Astuti, Guido. *Mos italicus e mos gallicus nei diologhi 'De iuris interpretibus' di Alberico Gentili.* Bologna, 1937.

Bohatec, Josef. *Calvins Lehre von Staat und Kirche mit besonderer Berücksichtigung der Organismusgedankens.* Breslau, 1937; reprint, Aalen, 1968.

Coing, Helmut. *Europäisches Privatrecht.* Vol. 1, *Älteres Gemeines Recht, 1500 bis 1800.* Munich, 1985.

Coing, Helmut, ed. *Handbuch der Quellen und Literatur der neueren europäischen Privatrechtsgeschichte.* Vol. 1, *Mittelalter 1100–1500: Die gelehrten Rechte und die Gesetzgebung,* Munich, 1973. Vol. 2, *Neuere Zeit, 1500–1800: Das Zeitalter des gemeinen Rechts;* pt. 1, *Wissenschaft,* and pt. 2, *Gesetzgebung und Rechtsprechung,* Munich, 1977.

Ius Romanum Medii Aevi. Milan, 1961–. A series of monographs on national legal traditions.

Kelley, Donald R. *Foundations of Modern Historical Scholarship: Language, Law, and History in the French Renaissance.* New York, 1970.

Kisch, Guido. *Erasmus und die Jurisprudenz seiner Zeit: Studien zum humanistischen Rechtsdenken.* Basel, 1960.

———. *Melanchthons Rechts- und Soziallehre.* Berlin, 1967.

Langbein, John H. *Prosecuting Crime in the Renaissance: England, Germany, France.* Cambridge, Mass., 1974.

Maffei, Domenico. *Gli inizi dell'umanesimo giuridico.* Milan, 1956.

Mazzacane, Aldo. *Scienza, logica e ideologia nella giurisprudenza tedesca del secolo XVI.* Milan, 1971.

Rowan, Steven. *Law and Jurisprudence in the Sixteenth Century: An Introductory Bibliography.* Sixteenth Century Bibliography, no. 26. Saint Louis, 1986.

———. *Ulrich Zasius: A Jurist in the German Renaissance, 1461–1535.* Frankfurt a.M., 1987.

Senior, William. *Doctor's Commons and the Old Court of Admiralty: A Short History of the Civilians in England.* London, 1922.

Strauss, Gerald. *Law, Resistance, and the State: The Opposition to Roman Law in Reformation Germany.* Princeton, 1986.

Watson, Alan. *Roman Law and Comparative Law.* Athens, Ga., 1991.

Wieacker, Franz. *Privatrechtsgeschichte der Neuzeit unter besonderer Berücksichtigung der deutschen Entwicklung.* 2d ed. Göttingen, 1967.

Wolf, Eric. *Grosse Rechtsdenker der deutschen Geistesgeschichte.* 4th ed. Tübingen, 1963.

STEVEN ROWAN

Canon Law

The Greek *kanōn* was a measuring rod or rule used by carpenters and masons. In the early church it was applied generally to indicate an officially approved standard, for example, the books recognized as divinely inspired scripture. In the fourth century, synods began to establish standards of organization and conduct for the Christian community by promulgating a series of canons or regulations. Ecclesiastical discipline was previously a matter of custom rather than of formal legislation. Second- and third-century documents such as the *Didache,* the *Traditio apostolica,* and the *Didascalia apostolorum,* belonging to a literary genre known as church orders, had recorded the traditions of a particular region, claiming that their practices had the authority of the collective apostolate. It is with the legislation of councils, however, that canon law may properly be said to begin.

Pre-Reformation. Within a century the first ecumenical council of Nicaea in 325 commanded enormous respect even beyond the boundaries of the Roman Empire and to this day finds almost universal acceptance among Christians. It enacted twenty canons concerning church structure (recognition of the province and of the incipient patriarchate), the clergy (mandatory dismissal of those who sin gravely or apostatize), public penance, the readmission of schismatics to the church, and some liturgical regulations. By the time of the Council of Chalcedon in 451 a chronological compilation of the canons of Nicaea and of four councils in Asia Minor, totaling slightly over one hundred canons, was in wide circulation and had even been translated into Latin. This core collection, greatly augmented and confirmed at the Council of Trullo in 692, remains to this day the fundamental law of the Eastern Orthodox churches. The scope of canon law had by then broadened to include texts of twelve Greek fathers, especially Basil, on matters of ecclesiastical discipline. John III Scholasticus, patriarch of Constantinople (565–577), systematically organized the canons under fifty "titles" or subject headings. Since in the East the emperor had been conceded the right to provide for the practical affairs of the church, John prepared a similar collection of imperial legislation. Later, when the ecclesiastical and civil legislation (*nomoi*) were integrated under the same titles, the collections were known as *nomocanons.* The *Nomocanon* of 883, divided into fourteen titles, serves as the source of law for all Orthodox churches. The most important modern printed collection of canons is *The Rudder* or *Pedalion*, originally compiled by two monks, published by the authority of the ecumenical patriarch at Leipzig in 1800. An English translation of the fifth edition appeared in 1908 and has since been reprinted.

In Rome about the year 500 Dionysius Exiguus made a more accurate Latin translation of the Greek corpus of canon law to which he added a large number of canons from several councils in North Africa. In a separate work he compiled about forty decretals of fifth-century popes (decretals being papal letters containing rulings in response to questions of discipline that had been addressed to the pope). Henceforth they were to be an increasingly important part of canon law. The two collections of Dionysius, known as the Dionysiana, were soon recognized as best embodying the Roman tradition and were transmitted in 774 by Pope Hadrian I to Charlemagne, who was seeking a uniform law for his empire.

After the dissolution of the Roman Empire, nevertheless, a consistent discipline throughout the West proved unachievable. The various nationalities developed their own peculiarities. For example, the penitentials, originating in Ireland and spreading to Britain and the Continent, caused confusion and, in some instances, corrupted the old law in permitting divorce. When in the mid-eleventh century a powerful reform movement, which had begun in the monasteries, succeeded in controlling the papacy, it was apparent that there were two masses of legal traditions, the Roman and the Franco-Germanic, which in numerous instances were incompatible.

In every field of human endeavor, but especially in theology and law, twelfth-century Europe witnessed a remarkable renaissance. Stimulated by the rediscovery of such works as the treatises of Aristotle and Justinian's *Digest*, scholars began a sophisticated analysis of what they had inherited from their Christian past. Using rules of interpretation and principles of textual criticism that were then being formulated, Abelard in *Sic et non* (1115–1117) applied his dialectical method to conflicting patristic texts in order to find a coherent theological tradition. With Abelard's work as an exemplar, Gratian in 1140 published his *Decretum* or *Concordance of Discordant Canons*, in which he sought to reconcile the contradictions in the legal patrimony.

Gratian inaugurated the classical period of canon law that was to last until the time of Joannes Andreae (d. 1348), who brought the scientific study of the subject to its fullest development. The appearance of the *Decretum*, along with the revival of Roman law scholarship in Bologna, stirred up an insatiable interest that led to the establishment of canon law faculties in the universities springing up all over Europe. Soon appeals began to pour in to Rome to settle disputed interpretations of the law or to provide for new contingencies.

The resulting papal decretals grew so numerous that after many private compilations had been made, Pope Gregory IX commissioned Raymond of Peñafort to prepare a definitive edition. Accordingly, the five books of the *Decretals* or *Extravagantes* (laws "wandering around" outside Gratian) of Gregory IX appeared in 1234, the first officially promulgated collection and destined to be the most important in the Roman Catholic church until superseded by the Code of Canon Law in 1917. The passage of time and the sophistication in legal studies ensured a ceaseless demand for papal resolution of difficulties. Over the next two hundred and fifty years, therefore, four additional collections of decretals were made. The *Liber sextus* of Boniface VIII (1298) and the *Constitutiones* of Clement V (1317) were officially commissioned, while the much smaller collections the *Extravagantes* of John XXII (1325) and the *Extravagantes communes* (1500) were compiled privately. In 1503 two Parisian printers published the *Decretum* of Gratian and the five collections of the decretals under the title *Corpus Iuris Canonici.* There can be no doubt that, for the most part, the canon law enshrined in the *Corpus* was universally observed throughout Western Christendom on the eve of the Reformation. There was a certain flexibility, of course, in that the law was subject to the interpretation of doctors learned in the law as well as to modification by local custom.

Reformation. The rallying cry of the reformers was *sola scriptura*, a call to restore the church to its primitive simplicity. The gospel, it was contended, had been obscured and the people confused by human inventions foisted upon them. "Ecclesiastical" had come to mean the same as "spiritual." Through such structures as the priesthood and the sacramental system a "yoke of tyranny" had been imposed upon the people. They were deprived of the liberty of the children of God and tricked into a "Babylonian captivity," controlled by the tyrant pope through an elaborate system of canon law.

It was one thing to champion freedom, but another to provide for the functioning of an institution. Every Reformation movement, save those on the left wing of the Reformation, was soon forced to deal with practical necessities such as the qualifications and succession of the leadership, the supervision of its members, and the conduct of worship. Of immediate concern was the regulation of marriage, which had been the exclusive preserve of the medieval Church. Replacing canon law, therefore, were the ecclesiastical regulations or ordinances formulated with the cooperation and sanction of the state. In effect, the legislative authority once wielded by pope and bishops was now exercised by the civil government.

Germany. At the very start of the Reformation, shortly before his definitive excommunication, on 10 December 1520 Martin Luther consigned to the flames the *Corpus Iuris Canonici* and other legal texts in the presence of the student body of the University of Wittenberg. In *De captivitate Babylonica ecclesiae* he wrote: "Neither pope nor bishop nor any other man has the right to impose a single syllable of law upon a Christian man." Yet ten years later Luther was quoting canon law on marital questions, and the Apology of the Augsburg Confession charged: "Our enemies falsely accuse us of abolishing good ordinances and church discipline. . . . if you look at it correctly, we are more faithful to the canons than our opponents are" (*Book of Concord* 15, 38–3). For lack of a legal doctrine and terminology of their own, many reformers, despite an initial basic rejection, fell back upon the traditional canon law and adopted it in many points.

As early as 1528 practical necessities impelled Philipp Melanchthon to draw up the *Unterricht der Visitatoren.* In it he treated church order, established the office of superintendent, regulated the conduct of public worship, and provided for enforcement through the ban or excommunication. In his opinion the civil authority as guardian of the two tables of the law was responsible for correct order in the church. After the Peace of Augsburg in 1555 the prince of a region was considered the *Summus Episcopus*, the legal successor of the Catholic bishops in his area. The secular authorities in Lutheran cities and territories served as executive bodies for establishing law in ecclesiastical matters, although the drafting of texts was done for the most part by theologians, which accounts for the fact that these ecclesiastical regulations usually lack juridical form and terminology. They dealt with a wide range of matters including the administration of property, marriage litigation, and the consistorial courts. The study of these ecclesiastical regulations is complicated since the secular authorities regulated church affairs under the civil law as well. A complete system of church law, *De Iurisprudentia ecclesiastica seu consistorialis*, was eventually published by Benedikt Carpzov in 1645. He systematically compiled statutes from ecclesiastical regulations, imperial law, and theological and juridical works; he also relied on the *Corpus Iuris Canonici* and the Roman law. Another notable jurist, Justus Henning Böhmer, among his many works published *Ius ecclesiasticum Protestantium usum modernum iuris canonici juxta seriem decretalium ostendens* (1714–1717).

Denmark, Norway, and Sweden. The Recess of the Diet of Copenhagen of 1536, which deposed the Catholic bishops and replaced them with superintendents, signaled the establishment of the Reformation in Denmark. A new church order appeared the next year, the *Ordinatio Ecclesiastica Regnorum Daniae et Norvegiae*, formulated on the model of the Saxon church order with the assistance of a close friend of Luther, Johannes Bugenhagen, city pastor at Wittenberg. The king was accorded an essential role in the promulgation of canonical statutes. Of considerable consequence was the marriage ordinance of 1582.

Norway accepted the Danish church ordinance at the assemblies of nobles, the diets of Oslo and Bergen, in 1539. The Reformation in Norway was consolidated through the special regulations of church affairs, which loosely resembled their Danish counterparts, promulgated under the authority of the king in 1607 and 1687.

In Sweden the first evangelical archbishop, Laurentius Petri, published in 1571 a "Book of Rites and Ceremonies," which was accepted by the clergy at the 1572 Synod of Uppsala and was subsequently confirmed by the king. In some matters the German ecclesiastical regulations served as models, but there were also many peculiarities in the Swedish system because of a strong emphasis on the Old Testament.

Switzerland. At the instigation of Huldrych Zwingli the Zurich city council promulgated in 1525 its first reform, the Order of the Matrimonial Tribunal, which was to consist of two pastors and four council members. The competence of the tribunal was expanded the next year to include all matters of morality. In 1532 Heinrich Bullinger, Zwingli's successor, drew up regulations for preachers and synods. The synod, composed of a burgomaster and eight members of the great council, was to meet biannually to report on the qualifications and performance of the pastors.

John Calvin persuaded the Geneva city council in 1537 to promulgate his *Articles concernant l'organisation de l'Église.* The articles provided for the maintenance of ecclesiastical discipline through a consistory composed of clergy and laity.

Because of opposition they were never enforced and Calvin was banished. He returned in 1541 to have the councillors accept his *Ordonnances ecclésiastiques*. The ordinances established four ecclesiastical offices: pastors, doctors, elders, and deacons. The elders, confirmed by the great council and really acting as its agents, were responsible for supervising the behavior of the congregation. In the 1561 definitive edition of the ordinances Calvin was able to achieve more independence of the congregation from the civil authorities. In it he referred to the third use of the law, its principal use with respect to believers in whose hearts the Spirit of God already flourishes and reigns. "For it is the best instrument for enabling them daily to learn with greater truth and certainty what that will of the Lord is which they aspire to follow, and to confirm them in this knowledge" (*Inst.* 2.7.11).

France. In France the first national synod of Huguenots issued in 1559 not only a profession of faith but also a *Discipline ecclésiastique* comprising forty articles. At the Synod of La Rochelle in 1571 this *Discipline* was revised to strengthen the authority of the pastors and was expanded to sixty-eight articles. The marriage law was generally based on the *Genevan Ordonnances ecclésiastiques* of 1561.

The Netherlands. Calvinism in the Netherlands was first constituted by fugitives outside the country, "the church under the cross," at the Assembly of Wessel in 1568 and the Synod of Emden in 1571. The ecclesiastical regulations of Geneva and Paris served as models. The "church reformed in accord with the word of God" was to be united with the state but not dependent upon it.

England. Unlike any other country in which the Reformation took hold, England maintained a clear continuity with the medieval canon law. If previously the law had had its reputed source in the pope, it now had its font and source in the king. It was argued that canon law had not had its force on the basis of papal authority, but from the fact that the king and people had freely accepted it and agreed to be bound by it. The clergy were required in the Act of Submission never to claim to enact in convocations "any new canons, constitutions, ordinances" without the assent and license of the king. R. C. Mortimer has well summarized the arrangement: "The King governs his subjects in part and on some matters through the civil law and the civil courts, in part and on other matters through the canon law and the spiritual courts. And when he wishes to change the law, he acts in the one case through Parliament, and in the other through the Convocations" (*Western Canon Law*, p. 59).

While both Parliament and convocations requested a revision of canon law, they stipulated that meanwhile the old canon law should remain in force. A commission was appointed but its draft was never approved by King Henry VIII. Another commission authorized by Parliament during the reign of Edward VI never completed its task. Under Elizabeth I an entire reconstruction was made and appeared in book form under the title *Reformatio legum ecclesiasticarum*, but she refused to have it promulgated. No general revision has ever been enacted. The queen did in 1575 authorize thirteen articles dealing with qualifications for the ministry, as she did a second series in 1585, and a longer series in 1597. In 1603 the three were compiled; with new articles added the total numbered 141. In the nineteenth and early twentieth century particular canons were amended; it was not until 1969 that the 1603 Code was completely revised. In the introduction to the compilation then published the archbishops of Canterbury and York wrote: "like that Code it presupposes both the common and statute law of England and the general pre-Reformation Canon Law of the Western Church, except where that Canon Law has been affected by contrary statute or custom in England" (*The Canons of the Church of England*, p. xi).

Though in the pre-Reformation period under the Tudors the competence of Christian courts had been significantly restricted, they still exercised jurisdiction over broad areas. Church courts heard all cases dealing with the contracting and annulment of marriages, the probation of wills not involving freehold property, the claims of defamation, the enforcement of contracts subscribed to by oath, and the collection of tithes. In the name of these courts action could be taken against those who violated public morality (such as by fornication) or the teaching of the church (such as by blasphemy or contempt of the clergy). Reformation statutes, except for prohibiting appeals to Rome, left the areas of ecclesiastical jurisdiction for the most part as they were in 1530.

The spiritual courts continued to function with surprising vigor and even progressed in developing their jurisprudence. The Elizabethan and Jacobean ecclesiastical lawyers, as Helmholz recently demonstrated, continued in the habits of the old Roman canon law. "They used the traditional literature constantly, and they 'kept up' with the masses of it being produced across the Channel. They preferred it in virtually every instance to authorities drawn from the English common law, applying the principles of the Roman canon law regularly in the causes that came before the ecclesiastical tribunals" (*Roman Canon Law in Reformation England*, pp. 154–55).

The Roman Catholic church. After many failed attempts the papacy at length succeeded in convening the Council of Trent (1545–63) to clarify the Roman Catholic position in response to the demands of the reformers. Ten of the conciliar sessions (4–7, 13–14, 21–25) enacted both doctrinal and disciplinary decrees. A collection entitled *Canones et decreta Concilii Tridentini* was officially edited at Rome in 1564. One of the most significant innovations was to invalidate clandestine or private marriages and to require that all marriages be celebrated in the presence of the parish priest.

A sharp break with classical canonical tradition came with the prohibition for anyone to publish commentaries, glosses, or any form of interpretation of these decrees. A special bureau was established in the Curia Romana, the Congregation of the Council, to make official clarifications whenever necessary.

The Council of Trent did not abrogate the old law but reestablished and supplemented it. Pope Gregory XIII set up a commission, the Correctores Romani, to review the text of the *Corpus Iuris Canonici.* The commission was charged to restore the original text of the authorities so that what had been corrupted would be emended and what was obscure would be explained in notes. A Roman edition of the *Corpus* was thus published in 1582. The pope forbade any changes whatever to be made in this official version. His action had the paradoxical effect of consigning all historical reconstruction of the text to Protestant scholars. Accordingly, modern editions were published by Justus Henning Böhmer (1747), Aemilio Ludovico Richter (1839), and the one ordinarily cited today by Aemilio Friedberg (1879).

In face of the Reformation challenge, the Roman Catholic church in its canon law as in its doctrine sought greater precision and conformity. The creativity that distinguished the great canonists of the Middle Ages was curtailed by limiting interpretation to an official body; canon law was to lapse into formalism for centuries. By contrast, the Protestants stifled canon law by subsuming it under secular law. Even if one acknowledged the practical necessity of canon law, the dialectic Luther had set up between law and gospel (no one is ever saved on the basis of the law, "the law always indicts") made it impossible for Protestantism to view canon law as anything but a human law unable to bind the Christian conscience. The reformers did acknowledge a threefold use of law, as articulated in the Lutheran Formula of Concord: (1) political, to maintain public order by restraining the unruly; (2) theological, to lead people to Christ through a knowledge of their sins; and (3) educational, to give guidelines for Christian living. In terms of contemporary thought one may say that the Catholic church tends to view canon law as applied or practical theology while Protestants tend to seek a theology of law.

BIBLIOGRAPHY

Berman, Harold J. *Law and Revolution: The Formation of the Western Legal Tradition.* Cambridge, Mass., 1983. Deals with the centralization of canon law circa 1050, then treats the emergence of secular law.

———. *Faith and Order: The Reconciliation of Law and Religion.* Atlanta, 1993.

Carlson, Eric. *Marriage and the English Reformation.* Cambridge, Mass., 1994.

Corecco, Eugenio. *The Theology of Canon Law: A Methodological Question.* Translated by F. Turvasi. Pittsburgh, 1992. Treats the divergence of Orthodox, Protestant, and Catholic theologies with respect to the nature of canon law.

Cranz, F. E. *An Essay on the Development of Luther's Thoughts on Justice, Law, and Society.* Cambridge, Mass., 1964.

Ellul, Jacques. *The Theological Foundation of Law.* Translated by M. Weiser. New York, 1960. A critique of classical and modern natural law theories in light of the scriptures from the Reformed church perspective.

Helmholz, R. H. *Roman Canon Law in Reformation England.* Cambridge, 1990. Traces the persistence of the traditional canon law from the mid-fifteenth century through the reign of James I.

Helmholz, R. H., ed. *Canon Law in Protestant Lands.* Berlin, 1992. A series of essays (most in English), treating Germany, the Dutch Republic, the Reformed Churches of France, Switzerland, post-Reformation England, Ireland, and colonial America.

Hesselink, John. *Calvin's Concept of the Law.* Princeton Theological Monograph Series, no. 30. Allison Park, Pa., 1992.

Honecker, Martin. "Kirchenrecht II: Evangelische Kirchen." In *Theologische Realenzyklopädie,* vol. 18, pp. 724–49. Berlin and New York, 1989. Surveys developments in Protestant areas of Europe through the nineteenth century; includes extensive bibliography.

Ingram, Martin. *Church Courts, Sex and Marriage in England, 1570–1640.* Cambridge, 1987. Primarily concerned with church courts; secondarily deals with aspects of sexual behavior and marriage.

Little, David. *Religion, Order, and Law: A Study in Pre-Revolutionary England.* New York, 1969.

Mortimer, R. C. *Western Canon Law.* London, 1953. Lectures of the bishop of Exeter given at the Berkeley campus of the University of California. A broad outline of the development of canon law in Western Christendom down to the Reformation with an additional chapter on canon law in England thereafter.

Pelikan, Jaroslav. *Spirit versus Structure: Luther and the Institutions of the Church.* New York, 1968. Treats the crisis brought about by the Reformation in the ordained priesthood, monasticism, the practice of infant baptism, the canon law, and the sacramental system.

Rowan, Steven W. *Law and Jurisprudence in the Sixteenth Century: An Introductory Bibliography.* Saint Louis, 1986.

JOHN E. LYNCH, C.S.P.

LAYNEZ, James. *See* Laínez, Diego.

LECLERC, Pierre (d. 1546), carder of wool who, in 1546, was elected to be the first minister of a Reformed congregation in Meaux, France. He was martyred in the same year. LeClerc and his congregation were a product of reform in the diocese of Meaux, formerly under Bishop Guillaume Briçonnet, although many in Meaux who were interested in reform remained Catholic. LeClerc was one of a number of ministers of artisan origins who led early French Protestant conventicles or congregations before the Reformed church organized and recruited pastors with formal education. He preached and administered the sacraments to a rapidly growing house church that met in the home of Étienne Mangin.

Jean Crespin, Protestant martyrologist, credited LeClerc with knowledge of scripture in French and recorded that on 8 September 1546, LeClerc and the members of his congregation who were present were apprehended by the lieutenant and provost of the city and imprisoned. They were sent before the Parlement of Paris. LeClerc was among fourteen of this group of approximately sixty-two men and women who were condemned to be tortured and burned alive and to have their possessions confiscated. They were returned to Meaux for the execution of their sentence. Eight of the fourteen, including LeClerc, refused to confess to a priest and had their tongues cut out before being burned to death. Others who had been apprehended with them, including LeClerc's wife, Martine, were ordered to watch the execution.

The so-called fourteen of Meaux became a part of a growing number of French martyrs who fueled the ardor of the evolving Reformed churches. Their treatment contributed to the desire for freedom of worship that led to the Wars of Religion in France (1562–1598).

BIBLIOGRAPHY

Crespin, Jean. *Histoire des martyrs persecutez et mis a mort pour la verite de l'evangile, depuis le temps des apostres iusques a present* (1619). 3 vols. Reprint, Toulouse, 1885–1889. The most readily accessible edition of Crespin's book containing the story of LeClerc.

———. *Histoire des vrays tesmoins de la verite de l'evangile, qui de leur sang l'ont signée, depuis Jean Hus iusques au temps present: Comprinse en VIII livres contenans actes memorables du Seigneur en l'infirmité des siens, non seulement contre les forces et efforts du monde, mais aussi a l'encontre de diverses sortes d'assauts et heresies monstrueuses* (1570). Reprint, Liège, 1964. Folios 160 verso-163 verso. This is a facsimile edition of the original.

JEANNINE E. OLSON

LEEUWEN, Denys van. *See* Denis the Carthusian.

LEFÈVRE D'ÉTAPLES, Jacques

(Lat., Faber Stapulensis; 1460?–1536), French humanist. He was born in Étaples in Picardy, the northern French province from which Guillaume Farel and John Calvin came. He was a student and then a professor at the Collège du Cardinal-Lemoine in Paris. Though a priest, he was never a doctor of theology, something his theologian adversaries would not hesitate to emphasize.

He is among the earliest and most celebrated figures of French humanism, one who truly applied himself to a return *ad fontes*. This return in his case was eclectic but unified by a vision of spiritual theology. One finds in him a confluence of various interests: philosophy, medieval spirituality, and patristics. During his voyage to Italy in 1492, he met the Aristotelian Barbaro, the Platonist Ficino, and Pico della Mirandola, who was attempting a synthesis of both traditions. On his return to France, Lefèvre became the "restorer" of Aristotle, annotating the whole of the latter's work, but he was also interested in hermetic writings and in Pseudo-Dionysius. He published the most mystical writings of the Middle Ages, for example those of Richard of Saint Victor, Ramon Lull, Ruysbroek, and Hildegard of Bingen. As for patristics, although he himself published *The Pastor* of Hermas, he had a circle of disciples working for him. These books, published by the first Parisian printers (W. Hopyl, J. Higman, H. Estienne, Josse Bade), are characterized by various degrees of editing, translation when called for, and annotation, according to the pedagogical method Lefèvre followed until the end of his life. This activity as editor culminated in the three volumes of the works of Nicholas of Cusa in 1514, in the production of which he was the chief architect surrounded by a team of scholars.

Lefèvre gradually abandoned this set of interests in order to devote himself exclusively to the Bible, doing so in three stages in which he successively became a commentator, a translator, and, together with his disciples, a preacher. In 1509, while residing at the abbey of Saint-Germain-des-Prés, he published, in synoptic form, five Latin versions of the psalter, the *Quincuplex Psalterium*, a work that both Martin Luther and Huldrych Zwingli are known to have annotated. In 1512 he commented on the Pauline epistles, and shortly thereafter a dispute over interpretation brought him into opposition with Erasmus. In 1521, at Meaux at the invitation of Bishop Guillaume Briçonnet, he commented on the four Gospels. In late 1525, following attacks by the Faculty of Theology of Paris, he took refuge in Strasbourg, during which time he composed a commentary on the "Catholic epistles"; published in 1527, it is the last work signed with his name. However, he had already begun a French translation of the Bible from the Vulgate, published at Antwerp in 1530. This text was largely, at least as concerns the New Testament, the inspiration for the famous translation composed by Pierre Robert Olivétan at the request of the Waldenses during the Synod of Chanforan (1532). Finally, at Meaux, Lefèvre together with his disciples composed a collection of homilies that are simple, pastoral, and "evangelical" in tone.

After having been tutor to the children of Francis I in Blois, Lefèvre finished his life at the court of Marguerite d'Angoulême in Nérac; it was there that he died in 1536. He made no statement of a break with the Church of Rome, but neither did he make any declaration—as he was apparently asked to do—of conformity to the doctrines of the Church of Rome.

According to Protestant historians Lefèvre was a proto-reformer, or rather, one of the first French-speaking reformers. Bèze inscribed his portrait in his *Icones* (1580). Such was the position taken by C. H. Graf (1842 and 1852), who based his judgments on the Pauline commentaries; by A.-L. Herminjard (1868); E. Doumergue (1899); J. Barnaud (1900 and 1936); N. Weiss (1919); H. Doerries (1925); K. Spiess (1930); J. Pannier (1935); and F. Hahn (1938). It was contradicted by the Catholic historians E. Amann (1926) and P. Imbart de La Tour (1944). The question was, so to speak, "deconfessionalized" by Richard Stauffer in 1967, in "Lefèvre d'Étaples, artisan ou spectateur de la Réforme?" (1980). Carlo Ginzburg attempted to cast Lefèvre as a "Nicodemite."

Sources of contention include Lefèvre's relations with the reformers, the facts concerning or legends surrounding his final years, and the exact content of his thought. Letters written to Farel in 1524 and 1525 show an admiration for Johannes Oecolampadius and Zwingli and mention works by Philipp Melanchthon, Oswald Myconius, and Otto Brunfels; Lefèvre met Martin Bucer, Wolfgang Capito, and Matthias Zell in Strasbourg. After 1525 there exists scarcely a trace of his opinions in writing, albeit that they were probably close to those of Marguerite d'Angloulême. Calvin's visit to Nérac for the purpose of meeting Lefèvre is mentioned only in the life of Calvin by Nicolas Colladon (*Corpus Reformatorum* 49, *Opera Calvini* 21, col. 57, Braunschweig, 1879). The story propagated at the beginning of the seventeenth century, according to which Lefèvre late in life expressed regret at not having the courage to break with Rome, seems scarcely probable. Bayle (*Dictionnaire*, vol. 2, pp. 469–470, Amsterdam, 1730) tends to doubt it. The commentaries of 1527 on the Catholic epistles probably present the final stage of Lefèvre's thought: writing at a time when confessional boundaries in France were not yet clearly defined, he steers a middle course, one that seems in keeping with his temperament and his ideal of harmony.

BIBLIOGRAPHY

Primary Sources

Lefèvre d'Étaples, Jacques. *S. Pauli Epistolae XIV ex vulgata. . . cum commentariis* (1512). Stuttgart, 1978.

———. *Quincuplex Psalterium* (1513). Geneva, 1979. See also the companion volume by Guy Bedouelle, *Le Quincuplex Psalterium de Lefèvre d'Étaples: Un guide de lecture,* Geneva, 1979.

———. *Epistres et Evangiles pour les cinquante-deux sepmaines de l'an* (1525). Edited by M. A. Screech. Geneva, 1965.

———. *Epistres et Evangiles pour les cinquante et deux dimanches de l'an* (1532). Edited by Guy Bedouelle and F. Giacone. Leiden, 1976.

Rice, Eugene F., Jr. *The Prefatory Epistles of Jacques Lefèvre d'Étaples and Related Texts.* New York, 1972.

Secondary Sources

Bedouelle, Guy. *Lefèvre d'Étaples et l'intelligence des écritures.* Geneva, 1976.

Ginzburg, Carlo. *Il Nicodemismo.* Turin, 1970.

Hughes, Philip Edgcumbe. *Lefèvre: Pioneer of Ecclesiastical Renewal in France.* Grand Rapids, Mich., 1984.

Rice, Eugene F., Jr. "The Humanist Idea of Christian Antiquity." *Studies in the Renaissance* 9 (1962), 126–160.

Stauffer, Richard. "Lefèvre d'Étaples, artisan ou spectateur de la Reforme?" In *Interprètes de la Bible.* Paris, 1980.

Guy Bedouelle

LEIPZIG. The largest city in Saxony, located at the confluence of the White Elster and Pleisse rivers, Leipzig has its origins in the seventh or eighth century. On the site of the West Slavic farming community called Lipsk (Lindenort, later Leipzig) a German settlement developed in the tenth century. Leipzig was first mentioned in 1115 and received its city charter in 1165. Located at the crossroads of important trade routes, one running from east to west and the other from north to south, Leipzig developed quickly into a center of trade. In 1497 Emperor Maximilian I confirmed the city's market rights. Beginning in 1500 there was a strong economic upswing, primarily because of the abundant yields from silver mining in the Erzgebirge and to book printing and trade. The Thomasschule, first mentioned in 1254, and the university, founded in 1409, became significant factors in the city's intellectual development. During these years, Leipzig overshadowed Nuremberg as a city of commerce.

The first public dispute over the Reformation was the Leipzig Disputation, held from 27 June to 17 July 1519 between Johannes Eck, Andreas Bodenstein von Karlstadt, and Martin Luther. Duke George had arranged this disputation despite the opposition of the university and Bishop Adolf of Merseburg. Luther's insistence on the exclusive authority of holy scripture over against papal claims to power made an impression on many listeners, who accepted and propagated Luther's thoughts.

Disputations became a weapon in overcoming those who represented the late medieval church. In Leipzig itself the evangelical movement began to gain ground. Despite prohibitions by the duke, which were formally enforced by the city council, the new ideas remained alive. Evangelical preachers were expelled, as were Sebastian Froschel in 1523 and Andreas Bodenschatz in 1524. To prevent the printing of Lutheran books, publishers and booksellers were kept under close scrutiny. The evangelical movement again surged around 1530. People from the city attended Lutheran worship services in neighboring villages. In 1533 the city council used metal tokens to keep track of those who made their traditional Easter Communion. About seventy or eighty burghers who insisted on receiving both bread and wine at the Lord's Supper were forced to leave the city. This expulsion marked the high point in the last fruitless attempts at suppression by the duke. Luther wrote two letters of consolation to those who had been expelled from Leipzig. The city became a symbol of resistance against the anti-Reformation church policy of George of Saxony. In 1534 and 1539 religious colloquies were held in Leipzig with the participation of Gregor Brück, Philipp Melanchthon, Martin Bucer, and Georg Witzel. Despite the efforts of some of the duke's councilors who were Erasmian in their outlook, these colloquies were unsuccessful.

In 1539 Duke Henry officially introduced the Reformation. With the participation of Luther, Melanchthon, and other Wittenberg theologians as well as Elector Johann Friedrich, solemn church services in Leipzig on Pentecost inaugurated the new religion. Justus Jonas, Caspar Cruciger (who was originally from Leipzig), and Friedrich Myconius went about the work of reordering the church in Leipzig.

The first superintendent was Johann Pfeffinger. The restructuring of the university posed major problems. Then, in March 1540, a bitter opponent of Luther's, Hieronymus Dungersheim of Ochsenfurt, died. The way was now open for reform of the university. Bernhard Ziegler and Alexander Alesius were appointed. Caspar Borner, together with Joachim Camerarius, energetically assumed responsibility for the reform of the entire university along Reformation and humanist lines. A Protestant territorial university eventually developed in Leipzig. In 1545 Luther visited Leipzig for the last time and dedicated the Paulinerkirche of the Dominicans as the university church (demolished in 1968). During the Schmalkald War the city managed to withstand a siege by Johann Friedrich in 1547.

At the end of 1549 the Albertine Landtag, representing the various classes, met to hold negotiations on the Interim. The articles on religion proposed to this body were published a short time later by Matthias Flacius Illyricus as the "Leipzig Interim," which became the starting point for lively controversies including Melanchthon and the Wittenberg theologians. In 1550 Pfeffinger touched off the Synergist Controversy. Only gradually was Leipzig theology able to move from the shadow of the Wittenberg theologians. The wrath of Elector August against the crypto-Calvinists in 1574 was particularly directed against the University of Wittenberg. Pfeffinger and Camerarius had died a short time earlier. In 1576 Nicholas Selnecker came to Leipzig as superintendent.

The Reformation fostered the economic and intellectual development of Leipzig, in particular through the reform of the university. Although the Schmalkald War and the aggressive foreign policy of Prince Elector Moritz of Saxony entailed major financial burdens, the new role of the Albertine Saxon electorate in the empire after 1547 also benefited Leipzig.

BIBLIOGRAPHY

Seifert, Friedrich. *Die Reformation in Leipzig*. Leipzig, 1883.

Wartenberg, Günther. "Leipzig Universität." In *Theologische Realenzyklopädie*, vol. 20, pp. 721–729. Berlin and New York, 1990.

Wustmann, Gustav. *Bilderbuch aus der Geschichte der Stadt Leipzig für Alt and Jung*. Vol 1. Leipzig, 1905.

GÜNTHER WARTENBERG

Translated from German by Robert E. Shillenn

LEIPZIG DISPUTATION. After what at first had been friendly relations between Johann Eck and Martin Luther, Eck came into increasing confrontation with the Wittenberg theologians. He criticized Luther's indulgence theses in his *Obelisci*. As a result, Andreas Bodenstein von Karlstadt involved Eck in a discussion on free will in his proposal for academic reform, *Apologeticae conclusiones* (9 May 1518). At the beginning of his work Karlstadt emphasized the preeminence of scripture over all other authorities. Contrary to Eck, he asserted that man with his natural powers could contribute nothing to receiving grace but could only passively accept grace as a gift.

In August Eck responded with three series of theses that were devoted to the doctrine of penance, the relationship of grace and free will, and indulgences. In his conclusion he challenged Karlstadt to a public disputation. On 29 December Eck ostensibly attacked Karlstadt with additional theses but, in fact, took aim at Luther. Until then Luther had mediated between Eck and Karlstadt. He now felt deceived and, formulating twelve theses, became a participant in the debate. Thus, Eck had achieved his goal. On 14 March 1519 Eck published an expanded version of his theses, which directly criticized Luther. As the proposed debate shifted to the issue of papal primacy, Karlstadt emphasized his obedience to the Roman church. In May, however, Luther added a thesis to his *Disputatio et excusatio F. M. Luther adversus criminationes D. Joh. Eccii*, in which he repeated an intentionally provocative conclusion: "That the Roman church was set above others is proven by the completely cold decrees of the Roman popes that have arisen in the last 400 years. In opposition to them stand the recognized historical accounts of 1100 years, the text of the Scripture, and the decree of the holy Council of Nicea." While intensively studying history and papal statutes to prepare himself for the disputation, Luther began to question whether the pope was the Antichrist or an apostle of the Antichrist.

The opponents agreed on Leipzig as the site of the disputation. Duke George of Saxony forced the university to agree to it, despite the determined will of its theologians, whom George thought of as fainthearted and lazy, and the prohibition of the disputation by Bishop Adolf of Merseburg, which he disregarded. Although Eck let the university know that he wanted to debate Luther, Duke George delayed permission for Luther to come until the beginning of the debate.

The debate took place in Leipzig at the Pleissenburg Castle, where there was a hall large enough to accommodate the audience. From 27 June until 3 July Karlstadt argued the activity of grace with regard to free will in the work of justification. Although Eck admitted to Karlstadt that without grace the human will was incapable of doing anything pleasing to God, he rejected the corollary that the will remained purely passive since God, who brought about the entire meritorious deed, did not do so in its totality.

On the day of Saints Peter and Paul (29 June), Luther preached in the disputation hall on the confession of Peter and unfolded the basic concepts of his ecclesiology. Christ has given to every Christian the office of the keys, which must serve the justification of the sinner by grace. For Luther the church consists not in a hierarchy directed by the pope but rather in a community of Christians united in faith and love.

From 4 to 8 July Eck and Luther debated the question that was decisive for the outcome of the disputation—whether the pope was *iure divino* the head of the church. Eck argued that Christ had established a monarchial order in his church and hence made the pope its head *iure divino.* Luther, on the contrary, held that Christ alone was head of the church. He did not reject the papacy but wanted to recognize it as *iure humano.*

The disputation not only deepened the disagreement over the primacy of the pope but also caused further differences to emerge. These differences found expression in the way citations were presented and interpreted. The debate took into account the demands of the humanists, as scholastic theologians played only a limited role and scripture and the church fathers a significant one. Luther reasoned also from tradition—that is, from church history (for example, that the Greeks were never subject to the pope), the church fathers, papal decretals, and conciliar decisions to the fifteenth century—subjecting all to the authority of the holy scripture. He disputed whether the pope could promulgate new articles of faith and contended that no Christian could be forced to believe anything beyond the scriptures unless it was a new revelation.

In his first involvement Eck had already labeled those who deviated from his opinion as heretics. Luther had maintained that among the tenets of Jan Hus, condemned by the Council of Constance in 1415, some had been Christian and biblical; Eck used the opportunity to present Luther as a defender of those "damned Hussites" and as a heretic (which persuaded Duke George to oppose Luther) and to reproach him for teaching that councils had erred. Luther protested repeatedly against that interpretation of his words.

From 9 to 13 July Eck and Luther dealt with the topics of purgatory, indulgences, and confession. On 14 and 15 July Eck and Karlstadt continued their discussion of free will.

Two notaries kept the minutes of the disputation. Luther wanted to circulate them in print form and to entrust them to the judgment of the public. Eck insisted on the opinion of the theology faculties. Duke George decided on 16 July that only theologians and canon law scholars could render a judgment on the issues. It was agreed to ask the universities of Erfurt and Paris for their opinion, which neither ever delivered.

More effective was the dissemination of the disputation through notes taken by members of the audience and released by three unofficial Erfurt printings. They gained Luther the endorsement of humanists and that of an emerging educated public. They also resulted in polemics with Duke George's court chaplain, Hieronymus Emser, and the Leipzig Franciscan Augustin Alfeld (1486–1535?), as well as condemnation from the theology faculties of Louvain and Cologne. Eck could not refute Luther from scripture but caused Luther to view the papacy more critically in addition to arousing support for Wittenberg theology. Eck, criticized and ridiculed, helped bring about in Rome a warning of excommunication against Luther.

[*See also* Eck, Johann; George, Duke of Saxony; *and* Luther, Martin.]

BIBLIOGRAPHY

Brecht, Martin. *Martin Luther: His Road to Reformation, 1483–1521.* Translated by James L. Schaaf. Philadelphia, 1985.

Iserloh, Erwin. *Johannes Eck, 1486–1543: Scholastiker, Humanist, Kontroverstheologe.* 2d rev. ed. Münster, 1985. See pp. 22–53.

Kähler, Ernst. "Beobachtungen zum Problem von Schrift und Tradition in der Leipziger Disputation von 1519." In *Hören und Handeln,* edited by Helmut Gollwitzer, pp. 214–229. Munich, 1962.

Seitz, Otto, ed. *Der authentische Text der Leipziger Disputation, 1519: Aus bisher unbenutzten Quellen.* Leipzig, 1903.

Selge, Kurt-Victor. "Der Weg zur Leipziger Disputation zwischen Luther und Eck im Jahr 1519." In *Bleibendes im Wandel der Kirchengeschichte,* edited by Bernd Moeller and Gerhard Ruhbach, pp. 169–210. Tübingen 1973.

———. "Die Leipziger Disputation zwischen Luther und Eck." *Zeitschrift für Kirchengeschichte* 86 (1975), 26–40.

HELMAR JUNGHANS

Translated from German by Susan M. Sisler

LEIPZIG INTERIM. *See* Interims.

LEO X (born Giovanni Damaso Romolo de' Medici; 1475–1521), *de facto* ruler of Florence (1512–1513), patron of arts and letters, and pope (1513–1521). Born in Florence the second son of Lorenzo de' Medici (the Magnificent; 1449–1492) and his wife, Clarice Orsini, he was groomed early on for an ecclesiastical career. Tutored by noted humanists in letters, he was enriched with numerous benefices, especially in Tuscany, and sent to the University of Pisa, where he earned in 1492 the doctorate in canon law (earlier conferred in 1489 as part of his father's strategy to make him appear better qualified for promotion to the cardinalate). His sister's father-in-law, Pope Innocent VIII, appointed him cardinal in 1489 but allowed him to function in that office only in 1492. His most important legation was under Julius II as head of the army of the Holy League that restored the Medici to power in Florence (1512).

Elected pope by the younger cardinals, he continued the policies of Julius II, seeking to exclude foreign influence from Italy but often allying with the empire and Spain against France. He succeeded in ending the Pisan schism (1513) and in negotiating at Bologna (1515) with Francis I a permanent abrogation of the Pragmatic Sanction of Bourges and a new concordat—something his ten predecessors had failed to achieve. To secure his position following an abortive plot to poison him, Leo packed the college of cardinals with thirty-one new appointments on 1 July 1517. In an effort to prevent Habsburg hegemony in Italy,

Leo pushed for the election of either Francis I of France or Frederick III of Saxony as emperor in 1519, but in the end he was forced to accept the unanimous choice of the electoral college, Charles V of the Habsburgs.

Leo promoted the interests of his family. With his assistance the Medici maintained their political control over Florence, passing it from his brother Giuliano (1479–1516), to his nephew Lorenzo (1492–1519), and then to his first cousin Giulio (1478–1534). He saw that his brother and nephew received new lordships and raised to the cardinalate three nephews and three cousins, the most important of whom was Giulio, his closest adviser. He appointed Giulio archbishop of Florence and prepared him as his eventual successor, the future Clement VII. To honor Giuliano and Lorenzo, Leo commissioned Michelangelo to carve their tombs in Florence.

Leo was known as a great patron of the arts. He was particularly fond of Raphael, who continued to work on the Stanze and painted the loggia of the papal apartments, designed the tapestries for the Sistine Chapel, painted Leo's portrait, and was put in charge of work on the new Saint Peter's basilica. By his support for humanists, poets, and scholars (giving notable support to the Sapienza University), Leo made Rome the cultural capital of Italy. His enthusiasm for music, hunting, and other diversions could mask his more serious concerns.

Leo did not neglect the various responsibilities of his office as pope. He faithfully and piously performed his liturgical functions. His concern for the preservation and propagation of the gospel is evident in his dealings with the Maronites and Ethiopians and in his support for the Portuguese missions. He tried to promote the defense of Christendom by organizing a crusade against the Turks. The Fifth Lateran Council (1512–1517), which he successfully brought to a close, registered in its decrees measures promoting peace among Christian princes, a crusade against the Turks, orthodox belief, and church unity and reform. His failure to enact more sweeping curial reforms was in large part the result of his dependence on the revenues the Curia Romana produced. To maintain a lifestyle he thought befitted his office and to finance his military operations, Leo exacted fees for promotions, increased the sale of venal offices, and went deeply into debt. The overarching concern of his pontificate was the preservation of papal power and the protection of papal prestige.

Leo X was slow to recognize the danger posed by Martin Luther. Early attempts were made to silence him, persuade him of his errors, or work out some compromise—and not alienate his overlord, Frederick of Saxony, whose support Leo X sought in order to prevent the election of Charles V as emperor. Luther's rejection of Roman primacy in the Leipzig debate in July 1519, which followed the imperial election and his condemnation by the universities of Cologne (30 August) and Louvain (7 November), led Leo to reopen his case in Rome. After a thorough review by three commissions of theologians and four consistories of cardinals, Leo issued on 15 June 1520 the bull *Exsurge Domine,* which demanded that Luther retract forty-one statements. When he refused to do so, the pope formally excommunicated him by the bull *Decet Romanum Pontificem* of 3 January 1521. In an effort to prevent Scandinavia from becoming Lutheran, Leo instructed in 1521 his nuncio, Giovanni Francesco Cina, to grant easy terms for an absolution to Christian II of Denmark for his various crimes. The pope also rewarded Henry VIII for his *Assertio septem sacramentorum* (1521) against Luther's teachings with the title "Defender of the Faith" on 26 October 1521. While Luther was concerned primarily with the sinner's trust in a loving and forgiving God and only indirectly with questions of church authority, Leo focused principally on the issue of papal power, as had his predecessors of the previous century. Leo X unexpectedly died in Rome of bronchial pneumonia on 1 December 1521 following celebrations over the expulsion of the French from Lombardy.

BIBLIOGRAPHY

Creighton, Mandell. *A History of the Papacy from the Great Schism to the Sack of Rome* (1897). New ed., 6 vols. Reprint, New York, 1969. Concentrates on political and cultural factors and assesses Leo as a skilled diplomat and churchman.

Hendrix, Scott. *Luther and the Papacy: Stages in a Reformation Conflict.* Philadelphia, 1981. Traces the evolution of Luther's thinking on Leo, from that of a kind but misinformed vicar of Christ to being the Antichrist himself.

Minnich, Nelson H. "The Healing of the Pisan Schism, 1511–13." *Annuarium Historiae Conciliorum* 16 (1984), 59–192. Based on archival research, it documents Leo's preoccupation with issues of papal power throughout the negotiations that ended the Pisan schism.

Pastor, Ludwig. *The History of the Popes from the Close of the Middle Ages.* 40 vols. Translated by Frederick I. Antrobus et al. London, 1891–1954. Volumes 7 and 8, based on the second German 1906 edition, remain the best account of Leo's pontificate.

Picotti, Giovanni Battista. *La giovinezza di Leone X.* Rome, 1981. Reprinted with a preface by Massimo Petrocchi and introduction by Cinzio Violante, this classic account of Giovanni de' Medici's childhood, education, and ecclesiastical career up to 1494 was originally published in 1928.

Rodocanachi, Emmanuel P. *Histoire de Rome: Le pontificat de Léon X, 1513–1521.* Paris, 1931. A study of the social, cultural, and ecclesiastical aspects of Rome under Leo X.

Setton, Kenneth. *The Papacy and the Levant, 1204–1571.* 4 vols. Memoirs of the American Philosophical Society, vols. 114, 127, 161, 162. Philadelphia, 1976–1984. Vol. 3, pp. 142–197, traces Leo X's efforts to organize a crusade against the Turks.

Thomas, Jules. *Le concordat de 1516: Ses origines, son histoire au 16e siècle.* 3 vols. Paris, 1910. Studies the practices prior to the Concordat of Bologna, the negotiations over the concordat, its contents, and its approval by both the Fifth Lateran Council and the Parlement of Paris.

Wicks, Jared. "Roman Reactions to Luther: The First Year (1518)." *Catholic Historical Review* 69 (1983), 521–562. Examines in detail the canonical procedures and theological responses of Mazzolini and Cajetan to Luther's writings.

Nelson H. Minnich

LEPANTO, BATTLE OF. Occurring on 7 October 1571, the Battle of Lepanto was a naval victory won by the Catholic League over the Ottoman Turks in the Gulf of Patras. Trumpeted throughout Christendom, it boosted the confidence of the Counter-Reformation and inspired countless monuments and works of art and poetry.

The victory obscured the loss of the war that erupted in 1570, when Venice refused the demand of Sultan Selim II to surrender Cyprus and turned to Pope Pius V in search of allies. Pius called for a crusade and forged through ten months of hard negotiation a Catholic League of Spain, Venice, and the papacy, to which the other Italian states also adhered. Philip II of Spain agreed to pay half the costs, Venice a third, and Pius a sixth. Because Spain and Venice needed papal approval to collect revenues from church sources, Pius bargained to achieve his ends. The allies concurred on saving Cyprus, but beyond that, Venice sought gains in the Aegean, while Philip wanted to conquer Algiers. Pius agreed to vest the supreme command in Philip II's illegitimate half-brother, John of Austria. On 24 May 1571 the league was proclaimed in Rome.

The Turks struck quickly in 1570 and by September overran all Cyprus save Famagusta, while the beylerbey of Algiers seized Tunis, a protectorate of Spain. An allied fleet under Pius's admiral sailed as far as Rhodes before the lateness of the season and the misgivings of Philip's Genoese admiral caused its return to port. Famagusta surrendered on 1 August 1571, but news of it had not reached Italy when, in mid-September, John of Austria took the league's armada—including more than 200 war galleys, six heavily gunned galleasses, and its train of storeships—to sea from Messina. The Ottoman fleet of nearly 300 galleys and galliots, anchored at Lepanto (Greek, Návpaktos) after a summer at sea, emerged to fight but suffered virtual annihilation.

The pope and Catholics in Spain and Italy offered *Te Deums* and castigated Protestants for their failure to fight the common foe of Christendom, accusing them of overtly or covertly aiding the Turks. They chided Emperor Maximilian II and the Germans for doing nothing and denounced the refusal of France to join the league because of its differences with Spain and treaties with the sultan. In France Catholic anger mounted as the queen mother Catherine de Médicis, the vacillating Charles IX, and the Huguenots worked to break the alliance of Spain and Venice. At the same time, lack of agreement among the allies allowed the Turks to crush Greek Christian uprisings prompted by the victory at Lepanto.

After the death of Pius, whose zeal held the league together, Venice in 1573 made a separate peace, using French offices, and saved Crete. The Ottomans, who gained Tunis and Cyprus, rebuilt their navy but never again terrorized the whole Mediterranean. Lepanto cost the navy prestige in İstanbul, while conflicts in the Caucasus with Persia caused the sultan to accept in 1578 a truce sought by Philip, who was forced to turn his chief efforts to the Netherlands and Atlantic wars. As Fernand Braudel remarks, after Lepanto the Mediterranean ceased being central to world history.

BIBLIOGRAPHY

Benzoni, Gino, ed. *Il Mediterraneo nella seconda metà del '500 alla luce di Lepanto.* Florence, 1974. A central work, with 23 contributions by leading scholars (13 in Italian, 6 in French, 2 in English, and 1 each in Spanish and German) that treat most aspects, including religious and cultural, and all sides of the battle, its preludes, and its consequences.

Braudel, Fernand. *The Mediterranean and Mediterranean World in the Age of Philip II.* 2 vols. Translated by Siân Reynolds. London and New York, 1976. Covers the diplomacy, battle, and campaign in great detail.

Guilmartin, John F. *Gunpowder and Galleys.* Cambridge, 1974. Brilliantly revises our understanding of galley warfare at Lepanto.

PETER O'M. PIERSON

LETTER OF MAJESTY. With this document Emperor Rudolf II granted religious liberties to the estates of Bohemia on 9 July 1609. The Protestant churches in the country, embracing a majority of the population and strongly represented among the noble estates, had previously enjoyed no constitutional guarantees, though Rudolf's father, Maximilian II, gave verbal endorsement to the Bohemian Confession submitted to him by the diet in 1575. As the local exponents of the Counter-Reformation gained ground from about 1600 under the ailing and irresolute Rudolf, the Protestant estates renewed their campaign. They were able to profit from the Hungarian insurrection under Stephen Bocskay, which yielded major religious concessions at the Peace of Vienna, and from the associated dynastic conflict between Rudolf and his brother Matthias.

By remaining loyal to Rudolf when that conflict reached its height in 1608, the Bohemians were poised to extract compensation from his crippled regime. Yet the king, however indecisive, could be stubborn, and some of his senior ministers were militant Catholics. Only after months of bargaining, during which the Protestants called the diet into session on their own initiative and threatened the use of force, did Rudolf yield; even then, his chancellor refused to sign the document.

The Letter of Majesty enacted the Bohemian Confession and extended the same protection to Protestant burghers and peasants. The Protestant estates were free to organize churches and to assume control of the existing Utraquist Consistory and the University of Prague. They were also empowered to choose thirty "defensors" as official guardians of their rights. During the next decade, both Lutherans and Bohemian Brethren worked hard to consolidate their position in the country. But Catholic obstruction precipitated the Defenestration of Prague and an armed revolt of the estates. With the collapse of this Protestant-led action at the Battle of White Mountain, the Habsburgs took immediate steps to abrogate the Letter of Majesty.

[*See also* Bohemia *and* Defenestration of Prague.]

BIBLIOGRAPHY

Gindely, Anton. *Geschichte der Ertheilung des böhmischen Majestätsbriefes von 1609*. Prague, 1858. Detailed account by the still unsurpassed political historian of the period.

Janácek, Josef. *Rudolf II a jeho doba*. Prague, 1987. Lively and authoritative modern treatment of Rudolf's reign.

R. J. W. EVANS

LEYDEN, Jan van. *See* John of Leiden.

L'HÔPITAL, Michel de (1505?–1573), chancellor of France from 1560 to 1568. His career illustrates the fate of a moderate caught between radical adversaries. While many contemporaries were swept away by overwhelming religious passion and factional enmity during the Wars of Religion (1562–1598), L'Hôpital strove to play the role of mediator between Catholics and Protestants. L'Hôpital was one of the few members of the royal council who, while sincerely wishing for religious uniformity, was convinced that the pacification of the kingdom hinged upon concessions to the Protestant party. But his policy of granting limited freedom of worship to Protestants, which he regarded as the only alternative to civil strife, aroused everyone's distrust. L'Hôpital's Catholic adversaries claimed that he was a secret Huguenot. They muttered "Dieu nous garde de la messe du chancelier," accusing L'Hôpital of going to Mass only to feign the Catholic belief. Protestant extremists, on the other hand, criticized the chancellor for irresolutely pleading for religious compromise. Suspicion about L'Hôpital's religion plagued him, despite his repeated refutation, throughout his chancellorship, and it seriously impeded the chancellor's pursuit of conciliatory religious policy.

L'Hôpital was born the eldest son of Jean de L'Hôpital, a personal physician of Constable Charles de Bourbon. When his father shared the fate of his master, who rebelled against Francis I in 1523 and fled France to serve Emperor Charles V, Michel was briefly thrown into jail but then went to Italy to study law at the universities of Padua and Bologna. Having returned to France in 1533, L'Hôpital began his public career in 1537 as *conseiller* at the Parlement of Paris—an office which his wife, Marie Morin, brought as dowry. L'Hôpital's political fortune began to blossom in 1550 when Marguerite of France, Henry II's sister, appointed him chancellor of her duchy in Berry. L'Hôpital also obtained the patronage of the powerful Guises.

L'Hôpital's relationship with the House of Guise is commonly misunderstood. Historians have amply discussed L'Hôpital's conflicts with Charles de Guise, the cardinal of Lorraine, especially their differences over religious issues during his chancellorship. L'Hôpital's early rapport with the Guises has been virtually ignored, however, perhaps because L'Hôpital's position as a client of the Guises seems inconsistent with the well-established portrayal of the chancellor as a heroic foe of the fanaticism that is often believed to represent the Guise faction. But the extensive and generous patronage of the Guises was vital in L'Hôpital's rise to power. The cardinal of Lorraine procured for L'Hôpital the office of *maître des requêtes* (1553) and exercised influence over his appointment to the presidency at the *Chambre des Comptes* (1555) and finally to the chancellorship of France (1560).

The essential aim of the royal court's religious policy in the early 1560s was to achieve a kind of forced religious compromise between Catholics and Protestants. L'Hôpital focused on finding a mean between persecution and toleration by drawing a line between political sedition and religious misbelief; thus, the Huguenots who resorted to violence should be punished, but the rest should be left in peace. L'Hôpital, addressing the Estates-General of Orléans on 13 December 1560, raised a fundamental question: "You say your religion is a true one, and I say mine is. Is it any more reasonable that I should adopt your opinion than you should adopt mine?" But the fiasco of the Colloquy of Poissy (1561) brought to an end the hope that the restoration of religious unity in the kingdom could be achieved by some form of concord or doctrinal compromise. The colloquy's failure convinced L'Hôpital that limited toleration of Protestants was the only way to escape prolonged anarchic confusion and crisis.

The Edict of Saint-Germain (January 1562) and the Edict of Amboise (March 1563) were the culmination of the policy of the separation of politics and religion, a theme that L'Hôpital consistently pursued during his chancellorship. Because of his defense of these toleration edicts, L'Hôpital has often been praised, anachronistically, as a sixteenth-century advocate of the freedom of conscience. Many historians have hailed him as a lonely apostle of toleration, driven off the stage of history by religious fanaticism. What L'Hôpital attempted to achieve, however, was not to guarantee religious freedom as a fundamental right but to stop religious hostilities and safeguard peace in the kingdom. L'Hôpital did not deny the unquestioned value of religious agreement. Yet he was also aware that, in the current situation, religious uniformity under Catholicism could not be achieved without endangering the state. L'Hôpital thus espoused the cause of toleration, less because of a moral or philosophic conviction than by way of the realization of the fundamental need for national unity and stability. L'Hôpital's toleration policy encountered, however, almost perennial resistance by the Parlement of Paris, a prominent champion of the orthodox religion. His religious policy also caused his estrangement from the cardinal of Lorraine, who never contemplated the possibility of legalizing Huguenot religious services in France.

L'Hôpital was a striking representative of Gallican royalists. He asserted that the Crown, not the pope, held control over the organization and discipline of the clergy in France and tried to resolve the problems of the French church on the national level. The Ordinance of Orléans (1561), drawn up by L'Hôpital on the basis of the *cahiers* of the Estates-General, was a clear reflection of his independent reform program for ecclesiastical institutions. L'Hôpital also attempted to create a reformed judicial structure. The main target of his reforms was venality of office, which he criticized for promoting the corruption of judges and the deterioration of administrative efficiency. In fact, L'Hôpital was one of the first statesmen in the sixteenth century who warned that the growing recalcitrance of the officeholders against the Crown, entrenched in their offices as a result of venality, was the main predicament of the monarchy. L'Hôpital's crusade against venality of office met strong opposition from the Parlement of Paris, and his judicial reforms failed to achieve much practical effect during his tenure. Yet his reform programs, epitomized in the Ordinance of Orléans, the Edict of Roussillon (1563), and the Ordinance of Moulins (1566), created precedents and arguments upon which reforming ministers in the seventeenth and eighteenth centuries could base their work.

While L'Hôpital stood accused by his adversaries, Catherine de Médicis was his closest ally and supporter. But Catherine grew increasingly impatient with the policy of conciliation and, when criticisms were heaped on the government for its seemingly vacillating attitudes, she was ready to hold her chancellor responsible for the ill-fated policy of toleration. L'Hôpital's disgrace in 1568 seemed to mark the end of any lingering hopes of resolving the unprecedented crisis of civil strife through peaceful means. L'Hôpital's misfortune was that his defense of religious moderation clashed with the religious idealism of the time. But, L'Hôpital's eloquent advocacy for toleration and the subordination of religion to civil policy inspired moderate Catholics. L'Hôpital was hence a spiritual precursor of the *politiques* party.

BIBLIOGRAPHY

Primary Sources

L'Hôpital, Michel de. *Michaelis Hospitalii, Carmina: Editio a prioribus diversa et auctior.* Edited by P. Vlaming. Amsterdam, 1732.

———. *Oeuvres complètes de Michel de L'Hospital.* 3 vols. Edited by P. J. S. Dufey. Paris, 1824–1825. Vols. 1 and 2 include L'Hôpital's speeches at the Estates-General and the Parlements, a few memoranda, scattered letters, and testament; vol. 3 is a collection of L'Hôpital's Latin poems, first published in 1585. Dufey also published *Traité de la réformation de la justice* in the two-volume *Oeuvres inédites de Michel de L'Hospital* (1826), but L'Hôpital's authorship of this work remains highly questionable. The political views expressed in the *Traité* are often irreconcilable with those expounded in L'Hôpital's public statements and other writings. See Neely's article.

———. *Poésies complètes du chancelier Michel de L'Hospital.* Translated by Louis Bandy de Nalèche. Paris, 1857.

———. *Discours pour la majorité de Charles IX et trois autres discours.* Edited by Robert Descimon. Paris, 1993. A critical annotated edition of the four major political discourses of L'Hôpital.

Secondary Sources

Amphoux, Henri. *Michel de l'Hôpital et la liberté de conscience au XVIe siècle.* Paris, 1900; reprint, Geneva, 1969. Often anachronistic, as the title suggests.

Atkinson, C. T. *Michel de L'Hospital.* London, 1900. One of the few biographies of L'Hôpital available in English.

Buisson, Albert. *Michel de L'Hospital, 1503–1573.* Paris, 1950. Provides a thorough bibliography; remains the most recent book published on L'Hôpital.

Dupré-Lasale, Émile. *Michel de L'Hospital avant son élévation au poste de chancelier de France.* 2 vols. Paris, 1875 and 1899. Based on extensive archival research, it unfortunately only covers L'Hôpital's pre-chancellor years.

Héritier, Jean. *Michel de L'Hospital.* Paris, 1943.

Kim, Seong-Hak. *Michel de L'Hôpital: The Political Vision of a Reformist Chancellor, 1560–1568.* Ph.D. diss., University of Minnesota, 1991.

Marie, Jean. *Essai sur la vie et les ouvrages du Chancelier Michel de L'Hospital.* Rennes, 1868.

Neely, Sylvia. "Michel de L'Hospital and the 'Traité de la Réformation de la Justice': A Case of Misattribution." *French Historical Studies* 14 (1986), 339–366. Convincingly refutes L'Hôpital's authorship of the *Traité*, which has been used by many historians as an important source in interpreting L'Hôpital's political ideas.

P. D. L. [Paul de la Faye de L'Hôpital]. *Quelques éclaircissements historiques et généalogigues sur M. de L'Hospital et sa famille.* Clermont-Ferrand, 1862. A polemical defense of L'Hôpital, written by a descendant of the chancellor.

Shaw, A. E. *Michel de L'Hospital and His Policy.* London, 1905.

Taillandier, A. H. *Nouvelles recherches historiques sur la vie et les ouvrages du chancelier de l'Hospital.* Paris, 1861. A thoughtful study, valuable for its use of archival materials.

SEONG-HAK KIM

LIBER BURSAE WITTENBERGAE. In 1546 Hungarian students at Wittenberg formed a loose national organization to provide assistance to Magyar students and to govern their academic, social, and spiritual life. Called the *Liber Bursae Wittenbergae* or the Hungarian *Coetus*, it was based on the model of the Hungarian Bourse at Kraków and governed by six articles. Membership in the *Coetus* was voluntary, but was restricted to those whose mother tongue was Hungarian. Throughout its history no German or Slovak from Hungary joined the *Coetus*, and not even all the Magyar students affiliated with it. The *Coetus* increased the distinction between the Magyars and the other nationalities from Hungary at Wittenberg. This was later reflected in the development of the Reformation in Hungary.

The *Coetus* was both a national and a confessional fraternity. In response to the growth of antitrinitarianism in Transylvania, the leaders of the *Coetus* revised *Regulae Vitae* in 1555 and, in 1565, added a confessional oath (*Confessio Formula Juramenti*) which repudiated antitrinitarianism. All who joined the *Coetus* were required to sign both the articles of incorporation and the oath to maintain the doctrine of the Holy Trinity before they were eligible for the substantial financial aid administered by the *Coetus*.

Melanchthon was held in high regard by the Magyars, and he showed a special interest in them and their kingdom. After his death in 1560, the majority of the members of the *Coetus* accepted the theological formulations of the Helvetic reformers, especially Bullinger and Calvin. This theological orientation of the *Coetus* eventually led to its demise. After Archduke August of Saxony sought to expunge Philippism and crypto-Calvinism from Wittenberg, the number of Magyars at Wittenberg declined. In 1613 the Hungarian *Coetus* closed and transferred its records to Hungary. By then, the majority of Magyar Protestants had accepted the theology of the Helvetic reformers.

BIBLIOGRAPHY

Stromp, Ladislaus. "Ungarn und Melanchthon." *Deutsch-evangelische Blätter*, n.s. 3 (1903), 727–746.

Szabo, Géza. *Geschichte des ungarischen Coetus an der Universität Wittenberg, 1555–1613*. Halle, Germany, 1941.

DAVID P. DANIEL

LIBERTINES. Applied disparagingly to people allegedly without moral restraint, the term *libertine* in the sixteenth and seventeenth centuries referred specifically to freethinkers, especially in religious matters. By the eighteenth century libertine came to lose its philosophical sense.

John Calvin (1509–1564) labeled as Libertines a group of pantheists associated with Quintin of Hainaut, a tailor whom he had encountered in France. These Libertines included Coppin of Lille, a Fleming who had propagandized around Lille; Bertrand of Moulins; Claude Perceval; and Anthony Pocquet, a former priest. To Calvin's consternation, Quintin found refuge at the court of Marguerite d'Angoulême (1492–1549) as doorkeeper-usher; Pocquet, as chaplain; and Perceval, as valet.

Encouraged by Valérand Poullain (26 May 1544) because of the growth of the Libertines at Valenciennes and by Guillaume Farel (2 October 1544), Calvin wrote his treatise *Contre la secte phantastique et furieuse des Libertins qui se nomment spirituelz* (Against the Fantastic and Raging Sect of the Libertines Who Call Themselves "Spirituals"; 1545). Libertines spread to Germany, the Low Countries, and Italy. Calvin attacked Libertines who spoke French, also called Quintinists, and described them as more pernicious than the papists; pantheistic and antinomian; denying the reality of evil, sin, and repentance; rejecting moral constraint; dissimulating; misinterpreting the Bible; denying the future resurrection; minimizing the humanity of Jesus and his suffering; and confusing the Holy Spirit with a diffuse indwelling spirit that permeates all things.

Calvin felt Libertines drew on heresies of the early church, Gnosticism, and Manichaeism. He considered them an Anabaptist sect that practiced community of goods and "spiritual" marriage. Scholars view Libertines as less licentious than Calvin did, heirs of medieval mysticism and pantheism.

Libertine was a term also used to describe Calvin's political opponents in Geneva, defeated in 1555, more accurately known as Perrinists after their leader, Ami Perrin. Though the two groups were distinct, some scholars suggest that spiritual Libertines influenced the Perrinists.

In the seventeenth century in France, Libertine, in a more general sense, described nonconformists to Christian orthodoxy and practice, precursors of the *philosophes* of the Enlightenment. Within that broad category *Érudits Libertins* were an elite group of freethinkers, not necessarily pantheist or anti-Catholic, which included Gassendi (Pierre Gassend, 1592–1655), priest and professor at Aix-en-Provence; François de la Mothe Vayer (1588–1672), tutor (1651) to Louis XIV (1638–1715); and Gabriel Naudé (1600–1653), doctor of Louis XIII (1601–1643).

Adversaries of Libertines assumed that free-living followed free-thinking. This dual understanding of "libertine" as theologically heterodox and morally reprobate continued in the seventeenth century.

BIBLIOGRAPHY

Busson, Henri. *La rationalisme dans la littérature française de la Renaissance, 1533–1601*. Paris, 1971.

Calvin, John. "Against the Fantastic and Furious Sect of the Libertines Who Are Called 'Spirituals.'" In *Treatises against the Anabaptists and against the Libertines*, edited and translated by Benjamin W. Farley. Grand Rapids, Mich., 1982. Translation with introduction summarizing content and historiography of the treatise.

———. "Contre la secte phantastique et furieuse des Libertins qui se nomment spirituelz" (Geneva, 1545); "Epistre contre un certain cordelier suppost de la secte des Libertins lequel est prisonnier à Roan" (1547). In *Ioannis Calvini Opera Quae Supersunt Omnia*, edited by Giulielmus Baum, Eduardus Cunitz, and Eduardus Reuss, vol. 7. Braunschweig, 1868. Two treatises of Calvin against Libertines. The second is addressed to the God-fearing in Rouen to warn them against a Franciscan attracted to Libertine teachings.

Jundt, Auguste. *Histoire du panthéisme populaire au moyen âge et au seizième siècle (suivie de pièces inédites concernant les frères du libre esprit. Maître Eckhart, les Libertins spirituels, etc.)* (1875). Reprint, Frankfurt a.M., 1964. Views the spiritual Libertines as heirs of medieval pantheism. Rejects Calvin's association of them with Anabaptism.

Spink, J. S. *French Free-Thought from Gassendi to Voltaire.* London, 1960. Traces Libertines from Calvin's use of the term for pantheists associated with Quintin of Hainaut to seventeenth- and eighteenth-century moral reprobates, free thinkers, and *philosophes*.

Verhey, Allen. "Calvin's Treatise 'Against the Libertines.'" Translated by Robert Wilkie and Allen Verhey. *Calvin Theological Journal* 15.2 (November 1980), 190–219. A translation of chapters 13–16 of the treatise, in which Calvin deals with God's providence and the determinism of the Libertines. The introduction summarizes the context and historiography of the treatise.

JEANNINE E. OLSON

———. "William Lily." In *Dictionary of National Biography,* edited by Leslie Stephens and Sidney Lee. Reprint, London, 1921–1922.

Trapp, J. B. "William Lily." In *Contemporaries of Erasmus,* edited by Peter G. Bietenholz and Thomas B. Deutscher, vol. 2. Toronto and London, 1986.

Verzeichnis der im deutschen Sprachbereich erschienenen Drucke des XVI. Jahrhunderts. Stuttgart, 1983–. See vol. 11, nos. 1746–1750.

MARIA DOWLING

LIEBER, Thomas. *See* Lüber, Thomas.

LILLY, William (c.1468–1522), English humanist. Though most famous as an influential Latin grammarian, Lilly is also notable, along with William Grocyn and Thomas Linacre, as one of England's earliest Greek scholars. After studies at Oxford, Lilly went on pilgrimage to Jerusalem. He studied at Rhodes, and then at Rome under Sulpizio and Pomponius Laetus. He settled in London about 1500 and became an intimate friend of Thomas More. With More he composed *Progymnasmata* (published in 1518 but composed much earlier), which were versions of Greek epigrams in Latin elegiacs. For More he translated Lorenzo Spirito's *Libro della sorte,* a work on divination by dice. His learning was praised by Bernard André (*Hymni Christiani,* 1517) and by Richard Pace (*De fructu qui ex doctrina percipitur,* 1517). Among his fifteen children was the scholar George Lilly, whose account of his father appears in Paolo Giovio's *Descriptio Britanniae* (1548).

William Lilly was the first high master of John Colet's humanist School of Jesus, formally founded at Saint Paul's Catherdral, London, in 1512. Among his pupils were Thomas Lupset and John Leland. For the school he composed two grammars, *Grammatices rudimenta* (c.1509) and *De octo orationis partium constructione libellus* (1513). At Colet's request Erasmus revised this last work. Lilly's two works formed the basis of Henry VIII's official grammar, *An Introduction of the Eight Parts of Speech* (c.1540); hence this book was known inaccurately as "Lilly's grammar." Lupton remarks that his fame as a grammarian is surprising considering the brevity of his work and speculates that much was probably due to his teaching methods. Lilly died before the Reformation crisis gripped England, and his religious opinions are unknown, though presumably they were conservative. He is significant because his grammatical works gave exegetical and polemical tools to both Catholic and Protestant divines.

BIBLIOGRAPHY

Alston, R. C., ed. *William Lily and John Colet: A Short Introduction of Grammer, 1549.* Menston, England, 1971.

Dowling, Maria. *Humanism in the Age of Henry VIII.* London, Sydney, and Dover, N.H., 1986.

Lupton, Joseph Hirst. *A Life of Dean Colet* (1887). Reprint, Hamden, Conn., 1961.

LINACRE, Thomas (c.1460–1524), pioneer in several fields of humanist study, most notably in medicine. Linacre was one of the few Englishmen who traveled to Italy for scholarship in the late fifteenth century. Between 1487 and about 1493 he studied Greek and Latin in Florence under Demetrius Chalcondyles and Angelo Poliziano; in Vicenza under Niccolò Leoniceno; and in Rome, where he met Ermolao Barbaro. In 1496 he received his medical degree from Padua University, and in 1497–1499 he helped the Venetian printer Aldo Manuzio with the first edition of Aristotle in Greek. Manuzio published Linacre's Latin translation of Pseudo-Proclus's *De sphaera* in 1499.

Back in England, Linacre was appointed physician to Henry VIII (1509) and to Henry's sister Mary (1514), and was Latin tutor to the king's daughter Mary (c. 1523). He composed four works of Latin grammar, two of which were popular on the Continent and were frequently reprinted.

Linacre used his Greek scholarship chiefly for medical studies; thus O'Malley calls him "the first English medical humanist." Between 1517 and 1523 he published Latin translations of six of Galen's works. His aim, as O'Malley shows, "was to help the practicing physician, and in consequence he decided to present those works of Galen which had application to clinical medicine." In 1518 Linacre founded the Royal College of Physicians in London with Henry VIII's support. He also established medical lectureships at Oxford and Cambridge.

Linacre numbered many eminent humanists among his friends: Erasmus, Guillamme Budé, Niccolò Leonico, John Colet, Thomas More, William Grocyn, William Latimer, and William Lilly. His religious opinions are unknown. He was an ordained deacon and a flagrant pluralist, confessing to Archbishop William Warham that his desire was to achieve leisure for a literary life. Thus he is typical of those pre-Reformation scholars who regarded church office as a source of income for study rather than as a spiritual or pastoral calling.

BIBLIOGRAPHY

Maddison, Francis, Margaret Pelling, and Charles Webster, eds. *Essays on the Life and Work of Thomas Linacre.* Oxford, 1977. Commemorative volume by Linacre College, Oxford; the fullest and most authoritative work on the subject.

O'Malley, C. D. *English Medical Humanists, Thomas Linacre and John*

Caius. Lawrence, Kans., 1965. Short, critical study focused chiefly on Linacre's medical interests.

Schmitt, Charles B. "Linacre, Thomas." In *Contemporaries of Erasmus*, edited by Peter G. Bientenholz and Thomas B. Deutscher, vol. 2, pp. 331–332. Toronto, Buffalo, and London, 1986. Concise and useful account of Linacre's career.

Verzeichnis der im deutschen Sprachbereich erschienenen Drucke des XVI. Jahrhunderts. Stuttgart, 1983–. See vol. 11, nos. 1762–1780.

MARIA DOWLING

LINCK, Wenceslaus (1482–1547,) theology professor at Wittenberg, friend of Martin Luther, popular preacher, and leader in early Reformation church organization. Born on 8 January in Colditz, Saxony, Linck began his studies at the University of Leipzig in 1498. The monastery at Waldheim, where he had become an Augustinian monk, sent him to Wittenberg in 1508 to continue his studies. He received his baccalaureate in 1504 and his master's degree in 1506. In 1511 he became one of four Augustinians to receive a doctorate at Wittenberg, inaugurating a new and significant contribution of this order. He remained at Wittenberg as prior and dean of the theology faculty.

In 1516 he made his first visit to Nuremberg to preach at Saint Vitus's. He was such a popular preacher that the humanist circle led by Staupitz, which included Willibald Pirckheimer, Lazarus Spengler, Albrecht Dürer, and several leading patricians, became known as Linck circle by the following year. The thirty sermons he preached in 1519 on the beatitudes are early examples of his reform message intended for a popular audience.

In 1518 he attended the Heidelberg Disputation and traveled with Luther and Johannes von Staupitz to the meeting with Cajetan in Augsburg. He replaced Staupitz as vicar-general in 1520 and in this capacity visited sixty-six of the German and Dutch monasteries of the order. Acting as vicar-general, he released monks from their vows at their request before he himself resigned from the order.

In 1522 the Altenburg city council called him to replace Gabriel Zwilling as preacher, and he assumed a leading role in the Reformation there. In 1525 he persuaded Elector Frederick III of Saxony to spare the peasants captured in the Peasants' War with the exception of two leaders. This is an early indication of his role as an advocate of peaceful resolutions to religious and political differences. At Altenburg Linck introduced Communion under both kinds and was married by Luther to Margarethe Schweizer. They had ten children, including a son who attended the University of Wittenberg.

Six months after the disputations in Nuremberg, the Nuremberg city council called him to a preaching position there. He was initially assigned the job of reforming the convent of the Sisters of Saint Clare, led by Caritas Pirckheimer. He, like the others before him, failed to sway her convictions and ceased his efforts when Philipp Melanchthon arrived to inaugurate the new gymnasium. He then assumed his duties as preacher of the New Hospital Church and custodian of its charitable endowments, a position he held until his death.

When Anabaptist preaching began to agitate Nuremberg, Linck assumed a moderate stance, advocating pastoral intervention to convert citizens to the right beliefs. To this end, he published with Andreas Osiander in 1528 a guide on how "Pastors should admonish and teach the people concerning the Anabaptists."

Among his many publications were catechisms, as well as paraphrases and annotations of the Old Testament. His work has been eclipsed by Luther's own editions, but it is worth noting that Linck wrote many of the introductions to Luther's publications. His later life indicates his importance in the ecclesiastical organization of the new church. He contributed to the agreement with Margrave George of Brandenburg-Ansbach that resulted in the church ordinance of 1533. The Nuremberg city council sent him and Osiander as representatives to the ecumenical colloquies at Worms. He died on 12 March 1547 and is buried in the cemetery of Saint John in Nuremberg.

Linck's importance lies in his relationships at Wittenberg with Luther, Staupitz, Georg Spalatin, and Melanchthon, all of whom were lifelong friends and correspondents. As Staupitz's successor as vicar-general of the German Augustinians, he permitted their dissolution in 1522 after allowing monks to be released from their vows. In Altenberg, Thuringia, from 1522 to 1524 and in Nuremberg from 1525 until his death, he was an important leader in the developing reform movement as adviser to both city councils, creator of educational and liturgical literature for youth, and reformer of the secularization of welfare. He is perhaps best known as a popular preacher who, Luther observed, could teach others how to preach. Some ninety extant sermons and sixteen translated or edited works are cited in *Bibligraphia Linckiana.*

BIBLIOGRAPHY

Primary Sources

Kolk, Helmich van der, ed. *Erbauungschriften: Eigene Schriften aus dem Jahren 1526–1536, nebst vier von Linck überseltzten bzw. neu herausgegebenen Schriften aus den Jahren 1524 und 1525.* Amsterdam, 1978. Available, and with modern print and critical notations with useful bibliography.

Pfeiffer, Gerhard, ed. *Quellen zur Nürnberger Reformationgeschichte.* Nuremberg, 1968. This brings together many scattered items mostly still only in manuscript form.

Reindell, Wilhelm, ed. *Werke.* Vol. 1. Marburg, 1894. Rare, but the only printed sources for his early works.

Scheurl, Christoph. *Christoph Scheurl's Briefbuch: Beitrag zur Geschichte der Reformation und ihrer Zeit.* Edited by Franz von Soden and J. F. K. Knaake. 2 vols. Aalen, 1962. First published at Leipzig, 1862.

Verpoorten, Alberg Meno, ed. *Sacra Superioris aevi analecta, in quibus variorum ad Venceslaum Lincum epistolae plures quam septuaginta. Ex tabulis Manuscriptis in lucem protulit.* Coburg, Germany, 1708. Contains correspondence not found in Luther's works.

Secondary Sources

Bendixen, R. "Wenzeslaus Link." *Zeitschrift für kirchliche Wissenschaft und kirchliches Leben* 8 (1887), 40–55, 72–79, 138–153.

———. "Linck, Wenzeslaus." In *Theologische Realencyclopedia*, vol. 18, 174ff. Leipzig, 1888.

Caselmann, Hermann Wilhelm. "Wenzeslaus Link's Leben für christliche Leser insgemein aus den Quellen erzählt." In *Das Leben der Altväter der lutherischen Kirche*, edited by Moritz Meurer, pp. 321–428. Leipzig, 1863.

Daniel, Charles. "The Significance of the Sermons of Wenzeslaus Linck." Ph.D. diss., Ohio State University, 1968. Contains many short quotations from the sermons translated into English.

———. "Hard Work, Good Work, and School Work: An Analysis of Wenzeslaus Link's Conception and Civic Responsibility." In *The Social History of the Reformation*, edited by L. P. Buck and J. W. Zophy, pp. 41–51. Columbus, Ohio, 1972. Emphasizes Linck's moral earnestness and educational attitudes.

Lorz, Jürgen. *Bibliographia Linckiana: Bibliographie der Gedruckten Schriften Dr. Wenzelaus Lincks, 1483–1547*. Nieuwkoop, 1977. Very helpful.

———. *Das reformatiorische Wirken Dr. Wenzeslaus Lincks in Altenburg und Nürnberg, 1523–1547*. Nuremberg, 1978. Important critical work. Contains correspondence to and from Linck and prints the ones not previously printed.

Reindell, Wilhelm. *Doktor Wenzeslaus Linck aus Colditz, 1483–1547: Nach ungedruckten und gedruckten Quellen dargestellt. Erster Teil.* Marburg, Germany, 1892. Now rare, but indispensable.

CHARLES E. DANIEL, JR.

LINDANUS, Wilhelmus (Dutch, Willem Damaszoon van der Lindt; 1525–1588), Catholic theologian, inquisitor, and bishop of Roermond and Ghent. He belonged to the new generation of clergy—the well-schooled, ardent defenders of Catholicism. Among the stimuli that moved him in this direction were his theological studies in Louvain and Paris and the influence of his mentor, Ruard Tapper. Lindanus's first chance to put zeal into practice came in 1557, when he was charged by the Spanish king to restore Catholic authority in Friesland and to prepare the province for the implementation of the decrees of the Council of Trent. He clashed often and bitterly with stubborn local authorities, including the Council of Friesland, long accustomed to independence of action; by 1560 they had compelled Lindanus to give up his efforts.

Soon afterward, however, Lindanus was named bishop of Roermond and inquisitor of Holland and Zeeland. Especially the latter assignment brought him into conflict with local authorities, owing to the confessional tensions of the time and his dogmatic, resolute approach. Yet Lindanus was no unbending, fanatical heresy hunter in the mold of Pieter Titelmans: his primary goal was (re)conversion. His protest against the obstacles that hindered the full functioning of the Inquisition led to his resignation of that post in 1565. During this early period Lindanus also wrote a number of pastoral handbooks, including a catechism and several hefty polemical works against calls for a reconciliation of Protestant-Catholic differences, namely by the Confession of Antwerp and Joris Cassander. As a theologian he came into conflict with the circle of Christoffel Plantijn, who published the Royal Bible.

Only in 1569 was Lindanus able, with the help of Fernando Álvarez de Toledo, duke of Alba, to take possession of his diocese. During the first seven years he displayed enormous energy, faithful to the model prescribed by Trent. In extraordinarily trying circumstances, he succeeded in making two visitations of his diocese, calling together five diocesan synods and giving clear shape to the organization of the diocese. The old hard-liner was, through personal contact with his flock, transformed into a true shepherd. He showed special care for the poor and for religious education. During this time Lindanus wrote not only apologetics but also pious meditations and sermons.

In 1576 the war with the northern Netherlands compelled him to flee Roermond. He remained active in church diplomacy, promoting especially a policy of cooperation between the church and Spain. The year 1587 saw Lindanus transferred to the bishopric of Ghent, but his episcopacy there was too short to make any real impact.

It was especially his obstinate character and apostolic zeal that made Lindanus a major figure. Many contemporaries regarded him as a saint, while others found him insufferable. An important biography by a near contemporary, the Carthusian Arnold Havens (Havensius), was published in 1609 and was based largely on Lindanus's lost autobiography. The last years and writings of Lindanus still await a historian.

BIBLIOGRAPHY

Beuningen, P. Th. van. *Wilhelmus Lindanus als inquisiteur en bisschop: Bijdrage tot zijn biografie, 1525–1576*. Assen, 1966. A biography of Lindanus to 1576, with further detail.

Havensius, Arnoldus. *Commentarius de erectione novorum in Belgio episcopatuum, deque iis rebus, quae ad nostram hanc usque aetatem, in eo praeclare gestae sunt*. Cologne, 1609. Contains the first biography of Lindanus.

Schmetz, Wilhelm. *Wilhelm van der Lindt (Wilhelmus Lindanus): Erster Bischof von Roermond, 1525–1588, Ein Beitrag zur Kirchengeschichte des Niederrheins und der Niederlande im 16. Jahrhundert*. Münster, 1926. A biography of Lindanus to 1569.

Verzeichnis der im deutschen Sprachbereich erschienenen Drucke des XVI. Jahrhunderts. Stuttgart, 1983–. See vol. 11, nos. 1923–1952.

Willemsen, M. A. H. "De werken van Wilhelmus Lindanus, eersten bisschop van Roermond." *Limburgs Jaarboek* 2 (1895), 204–233. Gives a description of the works of Lindanus.

MARIE JULIETTE MARINUS

Translated from Dutch by Craig Harline

LIPSIUS, Justus (also Joest Lips; 1547–1606), Flemish humanist, neo-Stoic, and Christian. Born at Overijsche, near Brussels, on 18 October 1547, Lipsius was the burgomaster's son and brought up as a Roman Catholic. He attended the Jesuit college at Cologne and the University of Louvain. Between 1568 and 1570 Lipsius served Cardinal Antoine Perrenot de Granvelle (1517–1586) as his secretary for Latin correspondence in Rome. Of crucial importance for Lipsius's intellectual development was his friendship with the French humanist Marc-Antoine Muret (1526–1585), whose interest in practical philosophy was accompanied by a predilection for the anti-Ciceronian style. The concise, terse, almost military language of Tacitus and Seneca would henceforth become known as the Lipsian style. Upon his return to Louvain, unsettled political and personal conditions made Lipsius leave the Southern Netherlands. In 1572, he was appointed to the chair of rhetoric and history at the Lutheran University of Jena. After only two years, however, he returned to Cologne to complete the first of his many editions of the *Taciti Opera* (1574), which brought the young scholar instant fame. A general amnesty enabled Lipsius to complete his law studies at Louvain in 1576, but, his religious orthodoxy in question, he decided to accept the chair of history at the newly founded Calvinist University of Leiden.

During his Leiden period (1579–1591). Lipsius published his two most influential works, which provided the philosophical and political underpinnings of neo-Stoicism, or the so-called Netherlands Movement. Lipsius set out to reconcile Roman Stoicism and Christianity, but the call for activity and perseverance clearly distinguished his neo-Stoic philosophy from its classical model. In *De Constantia* (1584) Lipsius taught that there was no real difficulty in reconciling the Stoic notion of *fatum* with the Christian emphasis on the free will as ordained by God. Influenced by Machiavelli, Badin, Guiccardini, and the sixteenth-century Spanish theological jurists, Lipsius in his *Politicorum* (1589) supported monarchy and moderate absolute government. Lipsius's postfeudal state was characterized by a princely ruler who knows how to blend the contrary elements of power and moderation and to impose discipline on himself, as well as on his subjects. Although Lipsius propagated freedom of conscience, his defence of the principle of "cuius regio eius religio" led to a public controversy with the Dutch spiritualist theologian Dirk Volkertszoon Coornhert (1522–1590). Lipsius subsequently left Leiden and made peace with the Jesuits at Mainz in 1591.

His return to Catholicism gained Lipsius a professorship of history and Latin at Louvain (1592), the post of royal historiography to Philip II (1594), and election as honorary member of the state council of Brabant (1605). He lost some of his intellectual independence, however, and was forced to rewrite part of his *Politica.* During these years Lipsius published two important treatises on the art of war, *De Militia Romana* (1595) and *Poliorceticon* (1596); issued two final expositions of Stoic philosophy, *Manuductionis ad Stoicam* (1604) and *Physiologiae Stoicorum* (1605); and edited Seneca's *Opera Omnia* (1605). He died on 23 March 1606 at Louvain. Neo-Stoicism was an international spiritual and intellectual movement that was able to cross the boundaries of the conflicting confessions during the most destructive phase of the age of the religious wars (1575–1650). To the citizens of the Republic of Letters, it provided a "third way" between the colliding forces of the Reformation and Counter-Reformation. As such, it constituted an intermediate stage in the secularization of society and the formation of the early modern state.

BIBLIOGRAPHY

Primary Sources

Lipsius, Justus. *Variarum Lectionum Libri Quattuor.* Antwerp, 1569.

———. *Taciti Opera.* Antwerp, 1574.

———. *De Constantia Libri Duo.* Antwerp, 1584.

———. *Politicorum sive Civilis Doctrinae Libre Sex.* Leiden, 1589.

———. *De Vna Religione Adversus Dialogistam Liber.* Leiden, 1590.

———. *De Militia Romana Libri Quinque.* Antwerp, 1595.

———. *Poliorceticon sive de Machinis, Tormentis, Telis, Libri Quinque.* Antwerp, 1596.

———. *Admiranda, sive De Magnitudine Romana Libri Quattuor,* Antwerp, 1598.

———. *Manuductionis ad Stoicam Philisophiam Libri Tres.* Antwerp, 1604.

———. *Physiologiae Stoicorum Libri Tres.* Antwerp, 1604.

———. *Monita et Exempla Politica Libri Duo.* Antwerp, 1605.

———. *Opera Omnia Philosophi Seneca.* Antwerp, 1605.

Secondary Sources

Bibliographie lipsienne: Oeuvres de Juste Lipse. 3 vols. Ghent, 1886–1888. Comprehensive list of all the contemporary editions of Lipsius's works.

Bireley, Robert. *The Counter-Reformation Prince: Anti-Machiavellianism or Catholic Statecraft in Early Modern Europe.* Chapel Hill and London, 1990. Important study on the international anti-Machiavellian tradition founded by Lipsius and the Italian political writer Giovanni Botero (1544–1617).

Croll, Morris W. *Style, Rhetoric and Rhythm.* Reprint, Woodbridge, Conn., 1989. Collection of essays dealing with Lipsius and Muret and the anti-Ciceronian, Atticist movement.

Gerlo, A. M., et al. *Iusti Lipsi Epistolae.* 3 vols. Brussels, 1978–1987. Lipsius's correspondence including his later changes and falsifications in his *Epistolarum Selectarum Centuria* published from 1586.

Gerlo, A., and H. D. L. Vervliet. *Inventaire de la Correspondance de Juste Lipse, 1564–1604.* Antwerp, 1968. Inventory of the correspondence of Lipsius, including 4,300 letters with more than 700 correspondents.

Morford, Mark. *Stoics and Neostoics, Rubens and the Circle of Lipsius.* Princeton, N.J., 1991. Impressionistic account of the relationship between the teachings of Lipsius and the work of the Flemish painter and diplomat Peter Paul Rubens (1577–1640).

Oestreich, Gerhard. *Neostoicism and the Early Modern State.* Cambridge, 1982. Critique of Dilthey and his disregard for the role of political Neostoicism in the constitutional development of the early modern state.

Saunders, Jason Lewis. *Justus Lipsius: The Philosophy of Renaissance Stoicism.* New York, 1955. Classical account of the life and works of Lipsius and analysis of Stoic ethical and physical theory.

Vervliet, H. D. L. *Lipsius's Jeugd, 1547–1578, Analecta voor een kritische Biografie.* Mededelingen van de Koninklijke Vlaamse Academie voor Wetenschappen, Letteren en Schone Kunsten van Belgie. Klasse der

Letteren, vol. 31, no. 7. Brussels, 1969. Deals with the "Brabant period" of Lipsius until his departure to Leiden.

MARCUS P. M. VINK

LISMANINO, Francisco (1504–1566), Italian prelate. Born on the island of Corfu in 1504 of half-Uniate and half-Roman parents, Lismanino was brought as a boy to Kraków. After completing studies in Italy, Lismanino entered the Franciscan order. In 1533, on the invitation of his Italian friends at Queen Bona Sforza's court at Kraków, Lismanino joined them in Poland. Appointed cantor (1538) and court preacher in Italian, Lismanino swiftly rose in influence as confessor to the queen and as superintendent of the Franciscan order in Poland, Lithuania, and Czech lands. He was the order's provincial head until 1554.

Meanwhile, Lismanino obtained a Paduan doctorate (1540) and received income from a Czech bishopric and as a professor at the Jagiellonian University. He was an adviser to the queen on such matters as liberalization and reformation of the church and aided in the choice of bishops. The queen gave him Bernardino Ochino's sermons to read.

Between 1550 and 1553 as royal confidant, Lismanino, twice a week after dinner, read privately to the king, Sigismund II Augustus, from John Calvin's *Christianae religionis Institutio* and discussed points of doctrine with him. In 1553 Lismanino left Poland as the king's agent to augment the royal library and also to visit foreign theologians, and on his return he was to report on all aspects of their churches. Apparently the king had a mind to introduce reform into the Polish church. While in Switzerland Lismanino was drawn to Heinrich Bullinger, who recommended him to Calvin. Calvin lobbied for Lismanino to join the reform movement. The books were sent for the royal library, but Lismanino stayed behind in Switzerland. He resided in Geneva from November 1554 until February 1555, married a Huguenot, and listened to Calvin's lectures on alternate weekdays.

In September 1555 the Reformed church at Pínczów elected Lismanino as co-superintendent. Lismanino accepted the invitation, arriving back in Poland at the end of March 1556. This angered the king, who abandoned any plans to reform the Polish church. The noble Stanisław Ivan Karniński protected him at Alexandrowice, some five miles west of Kraków. Meanwhile, the church at Pínczów in April 1556 called Jan Łaski to direct their affairs and invited Calvin and Théodore de Bèze to Poland. After more than a year in hiding Lismanino helped to revise the confession of the Bohemian Brethren (from 28 December 1556 to January 1557). Lismanino met Łaski at Kraków in February 1557. He received a cool reception then, as well as four months later in June at Włodzisław. Suspected of hidden Lutheran sympathies by Łaski's friends, Lismanino threatened to move to Kroliewiec to be with Pier Paolo Vergerio. Instead of this he went to meet Philipp Melanchthon at Wittenberg. Lismanino's Polish translation of Ochino's discussion of papal authority, *O Zwierzchnósci Papieskiej*, was published in 1558 in an effort to attract Lutheran landholders to Calvinism.

In 1558 Giorgio Biandrata joined the Protestant community in Minor Poland and became involved in a controversy with Francis Stancarus over the sole human mediatorship of Christ. Calvin's warnings about Biandrata in November 1558 were of little avail. In August 1559 Lismanino helped to produce a compact confession at Pínczów that responded to Stancarus. It was organized around the mediatorial triple office of Christ as prophet, priest, and king.

At Pínczów in 1560 Lismanino translated in part another of Ochino's writings—*Disputa intorno alla presenza del Corpo di Gesú Christo nel sacramento della Cena*—as the *Traiedyi o mszej*. With the death of Łaski on 8 January 1560, Lismanino and Biandrata assumed greater prominence as "secular seniors," or superintendents, of the Reformed churches. The Stancarus debate, however, had caused a tumult with the orthodox Reformed leaders, as Lismanino was attacked by Stancarus and Calvinists alike, both Polish and foreign. In 1561 Lismanino resigned. Caspar Cruciger, superintendent of the Reformed congregations in Minor Poland, released him from his functions, which included inspector of the churches, in October 1562.

Late in 1562 and early in 1563, Lismanino wrote his *Brevis explicatio doctrinae de sanctissima Trinitate,* which included collected patristic citations and comments of Thomas Aquinas. He added to it the Polish synodal statements at Kraków (1561) and Pínczów (1562) and a dedication to King Sigismund II Augustus. Published in Königsberg in 1565, it received a cool reception in Kraków and Lublin. Lismanino subsequently traveled and requested a permanent pension, which he received from Prince Nicholas Radziwill.

At the end of April 1566 Lismanino died in Kroliewiec from a fall into a well under mysterious circumstances. Was it the result of epilepsy, or did he commit suicide? This is uncertain since he was found in the well without his clothes. His situation at the time was none too pleasant, aggravated by his theological controversies, the unfaithfulness of his wife, and the payment of his pension in counterfeit money.

BIBLIOGRAPHY

Barycz, Henryk. "Meandry Lismaninowskie." *Odrodzenie i Reformacja w Polsce* 16 (1971), 37–67. Recent account of Lisamanino's itinerary as a reformer.

———. "Lismanin, Franciszek." In *Polski Słownik Biograficzny,* edited by Fabian Legendary and Alexander Lubomirski. Warsaw, 1972. Summary by leading authority on the Polish Reformation.

Lorenz, Heinz. *Italienische Protestanten und ihr Einfluß auf die Reformation in Polen während der beiden Jahrzehnte vor dem Sandomirer Konsens, 1570.* Leiden, 1974. Convenient summary of Lismanino's activities. Appendix 2 (pp. 100–104) contains the *Confessio de Me-*

diatore qeneris humani Jesu Christo Deo et homine from 10 August 1559 as drafted at Pińczów, along with a modern German translation.

Lubieniecki, Stanisław. *Historia Reformationis Polonicae . . . finitimis provinciis narrantur* (1685). Facsimile ed. Warsaw, 1971. Includes details from a history written by Stanisław Budziński, Lismanino's secretary. Also in English as *History of the Polish Reformation, with Nine Related Documents,* translated, edited, and illustrated by E. Morse Wilbur, Marek Wojsblum, and George H. Williams, Minneapolis, 1994.

Sandii, Christophori. *Bibliotheca Antitrinitariorum* (1684). Facsimile ed. Warsaw, 1967. Gives brief account on pp. 34–35 and lists letters and publications of 1563 and 1565.

Sippayłło, Maria, ed. *Acta synodolia ecclesiarum Poloniae reformatorum.* 2 vols. Warsaw, 1966–1972. Contains documents that Lismanino prepared and edited.

Williams, George H. *The Radical Reformation.* 3d ed. Kirksville, Mo., 1992. Contains numerous references to Lismanino as well as a partial English translation of the *Confessio de Mediatore generis humani Jesu Christo Deo et homine* of 10 August 1559.

Wotschke, Theodor. *Der Briefwechsel der Schweizer mit den Polen.* Leipzig, 1908. Letters of Lismanino and others, somewhat dated.

———. "Francisco Lismanino." *Zeitschrift der historischen Gesellschaft für die Provinz Posen* 28 (1910), 213–332. Point of departure for modern study.

Marvin W. Anderson

LITERACY. Protestantism is sometimes called "the religion of the book." Martin Luther, Philipp Melanchthon, and other reformers advocated the instruction of ordinary people so that they might achieve faith through a knowledge of God's word as embodied in the scriptures. The age of the Reformation saw the beginnings of a momentous shift from the closely restricted reading and writing of the Middle Ages to the mass literacy that Westerners have come to regard almost as a birthright. To understand the special importance of literacy in the Reformation, three questions need to be answered. What was "literacy" in early modern Europe? What effect did the Reformation have on the spread of literacy and its products, printed and written? And how did reading and writing influence religious life?

Early modern literacy was made up of several skills that are best seen as bands in a spectrum rather than discrete categories. Reading of print or writing was possible at two levels. Some people could decipher texts, read them aloud, and memorize them, though their personal understanding may have been questionable. Those with better education and a deeper immersion in printed and written culture could comprehend the text with greater precision and thus read and think silently to themselves. Reading, however, was not restricted to written or printed words alone. People could gather information and ideas from looking—interpreting pictures and prints in broadsheets and pamphlets or watching and participating in plays and processions. If they wanted to transmit their own thoughts other than through speech, they had to learn to write, or rather compose—an advanced skill that required considerable training and practice and that effectively marked "full" literacy for most people. The other, more common level of writing was, in fact, copying: writing without necessarily understanding. It was at this stage that people learned to sign their names on documents, and this ability is commonly used as an indicator that someone could read and understand printed and written texts in the venacular language. In other words, such a person was well along the road to full literacy. A small minority of men and an even smaller minority of women could also copy or compose in Latin, the international language of learning in the sixteenth century. Even those who had none of these skills were not culturally isolated, for they could listen—hear a priest's sermons or a friend reading aloud, as well as participate actively or passively in discussions with their peers. Religious conversion could come to those who only heard, saw, and memorized, and it is important not to regard their experience as inferior to that of friends and neighbors who read and wrote. By the same token, the understanding and facility of many of those "readers" should not be exaggerated.

It is known that this broad spectrum of skills existed and that few people were wholly "illiterate," even in 1500. But individuals unquestionably operated on different cultural levels depending on the range of literacy they possessed. If it is accepted that looking and listening were nearly universal, there are still the questions of who could read and write, how this changed over time, and what effect it had.

The century of the Reformation was a time of growing educational provision, and religion was at the heart of basic instruction. The number of schools grew dramatically, causing one historian to speak of an "educational revolution." For example, the duchy of Württemberg had 89 schools in 1520 compared with more than 400 by 1600, and across Germany in this period many rulers issued ordinances providing for or regulating elementary education. Catholics also expanded education. The first "school of Christian doctrine" was opened at Milan in 1536 to teach children the essentials of the Catholic faith. There were 28 such schools by 1564 and more than 120 in 1599.

Post-elementary education also expanded. Perhaps 1,000 new grammar schools were established in England from 1480 to 1660, while the Jesuits had set up an extensive and highly respected network of secondary education across Catholic Europe by 1650. In many parts of Europe both the number of colleges and universities and the percentage of young men attending institutions of higher education increased markedly. Separate seminaries existed to educate Italian clergy from the 1560s. One effect was a substantial growth in the number of parish clergy who were well educated. This development may in the long run have improved their ability to edify and educate their flocks, but religious flux and time lags meant the impact was not generally felt before the start of the seventeenth century. Formal education at all levels became more widely available, though not all the expansion can be attributed to religious changes. Political developments—the expanding state system with its need for trained officials—and burgeoning economic expansion also played vital roles.

Drives for education and the desire for learning had to overcome significant obstacles. Basic learning, such as instruction in the catechism (a set of questions and answers on central issues of faith that were to be memorized), was free, but beyond that education usually involved some cost. Because most rural families were poor and child labor was essential to their economic well-being, formal education was intermittent and brief. Thus, in practice, developments in schooling tended to favor the more privileged groups in society. Given their small disposable incomes, even those ordinary people who could read might find access to the printed word restricted by cost.

At the same time, the ideological assumptions of the age dictated that anything except basic religious instruction was inappropriate to certain social groups, such as women and the laboring classes. In other words, religious change certainly stimulated education and literacy, but it could not always overcome the secular constraints of an underdeveloped economy and a deeply traditional culture. This helps to explain why the expansion of literacy was often slow and uneven.

Religious authorities recognized the difficulties. They insisted that schools were not the only means of inculcating basic religious knowledge and that families could also be agents of the Reformation; fathers were charged with a responsibility to ensure godliness and morality among those under their roof. In a country that had few formal schools, the Swedish Lutheran church of the seventeenth century made home learning the core of a highly successful campaign of religious education.

The aim of basic education was to produce "passive" readers and memorizers. From an early date, reformers were on the horns of a dilemma. Reading books and pictures could help to inculcate the "correct" religious ideas, and illiterates were sometimes held to be "superstitious." But thinking about contents and writing down ideas might also introduce or perpetuate notions of which the mainstream churches, Protestant as well as Catholic, disapproved. Luther himself had advocated widespread reading and individual interpretation of the Bible in the early 1520s, but, shocked by the Peasants' War of 1525, he began to stress that the reformed faith should be explained to ordinary folk and that "safe" means of indoctrination, such as the catechism, should be sought. Secular authorities were also keen to prevent the spread of certain new ideas lest they interfere with order and stability within their territories. Luther's change of position highlights the important point that starting people on the road to full literacy opened up a so-called Pandora's box. Once men and women began to read, contemplate, and discuss the scriptures for themselves, it became impossible for the initiators of ideas to determine how they would be received and developed. The growing fragmentation of Protestantism even before Luther's death was partly attributable to this potential.

Educational expansion and rising literacy fed on and were nourished by the printed word. The spread of the word was helped enormously by the advent of printing by movable type in the mid-fifteenth century and its rapid expansion between then and 1600. Religious works in manuscript had circulated among heretics before and during the fifteenth century as part of a tradition of pious lay reading in the vernacular. Yet printing allowed a much wider dissemination of standard texts. Luther saw printing as "God's highest and extremest act of grace, whereby the business of the Gospel is driven forward" through the scriptures. Nearly 250 European centers had printing presses by 1500. Germany had print works in most major towns by 1520, and those produced an unprecedented outpouring of books—perhaps 300,000 copies of Luther's writings from 1517 to 1520. From the dawn of the Reformation, new religious ideas were available to the reading public. By 1530 perhaps 4,000 pamphlet titles had been produced in Germany, and throughout the sixteenth century as many as 200 million copies may have been turned out across Europe. They could be bought from publishers, shops, and stalls in towns as well as from itinerant peddlers in the countryside.

Between 40 and 50 percent of all editions of books published between 1460 and 1600 in the major cities of western Europe were religious. Religious works were normally the largest single category in a bookseller's stock. Not surprisingly, book ownership reflected the preoccupation with religion. Across Europe religious titles were dominant among books recorded in the inventories of the dead. In the sixteenth century the majority of those who left any books among their goods had only religious texts. The Bible was certainly among these, but in France and Germany during the sixteenth and seventeenth centuries it was far outnumbered by books of hours (portable books of private piety) and other modest devotional books of prayers and psalms. The English may have been particularly avid Bible owners and readers during the seventeenth century, but even at this date catechisms remained more common than Bibles as teaching aids in Dutch schools.

People could borrow works from friends (lending libraries did not exist until the eighteenth century), and there were cheap little pamphlets that might not be mentioned in documents. Restricted book ownership, however, was one sign of ordinary people's focus on "intensive" reading before the eighteenth century. They pored over, read out, and discussed a handful of works. More proficient, critical readers from the professional and noble classes owned a wider range of reading material, both secular (practical and recreational) and religious, and practiced more extensive reading. But among the peasants, craftsmen, and tradesmen who made up the majority of Europe's population, reading tastes were narrow and specific.

One problem in seeking more precise measures of reading and writing is that, in contrast to the contemporary world, extensive documentation of people's lives was rare three or four centuries ago. Nevertheless, it is clear that reading and writing were on the increase during the sixteenth and seventeenth centuries. Judged by the rather advanced skill of signing, the most pronounced early expansion occurred among the middle and upper class males in towns. In northern England the illiteracy of the gentry fell from about 30 percent in 1530 to almost nil in 1600, but that of day laborers stayed well above 90 percent during the same time period. One bridegroom in three could not sign Amsterdam's marriage register in 1630, compared with two-thirds of brides. Towns in seventeenth-century northern Italy were islands of extensive and high-quality literacy in a sea of rural backwardness.

The early years of the Reformation saw only gradual improvements in literacy. The drive for literacy was given fresh impetus by the Reformation, but it was not new, it was not unique to Protestantism, and its effects were felt only slowly. Seventeenth-century achievements were more substantial. The campaign to promote religious literacy in Scandinavia produced remarkable results. As late as the mid-seventeenth century only about one-third of adults were able to pass the church's tests of reading, but a century later more than four of five men and women could read. Sweden and Finland (one country in those days) are examples of areas where widespread literacy consolidated rather than caused religious change. In Denmark and Prussia it was not the Lutheran Reformation of the sixteenth century that brought about widespread literacy but the early eighteenth-century campaign waged by the Pietists with the help of the new "absolutist" rulers. Even so, one authority assigns critical-reading ability in the German lands to just 10 percent of the population as late as 1750.

Slowly and hesitantly, however, literacy was increasing. Did the expansion favor Protestants more than Catholics? The extensive literacy of the Dutch, Scots, and New Englanders in the eighteenth century stands alongside their commitment to Calvinism. The Catholic conservatism of rural France, Poland, and Spain cannot be divorced from deep illiteracy. But was it simply a question of faith? In the north of Ireland during the seventeenth century, Protestant farmers were better able to sign their names than Catholic ones, but they were also richer and lived in less remote areas. Protestants and Catholics, in fact, were not distributed equally among all sections of society. In seventeenth-century Poland virtually all the Calvinist minority were either nobles or town dwellers. Crude divisions between faiths, however, often break down under examination. Ability to sign was as common in staunchly Catholic northeastern France as it was in Protestant England at the end of the seventeenth century.

Some argue that Catholic and Protestant reformers had as much difficulty improving the outward conformity, moral behavior, literacy, and religious knowledge of ordinary people—that is, "Christianizing" them—as they did persuading them that one path to salvation was better than another. Qualitative evidence from rural Swabia in southwestern Germany suggests that even half a century after Luther's death ignorance of his message was still extensive. The same was true of some contemporary Calvinist areas of Germany and the Netherlands. This is known from visitations carried out by well-educated and theologically sophisticated churchmen, but because they had high expectations, it is important not to write off the masses as ignorant and irreligious merely on their say-so. The religious knowledge of many ordinary people may have seemed inadequate and erroneous, but it was appropriate to the lives they led and to the communal cultures that had shaped their minds. The values of family, neighborhood, and community—topics that cannot be understood simply through the study of religious literature—were important in determining which Protestant ideas were assimilated and how. Religion was part of everyday life for sixteenth-century people, even if they were less enthralled by its theological detail than the churches might have liked.

Yet, even using the broad criteria of looking, listening, reading, and memorizing, it cannot be said that all men and women had achieved the basic knowledge required by the Lutheran church. Judged by the same benchmark, achievements might have been just as good (or bad) in the staunchly Catholic Spanish kingdom of Castile. Those who appeared before the church courts for religious or moral transgressions were examined by the judges on their religious understanding. Just 40 percent of accused adults knew the Ten Commandments well in the 1560s and 1570s, but by the 1590s the figure rose to 80 percent, while the proportion thought to be crassly ignorant fell during the same time period from 50 percent to less than 10 percent. Dynamic Counter-Reformation Catholicism could produce results comparable with those of the Lutheran heartland.

The distinction between the faiths was more subtle than crude literacy rates suggest but no less important. Qualitative differences in the uses and importance of literacy distinguished Protestants from Catholics. Reading scripture was central to the reformed faith. Religious books were probably read more frequently among Protestants, and the very status of reading was special. Protestants tended to own more books on a wider variety of religious topics than their Catholic neighbors and to use them differently. Protestants accepted the overwhelming authority of what they knew or thought was in a religious book.

This does not mean that Catholicism should be condemned as obscurantist and antireading. The Catholic hierarchy wanted literacy to spread but in a controlled way, with the priest as intermediary in the process of understanding. Catholic leaders, however, seem to have regarded some types of reading as a threat rather than an invitation to sound beliefs. Indeed, it is plain that inability to read was construed by authorities in some areas—for example, Spain and Bohemia—as a sign of Catholic orthodoxy, immunizing one from contamination by Protestant ideas. Simply possessing a book was a sign of heresy. If illiteracy was equated by some with superstition, others, such as an Italian priest writing around 1530, could claim that "all literate people are heretics." In short, there is no conclusive proof of the direction of the relationship between Protestantism and literacy, but the bond was stronger than that between Catholicism and literacy.

Overall, religious change had direct and indirect effects on education and literacy. On the one hand, competing churches were anxious to provide instruction in their particular faith, establishing schools and other educational initiatives to "push up" men, women, and children toward God. This usually caused an increase in the supply of education, though the dominant faith sometimes tried to suppress instruction run by their opponents, as Protestants did in the late sixteenth-century Dutch province of Utrecht. The desire to create communities worthy of God encouraged adherents to Calvinism to provide or lobby for schooling, with profound results for the wider society in which they lived: seventeenth-century Scotland, the Netherlands, and pockets of east-central Europe, such as Transylvania, are examples. By the end of the seventeenth century the Protestant churches had made enormous headway in providing or guiding basic education and inculcating religious rote learning and low-level reading skills. Religious change also had indirect effects on literacy. The development of written and printed forms of languages as diverse as Slovene, Welsh, and a phonetic representation of Irish for evangelization and instruction stemmed primarily from religious needs. Moreover, Luther's vernacular writings helped to shape modern German, and modern French was influenced by the works of Calvin.

On the other hand, the ideological ferment of the Reformation and Counter-Reformation, coupled with economic development, created a strong demand for learning, both for spiritual enlightenment and for material advancement. This powerful force encouraged people either to seek out education or to teach themselves, possibly with help from literate friends and neighbors. Self-education was especially important for those living in isolated regions or coming from disadvantaged groups, such as women and the poor. Given the priorities of most educators, this demand, along with an appreciation of the potential of full literacy, probably had a more powerful impact on the spread of reading with understanding and of writing. The initial ideological fervor of the Reformation stimulated literacy by idealizing the pious reading laity, proffering an ideal of a theologically literate layperson. By fostering more extensive, more personal, and more private reading, Protestantism eventually altered the nature of literacy itself.

The Reformation broke on European societies with restricted reading and writing, and literacy spread only slowly in the first century of the reformed faith. Therefore, should the importance of print and writing on the reception and spread of Reformation ideas be questioned? That depends both on the period and the social group in question. First, the key figures of the early Reformation—not only theologians but the ordinary laity who were in the vanguard of Lutheran and Calvinist advances—should be considered. Literacy clearly helped the development of ideas among leaders of the reformed faith in its early years, as they read, wrote, and communicated with each other. Those who lobbied for the Reformation in such cities as Erfurt in the 1520s and 1530s or Edinburgh in the 1580s, as well as those who formed the core of Calvinist congregations in the towns of southern France around that date, came disproportionately from the ranks of merchants and professionals. They would already have been proficient in reading and writing thanks to their social backgrounds and business needs. They read the new ideas, saw their importance, and sought to implement them. Small wonder, then, that some historians see Protestantism as an "urban theology."

Particularly for Calvinists, literacy was almost a badge of membership: becoming literate and becoming religious were synonymous for believers to whom writing was as important as reading. Calvinists were encouraged to take their own notes of sermons for later perusal, and many late sixteenth- and seventeenth-century diaries were written by Calvinists for religious purposes. Indeed, during the sixteenth and seventeenth centuries Calvinism probably did more to encourage individuals to acquire the full spectrum of literacy—especially reading with understanding, copying, and composing—than did Lutheranism.

Reading and writing were much less important for the bulk of farmers, laborers, and the urban lower class, which formed perhaps 90 percent of the people in Europe. Most of them could not have read and understood Luther's more elaborate theological message in the early sixteenth century. Perhaps two out of every hundred were accomplished, comprehending readers, and they alone could have mopped up the entire output of Lutheran literature. Calvin's *Institutes* would probably have been far beyond all but this most accomplished group.

An important novelty of Lutheran writings was their availability in the vernacular rather than in Latin, the restricted language of scholarship. But a vernacular pamphlet in what was later to become standard French might as well have been in Latin to the millions of French men and women who spoke only a patois, or provincial language, such Breton, Flemish, Occitan, or Basque. There were no printed religious works in patois, Protestant or Catholic, before the mid-seventeenth century. The relatively low literacy of northern Irish Catholic farmers noted above was partly because they spoke Irish, whereas English was the language of education and functional literacy. Even type-faces could present a barrier. Many basic spelling books of the sixteenth century were printed in Gothic face, also known as "black letter" type. Regulations posted in German churches and courts conventionally used these characters, whereas literature was increasingly printed using the Latin type familiar to modern readers but accessible only to those with relatively advanced literacy.

Yet Lutheranism had the potential to be a mass movement speaking to all social classes. To understand how ideas spread, it is necessary to turn away from the written or printed word and look again at seeing and hearing. In the first decades of the Reformation, new ideas were conveyed to the masses through visual propaganda, which criticized abuses in the Catholic church and built up an alternative vision of salvation. Protestants replaced the visual piety of saints and relics with that of broadsheets. Rich in imagery, these broadsheets either consisted wholly of a picture or mixed words with woodcut or copperplate illustrations. Broadsheets were as numerous and easily available as printed books and pamphlets; because they were cheaper and because they were entertaining as well as edifying, they commanded larger audiences among the common people. Reformers, as well as the businessmen who made money catering to the demand for broadsheets and pamphlets, tailored the message to the medium. Even marriage "charters" or certificates carried religious messages in words and pictures in seventeenth-century France, and broadsheets continued to be an important means of communicating religious ideas in eastern Europe until the nineteenth century.

Books, pamphlets, and even broadsheets cost money. The spoken word was free, and it was also uniquely powerful, for verbal communication could be speedy, discrete, and fiery, whereas print and writing were slow, public, and possibly unemotive. Information could be transmitted only as quickly as a man on horseback could carry it (Germany had extensive trading networks), and print was therefore no faster than the spoken word. All early modern rulers and churches practiced censorship, and it was much easier to curb printed ideas than the spoken word. Written or printed forms certainly fixed expressions and ideas, but they were imperfect as a way of conveying the meaning or the fervent conviction of a speaker or writer.

It is not surprising, then, that written supplications from satellite villages of the major cities of Germany—asking first and foremost for evangelical preachers—testify to the preoccupations of ordinary Lutherans with the spoken rather than the printed word. The peasants from Lower Alsace (now along the border of France and Germany) who flocked to the city of Strasbourg did not need to be able to read and write in order to listen to sermons in the city's churches and cathedral. Nor was the flow one way. Charismatic preachers from the towns carried the Protestant message deep into the countryside, which was seen as a bastion of religious traditionalism. Informal meetings where religious works were read aloud and discussed were especially important for women, whose literacy was generally inferior to men's. If only one man or woman was literate in a village, he or she could read aloud or tell others the message of a pamphlet or broadsheet. The Bible—viewed as the living word of God as well as a text—was meant to be both heard and read. Reading was often a complement to visual literacy or the spoken word rather than a substitute for it. Pamphlets provoked oral debates, which in turn fed the printing presses. Print, writing, orality, and imagery interacted in a process of religious and cultural change.

Slowly but surely a profound transformation took place as literate means of communication came to dominate religious and cultural life. Printed literature had a substance and a permanence that oral communication lacked, and it could not so easily be ignored. Merely by circulating, Protestant pamphlets heightened awareness of the Reformation as an event, regardless of how widely they were read or understood. Symbolically as well as literally and in defense as well as in attack, the power of printed and written forms contributed to the Reformation.

The speed or the extent of the transformation again must not be exaggerated. The catechism was a powerful tool of religious instruction precisely because it bridged the oral-literate divide. Stage plays, music, and processions were still used to convey a religious message in southern and eastern Europe during the seventeenth century, by which time English Protestant leaders had turned decisively against traditional dramaturgy. Hymn singing remained for many Protestants a regular and primary expression of devotion and emotional religious experience. In the eighteenth century handwritten texts, singing, and community reading kept alive prohibited Protestant beliefs in parts of Bohemia, despite the efforts of the Counter-Reformation.

Medieval religion and the culture that surrounded it was based on images, symbols, and acts. It was visual, concrete, oral, and participative. By the seventeenth and eighteenth centuries the cultural universe of at least some social groups had become much more print-oriented, abstract, didactic, nonvisual, private, and silent. Reading privately allowed different and more varied interpretations than reading aloud in a group. By the late sixteenth century in England (although much later in eastern and rural southern Europe) people were moving from a culture based on orality and images to one based on print. An illustration is the way hybrid pamphlets, which combined a pictorial woodcut or engraving with text, were superseded by those made up of words alone. Society was also moving toward more private, introspective reading, where personal understanding was central, and the individual's relationship with God was increasingly mediated through the printed word.

This was the real legacy of literacy, for it became part of private religious faith, and it helped to restructure the mental world in which people lived. Paradoxically, the development of identifiably modern literacy—reading extensively with critical understanding and composing letters and literature—which was associated with religious change, ultimately meant impoverishing the skills of looking, listening, and talking, which had first given the Reformation substance among the people of early modern Europe.

What, then, is the connection between literacy and religious change during the Reformation? As with any historical issue relating to large groups of people, the solution is complex. By most criteria, literacy was restricted in pre-Reformation Europe. In all its forms literacy was far more widespread in 1720 than it had been in 1520. Its impact on the Reformation was profound, but religious change in turn affected both the demand for reading and writing and the supply of education. Literacy had more influence among certain types of Protestantism than others. Its power lay in symbolism as much as in literal content, and it was just one means of transmitting ideas. Reading and writing do not explain all the successes of Protestantism, while the reformed faith was not the sole reason for expanding education and literacy. The effects of both religious change and developing literacy were mediated by existing cultural forms, ideological assumptions, and material circumstances. The more widespread availability of writing and print did ultimately restructure thought, but the pace and depth of change varied considerably across Europe. Broadly defined, literacy was hugely important to the Reformation, but it should not be equated solely with schools, books, and book learning, nor understood in isolation from the wider context of early modern culture and society. Religious faith in the age of the Reformation was of the heart as well as the mind and of the ears as well as the eyes.

BIBLIOGRAPHY

Biller, P., and A. Hudson, eds. *Heresy and Literacy, c.100–c.1530*. Cambridge, 1994. Contains the most recent work on the antecedents of the Reformation.

Chartier, Roger. *The Cultural Uses of Print in Early Modern Europe.* Translated by Lydia G. Cochrane. Princeton, 1987. Collected essays of one of the principal cultural historians of Early Modern France. Important ideas, though not all about religious uses of literacy.

Chartier, Roger, ed. *The Culture of Print: Power and the Uses of Print in Early Modern Europe.* Translated by Lydia G. Cochrane. Oxford, 1989. Edited collection covering fifteenth to eighteenth century.

Collinson, Patrick. *From Iconoclasm to Iconophobia: The Cultural Impact of the Second English Reformation.* Reading, 1986. The 1985 Stenton lecture. A subtle and challenqing interpretation of intellectual and cultural change.

Graff, Harvey J. *The Legacies of Literacy: Continuities and Contradictions in Western Culture and Society.* Reprint, Bloomington, Ind., 1991. Dense but particularly good on humanist and early Protestant educational ideas.

Grendler, Paul F. *Schooling in Renaissance Italy: Literacy and Learning, 1300–1600.* Baltimore, 1991. Comprehensive overview in English of Italian developments. Part 4 particularly useful.

Houston, R. A. *Literacy in Early Modern Europe: Culture and Education, 1500–1800.* London, 1989. Unrivalled geographical coverage in a comprehensive and readable overview with an extensive bibliography.

Robinson-Hammerstein, Helga. *The Transmission of Ideas in the Lutheran Reformation.* Dublin, 1989. Important collection of conference papers on literate and oral communication.

Scribner, Robert W. *For the Sake of Simple Folk: Popular Propaganda for the German Reformation.* 2d ed. Oxford, 1993. Central text in English on the German lands, expanded and updated since its first appearance in 1981.

Watt, Tessa. *Cheap Print and Popular Piety, 1550–1640.* Cambridge, 1991. Only monograph in English to make a major contribution to debates on literacy and religion since work cited in Houston.

R. A. HOUSTON

LITHUANIA. Founded in the thirteenth century in the basins of the Nemunas (Neman) and Neris rivers, the Lithuanian state expanded during the fourteenth century into the territory occupied by the Eastern Slavs, thus forming the grand duchy of Lithuania (which would be divided between the Russian and Prussian empires at the end of the eighteenth century). The Union of Lublin of 1569 formed a confederation between Lithuania and the kingdom of Poland. The two countries had a common king, senate, and parliament but retained their separate territories, state officials, judicial systems, armies, and citizenship. In the mid-sixteenth century the grand duchy of Lithuania covered an area of about 550,000 square kilometers and had at least 3.7 million inhabitants. By the mid-seventeenth century it encompassed an area of about 300,000 square kilometers with a population of 4.5 million, composed of Lithuanians, Byelorussians, and Ukranians, as well as Polish and German settlers in the towns. Around 1550 the Lithuanians made up more than 1 million of the population and inhabited a compact area of about 80,000 square kilometers. In 1387 the Lithuanians adopted Catholicism. The Eastern Slavs were Orthodox, and the Tartars adhered to Islam. The Lithuanians spoke Lithuanian, but for writing official documents they used Latin, the office language of the Eastern Slavs, and from the mid-sixteenth century Polish as well. A part of the upper strata of society were bilingual.

Some of the western Lithuanians living close to the Baltic Sea—as well as the Curonians, Skalvians, Suduvians, Nadruvians, and Prussians living between the Nemunas, Pregel, and the lower reaches of the Vistula and Bebra rivers—were conquered by the Teutonic Knights in the thirteenth century. In 1525 the state of the Teutonic Order became the duchy of Prussia, where the Lutheran church was introduced between 1525 and 1529. The descendants of the conquered Baltic tribes and the Lithuanian settlers from the Lithuanian state constituted the majority of the rural population between the middle reaches of the Pregal and the lower reaches of the Nemunas in the Prussian duchy. This territory was called Lithuania Minor, which adopted the Lutheran faith as its state religion.

In the grand duchy of Lithuania the Reformation began in the 1530s among the higher nobility, the boyars, the clergy, and the townspeople. They were dissatisfied with the conservative character of the Roman Catholic church, its vast wealth exempt from taxes, the system of education (there were no secondary schools or university in Lithuania), and the incompetence of the ecclesiastic courts. They sought to separate the administration of the Lithuanian church from the church province of Poland, to modernize religion and church management, and to effect changes in the social structure. They profited from direct contact with the centers of the Reformation in Germany and Switzerland while studying at the universities of Basel, Leipzig, Wittenberg, Königsberg, Frankfurt an der Oder, and other cities, from the knowledge acquired from Reformation publications, and from the migration of Protestant clergy from Poland. The first period of the Reformation, extending from the 1530s to the 1550s, was Lutheran in character. A humanist secondary school was founded between 1539 and 1542 in Vilnius by some Lithuanian clergymen and teachers from the lesser gentry. They also prepared theological texts for print and translated some liturgical texts into the Lithuanian language. At this stage the supporters of the Reformation movement were not numerous, and the grand duchy of Lithuania supported the Catholic church. For this reason the first Lutherans had to emigrate to the Prussian duchy and work in Lithuanian churches, as well as at the University of Königsberg (founded in 1544) training pastors from among the local Lithuanians. The pastor Martynas Mažvydas (Martin Mosviolius) of Ragaine, who was from Lithuania, published in Köningsberg (under the sponsorship of Duke Albert of Brandenberg) the first book in the Lithuanian language, *Catechismusa prasty szadei* (The Simple Words of Cathechism; 1547). Together with his colleagues he prepared hymnbooks and other materials, thus introducing a model of written Lithuanian for public use. This marked the beginning of the history of literature in the Lithuanian language. In 1591 Jonas Bretkūnas (Johan Bretke) published the *Postile* and translated the whole of the Bible into Lithuanian.

The second period of the Reformation started in the 1550s, when Reformed teachings took hold. During the second half of the sixteenth century more than two hundred congregations were established in small and large towns and on manors. The most powerful families of the higher nobility of Lithuania and the boyars, such as the Radvilas, Šemetas, Narusevičius, Kenstortas, and Bilevičius, adopted Protestantism. In 1557 the Lithuanian Evangelical Reformed church, separate from that in Poland, came into being. It embraced all the congregations in the territory of the grand duchy of Lithuania, as well as the two provinces given over to the kingdom of Poland after 1569. Church administration was in the hands of the provincial synod of the Evangelical Reformed church, which convened annually in Vilnius. Standing apart from the Evangelical Reformed church in the 1560s were the Arians, who advocated antipedobaptist and antitrinitarian views. They formed the Church of Lithuanian Brethren with ten congregations, of which those in Vilnius, Naugardukas, and Iwie were the most vital. Toward the end of the sixteenth century the Arian congregations became fewer. Their views on the Trinity underwent an evolution from tritheistic to unitarian and a negation of Christ's divinity. Their social views evolved from prohibiting the use of serf labor to an acceptance of serfdom. Lutheran congregations were found in the major towns of Lithuania—Vilnius and Kaunas—as well as on some estates. All the rulers, however, were staunch Catholics. The privilege of 1568 proclaimed equal rights for the boyars confessing various Christian faiths in the grand duchy of Lithuania. The Warsaw Confederation of 1573 extended this toleration to the entire state of Poland-Lithuania. The act was included in the Lithuanian Statutes of 1588, which was valid until 1840.

The Counter-Reformation began in the second half of the sixteenth century, when the Catholic church sought to reform itself in the grand duchy of Lithuania according to the provisions of the Council of Trent. The course of Catholic reform was affected by the presence of the Reformation. Books in the Lithuanian language were prepared, the Jesuit order was invited into the country in 1569, a number of colleges and the University of Vilnius (1579) were founded, and the buildings and wealth of the churches were reclaimed through legal actions. Catholic candidates to official positions enjoyed the support of the king. Some of the families of the higher nobility and boyars were reconverted to the Catholic faith (e.g., one branch of the Radvilas, the dukes of Nesvyzius and Myras). Protestantism served as a bridge for some of the nobles of Slavic origin (the Sapiegas and the Vainas) to be converted from the Orthodox to the Catholic faith. At the end of the sixteenth century the adherents of the Evangelical Reformed church began to build churches and schools again. Evangelical Reformed congregations struck roots in the lands of the Radvila (the dukes of Biržai and Dubingiai in northern and central Lithuania, respectively), in the towns of Biržai and Kėdainiai, and in the lands of the Bilevičius, Šemetas, and Gruževskis families in Samogitia. At the end of the sixteenth century there were in the grand duchy of Lithuania about 190 congregations of the Evangelical Reformed church, about 10 congregations of the Evangelical Lutheran church, and a few Arian churches.

An agreement on joint action was reached by the members of the Evangelical Reformed and the Lutheran churches in the Polish and Lithuanian states at Sendomir in 1570. But the churches themselves remained separate. In

1599 members of the Evangelical Reformed church in the grand duchy of Lithuania concluded an agreement with the Eastern Orthodox believers, who had not signed the 1596 Brest Union. Active evangelical reformers Andrius Velanas and Adomas Rasius proposed reforming the social structure to reduce the isolation of the estates, increase the influence of individuals and the city population, and restrict the privileges of the boyars.

The activites of evangelical converts in the area of education and book publishing (the whole Bible was translated into Lithuanian in Oxford by Samuelis Beguslavas Chylinskis) as well as their endeavors in the sphere of intellectual life had an inspiring effect on Catholics and prompted them to rapidly introduce innovations: they founded new competing schools, prepared books for publication in Lithuanian, and maintained printing houses. The Reformation proved an active force promoting Lithuania's cultural development from the mid-sixteenth to the mid-seventeenth century. Despite the proclaimed equality of all Christian faiths, the church of the Evangelical Reformed in Vilnius was destroyed by fanatical crowds in 1591, 1611, 1639, and 1682. The library and the archives of the church were burned in 1611. By the 1640 edict of parliament (Seimas), the Vilnius church of the Evangelical Reformed was moved outside the wall of the city. From the 1630s the activities of the Protestants were restricted by edicts of parliament in the state of Poland-Lithuania. They were forbidden to build new churches or to seek converts from Catholicism to Protestantism. The rights of the Lutheran city population, especially in Vilnius, were protected by privilege of King Vladislav Vasa (1633). In accordance with the 1658 edict of parliament, Arians were expelled from the state. The Lithuanian economy was ruined by the wars with Russia and Sweden conducted in the mid-seventeenth century. The remnants of the Protestants managed to rebuild only a limited number of their churches. Those that were restored lasted until the Soviet occupation of Lithuania in the mid-twentieth century.

BIBLIOGRAPHY

Brakas, Martin, ed. *Lithuania Minor: A Collection of Studies on Her History and Ethnography*. New York, 1976. Covers Lithuanian national culture, names of places, geographical position.

Ivinskis, Zenonas. *Die Entwicklung der Reformation in Litauen bis zum Erscheinen der Jesuiten* (1569). Sonderdruck aus Forschungen zur osteuropäischen Geschichte, vol. 12. Berlin, 1967.

Kosman, Marceli. *Reformacja i Kontrreformacja w Wielkim Ksiestwie Litewskim w świetle propagandy wyzaniowej*. Wrocław, 1973. A comprehensive survey based on publishing activities in the sixteenth and seventeenth centuries. Overestimates the contribution of Polish activists to the reform movement in Lithuania.

Kot, Stanislaw. *La Réforme dans le grand-duché de Lithuanie: Facteur d'occidentalisation culturelle*. Annuaire de l'Institut de philologie et d'histoire orientales et slaves, vol. 12. Brussels, 1953. Studies local developments within the context of western Europe.

Lukšaitė, Ingė. *Lietuvių kalba reformaciniame judėjime XVIIa*. Acta Historica Lithuanica, vol. 5. Vilnius, 1970. A study of the use of the Lithuanian language in the seventeenth-century Evagelical Reformed church.

Musteikis, Antanas. *The Reformation in Lithuania: Religious Fluctuations in the Sixteenth Century*. East European Monographs. New York, 1988. Studies the reform movement in Lithuania and Prussia.

Puryckis, Juozapas. *Die Glaubenspaltung in Litauen in 16. Jahrhundert bis zur Ankunft der Jesuiten im Jahre 1569*. Fribourg, 1919.

Ulčinaitė, Eugenija, and Juozas Tumelis, eds. *Stanislovas Rapalionis*. Vilnius, 1986. Contains documents and articles by various authors on the activities of one of Lithuania's first Protestants.

Williams, George H. "Anabaptism and Spiritualism in the Kingdom of Poland and the Grand Duchy of Lithuania: An Obscure Phase of the Pre-History of Socinianism." In *Studia nad Arianizmem*, edited by Ludwik Chmaj, pp. 215–262. Warsaw, 1959.

INGĖ LUKŠAITĖ

Translated from Lithuanian by Birute Kiškyte

LITURGICAL CALENDAR. Like all calendars, the liturgical calendar is rooted in the seemingly universal assumption that time is uneven in quality; it acknowledges the seasonal rhythms of agricultural work, as well as days of particular meaning for Christian history. During the Middle Ages and in the sixteenth century, the liturgical calendar provided not only the framework for the annual schedule of liturgical celebration but also a system of reckoning time that was widely used in secular business.

Late Middle Ages. By the late Middle Ages the liturgical calendar comprised the weekly rhythm of worship on Sunday, the Lord's day, as well as two different annual cycles that set the feast days Christians would celebrate throughout the year. Feast days were uneven in importance and celebrated with varying degrees of solemnity. The seasonal cycle, called the Temporale, was set by the third century. Anchored in the life of Christ, it consisted of three great seasons—Christmas, Easter, and Pentecost—that defined for Christians their experience of Christ's life. The other cycle, called the Sanctorale, developed incrementally from late antiquity through the Middle Ages and varied somewhat from region to region. The Sanctorale's cadences were different from those of the Temporale; it was not anchored to a single life, with its specific, dramatic, and essential cycle, but to the lives of hundreds of saints.

The Temporale began with the first Sunday in Advent. Advent was defined in various ways during the Middle Ages, but by 1300 comprised the four Sundays that preceded Christmas. The liturgy of Advent commemorated Israel's anticipation of Christ's birth. Christians normally observed Advent with moderate penance, fasting, and abstinence from meat; clergy enjoined laypeople to refrain from marrying and sexual relations during the season. Christmas consisted of twelve days in the liturgical calendar, beginning on Christmas Eve (24 December), and concluding on the feast of the Epiphany (6 January). During this season Christians also celebrated the feast of Christ's circumcision (1 January). Throughout the Middle Ages Western Christians agreed that the anniversary of Christ's birth be observed on 25 December—liturgically, with a solemn Mass, and privately, with a festive meal and almsgiving. Elaborate public celebrations and lavish exchanges of gifts that have come to be identified with Christmas were virtually unknown before the late seventeenth century. The season between Epiphany and Easter held one major feast: Candlemas (2 February), identified for centuries as the Virgin Mary's purification following Christ's birth but increasingly also celebrated as Christ's presentation in the temple.

The next great season was Easter. This season was not fixed: reckoned in relation to the phases of the moon, following the ancient practice for Passover, Easter could fall anywhere between March 23 and April 26. The Easter season began formally with the first day of Lent. Lent was reckoned in two different ways at the beginning of the sixteenth century. According to the older manner, Lent comprised the forty-two days, or six weeks, preceding Easter Sunday. The reform of 1091 mandated a different manner of counting: the six Sundays of those six weeks were to be excepted, so that the total number of days preceding Easter Sunday in Lent was forty-six (forty plus the six Sundays). According to the new manner, Lent began on Ash Wednesday.

The Easter season was the most dramatic of the liturgical seasons. In the days immediately preceding Lent, the laity celebrated Carnival (Fastnacht or Fasnacht). Not a clerically sanctioned holiday, Carnival called attention to Lent, the excesses of Carnival underlining the austerities of Lent. During Carnival the laity danced, drank, and ate to excess and ridiculed the clergy and the ordering of their everyday lives. During Lent no one feasted on the Eucharist, which was withheld during the entire period; the pious, both lay and clerical, fasted, abstained from sexual relations, and gave up the pleasures of the flesh to concentrate on the penitence of their spirits. So, too, the contrast of Carnival and Lent was marked visually in the churches. On Ash Wednesday the altarpieces would be closed, the lights of the churches dimmed, and the colors quieted. Six Sundays marked the cadences of Lent: Invocavit, the first Sunday; Reminiscere; Oculi; Laetare; Judica, or Passion Sunday; and Palm Sunday.

Palm Sunday, which had its origins in Passover (*1 Cor.* 5:7–8) and had been celebrated since the fourth century, marked the beginning of Holy Week and Christians' final approach, after six weeks of purification, to the miracle of the Resurrection. In late medieval towns Christians reenacted Jesus' entry into Jerusalem by carrying palms in processions. On Maundy Thursday, four days later, laity and clergy commemorated the Last Supper by washing the feet of twelve humbler persons—for example, the poor, lepers, the handicapped, or choristers. At sunset of Maundy Thursday began the Easter triduum, the three days of Easter. At the conclusion of the Thursday service, the altar would be stripped of its decoration; all images and crucifixes would be covered until Easter vigil. On Good Friday, Christians commemorated Christ's crucifixion liturgically by venerating the cross and singing psalms of reproach. Extraliturgical commemorations included mystery plays dramatizing the crucifixion and popular rites of laying an effigy of Christ in a "grave" and keeping watch until Easter morning. Easter Sunday was an exuberant celebration of the Resurrection: all images, crosses, and crucifixes were unveiled, and the churches were lit up with candles, their colors once again exploding. Outside church laypeople stopped work, feasted on meat, and gave alms. Easter Sunday was further distinguished in the liturgical calendar: the Fourth Lateran Council (1215) had decreed that Christians must receive Communion once a year—on Easter. Christ's ascension into heaven following his resurrection was commemorated in the Feast of the Ascension, celebrated on the Thursday that fell forty days after Easter Sunday.

The third great season of the Temporale was Pentecost. The feast of Pentecost was celebrated fifty days after Easter. Like Easter, it had origins in a Jewish feast—in this case, Shavuot (*2 Cor.* 3:7–8). Pentecost commemorated the day when the Holy Spirit descended among Jesus' disciples as they prayed together following his ascension. On that day tongues of fire rested on the disciples, and "all of them were filled with the Holy Spirit and began to speak in other languages, as the Spirit gave them ability" (*Acts* 2:3–4). The day was celebrated with a solemn mass, frequently embellished by the ritual release of a white dove. The long season of Pentecost included one more major feast: Corpus Christi, apparently first celebrated in the early Middle Ages but declared by thirteenth- and fourteenth-century popes a more solemn feast commemorating Christ's presence in the Eucharist. During the late Middle Ages the evolution of an increasingly complex eucharistic theology was accompanied by increasingly elaborate liturgical celebrations of Corpus Christi that included citywide processions, public feasts, and mystery plays.

Over the Temporale was laid the second annual cycle, the Sanctorale. The Sanctorale comprised two levels of saints: those of universal importance to the life of the church, such as the Virgin Mary, John the Baptist, apostles, evangelists, early martyrs, church fathers, and founders of major religious orders; and those whose importance was local, immediate to a specific community, region, or country. The birth dates of saints were commemorated—John the Baptist on 24 June, Mary Magdalene on 22 July, Mark on 25 April, Luke on 18 October, Peter on 29 June. Also included were other dates of particular holiness, such as the conversion of Paul on 25 January, the Feast of Michael and the Angels on 29 September, and All Saints' Day on 1 November. The Virgin had her own cycle, which included commemoration of her conception (8 December), birth (8 September), and purification (2 February); the annunciation (25 March); and her assumption (15 August). Local holy men and women—those thought to have founded local Christian communities or whose relics were venerated locally—were celebrated in geographically restricted areas. The intensely local character of late medieval Christianity meant that such saints were often more cherished and elaborately commemorated than were those of universal relevance. The birthdays of saints Felix and Regula in Zurich, Geneviève in Paris, and John the Baptist in Florence were not only solemn liturgical feasts but also occasions on which communities celebrated local history and identity.

Sixteenth-Century Reforms. The liturgical calendar was not a focus of Protestant reform, but Protestant reform of worship altered the experience of the liturgical seasons. All Protestant churches retained the Temporale, marking the great seasons of Christmas, Easter, and Pentecost, but its cadences became less dramatic, less a force in the lives of Christians, for a number of reasons. Although Protestant reformers by no means agreed on the extent to which scripture should be the authority for the liturgy and liturgical calendar, even minimal adherence to a scriptural test for liturgical feasts—such as Martin Luther's—eliminated the more dramatic celebrations of the Temporale, and at the very least pruned many feasts from the Sanctorale. Protestant elimination of the cult of saints removed individual saints as the focus of liturgical commemoration. Most Protestant churches did not mark the Sanctorale cycle, although they continued to note dates by the names of persons they considered central to the work and mission of the early church: John the Baptist, the evangelists, the disciples, and the church fathers.

Protestant reformers placed greater emphasis on weekly worship, flattening the greater seasons as they brought the weekly rhythms forward. The Protestants' redefinition of worship itself, to focus upon the sermon and Communion more exclusively, had repercussions for the calendar. While retaining much of the structure of the medieval Mass, Luther shifted its emphasis to God's speaking to humankind, effectively bringing the sermon forward in the rhythm of the service. Huldrych Zwingli and John Calvin eliminated the medieval Mass altogether; for them God's speaking and the congregation's shared Communion dominated the liturgy. In calling for more frequent Communion, Luther and Zwingli leveled one of the dramatic rhythms of the Temporale cycle: although Easter would still be distinguished by offering the Eucharist, the drama of that event was diminished by the frequency of Communion in Protestant churches. Calvin sought weekly Communion in Geneva, but like Zwingli he had to compromise with the city council and agree to quarterly Communion services—a measurement tied not to the liturgical year but to the city's civil calendar. No more would the miracle of the Resurrection contrast dramatically with the preceding weeks of penance. Pared away would be certain of what Protestants called "medieval accretions"—all Marian feasts as well as the feasts of the Circumcision, Transfiguration, and Corpus Christi. All Continental Protestants, from the most conservative to the most radical, from Lutheran to Spiritualist and Anabaptist, eliminated much of the visual display (processions, vestments, and the sculpted, painted, and gilded images in churches) by which those rhythms were marked. No more would the seasons commemorating Christ's life be marked through excess—Carnival—then deprivation—Lent. Protestants even disapproved of special commemoration of Christmas, though it might be argued that the Genevan city council's declarations of Christmas and the Virgin's birthday as days of fasting and prayer implicitly acknowledged the traditional liturgical calendar and its powerful role in popular religious culture.

England provides a notable case study of the gradual transformation of the liturgical calendar under the pressure of successive church reforms, as well as more strictly political developments. Among Protestant churches the Church of England retained much more of the rhythm and cadences of the medieval liturgical calendar, although beginning in 1541 church authorities struggled to free their calendar of its "papist" roots. Throughout the turbulent Tudor and Stuart monarchies, the Civil War, and the Cromwellian reign, the liturgical calendar remained a focus of heated debate. As David Cressy has shown, political and church authorities were sensitive to the calendar's power to shape popular political and religious identity—evident in official acts to encourage celebration of anti-Catholic, anti-Continental festivals, such as Guy (or "Guido") Fawkes day and Armada defeat day. Moreover, legal and administrative business has continued to be transacted quarterly according to the feasts of Hilary, Easter, Trinity, and Michaelmas.

Although the Catholic church essentially retained the medieval liturgical calendar, Catholic practice was not untouched by sixteenth-century debates. Counter-Reformation popes insisted on their exclusive authority to shape the liturgical calendar. Indeed, sixteenth-century Catholicism's unquestioning acceptance of papal canonization of saints ensured that only Rome would add or subtract feasts from the church's calendar. Ironically, although Protestants and reformed Catholics alike considered the Catholic liturgical calendar "disorderly," it was late sixteenth-century popes who sponsored the calendar reform of the early modern period. Although not universally accepted in Europe until the late eighteenth century, the Gregorian calendar of 1582 brought modern astronomical and mathematical scholarship to bear on the thorny business of reckoning time—both sacred and profane.

[*See also* Festivals *and* Time.]

BIBLIOGRAPHY

Cressy, David. *Bonfires and Bells: National Memory and the Protestant Calendar in Elizabethan and Stuart England.* London and Berkeley,

1989. Protestant transformation of the liturgical calendar, including popular celebrations. Argues convincingly that after 1500 the English calendar gradually took on a national rather than religious character.

Denis-Boulet, Noële M. *The Christian Calendar.* Translated by P. J. Hepburne-Scott. New York, 1960. Historical sketch of the liturgical calendar; after 1500, Catholic developments only.

Jones, Cheslyn, Geoffrey Wainwright, Edward Yarnold, and Paul Bradshaw, eds. *The Study of Liturgy.* Rev. ed. Oxford, 1992. A collection of articles treating the Eastern and Western churches. Part 6 discusses the calendar.

Leith, John H. *An Introduction to the Reformed Tradition: A Way of Being the Christian Community.* Atlanta, 1977. Chapter 6 treats the liturgy in the Reformed tradition.

Perdrizet, Paul. *Le calendrier parisien à la fin du moyen âge: D'après le bréviaire et les livres d'heures.* Paris, 1933. Case study of the late medieval liturgical calendar in one diocese, with fully annotated edition of the Parisian calendar.

Phythian-Adams, Charles. "Ceremony and the Citizen: The Communal Year at Coventry, 1450–1550." In *Crisis and Order in English Towns, 1500–1700,* edited by Peter Clark and Paul Slack, pp. 57–85. Toronto, 1972. Probes the social meaning of the ritual calendar of Coventry; attention to strictly religious as well as more secular celebrations.

Righetti, Mario. *Manuale di storia liturgica.* 4 vols. 3d rev. and enl. ed. Milan, 1959–1966. Important history of the liturgy based on a broad definition of liturgy, emphasizing the period from early Christianity to Tridentine Catholicism. Liturgical calendar discussed in vol. 2, pp. 1–467. A rich store of information about the liturgical celebration of feasts and seasons.

White, James F. *Introduction to Christian Worship.* Rev. ed. Nashville, 1990. The most accessible survey of the structure and meaning of the liturgy, from early church to modern Protestantism. Provides brief summaries of historical origins for each dimension of worship.

Zerubavel, Eviatar. *Hidden Rhythms: Schedules and Calendars in Social Life.* Chicago, 1981. Attempts a "sociology of time." See especially chapter 3 on calendars as focus of communal identity and chapter 4 on sacred and profane time.

Virginia Reinburg and Lee Palmer Wandel

LITURGY. [*To survey the development of Protestant liturgy and the effects of the Reformation and the Counter-Reformation on Roman Catholic liturgy, this entry comprises two articles:* Protestant Liturgy *and* Roman Catholic Liturgy.]

Protestant Liturgy

Martin Luther may be said to have laid the foundations for liturgical reform as well as other aspects of the Reformation. As early as 1516, in a sermon on the third commandment, he stressed the importance of "hearing the word of God" over "hearing Mass." Medieval Christians did not lack for sermons. But preaching based on the scriptures, using a historical-grammatical heremeneutic, as opposed to preaching based on an allegorical interpretation of biblical texts or "fables," became the central practical reform that united the whole Protestant Reformation. The clear word of scripture revealed aberrations in teaching and abuses in practice.

In *De capitivitate babylonica* (1520) Luther attacked the heart of medieval religion: the sacramental system. He denied that there were seven sacraments and "for the moment" accepted only "baptism, penance, and the bread." He thought that the sacrament of the bread was held captive in three ways: the cup was withheld from lay communicants, the mystery of the Eucharist was rationalized with the dogma of transubstantiation, and the Mass was offered as "a good work and a sacrifice" (*opus bonum et sacrificium*) instead of being received as the gift of Christ to his church. The use of the Mass in the service of works righteousness (*Werkgerechtigkeit*), by which the faithful try to gain God's favor, could be corrected by preaching and teaching the gospel of justification by faith and by abolishing the "traffic" in masses (i.e., votive masses). But the assault on the Mass as a "sacrifice" had liturgical consequences for the *ordo missae* ("order of the Mass") itself since it involved a liturgical reorientation: the sacrament is not what the church offers to God (especially for special intentions in votive masses) but the gift of Communion that the faithful receive as "the last will and testament of Christ."

The consequence of the assault on the sacrifice of the Mass became clear when Luther undertook a revision of the Latin Mass in his treatise on the *Formula Missae et Communiones* (Form of the Mass and Communion for the Church at Wittenberg; 1523). His intention was not "to abolish the liturgical service of God completely, but rather to purify the one that is now in use from the wretched accretions which corrupt it and to point out an evangelical use." Little departure was made from the medieval rite until the offertory. "From here on," wrote Luther, "almost everything smacks and savors of sacrifice. And the words of life and salvation [the words of institution] are embedded in the midst of all it, just as the ark of the Lord once stood in the idol's temple next to Dagon. . . . Let us, therefore, repudiate everything that smacks of sacrifice, together with the entire canon, and retain only that which is pure and holy, and so order our mass." Accordingly, he deleted the offertory prayers (the "minor canon") and reduced the *canon missae* ("canon of the Mass") to the Preface, the words of institution (joined to the Preface by a *qui* clause in the style of a "proper" insertion), and the *Sanctus.* Luther thus placed the *Verba Christi* into the section of the Canon that was traditionally sung aloud (the Preface), instead of within the post-*Sanctus* prayers that were customarily recited silently by the priest while the choir sang the *Sanctus.* By retaining the elevation of the Host at the *Benedictus qui venit* ("Blessed is he who comes in the name of the Lord"), accompanied by the ringing of bells and genuflection, Luther managed to retain the most dramatic moment of the medieval Mass while effecting the most radical surgery on the Canon. In the section of the *Formula Missae* dealing with Communion practices, Luther recommended that the communicants announce their intention to receive the Sacrament, submit to a catechetical examination and private confession and absolution, and gather in the chancel for the Sacrament where they could make a public testimony. He also put out a plea for the composition of hymns that the entire congregation might sing.

Even as Luther was revising the Latin liturgy, a number of German liturgies were being published. Already in 1522 Wolfgang Wissenburger in Basel and Johann Schwebel in Pforzheim were holding services in German. That same year the Carmelite prior Kaspar Kantz prepared a German service for the use of his monks. In 1523/24 Thomas Müntzer published a German Mass, Matins, and Vespers with an original plainsong setting for use in Alstedt. An interesting German Mass with a revision of the Roman Canon appeared in Worms in 1524. In the same year German services were introduced in Reutlingen, Wertheim, Königsberg, and Strasbourg. The German Mass prepared by Diobald Schwartz for Strasbourg was an adaptation of the Roman rite. That same year Martin Bucer, who was to have enormous influence on Reformed liturgy, published his *Grund und Ursach*, which laid out an order for the celebration of the word and the Lord's Supper.

All of this activity in the production of vernacular liturgies created a confusing situation, and Luther's friends turned to him for guidance. This prompted Luther to prepare his own *Deutsche Messe und Gottesdienst* (German Mass and Order of Service; 1526). The *Deutsche Messe* was a song mass (*Lied Messe*) intended for village churches that lacked trained choirs. Luther substituted congregational hymns for parts of the Mass that had been sung by the choir: the Introit, Gradual, Nicene Creed, *Sanctus*, and *Agnus Dei*. This sparked similar efforts among German Lutherans, and soon metrical hymn versions of the *Kyrie*, *Gloria in excelsis*, and other canticles were also composed. The musical elements in the German Mass tradition compensated for such didactic elements as the catechetical paraphrase of the Lord's Prayer and the admonition to the communicants. The words of institution were still sung aloud, according to a tune provided by Luther. But the administration of the sacrament was brought into such close juxtaposition with the *Verba* that the bread was distributed immediately after the words over the bread, during which the German *Sanctus* was sung ("Isaiah, 'twas the prophet who did see"), and the cup was distributed immediately after the words over the cup, during which the German *Agnus Dei* ("O Christ, thou lamb of God") and other songs were sung.

The question has been raised as to whether Luther intended his German Mass to be a definitive order of service since it was his second and final example of revision of the Mass. That he was adverse to any kind of liturgical legalism, that he intended his Latin Mass to remain in use in towns and universities where trained choirs could sing plainsong or polyphonic settings of the texts, and that he gave his approval to later church orders which did not slavishly follow his own liturgical models argue against regarding the *Deutsche Messe* as the definitive Lutheran liturgy. But it gave impetus to the flowering of hymnody in the Lutheran Reformation. Luther himself wrote some thirty hymns, motivated others to write hymns, provided prefaces to several hymnals, and also encouraged the composition of liturgical art music.

Luther made two revisions of the order of baptism (1523, 1526). His first *Taufbüchlein* (Baptismal Booklet) was largely a translation of the medieval order of baptism as reflected in the Magdeburg Agenda of 1497. The second was a revision of the first, which omitted many of the redundant exorcism prayers and the baptismal anointing. Both orders included Luther's famous "flood prayer" (*Sintflutgebet*), which rehearses the history of salvation through water. Luther's orders retain the practice of immersion, the giving of a white robe, and a lighted candle. Luther's second *Taufbüchlein* served as a model for a number of Lutheran baptismal orders.

Lutheran Church Orders. Luther's personal influence as the charismatic leader of the Reformation carried great weight, but as the Reformation was officially adopted by princes for their territories and by city councils, it had to be regulated by church orders (*Kirchenordnungen*). These documents addressed matters of church polity, administration, congregational life, charitable institutions, schools, the calendar, and worship, and therefore effected a "revolution" in social life. Ecclesiastical and civic life became more thoroughly integrated even administratively with the establishment of consistories; monasteries were deserted and converted into schools, hospitals, orphanages, and so on; congregations exercised more authority over their affairs, including the calling of pastors; universal education of the young became an ideal; the number of holy days (and holidays) was reduced; public worship was increasingly in the vernacular; and private devotions in the home, including Bible reading, hymn singing, meal prayers, and morning and evening prayers were encouraged.

Many of the reformers were drawn into the task of drafting church orders. Johannes Bugenhagen prepared church orders for Braunschweig (1528), Hamburg (1529), Lübeck (1531), Pomerania (1535), Denmark-Norway (1537), Schleswig-Holstein (1542), and Hildesheim (1544). Justus Jonas prepared church orders for Wittenberg (1533) and for Duke Henry of Saxony (1539). Philipp Melanchthon was involved in preparing church orders for Mecklenburg (1540 and 1552, with Johannes Aurifaber and Johann Riebling) and for Archbishop Hermann von Wied of Cologne (1543, with Martin Bucer). An important church order for Brandenburg-Nuremberg (1533) was prepared by Johannes Brenz and Andreas Osiander. These church orders follow the model of the Saxon liturgies in which little is changed in the liturgy of the word from the pre-Reformation Mass, vernacular metrical hymns are used interchangeably with Latin chants, and the words of institution are juxtaposed with the administration of Holy Communion.

Some church orders were more traditional in retaining more of the pre-Reformation rites and customs; these include Brandenburg (1540), Pfalz-Neuburg (1543), and Austria (1570, prepared by David Chytraeus). In these church orders the words of institution were sung after the *Sanctus* and before the Lord's Prayer; sometimes intercessory or epicletic prayers were said silently by the celebrant during the singing of the *Sanctus*.

A third type of church order has been called "mediating," because it blended aspects of Lutheran and Reformed liturgies. These include Brenz's church orders for Württemberg (1553 and 1559), Bucer's church orders for Strasbourg (see below), and the church orders for Baden (1556), Rheinpfalz (1557), and Worms (1560). The church orders for Hesse (1532), Cassel (1539), Marburg (1574), and Nassau (1576) indicate some Reformed influence, but show strong individuality.

The Swedish church order (1571) prepared by Archbishop Laurentius Petri (the brother of Sweden's reformer, Olaus Petri), which was also used in Finland, was unique in defending the historical episcopate and arguing for an evangelical understanding of the eucharistic memorial and sacrifice. It provided propers and rubrics for the Swedish Mass of Olaus Petri (1531). The Swedish Mass faithfully followed the order of Luther's *Formula Missae*, including the words of institution within the Preface, so that in this tradition the *Verba institutionis* were part of the eucharistic prayer.

The use of congregational song led to the publication of song books or hymnals. The first Lutheran hymnal was the *Achtliederbuch* (Eight Song Book, Nuremberg, 1524), which included four hymns by Luther, three by Paul Speratus, and one anonymous hymn. Encouraged by Luther, hymns of catechetical, devotional, and liturgical character were written by Nikolaus Decius, Justus Jonas, Elizabeth Cruciger, Paul Eber, Lazarus Spengler, Paul Speratus, and many others. Hymnals appeared in quick succession, each one larger than the previous, including the Erfurt *Enchiridion* (1524), the Zwickau *Gesang Büchlein* (1525), and Joseph Klug's *Geistliche lieder* (Wittenberg, 1529; revised 1533). The *Geystliche lieder* published by Valentin Babst (Leipzig, 1545) is considered the most complete German hymnal of the period.

Luther also encouraged the production of liturgical art music. The reformer's friend and musical collaborator, Johann Walther, published the *Geystliches gesangk Buchleyn* (1524), which was a collection of polyphonic motets for choir based on chorales. *Cantionales* with plainsong settings of the chant-texts for choirs, numbering hundreds of pages, were also published, beginning with the *Cantionales ecclesiasticae* of Johann Spangenberg (Magdeburg, 1545), which Luther endorsed. The *Psalmodia* of Lucas Lossius (1553ff.), with a preface by Melanchthon, numbered eight-hundred pages and contained texts and plainsong melodies from pre-Reformation sources adapted for use in evangelical liturgy.

Bohemian Brethren. The Bohemian Brethren, who were the offspring of the Hussite movement in the fifteenth century, antedated Luther's Reformation. For the most part their congregations were located in remote forested regions of eastern Bohemia. Their use of vernacular congregational hymns in worship also antedated Luther's reforms. Hymnals were published in 1501, 1505, 1519, and 1541, although only the last survives. Edited by Johannes Horn (Jan Roh in Czech), it contains 481 songs set to some 300 melodies, surpassing in quantity any Reformation song book up to that time. A Brethren hymnal published in Germany, *Ein Neue Gesängbuchlein*, edited by Michael Weisse in 1531, influenced Lutheran song books.

Anabaptist Liturgy. The hymnals of the Bohemian Brethren provide a way of tracking the liturgical life of their communities. Even this kind of source is lacking among the adherents of the radical Reformation usually lumped together under the name "Anabaptist." While they agreed that "infant baptism" was unscriptural, subscribed to a memorialist view of the Eucharist, and stressed cross bearing and martyrdom as characteristic of Christian life, they also differed in other respects. Conrad Grebel regarded Thomas Müntzer's German Mass and orders of Matins and Vespers as contrary to New Testament forms and principles of worship. Grebel later clashed with Huldrych Zwingli in Zurich over whether Christian worship should try to replicate New Testament forms and practices; Grebel said yes, Zwingli said no. Zwingli's view prevailed and Grebel was banished from Zurich. While most Anabaptist leaders emphasized the church as a "pure, gathered community," Balthasar Hubmaier believed that this ideal could be reconciled with the idea of a territorial church, and experimented with this in the Austrian village of Waldshut. He provided in *Ein Form des Nachtmals Christi* (A Form of the Lord's Supper; 1527), which included a confession of sins, exposition of scripture, opportunity to question the preacher, self-examination in silent meditation on the passion of Christ, catechesis on the Lord's Supper and exhortation to living the Christian life, thanksgiving over the bread and cup with the words of institution, reception of the bread and cup in silence, further exhortation, and dismissal.

The frequency of celebration of the Lord's Supper varied widely among Anabaptist groups from weekly to only a few times a year. Among the followers of Menno Simons, footwashing was also an important sacramental observance. Typical Sunday services consisted of the exposition of scripture, exhortation, prayer, and hymn singing. Baptism was celebrated when someone asked to be baptized; but the consent of the community was required. A public form of penance was practiced that sometimes resulted in banishment from the community or in shunning. Marriage became important in Anabaptist communities, even though it was not regarded as a sacrament, because it was viewed as a covenant closely related to baptism. Problems arose when a member of the community married an unbaptized person or had a spouse who was shunned. Remarriage was practiced along with rebaptism.

Reformed Liturgy. The Reformed tradition emerged in several Swiss cantons and along the Rhine river in the early 1520s. The reformer of Zurich, Zwingli, published *De canone missae epichiresis* (An Attack on the Canon of the Mass; 1523) a few months before Luther's *Formula Missae.* This conservative work retained much of the Latin Mass but replaced the Canon with four Latin prayers: a thanksgiving, an invocation of the Holy Spirit to grant the benefits of Holy Communion, a memorial of the passion of Christ, and a prayer for worthy reception. More strongly influenced by Renaissance humanism than Luther, Zwingli objected to the illogical and repetitious character of the Canon of the Mass and appealed to patristic models in drafting his prayers. The emphasis on preaching in the Reformed tradition is evident in the institution of daily preaching services based on the medieval office of Prone.

In 1525 Zwingli provided a German service for the Lord's Supper, *Action oder Brauch des Herren Nachtmal* (Proceedings or Custom of the Lord's Supper). This specified that Holy Communion would be celebrated four times a year, that ministers would preside in clerical street garb rather than in liturgical vestments, and that the altar would be replaced with a Communion table from which the bread and wine were administered to the people in their seats using wooden trays and cups. Zwingli would have preferred an antiphonal reading of such texts as the *Gloria in excelsis* and the Apostles' Creed, but this was not countenanced by the city council so these texts were left for the ministers to recite. There also was no music or singing in worship in Zurich.

After 1525 it became evident that the Swiss reformers and the Lutherans held very different views of the Lord's Supper. Their debate came to an irreconcilable climax at the Colloquy of Marburg (1529). The debate centered on the real presence of Christ in the Sacrament and the interpretation of the *Verba Christi,* "This is my body." Luther argued for a literal interpretation, Zwingli for a spiritual one. The liturgical consequence of this was to reenact as closely as possible the original institution of the Lord's Supper. In some Reformed churches, notably in the Church of Scotland, communicants sat around the table to receive the bread and wine. The Reformed also emphasized the fellowship aspect of the Lord's Supper (the Christians' meal), and strove to include the whole congregation in the celebration (the reason for quarterly Communions); whereas the Lutherans emphasized the sacraments as "means of grace," and reception became an individual matter.

A more mediating theological position and liturgical practice was taken by Bucer in Strasbourg. Bucer had implemented there a German service of word and sacrament celebrated every Sunday (at least in the cathedral) with congregational singing of metrical psalms and canticles. This service began with a congregational confession of sins followed by words of pardon; then a psalm, hymn, *Kyrie,* or *Gloria* was sung and a collect for illumination was offered. A chapter of a Gospel was read, followed by a sermon. Alms were then collected and the Communion elements were prepared on the table while the Apostles' Creed was sung. The Communion office included intercessions, a consecration prayer, the Lord's Prayer, an exhortation, the words of institution, and the fraction. During the administration of the elements, psalms or hymns were sung. After a post-Communion collect, the *Nunc Dimittis* was sometimes sung, followed by the Aaronic benediction and dismissal.

John Calvin, after a brief sojourn in Geneva (from which he was expelled in 1538), ministered to the French congregation in Strasbourg and was greatly influenced by this German Reformed service, from which he prepared a French edition in 1540. When he was recalled to Geneva in 1541, he published an order of service similar to Bucer's, under the title *La forme des prières et chantz ecclésiastiques avec la manière d'administer les sacrements* (1542). Impressed by the singing of metrical psalms in the German congregation in Strasbourg, Calvin had Clément Marot provide metrical psalms for his French-speaking congregation in Strasbourg. When Calvin returned to Geneva, Marot continue working on the French Psalter. Marot died in 1544 and Théodore de Bèze completed the full Geneva Psalter in 1551. Calvin also secured the services of the composer Louis Bourgeois to provide tunes for these psalms. The complete French Psalter, *Psaumes de David* (1562), contained 125 tunes, 70 composed by Bourgeois.

Calvin was never able to institute weekly celebration of the Lord's Supper in Geneva. The city council preferred to remain in uniformity with other Swiss Reformed cities by celebrating the Lord's Supper four times a year. This affected the liturgical order. Calvin demonstrated that the full service required word and sacrament by using the pre-Communion for the typical Sunday service. Hence, the intercessions and Lord's Prayer (in paraphrase) concluded the liturgy of the word in Calvin's service. Also, Calvin moved the institution narrative to a place before the Consecration Prayer so that it would serve as a warrant for the celebration and not suggest an act of consecration.

This order was further adapted by John Knox, who was resident in Geneva during the reign of Queen Mary Tudor of England. He translated it into English and it became the rite of the Church of Scotland when *The Book of Common Order* supplanted *The Book of Common Prayer* in 1562. Knox supplied new intercessions and a new prayer of consecration. The influence of the 1552 *The Book of Common Prayer* is still detectable in the exhortation to communicants. Calvin's influence is evident in the fact that the pre-Communion remained the chief Sunday service when Holy Communion was not celebrated. The first Communion rubric in *The Book of Common Order* directed that Holy Communion be celebrated once a month, but in practice it was celebrated four times a year as in Geneva and Zurich. Lest these Communion times be associated with the church year, which was abolished, they were fixed on the first Sundays of March, June, September, and December. However, this does not imply a Zwinglian understanding of the Sacrament. The first Scottish Confession utterly damned "the vanity of those who affirm sacraments to be nothing else but naked and bare signs." The approved doctrine, set forth in the confession and in the Communion exhortation, was Calvinistic: "We spiritually eate the fleshe of Christ, and drinke his bloude; then we dwell in Christ, and Christ in us; we be one with Christ, and Christ with us."

Anglican Liturgy. England's leading liturgical reformer was Thomas Cranmer, archbishop of Canterbury (1533–1555). While visiting Nuremberg as King Henry VIII's envoy to the court of Emperor Charles V, Cranmer noted the liturgical changes that had been implemented (and later married the niece of the city's celebrated Lutheran pastor, Andreas Osiander). While Henry VIII broke relations with the pope over his divorce from Queen Catherine of Aragon, he remained theologically and liturgically conservative. The complete Bible was translated into English by Miles Coverdale and published abroad in 1535; it was revised in 1539 in an edition known as the "Great Bible," for which Cranmer provided a preface; it was ordered to be read at the Sunday offices and the Mass (1543, 1547). A new English primer was published in 1534 under Cranmer's direction. In 1548 Cranmer himself translated the Lutheran catechism of Justus Jonas into English. The general disarray of liturgical books throughout England gave Cranmer the excuse he needed to undertake a general liturgical revision. He revised the Sarum (Salisbury) Breviary and then worked on an English processional modeled on Luther's revision of the Great Litany, which appeared in 1544. The Cologne church order, prepared by Bucer and Melanchthon for Archbishop Hermann von Wied, was translated into English as *A Simple and Religious Consultation* (1547, revised 1548). Also in 1547 a *Book of Homilies* was authorized for use in each church as a basis for uniform teaching of the Christian faith.

Henry VIII died in 1547 and was succeeded by the ten-year-old Edward VI. Aided by the boy-king's Protestant counselors, reform proceeded more quickly. In January 1548 candles at Candlemas, ashes on Ash Wednesday, and palms on Palm Sunday were all suppressed. In March 1548 an order of Communion in English, based on material in the *Consultation* of Archbishop von Wied, was interpolated within the Latin Mass at the moment of Communion. It consisted of the use of one of two exhortations, confession and absolution, the "Comfortable Words," a "Prayer of Humble Access," the words of administration of the Sacrament, and a blessing. Communion was administered under both kinds.

This period of experimentation came to an end with the publication of *The Booke of Common Prayer and Administration of the Sacraments, and other Rites and Ceremonies of the Churche, after the Use of the Churche of England* (1549). This remarkable achievement, for which Cranmer was largely responsible, contained (all in English) a table of psalms, orders for Morning Prayer and Evensong, propers and lectionary for the church year (with epistles and gospels printed out), "The Supper of the Lorde and The Holy Communion, commonly called the Masse," the litany and suffrages, and orders for public and private baptism, confirmation, matrimony, the visitation of the sick, the Communion of the sick, the burial of the dead, the purification of women, a special order for Ash Wednesday, and a note on ceremonies. While there had previously been five liturgical traditions in England, an Act of Uniformity passed by Parliament decreed that the whole realm would have but one.

This first prayer book of King Edward VI was not just a translation and revision of the medieval use of Sarum; it drew upon several important German church orders. The fusion of Matins and Lauds to form an office of Morning Prayer and the fusion of Vespers and Compline to form an office of Evensong was modeled after the Calenburg and Göttingen church order (1542). In the order of Mass the Prayer Book uses whole psalms as introits, as in Luther's *Deutsche Messe.* In translating the Collects Cranmer sometimes worked from the texts in the German church orders as well as from the Latin originals. Phrases in the prayer "for the whole state of Christ's church," which took the place of the *Te igitur* in the Canon, are derived from van Wied's *Consultation*, as are the formulas taken over from the previously published Communion rite. The institution narrative is similar to the one in the Brandenburg-Nuremberg church order (1533). As in the Communion instructions in Luther's *Formula Missae*, the communicants are directed to go into the chancel during the offertory. The Order for Baptism was derived from the Cologne *Consultation*, which in turn had drawn upon Osiander's Order for Baptism from Nuremberg, which in turn had utilized Luther's second *Taufbüchlein.* The prayer book's Order for Public Baptism therefore resembles Luther's, including a translation of the "flood prayer." A catechism modeled on that of the *Consultation* was also included under the heading "Confirmation," which shows the influence of Bucer in that the rite of confirmation included a renewal of baptismal vows before the laying on of hands. The *Consultation* and other German church orders are among the sources for the Order of Marriage. The prayer book also made provision for the Communion of the sick from the reserved Sacrament on days when Holy Communion was celebrated, as in the Brandenburg church order (1540). Brandenburg is also the model for placing the burial of the dead within the structure of a prayer office. Thus, while there are other influences on the prayer book from patristic and medieval sources, the German church orders predominate—except for the eucharistic prayer, which is a superbly crafted revision of the Roman Canon.

No one seemed satisfied with the prayer book. It crystalized popular resentment that had been building against religious changes since the Pilgrimage of Grace in 1536. The clergy of Oxfordshire refused to use it, and riots and rebellions broke out in many counties. But some thought it had not gone far enough, and the Reformation proceeded apace. A new ordinal was published in 1550 based on Bucer's *De Ordinatione legitima ministrorum ecclesiae revocanda*, which placed occupants of ecclesiastical offices on the same spiritual plane as occupants of civil offices. In order to prevent priests from offering the sacrifice of the Mass using the new Communion service, the Council of Regents ordered the destruction of all altars throughout the realm on 23 November 1550, to be replaced with tables. Conservative bishops who would not countenance such measures, such as Stephen Gardiner of Winchester and Edmund Bonner of London, were imprisoned and replaced by more radical bishops such as Hugh Latimer and Nicholas Ridley. Cranmer also invited to England leading reformers from abroad. Martin Bucer was given a professorship at Cambridge and Peter Martyr Vermigli taught at Oxford. Melanchthon was also offered an Oxford professorship but was unable to accept it because of the crisis triggered by the Interim in Germany. Bucer especially, in his *Censura supra libro sacrorum seu ordinationis ecclesiae atque ministerii in regno Angliae* (1550), provided a thorough examination of the English prayer book with suggestions for revisions. (Vermigli also provided a "Censura," which failed to survive.)

A second prayer book was published in 1552, which reflected the influences of the radical bishops and the reformers from abroad. The number of holy days in the calendar was reduced. The Communion table was placed in the middle of the chancel so that communicants could be gathered around it, with the celebrant presiding "on the north side" facing some of the people. The *Kyrie* became a response to the rehearsal of the Ten Commandments. The prayer "for the whole state of Christ's church" was removed from the eucharistic prayer and placed at the offertory. The invitation, confession of sins, absolution, and comfortable words were relocated from before the administration of Holy Communion to before the *Sursum corda.* The Prayer of Humble Access was relocated from before the Communion to after the *Sanctus* so that the words of institution could lead directly to the distribution of the Sacrament. The "Lamb of God" was suppressed entirely. The element of thanksgiving was located after Communion, concluding with the *Gloria in excelsis* and a benediction. While the posture for receiving Communion remained kneeling, a rubric was inserted at John Knox's insistence, but over Cranmer's objections, that denied any sense of veneration of the elements (the so-called Black Rubric because it was a last-minute addition—rubrics are usually printed in red). The prayer of blessing the water and the anointing disappeared from the order for baptism. Communion from the reserved Sacrament was no longer an option in the Communion of the sick, although Holy Communion could be celebrated in the presence of the sick.

The 1552 prayer book was short-lived because the young King Edward died in 1553 and was succeeded by the Catholic Mary Tudor, the daughter of Henry VIII and Catherine of Aragon, who restored the Roman rite and deposed the leading reform bishops. Cranmer, Hooper, Latimer, and Ridley were imprisoned, tried for heresy, and burned at the stake in Oxford. Other leaders of the English Reformation took refuge on the Continent, especially in Reformed centers, such as Knox in Geneva.

In 1558 Elizabeth I, the daughter of Henry VIII and Anne Boleyn, succeeded Mary Tudor. Relations with the papacy were once again severed and *The Book of Common Prayer* was restored and imposed for use throughout the whole realm by the Act of Uniformity of 1559. The 1559 prayer book was essentially the 1552 prayer book, with the "Black Rubric" deleted. The formulas of administration from the two previous prayer books were joined together to make possible an expression of the sacramental union of the body and blood of Christ with the bread and wine. The Elizabethan prayer book thus reflected the policy of "comprehension" of Elizabeth's reign, designed to bring both Catholics and Puritans into one national church.

[*See also* Eucharist; Hymnals; Hymns; Mass; *and* Sacraments.]

BIBLIOGRAPHY

Blume, Friedrich, ed. *Protestant Church Music: A History.* New York, 1974. Chapter 1 deals exhaustively with the music of the Lutheran Reformation in Germany. Chapters 5–7 treat church music in the Reformed tradition, among the Bohemian Brethren, and in Scandinavia. Chapter 9 begins with the English Reformation.

The First and Second Prayer Books of King Edward VI. Everyman's Library, no. 448. London, 1968. Complete texts of the 1549 and 1552 editions of *The Book of Common Prayer.*

Jacobs, Henry E. *The Lutheran Movement in England during the Reigns of Henry VIII and Edward VI.* Rev. ed. Philadelphia, 1906. The most thorough analysis of Lutheran influences in England during the Reformation, especially on the 1549 *Book of Common Prayer.*

Kavanagh, Aidan. *The Concept of Eucharistic Memorial in the Canon Revisions of Thomas Cranmer, Archbishop of Canterbury, 1533–1556.* Saint Meinrad Archabbey, Ind., 1964. A doctoral dissertation which studies the changes in Cranmer's eucharistic beliefs and their affect on the prayer book revisions of 1552.

Luther, Martin. *Luther's Works.* Vol. 53, *Liturgy and Hymns.* Edited by Ulrich S. Leupold. Philadelphia, 1965. Translations of all of Luther's liturgical orders, prefaces to hymnals, and hymns.

Maxwell, William D. *The Liturgical Portions of the Genevan Service Book.* London, 1965. Translations of and commentary on Calvin's liturgy in Geneva.

———. *An Outline of Christian Worship: Its Developments and Forms.* Rev. ed. London, 1965. Also available as *History of Christian Worship,* Grand Rapids, Mich., 1982. A survey of the forms of worship in Christian history; old but still useful for Reformation liturgy, especially in the Reformed tradition.

Old, Hughes Oliphant. *The Patristic Roots of Reformed Worship* Zurich, 1975. An examination of the patristic ideal behind the liturgies of Zwingli, Oecolampadius, Bucer, Farel, Calvin and others within the Reformed tradition.

Pahl, Irmgard, ed. *Coena Domini.* Fribourg, 1983. See vol. 1. Critical edition and analyses of Reformation eucharistic texts. Articles are in the language of the liturgy.

Pipkin, H. W., and John H. Yoder, eds. and trans. *Balthasar Hubmaier: Theologian of Anabaptism.* Scottdale, Pa., 1989. Includes a translation of and commentary on "A Form of the Supper of Christ" (1527), which is the only extant Anabaptist liturgy from the Reformation era.

Poll, G. J. van de. *Martin Bucer's Liturgical Ideas.* Groningen, 1954. The only book-length treatment in English.

Reed, Luther D. *The Lutheran Liturgy.* 2d rev. ed. Philadelphia, 1975. Chapters 3–6 are a study and analysis of Luther's liturgical work, a categorization of the church orders, a synopsis of developments in Sweden, and a comparison of Anglican and Lutheran Reformation liturgies.

Sasse, Hermann. *This Is My Body: Luther's Contention for the Real Presence in the Sacrament of the Altar.* Minneapolis, 1959. A thorough examination of the background of Luther's doctrine of the real presence, Zwingli's sacramental theology and liturgical practice, the controversy between Luther and Zwingli, the text of the Marburg Colloquy, and the aftermath of the colloquy through Calvin and the Lutheran *Formula of Concord.*

Sehling, Emil, ed. *Die evangelischen Kirchenordnungen des XVI. Jahrhunderts.* Leipzig, 1902. Multivolume critical edition of all of the German Reformation church orders.

Senn, Frank C. *Liturgy: Catholic and Evangelical.* Minneapolis, forthcoming. The middle section is a survey and analysis of Reformation liturgies.

Thompson, Bard. *Liturgies of the Western Church.* Reprint, Philadelphia, 1980. Includes texts of the eucharistic liturgies of Luther, Zwingli, Bucer, Calvin, the first and second prayer books of Edward VI, and Knox.

White, James F. *Protestant Worship: Traditions in Transition.* Louisville, Ky., 1989. Portions of chaps. 3–6 on Lutheran, Reformed, Anabaptist, and Anglican worship deal with Reformation liturgies. White is especially interested in non-eucharistic worship, which was the more typical Sunday and weekday worship in all but a few traditions.

Wislöff, Carl F. *The Gift of Communion: Luther's Controversy with Rome on Eucharistic Sacrifice.* Translated by Joseph M. Shaw. Minneapolis, 1964. A perceptive examination of Luther's thought on eucharistic sacrifice as contrasted with medieval teaching, with some attention to the liturgical consequences.

Yelverton, Eric E. *An Archbishop of the Reformation: Laurentius Petri Nericius, Archbishop of Uppsala, 1531–73: A Study of His Liturgical Projects.* Minneapolis, 1959. The only monograph in English of the work of Archbishop Petri on the Swedish Mass and the 1571 Swedish church order.

Yelverton, Eric E., ed. *The Mass in Sweden: Its Development from the Latin Rite from 1531 to 1917.* Henry Bradshaw Society Collection, no. 57. London, 1920. English translation of the Mass of Olaus Petri and its subsequent evolution.

FRANK C. SENN

Roman Catholic Liturgy

In the mid-sixteenth century, the Roman liturgy resembled a garden so overgrown with plants from different times and places (and with a few weeds as well) that the original design of the Mass and the Divine Office was somewhat obscured. Devotional practices on the part of clergy and laity alike reflected an understanding of the Mass not as the communal action of a gathered assembly celebrating God's marvelous deeds in Jesus Christ, but rather as a private ritual performed by the priest for the benefit of a passive audience. Similarly, the Divine Office (the church's official prayer marking the hours of the day and night) had become the highly complex and exclusive preserve of clergy and religious known as the "breviary."

The impetus for the Council of Trent (1545–1563) to effect a reform of the liturgy came not only from the Protestant Reformers but also from many Catholics (like Desiderius Erasmus) who wanted order to replace chaos in liturgical practices. Although the council fathers decided that a revision of the breviary and missal was necessary, they realized that a council could not accomplish so complicated a matter as liturgical reform. Thus they set up a commission for this purpose in 1562. At their twenty-fifth session (1563), the council fathers entrusted the work of revision to the pope, Pius IV (1559–1565), and to his successor, Pius V (1566–1572). As a result, the Curia Romana were able to advance a claim that had been theirs since the time of Gregory VII (1073–1085): exclusive jurisdiction in liturgical practice. Theodor Klauser comments that "the period of episcopal independence in liturgical matters which stretches right back to the early Church was thereby first in principle and then also in practice brought to an end" (p. 118).

Roman Breviary. By the sixteenth century, there had been numerous calls for the reform of the Divine Office as contained in the *Roman Breviary.* Among the complaints: the almost complete suppression of the Sunday and weekday offices in favor of those of the saints (which were shorter); difficulty of reciting the entire Psalter in the course of a week; multiplication of such offices as the Little Office of the Blessed Virgin Mary and the Office of the Dead; substitution of legends, apocryphal stories, and texts of "dubious value" in place of scripture; complexity and confusion in ordos and calendars.

The mid-sixteenth century saw several attempted reforms of the breviary. Commissioned by Pope Leo X, Zacharia Ferreri recast the office hymns into Ciceronian Latin. A more extensive and radical reform was effected by Cardinal Francisco de Quiñones under the authority of Clement VII (1523–1534) and Paul III (1534–1549). The arrangement and content of the Quiñones Breviary (1535), often called the "Breviary of the Holy Cross" (after the cardinal's titular church), reflected its novel intention: to serve the individual cleric in private recitation. Thus most of the traditional choral and communal elements were excluded. This office, which was very popular because of its simplicity, influenced the work of Protestant reformers and *The Book of Common Prayer.* It was suppressed by Paul IV in 1558.

When the Council of Trent commissioned the papacy to

reform the breviary, the revisers considered a plan originally sketched out by Gian Pietro Carafa (the future Paul IV) in 1529. After Carafa became pope in 1555, he wished to purge the breviary of historical errors and literary defects while keeping the ancient structure and traditions of the office. He did not live to see the implementation of his reform. But reacting to the innovations in the Quiñones Breviary, the commission under Pius IV and Pius V was guided by three principles: (1) no essential part of the ancient *Roman Breviary* was to be removed; (2) the primitive form of the breviary was to be restored; (3) there was to be no difference between the text of the public office and the office recited in private.

Pius V's bull *Quod a nobis* (1 July 1568) promulgated such a breviary and abolished all its predecessors except those which had been in use for at least two hundred years. Like the subsequent missal of Pius V, his breviary became for all practical purposes the office of the Western church (except for the local so-called neo-Gallican breviaries in seventeenth- to nineteenth-century France). The breviary of Pius V, the first universal breviary, remained substantially unchanged until the *Liturgia Horarum* was approved by Paul VI in 1970.

Tridentine Reforms in the Mass. To tidy up the cluttered garden of the Mass, the commission set up by the Council of Trent first wielded the sickle. Yet in legislating "What Must Be Observed and Avoided in the Celebration of Mass" (17 September 1562), the council limited itself to correcting the more glaring abuses: avarice (e.g., insistent and involuntary exactions of stipends for masses), irreverence (e.g., striking the breast with great violence during the words *Nobis quoque peccatoribus* ["To us sinners also"] in the Roman Canon), and superstition (e.g., mass series for particular intentions and masses celebrated with a set number of candles). Proposals for correcting missals were listed in the first draft only, but were omitted in subsequent drafts due to limited time for debate. The second and third drafts condemned the *Missa sicca,* or "dry Mass" (a rite often used aboard ship, in which the consecration and Communion were lacking, and in which the Blessed Sacrament was shown to the congregation for adoration); yet the final text does not mention the "dry Mass" (perhaps because twelve council fathers defended the practice). Similarly, while a preliminary list of abuses condemned the deliberate celebration of a private Mass during the singing of a solemn Mass, or during the sermon, the final text forbade only masses in private homes or outside church, and at unseasonable hours.

In defending the ceremonies of the Mass against the criticism of the reformers, the Council of Trent used arguments from scripture, apostolic tradition, and human nature to support their use. Whoever proclaimed that these ceremonies, vestments, and external signs were provocation to impiety was declared anathema. The Roman Canon was declared free from doctrinal error; whoever wanted to eliminate the Canon because of its literary defects incurred an anathema. The council fathers defended recitation of the Canon in a low voice, declaring that this practice did not invalidate the essence of the Mass. They also defended the private Mass, stating that there is no essential difference between a public and private celebration of the Mass, even if there is no distribution of Communion. Yet the faithful were strongly encouraged to receive Communion at the masses they attended.

The Council of Trent did accomplish the limited task it set for itself: defending the Mass against the reformers' criticism and correcting abuses that were prevalent in its celebration. The members of the council did not seek to explore new theological territory regarding the Eucharist or its liturgical celebration, choosing instead to leave reform of the missal to the papacy.

Tridentine Missal. Some council fathers recommended that the commission preparing the new *Missale Romanum* leave unrestricted the right of dioceses to retain regional differences and regulate their own practices regarding the celebration of Mass. But the commission rejected this proposal, preferring instead to produce a uniform missal.

In his bull *Quo primum tempore* (14 July 1570), Pius V imposed this missal on all local churches and religious orders that could not claim to have used their own particular books for at least two hundred years; among those rendered exempt by this decree were the Ambrosian rite, the Dominican rite, and some dioceses in France. Further additions to and alterations in the missal, as in the breviary, were to be the exclusive concern of the papacy. This missal, the so-called Tridentine Missal or the Missal of Pius V, was the first to be officially published by the Holy See; as such it became a major part of the Counter-Reformation launched by the Council of Trent.

The aim of the commission that prepared this missal was to restore the Roman Mass "to the earlier norm and rite of the holy Fathers," for example, Gregory VII, who was seen as the defender of ancient Roman tradition, "standing . . . on the threshold of the period of centralization of Western liturgy" (Klauser, p. 126). The revisers believed that if the accretions and distortions that had come to mar the liturgical landscape since antiquity could be removed, and only the basic elements of the ancient Roman liturgy be retained, the new missal would be a beneficial imposition on all Western-rite Catholics.

Thus the major reforms in the missal of Pius V were directed at eliminating texts that contained dubious material. Only a few of the multitude of votive masses (those in honor of a particular saint or aspect of the life of Christ) were spared, and the use of these or any other mass formulary of various feasts as a votive mass was carefully regulated; Sunday masses could no longer be superseded by a votive mass.

Existing prefaces (the introductory, variable section of the

Roman Canon), especially those for saints' feasts, often contained legendary material; only eleven prefaces were included in the new missal.

Tropes (newly composed texts set to the existing music of the melismatic Gregorian chant for the proper and ordinary sung parts of the Mass) were judged parasitic and hence completely removed. Sequences, a special kind of trope written on the long musical ending of the Alleluia, survived, but greatly reduced in number: only four of the thousands of sequences in existence were included in the new missal.

The liturgical calendar of feasts and seasons was deliberately harmonized with that of the *Roman Breviary* published two years earlier. The number of saints' days was reduced so that 157 days were now free for other celebrations. This change lightened a burden that had been accruing during the years 800–1558, when almost three hundred saints' feasts were added to the calendar but none removed. Pius V's restraint in revising the sanctoral calendar was not matched by his successors, who added new saints' days.

Rubrics, now endowed with the force of law, took on as significant a role as the spoken text. Gestures and other ceremonies could no longer be added according to the inspiration of one's personal devotion, thus eliminating anything that might generate superstition or scandal. "Every word printed in black had to be uttered, every action printed in red had to be performed" (Howell, p. 288).

Limits and Significance of the Tridentine Liturgical Books. The Tridentine Breviary and Missal clearly did not constitute a complete break with the past. Rather, they constituted a reform that reached back into Roman tradition: the codification of traditional rubrics, the correction and excision of texts, and the securing of agreement between the missal and breviary (e.g., by means of the calendar common to both).

However, the aim of the commission to return to the eucharistic practice of ancient Rome was not completely achieved, nor could it be. Historical studies of the ancient liturgy were only in their infancy, and many valuable documents were yet to be discovered; the members of the commission knew almost nothing about liturgies antedating the tenth or eleventh centuries.

The most serious obstacle to reform of the Mass, one that the Missal of Pius V did not remove, was the understanding of liturgy that prevailed in the sixteenth century. Even though the Mass was held to be the worship of the entire church, the solemn High Mass closely resembled the celebration by the priest alone. While the rubrics in the Tridentine Missal indicate in minutest detail what the priest must do at Mass, the presence of the people is mentioned only twice (indeed, their presence was not considered necessary for the celebration). Because of this "defective concept of liturgy" (Howell, p. 287), passivity and unintelligibility remained the laity's malnutrition. But it must be observed that in the polemical era of the sixteenth century, such aids to popular participation as use of the vernacular would have seemed like capitulating to the demands of the Protestant reformers.

According to Joseph Jungmann, the most important innovation of the Tridentine Missal was to make this book standard throughout the West and to prohibit changes in it (*The Mass of the Roman Rite*, vol. 1, p. 138). Such standardization could have been possible only because of the development of printing, which made unity more convenient and economical than diversity. The Tridentine Missal and Breviary are significant because they were used for nearly four hundred years with almost no changes (except papal ones) but with a number of additions (e.g., feasts of newly canonized saints).

In response to sixteenth-century challenges to centuries-old Roman liturgical practices, the Breviary and Missal of Pius V centralized the liturgy in the authority of the Holy See and suppressed time-honored customs of regions and dioceses in view of what seemed a greater good—orthodoxy and unity—at the time. Yet these books also inaugurated a period of liturgical history described as a time of rigidity, stagnation, and rubricism. Theisen summarizes the liturgical aims of the Council of Trent: it "conceived its task as one of correction and purgation . . . The means it chose to accomplish these ends was the formation of a uniform missal. Thus, the words purgation, unification, rubrification, and fixation may well qualify the Tridentine work of Mass reform" ("The Reform of Mass Liturgy and the Council of Trent," p. 583).

Congregation of Sacred Rites. The institutional concerns reflected in the Tridentine liturgical books took another form in 1588, when Sixtus V established the Congregation of Sacred Rites (*Pro Sacris Ritibus et Caeremoniis*). The primary reason for establishing this congregation was for the purpose of reforming and correcting the liturgical books as need arose. It was responsible for implementing Trent's decrees regarding the public worship of the church.

Among the congregation's tasks were the following: vigilance for the observance of sacred rites; restoration and reform of ceremonies; revision and correction of liturgical books; regulation of the offices of patron saints; celebration of saints' feasts; canonization of saints; and resolution of controversies over precedence and other liturgical matters. This congregation completed the Tridentine reform by issuing authoritative editions of several liturgical books: the Roman Pontifical (rites reserved to the bishop) in 1596; the Ceremonial (episcopal ceremonies) in 1600; and the Roman Ritual (sacramental rites and blessings not reserved to the bishop) in 1614. Much of the congregation's attention was directed to issuing decrees on liturgical practices and responding to questions about these practices. In this way, centralization and uniformity in liturgical matters were maintained up to the Second Vatican Council (1962–1965).

Some might view Pius V, his successors, and the Congregation of Sacred Rites as villains who locked the Roman church into a liturgical straitjacket, thereby retarding the evolution of the Roman liturgy in such areas as artistic development and cultural adaptation. Yet Robert Cabié observes that Pius V was "a courageous innovator, and it is an almost unbelievable paradox that some should today be invoking his patronage to oppose a reform inspired by the same spirit as continued and brought to bear at the Second Vatican Council" (*The Church at Prayer,* vol. 2, p. 176). Modern liturgical reform, facing new challenges and using new resources, seeks to cultivate and invigorate the ancient garden that the Council of Trent, Pius V, and his successors so carefully tended in their time.

[*See also* Eucharist; Hymnals; Hymns; Mass; Sacraments; *and* Trent, Council of.]

BIBLIOGRAPHY

Batiffol, Pierre. *History of the Roman Breviary.* Translated by Atwell M. Y. Baylay. New York, 1898.

Baudot, Jules. *The Roman Breviary: Its Sources and History.* London, 1910.

Bossy, John. "The Mass as a Social Institution, 1200–1700." *Past and Present* 100 (1983), 29–61. Innovative study of the cultural meaning of the Mass.

Cabié, Robert. *The Church at Prayer.* Translated by Matthew J. O'Connell. Collegeville, Minn., 1986.

Crichton, J. D. *Christian Celebration: The Prayer of the Church.* London, 1976. Concise survey of the history, theology, and content of the church's liturgical prayer, from its origins to post-Vatican II reforms.

Freudenberger, Th. "Die Meßliturgie in der Volkssprache im Urteil des Trienter Konzils." In *Reformatio Ecclesiae: Beiträge zu kirchlichen Reformbemühungen von der Alten Kirche bis zur Neuzeit,* edited by R. Bäumer, pp. 679–698. Paderborn, 1980.

Gy, Pierre-Marie. *La liturgie dans l'histoire.* Paris, 1990. Concise popular history of the liturgy by one of its foremost historians.

Howell, Clifford. "From Trent to Vatican II." In *The Study of Liturgy,* pp. 285–294. Rev. ed. London and New York, 1992.

Jones, Cheslyn, et al., eds. *The Study of Liturgy.* Rev. ed. Oxford, 1992. Valuable collection of articles on the history of the liturgy from earliest times to the present; includes Catholic and Protestant liturgies.

Jungmann, Joseph A."Das Konzil von Trient und die Erneuerung der Liturgie." In *Das Weltkonzil von Trient: Sein Werden und Wirken,* edited by G. Schreiber, vol. 1, pp. 325–336. Freiburg, 1951.

———. "Liturgy on the Eve of the Reformation." *Worship* 33 (1959), 505–515.

———. *The Mass of the Roman Rite: Its Origin and Development.* Translated by Francis A. Brunner. 2 vols. Reprint, Westminster, Md., 1986. Classic, unmatched study of the Roman church's celebration of the Eucharist, from antiquity to the threshold of the Second Vatican Council.

King, Archdale A. *Liturgy of the Roman Church.* London and Milwaukee, 1957. Includes definitions of liturgical objects, rites, terms, and clerical offices.

Klauser, Theodor. *A Short History of the Western Liturgy: An Account and Some Reflections.* Translated by John Halliburton. 2d ed. Oxford, 1979. Very readable survey of important topics.

Kwatera, Michael. "Breviary." In *Dictionary of the Middle Ages,* pp. 370–373. New York, 1983.

Leroquais, Victor. *Les sacrementaires et les missels manuscrits des bibliothèques publiques de France.* 3 vols. Paris, 1924. Invaluable catalog of hundreds of medieval and early modern missals from all over Europe; illustrated.

Martinez, German. "Reform, Liturgical, History of." In *The New Dictionary of Sacramental Worship,* edited by Peter E. Fink, pp. 1066–1072. Collegeville, Minn., 1990.

Meyer, Hans Bernhard. *Eucharistie: Geschichte, Theologie, Pastoral.* Regensburg, 1989.

The Roman Breviary. Introduction by Fernand Cabrol. 4 vols. New London, Conn., 1936.

The Roman Missal in Latin and English for Every Day of the Year: In Conformity with the Latest Decrees. Introduction and liturgical notes by Fernand Cabrol. 9th ed., rev. & enl. New York, 1934.

Schroeder, Henry Joseph, trans. *The Canons and Decrees of the Council of Trent.* Rockford, Ill., 1978.

Theisen, Reinold Jerome. *Mass Liturgy and the Council of Trent.* Collegeville, Minn., 1965. An excerpt from the author's doctoral dissertation, this is the best work on the subject. Especially valuable presentation of the thinking that shaped the Tridentine reforms (e.g., views on the origin and immutability of the Roman canon).

———. "The Reform of Mass Liturgy and the Council of Trent." *Worship* 40 (1966), 565–583. A useful summary of the above.

Vogel, Cyrille. *Medieval Liturgy: An Introduction to the Sources.* Translated by William G. Storey and Niels Krogh Rasmussen. Washington, D.C., 1986. Comprehensive review of the ancient and medieval sacramentaries, ordos and pontificals, the stuff of which the Tridentine liturgical books were made.

MICHAEL KWATERA, O.S.B.

LOLLARDY. The term "Lollard"—related to the Middle English word for "mumble" and associated with biblical "tares" (weeds)—was used in England throughout the fifteenth century to denigrate followers of John Wycliffe (d. 1384). What Lollardy was or turned into in the sixteenth century is problematical. There are difficulties both in establishing what Wycliffe's heritage amounted to in 1500 and in discovering what became of Lollards in the course of the Reformation.

There is doubt about the strength of Lollardy during the first quarter of the sixteenth century. During this period, when episcopal investigations were undertaken with fresh vigor, many suspects were examined and some thirty-five heretics went to the stake. In 1511, under Archbishop Warham's initiative, there was concerted action in several dioceses, resulting in ten burnings and about 140 abjurations. A decade later, around 1521, when Bishop Longland of Lincoln undertook a major inquest, four hundred or so individuals were named, of whom six were burned and fifty abjured.

Now, as earlier, many individuals were accused whose deviancy was marginal but whose enthusiasm for scripture seemed dangerous. As a community of shared opinions and domestic religion, Lollardy was both more and less than doctrinal error. At its core lay a set of defined, inherited heresies; disbelief in Christ's corporeal presence in the Eucharist; rejection of the need for baptism and confession; denial of the value of pilgrimage, prayers to saints, or honoring of their images (with special aspersion of the Virgin). Oaths, fasting, and prayers for the dead were all attacked as unscriptural; holy bread, holy water, bells, organs, and church buildings were disparaged; papal pardons set at naught.

These negations of the church's rites were firmly grounded on biblical certainties, and Lollardy was above all a religion of vernacular scripture. Lollards were bound together by study of the Bible and other texts. Group meetings to read and hear, expound or learn, at well-guarded locations in houses or barns, as well as solitary readings in wood or field, were the central activity, and the most suspect. In their conventicles or schools, individuals might learn literacy as well as the salvation of the word. The term *known men* and *known women* used in trials was an old form of self-naming: the known of God were those who truly knew and followed his law.

The secreted texts were primarily books of the New Testament: the Gospels, the Epistles (especially the letter of James), and *Revelation*. There were also writings related to the Old Testament: works on the ten commandments and the ten plagues of Egypt, and a "book of Solomon." Such survivals as we have of other named English texts were mostly composed long before, suggesting that Lollards, if true to their inheritance, were also living on their past. Their prized texts have the appearance of a hoarded library, well thumbed, but not replenished. Wycliffe was still revered, but there is no proof that his authentic works or genuine views were known. His *Trialogus* was printed abroad in 1525 and had been imported into London by 1532, but it was the falsely attributed *Wycliffe's Wicket* and an unidentified "book called Wycliffe" that were read by sixteenth-century Lollards.

Late Lollardy suffered from its divorce from the universities. It had lost the intellectual momentum it possessed when led by clerks trained in the schools, and it is telling that no Lollard literature was printed until the Reformation was well under way. The character of Lollardy in this period is reflected in its leaders. John Stilman and Thomas Man, both burned in 1518, were looked up to by many, and the latter, whose ministry (shared with his wife) stretched from Colchester to Newbury and Amersham, was said to have converted six or seven hundred. Another famous apostle, likewise a layman, was John Hacker, who in the 1520s distributed texts and spread expertise in the gospel from London (center of the illicit booktrade) into Essex and as far as the Cotswolds. These lay missionaries could link scattered communities and win adherents, but they were not writing new books, originating fresh ideas, or gathering crowds at illicit sermons. Theirs was a ministry of subterfuge, of undercover teaching and book running. The days of challenging preaching tours were past—until restarted in the days of new Protestant initiatives.

Those listed as suspect were largely husbandmen and people involved in crafts and trades. It does not follow that they were poor. And undoubtedly men and women of wealth and standing sympathized with Lollardy and owned vernacular books that might prove fatally incriminating in the hands of artisans. In Colchester, Coventry, and London, Lollard connections extended into rich office-holding families, including mayors and their wives. Well-off heretics of less distinction were able to pay bribes of £20 to avoid public penance, or to burn books worth more than £65 to evade conviction—sums that were fortunes for most working people.

Lollard opinions had become deeply entrenched in parts of Kent, Essex, south Buckinghamshire, Berkshire, and Oxfordshire. Bristol was among the towns and cities with long heretical connections, and in some parishes the dominance of heresy was such that even curates and churchwardens were Lollard. These were closely knit communities. People might be born into as well as converted to Lollardy; Lollards intermarried, and certain families are known to have passed down both books and beliefs over several generations. Widely separated groups were associated, facilitating escapes at times of persecution.

Lollardy was a faith of house and household, whose church was the congregation of God's chosen, but Lollards we not separatists. Some individuals might absent themselves from church, but others received their annual Easter Communion in order to escape the stigma of heresy. There were those who served as holy water clerks or tended the very rood lights they mocked. If their forms of speech and behavior made Lollards recognizable (perhaps to outsiders as well as to fellow partisans), only the barest of hints—such as Bible readings at weddings—suggest they had alternative rites.

Heretics are made by laws as well as opinions. Lollardy still dominated the heretical map in 1533, when the power of the bishops to initiate heresy trials was replaced by secular indictments. During the later years of Henry VIII, with heresy for the first time defined by statute (in 1539), the searchlight focused on other kinds of offenders, and in 1547 the old anti-Lollard legislation was repealed. The regime of Mary Tudor put Lollardy back on the map, with the reinstatement of the fifteenth-century laws and orders for tracking down Lollardies. Perhaps this, rather than any resurgence of Wycliffite opinion, explains the inquiries of 1555 in Norfolk and York into Lollard heresy. By this time it is difficult for us, as it certainly was for contemporaries, to adjudicate between old heresy and new, but it may be that the eucharistic beliefs for which some died in this reign were more Lollard than Protestant. Finally, in 1559, legal provisions against the Lollards went for good, though until 1626 local officials still had to swear, on taking office, to eradicate all manner of heresies, errors, and Lollardies.

Although John Foxe drafted Lollards into his *Book of Martyrs* as godly ancestors of the Church of England, we cannot assume this, or any other, general line of descent. There was no necessary convergence between old heresy and new Protestantism. Those devoted to Saint James were not predisposed to enthusiasm for justification by faith, and knowledge of changes in Lutheran Germany might merely bolster old views. However, from the late 1520s we do know of exchanges of books and ideas, and there were Lollards who read new works and were affected by Lutheran doctrine. Joan Bocher, who in 1550 died as an Anabaptist, may not have been alone in making this credal transition after long commitment to Lollardy. At the same time a number of leading English reformers—including Tyndale, Bilney, and Latimer—may have been moved by and tried to promote essential features of the old Lollard program. That program entered the pool of reforming literature with the printing, in the 1530s and 1540s, of ten old Lollard English texts, preceded by Luther's 1528 edition of a Latin Lollard commentary on *Revelation*.

Coincidence of geography, family names, and religious opinions has led to claims of Lollard ancestry for Anglicans, Puritans, and Dissenters. However that may be, the Lollard's long-standing communities of scripturally oriented individuals, independent habits of thought, and vernacular religious literacy undoubtedly prepared the soil for another generation's Reformation planting. As a church without walls, Lollardy disappeared undenominated.

[*See also* Puritans.]

BIBLIOGRAPHY

Aston, Margaret. *Lollards and Reformers: Images and Literacy in Late Medieval Religion.* London, 1984. Collected articles on related themes including Wycliffe and Lollard texts in the Reformation period.

Brigden, Susan. *London and the Reformation.* Corr. ed. Oxford, 1991. Sets Lollard activity in London in the early sixteenth century richly in context.

Cross, Claire. *Church and People, 1450–1660.* Reprint, London, 1987. A very readable survey that gives due attention to Lollardy in the early Reformation.

Davies, Richard G. "Lollardy and Locality." *Transactions of the Royal Historical Society,* 6th series 1, (1991), 191–212. Indicates the importance of local roots and interconnected groups in the Lollard movement.

Davis, John F. "Lollardy and the Reformation in England." *Archiv für Reformationsgeschichte* 73 (1982), 217–237. Useful survey, but not helped by attaching term "evangelism" to English Reformation.

———. *Heresy and Reformation in the South-East of England, 1520–1559.* London 1983. Regional monograph with valuable case histories, partly drawn from unprinted sources.

Dickens, A. G. *Lollards and Protestants in the Diocese of York, 1509–1558.* 2d ed. London, 1982. A work of originality and insight, that put Lollardy on a fresh part of the map and is still very good reading.

———. "Heresy and the Origins of English Protestantism." In *Reformation Studies,* pp. 363–82, London, 1982. An essay that first appeared in 1964, this remains a useful summary.

Dunnan, D. Stuart. *The Preaching of Hugh Latimer: A Reappraisal.* Oxford, forthcoming. Includes consideration of the Lollard influences traceable in Latimer's preaching.

Gairdner, James. *Lollardy and the Reformation in England: An Historical Survey.* Reprint, New York, 1968.

Hill, Christopher. "From Lollards to Levellers." In *The Collected Essays of Christopher Hill. Religion and Politics in 17th Century England,* vol. 2, pp. 89–116, Brighton, 1986. A slightly revised version of an essay of 1978; postulates a continuous underground of dissent by accumulating examples of opinions and geographical locations.

Hope, Andrew. "Lollardy: The Stone the Builders Rejected?" In *Protestantism and the National Church in Sixteenth Century England,* edited by Peter Lake and Maria Dowling, pp. 1–35. London and New York, 1987. Most perceptive recent survey of Tudor Lollardy.

Hudson, Anne. *Lollards and their Books.* London and Ronceverte, W.Va., 1985. Collected articles, important for understanding fifteenth-century Lollardy and its manuscripts. Includes chapter on those printed in sixteenth century.

———. *The Premature Reformation: Wycliffite Texts and Lollard History.* Oxford, 1988. An invaluable comprehensive work, central to Lollard studies, embodying results of recent work and Hudson's research on Wycliffite writings. Concluding pages on 1520s and 1530s stress Lollard vitality and coherence.

Smeeton, Donald Dean. *Lollard Themes in the Reformation Theology of William Tyndale.* Sixteenth Century Essays and Studies, vol. 6. Kirksville, Mo., 1986. Argues the case for Wycliffite views having contributed to Tyndale's theology.

Spufford, Margaret, ed. *The World of Rural Dissenters, 1520–1725.* Cambridge, 1994. Brings economic sources to bear on groups of local dissenters, starting with Lollards of the Chilterns.

Thomson, John A. F. *The Later Lollards 1414–1520.* Oxford, 1965. Regional survey of those charged with Lollardy, largely from unprinted bishops' registers.

MARGARET ASTON

LONDON. Without a Reformation in London there could have been no Reformation in England. London was far larger than any other English town, comparable in size by the end of the sixteenth century with other European capitals, a seat of royal government and justice, a hub of international trade and finance. It was here that events of transcendent national importance occurred. Upon London's compliance depended the success of royal religious policies, but its loyalty was far from assured, for its population was notoriously volatile. London presented as great a challenge as any overmighty subject.

On the eve of the Reformation communal religious observance marked the autonomy of London, as of every city, and the Catholic faith united. Within that unity there was diversity, because London had over one hundred parishes, more than any other European city, a cathedral, thirty-nine religious houses, and perhaps as many as a hundred religious fraternities, parochial and transparochial. Each of these religious communities had its own traditions and engendered a particular loyalty. A community of heretics also lived in London, the Lollards, which may have been growing in size and influence at the beginning of the sixteenth century and which frightened the authorities. Yet it was not until the 1520s, when the Lollards joined forces with the reformers, that heresy fractured the Catholic community.

Some of England's first and most fervent evangelicals congregated in London and from there conducted their preaching and book-running campaigns. London had no university, but at the Inns of Court reform spread among lawyers who were to become prime movers of the English Reformation. London early became the center of a Protestant book trade. By the end of the 1520s the evangelicals were winning converts to the new faith, which already contained elements of reform more radical than Lutheranism; but persecuted and on the run, they were still a church under the cross, lacking patronage. The early infiltration of reform at court and the links between evangelicals at Court and in the City gave hope of future protection.

The political Reformation was made in London. The first petition against the "enormities of the clergy" in the Reformation Parliament was initiated by City interests, and London merchants and lawyers were at the vanguard of attempts to curb clerical powers. The power and wealth of Cardinal Thomas Wolsey, most evident in London, had been prejudicial to the entire clerical estate. When Henry VIII determined to break with Rome, London became the center of a propaganda campaign to promulgate the changes. From London pulpits, especially Paul's Cross, royal supremacy was declared and the pope denounced, and on London scaffolds the pope's defenders were destroyed. Sir Thomas More, perhaps London's most famous citizen, Bishop John Fisher, and the Carthusians were martyred in 1535.

Religious choices were demanded most immediately from Londoners, as successive royal policies transformed the church. The citizens became irrevocably divided in religion. From the 1530s the religious history of London was intimately linked with the struggle for power among contending factions at Court and in the council. The schism in the capital between the religious conservatives and the growing force of reformers, and the popular disturbance this schism engendered, underlay all the machinations in high politics and influenced the outcome. As he faced execution in 1553, John Dudley, duke of Northumberland, even claimed that he would have reversed the Reformation he had promoted during Edward VI's reign, but dared not because of the religious enthusiasm of the Londoners.

With the Reformation came unprecedented destruction. In 1532 the first religious house was dissolved in London, and by 1539 the rest had followed. In Edward VI's reign the parish churches, too, were transformed as images were removed. Londoners, who had venerated the shrines and the religious life, did little to prevent the desecrations. The enthusiasm shown at the restoration of Catholicism under Mary Tudor is evidence that very many regretted the destruction. Yet Mary's reign revealed also the continuing divisions among the citizens. Many went into exile to escape conformity or persecution, and more than a quarter of England's martyrs came from the capital.

Elizabeth's accession, and the prospect of a Protestant regime, were ostensibly greeted rapturously. But there were signs also of how many had been won back to the Catholic church under Mary or had never left it. During Elizabeth's reign London, like the rest of England, converted to Protestantism. Yet London became the center of the Catholic missionary movement to sustain the laity and to make converts in the country. It was the heartland, too, of the campaign by the "godly" for further reformation in the church. The stranger churches provided the model of a church fully reformed. Some of the more radical were driven into schism, but the presbyterian movement made surprisingly few converts in London, and only tiny bands of the godly moved into separatism. Transient and private congregations of religious radicals were a recurrent element in London religious life until the Civil War and beyond.

London's bishops often found themselves bound to impose religious policies of which they disapproved. London's conservatives in the 1530s had thought John Stokesley was on their side, and later London's Puritans believed Edmund Grindal "their own man." So, too, London's governors were not always in accord with the policies they were to enforce. As Elizabeth's reign progressed, advanced Protestants came to dominate City government. Their Reformed convictions were revealed in their practical godliness—their zeal to reform moral conduct and their attitudes toward poverty and charity.

London was "a mighty arm and instrument to bring any great desire to effect, if it may be won to a man's devotion," wrote London's great chronicler John Stow. When reformation was effected in London the realm followed, for the power of London's religious example was immense. The Reformation in London had been far more peaceful than in many other Continental cities, and London had escaped the fate of Paris. Rebellion and civil war had been averted—until the reforms of Bishop William Laud stirred the perennial religious divisions in London and helped determine the City's decision to declare for Parliament against the king in the English Civil War.

[*See also* England.]

BIBLIOGRAPHY

Archer, Ian W. *The Pursuit of Stability: Social Relations in Elizabethan London.* Cambridge, 1991. Study of London society and government.

Brigden, Susan. *London and the Reformation.* Rev. & corr. ed. Oxford, 1991. A study and an evocation of a community transformed by the Reformation.

Collinson, Patrick. *The Elizabethan Puritan Movement.* Oxford, 1990. Study of a movement among clergy and laity for further reform in the English church.

Davis, E. Jeffries. "The Transformation of London." In *Tudor Studies* (1924), edited by R. W. Seton-Watson, pp. 287–314. Reprint, New York, 1970. Study of the transformation of London in the wake of Reformation and dissolution.

SUSAN BRIGDEN

LORD'S SUPPER. *See* Eucharist.

LORIS, Heinrich. *See* Glareanus, Heinricus.

LORRAINE-GUISE, HOUSE OF. The history of the family of Lorraine-Guise is so interwoven into the skein of social, religious, and political complexity in sixteenth-century France that it is difficult to extricate it for specific consideration. At the outset it must be recognized that the history of this era was not driven by mass movements or high principles but by the interests of great families. As the reform movement was beginning in France in the second quarter of the sixteenth century, four great families dominated the power rivalries—the royal House of Valois and three other houses with royal lines in their histories: Montmorency, Albret-Bourbon, and the newly powerful Guise. The rapid rise of the Guises from the second quarter of the sixteenth century made them the new players in this league, much resented both for their recent origin and for their success.

When Claude of Lorraine, at the age of twelve, inherited the county of Guise in 1508, he also received two other counties, a marquisate, and four lordships. That was the beginning. His brother Jean, aged three, was made coadjutor of the bishop of Metz; at twenty years of age he was named cardinal of Lorraine, collecting archbishoprics, bishoprics, and abbeys—many of which he managed to pass on to relatives. In the middle of the century the House of Lorraine added a second cardinalate, that of Guise, and the Grand Priory of the Order of the Knights of Malta in France. The county of Guise was elevated to a duchy in 1527, and the former count of Guise was made a duke and peer of France—an enormous award as the titles, previously reserved for princes of the royal blood, gave him precedence over almost all the other nobles of France. Later the county of Aumale also was elevated to a duchy, as was the marquisate of Mayenne; and the family acquired the duchy of Chevreuse. The title of sieur of Joinville was raised to prince of Joinville, further enhancing the family's dignity. A Guise prince married into the Italian House of Este, which was of royal blood (Anjou); a daughter of Lorraine-Guise was married to the king of Scotland, and subsequently her daughter married the heir apparent to the French throne. Naturally, appointments to innumerable offices and honors accompanied the family's rise to glory. Even without the intrusion of the religious issue, the situation likely would have been explosive.

The First Generation. Claude of Lorraine (1496–1550), count and later first duke of Guise, was the second son of René II, duke of Lorraine. He took his first steps to favor and power on the battlefield, fighting with distinction beside Francis I at Marignano in 1515. Claude was then sent to the northern frontier to fight successfully against the English. In Italy, however, three of his brothers died in the service of Francis I. Claude was then named governor of Champagne and Burgundy in 1523. During the next two decades he continued to enjoy military successes for the Crown and won considerable popularity with the people of Paris, partly because of his dramatic personality, a trait that came to characterize the Guise princes, and also because he successfully defended the frontiers essential to the safety of Paris. Of his twelve legitimate children and one illegitimate son, only the most prominent can be mentioned here.

The Second Generation. Jean of Lorraine (1498–1550), cardinal of Lorraine, was René's third son. He was basically a political schemer who consolidated support for the Guises at court.

François of Lorraine (1519–1563), second duke of Guise, earned a distinguished military reputation and considerable popularity. Much was made of the mark of an almost-fatal wound on his face acquired in 1545 for which he was fondly nicknamed *le Balafré* ("Scarface"). It was Duke François and his brother Charles who entangled the Guises deeply in the French religious struggles. François grew up with escalating religious violence and matured in a period when the French Calvinists were developing congregations and even a loose national organization, and he came to despise them. In addition, political pressure was intense; it appeared that the hour of the Guises had come when Henry II died in 1559 and was succeeded by his son Francis II, who was married to Duke François's niece Mary. In 1560 the Guises crushed a fumbled coup d'état at Amboise involving Calvinist and possibly Bourbon plotting. But in December 1560 Francis II died and with him the Guise position behind the throne. As the next Valois prince, Charles IX, was a minor, the queen-mother, Catherine de Médicis, became regent. Catherine, an astute, intelligent, and endlessly patient woman, also possessed an implacable hatred for the ambition and arrogance of the Guises. François therefore found himself on the defensive as Catherine turned to the Bourbons and Montmorencys or anyone with the power to counterbalance the Guises.

It was the Guises who began the Wars of Religion with the Massacre of Wassy in 1562. François and his suite stumbled onto a Calvinist religious meeting; the resulting massacre opened three decades of bloody strife. A year later, in February 1563, François was gunned down by a Calvinist; whether, as his son and successor believed, the Calvinist leader Admiral Gaspard II de Coligny was involved has never been proved.

Charles of Lorraine (1524–1574), second cardinal of Lorraine, is usually considered the fount of political machinations in this generation of the Guises. He engaged in an endless match with Catherine de Médicis, attempting to sustain the Guise position at court while his older brother pursued military ventures.

Marie of Lorraine (1515–1560), eldest child of Claude, duke of Guise, married King James V of Scotland in 1538. Two sons of this marriage died in infancy, but a daughter, Mary, was born just after her father's death. Marie of Lorraine had the difficult task of trying to oversee her daughter's kingdom just as the Scottish Reformation erupted. Mary Stuart (1542–1587) was sent at the age of five to be brought up at the French court, in 1558 married the future Francis II, and in 1559 became queen consort of France. Francis II died in 1560, and a year later Mary Stuart returned to Scotland and her eventual tragic fate as Mary, queen of Scots.

The Third Generation. Henry of Lorraine (1550–1588), third duke of Guise, was the prince of Lorraine-Guise most prominently involved in the religious struggles in France. Though still only an adolescent when his father was killed in 1563, the new duke of Guise was permitted by the queen mother to assume some of his father's offices (Catherine dared not pick a quarrel with so powerful a clan), and in the late 1560s he acquired considerable military experience and wounds in the renewed civil wars. Though he showed no particular military talent, he earned a reputation for dashing bravery and became the hero of the young French nobility, as well as being idolized by the Paris crowd.

What role the duke of Guise had in orchestrating the events of 1572, a botched attempt to murder Admiral Coligny followed by the Saint Bartholomew's Day Massacre, has never been clearly established, though certainly he took part in the bloody work, especially in finishing off Coligny. While Guise wanted Coligny's death as atonement for the death of his father, too much may have been built on that. In 1575 Henry of Guise further strengthened his popularity with the Parisians by defeating an invading German force in the pay of the Huguenots. In that battle he received a deep wound to his left cheek and so inherited his father's nickname, *le Balafré*. Thus the Guise mystique continued to grow.

The Guises demanded and supported absolute Catholicism. For example, in the spring of 1576, attempting to calm the Wars of Religion, King Henry III made significant concessions to the Huguenots, a result of which was the formation of a Catholic League at Péronne in the north. The duke of Guise seized the opportunity and turned the movement into a national league under his direction.

In 1584 the death of the duke of Anjou resulted in the War of the Three Henrys: Henry Valois, king of France, Henry Bourbon, king of Navarre, and Henry, duke of Guise. The crisis came in 1588, when Henry III, fearing Guise's popularity, forbade him to enter Paris. Guise did so anyway, and when the populace heard a rumor that he had been arrested, it blocked the streets against the royal troops: this was the Day of the Barricades. Guise took command and cleared the streets, humiliating Henry III, who slipped out of Paris and fled to Chartres, leaving the capital to the duke of Guise. Henry III appeared to capitulate, but on 23 December, answering the king's summons, Guise entered the royal suite and was assassinated by the king's guards. His brother Louis, the cardinal of Lorraine, (1555–1588), was arrested and murdered in his cell the next day. A third brother, Charles, duke of Mayenne (1554–1611), barely escaped to Burgundy, where he was governor. Mayenne proved ineffective and the ascendancy of the House of Guise was ended. Henry III was himself assassinated by a Guisard, and thus Henry of Navarre emerged triumphant. In 1593 Navarre became a Catholic and in 1594 was crowned Henry IV of France. For the Guises, it was disaster. They had bound themselves to uncompromising Catholicism—military programs, unrelenting sectarian strife, and financial support from the king of Spain. Henry IV won over the moderate Catholics, mollified the Huguenots, and made peace with the King of Spain. The bases of the Guise position were wiped out.

The Last Generation. After this debacle of the 1590s the Guises were never again to know such influence and power. They continued to command respect and prestige during the seventeenth century, but the substance was gone. The senior male line died out in 1675. Some of the old titles were revived in the eighteenth century for Bourbon princes of the Condé branch, but the House of Lorraine-Guise was no more.

BIBLIOGRAPHY

Armstrong, Edward. *The French Wars of Religion: Their Political Aspects.* Oxford, 1904. Still useful, though older.

Isambert, François-André, et al., eds. *Recueil général des anciennes lois françaises.* 29 vols. Paris, 1822–1833.

Knecht, R. J. *The French Wars of Religion.* London and New York, 1989.

Michaud, Joseph F. *Biographie Universelle.* 45 vols. Reprint, Graz, 1966.

Romier, Lucien. *Royaume de Catherine de Médicis* (1922). 4th ed. Reprint, Geneva, 1978.

Rothrock, George A. *The Huguenots: A Biography of a Minority.* Chicago, 1979.

Salmon, J. H. M. *Society in Crisis: France in the Sixteenth Century.* London, 1975. The most important book on the subject in a generation; indispensible.

———. *The French Wars of Religion.* London and New York, 1989.

Sutherland, N. M. *The Massacre of St. Bartholomew and the European Conflict, 1559–1572.* London, 1973. Of far greater importance than its title suggests.

Thompson, James W. *The Wars of Religion in France, 1559–1576.* 2nd ed. New York, 1957.

George A. Rothrock

LOTTO, Lorenzo (c.1480–1556/57), Venetian painter.

Although a native of Venice, Lotto spent much of his career

elsewhere: in Treviso (1503–1506), in the Marches (1506–1512), and in Bergamo (1512–1525). Even after settling in Venice in 1525 he continued to work extensively for Marchigian and Bergamask customers, and in 1549 he returned to the Marches, spending his final years in Loreto.

Apart from his portraits—which are often melancholy and introspective in mood, with an exceptional psychological insight—Lotto's paintings are mostly religious in content: altarpieces, fresco decorations for chapels and oratories, and pictures for private devotion. The extraordinary spiritual intensity of these works, combined with an originality verging on eccentricity, has prompted critics from Bernard Berenson (1895) onward to speculate on the nature of the artist's religious attitudes and on his relationship with reforming currents within and outside the Catholic church. Further evidence on this matter is provided by Lotto's correspondence during the later 1520s with his patrons in Bergamo and in particular by his account book for the years 1538–1556, in which the artist records (among much else) the purchase of books of devotion, the names of his friends, and his gift to his nephew (in 1540) of portraits of Martin Luther and his wife.

The interpretation of this evidence has been controversial, with some recent critics seeing Lotto as a crypto-Protestant (Calí, 1980), and others insisting on his orthodoxy (Cortesi Bosco, 1980) and pointing to his close and lifelong contacts with the Dominican order. Yet there seems little doubt that Lotto was deeply sympathetic to the spirit of evangelism and of the pre-Tridentine Catholic reform, and in many ways he may be regarded as more directly and personally responsive than any other Italian painter of the period to the religious ferment of the early sixteenth century.

BIBLIOGRAPHY

Aikema, Bernard. "Lorenzo Lotto and the Ospitale de San Zuane Polo." In *Interpretazioni Veneziane: Studi di storia dell'arte in onore di Michelangelo Muraro*, edited by David Rosand, pp. 343–350. Venice, 1984. A recent study in English of an aspect of Lotto's relationship with the Catholic reform.

Berenson, Bernard. *Lorenzo Lotto* (1895). 4th rev. ed. New York, 1956. Although inevitably outdated, still the only monograph on Lotto in English.

Calí, Maria. "La 'religione' di Lorenzo Lotto." In *Lorenzo Lotto: Atti del Convegno Internazionale di Studi per il V Centenario della Nascita*, edited by Pietro Zampetti and Vittorio Sgarbi, pp. 243–277. Treviso, 1980. The most substantial of a number of discussions on aspects of Lotto's religion at the 1980 conference at Asolo.

Cortesi Bosco, Francesca. *Gli affreschi dell'Oratorio Suardi: Lorenzo Lotto nella crisi della riforma.* Bergamo, 1980.

PETER HUMFREY

LOTZER, Sebastian (also Weigelin; 1490?–1525?), German furrier, Reformation lay preacher, author of pamphlets in the Swabian imperial city of Memmingen, and scribe of the German Peasants' War. He hailed from a well-to-do, highly educated family of Horb, was apprenticed to the furrier trade, and moved to Memmingen, where he became a citizen and married the daughter of a merchant by the name of Weigelin. From 1521 his name appeared on the tax lists of Memmingen. His social standing was at the low end of the taxable citizens of the town.

His sympathies for the reform movement were probably motivated by social concerns and an emphatic partisanship for the poor. He acknowledged himself to be a follower of Martin Luther and endorsed his teaching on justification, his stress on scripture, and the notion of the priesthood of all believers. He studied the Bible, particularly Luther's translation of the New Testament, and concluded that true faith must prove itself, especially in the social order. Lotzer was familiar with the writings of other reformers and was directly influenced by his friend Christoph Schappeler, the minister of Memmingen.

In the spring of 1523 Lotzer published the first of his five pamphlets that emphatically endorsed Lutheran views. He became part of a group of laypersons who attempted to undertake reform in Memmingen. That same year he was admonished several times by the city council, but he continued to be active in opposing priests faithful to the old church. Whether he was directly involved in the dispute over the tithe in June and July 1524 and the disturbances in Saint Mary's Church on Christmas 1524 cannot be ascertained. In his writings he did, however, defend both actions and criticized the rich citizens who professed the true gospel but did not live accordingly.

The text of a sermon on *Matthew* 22:1–14 indicates that he publicly preached. Lotzer was among the participants, invited by the city council, in a disputation between Schappeler and the local Catholic priest in early January 1525. In his writings and sermons he primarily addressed the laity, urging them to appropriate the word of God through the Bible. He provided them with arguments to support their demand for a renewal of faith and society according to a social ethic based on the gospel. He clearly sided with the peasants.

When deputies from twenty-seven villages near Memmingen convened in the city, he drafted (24 February 1525) their petition to the city council. The basic ideas agreed with his own views: the divine word was to be the sole basis for all changes, including the relationship between peasants and the lords. A few days later the so-called Memmingen Articles were formulated, most probably by Lotzer. At the same time, he accepted the request of Ulrich Schmid, the leader of the peasants from Baltringen, to become their secretary. On their behalf he edited a summary of some three hundred individual grievances into twelve articles and supplied them with biblical justifications. As the Twelve Articles they became the most widespread program of the Peasants' War.

The demands, understood as expressions of divine law, were to be implemented without the use of force. After disagreement with the representatives of peasants from Allgäu and around Lake Constance, who insisted on the use of force, the moderate notions of Schmid and Lotzer carried the day and were reflected in the Memmingen Covenant of 7 March 1525. This moderate position became caught between the Swabian League, on the one hand, and the radical forces among the peasants, on the other, both of which rejected compromise. Armed insurrection ensued, eventually leading to the suppression of the peasants. In the middle of April 1525 Lotzer fled to St. Gall; nothing further about him is known.

BIBLIOGRAPHY

Arnold, Martin. *Handwerker als theologische Schriftsteller.* Göttingen, 1990. See pp. 145–193 for most recent summary of scholarship together with discussion of Lotzer's tracts.

Goetze, Alfred, ed. *Sebastian Lotzers Schriften.* Leipzig, 1902. Edition of five tracts as well as commentary; shows linguistic and substantive agreement with the Twelve Articles and identifies Lotzer's library sources.

ADOLF LAUBE
Translated from German by Hans J. Hillerbrand

LOUVAIN (Flem., Leuven). An ancient town in central Belgium, supposedly located where Julius Caesar once encamped, Louvain became prominent from the eleventh century, when the dukes of Brabant made it their seat. By 1423, when Duke John II founded the university there, Louvain was a flourishing center of the woolen industry. By 1517 Brabant, along with the other sixteen provinces in the Low Countries, had come under the dynastic suzerainty of the king of Spain, who, two years later, was elected Holy Roman Emperor as Charles V.

In 1518, with the publication at Basel of Luther's Latin *Lucubrationes* (Lucubrations), the theological faculty of the University of Louvain took its first formal notice of the reformer's work. In concert with their colleagues at Cologne, the Louvain theologians related certain allegedly heretical passages to Cardinal Cajetan, a learned theologian in his own right and at that time papal legate to Germany. When Cajetan declined to designate the texts shown to him as formal heresy, the two faculties let the matter rest until after the Leipzig Disputation involving Luther, Andreas Bodenstein von Karlstadt, and Johann Eck (July 1519). Then, in consequence of an invitation to universities to judge those proceedings, first Cologne and then Louvain issued condemnations of Luther's teachings.

On 7 November 1519 the doctors of Louvain pronounced statements contained in Luther's *Disputatio pro Declaratione Vertutis Indulgenturum* (Explanations of Indulgences), *Sermo de Triplici Justitia* (Sermon on Penance), and *Desem Praecepta Wittenbergensi praedicata populo* (Sermons on the Ten Commandments) to be false, scandalous, heretical, and proximate to heresy. A copy of *Lucubrationes* was solemnly burned. Before they took this step, however, the theologians prudently consulted their countryman and sometime colleague, Adrian Florensz Boeyens, cardinal of Utrecht (later Pope Adrian VI), who strongly endorsed their declaration. His letter of approval was appended to the condemnations of the two universities, published early in 1520. *Exsurge domine,* the papal bull excommunicating Luther that was promulgated the following 15 June reflected in many of its articles the Louvain formularies.

The university remained staunchly Roman Catholic in subsequent years, years that witnessed fierce confessional struggles across the whole of the Netherlands. At the end of the sixteenth century Cornelis Otto Jansen matriculated at Louvain, where, primarily because of the influence of Michel de Bay, the theological views later identified with Jansenism were in wide currency.

BIBLIOGRAPHY

Fife, Robert Herndon. *The Revolt of Martin Luther.* New York, 1957.

Jongh, H. de. *L'Ancienne faculté de théologie de Louvain au première siècle de son existence, 1432–1540.* Louvain, 1911.

Kidd, B. J. *Documents Illustrative of the Continental Reformation.* Oxford, 1911.

Noël, Léon. *Louvain, 1891–1914.* Oxford, 1915.

MARVIN R. O'CONNELL

LOYOLA, Ignatius. *See* Ignatius Loyola.

LUBBERTUS, Sibrandus (c.1555–1625), Frisian Calvinist theologian. He studied theology in Wittenberg, Geneva (with Théodore de Bèze), Marburg, and Neustadt an der Haardt. After a short period in the Reformed church of Emden he became the first professor of theology at the academy of Franeker, where he taught from 1585 until 1625. When Lubbertus was appointed to this important position, in the early days of the Frisian church, the States of Friesland complained of the lack of church ministers.

Lubbertus played an important role in the Calvinist church of Friesland, the officially privileged church of the province. He is the author of numerous, often polemical, theological works. He sought to defend orthodox Calvinist theology in the academy and in the larger Calvinist world. He launched many polemics against the Socinians (in his book *De Jesu Christo Servatore*; 1611), the Arminians (the Dutch Contra-Remonstrants) and the Roman Catholics. Throughout his scholarly life Lubbertus disputed with the Roman Catholic Roberto Bellarmino, resulting in his book *De principiis Christianorum dogmatum.* The main theme of Lubbertus's life was his controversy with Rome. He was additionally involved in theological controversies with Petrus Bertius, Conradus Vorstius, Hugo Grotius, and the Polish theologian Maccovius.

Lubbertus had many friends among orthodox Calvinists, including Ubbo Emmius, Isaac Casaubon, Franciscus Gomarus, Menso Alting, and Zacharius Ursinus. He served the Reformed church in many ways, and his advice was often requested in matters such as appointments of ministers, the synods of the church, academic disputes and academic discipline and the reformation of the church in the province of Groningen (after 1594). After the death of Gomarus, Lubbertus was considered the leading theologian of the Contra-Remonstrants. In the *Respublica litteraria et christiana* the Calvinists in Europe considered Lubbertus one of their leaders as well. Contemporaries and scholars had different opinions about this severe Calvinist. Most scholars agree that Lubbertus's works are in general systematic works defending the true Calvinist creed, instead of presenting new ideas.

BIBLIOGRAPHY

Woude, C. van der. *Sibrandus Lubbertus: Leven en werken, in het bijzonder naar zijn correspondentie.* Kampen, 1963. Interprets all the relevant sources and works of Lubbertus. Although overly sympathetic the most important biography.

WIEBE BERGSMA

LÜBECK. In the fourteenth and fifteenth centuries this wealthy commercial city was, as head of the Hanseatic League, a dominant power in the Baltic region. In the sixteenth century, however, the city experienced a gradual decline, owing politically to the rise of Denmark and Sweden and economically to the success of the Dutch and the disintegration of the Hanseatic League.

Before 1520 Lübeck was also a center of culture (architecture, painting, and wood carving) and of printing. Since the bishop of Lübeck exerted hardly any influence in the city, ecclesiastical sovereignty resided in the cathedral chapter, which cooperated closely with the aristocratic council. Both of these conservative forces successfully suppressed all reform tendencies until 1528. Stimulated by pamphleteering and peripatetic preachers from outside the city, an evangelical movement had begun to emerge after 1520 in circles of well-to-do citizens. Not until 1528 did the local preachers play a greater role as disseminators of the new message. The citizens of Lübeck gave the decisive impetus to the Reformation in 1529/30. Working together were the political pressure of citizens in the approval of a special tax, which was important for the city council, as well as religious disturbances. On 1 July 1530 a sudden, radical change in the structure of the church was settled. At the same time, a political revolution took place through citizen participation in the council's government of the city. The church order of 31 May 1531, drafted under the direction of Johannes Bugenhagen, brought the complete reorganization of worship, the clergy, the schools, and the care of the poor. This reorganization was under the leadership of the community and followed the spirit of the evangelical movement.

There were no prominent theologians in Lübeck. Hermann Bonnus was superintendent from 1532 to 1535. After conflicts with the Dutch, the citizens' council under Jürgen Wullenwever called for another war against Denmark in 1534. The consequence of their defeat in 1535 with regard to the internal politics of Lübeck was that the old aristocratic city council was restored and the participation of the citizens in church matters ended. Until the rejection of the Augsburg Interim (1548–1552), the possibility of re-Catholicization existed. Lübeck took a leading role in the rejection of the Augsburg Interim in northern Germany, just as it had done during the doctrinal disagreements within Lutheranism. The ecclesiastical administration was strictly Gnesio-Lutheran. In 1560 it created a *corpus doctrinae* for Lübeck, and after 1574 the city was committed to the Formula of Concord. The city became a stronghold of Lutheran orthodoxy until the eighteenth century. Calvinists, spiritualists, and Catholics were not tolerated. The cathedral chapter became largely Protestant and continued as such until 1804. The diocese of Lübeck, with its residence in Eutin, was opened to the Reformation by Eberhard von Holle in 1566 and adopted the *Book of Concord* in 1580. It was not secularized but had strong ties with the House of Schleswig-Holstein Gottorf. From 1648 to 1803 the diocese was the only completely Protestant prince-bishopric in the empire.

[*See also* Denmark.]

BIBLIOGRAPHY

Hauschild, Wolf-Dieter. *Kirchengeschichte Lübecks.* Lübeck, 1981.
Hauschild, Wolf-Dieter, ed. *Lübecker Kirchenordnung von Johannes Bugenhagen, 1531.* Lübeck, 1981.
Jannasch, Wilhelm. *Reformationsgeschichte Lübecks vom Petersablaß bis zum Augsburger Reichstag, 1515–1530.* Lübeck, 1958.
Savvidis, Petra. *Hermann Bonnus, Superintendent von Lübeck, 1504–1548.* Lübeck, 1992.

WOLF-DIETER HAUSCHILD
Translated from German by Susan M. Sisler

LÜBER, Thomas (known as Erastus; also Lieber; 1524–1583), Swiss Reformed theologian, physician, and church politician. Born in Baden (Aargau), Switzerland, on 7 May 1524, Lüber was the son of poor peasants. He began to study theology in 1540 at the University of Basel, where he changed his name to Greek (Erastus) according to prevailing humanist fashion. He left Basel because of the pestilence and then studied philosophy and medicine at Bologna and Padua. After nine years in Italy he became the personal physician of the dukes of Henneberg; in 1558 he was appointed physician of Elector Otto Heinrich of the Palatinate and simultaneously professor of medicine at Heidelberg. He published a number of writings against Paracelsus's natural philosophy and his specific methods of treatment and from 1577 favored the death sentence for witches.

As spiritual counselor of the elector of the Palatinate, especially Frederick III, he participated actively in the discussion on the introduction of the Reformed faith. He was a strict partisan of the Zwinglian view of reform, which he expressed especially in his views of the Lord's Supper and of society. He became a close friend of Huldrych Zwingli's successor in Zurich, Heinrich Bullinger. In Heidelberg he agitated against the Lutheran superintendent and professor of theology Thomas Hesshussen by seeking to have Zwinglian partisans appointed to the theology faculty. Elector Frederick III appointed him a member to the consistory. At his behest Lüber participated in the religious colloquies between Lutheran and Reformed theologians in Heidelberg (1560) and Maulbronn (1564). The Zwinglian view of the Lord's Supper is delineated in his tract *Vom Verstand der Worte Christi: Das ist mein Leib* (Heidelberg, 1565). A Strasbourg theologian, Johannes Marbach, violently attacked the book, prompting Lüber's defense. Especially pertinent was his disagreement with Calvinist views concerning the power and authority of the church, church order, and church discipline. After 1560 Calvinists at the University of Heidelberg, led by Kaspar Olevianus, attempted to introduce presbyterianism and Calvinist church discipline. Lüber and several members of the philosophy faculty unsuccessfully protested. In 1570 Elector Frederick III introduced presbyterianism and church discipline, including the ban. Because of his correspondence with the Transylvanian antitrinitarian Johannes Sylvanus, who was later executed in 1572, Lüber lost the elector's favor and was banned until 1576. Since he did not subscribe to the Formula of Concord, he lost his office in 1580 and returned to Basel as professor of medicine. Shortly before his death (1 January 1583) he also received the chair in moral philosophy. After his death an article of his was published concerning church discipline and presbyterian church order based on his correspondence with Théodore de Bèze. As a result, Bèze took a position critical of Lüber and thus publicized their controversy.

In the seventeenth century an English sect called itself Erastian. Up to the present day in England and in Scotland the demand for a state church with no claim to ecclesiastical autonomy is called "Erastianism." Lüber, however, always saw the Zurich model as his ideal.

BIBLIOGRAPHY

Primary Source

Lüber (Erastus), Thomas. *The Theses of Erastus Touching Excommunication.* London, 1844.

Secondary Sources

Bonnard, Auguste. *Thomas Eraste, 1524–1583, et la Discipline ecclésiastique.* Thesis, Université de Lausanne, 1894. Includes a list of Lüber's writings and makes thorough use of the original sources. Still the basic study of the life and work of Lüber.

Wesel-Roth, Ruth. *Thomas Erastus: Beitrag zur Geschichte der reformierten Kirche und zur Lehre von der Staatssouveränität.* Lahr, Germany, 1954. Comprehensive treatment of Lüber's notions of the relationship between church and state.

SIGRID LOOẞ

Translated from German by Hans J. Hillerbrand

LUIS DE LEÓN (1527/28–1591), Spanish Augustinian friar. He was born in Belmonte (province of Cuenca, Spain) 1527/28 and died in 1591 in Madrigal de las Altas Torres. As a professor at the University of Salamanca after 1561, his originality and his character, which was introverted and remote from the "vain world's uproar," gave rise to enemies and rivals, who denounced him to the Inquisition. Tried as a suspected heretic and imprisoned in 1572, he was acquitted in 1576 and returned to the university. Resuming his lectures, he reportedly began as "we were saying yesterday. . . ."

The inquisitorial proceedings made manifest his moral integrity, his orthodoxy, and his scientific sense of modern biblical exegesis based on three criteria: scholastic theology as introduction, the doctrines of the holy fathers as hermeneutical rule, and knowledge of the Greek and Hebrew languages. Humanist, poet, scripturist, Luis de León sings of peace, starry nights, silence, and his love of music. As a poet he is one of the finest bards of the sixteenth century. His most famous prose works are *De los Nombres de Cristo,* which is a Christology based on the archetype of the names that the Bible (Old and New Testaments) gives to the Messiah, and *La perfecta casada,* a commentary on chapter 26 of *Ben Sira.*

He also played a leading role in the reform of his Augustinian order with his sermon in the chapter meeting at Dueñas in 1587 and with his edition of the Constitutions, and he was elected provincial (major superior) of the reformed branch of the Augustinians. The principal emphases of Luis de León as a religious man and an exegete were orthodoxy, as demonstrated before the Inquisition; scientific criticism in the study of the sacred scripture without confining himself to the Vulgate, which had its limitations; reforming fervor within the Augustinian order to which he belonged; and imitation of Christ.

BIBLIOGRAPHY

Primary Source

Luis de León. *Obras completas.* Edited by Felix García. 5th rev. ed. Madrid, 1991.

Secondary Sources

Bell, A. F. G. *Luis de León: A Study of the Spanish Renaissance.* Oxford, 1925.

Coster, Adolphe. *Luis de León.* New York, 1921–1922.

Martinez Cuesta, A. "El movimiento recoleto en los siglos 16 y 17." *Recollectio* 5 (1982), 5–47.

Welsh, R. J. *Introduction to the Spiritual Doctrine of Fray Luis de León.* Washington, D.C., 1951.

ALVARO HUERGA

LUKE OF PRAGUE (also Lukáš Pražský; 1460?–1528), bishop (senior) of the Bohemian Brethren (Unity of Brethren) and a distinguished theologian. Born in Prague around 1460 into a Hussite (Utraquist) family, Luke studied in the faculty of arts of Charles University, where he obtained his baccalaureate in 1481. Luke joined the circle of the so-called Prague Brethren (Pražští bratří) of the Bohemian Brethren, which was under the spiritual leadership of the congregation in Lenešice, near Louny. Jan Černý and Lawrence Krasonický, later outstanding personalities of the Bohemian Brethren, were also brought into the circle by Luke of Prague. Luke left Prague for a large congregation in Litomyšl, where he finally joined the Bohemian Brethren and went through the stages of its priesthood. In 1490 he was elected a member of its highest leading body, the "Closed Council." At that time a controversy between a "small branch" and "great branch" broke out inside the Unity of Brethren. It concerned the significance of scholarship, theology, and education for the church. Luke supported the "great branch," with which he identified himself.

At the end of the fifteenth century the Bohemian Brethren assumed that somewhere in the world it was possible to find a surviving ancient apostolic church—which, according to them, was not as deformed as the Roman church—and sought to find it. Luke of Prague went to the Balkans and Greece. During his journey he acquired considerable theological experience and contacted both the Orthodox church and the remains of the Bogomils. The asceticism and austerity of Eastern monasticism did not appeal to him, and he saw the Christian life as a following of Jesus Christ in self-sacrifice for others. His first writing, *Bárka* (The Barge; 1493), presented these ideas.

In 1494 Luke became a preacher in Mladá Boleslav, the largest congregation of the Bohemian Brethren. Afterward he set off to western Bohemia, where he consolidated congregations disrupted by the activity of the "small branch." After the separation of the "small branch" from the brethren in 1496, Luke wrote *O příčinách rozdělení* (On the Cause of Separation). Around 1497–1498 Luke journeyed to Italy, visited Bologna and Rome, met in Pra del Forne representatives of the Waldensian church council, and was present at Girolamo Savonarola's burning. After the death (1500) of Matthew of Kunvald, Luke of Prague and Ambrosius of Skuteč were elected bishops of the brethren, joining bishops Tůma of Přelouč and Elias of Chřenovice.

In 1501 Luke prepared an agenda for the ordination of priests, which later became part of the *Zprávy kněžské* (Ceremonies of Priests). In 1501 he also prepared the first hymnbook for the brethren. Around 1501 Luke prepared his *Otázky dětinské* (Juvenile Questions), which provided religious teaching for children. He also wrote *Otázky větší* (Bigger Questions), a reference book for religious education. Luke was entrusted with apologetic tasks and the public defense of the Bohemian Brethren. When the existence of the brethren was endangered in 1503, Luke wrote *Počty z víry* (The Testimony of Faith) and an apologetic *List k ospravedlnění a osvědčení* (Letter for Justification and Certification). It was adapted and printed as late as 1542. Between 1505 and 1510 Luke also debated the Catholic monk Wolfgang Bosák in print.

When the persecution of the Bohemian Brethren increased again in 1507–1508, Luke of Prague prepared the *Konfese* (Confession) of 1507. It was intended to present the brethren as true Christians to King Vladislav II. The confession, however, did not persuade the king, and Luke himself was persecuted. For a time he had to leave the Boleslav congregation and go into hiding, during which period he wrote his greatest theological work, *O obnovení církve svaté* (On the Renewal of the Holy Church). In it he wrote that God's law is a measure of renewal, and Jesus Christ is its continual teacher. For renewal an unceasing contact with holy scripture is necessary. In 1510 he wrote the booklet *O spravedlnosti z víry* (On the Justification from Faith) and a more extensive work, *O pokání* (On Repentence). In 1511 he sent the confession of the brethren to Desiderius Erasmus, but this mission did not bring the desired results. It did, however, contribute to greater recognition of the Bohemian Brethren abroad.

In 1515 Luke of Prague was arrested in Janovice on the Úhlava River by the nobleman Jan Suda of Řeneč and was released only after a long internment. After the death of Tůma of Přelouč, Luke was elected a judge of the brethren (1518), and he became the head of the "Closed Council." After Martin Luther's emergence, the brethren established contact with him. In 1522 Luke of Prague sent Jan Roh to Luther with translations of *Otázky dětinské, Konfese,* the Apology, and *O pravdě vítězné* (On the Victorious Truth). Luther criticized some of the positions of the brethren and wrote for Luke the tract *Von aubeten des Sakraments des heyligen leychnams Christi* (On the Eucharist). Luke offered as a response *Odpověď Bratří na spis M.Luthera, co by se mu při Bratřích vidělo za pravé* (The Reply of the Brethren to Luther's Writing, That He Might See the Brethren as Just; 1523), which restated the basic standpoint of the brethren and their acceptance of seven sacraments and the celibacy of priests. Formally Luther and Luke reconciled as a result of the mediation of their messengers, Roh and Michael Weiss, who in 1524 visited Wittenberg. In other writings—*O stavu svobodném* (On Celibacy), *Spis ku poznání zákona a milosti* (Recognition of the Law and Grace), and *Spis o lásce* (On Love)—Luke did not attack Luther personally but criticized his opinions. In the 1520s several factions abandoned the brethren, against which Luke wrote *O úvodu Jednoty bratrské* (On the Origin of the Unity of Brethren) and convened a synod in 1526 to be held in Mladá Boleslav. At the synod he gained approval for changes in the liturgy, ordination, the fast, and the calendar, which he had been introducing since 1500. The changes were published in two volumes entitled *Zprávy při službách úřadu kněžského v Jednotě bratrské* (Ceremonies Performed by the Priests of the Unity of Brethren). The collection also includes the most important decrees of the brethren synods up to 1526. Luke's theological testament is the work *O pravdě a pravé jistotě Božího spasení* (On the Truth and True Certainty of God's Salvation; 1528), and shortly before his death on 11 December 1528, he wrote a *Výzva* (Challenge) for the "Closed Council," in which he entrusted the Bohemian Brethren to their elders. Luke clearly formulated the teaching of the Bohemian Brethren, established their contacts, and contributed to the recognition of the brethren abroad.

BIBLIOGRAPHY

Molnár, Amadeo. *Bratři a král.* Prague, 1947. Edition of Luke's letter to King Vladislav II of 1507.

———. *Bratr Lukáš, bohoslovec Jednoty.* Prague, 1948. The basic biography. Luke's most important works are included in an appendix.

———. "Études et conversion de Luc de Prague." *Communio viatorum* 3 (1960), 255–262.

———. "Luc de Prague devant la crise de l'Unité des années 1490." *Communio viatorum* 4 (1961), 316–324.

———. "Luc de Prague édifiant la communauté, 1498–1502." *Communio viatorum* 5 (1962), 189–200.

———. "Luc de Prague à Constantinople." *Communio viatorum* 4 (1961), 192–201.

———. "Pasteur dans la tourmente: Luc de Prague." *Communio viatorum* 6 (1963), 276–286.

———. "Les premières années de Luc de Prague au sein de l'Unité." *Communio viatorum* 4 (1961), 83–89.

———. "Die kleine und die große Partei der Brüderunität." *Communio viatorum* 22 (1979), 239–248.

———. "Luther und die böhmischen Brüder." *Communio viatorum* 24 (1981), 47–58.

Skalský, Gustav Adolf. "Bruder Lukas von Prag und die 'Anweisungen für die Priester' vom Jahre 1527." *Zeitschrift für Brüdergeschichte* 2 (1908), 1–44.

Vindi, Rudolf. "Bratra Lukáe Pražského učení o eucharistii." In *Věstník královské české společnosti nauk 1921–1923*, pp. 8–74. Prague, 1923.

JAN BLAHOSLAV LÁŠEK

LUNGE, Vincens (1486?–1536), leader in the movement for Norwegian self-government in its dynastic union with Denmark. Of Danish noble stock, Lunge received a humanistic education at several European universities, earning a doctorate. Upon returning to Copenhagen, he served briefly as professor of law and rector of the university.

After the Danes ousted King Christian II (r. 1513–1523) in favor of his uncle, Frederick I (r. 1523–1533), Lunge was sent north to encourage the Norwegian council of state to elect Frederick king of Norway. Upon arriving in Norway, Lunge became a member of this council through marriage to a Norwegian noblewoman. When the council convened, its president, Archbishop Olav Engelbrektsson of Trondheim, and Lunge emerged as leaders. The two cooperated because they each believed their personal goals would be reached through Norwegian self-rule—Engelbrektsson wanted to maintain the integrity of the Catholic church; Lunge sought personal power and wealth. Together they led the council to elect Frederick, but with the stipulation that he accept a royal charter that would leave Norway's internal affairs in the hands of the council. Lunge took the charter to Frederick in Denmark and convinced the king to accept its terms in 1524.

The continued pursuit of their personal goals soon alienated Lunge from Engelbrektsson. In 1527 Lunge gave his support to the *Daljunker* (a young nobleman from Dalarne, Sweden), a pretender to the throne of Sweden, who claimed to be Nils the son of Sten Sture, the late regent of Sweden. Consequently, Frederick, who was allied with Sweden, removed Lunge from governorship of the fortress of Bergen in western Norway but then gave him the rich Nonneseter monastery. Thereafter Lunge recognized that he could gain power and property only through collaboration with the Danes. His acquisition of monastic property and his support of Lutheranism in Bergen and in his own family further alienated him from Engelbrektsson.

After Frederick's death in 1533 and the accession to the Danish throne by his Lutheran son, Christian III (r. 1536–1559), Lunge and several others were sent to Trondheim to secure Christian's election as king of Norway. Engelbrektsson responded by arousing a mob, which on 3 January 1536 murdered Lunge and jailed his colleagues. Within a year Christian declared Norway to be a Danish province.

BIBLIOGRAPHY

Bull, Edv. *Vincens Lunge.* Kristiania (Oslo), 1917. Available in the United States only at the University of Minnesota; useful because it depicts Lunge's life by quoting many of his letters in full.

Christopherson, Kenneth Eugene. "Norwegian Historiography of Norway's Reformation." Ph.D. diss., University of Minnesota, Minneapolis, 1972. Discusses Lunge's role as it evaluates the way in which Norwegian historians interpreted his actions. An extensive bibliography is very helpful.

Koht, Halvdan. *Vincens Lunge contra Henrik Krummedige, 1523–1525.* Oslo, 1950. These two works in Koht's series Kriseår i Norsk Historie give a detailed picture and interpretation of the history of the Reformation in Norway during the time when Vincens Lunge was most active.

———. *Olav Engelbriktsson og Sjølvstendetapet, 1537.* Oslo, 1951.

Willson, Thomas. *Church and State in Norway: From the Tenth to Sixteenth Century*. London, 1903. Dated, but the only work in English that gives a detailed account of the events. Willson's bias in favor of the historic episcopate is evident throughout.

JOHN E. QUAM

LUSATIA. Known in German as Lausitz, Lusatia is the region in the southeast corner of present-day Germany, east of the Elbe River and west of the Neisse River. Historically, Lusatia was divided into two parts: Upper and Lower Lusatia, the latter to the west of Silesia. Both were settled by Slavic tribes, from which the region received its name. In the Middle Ages Lusatia became part of the bishopric of Meissen. Economically, the region was known for wool and linen weaving with only a few trades and artisan guilds. Important for the social history of Lusatia was the emergence and development of large estates.

In the early sixteenth century Lusatia was affected by the Reformation. In 1526 Lower Lusatia became part of the Habsburg possessions of Ferdinand I and thereby became related to the Bohemian crown lands. This implicated Lusatia in the controversies of the Reformation. Lutheran ideas reached Lusatia quickly, though at different places with different impact. The old views, customs, and notions were only slowly replaced by the new messages. The Lutheran teaching spread foremost in the towns, with their German-speaking population. Its impact in the rural areas, where the vernacular language was Sorbic, was slow and faced greater difficulties. Lutheran notions also spread among monastic possessions. The foremost representative, Abbot Henry, did not hinder the dissemination of the new teaching. The Reformation caused the ecclesiastical foundations in various places to disappear. In 1618, when the estates of Upper Lusatia participated in the election of Elector Frederick of the Palatinate as king of Bohemia, Elector John George I of Saxony occupied, by order of Emperor Ferdinand II, both parts of Lusatia. In 1620 Lower Lusatia joined the Protestant King Frederick. By order of the emperor, electoral Saxony thereupon occupied Lusatia. Both parts of Lusatia became, in the Peace of Prague (1635), part of electoral Saxony even though Bohemia retained formal sovereignty.

BIBLIOGRAPHY

Bönhoff. "Die Einführung der Reformation in den Parochien der sächsischen Oberlausitz." *Beiträge zur sächsischen Kirchengeschichte* 27 (1913), 132–178.

Kadisch, Karl. *Die Reformation in der Lausitz*. Bautzen, Germany, 1867.

Lehmann, Rudolf. "Niederlausitz und Oberlausitz in vergleichender geschichtlicher Betrachtung." *Jahrbuch für die Geschichte Mittel- und Ostdeutschlands* 7 (1958), 93–133.

Scheuffler, Heinrich Johann. *Einführung und Schicksal der Reformation in der Oberlausitz*. Barmen, Germany, 1881.

KRISTINA HÜBENER

LUTHER, Katharina (maiden name, von Bora; 1499–1552), Martin Luther's wife. She was born of an impoverished Saxon noble family in Lippendorf near Leipzig. After her mother's early death she was first raised at the Benedictine convent of Brehna, and later at the Cistercian convent of Nimbschen near Grimma (duchy of Saxony). In 1515 she became a nun at the convent of Nimbschen. In 1523 she was one of the twelve nuns whose escape from the convent Luther himself had organized, an act he justified afterward in programmatic fashion in the paper "Ursache und Antwort, daß Jungfrauen Klöster göttlich verlassen mögen" (Cause and Reply, That Virgins May Leave Convents with Divine Consent). Katharina's fate also makes evident how difficult it was to provide for nuns who had left the convent. Nothing came of her engagement with Hieronymus Baumgärtner, son of a patrician family from Nuremberg. Another suitor was turned down (with good reason) by this self-confident woman. She wanted Nikolaus von Amsdorf or Luther himself. The latter, however, was not considering marriage, much less to Katharina.

The wedding of the two, which took place on 13 June 1525, shortly after the Peasants' War, came as a surprise even to some of Luther's friends. For centuries the marriage between a monk and a nun had encountered by far the harshest criticism and fostered the vilest gossip in Catholic religious circles. By contrast, within Protestantism this marriage was held up as a model for the clergy. This marriage of a bourgeois and an aristocrat, an occasional occurrence during the time of the Reformation, was probably legitimized in social terms by Luther's status as a professor. It became a successful marriage of two strong partners who nonetheless needed to come to terms with each other. Luther called Katharina "the morning star of Wittenberg," whom he would not give up for anything, but due to her driving energy he also called her "Mister Kate." She was well aware of her husband's greatness, and even their last letters express their mutual and warm affection. Katharina's scholastic and spiritual education was sufficient to enable her to follow Luther's thoughts and innovations. She strived to perfect her knowledge of the Bible and of the catechism. She raised objections to difficult theological deliberations using good common sense.

The marriage produced three boys and three girls, one of whom died early. Another child, Magdalena, died at the age of 13 and was deeply mourned by her parents. Katharina energetically took on the management of the growing household in the former Augustinian monastery. This was not an easy task considering that neither she nor Luther had any wealth and that Luther's professorial salary, including the remunerations in kind, was not sufficient (as his "domestic budget" indicates) to cover all expenses, strained by the large number of guests and his heedless generosity. For this reason Katharina ran a hostel for paying students. Significantly, most of the critical comments about her were made by Veit Dietrich, the manager of the hostel for many years. The food supplies came in part from gardens in Wittenberg that had been acquired at Katharina's instigation, as well as from the farm Zöllsdorf, a former property of the Bora family. In her striving for ownership and cultivation of land, one still detects a bit of an attitude of aristocracy, which naturally was viewed critically by the chancellor of the electorate of Saxony, Gregor Brück. In his will Luther sought to assure Katharina's livelihood, but after his death she suffered economic hardship owing to the turbulence of war. As a result of the plague in Wittenberg, she meant to migrate to Torgau in 1552, but during the voyage she had an accident and died. Her tombstone is located in the town church of Torgau.

BIBLIOGRAPHY

Deutler, Clara Louise. *Katherine Luther of the Wittenberg Personage.* Philadelphia, 1924.

Junghans, Helmar. "Luther in Wittenberg." In *Leben und Werk Martin Luther's von 1526 bis 1546*, edited by Helmar Junghans, 2 vols., pp. 11–37, 723–732. Berlin, 1983.

Kroker, Ernst. *Katharina von Bora: Martin Luther's Frau.* 16th ed. Berlin, 1983.

MARTIN BRECHT

Translated from German by Wolfgang Katenz

LUTHER, Martin (1483–1546), reformer and theologian. The world-historical event of the Reformation was triggered and substantially shaped by the monk and professor Martin Luther. His religious struggle over a "gracious God," his existence "between God and the Devil" (Oberman), led to a schism within Western Christendom and to the emergence of Protestant churches. In the process, Luther himself remained in a peculiar way a figure suspended between the Middle Ages and the modern era. Luther's reform work, carried out in the context of other political, social, scholarly, and intellectual changes leading to the modern age, influenced these changes and, in turn, was influenced by them.

From Youth to Professor of Theology. Luther was born in Eisleben and spent his childhood in neighboring Mansfeld, where his father ran a small business mining copper-bearing shale. In accordance with the circumstances of the times, his upbringing in a family with many children was strict. But one can hardly explain Luther's complicated development as an adult by reference to a problematic childhood, as Eric Erikson argued. Martin attended school in Mansfeld and Magdeburg, where he lived with the Brethren of the Common Life, and in Eisenach, where he was part of a devout circle of students who probably instilled in him a deep sense of piety.

It was his father's wish for Luther to become a lawyer. Accordingly he enrolled at the University of Erfurt in 1501 and four years later completed the prerequisite studies of liberal arts with a master's degree. At the beginning of his subsequent study of law symptoms of a crisis began to emerge that included a fear of death and questions about the purpose of life. During a trip in the summer of 1505 when a bolt of lightning struck him down, he vowed: "Help me, Saint Ann, I will become a monk." He determined to devote the rest of his life to the service of God. Thus, much against the will of his father, he joined the large monastery of the Observant Augustinian friars in Erfurt. One year later he took his monastic vows and set about becoming a priest and later a student of theology.

Although Luther was an extremely conscientious monk, he did not have the assurance of living up to God's strict demands. As a priest when he was celebrating Mass he did not feel pure enough to be able to face God, even as he saw Christ only as the judge. The scrupulous practice of confession brought only temporary relief. Lasting well into his time in Wittenberg, these anxieties (*Anfechtungen*) resulting in what was considered particularly sinful, namely, doubts about his own salvation, led Luther to lose faith in monastic life—generally considered a safe path to salvation—and in the common notion of work-righteousness. This conflict fueled the energy for reform. In his theological studies, which he completed with uncommon speed, Luther was shaped by nominalism, the prevalent school of thought in Erfurt. This school of thought held that if one strives with all one's might, God will not deny his grace. Luther formulated critical notions about the predominant influence of Aristotle in theology. A particular characteristic was his early and strong interest in the Bible, which he nurtured through intense prayer and meditation. In 1510/11 Luther was sent to Rome on business for the Observant Augustinian friars. He made ample use, although not to his complete satisfaction, of the Holy City's abundant availability of grace and indulgences. The lax piety in Rome and secularization of the papal court did not particularly irritate him; the mission itself was unsuccessful in that the special policies of the Observants were not endorsed by the curia. When Luther afterward no longer agreed with the policies of the Erfurt monastery, Johannes von Staupitz, vicar of the German Observant Augustinian friars, transferred him to the monastery in Wittenberg.

Staupitz himself held a professorship in Bible at the new university in Wittenberg, from which, however, he intended to resign. He thought of Luther, who in 1512 was awarded the doctorate in theology, as his successor. Luther was at first reluctant but eventually assumed the professorial chair. Later he relied again and again on the authority of the office of teacher thereby conferred on him as justification for his reforming work. Two years later Luther was appointed preacher at the town church of Wittenberg, an ecclesiastical responsibility he fulfilled for the remainder of his life and one that he considered as important as his professorship.

Luther's first lectures on the *Psalms* as well as on *Romans*, *Galatians*, and *Hebrews* (1513–1518) illustrate the evolving theology of the young professor. Hermeneutically, he adhered at first to medieval conceptualizations, but he already emphasized the literal sense of the Bible, which was understood to express Christ, while also making use of the philological resources provided by biblical humanism. In his lectures on *Galatians* he arrived at the important distinction between law and gospel as the two ways in which God is revealed. Theologically, Luther had drawn this important conclusion from his experiences: humans must declare themselves sinners before God and reach conformity with the crucified Christ; only then are they able to accept their situation before God. Luther found this theology of humility confirmed in German mysticism (Johannes Tauler and the *Theologia deutsch*) and in Augustine's anti-Pelagian writings. At the same time, he became increasingly aware that his views were in opposition to nominalism. In addition to this theology of humility he began to understand that God offers righteousness through Christ. Some scholars have seen this awareness as the decisive turning point in Luther's theology. But for the time being Luther remained undecided, probably because he was reluctant to abandon the strict theology of humility.

The Breakthrough of Reform, 1517–1521. The Reformation consisted of a multifaceted ecclesiastical, theological, academic, and political set of events. Its trigger was a dispute over the selling of indulgences. The rebuilding of Saint Peter's basilica in Rome was to be financed through a plenary indulgence, which, in return for a payment of money, promised the living and the dead the remission of ecclesiastical penalties for sins and thereby possibly the avoidance of purgatory. In Germany Archbishop Albert of Mainz was persuaded to authorize the sale of indulgences in his territories by allowing him to use part of the revenue to pay off the debts he had incurred in taking over the archdiocese of Mainz. In the context of his pastoral responsibilities Luther came in contact with the Dominican Johann Tetzel, who was selling the Saint Peter's indulgences near Wittenberg. Luther repudiated the practice because it undermined the seriousness of penance and competed with the preaching of the gospel and acts of charity. Since the church had not promulgated a doctrine on indulgences at that time, Luther, as a professor, saw himself entitled to discuss the topic critically. On 31 October 1517 he presented his objections in a letter to Archbishop Albert of Mainz and enclosed in it ninety-five "Theses on the Power of Indulgences," which were meant as the subject of a disputation at the University of Wittenberg. The posting of the theses on the door of Wittenberg's castle church was first reported by Philipp Melanchthon after Luther's death. Since the theses as subject of an academic debate would have had to be published in one way or another, however, the scholarly dispute about the actual posting of the theses, pursued mainly by Erwin Iserloh in 1966, is largely irrelevant. The theses deployed their explosive effect after they had been printed at the end of 1517, and a bit later when Luther had elaborated his views in German as well.

The theses on indulgences can be understood as an expression of a strict theology of humility. According to Luther's own account, a decisive theological breakthrough must have occurred in the spring of 1518 that—befitting the location of his study—is also referred to as the "tower experience" (*Turmerlebnis*). In struggling to understand *Romans* 1:17 Luther realized that God's justice did not consist of a demand but a gift given by God to humans out of grace, which must be received through faith. Therein lay the message of the Reformation. In its consequences it was bound to lead to a virtually complete restructuring of theology and to a conflict with an ecclesiastical system that placed much emphasis on works.

In December 1517 Archbishop Albert forwarded the theses on indulgences to Rome because he saw in them a challenge to papal authority. Counter to Luther's intentions the matter thus escalated into a conflict over ecclesiastical authority. In the summer of 1518 Luther was summoned to Rome, first because of suspicion of heresy, later because of allegations of rampant heresy. At this point the "Luther case" became enmeshed with politics. At the Diet of Augsburg in 1518 the succession of Emperor Maximilian was under discussion. The Papal Court sought to prevent the election of Maximilian's nephew Charles, and therefore solicited the support of Luther's sovereign, Elector Frederick III of Saxony. Hence, Frederick was able to arrange for Luther's examination by the papal legate Cajetan to be conducted in Augsburg instead of in Rome. Luther contested the biblical justification of indulgences, refused to retract, and finally appealed to a papal council.

Since Rome at first did not take vigorous action against Luther (because of the electoral complications just noted) the dispute played itself out in the academic realm, in which a professor from Ingolstadt, Johann Eck, had begun to oppose Luther. The conflict came to a head in the summer of 1519 at a disputation in Leipzig. Eck forced Luther to declare that not only the pope but also councils could be in error. Therefore scripture remained the sole norm of teaching, alongside righteousness by faith, the second pillar of Luther's principle. Eck regarded his maneuver as a great success, but the learned humanist public saw Luther as the victor.

Displaying admirable creativity and profiting from the linguistic skills he had acquired in the meantime, Luther began to develop a far-reaching reform program, which he set forth in numerous pamphlets. (Luther, indeed, became the most published author of the century.) At the University of Wittenberg Scholasticism was replaced by the study of Greek and Hebrew, as well as by biblical exegesis. Luther recruited the young humanist Philipp Melanchthon to Wittenberg; he became his most important colleague. Luther's commentaries on *Galatians* and on the *Psalms* were soon considered the most dependable interpretations of these books. His "Sermon von der Bereitung zum Sterben" (Sermon on the Preparation for Dying; 1519) set out a new "art of dying" centered on Christ. His "Sermon vom Wucher" (Sermon on Usury; 1520) marked the beginning of Luther's increasingly critical assessments of prevailing economic practices. In addition, Luther re-evaluated the status of marriage in relation to celibacy, which heretofore had been considered a superior state. His "Sermon von den guten Werken" (Sermon on Good Works; 1520) linked all Christian behavior to faith and redefined the ordinary vocation as a new way of rendering godly service to one's neighbor. Luther collected his general reform proposals concerning the church in his pamphlet *An den christlichen Adel deutscher Nation von des christlichen Standes Besserung* (To the Christian Nobility of the German Nation Regarding the Improvement of the Christian Estate; 1520). On the basis of the concept of a common ministry shared by all the baptized, he called on the Christian authorities to carry out reform within the church and in society. Particularly sensational was *De Captivitate Babylonica Ecclesiae Praeludium* (On the Babylonian Captivity of the Church; 1520), with its definition of the sacraments as divine promises linked to visible signs. Luther reduced the seven sacraments to baptism and Communion, and the notion of the sacrifice of the Mass he repudiated as an abomination. These notions implied the dissolution of the church as a sacramental institution. Finally, *Von der Freiheit eines Christenmenschen* (On the Freedom of a Christian; 1520), arguably his most famous writing, expounded on the one hand the Christ-given inner freedom from sin, death, and devil, and on the other defined the Christian life as service to one's neighbor.

After the election of Charles V as emperor, and with Eck's prodding, the Roman proceedings against Luther resumed. In the summer of 1520, they led to the drafting of a papal bull that threatened Luther with excommunication and rejected some forty-one sentences culled from his writings. Luther not only responded to it in print but also burned a copy of the bull, together with a copy of canon law, on 10 December 1520. In so doing he broke publicly with the legal system of the church. The ecclesiastical ban would now have been followed by a ban of the empire as a secular measure. At his election, however, Charles V had promised not to ban anyone without a legal hearing. Accordingly, protests from the pope notwithstanding, Luther was cited to the Diet of Worms in 1521, but only for the purpose of retraction. In an appearance of great historical import, Luther refused to retract, claiming that his conscience was bound by common reasoning and scripture. Subsequent to the recess of the diet, in the Edict of Worms the emperor put Luther and his followers under the ban. This measure yielded only partial success. Soldiers of Frederick III of Saxony staged a mock assault on Luther during his return trip from Worms and arranged his hiding at Wartburg castle.

The Spread of Reform. At this critical juncture in the Reformation Luther needed to disappear from public view, not only because of political threats but also because anticlerical sentiment was increasing. Above all, a practical reform program had to be undertaken. In his solitude at Wartburg Luther made a threefold contribution to its implementation. In his *De votis monasticis indicium* (On Monastic Vows) he supplied a theological justification for the view that monastic life is not a higher form of Christian faith and that it contradicts the righteousness of faith as well as Christian liberty. Wherever the Reformation was influential this view led to the virtual collapse of monasticism and thus to momentous changes in church life. In 1523 Luther also advocated the closing of convents. While at Wartburg castle Luther completed the Christmas and Advent sections of his *Church Postil*, a collection of exemplary sermons that became one of Luther's most well-known and most widely used writings. As a result (as well as through the numerous printings of individual sermons) Luther became the most influential preacher of his time. At the suggestion of Melanchthon, Luther translated the New Testament into German in a matter of eleven weeks at Wartburg in order to enable laypersons to have direct access to "God's word." The German New Testament (*Das Newe Testament Deutsch*) appeared in 1522. In embarking on the translation of the Bible Luther accepted one of his most ambitious tasks, which occupied him until the end of his life. Not until 1534 did he complete the translation of the entire Bible, with the assistance of his colleagues in Wittenberg. Constant efforts went into the improvement of this work. Luther succeeded in creating the standard German translation of the Bible for centuries to come, which deeply influenced the German language. Rival undertakings by Catholics (Hieronymus Emser, Eck, Johann Dietenberger) were merely modifications of his work. The Lutheran Bible strongly influenced the Low German, Scandinavian, and English Bible translations. In comparison to medieval translations, Luther's was linguistically superior in its readability. Through its prefaces and marginal notes it sought to buttress a Protestant understanding of the Bible.

Without Luther's presence, difficulties arose in Wittenberg when attempts were made to introduce reform. Against the will of the conservatives and the elector, Andreas Bodenstein von Karlstadt celebrated an evangelical Communion for the first time on Christmas of 1521. A new church order was promulgated and iconoclasm ensued. As a result of these disturbances in Wittenberg, Luther's conservative friends implored him to leave Wartburg. In his "Invocavit" sermons (March 1522) Luther opposed almost all of the innovations of the new church order on the grounds that it was necessary to consider the "weak."

Luther did not reject the new order, but he saw no other way than to proceed more cautiously. He granted the congregation the rights to pass judgment on doctrine, to appoint evangelical preachers, and to manage its property. Luther wrote a baptismal ceremony in German and a slightly altered Latin liturgy (*Formula Missae*, 1523). His effort to create new German hymns (psalms, catechetical, and festival hymns) proved to be exceedingly successful and became the beginnings of an evangelical hymnal.

In 1524 Luther urged town councils to establish schools. Later he admonished parents to allow their children to attend those schools. He wanted to provide an educated younger generation for the church as well as for society—even education for girls was intended. His appeal was successful. A Protestant school system developed that was far superior to its Catholic counterpart.

In 1526 Luther began to undertake, under the aegis of Prince Elector John, a comprehensive reorganization of the Saxon church. In addition to the Latin Mass he created a "German Mass." In its preface he mentioned the possibility of holding spontaneous worship in people's homes for those "who seriously wanted to be Christians," but granted that it was not yet possible to do so. He saw a particularly urgent problem in guaranteeing the financial support of pastors and parishes. Since the bishops had failed to endorse the new ecclesiastical order, Luther appealed to the prince elector to implement "as a duty of love" those reforms by constituting a visitation commission comprised of theologians and government officials. This temporary arrangement was not aimed at state rule of the church although it later led to the governance of the church by secular authorities.

The superintendents, the pastors of the large town parishes, were originally to act as bishops, an office that Luther strove to preserve. During the visitations and in other connections Luther had the sobering experience of how profoundly difficult it was to replace the collapsing old order with a new piety and a new ecclesiastical morality. Therefore, in 1529 he sought to counteract widespread religious ignorance by writing the Small Catechism and the Large Catechism (for pastors). The Small Catechism—with its characteristic sequence of Decalogue (law), creed, Lord's prayer, baptism, Communion, and power of the keys, with related prayers and a summary of the duties of domestic life, all in concise and memorizable format—has probably become the most widespread and most effective text of Luther and Lutheranism.

Luther's reflections on order also included his assessment of the basic relationship between the realm of the secular and the realm of the divine, which he developed in *Von weltlicher Obrigkeit, wieweit man ihr Gehorsam schuldig sei* (Secular Authority and the Obedience One Owes It; 1523). He wrote the tract when Catholic ducal Saxony prohibited and threatened to confiscate his writings. According to Luther, the role of secular authority consisted in preserving external peace. Christians take part in this task out of love for others. The authorities must not intrude into one's relation to God with respect to matters of conscience and salvation because they have no competence to do so. This notion was Luther's contribution to freedom of conscience. Political power serves to maintain the secular order, not to ensure salvation. It has no autonomy independent of the norms of the word of God; however, Luther himself was not always entirely in conformity with this principle. In addition to the concept of two kingdoms, Luther later also propounded the notion of the three estates—family (economy), state, and church—which, theologically, were not clearly distinguished. Although Luther recognized the authority of political decisions, he raised objections to such decisions if he deemed it theologically necessary.

Crises of the Lutheran Reformation. Until 1523/24 the reform movement was shaped mainly by Luther. A series of divisions occurred subsequently that resulted in the diversity of the movement of reform. It became apparent that Luther's message could be received in different ways. Luther himself saw these disagreements as the work of the devil rising up against the newly unfolding gospel. Disagreements between Luther and Karlstadt had already hinted at this turn of events, which became more intense when Thomas Müntzer began to introduce a harshly anticlerical reform in Allstedt (1523) motivated by a mystical commitment to atonement and a prophetic claim to an eschatological sense of mission. This reform was directed toward the elimination of all things profane and all godlessness, even if force was necessary to achieve that end. Luther pushed to have Müntzer expelled from Saxony as a revolutionary.

The demands of the insurgent peasants in 1525 had a biblical foundation and included the free exercise of evangelical preaching, the abolition of the tithe, as well as the abolition of serfdom, which was deemed irreconcilable with human redemption through Christ. Although the Peasants' War was clearly influenced by the Reformation, Luther repudiated the peasants. His critique of the social injustice of the feudal lords notwithstanding, he declared that the peasants' disobedience toward the authorities was wrong and that the intermingling of personal Christian freedom and social freedom was erroneous. Here he saw Müntzer's influence at work, since he had become involved in the uprising in Thuringia. Luther warned the peasants several times to reach a peaceful settlement. When the peasants' uprising threatened to turn into bloody chaos, Luther, in his tract *Wider die räuberischen und mörderischen Rotten der Bauern* (Against the Murderous and Plundering Hordes of the Peasants), urged the authorities to exhaust all peaceful means but to crush the uprising by force if necessary. Luther's tracts on the Peasants' War scarcely influenced the course of events, but they compromised his reputation permanently. After the swift defeat of the peasants and the severe persecution that followed, criticism welled up in his own ranks as well. Luther maintained his point of view, particularly as regards Müntzer, who in the meantime had been executed; Luther could not bring himself to strike a conciliatory note. The

Peasants' War did not lead him to waver in his work of reform. Shortly after the war, to demonstrate that he stood firm in his cause, he married the former nun Katharina von Bora, although he did not expect to live much longer.

Even before the Peasants' War a conflict between Luther and the humanist Desiderius Erasmus of Rotterdam had broken out. Luther had realized as early as 1516 that his notion of justification could not be reconciled with Erasmus's moralism. Erasmus kept a distance from Luther, who to him was too impetuous. At first, however, he expressed empathy for Luther's critique of the church. This neutrality aided the cause of reform. In the long run Luther's efforts to keep Erasmus out of the controversy were unsuccessful. In 1524 Erasmus agreed to attack Luther theologically in *De Libero Arbitrio Diatribe* (On the Freedom of the Will). The central question at issue was whether humans were able to contribute to their salvation or whether this was entirely foreordained by divine predestination. Erasmus wanted to leave salvation almost entirely up to divine grace, but at the same time he wanted to emphasize a person's moral motivation; beyond that he did not want to speculate about such elusive questions as predestination. After a year's hesitation Luther replied with *De Servo Arbitrio* (On the Bondage of the Will). Driven by the deepest insights of his faith, he insisted on clarity about the human will and on the certainty of salvation according to God's merciful grace. In his response he addressed such daunting problems as God's inscrutability and the origin of evil. Although the dispute was not conducted dogmatically but exegetically in terms of understandings of specific biblical passages, *De Servo Arbitrio* is probably Luther's most significant theological tract. It did not end the dispute, which years later flared up once again. Not even the rudiments of agreement were attained. Quite to the contrary, Luther's mistrust of Erasmus's smooth formulations increased more and more. But the break with Erasmus did not mean a total dismissal of humanism, to which Luther owed a great deal and to which many of his followers, most notably Melanchthon, remained indebted. But Luther's harsh alternatives did not even succeed in convincing his colleagues in Wittenberg. These were the causes of subsequent disputes and discord within Lutheran theology.

The most difficult, protracted, and important conflict among the reformers concerned the Lord's Supper. Widespread dispute regarding the real presence of Christ's body and blood in the Lord's Supper probably existed both in mystical spiritualism and in humanism. By contrast, Luther never shared such discontent, given his commitment to the objective effect of God's word. Already in 1523 he was opposed to the rendition of the word *est* ("is") in the words of institution as *significat* ("signifies"), which had been proposed by the Dutch humanist Cornelis Henricxzoon Hoen. In his tract *Wider die himmlischen Propheten von den Bildern und Sakrament* (Against the Divine Prophets of the Images and Sacrament; 1524/25) Luther opposed Karlstadt's devaluation of the spoken word and the Sacrament in favor of mystic inwardness. Expelled from Saxony, Karlstadt found acceptance for his ideas in Strasbourg and Basel. At the same time Huldrych Zwingli advocated a symbolic interpretation of the words of institution, and he became Luther's main opponent in the ensuing conflict. In addition to disagreements over the words of institution and thereby the real presence of Christ's body and blood in the sacrament, the issue increasingly became a christological one. In Luther's opinion Christ's humanity is part of his divine nature, for both are joined in one person (*communicatio idiomatum*). Therefore Christ can be present in the Supper through his suffering and death.

In 1528 Luther sought to end the dispute with the formidable tract *Vom Abendmahl Christi. Bekenntnis* (On Christ's Communion. Confession). Subsequently, other efforts to resolve the conflict became more significant. During the Colloquy of Marburg, arranged by Philipp of Hesse in October 1529, where Luther argued against Zwingli, Johannes Oecolampadius, and Bucer, no agreement on the question of the real presence was reached, and Luther refused to recognize the opposing party as brothers. Bucer, who had always suggested the spiritual but not the bodily presence of Christ in the Lord's Supper, nonetheless continued to strive for Protestant unity. After difficult negotiations, in 1536 he and several southern German Protestant towns, but not the Swiss, recognized in the Wittenberg Concord that even the "unworthy" would receive the body and blood of Christ through Communion. In effect, Luther had enforced his view that the objectivity of the sacrament of Communion is independent of its recipient.

Consolidation of the New Church. As with any revolution, the problems of consolidation arose for the Reformation as well. Admittedly, this phase is not as spectacular as the earlier stages, but one must not depreciate Luther's later accomplishments, as has frequently been the case. At the Diet of Augsburg in 1530 when Charles V attempted to reach an agreement with the Protestants, Luther, still under the ban at Coburg, participated from afar in an advisory function. He criticized the Augsburg Confession, written by Melanchthon, because of its emphasis on the commonalities with the traditional faith. Luther astutely realized that agreement with the Catholics could not be reached, and therefore he called for religious peace despite existing differences of faith. Not without reservations, he consented to the Protestant defense alliance known as the Schmalkald League, although it was difficult to reconcile this stance with obedience toward the emperor. His efforts were essentially directed at keeping peace.

Luther did not expect the religious controversy to be resolved through the ecumenical council in 1537. His Schmalkald Articles, drawn up for this purpose, define the disagreement of the Protestant and Catholic churches: the doctrine of justification, the "article that makes or breaks the church." The multiple postponements of the council confirmed Luther's view regarding Rome's reluctance in matters of reform. In numerous writings, especially *Von den Konziliis und Kirchen* (Of the Councils and Churches; 1539), he elaborated on the difference between the true and the false church. When the pope urged the emperor to wage a religious war against the Protestants, Luther was aroused to tremendous wrath, which he vented in *Wider das Papsttum zu Rom vom Teufel gestiftet* (Against the Papacy in Rome Founded by the Devil; 1545).

In the context of his teaching Luther produced interpretations of *Galatians*, the *Psalms*, and *Genesis*, which for a long time to come wielded significant theological influence. In the 1530s disputations were reintroduced in Wittenberg. The theses for these disputations often provide the most precise formulations of Luther's central theological notions. Here Luther discussed scholarly differences in Wittenberg, such as the dispute over the continued validity of the law with Johann Agricola, who wanted to eliminate the remaining tension between the law and the gospel.

Luther's anti-Semitism warrants mention. He had originally shared the general Christian anti-Jewish attitude, but later advocated the civic emancipation of Jews since it represented the only hope of their conversion. Unpleasant personal experiences, his disagreement with the rabbinical interpretation of the Old Testament, and (probably untrue) information about Jewish agitation against Christianity aggravated him to such an extent that from the 1530s onward he regarded the coexistence of Christians and Jews as no longer possible. In *Von den Juden und ihren Lügen* (On the Jews and Their Lies; 1543) he demanded their banishment and the destruction of their homes, synagogues, and books. Luther's driving motivation came from his conviction that the Jews had violated faith in Christ. But precisely on those grounds his advocacy of the use of force against Jews cannot possibly be justified.

Luther continued to be involved in the reform politics of electoral Saxony, but his advice was not always heeded. He occasionally became occupied with the problems of other Lutheran territories, for example, when reform was instituted in the duchy of Saxony and in the electorate of Brandenburg (1539), in which his influence was limited. Regarding the bigamy of Philipp of Hesse Luther soon had to realize that his consenting "counsel of confession" had been a grave misjudgment that he had made on the basis of insufficient information. Not to be underestimated are Luther's letters of recommendation for pastors and schoolteachers as well as his advice to pastors regarding the often difficult situations within congregations. Personal contacts and correspondence took place with numerous followers of the Reformation in almost all European countries. In this respect Luther exerted his greatest influence on the Scandinavian countries. On the whole Luther never saw himself as the great strategist of the Reformation; instead, his abiding concern was the preaching of the gospel.

With the outbreak of Meniere's disease in 1527, Luther's health weakened. In 1537 kidney stones threatened his life. He felt increasingly weary of life, even though his energies continued to be formidable. In 1546 he successfully mediated in a controversy between the counts of Mansfeld, and he died in the course of that effort in his native city of Eisleben. He was interred in the castle church in Wittenberg. His friends mourned the departed "charioteer of Israel." They were conscious of the incisive changes in theology, church, piety, society, and politics that he had effected. On that occasion Melanchthon did not conceal the tensions in Luther's rich personality: his furious polemicism that at times knew no bounds and his defiant stubbornness whenever he was suspicious and saw the devil at work. Nonetheless, many positive qualities must be mentioned: the precision of his mind and the ability to modulate his formulations; the ability to listen, which undoubtedly related to his musical talents (and made Luther a poet); his delight in the gift of life and creation; his conviviality, of which his *Tischreden* (Table Talks) are the magnificent witness; and his carefree liberality and childlike trust in God that allowed him to go his way despite all temptations. Luther never saw himself as a saint, but as a beggar and a sinner who depended on God's mercy. In this fashion, he was able to live with his own contradictions.

Legacy and Reception. That Luther was a figure of world-historical significance is shown by the fact that historical reflection to this day has not been able to free itself from preoccupation with him. This reflection is as multifarious as was he himself. All of the Reformation was molded by him more than by any other. This also applies to his adversaries within Protestantism, and even Catholicism did not remain unaffected by Luther's influence. Lutheran orthodoxy attributed to him a special divine calling. On 31 October 1617, the centennial of the assumed date of the posting of the theses, festivities to commemorate the Reformation were held for the first time. Pietism rediscovered in Luther's faith a vivacity that affected even ethical activities, but at the same time it attempted to extend his reformation of doctrine to include a reform of life. The Enlightenment relied on Luther as the critical searcher after truth. Luther's contribution to the German language, already recognized in the baroque period, was particularly emphasized in the period of German classicism. Since the beginning of the nineteenth century Luther has been fashioned into a national hero. The culmination to this view was represented by the inscription of Luther into a German history of calamities that can be traced to Hitler, as argued by, among others, Thomas Mann. The Catholic image of Luther up until the twentieth century has been marked by the nasty *Commentaria de Actis et Scriptis Martinis Lutheri* (On the Acts and Writings of Martin Luther; 1549) by Johannes Cochlaeus.

The more reasonable Catholic appraisal of Luther introduced by Joseph Lortz (1939/40) represented an integral part of an overall ecumenical rapprochement. Karl Marx and Friedrich Engels subsumed the Reformation under the history of revolutions. They judged the role played by Luther as partly positive and, because of his opposition to the peasants, partly negative. This ambivalence has shaped Marxist historiography.

As a result of the critical edition of Luther's works published since 1883, a new engagement with Luther's theology has ensued in Germany, Scandinavia, and the United States as well, which has partly denominational, partly critical-historical roots. For a while this interest was biased either in favor of the young Luther or in favor of Lutheran theology. Now both tendencies have been balanced. But the intensity of Luther scholarship has decreased.

The reception of Luther in the United States cannot be easily told. It depended on the respective groups supporting it, and they varied in their assessments. In the early nineteenth century Luther was seen from the points of view of the Enlightenment and Romanticism. Anti-Catholicism used him for its purposes. He found an enduring but not unvarying interest among American Lutherans. By 1883 he appears to have been integrated into American history largely as a heroic figure. Under the influence of professional historical inquiry a process of distancing occurred in which Luther's impact on the modern world was both appraised and relativized. One problem of contemporary scholarship consists in continuing to understand the religious and theological impulses in Luther's work.

BIBLIOGRAPHY

Primary Sources

D. Martin Luthers Werke: Kritische Gesamtausgabe. Weimar, 1883–.

Pelikan, Jaroslav, and Helmut T. Lehmann, eds. *Luther's Works.* 55 vols. Saint Louis, 1955–1986.

Walch, Johann Georg, ed. *D. Martin Luthers sämtliche Schriften.* 23 vols. Saint Louis, 1881–1910. All texts in German; also contains additional sources.

Secondary Sources

Aland, Kurt. *Hilfsbuch zum Lutherstudium.* 3d rev. ed. Witten, 1970. Important guide to the Luther editions.

Althaus, Paul. *The Theology of Martin Luther.* Translated by Robert C. Schulz. Philadelphia, 1966.

———. *The Ethics of Martin Luther.* Translated by Robert C. Schulz. Philadelphia, 1972.

Archiv für Reformationsgeschichte. Literaturbericht. Gütersloh, 1972–. A review of the literature published annually.

Bainton, Roland H. *Here I Stand: A Life of Martin Luther.* Reprint, Nashville, 1990. The most popular of the older Luther biographies.

Bornkamm, Heinrich. *Luther in Mid-Career, 1521–1530.* Translated by E. Theodore Bachmann. Philadelphia, 1983.

Brecht, Martin. *Martin Luther.* Translated by James L. Schaaf. 3 vols. Philadelphia, 1985–1992.

Brecht, Martin, Karl-Heinz zur Mühlen, and Walter Mostert. "Luther, Martin I-III." In *Theologische Realenzyklopädie,* vol. 21, pp. 513–594. Berlin, 1991. On the life, theology, and significance of Luther, with bibliographical overviews.

Ebeling, Gerhard. *Luther: An Introduction to His Thought.* Translated by R. A. Wilson. Philadelphia, 1970.

Erikson, Erik H. *Young Man Luther: A Study in Psychoanalysis and History.* Reprint, New York, 1993. The most widely discussed psychohistorical work on Luther.

Gritsch, Eric W. *Martin, God's Court Jester: Luther in Retrospect.* Reprint, Ramsey, N.J., 1991.

Iserloh, Erwin. *Luther zwischen Reform and Reformation.* Münster, 1966.

Junghans, Helmar. *Leben und Werk Martin Luthers von 1526–1546.* 2 vols. Berlin, 1983. The important anthology commemorating the Luther anniversary.

Kittelson, James M. *Luther the Reformer: The Story of the Man and His Career.* Minneapolis, 1986.

Lehmann, Hartmut. *Martin Luther in the American Imagination.* Munich, 1988.

Lohse, Bernhard. *Martin Luther: An Introduction to His Life and Work.* Translated by Robert C. Schulz. Philadelphia, 1986.

Lutherjahrbuch. Göttingen, 1919–. Annual publication including the most comprehensive bibliography on Luther.

Manns, Peter. *Martin Luther: An Illustrated Biography.* Translated by Michael Shaw. New York, 1982.

Oberman, Heiko A. *Luther: Man between God and Devil.* Translated by Eileen Walliser-Schwarzbart. New Haven, 1986.

Todd, John M. *Luther: A Life.* London, 1982.

MARTIN BRECHT

Translated from German by Wolfgang Katenz

LUTHERANISM.

[*This entry comprises two articles. The first is an overview of the history, teachings, leadership, membership, and practices of Lutheranism during the sixteenth century; the second focuses on the development of a distinctively Lutheran theology during the same period.*]

An Overview

When Luther stood before the Diet at Worms in 1521 he recounted his discovery of the gospel and insisted that he was really not alone, for he stood with the prophets, evangelists, apostles, and fathers of the church. Less than a decade later at the Diet at Augsburg in 1530, many imperial cities and territories had embraced the cause of the new gospel. Luther was always adamantly opposed to naming his evangelical revival within the *una sancta catholica,* the one holy catholic church, after himself. "I was not crucified for anyone," he wrote (WA 8.685), but his opponents, some of them ferocious enemies, bestowed the name "Lutheran" on his message and his movement for a restored Christianity within the church.

The words "Lutheran" and "Lutheranism" refer to the working out of the meaning of his religious message. Luther himself declared, "This is my teaching, that it allows God to be God!" (WA 17.1.232.9–10). Lutheranism refers to the religious and ecclesiastical tradition related to Luther's own religious experience and his biblical studies as a professor of exegesis. Luther himself was fairly indifferent to ecclesiastical structures and liturgical forms. He could work well with congregational churches, the councils of imperial and other free cities, or with evangelical princes, as long as they favored the cause of the new gospel. The idea of a distinctive "Lutheran" church emerged only gradually during the course of the sixteenth century. It was not established in a legal sense until the nineteenth century in connection with the old Prussian Union and the Hohenzollern mandated state church combining a Calvinist minority and a Lutheran majority in the Prussian state church.

In the sixteenth century Elector Frederick III of Saxony was the first to set up an organization of the new church. During the following decades, many church orders Lutheran in character were adopted in cities and territories. From the very beginning Lutheranism was the leading form of Reformation Christianity in Germany and especially in Scandinavia; Calvinism and the radical Reformation of the Anabaptists, spiritualists, and evangelical rationalists remained a small minority.

Until 1580 Lutheranism was in the ascendancy within the Holy Roman Empire, and Calvinism was restricted to smaller areas on both sides of the Rhine, the Palatinate, the Netherlands, as well as in a few small states such as Lippe-Detmold and Anhalt. Zwinglianism exercised initially some limited influence in southwest Germany, in territories such as Württemberg, an area turning increasingly Lutheran, though in liturgical forms and ecclesiastical structure it retained Swiss Reformed elements. These things did not just happen, for the reformer Johannes Brenz, who once had to flee for his life to France, led the Reformation movement in that territory, with the guidance of Duke Ulrich, who reestablished himself in power, having replaced the Habsburgs. Most of the imperial and free cities as well as princely territories became and remained Lutheran. The most important of these were electoral and ducal Saxony, Hesse, Brandenburg, Pomerania, Mecklenburg, Prussia, the Guelph dukedoms, the Franconian margravates, Württemberg, and parts of Silesia. The imperial and Hanseatic cities that became entirely or in large part Lutheran included Hamburg, Bremen, Stralsund, Lübeck, Frankfurt am Main, Strasbourg, Ulm, Danzig, Nuremberg, and in part Augsburg.

The spread of Lutheranism was usually accompanied by a sense of hostility to the clergy, viewed as corrupt and exploitative, and to the ecclesiastical hierarchy, especially the local bishop, who was consequently often driven out of the city, such as the bishop of Constance. Sometimes an active reform group, such as the followers of Johannes von Staupitz in Nuremberg, accepted Luther's program for reform. The city council would appoint or at least tolerate evangelical preachers, who prepared the populace for the changes to come. In Nuremberg, for example, the council and the city secretary, Lazarus Spengler, worked with the evangelical preacher Wenceslaus Linck for reform. In Constance the preacher Johannes Zwick played a key role in turning the city evangelical, though the Habsburg armies soon took the city by force and reestablished Catholicism. In the south the cities that turned Lutheran included Esslingen, Reutlingen, Memmingen, Lindau, Regensburg, and, as mentioned, Nuremberg and Augsburg, and in the north, as mentioned, Magdeburg, Erfurt, Halberstadt, as well as Stralsund, Danzig, and Bremen.

One of the major territories within the empire to turn Lutheran was East Prussia, where the grandmaster of the Teutonic Knights, Albert von Hohenzollern, on Luther's advice, secularized the land as a duchy under the overlordship of the king of Poland. His marriage to the daughter of King Frederick I of Denmark contributed to the spread of the Reformation in that country. In 1535 Pomerania in the north was given a Lutheran church order prepared by Luther's colleague and the pastor of the city church in Wittenberg, Johannes Bugenhagen. In 1539 Elector Joachim II reformed Brandenburg, though he kept the episcopal constitution intact until 1543. The territorial conversion that brought the greatest relief to the Wittenberg reformers was the adoption of the Reformation by ducal Saxony, which turned to Lutheranism in 1539. Duke George had been Luther's most dedicated princely enemy, but in that year he died. His successor, Duke Henry, in 1539/41 quickly introduced the Reformation. Luther preached the festive Reformation sermon, celebrating the joining by the "other half" of Saxony with the Reformation movement, and in the very same hall in Leipzig where he had debated Johann Eck in 1519. Subsequently part of the Palatinate and Braunschweig-Wolfenbüttel and other states became Lutheran. Indeed, the entire northwestern part of the empire came close to turning Protestant, for even the archbishop of Cologne, Hermann von Wied, showed Protestant leanings. He called on Martin Bucer and Philipp Melanchthon to help reform his archdiocese, one of three great sees of the "Bishop's Alley," Mainz, Trier, and Cologne. But once again the Habsburgs with their Spanish armies intervened, and Wied was deposed when the armies of Emperor Charles V forced the Protestant Duke William of Cleves to re-Catholicize his territories. That part of Germany has remained Catholic to the present time.

Outside the empire the most important conversions to Lutheranism took place in the Scandinavian countries and were for the most part imposed from above. As early as the 1520s and 1530s the ideas of the Reformation reached the northland. The king of Denmark, Christian II (r. 1513–1523), attempted to introduce the Reformation into his country with the hope of joining Sweden to form a strong, consolidated state. But the opposition of the Swedish aristocracy and of the Danish clergy and nobility was formidable, and he was forced to flee the country. His successor was King Frederick I (r. 1523–1533), who was well disposed toward the Reformation. He had the precedent of his son-in-law Albert of Prussia, but he had to compromise with the conservative nobility, who resisted a break with the old church. Only with the reign of Christian III (1533–1559) was a complete Reformation possible, with the introduction of a Lutheran church order, prepared by Luther's colleague Bugenhagen. The seven bishops became superintendents and the king became the head of the church as supreme bishop. The Augsburg Confession was later adopted as the official creedal statement.

In Sweden the drive for independence from the Danes between 1521 and 1523 led to an alliance of nationalism and Lutheranism. The new king, Gustavus Vasa (r. 1523–1560), was crowned by the Swedish diet at Strengnäs on 7 June 1523, a hero of the struggle for independence from the Danes. He was personally inclined toward Lutheranism and believed that its introduction as a national religion would add cohesion to the independence movement. In 1527 at Västerås he had the diet transfer church property to the king and allow evangelical preaching. As was true of many areas in rural Germany, it took another generation for Lutheranism to saturate the country. That Sweden became and remained staunchly Lutheran was of great political and military importance during the centuries that followed, considering, for example, the role of Gustavus Adolphus in the Thirty Years' War (1618–1648).

Finland, a territory of Sweden, also embraced the Lutheran evangelical movement. Michael Agricola (1510–1557) was the major Finnish reformer. He had studied and taught at Wittenberg, translated the New Testament, the *Psalms*, and a number of the prophets into Finnish, following Luther's rendition. Just as Luther's Bible was important for the early modern German language, Agricola's translation helped to develop Finnish as a literary language.

Lutheranism spread also to the Baltic states of Lithuania, Latvia, and Estonia. Albert of Brandenburg's move as grandmaster of the Teutonic Order in East Prussia in 1525 to secularize and turn his territories Lutheran served as a trigger for the Baltics, where the order since the medieval conquests had been a dominant force. But in the Baltics, in contrast to Scandinavia, the Reformation was more a matter of the penetration and dissemination of religious ideas than of imposition from above. The center of Lutheranism in the Baltics was the city of Riga, the capital of Latvia, where there had been Lutheran influence as early as 1523, as German Lutheran merchants proved to be active missionaries for the evangelical cause. In 1539 an evangelical archbishop was elected. In 1561 the master of the Livonian Brethren of the Sword in Courland became a Lutheran and turned his territory into a secular duchy, which he held as a fief under the king of Poland.

Within the Habsburg lands Lutheranism was suppressed, especially by Emperor Ferdinand, brother and successor of Charles V. Nevertheless, Lutheranism made astonishing progress. In Hungary the cities with a large German population turned Lutheran, as well as many of the Magyar landed magnates, including the family of János Zápolya, the king under the Turkish hegemony. Mátyás Bíro Dévay, a Wittenberg student and friend of Melanchthon, was the most influential reformer. After his exile to Switzerland he returned in 1543 to lead the Reformed movement in the direction of the Helvetic Confession, and, during the following decades, Hungary moved to a more explicit Calvinist line.

In Austria the chief centers of Lutheranism were in cities and urban areas, such as Graz and Klagenfurt, but prominent members of the landed nobility also turned Lutheran, and for a time it seemed that Austria might outflank Catholic Bavaria under the Wittelbachs and turn Lutheran. Once their struggles with the French and Turks abated, the Habsburgs harshly persecuted the Protestants and reestablished a Catholic preponderance in Austria.

At the outset of the Reformation movement Lutheranism had a critical role to play also in western Europe, France, the Netherlands, England, and even slightly in Scotland. In France German Lutheran merchants smuggled in pocket-sized testaments and slim copies of Luther's writings, especially the three famous treatises of 1520. The importance of Luther for the young Calvin is a story often told. Calvinism became the dominant force within French Protestantism. After initial influences in the Netherlands under the dark shadow of the Habsburgs, Lutheranism gave way to Calvinism and the Dutch Reformed church reflected Zwinglian, but then definitively Calvinist, religious solutions and proclamations, as at the Synod of Dordrecht (1618).

Lutheranism was plagued from the outset by doctrinal controversies. The question of authority has been labeled the Achilles' heel of Protestantism, but Luther's assertion was that Christ is the head of the church and that the scriptures are the source and norm of all teaching. Too much has been made of the inner-Lutheran doctrinal controversies, for they proved not to be divisive nor did they undermine the basic Lutheran affirmations.

The antinomian controversy had to do with the third use of the law. Luther had maintained that the law of God, "thou shalt and thou shalt not," the natural law reflected in the Decalogue and even in pagan legal codes, was forever valid. The law of God was binding as a rule, as a mirror revealing one's defectiveness, and for the Christian's life as well as for the life of the unbeliever, for the Christian here on this earth remains a sinner in fact, though declared righteous in God's eyes as forgiven. In the antinomian controversy, which ran on from 1527 to 1556, some, such as Johann Agricola, felt that Christians as good and well-meaning persons no longer needed the law but would follow the direct impulses from the Holy Spirit. Finally Luther ceased trying to explain to his colleague and once wrote, "Grickel bleibt Grickel!" (Agricola is still merely Grickel).

The adiaphora controversy from 1548 to 1555 had to do with matters that were absolutely essential or merely peripheral for the Christian, for dogmatic correctness, faith, and church practice. The Philippists, followers of Philipp Melanchthon, assumed a more yielding posture, defending the Leipzig Interim and the reintroduction of "Romish" ceremonies into the Lutheran Reformed church. They were opposed by the champions of "genuine Lutheranism" (Gnesio-Lutherans) led by Matthias Flacius Illyricus, a leader of the conservative party, whose strongholds were Magdeburg and the University of Jena, founded in 1547 by the sons of the elector of Saxony, John Frederick. The Jena school adamantly opposed the modified Lutheranism and unionistic tendencies of the Philippists in Wittenberg and Leipzig. Flacius Illyricus declared that "nothing is an *adiaphoron* in the case of confession and offense," from which followed the Majorist controversy, Synergist controversy, Flacian controversy, crypto-Calvinist controversy, and others.

Between the Philippists and the Gnesio-Lutherans a group of theologians who can be thought of as a "center party" moved ahead, as constructive people must always do. They had not been conspicuously involved on the acrimonious level of the controversies, but came to the fore when the time for reconciliation and for a positive doctrinal statement had arrived. They produced the Formula of Concord (1577), followed by the *Book of Concord* (1580), which contained the ecumenical creeds, Luther's writings such as the Schmalkald Articles, and the general Lutheran confessions such as the Augsburg Confession of 1530 and the Apology of the Augsburg Confession. Among the most prominent men in the framing of the Formula of Concord, which was intended to "restore a true and godly peace" to the evangelical church, were Johannes Brenz, Jakob Andreae, Martin Chemnitz (nicknamed the "second Martin"), Nicholas Selnecker, and David Chytraeus. It is generally estimated that at least two-thirds of the Protestants within the empire eventually subscribed to the formula and to the *Book of Concord.* In Scandinavia there was more reluctance to sign, and many preferred to hold merely to the Augsburg Confession without further doctrinal statements.

The Formula of Concord devoted specific articles to the various deviations that had resulted in doctrinal controversies and addressed the problems effectively to the satisfaction of most theologians. Historians have understandably been attracted by the theological pyrotechnics of controversy and conflict resolution, but the Lutheran "ethos" remained unaffected in practical church life in parish churches in untold villages and the growing urban centers.

The decades that followed have traditionally been characterized by historians as the age of orthodoxy. This age began in the final decades of the sixteenth century, reached its apogee during the seventeenth century, and lasted well into the eighteenth century. While the period has been depicted as that of a new Protestant scholasticism with a rebirth of Aristotelian dialectic, a certain corrective is needed. Many of the most formidable figures were also religiously creative, composing hymns, religious poetry, and devotional books. Names known to scholars of the period include Michael Walther, August Pfeiffer, Erasmus Schmidt, Abraham Calov, Johann Gerhard, and Johann Andreas Quenstedt. Men such as the hymnist Paul Gerhard, Martin Rinckart, Paul Flemming, and Johann Sebastian Bach were nourished in this orthodox Lutheran environment.

As the century progressed, Lutheranism came to be defined in part by the doctrinal contrast to Calvinism, united with Zwinglianism in the *Consensus Tigurinus* in 1549. Several points of doctrinal difference were discussed and became divisive, including Calvin's doctrine of grace and double election, and the spiritual presence of Christ in the Sacrament of the Altar. While for Luther forms of worship and ecclesiastical structure were not biblically determined and were therefore of secondary importance, Calvin stressed the independence of the church from the state and preferred a form of church government analogous to what developed as Presbyterianism. In 1577 some Lutheran theologians expressed surprise that the Calvinists were so quiescent, but the following decades witnessed the unfolding of their opposing positions, and sharp polemics helped to define and to articulate the Lutheran theological positions.

[*See also* Augsburg Confession; Formula of Concord; Gnesio-Lutherans; Philippists; *and* Wittenberg Concord.]

BIBLIOGRAPHY

Bergendoff, Conrad. *The Church of the Lutheran Reformation: A Historical Survey of Lutheranism.* Saint Louis, 1967.

Elert, Werner. *Morphologie des Luthertums.* 2 vols. Munich, 1958. Volume one, concerning theology, is available in English as *The Structure of Lutheranism,* translated by Walter A. Hansen, preface by Jaroslav Pelikan, Saint Louis, 1962.

Kolb, Robert. *Andreae and the Formula of Concord: Six Sermons on the Way to Lutheran Unity.* Saint Louis, 1977.

Scaer, David P. *Getting into the Story of Concord: A History of the Book of Concord.* Saint Louis, 1977. Useful introduction to the development of the Formula of Concord, so critical for Lutheranism in the sixteenth century.

Spitz, Lewis W. "The Lutheran Reformation." In *The Protestant Reformation, 1517–1559,* pp. 59–144. New York, 1985. Lutheranism in a larger historical context.

Triglot Concordia: The Symbolical Books of the Evangelical Lutheran Church. Saint Louis, 1921. Contains an excellent introduction by F. Bente; presents the texts in Latin, German, and English. The most venerable edition of Lutheran confessional writings.

LEWIS W. SPITZ

Theology

Although Lutheran theology and Luther's theology must be distinguished, the former is unthinkable without the latter, and later Lutheran theology shows Luther's influence even where its shape was altered by other currents of thought. Medieval theology certainly influenced the way in which Luther's followers absorbed and processed his ideas. Also influential were his colleagues and followers in the first half of the sixteenth century, above all Philipp Melanchthon and Johannes Brenz, and students and disciples in the latter half of the century, for example, Martin Chemnitz and Nicholas Selnecker.

Luther's theology grew out of his Ockhamist background, his study of the scriptures as a university professor who used the tools of biblical humanism, and his own personal crisis over his relationship with God. Although scholars have intensely but inconclusively debated the dating and the definition of his "evangelical breakthrough," it centered upon his formulation of the doctrine of justification by grace through faith, based upon his "distinction between the two kinds of righteousness," with its corollary in the proper distinction of law and gospel. This doctrine of justification was closely tied to his understanding of the word of God and particularly of its nature as gospel promise, which elicits faith, and to his definition of faith as *fiducia* or trust. Vital for his theology was also his understanding of the "means of grace" and of God's action through the several forms of his word.

Luther anchored his theology in a belief that God is creator and that human creatures have fallen into sin. He defined sin primarily in relational terms. At its root, sin is "failing to fear, love, and trust in God above all things" (Small Catechism), a broken relationship with the creator of human life.

Inheriting sinfulness from Adam and Eve, sinners are born, according to Luther, with wills completely bound to oppose God and to flee from him. Luther was convinced that the fallen cannot by their own reason and strength return to faith in God. Only the Holy Spirit can turn sinners from their sinfulness and re-create them as children of God. Rejecting a doctrine of double predestination because it stood outside his distinction of law and gospel, Luther taught that God chose his own elect people before the foundation of the earth but that responsibility for damnation falls upon the sinner. The elect rest upon the assurance of their righteousness in God's sight, his choice of them and love for them, as they have received it in the means of grace.

Luther distinguished what makes human creatures righteous in God's sight from that which makes them righteous in relationship to other human beings. In this dimension of human life, "proper" (one's own) righteousness means carrying out God's commands through the human performance of deeds of love. In relationship to God, righteousness is always a gift of the creator, who freely, without condition bestows a right relationship between himself and the sinner on the basis of his unconditional favor. Luther taught that this bestowal comes through the creative word of God, which bestows God's promise. Trust is the only possible response to a promise, and so trust is the instrument that appropriates God's favor by being given this promise of forgiveness of sins, life, and salvation. By faith believers are totally righteous in God's sight even though they still experience sinfulness in every corner of life (*simul justus et peccator*).

The gospel that justifies sinners consists solely of the work of Jesus Christ, truly God and truly a man. Luther emphasized the unity of the divine and human natures in the one person of Christ and understood the ancient doctrine of the communication of attributes to mean that these two natures are so united in the person that they share their characteristics even though they remain totally distinct from each other. This person, the second person of the Trinity, Jesus of Nazareth, obeyed the will of God the Father and took the sins of all humankind into his substitutionary, sacrificial death, which abolished sin for God's elect children. Jesus then rose from the dead to bestow upon those whom God justifies through the word of forgiveness a new life, righteous in God's sight for Christ's sake. Luther depicted Christ's triumph over Satan, hell, the law, and sin as a "magnificent duel," and he understood the justification of the sinner as a "joyous exchange" of human sinfulness for his own righteousness.

The benefits of Christ's work are conveyed to God's children through the action of the word of God, specifically in the form of the gospel. Luther defined the word of God in terms of God's prescription for human life, which he labeled law, and his gift of righteousness, or the identity of a child of God, a gift that comes to sinners only through the action of forgiveness for the sake of Jesus Christ, which he labeled gospel. The working principle of his theology was the proper distinction between these two, law being applied to those who were secure in their sinfulness, gospel being bestowed upon those who were being turned in repentance from false gods and false actions.

For Luther God's message for humankind is found authoritatively in the scriptures, the word of God, but he also emphasized that this word must be delivered in what he called the *viva vox evangelii* ("living voice of the gospel"), the application of the forgiveness of sins to the lives of the repentant, in preaching, absolution, and Christian conversation. God's word also delivers forgiveness and life in sacramental form. Because they did not combine material elements with a promise instituted by Christ, he rejected marriage, confirmation, ordination, and extreme unction as sacraments, and saw absolution as a continuation of baptism. He retained only baptism and the Lord's Supper as sacraments because they combined material elements with the institution of Christ for the delivery of the promise of forgiveness of sins. Baptism, as God's instrument to bury sinners and bring them to new life in Christ, formed a central theme in Luther's proclamation, and the Lord's Supper as the means whereby God forgives sins and bestows community and life upon his people also played a vital role in Luther's piety.

Luther criticized not only medieval sacramental teaching

and practice, particularly the view of the Mass as a repetition of the sacrifice of Christ anew, transubstantiation, and Communion in both kinds. He also rejected "sacramentarian" doctrines of the Lord's Supper, which denied the real presence of Christ's body and blood under the bread and wine. Luther insisted that his body and blood are "sacramentally" present, to be partaken through the mouth, even by the impious (who, however, without faith do not receive the benefits of Christ's bodily presence, which God's word effects). His argument was based upon a literal interpretation of the words of institution and a christological argument that employed the communication of attributes. He emphasized the proper use of the Lord's Supper as the gift of forgiveness and strengthening for faith.

The gospel frees sinners from sin, death, the power of the devil, and the accusation of the law so that they may live a life bound to loving the neighbor. From faith flow the fruits of faith in the good works of daily living. For Luther the daily Christian life was to be lived out of the regular use of the means of grace and in service to the neighbor. The former was possible through use of God's word, conveyed to the illiterate through the memorized catechism, to the literate through Bible reading, hymns, and devotional literature. The conversation of God's "real children" with their "real Father" in prayer inevitably resulted from this use of the word. For Luther, service to the neighbor took place within God's structure for human life as expressed in the three "estates" of medieval social theory. He believed that all people were assigned by God to offices, or responsibilities, within the network of human life in situations of family and occupation, society or the political sphere, and the church. Christians recognize these responsibilities as callings or vocations from God, who provides for his creation through human beings, who serve as his masks, as they provide love and care for others.

Sixteenth-century Lutheran theology developed under the influence of the parish-level proclamation of Luther's central theme of the consolation of troubled consciences through the gospel of the forgiveness of sins through Christ's death and resurrection in sermons, catechetical literature, a rich and growing hymnic tradition, and devotional literature of other kinds. It also developed in the process of argument over the correct definition of Luther's and the Bible's intended message. Even before his death Luther's followers began to argue among themselves for the proper interpretation of his theology. An early student of Luther, Johann Agricola, disagreed with Luther's Wittenberg colleague Melanchthon and with Luther himself in the late 1520s and 1530s over the role of the law in the Christian life, banishing its use from the life of the Christian. The Wittenbergers instead insisted that the whole life of the believer is a life of repentance, to which the law continues to call even the Christian throughout earthly life. Tensions rippled below the surface between Melanchthon and some colleagues and students during the 1530s and 1540s on a variety of subjects, including the necessity of good works, the role of the will in conversion, the relationship between evangelicals and the papacy, and the definition of the presence of Christ in the Lord's Supper.

These tensions broke into public controversy in the wake of the Schmalkald War and the Augsburg and Leipzig Interims. Two parties formed among Melanchthon's and Luther's students, later named, respectively, "Philippists" and "Gnesio-Lutherans" by scholars, the former representing a more conservative posture from a medieval point of view, the latter more radical in their following Luther's emphases. Both parties wanted to preserve Luther's teaching, and both parties were heavily influenced by Melanchthon's theological method and the content of his teaching. From about 1550 to the 1570s they engaged in a series of controversies aimed at defining Luther's doctrinal legacy.

The first of these disputes over the proper interpretation of Luther's legacy, the adiaphora controversy, concerned the right of secular government to interfere in the life of the church, the importance of ceremonies in conveying the faith, and the necessity of clear confession of the faith in times of persecution.

Some of these controversies revolved around questions relating to justification through faith, others around the Lord's Supper and related questions. Andreas Osiander, reformer in Nuremberg, then leader of the church in East Prussia, reflected his Cabbalistic background in his teaching that the saving righteousness that believers receive by grace through faith consisted not in Christ's obedience to the Father in his death and resurrection but rather in the indwelling divine nature of Christ. Philippists and Gnesio-Lutherans alike rejected this view, defending the righteousness of relationship established by the atoning work of Christ.

The Philippist Georg Major, professor in Wittenberg, defended the thesis, "good works are necessary for salvation." Most contemporary Lutherans rejected this formula while affirming the necessity of good works in the Christian life. In related disputes some Gnesio-Lutherans objected to Melanchthon's "third use" of the law as a guide for Christian decision making, arguing that Christians do good works out of a "free and merry spirit," without the law playing a role in their producing the fruits of faith "in so far as they are in Christ."

Some Philippists taught a "synergism" in which the human will was said to have to accept God's grace before it could take effect in believers' lives. Their opponents taught that the Holy Spirit changes hearts and wills apart from human consent as he brings the sinner to trust the gospel. Related to this controversy was another over the definition of Original Sin. The Gnesio-Lutheran Matthias Flacius Illyricus defended the proposition that Original Sin is the formal (though not the material) essence or substance of fallen human creatures, whose sinfulness has recast them in the image of Satan. The Philippists and moderate Gnesio-Lutherans rejected this position. Without public controversy related tensions tested Luther's "broken" doctrine of predestination or election, which affirmed that God's choice of believers to be his own comforts them with the assurance that nothing can separate them from God's love.

Some Philippists, mistakenly called "crypto-Calvinists" because their working out of elements in Melanchthon's theology led them to a point of view similar to that of the Calvinists, developed a range of definitions of the real presence of Christ in the Lord's Supper and the relationship of the two natures of the person of Christ. These definitions caused controversy with Gnesio-Lutherans and finally with other Philippists. The group gathered around Brenz in Swabia, later led by Jakob Andreae, insisted that Christ's human nature was everywhere present (thus they were called "Ubiquitists" by their foes), arousing opposition among the Saxon Philippists and disagreement with many Gnesio-Lutherans, who shied away from this kind of defense of the real presence. Some Philippists professed Luther's doctrine of the real presence but rejected his christological defense of it; others taught a real presence of Christ, apprehended through faith but not to be partaken by the mouth, and certainly not by the impious. In 1577 an attempt to settle these controversies, the Formula of Concord, reconciled part of German Lutheranism but failed to integrate some Philippists because the Formula taught that the body and blood of Christ are truly sacramentally present under the bread and wine, and that the communication of attributes enables the human nature of Christ to be present wherever, whenever, and in whatever form God wills, thus making possible the real presence.

These controversies, and the attempt of the Formula of Concord to solve them, left a legacy for the Lutherans of later centuries that included the *Book of Concord* as a measure of correct teaching, but that also left unresolved some questions, which demanded further attention in the period of "orthodoxy."

BIBLIOGRAPHY

Adam, Alfred. *Lehrbuch der Dogmengeschichte.* Vol. 2. Gütersloh, 1981.

Andresen, Carl, ed. *Handbuch der Dogmen- und Theologiegeschichte.* Vols. 2 and 3. Göttingen, 1980 and 1984.

Gritsch, Eric. *Lutheranism: The Theological Movement and Its Confessional Writings.* Philadelphia, 1976.

Haegglund, Bernd. *History of Theology.* Saint Louis, 1968.

Ratschow, Carl Heinz. *Lutherische Dogmatik zwischen Reformation and Aufklärung.* Gütersloh, 1964.

ROBERT KOLB

LUTHER RENAISSANCE is the name usually given to a movement in Germany during the interwar era, the chief aim of which was to demonstrate the relevance of Martin Luther's theology to the modern world. It was part of a larger "back-to-Luther" movement in Protestant Europe that had its roots in the works of the Göttingen theologian Albrecht Ritschl (1822–1889), who, in the words of Wilhelm Herrmann (1846–1922), "had the power to rescue Luther's work from that ruin into which it had fallen." The Luther Renaissance included, but was not identical with, the school of Luther studies founded by Karl Holl (1866–1926), from 1906 professor of church history at Berlin. The reputations of both the Holl school and the larger German Luther Renaissance were permanently scarred by Ernst Wolf (1902–1971), who in 1946 accused Holl and his disciples of "using Luther against Luther" and of preparing the way for Adolf Hitler.

Karl Holl was a Swabian and a native of Tübingen, where he taught from 1900 until 1906. Although his prewar reputation rested on work in patristic and Eastern Orthodoxy, he is now remembered chiefly for his collected studies on Martin Luther, the publication of which in 1921 (rev. ed. 1923) came, Hans Lietzmann (1875–1942) wrote, "like a mighty revelation." Holl's reputation as a Luther scholar did not rest, as is often alleged, on his shift from older editions to the newer Weimar edition of Luther's works—to which Holl did not shift until the mid-1910s—but on his interpretation of Luther's thought. It is nonetheless true that careful philological and historical criticism of the sources, a hallmark of Holl's school, also formed a parallel between Luther studies after Holl and "the quest of the historical Jesus, and the attempt to separate historic Christianity from creative Christian tradition." (Rupp, p. 29). Contemporary testimonies agree that Holls' impact on Luther studies lay in his ability to make Luther's thought and personality relevant to the postwar situation of German Protestant Christians.

The tradition of Luther scholarship founded by Holl operated on several general principles. First, the basis of all study of Luther must be the exact historical and philological examination of the sources in the best available editions. Second, Luther must be seen in the context of the entire spiritual development of the West, which reveals his relevance to many modern problems, because he was the first to raise them. And third, Luther's understanding of religion was modern, not medieval, because of its theocentrism, its theology of conscience, and its radically personal ethics. The latter principle came under immediate attack, chiefly by Friedrich Gogarten (1887–1967), who criticized Holl for slighting Luther's Christocentrism and overemphasizing his ethical ideas.

Holl's major controversy with Ernst Troeltsch (1865–1923) concerned Luther's modernity, a debate that marked a major stage in the disintegration of liberal Protestant theology in Germany. Holl was a theological liberal; his academic patrons, Adolf von Harnack (1851–1930) and Adolf Jülicher (1857–1938), were liberals of the first water; and he belonged to the premier liberal theological circle, the

"Friends of the *Christliche Welt.*" Before 1914 Holl's scholarly interests ranged very broadly, and he developed strong interests in Calvin and in ideas of Leo Tolstoy (1828–1910). His first doubts about liberalism arose not from Luther studies but from a controversy about Luther's relationship to the modern era.

Holl journeyed to the meeting of the Historians' Association (*Historikertag*) at Stuttgart in 1906 for the express purpose of meeting Troeltsch. He heard his fellow Swabian inaugurate a sweeping deconstruction of traditional Protestant Christianity, arguing that Luther and Lutheranism were medieval and unoriginal, that Calvin, the sects, and spirituals first made Christianity relevant to the modern world, and that the modern age began with the Enlightenment in England and France, not with the German Reformation. Troeltsch's radical modernism proved deeply troubling to Holl, not only because he had already begun to read in the sources of traditional Protestant Christianity, but also, and perhaps more so, because of his deep hatred for Catholicism.

Holl belonged to a generation of German Protestants who lived to see the euphoria of 1871, when Bismarck seemed to complete what Luther had begun, give way to the doubts of the early 1890s, when the philosopher Wilhelm Dilthey (1833–1911) warned that the Protestant contempt for ideas would serve it ill against its two foes, social democracy and Catholicism, the political advantages of which consisted "not only in naturally powerful emotions, but also in closed systems of thought" (Wilhelm Dilthey, *Weltanschauung und Analyse des Menschen seit Renaissance und Reformation*, 7th ed., *Gesammelte Schriften*, vol. 2, Stuttgart and Göttingen, 1964, p. 92). Holl may have at this time doubted the future of Protestant theology—he thought of abandoning it for philosophy—but he hated Catholicism, which, he wrote to a friend, "is our worst enemy, and we shall never be rid of it." The son of a Catholic convert to Lutheranism, Holl had been fascinated by Catholicism during his student days. Later, however, he came to despise its "superstitions" and fear its political power.

This background, plus the savage confessional controversies aroused by the medievalist Heinrich Denifle's (1844–1905) scholarly but intemperate treatment of Luther, help to explain why Holl turned to the Protestant reformers, mainly to Calvin at first, and rejected Troeltsch's modernist consignment of historic Lutheran Christianity to history's dustbin. Yet his reaction proceeded from shared assumptions, for Holl's initial reply to Troeltsch built not on a radical, post-liberal theology, but on the familiar ground of what was called "cultural Protestantism." In *The Cultural Significance of the Reformation* (1911), he argued that Luther's thought gave a decisive impulse to many of the most progressive and creative developments in modern (particularly but not exclusively German) culture. Although he shared Troeltsch's method, Holl rejected his dissection of the Reformation into progressive/Calvinist/Western and regressive/Lutheran/German components and shifted the argument, instead, back to the familiar terms of Reformation vs. Middle Ages.

Then came the Great War, which radically altered Holl's perception of national community and the possibilities for theologizing in the modern age. By 1916 or 1917—the year of the war's political crisis and the Reformation jubilee—Holl completed his break with liberalism—in company with a great number of other liberals and former liberals. They moved toward the nation, for by far the most popular theme in the flood of writings on Luther in the anniversary year 1917 was "Luther and Germany." Holl shared this new sense of national community—he broke politically with the liberals and later joined the Fatherland party—but the war years also fostered his breakthrough to a new theology.

The war's impact on Karl Holl is readily grasped in two great pieces, his jubilee address *What Did Luther Understand by Religion?* (1917) and his study *The Reconstruction of Morality* (1919). While most jubilee celebrators of Holl's generation waxed eloquent on Lutheran Christianity and German identity, Holl embarked on a far more radical task of exposing in Luther's theology the foundations of an understanding of religion that was both radically personal and communitarian. His new vision, which did not rest on the identification of Luther with Wilhelmine culture, spoke with great eloquence to a younger generation of Protestants, for whom the war had destroyed the Wilhelmine content of "modernity." In his new and revised studies on Luther, Holl set out to prove, based on the reformer's writings alone, that Luther's discovery of the gospel led to his formulation of "a magnificent outline of a strictly religious morality" and showed "with some success that a doctrine of morality of the highest type is possible precisely, in fact exclusively, on the basis of religion. For only here, where individuals may regard themselves as tools of God, does duty receive its completely pure form, in which a strict sense of obligation is combined with a complete consciousness of freedom." Despite the decline of Lutheranism after Luther, "if we today compare subsequent ethical thought—right down to Nietzsche—with Luther's, there is scarcely a question that can be mentioned which Luther did not already raise; nor have his solutions thus far been surpassed" (Holl, 1979, pp. 137–138). In Luther, therefore, Holl discovered that of which he had long despaired, the basis for a post-liberal theology.

Holl linked his peculiar discovery, Luther's radically personal religion, to the more general wartime message of Luther studies, the church as national community, an idea that gained great power in the postwar period of disestablishment of the Protestant churches. Holl thus shared the tendency to marginalize both pietism and orthodoxy and to disdain the traditions of the Lutheran state churches in favor a new, national sense of the church as the nation before God, unmediated by the state. On this ground the great rivals were the socialists, and when Holl lectured in March 1922 at Wittenberg on "Luther and the Enthusiasts," he hammered away at social democracy in the guise of Thomas Müntzer, just as he had attacked Catholicism in the dress of the Middle Ages.

In summary, Karl Holl's odyssey reveals how the Luther Renaissance was born out of the Protestant predicament in late Wilhelmine Germany, which the Great War brought to its crisis. The elements of this situation included the collapse of biblical studies and the crisis of liberal theology; the political vigor of Catholicism; and the rise of social democracy, which supplied itself with members and votes mainly at Protestant Germany's expense. Holl, together with Troeltsch and other liberals, experienced the disintegration of the common Ritschlian heritage on the horns of this Protestant dilemma, but he refused to follow Troeltsch from liberalism toward modernism. Then, in the spiritual turmoil of the Great War, Holl found in Luther's writings the language for radical solutions to the crisis of liberalism: Luther's radical personalism to overcome the crisis of religion; Luther's concept of the church as national community to overcome the threat of a state without God. To his own school and to Protestant Christians of the interwar era in general, Holl bequeathed hope, the expectancy of a coming age in which one could be Christian, Protestant, modern, and German.

Although few established scholars accepted Holl's view of Luther, the times favored radical new approaches. Embattled by their two old foes, Catholicism and social democracy, and by a hostile state, younger Protestant thinkers turned to revolutionary Christian nationalism, and some of Holl's students assumed prominent places among those Christian nationalist thinkers whom Klaus Scholder has called "the folkish theologians." Two of them, Emanuel Hirsch (1888–1972) and Heinrich Bornkamm (1901–1978), were moving by the end of the 1920s toward a convergence with National Socialism. Hirsch, much the broadest, most radical, and most interesting member of the Holl school, moved from Christian nationalism through German Christianity into the National Socialist party. Although postwar dismissal from his Göttingen professorship began decades of isolation and astounding productivity, few of his nearly eighty writings in the Reformation field (including two volumes of studies on Luther, 1954) made a lasting impact. Bornkamm, by contrast, did not join the party, retained his professorship, and after 1945 published his principal works on Luther, chiefly his massive *Martin Luther in Mid-Career* (1979). Some other members of the Holl school—a term they did not willingly use in public—such as Fritz Blanke of Zurich and Walther Eltester and Hanns Rückert, both of Tübingen, did not concentrate on Luther at all.

The nonidentity of the "Holl school" and "Luther Renaissance" is further confirmed by the fact that some of the most violently nationalistic writers on Luther during the 1920s, such as Otto Scheel (1876–1954) and Gerhard Ritter (1900–1967), were not students of Holl at all. Nor was the theologian Paul Althaus (1888–1966), whose theology of the "orders of creation" lent important support during the later 1920s to those who hoped that national socialism would open the way for a modernized Protestant Christianity to become the German national religion. Like Bornkamm, Althaus survived professionally to produce influential writings on Luther after 1945, notably *The Theology of Martin Luther* (English, 1966) and *The Ethics of Martin Luther* (1965; English, 1972).

The German Luther Renaissance was the most important element of a much broader "back-to-Luther" movement in European Lutheranism. Its Swedish counterpart developed from roots around 1900 along a quite different track, one less overtly political and more highly theological than the German movement. The unproblematical identity of church and nation in Sweden—the German Protestants' dream—allowed Luther studies to become more speculative and to focus on specifically cultural problems such as secularization. The work of the major Swedish Luther scholars of the interwar era—Anders Nygren, Ragnar Bring, and Gustav Aulen—avoided the Holl school's philological obsession and concentration on the young Luther's "breakthrough" by pursuing "motif-research," the search for coherent underlying concepts to serve twentieth-century theologizing.

The most curious tributary of the Luther Renaissance is represented by the work of Joseph Lortz (1887–1975), a Catholic priest of Luxembourg origin who became professor at Braunsberg (1929), Münster (1935), and Mainz (1950). Like the Protestant "folkish theologians," Lortz aimed to foster solidarity between the church and the Nazi party, of which he was a member from 1933 until 1944. He announced this goal in a programmatic final chapter to his general history of the church (1933). Then, his two-volume *Reformation in Germany* (1939; English, 1968–1969) acclaimed, against a background deeply critical of the pre-Reformation church's state of moral decay and theological confusion—for which he blamed nominalist scholasticism and Erasmian humanism—Luther's moral seriousness and theological acumen. Luther had been led astray, Lortz thought, by the very corrupt theology that made his protest necessary and understandable. Unlike his Protestant counterpart Hirsch, who hated Catholicism to a fanatical degree, Lortz strove for ecumenical peace between the German confessions, a popular stance in many pro-Nazi Christian circles. To a great degree, Lortz revived a German Catholic view of Luther that had been represented by Johann Ignaz von Döllinger (1799–1890), the Munich theologian who had been excommunicated for his opposition to Vatican I; but the harsh Catholic critiques of Luther that had been delivered in the meantime by Heinrich Denifle and Hartmann Grisar (1845–1932) lent Lortz's irenic work a sensational quality in 1939. In the postwar era, Lortz's ecumenism—

shorn, naturally, of its nationalist agenda—became extremely influential in Christian ecumenical circles beginning in the 1950s. His writings on the Reformation remain significant chiefly for their programmatic character.

We cannot yet assess the historical importance of the Luther Renaissance; not only are many documents still inaccessible, but we lack a general history of the "back-to-Luther" movement of which the Luther Renaissance was only one, if the most dramatic, part. The movement's most questionable scholarly consequence, its obsessive emphasis on the theology of the young Luther, surely contributed to the fact that no full scholarly biography of Luther was published in German between Julius Köstlin's (1875; English, 1883) and Martin Brecht's (1981–1987; English, 1985–1992). Now that Luther's thought and biography have been reunited, and now that the Weimar edition of Luther's *Works* is complete, the Luther Renaissance belongs to history.

BIBLIOGRAPHY

Boehmer, Heinrich. *Luther and the Reformation in the Light of Modern Research.* London, 1930.

Carlson, Edgar M. *The Reinterpretation of Luther.* Philadelphia, 1948.

Holl, Karl. "Martin Luther on Luther" (1903). In *Interpreters of Luther: Essays in Honor of Wilhelm Pauck,* edited by Jaroslav Pelikan, pp. 9–34. Philadelphia, 1967.

———. *The Cultural Significance of the Reformation* (1911). Edited by Wilhelm Pauck. Reprint, New York, 1962.

———. *What Did Luther Understand by Religion?* (1917). Edited by James Luther Adams and Walter F. Bense. Philadelphia, 1977.

———. *The Reconstruction of Morality* (1919). Edited by James Luther Adams and Walter F. Bense. Philadelphia, 1979.

Kupisch, Karl. "The Luther Renaissance." *Journal of Contemporary History* 2.4 (Oct. 1967), 39–49.

Lotz, David W. *Ritschl & Luther: A Fresh Perspective on Albrecht Ritschl's Theology in the Light of His Luther Study.* Nashville, 1974.

Pauck, Wilhelm. "The Historiography of the German Reformation during the Past Twenty Years." *Church History* 9 (1940), 305–340.

Robinson, James M., ed. *The Beginnings of Dialectical Theology.* Richmond, 1968.

Rupp, E. Gordon. "The Luther of Myth and the Luther of History." In *The Righteousness of God: Luther Studies,* pp. 3–36. London, 1953.

Scholder, Klaus. *The Churches and the Third Reich.* Translated by John Bowden. 2 vols. London, 1987–88.

Troeltsch, Ernst. *Protestantism and Progress: A Historical Study of the Relation of Protestantism to the Modern World* (1912). 2d ed. Reprint, Philadelphia, 1986.

THOMAS A. BRADY, JR.

LUTHER'S CATECHISMS. Originally written for two different audiences, Luther's catechisms share the same structure and theological assumptions, although diverging in size and use. The Small Catechism (1529) was written for parents to use in the instruction of their children; the Large Catechism (1528–1529) was prepared for pastors and teachers for their own instruction as well as that of parents. The Small Catechism quickly became, with the Augsburg Confession, one of the most influential documents of Lutheranism.

The late 1520s were a critical time in the Lutheran reform. Apocalyptically driven, hoping for a conciliar settlement that would honor scriptural priority and renew the church's preaching, Luther and his followers had initially pursued their movement of reform rather spontaneously, seeing no need for long-term planning or political considerations. In 1526 the situation changed. Emperor Charles V had covened a diet at Speyer to deal with the blatant ineffectuality of the Edict of Worms. Further conflicts with Süleyman I made it impossible for Charles himself to attend. Strong reform sentiment as well as jealeously guarded territorial autonomy prompted a recess of the diet, and the reformers subsequently interpreted this as giving them a local option clause—the freedom legally to reform the churches in their territories.

Intent on dealing with the religious and theological life of the congregations themselves, Luther in 1526 proposed he use an ancient practice for the furtherance of reform: church visitations. Committees that included theologians as well as lawyers and other government officials would visit the parishes, assessing the conditions within them and making recommendations for reform. The conditions the parish visitators found were appalling, especially to a humanist as sensitive as Philipp Melanchthon, who was anxious about public morality. Drunkenness, fornication, spiritual indolence, and ignorance were found to be widespread among the clergy as well as the laity.

Alarm over these findings led to the first public controversy within Lutheran reform. Anxious to redress the circumstances, Melanchthon in his drafts of the "Instructions to Parish Visitors" proposed moral reform on the basis of the Ten Commandments. A long-time friend and colleague of his and Luther's, Johann Agricola, objected stridently, insisting that the gospel, the message of God's grace in Christ, would bring about the required changes. The resulting conflict, extending through the summer into the fall of 1528, required Luther to reflect on the role of the law and the gospel in public life.

"Catechism" as a form of instruction for children and others was an old medieval tradition. For example, Augustine wrote an *Enchiridion,* or handbook, to the Christian life. Many of the numerous other catechisms included the Apostles' Creed, the Lord's Prayer, and other forms of devotion. Early in the German Reformation Luther encouraged his friends, including Melanchthon and Agricola, to write catechisms but was dissatisfied with the results. In 1528–1529 he put his own hand to it, writing the two documents that he later named together as the "Catechism," identifying them with *De servo arbitrio* (The Bondage of the Will) as the best he had written.

Luther's conservative nature is evident in the structure of the work. He took as the basis the Ten Commandments, traditionally used for moral instruction in Catholicism; the Apostles' Creed, since the time of Charlemagne the primary statement of faith in the Western church; and the Lord's Prayer, the prayer most commonly used in the church. These three Luther himself often referred to as the "Catechism," considering them the primary instruction in matters of faith.

To these three parts Luther added statements on the sacraments of baptism and the Lord's Supper. Shortly after the catechism was published—the Small Catechism having been printed on large sheets to be hung in family kitchens—sections were added on the office of the keys and on confession and absolution. Later additions include daily prayers and a table of duties.

The innovation in Luther's catechism, controversial among Lutherans as well as with other traditions, was its structure. The Ten Commandments were first, followed by the Apostle's Creed, the Lord's Prayer, baptism, confession and absolution, and the Lord's Supper. Explaining himself, Luther appealed to experience, arguing that people must first of all know what to do and to leave undone (the commandments) before learning of the help God gives (the Apostles' Creed) and how to seek and obtain such help (the Lord's Prayer).

This argument reflected Luther's settlement of the controversy between Melanchthon and Agricola. Luther thought that the believer is free from the claims of the law. But invoking the natural law tradition, with his own modifications, he also affirmed that the requirements of creaturely life condition all relationships. The Ten Commandments sum up the minimum requirements of daily life in relation to God (the first three commandments) and the neighbor (the remaining seven). Thus "you shall" and "you shall not" are not voluntaristic appeals to a particular religious code of behavior; they are an indication of what life itself demands.

Within the context of these demands, summed up in the first article of the Apostles' Creed, Christ's work occurs, making the believer "glad and content" to be a creature once more, subject to the work of the Spirit in bringing about the confession of both sin and faith. It is from this context that the believer calls out in prayer, appealing to God for help, living with the demands while at the same time hearing the promise of God's sustaining grace in Christ.

The Small Catechism's spare elegance and directness quickly won it a commanding place in the Reformation and the Lutheranism that followed. It has been translated into all the languages of the Lutheran church and memorized by generations of children, including Johann Sebastian Bach, who wrote a musical exposition of it.

In the sixteenth and into the seventeenth century, the Large Catechism was commonly read as part of Lutheran services in Germany. Despite its larger size, it has always been the lesser used of Luther's catechisms.

[*See also* Catechisms.]

BIBLIOGRAPHY

Aland, K. *Der Text des Kleinem Katechismusin der Gegenwart.* Gütersloh, 1954.

Girgensohn, Herbert. *Teaching Luther's Catechism.* Philadelphia, 1959.

Meyer, Johannes. *Historischer Kommentar zu Luthers Kleinem Katechismus.* Gütersloh, 1929.

Reu, Johann Michael. *Dr. Martin Luther's Small Catechism: A History of Its Origin, Its Distribution and Its Use* (1929). Reprint, Saint Louis, 1980.

James Arne Nestingen

LYDIUS, Martinus (c.1539–1601), Dutch Reformed minister and professor of theology. Born in Lübeck, where his parents, who were originally from Deventer in Overijssel, lived as refugees, Lydius studied theology at Tübingen from 1560; unable to support the Lutheran doctrine of the Eucharist, he moved to Heidelberg in 1565. Here he received the post of master in the Collegium Sapientiae. After the Lutheran Ludwig VI succeeded the Reformed Frederick III as elector of the Palatinate, Lydius had to resign his post. During the next four years he worked as a minister in the refugee church of Frankfurt and in the church of Antwerp. From 1580 to 1585 he served the church of Amsterdam, and from 1585 until his death he was professor of theology at the newly founded university of Friesland at Franeker.

Little is known of Lydius's work as a pastor. In Amsterdam, where he was appointed soon after the city went over to the Prince of Orange in 1578, he was one of the four ministers in a well-organized church, and soon he was involved in ecclesiastical affairs outside the town. He was a member of the general synod of Middelburg in 1581, and in 1582 he presided over the synod of the province of Holland, which decided to excommunicate the Leiden minister Caspar Coolhaes.

Thus it is sufficiently clear that Lydius belonged to the small group of well-trained and decidedly Reformed ministers of the time. Nevertheless, personally he was a peace-loving man, and therefore was often called to reconcile the many conflicts of the 1580s, activities which continued in his Franeker years. These conflicts always involved two major issues: first, the frictions between decidedly Reformed, sometimes Calvinist ministers, and those ministers who adhered to a broader, sometimes Reformed, but not Calvinist Reformation movement; and second, relations between church and state. The questions were intertwined, in that the Calvinists demanded a larger degree of autonomy for the church than the others did. During dispute between Jacobus Arminius and his colleague Petrus Plancius at Amsterdam, a conflict with far reaching consequences, Lydius asked his friend Wtenbogaert to mediate.

In 1585 Lydius was offered posts at the universities of Leiden and Franeker; he preferred the latter, and taught there until his death. Nothing is known of his studies, except that he left behind manuscript studies that are now lost on the Old Testament.

A manuscript, *Apologia Erasmi*, most probably from 1596, defends Erasmus against charges of all kinds of heresies, especially against the accusation of Arianism. The study is well documented, thoroughly citing Erasmus's *Collected Works*, and the defense of Erasmus is without doubt its first aim. However, there is a second objective. The author emphasizes that Erasmus lived in the first phase of the Reformation era. Those who even at the end of the sixteenth century refuse to make their choice for the Reformed church, the "neutrals," have to consider the difference between Erasmus's times and their own, in which the differences have become sufficiently clear. The study is consequently a manifestation of the church's combat against lack of religious commitment. It was not printed until 1706, in the then-new edition of Erasmus's works.

BIBLIOGRAPHY

Evenhuis, R. B. *Ook dat was Amsterdam*. Amsterdam, 1965. Vol. 1, pp. 151–169, covers the Amsterdam Reformed church, especially Lydius.

Nijenhuis W. "Riskante Toleranz: Martinus Lydius' 'Apologia pro Erasmo.' " In *Reformierte Erbe*, vol. 2, pp. 245–261. Zurich, 1993.

Woude, C. van der. "Lydius, Martinus." In *Biografisch Lexicon voor de Geschiedenis van het Nederlandse Protestantisme*, edited by D. Nauta, et al., vol. 1, pp. 146–148. Kampen, Netherlands, 1978. Excellent biographical dictionary; includes a full bibliography.

CORNELIS AUGUSTIJN

LYON.

LYON. In the sixteenth century Lyon was a city of considerable importance. The third-largest city in France and a hub of commerce, manufacturing, and finance, the southeastern French municipality was a pole of attraction for immigrants and a cultural center as well, with influential poets and a number of significant publishers. Not surprisingly, it was also vital for the Reformation.

The first signs of the Reformation in Lyon date to the early 1520s, when it is clear that religious reform had won over a small number of supporters in the city. The French court, which began a long stay in Lyon in August of 1524, brought additional sympathizers in the entourage of the king's sister, Marguerite d'Angoulême. There were also preachers favorable to reform, beginning with the Dominican Aimé Maigret in 1524. Yet in the 1520s the Reformation in Lyon was not a large, organized movement. The number of adherents was still tiny, and they seemed hesitant to act without Marguerite's protection.

Despite repression, the Reformation gained ground in Lyon, particularly in the late 1540s and the 1550s. In 1546 a Reformed church was established, and in 1560 a Calvinist consistory: Protestantism in Lyon would remain Calvinist, with essentially no Anabaptist proselytizing. By the early 1560s, the Calvinists were benefiting from a relaxation of religious persecution. For the first time, they began to worship in public within the walls of the city, and by 1562 their numbers swelled to perhaps one-third of Lyon's population.

These Calvinists, we know from the work of Natalie Davis, came from all social classes except the very poor. But at each social level Calvinism was particularly strong in certain groups. Among these groups—the list here is not exhaustive—were the literate, the city's foreign immigrants, and the practitioners of newer and more skilled professions and trades, such as journeymen printers.

What then explains Calvinism's complex appeal? To begin with, Calvinism may have fed upon disenchantment with Catholic ritual, evident even among those who remained within the church. It may also have played upon widespread hostility to the clergy and the church's powers. Admittedly, the feelings of hostility to the clergy were shared—in varying degrees in different social groups—by Protestants and Catholics alike; indeed, many Catholics disliked the clergy and yet remained within the church. But having denounced the clergy and the church's powers in sermons and writings since the 1520s, the Protestants were particularly well placed to exploit the enmity toward the clergy.

The anticlerical attacks may have been particularly effective among vocational groups such as the journeymen printers, for the attacks stressed how demeaning the Catholic clergy were to the laity. As Natalie Davis has argued, that message had an obvious appeal to the printers, whose novel skills gave them pride in their calling and made them resentful of ecclesiastical tutelage. As for Calvinism's strength among Lyon's immigrants, it derived—so Davis maintains—from the structure of traditional Catholicism. Lyon's Catholic parishes did little to integrate newcomers, and the very rituals and images of traditional Catholicism frustrated the assimilation of foreigners. A local shrine, for instance, might be full of meaning for a native of Lyon, but not for a newcomer. Calvinism, by contrast, had swept away all the shrines and locally rooted rituals as well. It could thus put immigrants on the same footing as natives and unite them both in a shared urban piety.

As the first War of Religion approached, relations between Catholics and Protestants worsened in Lyon. Fearing a massacre, the local Calvinists entered into contact with Huguenot military leaders, and in April of 1562 they seized control of Lyon by force. Once in power, they purged the city council of Catholics and replaced them with Protestants. Banning the Catholic Mass and imposing Reformed services on Catholics, they destroyed relics, remade churches, and built streets through cloisters.

With military help from Huguenot armies, the Calvinists held the city until June of 1563. The Catholic clergy and many Catholic authorities had fled during the Protestant takeover; upon their return, they were outraged to find their churches "polluted" and were eager for revenge. To preserve a fragile truce between the two hostile camps, the Crown intervened in city council elections, but it was not long before the city government's tradition of religious neutrality foundered beneath a wave of extremism. The Crown's representatives shifted their support to the Catholic cause, and as moderates on both sides retreated from city government, the Crown allowed hard-line Catholics to take over the city council.

The result was violence and retaliation against the Protestants. In 1565, for example, a Huguenot attack on a traditional Catholic festival provoked a riot; in the aftermath, three Protestant ministers were expelled, including the chief pastor of the Reformed church in Lyon, the popular preacher Pierre Viret. Worst of all for the Protestants was an appalling massacre in 1572. Committed with the complicity of the city council and perhaps even the royal governor, it repeated, after a delay of several days, the tragic events of the Saint Bartholomew's Day Massacre in Paris.

Faced with such persecution, Lyon's surviving Calvinists fled or converted. Surprisingly, not all of the conversions were forced; indeed, some were undertaken sincerely, for reasons unrelated to the persecution. Calvinist journeymen printers, for example, grew disillusioned with the increasingly hierarchical administration of the Reformed church and its harsh moral discipline. Ultimately, the Reformed community they left behind was reduced to a tiny minority in Lyon.

Meanwhile, the Catholic church in Lyon was itself changing. The first efforts toward Catholic reform in Lyon date back to the 1520s and early 1530s, when the Dominican Sante Pagnini, a humanist and student of Savonarola, preached against Protestants in Lyon and advocated a reform of poor relief. In 1528 Lyon was the site of a provincial church council. But it was not until after midcentury—and particularly after the Catholic return in 1563—that the Counter-Reformation made significant headway. Beginning in the 1550s, the canons in Lyon's collegiate churches began to correct the behavior of the lower clergy. About the same time, Catholic preaching revived thanks to clergymen from Lyon's older mendicant houses and from the new orders established after the 1550s—the Minims, the Capuchins, and the Jesuits. Catholic preachers included such notable figures as the Jesuits Edmond Auger and Antonio Possevino, and they did not hesitate to challenge the Calvinists, either in the pulpit or in print. Indeed, preachers such as Auger added considerably to the growing literature of religious debate published in Lyon in the 1560s by Catholics and Protestants alike.

The Counter-Reformation also involved the Catholic laity, particularly the lay elite. They gave increasing amounts of money to the church, encouraged the revival of Catholic preaching, and joined new devotional confraternities that were founded in Lyon beginning in the late 1570s. And once in control of the city council, the Catholic elite took a number of steps in favor of the Counter-Reformation. Between 1565 and 1567 the council placed the Jesuits in charge of Lyon's secondary school—a break with an old tradition of secular control—and in the 1570s they subsidized the Catholic preaching orders in order to "further the Catholic religion."

Not surprisingly, some of Lyon's most zealous Catholics were ardent supporters of the Catholic League, the anti-Protestant alliance that grew into a revolution against the monarchy. Such zealots were compromised when the league collapsed in the 1590s, but the Counter-Reformation in Lyon was not slowed. Indeed, during the first half of the seventeenth century, Lyon added a dozen churches and a score of religious orders for men and women. At the same time, devout members of the lay elite continued to play a prominent role in the local Counter-Reformation. They poured money into the new religious institutions and into the new *hôpital-général*, where from the 1620s on the poor were locked up to work and pray.

Devout laymen also joined a number of new confraternities and religious associations, the most important of which was a chapter of the Company of the Holy Sacrament, established in 1630 in Lyon. A secret society with sister chapters throughout France, it united clerics, officials, and members of the urban elite to perform "good works." It was in fact involved in nearly every social and religious reform after the 1630s. Its members created schools, helped organize confraternities, and founded a wide variety of charities in Lyon. They even played a major role in the establishment of Lyon's seminaries—the sort of reform usually attributed to Counter-Reformation bishops.

In the company's good works, and in the actions of Lyon's clergy as well, one detects the distinctive ethic and piety of the late Counter-Reformation. The poor and the unfortunate certainly benefited from the charitable undertakings, but they had to endure a heavy discipline that accompanied the good works. If the evidence from Lyon can be trusted, Catholic piety itself was placing increasing stress on order, self-control, and the proper internal attitude. In Lyon, as elsewhere, the Counter-Reformation now frowned on traditional religious festivities, and Catholicism lost part of its social dimension in the process.

[*See also* Marguerite d'Angoulême *and* Viret, Pierre.]

BIBLIOGRAPHY

Baudrier, Henri-Louis, Julien Baudrier, and Georges Tricou. *Bibliographie lyonnaise, recherches sur les imprimeurs, libraires, relieurs et fondeurs de lettres à Lyon au XVIe siècle.* (1896–1952). 13 vols. Reprint, Paris, 1964–1965. Important source regarding the city's printers. Also useful bibliography of Protestant and Catholic pamphlets and religious works.

Davis, Natalie Zemon. "The Sacred and the Body Social in Sixteenth-Century Lyon." *Past and Present* 90 (1981), 40–70. Calvinism's social appeal and the Reformation's implications for urban life.

———. *Society and Culture in Early Modern France.* Reprint, Cambridge, 1987. Essential for all aspects of the local Reformation.

Gadille, Jacques, ed. *Le diocèse de Lyon.* Histoire des diocèses de France, 16. Paris, 1983.

Gascon, Richard. *Grand commerce et vie urbaine au XVIe siècle: Lyon et ses marchands.* 2 vols. Paris, 1971. Social and economic background plus a narrative of political and religious events from mid-century to the Catholic League.

Gutton, Jean-Pierre. *La société et les pauvres: L'exemple de la généralité de Lyon, 1534–1789.* Paris, 1971. The effect that the Counter-Reformation had on poor relief.

Hoffman, Philip T. *Church and Community in the Diocese of Lyon, 1500–1789.* New Haven, 1984. The Counter-Reformation in Lyon.

Hours, Henri. "Procès d'hérésie contre Aimé Maigret." *Bibliothèque d'humanisme et renaissance* 19 (January 1957), 14–43. Useful appraisal of the early Reformation in Lyon.

Kleinclausz, Arthur, ed. *Histoire de Lyon.* 3 vols. Reprint, Marseille, 1978. The chapters by Roger Doucet in the first volume are still the most detailed narrative, but portions need revision in the light of more recent scholarship.

Martin, Odile. *La conversion protestante à Lyon, 1659–1687.* Geneva, 1986. The later history of Protestantism in Lyon.

PHILIP T. HOFFMAN

M

MACHIAVELLI, Niccolò (1469–1527), citizen and middle-ranking official of Florence who became the foremost political philosopher and a leading historian of the Italian Renaissance. Among his best-known works are *Il principe* (The Prince), source of his enduring fame; *Discorsi sopra la prima deca di Tito Livio* (Discourses on the First Ten Books of Titus Livy); *Dell'arte della guerra* (The Art of War); and *La mandragola,* this last considered by many the finest Italian Renaissance play. In 1494 Machiavelli, who came from a minor aristocratic family, took service with the Florentine republic (1494–1512), which had been established following the expulsion of the Medici family. He rose through the bureaucracy as far as social status and modest means would allow, eventually serving as an ambassador and secretary to the Council of Ten, in which capacity he tried to institute a citizen's army in Florence. With the expulsion of the French from Italy in 1512, the republic collapsed, and Machiavelli lost his position.

Forced into retirement, Machiavelli devoted the rest of his life to his writings, most of which originally circulated in manuscript and appeared in print only after his death. The relatively few passages on religion that one finds in his work show an author who cared little for theological truth but instead valued religion primarily as an instrument of social control and a means of inculcating civic virtue. Machiavelli considered both ancient paganism, with its emphasis on this world, and Islam as more conducive than Christianity to inspiring such virtue. He thus advocated a reformed brand of Christianity that would place more emphasis on this world and less on the next. Machiavelli shared with Protestant leaders a lively antipapalism, owing partly to the immorality of Rome but mainly to the papacy's having kept Italy divided. This comes through in *Discorsi* but not in *Il principe,* a pamphlet-length work written around 1513 in hopes of winning employment from the newly restored Medici, whose current head was Pope Leo X. Machiavelli's writings, like those of his Protestant contemporaries, consistently appeared on the Index of Prohibited Books.

BIBLIOGRAPHY

Primary Source

Machiavelli, Niccolò. *Chief Works and Others.* Translated by Allan H. Gilbert. 3 vols. Reprint, Durham, N.C., 1989.

Secondary Sources

Gilbert, Felix. *Machiavelli and Guicciardini: Politics and History in Sixteenth-Century Florence.* Reprint, New York, 1984.

Grazia, Sebastian de. *Machiavelli in Hell.* Reprint, New York, 1994.

Hale, J. R. *Machiavelli and Renaissance Italy.* Reprint, Harmondsworth, 1972.

Meinecke, Friedrich. *Machiavellism: The Doctrine of Raison d'Etat and Its Place in Modern History.* Reprint, Boulder, Colo., 1984.

L. J. ANDREW VILLALON

MAÇON, Jean le. *See* La Rivière.

MAGDEBURG. In 1524 an evangelical constitution for the churches of Magdeburg, a north German archiepiscopal city on the river Elbe, was drawn up by the Augustinian prior Melchior Mirsch. By the sixteenth century Magdeburg was already relatively independent of ecclesiastical control; on a secular level, the Reformation promised full exercise of the liberties granted, according to tradition, in A.D. 955 by the city's founder, Emperor Otto I. The city's chief reformer, recommended by Luther, was Nikolaus von Amsdorf, called by Saint Ulrich's church in 1524. With firm support in the old city, he did successful battle against the canons of the cathedral chapter and against the Magdeburg archbishop Albrecht of Hohenzollern. The unpopularity of the archbishop was based in part on the sale of indulgences to finance pluralism: he was also bishop of Halberstadt and Mainz. Among Amsdorf's priorities was education; early rectors of the Johannesschule were Caspar Cruciger and Georg Major, both subsequently professors at Wittenberg.

When Emperor Charles V neglected to subdue the city after his 1547 defeat of the Schmalkald League, Magdeburg became the last redoubt for the defeated military chieftains and the rallying point for outspoken defenders of Luther, the Gnesio-Lutherans: Amsdorf, Matthias Flacius Illyricus, Erasmus Alber, and Nikolaus Gallus. Gallus was the author of the 1550 *Confessio et apologia pastorum et reliquorum ministrorum ecclesiae Magdeburgensis* (Confession, Instruction, and Warning), whose doctrine of the obligation of "lesser magistrates" to military resistance against imperial power in defense of religion influenced the plotters of the 1552 Princes' Revolt, served as a central document in the unsuccessful struggle of Flacius's party for freedom of the church against early German absolutism, and (via Théodore de Bèze) was influential in political resistance movements among Calvinists—French Huguenots, Dutch revolutionaries, and English Marian exiles.

A flood of pamphlets by Flacius, Gallus, Amsdorf, and Alber before and during the 1550–1551 siege of Magdeburg helped earn for the city the title *Unseres Herrgotts Kanzlei* (Our Lord God's Chancery) and credit for the survival of the Reformation. In retrospect, the siege, ostensibly on behalf of the emperor, was a duplicitous maneuver by Elector Moritz of Saxony to assemble troops for the Princes' Revolt against the emperor. Nevertheless, the Magdeburgers' defense of the Augsburg Confession and traditional political freedoms counts as the last time the voice of the people was heard in Germany until the eighteenth century.

After the 1552 Treaty of Passau assured the political survival of the Reformation, the government of Magdeburg became an official sponsor of the thirteen-folio history of the church called the *Magdeburg Centuries*, the first comprehensive church-historical work since Eusebius of Caesarea in the fourth century. It was an unprecedented team effort of the city's clergy and others, organized by Flacius. The basis for the modern restriction of the word to "one hundred years," the work itself has been called meaningless as a principle of periodization. The sections, however, organized around topics (*loci communes*), were meant simply to organize a cornucopia of original sources chosen to demonstrate the catholicity of the Reformation.

[*See also* Flacius Illyricus, Matthias; Holy Roman Empire; Interims; Saxony; *and* Schmalkald War.]

BIBLIOGRAPHY

Brandi, Karl. *Deutsche Geschichte im Zeitalter der Reformation und Gegenreformation.* 4th ed. Munich, 1969.

Cargill, Thompson, W. D. J. "Luther and the Right of Resistance to the Emperor." In *Church, Society and Politics*, pp. 159–202. Oxford, 1975. Challenges the notion that Luther encouraged only political passivity.

Diener, Ronald. "The *Magdeburg Centuries:* A Bibliothecal and Historiographical Analysis." Diss., Harvard Divinity School, 1979. Detailed, with original sources in English translation.

Gilmont, Jean-François. "Flacius Illyricus." In *Dictionnaire d'histoire et de géographie ecclésiastique*, vol. 17, pp. 311–316. Paris, 1971. Includes the best summary of the *Centuries* enterprise.

Hoffman, Friedrich Wilhelm. *Geschichte der Stadt Magdeburg.* Revised by G. Hertel and Friedrich Hülsse. Magdeburg, 1885.

Hülsse, Friedrich. *Die Stadt Magdeburg im Kampfe für den Protestantismus während der Jahren 1547–1551.* Schriften für das Deutsche Volk 17. Halle, 1892.

Kolb, Robert. *Nikolaus von Amsdorf, 1483–1565.* Nieuwkoop, 1978. The best source in English on Magdeburg's reformer.

Olson, Oliver K. "Theology of Revolution: Magdeburg, 1550–1551." *Sixteenth Century Journal* 3.1 (1972), 56–79. Argues that the strict Lutheran Magdeburg Confession led to armed resistance.

Scheible, Heinz. *Die Entstehung der Magdeburger Zenturien.* Schriften des Vereins für Reformationsgeschichte 183. Gütersloh, 1966. The standard work on the preparation of the *Magdeburg Centuries.*

Schoenberger, Cynthia Grant. "The Confession of Magdeburg and the Lutheran Doctrine of Resistance." Diss., Columbia University, 1972.

OLIVER K. OLSON

MAGDEBURG CONFESSION. *See* Resistance Theory.

MAGIC assumed protean forms in Reformation Europe, nearly all of which came under attack from various religious reformers. From erudite *magi*—the court astrologers, Hermeticists, and occultists such as Heinrich Cornelius Agrippa and Giovanni Battista Della Porta—down to the small army of uneducated local magicians across Christendom—cunning folk, *wahrsagers, curanderos, devins-guérisseurs*—all fell under suspicion of illicit practices. There were, of course, significant differences between Protestant and Catholic styles of attack, with the former usually being somewhat more radical in theory but the latter boasting a better system of ecclesiastical repression. Neither, however, was particularly effective.

At the summit of the occult arts, astrology was usually considered a science rather than a superstition. The Renaissance saw many famous practitioners, from Nostradamus to John Dee. Ambiguity about its genuine predictive value and its possible conflicts with divine providence ran deep among both Protestants and Catholics. Even John Calvin, in his treatise condemning judicial astrology, acknowledged that "there is some conformity *(convenance)* between the stars or planets and the disposition of human bodies." The Spanish theologian Pedro Ciruelo explained its abuses in 1530: "The astrologer who attempts to employ the stars to penetrate the heart and will of man is superstitious and has an alliance with the Devil; it . . . must be punished as a type of necromancy." Eventually it was; Pope Sixtus V issued a bull prohibiting it in 1586. In Spain the University of Valencia accordingly suppressed its chair of astrology; its holder, however, reemerged as a professor of astrology in 1591–1593 and again from 1608–1613, serving in the interval as professor of astronomy. At least six of his students were subsequently punished by four different tribunals of the Spanish Inquisition. In contrast, London's Society of Astrologers heard sermons from invited guests, five of which were subsequently published, at its annual banquets between 1649 and 1658.

Less scientific types of magic were easier to condemn as more or less disguised forms of necromancy or superstitious relics of paganism. Both erudite and popular magic tended to invoke supernatural spirits for one of three main purposes: divination, healing, or spells to produce either love or wealth. In their tracts and sermons, Protestants censured all such activities, to which they added such Catholic practices as exorcism and transubstantiation, as "conjuring." A Catholic spokesman such as Ciruelo could explain that "although necromancy is not a formal heresy, it is close to being one" and could condemn those "curious and undisciplined men" who employ "diabolical arts and superstitious practices." Protestantism, however, went much further in its disapproval of anything mysterious or miraculous and "presented itself as a deliberate attempt to take the magical elements out of religion" (Thomas, pp. 75–76).

Protestants often lacked the practical means to enforce their prohibitions of magical practices. Their legislation seemed ferocious: the English Parliament in 1563 declared conjuring of spirits, love magic, divination for lost goods or hidden treasures, and even alchemy to be felonies. White magic was similarly declared a capital crime in Lutheran Saxony nine years later. Even so, indictments were remarkably few and punishments mild: of 503 people accused of witchcraft at the Essex circuit court, only eleven were magicians who had tried to locate buried treasure or lost property. Meanwhile, two dozen people were charged with divination or superstitious healing in Essex's ecclesiastical courts, while three dozen were charged with employing them; most culprits received small fines. Such toothless institutions rarely humiliated and never effectively inhibited England's "cunning folk," and they did not even punish seventeenth-century Oxford undergraduates who held magical séances or publicly debated the efficacy of love philters. Even the most famous Protestant system of ecclesiastical censure, the consistory of Geneva, excommunicated relatively few people during the 1560s for "superstition," and when it did, it was usually for consulting nearby Catholic diviners or exorcists. Detailed edicts against all forms of divination, read from hundreds of pulpits in French Switzerland in 1599, 1610, and 1640, resulted in only a handful of trials. In general, Protestants arrested white witches only when their activities seemed fraudulent or otherwise harmful.

Catholics were less sweeping in their attack on magical superstitions but had more effective means of punishing them. In Northern Europe the secular Catholic court systems resembled those of the Protestants—a mere half-dozen necromancers, some educated, others illiterate, appear in the records of Lorraine or Franche-Comté—but the great Mediterranean Inquisitions took illicit magic far more seriously. The Venetian Holy Office, like other branches of the Roman Inquisition, spent most of its energy after 1580 in repressing superstitions rather than Protestantism. As the papal nuncio reported, "those [matters] which have taken up most time are the superstitious use of incantations" generally "accompanied by activities which made them matters for the Inquisition, such as the adoration of demons, the recitation of prayers, the burning for magical purposes of. . . substances which give off sweet or foul odors." The nuncio pointed out that these incantations "did not arise from any inclination towards heresy; rather, they were directed towards two ends, love and gain, which wield great power over empty-headed people." More than five hundred accusations of illicit magic and superstition fill its records across the next seventy years; 70 percent of the defendants were women and almost 20 percent were clerics. They stood accused of divination by casting beans; of using water bowls or sieves to find lost objects, including absent lovers; of baptizing magnets in order to locate hidden treasures; and of casting potent love spells, such as the "hammer," which involved burning pieces of broken Venetian glass or even roasting a statue of Christ over a slow fire in order to arouse passion. Only a handful of monks, suspected of using consecrated objects for necromancy, were tortured; four were sent to the galleys, but none was killed.

After the Council of Trent a whole gamut of activities—ranging from elaborate necromancy with explicit invocation of devils by clergy (once performed for Benvenuto Cellini in the Roman Colosseum) down to superstitious curative charms recited by illiterate old women—came under investigation throughout the Mediterranean. The Spanish Inquisition seemed much harsher toward clerical necromancers than the Venetians were. A half-dozen death sentences against necromancers at Saragossa are known to have occurred between 1511 and 1537, years when the historical Doctor Faustus wandered through Germany bothered only by accusations of pederasty. The Palermo Inquisition subsequently sent fifty Sicilian magicians to the galleys between 1570 and 1640. One Sicilian cleric in minor orders was sentenced to six years in the galleys for necromancy in 1586 by the Spanish Inquisition, convicted by the Roman Inquisition ten years later, and sentenced again at Palermo to seven years at the oars for sacrilegious magic in 1604, but he then made a successful astrological prediction and became personal "philosopher" to a cardinal in 1610; however, the Palermo tribunal condemned him a third time in 1621 for practicing astrology and exiled the old man to a remote island. The Portuguese Inquisition, although less preoccupied with magic, discovered the spells used by a widow who had invoked even "Lucifer and his wife" in a successful attempt to win her son a position as chaplain in the household of Portugal's inquisitor general.

For much different reasons magical healers came under suspicion and even risked death. Healers believed they had special gifts that clients could use, but many of them employed such superstitious practices as invoking saints (in Protestant lands) or uncanonical saints (in Catholic lands). Clerics and demonologists viewed them as sinister figures, necromancers employing demons to conjure away spells they had cast. Because it was widely accepted that anyone who could lift spells could also cast them, some healers came under both popular and clerical suspicion; local courts then arrested, tortured, and executed them for black witchcraft. Their judges occasionally employed natural magic themselves, forcing one suspected witch to wear a chaplet "made from an herb named *fuga demonum,*" while another was given holy water to drink during her interrogation; neither confessed.

During the scientific revolution and the Enlightenment, while witchcraft trials gradually ended across Europe and astrology lost its intellectual prestige, popular magic endured. Although Geneva banished a *devineresse* as late as 1735, English bishops had stopped inquiring about popular divination at their visitations after 1660, while Spanish and Roman inquisitors arrested few magicians after the mid-seventeenth century. Such activities were no less common than before, merely less dangerous. If it is easy to find connections between the magical practices of medieval and Reformation Europe, it is equally easy to discover continuities between sixteenth- and twentieth-century magic. In 1951 Etienne Delcambre wrote, "Even today, magical healers (still numerous in the Vosges forests) deny they are witches; and today as formerly, clergymen regard them with suspicion" (Delcambre, p. 216). The most important change in modern magic is not its decriminalization but its democratization: mass literacy, plus the removal of astrology and alchemy from the canonical list of sciences, has largely erased the traditional line separating high from low magic. Do-it-yourself handbooks of magic, or *grimoires,* have proliferated since the eighteenth and especially the nineteenth centuries. The road from Doctor Faustus to contemporary occultism leads through the printers of Calvinist Geneva, one of whom produced a deluxe edition of Europe's best-known magical handbook, the *Clavicula Salomonis* (Solomon's Key), in 1762, complete with drawings of the Devil by a local artist.

BIBLIOGRAPHY

Ciruelo, Pedro. *A Treatise Reproving All Superstitions and Forms of Witchcraft.* Rutherford, N.J., 1977.

Delcambre, Etienne. *Les devins-guérisseurs dans la Lorraine ducale: Leur activité et leurs méthodes.* Nancy, 1951.

Kieckhefer, Richard. *Magic in the Middle Ages.* Cambridge, 1989.

Martin, Ruth. *Witchcraft and the Inquisition in Venice, 1550–1650.* Oxford, 1989.

Thomas, Keith. *Religion and the Decline of Magic.* London, 1970.

E. WILLIAM MONTER

MAGISTRACY.

[*This entry comprises three articles dealing with the role and authority of magistrates during the sixteenth century in the British Isles, Germany and the Low Countries, and France. For a related discussion, see* Secular Magistrate, Office of.]

The British Isles

The early establishment of the royal supremacy over the Church of England dictated much of the course of British debates over the role and authority of Christian magistrates. Henry VIII had intended to control his church right from the beginning of his reign; that the supreme headship was not established until 1534 was something of an accident. The papal church with the monarch in place of the pope remained the administrative structure of the *ecclesia anglicana,* except for a brief period under Mary Tudor. The monarch combined both secular and ecclesiastical authority, limited only by his or her inability to perform the clergy's sacral functions. The Crown's agents continued to be the bishops and, though the royal supremacy itself was almost never openly questioned, the extent of the bishops' authority became a central issue for those who wished further reformation. In the name of discipline, these presbyterians and congregationalists proposed the abolition of the bishops and their replacement by a more broadly based clerical enforcement of morality on either a national (presbyterian) or a local (congregationalist) scale. They also favored the separation of secular and ecclesiastical authority. Defenders of the established order, too, could support more rigorous discipline requiring cooperation between religious and secular authorities.

Henry's aspirations to supreme authority over the church in England appeared very early in his reign. In 1515 in the Standish Affair, he told defenders of clerical privilege that "by the ordinance and sufferance of God, we are king of England, and kings of England in time past have never had any superior but God only." At roughly the same time, Henry exercised a nearly complete superiority over the conquered church of Tournai, virtually excluding the pope's authority. Yet Henry apparently needed the stimulus of Clement VII's refusal to grant him a divorce to proceed to the institutionalization of his supremacy. By a series of acts in 1534, probably coordinated from the beginning, Henry induced Parliament to make him supreme head of the church (initially "as far as the law of Christ allows," but that qualification was quickly and quietly dropped). Not at all coincidentally, England at the same time became a fully fledged empire, with Henry drawing on Byzantine precedents to support his new claims. As far as he was concerned, England was a theocracy.

Sir John Neale once argued that the Elizabethan Settlement was constructed by returned exiles putting into practice the latest Continental principles. Although that theory is now discredited, it would be safer to make a similar argument about the Reformation under Edward VI. It was heavily influenced by exiles from the Continent, chief among them Martin Bucer and Peter Martyr Vermigli, both forced to leave the empire in 1549–1550. Since Thomas Cranmer, the archbishop of Canterbury, had a good deal of sympathy for both men's theology, major changes in religious and secular authority were bruited, though not much happened apart from further depredations on church property. Bucer wrote and dedicated to Edward *De regno Christi*

(1550), in which he argued for reformation through royal supremacy. This entailed the reduction of bishops to strictly religious authorities and the shedding of all their secular involvements. The king had the responsibility for further reform, which he was to put through by means of a special council for religious affairs. The council was especially to see to the introduction of a comprehensive discipline, which was to be supervised by the bishops—acting mainly through example—together with the rest of the clergy. Secular magistrates also had a placc in Bucer's new comprehensive system of surveillance and in addition retained a good deal of authority, especially the power to punish with death. In his attempt to delineate the secular and religious spheres, however, Bucer wound up with a complex codependency, which would probably have led to stalemate if put into practice. Thus, by trying to sit on both sides of the fence, Bucer simultaneously gave aid and comfort to the old order and to the new.

Both Bucer's and Vermigli's ideas show up prominently in one of the most important of broken Tudor monuments, the *Reformatio legum,* a proposed new code of canon law. Drawn up by a committee sponsored by Cranmer in 1552, it never gained official sanction. It stoutly defended against the Anabaptists the existence of Christian magistrates and their coercive authority. The bishops, too, retained most of their former jurisdiction—over heresy and blasphemy and the appointment of preachers, for instance—and both magistrates and bishops explicitly derived their power from the king. Yet at the same time, the *Reformatio* set up a congregational model of discipline, grounded in elders and their frequent consultation with ministers, a system that closely resembled the Genevan presbytery. Jan Łaski's foreigners' church in London set another example of a similar cooperative organization. The royal supremacy could cover a wide variety of forms of ecclesiastical polity.

When Mary Tudor succeeded her brother in 1553, Protestant experiments were immediately put on hiatus, but oddly enough Mary returned to a form of church government almost identical to Henry's first version; that is, although she renounced the headship, her church was ruled through a permanent papal legate, Reginald Pole, just as Henry had used Thomas Wolsey for fifteen years. Whatever his attitude toward the papacy, Pole's view of the bishops was virtually identical to Bucer's and that of the *Reformatio*: they were to rule by example rather than the brute exercise of jurisdiction and, if anything, to bear even more responsibility for previous failures. Mary's and Pole's efforts to return England to Rome produced more dramatic effects than Henry's original separation had, whether in the fires of Smithfield or—more important here—several waves of exiles. Although hardly the "wolves of Geneva" or anything like the organized party they used to be portrayed as, the exiles largely shaped discussions of magistracy for the rest of the century.

They wrestled particularly with two issues: the subject's right of resistance and the form of religious organization. On the first point John Ponet, who had been bishop of both Rochester and Winchester under Edward, put forward in his *Short Treatise of Politic Power* (1556) a radical defense of any private subject's right to resist tyranny, even through tyrannicide. Most of Ponet's contemporaries, especially Lutherans in the empire, had limited legitimate resistance only to those magistrates whose constitutional position allowed it, and Ponet was among the few to defend tyrannicide. John Knox, the fiery Scottish exile whose experience as a French galley slave did not endear him to any form of what he took to be religious tyranny, and Christopher Goodman (*How Superior Powers Ought to be Obeyed,* 1558) joined Ponet. Ponet and Goodman's theories were rooted in the contention that God chose magistrates, but magistrates were to be obeyed only insofar as they observed God's laws. This point would become a fundamental tenet of the more radical Puritans. Equally important, the various exile communities, especially those in Frankfurt am Main and Geneva, wrangled almost endlessly over the proper form of church government. Significantly for the history of Anglicanism, the conflict at Frankfurt was settled by an appeal to the local magistrates, who expelled Knox. The alumni of this congregation would mostly become defenders of the Elizabethan Settlement.

After his expulsion Knox and some other Englishmen went to Geneva, where they absorbed a nearly unadulterated Calvinist view of the church. It depended on discipline, and in its establishment the secular magistrate still played a vital role. Knox, as he always did during Mary's reign, argued a more radical line, going so far as to claim that "princes . . . [should] be compelled also to reform their wicked laws," perhaps by their godly subjects. But Knox and the other radicals made a crucial blunder by fulminating against female rule, and when Elizabeth succeeded Mary in 1558, they found themselves largely without influence in England. Knox, at least, has usually been thought to have found success instituting a rigorously presbyterian system in Scotland. Officially the Parliament of 1560 established that new order, but because of the continued existence of the hierarchy (and later James VI's strong preference for episcopacy), the vagaries of Scottish politics, and recent evidence that the vaunted discipline of the consistory really was not very rigorous after all, there is room for doubt about the degree of Knox's impact in his native land.

Elizabeth probably intended from the first both to restore the royal supremacy and to establish some kind of Protestant church. Both provoked contention in Parliament, although the opposition does not seem to have thrown up considerations of magistracy on either point. Once the bishops' resistance was broken early in 1559, the supremacy came back into existence, with Elizabeth styling herself "supreme governor," partly to allay concern about a woman acting as head of the church. Although most of the exiles had by then officially repudiated any form of private resistance, that did not mean that they forbore to ask Elizabeth for further reformation of her church. One of them, Laurence Humphrey, brought out in late 1559 *De religionis conservatione et reformatione vera* (dedicated to Francis Russell, who had been in exile mainly in Italy), which demanded more discipline and drew a sharp line between the coercive powers of church and state, arguing that neither must interfere in the affairs of the other. Humphrey also argued in favor of an elective monarchy restrained by Parliament, a point he made in another treatise, *Optimates* (1559; English translation, 1563), which was explicitly (and more dangerously) aimed at the nobility.

By the late 1560s lines had hardened. During the Vestiarian Controversy in 1566, Anthony Gilby, a protégé of Henry Hastings, earl of Huntingdon, argued forcefully that the prince must defend the church, but that subjects also were obligated to "restrain the prince's authority to bounds and limits" drawn from scripture. The conclusions John Bartlett put forward in his *Fortress of Fathers* were blunter yet. Drawing on a wide variety of ancient fathers and contemporary Continental reformers, Bartlett argued for the abolition of episcopacy; for a commonwealth rooted in evangelical laws (here he cited Philipp Melanchthon's authority); for a sharp distinction such as Vermigli had drawn (based on the same Aristotelian argument) between magistrates and clergy so that the prince could not be head of the church (although spiritual power had to be subject to the temporal in worldly affairs, and the prince still kept an obligation to oversee and reform the church); and, finally, in another rigorously Aristotelian argument following Ponet and Goodman, for the view that magistrates were chosen by God and that therefore people "are subject to the magistrate no further than belongeth unto his vocation and office" and must obey God first. In February 1570 Edward Dering actually put most of these same points to the queen herself in a famous speech. He concluded that "if princes and magistrates will be still rebellious [to God's will], what is that to us?"

Between 1570 and 1572 Thomas Cartwright systematized the presbyterian program and engaged in a famous debate with John Whitgift, defender of what Peter Lake calls the conformist position and later archbishop of Canterbury. In the Admonition Controversy Cartwright and Whitgift agreed that the temporal and ecclesiastical worlds were in theory distinct but about little else. Whitgift claimed that the visible church had to be subject to secular authorities, a point made in large part to defend the prince's headship. This, of course, effectively collapsed the church into the state. Cartwright, instead, vehemently preserved the gap between them. Only the state had coercive powers, and presbyterianism was the only form of government allowable in the domain of conscience, the church. Magistrates were all equally subject to spiritual sanctions, but this had no effect on their temporal authority; in fact, the institution of uniform discipline would enhance it. Ministers were to be consulted on any issue within their competence, and their expert advice ought to resolve the problem. In common with Vermigli, but against Whitgift's monarchial views, Cartwright argued that the church was a mixed polity and that therefore ministers ought to be elected.

For the rest of Elizabeth's reign, presbyterians reworked the positions staked out in the 1560s and 1570s, usually weaving back and forth more or less simultaneously between the more conservative and more radical ends of their spectrum of ideas of magistracy. Much the same is true of Richard Hooker, the greatest of the conformist thinkers, in his *Of the Laws of Ecclesiastical Politie* (published between 1593 and 1662). Hooker was an even more thoroughgoing Aristotelian than Vermigli or Bartlett and shared with them some of the same fundamental principles, especially the primacy of the community. Like Ponet and Goodman, he stressed the role of consent but left subjects with no right of resistance to tyrannous magistrates. Instead, he strongly supported a virtually total "chiefty" or "principality" of "ecclesiastical dominion" for the English monarch. Although he demanded that bishops make decisions in concert with their clergy, he also left them the principal role in enforcing law. Introducing his famous version of the mean, Hooker declaimed in favor of "prelacy, the temperature of excesses [i.e., the mean] in all estates, the glue and solder of the public weal." Hooker based his case on somewhat the same premise as Whitgift had, that secular and ecclesiastical society were identical. This led him to attack head-on the central Puritan claim that the standard of ecclesiastical polity had to be the early church, because that denied present communities the right to legislate.

The greatest significance of the development of magistracy in the British Isles—and hence of the development of the Tudor monarchy—lies in the determinative role of the royal supremacy. The story may almost seem as simple as saying that once Henry VIII decided to claim his full rights over the church and relatively easily persuaded Parliament to help him, the only question of significance became the monarch's attitude.

In fact, the challenge of presbyterian and even separatist forms of magistracy was more profound but much less well documented than the wishes of princes and parliaments. Real English magistrates, with the justices of the peace in the forefront, were increasingly drawn into enforcing new modes of discipline, from the regulation of wages to the poor laws. All these responsibilities might fit nicely with reformed notions of discipline, especially since both justices of the peace and elders were local authorities. Theories of resistance may look more striking in retrospect, but Hooker's stress on the role of communities and on coordination between secular and religious magistrates more accurately summarizes most of his century's theory and practice of magistracy.

[*See also* Secular Magistrate, Office of.]

BIBLIOGRAPHY

Allen, J. W. *A History of Political Thought in the Sixteenth Century.* London, 1928. See especially pt. 2: "England."

Bucer, Martin. *Martini Buceri Opera Latina.* Vol. 15, *De Regno Christi.* Edited by François Wendel. Paris, 1955.

Collinson, Patrick. *The Elizabethan Puritan Movement.* Reprint, New York and London, 1982. A pioneering social and political history that also has much to say in general terms about Puritan religio-political beliefs. To be read in conjunction with Knappen and Lake.

Guy, John. *Tudor England.* Reprint, Oxford and New York, 1990. A recent synthesis, especially helpful on political matters, with good bibliography.

Hill, W. Speed, gen. ed. *The Folger Library Edition of the Works of Richard Hooker.* 6 vols. Cambridge, Mass., and Binghamton, N.Y., 1977–1993. The standard text, replacing Keble.

Kingdon, Robert M. "The Political Thought of Peter Martyr Vermigli." In *Peter Martyr Vermigli and Italian Reform,* edited by Joseph C. McLelland, pp. 121–139. Waterloo, Ont., 1980.

Knappen, M. M. *Tudor Puritanism: A Chapter in the History of Idealism.* Chicago, 1939. The subtitle reveals Knappen's slant, but his arguments still deserve careful consideration.

Lake, Peter. *Anglicans and Puritans? Presbyterianism and English Conformist Thought from Whitgift to Hooker.* London, 1988. The standard treatment.

Loades, D. M. *The Oxford Martyrs.* New York, 1970. See pp. 89–100 for Hugh Latimer's ideas of magistracy.

Mayer, Thomas F. "Tournai and Tyranny: Imperial Kingship and Critical Humanism." *Historical Journal* 34 (1991), 257–277. The most recent contribution to uncovering the roots of Henry's theocracy.

Skinner, Quentin. *The Foundations of Modern Political Thought.* Vol. 2, *The Age of Reformation.* Cambridge, 1978. Especially good on Ponet, Goodman, and Knox in Continental context.

Spalding, James C., ed. *The Reformation of the Ecclesiastical Laws of England. 1552.* Sixteenth Century Essays and Studies, vol. 19. Kirksville, Mo., 1992. The introduction should be used with care.

Trinterud, Leonard J., ed. *Elizabethan Puritanism.* New York, 1971. A comprehensive collection of sources with fine commentary.

THOMAS F. MAYER

Germany and the Low Countries

Reformation scholars writing in English have followed George H. Williams in distinguishing between the churches of the magisterial Reformation, established by state authority, and the radical Reformation, whose leaders rejected the traditional medieval notion of a *corpus Christianum* embracing both state and church. More recently the concept of confessionalization put forward by German scholars focuses on the degree to which ministers or priests of the church functioned as agents of the state, not merely in Lutheran and Reformed territories but also in Catholic regions. Thus, the Catholic church and its main Protestant rivals shared a belief in the unity of the body social and political, on the basis of which each of the churches made its peace with the rising modern state. Yet a new Protestant clergy, which gingerly asserted its influence over layfolk rejoicing in their recent emancipation from clerical authority, faced somewhat different problems than did a Catholic hierarchy reinvigorated in the wake of the Council of Trent. Similarly, a theology of Christian society that started from Martin Luther's dichotomy between the two kingdoms could not so easily justify an autonomous church polity with its own coercive powers, as could a traditional Catholic theology that started from the *analogia entis* (analogy of being). Finally, when faced with the all-encompassing ambition of the emerging modern state, Catholic bishops had at least the option of appealing to the nearest papal nuncio; in most cases a Protestant superintendent or *Antistes* could only invoke the moral authority of church leaders in other territories. For a variety of reasons, then, debates within the churches of the Reformation about the proper authority of the Christian magistrate raised a series of questions for which there were no ready-made answers: Must a Christian magistrate or prince suppress heretical or dissenting belief or enforce participation in the worship of the established church? What are the proper limits of the magistracy's responsibility for public morals? What role do magistrates have in appointing ministers for the church or overseeing its affairs? Does a Christian magistracy fail in its duty by not asserting itself on behalf of true Christians in other territories? This article touches on the various contexts in which the church-state doctrines of the leading Continental reformers emerged and sketches some of the principal conflicts over the role of magistrates during the second half of the sixteenth century, focusing on Germany and the Netherlands.

Emergence of Church-State Doctrines. As formulated in *Von weltlicher Oberkeit* (1523), Luther's doctrine of the two kingdoms tells the magistrate what he may not do in matters of faith, not what he may or should do. The treatise is based on sermons preached at the court of Duke John of Saxony, younger brother of the staunchly Catholic Duke George, and the sermons in turn were directed against princely mandates commanding confiscation of all copies of Luther's German New Testament. In a nutshell, subjects must refuse obedience to the prince when he wrongfully seeks to extend his God-given coercive power into the realm of faith. Almost at once, however, even though Luther feared what might happen if churches were governed by princely courts, he himself was compelled to call upon the prince to use his authority to protect and sustain the new faith. Each such request or concession to princely powers was tempered by a caveat: although princes must allow the tares of false doctrine to be sown freely, they must suppress false preaching that incites violence; even though princes must not force their subjects to accept the gospel, they must suppress manifest blasphemy against God, including the impious Catholic Mass; princes must authorize visitation of churches in their lands for the removal of unsuitable pastors, but they do so only because of the necessity of the moment (i.e., Luther's concept of the prince as *Notbischoff*). One may summarize by saying that Luther granted the prince a *jus reformandi,* as provided for in imperial law, but not a *cura religionis*—that is, an authority over the church inherent in his God-given office as a temporal ruler.

Yet both the majesty of the prince and the urgent organizational needs of the nascent church were in conflict with Luther's subtle distinctions. Also, the continued growth of sectarian movements, especially Anabaptism, confronted Luther and his followers again and again with a choice between allowing the people to be seduced by false doctrine and granting more authority to magistrates and princes. In 1530 an anonymous citizen of Nuremberg provoked a minor storm with a memorandum citing Luther's doctrine of the two kingdoms in support of his argument that magistrates had no authority to suppress religious dissent; referring to the now peaceful coexistence of various churches in Bohemia, the author also questioned the connection Luther and others had assumed between heresy and rebellion. In response, three preachers—Johannes Brenz, Andreas Osiander, and Wenceslaus Linck—penned treatises, two of which worked out (in James Estes' phrase) a more solid basis for intolerance: heresy must be suppressed not because it was necessarily seditious but because it was an offense against the honor of God. What Eike Wohlgast has called "Wittenberg theology" was moving in the same direction. A 1531 memorandum prepared by the theology faculty treats rejection of the public ministry of the word as an example of the "blasphemy" that a good prince is duty-bound to suppress. Taking this line of development one step further, Philipp Melanchthon, followed by Brenz, proposed that the prince was a "special member" (*praecipuum membrum*) of the church and that his office embraced responsibilities for both tables of the law—that is, for the honor of God, as well as for the good order of the commonwealth. *Cura religionis* was taking on a Lutheran garb.

Huldrych Zwingli and Heinrich Bullinger started from quite different premises, formulated in quite different circumstances. Zwingli was appointed *Leutpriester* of the Grossmünster in Zurich by the town council in 1518, just as Bullinger's father was appointed *Leutpriester* of Bremgarten (1506) in the same way. Indeed, the so-called *Pfaffenbrief,* extorted from Bishop Hugo van Hohenlandenburg (1496–1529) by priests in the Swiss portion of the diocese of Constance, made the control of certain benefices by local magistrates a matter of principle. It is at least congruent with this background that Zwingli and (even more) Bullinger envisioned the Christian commonwealth as bound by a covenant with God under the leadership of Christian magistrates, just as in ancient times the kings of Judah were the sole "heads" of God's covenanted people. Thus, for Zwingli, unlike Luther, the Christian did not have a dual identity as a believer and as a subject of the temporal order: "The Christian man is nothing but a good and faithful citizen, and the Christian city is nothing other than a Christian church" (*Zwinglis Werke,* XIV, 424.20ff.). Under pressure from Saxon jurists, Luther admitted that an imperial prince might rightly defend himself against aggression from the emperor, but he consistently regarded preventive war, even in a just cause, as a sinful want of trust in God's governance of the world.

Zwingli, an ardent Swiss patriot, penned a memo just before the Second Kappel War (1531) urging that the fiercely Catholic cantons of inner Switzerland be *usgerütet* ("stripped of their autonomy") if they did not agree to allow free preaching of the gospel. In 1528 he had persuaded Zurich's town council to create a new secret council (with Zwingli himself as one of six members), which now took over the foreign policy advisory role formerly exercised by guild representatives assembled in the great council. Because the secret council inspired Zurich's hard-line stance in the First and Second Kappel Wars and was thus blamed for the debacle in which hundreds of men, including Zwingli (1531), perished, the reformer's political activism unwittingly imperiled the future of the new church. Rumors of a Catholic restoration in Zurich proved to have no foundation, but a protest against recent developments, formulated in a rural area of the canton (the so-called *Meilener Verkommnis*), was soon accepted as the basis for a *Pfaffenbrief* (1532) agreed to by the city and its *Landschaft:* the secret council was to be abolished, and ministers were to confine themselves to preaching the gospel without interfering in worldly affairs. It was just at this moment that Bullinger was accepted by the town council as Zwingli's successor. The new *Antistes,* backed by his fellow ministers, refused to swear to the *Pfaffenbrief* until the council agreed to a clarification: ministers would stay out of politics but would be free to preach on what scripture teaches about worldly authority. Meanwhile, the continued presence of Anabaptism strengthened the hand of civil power in Zurich as well. Whatever hesitations Zwingli may have had about coercion in matters of faith were soon forgotten under Bullinger.

In Lutheran territories, then, what started out as a doctrine restricting the competence of the *Oberkeit* in religious matters was gradually reconfigured to become a limited charter for the prince's authority as the *praecipuum membrum ecclesiae.* In Zurich a doctrine that embraced the magistracy's *cura religionis* at the very outset was rather suddenly reconfigured by the conscious rejection of the theocratic tendencies, which, so long as Zwingli lived, gave the church a certain autonomy vis à vis the town council. In both cases control of the church by the magistracy or prince grew more visible. There was thus a real possibility that the church might be wholly absorbed into civil society, whose norms were, of course, not those of the gospel. This danger provides the background for the emergence of yet another Protestant vision of the Christian polity, this one formulated by Martin Bucer and John Calvin. Like Luther, Bucer and Calvin distinguished between the realm of worldly authority and the realm of faith, which made it impossible for the church to be viewed as a mere aspect of civil society; like Zwingli and Bullinger, they understood the gospel itself as a law (for true Christians), which made it easier to envision church and magistracy working together to build a Christian commonwealth. For much of his career as reformer of Strasbourg, including the period when Calvin served as pastor of the French refugee church (1538–1541), Bucer was frustrated by Christian magistrates who dealt gently with Anabaptist dissidents and showed themselves lukewarm in the cause of godly discipline among the people. In the years before the Augsburg Interim forced him into exile (1547), he argued in vain that the power of excommunication should be vested with the church, not the magistrates. He also obtained permission for pastors and elders (*Kirchenpfleger*) in two of the city's parishes to form small voluntary groups of believers, which were to show by example what a "true Christian community" would be like. In the former respect, if not the latter, he pointed the way for Calvin in Geneva.

Calvin readily accepted magisterial supervision of the affairs of the church, as was consistent with his own principles. Whereas Luther granted *cura religionis* to the civil government either not at all or only as a temporary measure, Calvin believed that the office of magistrate as established by God entailed responsibility for observance of both tables of the law and hence for the promotion of true religion and the suppression of heresy. It did not trouble him that the city council approved candidates for the ministry (none was, in fact, rejected by civil authorities during his lifetime), nor that elders were chosen from among the magistrates, nor that meetings of the consistory were presided over by a town syndic. Since magisterial authority over the church was by this time a common heritage of the Reformation in Switzerland, he could not have refused Geneva's government such a role even if he had wanted to do so. The critical point was that Calvin would not suffer the magistrates to define the religious duties of church members as distinct from the religious duties of citizens and *habitants*. Thus, he and the magistrates were in perfect agreement (1537) that all citizens and *habitants* must be obliged to swear to a Reformed confession of faith on pain of expulsion from the city. But he shook the dust of Geneva from his feet and sought exile in Strasbourg (1538–1541) rather than acquiesce to the syndics' demand that all who presented themselves should freely be admitted to the Lord's Supper, as was the practice in Bern (and Zurich). The syndics were concerned with civic unity, but Calvin was concerned lest it be said, "*cum Dei contumelia*," that wicked and sinful folk were included in God's holy church (1559, *Institutio*, IV.xii.5, language on this point dating from 1536 edition). (In the Lutheran camp, by contrast, even a strong advocate of church discipline such as Brenz believed it was better to risk an unworthy Communion than to despise a contrite heart.)

This deep concern for the reputation of God's holy church explains Calvin's long struggle to resolve ambiguities in the *Ordonnances Ecclesiastiques* of 1541; after his enemies in Geneva launched an unsuccessful coup (1555), it was accepted by all that ultimate control of excommunication lay with the church, not the syndics. As need required, Calvin could also fend off what he considered unwarranted interference from the magistrates with creative exegesis; when the syndics demanded to be consulted before a sensitive matter was broached from the pulpit, Calvin replied that scripture dictated the reverse order of procedure ("Go and announce it to my people, go into the house of the King"). By 1560, not long before his death, Calvin had the satisfaction of seeing the syndic who presided at consistory meetings appear without his staff of office, signifying that he came as an official not of the city but of the church. The autonomous church that Calvin built was no less a legacy for the future than his 1559 *Institutio*. If detractors caught a whiff of new popery in Geneva, Calvin's supporters understood that a church that had the capacity to define its own boundaries was in no danger of being absorbed by the state.

Conflicts over the Role of Magistrates. What makes the intra-Protestant conflicts of the second half of the sixteenth century difficult to sort out is that enemies on one issue were often allies on another. In this case the principal debates about the proper role of magistrates in church affairs pitted admirers of Zurich and Geneva against one another, despite the fact that Calvin and Bullinger had recently achieved a hard-won agreement on the Eucharist. Menna Prestwich believes that the united front presented by the Consensus Tigurinus (1549) facilitated the expansion of Reformed Protestantism within the empire. The Consensus Tigurinus also made a favorable impression on Melanchthon, whose Augustana Variata (1541), unlike the original Augsburg Confession of 1530, was deemed acceptable in Reformed circles. Philippists and partisans of the Reformed cause were drawn still closer together by orthodox-Lutheran polemics on the Eucharist after 1550, as well as by their common efforts to have the Variata (and hence the churches that could subscribe to it) recognized in the empire as legitimate under the terms of the 1555 Peace of Augsburg. In these circumstances neither Calvin nor Bullinger had any good reason to make an issue of questions of ecclesiastical polity that divided Zurich from Geneva. In these circumstances, too, it made sense for those who desired what they saw as a more complete Reformation to draw their inspiration from Geneva and Zurich indifferently. Thus, A. Th. van Deursen believes that Bullinger may have been the most widely read author during the formative period of the Dutch Reformed church, whose Calvinist character was fully apparent by about 1600. Indeed, even among those who considered themselves followers of Calvin, there were potential conflicts that could come to light only under circumstances far different from those prevailing in Geneva. To appreciate

A. C. Duke's point about unresolved differences that "lay buried like a time-bomb" in nascent Reformed communities, it may suffice to note that Jacobus Arminius had been a prized pupil of Théodore de Bèze.

Among German Lutheran territories that subsequently adopted a Reformed confession, the Rhine Palatinate under Elector Frederick III (r. 1559–1576) was the earliest and politically the most important. By all accounts the local population was strongly attached to the Lutheranism introduced by Frederick II (r. 1544–1556), with a marked dislike for pastors with Swiss accents and for their practice of breaking bread in Communion. But the staunchly Lutheran church superintendent Tilemann Hesshus paved the way for his own dismissal, first by threatening to excommunicate the prince's chief councillor and then by moving against suspect theological promotions in a way that allowed his enemies at the university, including the politically astute Swiss professor of medicine Thomas Lüber (Lat., Erastus; 1524–1583), to raise the issue of academic freedom. Frederick III and his advisers were thus free to move toward the Reformed camp, even as debates over the direction of the territorial church intensified among members of his *Kirchenrat* (which for a time included both Lüber, who corresponded regularly with Bullinger, and the ardent Calvinist Pierre Robert Olivétan). Both the famous Heidelberg Catechism and the *Kirchenordnung* of 1563 were of a clearly Calvinist inspiration and thus called for discipline to be vested with a church body. But the implementing legislation issued the following year by the *Kirchenrat* merely empowered pastors to report persons causing scandal to local judicial officers and, if these failed to act, to the *Kirchenrat*. In time, as the elector embraced an aggressively Protestant foreign policy, "disciplinarians" gained control of the *Kirchenrat* but not the university. Hoping to ward off the creation of presbyteries, or boards of elders vested with disciplinary authority, Lüber in 1568 circulated, but did not publish, a treatise on excommunication, which he then revised by incorporating his responses to criticisms from Bèze and others. The *Kirchenzuchtordnung* of 1570 was at least a partial victory for the antidisciplinarians because, although boards of elders were to be created, they had no authority even to scold sinners in public, and excommunication was reserved to territorial officials, acting with the consent of the prince. But Lüber himself lost credit through his association with two pastors condemned for Arianism, which enabled his foes to have him placed under the ban of the church in 1573.

The debate over Lüber's *Explicatio gravissimae quaestionis utrum excommunicatio mandato nitatur Divino, an excogitata sit ab hominibus* resonated far beyond the borders of the Palatinate. After provoking much discussion in manuscript form, the treatise was published anonymously in England in 1589, possibly at the behest of Archbishop John Whitgift (c.1530–1604), who endorsed the author's contention that the sovereignty of the prince extended to the church. It was in the chapter "De munere et distinctione Magistratus" that Lüber developed his thesis that "one and the same magistrate is called holy (*sacer*) inasmuch as he governs and disposes sacred matters according to Scripture, and political (*politicus*) inasmuch as he governs profane affairs according to the laws." Two heads in one body are unnatural, and the *divisio rectionum* that existed among the early Christians was a reflection of passing circumstances, since the empire was then pagan. From this conception of magisterial authority, it follows that excommunication is part of the magistrate's criminal jurisdiction, as it extends to blasphemy and other offenses against God. Hence, Lüber is harshly critical of the Calvinist (and Roman Catholic) idea that there is a divinely ordained form of ecclesiastical polity; this error has the effect of placing the magistrate under the control of the church and encouraging subjects to rebel against divinely ordained authority. In Lüber's view God has nowhere provided subjects with arms against the magistrate.

The best-known reply to Lüber, Bèze's *Tractatus Pius* (requested by the Synod of La Rochelle in 1571 but not published until 1590, following the appearance of Lüber's treatise), asserts that it is officers of the church, not magistrates, who are called to make judgments based on divine law. Bèze knew full well that Lüber's ideas were endorsed at the time by Bullinger and defended by Rudolf Gwalther, who was to succeed Bullinger as *Antistes* in Zurich, but he professed in the published version of his treatise to distinguish between the theories of Lüber, who in his view opposed excommunication in principle, and the practice of Zurich, whose leaders were merely fearful of the abuses of excommunication. For an implied critique of Lüber's views on the obedience due magistrates, one may look also to Bèze's *Du Droit des Magistrats* (1574), even though it arises from a wholly French context having to do with Bèze's involvement in negotiations with Huguenot refugees in the wake of the Saint Bartholomew's Day Massacre (1572). Bèze develops here the principle that was barely mentioned by Calvin in the last section of his 1559 *Institutio*, namely that "inferior magistrates" have not merely the right but the duty to resist the tyranny of their superiors.

Whereas Calvinism in the empire was usually established by princely fiat (as in the Palatinate under Frederick III and again under Johann Casimir [1583–1592] after a Lutheran interval under Ludwig VI), in the Netherlands and in parts of France it was established in the wake of revolutionary movements. The Dutch Reformed church was in the peculiar position of being chartered by the government but not established in the usual sense. During the long war for independence Dutch burghers were deeply divided about whether their struggle was in defense of traditional liberties or on behalf of true religion. Both the States General and the states of the several provinces identified "the Christian evangelical religion" as the sole religion that might be practiced in public and as the beneficiary of the appropriated wealth of the Catholic church. But citizens were free to practice in private whatever religion they might wish (except for the large Catholic population, for whom the benefits of benign neglect by the government came a bit more slowly). Moreover, the Reformed church, threatened here more than elsewhere by competition from vigorous if fissiparous Anabaptist communities, cared more about purity than about numbers, admitting to Communion only those who submitted themselves to church discipline—rarely more than 10 percent of the population of any given locality before 1600. (Those who attended services but did not seek to be accepted as communicants were known as *toehoorders*—i.e., "listeners.") Yet town governments, animated by a traditional sense of the town as a community under God, expected the clergy of the new church to serve the religious needs of the entire town. Ministers could, in fact, meet some of these expectations without difficulty (e.g., the baptism of infants, regardless of their parents' confession), but where magistrates expected the church to be a unifying force among the citizenry, they and their dominies could be on a collision course. Particularly in the heavily urban province of Holland, magistrates having a problem with refractory clerics could get a sympathetic hearing in the States of Holland, whose subordination to the States General was not much more than theoretical. Conversely, an embattled dominie could rely absolutely on the support of his classis, a regional assembly dominated by the clergy, which became the vital organizational nucleus of the Reformed church. But though either side in such conflicts could appeal to its own higher authority, appeals led only to further debate; in a society built on loosely structured consensus, neither the States of Holland nor a provincial synod of the Reformed church was eager to press its authority too far. Thus, in the decades prior to the climactic national Synod of Dordrecht (1618–1619), protracted battles between what can properly be described as conflicting visions of Christian society echoed up and down the land.

In the more interesting of these local conflicts—as at Leiden (Holland) and Utrecht (in the province of the same name)—differences between Zurich and Geneva can be recognized as one strand among many. Leiden was one of many towns where a popular preacher strongly supported by the magistrates—in this case Caspar Coolhaes—was at loggerheads with other dominies in his regional classis. Coolhaes angered his colleagues by proclaiming that the Apostles' Creed was creed enough for good Christians (no need, in other words, for the Belgic Confession) and that the church, acting separately from the magistrates, had no authority to make decisions that were binding on its members. On the other hand, the town council was more than content with a preacher who not only drew large crowds but also argued that preachers must not divide the community into rival doctrinal camps and backed the magistrates in their determination to control both the membership and the activities of the consistory. Coolhaes drew some of his latitudinarian views from the spiritual reformers (his writings include an apologia for Sebastian Franck), but he also translated some of the works of Gwalther, and Jan van Hout, a town secretary, appealed to the example of Zurich in a pamphlet defending the magistrates (and their support of Coolhaes) against the attacks of the classis. The immediate conflict was resolved in a compromise (1582) that forced both Coolhaes and his chief detractor in Leiden to resign their pulpits, but the magistrates did not soften their position and continued long afterward to rule the local church with a strong hand.

Hubert Duifhuis (c.1531–1581) had been a Catholic pastor in Rotterdam and at Utrecht's Saint Jacob's Church (1574), but after a brief exile he returned as a Reformed pastor of the latter church in 1578. Noting that Jesus admitted Judas to the Last Supper, Duifhuis offered the Eucharist in his church to all who presented themselves, and he denounced the whole Calvinist system of church discipline as a form of tyranny. Following Duifhuis's death sympathetic magistrates ensured the succession of like-minded preachers and not only at the Jacobskerk; indeed, it was not until 1605 that Utrecht's Calvinist party was able to establish an effective church discipline in all of the city's parishes. To orthodox Calvinists, men such as Duifhuis and Coolhaes, as well as their supporters, were godless "Libertines" of the same ilk as those denounced by Calvin himself. Concerning their own convictions, recent scholarship has tended to emphasize spiritualist influences, as may be seen in Duifhuis's membership in the underground movement known as the Family of Love. Yet Zurich was always in the background as the unimpeachably godly model of how church and civic community could be of one accord. It was because Utrecht Libertines had cited the example of Zurich that the Calvinist Johannes Wtenbogaert made a side trip to Zurich on his way back to Utrecht from Geneva to obtain a letter from Gwalther himself denouncing the Jacobskerk congregation.

These few abbreviated case histories may serve to illustrate how sharply differing conceptions of the magistrate's role in the church were fought out among Reformed Christians, even as church leaders in Geneva and Zurich studiously refrained from denouncing one another. Can it be said, then, that a given vision of the proper role of magistrates may be inferred from a given theological stance, whether Calvinist, Zwinglian, Lutheran, or Tridentine Catholic? The obvious difficulty with this way of thinking is that ongoing research has undermined every known effort to draw putatively necessary connections between a particular theology and a particular form of social or political organization. For example, Calvinism may seem a theology of revolution if one looks to the French monarchomachs (like Bèze), but not if one looks to the Second Reformation in Germany. Post-Tridentine Catholic theology may seem ready made for would-be absolute monarchs until one sees how theorists for the French Catholic League outdid Huguenot monarchomachs in setting limits to royal power. Lutheranism may look like a theology for princes if one focuses on the era of the Peasants' War, but not if one looks to Magdeburg holding out against Charles V in the first Schmalkald War (an example cited in later Calvinist resistance theories) or examines, as Heinz Schilling has done, the links between Lutheranism and movements to preserve communal autonomy in north Germany in the latter part of the sixteenth century. In the end even a good Hegelian must eschew the fantasy that ideas have consequences in and of themselves and recognize that ideas or doctrines are efficacious only as filtered through some combination of personal, local, and social circumstances. Thus, Brenz was as much a Lutheran as Hesshus, even though the former drafted a church ordinance (for Württemberg) that reserved the power of excommunication to the prince, while the latter, as church superintendent (in the Palatinate), threatened to excommunicate the prince's chief adviser. Bèze, in Geneva, accepted an arrangement under which pastors were subject to the "predominantly civil" authority of lay elders, but for Lambert Daneau, Bèze's erstwhile colleague, the magistrates of Leiden (the supporters of Coolhaes) were not properly Christian and hence had no competence at all in the affairs of the church. The Reformed clergy of Dordrecht (Holland) happily agreed to the participation of a staunchly Calvinist magistracy in the selection of church elders, but their confreres in nearby cities (including Leiden and Utrecht) fiercely opposed similar powers in the hands of magistrates who were distinctly less well disposed to their cause. The simple fact is that a doctrine of any significance is and must be polyvalent in terms of its potential for fruitful combination with a variety of political settings.

Yet the historical imagination, in its quest to integrate the phenomena under review into some coherent picture of the past, needs to return again and again to the process by which historical actors seek to integrate their own situation into some coherent picture of the world. With regard to debates among Reformed Christians about the religious functions of magistrates, it does seem that different visions of the body politic were congruent with a preference for the theology of Zurich or Geneva. For example, Schilling finds that Germany's Second Reformation was in some ways more Erastian than Calvinist, as evidenced by the fact that models of Christian society put forward by theologians in Germany's Reformed territories were marked by a "Zwinglian" or Erastian emphasis on the functions of the supreme magistrate rather than by a characteristically Calvinist stress on the prerogatives of "inferior magistrates." Two American scholars, John Elliott and Benjamin Kaplan, both make a related point about church-state conflicts in the early Dutch republic. Here Libertine preachers and pamphleteers endeavored to defend both the spiritual unity of the urban community and its autonomy vis à vis higher levels of government; in doing so they sometimes appealed (not surprisingly) to Zurich and its theology. Conversely, the Calvinist party emphatically rejected the idea of the spiritual unity of the town put forward by magistrates who hoped to see an all-encompassing "people's church"; in the early seventeenth century Calvinists also set themselves against urban autonomy by their constant calls for a national synod and by their support for the house of Orange in opposition to urban "particularism."

Thus, Zurich theology was consonant with the notion of the seamless unity of a Christian body ruled by a single magistracy, just as Geneva theology, featuring a church that defined its own boundaries, suited the needs of those who envisioned the seamless unity of a Christian community within a divided body politic. An observation of this kind makes no claim to exhaust either the political possibilities of a given theology or the potential theological affinities of a given political situation. But it may serve to illustrate how arguments about the role of Christian magistrates were, in fact, arguments about the inner nature of that Christian polity, whose essential unity had been, since the time of Constantine, presumed by theologians and political writers of almost all persuasions.

[*See also* Secular Magistrate, Office of.]

BIBLIOGRAPHY

Baker, J. Wayne. *Heinrich Bullinger and the Covenant: The Other Reformed Tradition.* Athens, Ohio, 1980.

Berg, A. J. van den. "Herman Herberts, c.1540–1607, in conflikt met de gereformeerde kerk." In *Kerkhistorische Opstellen aangeboden aan Prof. dr. J. van den Berg,* edited by C. Augustijn et. al., pp. 20–29. Kampen, 1987.

Blanke, Fritz, and Immanuel Leuschner. *Heinrich Bullinger: Vater der reformierten Kirche.* Zurich, 1990.

Bonger, H. *Leven en Werk van Dirk Volkertszoon Coornhert.* Amsterdam, 1978.

Brecht, Martin. *Martin Luther: His Road to Reformation.* Translated by James Schaaf. Philadelphia, 1985.

Deursen, A. Th. van. *Bavianen en Slijkgeuzen: Kerk en Kerkvolk ten Tijde van Maurits en Oldenbarnevelt.* Assen, 1974.

Duke, Alastair. "The Ambivalent Face of Calvinism in the Netherlands." In *International Calvinism, 1541–1715,* edited by Menna Prestwich, pp. 109–133. Oxford, 1985.

Elliott, John Paul. "Protestantization in the Northern Netherlands: A Case Study; The Classis Dordrecht, 1572–1640." Ph.D. diss., Columbia University, 1990.

Estes, James Martin. *Christian Magistrate and State Church: The Reforming Career of Johann Brenz.* Toronto, 1982.

Fasolt, Constantin. *Council and Hierarchy: The Political Thought of William Durant the Younger.* Cambridge, 1991.

Fatio, Olivier. *Nihil pulchrius ordine: Contribution à l'étude de l'établissement de la discipline ecclésiastique aux Pays-Bas ou Lambert Daneau aux Pays-Bas, 1581–1583.* Leiden, 1971.

Gelder, H. A. Enno van. *Getemperde Vrijheid.* Assen, 1972.

Hammann, Gottfried. *Martin Bucer, 1491–1551: Zwischen Volkskirche und Bekenntnisgemeinschaft.* Wiesbaden, 1989.

Hoffmann, H. Edler van. "Das Kirchenverfassungsrecht der niederländischen Reformierten bis zum Beginn der Dordrechter National-synode von 1618/1619." In *Kirche und gesellschaftlicher Wandel in deutschen und niederländischen Städten der werdenden Neuzeit,* edited by Franz Petri, pp. 203–217. Cologne, 1980.

Höpfl, Harro. *The Christian Polity of John Calvin.* Cambridge, 1982.

Kamphuis, J. *Kerkelijke Besluitvaardigheid: Over de bevestiging van het gereformeerd kerkverband in de jaren 1574 tot 1581/2 ondanks de oppositie . . . van het . . . indifferentisme zoals deze . . . vanuit Leiden werd gevoerd.* Groningen, 1970.

Kaplan, Benjamin Jacob. "Calvinists and Libertines: The Reformation in Utrecht, 1578–1618." Ph.D. diss., Harvard University, 1989.

Kingdon, Robert M, ed. *Théodore de Bèze: Du droit des magistrats.* Geneva, 1970.

Locher, Gottfried W. *Die Zwinglische Reformation im Rahmen der europäischen Kirchengeschichte.* Göttingen, 1979.

Maruyama, Tadatake. *The Ecclesiology of Theodore Beza.* Geneva, 1978.

Nijenhuis, W. "Variants within Dutch Calvinism in the Sixteenth Century." *Acta Historiae Neerlandicae* 12 (1979), 48–64.

Pettegree, Andrew. *Emden and the Dutch Revolt.* Oxford, 1992.

Press, Volker. *Calvinismus und Territorialstaat: Regierung und Zentralbehörden der Kurpfalz, 1559–1619.* Stuttgart, 1970.

Prestwich, Menna, ed., *International Calvinism, 1541–1715.* Oxford, 1985.

Schilling, Heinz. *Konfessionskonflikt und Staatsbildung: Eine Fallstudie über das Verhältnis von religiösem und sozialem Wandel in der Frühneuzeit am Beispiel der Grafschaft Lippe.* Gütersloh, 1981.

———. *Religion, Political Culture, and the Emergence of the Early Modern State.* Leiden, 1992.

Spaans, Joke. *Haarlem na de Reformatie: Stedelijke Cultuur en Kerkelijk Leven, 1577–1620.* The Hague, 1989.

Steinmetz, David. *Luther in Context.* Bloomington, Ind., 1986.

Tukker, C. A. *De Classis Dordrecht van 1573 tot 1609.* Leiden, 1965.

Visser, Derk, ed. *Controversy and Conciliation: The Reformation and the Palatinate, 1559–1583.* Allison Park, Pa., 1986.

Wesel-Roth, Ruth. *Thomas Erastus.* Lahr, Germany, 1954.

Williams, George H. *The Radical Reformation.* 3d ed. Kirksville, Mo., 1992.

Wohlgast, Eike. *Die Wittenberger Theologie und die Politik der evangelischen Stände.* Gütersloh, 1977.

JAMES D. TRACY

France

The magistrates played an important part during the Reformation owing to their public functions in the spheres of administration, jurisdiction, and politics. Until the mid-sixteenth century they endeavored—with a few exceptions—to repress the new ideas, which they rejected as being heretical. Thereafter, especially from the 1560s onward, their opinions concerning the "allegedly Reformed religion" were divided: while the majority remained attached to the traditional religion, another faction, numbering the most open-minded persons, tried to legitimize the Reformed worship and to grant it an official status sanctioned by royal edicts.

Royal and Temporal Jurisdiction. At the time of the Reformation France was a hereditary monarchy, with the sovereignty exclusively vested in the king. In the exercise of his power the monarch was assisted by various counselors: the princes "of the royal blood" and the peers of France, lay or ecclesiastical; the general officers of the Crown such as the *Connétable*, the *Grand Chambellan*, the *Grand Maître*, the chancellor, and the four marshals of France; and the legists, formerly called *magistri curiae*, *magistri tenetes parlamentum*, or magistrates. These three formed the King's Council, also called the Privy or Strict Council, or the *Conseil des Affaires* (divided into *Conseil d'État*, *Conseil des Parties*, and *Conseil des Finances*), which administered all matters of state and in particular exercised the legislative power. After the king, the chancellor stood at the top of the hierarchy as a sort of first magistrate of the realm. He was appointed by the king, his office being neither purchasable nor hereditary, and he was entitled to preside over all sovereign courts. Another office of high responsibility was that of the secretary of state, who was related to all financial and political matters and therefore played an essential role in the government of the country.

One of the foremost prerogatives of sovereignty lay in the administration of justice. The king was above all a judge; he was the source of the law inasmuch as the essential attribute of royalty consisted in the personal exercise of justice. In this capacity he delegated the administration of justice to the magistrates who sat in the sovereign courts (*Cours des Aides*, *Chambres des Comptes*), in the presidial courts, bailiwicks, seneschalsies, provostships, as well as in the other royal jurisdictions, especially in the parlements. The Parlement of Paris, the first to be established and the most important one (the model for the provincial parlements) was composed of the *Grand Chambre* (the superior jurisdiction of appeal), the *Chambre des Enquêtes*, the *Chambre des Requêtes*, and the *Chambre de la Tournelle* (reserved for criminal cases and lèse-majesté, including some cases of heresy). These permanent chambers were supplemented by other chambers, depending on the circumstances (for instance, the *Chambres "mi-parties,"* composed of an equal number of Catholic and Protestant counselors, which supervised the application of the edict of pacification after 1576; later they were called *Chambres de l'Édit*, being in charge of the application of the Edict of Nantes of 1598 in the parlements of Paris, Bordeaux, Grenoble, and Toulouse; they were suppressed by Louis XIV in 1669). The presidents of the several chambers had a superior in the first president, who was the head of the parlement and chaired it when all the chambers were in session. The president's role was especially important for the interests of the Crown; the same can be said of the advocates general and attorneys general. They were the intermediaries between the parlement and the king, together with the king's entourage and the chancellor, who held the first rank. In order to ensure the discipline of the judicial company, all the chambers periodically gathered behind closed doors on Wednesdays (the *Mercuriales*), and the attorney general or advocate general would deliver a speech to call attention to possible negligences, disobediences, and abuses; the culprits were denounced to the king, deprived of their office, and in serious cases prosecuted.

The ways of appointing new magistrates varied in the course of time. At first the king would appoint the officers of justice. Later the members of parlements themselves appointed their presidents as well as the counselors. From the fifteenth century onward, however, another system took precedence with the practice of purchasing offices. Although it was condemned by several edicts of Charles VII and Louis XII, the "venality of offices" was widely practiced under Francis I and Henry II, who managed thereby to replenish the royal treasury. The same practice prevailed under Henry III (notwithstanding the Ordinance of Blois of 1579) and Henry IV, as the offices became hereditary. In spite of this venality, new candidates were usually requested to fulfill some conditions: to be male, to be physically able to carry out the responsibilities, to be of legitimate birth, to be preferably of a family of magistrates (the *noblesse de robe*), to possess a personal fortune, and to give evidence of their morality. As to age, the counselors had to be at least twenty-six years old (after 1579), while the presidents of the parlements had to be at least thirty under Francis I and Henry II, and forty under Henry III. The presidents and counselors therefore demanded that the candidates pass a rigorous examination (under the edicts of 1546, 1566, and 1579), although it focused on Roman law rather than on the judicial practices based on the customs of the realm. French "nationality" was not required (time and again, under Francis I, Italian jurists from Milan, Genoa, Turin, or Naples were appointed counselors). Thus the Parlement of Paris numbered a hundred members—the presidents and lay or cleric counselors—and this number increased during the sixteenth century through the creation of new offices.

The parlements enjoyed considerable powers, being invested with political, administrative, and judicial authority, and being therefore competent in private and public law. In public law their foremost prerogative was to verify the edicts, the ordinances, and all the royal acts before publishing and "registering" them, that is, before they could be executed. Although the legal effects of registration were confined to the jurisdiction of the parlement concerned, registration by the Parlement of Paris was enough for the act to be executed. The Parlement of Paris thus had the right to modify the legal text and could even refuse to register it. It exercised this right above all to maintain the king's sovereignty (against encroachments by papal authority), to preserve the public good (with respect to fiscal edicts), and to defend religious unity, which was considered the condition and the basis of the unity of the state (as against the tolerance of other religions that were introduced in turn by the edicts "of pacification" during the Wars of Religion). In case of rejection, the parlement justified its position through "remonstrances" whereby it expressed its right to control the king's legislative activity and hence its solicitude for the interests of the state. The king could in such cases either accept the modifications or enforce the registration of the edicts without change through *lettres de jussion*; in extreme cases he could even go to the parlement in person, preside over it with his chancellor, and require the registration upon his authority (*lit de justice*). The magistrates then deferred to the king's majesty, which was the source of the law (*adveniente principe cessat magistratus*), and submitted to his authority; but they approved his edict only by adding the formula *lecta et publicata de expresso mandato domini regis* (read and published by express order of the king), in order to show that the law was published against their opinion. Far from being superfluous, such formulas often weakened the coactive force of the law and thereby also the subjects' obligation to obey it.

Ecclesiastical or Spiritual Jurisdiction. During the sixteenth century, the Gallican church, while having its own "liberties" with regard to the Roman Catholic church, depended on the king, who, under the Concordat of Bologna of 1516, had the right to invest newly instituted bishops. In parallel with the royal jurisdiction, ecclesiastical jurisdiction took shape with its clerical judges and its tribunals, having long ago obtained the *privilegium fori*. However, secular justice was entitled to annul any decision of the ecclesiastical authorities that it deemed abusive (*appel comme d'abus*). Ecclesiastical jurisdiction related in principle to the persons of the church, the clerics, and also to the poor, the sick, and the widows, and extended to all religious matters pertaining to ecclesiastical discipline, the maintenance of order in places of worship, and the sacraments, including those which also touched on civil matters such as marriage (engagement, separation, adultery). The bishop, who in ecclesiastical matters also acted as judge, delegated his right of justice to the "official," a graduate in theology and canon law, who judged with the assistance of assessors who were experts in law (*juris periti*).

Until the fourteenth century ecclesiastical jurisdiction had progressively extended its role in areas in which both jurisdictions applied (*mixti fori*, such as oaths, contracts, testaments, benefices, etc.), and it entered into competition with royal jurisdiction which sought to regain all cases directly or indirectly related to the temporal sphere. This was the case with offenses concerning faith or religion, such as heresy, witchcraft, or blasphemy, which endangered the public order and the security of the state, and which were punishable as crimes of lèse-majesté. Toward the end of the fourteenth century the difference between the two jurisdictions found expression in the distinction between "common (i.e., ordinary) offenses," which fell within the prerogatives of ecclesiastical justice, and "privileged cases" (named after the privilege of intervention of the temporal authority), that is, offenses committed by clerics, which lay within the cognizance or jurisdiction of royal justice. Little by little the concept of "privileged case" was extended to common crimes that were punished not by the church but by secular justice.

Such was the case with the crime of heresy, which was

handled according to the procedures of the Inquisition. The inquisitional authority (i.e., the bishop in the first phase; the pope's legate in the second phase; the monastic orders, Franciscans and Dominicans, in the third phase) ordered the suspect to be arrested by their officers, whereupon the inquisitorial tribunal inquired into and judged the case. If the accused was convicted of the crime of heresy he or she was anathematized and excommunicated, and the tribunal handed (literally "abandoned," *reliquit*) him or her over to the secular judge, with the formal request to spare him or her mutilation and death (following the principle *Ecclesia abhorret a sanguine*). Once the accused was abandoned to the "secular arm," the temporal judge was under the obligation to pronounce and to execute the capital punishment. This practice was maintained until the fourteenth century, when the right to arrest the accused was withdrawn from the church's judge and given to the royal justice. The parlements insisted that the inquisitorial judges were dependent on royal jurisdiction. The Sorbonne also took an increasing part in the sentences that were pronounced against heretics. However, the activity of the inquisitorial tribunals, which had been intense during the thirteenth century in the south (Pamiers, Toulouse, Carcassonne), less so in the north (Cambrai, Douai, Lille, Arras) and the center (Paris, Orléans, Mâcon, Tours), declined toward the end of the fourteenth century, although it was still noticeable at the end of the fifteenth century during the "crusade" against the Waldensians in Piedmont in 1488 (Louis XII thereafter tried with mandates given at Lyon on 12 October 1501 to redress the wrongs that had been inflicted).

After this period of decline of inquisitorial activities, the conflict between ecclesiastical and secular jurisdictions, which significantly manifested itself in matters of heresy, entered a new phase of rivalry during the sixteenth century. This was partly because of the double meaning of the concept of heresy derived from the inquisitorial tradition: "simple" heresy on the one hand, namely, erroneous religious opinion (as distinguished from or in conflict with the opinion of the Catholic church) that constituted an offense prosecuted by the church; on the other hand heresy aggravated by the crime of sedition (against the realm or the established order), which was tantamount to the offense of lèse-majesté and was a "privileged case" falling under the jurisdiction of royal justice.

Significance for Religion and the Reformation. The king was the protector of the catholic-apostolic-Roman faith. This was the first of the three oaths he had to take when he was anointed (with the second oath he promised to treat his subjects with justice and equity; with the third one, to abolish bad laws and to promulgate only just and good ones). After the fourth Lateran Council (1215) a fourth precept was added: "to exterminate the heretics from his realm" (*de haereticis de regno suo extirpandis*). On the basis of this fourth oath each king of France was proclaimed "the eldest son of the church" and was consecrated as "the Most Christian King." In his capacity as supreme magistrate of the kingdom, he was the foremost defender of traditional religion.

With the coming of the Reformation, the lay jurisdiction and notably the parlements were the first to defend the old religion. To repress the "Lutheran" heresy, the legislators did not need to invent new strategies or institute new repressive organs (the legislation concerning the Inquisition had, despite its decline, never been repealed). They followed therefore traditional patterns, which in all their diversity complemented one another; indirectly, they dealt with blasphemy, prohibited the carrying of firearms and illegal gatherings, and censured books. They directly attacked heresy proper.

Blasphemy. Numerous laws against blasphemy that had been promulgated between 1182 and 1514 provided for severe punishment against whoever swore on the name of God (extending from fines to piercing—if not cutting—the tongue with a hot iron). Edicts of February 1524, October 1535, March 1545, 1560, February 1566, December 1571, October 1572, March 1579, and April 1594 were directed first against the Lutherans, then against the Reformed, both of whom slandered the Virgin Mary and the saints.

Carrying of arms. The law against carrying arms, of which two or three were promulgated in the fourteenth and fifteenth centuries, became more numerous and severe by the sixteenth century (1532, 1539, 1546, 1548, 1549). The law of 1546 even provided for the death penalty. Their number increased after the 1550s (December 1558, July 1559, December 1559), especially after the Conspiracy of Amboise, which revealed to what degree the Huguenots were capable of recruiting men, of equipping them with arms, and of setting up a hierarchically organized network throughout the entire kingdom. The prohibition of carrying firearms, pistols, and arquebuses, under pain of confiscation and, in some cases, of death, were reiterated by edicts of August 1560, January 1561, October 1561, August 1563, February 1566, and April 1598. In order to discover plots and to avoid uprisings, revolts, and open war, the legislators often included in the same laws prohibitions against unlawful gatherings.

Unlawful gatherings. During the sixteenth century, the prohibition of unlawful gatherings, gathering of armed people and gatherings at night, which was intended to prevent agitations and conspiracies (October 1532, May 1539, August 1546), also included meetings for the celebration of worship "in the Genevan way," which were suspected by the authorities to have subversive ends (September 1559: "razing of houses where meetings are held"; November 1559: death penalty against unlawful religious gatherings). It was also to this end that the Edict of 1561 was promulgated, although it brought about a change since religious meetings were considered different from armed gatherings.

The change became evident after the Edict of January 1562, which made the meetings for Reformed worship legal. In February 1566 one of the several legislative measures against unlawful gatherings prescribed that the meetings for worship be attended by a counselor of the parlements, a seneschal, or another royal officer.

Censorship of books. The diffusion of books had been one of the most efficient means of propagating the Reformation. The authorities soon realized the need for legislating in order to censor the printing, display, and selling of books containing—according to an order of the Parlement of Paris of 1 July 1542—"new doctrines, Lutheran, and others, against the Catholic faith of our holy mother the Church, and among others a book entitled *Institutio religionis Christianae, authore Alcuino*, and in vulgar language: the 'Institutes of the Christian Religion' composed by John Calvin." The Parlement of Paris, in close collaboration with the Sorbonne, adopted radical measures to stop the heresy from spreading. The letters patent of 13 January 1535, and the edicts of 16 July 1535, 28 December 1541, 19 July 1542, 11 December 1547, 27 June 1551, and May 1560 provided for severe measures that nonetheless proved insufficient. The same can be said, with respect to France, of the Index of Prohibited Books. The Sorbonne drew up a first list in 1545, well before the first official Index was published by Pope Paul IV in 1559.

Legislation against Heresy. It is impossible to understand historically the legislation against heresy and religious dissent in the sixteenth century if one does not make a clear distinction between the reigns of Francis I and Henry II on the one hand, and the reigns of Francis II, Charles IX, and Henry III on the other. The reason for this distinction lies in the history of the concept of heresy, which around 1560 underwent a change both in the opinion of certain intellectuals exercising public functions (clerics, representatives of the third estate, etc.) and in the conception of many magistrates, as is discernible in the formulation of edicts in this field. This change first manifested itself at the Council of Fontainebleau (21–26 August 1560) in the speeches of Jean de Montluc (bishop of Valence and Die), Charles de Marillac (bishop of Vienne), and, surprisingly, in the intervention of Charles de Guise, the formidable cardinal of Lorraine and one of the three inquisitors of the kingdom. The cardinal spoke no more of "heretics" to designate the dissidents and drew a clear distinction between the seditious ("disturbers of the people and the kingdom") and the faithful (those who "go to the sermon without arms" to sing the psalms). With respect to the latter, the king should no more proceed "by way of punishment of justice" or by rigorous pains, but should think of "defending" them. Meanwhile the authors of pamphlets distinguished between "Huguenots of the state" and "Huguenots of the church." Even on the level of legislative terminology the dissidents were preferably called (except during the Catholic League) "misled of faith" rather than heretics, while later they were named those of the "allegedly Reformed religion."

Reigns of Francis I and Henry II. The magistrates showed all along a real preoccupation for the maintenance of the traditional faith and for the religious unity of the kingdom. The first legislative measures aimed at the repression "without appeal" of the "Lutheran" heresy was enacted on 10 June 1525 (during the absence of Francis I—then a prisoner—under the regency of his mother, Louise of Savoy) by way of letters patent incorporating the bull of Clement VII of 17 May 1525. Following tradition, a mixed inquisitorial commission was set up, composed of counselors of the Parlement of Paris (Jacques de La Barde, André Verjus, and Nicolas Clerc, a doctor of theology) and a clergyman (Guillaume Chesne, doctor of theology and parish priest of Saint-Jean-en-Grève). On 29 December 1530 all the officers of the kingdom (magistrates of the parlements, the bailiffs, and the seneschalsies) were ordered by letters patent given at Saint-Germain to assist the "inquisitors of the faith" (the pope's "delegated judges") in apprehending and condemning the heretics. This was followed by two royal letters of 10 December 1533, ordering parlement to register two papal bulls (of 30 August and 10 November 1533) for the extirpation of the heresy and the Edict of Paris of 29 January 1535 ("perpetual and irrevocable").

A first sign of tolerance appears in the Edict of Coucy of 16 July 1535, in which the king granted amnesty ("grace and mercy") and invited the emigrated "sectators" to return to the kingdom on the condition that they recant. The Declaration of Lyon of 30 May 1536 had a similar content, although the king by letters patent drawn up on the following day replaced Valentin Lievin by another Dominican, Mathieu Ory, as "one of the inquisitors of the faith," but with powers extended to the whole kingdom.

While up to that time the royal jurisdiction had confined itself to its traditional role of judging privileged cases and cases on appeal, it suddenly took the lead in matters of heresy by the Edicts of Paris of 16 December 1538 and 24 June 1539, and above all by the Edict of Fontainebleau of 1 June 1540. By these edicts the king ordered that all royal officers of the sovereign courts and the provinces should "indifferently and concurrently have the power of inquisition, information, verification, and cognizance" as regards heresy against all persons "of whatever quality or condition." Anxious to make the legal proceedings more expeditious, the legislator emphasized that heresy was tantamount to sedition (and was, therefore, directly within the jurisdiction of the royal judges), for "such errors and false doctrines contain in themselves the crime of divine and human lèse-majesté, sedition of the people, and disturbance of our realm and public peace." In order to obtain a better definition of the concept of heresy, which was not clear although it constituted the basis of the instruction and the proceedings, the Sorbonne drew up a list of twenty-five articles of faith to provide the magistrates with a doctrinal table with which they could compare the declarations of the accused. These articles were included in the Edict of Paris of 23 July 1543. These enactments revived the conflict of competence between ecclesiastical and secular jurisdictions, for the judges of the church deemed themselves dispossessed of their prerogatives (notwithstanding article 9, which confirmed their customary right to sue heretics accused of "common offenses").

During these theoretical controversies an event took place that shocked public opinion and compromised the credibility of the magistracy: the repression, and then the "massacre," of the Waldensians of Cabrières and Mérindol in 1545. The decision of 18 November 1540 of the Parlement of Aix—the famous Barthélémy of Chasseneux being on the bench—had authorized the persecution that had been stayed by the intervention of Cardinal Jacopo Sadoleto. The king then ordered its execution on 1 July 1545, upon the insistence of Cardinal François de Tournon. After lengthy proceedings, begun in 1550, the Parlement of Paris condemned those responsible for these excesses.

Henry II inherited this state of co-belligerency against heresy, which united the magistrates of all administrative and judicial levels, the clergy, the Sorbonne, and the inquisitors of the faith. The Parlement of Paris distinguished itself by the number of decisions it rendered against Protestants as well as by its judicial activity in the newly established criminal court known as the *Chambre ardente* (8 October 1548–10 January 1550). The first years of the reign therefore witnessed an intense legislative activity against the heretics through the edicts of Fontainebleau (11 December 1547 and 11 February 1550) and of Paris (19 November 1549), the letters patent of Saint-Germain of 22 June 1550, which gave full powers to the inquisitor general of the faith, Ory, and the great Edict of Châteaubriant (27 June 1551), which sought to specify the procedures against the heretics. So-called simple heresy was reserved to the ecclesiastical jurisdiction, while the civil jurisdiction (sovereign courts and presidential judges) had the charge of "the identification, punishment, and correction" of all violations of the edicts on heresy issued by Francis I and his successor. This increasing severity, which sought to stop the dissemination of the new ideas and to counteract the iconoclastic fury, culminated in the Edict of Compiègne (24 July 1557), which ordered against the heretics the "penalty of death, our judges having no power whatsoever to remit or to moderate the punishment," and in the letters patent of Ecouen (2 June 1559), which demanded support of the judges "actively and if need be even with armed force."

However, this did not resolve the jurisdictional conflict between the judges of the church and the judges of the king. The Remonstrances of November 1549 as well as the ensuing protestations express the persistent preoccupation of the magistrates, especially those of the Parlement of Paris, who asked the king to specify "the right of the royal and ecclesiastical judges to have joint jurisdiction" of the cases of heresy. In France, they argued, there was only one king, and he was the sole sovereign of justice. To leave the judgment of the heretics to the church, reserving only its execution to the secular judge, amounted to jeopardizing the king's full sovereignty. The same argument underlies the opposition of the counselors of the parlement to reinstate in France the tribunals of the Inquisition, which would enhance the power not only of the Gallican but also of the Roman church at the expense of the royal authority.

Reigns from Francis II to Henry IV. Francis II, assisted by his counselors, was anxious to ensure the continuation of this religious policy, especially with respect to unlawful gatherings (edicts of Villers-Cotterêts, 4 September; of Blois, 9 and 14 November 1559; of Amboise, February 1560) and the carrying of arms (Edict of Chambord, 17 December 1559). In order to reduce the penalties against "the sectators of the new opinions," the "irrevocable" Edict of Romorantin (May 1560) ordered that the jurisdiction over the crime of heresy and the repression of unlawful gatherings be again conferred (as it had been before 1530) on the ecclesiastical courts, while the royal jurisdiction should only become involved if requested by the judges of the church. A declaration of 6 August 1560 specified in this respect that presidial judges had "concurrent and preferential jurisdiction" over crimes of heresy. The changes in the priorities to be granted either jurisdiction were to continue until the royal magistrates brought within their competence all the matters concerning the Reformation, leaving to the ecclesiastical judges the jurisdiction over clerics promoted to holy orders.

Apart from this decline of the inquisitorial institution, one notices a new orientation in religious policy when Catherine de Médicis, the queen mother, began to take an active part in government. A new era began in March 1560 with the Edict of Amboise, an edict of amnesty providing for "pardon, remission, and general absolution"—abjuration not being required—for those who had been accused "concerning matters of faith and religion," except for the preachers and conspirators who had been embraced at Amboise. This edict characterized the government's religious policy that was henceforth to face the dilemma of either maintaining religious unity or granting the Reformed religion a provisional tolerance (i.e., concord or tolerance?). The magistrates of the kingdom tended to remain coherently respectful of its fundamental laws, the first of which was the maintenance of religious unity (the principle being that any change in religion inevitably brought about a change in the kingdom). Most of them advocated moderate punishment of the dissidents, but they were opposed to tolerating public worship other than that of the Catholic church. This is evidenced by the remonstrances against the edict of 17 January 1562, whose registration the parlements had prevented until 6 March, when it yielded to the king's orders, specifying that the edict was published, "however, without approbation of the new religion, all only provisionally and until the king has ordained otherwise." From then on the parlements became the main lay defenders of the traditional faith and often came into conflict with the sometimes tolerant, sometimes rigorous attitude of Charles IX.

This conflict between the King's Council and the parlements during the Wars of Religion appeared especially in the legislative activity, which speaks volumes as to the alternation between measures of tolerance (duality of religions) and measures of concord (religious conformity). This legislative activity manifested itself in a prolific production of edicts, letters patent, declarations interpreting the edicts, remonstrances against edicts, and so on. The Toleration Edict of 17 January 1562 was not yet law, when on 14 February a declaration of concord appeared specifying that the King's Council had not seen fit, for whatever reason, to recognize two religions within the realm. On 25 February the parlement refused to pass the Edict of Toleration and proposed renewed recourse to repressive measures (of forced concord) against the "seditious." No sooner was the Edict of Toleration (with additional clauses of concord) passed by parlement on 6 March, than (on 11 April) a royal declaration of concord appeared forbidding the presence of Protestant assemblies in the city of Paris and even in the suburbs. This declaration was registered by the parlement on 14 April with the proviso that the concessions of tolerance were to be strictly temporary. On 21 April, in its reply to the declaration of the prince of Condé, the parlement stressed that the Edict of Toleration was no more than a temporary expediency, and that there was no question of any innovations in matters of religion (in other words, it was an affirmation of concord). This burst of feverish activity (ignored by historians so far) shows to what extent preoccupation with concord made for a desire to wipe out the slightest measures of tolerance.

One can study the alternation through the major legislative events of the period. The Toleration Edict of Amboise (19 March 1563, the end of the first War of Religion) was dampened by the declarations of 14 December 1563 and 24 June 1564, which limited the number of places of worship and forbade all Protestant religious practice in royal residences. The next instance of alternation is even more striking. The Toleration Edict of Longjumeau (23 March 1568, end of the second War of Religion) was revoked and replaced on 28 September by the Edict of Saint-Maure-les-Faussés, which imposed the confession of the Roman Catholic religion on all the subjects of the realm. This edict of concord, in addition, considered itself "perpetual and irrevocable." In 1570 the enforcement of the Edict of Saint-Germain (end of the third War of Religion) of 8 August was rendered less effective by the prohibition of Protestant schools on 4 October. It was finally rendered null and void on 28 August 1572 (four days after the Saint Bartholomew's Day Massacre) by a declaration that forbade temporarily all Protestant religious gatherings. Any tolerance still remaining was neutralized by the edict of 24 October 1572 against those "who blaspheme the name of the Virgin and the saints" (i.e., the Huguenots). In 1573 the Edict of Pacification of 2 July (fourth War of Religion) was counterbalanced by the edict of 10 September 1574 against blasphemers. Between 1576 and 1580 a series of edicts and treaties (Peace of Beaulieu, Edict of Poitiers, Treaty of Nérac, Treaty of Fleix) stabilized and specified the status of tolerance. This series was followed inevitably by a further long series of treaties, declarations, and edicts between 1585 and 1588, the object of which was to reinstate concord in the most drastic forms: abjurations were to be made as soon as possible, all negotiation with heretics was forbidden. The Edict of Union of 1588 was sanctioned as basic and irrevocable law of the realm. The accession of Henry IV led to a lessening of severity. However, it is worth remembering that the alternation of concord and tolerance did not stop with the Edict of Nantes (1598). By that time, moreover, royal justice had taken precedence in matters of religious dissent over ecclesiastical justice, whose jurisdiction henceforth extended only to clergy and to cases concerning doctrine.

Principal Figures. The magistrates did not remain indifferent to the ideas propagated by the Reformation. Francis I, Henry II, and, even more vehemently, the subsequent kings, including Henry III, time and again complained about the spirit of "connivance and dissimulation" that dominated their parlements and other courts of justice, where the magistrates tended to show too much clemency toward the heretics and the other dissenters. By the edict of 23 March 1543, an oath and a profession of the Catholic faith were required from all the members of the magistracy: presidents, *maîtres des requêtes*, counselors, the *gens du roi*, registrars, notaries, ushers, clerks, and so on. Similar strictures were applied to the ecclesiastical judges. This was the reason why parts of the ecclesiastical jurisdiction were transferred to the supposedly more rigorous royal judges. Apart from that it is hardly possible to characterize the opinions of the magistrates relating to the Reformation, except in general terms through representative cases. The King's Council and the Parlement of Paris suggest the variety and cleavage of the position concerning religion in the entire kingdom.

An illustration is the case of the chancellors, whose opinions were decisive for the fate of the Reformation. Antoine Duprat, Antoine Dubourg, Mathieu de Longuerue, Guillaume Poyet, François de Montholon, François Evraut, Jean Bertrand (who was minister of justice), and François Olivier, who succeeded each other in the office of chancellor from Francis I to Charles IX, all maintained a common course of unrelenting defense of the monarchical traditions, of which the Catholic religion was in their opinion the indispensable basis. Michel de L'Hôpital's rise to power was of major historical importance because of his legislative innovations that marked an opening to the principle of religious tolerance. He nonetheless had great difficulties in adapting these novelties to the legal reality of France, which was averse to a program of tolerance contradicting its entire institutional history that centered on concord as a necessary condition for the exercise of national sovereignty. This was the real reason why L'Hôpital was dismissed from favor in 1568 and sent back to his estates. Jean de Morvilliers, bishop of Orléans, who succeeded him as minister of justice, was a moderate advocating religious conciliation rather than conceding measures of tolerance, whereas René de Birague̦s, Philippe Hurault de Cheverny, François de Montholon, Charles de Bourbon (head of the council), Philippe Hurault de Cheverny (for the second time), and Pomponne de Bellièvre followed faithfully, within the limits of their own options, the line of the government.

This line was uncertain, to be sure; it characterized what was perhaps the deepest crisis in the history of the magistracy in France. At the height of this crisis, in February 1589, Henry III saw himself compelled to dismantle the glorious monarchical institutions by revoking the parlement, the *Chambre des Comptes*, the *Cour des Aides*, the chancery, and all the offices of judicature of Paris, Orléans, Amiens, Abbeville, and other cities declared to be rebellious. The Parlement of Paris and the *Chambre des Comptes*, both composed of councillors and presidents loyal to the king, were transferred to Tours ("owing to its great faithfulness"), while the majority of the members of parlement living in Paris had sworn an oath to the Catholic League (Louis de Brège, bishop of Meaux, being minister of justice). For five years, mainly because of divergent religious opinions, the French institutions were in an anomalous and chaotic situation, which was to be remedied by Henry IV.

Among the counselors who sided with the Reformation, whose number is uncertain, the main figure was the deacon Anne Dubourg (nephew of Chancellor Antoine Dubourg), who at the famous *Mercuriale* of 10 June 1559 was committed for trial with other colleagues: Paul de Foix, Loys Du Faur, Eustache de la Porte, Anthoine Fumée, Nicholas Du Val, Guillaume Violle, and Arnaud Du Ferrier, the president of inquiries. While these, with the exception of the last, were ultimately reinstated in their functions, Dubourg was sentenced to death and executed on 23 December 1559. (The sentence was passed by a special council named by Henry II, comprised of Eustache Du Bellay, bishop of Paris; Antoine de Mouchy, Inquisitor of the Faith; the president of Saint-André; counselors Jean de Mesmes, Louis Gayant, and Robert Bouette. The judge, President Anthoine Minard, was assassinated on 12 December.) An important role was played among Reformed magistrates by Jean de Coras, the presumed author of the *Question politique* (1568).

Among the majority of moderate members of parlement who were in favor of a concord with the Reformed, mention must be made of Pierre Séguier (1504–1580), ancestor of a dynasty of magistrates who became famous for having dissuaded the king in 1555 from reinstating the tribunal of the Inquisition; Étienne Pasquier, counselor of the Parlement of Paris, author of *Les Recherches de la France* (1560); and his colleague Guillaume Du Vair, the eloquent and courageous author of numerous addresses before the "Ligueur" Parlement of Paris (1589–1592).

A great number of magistrates, faithful to the monarchical and Catholic tradition of the kingdom, showed themselves rigorous and intransigent throughout their careers: the First Presidents of the Parlement of Paris, Jean de Selve (1521–1529), Pierre Lizet (1529–1550), Gilles Le Maistre (1551–1562), Christophle de Thou (1562–1582), Achille de Harlay (1582–1611), and Jean Bégat, president of the Parlement of Burgundy, author of the remarkable *Remontrances au Roi sur l'Édit de Pacification* (1563). The same can be said of the secretaries of state, especially those who had been close to Catherine: Guillaume Bochetel, Cosme Clausse, Jean Du Thier, Claude de Laubespine (d. 1567), Jacques Bourdin, Florimond Robertet (lord of Alluye), Claude de Laubespine (d. 1570), Simon Fizes, Nicholas de Neufville (lord of Villeroy), Pierre Brulart, and Claude Pinart.

[*See also* Secular Magistrate, Office of.]

BIBLIOGRAPHY

Chénon, Emile. *Histoire générale du droit français, public et privé, des origines à 1815.* 3 vols. Paris, 1926.

Coquille, Guy. *Institution av droict des François.* Paris, 1630.

Douchet, Roger. *Les institutions de la France au XVIe siècle.* 2 vols. Paris, 1948.

Fontanon, Antoine, ed. *Les edicts et ordonnances des rois de France depvis Lovys VI, dit le gros.* 4 vols. Paris, 1611.

Fustel de Coulanges, Numa Denis. *Histoire des institutions politiques de l'ancienne France.* 6 vols. Paris, 1888–1901.

Isambert, M., et al., eds. *Recueil général des anciennes lois françaises.* Vols. 11–15. Paris, 1827–1829.

La Roche Flavin, Bernard de. *Treize livres des Parlemens de France.* Bordeaux, 1617.

Loyseau, Charles. *Cinq livres des droits des offices.* Cologne, 1613.

Maugis, Édouard. *Histoire du Parlement de Paris: De l'avènement des rois Valois à la mort d'Henri IV.* 3 vols. Paris, 1913–1916.

Rebuffi, Pierre, ed. *Edits et ordonnances des rois de France depuis 1226.* Lyon, 1575.

Rousselet, Marcel. *Histoire de la magistrature française, des origines à nos jours.* 2 vols. Paris, 1957.

Tanon, L. *Histoire des tribunaux de l'Inquisition en France.* Paris, 1893.

Turchetti, Mario. "Religious Concord and Political Tolerance in Sixteenth- and Seventeenth-Century France." *Sixteenth Century Journal* 22 (1991), 15–25.

Mario Turchetti

Translated from French by Peter Haggenmacher

MAGNUS, Olaus (1490–1557), Swedish historian and geographer. Olaus and his brother, Johannes Magnus (1488–1544), were both appointed Roman Catholic archbishops of Uppsala, but neither were able to occupy the office because of the Lutheran Reformation in Sweden.

Olaus, the younger of the brothers, was one of the foremost geographers of the Renaissance. His extensive knowledge of the Arctic region from Greenland to Russia led him to produce one of the most accurate maps of his time. Known as "Carta marina," it was published in Venice in 1539. Thought to have been lost, a copy was discovered in 1886 in the Munich Royal Library. Toward the end of his life, Olaus also published his *Historia de gentibus septentrionalibus* (History of the Northern People; 1555) in which he depicted the social and political life of Scandinavia, its topography, minerals, and animal life. For many years, Olaus's eyewitness accounts served as the primary source for European knowledge of Scandinavia. The *Historia* was also intended as a commentary on his famous "Carta marina" map.

While Olaus was busy working on his description of sixteenth-century Scandinavian society and topography, he was also editing his older brother Johannes's massive history of the Swedish kingdom, *Historia de omnibus gothorum sueonumque regibus* (History of All the Gothic and Swedish Kings) which he published in Rome the year before his own *Historia.* Unlike Olaus's work, which describes a transverse section of sixteenth-century Scandinavian society, Johannes's work gives a running account from the dawn of Swedish history to an apology for the sixteenth-century Roman Catholic church in Sweden. In doing so, Johannes revived Jordanes's sixth-century contention that the Goths, who were invading the Roman Empire at the time, had stormed out of prehistoric Sweden into the pages of European history. In 1432 the Swedish bishop Ragvaldi had resurrected the claim of a Gothic-Swedish relationship at the Council of Basel. Johannes popularized this theory in his *Historia* during the sixteenth century. In the seventeenth and eighteenth centuries, nationalistic Swedish historians championed this theory of Swedish origins in order to enhance their nation's image as a great power. Most historians today reject the hypothesis of a Gothic-Swedish connection.

Both Magnus brothers are tragic figures. Born in Linköping, recipients of the finest Renaissance education possible, they were destined for the highest ecclesiastical office in Sweden. But the inroads of the Reformation and their loyalty to Rome forced them into exile, and they lived the major part of their adult lives in Danzig and Rome, from where they sought to stem the Lutheran advance in Scandinavia. But as ardent Swedish patriots, they wrote of their homeland with love, fervor, and fantasy.

BIBLIOGRAPHY

Primary Sources

Magnus, Johannes. *Historia de omnibus Gothorum Sveonumque regibus.* Rome, 1554.

Magnus, Olaus. *Historia de gentibus septentrionalibus.* (1555). Facsimile ed. Copenhagen, 1972.

——— *Historia om de nordiska folken i svensköversättning.* 4 vols. Edited by John Granlund. Uppsala, 1976.

Secondary Sources

Johannesson, Kurt. *The Renaissance of the Goths in Sixteenth-Century Sweden: Johannes and Olaus Magnus as Politicians and Historians.* Berkeley, 1991.

Lynam, Edward. *The Carta Marina of Olaus Magnus.* Jenkintown, Pa., 1949.

TRYGVE R. SKARSTEN

MAIER, Johann. *See* Eck, Johann.

MAINZ.

On the eve of the Reformation three fundamental factors characterized Mainz. First, Emperor Maximilian I had plans for a reform of the Holy Roman Empire. The establishment of ten imperial defense districts made Mainz a kind of capital of the empire, already implied by the fact that the imperial archchancellor, who was the elector of Mainz, had his principal seat there.

Second, the city constantly struggled for emancipation from its ecclesiastical overlord. This struggle climaxed in 1462 when two rival princes, Adolf II of Nassau and Dieter von Isenburg, fought for the electorate. The majority of the citizens sided with von Isenburg, whom they trusted to respect the liberties of Mainz. Nevertheless Adolf conquered the city on 28 October 1462. This proved to be a major factor in the attempt toward a reformation. As a consequence of the fact that eight hundred citizens had to emigrate, Mainz lacked a city aristocracy strong enough to implement reform or to pursue the status of free imperial city.

Third, the question whether a reformation movement could successfully take place in Mainz was shaped by the impending Peasants' War and Knights' Revolt. As a result Elector Cardinal Albert of Brandenburg severed all links with the Reformation movement and embraced the cause of Catholic church reform. By that move he escaped the fate of his colleague Hermann von Wied, who was deposed as elector of Cologne. After the defeat of the city in 1462, Emperor Maximilian gave up all imperial rights to Mainz in order to get the vote of Elector Berthold von Henneberg in the imperial election. As a consequence, in 1486 Mainz became by imperial declaration the capital of the electorate of Mainz. In the same year Hesse inherited the county of Katzenellenbogen and thus became the rising power on the middle Rhine, close to the city gates of Mainz. Partly as a result of the religious differences between Hesse and Mainz, Nuremberg was able to establish itself as the seat of the imperial regiment. The strategic presence of Hesse near the electoral capital had an impact on reform in Mainz. Out of fear for the knights, Mainz stayed neutral in the war against Franz von Sickingen, which annoyed Hesse even more. Cardinal Albert was forced to buy peace from the princely alliance led by Hesse at a cost of 25,000 gold guilders.

Luther's Ninety-five Theses created a financial disaster with respect to the indulgences with which Cardinal Albert hoped to pay back his debts to the papacy and the banks. Although the Reformation caused him great embarrassment, Albert stayed neutral in the ensuing theological battle. This neutrality was also the result of the humanist circle at his court, in which the later reformers of Strasbourg, Wolfgang Capito and Caspar Hedio, played a leading role. Because of this constellation the theology faculty in Mainz refused to condemn Luther's theses. Not only did Reformation preaching take place at the church of Saint Ignaz, but the printer Johannes Schöffer even printed Luther's writings in 1520 and 1523. Capito had been won over by Luther in 1518. At the time of the Frankfurt am Main election of Emperor Charles V, Capito was in personal contact with Elector Frederick III of Saxony and Georg Spalatin. In the spring of 1520, Albert invited Capito to become cathedral preacher in Mainz. At that time Capito corresponded with Luther and boycotted the papal verdicts against Luther. Capito continued to broaden the Reformation basis and reported to Luther about Johann Eck's and Thomas Murner's activities and the burning of Luther's books at Mainz. In support of Luther, Capito had retained contact with the Cologne humanist Hermann von dem Busche, who came to Mainz in order to play an important role in Nuncio Girolamo Aleandro's disastrous auto-da-fe of Luther's writings. His appearance in Mainz was thought to be the breakthrough for the Reformation in the city. Von dem Busche brought along with him quite a few students, who spit in Aleandro's face and would have stoned Aleandro if the prince abbot of Fulda had not prevented it. As a result of this event no further attempt was made to burn Luther's writings.

The religious and social unrest of the city of Erfurt, which was deeply influenced by Luther, forced Albert into an anti-Saxon coalition in order to retain his possession, a move that also had religious consequences. In the following years Albert was content to be a humanist patron of arts, whereas his Catholic reform position gave way gradually to the spirit of the Counter-Reformation, which could not take hold in Mainz until his death in 1545.

BIBLIOGRAPHY

Brück, A. Ph. "Die Mainzer Domprediger des 16. Jahhunderts." *Jahrbuch für Hessische Landesgeschichte* 10 (1960).

Herrmann, F. *Die evangelische Bewegung zu Mainz im Reformationszeitalter.* Mainz, 1907.

Kalkhoff, P. *Wolfgang Capito in Dienste Erzbischof Albrechts von Mainz.* Berlin, 1907.

Kittelson, James M. *Wolfgang Capito.* Leiden, 1975.

Roth, F. W. "Beiträge zur Geschichte des Erzbischofs Albrecht II. von Mainz 1514–1545." *Historisch-politische Blätter für das katholische Deutschland* 10 (1896).

Schrohe, H. "Bilder aus der Mainzer Geschichte." In *Hessische Volksbücher*, no. 48. Friedberg, 1922.

Ulrich Michael Kremer

MAJOR, Georg (1502–1574), German Lutheran theologian and professor at the University of Wittenberg. Major left his native Nuremberg in 1511 to become a choir boy in Wittenberg, where he completed university studies in 1529. In 1528 he married Margarethe von Mochau; they had twelve children. After serving as school rector in Magdeburg, he returned to Wittenberg as preacher in the castle church (1537), assessor of the Wittenberg consistory, and professor of theology (1545). In 1546 he represented the Wittenberg faculty at the second Colloquy of Regensburg.

Although he contributed a satirical piece to the Schmalkald League's propaganda campaign against Emperor Charles V, he followed Philipp Melanchthon into the service of Elector Moritz of Saxony following the Schmalkald War and became deeply involved in the formulation of the Leipzig Interim. His defense of this document led him into a disagreement with Nikolaus von Amsdorf, his friend from their service together in Magdeburg, over Major's use of the phrase "good works are necessary for salvation" (1551). The resulting "Majoristic controversy" plagued Major for more than a decade. He attempted to deny that he had used the phrase and to explain it away as he replied to attacks from Amsdorf, Matthias Flacius Illyricus, Nikolaus Gallus, Joachim Westphal, and others. Neither side in the dispute recognized that differing definitions of terms, as well as different theological agendas, were separating them. Major defined good works as all that the Christian does, including trust the gospel, and he defined salvation as the whole of the saved (*selig*) life, not just the act or event of becoming saved or a child of God. Major did not teach that good works merit salvation. Some of his followers, in defending him, later seemed to veer in that direction, however. The Formula of Concord, article 4, rejected the phrase.

Major left Wittenberg briefly to assist Georg von Anhalt in Merseburg (1547) and to serve as ecclesiastical superintendent in Mansfeld County (1552–1553), where he was dismissed by the Gnesio-Lutheran Count Albrecht upon the count's return from imperial imprisonment. In 1551 Major translated into German the *Repetition of the Saxon Confession.* Though not a particularly skilled theologian, he led the Wittenberg faculty from 1560, after the deaths of Johannes Bugenhagen and Melanchthon, and was marginally involved in the "crypto-Calvinist" controversy over the Lord's Supper as his own health failed and death approached. His schoolbooks on the psalms, the catechism, classical texts, and grammar and rhetoric, as well as a school play on Jacob and his sons and his collection of the wisdom of the church fathers (prepared at Luther's instigation in 1544), all demonstrate his absorption of Melanchthon's humanistic interests. His *De origine et autoritate verbi Dei* (1550) presents the developing Lutheran concepts of the verbal inspiration of scripture and the catholic consensus of the ancient church. He edited several volumes of the Wittenberg edition of Luther's works. His attack on antitrinitarians, *Commonefactio ad ecclesiam catholicam . . . de . . . blasphemiis Samosatencis* (1569), traced the trinitarian teaching of the church from Adam through the ancient church councils to his own era. His lectures on Paul's epistles and his postils on epistle and gospel lessons provided detailed treatment of those texts. Major typifies the "epigones" of his generation, a man touched by the greatness of Melanchthon and Luther but unable to continue their work with insight and good leadership.

BIBLIOGRAPHY

Kolb, Robert. "Georg Major as Controversialist: Polemics in the Late Reformation." *Church History* 45 (1976), 455–468. Assessment of personal factors in Major's defense of his proposition on good works.

Peterson, Luther David. "The Philippist Theologians and the Interims of 1548: Soteriological, Ecclesiastical, and Liturgical Compromises and Controversies within German Lutheranism." Ph.D. diss., University of Wisconsin, 1974. Thorough study of the sources, with much material relating to Major.

Scheible, Heinz. "Major, Georg." In *Theologische Realenzyklopädie*, edited by Gerhard Müller, vol. 21, pp. 725–730. Berlin and New York, 1991. Thorough overview of Major's life and significance.

ROBERT KOLB

MALDERUS, Joannes (Flem., Jan van Malder; 1562–1633), theologian, and fifth bishop of Antwerp. After theological studies Malderus taught sixteen years at the University of Louvain, specializing in the interpretation of Thomas Aquinas' *Summa theologiae.* Three groups of his lectures were published in 1616, 1624, and 1634. In 1611 this pious and prudent man was consecrated bishop of Antwerp.

His twenty-two-year episcopacy was of special importance for the diocese, for during this time he formulated and promulgated rules and statutes on every conceivable aspect of religious life. This codification was due to the administrative gifts of Malderus and to the mind of his chief secretary, the legal thinker Franciscus Zypaeus. The standards established remained in effect for decades—in 1643 they were published posthumously in book form as *Ordinationes dioecesanae Antverpienses.* They reveal that Malderus was a meticulous administrator who wished to control the shape of religious life down to its smallest detail.

This zeal for standards was matched by his fervor for pastoral care. Malderus maintained frequent personal contact with his clergy. Like his predecessors, he especially promoted the Jesuits. He also attached great importance to religious education and wrote in his own hand a catechism-like text for adults. By every possible means he tried to convert Protestants and Jews within the diocese. The conflicts within Calvinism in the northern Netherlands between 1611 and 1619 interested him extremely; he hoped for rapprochement with the Arminians, who were banned as a result of this conflict, and published in 1620 a polemical work on the affair. He also began a battle against prostitution in Antwerp.

At the end of his life he published a few more short works: a tract on the sacrament of confession (1628), a commentary on the *Song of Songs* (1630), and theological meditations (1630). The primary contribution of Malderus, however, was his form-giving systematization of religious norms, which promoted the establishment and persistence of the post-Tridentine church in his diocese. Thanks to the journal he kept, we know that these norms were developed in consultation with those expected to live by them and were based upon years of practical experience.

BIBLIOGRAPHY

Clerq, Carlo de. "Kerkelijk leven." In *Antwerpen in de 17de eeuw*, edited by Genootschap voor Antwerpse Geschieden, pp. 16–35. Antwerp, 1989. Concentrates on his activities as bishop.

Haeghen, Ferdinand van der. *Bibliotheca Belgica: Bibliographie générale des Pays-Bas.* 2d ed., 6 vols. Brussels, 1979. Describes the works of Malderus.

Ram, P. F. X. de. *Synodicon Belgicum sive acta omnium ecclesiarum Belgii.* 3 vols. Louvain, 1828–1858. Gives most of his instructions for religious life.

MARIE JULIETTE MARINUS
Translated from Dutch by Craig Harline

MALDONADO, Juan (Lat., Johannes Maldonatus; Fr., Jean Maldonat; 1533–1583), Spanish Jesuit, theologian, and exegete. Born in Fuente del Maestro, he studied at the University of Salamanca, joined the Society of Jesus in Rome in 1562, and was ordained in 1563. Following his ordination his superiors sent him to Paris, where he initially taught philosophy and then in 1565 began a series of lectures on theology at the Jesuit college. In both his lectures and his pastoral work, particularly at Poitiers in 1570, Maldonado was an adversary of Protestantism, but his involvement in theological controversies on the validity of Calvinist baptism and of mixed marriages between Catholics and Protestants and especially on the Immaculate Conception gained him enemies among the Catholic theologians at the Sorbonne. His views on the Immaculate Conception received vindication from the bishop of Paris and the papacy, but these controversies contributed to the conflict between the Society of Jesus and the University of Paris, a conflict that continued for so long that the Jesuit historian James Brodrick (*The*

Progress of the Jesuits, London, 1946) has called it the "'Hundred Years' War of the Jesuits."

As official visitor to the Jesuit province of France between 1578 and 1580, Maldonado initiated a number of pedagogical reforms, and then late in 1580 he returned to Rome, where he assisted in the preparation of the Jesuit educational program, the *Ratio Studiorum.* He died in Rome on 5 January 1583. The publication of his writings occurred posthumously, the first and the most important being his commentaries on the four gospels, which went through many editions. With the exception of this work of exegesis, subsequent theologians rarely consulted his work.

BIBLIOGRAPHY

Maldonado, Juan. *Commentarii in quattor evangelia.* 2 vols. Pont-à-Mousson, France, 1596–1597.

Martin, A. Lynn. *The Jesuit Mind: The Mentality of an Elite in Early Modern France.* Ithaca, N.Y., 1988. Devotes considerable attention to Maldonado and contains a portrait of him.

Schmitt, Paul. *La réforme catholique: Le combat de Maldonat, 1534–1583.* Paris, 1985. Too much a history of the times, not enough attention to the career of Maldonado.

A. LYNN MARTIN

MALMØ. At the beginning of the sixteenth century, the Danish town of Malmø, with a population of around seven thousand, was rivalled only by Copenhagen as the most important city in Scandinavia. When evangelical ideas began to reach the city, Malmø had recently grown rapidly and was able to exercise some independence and influence within the Danish kingdom.

A number of social and economic problems faced the city as a consequence of its growth. As a walled and fortified city only a limited number of plots and buildings were available to its citizens. This situation was aggravated by the Catholic church's ownership of about one-third of all properties in the city. Since the church was exempted from tax while capitalizing on a booming property market in which it benefited from issuing ever-shorter leases, it proved fertile soil for a growing anticlericalism among the burghers. Furthermore, Malmø belonged to the archbishopric of Lund, which, since the death in 1519 of its last consecrated archbishop, had remained in a state of disarray.

In the early 1520s evangelical ideas gained ground primarily among the many German or German-speaking merchants in Malmø, not least through their close trade links with Lübeck, Rostock, and Stralsund. In May 1527 the first Danish evangelical preacher, Claus Mortensen, commenced preaching in the city. Mortensen appears to have arrived on the invitation of Malmø's leading mayor (of the four who served at any given time), Jørgen Kock. The magistracy wanted Mortensen to gauge the popularity of the evangelical message. Early in 1528 Mortensen was able to take over one of the city's main churches in order to accommodate his growing number of followers. By then Malmø had acquired a second evangelical preacher, and the magistracy led by Kock had made sure that the two monasteries in the city were close to collapse. In October that year Kock managed to obtain a royal privilege allowing the magistracy to use the monasteries for a hospital and a new town hall.

Apart from the intervention of the elected archbishop of Lund in 1528, the reformation in Malmø, promoted by the magistracy and supported by the king, progressed relatively unhindered; by 1530 the city was fully reformed. Paradoxically, rather than a setback for the evangelical movement through the enforced exile of the city's evangelical preachers, the archbishop's interference eventually proved beneficial. The two "compromise" candidates invited to replace the exiles, Frans Vormordsen and Peter Laurentsen, whom the elected archbishop evidently considered Erasmian Catholics, turned out to be leading protagonists of the Danish Reformation, providing the evangelical movement in Malmø with the dedicated religious leadership it had hitherto lacked.

After a final violent confrontation with the Catholic minority in the city during the autumn of 1529, the evangelical party was victorious, and in January 1530 Laurentsen published *Malmøbogen,* describing the changes brought about by the Reformation. The Mass had been abolished and the properties of the Catholic church had been confiscated, providing the economic basis for the new Protestant order: salaries for ministers, poor relief, a hospital, a school, and an academy. Much has been made of the southern German, as opposed to the Lutheran, inspiration for the Malmø reformers, but like so many of their German colleagues their Protestantism is best described as evangelical.

BIBLIOGRAPHY

Grell, Ole Peter. "The City of Malmø and the Danish Reformation." *Archiv für Reformationsgeschichte* 79 (1988), 311–340. Detailed study of the significance of Malmø for the Danish reformation.

———. "The Emergence of Two Cities: The Reformation in Malmø and Copenhagen." In *The Danish Reformation against Its International Background,* edited by Leif Grane and Kai Hørby, pp. 129–145. Göttingen, 1990. A comparative study of the early reformation in the two cities.

OLE PETER GRELL

MANDENMAKER, Jan Arendszoon (c.1535–1573), Dutch Reformed preacher. He was born in Alkmaar, a town in the northern part of the county of Holland. In the 1550s he and Pieter Corneliszoon (later a Calvinist preacher in Holland) were journeyman basketmakers (*mandenmakers*) working under master Allard Gerritszoon, who, along with both his workmen, was influenced by the heterodox ideas of Cornelis Cooltuyn. In these years all three basketmakers acted as preachers. On Cooltuyn's recommendation, Mandenmaker received from the refugee church in Emden a roving commission to serve the Reformed throughout Holland; by 1561 he was known to the Netherlands congregation in London as *Verbi Dei minister in Hollandia.* Early in 1566 he had to flee to Kampen, in Overijssel, where his preaching was soon banned.

After the regent Margaret of Parma temporarily mitigated prosecutions for heresy (April 1566), many Reformed preachers conducted open-air services in fields outside the towns (hedge preaching), beginning in Flanders on 26 May. On 8 July six distinguished Amsterdammers held a meeting outside the jurisdiction of their city and authorized Mandenmaker to organize hedge preaching in Holland, starting with a service outside the jurisdiction of Hoorn on 14 July. Until the end of August Mandenmaker was at work in northern Holland and in the province of Utrecht; his sermons, lasting at least three hours, were given before crowds numbering as much as four to five thousand people, according to the sources. Following the wave of iconoclasm that swept across the Low Countries from 10 August, Mandenmaker preached for two weeks in September in the provinces of Overijssel and Gelderland. In a few places his sermons were followed immediately by image-breaking, though he did not directly incite crowds to this end. When a church inside Amsterdam was placed at the disposal of the Reformed, the congregation called as its ministers Mandenmaker and another hedge-preacher, Pieter Gabriel. On 15 December a congregation of one thousand persons celebrated the Lord's Supper here for the first time.

The tide turned in the spring of 1567. The regent regained her power by force of arms, and at the end of April Reformed churches were closed everywhere. Mandenmaker and Gabriel joined those who fled to Emden and acted there as the "ministers of the dispersed congregation of Amsterdam." To settle differences among Reformed refugees from many provinces, Flemings and Brabanders sought general acceptance of some "formulas of unity," but the Holland contingent, led by Mandenmaker and Gabriel, abhorred all such formulas, fearing a new kind of religious constraint. When the Synod of Emden in 1571 adopted the Belgic Confession and the Heidelberg Catechism as standards for all, the Hollanders at last resigned themselves "for unity's sake."

In Holland these decisions were put into practice after 1 April 1572, when the Revolt of the Netherlands gained a foothold there. Mandenmaker did not at first join the refugees returning to Holland, since Amsterdam remained loyal to the central government in Brussels until 1578. In January 1573, however, he and his erstwhile colleague Pieter Corneliszoon were called as ministers to Alkmaar, Mandenmaker's birthplace. Here Mandenmaker presided over a provincial synod that sanctioned many decisions taken at Emden. He fell mortally ill during the siege of the city by Spanish troops and died on 28 August 1573.

Mandenmaker was not a learned theologian or even an educated man, but he was respected for his piety. He was eloquent, even charismatic, and he knew the scriptures thoroughly. Opponents who suspected him of preaching from a memorized text came to a different view after debating him. Since he believed that the Reformation had purged the one, holy, Catholic, and apostolic church but had not abandoned it, he adopted a lenient attitude toward Lutheranism; Lutherans and Calvinists should be members of the one restored church. At the end of 1566 he even declared himself willing to accept the Augsburg Confession in regard to consubstantiation. His desire to restore the worldwide *una sancta* also formed the background for his Emden conflict with the champions of creedal formulas.

Mandenmaker may have been married twice. In 1560 a woman named Sijtje Gerritsdochter made, just before her death, her last will in favor of her husband Jan Aerntsz, who might have been the same man. In this will no children were mentioned. Later Mandenmaker's wife and children are mentioned in other sources; all of them fled together with him to Emden and were present at his deathbed. His son Mattheus Janszoon appears in other sources.

BIBLIOGRAPHY

Duke, Alastair. *Reformation and Revolt in the Low Countries.* London and Ronceverte, W.Va., 1990.

Evenhuis, R. B. *Ook dit was Amsterdam.* Vol. 1, *De kerk der hervorming in de gouden eeuw.* Amsterdam, 1965. See pp. 51–76.

Fruin, R. "De voorbereiding in de ballingschap van de Gereformeerde kerk van Holland." In *Verspreide Geschriften,* edited by R. Fruin, vol. 2, pp. 235–276. Haarlem, Netherlands, 1900.

Nauta, D., J. P. van Dooren, and O. J. de Jong, eds. *De synode van Emden, Oktober 1571.* Kampen, Netherlands, 1971.

Rogge, H. C. "Jan Arentszoon en de prediking der hervorming in Noord-Holland, inzonderheid buiten en in Amsterdam." *Kalender voor de Protestanten in Nederland* 4 (1859), 79–121.

Vis, G. N. M. *Jan Arentsz, de mandenmaker van Alkmaar, voorman van de Hollandse reformatie.* Hilversum, 1992.

S. Groenveld

MANTZ, Felix (d. 1527), cofounder of Zurich Anabaptism and its first martyr. Mantz was the illegitimate son of a Zurich canon, well educated in Latin, Greek, and Hebrew. An early supporter of Huldrych Zwingli, he soon joined the radical opposition. He was one of the cosigners of the letters to Thomas Müntzer of 5 September 1524 in which the pro-Reformation radicals expressed their disappointment in the official Reformation led by Zwingli and implemented by the Zurich government. He and Andreas Castelberger, a bookseller belonging to the Zurich radical group, supervised the publication in Basel of six of Andreas Bodenstein von Karlstadt's tracts against Luther in October and November 1524. These published writings of Karlstadt opposed Luther on the pace of the Reformation and on the Lord's Supper, but, because Johannes Oecolampadius intervened with the printer, they did not include a tract, highly regarded by Mantz, in which Karlstadt opposed the baptism of infants. Mantz and Castelberger distributed more than five thousand copies of Karlstadt's works among their supporters in Zurich and its territories.

In December Mantz submitted a *Protestation* against infant baptism to the Zurich council; with its mixture of High German and Swiss German, it suggests some dependence on Karlstadt's works, although it is probably well not to exaggerate Karlstadt's literary or theological influence on the emergence of the issue of believers' baptism in the Zurich reformation. The Zurich radicals emphasized the literal reenactment of baptism and the Lord's Supper as described in the New Testament, while the Saxon radicals with whom they sought contact were most of all concerned that external sacramental ceremonies should not be allowed to eclipse the work of the Holy Spirit in the individual believer.

In any case, the issue of infant baptism became the focus of controversy between Zwingli and the radicals. It was the subject of a disputation in the Zurich council chamber on 17 January 1525, in which Mantz, Conrad Grebel, and the rural priest Wilhelm Reublin presented the case for the baptism of mature believers only. The council declared Zwingli the winner of the debate and enjoined Grebel and Mantz to cease holding meetings with their followers. They replied shortly afterward by initiating the baptism of adult believers in defiance of the authority of the Zurich government. This event is conventionally accepted as the beginning of Anabaptism.

A good deal of our knowledge of Mantz's two-year career as an Anabaptist comes from the court records of the Zurich government's efforts to suppress the movement. Even through this distorted medium it is evident that Mantz played a prominent role in articulating the distinctive early Anabaptist beliefs. He gave a succinct statement of Anabaptist nonresistance that predated the Schleitheim Articles: "no Christian should be a government official, nor judge with the sword, nor kill or punish anyone." Within weeks of the first adult baptisms he described how he instructed the newly baptized in "love, unity, and community of all things, like the apostles in Acts 2," thus initiating the preoccupation with community of goods that is much more general in early Anabaptism than is customarily recognized.

Mantz worked actively to spread the new baptism, usually accompanied by Grebel, George Blaurock, or both of them. He went to the territories of Basel, Graubünden, Appenzell, St. Gall, Schaffhausen, and the Grüningen territory in the Zurich highland. Particularly in the last three areas, he found himself in the midst or the immediate aftermath of the peasant uprisings that had severely damaged the authority of both government and Zwinglian pastors, who raised questions in their sermons about the practice of infant baptism and the collection of tithes but hurriedly drew back when rebellion seemed imminent.

The Zurich government became increasingly frustrated by the Anabaptist leaders, who could be silenced neither by successive public disputations nor recurrent imprisonments. On 7 March 1526, Mantz, Grebel, and Blaurock were sentenced to imprisonment on bread and water "until they die and decay," with the stipulation that continuation of baptismal activity would be punished by drowning. Two weeks later the prisoners succeeded in a jailbreak. When Mantz was rearrested in December 1526 the Zurich magistracy proceeded to carry out its threat. Unlike his fellow prisoner Blaurock, Mantz had broken his *Urfehde*, a solemn oath not to continue the new baptism; thus he was singled out. On 5 January 1527, he was pushed, hands and feet bound, from a boat into the Limmat, thereby becoming Zurich's first and most prominent Anabaptist martyr.

BIBLIOGRAPHY

Harder, Leland, ed. *The Sources of Swiss Anabaptism: The Grebel Letters and Related Documents.* Classics of the Radical Reformation, vol. 4. Scottdale, Pa., 1985. Includes English translations of Mantz's *Protestation*, one of his judicial interrogations, and an account of his martyrdom.

Krajewski, Ekkehard. *Leben und Sterben des Zürcher Täuferführers Felix Mantz.* Kassel, 1957. This biography works from a "free church" perspective but undertakes to bring Mantz out from under Conrad Grebel's shadow. The best source of detailed information.

Pater, Calvin Augustine. *Karlstadt as the Father of the Baptist Movements: The Emergence of Lay Protestantism.* Toronto, 1984. An important part of Pater's argument that the first Anabaptists in Zurich were followers of Karlstadt is his hypothesis that Mantz's *Protestation* was based on Karlstadt's *Von dem Tauff.*

Schmid, Walter. "Der Autor der sogenannten Protestation und Schutzschrift von 1524/1525." *Zwingliana* 9 (1950), 139–149. Schmid, coeditor of the Zurich Anabaptist sources, demonstrates on linguistic grounds that the *Protestation*, previously thought to be a work of Conrad Grebel, was authored by Mantz.

Stayer, James M. "Saxon Radicalism and Swiss Anabaptism: The Return of the Repressed." *Mennonite Quarterly Review* 67 (1993), 5–30. Emphasizes the different motives behind opposition to infant baptism that divided the early Swiss Anabaptists from Karlstadt and Müntzer, despite their appearance of agreement.

Zorzin, Alejandro. "Karlstadt's 'Dialogus vom Tauff der Kinder' in einem anonymen Wormser Druck aus dem Jahr 1527: Ein Beitrag zur Karlstadtbibliographie." *Archive for Reformation History* 79 (1988), 27–58. Claims the identification of a tract printed in 1527 at Worms as Karlstadt's dialogue criticizing Luther's advocacy of infant baptism. Since the themes of this dialogue are unlike Mantz's *Protestation*, Zorzin regards Pater's hypothesis of Mantz's *verbal* dependence on Karlstadt as "unsustainable."

JAMES M. STAYER

MANUEL, Niklaus (also Niklaus Manuel Deutsch; 1484–1530), Swiss painter, poet, politician, mercenary soldier, and pioneer of the Reformation. Born in Bern, Manuel most likely received his early training in glass painting. He evidently spent his journeyman's *Wanderjahre* in south Germany, for his paintings display artistic influences from that region. Upon his return Manuel married a local woman of good family and shortly thereafter (1510) was named to the large council of the Bern city government. He supplemented his income with military service, participating in at least two Italian campaigns (1516, 1522). During the years 1523–1528 he held the office of *Landvogt* ("bailiff") over a rural district belonging to Bern. In April 1528 he was elected to the small council, the true governing body of the city. Soon he emerged as a leading member of that elite group. He specialized in diplomacy and ably represented both his community and the Protestant cause at more than thirty diets and conferences during the last two years of his life. He promoted religious peace and conciliation within the Swiss Confederation, in contrast to the intransigence displayed by Zurich under Huldrych Zwingli's leadership.

About thirty of Manuel's paintings survive, all of them probably created before he joined the reform movement. Representative works include the *Beheading of John the Baptist*, the *Temptation of Saint Anthony*, and the *Judgment of Paris*. His once-famous wall paintings in the Dominican cloister in Bern depicting the Dance of Death are known only from copies, but numerous drawings, many on military subjects, remain and testify to his skill as a draftsman. Manuel's literary efforts have won him recognition as one of the most effective popular writers of the Reformation. He concentrated on carnival plays and dramatic dialogues attacking financial abuses of the Roman church.

BIBLIOGRAPHY

Abbé, Derek van. "Niklaus Manuel of Bern and His Interest in the Reformation." *Journal of Modern History* 24 (1952), 287–300. Analyzes Manuel's dramatic writings and their effectiveness as propaganda.

Niklaus Manuel Deutsch: Maler, Dichter, Staatsmann. Exhibition catalog, Kunstmuseum, Bern. Bern, 1979. Thoroughly covers his art, career, and writings; heavily illustrated.

Parshall, Linda B., and Peter W. Parshall. *Art and the Reformation: An Annotated Bibliography.* Boston, 1986. See items 1085–1101.

CARL C. CHRISTENSEN